READINGS IN ETHICS

Compiled and Edited

By

J. F. Leibell, Ph. D.

Lecturer on Ethics

LOYOLA UNIVERSITY PRESS
Chicago, Illinois
1926

COPYRIGHT, 1926
BY
LOYOLA UNIVERSITY
CHICAGO, ILL.

Composed and printed by
LOYOLA UNIVERSITY PRESS
Chicago, Illinois, U. S. A.

PREFACE

Selected readings have become a well-established element in the apparatus of college teaching. The reason is obvious. However earnest and intelligent a student may be, he cannot obtain an adequate grasp of a subject from the class text-book, nor from the instructor's lectures. On many topics, the exposition found in the manual, or heard in the classroom, is not sufficiently clear, or sufficiently comprehensive. This is no reflection upon either manual or instructor. It is merely a recognition of human limitations.

Hence, the student requires collateral reading, even though none of the supplementary authors that he consults may be as satisfactory, taken by itself, as his class text or class notes. Each additional source provides a new viewpoint, or a new emphasis, or a better understanding of some fact or doctrine. While the class text-book might yield the same results to the student who gave it deeper study, the average student obtains such results more interestingly and more easily through the medium of outside reading. The mere provision of a different treatise is a distinct help. When the additional reading matter presents the views, not of one, but of many authors, the advantage is multiplied.

Collateral reading texts are numerous in most of the college disciplines: for example, history, sociology, politics, and economics. Curiously, however, we have had nothing of this sort in English for the use of our classes in ethics. Nevertheless, ethics is one of the subjects that requires much and varied reading and study in order to produce satisfactory and comprehensive understanding. Teacher, as well as student, will readily agree with this statement.

Ethics proceeds with due respect for, but without intrinsic dependence upon, revelation and ecclesiastical enactment. Reason, arguing from naturally known facts, is the tool it employs in shaping its conclusions. Hence the compiler is to be commended for having sought the testimony of authorities who have reasoned well, irrespective of their religious affiliations. If the Church can claim as hers the majority of those whose names appear, the explanation is to be sought in the fact that the Church has for twenty centuries been vitally interested in the welfare of society and the ethical improvement of the individual. Selections referring to the theory and practice of the Church are to be received for their historical and their purely ethical value. The scope of this work is ethical, not dogmatic. Its primary advantage is to provide the student with a substitute for the library. The range of readings is sufficiently wide on each topic to render unnecessary the consulting of a great number of ethical treatises.

Naturally, the volume will fail to conform in all respects with all the conceptions of an ideal text which may be held by all its readers. Any work of this kind presents a wide opportunity for differences of view as regards quantity, selections, authors, and the relative amount of space assigned to various topics. In the opinion of the writer of these paragraphs, the book can fairly lay claim to certain valuable qualities. In the first place, it is comprehensive. Vast as is the field of ethics, every important section of it is represented by one or more selections. It is likewise representative in the sourcs from which it draws. All the important viewpoints that are to be found among Catholic ethical writers are reflected in its pages. The postulates of ethics, and the relations between ethics and the cognate sciences receive due attention. Since ethics is a practical science, since its main benefit to students is to afford guidance for their own conduct, the compiler has wisely included a generous amount of readings on the practical phases, relations, implications, and applications of ethical truth. Witness: the selections on "Anger" and on "Habit", in the section on Human Acts; on "Health", "Gambling", and "Stock Speculation", in the section on Rights and Duties; on "Labor Unions", "Strikes", "Co-operation", and "Wages", in the section on Property; on "Birth Control" and "The Christian Home", in the section on the State. The prominence of recent magazine articles is an

PREFACE

indication at once of the attention given to practical questions and to the up-to-dateness of the volume.

While the writer of this preface has studiously avoided the language of exaggeration, he would be somewhat less than just if he did not record his judgment that the student who conscientiously reads this book in connection with the classroom work will acquire much more than the dry bones of the subject. He will have a grasp of ethics which will be a source of intellectual satisfaction, a stimulus to continued interest in the subject, and a special equipment for the solution of his own problems of conduct.

JOHN A. RYAN.

Washington, D. C.

TABLE OF CONTENTS

General Ethics

I. Introduction

1. The Purpose of Ethics, *Aristotle* 1
2. Definition and Scope of Ethics, *Victor Cathrein* 3
3. The Necessity of Ethics, *Vincent McNabb* 6
4. The Golden Mean in Philosophy, *Charles S. Devas* 11
5. Methods of Ethics, *Michael Cronin* 13
6. History of Ethics, *Victor Cathrein* 19

II. The Postulates

7. The Necessity of Postulates, *Henry S. Spalding* 35
8. Postulates, *Timothy Brosnahan* 36
9. Arguments in Proof of the Existence of God
    (a) The Prime Mover, *Saint Thomas Aquinas* 39
    (b) Teleological Proof, *Bernard Boedder* 48
    (c) Argument from Conscience, *George H. Joyce* .. 57
    (d) The Common Consent of Mankind, *T. J. Walshe* 66
10. Why Some Do Not Believe in God, *Joseph Rickaby* ... 69
11. Immortality of the Soul, *Michael Maher* 71
12. Freedom of the Will, *Michael Maher* 89
13. Freedom, *John G. Vance* 98
14. Determinist Theories, *Cardinal Mercier* 106
15. Morality Without Free Will, *Joseph Rickaby* 111
16. Certitude, *Michael James Ryan* 120
17. The Illative Sense, *Cardinal Newman* 129

III. Human Acts

18. The Norm of Morality, *Thomas Slater* 155
19. The Norm of Moral Rectitude, *Victor Cathrein* 156
20. Human Acts, *Walter H. Hill* 162
21. The Moral Determinants of an Action, *Michael Cronin* 165
22. Are There Any Indifferent Acts?, *Michael Cronin* 168
23. The Highest Good, *Michael F. Dinneen* 171
24. The Last End, *Etienne Gilson* 174
25. Happiness, *Charles C. Miltner* 182

26. Hindrances to Accountability, *Michael Cronin* 191
27. Does the End Justify the Means?, *John Gerard* 193
28. The Passions, *Arthur Devine* 207
29. Fear and Anger, *Michael Maher* 210
30. Anger, *Saint Francis de Sales* 211
31. Virtue, *Augustine Waldron* 213
32. Virtue, the Soul's Greatness, *Anscar Vonier* 221
33. Charity, *John A. Ryan* 221
34. The Place of Charity in Present Society, *John A. Ryan* 223
35. Who Is My Neighbor?, *William J. Kerby* 227
36. The Cardinal Virtues, *Joseph Rickaby* 236
37. Perfect Virtues Are Never One Without the Other, *Saint Francis de Sales* 241
38. True Conceptions of Welfare, *John A. Ryan* 245
39. False Conceptions of Welfare, *John A. Ryan* 258
40. Vice, *Joseph F. Delany* 269
41. Punitive Sanction, *Joseph C. Sasia* 270
42. Ethical Implications of the Law of Habit, *William James* 272
43. The Limitations of Habit, *John MacCunn* 279
44. Ethics and Character, *Michael Maher* 283
45. Character, *Timothy Brosnahan* 284
46. The Nature of Character, *Robert Swickerath* 285
47. The Value of Character, *Ernest R. Hull* 288
48. The Importance of Character, *Robert Swickerath* 289
49. Personality, *Howard C. Warren* 291
50. Personality in Life, *Robert Kane* 293

IV. LAW

51. The Nature of Law, *Thomas Slater* 301
52. The Effects of Law, *Saint Thomas Aquinas* 302
53. Classification of Laws, *Victor Cathrein* 303
54. Major Divisions of Law, *Francis P. Le Buffe* 306
55. The Eternal Law, *Joseph Rickaby* 313
56. The Natural Law, *Walter McDonald* 317
57. The Natural Law, *Victor Cathrein* 320
58. The Precepts of the Natural Law, *Joseph Rickaby* .. 323
59. Moral Law, *Timothy Brosnahan* 325
60. The Moral Obligation of Civil Law, *John A. Ryan* .. 326
61. Synderesis, *Thomas Slater* 341
62. The Moral Faculty, *Michael Cronin* 342
63. Conscience, *Cardinal Newman* 344
64. Conscience, *Ernest R. Hull* 349
65. Can Conscience Develop and Decay?, *Michael Cronin* 352
66. The Prohibition Laws and Conscience, *John A. Ryan* .. 355

TABLE OF CONTENTS

67. Is National Prohibition in Accord With Sound Ethics?, *Philip E. Burkett* 356
68. Probabilism, *Joseph Rickaby* 360
69. The Nature of Sin, *Thomas Slater* 365
70. The Malice of Sin, *Cardinal Manning* 367
71. Why Men Sin, *Ernest R. Hull* 367
72. Philosophical Sin, *Arthur Charles O'Neill* 373
73. Utilitarianism, *James J. Fox* 375
74. Altruism, *Timothy Brosnahan* 380
75. The Kantian Ought, *Timothy Brosnahan* 383

SPECIAL ETHICS

V. RIGHTS AND DUTIES

76. The Basis and Justification of Rights, *John A. Ryan* .. 405
77. Duty, *James J. Fox* 420
78. Contract, *Thomas Slater* 427
79. Revelation, *Timothy Brosnahan* 432
80. Obligation to Worship God, *Orestes A. Brownson* .. 432
81. Religious Indifferentism, *James J. Fox* 439
82. Authority in Religion, *Wilfrid Parsons* 446
83. The Malice of Scandal, *Achille Van der Heeren* ... 450
84. The Right to Moral Integrity, *Timothy Brosnahan* . 451
85. Virtue and Vice in Matters of Toilet, *Saint Thomas Aquinas* 452
86. Morality and Art, *Wilfrid Parsons* 454
87. Suicide, *Achille Van der Heeren* 457
88. Duties Toward the Body, *Charles C. Miltner* 463
89. Preservation of Life, *Thomas Slater* 474
90. The Ethics of Intoxication, *Ernest R. Hull* 474
91. Health and Holiness, *Francis Thompson* 480
92. Games and Sports, *Saint Thomas Aquinas* 482
93. Body Training and Temporal World Forces, *William J. Lockington* 483
94. Homicide, *Joseph F. Delany* 487
95. Homicide, Excusable and Felonious, *J. Harding Fisher* 490
96. Self-Defence, *James J. Fox* 494
97. Ethics of the Ouija Board, *James F. Barrett* 496
98. The Wrongfulness of Duelling, *Victor Cathrein* ... 498
99. May the State Kill?, *Paul L. Blakely* 502
100. Killing the Wounded, *Ernest R. Hull* 505
101. Vivisection, *John S. Vaughan* 507
102. Betting, *Thomas Slater* 513
103. Gambling, *Thomas Slater* 514
104. The Moral Aspects of Speculation, *John A. Ryan* . 517

105. The Malice of a Lie, *J. Harding Fisher* 528
106. The Doctrine of Lying and Equivocation, *Joseph Rickaby* 533
107. Lying and Equivocation, *Cardinal Newman* 543
108. The Obligation of Veracity, *Reginald Middleton* 555
109. The Loan of Money, *Michael Cronin* 565
110. The Church and the Money Lender, *Henry Irwin* 568
111. The Just Price, *Patrick Cleary* 570
112. The Ethics of Just Prices, *Joseph Husslein* 572
113. Morality of Monopolistic Prices, *Joseph Husslein* 576

VI. Property

114. The Doctrine of Property, *John A. Ryan* 583
115. Property and Socialism, *Pope Leo XIII* 592
116. Socialism, *Peter Finlay* 596
117. Socialism and Religious Orders, *Bernard Vaughan* 611
118. Henry George and the Single-Tax Theory, *Charles S. Devas* 613
119. The Ethics of Labor, *Father Cuthbert* 615
120. Social Reform, *William von Ketteler* 631
121. The Condition of Labor, *Pope Leo XIII* 639
122. Industrial Democracy, *John A. Ryan* 646
123. A Modern Gild Program, *Joseph Husslein* 662
124. Industrial Relations, *Joint Pastoral of the Archbishops and Bishops of the United States, 1919* 667
125. Rights and Duties of the Unions, *J. Alfred Lane* 674
126. Relations Between Employers and the Employed, *Cardinal O'Connell* 681
127. A Living Wage by Law, *John A. Ryan* 687
128. Family Endowment, *J. E. Canavan* 699
129. A New Method of Wage Distribution, *Virginia M. Crawford* 704
130. Co-operation a Partial Solvent of Capitalism, *John A. Ryan* 715
131. The Ethics of Strikes, *Joseph J. Ayd* 735

VII. Society

132. Society, *Charles Macksey* 743
133. The Theory of Hobbes, *Michael Cronin* 756
134. Rousseau's Social Contract, *Charles Macksey* 759
135. Marriage, *John A. Ryan* 763
136. The Principles of the Marriage Bond, *Charles Macksey* 777
137. The Evils That Flow from Divorce, *Pope Leo XIII* 778

TABLE OF CONTENTS

138. Divorce, *Joint Pastoral of the Archbishops and Bishops of the United States, 1919* 779
139. Divorce Legislation in the United States, *John A. Ryan* 780
140. Woman's Influence, *Joint Pastoral of the Archbishops and Bishops of the United States, 1919* 788
141. Woman in Society, *John L. Spalding* 789
142. One Moral Law for Men and Women, *Margaret Fletcher* 792
143. The Attitude of the Church Toward Women, *Margaret Fletcher* 793
144. Equal Rights Amendment, *National Council of Catholic Women* 794
145. The Indispensability of the Ascetic Ideal, *F. W. Foerster* 796
146. Celibacy, *C. Kegan Paul* 820
147. Birth Control, *John M. Cooper* 822
148. The Essential Fallacies of Malthusian Teaching, *Halliday G. Sutherland* 827
149. Duties Resulting from the Marriage Relation, *Rene L. Holaind* 841
150. The Duty of Caring for the Child, *Michael Cronin* .. 845
151. Discussion of the Rights of the State to Educate, *James A. Burns* 848
152. The Catholic Attitude on Education, *Joint Pastoral of the Archbishops and Bishops of the United States, 1919* 849
153. The Right to Educate, *Victor Cathrein* 855
154. The State and Education, *Michael Cronin* 856
155. Rights and Duties Regarding Education, *James Conway* 860
156. The State's Power to Regulate Education, ... 870
157. The Educational Fact, *Timothy Brosnahan* 871

VIII. STATE

158. The Christian Home, *Cardinal Gibbons* 887
159. The Origin and Rights of Sovereignty, *Charles Macksey* 895
160. The Moral Origin of Civil Authority, *Cardinal Billot* 900
161. Political Theories of Saint Thomas, *Leo F. Hughes* . 905
162. The Democracy of Saint Thomas, *Alfred O'Rahilly* ... 913
163. Suarez and Democracy, *Alfred O'Rahilly* 925
164. The Right of Self-Government, *John A. Ryan* 933
165. The Sovereignty of the People, *Alfred O'Rahilly* ... 944
166. The Best State, *Michael Cronin* 971
167. Patriotism, *Thomas Slater* 974

168.	Practical Patriotism, *William Turner*.............	978
169.	Legislators, *Rene L. Holaind*....................	983
170.	The Functions of Government, *Woodrow Wilson*	987
171.	The Duties of the Citizen, *John A. Ryan*	987
172.	Woman Suffrage, *J. W. Dawson*..................	1002
173.	International Law, *Walter George Smith*..........	1010
174.	International Law, *Timothy Brosnahan*............	1015
175.	The Law of Nations, *Alfred O'Rahilly*............	1016
176.	War, *Charles Macksey*...........................	1032
177.	War, *Alfred O'Rahilly*...........................	1044
178.	Air-Raids, the Sinking of Merchant Vessels, and Reprisals, *Michael Cronin*......................	1053
179.	The Bombardment of Towns and Reprisals, *Walter McDonald*	1055
180.	International Relations, *Joint Pastoral of the Archbishops and Bishops of the United States, 1919*....	1059
181.	International Peace, *John A. Ryan*................	1062
182.	Efforts Towards Peace, *Charles Plater*.............	1070

ACKNOWLEDGMENT

The compiler wishes to acknowledge indebtedness to the authors whose works have enriched the following pages. To the various publishers thanks are rendered for courteous permission to use the excerpts. Sincere gratitude is due to Reverend John H. Fasy, S. J., of Fordham University, to Reverend John A. Ryan, D. D., of the Catholic University, and to Reverend John M. Cooper, D. D., of the Catholic University, for valuable suggestions and generous help.

J. F. L.

Washington, D. C.
June 19, 1926

ACKNOWLEDGMENT

The compiler wishes to acknowledge indebtedness to the authors whose names have enriched the following pages. To the various publishers thanks are tendered for courteous permission to use the excerpts. Thanks particularly are due to Reverend John H. Fasy, S. J., for hand corrections, to Reverend John K. Ryan, Ph.D., of the Catholic University, and to Reverend John M. Cooper, D. D., of the Catholic University, for valuable suggestions and generous help.

F. F. K.

Washington, D. C.
June 15, 1926.

PART ONE
GENERAL ETHICS

INTRODUCTION

Good is the aim of every action

∴ The aim of a subordinate act is subserviant to the aim of its principal

∴ There must be one great principal aim: the "supreme good."

∴ The "supreme good" must be the aim of all our actions.

1

THE PURPOSE OF ETHICS

ARISTOTLE [1]

Every art, and every scientific inquiry, and similarly every action and purpose, may be said to aim at some good. Hence the good has been well defined as that at which all things aim. But it is clear that there is a difference in the ends; for the ends are sometimes activities, and sometimes results beyond the mere activities. Also, where there are certain ends beyond the actions, the results are naturally superior to the activities.

As there are various actions, arts, and sciences, it follows that the ends are also various. Thus health is the end of medicine, a vessel of shipbuilding, victory of strategy, and wealth of domestic economy. It often happens that there are a number of such arts or sciences which fall under a single faculty, as the art of making bridles, and all such other arts as make the instruments of horsemanship, under horsemanship, and this again as well as every military action under strategy, and in the same way other arts or sciences under other faculties. But in all these cases the ends of the architectonic arts or sciences, whatever they may be, are more desirable than those of the subordinate arts or sciences, as it is for the sake of the former that the latter are themselves sought after. It makes no difference to the argument whether the activities themselves are the ends of the actions, or something else beyond the activities as in the above mentioned sciences.

If it is true that in the sphere of action there is an end which we wish for its own sake, and for the sake of which we wish everything else, and that we do not desire all things for the sake of something else (for, if that is so, the process

---

[1] *The Nicomachean Ethics of Aristotle*; translated by J. E. C. Welldon, M. A. (Macmillan and Company, London.)

will go on *ad infinitum,* and our desire will be idle and futile), it is clear that this will be the good or the supreme good. Does it not follow then that the knowledge of this supreme good is of great importance for the conduct of life, and that, *if we know it,* we shall be like archers who have a mark at which to aim, we shall have a better chance of attaining what we want? But, if this is the case, we must endeavor to comprehend, at least in outline, its nature, and the science or faculty to which it belongs.

It would seem that this is the most authoritative or architectonic science or faculty, and such is evidently the political; for it is the political science or faculty which determines what sciences are necessary in states, and what kind of sciences should be learnt, and how far they should be learnt by particular people. We perceive, too, that the faculties which are held in the highest esteem, e. g., strategy, domestic economy and rhetoric, are subordinate to it. But as it makes use of the other practical sciences, and also legislates upon the things to be done and the things to be left undone, it follows that its end will comprehend the ends of all the other sciences, and will therefore be the true good of mankind. For although the good of an individual is identical with the good of a state, yet the good of the state, whether in attainment or in preservation, is evidently greater and more perfect. For while in an individual by himself it is something to be thankful for, it is nobler and more divine in a nation or state.[2]

These then are the objects at which the present inquiry aims, and it is in a sense a political inquiry. But our statement of the case will be adequate, if it be made with all such clearness as the subject matter admits; for it would be as wrong to expect the same degree of accuracy in all reasonings as in all manufactures. Things noble and just, which are the subjects of investigations in political science, exhibit so great a diversity and uncertainty that they are sometimes thought to have only a conventional, and not a natural existence. There is the same sort of uncertainty

---

[2] According to Aristotle, ethics is but a part of politics, or social science. Aristotle never speaks of ethics as a separate science, but only of "the study of character," or "our discussions of character". His politics are ethical, and his ethics political or social. —*Editor's note.*

in regard to good things, as it often happens that injuries result from them; thus there have been cases in which people were ruined by wealth, or again by courage. As our subjects then and our premises are of this nature, we must be content to indicate the truth roughly and in outline; and as our subjects and premises are true generally *but not universally*, we must be content to arrive at conclusions which are only generally true. It is right to receive the particular statements which are made in the same spirit; for an educated person will expect accuracy in each subject only so far as the nature of the subject allows; he might as well accept probable reasoning from a mathematician as require demonstrative proofs from a rhetorician. But everybody is competent to judge the subjects which he understands, and is a good judge of them. It follows that in particular subjects it is a person of *special* education, and in general a person of universal education, who is a good judge. Hence the young are not proper students of political science, as they have no experience of the actions of life which form the premises and subjects of the reasonings. Also it may be added that from their tendency to follow their emotions they will not study the subject to any purpose or profit, as its end is not knowledge but action. It makes no difference whether a person is young in years or youthful in character; for the defect *of which I speak* is not one of time but is due to the emotional character of his life and pursuits. Knowledge is as useless to such a person as it is to an intemperate person. But where the desires and actions of people are regulated by reason the knowledge of these subjects will be extremely valuable.

2

DEFINITION AND SCOPE OF ETHICS

Victor Cathrein[1]

Many writers regard ethics as any scientific treatment of the moral order and divide it into theological, or Christian, ethics (moral theology) and philosophical ethics (moral philosophy). What is usually understood by ethics, how-

---

[1] *Catholic Encyclopedia,* vol. v, pp. 556.

ever, is philosophical ethics, or moral philosophy, and in this sense the present article will treat the subject. Moral philosophy is a division of practical philosophy. Theoretical, or speculative philosophy has to do with being, or with the order of things not dependent upon reason, and its object is to attain by the natural light of reason a knowledge of this order in its ultimate causes. Practical philosophy, on the other hand, concerns itself with what *ought to be,* or with the order of acts which are human, and which, therefore, depend upon our reason. It is also divided into logic and ethics. The former rightly orders the intellectual activities and teaches the proper method in the acquirement of truth, while the latter directs the activities of the will; the object of the former is the true; that of the latter, the good. Hence ethics may be defined as the science of the moral rectitude of human acts in accordance with the first principles of natural reason. Logic and ethics are normative and practical sciences because they prescribe norms or rules for human activities, and show how, according to these norms, a man ought to direct his actions. Ethics is pre-eminently practical and directive; for it orders the activities of the will, and the latter it is which sets all the other faculties of man in motion. Hence to order the will is the same as to order the whole man. Moreover, ethics not only directs a man how to act if he wishes to be morally good, but sets before him the absolute obligation he is under of doing good and avoiding evil.

A distinction must be made between ethics and morals, or morality. Every people, even the most uncivilized and uncultured, has its own morality or sum of prescriptions which govern its moral conduct. Nature has so provided that each man establishes for himself a code of moral concepts and principles which are applicable to the details of practical life, without the necessity of awaiting the conclusions of science. Ethics is the scientific or philosophical treatment of morality. The subject-matter proper of ethics is the deliberate, free actions of man; for these alone are in our power, and concerning these alone can rules be prescribed, not concerning those actions which are performed without deliberation, or through ignorance or coercion. Besides this, the scope of ethics includes whatever has reference to free human acts, whether as principle or cause of action (law, conscience, virtue), or as effect or circumstance of action (merit, punishment, etc.). The particular aspect (formal aspect) under which ethics considers free acts is that of their moral goodness or the rectitude of order involved in them as human acts. A man may be a good artist or orator and at the same time a morally bad man, or, conversely, a morally good man and a poor artist or technician. Ethics has merely to do with the order which relates to man as man, and which makes of him a morally good man.

Like ethics, moral theology also deals with the moral actions of man; but unlike ethics, it has its origin in supernaturally revealed truth. It presupposes man's elevation to the supernatural order, and, though it avails itself of the scientific conclusions of ethics, it draws its knowledge for the most part from Christian Revelation. Ethics is distinguished from the other natural sciences which deal with moral conduct of man, as jurisprudence and pedagogy, in this, that the latter do not ascend to first principles, but borrow their fundamental notions from ethics, and are, therefore, subordinate to it. To investigate what constitutes good or bad, just or unjust, what is virtue, law, conscience, duty, etc., what obligations are common to all men, does not lie within the scope of jurisprudence or pedagogy, but of ethics; and yet these notions and principles must be presupposed by the former, must serve them as a groundwork and guide; hence they are subordinated to ethics. The same is true of political economy. The latter is indeed immediately concerned with man's social activity, inasmuch as it treats of the production, distribution, and consumption of material commodities, but this activity is not independent of ethics; industrial life must develop in accordance with the moral law and must be dominated by justice, equity, and love. Political economy was wholly wrong in trying to emancipate itself from the requirements of ethics. Sociology is at the present day considered by many as a science distinct from ethics. If, however, by sociology is meant a philosophical treatment of society, it is a division of ethics; for the inquiry into the nature of society in general, into the origin, nature, object, and purpose of natural societies (the family, the state) and their relations to one another forms an essential part of ethics. If, on the other hand, sociology be regarded as the aggregate of the sciences which have reference to the social life of man, it is not a single science, but a complexus of sciences; and among these, so far as the natural order is concerned, ethics has the first claim.

3

THE NECESSITY OF ETHICS

Vincent McNabb[1]

For the purpose of stimulating thought on a subject worthy of our thinking let me set down some detached ideas:

Philosophy is largely in ill odor because it has ceased to be Ethics and has become Metaphysics.

In the classical days of Grecian philosophy the dominant subjects were Logic and Ethics; indeed there were no other subjects in the higher ways of thought.

Logic was a science that put order into a man's mental activity. Ethics was a science that put order into a man's moral activity. Logic had sway over the mind; Ethics over the will. Grecian education was based on liberal schooling in these two noble sciences; and gave us many masters of sublime thought and noble wisdom.

But nowadays the science of Ethics has largely disappeared from the Schools. Its place has been taken by Metaphysics. Even Logic has outgrown itself. Far from being what it once was, to wit, a practical science or art that put order into a man's thoughts, it has become but an outwork of subtle Metaphysics, only calculated to put disorder into a man's thoughts.

Practical Logic might still be sought and taught by many in the Universities if only it was practical. But it has become so abstruse that its chief achievement is to discourage thinking.

In the olden days just as men began blacksmithing by learning the processes of blacksmithing, so they began the craft of thinking by learning in outline the processes of

[1] *From a Friar's Cell*, pp. 159-167. (P. J. Kenedy and Sons, New York.)

thinking. Of late, however, these processes have become so subtle that logic instead of being suited to introduce thought is almost more calculated to stifle thought. The scientific way of teaching smithing is to make the student know the processes say of wielding a hammer, beating a rivet, fashioning a horseshoe. If the university methods were to obtain, the would-be smith would spend several years studying the chemistry of the hammer and rivet and the natural history of the horse!

The strange fate that has befallen Logic has also befallen Ethics; but has befallen it in another way. Logic is now largely ignored because it has been taught too much; Ethics, because it has been taught too little. Even such a book as Green's *Prolegomena to Ethics,* whilst seeming to weaken this statement, really strengthens it. The fault of this *Prolegomena to Ethics,* as the author would be the first to admit, is that there is too much Prolegomena and too little Ethics. If one may use a "bull," it is not Ethics, but the Metaphysics of Ethics.

Add to this that for the most part Ethics has been handed over to the care of the theologians. It has become "moral theology." In consequence, the ordinary university student does not feel called to supplement his over-stocked syllabus with a course in theology!

Again Ethics has provided so many sites for disagreement that it has become embittered with controversy. It has almost become the "Apologetics of Ethics," and a science is *in extremis* when it has become Apologetics.

Yet this lack of Ethics is a serious want in all liberal or university education. The chief schools in a modern university are Theology, Medicine, Law, and (for want of a better name I shall call) Pedagogy. It need not be urged, for it goes without saying that Ethics is of supreme importance for the theologian. Yet it is hardly of less importance for the doctor, lawyer, teacher. Nowadays it is the moral aspects of medical science that are of supreme importance. Doctors are already crossing the frontiers of their medical science into Ethics, with little or no ethical training.

Lawyers, too, are drafting and interpreting laws with little or no reference to the eternal laws of Ethics.

Speaking accurately, Ethics is not a science, nor yet an art, but a life. There is a "Science of Ethics." This necessarily is a science, but the essential Ethics is a life.

To explain. A science is what the Scholastics call an intellectual habit. The nature of intellectual habits has not yet been sufficiently analyzed, that we may venture on any lengthy explanation. But it may be good enough to say that an intellectual habit like the science of algebra, geology, botany, history, consists in a number of accurate facts, a number of general principles, and a certain intellectual power and ease in seeing facts in principles and principles in facts.

An art is different. Whilst it includes certain intellectual habits, it requires certain qualities of mind or hand which are creative. Thus the art of the painter is not merely an intellectual knowledge of the principles and technique of painting, but an intellectual power of conceiving pictures and a hand power of carrying out the pictures conceived.

But Ethics is something still more than a science or an art. It is not mere organized knowledge, though it is accompanied by organized knowledge. It is not a mere eye and hand power to make external things or carry out practical ideas. It is above all a practical power for controlling the human will for good or evil in all matters where the human will may enter for good or evil. Its aim is not to make good scientific judgments or to make good artistic products but to make good men. Ethics then differs from art inasmuch as its product is not an external thing but an internal state; and from science, inasmuch as this internal state is not a faithful copy of some external thing but, as it were, a definite attitude toward things for good or evil.

To those who have grasped these truths, what has been said will probably be clear; to those who have not grasped these truths, what has been said will be almost unintelligible. Yet the obscurity is but a proof of the thesis which these words are aimed at developing. For it is evident that the seat of science is the intelligence and the seat of Ethics is the will. It need hardly be proved that the intelligence is not the will; their processes are not identical. Moreover, one process of intelligence is not identical with another. Ratiocination or reasoning is not like intuition; the secondary is not like the primary.

Hence just as it is never quite satisfactory to express the greater in terms of the less or the primary in terms of the secondary, so it can not be satisfactory to express processes of the will in terms of the processes of the intelligence. Neither intuitions nor desires act syllogistically.

If, then, Ethics is essentially and primarily a quality of the will, and, as we have called it, a life, it is not fully expressed in terms of a science. We do not deny that there is a science of Ethics; though we deny that Ethics is essentially and primarily a science. But we urge that even as a science, and especially as a life, it differs very materially from all essential sciences.

Thus it is futile to attempt to prove by reasoning the validity of our intuitions; for the very fact that our reasons rest on the validity of our intuitions. Reason can show only that the arguments against the validity of the intuitions are "Not proven;" and can protest that if this validity of intuitions is not assumed, reason itself can make no headway.

In the same way it would seem futile to attempt to prove the validity of our ethical intuitions, or, as to be more accurate, our moral instincts. No science proves its principles; all that it can do is to verify its principles.

No merely intellectual process, and especially no mere ratiocinative process is adequate to a moral or ethical activity. Ethical principles must not be merely thought about and reasoned about; they must be lived. Indeed, these principles have received a more vital evolution in the heart of some ploughman who lives them without knowing them than in the mind of some philosopher who knows them without living them.

This was the final fault of Greece, that it made Ethics a science and not a life. In the end it died, not for want of knowledge, but for want of life. As we sometimes say of the dead, "His mind was clear up to the last." Had thought been life, Greece would never have known the tomb.

In modern times there is much arguing about Ethics. People hotly dispute about the Decalogue. The discussion is heartening inasmuch as it betokens interest; but it is disheartening inasmuch as it is discussion and reasoning. It seems to be quietly assumed by the men on the right and the wrong side of the discussion that it is quite relevant to argue about Ethics. This assumption is probably an immense error and, therefore, an immense crime.

For example. Hot discussions rage about the simple commandment "Thou shalt not commit adultery," with its implicit restraint on other sexual indulgences. Few monthly magazines of the weightier sort lack monthly articles showing by many cogent reasons that this commandment is antiquated; and that having been adapted to an earlier stage of civilization it is unfitted for to-day.

By such a writer and by the ordinary writer of an answering article it is assumed that we can prove the validity or invalidity of these ethical intuitions. But, as we have said before, the ethical intuitions are not patient of rational proof or disproof. If a writer attempts to prove that the doctrine of the Trinity is absurd, our apologetic does not take the form of attempting to prove the Trinity, for we know that it can not be proved. It can be believed only on its being declared by competent authority.

Though reason has not the power to prove or disprove the intuitions or principles of Ethics, reason has (1) protective and (2) explanatory duties toward Ethics. It must (1) protect Ethics against the attacks of reason. Arguments seemingly powerful against ethical principles must be shown to be a mere seeming. Reason must be sent in pursuit of reason. Again and again it will turn out that the very arguments used to deny our ethical instincts turn out to their help.

(2) Reason must explain Ethics: in other words, reason must state Ethics in terms of reason in order to reconcile reason; just as a man must explain his wares in Chinese if he wants to barter them with the Chinese.

How futile, then, seem the many attempts to give a logical, that is, a ratiocinative evolution of Ethics. Yet it is being attempted day after day. Now one thinker, and now another, attempts to evolve Ethics from some one principle. The assumption of such an attempt is an original fallacy. This is all the more patent when the attempted activity starts from and rests upon an intellectual activity such as consciousness. Assuredly, as St. Thomas accurately puts it, the intellect moves the will "specificative;" and the will moves the intellect "effective." These truths are simple in their truth. But it is a constructive fallacy to assume that, granted such an intellectual concept as "consciousness," one can evolve the "Science of Ethics."

Such an evolution of Ethics would have as much relation to reality as the mathematical and mechanical thinking of the Utilitarians had with Political Economy. Their thoughts were a paper science; Political Economy is the life of flesh and blood.

4

THE GOLDEN MEAN IN PHILOSOPHY

Charles Stanton Devas[1]

Indeed in philosophy as elsewhere it is ever the golden mean proclaimed by the genuine voice of Christianity. The claims of explicit reasoning, of criticism and argumentation, are not rejected, only put in their proper place as part of a whole, an assistant towards attaining the truth and an excellent negative test, but not the supreme teacher. We must recognize that faith and tradition and unconscious inference are also our informants; that we are not self-sufficing in regard to knowledge, but must cling to others, accept their witness and authority, admit in many things the *consensus humani generis,* nay that the *vox populi* is the *vox Dei,* or perish in our willful individualism. But then testimony is not everything; and if rationalism is an exaggeration on one side, so is traditionalism on the other. To say we can adequately express in words all valid inferences, is to fall from our middle way, as though there were not many of the most valuable of them and most practical, nay the very principles of reason and morality, too subtle or too obscure or too complex for statement. But we fall equally on a different side, if we scoff at logic, deny the validity of words, or the use of definitions, and reduce science, sacred and profane alike, to a condition of mist.

Similarly the Church keeps the golden mean between the materialism that will not recognize the higher and spiritual side of man, and a miscalled idealism that is so enamored of the higher side as to ignore the reality of the lower;

[1] *The Key to the World's Progress,* pp. 76-80. (Joseph F. Wagner, New York.)

she will not allow the crude realism (like that of Tertullian) which confuses the corporal with the real; nor again the nominalism which transmutes all super-sensual things into mental products, merely distinguished by the name; rather she chooses the middle course and unites a true idealism with a true realism. Indeed, from the time of St. Augustine, the central figure in history, who was the heir of all ancient wisdom, the starting point of all new, the Church has handed down with unbroken continuity a *philosophia perennis*, ever growing more comprehensive and gaining force from every controversy, those yielding perhaps the greatest contribution who have been in appearance, from Porphyry to Kant, her greatest opponents.

And thus we must expect an intellectual conflict between the Church and the world. The intellectual position known as the spirit of the age (*der Zeitgeist*) incessantly varying with the age, displays amid many variables one constant character of opposition to the Church. This is to be expected, because contemporary science and the fashions of the day are inevitably defective and distorted; not wholly wrong, but mingling together extravagance and good sense, and presenting a teaching that can not claim our assent till the dross be separated from the gold. This is done by degrees, and then, after having molded, leveled, checked, and corrected the new ways of science or life, the Church adopts in tranquility and assimilates what at last has been proved to be sound theory and wholesome practice. Only this tardy Concordat is no bar to a similar conflict beginning over again. We smile now at the thought that the study of Greek literature, and Homer in particular, could seriously imperil the Christian faith; we are in no danger of being so impressed by the majestic structure of the Roman law as to think it an oracle of heaven and give the name of priests to its lawyers; we no longer hold it of vital importance to eschew Gothic barbarism, to write Ciceronian Latin, and to conform our lives to an imaginary picture of Roman or Greek civilization; we are little touched by the eighteenth century repugnance to enthusiasm; indeed, think little worth having that fails to enkindle it; even the ideals of our own fathers set forth in the political and economic liberalism of barely fifty years ago, appear to us empty and unreal; yet in the fourth century, in the twelfth, in the fifteenth, in the eighteenth, in the nineteenth, the Church had to face these overmastering views of learning and living, and mold them to her purposes. And are we to expect our own time to be without its favorite notions, its shibboleths, its presuppositions, its exaggerations, its distortion of the relative magnitudes of truths and duties? The more completely we are the children of our own age the more behind the age will the Church appear; yet might equally be called before the age, which is but a transitory phase of human thought and imagination encompassed by a more than human society that is eternal.

How pitiable, then, the lack of knowledge, how gross the self-deception of those who take occasion of this chronic discord between the Church and the world to make shipwreck of their faith. Instead of possessing their souls in peace, instead of knowing when it is the time to wait and be silent, they press forward sword in hand for an instant solution, demand an immediate triumph, cannot suffer with Christ or endure the appearance of uncertainty and defeat. And as the Church fails to support them, they must needs reform the Church, who in her essence is irreformable; and forgetting that the first reform must be within themselves, they raise, all laden with their infirmities, the standard of revolt; and because they cannot see the immediate solution of some antinomy, they leave the realm of tempered light for the realm that is forever darkened by irreconcilable contradictions.

5

METHODS OF ETHICS

Michael Cronin [1]

The methods employed by various ethicians in the development of this science may be conveniently reduced to three. First, methods are either intuitive or inferential—that is, moral truths are either represented as known di-

---

[1] *The Science of Ethics,* pp. 14-23. (Benziger Brothers, New York City.)
The edition of *The Science of Ethics,* by Michael Cronin, used throughout this book is Vol. I, 1909; Vol. II, 1917.—*Editor.*

rectly and immediately without reasoning, or they are represented as knowable through reasoning alone. Secondly, the inferential method is either one of induction or of deduction—that is, the ethician either starts from experience and builds up the general moral proposition, from particular truths, or he represents particular moral truths as deducible from the more general self-evident moral principles. Speaking broadly then, the methods recognized by different ethicians are the intuitive, the inductive or *à posteriori,* and the deductive or *à priori.*

The intuitive method represents moral truths as knowable immediately by direct perception. Now, in general, there are possible two modes of intuition—intuition by sense and intuition by intellect. Accordingly, intuitional moralists may be divided broadly into two classes—those who attribute the knowledge of moral truths to a sense which they call the moral sense, and those who attribute it to intellect. To the former class belong Reid, Shaftesbury and Hutcheson, to the latter, the Intellectual moralists Cudworth and Clarke. Again, the "moral sense" theory is a theory either of an "inner" sense or of an "outer." An "inner" sense, it is claimed, discovers the moral law within a man himself by introspection. In this way Hume may be regarded as a sense intuitionist. The moral sense as "outer" is represented as sensible to the morality of other men's acts as well as of our own, and as such its action is said to be akin to that of our other ordinary outer senses.

It is not so easy to mark off the various methods of "intellectual" Intuitionism. In one way even the defenders of the inferential method are all, to some extent, Intellectual Intuitionists, for they insist that the process of reasoning must begin with intuition of some kind, that we cannot reason back *in infinitum.* Indeed, every moralist recognizes the need of intuition at some stage or other in the determination of moral truths. But between the inferential theory and the theory of the "Intellectual Moralists" we may at least draw a distinction of degree, as regards the number of intuitions they each admit. Intuitional Moralists as a rule regard all the general moral principles, or at least those simpler truths which all civilized men know of, like "justice is to be done," "drunkenness to be avoided," "the truth to be told," "superiors to be obeyed," as judgments of intuition. Those who follow the inferential method insist that the great body of these same moral principles, including the many principles which are generally accepted by civilized men, need to be proved; but they admit that we must fall back somewhere in our reasoning on self-evident truths. This second class of writers are not usually described as intuitionists.

The *à posteriori or inductive method* may be defined in a general way as that method which bases the general principles of moral science, if not exclusively, at least mainly on experience. It is the method adopted, for instance—(1) by the hedonists and utilitarians, for whom moral good and evil are determined by the pleasurable and painful consequences of acts, pleasure and pain being plainly matters of experience. (2) By evolutionists, in so far as they lay claim to discover the moral law in the general line of development that may be observed in the past history of men and things. This also is an appeal to experience. (3) It is used by all who discover the moral laws by comparison of the various types of character and sentiment that have come prominently before the world in the course of history, and that have aided its progress. As so employed, it is sometimes known as the historic method; but this kind of historic method must be carefully distinguished from (4) the *historic* method proper (also a method of empiricism), which bases moral judgments on the examination of the development of history as a whole, and not on the accidental appearance of individual types.

We find some difficulty in bringing the various forms of this historic method under one formula or principle, so different and apparently so opposed are the accounts that are given of it by different ethical writers of the historical school. Thus some, like M. Levy Bruhl, regard the historic method as purely positivistic and descriptive. They maintain that it is the business of ethics to give the history of human customs and of the moral views of different nations as expressed in these customs; also, to discover from an examination of these views and customs the law that has regulated their occurrence and succession. They also expressly declare that all these customs and views, though opposed to one another, *are equally natural and true,* since they are all necessary stages in the evolution of mind and of society. On the other hand, some, like Professor Wundt, who often speaks of ethics as the study of the "social historic phenomena" and describes the historic method as the right method of ethics, would seem to imply that the object of ethics is not merely to correlate the customs of nations and discover the law of their succession, but to distinguish what is natural and good in them and in law from what is unnatural and bad. Wundt, for instance, suggests a distinction between valid and invalid moral law when he speaks of the "universally valid contents of morality," and between "natural" and "unnatural" when he describes the moral laws as founded on "uniformity in human nature," or on "certain moral impulses which are in essence always and everywhere the same"; and he even gives as one characteristic of the moral laws (and, therefore, of course, as a criterion by which they are to be distinguished from immoral laws) the fact that the former kind afford "enduring satisfaction."

These, we say, are seeming differences between the forms of the historic method adopted by M. Levy Bruhl and Professor Wundt and their respective schools. Yet, though seemingly so different in their purpose and suppositions, these methods, we claim, are fundamentally one and the same, for they depend both upon a view of morals which so many evolutionists maintain and defend—namely, that there is no *à priori* rightness and wrongness, that distinctions of right and wrong do not exist outside the customs and views of different peoples, that the moral law, in so far as such a thing exists at all, is discoverable not by reasoning but by the study of the views and customs of nations, and that all views of "good" and "evil" that have gained anything like wide acceptance are necessarily right and true even though our reason cannot prove them.

At this point it will be well to call the reader's attention to one particular form of the inductive method, a form to which, we may say at once, we shall rigorously refuse a place in this science—namely, the method of "induction through moral instances," or the establishment of general moral truths through particular cases of the general truth. An example of this method would be the establishment of the general proposition "all lies are bad" by finding that this, that and the other lie were bad, or that "murder is bad" because the murder of this, that and the other man was bad. This method, as we have said, cannot be admitted into ethics. We do not know that the lie in general is bad on the ground that many particular lies are bad. On the contrary, we can only know that a particular lie is bad through knowing that the lie of its nature, and therefore of itself and in general, is bad. Induction through instances has an undoubted value in the physical sciences, for the physical sciences are concerned solely with objects and qualities that fall under the senses. We see, for instance, with our eyes that this and that piece of gold are yellow, and thus we can argue from many single instances to the general proposition that "gold is yellow." But such a form of argument is quite inapplicable in Morals. For, individual lies are not labelled "good" or "bad." We have to discover their moral quality by the use of reasoning, and in establishing their moral quality we argue on the strength of premisses that are quite of general application.

The *à priori method.*—The deductive or *à priori* method is that which deduces all moral truths from certain broad moral principles that have either the force of analytic judgments themselves or may be reduced to judgments that are analytic. As there are schools of ethics that adopt only the *à posteriori* method, so there are ethical schools that adopt the *à priori* method exclusively, and make no appeal, or at least aim at making no appeal whatsoever to experience in the building up of their science.

The following are instances of the *à priori* ethical method: (a) The geometric method of Spinoza, in which proposition is drawn from proposition exactly as in Euclid, without any appeal to experience, or any admixture of probable reasoning—the last conclusions being, it is contended, quite as certain as the axioms from which they are drawn, whatever be the number of intervening propositions; (b) the transcendental or abstract *à priori* method, in which all moral truths are deduced from some *one* original speculative truth, such as "I find myself willing" (Fichte), or "I am free" (Hegel), which one proposition, it is contended in each case, is just the abstract expression of the whole moral order, the manifold laws of which are derived from the first principle by pure *à priori* reason alone; (c) the Ideal *à priori* method of Plato in his "Laws," and of More in his

"Utopia," in which conduct is regulated not by what is good and obligatory for real men, but by an abstract ideal of what is best or might be best for us under conditions that are superhuman. . . .

As the present work proceeds and the moral laws and their many applications come before us for consideration, it ought to become plain to the reader that the method of ethics is a mixed one, that it is partly *à priori* or deductive, and partly empirical. Ethics is primarily and in the main a *deductive* science, that is, it is a science in which the morality of particular acts is deduced from general moral propositions. For ethics is a practical science, and therefore its aim is to direct men aright in the concrete circumstances of real life. Hence the primary and essential method of ethics will be that by which our reason determines the individual duty in individual circumstances. Now, in order to determine the morality of any particular act, it is necessary to bring together certain general moral principles such as will suit the circumstances of the act in question, and from a consideration of those principles we are able to determine deductively the individual duty. Hence the method of ethics is primarily and in the main deductive.

But it is in the establishment of the general principles themselves that reason has to fall back to a large extent on experience. For we can only establish the general moral laws by a consideration of the natural human appetites and their objects, and this latter it is evident is largely a matter of experience. We must, therefore, acknowledge that experience is a necessary part of the method of ethics. Thus we know that society is a natural necessity, because we know that there is in man a natural appetite for society and for certain things that can only be achieved in society, and because, allied to the natural appetite for society, there is also a special natural faculty—namely, speech—which has no other natural purpose than the attainment of certain social ends. Now, the discrimination of these faculties and their objects is the work to a large extent of experience, and, therefore, experience is a necessary factor in the establishment of the general moral principles. We should mention, however, that this experimental factor which plays so important a part in the determination of the general moral principles is no bar to the certitude required of the science of ethics. For the experience that we suppose in ethics is no narrow experience, but one so broad and universal that there can be no error nor risk of error in following it. The method, therefore, of ethics is in the main deductive. But it presupposes experience, for in the establishment of its general principles it must rely upon experience.

6

HISTORY OF ETHICS

Victor Cathrein [1]

The history of ethics is concerned solely with the various philosophical systems which in the course of time have been elaborated with reference to the moral order. Hence the opinions advanced by the wise men of antiquity, such as Pythagoras (582-500 B. C.), Heraclius (535-475 B. C.), Confucius (558-479 B. C.), scarcely belong to the history of ethics; for though they proposed various moral truths and principles, they did so in a dogmatic and didactic, and not in a philosophically systematic manner. Ethics properly so called is first met with among the Greeks, i. e., in the teaching of Socrates (470-399 B. C.). According to him, the ultimate object of human activity is happiness, and the necessary means to reach it, virtue. Since everybody necessarily seeks happiness, no one is deliberately corrupt. All evil arises from ignorance, and the virtues are one and all but so many kinds of prudence. Virtue can, therefore, be imparted by instruction. The disciple of Socrates, Plato (427-347 B. C.), declares that the *summum bonum* consists in the perfect imitation of God, the Absolute Good, an imitation which cannot be fully realized in this life. Virtue enables a man to order his conduct, as he properly should, according to the dictates of reason, and acting thus he becomes like unto God. But Plato differed from Socrates in that he did not consider virtue to consist in wisdom alone, but in justice, temperance, and fortitude as well, these constituting the proper harmony of man's activities. In a sense, the State is man writ large, and its function is to

[1] *Catholic Encyclopedia*, Vol. V, pp. 557-561.

train its citizens in virtue. For his ideal State he proposed the community of goods and of wives and the public education of children. Though Socrates and Plato had been to the fore in this mighty work and had contributed much valuable material to the upbuilding of ethics; nevertheless, Plato's illustrious disciple, Aristotle (384-322 B. C.), must be considered the real founder of systematic ethics. With characteristic keenness he solved, in his ethical and political writings, most of the problems with which ethics concerns itself. Unlike Plato, who began with ideas, as the basis of his observations, Aristotle chose rather to take the facts of experience as his starting-point; these he analyzed accurately, and sought to trace to their highest and ultimate causes. He sets out from the fact that all men tend to happiness as the ultimate object of all their endeavors, as the highest good, which is sought for its own sake, and to which all other goods merely serve as means. This happiness cannot consist in external goods, but only in the activity proper to human nature—not indeed in such a lower activity of the vegetative and sensitive life as man possesses in common with plants and brutes, but in the highest and most perfect activity of his reason, which springs in turn from virtue. This activity, however, has to be exercised in a perfect and enduring life. The highest pleasure is naturally bound up with this activity, yet, to constitute perfect happiness, external goods must also supply their share. True happiness, though prepared for him by the gods as the object and the reward of virtue, can be attained only through a man's own individual exertion. With keen penetration Aristotle thereupon proceeds to investigate in turn each of the intellectual and moral virtues, and his treatment of them must, even at the present time, be regarded as in great part correct. The nature of the State and of the family were, in the main, rightly explained by him. The only pity is that his vision did not penetrate beyond this earthly life, and that he never saw clearly the relations of man to God.

A more hedonistic turn in ethics begins with Democritus (about 460-370 B. C.), who considers a perpetually joyous and cheerful disposition as the highest good and happiness of man. The means thereto is virtue, which makes us independent of external goods—so far as that is possible—and which wisely discriminates between the pleasures that are to be sought after and those that are to be shunned. Pure Sensualism or Hedonism was first taught by Aristippus of Cyrene (435-354 B. C.), according to whom the greatest possible pleasure, especially sensual pleasure, is the end and supreme good of human endeavor. Epicurus (341-270 B. C.) differs from Aristippus in holding that the largest sum total possible of spiritual and sensual enjoyments, with the greatest possible freedom from displeasure and pain, is man's highest good. Virtue is the proper directive norm in the attainment of this end.

The Cynics, Aristhenes (444-369 B. C.) and Diogenes of Sinope (414-324 B. C.), taught the direct contrary of Hedonism, namely, that virtue alone suffices for happiness, that pleasure is an evil, and that the truly wise man is above human laws. This teaching soon degenerated into haughty arrogance and open contempt for law and for the remainder of men (Cynicism). The Stoics, Zeno (336-264 B. C.), and his disciples, Cleanthes, Chrysippus, and others, strove to refine and perfect the views of Aristhenes. Virtue, in their opinion, consists in man's living according to the dictates of his rational nature, and, as each one's individual nature is but a part of the entire natural order, virtue is, therefore, the harmonious agreement with the Divine Reason, which shapes the whole course of nature. Whether they conceived this relation of God to the world in a pantheistic or a theistic sense, is not altogether clear. Virtue is to be sought for its own sake, and it suffices for man's happiness. All other things are indifferent and are, as circumstances require, to be striven after or shunned. The passions and affections are bad, and the wise man is independent of them. Among the Roman Stoics were Seneca (4 B. C. – A. D. 65), Epictetus (born about A. D. 50), and the Emperor Marcus Aurelius (A. D. 121-180), upon whom, however, at least upon the latter two, Christian influences had already begun to make themselves felt. Cicero (106-43 B. C.) elaborated no new philosophical system of his own, but chose those particular views from the various systems of Grecian philosophy which appeared best to him. He maintained that moral goodness, which is the general object of all virtues, consists in what is becoming to man as a rational being distinct from the brute.

Actions are often good or bad, just or unjust, not because of human institutions or customs, but of their own intrinsic nature. Above and beyond human laws, there is a natural law embracing all nations and all times, the expression of the rational will of the Most High God, from obedience to which no human authority can exempt us. Cicero gives an exhaustive exposition of the cardinal virtues and the obligations connected with them; he insists especially on devotion to the gods, without which human society could not exist.

Parallel with the above-mentioned Greek and Roman ethical systems runs a sceptical tendency, which rejects every natural moral law, bases the whole moral order on custom or human arbitrariness, and frees the wise man from subjection to the ordinary precepts of the moral order. This tendency was furthered by the Sophists, against whom Socrates and Plato arrayed themselves, and later on by Carneades, Theodore of Cyrene, and others.

A new epoch in ethics begins with the dawn of Christianity. Ancient paganism never had a clear and definite concept of the relation between God and the world, of the unity of the human race, of the destiny of man, of the nature and meaning of the moral law. Christianity first shed full light on these and similar questions. As St. Paul teaches (Rom. ii, 24 sq.), God has written His moral law in the hearts of all men, even of those outside the influence of Christian Revelation; this law manifests itself in the conscience of every man and is the norm according to which the whole human race will be judged on the day of reckoning. In consequence of their perverse inclinations, this law had to a great extent become obscured and distorted among the pagans; Christianity, however, restored it to its pristine integrity. Thus, too, ethics received its richest and most fruitful stimulus. Proper ethical methods were now unfolded, and philosophy was in a position to follow up and develop these methods by means supplied from its own store-house. This course was soon adopted in the early ages of the Church by the Fathers and ecclesiastical writers, as Justin Martyr, Irenaeus, Tertullian, Clement of Alexandria, Origen, but especially the illustrious Doctors of the Church, Ambrose, Jerome, and Augustine, who, in the exposition and defense of Christian truth, made use of the principles laid down by the pagan philosophers. True, the Fathers had no occasion to treat moral questions from a purely philosophical standpoint, and independently of Christian Revelation; but in the explanation of Catholic doctrine their discussions naturally led to philosophical investigations. This is particularly true of St. Augustine, who proceeded to thoroughly develop along philosophical lines and to establish firmly most of the truths of Christian morality. The eternal law (*lex aeterna*), the original type and source of all temporal laws, the natural law, conscience, the ultimate end of man, the cardinal virtues, sin, marriage, etc., were treated by him in the clearest and most penetrating manner. Hardly a single portion of ethics does he present to us but is enriched with his keen philosophical commentaries. Later ecclesiastical writers followed in his footsteps.

A sharper line of separation between philosophy and theology, and in particular between ethics and moral theology, is first met with in the works of the great Schoolmen of the Middle Ages, especially of Albert the Great (1193-1280), Thomas Aquinas (1225-1274), Bonaventure (1221-1274), and Duns Scotus (1274-1308). Philosophy, and, by means of it, theology reaped abundant fruit from the works of Aristotle, which had until then been a sealed treasure to Western civilization, and were first elucidated by the detailed and profound commentaries of Bl. Albert the Great and St. Thomas Aquinas, and pressed into the service of Christian philosophy. The same is particularly true as regards ethics. St. Thomas, in his commentaries on the political and ethical writings of the Stagirite, in his "Summa contra Gentiles" and his "Quaestiones disputatae," treated with his wonted clearness and penetration nearly the whole range of ethics in a purely philosophical manner, so that even to the present day his works are an inexhaustible source whence ethics draws its supply. On the foundations laid by him the Catholic philosophers and theologians of succeeding ages have continued to build. It is true that in the fourteenth and fifteenth centuries, thanks especially to the influence of the so-called Nominalists, a period of stagnation and decline in philosophy set in, but the sixteenth century is marked by a revival. Ethical questions also, though largely treated in connection with theology, are again made the subject of careful investigation. We mention as examples, the great theologians, Victoria, Dominicus Soto, L. Molina, Suarez, Lessius, and De Lugo. Since the sixteenth century special chairs of ethics (moral philosophy) have been erected in many Catholic universities. The larger, purely philosophical works on ethics, however, do not appear until the seventeenth and eighteenth centuries, as an example of which we may instance the production of Ign. Schwarz, "Institutiones juris universalis naturae et gentium" (1743).

Far different from Catholic ethical methods were those adopted by Protestants. With the rejection of the Church's teaching authority, each individual became on principle his own supreme teacher and arbiter in matters appertaining to faith and morals. True it is that the Reformers held fast to Holy Writ as the infallible source of revelation, but as to what belongs or does not belong to it, whether, and how far it is inspired, and what is its meaning—all this was left to the final decision of the individual. The inevitable result was that philosophy arrogantly threw to the winds all regard for revealed truth, and in many cases became involved in the most pernicious errors. Melanchthon, in his "Elementa philosophiae moralis," still clung to the Aristotelian philosophy; so, too, did Hugo Grotius, in his work, "De jure belli et pacis." But Cumberland and his follower, Samuel Pufendorf, set out along other devious paths in matters ethical, inasmuch as they identified moral goodness with the utilitarian interests of human society. Pufendorf, moreover, assumed with Descartes, that the ultimate ground for every distinction between good and evil lay in the free determination of God's will, a view which renders the philosophical treatment of ethics fundamentally impossible. Quite an influential factor in the development of ethics was Thomas Hobbes (1588-1679). He supposes that the human race originally existed in a rude condition (*status naturae*), in which every man was free to act as he pleased, and possessed a right to all things, whence arose a war of all against all. Lest destruction should be the result, it was decided to abandon this condition of nature and to found a state in which, by agreement, all were to be subject to one common will (one ruler). This authority ordains by the law of the State, what is to be considered by all as good and as evil, and only then does there arise a distinction between good and evil of universal binding force on all. The Pantheist Baruch Spinoza (1632-1677) considers the impulse to self-preservation as the foundation of virtue. Every being is endowed with the necessary impulse to assert itself, and, as reason demands nothing contrary to nature, it requires each one to follow this impulse and to strive after whatever is useful to him. And each individual possesses power and virtue just in so far as he obeys this impulse. Freedom of the will consists merely in the ability to follow unrestrainedly this natural impulse. Shaftesbury (1671-1713) bases ethics on the affections or inclinations of man. There are sympathetic, idiopathic, and unnatural inclinations. The first of these regard the common good, the second the private good of the agent, the third are opposed to the other two. To lead a morally good life, war must be waged upon the unnatural impulses, while the idiopathic and sympathetic inclinations must be made to harmonize. This harmony constitutes virtue. In the attainment of virtue the subjective guiding principle of knowledge is the "moral sense," a sort of moral instinct. This "moral sense" theory was further developed by Hutcheson (1694-1747); meanwhile, "common sense" was suggested by Thomas Reid (1710-1796) as the highest norm of moral conduct. In France the materialistic philosophers of the eighteenth century—as Helvetius, de la Mettrie, Holbach, Condillac, and others—disseminated the teachings of Sensualism and Hedonism as understood by Epicurus.

A complete revolution in ethics was introduced by Immanuel Kant (1724-1804). From the wreck of pure theoretical reason he turned for rescue to practical reason, in which he found an absolute, universal, and categorical moral law. This law is not to be conceived as an enactment of external authority, for this would be heteronomy, which is foreign to true morality; it is rather a law of our own reason, which is, therefore, autonomous, that is, it must be observed for its own sake, without regard to any pleasure or utility arising therefrom. Only that will is morally good which obeys the moral law under the influence of such a subjective principle or motive as can be willed by the individual to become the universal law for all men. The followers of Kant have selected now one now another doctrine from his ethics and combined therewith various pantheistical systems. Fichte places man's supreme good and destiny in absolute spontaneity and liberty; Schleiermacher, in co-operating with the progressive civilization of mankind. A similar view recurs substantially in the writings of Wilhelm Wundt and, to a certain extent, in those of the pessimist, Edward von Hartmann, though the latter regards culture and progress merely as means to the ultimate end, which, according to him, consists in delivering the Absolute from the torment of existence.

The system of Cumberland, who maintained the common good of mankind to be the end and criterion of moral conduct, was renewed on a positivistic basis in the nineteenth century by Auguste Comte and has counted many adherents, e. g., in England, John Stuart Mill, Henry Sidgwick, Alexander Bain; in Germany, G. T. Fechner, F. E. Beneke, F. Paulsen, and others. Herbert Spencer (1829-1903) sought to effect a compromise between social Utilitarianism (Altruism) and private Utilitarianism (Egoism) in accordance with the theory of evolution. In his opinion, that conduct is good which serves to augment life and pleasure without any admixture of displeasure. In consequence, however, of man's lack of adaptation to the conditions of life, such absolute goodness of conduct is not yet possible, and hence various compromises must be made between Altruism and Egoism. With the progress of evolution, however, this adaptation to existing conditions will become more and more perfect, and consequently the benefits accruing to the individual from his own conduct will be most useful to society at large. In particular, sympathy (in joy) will enable us to take pleasure in altruistic actions.

The great majority of non-Christian moral philosophers have followed the path trodden by Spencer. Starting with the assumption that man, by a series of transformations, was gradually evolved from the brute, and therefore differs from it in degree only, they seek the first traces and beginnings of moral ideas in the brute itself. Charles Darwin had done some preparatory work along these lines, and Spencer did not hesitate to descant on brute ethics, on the pre-human justice, conscience, and self-control of brutes. Present-day Evolutionists follow his view and attempt to show how animal morality has in man continually become more perfect. With the aid of analogies, taken from ethnology, they relate how mankind originally wandered over the face of the earth in semi-savage hordes, knew nothing of marriage or the family, and only by degrees reached a higher level of morality. These are the merest creations of fancy. If man is nothing more than a highly developed brute, he can not possess a spiritual and immortal soul, and there can no longer be question of the freedom of the will, of the future retribution of good and evil, nor can man in consequence be hindered from ordering his life as he pleases and regarding the well-being of others only in so far as it redounds to his own profit.

As the Evolutionists, so too the Socialists favor the theory of evolution from their ethical viewpoint; yet the latter do not base their observations on scientific principles, but on social and economical considerations. According to K. Marx, F. Engels, and other exponents of the so-called "materialistic interpretation of history," all moral, religious, juridical, and philosophical concepts are but the reflex of the economical conditions of society in the minds of men. Now these social relations are subject to constant change; hence the ideas of morality, religion, etc., are also continually changing. Every age, every people, and even each class in a given people forms its moral and religious ideas in accordance with its own peculiar economical situation. Hence, no universal code of morality exists binding on all men at all times; the morality of the present day is not of Divine origin, but the product of history, and will soon have to make room for another system of morality. Allied to this materialistic historical interpretation, though derived from other sources, is the system of Relativism, which recognizes no absolute and unchangeable truths in regard either to ethics or to anything else. Those who follow this opinion aver that nothing objectively true can be known to us. Men differ from one another and are subject to change, and with them the manner and means of viewing the world about them also change. Moreover, the judgments passed on matters religious and moral depend essentially upon the inclinations, interests, and character of the person judging, while these latter in turn are constantly varying. Pragmatism differs from Relativism inasmuch as that only is to be considered true which is proven by experience to be useful; and, since the same thing is not always useful, unchangeable truth is impossible.

In view of the chaos of opinions and systems just described, it need not surprise us that, as regards ethical problems, scepticism is extending its sway to the utmost limits, in fact many exhibit a formal contempt for the traditional morality. According to Max Nordau, moral precepts are nothing but "conventional lies"; according to Max Stirner, that alone is good which serves my interests, whereas the common good, the love for all men, etc., are but empty phantoms. Men of genius and superiority in particular are coming more and more to be regarded as exempt from the moral law. Nietzsche is the originator of a school whose doctrines are founded on those principles. According to him, goodness was originally identified with nobility and gentility of rank. Whatever the man of rank and power did, whatever inclinations he possessed, were good. The down-trodden proletariat, on the other hand, were bad, i. e., lowly and ignoble, without any other derogatory meaning being given to the word *bad*. It was only by a gradual process that the oppressed multitude through hatred and envy evolved the distinction between good and bad, in the moral sense, by denominating the characteristics and conduct of those in power and rank as bad, and their own behavior as good. And thus arose the opposition between the morality of the master and that of the slave. Those in power still continued to look upon their own egoistic inclinations as noble and good, while the oppressed populace lauded the "instincts of the common herd," i. e., all those qualities necessary and useful to its existence—as patience, meekness, obedience, and love of one's neighbor. Weakness became goodness, cringing obsequiousness became humility, subjection to hated oppressors was obedience, cowardice meant patience. "All morality is one long and audacious deception." Hence the value attached to the prevailing concepts of morality must be entirely rearranged. Intellectual superiority is above and beyond good and evil as understood in the traditional sense. There is no higher moral order to which men of such calibre are amenable. The end of society is not the common good of its members; the intellectual aristocracy (the over-man) is its own end; in its behalf the common herd, the "too many," must be reduced to slavery and decimated. As it rests with each individual to decide who belongs to this intellectual aristocracy, so each one is at liberty to emancipate himself from the existing moral order.

In conclusion, one other tendency in ethics may be noted, which has manifested itself far and wide: namely, to make morality independent of all religion. It is clear that many of the above-mentioned systems essentially exclude all regard for God and religion, and this is true especially of materialistic, agnostic, and in the last analysis, of all pantheistic systems. Apart also from these systems, "independent morality," called also "lay morality," has gained many followers and defenders. Kant's ideas formed the basis of this tendency, for he himself founded a code of morality on the categorical imperative and expressly declared that morality is sufficient for itself and therefore has no need of religion. Many modern moral philosophers—Herbart, Eduard von Hartmann, Zeller, Wundt, Paulsen, Ziegler, and a number of others,—have followed Kant in this respect. For several decades practical attempts have been made to emancipate morality from religion. In France religious instruction was banished from the schools in 1882 and moral instruction substituted. This tendency manifests a lively activity in what is known as the "ethical movement," whose home, properly speaking, is in the United States. In 1876 Felix Adler, professor at Cornell University, founded the "Society for Ethical Culture" in New York City. Similar societies were formed in other cities. These were consolidated in 1887 into the "Union of the Societies for Ethical Culture." Besides Adler, the chief propagators of the movement by word of mouth and writing were W. M. Salter and Stanton Coit. The purpose of these societies is declared to be "the improvement of the moral life of the members of the societies and of the community to which they belong, without any regard to theological or philosophical opinions." In most of the European countries ethical societies were founded on the model of the American organization. All these were combined in 1894 into the "International Ethical Association." Their purpose, i. e., the amelioration of man's moral condition, is, indeed, praiseworthy, but it is erroneous to suppose that any such moral improvement can be brought about without taking religion into consideration. In fact many members of the ethical societies are openly antagonistic to all religions, and would, therefore, do away with denominational schools and supplant religious teaching by mere moral instruction. Even upon purely ethical considerations, such attempts must be unhesitatingly rejected. If it be true that even in the case of adults moral instruction without religion, without any higher obligation or sanction, is a nonentity, a meaningless sham, how much more so is it in the case of the young? It is evident that, judged from the standpoint of Christianity, these efforts must meet with a still more decided condemnation. Christians are bound to observe not only the prescriptions of the natural law, but also all the precepts given by Christ concerning faith, hope, love, Divine worship, and the imitation of Himself. The Christian, however, knows that without Divine grace and hence without prayer and the frequent reception of the sacraments, a morally good life for any considerable length of time is impossible. From their earliest years, therefore, the young must not only receive thorough instruction in all the Commandments, but must be exercised and trained in the practical use of the means of grace. Religion must be the soil and atmosphere in which education develops and flourishes.

While, among non-Catholics ever since the Reformation, and especially since Kant, there has been an increasing tendency to divorce ethics from religion, and to dissolve it into countless venturesome and frequently contradictory systems, Catholics for the most part have remained free from these errors, because, in the Church's infallible authority, the guardian of Christian Revelation, they have always found secure orientation. It is true that toward the end of the eighteenth, and at the beginning of the nineteenth century, Illuminism and Rationalism penetrated here and there into Catholic circles and attempted to replace moral theology by purely philosophical ethics, and in turn to transform the latter according to the Kantian autonomy. This movement, however, was but a passing phase. With the reawakening of the Church's activity, fresh impetus was given to Catholic science, which was of benefit to ethics also and produced in its domain some excellent fruits. Recourse was again had to the illustrious past of Catholicism, while, at the same time, modern ethical systems gave occasion to a thorough investigation and verification of principles of the moral order. Taparelli d'Azelio led the way with his great work, "Saggio teoretico di diritto naturale appoggiato sul fatto" (1840-43). Then followed in Italy, Audisio, Rosmini, Liberatore, Sanseverino, Roselli, Zigliara, Signoriello, Schiffini, Ferretti, Talamo, and others. In Spain this revival of ethics was due to, among others, J. Balmes, Donoso Cortés, Zefirio Gonzalez, Mendive, R. de Cepeda; in France and Belgium, to de Lehen (Institutes de droit naturel), de Margerie, Onclair, Ath, Vallet, Charles Périn, Piat, de Paschal, Moulart, Castelein; in England and America, to Joseph Rickaby, Jouin, Russo, Holaind, J. J. Ming. In German-speaking countries the reawakening of Scholasticism in general begins with Kleutgen (Theologie der Vorzeit, 1853; Philosophie der Vorzeit, 1860), and of ethics in particular with Th. Meyer (Die Grundsätze der Sittlichkeit und des Rechts, 1868; Institutiones juris naturalis seu philosophiae moralis universae, 1885-1900). After them came A. Stöckl, Fred Walter, Moy de Sons, C. Gutberlet, Fr. J. Stein, Brandis, Costa-Rossetti, A. M. Weiss, Renninger, Lehmen, Willems, V. Frins, Heinrich Pesch, and others. We pass over numerous Catholic writers who have made a specialty of sociology and political economy.

THE POSTULATES

7

THE NECESSITY OF POSTULATES
Henry S. Spalding [1]

A postulate is a premise which a given science assumes as proved. It is a starting point. Not only can it be proved, but it has been proved. To prove it again would be a waste of time and energy; to prove it again would be unscientific; to prove every postulate again would be so to limit and restrict human endeavor that progress in any of the sciences would be impossible. Suppose that the class actually asked to be sent to the islands of Yap and Guam to prove to themselves that the islands really exist. Let us further suppose that Congress was asked for a special appropriation to defray the expenses of the voyage. Do you not imagine that the students after making such a request would be dismissed from Annapolis as mentally deficient? This is only stating in other words that common sense dictates the necessity of postulates. Postulates are required not only in scientific treatises but in the action of daily routine. We admit the existence of persons and nations, of rivers and mountains.

Let us further prove the necessity of postulates by a reference to the abstract science of mathematics. No one will for a moment question the proofs of numerous propositions in geometry. These propositions once proved become the postulates of the practical sciences,—surveying, architecture, and astronomy. In every movement of his instruments and in every calculation of results, the surveyor relies on his knowledge of mathematical formulae and deductions. Their use becomes a habit; and yet they cannot be neglected. What sorry results would be his, if he set aside the elementary application of the propositions in

---

[1] *Introduction to Social Service*, pp. 20, 21. (Heath and Company, Boston.)

regard to triangles. Buildings would be unsafe and unsightly structures if the architect had not the abstruse and unchanging laws of mathematics to guide him; and in astronomy, if the simple rules in regard to the measurement of angles were neglected, clocks and watches would be useless, and uncharted ships would sail uncharted seas.

There must be postulates. Everyday action demands them; no science can be without them. Moreover, it is useless to admit the necessity of postulates and then fail to use them in any given science.

8

POSTULATES

Timothy Brosnahan [1]

Postulate, a premiss which a given science claims as valid without demonstrating it; not because it cannot be demonstrated, but because the demonstration of it belongs to a science other than that which uses it. A Postulate differs from an hypothesis. Confusion in the modern acceptation of the term, postulate, is due to prevalent theories of knowledge. Every science has need of the external assistance of other sciences and is their debtor for postulates. Ethics which is concerned with the highest and most far-reaching activity of man must impetrate largely from other sciences, of which man is the subject.

The Cosmological Postulate. Any ultimate explanation of the cosmos must start, either from sheer nothing, or sheer actuality, i. e., the universe either sprang from nothing and become what it is through some process of creative evolution or it was produced by a being of sheer actuality. The first is untenable initially and progressively; the second demands a being of sheer actuality from the fact that there is any being at all. The existence of the universe, therfore, postulates: (*a*) a *necessary self-existing being,* possessing the plentitude of being, and specifically, in the transcendent degree, the intellectual attributes of mind and the moral attributes of will; (*b*) this being is the efficient, archetypal

---

[1] *Digests of Lectures on Ethics,* pp. 12-17. (John Murphy Company, Baltimore.)

and final cause of all other beings, which are, consequently, analogues of sheer actuality; (*c*) such beings are *contingent*, i. e., owe nature and existence, endurance in existence, and activity of nature to the Self-existing Being; and are necessarily images of the Creator's archetypal ideas; (*d*) the Self-existing Being bestowed existence on contingent being *freely* and for a purpose, though not from a motive; (*e*) the only conceivable purpose of a Self-existing Creator is to communicate being in such a way as to manifest his own perfections.

The Psychological Postulates are: *Freedom*, a logically necessary and immediate antecedent of the moral act; *immortality*, a necessary though remote consequence.

Freedom. Variety of meanings. Generically it means immunity from *necessity*. Necessity may arise from causes *extrinsic* to the agent: (*a*) *physical*, when the agent is constrained by force to an action that is incongruous to native appetency, or restrained from an action that is congruous thereto—*necessity of co-action;* (*b*) *emotive*, when an end is absolutely wished, for whatever reason, the will, of necessity, wishes the *means* to the end, or when an end is authoritatively assigned by a superior, the will is subject to the necessity of conforming its action to the command of the superior—Emotive or Moral necessity. The will cannot be subject to the first necessity in its elicited acts; it may be subject to the second necessity.

Necessity may arise from causes *intrinsic* to the agent. Inherent in every nature there is a tendency or motive power that specifies it. It is as much an attribute of intellect as it is of matter, as distinctive of will as of a magnet. This necessity is called by the Schoolmen the *necessity of specification*. It does not drive the faculty to action, but when tendency is actuated, it determines its specific functions and defines its range of operations. In cognitive beings the appetitive tendency is enacted by sensuous and intellectual apprehension. The *necessity of actuation* is had when a faculty in presence of its proper object duly and rightly proposed cannot withhold action. The will is always subject to the necessity of specifications; and to the necessity of actuation, when the object presented to it is absolute good, or good without qualification.

The cases in which freedom is claimed for the will are when the object, either has not and is seen not to have a necessary connection with the specific satisfaction of the will's inherent tendency to good as such; or if it have such a connection is presented through false apprehension as not having it. The attitude of the will towards qualified good is similar to the attitude of the intellect towards probable truth.

The theory of free-will is not a theory of pure indeterminism. The will even when freely acting, acts from a motive and for a purpose. The casualty of motive is not reducible to the attractive power of a physical force; it is peculiar to the faculty that is moved by cognition. The will, as every faculty, needs the stimulation of some cause distinct from itself before it can act. This cause, an object present in consciousness, and known to be desirable, arouses a will-movement towards the object. This *first act* is necessary. If other and undesirable aspects of the known object come into consciousness (as normally happens, unless the will is hurried into action either by the suddenness with which the object is presented or the intensity with which it attracts) a conflicting will-movement away from the object is aroused. The will concurs or refuses concurrence with one or other of these movements. In this *second act* the will is not necessitated. Though it could not consent to either will-movement but for a motive, its consent is not compelled by either motive.

Immortality. The individual soul or the spiritual principle in man, by which he is a rational and a moral being, will survive the dissolution of the body, and continue endlessly to lead a life of intellectual and moral activity. But the soul is *not immortal of its essence,* as is the Creator; it never ceases to be a contingent being. It is *naturally immortal,* in the sense that the purpose for which it was created, stamped on its highest faculties and tendencies, demands its conservation in endless existence.

The Anthropological Postulate. Every created being has its own mode of operation, and an innate inclination to perform those operations that agree with its nature and fix its place in the scheme of the universe. As we ascend in the grade of being these modes of operation become many and complex; are performed by different faculties, each having its own natural inclination. All the faculties of a being are radicated in the same nature; their inclinations are co-ordinated with one another, and subordinated to a dominant inclination, which manifests the inclination of the unitary nature. This inclination of the unitary nature we call *natural appetency*. Man is a composite being in whom are found appetencies analogous to those characterizing inferior creatures; he is a microcosm. These are subordinated to the good of his unitary nature through mind, i. e., intellect and will. As each separate faculty has its appetency for what is connatural to it, so his nature has its natural appetency for its good.

This latter appetency manifests itself in four fundamental directions; (a) In common with all creatures, he has an inclination to resist dissolution, i. e., to *self-preservation;* (b) In common with all animals, he has an inclination to perpetuate his species, to care for and educate progeny; (c) As an intellectual being, he has an inclination to know the source and purpose of his existence; (d) As a social being he has an inclination to live in the communion of thought and endeavor with his fellowman. This latter inclination has universally actuated itself in three distinct natural societies; domestic, civil and religious; through which the objects of the three first inclinations are more securely and adequately realized.

Other inclinations of our nature are extensions, derivations, or complexes of these.

9

ARGUMENTS IN PROOF OF THE EXISTENCE OF GOD

(A) THE PRIME MOVER
St. Thomas Aquinas[1]

Having shown, then, that it is not futile to prove the existence of God, we may proceed to set forth the reasons whereby both philosophers and Catholic doctors have proved that there is a God. In the first place we shall give the

---

[1] *Summa contra Gentiles,* vol. i, pp. 23-33; trans. by English Dominican Fathers. (Burns, Oates and Washbourne, London.)

arguments by which Aristotle sets out to prove God's existence; and he aims at proving this from the point of view of movement, in two ways.

The first way is as follows: Whatever is in motion is moved by another; and it is clear to the sense that something, the sun, for instance, is in motion. Therefore, it is set in motion by something else moving it. Now that which moves it is itself either moved or not. If it be not moved, then the point is proved that we must needs postulate an immovable mover: and this we call God. If, however, it be moved, it is moved by another mover. Either, therefore, we must proceed to infinity, or we must come to an immovable mover. But it is not possible to proceed to infinity. Therefore, it is necessary to postulate an immovable mover.

This argument contains two propositions that need to be proved, namely; that *whatever is in motion is moved by another,* and that *it is not possible to proceed to infinity in movers and in things moved.*

The first of these is proved by the Philosopher in three ways. *First,* thus. If a thing moves itself, it must needs have the principle of its movement in itself, else it would clearly be moved by another. Again, it must be *moved primarily,* that is, it must be moved by reason of itself and not by reason of its part, as an animal is moved by the movement of its foot, for, in the latter way, not the whole but the part would be moved by itself, and one part by another. Again, it must be divisible and have parts, since whatever is moved is divisible, as is proved in 6 *Phys.*

These things being supposed, he argues as follows: That which is stated to be moved by itself is moved primarily. Therefore, if one of its parts is at rest, it follows that the whole is at rest. For if, while one part is at rest, another of its parts were in motion, the whole itself would not be moved primarily, but its part which is in motion while another is at rest. Now nothing that is at rest while another is at rest, is moved by itself: for that which is at rest as a result of another thing being at rest must needs be in motion as a result of the other's motion, and hence it is not moved by itself. Hence that which was stated to be moved by itself, is not moved by itself. Therefore, whatever is in motion must needs be moved by another.

Nor is this argument traversed by the statement that might be made, that, supposing a thing moves itself, it is impossible for a part thereof to be at rest, or, again, by the statement that to be at rest or in motion does not belong to a part except accidentally, as Avicenna quibbles. Because the force of the argument lies in this, that if a thing moves itself primarily and of itself, not by reason of its parts, it follows that its being moved does not depend on something; whereas, with a divisible thing, being moved, like being, depends on its parts, so that it can not move itself primarily and of itself. Therefore, the truth of the conclusion drawn does not require that we suppose as an absolute truth that a part of that which moves itself is at rest, but that this conditional statement be true that *if a part were at rest,* the whole would be at rest. Which statement can be true even if the antecedent be false, even as this conditional proposition is true: *if a man is an ass he is irrational.*

Secondly, he proves it by induction, thus. A thing is not moved by itself if it is moved accidentally, since its motion is occasioned by the motion of something else. Nor, again, if it is moved by force, as is manifest. Nor if it is moved by its nature like those things whose movement proceeds from themselves, such as animals, which clearly are moved by their souls. Nor if it is moved by nature, as heavy and light things are, since these are moved by their generating cause and by that which removes the obstacle to their movement. Now whatever things are in motion are moved either *per se,* or accidentally; and if *per se,* either by force or by nature: and if the latter, either by something in them, as in the case of animals, or not by something in them, as in the case of heavy and light bodies. Therefore, whatever is in motion is moved by another.

Thirdly, he proves his point thus. Nothing is at the same time in act and in potentiality in respect of the same thing. Now whatever is in motion, as such, is in potentiality, because motion is *the act of that which is in potentiality, as such.* Whereas, whatever moves, as such, is in act, for nothing acts except in so far as it is in act. Therefore, nothing is both mover and moved in respect of the same movement. Hence nothing moves itself.

We must observe, however, that Plato, who asserted that every mover is moved, employed the term *movement* in a more general sense than Aristotle. For Aristotle took movement in its strict sense, for the act of a thing that is in potentiality as such, in which sense it applies only to divisible things and bodies, as is proved in 6 *Phys.* Whereas, according to Plato, that which moves itself is not a body; for he took movement for any operation, so that to understand or to think is a kind of movement, to which manner of speaking Aristotle alludes in 3 *De Anima.* In this sense, then, he said that the first mover moves itself, in as much as it understands, desires and loves itself. This, in a certain respect, is not in contradiction with the arguments of Aristotle; for it makes no difference whether, with Plato, we come to a first mover that moves itself, or with Aristotle to something first which is altogether immovable.

He proves the other proposition, namely, that *it is impossible to proceed to infinity in movers and things moved,* by three arguments.

The *first* of these is as follows: If one were to proceed to infinity in movers and things moved, all this infinite number of things would necessarily be bodies, since whatever is moved is divisible and corporeal, as is proved in 6 *Phys.* Now every body that moves through being moved is moved at the same time as it moves. Therefore, all this infinite number of things are moved at the same time as one of them is moved. But one of them, since it is finite, is moved in a finite time. Therefore, all this infinite number of things is moved in a finite time. But this is impossible. Therefore, it is impossible to proceed to infinity in movers and things moved.

That it is impossible for the aforesaid infinite number of things to be moved in a finite time, he proves thus. Mover and moved must needs be simultaneous; and he proves this by induction from each species of movement. But bodies cannot be simultaneous except by continuity or contact. Wherefore, since all the aforesaid movers and things moved are bodies, as proved, they must needs be as one movable thing through their continuity or contact. And thus one infinite thing would be moved in a finite time, which is shown to be impossible in 6 *Phys.*

The *second argument* in proof of the same statement is as follows: In an ordinate series of movers and things moved, where, namely, throughout the series one is moved by the other, we must needs find that if the first mover be taken away or cease to move, none of the others will move or be moved: because the first is the cause of movement in all the others. Now, if an ordinate series of movers and things moved proceed to infinity, there will be no first mover, but all will be intermediate movers as it were. Therefore, it will be impossible for any of them to be moved; and thus nothing in the world will be moved.

The *third argument* amounts to the same, except that it proceeds in the reverse order, namely, by beginning from above, and it is as follows: That which moves instrumentally, cannot move unless there be something that moves principally. But if we proceed to infinity in movers and things moved, they will all be like instrumental movers, because they will be alleged to be movers, and there will be nothing by way of principal mover. Therefore, nothing will be moved.

We have thus clearly proved both statements which were supposed in the first process of demonstration whereby Aristotle proved the existence of a *first immovable mover*.

The *second way* is as follows: If every mover is moved, this statement is true either in itself or accidentally. If accidentally, it follows that it is not necessary, for that which is accidentally true is not necessary. Therefore, it is a contingent proposition that no mover is moved. But if a mover be not moved, it does not move, as the opponent asserts. Therefore, it is contingent that nothing is moved, since, if nothing moves, nothing is moved. Now, Aristotle holds this to be impossible, namely, that at any time there be no movement. Therefore, the first proposition was not contingent, because a false impossibility does not follow from a false contingency. And, therefore, this proposition, *Every mover was moved by another* was not accidentally true.

Again, if any two things are found accidentally united in a certain subject, and one of them is to be found without the other, it is probable that the latter can be found without the former; thus, if *white* and *musical* are found in Socrates, and *musical* without *white* is found in Plato, it is probable that it is possible to find *white* without *musical* in some subject. Accordingly, if mover and moved be united together in some subject accidentally, and it be found that a certain thing is moved without its being a mover, it is probable that a mover is to be found that is not moved. Nor can one urge against this the case of two things, one of which depends on the other; because those in question are united, not *per se,* but accidentally. If, however, the aforesaid proposition is true in itself, again there follows something impossible or unfitting. For the mover must needs be moved either by the same kind of movement or by another kind. If by the same kind, it follows that whatever causes alteration must itself be altered, and, furthermore, that the healer must be healed, that the teacher must be taught, and in respect of the same science. But this is impossible, for the teacher must needs have science, while the learner must needs not have it, and thus the same will be possessed and not possessed by the same, which is impossible. And if it be moved by another kind of movement so that, to wit, that which causes alteration be moved in respect of place, and that which moves in respect of place be increased, and so on, it will follow that we can not go on indefinitely, since the genera and species of movement are finite in number. And thus there will be some first mover that is not moved by another. Unless, perchance, someone say that a recurrence takes place in this way, that when all the genera and species of movement have been exhausted, a return must be made to the first; for instance, if that which moves with respect of place be altered, and that which causes alteration be increased, then, again, that which is increased be moved in respect of place. But the consequence of this will be the same as before, namely, that which moves by one kind of movement is itself moved by the same kind, not immediately, indeed, but mediately. It remains, therefore, that *we must needs postulate some first mover that is not moved by anything outside itself.*

Since, however, given that there is a first mover that is not moved by anything outside itself, it does not follow that it is absolutely immovable, Aristotle proceeds further, saying that this may happen in two ways. First, so that this first mover is absolutely immovable. And if this be granted, our point is established, namely, that there is a first immovable mover. Secondly, that this first mover is moved by itself. And this seems probable; because what is of itself is always prior to what is of another; wherefore, also in things moved, it is logical that what is moved first is moved by itself and not by another.

But, if this be granted, the same consequence follows. For it cannot be said that the whole of that which moves itself is moved by its whole self, because then the absurd consequences mentioned above would follow, namely, that a person might teach and be taught at the same time, and in like manner as to other kinds of movement; and again that a thing would be at the same time in act and in potentiality, since a mover as such, is in act, while that which is moved is in potentiality. It remains, therefore, that one part thereof is moved only, and the other part moved. And thus we have the same conclusion as before, namely, that there is something that moves and is itself immovable.

And it cannot be said that both parts are moved, so that one is moved by the other; nor that one part moves both itself and the other; nor that the whole moves a part; nor that part moves the whole, since the above absurdities would follow, namely, that something would both move and be moved by the same kind of movement, and that it would be at the same time in potentiality and in act, and, moreover, that the whole would move itself not primarily but by reason of its part. It remains, therefore, that in that which moves itself, one part must be immovable, and must move the other part.

Since, however, in those things among us which move themselves, namely, animals, the part which moves, namely, the soul, though immovable of itself, is, nevertheless, moved accidentally, he goes on to show that in the first mover, the part which moves is not moved neither of itself nor accidentally.

For in those things which among us move themselves, namely, animals, since they are corruptible, the part which moves is moved accidentally. Now those corruptible things which move themselves must needs be reducible to some first self-mover that is everlasting. Therefore, that which moves itself must have a mover, which is moved neither of itself nor accidentally.

It is clear that in accordance with this hypothesis, some self-mover must be everlasting. For if, as he supposes, movement is everlasting, the production of these self-movers that are subject to generation and corruption must be everlasting. But no one of these self-movers, since it does not always exist, can be the cause of this everlastingness. Nor can all of them together, both because they would be infinite, and because they do not exist all together. It follows, therefore, that there must be an everlasting self-mover, that causes the everlastingness of generation in these lower self-movers. And thus its mover is not moved, neither of itself nor accidentally. Again, we observe that in self-movers some begin to be moved anew on account of some movement whereby the animal is not moved by itself, for instance, by the digestion of food or a change in the atmosphere, by which movement the mover that moves itself is moved accidentally. Whence we may gather that no self-mover, whose mover is moved *per se* or accidentally, is always moved. But the first self-mover is always in motion, else movement could not be everlasting, since every other movement is caused by the movement of the first self-mover. It follows, therefore, that the first self-mover is moved by a mover who is not moved, neither *per se* nor accidentally.

Nor is this argument rebutted by the fact that the movers of the lower spheres cause an everlasting movement, and yet are said to be moved accidentally. For they are said to be moved accidentally not by reason of themselves, but by reason of the things subject to their motion, which follow the motion of the higher sphere.

Since, however, God is not part of a self-mover, Aristotle goes on in his *Metaphysics* to trace from this motor that is part of a self-mover, another mover altogether separate, which is God. For, since every self-mover is moved through its appetite, it follows that the motor that is part of a self-mover, moves on account of the appetite for some appetible object. And this object is above the motor in moving, because the appetent is a moved mover, whereas, the appetible is a mover altogether unmoved. Therefore, *there must needs be a first mover separate and altogether immovable, and this is God.*

Now two things would seem to weaken the above arguments. The *first* of these is that they proceed from the supposition of the eternity of movement, and among Catholics this is supposed to be false. To this we reply that the most effective way to prove God's existence is from the supposition of the eternity of the world, which, being supposed, it seems less manifest that God exists. For if the world and movement had a beginning, it is clear that we must suppose some cause to have produced the world and movement, because whatever becomes anew must take its origin from some cause of its becoming, since nothing evolves itself from potentiality to act, or from non-being to being.

The *second* is that the aforesaid arguments suppose that the first moved thing, namely, the heavenly body, has its motive principle in itself, whence it follows that it is animated; and by many this is not granted.

To this we reply that if the first mover is not supposed to have its motive principle in itself, it follows that it is immediately moved by something altogether immovable. Hence, also, Aristotle draws this conclusion, with an alternative, namely, that either we must come at once to a first mover immovable and separate, or to a self-mover from which again we come to a first mover immovable and separate.

The Philosopher proceeds in a different way in 2 *Metaph*. to show that it is impossible to proceed to infinity in efficient causes, and that we must come to one first cause, and this we call God. This is how he proceeds. In all efficient causes following in order, the first is the cause of the intermediate cause, and the intermediate is the cause of the ultimate, whether the intermediate be one or several. Now if the cause be removed, that which it causes is removed. Therefore, if we remove the first the intermediate cannot be a cause. But if we go on to infinity in efficient causes, no cause will be first. Therefore, all the others which are intermediate will be removed. Now this is clearly false. Therefore, we must suppose *the existence of a first efficient cause*. And this is God.

Another reason can be shown from the words of Aristotle. For in 2 *Metaph*. he shows that those things which excel as true excel as beings; and in 4 *Metaph*. he shows that there is something supremely true, from the fact that we see that of two false things one is falser than the other, wherefore, it follows that one also is truer than the others. Now this is by reason of approximation to that which is simply and supremely true. Wherefore, we may further conclude that *there is something that is supremely being.* And this we call God.

Another argument in support of this conclusion is adduced by Damascene from the government of things, and the same reasoning is indicated by the Commentator in 2 *Phys.* It runs as follows: It is impossible for contrary and discordant things to accord in one order always or frequently except by someone's governance, whereby each and all are made to tend to a definite end. Now we see that in the world things of different natures accord in one order, not seldom and fortuitously, but always or for the most part. Therefore, it follows that there is *someone by whose providence the world is governed.* And this we call God.

(B) TELEOLOGICAL PROOF
Bernard Boedder [1]

The Argument from Design is built upon the fact that material things do constantly and in a most complex way group themselves together into well-ordered wholes and systems. This fact cannot be explained sufficiently otherwise than by admitting an Intelligence presiding over nature's works, designing and adapting means to ends with foreknowledge of eventual results. That the Intelligence we speak of is self-existent, we cannot directly prove by this argument. We shall have to supplement the deficiency in this regard by the argument of a First Cause. Yet, considered apart from it, the argument from Design is, in itself, a striking refutation of materialism, whether in the shape of a fortuitous mechanical concurrence of atoms, or in the monist's mystic vision of the undifferentiated developing into the differentiated and individualized.

The order which prevails throughout the visible world has excited the attention of thinkers from the very dawn of philosophy. According to Cicero, Thales, the leader of the Ionian school, held God to be that Intelligence which out of water forms all beings. Anaxagoras believed, likewise, in a Superior Reason pervading the whole of nature.

---

[1] *Natural Theology,* pp. 46-62. (Longmans, Green and Company, New York. With permission.)

Plato attributed the harmonious order of celestial and terrestrial bodies to a designing mind; and Aristotle, at the end of the twelfth book of his *Metaphysics*, concludes from the unity of the order in the physical world to the unity of its Ruler. The same argument was treated more fully by the Stoics, a fine specimen of whose reasoning is preserved by Cicero in the second book of the *De natura Deorum*.

To say nothing of scholastic philosophers, Bacon held it for absolutely certain, that the attributes of God, and particularly His wisdom and His ruling providence, are traceable in creation. Leibnitz expressed it as his persuasion, that the material elements of the world, considered in themselves, are capable of quite another order than that by which they actually are connected; whence he concludes that the realization of this one order out of many possible orders must be attributed to the determining mind of God. Kepler's reverence for the Author of Nature is well known. Newton concludes his *Scholia* with a *scholion generale* in praise of the Creator, whose infinite wisdom in arranging the solar system had struck him with admiration. "This most elegant contrivance, consisting of the sun, planets, and comets," he says, "could not originate but by the design and power of an intelligent Being." What this great astronomer saw so clearly, the great biologist of modern time, Charles Darwin, felt instinctively and "with overpowering force," although he did not care to draw the conclusion suggested to common-sense by his own observations. Let us add here that although John Stuart Mill doubted whether the Darwinian principle of the "survival of the fittest" be not able "to account for such truly admirable combinations as some of those in nature," he was, nevertheless of opinion, "that it must be allowed that in the present state of our knowledge, the adaptations in nature afford a large balance of probability in favour of creation by intelligence."

Of far more weight, however, than Mill's timid admission of a large balance of probability is the firm conviction of many of the best scientific men of our own century, that it is absolutely impossible to explain the adaptations we meet with in all departments of nature, otherwise but by intelligence and design. St. George Mivart tells us that the cause of the phenomenal universe "must be orderly and intelligent, as the first and absolute cause of an orderly series of phenomena which reveals to us an objective intelligence in the bee and the ant, which is not that of the animals themselves, and which harmonizes with and is recognized by our own intellects." Dr. W. B. Carpenter, after having given us in his *Vegetable Physiology* a highly interesting chapter on the Secretions of Plants, pauses to contemplate with his readers "the important inferences which may be drawn from the foregoing details, in regard to the Power, Wisdom, and Goodness of the Almighty Designer."

With the two great biologists just mentioned, A. R. Wallace, in the work already quoted above, agrees at least to a certain extent. According to him, the "three distinct stages of progress from the inorganic world of matter and motion up to man, point clearly to an unseen universe—to a world of spirit, to which the world of matter is altogether subordinate."

No less pronounced statements in favour of the existence of an intelligent arranger of the universe came from other quarters of modern science. "Overpowering proofs of intelligence and benevolent design," said Sir William Thomson some years ago, "lie around us, showing to us through nature the influence of a free-will, and teaching us that all living beings depend upon one ever-acting Creator and Ruler." Two years later, Sir William Siemens repeated the same judgment in these words: "We find that all knowledge must lead up to one great result, that of an intelligent recognition of the Creator through His works."

At the same conclusion which English scientists drew from the order of nature, the French astronomer, Faye, in his work, *Sur l'origine du monde* (Paris, 1884), arrived from the consideration of the human mind. After having stated that human intelligence must owe its origin to an intelligence higher than human, he thus continues: *"Plus l'idée qu'on se fera de cette intelligence suprême sera grande, plus elle approchera de la vérité."*

But what seems to us the best extrinsic evidence of the great strength of the argument from design, is the fact that such a judge of the value of arguments as Kant thinks it a blameable imprudence not to conclude from the order of nature to an intelligent designer. "This proof," he says, "will always deserve to be treated with respect. It is the oldest, the clearest, and most in conformity with human reason. It gives life to the study of nature, deriving its own existence from it, and thus constantly acquiring new vigour. It reveals aims and intentions, where our own observation would not by itself have discovered them, and enlarges our knowledge of nature by leading us towards that peculiar unity, the principle of which exists outside nature. This knowledge reacts again on its cause, namely, the transcendental idea, and thus increases the belief in a Supreme Author to an irresistible conviction. It would, therefore, be not only extremely sad, but utterly vain, to attempt to diminish the authority of this proof. Reason, constantly strengthened by the powerful arguments that come to hand of themselves, though they are no doubt empirical only, cannot be discouraged by any doubts of subtle and abstract speculation. Roused from all curious speculation and mental suspense, as from a dream, by one glance at the wonders of nature and the majesty of the cosmos, reason soars from height to height till it reaches the highest, from the conditioned to conditions, till it reaches the supreme and unconditioned Author of all." Later on, Kant refers to the objection that we must not argue from the need of foresight in human workmanship to a similar need in nature. His answer is: "We cannot do better than follow the analogy of these products of human design, which are the only ones of which we know completely, both cause and effect. There would be no excuse, if reason were to surrender a causality which it knows, and have recourse to obscure and indemonstrable principles of explanation, which it does not know."

It is true that Kant, while granting thus much, has, nevertheless, some speculative difficulties against the argument from Design. We shall treat of these later. For the present we are satisfied with knowing that one of the most acute leaders of modern thought, forced by the voice of reason, bears testimony to the great truth that "the heavens show forth the glory of the Lord," that "by the greatness of the beauty and of the creature, the Creator of them may be seen so as to be known thereby," and that "the unknown God" "left not Himself without testimony, doing good from Heaven, giving rains and fruitful seasons, filling our hearts with food and gladness."

We now proceed from authority to argument.

Order is the adaptation of diverse things to one definite result. Order of simple coexistences is called *statical;* order of motions and activities is called *dynamical.* Thus, for instance, in a well-arranged library we have statical order, in machinery not only statical, but also dynamical. These definitions supposed, it cannot be doubted that the visible universe in all its parts bears marks of a most varied and beautiful order. Darwin was so struck by this complex final order, that he did not hesitate to pronounce "nature's productions far truer in character than man's productions;" and to maintain that they are "infinitely better adapted to the most complex conditions of life, and plainly bear the stamp of far higher workmanship."

Any good popular treatise on astronomy and physiology will serve as a rich source of illustrations bearing on the truth of these statements, nor is there anyone who will be foolish enough to dispute them. It must, however, be carefully noted, that we do not as yet affirm that *everything* in this world is well-ordered, nor do we say that there is *a universal combination of things for the fulfilment of one common purpose.* Were we to claim all this, we should indeed be claiming only what, if rightly understood, is most true. But so far-reaching a proposition is not necessary for the argument from Design, nor would it be sufficiently warranted until we have carried our inquiry further.

Confining, therefore, our attention to those manifestations of order which are obvious to everyone who cares for the study of the workings of nature, we ask: How did these orderly arrangements, their harmony, beauty, and usefulness, come to be? May we suppose, with Epicurus, that they are the effect of chance? in other words, that they are owing to an accidental concurrence of atoms, moving in infinite space, and meeting one another in such a way as to form, after many failures, various kinds of inanimate and animate bodies? Such an hypothesis would be not only inadequate to account for the laws and results of chemical combinations, and for the origin of life; it would be intrinsically absurd, conflicting with the universality of the Principle of Causation, inasmuch as this fortuitous concurrence would be an uncaused concurrence. There must, then, have been a cause of the formation of the heavenly orbs and their arrangement in systems: a cause, again, which, on our earth, grouped together the elements into organized structures, moving, growing, repairing themselves, and reproducing their kind according to definite laws. Where shall we find this cause? It must either be inherent in the elements of matter, or it must be something outside these. If it is outside matter, it can only be a mind, understanding and designing the order of matter. But will not the inherent forces of matter suffice to explain this complex order? Let us see.

In the first place, the inherent forces of matter cannot be appealed to as the cause of the order prevailing in the inorganic world. We know that material elements produce different effects according to their different collocations in regard to one another. Consequently, each effect is the natural outcome of a previous disposition of the parts of matter. This being so, every orderly effect is due to a pre-arrangement of particles suitable to the production of such an effect. That is, the order which is worked out by the elements of matter, presupposes order in the combination of the working elements. Thus the question of order in the world of inanimate matter is thrown back to the origin of that combination of elements which generated order.

Nor do we escape the necessity of seeking a cause external to the combinations themselves, by pleading the possibility of an eternal series of combinations. In the first place, eternal succession is a self-contradictory conception. Succession implies links of a series, it is constituted by the continuous addition of link to link. Now links added to one another are always numerable. Links of a series must always be in some number, however immense the number may be. But to be in some number, is to be finite: for every number is made up of finite unities. Thus eternal succession would be essentially finite, because it was succession, and yet infinite because eternal.

In the second place, even if eternal succession were possible, it would furnish no explanation of the phenomenon of orderly combination which the world exhibits: any more than infinite extension of a chain hung in air would supply the want of supports for it. Consequently, although we have nothing to say against the assumption made by astronomers, that our cosmic system resulted from the condensation and division of a primitive rotating *nebula;* yet we cannot admit this *nebula,* without observing that there must have been a *first* arrangement of the material elements which constituted it, one which already contained in germ the present system, or else the said system could never have resulted from it. Now this first arrangement was neither the effect of the forces of matter, nor was it essential to matter. Had it been the effect of material forces, it could not possibly have been the first disposition of matter, but was rather the effect of a preceding disposition of the elements. Again, had it belonged essentially to matter, it could not have yielded to another disposition so long as matter existed, and thus the present cosmic system could never have been formed. Therefore, if we would explain the origin of that system without violation of reason, we are forced to say that its first beginning, nebular or otherwise, is due to an intelligent cause.

If the forces of matter are inadequate to explain the order of the inorganic world, much less can they account for the existence of life and the orderly relations which exist between animate and inanimate beings.

Whence comes the adaptation of inanimate nature to the support of life? The natural tendency of brute matter cannot explain it. The relation of brute matter to life is accidental to its nature. Whence, then, did the relation originate? No satisfactory answer to this question can be given except this: that an Intelligent Ruler of this world arranged the material elements of which the universe is built up in such a way that they gradually became adapted to the service of living beings whose existence he intended and foresaw. This answer must be insisted upon all the more from the fact that man, the most noble being on earth, finds it rich with an innumerable multitude of things accommodated to his bodily and mental wants. As we have proved before, the soul of man is not the outgrowth of matter, but the work of an intelligent Creator only. No evolution of matter, of plants, and of animals, could culminate in the existence of man, composed of a human soul and a human body; and yet matter and life inferior to man, conspire to furnish him what he needs for the maintenance of his body, and to help him in the cultivation of his intellect. Certainly no reasonable explanation of this great fact can be given but by recurring to an intelligent mind, superior to man and the irrational world, which arranged the latter, ere man was created, with a view to prepare him a fit dwelling-place.

We have then seen hitherto that the adaptations to one another which connect the various groups of beings in the macrocosm of the universe must be attributed to a Designing Mind. The same conclusion we arrive at by pondering the order prevailing in the microcosm of each living organism, from the tiniest unicellular plant up to the most highly organized animal. Just as in scientific inquiry, the further that it proceeds, the more it becomes evident that brute matter by its own forces alone never develops into organized living structures; so, when we look at the subject from a metaphysical point of view, we are forced to maintain that the vast differences which separate the natural tendencies of living bodies from those of lifeless matter, are a sufficient evidence of the impossibility of a natural evolution of the latter into any species of the former. And with this conclusion coincides the verdict of scientific experience.

Mr. St. George Mivart speaks on this point with authority. He says:

"That there is an absolute break between the living world and the world devoid of life, is what scientific men are now agreed about—thanks to the persevering labors of M. Pasteur. Those who affirm that though life does not arise from inorganic matter now, nevertheless it did so 'a long time ago,' affirm what is at the least contrary to all the evidence we possess, and they bring forward nothing more in favor of it than the undoubted fact that it is a supposition which is necessary for the validity of their own speculative views. There is, then, one plain evidence that there has been an interruption of continuity, if not within the range of organic life, yet at its commencement and origin. But we go further than this, and affirm, without a moment's hesitation, that there has, and must necessarily have been, discontinuity within the range of organic life also. We refer to the discontinuity between organisms which are capable of sensation and those which do not possess the power of feeling. That all the higher animals 'feel' will not be disputed. They give all the external signs of sensitivity, and they possess that special organic structure—a nervous system—which we know supplies all our organs of sensation. In the absence of any bodily mutilation, then, we have no reason to suspect that their nervous system and organs of sense do not act in a manner analogous to our own. On the other hand, to affirm that the familiar vegetables of our kitchen-gardens are all endowed with sensitivity, is not only to make a gratuitous affirmation, but one opposed to evidence, since no vegetable organisms possess a nervous system, and it is a universally admitted biological law, that structure and functions go together. If, then, there are any organisms whatever, which *do not* feel, while certain other organisms *do feel* (as a door must be shut or open), there is, and must be, a break and distinction between one set and the other."

What then was it which gave birth to organic life? To say it had no beginning, but that from eternity there existed one or several series of living organisms, would involve the postulate of succession without beginning, which we have proved to be self-contradictory. But, if organic life can neither be considered as an effect of the forces of dead matter, nor have the source of its own existence within itself, we cannot reasonably explain its origin except by admitting that an intelligent Being, ruling over the matter of our earth, first put into it the germ of life, although we are not able to point out *when,* and *in what way,* this influence was exercised. Hence, the countless living organisms that people our globe are the realizations of ideas conceived by an immaterial superhuman Intelligence. This Intelligence drew the plans on which they are built, foresaw the stages of evolution, through which they run with so astonishing a regularity, furnished them with a multitude of skilfully-contrived organs, and adapted their whole structure to the environment in which they are placed.

That the Ruler in whose mind the order of the world originated is a self-existing Intelligence, and consequently a personal God, does not follow immediately from the fact that the order of the world must be the work of a superhuman Intelligence. What does, however, follow immediately is that the Intelligence which rules the physical world is so vast that no human understanding and wisdom can be compared with it. For many ages the cleverest of men have been occupied in studying the relations that exist between the different parts of living beings, and between these parts and their functions, and yet there is no man who understands completely the mysteries hidden even in one living cell. Far indeed then above human comprehension must be the excellence of that Mind whose ideas were the models after which the universe was fashioned, with its wealth of marvels and complexity of order.

If, however, we would show that the order of the world is due, not only to an Intelligence far exceeding all intelligence of man, but ultimately to a self-existent Intelligence—in other words, to a personal God, we must go back to the argument of the First Cause. Either the intelligent mind who designed the order of our world is dependent upon a series of other minds without beginning, or it depends upon a first mind, or it is itself the first mind. The first alternative is absurd, because it implies a series of causes produced without a self-existent cause to produce them; therefore, either the second or the third must be admitted. But this is equivalent to an admission that the order of the world depends upon an intelligent, self-existent cause; for the cause of order must also, at least mediately, be the cause of order itself.

(C) ARGUMENT FROM CONSCIENCE
GEORGE H. JOYCE [1]

Since man is possessed of intelligence, he recognizes that certain actions are comformable to his rational nature and that others are at variance with it. He sees, for instance, that gluttony, cruelty, lust, and the infringement of the rights of others, are contrary to the order of reason; that in so far as a man allows the lower part of his nature, his passions, to dominate him, or disregards the law of justice which bids him give to each his due, he is doing violence to that element in him which makes him a man. In other words, these actions are *evil*, and, contrariwise, temperance, kindness, continence, and justice are *good*. And this distinction between good and evil has regard purely to our nature as moral agents; it is entirely irrespective of any

---

[1] *Principles of Natural Theology*, pp. 153-166. (Longmans, Green and Company, New York. With permission.)

question as to whether the act results in a balance of pleasure or of pain. Those acts are good which befit us as rational beings; those are evil which are repugnant to our nature in this respect. The supreme rule of conduct is to do what is morally good and avoid all that is morally evil. The ethical standard thus imposed is clear enough as regards its broad outlines. All men can see sufficiently for the general direction of life what acts are conformable to reason and what are not. The primary precepts of the moral law, as the Scholastic philosophers said, do not admit of mistake. It is, of course, the case that on points of detail there will be numerous differences of opinion. Problems of this kind are bound to arise, since it is frequently no easy matter to judge of the application of a general principle to a particular case. All will own that obedience to lawful authority is ethically right. But the precise limits within which obedience is due alike as regards the state and as regards the family in this or that individual instance may be an extremely delicate point to settle. Sometimes, too, it happens that what once was a right action ceases to be so owing to change of circumstances. Thus it comes about that what was universally recognized as a duty is afterwards viewed as a breach of the moral law. Moreover, occasionally the force of custom is so strong that great numbers of men form an erroneous judgment on some matter which to the unprejudiced mind is plain enough. The Chinaman who commits infanticide may do so without realizing that the act is evil. But difficulties and discrepancies such as these do not alter the broad fact on which we are insisting, that all men without exception can and do distinguish between moral good and moral evil. Were a man incapable of distinguishing these, he would have no just claim to the name of man, for he would be destitute of that light of reason which is man's prerogative above the brutes.

It is, further, a patent fact not admitting of denial or question that men feel the moral law to be *obligatory*. They recognize it as a force which *binds* them. Its prescriptions are no mere norm for the realization of life at its best. They come as authoritative commands; and to slight those commands is to fail in a duty which we *owe*. If we act thus, we are conscious that retributive justice pronounces us deserving of punishment. *Necessity* is a primary characteristic of the moral law. The meaning of this word should be carefully weighed. The necessary is that which *must* be. We sometimes speak of physical laws as necessary. Yet it may be questioned whether we are justified in using the term in their regard. The mind does not recognize any reason in the nature of things why such and such an antecedent *must* be followed by such and such a consequent. Experience shows us that the fact *is* so, not that it *must be* so. On the other hand, mathematical relations are necessary; the square on the hypotenuse *must* be equal to the squares on the containing sides. But the necessity with which we are concerned is not mathematical; it is moral. It signifies that our will is bound by an obligation which is not conditional but absolute; that we have no choice in the matter; that no alternative course is open, which we are free to adopt if we will. It declares that we are face to face, not with a counsel, but with a command.

This sense of moral obligation cannot be resolved into a perception of expediency, notwithstanding that many have sought so to explain it. In England, Mill and Spencer, though differing on many points, were at one on this, that the sole basis of morality is expediency; that the moral law is simply the generalized result of what experience has shown to be conducive to the public utility. Right, they held, is not absolute but relative. It is determined by the needs of the species, which are essentially variable; of no action whatever can it be affirmed that it is essentially and unalterably evil or good. Such an explanation of the moral law is manifestly inadequate, inasmuch as it wholly fails to account for that binding force which is its essential characteristic. Obligation and expediency are incommensurables; the one cannot be reduced to the other. That an act will in the long run contribute to the material welfare of the community is certainly a reasonable motive of action. It is not, and can never be, an obligation—an absolute imperative with power to bind my will. Expediency affords no account of the word "ought." The conviction expressed when we acknowledge that we ought to do this or that, could never spring from that source. It cannot give it, for it has not got it to give.

Law implies a lawgiver. We cannot have a command without a superior who issues the command. It is true that Kant declared the reason to be autonomous, and maintained that its precepts must be self-imposed. He contended that unless they were regarded in this light they lacked the essential quality of moral laws; that to treat them as commands coming from an external source was to deprive them of their moral character. But, though many writers have adopted his views on this point unquestioningly, the position is altogether untenable. There can be no obligation where there are not two persons concerned—a superior having authority and a subject who owes obedience to his ommands. No man can impose a law upon himself. For law binds the will, and so long as no superior authority commands us, we remain at liberty to choose either alternative. I cannot owe a debt to myself. If the moral law binds us, as we know that it does, this can only be because it comes to us from one who can claim the duty of obedience from us. An essential note of morality is lacking unless we recognize that the command is imposed by an external authority, and yield obedience to it as such.

This is not to say that the moral law is arbitrary. We have seen that it is not so; that it is revealed to us by reason as the rule of life involved in our rational nature. It is *natural* law. But only if there be an authority who commands me to observe the natural order, does it acquire the character of *law*.

If, then, we ask who it is who thus commands, there can be but one answer. The moral law, as we have seen, has the note of necessity. The authority who imposes it must then be final. Only when a command issues from the supreme and ultimate authority is it in the strict sense necessary. The lawgiver who commands me is, then, the source and fountain of morality, the supreme arbiter of right and wrong. But he who possesses these attributes is God.

The proof which we have here sought to enforce is finely expressed by Butler, in language every phrase of which bears witness to his conviction of the argument. His words are all the more weighty, since no point of style is more characteristic of this great thinker than his cautious accuracy of statement and his care to avoid aught that savors of rhetorical exaggeration.

"There is," he writes, "a principle of reflection or conscience in every man, which distinguishes between the internal principles of his heart, as well as his external actions; which passes judgment upon himself and them; pronounces determinately some actions to be in themselves just, right, good; others to be in themselves evil, wrong, unjust; which without being consulted, without being advised with, magisterially exerts itself, and approves or condemns him the doer of them accordingly; *and which, if not forcibly stopped, naturally and always, of course, goes on to anticipate a higher and more effectual sentence, which shall hereafter second and affirm its own.*"

It has sometimes been urged that it is impossible to feel the sense of obligation before we are aware of a lawgiver; that no man can recognize that he owes the duty of obedience, unless he already knows for certain that someone makes this claim upon him. The argument, it is contended, which professes to prove the existence of God from the consciousness of obligation is manifestly fallacious; the conclusion is presupposed in the premises. We imagine we are demonstrating God's existence, whereas it is really assumed without proof. The objection has, it is true, a *prima facie* speciousness; but this is all. It amounts to no more than that it is not easy to see how the sense of obligation can arise; it is wholly *a priori*. On the other hand, we have but to appeal to our own experience to convince ourselves that in point of fact the sense of obligation arises spontaneously in the mind so as to afford us the basis of a legitimate argument for the existence of a lawgiver. When faced with the alternatives of right and wrong, we are immediately aware that we *ought* to choose the right. And this consciousness of duty owed is attested no less unmistakably by the character of the feelings which are consequent upon our actions. A breach of the moral law arouses in us certain affections of the mind such as shame, self-reproach, remorse, which necessarily involve the presence of obligation. Cardinal Newman, when dealing with this argument in *The Grammar of Assent*, has given an admirable description of the emotions occasioned by the commission of some evil act in one whose moral sense is not yet blunted by wrongdoing. He writes, "No fear is felt by anyone who recognizes that his conduct has not been beautiful, though he may be mortified at himself, if, perhaps, he has thereby forfeited some advantage; but if he has been betrayed into any act of immorality, he has a lively sense of responsibility and guilt, though the act be no offence against Society—of distress and apprehension, even though it may be of present service to him—of compunction and regret, though in itself it be most pleasurable—of confusion of face though it may have no witnesses. These various perturbations of mind, which are characteristic of a bad conscience, and may be very considerable—self-reproach, poignant shame, haunting remorse, chill dismay at the prospect of the future—and their contraries when the conscience is good, as real, though less forcible, self-approval, inward peace, lightness of heart, and the like, constitute a generic difference between conscience and our other intellectual senses" (p. 105). The value of this argument is strikingly attested by the great writers of classical antiquity. Not a few of these affirm, as beyond all possibility of question, the existence of a law, rooted in the very nature of man, immutable, universal in its obligation, and independent of all human authority. No earthly ruler, however absolute his sway, has, they declare, the power to change or override what this law prescribes, for it is divine in origin, and is imposed upon us by God Himself. Lactantius has preserved for us a passage from Cicero's lost work, *De Republica,* which is, perhaps, the most remarkable of these. It runs as follows:

"There is a true law, right reason, consonant to nature, coextensive with the race of man, unchanging and eternal. . . . It is not allowed us to make any alteration in that law; we may not take away any least portion of it; nor can we repeal it as a whole. Neither senate nor people have power to release us from our obligation in its regard. We need not search for someone to explain or interpret it. We shall not find one law at Rome, another at Athens; one now, another hereafter; but that law, one, everlasting and immutable, is binding on all races and at all times; and there is one common Master and Lord of all, God. He it is who drew up this law, determined its provisions, and promulgated it."

Yet our claim that man cannot fail to refer the moral law to a Divine authority, is not allowed to pass unchallenged. Appeal is made to the notions prevalent among uncivilized and barbarous races as, e. g., the Australian aborigines. More is to be learnt, it is contended, from these backward peoples than from civilized man, since they exhibit human nature in its primitive condition. We are assured by certain anthropologists that amongst these races morality is merely tribal custom, and that it is destitute of supernatural sanction. Thus Messrs. Spencer and Gillen, speaking of the precepts forming the moral code of the tribes which they describe, declare that "in no case whatever are they supposed to have the sanction of a supernatural authority." A closer investigation has shown, however, that the statement thus confidently made was based on insufficient knowledge; that on this point the native had not fully communicated his beliefs to the European. Those who have acquired a deeper insight into the mentality of these tribes, assert unhesitatingly that the Australian, no less than the civilized man, sees in the moral law the command of a Divine Being.

It may very likely be objected that, were the obligation of the moral law really inexplicable apart from a belief in God's existence, then those who deny the latter would as a consequence repudiate the former; that this, however, is most certainly not the case, for many of those who reject all belief in a Deity are forward to acknowledge the binding character of duty, and vehement in asserting that they recognize to the full the imperative nature of its commands. This is true. And it is natural that it should be so, even though it be the case that they have deprived themselves of all reasonable basis for such an attitude. Those who enunciate a revolutionary principle do not usually recognize all that is contained in it. It is left to those who come after to draw the conclusions and apply them to the conduct of life. Our militant rationalists have been educated to regard the moral law as binding. They grew up in a society where men's opinions on these matters were determined by that Christian tradition, which, for so many centuries, governed European thought. From their earliest years they were taught, in common with their fellows, to regard the law of right as obligatory. It has not entered into their minds to question that early teaching, or to scrutinize very closely the grounds of that obligation. They accept it as self-evident, and overlook the important fact that the reverence for the moral law, which Christian teaching enjoined, was based on the conviction that it is the authentic voice of God speaking within the soul. If there be no God, then no adequate ground for an obligation properly so called—for a moral necessity—exists; the sole authority to which a man owes obedience is the state. He may, it is true, see that of two courses of action open to him the one is more, the other less desirable. In this he has a motive for choice. But, as we have said above, a motive and an obligation are not the same thing. Be this, however, as it may, even if the champions of materialism fail to realize the consequences of the principle which they have adopted, their disciples will draw the inevitable conclusion. And, human nature being what it is, we may rest assured that this conclusion will be reduced to practice. Under any circumstances the passions chafe under the restraints of the moral law, and are always tending to break loose from its control. If it be deprived of that which alone gives it its constraining force, its power to rule us will be at an end; the sole barrier to the domination of passion will have been removed. In view of these facts the rapid spread of materialism suggests to thoughtful minds some very grave apprehensions for the future.

The point which we have been considering leads us naturally to the argument from the need of a sanction to the moral law. The argument is so closely connected with that from conscience, that they may conveniently be treated in the same section.

We have already urged that the distinction between good and evil is fundamental; that the goodness of an action is altogether independent of the question whether or not it will in the long run result in a balance of pleasure to the doer or to the community; and, further, that the life of virtue is the only life which befits man as a rational being. This, we maintain, is not merely the spontaneous affirmation of reason, but the verdict of all philosophy worthy of the name. Yet in the face of these truths the realities of life present us with a strange spectacle. The forces which, in human society, make for evil are so strong, that the practice of virtue is seen often enough to involve a man in temporal misfortune. There is no need to develop a theme which is a matter of universal experience. In a world where fraud, vindictiveness and treachery are so prevalent, the man who follows after justice does not compete with his rivals upon equal terms. His faithfulness to the law of right puts him at an overwhelming disadvantage. The prizes of life tend to fall to those who are devoid of scruples. These, as a rule, are the men who "prosper in the world and have riches in possession." Even in those cases in which a man, in spite of this handicap, attains some measure of success, the practice of virtue entails tremendous sacrifices. Purity, forgiveness of injuries, integrity, are possessions which are dearly bought. They involve an uphill struggle with our lower nature, which only ends with death. Those who purpose to be faithful to the moral law must be prepared to act directly counter to their comfort and expediency, not once or twice, but again and again; and so far as this existence is concerned, to forego in most cases all hope of a compensating advantage. It is impossible for human reason to acquiesce in this state of things. It refuses to believe that where the moral law is concerned, the universe lapses into chaos. In all other regards the mind of man recognizes the presence of order in the world. In so far as that order holds sway, things attain their perfection; it is the violation of order which involves them in catastrophe. To suppose that, when we are concerned, not with physical, but with moral law this should become otherwise, that in that sphere alone the path of order should be the road to ruin, and the contempt of order the path leading to success, is to put inconsistency at the very heart of things. It is to affirm that the universe is at the same time rational and irrational, and, what is still more incredible, that it is rational as regards what is inferior, irrational as regards its higher element. This our minds unhesitatingly reject as an impossibility. But, in this case, there is but one conclusion to be drawn. It is that the end is not yet; that the wrong of this life will be righted in another; that in due time the just will be rewarded and the wicked punished. But those who grant this must go further. They must admit that there exists a Supreme Ruler of the world who has imposed the moral law upon us as His command,

and has attached adequate sanctions to its observance; and that at His tribunal the actions of all men will be judged. They must allow, likewise, that He possesses the attributes requisite for such an office; that the secrets of all hearts are open to Him, and that He can judge infallibly regarding the merit or demerit of every thought, every word and every action that has ever been. To hold this is to affirm the existence of God.

(D) COMMON CONSENT OF MANKIND

T. J. WALSHE [1]

Regarding the existence of God, an appeal is sometimes made to the probative value of the testimony of mankind, and the following syllogism formulated:

The universal testimony of mankind in regard to a belief, upon which it is competent to pass judgment, is a criterion of truth.

But such universal testimony gives support to the existence of God—a belief upon which men are competent to pass judgment.

Therefore, God exists.

The major premiss is undoubtedly true. St. Thomas reminds us that an erroneous opinion comes from some accidental defect of intelligence, and cannot, therefore, be universal. Aristotle's judgment is similar: "That which all men instinctively hold to be true is a truth of Nature." But a twofold doubt arises in connection with the minor premiss:

1. With the exception of primary principles intuitively perceived, the statements which universal testimony supports are statements capable of being proved by reason. In face of this fact can it be said that universal testimony has a separate probative value? Is it not rather the case that universal testimony is the *result* of the fact that human reason perceives the truth of these statements?

2. Is the question of the existence of God one upon which it is really within the competence of *all* men to adju-

---

[1] *The Principles of Christian Apologetics*, pp. 47-50. (Longmans, Green and Company, New York. With permission.)

dicate? And is the consent really unanimous, i. e., do *all* men attest the *same* truth in the *same* sense?

These objections, however, disappear if the testimony of mankind be regarded, not as a separate proof, but as confirmatory of the rigorous metaphysical argument. And the confirmation is strong. Rome, Greece, Persia, India, Germany, Scandinavia, in the past—the Kelts, Slavs, Chinese, Egyptians, Ninivites, Chaldaeans, in the heyday of their power, and the races which cover the face of the earth at the present time—all agree as to the existence of God, whatever their differences of view regarding His nature. "Nowhere," wrote Quatrefages in *L'Espèce Humaine,* "is there a race, or an important division of a race, without belief in God."

It is time now to consider certain objections raised against the doctrine of God's existence. The assertion has been made, that such belief is due to the prejudices of education, or to the influence of legislators and priests, or to the vague fear which the mystery of life engenders. It is a wellknown fact, however, that prejudices change and disappear, and cannot account for a belief which has been and continues to be universal. Nor can any record be found of the imposition of such belief by either legislators or priests. The office of the priesthood is the effect of the belief, and not the cause. To say that the greatest minds of the human race have been actuated by fear in the adoption of religious belief is equivalent to a denial of the value of human thought and character.

But the universality of the belief has been impeached. Certain savage tribes, and many men of science do not believe in the existence of God. The statement as to the atheistical tribes should be met by an unqualified denial. Even the most barbarous—the Mincopies of the Andaman Islands, the Pygmies and Hottentots of Africa—err in this matter by excess and not by defect. When we speak of "men of science," we pass over those who have been justly called "les fanfarons petits-maitres de la Science"—the blustering coxcombs of Science—and we quote, before giving the full statistics, the testimonies of Lord Bacon, Pasteur, Brunetière, Lord Kelvin and others. "A profound knowledge of Science brings us back to God," is the judgment of him whose name is so honourably associated with the advance of Inductive Science. "C'est pour avoir réfléchi et étudié beaucoup que j'ai gardé une foi de Breton; si j'avais réfléchi et étudié davantage j'en serais venu à une foi de Bretonne." So wrote Pasteur in the "Revue des Questions Scientifiques" (T. XXXIX, p. 385). Brunetière's witness is not less explicit: "The more I have studied and seen, the longer I live and experience the trials of life, the greater the emphasis and conviction with which I declare myself a Catholic." It is most interesting to note the roads whereby great leaders in Science, Art and Literature have returned to the Church and Faith of their youth; Huysmans by the route of medieval art; Coppée by the royal road of suffering; Pasteur's faith was confirmed by the study of natural science; Brunetière was led back through the study of philosophy and literature; Bourget, through the investigation of sin and its consequences. The routes differ, but they all converge to a centre—the home of Unity and Peace. And Lord Kelvin's theistic witness has been expressed in the following words: "Overpoweringly strong proofs of intelligent and benevolent design lie around us . . . showing to us through nature the influence of a free-will, and teaching us that all living things depend on one everlasting Creator and Ruler." Dr. Dennert's chart records the religious views of the greatest men of Science from the fifteenth to the nineteenth centuries. The class of "non-theists" in the chart embraces those authorities in whose works appear no definite theistic views, as well as those who explicitly held atheistic views.

	Theists	Non-theists	Total
XV to XVII centuries	79	3	82
XVIII century	39	16	55
XIX century	124	39	163
	242	58	300

A final objection is drawn from the prevalence at all times of Polytheism. It will be sufficient to state here that the testimony of the greatest mythologists emphatically supports the statement that Monotheism was the original belief. Corruption of belief and decadence of nations came later. Such is the contention of Pritchard in his "Egyptian Mythology," of Grimm in his "Germanic Mythology," of

Müller in "Orchomenus," of Franck, "Oriental Studies," and of Darmesteter in his "Aryan Mythology." Thus the testimony of mankind—whether the races be civilised or barbarous—gives strong confirmatory proof of the doctrine of Theism.

10

WHY SOME DO NOT BELIEVE IN GOD

Joseph Rickaby [1]

You ask me how it is that if the existence of God our Creator can be proved to a certainty, so many intellectual men remain unconvinced. I reply that by aid of one proof or another, sundry proofs appealing to sundry minds, most intellectual men do arrive at some conviction of the being of God, however they may differ as to His nature. You have heard what Jowett said, walking in the quadrangle of Balliol with a newly arrived freshman, who, thinking to please the Master, told him that he had searched and found no God anywhere: "Well, Mr. X., unless you have found a God by half-past four this afternoon, you leave this College." Jowett was right: God can be found; and by most men, with greater or less success, He is actually found. Still, you say, there is a considerable residue, and in our day an increasing residue, of men who do not find Him. For this there are many reasons. One reason, often alleged, and, doubtless, rightly alleged in many cases, is some moral obliquity, pride, sensuality, or the like, perverting the judgment. But I spare you that well-worn topic. I want to set before you a reason, assigned by our Saviour Himself. Take out your New Testament, and read St. John vi. 41-45, 64, 65. You will say, this *drawing,* this *gift* of the Father, refers to the actual grace which is requisite to faith, but that we are not now discussing faith in revelation, we are discussing the natural certitude about God attainable by reason. Quite so, but he who rejects God's call to faith is apt to be scornful of reason also; he who will not be a Christian, when he might have been, will

[1] *Studies on God and His Creatures,* pp. 75-78. (Longmans, Green and Company, New York. With permission.)

make a very feeble-kneed Deist. But I am anxious to keep the argument out of the region of the supernatural, and remain, as a philosopher should, *in puris naturalibus*. Even in the natural order, then, so good theologians aver, there is such a thing as "natural grace." Even in the natural order, it is no apparent impossibility for God Himself to speak direct to the human soul, and not leave it to be impressed solely by contact with creatures. St. Thomas, you will remember, makes direct communications from God a necessity for the angels to have any knowledge at all of the facts of creation; yet, surely, such knowledge naturally befits the angel. So, then, there are natural locutions of God to angels; so, also, to men (*Summa*, i a, q. 55, art. 2). In the present supernatural order, actual grace is necessary for man to observe the natural law uniformly and thoroughly; so the Council of Trent rules, Sess. vi., canon 22; and the Council of Carthage (A. D. 418), canon 5. And St. Paul speaks of the perfect observance of the law as *what the law could not do, in that it was weak through the flesh* (Rom. viii, 3). But in all sound theology it must be assumed that man in the state of pure nature would not be stronger to observe the law of rectitude than man is now. Locutions from God, or "natural graces" (they are natural merely, and not supernatural, because they do not lead up to any beatific vision, or face-to-face contemplation of God in heaven), are, then, necessary for man to exist as a moral being even in the state of pure nature; they are needs of man as man. If the will needs these natural graces, these divine locutions, the intellect needs them also; the intellect, to know its Master, the will, to serve Him. Thus in any case it *is not a mere matter of proofs,* when there is question of man arriving at and holding fast to the philosophic cognition of God. When proofs have led the enquirer a certain way, he comes within the sphere of divine locutions. These locutions do not instruct him, they are not revelations, but they press upon the mind the arguments which reason has already found for believing in God. Some men listen to God and believe; others disobey those inner divine voices, and, turning their backs upon Him who has spoken to them, they fall to quarrelling with arguments. They cavil at the process of Reason proving a God, because they stop the ears of their intelligence to the Voice, speaking within, which bids them accept the demonstration. Read St. John again, xii, 37-48; also St. Paul, Acts xxviii, 24-27; and apply those texts, first, to the actual world, of which they are spoken, then to the world of philosophers and speculative divines, and to the divine locutions which would be given even in the state of pure nature. Some men listen to the call of God, and find Him; the reason why others miss Him is because they do not listen to His call.

11

IMMORTALITY OF THE SOUL

MICHAEL MAHER [1]

Although rigid demonstration of a future life presupposes the existence of a Divine Ruler,—for were there no God, the present question would be idle and meaningless,—still it is worthy of note that some of the proofs of immortality are amongst the most forcible arguments for the existence of the Deity. Anyhow, the considerations to be advanced here are of a purely rational character, and prescind altogether from the assured certainty of an everlasting life which we have guaranteed by Revealed Religion.

Teleological Argument.—Our first proof will be that deduced from the nature of the faculties, aspirations, and yearnings of the human mind, and the manner in which they point to another sphere of existence in which they are designed to enjoy their appropriate objects. Notwithstanding the seeming success which temporarily marked the first assault of the theory of *natural selection* on the doctrine of final causes, it is now becoming more and more evident every day that the attempt to explain the universe and all it contains in a purely mechanical fashion, as the fortuitous outcome of the collision of blind forces, has completely failed; and that the theory of Evolution is hopelessly incompetent to solve even the simplest biological problems without ultimately falling back on a teleological conception of the world. At all events, evolutionists themselves are fully as insistent as pre-Darwin physiologists on the axiom

---

[1] *Psychology*, pp. 526-543. (Longmans, Green and Company, New York. With permission.)

that there is *no organ without its function,* that no activity or faculty is to be found in the kingdom of organic life which has not its fitting object, its appropriate end to serve. The eye would never have been developed unless there were in existence light and material objects to be seen. The mechanism of the ear would never have been evolved save to operate in a universe of sound. The senses of smell and taste exist only because there are real stimuli to exercise them. And each instinct discovered in the animal kingdom points infallibly to some real object by which it is to be gratified. "Everywhere in nature there is evident the law of correlation, of finality of harmonious reciprocity, of appeasement of real needs, and satisfaction of natural tendencies." [2] Even the rudimentary organ is held to establish conclusively the reality of the past or future occupation for which the member was made. In fact, all the evidence gathered in behalf of Evolution, when impartially viewed from a larger and higher standpoint, merely confirms the main thesis of Natural Theology that the Author of the world is a Being of infinite wisdom who governs it in harmony with *reason* and according to *law.* If we now turn to Psychology for an accurate account of our mental aptitudes and tendencies, we shall learn that the Mind is the subject of activities and powers rising altogether above the needs of the present life; and that it exhibits talents and aspirations which find not their proper satisfaction here, but stretch out beyond the present existence, demanding a future state in which they may attain adequate realization.

Aspirations of the Intellect.—Man alone, of all creatures upon earth, has the power of looking back into the past and forward into the future. His mind, by the indwelling energy of its peculiar nature, strains and gazes out across distant epochs of time. Unlike that of the mere animal, its interest is not confined to the present *Now.* It naturally rises to the concept of *endless duration.* The mystery which surrounds this notion has ever been a stimulus to thought and speculation. It lies at the source of man's most universal and deep-seated intellectual cravings; whilst the most ardent admirers of the sagacity of the lower animals do not venture to suggest that the idea of a never-ending future exercises their intelligence

---

[2] Cf. J. Knabenbauer, S. J., *Das Zeugniss des Menschengeschlechtes für die Unsterblichkeit der Seele,* p. 5.

or troubles their peace of mind. There is a similar attraction for the intellect in the notion of *space*. Thought is conscious of the power and the impulse to transcend the physical boundaries and impediments which fetter the bodily frame. It feels that, unlike material energies, it can in an instant reach out and soar beyond the utmost frontiers of the created universe. The conception of the *possible,* the *necessary,* the *universal,* as the schoolmen insisted, is the special fruit of man's intellect. The more the human mind is developed and perfected, the more it feels its affinity with realities which lie behind and beyond sensible experience.[3] Higher rational activity, in fact, proclaims that the true and sufficient object of the yearnings of the soul must lie beyond the confines of this life circumscribed by corporeal conditions. If every organ has its fitting function, and every instinct its appropriate object, it is incredible that the highest aspirations of reason should be aimless, and the noblest energies of man should be ever emptying themselves into a void.

This same line of reasoning is accepted by as thorough-going an evolutionist as A. R. Wallace. He has written thus: "Those faculties which enable us to transcend time and space, and to realize the wonderful conceptions of mathematics and philosophy, or which give us an intense yearning for abstract truth (all of which were occasionally manifested at such an early period of human history as to be far in advance of any of the few practical applications which have since grown out of them), are evidently essential to the perfect development of man as a spiritual being, but are utterly inconceivable as having been produced through the action of that law (of Natural Selection) which looks only, and can look only, to the immediate material welfare of the individual or the race. The inference I would draw from this class of phenomena, is that a superior intelligence has guided the development of man in a

---

[3] Cf. Piat: "Notre pensée n'est pas close, comme celle des bêtes, dans une portion déterminée du temps et de l'espace; son élan natif l'emporte plus loin: de quelque manière qu'elle s'exerce, de quelque côté qu'elle se tourne, c'est toujours de l'Eternel qu'elle a en perspective. Or il y a quelque chose de significatif dans cette excellence de notre esprit. En face de l'éternité le temps ne compte pour rien. Si longtemps que nous ayons vécu, tout nous a encore manqué lorsque nous venons à mourir, si nous mourons tout entiers. Quand nous sortons de la vie, l'adaptation de notre pensée à son milieu connaturel n'a pas commencé; il reste entre notre idéal et nous une disproportion radicale. Il faut donc, pour que la finalité soit satisfaite, que notre existence se prolonge à l'indéfini." (*Destinée de l'Homme,* p. 159. Paris, 1898.)

definite direction and for a special purpose." (*On Natural Selection,* p. 359.)

Yearning of the Will: *Insatiate desire of Happiness.*—But the intellect is not the only faculty which speaks to us of another life; the conative side of man's being insists not less urgently on the same truth. In each living creature the collective tendencies which issue from its internal constitution form the complete expression of its *nature* or *essence,* and manifest the end which it is designed to realize. The specific tendency of the human being is *rational appetency.* This is the characteristic outpouring of man's being; through it, his true self-realization is to be accomplished. But since rational appetency follows upon intellectual cognition, and since this latter activity tends towards the universal and the infinite, ever insatiably conceiving better and more perfect objects than those presented by experience, so rational desire can never rest content with the goods and pleasures of this life.

We are not dependent, however, on abstract reasoning for the establishment of this fact. Our own consciousness, along with the sages, poets, and philosophers of every age, all iterate the same truth. There is implanted in our nature a yearning for happiness which can never be satisfied in our present sphere. This rational instinct exhibits itself in the lowest and hardest conditions of human existence; but the wealth, the comforts, the luxuries, the art and the science which civilization brings, are impotent to appease it. The power of conception ever exceeds the present reality. With each successive stage of mental development the craving becomes more and more conscious of itself, and it grows and expands, proclaiming ever more clamorously that it is not to be satiated with any finite creature. The brute animal lives normally in a state of content. Its faculties and instincts find their proper nutriment, and it is satisfied. But for man "the eye is not satisfied with seeing, nor the ear filled with hearing." Though master of the rest of creation, he is condemned throughout this life by the very constitution of his rational nature to be *un-*satisfied with his lot! Is it possible, that of all living beings on earth, man alone—and in his highest powers—is to be aimlessly dis-proportioned and mis-adapted to his environment? Is this highest of rational instincts destined to be universally frustrated? Are the loftiest and best yearnings of the noblest and best work in this rational universe to be for ever vain and illusory? and more vain and disappointing *precisely in proportion as by moral and intellectual culture he developes and perfects his highest faculties?*[4]

Ethical Argument.—It is, however, from the department of *Ethics* that reason puts forth the most irresistible demand for a future life.[5] Morality is an essentially *rational* phenomenon. The reality of right and wrong, of duty and virtue, of merit and responsibility, are amongst the most certain convictions of our rational nature. That what is seen to be clearly wrong *must not* be done, notwithstanding the temporal disadvantages which may ensue, is an axiom to which the intellect gives complete assent, however feeble the will may be in actual practice. But in the judgment that conduct entailing a sacrifice *ought* to be pursued, there is implied the further judgment that it cannot be ultimately *worse for the agent himself* to do that which is right. Our intellect, in fact, affirms that right conduct is always *reasonable*. The supposition that virtue can finally result in a maximum of misery for the agent; or that wickedness may effect an increase in the total quantity of his personal happiness is seen to be in conflict with reason, and to be destructive of all morality. It is impossible that perfect and fully enlightened reason can recommend us *to do* that which conscience categorically *forbids*. But if so, our permanent real interests cannot be injured by right conduct. *Duty cannot be in irreconcilable war with rational self-love.*

In the concrete.—The issue becomes clearer when we face the question in the concrete. Can it be equally well in the end for the successful swindler who amasses a fortune

---

[4] "Il faut donc ou que l'homme soit dans la nature un monstre incompréhensible ou qu'il y ait pour lui quelque chose de plus que la nature. Il faut ou que la vie de l'homme n'ait aucun sens et n'en puisse jamais avoir . . . qu'elle devienne de plus en plus intolérabie au fur et à mesure, que se déployant davantage, elle enferme plus de raison; il faut que la vie de l'homme soit impossible en droit ou qu'on la conçoive comme la première étape d'une évolution commencée qui doit s'achever ailleurs. Si tout finit avec le dernier soupir, l'homme est un être manqué; il est tel par nature; il l'est d'autant plus qu'il touche de plus près à son point de maturité. Or il n'est pas rationnel de croire à une antinomie aussi profonde: on ne peut admettre que cette même finalité qui s'accuse si visiblement dans toutes les espèces inférieures, s'arrête brusquement au plus haut degré de la vie et y fasse à jamais défaut." (Piat, op. cit. pp. 192, 193. Cf. Martineau, *A Study of Religion*, Bk. IV.)

[5] The ethical proof, resting on *divine purpose* in the world, is itself *teleological*, but is conveniently separated from the former proof.

by the plunder of his clients, and for the upright man who honestly struggles through a life of poverty, and resisting temptation, dies in want? Can it be ultimately the same for the forger or slanderer and the innocent man, whose life he has ruined? Is there to be no difference, when the last breath is breathed, between the murderer and his victim, the adulterer and the chaste, the martyr or the saint and his malicious persecutor? History affords plenty of examples of bad men, with hardened conscience, prosperous to the end of their lives, and of virtuous men who, owing to their honesty, have died with the stamp of failure on their earthly career. Our whole rational moral nature affirms that this cannot be the final outcome of things; that it cannot in the last resort be as well or better for those who violate the principles of justice, and those who faithfully observe the moral law seeking to conform their conduct to the ideal of right and holiness. *The first postulate of physical science is that the universe is rational.* Its most fundamental axiom, the *law of uniformity,* is based on this assumption. *Would it be a rational universe if vice is to be rewarded and virtue to be punished in the end?* Is it a rational universe if the moral life of mankind be founded on an *illusion?* Can the holiness of the world's saints, the virtues of its best heroes, the moral life of the mass of mankind, have had their source and origin, their never-failing food and support in one huge hallucination?

Professor Sidgwick merely expressed this truth in the most moderate terms when, after all decorous hesitations and qualifications and sub-qualifications, he conceded that "the existence of a Supreme Being who will adequately reward me for obeying this rule of duty or punish me for violating it," is "a matter of life and death to the Practical (Moral) Reason," and finally concluded with the truest philosophical statement in his work. "The whole system of our beliefs as to the intrinsic reasonableness of conduct must fall . . . without a belief in some form or other that the Moral Order which we see imperfectly realized in the actual world is yet actually perfect. If we reject this belief, we may, perhaps, still find in the non-moral universe an adequate object for the Speculative Reason capable of being in some sense ultimately understood. But the Cosmos of Duty is reduced to a Chaos, and the prolonged effort of the

human intellect to frame a perfect ideal of rational conduct is seen to be foredoomed to inevitable failure."[6]

Immortality makes Morality always reasonable.—On the other hand, if the present life be, as the Schoolmen taught, only the antechamber to eternity; if the happiness of Heaven means the perfection of man's highest powers and the satisfaction of his highest aspirations in a blissful union with the infinite source of all beauty and all good by contemplation and love; and if a life of virtue here consists in the perfecting of our nature and the preparation of it for that union with God, then we have an adequate foundation for all our ethical notions. And we are provided with an ideal of moral life and a conception of man's end, which explain and harmonize our ethical conceptions among themselves, and their relations with the facts of our temporal life.

Actual sanctions imperfect.—It is true, of course, that the present life is not devoid of moral sanctions, that extreme courses of vice generally meet with retribution, and that, as a rule, honesty is the best policy—at least where the police system is efficient. But it cannot be seriously pretended that this is always the case; and still less that each individual act of virtue, and every noble sacrifice for the sake of duty gains its just recompense. It is indisputable that in the lives of the great majority of men a certain judicious mixture of unscrupulousness would secure to the agent an increase in the dividend of the sources of happiness. It is urged also that the sanctions of conscience and of public opinion, compensate for all other deficiencies. We should be very sorry to unduly depreciate the value of a good conscience; but the assertion cannot stand the test of experience. It is generally only in the virtuous that conscience is sensitive; and good men probably suffer sharper pangs for smaller faults than the wicked do for grievous crimes. Indeed, the more abandoned the criminal, the fainter the internal moral chiding becomes; whilst agreeable elation or complacent self-satisfaction over his meritorious performances is not a kind of pleasure in which the truly virtuous man is wont to indulge. Finally, if belief in a future retribution be recognized as illusory, both the *menace* and the *promise* which make up the chief part of the sanction of conscience are annihilated.

---

[6] *Methods of Ethics* (Edit. 1874), Bk. IV. c. vi.; cf. also Balfour, *Foundations of Belief*, pp. 339-354; and Mallock, *Is Life Worth Living?* c. ix.

The claim put forward on behalf of public opinion as an adequate supplementary sanction is equally invalid. For, firstly, the censure of society cannot reach secret sins and a very large part of man's moral life; whilst it is extremely likely to err regarding *motives* on which the *goodness* or badness of conduct essentially depends. Secondly, the only public opinion for which the individual cares is that of his own class or neighborhood; and this not infrequently is opposed rather than favorable to virtuous actions.

Formal Theistic Proof.—Formally assuming the existence of God as independently established in Natural Theology, the argument for a future life may now be thus enunciated: An infinitely wise and benevolent God could not have implanted in all men a yearning for happiness whilst intending this natural desire to be necessarily, finally, and universally frustrated. Nor could He as a just and holy legislator have imposed upon mankind His Moral Law whilst leaving it incomplete and imperfect through defective sanction. But if there be no future life for man, God has done this: hence we are bound to conclude that God has designed to continue the soul's conscious existence after death.

Argument from Universal Belief.—Another argument upon which much stress has always been laid is the practical universality of the belief in a future life. Such a conviction in opposition to all sensible appearances must spring, it was urged, from man's rational nature, and must be allowed to be true unless we are prepared to hold that man's rational nature inevitably leads him into error in a matter of fundamental importance to his moral life. To admit this, it was argued, logically leads to scepticism. Adequate treatment of this argument would require considerable space.

Scholastic Metaphysical or Ontological Argument.—In addition to the arguments just given, the schoolmen deduced a proof of the soul's future preservation from its nature as a simple spiritual being. This ontological demonstration, it must be admitted, has not the persuasiveness with the modern mind which it possessed in the schools. Nevertheless, when properly understood, its defensive value is considerable. It enables the spiritualist to meet all materialistic attacks by showing that the subject of our conscious life is constructed to resist the destructive agencies which corrupt material beings; and it furnishes a conception by which a future life becomes more intelligible. We shall briefly state it in its scholastic shape.

By *death* is understood cessation of life in living beings. Such cessation of life might conceivably be brought about by either of two causes: *annihilation* of the living being, or *corruption* of its vital principle. *Annihilation* means the reduction of the object into absolute nothingness A creature is, strictly speaking, *annihilated* only when it so ceases to be that no element of it remains A being is said to be *incorruptible* when it is incapable of perishing either by dissolution into the constituent parts or elements which may compose it, or by destruction of the subject in which it inheres or upon which it depends for its existence. *Corruption* from the philosophical point of view may thus in scholastic language be of either of two kinds, *corruptio per se,* essential corruption, or *corruptio per accidens,* accidental corruption.[7] In corruption *per se* there is a dissolution of the being into its component principles, as in the death of a man and the combustion of firewood. A being was said to suffer corruption *per accidens* when put an end to *indirectly* by the destruction of the subject on which it depends. An *accident* perishes in this way when the subject in which it inheres is broken up or changed in such a manner as to be no longer a fit support for it, as in the case of the disappearance of the shape and color from a ball of melting snow or butter. According to the opinion most commonly received among the schoolmen, the extinction of the vital activity of brute animals and plants is an instance of *corruptio per accidens.*

Now the Ontological argument claims to prove three propositions: (A) that the human soul is both *per accidens* and *per se* incorruptible; (B) that it can be annihilated neither by itself nor by any other creature; (C) that no sufficient reason can be assigned for supposing that God will ever annihilate it. It should be clearly understood that Almighty God could by an exercise of His absolute power[8] annihilate the human soul

---

[7] "A Being is *incorruptible* if it does not contain within itself a principle of dissolution; it is *indestructible* if it can resist every external power tending to destroy or annihilate it. If the destructible and incorruptible Being is endowed with life, it is called *immortal.*" (Kleutgen, *Phil. d. Vorzeit,* § 844.) The significance of these terms varies slightly with different writers. Kleutgen points out that annihilation is always possible to God by the mere withdrawal of His conserving act.

[8] The phrase *potentia absoluta* denotes the range of the Divine Power abstracting from all self-imposed decrees. Within its sphere is included the production of anything not involving a contradic-

or any other creature. For *every* creature continues to *exist* and *act* only in virtue of the constant *conservation* and *concurrence* of God. But the argument proves that the soul is fitted in its nature to survive, and that God is the only Agent by whom its destruction could be accomplished.

(A) *The Soul is incorruptible.*—It has been already demonstrated (1) that the soul is a substantial being, (2) that it is simple or indivisible, (3) that it is spiritual or not intrinsically dependent on the body for its action or existence. (c. xxi.) But a simple substantial being is incapable of corruption *per se,* for it is not composed of distinct parts or principles into which it might be resolved; and a spiritual substance is exempt from corruption *per accidens,* since it does not intrinsically depend on the body for its existence. Therefore the human soul is incapable of corruption in either of these alternative ways. Incorruptibility is thus a consequence of immateriality. If the mind were a function of the brain, or an aspect of nervous processes, then dissolution of the organism would necessarily involve destruction of the soul. The refutation of these hypotheses in our first three chapters has, consequently, removed the chief argument against the possibility of a future life.

(B) *The Soul cannot be annihilated either* (1) *by itself or* (2) *by any creature.*—Annihilation is the reduction of something to nothing. But this result cannot be the effect of any *positive* action; for every positive action must terminate in a positive reality. A positive act, other than that of creation, can only *change* the state of the materials upon which it operates. It cannot make them disappear altogether. Any action accordingly, whether of the soul itself or of another creature, could at most effect merely a change or modification in the soul. Annihilation is possible only by the withdrawal of the conserving or creative power which has sustained the being in existence. Now, as creation and conservation in existence pertain to God alone, He only can cease to preserve; and, therefore, He alone can annihilate. The argument has been thus concisely stated: "Inasmuch as it is a simple spiritual substance, the soul can come into existence only through the creative act of God; and, therefore, only through annihilation by God can it perish. Annihilation consists in the refusal of any further creative conservation: accordingly, He alone who preserves and sustains a being can let it sink back into nothing.

tion, such as would be, *e. g.,* a square circle. *Potentia ordinata* signifies the range of God's power as conditioned by His free decrees. Thus, if God has once promised a particular reward on the fulfilment of a certain condition, He cannot henceforward retract.

In fact, no created force can subdue Omnipotence exercising creative conservation, so as to reduce into nothingness that which God preserves in existence. Divine creation and conservation consists merely in the effective volition that something *be*. Now, either God wills that the soul exists longer, or He does not will it. If He wills it, then His will can be overcome by no finite power. If He does not will it, then it ceases of itself to exist without any other agency being cause of its cessation. Consequently, the soul can in no way be destroyed by any finite power." [9]

(C) *There is no reason to suppose that the Soul will ever perish.*—It has been now proved by the ethical and teleological arguments that the soul will not perish at death, and by this ontological argument that it is of its own nature incorruptible, and that it can be destroyed neither by itself nor by any created being; it only remains to be shown that there is no ground for supposing that God will ever annihilate it. The ultimate end and purpose for which the Almighty conserves the soul in existence is His own extrinsic glory, both objective and formal.[10] But this end remains for ever; therefore the act of conservation ought to be everlasting.

The only conceivable grounds which can be suggested for the cessation of God's preserving action are, (*a*) the incapacity of the soul to act when separate from the body, with its consequent inability to apprehend, to praise, or to love God, and (*b*) the unworthiness of the souls of the wicked to exist. As regards (*a*), the ethical argument proves that the soul must live at least for a time after death, and be capable of experiencing reward or punishment. It must, therefore, be endowed with intelligence and will, and so be capable of contributing to the formal glory of God. The mode, however, of its action, following the mode of its existence, must be different from that of its present state. (*b*) As for the wicked, it is at least *possible* that they may be preserved for ever to vindicate by their punishment the justice and offended majesty of God; though that this is a *fact* cannot be proved by *philosophy* alone. For, absolute

---

[9] Gutberlet, *Die Psychologie*, pp. 314, 315.
[10] The *extrinsic* or *external* glory of God is that given to Him by His creatures; *intrinsic* or *internal*, is that afforded by Himself. The former is finite, the latter infinite. Both kinds may be either *objective* or *formal*. The *objective* glory of God is that conferred by the mere existence of His perfections, whether manifested in Himself or in His works. The latter is compared to that reflected on the painter by his pictures. The *formal* glory of God consists in the recognition and acknowledgment of the Divine excellences, whether by Himself or by created intelligences.

certainty of eternal punishment, as of everlasting reward, is afforded us only by the infallible testimony of Holy Writ. The *congruity* of such unending punishment was deduced by scholastic theologians from consideration of the infinite majesty of the Person offended, and the infinite claims which He possesses over His creatures. The rebellion and ingratitude of the creature constituting an offence under a certain aspect infinite was held to be—even in the light of pure reason—not unfittingly punished by a penalty finite in intensity but unlimited in duration. The adequate treatment, however, of this difficulty would lead us into the territory of dogmatic theology.

Objections against the doctrine of a Future Life.—As the proofs of Immortality are nowadays attacked from various standpoints, it is most desirable to define accurately how much each can really establish. A want of clearness and precision on this point is not infrequently exhibited by defenders of a future life; and they sometimes forget that the use of an unsound argument, or the misuse of a sound one, has often seriously damaged a good cause. To us it seems best to admit frankly that whilst each of the ordinary proofs has some special merit, it is also subject to some particular defect or limitation; and that it is only by their collective combination that the complete doctrine can be satisfactorily established.

(1) *The ethical argument* demonstrates that there must be a future *conscious existence;* but it hardly proves that this must last *for ever.* For it would be difficult to show that God could not adequately reward and punish virtue and vice in a finite period. (2) The *teleological argument* also proves a future conscious existence in which the higher aspirations of Intellect and Will can be satisfied. And although it may not rigidly demonstrate that the future life must be *endless,* it points to that conclusion, at least in the case of the *good.* But it is more complex than the previous argument: it presupposes the formal establishment of the *law of finality* by Natural Theology or Science; and so its persuasive power is less. Further, respecting the future existence of the *wicked,* its logical force is distinctly weaker. (3) The argument from *universal belief* is subject to these same limitations. All three proofs merely establish the *fact* of a future existence. None of them suggest *how* this is to be reconciled with the tendency to decay witnessed in all living organisms. They simply leave us with the *antinomy*

or seeming conflict between experience and reason unsolved. (4) Here the *ontological argument* comes to our aid. It removes the conflict by showing that the objections based on the corruption of material beings lose their force when directed against the subject of thought and self-consciousness. It also shows that continuity of existence is *natural* to the soul; that is, that the soul is *apt* to endure, and that it is not liable to destruction by any created agency. But since this continuity of existence is a contingent fact, depending on the free-will of God, the simplicity or spirituality *alone* cannot prove that this continuity will be certainly realized. To secure this recourse must be had to some form of the *teleological* argument. Further, since in our experience consciousness is liable to interruptions; and since, as far as our knowledge goes, mental states are always accompanied by cerebral changes, the ontological argument, without still further help from teleology, would be unable to prove that the soul will be capable of eliciting conscious acts when separate from the body.

1. The answer to sundry difficulties will now be comparatively easy. Thus, for example, Professor James writes: "The substance (of the soul) must give rise to a stream of consciousness continuous with the present stream, in order to arouse our hope, but of this the mere persistence of the substance *per se* offers no guarantee. Moreover, in the general advance of our moral ideas, there has come to be something ridiculous in the way our forefathers had of grounding their hopes of immortality on the simplicity of their substance. The demand for immortality is nowadays essentially *teleological*. We believe ourselves immortal because we believe ourselves *fit* for immortality." *Principles of Psychology,* vol. i, p. 348.

It may be replied that the demand for immortality was teleological eight centuries ago in the time of Aquinas, and long before in that of Plato. The philosophers of the middle ages insisted much upon the *contingent* character of all created things. Not one of them would have put forward the simplicity of the soul as an argument for continuity of existence *except on teleological grounds*—as indicative of the intention of a wise and good God. It is an essential tenet of the scholastic philosophy (1) that the continuous existence of every creature depends on its free *conservation* by God and (2) that all its operations require the free *efficient concurrence* of the Divine Being. But all inferences as to the future free actions of God must necessarily be based on the doctrine of finality. For the persistence, then, both of "the stream of consciousness" and of the substance of the soul, the schoolmen had to argue from the "providentia divina" or the "consilium Dei," which is merely the Latin for *theistic teleology*. But in proving the soul to be a simple immaterial being, and thus exempt from corrupting agencies, they believed they showed its conservation to be natural or in harmony with reason; whilst to them it would be evidently incompatible with Divine Wisdom to preserve in existence an inert soul devoid of action and consciousness.[11]

2. The same answer destroys the force of **Kant's** famous objection based on what he calls "the *intensive quality*" of the soul, which he thus stated: "The supposed substance (of the soul), if not by decomposition, may be changed into nothing by gradual loss (*remissio*) of its powers, consequently, by *elanguescence*. For consciousness itself has always a degree which may be lessened, consequently, the faculty of being conscious may be diminished, and so with all the other faculties."[12]

---

[11] As an "encyclopaedic ignorance" of scholastic philosophy widely prevails in English psychological literature of the present day, a few citations may be useful to show that the teleological argument was appreciated by St. Thomas. That all creatures are *contingent* he proves thus: "Hoc, igitur, quod Deus creaturae esse communicat, ex Dei voluntate dependet; nec aliter res in esse *conservat*, nisi inquantum eis *continue influit* (infundit) esse, ut dictum est; sicut ergo antequam res essent, potuit eis non communicare esse, et sic eas non facere; ita postquam jam factae sunt, potest eis non influere esse; et sic esse desinerent, quod est, eas in nihilum redigere." (*Sum*. 1. q. 104. a. 3.) But the soul is *designed* to exist forever: "Unumquodque naturaliter suo modo esse desiderat; desiderium autem in rebus cognoscentibus sequitur cognitionem; sensus autem non cognoscit esse, nisi sub hic et nunc; sed intellectus apprehendit esse absolute, et secundum omne tempus; unde omne habens intellectum naturaliter desiderat esse semper; *naturale autem desiderium non potest esse inane;* omnis igitur intellectualis substantia est incorruptibilis." (*Ib.* q. 75. a. 6.) Again: "Impossibile est *naturale desiderium* esse inane; *natura nihil facit frustra*. Sed quodlibet intelligens naturaliter desiderat esse perpetuum, non solum ut perpetuetur secundum speciem, sed etiam individuum." (*Cont. Gent.* Lib. II. c. 55. Cf. *Ibid.* c. 79. ad. 4.)

[12] *Critique of Pure Reason* (Meiklejohn's Translation), p. 246.

Undoubtedly if God ceased to conserve the soul it would at once cease to exist; and whether this happened suddenly or after a gradual waning of its activity, matters not a whit. But it would be in conflict with the wisdom of God to suppose that He could conserve the soul in an inert, unconscious condition, devoid of all activity. Further, the argument from Ethics, and the desire of happiness, in so far as they establish anything, prove that the future existence must be *conscious*. Kant seems to suppose that continuous conscious existence is deduced by the ontological argument as a necessary result of the simplicity of the soul, *apart from and independently of the divine conservation and concurrence*. The argument may have been employed in this illegitimate way by deists—certainly not by the schoolmen. For them the aspirations of the intellect, the desire of happiness and the simple immaterial constitution of the soul, which secures its immunity from corruptive agencies, were all so much teleological evidence of God's design to continue the soul's existence and to supply His efficacious concurrence requisite for its conscious activity in the future.

3. A disembodied spirit, it is affirmed, cannot be pictured by the imagination. "A spirit without a body," Buchner assures us, "is as unimaginable as electricity or magnetism without metallic or other substances." Science also refutes our doctrine. "Physiology," says Vogt, "decides definitely and categorically against individual immortality, as against any special existence of the soul." Again Buchner: "Experience and daily observation teach us that the spirit perishes with its material substratum." To observations of this sort we may reply that (*a*) as far as imagination goes we cannot picture the soul *with* the body. Neither can we imagine God, nor the ultimate atoms of matter. (*b*) The comparison of the soul to bodiless electricity is a complete misrepresentation of our knowledge of mind. Electricity and magnetism, as we have already pointed out, are presented to us only through sensible *movements*, whilst we have an immediate consciousness of the simple nature of mental energy. (*c*) Vogt's assertion is simply as false as his other dictum, borrowed from Cabanis, that "thought is a secretion of the brain." Physiology can say nothing more than that the action of the soul during this life is affected by the condition of the brain. (*d*) The final statement cited from Buchner is equally untrue. We most certainly cannot observe or experience the death of the soul; and we trust our arguments have shown that we may infer the contrary.

4. "The soul is born with the body, it grows and decays with the body, therefore, it perishes with the body." [13] Modern

---

[13] Lucretius, *De Rerum Natura*, Lib. III, vv. 446, seq.

science has added very little to the argument stated with so much power by the Latin poet. Now, we have repeatedly pointed out that in the Scholastic system the human soul is *extrinsically* dependent on the body which it informs. Such a condition would completely account for all the correspondence observed, whilst *intrinsic* or essential independence remains. Such *intrinsic* independence combined with extrinsic *dependence* is thus advocated by Ladd: "That the subject of the states of consciousness is a real being, standing in certain relations to the material beings which compose the substance of the brain, is a conclusion warranted by all the facts. That the modes of its activity are correlated under law with the activities of the brain-substance is a statement which Physiological Psychology confirms: one upon which, indeed, it is largely based. . . . *All physical science, however, is based upon the assumption that real beings may have an existence such as is sometimes called 'independent,' and yet be correlated to each other under known or discoverable laws.* If this assumption could not be made and verified, all the modern atomic theory would stand for nothing but a vain show of abstractions. Upon what grounds of reason or courtesy—we may inquire at this point—does Materialism decline to admit the validity of similar assumptions as demanded by mental phenomena?" (*Physiological Psychology*, p. 607.)

The soul, moreover, as will be proved in a later chapter, is *created*, not derived, like the body, from the parents. It does not grow in the sense of being *quantitatively* increased; but, conditioned by the efficiency of the brain and sensory organs, it gradually unfolds its capabilities. It does not really decay with bodily disease, although since its sensuous operations are immediately dependent on the instrumentality of the organism, it must naturally be affected by the health of the latter. The argument can also be inverted. In many instances the mind is most powerful and active in the decrepit frame of the old; and at times, in spite of dreadful havoc from bodily disease, intelligence may survive in brilliant force to the last.

5. The argument from universal belief has been attacked on the ground that some peoples, and many individuals, both philosophers and non-philosophers, do not judge there is any future life. It may be observed in answer, that whenever the proof from universal consent is invoked, it only presupposes a *moral* universality. As regards the nations or tribes who have been asserted to believe in no future life, advancing knowledge does not confirm such a statement. The greatest care is required in interrogating savages regarding their religious opinions. Inaccuracy in this respect has often caused the

ascription of atheism to tribes later on proved to possess elaborate systems of religion and hierarchies of gods. Future annihilation, asserted to be a cardinal doctrine of Buddhism, is by the vast majority of the disciples of that sect understood to be not a return to absolute nothing, but an ecstatic state of peaceful contemplation.[14]

Final Objection.—There remains one sweeping objection which strikes at all the proofs alike. The insatiate desire for happiness, the intellectual demand for final equity, the seeming aptitude of an immaterial soul to survive, it is roundly asserted, afford *no guarantee that they will be realized.* The mind's inferences to the ultimate perfecting and setting right of things need not be valid; our intellectual craving for completeness, harmony, or symmetry in the universe does not prove their objective reality.

The answer is that the postulate here is not merely the satisfaction of some particular impulse. If those exigencies of our reason which demand a future life are doomed to disappointment, then there is an utter and enormous failure which involves radical perversity in the constitution of things. Science and Natural Theology alike assume as first principle and starting-point the *rationality* of the universe. But if there be no future life, then the fundamental principles of morality are in irredeemable conflict with the just claims of reason: the fount of seeming law, order, and finality is hopeless discord and senseless strife: the most imperious affirmation of our rational moral nature is one prolonged fraud: the ethical life of man, all that is highest and greatest in this world—that which alone is truly *good*—is a meaningless chaos. Intrinsic contradiction, absolute irrationality is the last answer both of science and philosophy!

It is true that some naturalistic writers adopt a lofty tone on this subject. The old-fashioned view of life and morality, they assure us, was base and ignoble. Virtue, we are told, is its own sufficient reward. Profound contempt is expressed for "the pains and penalties argument" of Christian philosophy. The doctrine of rewards and punishments is an "immoral bribe." Right conduct, we are informed with an unctuous austerity, ceases to be worthy

---

[14] On this argument, see Knabenbauer, op. cit.

of approval if the prospect of thereby attaining everlasting happiness is allowed to enter as a motive.

The academic philosopher from the university professorial chair—enjoying a comfortable income and agreeable occupation—may sneer at the moral convictions of human nature; but to the thoughtful man who gravely looks the stern realities of actual life in the face and contemplates the suffering of multitudes of mankind, such language must seem the most flippant and unworthy trifling. If this life be but a passing period of probation, and if there be a future state and an infinitely good and just God who will there apportion to all their just award, then difficult and obscure though the problem of existence be, *a rational solution is possible.* But if, instead, the universe be naught but an iron mechanism—whether idealistic or materialistic matters little—aimlessly and remorselessly grinding out tears, and pain, and sorrow; and if, when once this frail thread of conscious life is cut, all is over; then, for vast numbers of human beings hopeless pessimism is the only creed—and often and often suicide the most rational practical conclusion!

Here is a picture: "I think," says the poor dying factory girl, "if this should be the end of all, and if all I have been born for is just to work my heart and life away, and to sicken in this dree place, with those mill-stones always in my ears, until I could scream out for them to stop and let me have a little piece of quiet, and with the fluff filling my lungs, until I thirst to death for one long, deep breath of the clear air, and my mother gone, and I never able to tell her again how I loved her, and of all my troubles,—I think, if this life is the end, and that there is no God to wipe away all tears from all eyes, I could go mad." [15]

---

[15] Cited in the *Grammar of Assent*, p. 312.

12

FREEDOM OF THE WILL

Michael Maher [1]

Free-will defined.—Will, or Rational Appetency in general, may be described as *the faculty of inclining towards or striving after some object intellectually apprehended as good;* but viewed strictly as a free power, it may be defined as the *capability of self-determination.* By *self* is meant not the *series of my mental states,* nor the *conception* of that series, but the *abiding real being* which is *subject* of these states. By *Free-will* or *Moral Freedom,* then, we understand that property in virtue of which a rational agent, when all the conditions required to elicit a volition are present, can either put forth or abstain from that volition.

Scholastic Terminology.—The schoolmen here, as usual, distinguished terms with more accuracy and precision than their successors. They defined *spontaneous* acts, as *all those which have their source within the agent, e. g.,* the movements of the roots of a plant, as well as the impulsive or the fully deliberate actions of men. Such acts merely exclude *coaction.* The schoolmen further distinguished two forms of *voluntary* action. Voluntary acts in a *wider sense* they defined as "those proceeding from an internal principle (*i. e.,* spontaneous) *with the apprehension of an end."* Only voluntary acts in the *strict sense* were held to be free, or *deliberate.* These latter imply not only an apprehension of the object sought, but a self-conscious advertence to the fact that we are seeking it, or acquiescing in the desire of it. The spontaneous or impulsive acts of man which are the outcome of his nature are voluntary in the lax sense, but non-voluntary in the stricter signification. The term *actus humanus*—human action—was confined to *free* or *deliberate* acts: *actus hominis* designated all indeliberate actions of man. Further, the term *liberty* was carefully distinguished. *Physical liberty* means immunity from physical compulsion or restraint (*necessitas coactionis*). The unbridled horse is in this sense free, whilst the prisoner in a cell is not. *Moral Liberty, or Freedom of Will* (*libertas arbitrii*) signifies

---

[1] *Psychology,* pp. 395-404. (Longmans, Green and Company, New York. With permission.)

immunity from necessitation by the agent's nature (*necessitas naturae*). In this latter sense the prisoner is free, but the horse is not. When Locke defines free-will as *the power to do what I choose,* he confounds moral and physical liberty. The latter in the case of human beings is also called *personal freedom.*

Problem stated.—Now the question at issue is not whether man can choose or will without *any* motive whatsoever. Such a choice would be irrational and impossible, because volition implies the embracing of an object *intellectually apprehended as a good.* But any object of thought apprehended *as good* or *desirable* is thereby a *motive soliciting the will*—whether it be ultimately preferred or not. Attacks of determinists on "the theory of *motiveless* volition" are, therefore, completely irrelevant. No accredited defender of free-will teaches that man can choose or will without any motive. St. Thomas would have described such a view as self-contradictory and absurd. *Nihil eligitur nisi sub specie boni*—"Nothing is willed except under the appearance of good," was a universally received axiom in the schools. Free-will implies not choice *without* motive, but choice *between* motives. If there be but *one* motive within the range of intellectual vision, the volition in such circumstances is not *free,* but *necessary.* Equally unjustifiable is it to represent the doctrine of Indeterminism as a theory of *causeless volition.* The *mind* or the *self* is the cause. Again, the question is not whether *all* actions of man are free, but whether *any* action is so. In the words of Dr. H. Sidgwick: "Is my voluntary action at any (every) moment determined by (1) my character (*a*) partly inherited (*b*) partly formed by past feelings and actions, and (2) my circumstances or the external influences acting on me at the moment? or not?" Or, in those of Dr. Martineau: "In exercises of the will (*i. e.,* in cases of choice) is the mind *wholly* determined by phenomenal antecedents and external conditions; or does itself also, as *active subject* of these objective experiences, play the part of determining Cause?" Or, to put it otherwise: Given all the prerequisites for a volition except that act itself, does it necessarily follow? Or, finally, in the language of Professor James: "Do those parts of the universe already laid down absolutely appoint and decree what the other parts shall be?[2] *Determinists* or *Necessarians* answer in the affirmative; *Libertarians,* or *Anti-determinists* or *Indeterminists* say, No.

We allow most readily, first, that a very large part of man's daily action is *indeliberate,* and, therefore, merely the resultant of the forces playing upon him; secondly, that even where he acts deliberately, and exerts his power of free choice, he is *influenced* by the weight of the motives attracting him to either side; and, finally, as a consequence of this, we grant that a being possessed of a perfect knowledge of all the forces operating on a man would be able to prophesy with the greatest probability what course that man will take. But, on the other hand, we hold that there are many acts of man which are not simply the resultant of the influences working upon him; that he can, and sometimes does set himself against the aggregate balance of motive, natural disposition, and acquired habit; and that, consequently, prediction with absolute certainty concerning his future free conduct would be impossible from even perfect knowledge of his character and motives. Such is the thesis we defend. Whether it be called the doctrine of *free-will,* of *moral liberty,* of *indeterminism,* or of *contingent choice,* seems to us of little moment. But it is of the utmost importance that the precise point of the dispute should be understood, and the gravity of the issue realized. For this reason we have formulated the question in so many ways.

Fatalism and Determination.—There is a marked tendency among recent opponents of free-will to shrink from the use of such "hard" terms as necessity, fatality, and the like, adopted by their more courageous and more logical predecessors. We have now-a-days, as James says, "a soft determinism which says that its real name is freedom." (Op. cit. p. 149.) These efforts to change the meaning of the terms employed in the controversy can only confuse the student by obscuring the fundamental difference between the rival doctrines, which involve profoundly opposed conceptions of the universe. Mill (*Logic,* Bk. VI. c. ii. § 3, n. 3) sought to make a distinction between *Determinism* and *Fatalism.* The latter doctrine holds, he teaches, that all our acts are determined by *fate* or external circumstances,

---

[2] Cf. Sidgwick, op. cit. p. 46; Martineau, *Types,* p. 188; James, *The Will to Believe* (1898), p. 150.

independently of our feelings and volitions. Determinism, on the contrary, maintains that action is determined by feeling. *In practice,* then, they will certainly differ. The *determinist* may seek to arouse good desires in himself or others; the *fatalist* will abandon the attempt as useless. But, *logically,* fatalism flows from determinism. In connexion with this point Mill falls into one of his frequent inconsistencies, teaching that "our character is in part amenable to our will." (*Exam.* p. 511.) Our character is, of course, merely the result of inherited constitution and personal acts. The former is obviously beyond our control, and, according to Mill, the latter have all been inevitably predetermined by antecedent character and external influences, until we reach infancy, where, of course, there was no freedom at all. The desire to "alter my character" or to improve myself must, in the determinist theory, have ever been *as independent of* me, as *completely given to* me, as the shape of my nose.

The arguments usually adduced to establish the Freedom of the Will are threefold. They have been called the psychological, the ethical, and the metaphysical proofs respectively. The first of these appeals to the direct testimony of consciousness. The second is indirect in character, being based on the analysis of certain mental states—ethical concepts. The third is a more complex deduction from the nature of higher mental activity. We shall begin with the second as its demonstrative force is, to some minds, clearest.

Argument from Ethical Notions: Obligation.—"Thou canst for thou oughtst." The inference which Kant thus draws is perfectly just; though he erroneously interprets it, and confines liberty to the *noumenal world,* whilst conceding the "empirical self" and the phenomena of experience to the rule of a rigid determinism. If I am really bound *hic et nunc* to abstain from an evil deed, then it must at some moment be really possible for me that this deed shall not occur. The existence of *moral obligation* is at least as certain as *the uniformity of nature*—the assumption or postulate on which all the propositions of physical science rest. The conviction that I am bound to abstain from evil is not a *generalization* from an imperfect and limited experience, but an immediate and universal judgment of mankind. The moral law lies at the foundation of practical social life. *Right conduct is not merely a beautiful ideal which attracts me. It commands me with an absolute authority.* It obliges *me unconditionally.*³ Whatever be my own feelings or desires, I remain in each act categorically bound to do right and to avoid wrong. At the same time it is a patent fact that the moral law is not always observed. But if the moral law obliges me at all times it must be really within my power on those occasions when I disobey it. To suppose that I can be really and unconditionally bound to perform an act which is now, and has ever been, for me *absolutely impossible,* is utterly irrational. For instance, a dishonest director or promoter of a bubble company, is elaborating a plan to amass a fortune by the plunder of several hundred poor people. Suppose his moral sensibility is not as yet altogether obliterated, and that he adverts to the fact that his evil scheme is a piece of cruel and nefarious swindling. He feels that it is *wicked* and *wrong*—that he *ought not* to proceed with it. Involved in this consciousness of the present *obligation* is the conviction that he *can* abstain from his evil course. Are both the persuasion that he *ought* and that he *can* an illusion? In the determinist theory no other volition or choice than those actually elicited were really possible to that man throughout his entire past life, and the present criminal choice is inexorably determined by the equally inevitable choices that have gone before.

Remorse and Repentence.—Let us now examine the character of another mental state: If I have voluntarily yielded to some evil temptation, or knowingly done a wrong act; if I have been deliberately unjust, unkind, or dishonest, especially if I believe my act to have been grievously sinful; when I reflect upon it I am keenly conscious that my conduct was *blameworthy.* I *condemn* myself for it, I feel *remorse* for it, I judge that I ought to *regret* it, that I am bound to *repent* it.

³ Léon Noël states this argument well: "Si nous n'étions pas libres, *le bien* nous apparaîtrait comme un *idéal* nous manifestant sa beauté et solicitant notre amour. Il serait le terme d'une tendance analogue à l'admiration esthétique. . . . Ce n'est pas ainsi que *le bien* s'offre à nous. Il ne nous présente pas un *idéal,* attendant, pour nous entraîner à l'action, qu'il lui réponde un attrait assez puissant. Il nous apparaît sous la forme austère du *devoir,* nous *imposant* une loi à accomplir *toujours,* quelles que soient nos dispositions et nos tendances. Pour qu'un sentiment pareil ne soit pas absurde, il faut que nous soyons *libres.* L'impératif absolu du *devoir* suppose une puissance supérieure à toutes les circomstances, n'ayant besoin que d'elle-même pour lui obéir." (*La Conscience du Libre Arbitre,* p. 165.)

But for acts that have not been thus deliberately performed I do not in this way *blame* myself, even though they may have resulted in far more serious injury to others or to myself. Of course I wish that even involuntary actions of mine which may have occasioned harm had not happened; but I do not deem them *culpable;* and I judge that I am not bound to *repent* them. The sentence of self-condemnation and the pain of remorse present in the former and absent from the latter cases are due to the assurance that the former were *mine* in the strictest sense, that I *freely* did them—that, *unlike the latter,* they were *not* the inevitable outcome of my nature and circumstances, that I *could* have done otherwise. Furthermore, this clear distinction is confirmed by the universal judgment of mankind, which asserts that it is right to have remorse and to blame myself for the evil deliberately done *which I could have avoided,* but not for those acts which were not deliberate, and, *therefore, not in my power.* But if determinism be true, *both classes of acts were equally the inevitable outcome* of my nature and circumstances. If the reader will think out the strictly logical consequences of determinism he will see that, according to that theory, it is just as rational to indulge in remorse and self-condemnation for an attack of heart-disease or for being caught in a railway accident as for having committed an act of perjury.

The determinist—who invariably claims exclusive monopoly of the scientific attitude of mind—refuses to *think;* and, instead, vehemently insists that injustice is done his theory, that there is a profound difference between the two cases, that feelings of sorrow, desires, and purposes of amendment, are useful to prevent future perjuries, but not for the avoidance of railway collisions. This is very true, but equally irrelevant to the point at issue—the *rationality* of *remorse* and *self-condemnation* for our past *voluntary* acts. If all my past acts, whether deliberate or indeliberate, alike inevitably resulted from my nature and circumstances, it is not virtue but irrational folly to indulge in remorse for sin, and it is mendacious to teach that it is right and reasonable to repent of a crime which we believe to have been as unavoidable as an earthquake. Professor James writes on this topic with his wonted vigour. "Some *regrets* are pretty obstinate and hard to stifle,—*regrets* for acts of wanton cruelty or treachery, for example, whether performed by others or by ourselves. Hardly anyone can remain *entirely* optimistic after reading the confession of the murderer at Brockton the other day; how, to get rid of the wife whose continued existence bored him, he enveigled her into a desert spot, shot her four times, and then as she lay on the ground and said to him, 'You didn't do it on purpose, did you, dear?' replied, 'No, I didn't do it on purpose,' as he raised a rock and smashed her skull. Such an occurrence with the mild sentence and self-satisfaction of the prisoner, is a field for a crop of regrets, which one need not take up in detail. We feel that though a perfect *mechanical* fit for the rest of the universe, it is a bad *moral* fit, and that something else would have been really better in its place. But for the deterministic philosophy the murder, the sentence, and the prisoner's optimism were all necessary from eternity; and nothing else for a moment had a ghost of a chance of being put into their place. To admit such a choice, the determinists tell us, would be to make a suicide of reason; so we must steel our hearts against the thought. . . . (Yet) Determinism in denying that anything else can be instead of the murder, virtually defines the universe as a place in which what *ought* to be is *impossible*." (Op. cit, p. 61.) But it is in the name of reason—in order to conceive the universe as a *rational* whole—to satisfy the postulate of uniformity of causation, that determinists deny free volition!

Merit and Desert.—Closely related to the mental states just discussed are the conceptions of *merit* and *desert*—notions embodied in all languages, and engrained in the moral consciousness of mankind. When I have struggled perseveringly against a difficult temptation, or made some deliberate sacrifice in the cause of virtue, I feel that my act is *meritorious,* that I have *deserved* a reward. I may see no prospect throughout my life of receiving the recompense. But I am none the less assured that I have established a *right* to it, that such a recompense is *just*. And this I judge to be so *because* I believe the act to have been *free*. For if not, even though the act had been far more painful to myself, and far more useful to mankind, I deem that I have not this claim. The good accomplished unwittingly or involuntarily, however *useful,* is not *meritorious* on the part of the agent; praise or esteem which I may receive for it I recognize in my heart to be *undeserved*.[4]

[4] Cf. G. L. Fonsegrive: "Quand on dit, en effet, qu'on a mérité une récompense ou une punition, on veut dire non pas seulement que nécessairement il résultera de l'acte accompli un plaisir ou une douleur, mais qu'on s'est créé des droits soi-même à ce plaisir ou à cette douleur. Cela est si vrai que nous regarderions tous comme injustes une récompense ou une punition qui seraient les conséquences d'une action accomplie par nous sans notre assentiment intérieur." (*Essai sur le Libre Arbitre,* p. 509.)

Now this judgment is primarily *inward*. It is a *retrospective* sentence pronounced by my reason on my *deliberate* actions—or rather on *myself* as exerting them. I do not, as some determinists seem to imply, esteem these acts because they are evidence to me of the *valuable character* which I possess. The very reverse is often conspicuously the case, as when the drunkard, striving to reform, measures the merit of his painful resistance by the very badness of that formed character which the violence of his temptation reveals. Still less is the sense of merit due to the experience that good actions have been rewarded and evil acts punished in the past. From a very early age the child shows, in its feeble way, that it can clearly distinguish between *deserved* and *undeserved* punishment. "I could not help it," is the invariable excuse; and when the child really *believes* that this was the case, he is convinced that the punishment is *unjust*. This same retrospective judgment as to the merit or demerit of free action, and their absence from actions similar in effects but involuntary in origin, is confirmed by the general sense of mankind both cultured and uncultured.

Retribution.—The truth is, the idea of *moral retribution* is incompatible with Determinism. That theory is compelled to maintain that the notion of the *restitution of violated right order through expiatory suffering* is a childish delusion. Punishment is purely preventive. Praise and blame are not *just awards* for self-sacrifice in the *past*, but *judicious incentives* for anticipated *future* services. Gratitude is, not in jest but in earnest, "a delicate sense of favors to come."

Responsibility.—For acts done by me with advertence to the fact that I was doing them, and with a consciousness of their moral quality, I judge myself *accountable*. Their goodness or badness I consider to be rightly *imputed* to *me*. If good the *praise,* if evil the *blame* is *mine*. But actions performed by me inadvertently, or without cognizance of their moral quality, I pronounce with equal certainty *not* to be justly imputable to *me*. They are not truly *mine;* and it is not right that I should have to *answer* for them. The meaning and ground of this distinction is that I am convinced the former acts were *free* in the strict sense; that I had real power to have chosen the other course; whilst the latter were there and then inevitable—the necessary resultant of my character and the forces playing on me. This ethical conception is so important that it is desirable to scrutinize it closely:

Notion of Responsibility Analyzed.—Responsibility in the fullest sense pre-supposes: (1) A justly binding authority. (2) Knowledge in the agent of the just will of this authority—of the rightness or wrongness of the act. (3) Power either to perform or abstain from the act. If any of these be absent, responsibility in the full sense no longer exists. Be it noted that the reality of my responsibility or of my duty does not rest ultimately on the mere fact that the badness or goodness of the deed actually *moves* my will. Even were my will hardened by crime so as to become insensible to the charms of virtue or the foulness of vice, both obligation and responsibility would remain real, so long as I intellectually apprehended the act to be my *duty*. But most important of all, the act must be really *mine*—really within my power to perform or to omit. If not, my reason affirms, I cannot be *answerable* for it. Imperfect knowledge, fear, sudden passion—in so far as these conditions were themselves outside of my control—all diminish responsibility, precisely in proportion as they diminish freedom. I may have communicated the plague to an entire city, or poisoned my father and mother, and though plunged in grief over the terrible misfortune, I may retain the clearest conviction that I am not *responsible* for the calamity, that I am not morally *guilty* of the act, that I cannot be *justly* punished for it, *because I know it was not my free act,* because I am sure that *I could not have helped it.* I apply this same criterion to the conduct of other men, and I am quite certain that mankind at large would endorse my judgment. I may of course have been guilty of voluntary carelessness, or imprudence which resulted in the act. If so, I am accountable just in so far as this final act was voluntary or free *in causa*—in its original cause. That is, my responsibility is measured by the distinctness with which the final disastrous act could have been foreseen by me as likely to result from my earlier faults, and the facility with which these could have been avoided. It is because the maniac and the somnambulist are inevitably determined by their nature and the forces acting on them, that we judge them unaccountable for any harm which they may have caused. We take measures to prevent their innocently doing further evil; and we may even apply painful remedies to deter them in the future; but we do not judge them deserving of *blame* or moral *censure*. We deem them *irresponsible* agents. Responsibility is therefore not the "consciousness of the *solidarity* of our mental life," that is, the conviction that certain acts, *as a matter of fact,* physically entail certain painful consequences; nor the knowledge that the *law* visits certain transgressions with particular penalties. It implies that I am *justly* punishable for a past *free* act, and *only* for a *free* act.[5]

13

FREEDOM

JOHN G. VANCE [1]

What do we mean by freedom? And what is the will? Freedom looks at first sight like a wholly negative conception. It seems to imply only the absence of compulsion. A state is politically free when it can, without revolution, make or unmake its government, or when it is not compelled to accept a particular government by the enactments of constitutional law. An individual is free who can determine his own actions and movements in self-regarding matters without the intervention of some *force majeure.* An individual on the other hand, is not free to leave, unaided, the earth's surface. He suffers the compulsion of physical law. A chemical atom, too, is determined. It has no say as to whether it will be combined with others to form water or hydrogen peroxide. Nor on being combined can it resist disintegration, once the necessary energy is applied.

---

[5] Professor Alexander, who attacks the doctrine of Free-will in his Chapter on Responsibility, writes: "Responsibility depends on two things. First that a man is capable of being influenced by what is right, that he can feel the force of goodness; and second that *whatever he does is determined by his character.*" (*Moral Order and Progress,* p. 335.) Now if every human act is thus absolutely determined by character, how can I justly pronounce the Brockton murderer, mentioned above, to be worthy of *reprobation* rather than *pity;* or the man who perseveringly struggles against temptation to be *meritorious?* The *character* and every *volition* of each throughout his life were alike inexorably predetermined for him by his inherited organism and environment. Neither of these men have ever had for a second in their lives the *real power of making a different choice* than that which they have made. Again, Mill's statement that responsibility means "the knowledge that if we do wrong we shall *deserve* punishment," is plausible only because it explains one *free-will* term by another.

[1] *The Dublin Review,* July, 1919.

Chemical atoms are compelled by external agencies; they are not free.

Yet in spite of the negative appearance, freedom is something profoundly positive. Men do not die to defend negations; and many have died in the cause of freedom. It means the positive power of self-determination—a term long used by philosophers before it grew to be a by-word of European politics. In the absence of compulsion from without, the free State determines its own government and policy. In the absence of compulsion from without, the free individual arranges the affairs of his own private life. Freedom thus implies first, the absence of determining, necessitating forces from without, and secondly, the power of making and unmaking, of pursuing the path of national or individual choice. It means the power to live, expand and grow according to intrinsic desire or purpose, not necessarily uninfluenced or unimpeded, but certainly undetermined by any extrinsic fiat or order or force that could summarily arrest the inner development.

From freedom we turn to the will. What is the human will? Just one of our characteristic operations which shows itself in desire and in delight. We are led to do things, to take food and drink, to move from place to place, to adapt and fix the whole course of our actions which move, now slowly, now quickly, sometimes disjointedly, sometimes continuously, sometimes along the curve, often down the tangent, by our desires. In most things, great and small, we can easily unearth the desire, the tendency towards the satisfaction of some wish or craving, which shows the will in action. On the attainment of our wish, desire gives way to delight. We rejoice in what we hold or possess, in the power acquired, or in the means at our disposal. Desire shows the action of the will in urging us forward; delight shows the action of the will in possession. We delight in what we have; we desire what we have not.

So much for freedom and the will. Now what do we mean by freedom of the will? Nothing in the world is easier to misunderstand, and not a few philosophers have added to the natural obscurity an "artificial fog" of their own. (1) We do not mean that we can suddenly undo or uproot the whole past, and begin again as though nothing had happened. The past is irrevocable; it "eats" into the present. What's done is done without remedy and it may be without regard. The past beyond all question impels us. When we say that the will is free, we only mean that it does not necessarily compel us. (2) We do not mean that at any moment we can do just as we wish. We cannot add to our stature, cure a lingering disease, nor fly through the blue. We have no control over multitudes of physiological processes in our own bodies. As extended bodies we obey the laws of matter. When we assert freedom, we only mean that, beyond this ring of determination, lies a limited but important sphere of action, in which we are not necessarily compelled. (3) We do not mean that our wills have some secret fund of energy which, once liberated, can secure an otherwise impossible result. Our wills simply dispose of the energy stored in our bodies; they are dispositive and not productive agents. We may will something with extreme tenacity and vigor. If we do not possess the vital energy for its accomplishment, then our willing is doomed to failure. Witness a convalescent after a period of high fever. He wills, on rising, to walk across the room. The energy failing, he sits on his bed and smiles feebly at his impotence. His will cannot supply the deficient energy. Doubtless a vehement desire may lead to a full use of all our reserve strength; it cannot, however, create energy. The will is a dispositive and not a productive agent. (4) From the multitude of other considerations we single out just one further instance of what we never mean. In talking of freedom we never suggest that we do actually as a rule choose freely. Free acts are very rare. Habit is strong and forges iron bands. Apart from habit, we very often allow our nature, character or temperament to decide our actions. Sometimes we give rein to the dominant impulse of the moment, or under stress of passion we "let fly." It is easy to give way, and difficult to resist. Our native inertia does the rest. There are thus hundreds of cases in ordinary life, in which we are frankly and absolutely determined by our convictions, by our personal ideals, by acquired habits of thought and will, by acquired or inherited tendencies, or even by the feeling, impulse or passion of the moment. Free acts we repeat, are rare, and no sane doctrine of freedom will attempt to deny so obvious a truth. All that we assert is that it is of the nature of the will to be free; that the will *need* not necessarily be determined in choosing between alternatives; that however much it may be influenced or impelled, it need not *necessarily* suffer compulsion. Where determination takes place in the healthy normal individual, it is due to his inertia in not asserting his freedom.

We may, in conclusion, note an interesting corollary. Beyond all question, conscience can after a time be blunted or seared; after having often sounded in vain, the categorical imperative is at length mute. Why? Because in practice the man is no longer free. Gradually by repeated wrong-doing, he has lost his natural power of resistance. He has surrendered his freedom to a bad habit. In the absence of any practical freedom of action, conscience ceases to assert its commands. Its operation would be useless. Only after some radical transformation will its voice be heard again, asserting the law of our nature and the truth of our own freedom at one and the same time. Once again, it is only too clear that the commanding judgment of conscience only sounds where there is a possibility of disobedience. We end where we began. . . .

In presence of an object which would satisfy us wholly and fully, we should cease to be free, or rather, we should be as determined as any physical body that clings perforce to the earth's surface. The facts are these. There lies in us, deep down, a commanding, indeed overriding, desire for happiness. We as individuals may seek our happiness very differently. Some may follow the enticements of sense, others may rejoice in intellectual pursuits, mathematics, philosophy, or science. Some may seek their great happiness in religion, in marriage, while others will follow some work of philanthropy, some effort to do good in individuals, a class, or a nation. Whatever we do, whatever our professed or actual code of conduct, we are all dominated by an imperious, deep-set, inalienable desire for happiness. To an object which would fulfil that craving of our whole nature, we should rush as precipitately and as determinately as a small needle to a high power magnet. Here, then, once again is a standard of comparison, a test case of an action, obviously determined.

"But," a not unfriendly critic may say, "you have chosen an impossible test-case. You say, with truth, that we are never lastingly and completely satisfied. How, therefore, find a case where the impossible condition of absolute full happiness is realized?"

The effort is not so hopeless as it appears. Let us think for a moment of the phenomenon of infatuation. A boy of eighteen or nineteen becomes infatuated, let us say, with a girl. Infatuations are not always those of men for women or *vice versa*. We only choose the instance because it is more typical and more obvious. What happens? He dreams of her, longs to be in her company, frets at her absence, devotes leisure, income, life—all that he possesses and all that he is—to her service. He anticipates her wishes, satisfies her caprices. As we who are older look on, we think of the inevitable awakening. While the fretful, devoted spell lasts, however, the boy dreams that absolute lasting happiness is to be obtained by marrying the girl whom he adores. In his mind there is no conceivable drawback, no admitted disadvantage. All is rosy and golden and blue. He is prepared to sacrifice income, profession, home, parents, friends. He will be ostracized by the world? "What matter," he says, "provided we are together?" Life is fraught with many sorrows? "Not in her company," comes his quick reply. When a few years have passed the old longing for kindred, home and friends will assert itself? "Never, provided I have her," he says. Nothing matters then, in heaven or on earth, except this girl? "Nothing."

The case stated is one of clear infatuation. Is the boy free to decide against the proposed course? Not in the very least, so long as the infatuation lasts. If any argument, principle or statement of fact can shake his belief that complete happiness is to be attained by his precipitate course, then he may be free to revoke his decision, or to decide again freely. While under the spell of the illusion he is absolutely and completely determined. His whole nature is bound to crave for a full and lasting happiness; that is an irrevocable law of his being. If he is persuaded that the unsullied happiness for which he spontaneously and deeply longs is to be secured by the suggested marriage, then that marriage becomes automatically the object of his whole life, the determined goal of all his strivings. Here, we have given an unequivocal case of determination which is strangely unlike the ordinary events of our lives. As a rule, we see and acknowledge the fact that nothing can fill the measure of our capacity for longing. We desire things vehemently without being blind to their disadvantages. We deliberate, weighing pros and cons. Life is not made up of infatuations, though illusions be not spared.

A free act must be preceded by some deliberation, however short. If there be no deliberation, the act may be instinctive, reflex, impulsive, habitual, temperamental, but not free. In the course of our deliberation, we sum up the advantages and drawbacks of a particular action. The advantages one by one impel us to act. The disadvantages one by one repel us. How different such a mixture of allurement and repulsion from a determined compulsory act! There is almost as much difference as between the heavy thud of falling masonry and the flight of a sky-lark now soaring high, now sinking low over the corn-fields.

We may sum up briefly. Apart from the rare cases of infatuation, we men never even think that anything to be seized, held or seen, here and now, can ever assuage every desire and satisfy our unslaked thirst for happiness. We love, but we criticize. We reject, but we look backward. How then can we be necessarily compelled by actions or objects which leave us expectant of some disappointment? The answer rings out with the clearness of a bugle-call. We are not determined; we are free.

Of the many difficulties of critics, we select the one which seems to us the most insistent and also the most reasonable for comment. "Granted all your analysis of motives, pros and cons, and the whole paraphernalia of deliberation," a critic may urge, "there yet remains one distasteful truth. The strongest motive carries the day. The period of deliberation is no more than a tilting-ground, where motives try their strength. The vanquished motives disappear. The victor remains and summarily drives the will to act. Why, therefore, dream of freedom? We are compelled by the strongest motive."

Set out in this forcible and almost algebraic manner, the difficulty seems seductive if not crushing. Our whole structure seems to sway unsteadily. Once again we seem to hear those unforgettable, mocking words: "freedom is only the dream of the falling sand."

We turn to reflect. The strongest motive wins. Obviously; but what gave it its strength? Motives are not like motor-engines or rifle magazines formed and fashioned ready-made. Nor are they something wholly external to us, driving us to action. They are our own inalienable property; nothing more, in fact, than our own ideas, judgments, principles, viewed as stimuli to action. The strength which they have comes from us, from our beliefs, convictions, our principles of conduct or code of honor, and from our own experience. Why, therefore, speak of them as external driving forces?

And then again, the strongest motive wins. How do you know that it is the strongest? Because it wins? Is not that rather like the old "survival of the fittest," long since modified to the "survival of the survivors"? Similarly modified, the statement runs "the winning motive wins." This we admit, without any reluctance. Why then is it the winning motive? Because, in a free act, the mind and will have decided that it alone shall have action-working power.

Let us put the same thing in a more graphic and less analytic manner. A bachelor is living with his aged mother, who depends upon him. He falls in love with a woman, and is sure of her consent to a proposal of marriage. He desires vehemently to settle down in his own home. He could make his mother a small allowance, but she could not live alone. Nor could she live with his wife of whom she disapproves. One evening he sits down to turn the matter over and to decide once and for all. As he starts, the strongest motive is surely his great desire to marry. The happiness, satisfaction, and freedom of it all seems to him like a midnight summer's dream. Temperament, nature, character, and his love for the woman, all drive him to decide in favor of marriage. Against the proposal, there is only one pale weak judgment, "don't be mean or dishonorable to your mother." He talks this judgment down, argues about it, builds castles in Spain, only to find the thought repeated, "don't desert your mother." The problem is difficult; the debate long. His own future—the years creep on apace—must be thought of. His mother is a querulous, bad housekeeper. Motives in favor of marriage pile themselves mountains-high in his mind. If strength be anything measurable, they are strong enough to effect a hundred decisions. And yet, after hours of alternate calm and fretfulness, cynicism and tenderness, of hope and despair, the day breaks to find his decision fixed. He will sacrifice his own prospects and live with his mother. What gave the pale, weak motive the power of effecting the decision? There has been an obvious resistance to a strong and attractive motive, an effort to which the most cynical of men would bow in respect. Is such a decision against all impulse, all prospects, all feelings and all soaring hopes, as determined as the path of a cannon-ball? If not, it must be free. Instances of such actions performed against overwhelming impulse and desire cry out against the doctrine of determinism.

The theme is endless, but we have done. We have attempted to state the meaning of the much-abused doctrine of freedom, to give a proof in terms of the insistent facts of conscience and remorse, and to clinch that proof by an appeal to experience. We can never be fully and lastingly satisfied by any finite object. Were we so satisfied we should be necessitated. As we are not satisfied, we are not determined *de lege* but *de facto*. It is of the nature of of our wills to be free.

This freedom, upon which our greatness depends, cannot be entirely lost. The steel will remain though the rust eats in. It were well, however, that the steel should be bright, that the weapon should be ready. Of what use is the bayonet that buckles up at the moment of the charge? Or of the sword that snaps as it leaves the scabbard? Freedom, indeed, is ours. To realize our freedom, however, we need to do many a battle, to resist the towering strength of feeling, and the surging impulses that guide so much of our lives. The test of great men is that they should be free men.

14

DETERMINIST THEORIES

Cardinal Mercier [1]

Determinism is the theory that the will is not free and that all our acts, even including those apparently free, are adequately and inevitably determined by their antecedents. According to the nature of the antecedents which are held to account for our actions is determinism to be variously denominated. *Mechanical* determinism is not distinguishable from fatalism; it makes the will a material force subject like everything else to inexorable mechanical laws. *Physiological* determinism likens even our noblest volitions to reflex action. Lastly *psychological* determinism is the theory that the will necessarily follows the strongest motive, or what is presented to it as the greatest good.

The first two determinist theories are sufficiently disproved by all that has already been said in support of the freedom of the will and they do not require to be specially reviewed here. Psychological determinism owing to the plausibility given to it by Leibniz calls for more particular attention. According to him the will is bound to seek the greatest good offered to it, since to conceive it as making a positive choice whilst indifferent, without being moved by the strongest motive, is to attempt to deny the principle of sufficient reason. The *principle of sufficient reason* on which psychological determinism is grounded, is thus formulated by Leibniz: "Nothing can be true or real for which there is not a sufficient reason of it being so."

To assert that the will is always dominated, consciously or unconsciously, by the prevailing motive, is, if not tautological, an entirely gratuitous statement. It may happen, as indeed it does happen, that a choice has to be made between two good things that in themselves are absolutely equivalent. Who will doubt that between two glasses of water, between two sovereigns, between two roads of exactly the same length and leading to the same place, the will is ob-

---

[1] *A Manual of Modern Scholastic Philosophy*, Vol. I, pp. 272-277. (B. Herder Book Company, St. Louis.)

jectively swayed in neither direction? In such circumstances, inability to choose would remind us of the ass in the proverb which died of starvation between two pecks of oats. As the theory of Leibniz stands contradicted by facts, it remains only to consider his criticism that our theory is a contradiction of the principle of sufficient reason.

The value of Leibniz's criticism will best be gauged by an example. The two glasses of water we supposed to be exactly similar and equally desirable in every respect are objectively equal motives. If I reach out my hand to the one on the left instead of the one on the right, the sole reason for my action, since it can not be in any objective quality attaching to one and not to the other, must be my desire to act; I am actuated by my desire to act (to take a glass) which can be realized only on the condition of my making a choice and taking one. My choice, then, which is without an objective motive, has its sufficient reason in something subjective, in my own desire to exercise my will.

All difficulty will vanish as soon as it is remembered that the freedom of the will resides formally not in the selection between different goods (freedom of specification) but in the volition, or rather the self-determination to move towards it (freedom of exercise). Determinists who bring forward the above objection make the mistake of asserting that when the will is presented with two unequal motives, it is compelled to choose the better, an assertion which is only partly true, as can be seen from the example of an artist who is offered the choice of two pictures of unequal value. The act of *preference,* as such, is undoubtedly not free, for it is physically impossible for the will not to prefer that good which the practical reason judges *hic et nunc* to be on the whole the better. Thus if the deliberative faculty be concentrated upon the *relative* artistic value of the two pictures, the will can not but prefer the one which is judged the better. Yet if attention is not paid to the superiority of one over the other, so that each is presented *separately* to the will as a particular good which may be chosen because a good and rejected because not the universal good, then a basis for choice exists; the better picture may freely be chosen or rejected as also may the inferior one, seeing that in itself it too is a particular good, yet only a particular good. Of course the man would be foolish to choose the less good, but it is consistent with our explanation to assert that he is free to be foolish; he may refuse to allow attention to be paid to the objective considerations that would change the course of his conduct were he acting reasonably, and instead, if he so will, he may say, 'Stat pro ratione voluntas.' In our explanation, to sum up, choice is founded on the freedom of exercise, the freedom of willing an act or of abstaining from willing it.

Moral liberty is freedom exercised in respect of *moral* acts, i. e., acts considered in relation to the end of our rational nature. Sometimes moral liberty is defined as "the power of choosing between good and evil." In point of fact human liberty does verify this definition, inasmuch as man can choose evil; but, strictly, moral liberty does not imply the power of choosing evil. This power is an imperfection, just as the power of self-deception is an imperfection in our reason.

A man chooses evil under the guise of apparent good. Such an unfortunate action is possible on acount of his possession of many faculties each of which has a different proper object; what is the real good of one is not necessarily that of another—as is manifest in the case of the higher and lower appetites, where what is truly the pleasure of the lower is sometimes not at all the good of man as he is a rational being.

When the will seeks an inferior good in place of what is upright, it violates the law of its nature, thereby acting inconsistently with right order and abusing its liberty. Hence a moral evil is called a defect, unrighteousness, a fall.

Since the liberty to commit evil is an imperfection of the will, to claim it as a right either for one's self or for others is manifestly absurd. When, therefore, a legitimately constituted authority, acting within the limits and observing the precautions demanded by prudence, takes measures to prevent in the family or in society vice or error leading to vice, it is protecting moral liberty and in no way curtailing it. Unbridled liberty is no true liberty but only *license,* a counterfeit of it.

Two sets of facts are adduced by the determinists against the freedom of the will:

1. An irresistible propensity to crime to be met with in criminals.

2. The uniformity and constancy of certain moral facts.

3. A further objection is drawn from the impossibility of reconciling free will with the law of the conservation of energy.

These three objections require to be briefly noticed.

1. We admit that under certain influences—heredity, alcohol, vicious habits, etc.,—responsibility is in a large number of cases *lessened,* and indeed so much lessened that it is probable it is not sufficient, or is no longer sufficient, to justify their being called criminals. This granted, it is surely very arbitrary to make the exception a rule and to deny responsibility for all because there are some who are not responsible; as arbitrary as to deny that man is rational because some men are deficient in reason.

2. The second objection runs thus: If the individuals composing the social body were free, their moral acts would vary; yet statistics of such moral events as marriages, illegitimate births, crimes, suicides,[1] etc., show a remarkable constancy, which therefore proves that the moral acts considered to be free are as subject to laws as physical events.

To this we reply in the first place that all acts performed by man are not free. Only those acts are free which are the fruit of reflection. A very large percentage of acts then, even in the most serious life, are not free because done without thought; a large percentage are suggested simply by the imagination, controlled by passion or self-interest, or are due to routine. In the second place, it is a mistake to imagine that free acts are purely arbitrary, proceeding from a will that acts without purpose. Truly, man may be unreasonable if he like. But in point of fact, in by far the majority of cases, men are not unreasonable, but allow themselves to be actuated by a purpose. Thus, not to speak of the last intention—the seeking after supreme happiness—the instinct of self-preservation, the instinct of propagation, the natural love of parents for children, of children for parents, the striving for well-being, or for personal interest, are all so many motors to the will to which it generally responds without making a deliberate choice.

---

[1] The number of suicides recorded in France between 1849 and 1860 is as follows: 3583, 3596, 3598, 3676, 3415, 3700, 3810, 4189, 3967, 3903, 3899, 4050.

It follows that in apparently similar circumstances men will for the most part be led by the same intentions, so that it is in reality the similar spontaneous desire which accounts for men acting in many instances in a uniform and constant fashion.

It must be observed that this relative constancy and approximate uniformity in no way excludes liberty, for every act induced by a spontaneous intention may be the subject for a deliberation either concerning the motives for which it shall be done or concerning the manner or time. Thus we are no doubt each of us free to travel tomorrow or to stay at home; yet it is absolutely certain that, when tomorrow comes, of the number who have a reason to travel many will freely decide to do so and the number of people traveling by train will be approximately the same tomorrow as on any other day of the year.

Finally, the constant and uniform manner of action of men certainly allows us to deduce laws akin to physical laws, but as their actions are free they are called by the special name of *moral laws*.

3. The materialistic determinist makes it his objection against free will that it would militate against the constancy of the energy of the universe.[1] If the will, they argue, were to cause other bodily movements besides those which would occur if the organism were subjected exclusively to the action of material forces, it would thereby introduce so much more energy into the universe and necessarily destroy the constancy of the total energy.

The answer to this is very simple: the will is not an efficient cause producing mechanical effects. All that the will does is to direct the power of local movement possessed by the organism to some action. This effect does not require the expenditure of any active force, for the action of the will is not transitive, having an external effect, but is immanent. All the energy that is put forth externally

---

[1] Lavoisier's well-known axiom is: "Nothing is ever lost or created in nature." This principle, which was enunciated originally by its author, in reference to the conservatism of mass, applies also to the conservatism of the energy of the universe. So applied, it means that of the quantity of energy displayed under the various forms of mechanical movement—sound, heat, light and electricity—whilst one form may give place to another form, *the sum total in the universe remains constant.*

comes from the sensitive appetite, and the locomotive faculty, which are material faculties subject to the law of the conservation of energy.

15

MORALITY WITHOUT FREE WILL

Joseph Rickaby [1]

There is a philosophy which resolves the universe into a process of divine thought flowing on irresistibly. In this philosophy everything happens *a priori:* everything that happens is a foregone conclusion, following necessarily upon what happened before; there is no room anywhere, whether in God or man, for what Catholic divines understand by free will. To be sure, this philosophy speaks of free will, meaning thereby the choice of a man of good character, acting according to his character, and not driven out of his ways of characteristic goodness by the force of temptation; such a one, so doing, is said to act up to his "real self," and thereby to act "freely." In all this, determinism lurks; for the good character, taking its free and unimpeded course, determines the resultant action, as surely and as masterfully as a river, unchecked by a dam, rolls on its course towards the ocean. All pantheism involves determinism. Plato, following Socrates, from first to last is a thorough determinist; he always assumes that to know good is to do it; he never contemplates the case of a man looking away from the good that he knows, or failing to regard it steadily.[2] I refrain

---

[1] *Political and Moral Essays,* pp. 249-265. (Benziger Brothers, New York City.)

[2] "No one is willingly wicked: only through a bad habit of body and unscientific rearing does the bad man go bad," Plato, *Timæus,* 86 D, E; cf. *Laws,* 886 A, B. Aristotle, *Nic. Eth.,* III. 1114 *a* (c. vii.), corrects Plato: he admits that no man intends to form to himself a wicked character, but he says that man does choose to do acts which of themselves go to the formation of such a character; and he thinks that the character thus formed is irresistible. Aristotle seems to consider that man is free, not in the main purpose of life (βούλησις), but in the choice of means thereto (προαίρεσις), so far as this choice is not determined by some previously formed character (ἦθος), or habit (ἕξις), whether of virtue (ἀρετή),

from all reference to St. Augustine and Pelagianism and Calvanism and Jansenism, to the effects of the fall, the corruption of nature, and *gratia victrix*. I deal with philosophical determinism only, without theological complications.

There is what is called "hard determinism" and "soft determinism." The *soft* is as genuine determinism as the *hard* variety. You may wrap a millstone in a cloth, but it remains a millstone. *Hard* determinism, now gone out of fashion, makes the motion of the will like the motion of a material particle under mechanical forces, wholly determined from without, without the set and form of the will itself having any influence on the movement. If *hard* determinism were right, man would be like a weathercock, the sport of every wind of impulse that blew. But obviously man has something in him which often resists present solicitation. Men behave differently under the same temptation: one man yields, another holds out. There is something which carries a man above his surroundings, or haply sinks him below them. This is said to be "character." Character is partly inherited, partly acquired; partly a physical, partly a mental, property. If the *hard* determinist ignored character,—I am not so sure that he did,—the *soft* determinist at any rate makes the most of it. But character in his view is but the result of past circumstances, a sort of conglomerate of past circustances. It is ancient circumstance, crystallised and preserved and still effectual. Thus, in the view of *soft* determinism, man is the creature of circumstances, present and past. He is led about by a chain of circumstance, many links of which were forged before he was born. No other view is possible upon the hypothesis of blind evolution. Man, then, in this *soft* determinist view, has the attribute of *spontaneity*, inasmuch as many of the things that he does are not done against the grain; he is not reluctant to do them, not coerced, bullied, threatened, deluded, or deceived; he really wishes to do them, and has his eyes open, and is free from the compulsion of his fellow-men in the trans-

or of vice (κακία). I do not think that Aristotle supposes *all the choices* (προαιρέσεις) of any man to be determined by his character or habits. Aristotle, it seems to me, does stand for a limited play of free will, especially in the young and unformed.

action. But though he has this *freedom from compulsion,* as it is called, he has not that *freedom of indifference,* in which free will is placed by Catholic divines. What he wills and wishes to do, he cannot but will and wish to do, with the character that he has. And that same character was made *for him,* not really *by him.* It is a natural growth of the circumstances of his past history. It follows the law of causation, or of invariable and unconditional sequence, as much as any other physical phenomenon, say the stratification of some particular rock.

Under much contradiction, the Christian Church has always taught the doctrine of free will. *Hard* determinism is heresy, and *soft* determinism is no better. The doctrine of the Church has formed the thoughts of men even outside her communion. We have learnt to think in terms of free will. If determinism shall pass from the lecture room to the market-place, our thought and our speech on all moral subjects will undergo a vast change. The change may be compared to the proposed change from the present system of private capital to socialism. One has to think oneself into determinism as into socialism. In either case, more remains than might have been expected. The change is not so much on the surface of things as in the underlying principle. And first of what remains of our present moral system, when it comes to be worked on determinist principles.

The ten commandments remain unchanged.[3] The list of virtues and vices remains unchanged. The ethical motives for virtue and against vice remain unchanged. The State continues to frame laws, commanding and forbidding the same things as before. The same conduct is praised and rewarded, or blamed and punished, as before, albeit not quite with the same intention. The portraits of the good man and of the bad man respectively have lost none of their external lineaments. The one is still self-controlled and self-denying, brave, loving, magnanimous, and just. The other remains a sensualist, cruel and cowardly, frivolous, idle, heartless, and untrustworthy. Nero is still bad, and Paul

---

[3] The determinist is likely to be also a pantheist. Pantheism, as it alters men's other relations to God, may also alter their worship of Him. But I leave pantheist worship to its own evolution.

good. The exigencies of human nature and of human society have not lost their value. The good and happiness of the individual, and the prosperity of the society to which he belongs, require of him the same conduct as heretofore. Goodness has not become less profitable, nor wickedness less detrimental and deplorable, now that both are recognised necessities. Wickedness is what it was in every respect save one; and the same deeds are wicked that were wicked. Goodness has lost only one of its attributes. Formerly the good man did what it befitted a man to do, having at the same time in the very act and circumstances of his well-doing the power to swerve from goodness: still he does the same things, but, further, it is to be noted that, with his character and circumstances, he cannot help doing them. And conversely of the wicked man, who is rightly enough pronounced by the determinist a dangerous, disgusting, and offensive animal. Ugly conduct fits in with the determinist hypothesis as well as ugly architecture.

We praise a flower, or a gun, or the "points" of a horse. There would be no difficulty in praising in that way a man in whose conduct we recognised no free will. Still, he might be to us a grand fellow, a very useful creature. We might further encourage him with prospective praise, as an inducement to serve us still better, much in the same way that a driver pats his horse and utters kind cries to it on a hard road. Such praise, however, and the corresponding blame, cannot be called *moral approbation,* and *reprobation.* This is more apparent in the case of blame. We blame stupidity, but we have a very different censure for malice. We are angry with stupidity, only as we imagine it to contain an element of wilfulness, or carelessness, which approaches very near to malice. To the determinist, a malicious offender could not but have been malicious in the past; there is no use being angry with him; the only thing to do is to devise and apply new motives in order to his cure. This may be done by instructing him; it may also be done by punishing him. Determinist punishment is always prospective, never retrospective. It is inflicted in prospect either of the amendment of the offender, by supplying him with new motives, which shall "make him help" what he rightly pleads he "could not help" before, or else of deterring the community from imitating such socially harmful conduct, as when we hang a man for murder. No consideration of suffering as expiatory of wrong-doing, no idea of retribution, must ever enter into the calculations of the determinist. The determinist must adopt the Stoic profession of never being angry. Anger, says Aristotle, is a desire of vengeance; but there is no vengeance for the determinist, as there is no retributive punishment. He must punish with the calmness of a surgeon performing an operation; or if he assumes an outward mien of anger, it must be for the humane purpose of creating new motives in the breast of the culprit and backing up his infirmity. Believing that men are literally "made better," that is, are made to act better in future by reprehension and punishment, the determinist will not stint them of these beneficial applications. He will not spare the incapable, where he believes that punishment will amend them. He will not accept the usual distinction between incapacity and crime, as between an incapable commander and a treacherous one. To him it is all incapacity, "crime" being incapacity of will, and "incapacity," commonly so called, being incapacity of understanding. He will punish the former more severely than the latter, only in so far as it appears to him more amenable to the motive of punishment. His distinction will be drawn between "curable" and "incurable" incapacity, whether of will or of understanding; and so far as the traitor is more responsive to punishment, or to bribery, than the blockhead, he will consider him the better man of the two. The phrase, "not merely a crime but a blunder," will come well from his mouth. The Carthaginian practice of crucifying unsuccessful generals must have been stimulating to persons in command to do their best. A good precedent for determinists likewise is the execution of Admiral Byng, shot, as Voltaire remarked, *pour encourager les autres*. The determinist will fully enter into the definition given by Dr. Alexander Bain in his work on *The Emotions and the Will*, that "responsibility is punishability." The determinist will go on further to define *punishability*, "a liability to painful inflictions, and thence to fear, as a motive to ensure better conduct in future."

The proceedings of a man-eating tiger in a lonely Indian village, where with his huge shoulders he overthrows frail walls and doors at night, and devours the sleeping inhabitants, are fearfully destructive, but we should never call them *disgraceful*. They excite no moral reprobation; what else could such a creature be expected to do? You do not argue with a tiger; you shoot him, or get out of his way. But the doings of a thug, an assassin who kills as many men as a tiger, are called *disgraceful*. The reason of this, the determinist tells us, is because the assassin is open to argument; or if the professed assassin is not, at least novices and aspirants to the craft are so open: by calling the assassin's doings *disgraceful, criminal, wicked,* you diminish the chance of assassinations in future. Assassins, in fact, can be talked to, though tigers can not; and talk is prophylactic. This is all very true. It is useful to talk of thuggism as "disgraceful conduct," and to kindle moral sentiment against murder. But is thuggism truly and really *disgraceful,* when, to parody Watts's hymn, "nature has made thugs so," any more than the tiger's practice of preying upon human kind, once it has learnt that fatal trick, carries with it any stigma of *disgrace?* The tiger is not more thoroughly determined by causative agents than the thug, so the determinist must allow. The use of terms of moral censure in speaking of human criminals, then, is a mere *façon de parler,* adopted because such language is useful, not because it is true. It is an exemplification of the Platonic γενναῖον ψεῦδος, the "noble lie" told to the people by their rulers for purposes of government. The sentiment of moral disapprobation has the ground cut from under it when it is thus explained. Were determinism generally accepted, this sentiment would disappear, and give place to the very different sentiments of dislike and dread of a wicked man, exactly the sentiments with which we regard a "man-eater" in the jungle.

With this there perishes the notion that moral evil is worse than all other evil, that sin is more to be avoided than any amount of suffering: the sentiment, *malo mori quam foedari,* "death rather than moral defilement," becomes inane and foolish. Moral evil no longer dwells in a category apart from other evil. It is henceforth definable as *a public nuisance, open to treatment by motives.* And as motives are cheap, terms of reproach plentiful, and rods grow on every bush, this peculiarity of moral evil, that it is remediable by motives, is rather in its commendation. A small-pox patient in a crowded neighbourhood is a nuisance harder to deal with than the perjurer or the bigamist, and may set the determinist philosopher musing whether he be not on the whole the worse man. This is utilitarianism indeed, but not moral philosophy.

With the sentiment of moral reprobation and righteous indignation in regard to other men's sins goes the sentiment of remorse for our own. What we really believe we could not have helped, as matters stood, e. g., the loss of a piece of luggage in travelling, we regret indeed, and are annoyed at; but we do not feel any remorse over it, not even though the lost trunk contained some precious article solemnly entrusted by a friend to our care. Such reflections as *I could not help it, It was not my fault,* are a salve against remorse. So long as we honestly believe that we took all the care that we possibly could under the circumstances, the poignancy of our regret never passes into remorse. A man who lays the unction of determinism to his heart, even *soft* determinism, should believe that in every circumstance of his past history he has done the best thing that he could possibly have done there and then; that he is the best man that, with his inherited character and under such circumstances as have been his, he possibly could have been, and so are all other men the best men possible; that, in fact, we are living in the best of all possible worlds, because it is the only world that could have been so far, though we hope there is a better time coming. If still the determinist feels remorse for some harsh word or deed of unfaithfulness, it is because his conscience is stronger than his philosophy. He ought to be, like the ideal sage of Stoicism, a man above remorse and incapable of sin. Above remorse, but not above regret for what was inevitable in the past but may perhaps be prevented in future.

The nonconformist conscience affords us occasional surprises of hatred of religion in the name of religious liberty. The determinist conscience will also conduct humanity into pastures new and strange. The study of the determinist will be, not so much "what I ought to do," as "what I feel carried to," "what is consistent with my character under the present weight of motives." Were I a determinist, I should feel a certain sense of degradation and helplessness, as though I were no longer master of my human acts, but were reduced to the *rôle* of a spectator of the goings on at the domestic hearth of my own soul. Instead of *I will*, I should be apt to say *I feel I must;* while *I won't* would subside into *just at present I can't*. And when the deed was done, my judgment on the sinfulness of it would take the form, *However deplorable, what else could I have done?* I think I should even cease to speak and act in the first person, and employ the third instead, as children do before they come to the use of reason and before their will is free. In this habit of mind I should still retain *consciousness,* but old-fashioned *conscience* would have fled with the sense of remorse, of personality, of agency of my own, and of that self-application which is a function of intelligence.

I believe, however, that the consciousness of the *ego* in man is a consciousness of free will, and carries conscience with it. But, like other truthful witnesses, this witness of consciousness to free will easily breaks down under cross-examination, and then goes discredited. It is a witness to the *fact*, τὸ ὅτι, of free will, not to τὸ διότι, or the *how*. Time, space, self, free will, simple things enough as common experience presents them,[4] become a perplexity and a puzzle when we try to draw them out scientifically. I have no purpose of doing so. So far as I may theorise on the subject, I should say that an act of free will is not a reaching out to the absent, but a clutching and sustaining of something already present in consciousness,—an actuation, endorsement, and personal acceptance of some affection that has arisen in the mind spontaneously by the necessary workings of causation. *The spontaneous is necessary.* In other words, *soft* determinists, who admit nothing beyond spontaneity, are true determinists. Free will is something beyond spontaneity.

It remains to study the effects of determinism on the "plain man." The plain man may profess determinism as

[4] Did ever any catechist find it necessary to tell any child what free will meant?
"One of the first experiences of an infant is that of his willing and doing; and, as time goes on, one of the first temptations of the boy is to bring home to himself the fact of his sovereign arbitrary power, though it be at the price of waywardness, mischievousness, and disobedience" (Newman, *Grammar of Assent*, p. 66, ed. 1895).

some profess Christianity, without its having any appreciable effect upon his conduct. He may be a determinist when he opens a book, and a vigorous assertor of free will in his business hours and his ordinary conversation. I am thinking of the plain man when he becomes a practising determinist. A whole nation may agree some day to teach morality independently of religion. Up to a certain point the thing is possible,—I do not say possible in the concrete, but theoretically and in the abstract possible,—in so far as ethics are a science in their own right, distinct from theology. When ethics are thus adopted, no longer as a mere speculative study, but as the sole guide of action, it will become a serious question for school authorities whether they shall teach determinist ethics, and hazard the effect of such teaching upon the minds of the million. It is to be feared that the effect would be the sending out of a multitude of human beings, pretending to be determined by "character," and really having no character, because they never use their wills as their own,—young men and women of an emotional, passive temperament, drifting about under every wind of impulse and every breath of sensational excitement. Most of these *soft* determinists, to borrow a metaphor from Plato, would prove mere stingless drones, their own worst enemies. Some of them, however, would develop cruel stings; and now and then a *soft* determinist, grown into what Plato calls "a walking drone with a sting," would commit a crime big enough to amaze the world.[5]

But are not Orientals generally determinists, and have not great men and great empires arisen in the East, and that under the conscious influence of determinist and fatalistic principles? No doubt. But the great men and empire-builders of the East were determinists and something more: they were strong theists. They believed that they had a mission from Heaven to go forth and conquer. They were

---

[5] "These winged drones have been fashioned by Providence all without stings; but as for those drones that go about afoot, while some of them are stingless, others have got awful stings. For the former sort is reserved the life of a tramp and the old age and death of a pauper; but of the number of stinging drones are all who bear the name of belonging to the criminal class" (Plato, *Republic,* VIII. 552 C).

men of prayer and prophecy. They had the strength of religion, albeit a false religion, at their back. They were determinists and fanatics to boot. And thus much of the great men of the East. But it may be doubted whether the mass of Oriental populations have not lost in vigour by their determinism, degenerating into apathy, indolence, and submission to preventable calamities, whether visitations of nature or the tyranny of princes. Western determinism, prompted by a belief in pantheistic evolution, will derive no support from any religion that can stir the soul. It will be a gloomy, godless, mechanical affair.

16

CERTITUDE

MICHAEL JAMES RYAN [1]

The word *certitude* indicates a state of mind and a quality of a proposition, according as we say, "I am certain," or "It is certain." This distinction is expressed in the technical language of philosophy by saying that there is subjective certitude and objective certitude. It is worthy of notice, as regards the use of English terms, that Newman reserves the term *certitude* for the state of mind, and employs the word *certainty* to describe the condition of the evidence of the proposition. Certitude is correlative to truth, for truth is the object of the intellect. Knowledge means knowledge of truth; and hence we are in the habit of saying simply of a proposition that "it is certain" to express that it is true, and that its truth is so evident as legitimately to produce certitude. Certitude is contrasted with other states of mind in reference to a proposition: the state of ignorance, the state of doubt, and the state of opinion. The last-named signifies, in the strict use of the term, the holding of a proposition as probable, although in common parlance it is loosely used in a wider sense, as in speaking of a man's religious opinions, meaning not his speculations or theories about religious questions, but his dogmatic convictions. Certitude is such an assent to the truth of a proposition as excludes all real doubt. Here it is

[1] *Catholic Encyclopedia*, Vol. III, pp. 539-542.

proper to reserve a distinction between merely undoubting assent, i. e., the mere absence of doubt, and an assent that positively excludes doubt, an assent with which doubt is incompatible. Thus one may give to a statement in the morning newspaper an undoubting assent and credence, yet readily withdraw that assent if the statement be contradicted in the afternoon papers. Such assent, though undoubting, is not certitude. But there is a kind of assent from which doubt is not only in fact absent but absent of necessity, because such assent and doubt are incompatible. Such is the assent which one gives to the truth that he really exists, and that he feels well or ill, or to the truth of the proposition that it is impossible for a thing in the same respect both to be or not to be, or to the moral law, the existence of God, and the immortality of the soul. Of these truths we are *certain,* and such assent is properly called certitude. Certitude differs from opinion in kind, not in degree only; for opinion, that is assent to the probability of a proposition, regards the opposite proposition as not more than improbable; and therefore opinion is always accompanied by the consciousness that further evidence may cause a change of mind in favor of the opposite opinion. Opinion, therefore, does not exclude doubt; certitude does. It has been disputed among philosophers whether certitude is susceptible of degrees, whether we may rightly say that our certitude of one truth is greater than our certitude of another truth. In Zigliara's judgment, this question may easily be solved if a distinction is made between the exclusion of doubt (in which our various certitudes of different truths are all equal, and by which they are all equally marked off in kind from opinion) and the positive firmness of assent, which may be more intense in one case than in another, though in both it be equally true that we are certain. And, in fact, if we examine experience on this point, it is clear that our certitude of a self-evident truth, e. g., of the axioms of geometry, is greater than our certitude of a proposition demonstrated by a long and complex series of proofs, and that our certitude of such a fact as our own existence or our own state of feeling (gladness or health) is greater than our certitude of the existence, for instance, of a republican form of government in this country, though we are certain in both cases. We are more certain when we assent to a truth as certain which falls in with our inclination than when we are forced to a conviction. It should be noted, too, that in the common opinion of theologians, there is a greater certitude in Divine faith than in any human science.

There are several kinds of certitude. In the first place, it is divided into physical, metaphysical, and moral certitude. Metaphysical certitude is that with which self-evidently necessary truth is known, or necessary truth demonstrated from self-evident truth. The demonstrative sciences, such as geometry, possess metaphysical certitude. The contingent fact of one's own existence, or of one's present state of feeling, is known with metaphysical certitude. Physical certitude is that which rests upon the laws of nature. These laws are not absolutely unchangeable, but subject to the will of the Creator; they are not self-evident nor demonstrable from self-evident truth; but they are constant, and discoverable as laws by experience, so that the future may be inferred from the past, or the distant from the present. It is with physical certitude that a man knows that he shall die, that food will sustain life, that electricity will furnish motive power. Astronomers know beforehand with physical certitude the date of an eclipse or of a transit of Venus. Moral certitude is that with which judgments are formed concerning human character and conduct; for the laws of human nature are not quite universal, but subject to occasional exceptions. It is moral certitude which we generally attain in the conduct of life, concerning, for example, the friendship of others, the fidelity of a wife or a husband, the form of government under which we live, or the occurrence of certain historical events, such as the Protestant Reformation or the French Revolution. Though almost any detail in these events may be made a subject of dispute, especially when we enter the region of motives and try to trace cause and effect, and though almost any one of the witnesses may be shown to have made some mistakes or misrepresentation, yet the occurrence of the events, taken in the mass, is certain. Father John Rickaby (*First Principles of Knowledge*) observes that certitude is not necessarily exclusive of all misgiving whatsoever (such as the thought of the bare possibility that we may be mistaken, for we are not infallible), but of all solid, reasonable misgivings. The term *moral certitude* is used by some philosophers in a wider sense, to include an assent in matters of conduct, given not on purely intellectual grounds of evidence, but through the virtue of prudence and the influence of the will over the intellect, because we judge that doubt would not be wise. In such a case, we know that an opinion or a course of action would be right, as a rule, let us say, in nine cases out of ten, though we cannot shut our eyes to the possibility that the particular case which we are considering *may* be the exceptional case in which such a judgment would be wrong. Other philosophers say that in such a case we are not certain, but only judge it wise to act as if we were certain, and put doubts aside because useless. But it seems clear that in such a case we are certain of something, whether that something be described as the truth of a proposition or the wisdom of a course of action. This certitude might, perhaps, better be called practical certitude, since it mainly concerns action. Hence, it is said that in cases in which it is necessary to act, in which great issues are involved, and yet the evidence, when logically set forth, would seem to amount to no more than a higher probability for one course than for another, the standard of judgment, or criterion, is the *judicium prudentis viri,* the judgment of a wise man, whose mind is unclouded by passion or prejudice, and who has some knowledge derived from experience of similar cases. Such a judgment is totally different from the spirit of the gambler's throw, which is reckless not only of certainty but even of probability.

Certitude is likewise divided into natural certitude (termed also direct, or spontaneous) and philosophical. Natural certitude is that which belongs to "common sense," or the spontaneous workings of the judgment, which is common to all men not idiots or insane. This certitude belongs chiefly to self-evident truth and to the truths necessary for the conduct of life, e. g., the existence of other beings besides ourselves, the duties existing between husband and wife, parents and children, the existence of a Supreme Being deserving of reverence. To these and similar truths the mind comes with certitude, without any special education, in the ordinary course of life in human society. Philosophical (or scientific) certitude is that which results from a process of reflection, upon an analysis of the evidence for and against our convictions, a perception of the reasons which support them and of the objections which may be urged against them, together with an examination of the powers and the limits of the human intelligence. The term natural certitude is sometimes used in another sense, in contradistinction from the certitude of Divine faith, which is supernatural certitude, and which, according to theologians generally, is greater than any degree of certitude to be had in science, because it rests not upon human reason, which is liable to be mistaken, but upon the authority of God, who cannot err. (St. Thomas, Summa, 1, Q. i, a. 5.)

A great part of philosophy is taken up with the questions whether certitude is possible, what is the extent of the sphere of certain knowledge, and by what tests or criteria truth may be certainly distinguished from falsehood, so that we may know when we have a right to be certain. A few philosophers have in ancient and modern times, seriously or not, denied the possibility of attaining certitude on any subject whatsoever, and professed universal scepticism. Such are Nicholas of Cusa, Montaigne, Charron, and Bayle, the last of whom aimed at producing the impression that everything is disputable by showing that everything is disputed. Literally universal scepticism is impossible, for it is a profession of knowledge to assert that nothing can be known, and to believe that there can be no belief. It is thus a contradiction in terms. A sceptic should in consistency be sceptical as to his own scepticism; but no attention would be given to such a sceptic unless as one attends, for amusement, to a jester. Nevertheless, universal scepticism may practically produce pernicious consequences, because its universality is overlooked, and its arguments are viewed as if they applied only to some particular sphere in which the reader (if it so be) is tempted to doubt. Thus, sceptical objections against the principle of causation may be employed against the proofs for the existence of God, while the reader is not warned and does not remember that they would equally avail against taking food and sleep for the restoration of strength, or against the anticipation that the sun will rise to-morrow. It should be added that some Christian apologists, in endeavoring to prove the necessity of Divine revelation, have used language differing but little from that of scepticism, to the disparagement of human reason. A noted example is Huet, "Traité de la faiblesse de l'esprit humain" (Paris, 1723).

What is more common than a profession of universal scepticism is a scepticism as to the possibility of philosophic certitude. Many who have no doubt as to natural certitude, or the certitude acquirable by "common sense," the natural, spontaneous action of the unsophisticated mind, regard philosophy as more apt to open questions than to settle them, and to raise objections than to solve them. This seems to have been the position of Pascal, who says: "Reason confounds dogmatists, and nature confounds sceptics;" and, "the heart has reasons of its own which the understanding does not know." This seems to have been the position also of a very different man, David Hume, who says: "Fortunately, since reason is incapable of dispelling these clouds, nature herself suffices for that purpose and cures me of this philosophical delirium" (Treatise on Human Nature, I, 297). He said to a friend who spoke to him concerning the future life and the existence of God: "Though I throw out my speculations to entertain the learned and metaphysical world, yet in other things I do not think so differently from the rest of the world as you imagine." And he gives his idea of scepticism in a remark upon Berkeley's arguments against the real externality of the sensible world: "That these arguments are in reality merely sceptical appears from this, that they admit of no answer, and produce no conviction; their only effect is to cause that momentary amazement and irresolution and confusion which is the result of scepticism." (Inquiry concerning Human Nature, ch. xii, note 4.) Kant's system, which denies that the speculative reason can attain to real knowledge, and admits only practical certitude, and, consequently, denies the possibility of any system of metaphysical philosophy is virtually the same view. It is needless to say that, in a philosopher, such a view is self-contradictory. Kant's "Critique of Pure Reason," as well as his other works, was an exercise of the speculative reason. If certitude of knowledge is not obtainable on any subject by the speculative reason, how could he indulge in such positive and dogmatic propositions? If we consider this view of philosophy, as it is held by some men of sense and virtue, who point to the disputations and wranglings of philosophers, the variety of opinions, the number of infidel philosophers, and the general suspicion felt by earnestly religious people, the answer to it is, that this view has some measure of truth, but is a great exaggeration. It is quite true that philosophical inquiries concerning morals and religion, if not conducted with proper moral dispositions, are likely to terminate in doubt. If there be any bias, whether conscious or unconscious, against the obligations of morality and religion, there can, of course, be only one issue. If the understanding seeks to know everything; if it rejects facts, however well attested, because it does not see *how* they can be so; if it will accept no truth, however firmly demonstrated, unless the harmony with every other part of a system can be made clear; if it claims to see through and through the universe, and its origin and its end; if it refuses to submit to mystery, or to acknowledge that it is limited; and, if because it can not know everything, it will proudly not consent to know anything, of course, with such a disposition, philosophizing cannot issue in philosophic certitude. But that is not the fault of philosophy, nor of reason; and the abuse cannot take away the use, but only be a warning against the misuse of philosophy.

"Methodic doubt," that is, provisional doubt of every truth, was put forward by Descartes as the proper course for the discovery of truth. This philosopher teaches that in order to be certain of the truth of our convictions we should begin by doubting everything except one thing: "I think, and therefore I am." He professes to hold that every other truth may be doubted and needs proof. He suggests that we may doubt whether we can discover the truth on any other point whatsoever, for it may appear possible that we have been created by a malign or mischievous being, who so constituted our mind that we must be invariably mistaken. The Cartesian method is self-contradictory. To make the supposition that possibly the human intellect cannot know the truth on any point whatsoever, is to assume that this supposition may be true, and that there is such a thing as truth, and that it can be known. To attempt to disprove the supposition, to undertake to show the veracity of the cognitive faculties, presupposes their veracity or power of knowing the truth on some points at least. In fact, Descartes proved the veracity of the cognitive faculties from the veracity of God. The veracity of God, however, is known as the result of a demonstration of some length and complexity; and the undertaking of such demonstration shows a previous belief in the power of the mind to discover the truth. In fact, the very doubt on such a subject is a self-contradiction; for doubt as well as certitude is correlated to truth. To doubt whether a particular view may not be false is to suspect that the opposite may be true. To doubt that the intellect can know any truth is to question whether it may not be true that we are ignorant. But this implies that there is such a thing as truth, and that the truth, at least about our own power of knowing, can be discovered. Without such a presupposition, thought cannot be carried on at all. Nor is it a blind supposition, or animal instinct. For in the perception of first principles, or truths evident by their own light, there is implicit the perception that there is such a thing as truth and knowledge. The error in Descartes' method is its exaggeration. It is wise to be on our guard against the prejudices, or opinions, peculiar to a particular time and place, the place of birth or education, the class or party to which our early associations have attached us; but the principles which are self-evident, or which are accepted by the human race, should be exempted from doubt. It must be remembered, too, that the Church teaches that a Catholic cannot without sin entertain doubts against the Faith; though, of course, he may lawfully doubt whether it is true that a particular doctrine is taught by the Church, or whether he has correctly apprehended what the Church intends to teach, and whether a particular teacher expounds it correctly; or, again, he may investigate the evidences of Christianity and of Catholicism, and may doubt whether a particular argument is valid proof. But the method of doubt, taken as a whole, has been condemned by the Church.

Since, then, some things can be known with certitude, some things can be seen to be probable, and some things must remain forever a matter of doubt; and since the human reason is liable to error, the need has been felt for some criterion or criteria by which we may know that we really know, and by which genuine certitude concerning the truth may be distinguished from the spurious certitude of delusion.

The proper test of truth is evidence, whether the evidence of a truth in itself or by participation in the evidence of some other truth from which it is proved. Many truths, indeed, have to be accepted on authority; but then it has to be made evident that such authority is legitimate, is capable of knowing the truth, and is qualified to teach in the particular department in which it is accepted. Many truths which are at first accepted on authority, may afterward be made evident to the reason of the disciple. Such, in fact, is the ordinary way in which learning and science are acquired. The error of Bonald's system of Traditionalism (which was condemned by the Church) consists in its exaggeration, in its maintaining that the truths of natural religion are known solely on authority, that each generation simply inherits them from the preceding, and that unless they had been revealed to the first parents of the race, human reason never could have discovered them.

If we take the cognitive faculties, one by one, the senses are not in themselves deceived concerning their proportionate object, but, owing to circumstances, they are so liable to deception that they need the vigilant supervision of the reason. The nature of sensible phenomena is not their object, but that of the reason. It should be remembered, however, that the scientific theories concerning the nature of sound, of color and light, and of heat, have been thought out by the aid of data furnished by the senses, and, therefore, confirm the trustworthiness of the senses within certain limits. That men of science have no doubt as to the reality of extension, figure, movement, and space, any more than of force, is shown by their discussions concerning atoms, electrons, and ions. Consciousness is infallible as to the fact of its present states, e. g., that I am feeling warm, or well, or that I am thinking. The memory often errs, but often is trusted with certitude. Reason, within a narrow sphere, is infallible, viz., in the perception of self-evident truth, e. g., that whatever is *is*, that every movement or change must have a cause, that things equal to the same are equal to each other. Truths which are clearly and easily deducible from self-evident truth share in their certitude. Next to such certitude, we may place the certainty of truths affirmed by the whole human race, especially as regards practical principles. "That which seems to all men, this we say *is*; and he who rejects this ground of belief will not easily assign a more solid one" (Aristotle, Ethics, X, ii). Universal consent is not, however, the sole criterion. To make it such was the error of Lamennais. Besides the truths resting on self-evidence (or easy deduction from it) and those resting on the authority of the human race, there is a considerable body of truth which each man of average intelligence comes to know with certitude in the course of his life. Most of these truths are first learned upon authority and afterwards verified by one's own reflection of experience. It may even be said that a practical Christian in the course of his life has by experimental verification an additional moral certitude of the truth of revelation, since he has experience of the power of the Christian religion to sustain the soul against temptation and to strengthen every virtuous and noble aspiration.

17

THE ILLATIVE SENSE

Cardinal Newman [1]

Certitude is a mental state; certainty is a quality of propositions. Those propositions I call certain, which are such that I am certain of them. Certitude is not a passive impression made upon the mind from without, by argumentative compulsion, but in all concrete questions (nay, even in abstract, for, though the reasoning is abstract, the mind which judges of it is concrete) it is an active recognition of propositions as true, such as it is the duty of each individual to exercise for himself at the bidding of reason, and when reason forbids, to withhold. And reason never bids us be certain except on an absolute proof; and such a proof can never be furnished to us by the logic of words, for as certitude is of the mind, so is the act of inference which leads to it. Every one who reasons, is his own centre: and no expedient for attaining a common measure of

---

[1] *Grammar of Assent*, pp. 344-377. (Longmans, Green and Company, New York.)

minds can reverse this truth; but then the question follows, is there any *criterion* of an act of inference, such as may be our warrant that certitude is rightly elicited in favor of the proposition inferred, since our warrant cannot, as I have said, be scientific? I have already said that the sole and final judgment on the validity of an inference in concrete matter is committed to a mental faculty, which I have called the Illative Sense, a use of the word "sense" parallel to our use of it in "good sense," "common sense," a "sense of beauty," etc.,—and I own I do not see any way to go farther than this in answer to the question. However, I can at least explain my meaning more fully; and therefore I will now speak, first of the sanction of the Illative Sense, next of its nature, and then of its range.

§ 1. The Sanction of the Illative Sense

We are in a world of facts, and we use them; for there is nothing else to use. We do not quarrel with them, but we take them as they are, and avail ourselves of what they can do for us. It would be out of place to demand of fire, water, earth, and air their credentials, so to say, for acting upon us, or ministering to us. We call them elements, and turn them to account, and make the most of them. We speculate on them at our leisure. But what we are still less able to doubt about or annul, at our leisure or not, is that which is at once their counterpart and their witness, I mean, ourselves. We are conscious of the objects of external nature, and we reflect and act upon them, and this consciousness, reflection, and action we call our own rational nature. And as we use the (so called) elements without first criticizing what we have no command over, so is it much more unmeaning in us to criticize or find fault with our own nature, which is nothing else than we, instead of using it according to the use of which it ordinarily admits. Our being, with its faculties, mind and body, is a fact not admitting of question, all things being of necessity referred to it, not it to other things.

If I may not assume that I exist, and in a particular way, that is, with a particular mental constitution, I have nothing to speculate about, and had better let speculation alone. Such as I am, it is my all; this is my essential stand-point, and must be taken for granted; otherwise, thought is but an idle amusement, not worth the trouble. There is no medium between using my faculties, as I have them, and flinging myself upon the external world according to the random impulse of the moment, as spray upon the surface of the waves, and simply forgetting that I am.

I am what I am, or I am nothing. I cannot think, reflect or judge, without starting from the very point which I aim at concluding. My ideas are all assumptions, and I am ever moving in a circle. I cannot avoid being sufficient for myself, for I cannot make myself anything else, and to change me is to destroy me. If I do not use myself, I have no other self to use. My only business is to ascertain what I am, in order to put it to use. It is enough for the proof of the value and authority of any function which I possess, to be able to pronounce that it is natural. What I have to ascertain is the laws under which I live. My first elementary lesson of duty is that of resignation to the laws of my nature, whatever they are; my first disobedience is to be impatient at what I am, and to indulge an ambitious aspiration after what I cannot be, to cherish a distrust of my powers, and to desire to change laws which are identical with myself.

Truths such as these, which are too obvious to be called irresistible, are illustrated by what we see in universal nature. Every being is in a true sense sufficient for itself, so as to be able to fulfil its particular needs. It is a general law that, whatever is found as a function or an attribute of any class of beings, or is natural to it, is in its substance suitable to it, and subserves its existence, and cannot be rightly regarded as a fault or enormity. No being could endure, of which the constituent parts were at war with each other. And more than this; there is that principle of vitality in every being, which is of a sanative and restorative character, and which brings all its parts and functions together into one whole, and is ever repelling and correcting the mischiefs which befall it, whether from within or without, while showing no tendency to cast off its belongings as if foreign to its nature. The brute animals are found severally with limbs and organs, habits, instincts, appetites, surroundings, which play together for the safety and welfare of the whole; and, after all exceptions, may be said each of them to have, after its own kind, a perfection of nature. Man is the highest of the animals, and more indeed than an animal, as having a mind; that is, he has a complex nature different from theirs, with a higher aim and a specific perfection; but still the fact that other beings find their good in the use of their particular nature, is a reason for anticipating that to use duly our own is our interest as well as our necessity.

What is the peculiarity of our nature, in contrast with the inferior animals around us? It is that, though man cannot change what he is born with, he is a being of progress with relation to his perfection and characteristic good. Other beings are complete from their first existence, in that line of excellence which is allotted to them; but man begins with nothing realized (to use the word), and he has to make capital for himself by the exercise of those faculties which are his natural inheritance. Thus he gradually advances to the fulness of his original destiny. Nor is this progress mechanical, nor is it of necessity; it is committed to the personal efforts of each individual of the species; each of us has the prerogative of completing his inchoate and rudimental nature, and of developing his own perfection out of the living elements with which his mind began to be. It is his gift to be the creator of his own sufficiency; and to be emphatically self-made. This is the law of his being, which he cannot escape; and whatever is involved in that law he is bound, or rather he is carried on, to fulfil.

And here I am brought to the bearing of these remarks upon my subject. For this law of progress is carried out by means of the acquisition of knowledge, of which inference and assent are the immediate instruments. If, then, the advancement of our nature, both in ourselves individually and as regards the human family, is to every one of us in his place a sacred duty, it follows that that duty is intimately bound up with the right use of these two main instruments of fulfilling it. And as we do not gain the knowledge of the law of progress by any *à priori* view of man, but by looking at it as the interpretation which is provided by himself on a large scale in the ordinary action of his intellectual nature, so too we must appeal to himself, as a fact, and not to any antecedent theory, in order to find what is the law of his mind as regards the two faculties in question. If then such an appeal does bear me out in deciding, as I have done, that the course of inference is ever more or less obscure, while assent is ever distinct and definite, and yet that what is in its nature thus absolute does, in fact, follow upon what in outward manifestation is thus complex, indirect, and recondite, what is left to us but to take things as they are, and to resign ourselves to what we find? that is, instead of devising, what cannot be, some sufficient science of reasoning which may compel certitude in concrete conclusions, to confess that there is no ultimate test of truth besides the testimony borne to truth by the mind itself, and that this phenomenon, perplexing as we may find it, is a normal and inevitable characteristic of the mental constitution of a being like a man on a stage such as the world. His progress is a living growth, not a mechanism; and its instruments are mental acts, not the formulas and contrivances of language.

We are accustomed in this day to lay great stress upon the harmony of the universe; and we have well learned the maxim so powerfully inculcated by our own English philosopher, that in our inquiries into its laws, we must sternly destroy all idols of the intellect, and subdue nature by co-operating with her. Knowledge is power, for it enables us to use eternal principles which we cannot alter. So also is it in that microcosm, the human mind. Let us follow Bacon more closely than to distort its faculties according to the demands of an ideal optimism, instead of looking out for modes of thought proper to our nature, and faithfully observing them in our intellectual exercises.

Of course I do not stop here. As the structure of the universe speaks to us of Him who made it, so the laws of the mind are the expression, not of mere constituted order, but of His will. I should be bound by them even were they not His laws; but since one of their very functions is to tell me of Him, they throw a reflex light upon themselves, and, for resignation to my destiny, I substitute a cheerful concurrence in an overruling Providence. We may gladly welcome such difficulties as there are in our mental constitution, and in the inter-action of our faculties, if we are able to feel that He gave them to us, and He can over-rule them for us. We may securely take them as they are, and use them as we find them. It is He who teaches us all knowledge; and the way by which we acquire it is His way. He varies that way according to the subject-matter; but whether He has set before us in our particular pursuit the way of observation or of experiment, of speculation or of research, of demonstration or of probability, whether we are inquiring into the system of the universe, or into the elements of matter and of life, or into the history of human society and past times, if we take the way proper to our subject-matter, we have His blessing upon us, and shall find, besides abundant matter for mere opinion, the materials in due measure of proof and assent.

And especially, by this disposition of things, shall we learn, as regards religious and ethical inquiries, how little we can effect, however much we exert ourselves, without that blessing; for, as if on set purpose, He has made this path of thought rugged and circuitous above other investigations, that the very discipline inflicted on our minds in finding Him, may mould them into due devotion to Him when He is found. "Verily Thou art a hidden God, the God of Israel, the Saviour," is the very law of His dealings with us. Certainly we need a clue into the labyrinth which is to lead us to Him; and who among us can hope to seize upon the true starting-points of thought for that enterprise, and upon all of them, to understand their right direction, to follow them out to their just limits, and duly to estimate, adjust, and combine the various reasonings in which they issue, so as safely to arrive at what it is worth any labor to secure, without a special illumination from Himself? Such are the dealings of Wisdom with the elect soul. "She will bring upon him fear, and dread, and trial; and She will torture him with the tribulation of Her discipline, till She try him by Her laws, and trust his soul. Then She will strengthen him, and make Her way straight to him, and give him joy."

§ 2. THE NATURE OF THE ILLATIVE SENSE

It is the mind that reasons, and that controls its own reasonings, not any technical apparatus of words and propositions. Great as are the services of language in enabling us to extend the range of our inferences, to test their validity, and to communicate them to others, still the mind itself is more versatile and vigorous than any of its works, of which language is one; and it is only under its penetrating and subtle action that the margin disappears, which I have described as intervening between verbal argumentation and concrete conclusions. It determines what science cannot determine, the limit of converging probabilities, and the reasons sufficient for a proof. This power of judging about truth and error in concrete matters, I call the Illative Sense, and I shall best illustrate it by referring to parallel faculties, which we commonly recognize without difficulty.

For instance, how does the mind fulfil its function of supreme direction and control, in matters of duty, social intercourse, and taste? In all of these separate actions of the intellect, the individual is supreme, and responsible to himself, nay, under circumstances, may be justified in opposing himself to the judgment of the whole world though he uses rules to his great advantage, as far as they go, and is in consequence bound to use them. As regards moral duty, the subject is fully considered in the well known ethical treatises of Aristotle. He calls the faculty which guides the mind in matters of conduct, by the name of *phronesis,* or judgment. This is the directing, controlling, and determining principle in such matters, personal and social. What it is to be virtuous, how we are to gain the just idea and standard of virtue, how we are to approximate in practice to our own standard, what is right and wrong in a particular case, for the answers in fulness and accuracy to these and similar questions, the philosopher refers us to no code of laws, to no moral treatise, because no science of life, applicable to the case of an individual, has been or can be written. Such is Aristotle's doctrine, and it is undoubtedly true. An ethical system may supply laws, general rules, guiding principles, a number of examples, suggestions, landmarks, limitations, cautions, distinctions, solutions of critical or anxious difficulties; but who is to apply them to a particular case? whither can we go, except to the living intellect, our own, or another's? What is written is too vague, too negative for our need. It bids us avoid extremes; but it cannot ascertain for us, according to our personal need, the golden mean. The authoritative oracle, which is to decide our path, is something more searching and manifold than such jejune generalizations as treatises can give, which are most distinct and clear, when we least need them. It is seated in the mind of the individual, who is thus his own law, his own teacher, and his own judge in those special cases of duty which are personal to him. It comes of an acquired habit, though it has its first origin in nature itself, and it is formed and matured by practice and experience; and it manifests itself, not in any breadth of view, any philosophical comprehension of the mutual relations of duty towards duty, or any consistency in its teachings, but it is a capacity sufficient for the occasion, deciding what ought to be done here and now, by this given person, under these given circumstances. It decides nothing hypothetical, it does not determine what a man shall do ten years hence, or what another should do at this time. It may indeed decide ten years hence as it does now, and decide another case now as it decides the case which is before it; still its present act is for the present, not for the distant or the future.

The law of the land is inflexible, but this mental rule is not only minute and particular, but has an elasticity, which, in its application to individual cases, is, as I have said, not studious to maintain the appearance of consistency. In old times the mason's rule which was in use at Lesbos was, according to Aristotle, not of wood or iron, but of lead, so as to allow of its adjustment to the uneven surface of the stones brought together for the work. Such is the philosopher's illustration of the nature of equity in contrast with law, and such is that *phronesis*, from which the science of morals forms its rules, and receives its complement.

In this respect of course the law of truth differs from the law of duty, that duties change, but truths never; but, though truth is ever one and the same, and the assent of certitude is immutable, still the reasonings which carry us on to truth and certitude are many and distinct, and vary with the inquirer; and it is not with assent, but with the controlling principle in inferences that I am comparing *phronesis*. Therefore it is that I say that as regards conduct, the rule for one man is not always the rule for another, though the rule is always one and the same in the abstract, and in its principle and scope. To learn his own duty in his own case, each individual must have recourse to his own rule; and if his rule is not sufficiently developed in his intellect for his need, then he goes to some other living, present authority, to supply it for him, not to the dead letter of a treatise or a code. A living, present authority, himself or another, is his immediate guide in matters of a personal, social, or political character. In buying and selling, in contracts, in his treatment of others, in giving and receiving, in thinking, speaking, doing, and working, in toil, in danger, in his recreations and pleasures, every one of his acts, to be praiseworthy, must be in accordance with his practical sense. Thus it is, and not by science, that he perfects the virtues of justice, self-command, magnanimity, generosity, gentleness, and all others. *Phronesis* is the regulating principle of every one of them.

These last words lead me to a further remark. I doubt whether it is correct, strictly speaking, to consider this *phronesis* as a general faculty, directing and perfecting all the virtues at once. So understood, it is little better than an abstract term, including under it a circle of analogous faculties, severally proper to the separate virtues. Properly speaking, there are as many kinds of *phronesis* as there are virtues; for the judgment, good sense, or tact which is conspicuous in a man's conduct in one subject-matter is not necessarily traceable in another. As in the parallel cases of memory and reasoning, he may be great in one aspect of his character, and little-minded in another. He may be exemplary in his family, yet commit a fraud on the revenue; he may be just and cruel, brave and sensual, imprudent and patient. And if this be true of the moral virtues, it holds good still more fully when we compare what is called his private character with his public. A good man may make a bad king; profligates have been great statesmen, or magnanimous political leaders.

So, too, I may go on to speak of the various callings and professions which give scope to the exercise of great talents, for these talents also are matured, not by mere rule, but by personal skill and sagacity. They are as diverse as pleading and cross-examining, conducting a debate in Parliament, swaying a public meeting, and commanding an army; and here, too, I observe that, though the directing principle is called by the same names—for instance, sagacity, skill, tact, or prudence—still there is no ruling faculty leading to eminence in all these various lines of action in common, but men will excel in one of them, without any talent for the rest.

The parallel may be continued in the case of the Fine Arts, in which, though true and scientific rules may be given, no one would therefore deny that Phidias or Rafael had a far more subtle standard of taste and a more versatile power of embodying it in his works than any which he could communicate to others in even a series of treatises. And here again genius is indissolubly united to one definite subject matter; a poet is not therefore a painter, or an architect a musical composer.

And so again, as regards the useful arts and personal accomplishments, we use the same word "skill," but proficiency in engineering or in shipbuilding, or again in engraving, or again in singing, in playing instruments, in acting, or in gymnastic exercises, is as simply one with its particular subject-matter, as the human soul with its particular body, and is, in its own department, a sort of instinct or inspiration, not an obedience to external rules of criticism or of science.

It is natural, then, to ask the question, why ratiocination should be an exception to a general law which attaches to the intellectual exercises of the mind; why it is held to be commensurate with logical science; and why logic is made an instrumental art sufficient for determining every sort of truth, while no one would dream of making any one formula, however generalized, a working rule at once for poetry, the art of medicine, and political warfare?

This is what I have to remark concerning the Illative Sense, and in explanation of its nature and claims; and, on the whole, I have spoken of it in four respects,—as a mental exercise, as it is found in fact, as to the process it uses, and as to its function and scope.

First, as an exercise of mind, it is one and the same in all concrete matters, though employed in them in different measures. We do not reason in one way in chemistry or law, in another in morals or religion; but in reasoning on any subject whatever, which is concrete, we proceed, as far, indeed, as we can, by the logic of language, but we are obliged to supplement it by the logic of thought; for forms by themselves prove nothing.

Secondly, it is, in fact, attached to definite subject-matters, so that a given individual may possess it, in one department of thought, for instance, history, and not in another, for instance, philosophy.

Thirdly, it proceeds, in coming to its conclusion, always in the same way, by a method of reasoning, which I have considered as analogous to that mathematical calculus of modern times, which has so wonderfully extended the limits of abstract science.

Fourthly, in no class of concrete reasonings, whether in experimental science, historical research, or theology, is there any ultimate test of truth and error in our inferences besides the trustworthiness of the Illative Sense that gives them its sanction; just as there is no sufficient test of poetical excellence, heroic action, or gentlemanlike conduct, other than the particular mental sense, be it genius, taste, sense of propriety, or the moral sense, to which those subject-matters are severally committed. Our duty in each of these is to strengthen and perfect the special faculty which is its living rule, and in every case as it comes to do our best. And such, also, is our duty and our necessity, as regards the Illative Sense.

§ 3. The Range of the Illative Sense

Since ratiocination, viewed in itself, is an instrumental faculty, though, in fact, ever embodied and acting in some definite subject-matter, such, also, is the Illative Sense, which is its virtue or perfection. It is only concerned with the soundness of the reasoning; but for the truth of the conclusion we must have recourse to the truth of the premises. It is a capacity of entering with instinctive correctness into principles, doctrines, and facts, whether they be true or false, and of discerning promptly what conclusion from them is necessary, suitable, and expedient, if they are taken for granted; and this, either by means of a natural gift, or from long habituation to those various circumstances. Thus, when Laud said that he did not see his way to come to terms with the Holy See, "till Rome was other than she was," no Catholic would admit the sentiment; but any Catholic might understand that it was just the judgment consistent with Laud's actual condition of thought and cast of opinion, and that any other judgment would have argued a defect in his capacity for judging. This intimate understanding of an assemblage of intellectual data, of our position of mind towards particular questions, and of the relations of our own position towards other conceivable stand-points, is the first and last of the faculty or talent, which I call the Ratiocinative or Illative Sense, being parallel to *phronesis* in conduct, and to taste in the Fine Arts.

As in the instance just given, it is more commonly engaged on particular questions, and categorical answers, than on conclusions which are general or probable, and as such I have mainly considered it; but it is the regulating principle of all reasoning in the concrete. As to general propositions, these are certainly not concrete, but abstractions; however, they need not be so considered, as regards their scope; but as convenient modes of expressing by anticipation a judgment about definite concrete things, as they come before us. Thus, if I say, "*Most* Englishmen are brave," this general enunciation is but a comprehension of a series of individual cases, provisionally thrown, till wanted, into the shape of a formula, and, in order to receive a real meaning, must be translated into the particular proposition, "This, that, or the other Englishman, who comes before us, the *individuum vagum*, is *probably* brave."

However, with whatever explanation, the Illative Sense is employed on reasonings from primary facts, as well as directed towards personal issues. And thus it is the instrument of induction from particulars, and determines what are general laws, and what conclusions cannot reach beyond bare probability. I have already ventured to say that our belief in the extended material world follows on an inference from our perception of particular objects through their phenomena, as those phenomena actually come before us, or even (as I might say) from our experience of the sensible phenomena of self. It is by the Illative Sense that we come to this conclusion, which no logic can reach; and so, again, it is by the Illative Sense that we reason out, from the data we possess, that nature is uniform, and it is by a defect in that sense, that we go on farther to pronounce, if we pronounce, the laws of nature to be invariable. Its range, then, is commensurate with the actual range of our intellect, till we arrive at experiences of whatever kind; and, even as regards experiences, it is of use in discriminating real from apparent, in resolving apparent into their elements, and in determining the value and application of those which are real. It must be recollected, too, that the first springs of thought are so obscure, that at times experiences and reasonings may be indistinguishable from each other; and sometimes it may be impossible to say whether an apparent first principle is an elementary truth, or rather the exhibition of some sensation or sentiment in the shape in which the Illative Sense represents it to us.

Hence it is, that nothing I have been saying about the instrumental character or the range of the Illative Sense, interferes with its being, as I have considered it, a personal gift or habit; for, being in fact ever embodied in some definite subject-matter, it is personal because the discernment of the principles connected with that subject-matter is personal also. Certainly, however we account for it, whether we say that one man is below the level of nature, or another above it, so it is that men, taken at random, differ widely from each other in their perception of the first elements of religion, duty, philosophy, the science of life, and taste, not to speak here of the differences in quality and vigor of the Illative Sense itself, comparing man with man. Every one, in the ultimate resolution of his intellectual faculties, stands by himself, whatever he may have in common with others; and One only is his ultimate judge. Not as if there were not an objective standard of truth; but that individuals, whether by their own fault or not, variously apprehend it. Thus one man deduces from his moral sense the presence of a Moral Governor, and another does not; in each case there may be an exercise, and a sound exercise, of the Illative Sense; but the one recognizes the principle of conscience in his moral sense, and the other does not recognize it,—the illative sence of the one is employed upon and informed by the emotions of hope and fear and the sense of sin, whereas the other discerns the distinction of right and wrong in no other way than he distinguishes light from darkness, or beautifulness from deformity. That is (identifying the apprehension of the subject-matter with the faculty using it), we might say that the one man had the Religious Sense, and the other the Moral.

Thus the Illative Sense has its exercise in the starting-points as well as in the final results of thought; but not only so, but further still, whenever an inquiry or discussion is long and complex, then it is ever in request, and exerts an influence at every turn, in relation to those various affluents of argument, which are continually flowing in, and augmenting the volume and the force of the whole in its way to a final conclusion. Any investigation whatever, which we light upon, will suffice to show how impossible it is to apply the cumbrous apparatus of verbal reasoning to its continuous necessities, and how imperative it is to fall back upon that native good sense (that is, the action of our illative judgment upon our personal view of things) which legitimately trusts itself, because there is nothing else given to it to trust.

There has been, for instance, a great deal written of late years, on the subject of the state of Greece and Rome during the pre-historic period; let us say before the Olympiads in Greece, and the war with Pyrrhus as regards Rome. Now, in a question like this, it is plain that the inquirer has first of all to decide on the point from which he is to start in the presence of the received accounts; on what side, from what quarter he is to approach them; on what principles his discussion is to be conducted; what he is to assume, what opinions or objections he is summarily to put aside as nugatory, what arguments, and when, he is to consider as apposite, what false issues are to be avoided, when the state of his arguments is ripe for a conclusion. Is he to commence with absolutely discarding all that has hitherto been received; or to retail it in outline; or to make selections from it; or to consider and interpret it as mythical, or as allegorical; or to hold so much to be trustworthy, or at least of *primâ facie* authority, as he cannot actually disprove; or never to destroy except in proportion as he can construct? Then, as to the kind of arguments suitable or admissible, how far are tradition, analogy, isolated monuments and records, vague reports, legends, the facts or saying of later times, language, popular proverbs, to tell in the inquiry? what are marks of truth, what of falsehood, what is probable, what suspicious, what promises well for discriminating facts from fiction? Then, arguments have to be balanced against each other, and then, lastly, the decision is to be made, whether any conclusion at all can be drawn, or whether any till certain issues are tried and settled, or whether a probable conclusion or a certain. It is plain how incessant will be the call here or there for the exercise of a definite judgment, and how that judgment will be in accordance with the intellectual complexion of the writer.

This might be illustrated at great length, were it necessary, from the writings of any of those able men, whose names are so well known in connexion with the subject I have instanced; such as Niebuhr, Mr. Clinton, Sir George Lewis, Mr. Grote, and Colonel Mure. These authors have severally views of their own on the period of history which they have selected for investigation, and they are too learned and logical not to know and to use to the utmost the testimonies by which the facts which they investigate are to be ascertained. Why, then, do they differ so much from each other, whether in their estimate of those testimonies or of those facts? because that estimate is simply their own, coming of their own judgment; and that judgment coming of assumptions of their own, explicit or implicit; and those assumptions spontaneously issuing out of the state of thought respectively belonging to each of them; and all these successive processes of minute reasoning superintended and directed by an intellectual instrument far too subtle and spiritual to be scientific.

What was Niebuhr's idea of the office he had undertaken? I suppose it was to accept what he found in the historians of Rome, to interrogate it, to take it to pieces, to put it together again, to rearrange and interpret it. Prescription together with internal consistency was to him the evidence of fact, and if he pulled down he felt he was bound to build up. Very different is the spirit of another school of writers, with whom prescription is nothing, and who will admit no evidence which has not first proved its right to be admitted. "We are able," says Niebuhr, "to trace the history of the Roman constitution back to the beginning of the Commonwealth, as accurately as we wish, and even more perfectly than the history of many portions of the middle ages." But "we may rejoice," says Sir George Lewis, "that the ingenuity or learning of Niebuhr should have enabled him to advance many novel hypotheses and conjectures respecting the form of the early constitution of Rome, but, unless he can support those hypotheses by sufficient evidence, they are not entitled to our belief."

"Niebuhr," says an intimate relative of my own, "often expresses much contempt for mere incredulous criticism and negative conclusions; . . . yet wisely to disbelieve is our first grand requisite in dealings with materials of mixed worth." And Sir George Lewis again, "It may be said that there is scarcely any of the leading conclusions of Niebuhr's work which has not been impugned by some subsequent writer."

Again, "it is true," says Niebuhr, "that the Trojan war belongs to the region of fable, yet undeniably it has an historical foundation." But Mr. Grote writes, "If we are asked whether the Trojan war is not a legend . . . raised upon a basis of truth, . . . our answer must be, that, as the possibility of it cannot be denied, so neither can the reality of it be confirmed." On the other hand, Mr. Clinton lays down the general rule, "We may acknowledge as real persons, all those whom there is no reason for rejecting. The presumption is in favor of the early tradition, if no argument can be brought to overthrow it." Thus he lodges the *onus probandi* with those who impugn the received accounts; but Mr. Grote and Sir George Lewis throw it upon those who defend them. "Historical evidence," says the latter, "is founded on the testimony of credible witnesses." And, again, "It is perpetually assumed in practice, that historical evidence is different in its nature from other sorts of evidence. This laxity seems to be justified by the doctrine of taking the best evidence which can be obtained. The object of [my] inquiry will be to apply to the early Roman history the same rules of evidence which are applied by common consent to modern history." Far less severe is the judgment of Colonel Mure: "Where no positive historical proof is affirmable, the balance of historical probability must reduce itself very much to a reasonable indulgence to the weight of national conviction, and a deference to the testimony of the earliest native authorities." "Reasonable indulgence" to popular belief, "deference" to ancient tradition, are principles of writing history abhorrent to the judicial temper of Sir George Lewis. He considers the words "reasonable indulgence" to be "ambiguous," and observes that "the very point which cannot be taken for granted, and in which writers differ, is, as to the extent to which contemporary attestation may be presumed without direct and positive proof, ... the extent to which the existence of a popular belief concerning a supposed matter of fact authorizes the inference that it grew out of authentic testimony." And Mr. Grote observes to the same effect: "The word *tradition* is an equivocal word, and begs the whole question. It is tacitly understood to imply a tale descriptive of some real matter of fact, taking rise at the time when the fact happened, originally accurate, but corrupted by oral transmission." And Lewis, who quotes the passage, adds, "This *tacit understanding* is the key-stone of the whole argument."

I am not contrasting these various opinions of able men, who have given themselves to historical research, as if it were any reflection on them that they differ from each other. It is the cause of their differing on which I wish to insist. Taking the facts by themselves, probably these authors would come to no conclusion at all; it is the "tacit understandings" which Mr. Grote speaks of, the vague and impalpable notions of "reasonableness" on his own side as well as on that of others, which both make conclusions possible, and are the pledge of their being contradictory. The conclusions vary with the particular writer, for each writes from his own point of view and with his own principles, and these admit of no common measure.

This, in fact, is their own account of the matter: "The results of speculative historical inquiry," says Colonel Mure, "can rarely amount to more than fair presumption of the reality of the events in question as limited to their general substance, not as extending to their details. Nor can there, consequently, be expected in the minds of different inquirers any such unity regarding the precise degree of reality, as may frequently exist in respect to events attested by documentary evidence." Mr. Grote corroborates this decision by the striking instance of the diversity of existing opinions concerning the Homeric Poems. "Our means of knowledge," he says, "are so limited, that no one can produce arguments sufficiently cogent to contend against opposing preconceptions, and it creates a painful sensation of diffidence, when we read the expressions of equal and absolute persuasion with which the two opposite conclusions have both been advanced." And, again, "there is a difference of opinion among the best critics, which is probably not destined to be adjusted, since so much depends partly upon critical feeling, partly upon the general reasonings in respect to ancient epical unity, with which a man sits down to the study." Exactly so; everyone has his own "critical feeling," his antecedent "reasonings," and, in consequence, his own "absolute persuasion;" and who, whether stranger or friend, is to reach and affect what is so intimately bound up with the mental constitution of each?

Hence the categorical contradictions between one writer and another which abound. Colonel Mure appeals in defence of an historical thesis to the "fact of the Hellenic confederacy combining for the adoption of a common national system of chronology in 776 B. C." Mr. Grote replies: "Nothing is more at variance with my conception,"—he just now spoke of the preconceptions of others,—"of the state of the Hellenic world in 776 B. C., than the idea of a combination among all the members of the race for any purpose, much more for the purpose of adopting a common national system of chronology." Colonel Mure speaks of the "bigoted Athenian public;" Mr. Grote replies that "no public ever less deserved the epithet of 'bigoted' than the Athenian." Colonel Mure also speaks of Mr. Grote's "arbitrary hypothesis;" and, again (in Mr. Grote's words), of his "unreasonable scepticism." He cannot disprove by mere argument the conclusions of Mr. Grote; he can but have recourse to a personal criticism. He virtually says, "We differ in our personal view of things." Men become personal when logic fails; it is their mode of appealing to their own primary elements of thought, and their own illative sense, against the principles and the judgment of another.

I have already touched upon Niebuhr's method of investigation, and Sir George Lewis's dislike of it; it supplies us with as apposite an instance of a difference in first principles as is afforded by Mr. Grote and Colonel Mure. "The main characteristic of his history," says Lewis, "is the extent to which he relies upon internal evidence, and upon the indications afforded by the narrative itself, independently of the testimony of its truth." And, "Ingenuity and labor can produce nothing but hypotheses and conjectures, which may be supported by analogies, but can never rest upon the solid foundation of proof." And it is undeniable, that, rightly or wrongly, disdaining the scepticism of the mere critic, Niebuhr does consciously proceed by the high path of divination. "For my own part," he says, "I *divine* that, since the censorship of Fabius and Decius falls in the same year, that Cn. Flavius became mediator between his own class and the higher orders." Lewis considers this to be a process of guessing; and says, "Instead of employing those tests of credibility which are consistently applied to modern history," Niebuhr, and his followers, and most of his opponents, "attempt to guide their judgment by the indication of internal evidence, and assume that the truth is discovered by an occult faculty of historical divination." Niebuhr defends himself thus: "The real geographer has a tact which determines his judgment and choice among different statements. He is able from isolated statements to draw inferences respecting things that are unknown, which are closely approximate to results obtained from observation of facts, and may supply their place. He is able with limited data to form an image of things which no eye-witness has described." He applies this to himself. The principle set forth in this passage is, obviously, the same as I should put forward myself; but Sir George Lewis, though not simply denying it as a principle, makes little account of it, when applied to historical research. "It is not enough," he says, "for an historian to claim the possession of a retrospective second-sight, which is denied to the rest of the world—of a mysterious doctrine, revealed only to the initiated." And he pronounces that "the history of Niebuhr has opened more questions than it has closed, and it has set in motion a large body of combatants, whose mutual variances are not at present likely to be settled by deference to a common principle."

We see from the above extracts how a controversy, such as that to which they belong, is carried on from starting-points, and with collateral aids, not formally proved, but more or less assumed, the process of assumption lying in the action of the Illative Sense, applied to primary elements of thought respectively congenial to the disputants. Not that explicit argumentation on these minute or minor, though important, points is not sometimes possible to a certain extent; but it is too unwieldy an expedient for a constantly recurring need, even when it is tolerably exact. Should it be objected, apropos of the particular case, that the instinctive reasoning, on which I have been dwelling, is not worth much, since it has not brought disputants into agreement, I answer that I profess to be stating facts, not devising an optimism; also, that it is not the fault of the Illative Sense, that men differ in first principles. Moreover, it must be recollected that the controversy is still in its beginnings; and there is no reason for deciding that it will not lead in the event to a unanimous conclusion of some kind, that is, either to an assent to one particular view of the history as the true one, or else to a conviction that no true view is attainable, the existing data for proof being insufficient to overcome the intellectual contrarieties of individual disputants.

In illustration, I will mention under separate heads some of those elementary contrarieties of opinion, on which the Illative Sense has to act, discovering them, following them out, defending or resisting them, as the case may be.

1. As to the statement of the case. This depends on the particular aspect under which we view a subject, that is, on the abstraction which forms our representative notion of what it is. Sciences are only so many distinct aspects of nature; sometimes suggested by nature itself, sometimes created by the mind. (1) One of the simplest and broadest aspects under which to view the physical world is that of a system of final causes, or, on the other hand, of initial or effective causes. Bacon, having it in view to extend our power over nature, adopted the latter. He took firm hold of the idea of causation (in the common sense of the word) as contrasted to that of design, refusing to mix up the ideas in one inquiry, and denouncing such traditional interpretations of facts as did but obscure the simplicity of the aspect necessary for his purpose. He saw what others before him might have seen in what they saw, but did not see as he saw it. In this achievement of intellect, which has been so fruitful in results, lies his genius and his fame.

(2) So again, to refer to a very different subject matter, we often hear of the exploits of some great lawyer, judge or advocate, who is able in perplexed cases, when common minds see nothing but a hopeless heap of facts, foreign or contrary to each other, to detect the principle which rightly interprets the riddle, and, to the admiration of all hearers, converts a chaos into an orderly and luminous whole. This

is what is meant by originality in thinking: it is the discovery of an aspect of a subject-matter, simpler, it may be, and more intelligible than any hitherto taken.

(3) On the other hand, such aspects are often unreal, as being mere exhibitions of ingenuity, not of true originality of mind. This is especially the case in what are called philosophical views of history. Such seems to me the theory advocated in a work of great learning, vigor, and acuteness, Warburton's "Divine Legation of Moses." I do not call Gibbon merely ingenious; still his account of the rise of Christianity is the mere subjective view of one who could not enter into its depth and power.

(4) The aspect under which we view things is often intensely personal; nay, even awfully so, considering that, from the nature of the case, it does not bring home its idiosyncrasy either to ourselves or to others. Each of us looks at the world in his own way, and does not know that perhaps it is characteristically his own. This is the case even as regards the senses. Some men have little perception of colors; some recognize one or two; to some men two contrary colors, as red and green, are one and the same. How poorly we appreciate the beauties of nature, if our eyes discern, on the face of things, only an Indian-ink or a drab creation!

(5) So again, as regards form: each of us abstracts the relation of line to line in his own personal way—as one man might apprehend a curve as convex, another as concave. Of course, as in the case of a curve, there may be a limit to possible aspects; but still, even when we agree together, it is not perhaps that we learn one from another, or fall under any law of agreement, but that our separate idiosyncrasies happen to concur. I fear I may seem trifling, if I allude to an illustration which has ever had a great force with me, and that for the very reason it is so trivial and minute. Children, learning to read, are sometimes presented with the letters of the alphabet turned into the figures of men in various attitudes. It is curious to observe from such representations, how differently the shape of the letters strikes different minds. In consequence I have continually asked the question in a chance company, which way certain of the great letters looked, to the right or to the left; and while nearly every one present

had his own clear view, so clear that he could not endure the opposite view, still I have generally found that one-half of the party considered the letters in question to look to the left, and the other half thought they looked to the right.

(6) This variety of interpretation in the very elements of outlines seems to throw light upon other cognate differences between one man and another. If they look at the mere letters of the alphabet so differently, we may understand how it is they form such distinct judgments upon handwriting; nay, how some men may have a talent for decyphering from it the intellectual and moral character of the writer, which others have not. Another thought that occurs is, that perhaps here lies the explanation why it is that family likenesses are so variously recognized, and how mistakes in identity may be dangerously frequent.

(7) If we so variously apprehend the familiar objects of sense, still more various, we may suppose, are the aspects and associations attached by us, one with another, to intellectual objects. I do not say we differ in the objects themselves, but that we may have interminable differences as to their relations and circumstances. I have heard say (again to take a trifling matter) that at the beginning of this century, it was a subject of serious, nay, of angry controversy, whether it began with January, 1800, or January, 1801. Argument, which ought, if in any case, to have easily brought the question to a decision, was but sprinkling water upon a flame. I am not clear that, if it could be fairly started now, it would not lead to similar results; certainly I know those who studiously withdraw from giving an opinion on the subject, when it is accidentally mooted, from their experience of the eager feeling which it is sure to excite in some one or other who is present. This eagerness can only arise from an overpowering sense that the truth of the matter lies in the one alternative, and not in the other.

These instances, because they are so casual, suggest how it comes to pass, that men differ so widely from each other in religious and moral perceptions. Here, I say again, it does not prove that there is no objective truth, because not all men are in possession of it; or that we are not responsible for the associations which we attach, and the relations which we assign, to the objects of the intellect. But this it does suggest to us, that there is something deeper in our differences than the accident of external circumstances; and that we need the interposition of a Power greater than human teaching and human argument to make our beliefs true and our minds one.

Next I come to the assumption of first principles in a course of reasoning, and the exclusion of propositions, of whatever kind. Unless we had the right, when we pleased, of ruling that propositions were irrelevant or absurd, I do not see how we could conduct an argument at all; our way would be simply blocked up by extravagant principles and theories, gratuitous hypotheses, false issues, unsupported statements, and incredible facts. There are those who have treated the history of Abraham as an astronomical record, and have spoken of our Adorable Saviour as the sun in *Aries.* Arabian Mythology has changed Solomon into a mighty wizard. Noah has been considered the patriarch of the Chinese people. The ten tribes have been pronounced still to live in their descendants, the Red Indians; or to be the ancestors of the Goths and Vandals, and thereby of the present European races. Some have conjectured that the Apollos of the Acts of the Apostles was Apollonius Tyaneus. Able men have reasoned out, almost against their will, that Adam was a negro. These propositions, and many others of various kinds, we should think ourselves justified in passing over, if we were engaged in a work on sacred history; and there are others, on the contrary, which we should assume as true by our own right, and without which we could not set about or carry on our work.

However, the right of making assumptions has been disputed; but, when the objections are examined, I think they only go to show that we have no right in argument to make any assumption we please. Thus, in historical researches, it seems fair to say that no testimony should be received, except such as comes to us from competent witnesses, while it is not unfair to urge, on the other side, that tradition, though unauthenticated, being (what is called) in possession, has a prescription in its favor, and may, *primâ facie,* or provisionally, be received. Here are the materials of a fair dispute; but there are writers who seem to have gone far beyond this reasonable scepticism, laying down as a general proposition that we have no right in philosophy to make any assumption whatever, and that we ought to begin with a universal doubt. This, however, is of all assumptions the greatest, and to forbid them is to forbid it. Doubt itself is a positive state, and implies a definite habit of mind, and thereby necessarily involves a system of principles and doctrines of its own. Again, if nothing is to be assumed, what is our very method of reasoning but an assumption? and what our nature itself? The very sense of pleasure and pain, which is one of the most intimate portions of ourselves, inevitably translates itself into intellectual assumptions.

Of the two, I would rather have to maintain that we ought to begin with believing everything that is offered to our acceptance, than that it is our duty to doubt of everything. This, indeed, seems the true way of learning. In that case, we soon discover and discard what is contradictory; and error having always some portion of truth in it, and the truth having a reality which error has not, we may expect, that when there is an honest purpose and fair talents, we shall somehow make our way forward, the error falling off from the mind, and the truth developing and occupying it.

HUMAN ACTS

18

THE NORM OF MORALITY

Thomas Slater [1]

As men have differed and do differ widely in their views as to the meaning of human life and as to man's destiny, they naturally have differed and do differ widely in deciding what is the rule of human conduct. The rule of evolutionary ethics will be the survival of the fittest; in other systems it will be progress, or the greatest progress of the greatest number, or pleasure, or the categorical imperative of the individual reason. Even among Catholic philosophers and divines there is some difference of opinion as to what constitutes the fundamental norm of morality. Practically the different opinions come to much the same, especially as there is greater agreement among Catholics as to what are the formal and proximate rules of morality. The teaching of St. Thomas and many others seems to be that the fundamental norm of morality is rational human nature as such. Good in general is that which is conformable to the being whose good it is; and so morally good actions will be such as are conformable to the rational nature of man considered in itself and in all its relations. Man's intellect can know man himself, the existence of God and our relation to Him, our relations to other human beings, and to the world round about us; knowing these things, our reason can tell what actions are becoming and what unbecoming to such a nature. Moreover, reason tells us that although we have the physical liberty to do wrong, we are nevertheless under a moral obligation to abstain from it. Our most wise, and good, and provident Creator, who has given us our nature and placed us in the position which we hold, cannot be indif-

---

[1] *Moral Theology,* Vol. I, pp. 41-42. (Benziger Brothers, New York City.)

ferent as to the manner in which we conduct ourselves. The still, small voice of conscience is there to tell us what is right, in the name of God whose herald it is, to approve of what we do well, and to condemn what we do ill. The fundamental norm of right conduct then is man's moral nature; morally right conduct is conduct in conformity with man's nature in itself and in all its relations. This constitutes right order in the moral world, which God the Creator and provident Ruler of the universe cannot but will us to observe, and this divine Will or Reason bidding us to observe right order and prohibiting its violation is the eternal law of God, the formal objective rule of morality. Human reason, applied to conduct, or conscience, is the formal subjective rule which makes known to us and applies the objective rule.

19

THE NORM OF MORAL RECTITUDE

Victor Cathrein [1]

Since there is an intrinsic difference between good and bad actions in many cases, there must be a reason for this distinction, which reason is not merely subjective and variable but also objective and invariable. This objective reason, as a rule or criterion for judging the right and wrong of human actions, is called the norm of morality.

The proximate norm for moral good and moral evil for man is his rational nature as such. The ultimate and universal norm is the divine Essence.

A moral act is one which is done freely with attention to the norm of rectitude, or to the right and wrong of the object. According as the object is good or bad the act itself becomes right or wrong. Therefore the goodness or badness of the object is prior to the goodness or badness of the act. The correct understanding of this distinction between the goodness of the object and the goodness of the act, or in other words, between objective goodness on the one hand and subjective or formal goodness on the

---

[1] Adapted from *Philosophia Moralis*, pp. 79-86. (B. Herder Book Company, Friburg and St. Louis.)

other, is very necessary for the whole of this treatise. In order the better to grasp the difference, the following explanation should be kept in mind: There are two ways in which a thing may be suitable or good for man—either as an object or as an act. Hence there is a double goodness—objective and subjective. The good which is attached to the object of a human act makes it worthy of man's reasonable love. The good which is found in the human act itself makes the doer for the time being morally good.

Before a man acts well or ill, and hence before he becomes subjectively or formally good or bad, his intellect must propose an object as good or bad. This goodness or badness, which belongs to the object thus considered, and which is the reason that the will becomes good or bad for embracing it, is called objective goodness. For true objective goodness, it is not necessary that the object should really exist; it is sufficient that it be considered by the reason and proposed to the will as an object. On the other hand, that goodness which the act derives from the object, and in virtue of which man becomes formally good or evil, is called formal goodness. This is real only when the will acts freely. From what has been said it is clear that the fundamental question in discussing the norm of rectitude is this: What is the rule or criterion whereby the goodness or badness of an object can be decided? Observe that we are not seeking the subjective norm which manifests to us objective goodness or badness—the subjective norm is evidently reason—but we are investigating the objective norm which enables reason to decide the goodness or badness of the object. Neither do we seek a mere *material* norm which only points out what is good and what is bad without explaining why; we want the formal norm which shows the intrinsic reason of right and wrong. The material norm would be, for instance, the will of God commanding or forbidding.

We hold that the objective norm of morality is rational nature as such, that is, as it is rational. This nature must be studied *completely*.

(a) According to all its parts, rational, sensitive and vegetative, provided the inferior powers be considered as under the control of reason and thus rational by participation.

(b) According to all the relations which man has with other beings. Man excels brutes and plants and organic things, and is their immediate end. He has relations also with God, his Creator and Lord. He must seek him as his last end, love him as the Supreme Good, and thank him for countless favors. In man himself reason is superior to sense, the soul to the body, so that the inferior part must serve the superior as its end. The most important of these relations is that of man to God, his Creator and last end, and all other relations must be subordinated to that.

(c) Human nature can be viewed in the abstract or in the concrete: in the abstract as a species, and in the concrete, with all its individuating notes. In both ways rational nature is a norm. If it be considered as a species, then from it are derived those immutable rules which apply to all men alike. If it be viewed in the concrete, then it serves as a guide to apply general principles to particular cases. For example, from human nature viewed in the abstract, is derived the rule that temperance is to be observed, which means that in the use of pleasant things, the inferior part must be regulated by the superior, that is, by the rational part of man. This principle is absolutely immutable, and holds good for all men in all circumstances. But what the rule of temperance requires in the concrete is to be decided by human nature as it exists in the individual. The law of temperance varies with individuals, times and places. It prescribes different amounts for different persons and even for the same person at different times.

The goodness of an object with respect to man is certainly goodness of some kind. It must contain the notion of suitableness or desireableness. Indeed, all admit that the honest good (*bonum honestum*) is most desirable. This presupposed, we argue as follows:

An object may be fitting or desirable for man in three ways: not for its own sake, but as a means to compass something else (*bonum utile*); for its own sake as an end to give pleasure and quiet the appetite (*bonum delectabile*); for its own sake inasmuch as it is desirable for man, prescinding from the pleasure which it produces (*bonum honestum*). But the first two do not suffice for moral good. The third does. Therefore, moral good is any good which is desirable for man on its own merits and for its own sake. But what is thus desirable for man is to be decided by considering rational nature as such. Therefore, this is the proximate norm of morality. In order to determine what habits befit and do not befit human nature, all we have to do is to compare an object (an action or a thing) with human nature, and see whether it be suitable and proper or not.

As to the useful good, evidently it is not sufficient to constitute moral good, which, as all allow, is desirable for its own sake. In the next place, whether the useful as such, be morally good or not depends on the end to which it is referred. This will be clearer when we come to treat of utilitarianism. The pleasurable good, which is contradistinguished from the honest, is delightful for the senses, and, therefore, something common to man and brute. Consequently, it cannot suffice of itself for moral good which is proper to man. Besides, the common sense of mankind admits that pleasurable things are often disgraceful, vile and injurious. All honest good, on the other hand, that is, a good which is fitting for man, is sufficient for moral good. Every nature has an inborn inclination for its true good. But human nature is one and that rational; that is, it derives its species from the rational soul. Therefore, whatever is really good for man, inasmuch as he is a rational being, must be morally good. If man in pursuing the true good to which he is naturally inclined, did morally wrong, the defect would be traceable to the Author of nature, God himself.

God directs all things to their appointed ends by giving them an inborn inclination to the good which suits their specific nature. The same principle applies to man. But the specific nature of man is rational. Therefore, the good proper to him is one which suits him as a rational being; and, consequently, this rational nature is the rule which enables us to decide what is simply good for him as man.

The norm of morality should possess the following characteristics:

1. It should be such that from it the same rules of morality may be derived for all men.

2. These rules should be immutable, and yet elastic enough to admit of various applications according to a variety of circumstances.

3. It should be a norm which is constantly present and manifest to all men.

4. It should be a norm from which all the rules of morality can be derived.

Human nature, though it varies in the concrete, is common to all men and immutable in the abstract; i. e., in the essentials. It is specifically the same, individually variable, essentially alike, yet accidentally different. It is manifest to all men, for every man who possesses the use of reason knows that he is a rational being, and, consequently, more than a real animal. All the principles of morality can be readily derived from a consideration of human nature in all its manifold relations, with his fellow-men, with inferior beings, with himself and with his Creator.

Man is a social being, and, consequently, whatever is necessary for social intercourse is natural and proper for him. It is, therefore, natural to man to preserve what he has and to refrain from injuring his fellow-men. Hence theft, homicide, adultery, and false witness are wrong, as being forbidden and condemned by his social nature.

Inferior things are given to man to be used for the needs of life. Consequently, there is a definite measure which determines the use of such things, and which is, therefore, in keeping with human life. Accordingly, it is good for man to observe that measure, and bad to ignore it, such as excess in food and drink.

The body is for the good of the soul, and the lower for the sake of the higher powers. Hence the material part of man should be a help and not an impediment to the spiritual, a means to an end, an instrument for a higher good. Consequently, whatever tends to subject the higher to the lower nature, to gratify the passions at the expense of the soul, is disordered and essentially wrong, whereas, the converse is always right and proper and good. Thus, intoxication, gluttony, and impurity, which impede or destroy the use of reason and subject it to the passions, are always and everywhere wrong.

Whatever directs a person to his natural and proper end is proper, befitting and good; and the contrary is unbecoming and wrong. Since God is man's ultimate end, all those acts which are calculated to increase in man the knowledge and love of God, are naturally right; whereas, their opposites, such as blasphemy, contempt of God, and disobedience are naturally bad for man.

Human nature, like every other nature, derives its intelligible truth, necessity and immutability from the divine Essence. Therefore, the divine Essence is the exemplary cause of all things, is the ultimate norm of rectitude, not alone for man but for all beings without exception, even for God himself in so far as a norm can be applied to Him. If I ask why God cannot lie, cannot break His word, and why, on the other hand, He can create and reward man, the last assignable reason is because the one set of actions is unworthy of His infinitely perfect nature and the other is in harmony with it. It is eminently fitting, though not necessary, that a Being of infinite goodness should share His blessings with creatures.

Moral rectitude perfects man, for an action befitting a nature is the perfection of that nature. Every good deed leads to man's last end, for it contributes at least to the objective, extrinsic glory of God. Since man is an image and likeness of God in virtue of his nature by the very fact that he acts in conformity with that nature and perfects it, he develops in himself the image of God. Moreover, human nature in the physical order is the expression of the eternal law. As God directs all creatures to their proper end by means of their specific natures, so too, in the case of man. Therefore, when man follows the impulse of his rational nature as such, he is observing the eternal law, and thus he merits beatitude.

Objective goodness may be defined as the fitness or appropriateness of an object for rational nature as such. It is important, however, to observe that goodness does not consist in a mere relation between object and standard, but in the perfection of the thing itself as connoting rational nature, by which that perfection is measured. This objective goodness affords an easy explanation of objective badness and objective indifference. Objective badness and objective goodness are contraries. Objective indifference postulates two qualities in the object: a certain degree of fitting and desirable good and the absence of either rectitude or badness.

20

HUMAN ACTS

Walter H. Hill[1]

Man has some actions which are specifically the same that minerals have; v. g., to gravitate towards the earth's centre, to reflect light, etc.; it is evidently not by such actions that he differs from the mineral. He has, also, actions which are essentially the same in him and the vegetable, v. g., growth by intus-susception and assimilation of nutriment; and, similarly, he has sensible actions which are identical with those of brute animals; as to see, hear, suffer bodily pain, etc. Hence, none of these actions common to him and the three inferior forms of material beings are *per se human;* for that is not *human* by which he agrees with those different natures; but that is human by which man is specifically or essentially superior to them, and differs from them. What are the perfections by which man is elevated in his actions above them? The peculiar perfections of man, are his intellect or reason, and his will. It follows from these distinctions, then, that only those actions are specifically and properly human, which proceed from man's rational nature; that is, from his intellect and will.

The empire of reason does not extend over all things, but over a few only; of those things or beings which man knows, many both without and within himself are not subject to his control; nay, even not all action of his reason and will can be controlled by him; v. g., his reason necessarily assents to the evident truth, and his will necessarily loves what is presented to it as good in general, or as simply good. Since this kind of action in the reason and will is merely natural, just as the action of material substance is also merely physical and natural in its species,

[1] *Moral Philosophy,* pp. 41-45. (John Murphy and Company, Baltimore.)

it is of man physically, but it is action comprehended under the general physical law of created nature, of which he is not master. It is clear, then, that only that action is properly and adequately human, which is *deliberately* willed, and which, therefore, proceeds both from the intellect and the will, as having empire over it. Of indeliberate acts in his faculties, man, as a substantial and living nature, is the principle, to be sure; but as he has not dominion over them, they are not properly termed human, since they are not completely his actions, as lord over them. It may be said, then, that a human action is one which is deliberately put or elicited by the will. It is entirely man's act, for, over it, he is master.

The action of the will by which it tends to good in general, and, therefore, to any particular good, when first offered to it precisely as good, is variously termed its necessary action, natural action, spontaneous action, according to the respect under which it is considered; but it is, indeed, the same operation of the will which is thus differently named. Such action of the will is also termed *voluntary*, inasmuch as it is physically from the will, or the will is the principle that elicits it, although it is not subject to the will, or under its control.

The will, as capable of freely choosing, is termed in the Latin language, "liberum arbitrium;" for, the power to choose was defined to be a "faculty of reason and will;" because this elective power in the will, or its power to choose, connotes reason also; or, it implies both intellect and will; and hence, *free choice*, in the very nature of things, is a deliberate act, since it necessarily supposes comparison to have been made.

When an act is considered as put by a power, or as coming intrinsically from the power as the living principle that caused it, such power is said to *elicit* that act, and the act itself is termed an *elicited* act; hence, an "elicited act" is one which is immediately put by a living power; non-living things are not said to *elicit* acts. Again, man's members, both his external and internal senses, and even the intellect itself, are all in some manner subject to his will; and, as everyone knows by experience, they can be made to act, or can be directed in their action, by the reason and the will; v. g., when the hand reaches for the pen, and then writes down your thoughts; when you call before the imagination the scene which you wish to contemplate or describe; both the hand and the imagination, in such actions, obey the will, and their acts are termed *commanded* acts, or, with Hale, they may be appropriately styled "imperate acts." An imperate act, therefore, is the act of any member or faculty of man which it puts in obedience to his will; the act is in itself elicited by the power which puts it; but it is elicited by command of the will.

The multiplied distinctions in the facts of the will that are made by theologians are useful for a thorough analysis of its nature; but ethics or moral philosophy is primarily and directly concerned only with those actions of man which are *deliberate,* and, therefore, free.

Deliberation, and election or choice, regard the means to the ultimate end or beatitude, not that beatitude itself, as already observed. Man's most perfect action in this life is that by which he freely chooses the means to his future beatitude; his most perfect act in his bliss, is that by which he contemplates and loves God.

To the preceding definitions and explanations it may be objected thus: "When man actually possesses beatitude, the will must love the object necessarily, not deliberately or freely; but only a deliberate act of the will is a human act; therefore, the act of the will in loving the chief good in beatitude will not be a human act; but this seems not to be admissible."

Observe that deliberation implies, under different respects, both perfection and imperfection, as before explained; that man, while on earth, is concerned only about the means to his perfect beatitude, and, by consequence, all *deliberate* action regards an imperfect object, or a perfect object, only as imperfectly understood. Hence, distinguish the minor, "only a deliberate act of the will is specifically a human act," when it regards the means to beatitude, is true; but not when it is the act of possessing the perfect object of beatitude. It will then be really a necessary action; yet it will still be specifically and most perfectly human, because it will be elicited by the intellect and will, acting according to the complete perfection of their nature. Beatitude does not change man's nature, but perfects it, enabling it to operate in the most perfect manner; i. e., to contemplate and love good that is an absolutely perfect object.

It may be objected further: "In order for an action to be properly styled human, it should, according to the explanation given, be put by man as man, and not by man taken according to a part only of his definition; but the acts of the soul in beatitude are of the soul as separated from the body; therefore, either those acts will not be acts of *man,* or else the body must rise again, both of which propositions are philosophically false." Man is such principally and preeminently by means of his soul; and his actions are said to be his, whenever they are deliberate, because all action is attributed chiefly to the formal principle in a being. Besides, if some proof for the resurrection of the body can be founded on the very nature of man as a complete being, this contradicts no genuine conclusions of philosophy; for, philosophy does not teach that there will be no resurrection of the body.

21

THE MORAL DETERMINANTS OF AN ACTION

Michael Cronin [1]

The moral determinants of an action are all those things that go to make an action good or evil, better or worse. The principal moral determinants enumerated by the Scholastics are three—the object, the end, and the circumstances. These determinants may be more easily understood from an example than by their definition. We shall take as our example the case of a complete human act having an inner and an outer element. In murder the *act* whose morality is in question is the act of killing. The *object*—that is, the *formal moral* object of this act—is a person over whom I have no authority—someone who is not subject to me. The *circumstances* are that I do the deed at such a time, place, and so forth. The *end* is that which I purpose gaining by the act—for instance, satisfaction for some wrong or the obtaining of money.

[1] *The Science of Ethics,* Vol. I, pp. 94-97. (Benziger Brothers, New York City.)

The object is the specifically moral factor in all acts. It is that which specifies the act, which gives it a name and puts it in a class. Thus to destroy the life of another is homicide. To take the goods of another is stealing—that is, these acts are put by their respective objects into a particular moral species, to which we attach a particular name. It is with the consideration of the objects of acts, therefore, that the science of Ethics is particularly concerned. For it is through the consideration of objects that the code of general laws is constructed, which to Ethics are what the general physical laws are to Physics.

Now, if the object of an act is bad the act itself is bad; but if the object is good the act may still not be good, for we have still to consider the circumstances and the end or the *finis operantis*.

The circumstances. In every individual act, besides the *specific* moral character which depends on object, there is also an *individual* moral character which depends on circumstances. Thus, it is worse to murder one's father than to murder a stranger, and worse to steal ten pounds than five. Now, an act should be good not only in its object but in its circumstances. For morality denotes, as we have already seen, a certain fulness of being, and to have fulness of being means, not merely to be in a certain species, but to have suitable individual characteristics as well. So the individual moral act has its circumstances as well as its object, which should all be good. Still, not every circumstance counts in the morality of the act. And of those that do count some only increase or diminish the morality, as in the examples given, whilst others add on a specifically new moral relation to that which results from the object. Thus to steal six pounds is only *worse* than to steal five; but to kill a father is not only homicide but patricide. The fact that this is one's father adds on a specifically new crime.

How the circumstances affect the morality of an act: The circumstances give rise to a twofold law in action: (a) first, a negative law—there must be no bad circumstances; (b) second, a positive law—every circumstance that is necessary for the due performance of the act—that is, for the attainment of the natural end of action—must be present, else the act is not good. Now, in regard to this second point, it is to be noted that sometimes the attainment of the natural end of an act does not depend wholly on that which the *agent* does, nor does it follow immediately on the performances of his action, but requires along with the action of the agent a subsequent process also with which the agent has nothing to do, and which depends altogether on nature. Now, in such cases, provided that all the circumstances necessary for the due performance of *our own* share of the act are present, the act is lawful, and it is lawful even though nature should afterwards fail in the work proper to her, thus preventing the accomplishment of the natural end. This principle is of importance in connection with many difficult moral problems which readers of Moral Theology will have no difficulty in recognizing.

The end aimed at (*finis operantis*[2]) is the original source of the whole act, for the act that we do, with its object and its circumstances, is nothing more than means to the realization of the end aimed at. And as a man intends the end more than the means, so the end is, in one sense, the principal moral element in the act. Still the object and circumstances have their own morality apart from the end aimed at, and unless the object and circumstances are good the act is bad in spite of the fact that the end aimed at may be most praiseworthy. This is expressed by saying that *the end does not* justify the means. By the means we wish to signify all that we do in order to attain our end. A good end could not justify an act or a means which is in itself bad.

Hence to take a bad means to a bad end is to commit two crimes, whilst to take a bad means to a good end or a good means to a bad end is one crime.

---

[2] The end aimed at, though part of the *object* of the inner will, is the principal circumstance in relation to the external act. Thus the end aimed at (for instance, riches or revenge) is a circumstance of the act of stealing.

22

ARE THERE ANY INDIFFERENT ACTS?

MICHAEL CRONIN [1]

It is not our intention here to give a full account of the heated controversy to which this question of moral indifference has given rise. But it will be necessary to quote Aquinas' view at full length. In opposition to Scotus, who maintains that there can be morally indifferent acts, St. Thomas distinguishes between acts considered specifically and acts *in individuo* or in their individual circumstances, and affirms that *in specie*—that is, considering the act apart from the circumstances—there can be indifferent acts; but that *in individuo*—that is, considering the act with its concrete circumstances, and in particular the end for which the act is done—no act can be morally indifferent.

This view, it seems to us, is the logical and the correct view, as we hope to make clear to the reader, following Aquinas' reasoning on the subject. That acts can be morally indifferent apart from their circumstances, and considered in their mere specific nature, is self-evident. To lift up a straw from the earth, to think, to shout, are in themselves neither good nor evil, for they neither help nor retard the attaining of our final end. Such acts may be made either good or bad according to the circumstances and the intention with which we do them. But, concerning individual acts, we may divide St. Thomas' teaching into two parts. He claims (a) that without considering the question of the end aimed at, and taking account merely of the other concrete circumstances, the human act can be shown to be *very nearly always* morally good or bad; (b) that when we take into account the end of the will, the individual act is not merely practically always, but always and necessarily, either good or bad.

(a) On the first point Aquinas' position is as follows: A good act is one that leads to the final perfection of a man. Now, just as in the case of any particular organism developing towards a certain perfection—say the human

---

[1] *The Science of Ethics*, Vol. I, pp. 97-101. (Benziger Brothers, New York City.)

body—practically no interference with it is possible which would not affect it either for good or for evil in relation to its final perfection, so no human act is possible that would not in some way affect us as regards our final perfection.

An organism will always be affected for good or for evil by any movement or action of its inner powers. This, we fancy, should be clear from all we know of organisms and their mode of action. But a human act always involves the exercise of the inner powers of the human organism, and hence it must affect the organism well or ill in relation to its end.

Again, from a mathematical point of view, we may gain even a clearer view of the same conclusion, and, perhaps, also the reason why a purely indifferent act is so very difficult of realization. For, supposing that each of the circumstances that make up the individual act could be either good, bad, or indifferent, the chance is exceedingly small that all together will belong to the indifferent class. If there are seven circumstances in the act, the chances against these circumstances and the object being all indifferent are one divided by "three to the power eight," which is a very small chance indeed.

(b) Let us now take up St. Thomas' second point of view—that is, the point of view of the end aimed at by the individual. From this point of view, as we have said, it becomes certain that not only in most cases, but in absolutely every case, the individual act is either good or bad.

For the object which we seek can be either morally good, morally bad, or morally indifferent. If the object is morally good it is plain that our act is morally good. If the object is morally bad it is equally plain that our act is morally bad.

But what, now, if the object is morally indifferent? In that case we maintain that the act by which we pursue such an object is, if free and deliberate, a morally good act.

Before attempting a proof of this proposition we must show what is required in order that an act be morally good. An act is morally good when the object of the act is not only referrible, but is also referred or directed to the final end by the human will—that is, when it is sought as leading to the final end. Now, an object is *referrible* to the final end when it does not oppose the final end, or when it is not morally evil. And since it is supposed in our present question that the object is morally indifferent, the sole remaining condition of the morally good act is that this object, which in itself is morally indifferent, be *referred* by the will to the final end. As Aquinas says, a rational being is bound to seek a *finis debitus,* but a *finis* is *"debitus"* in so far as it leads us to our final end, which is, as we saw, the perfect good. This reference to the final end is the natural order for a rational being, and, therefore, it is the good and the right order.

Now, we contend that if any object or end be morally indifferent the act of the will which desires that object is a morally good act. And for the following reason: Every end is, in so far as it is an end, a good, also, since it satisfies some appetite or desire. *Bonum et finis convertuntur.*

Now, it is impossible that the will in seeking that good should not seek it in reference to our final end, which is the perfect good. For, since the will itself is fixed on the final end, it follows that every imperfect good that it seeks is *sought as an instalment* of the perfect good. As Aquinas writes—"Omnis inchoatio perfectionis ordinatur in perfectionem consummatam, quae est per ultimum finem" (a principle of the greatest importance in our science). Hence, naturally, every intermediate or particular end is directed to and is sought as leading to the final end ("omnia quae homo appetit appetit propter ultimum finem"). This direction of particular ends to the ultimate end on the part of the will may not be conscious and *actual;* "non oportet," he writes, "ut semper aliquis cogitet de ultimo fine quandocumque appetit vel operatur; sed virtus primae intentionis quae est respectu ultimi finis manet in quolibet appetitu cujuscumque rei, etiamsi de ultimo fine actu non cogitetur; sicut non oportet quod qui vadit per viam in quolibet passu cogitet de fine." From this we see that everything that we seek is at least *virtually* referred to the final end; and if the particular end be, as we have supposed all along, without evil, if it be a natural or physical good, and, therefore, *referrible* to the final end, the act that seeks that end is necessarily a morally good act, since in seeking that end it seeks it as a means to our ultimate good, the moral good being that which is sought by our wills and appetites, or which perfects one, in relation to his final end.

Hence, even where the object is morally indifferent, the act of the will is morally good, and, consequently, all individual deliberate acts are either morally good or evil. There are no indifferent acts *in individuo.*

23

THE HIGHEST GOOD

Michael F. Dinneen [1]

We always act with a view to some good. "The good is the object which all pursue, and for the sake of which they always act," says Plato (Republic, I, vi). His disciple Aristotle repeats the same idea in other words when he declares (Ethics, I, i) that the good is "that which all aim at." This definition is, as St. Thomas observes, à posteriori. Yet, if appetibility does not constitute goodness, still it is our only means of identifying it; in practice, the good is the desirable. But experience soon teaches that all desires cannot be satisfied, that they are conflicting, and that some goods must be foregone in order to secure others. Hence the necessity of weighing the relative value of goods, of classifying them, and of ascertaining which of them be procured even at the loss of others. The result is the division of goods into two great classes, the physical and moral, happiness and virtue. Within either class it is comparatively easy to determine the relation of particular good things to one another, but it has proved far more difficult to fix the relative excellence of the two classes of virtue and happiness. Still the question is of supreme importance, since in it the reason and final destiny of our life is involved. As Cicero says (De Finibus, v. 6), "Summum autem bonum si ignoratur, vivendi rationem ignorari necesse est." If happiness and virtue are mutually exclusive, we have to choose between the two, and this choice is a momentous one. But their incompatibility may be only on the surface. Indeed, the hope is ever recurring that the

---

[1] *Catholic Encyclopedia*, Vol. VI, pp. 640-642.

sovereign good includes both, and that there is some way of reconciling them.

It has been the task of moralists to sift the conditions on which this may be done. (1) Some would reduce virtue to happiness; (2) others teach that happiness is to be found in virtue; (3) but, as both these solutions are ever found to be in contradiction with the facts of life, the consequent vacillations of opinion can be traced throughout the history of philosophy. In the main, they can be classified under three heads, according as one or the other predominates, or both are made to blend, viz., (1) Eudaemonism or Utilitarianism, when the highest good is identified with happiness; (2) Rational Deontologism, when the highest good is identified with virtue or duty; (3) Rational Eudaemonism, or tempered Deontologism, when both virtue and happiness are combined in the highest good. . . . Christian Philosophers, in dealing with the problem of the highest good, have necessarily kept in view the teachings of Faith; still, they base their solution of it on motives of reason. Their system is neither strictly deontologico-rational, nor yet altogether eudaemonistic, but a consistent blending of both. The ultimate end of man is to be placed in perfect rational activity, in ultimate perfection, and in happiness, not as in three different things, but as in one and the self-same, since the three conceptions are resolvable into one another, and each of them denotes a goal of human tendency, a limit beyond which no desire remains to be satisfied. Though they differ somewhat in their several ways of formulating it, at bottom they all agree: (1) that in the blissful possession of God is to be found the rightful object of reason (man's deontologico-rational end), and of free will (his eudaemonistic end); (2) that this eudaemonistic end—the perfect satisfaction of the will in the possession of God—is not merely an accidental result of the former, but is the positive determination of God, the author of our nature; (3) that this eudaemonistic end may not be intended by the will for its own sake, to the exclusion of the deontologico-rational end, which, by its nature, it presupposes, and to which it is subordinated.

It is St. Thomas Aquinas who best harmonizes this system with revelation. His teaching may be summarized thus: (a) man's highest happiness does not consist in pleasure, but in action, since, in the nature of things, action is not for pleasure, but pleasure for action. This activity, on which man's happiness rests, must, on the one hand, be the noblest and highest of which his nature is capable, and, on the other, it must be directed toward the noblest and the highest object.

(b) This noblest and highest object of human activity is not that of the will, which merely follows upon and is conditioned by knowledge; it must rather be knowledge itself. Consequently, the highest happiness of man consists in the knowledge of the highest truth, which is God. With the knowledge of God must, of course, be joined the love of God; but this love is not the essential element of perfect happiness; it is merely a necessary complement of it (Summa Theol., I-II, Q. iii, a. 2, c; Con. Gen., III, xxv, xxvi).

(c) Since the knowledge of God can be acquired in three ways—by demonstration, by faith, and by intuition—the further question arises; which of these three kinds of knowledge is the foundation of man's highest happiness? Not knowledge by demonstration, for happiness must be something universal and attainable by all men, whereas only a few can arrive at this knowledge by demonstration; neither can knowledge by faith be a basis for perfect happiness, seeing that this consists chiefly in the activity of the intellect, whilst in faith the will claims for itself the principal part, inasmuch as the will must here determine the intellect to give assent. Consequently, happiness can consist only in the intuitive knowledge of God; and since this is attainable only in the next life, it follows that the ultimate destiny of man—and hence his highest good—reaches beyond time into eternity. It must be everlasting, otherwise it would not be perfect (Con. Gent., III, xxxviii, sqq).

(d) This end is not merely a subjective one which the reason imposes upon itself. Just because it is an activity, it involves relation to some external object. The intellect essentially represents a truth distinct from itself, as the act of the will is an inclination towards some good not identical with itself. The truth to be represented, therefore, and the good to be attained or possessed, are objects to which happiness refers as to further ends, just as the image has reference to a model and motion to a goal. Truth, therefore, and good are objective ends to which formal happiness corresponds as a subjective end. The absolutely ultimate end, therefore, is in the objective order, beyond which nothing remains to be known and desired, and which, when it is known and possessed, gives rest to the rational faculties. This can be nothing else than the infinite truth and the infinite good, which is God. Hence the system is not a purely deontologico-rational one, constituting the reason a law to itself, the observance of which law would be the highest good.

(e) Still less is it purely eudaemonistic, since the ultimate end and highest good does not coincide with subjective happiness as Hedonism teaches, but with the object of the highest acts of contemplation and love. This object is God, not merely as beatifying us, but as the Absolute Truth and Goodness, infinitely perfect in itself.

24

THE LAST END

Etienne Gilson [1]

Since all creatures, even those devoid of intellect, are ordered towards God as to their last end, and since all things attain to their last end in the measure of their participation in His likeness, creatures endowed with intelligence cannot but attain to it in a manner peculiar to them, namely, by the operations proper to them as intelligent creatures and with a knowledge of their end. It is therefore evident that the last end of an intelligent creature is to know God. This conclusion is inevitable and other arguments, equally direct, confirm us in the sense of its necessity. We shall reach, however, full conviction only when we have understood the way in which this last end gathers up and organises all the intermediate ends and how all particular happiness is nothing but the premiss to this beatitude.

[1] *The Philosophy of St. Thomas Aquinas*, pp. 258-266. (B. Herder Book Company, St. Louis.)

Man, as a being endowed with will and freedom, acts always, as explained earlier, with the view to an end which imparts to his acts their specific quality; which means that his acts arrange themselves under diverse species according to the ends which constitute both their principles and completion. But there is no doubt that, besides the multiplicity of particular ends, a last end of human life, taken in its totality, exists. For the ends are ordered and willed for the sake of each other; unless, therefore, a final end existed, we would have to regress *ad infinitum* in the series of ends; just as in the series of movers and moved things, if it were infinite, nothing would be desired and no action could ever be completed. Every action takes its starting-point from an end and comes to rest in it; the existence of a final end must, therefore, be necessarily admitted. It is apparent, moreover, that all that man wills he wills in view of this last end. The last end moves the appetite in the same manner in which the first mover moves all other moveable things. Now, it is evident that when a secondary thing imparts movement, it can do so only inasmuch as it has itself been set in motion by the first Mover. In the same way, consequently, the secondary ends are desirable and move the appetite only in so far as they are ordered towards the last end which is the first of all desirable objects. Wherein consists this last end?

A search for the aspects under which men conceive it, would discover the most diverse and strange notions. Wealth, health, power, etc., all the goods of the body in short, have been considered as constituting the Supreme Good and last end. But these are only so many palpable errors. For man himself cannot be the last end of the universe; he is but a particular being, ordered, like all the others, in view of a superior end. The satisfaction and preservation of his body therefore cannot form the Supreme Good and last end. And even if it were conceded that the end of reason and of the human will were the preservation of the human being, it would not follow therefrom that the last end of man consists in some bodily good. For the human being is composed of body and soul, and though it is true that the being of the body depends on the soul, it is not true that conversely the being of the soul depends on the body. On the contrary, the body is ordered in view of the soul, as matter is ordered in view of the form. In neither case, therefore, could the last end of man which is beatitude, be identified with some good of the corporeal order.

Does it consist in pleasure or some other good of the soul? If we mean by "beatitude" not the attainment or possession of beatitude—which indeed pertains to the soul—but what actually beatitude consists in, it must be said that beatitude is none of the goods of the soul, but subsists outside of, and infinitely above, the soul. "Happiness is something belonging to the soul, but that which constitutes happiness is something outside the soul." It is in effect impossible that the last end of man could be his soul or anything whatever belonging to it. The soul, considered in itself, is only in potency; its knowledge and its virtue are in need of being brought from potency to act. But, whatever is in potency is to its act, as the incomplete is to the complete; potency exists only in view of the act. It is therefore clear that the human soul exists in view of some other thing and that, consequently, it is not its own last end. But it is yet far more evident that no good of the human soul constitutes the Supreme Good. The Good which is the last end can only be a perfect good which fully satisfies the appetite. Now, human appetite which is the will, tends, as was shown before, to the universal good. On the other hand, it is obvious that every good inherent in a finite soul such as ours is, by that very fact, but a finite and participated good. It is consequently impossible for any of these goods to constitute the Supreme Good of man and to become his last end. It may consist only, as just stated, in a perfect good, fully satisfying the appetite—it would not, in fact, be the last end if, once attained, it left anything to be desired—and since nothing can fully satisfy the human will except the universal good which is its proper object, it follows of necessity that every created and participated good is incapable of constituting the Supreme Good and last end. Human beatitude consists therefore in God alone, as in the first and universal good and the source of all other goods.

With this knowledge of what beatitude consists in, let us consider what is its essence. The exact meaning of the question is this: the term "end" may have two senses. It may mean an actual thing which it is desired to obtain;

thus money is the end pursued by the miser; but it may also mean the acquisition or possession or finally the enjoyment of what is desired; thus the end which the miser seeks is the possession of money. These two senses must be carefully kept apart in considering beatitude. We know what it is in the first sense, namely, the uncreated Good which we call God who alone in His infinite goodness is able to satisfy perfectly the will of man. But what beatitude consists in, taken in the second sense, is a matter that has now to be examined.

It seems at first sight that, viewed under this aspect, beatitude is a created good. Doubtless the cause or object of beatitude is, as just established, something uncreated. But the essence itself of beatitude, i. e., the acquisition and the enjoyment by man of the last end, is necessarily something human, and consequently something created. We may add that this something is an operation and an act, since beatitude constitutes the highest perfection of man and perfection implies an act, as potency implies imperfection. Lastly, this operation belongs to the human intellect to the exclusion of every other power of the soul. For it cannot be claimed that beatitude could be reduced to an operation of the sensitive soul; we have shown that the very object of beatitude does not consist in bodily goods, and these are the only goods which are accessible to the sensitive operations of the soul; they are consequently completely incapable of conferring beatitude. It appears, on the other hand, that of the intellect and the will, which are the rational part of our soul, the intellect is the only power capable of grasping directly the object of our beatitude and of our last end. For we must distinguish, within beatitude, what constitutes the very essence of it, from the delight which is certainly always linked with it, but is in the last resort only a mere accident of it. In view of this, it becomes clear that beatitude cannot consist essentially in an act of will. For all men desire, it is true, their last end, the possession of which represents in their eyes the supreme degree of perfection and therefore beatitude; but it is not for the will to apprehend any end. The will tends to absent ends when it desires them, and to present ends when it delights and finds rest in them. But to desire an end would not seem to be the same as apprehending it; it means simply moving towards it. And as regards the delight, this arises in the will only by reason of the very presence of its object. In other words, the will rejoices in an object only on condition that it is present, and it must not be argued, as if the object became present, simply because the will delights in it. The essence itself of the beatitude consists accordingly in an act of the intellect; only the delight accompanying it can be considered as an act of the will.

These arguments all presuppose the principle that if beatitude is attainable by a human operation, it could be attained only by the most perfect and highest operation. This same principle enables us to assert further that beatitude must consist in an operation of the speculative intellect rather than of the practical intellect. For the most perfect power of the intellect is that of which the object is the most perfect, viz., the essence of God. Now this essence is the object of the speculative, not of the practical intellect. The act constituting beatitude must therefore be of a speculative nature, and this amounts to saying that this act must consist in contemplation. Still, its object remains to be determined. Would this contemplation as the source of beatitude consist, for example, in the study and consideration of the speculative sciences? To reply to this question, we must distinguish between two beatitudes accessible to man, the one perfect, the other imperfect. The perfect beatitude is that which attains to the true essence of beatitude; imperfect beatitude does not reach this, but participates, at some particular points, in some of the characters peculiar to true beatitude. Now, it is certain that true beatitude cannot be reduced in its essence to a knowledge of the speculative sciences. In our study of speculative sciences, the range of our vision cannot extend beyond the first principles of the sciences, for the whole of every science is virtually contained in the principles whence it is deduced. But the principles of speculative science are known to us only by means of sensible knowledge; the study of these sciences cannot therefore carry our intellect beyond the point to which the knowledge of sensible things can advance it. All that is needed therefore is to consider whether the knowledge of the sensible could constitute the highest beatitude of man, i. e., his highest perfection. The answer is evidently in the negative. The higher cannot find its perfection in what is inferior to it as such. The lower can contribute to the perfection of the higher only in so far as it participates, however inadequately, in a reality beyond, and which is even beyond that, to the perfection of which it contributes. It is evident, for example, that the form of a stone or of any other sensible object is inferior to man. If, therefore, in sensible knowledge, the form of a stone confers some perfection on the human intellect, it does so not inasmuch as it is simply the form of a stone, but in so far as this form participates in some reality of a higher order than the human intellect—say, the intelligible light or something else of that kind. All knowledge capable of imparting some perfection to the human intellect presupposes therefore an object superior to the intellect, and this is eminently true of the absolutely perfect human knowledge which the beatific contemplation would confer on it. Here we gather the fruits of the conclusions which we have reached earlier concerning the value and range of human knowledge. Its proper object is the sensible; the human intellect cannot therefore find its beatitude and highest perfection in the study of the sensible to which the speculative sciences are limited. But it may find there the imperfect beatitude, the only one accessible to us here on earth. Just as the sensible forms participate in some resemblance to the higher substances, so the study of the speculative sciences is a sort of participation in the true and perfect beatitude. For by them our intellect is brought from potency to act, even though they cannot bring it to its full and ultimate actuality.

This means that the essential and true beatitude is not of this world; it can only be found in the full view of the essence of God. In order to see the truth of this conclusion, it is important to keep the following two principles in mind. The first is that man is not perfectly happy as long as there is something to be desired and searched for. The second is that the perfection of a power of the soul is always measured by the nature of its object. Now, the object of the intellect is *quod quid est*, i. e., the essence of a thing. The perfection of the intellect is consequently measured by the more or less deep knowledge of the essence of its object. If, for instance, a given intellect knows the essence of a certain effect without this knowledge enabling him to know the essence of its cause, one might say that it knows the existence of the cause, but not its nature, the *an sit,* but not the *quid est;* in short, it could not be straightway said that it knows the cause. A natural desire therefore subsists in that man who knows that the effect has a cause, to know what that cause is. This is the source of curiosity and of that "wonder" which, according to the Philosopher, is at the root of all enquiry. Someone seeing an eclipse of the sun judges at once that this phenomenon has a cause; but since he is ignorant of the cause, he wonders, and because he wonders searches for it; and this search will only end when he discovers in its very essence the cause of the event. Let us now recall what the human intellect knows of its Creator. We saw that strictly speaking, it knows no other essences but those of a few sensible and created objects, and that it advances from this knowledge to that of the existence of God, but without ever attaining to the essence of the first Cause, in its perfection. Man, therefore, feels the natural desire to know fully and to see directly the essence of this cause. But he desires beatitude naturally, though he does not, *qua* man and without the light of Revelation, know what beatitude is; at least he knows it only to the extent to which God can be known by starting from sensible things. He will therefore never reach his last end and his highest perfection except by his union with God, the only object whose contemplation can entirely satisfy the highest powers of his soul and raise him to complete perfection.

This beatitude, transcending man and nature, is, however, no adventitious term invented in order to harmonize morality with religion; there is, between terrestrial beatitude, accessible to us in this life, and the celestial beatitude to which we are called, an intimate harmony and almost continuity. The last end is not the negation of our human ends; on the contrary, it gathers them up in sublimating them, and conversely our human ends are like so many partial imitations and imperfect substitutes of our last end. There is not a single thing of those that we desire, the desire for which, if interpreted and regulated by reason, is not capable of receiving a legitimate meaning. We desire in this life health and the goods of the body; but health and bodily perfection are in fact conditions favorable to the operations of knowledge by which we reach the most perfect human happiness. We desire in this life external goods, such as wealth; but the reason is that it allows us to live and to achieve the operations of contemplative as well as active virtue; if wealth is not essential to beatitude, it may be at least its instrument. We desire here even the company of our friends and we are right, for as a matter of happiness in this present life, a happy man has need of friends; not to make use of them; the wise man suffices unto himself; not to derive pleasure from them; the wise man finds his perfect pleasure in the exercise of virtue; but in order to have the material for the very exercise of virtue. His friends serve him as the recipients of his benevolence, and for the expansion of the perfection of his goodness. Conversely, we said, all goods are ordered and sublimated in the celestial beatitude. Even seeing God face to face in the beatific vision, even when the soul has become like some separate intelligence, the beatitude of man is not that of a soul wholly separated from its body. This combination we find again even in the glory of heaven itself: "For, since it is natural for the soul to be united to the body, it is not possible for the perfection of the soul to exclude its natural perfection." The body *before* beatitude is the minister of the soul and the instrument of such inferior operations, as smooth our path to it; *in* beatitude, the soul, on the contrary, in rewarding its servant, confers upon it incorruptibility and allows it to share in its immortal perfection: "From the happiness of the soul there will be an overflow on the body, so that this too will obtain its perfection." Reunited with this hitherto animal body, now spiritualized by the soul's glory, the soul has no further use for the material goods which had been disposed here below for the sake of our animal existence; it has no need even of friends other than God who comforts it out of His eternity, truth and love. Yet perhaps it is not forbidden us to think that the joy of heaven is not a solitary joy and that celestial beatitude, fulfilled in the vision which the Blessed enjoy of their mutual happiness, is further enhanced by eternal friendship. Thus the thought of St. Thomas prolongs nature into the supernatural, for having assigned the description of man as a whole, not only of the human soul, to philosophy as its object, it outlines the destiny, not of the soul alone, but of the whole man. The beatitude of the Christian, as conceived by St. Thomas, is the beatitude of man in his entirety.

25

HAPPINESS

Charles C. Miltner [1]

NATURE AND KINDS OF HAPPINESS. It is a matter of common experience that we are happy when we possess what we want; unhappy when we cannot get what we want. In a general way, then, happiness is desire satisfied by the possession of some good. The reason why many are unhappy is because they desire so many things which they are not only unable to get, but which they in no way need. Our needs are infinitesimal to our wants.

There are, as everyone knows, degrees of happiness. Greater satisfaction, more lasting contentment, results from the possession of some things rather than others. But it is safe to say that none of us has been perfectly happy, because nothing that we have ever possessed was capable of fully and permanently satisfying our desires.

Perfect happiness, therefore, can come only from the possession of a good, perfect in every way. Such a good must obviously be desirable in and for itself. It cannot be a means to an ulterior good. It must be fully and permanently satisfying. These attributes are implied in the following classical definitions: "A state rendered perfect by the accumulation of all goods" (Boethius); "The perfect possession of good things, free from all evil" (Cicero); "The plentitude of all good things that may be hoped for" (St. Augustine).

The first of these definitions, by calling perfect happiness a state or act of possession, emphasizes the subjective element; the last two stress the goods to be possessed, or the objective element. This makes clear the distinction between subjective and objective happiness, a distinction concerning which more will be said later. The object possessed, since it may be a good proportionate to man's nature (health), or one which transcends his natural powers (God), grounds the further distinction of happiness respectively into natural and supernatural.

[1] *The Elements of Ethics*, pp. 34-49. (The Macmillan Company, New York City.) By permission of the publishers.

THE DESIRE FOR HAPPINESS. It scarcely needs to be proved that all men desire happiness. It is universally the craving of the human heart, the object we hope to attain in all our multitudinous activities. One cannot desire to be miserable, unless perchance he consider that enduring his misery be a greater happiness than attempting to escape from it.

We can desire only what we know, and we can know only what exists. Hence it follows that the object of the will, of which desire is an act, is an existing thing considered beneficial to us, that is, a good. We have already shown that man's highest good is his last end; that in all his acts it is this end which, at least virtually, is his goal, and that, in its possession consists his happiness. We may conclude then that the desire for happiness is *essential to man's nature*.

Even if one should desire to do evil, he always does so with the persuasion that here and now, under the circumstances that actually prevail, it is good so to act. "It is the judgment of all men who can in any way use their reason," says Saint Augustine, "that everybody wishes to become happy."

This argument is valid of course only with regard to happiness in general. It does not mean that all men know and therefore desire that particular supreme good in which perfect happiness is found. The following quotation from Saint Thomas makes the point clear:

"Happiness may be viewed in two aspects: in one way according to the general notion of happiness, and under that aspect it needs must be that every man wishes for happiness. The general notion of happiness is that of perfect good. Now, as good is the object of the will, a man's perfect good is that which entirely satisfies his will. Hence to desire happiness is nothing else than to desire that the will be satisfied, a thing which everyone wants. In another way we may speak of happiness in special detail, having regard to that wherein happiness consists; and in that regard not all men have knowledge of happiness, because they do not know to what thing the general notion of happiness applies; and consequently so far forth not all men wish for happiness." [2]

[2] Rickaby, *Aquinas Ethicus*, vol. i, p. 39.

It may have occurred to the reader that very little of this philosophizing about the last end and happiness and perfect good seems to fit in with our actual state of mind as we go about our daily round of duties. It seems altogether too academic and out of harmony with our contention that Ethics is a practical science.

Of course, did this doctrine of final end of human acts and the necessity of always acting from a motive mean that we had always explicitly to seek happiness in all our acts; if, before acting, we should have to pause and say to ourselves, at least mentally, "Now, I am going to do this in order to become happier"—then there would be some grounds for the charge made above. But this is not our contention. For, though one may and sometimes does so frame his intention, it is by no means the rule.

The rule in this matter seems to be that when one is in a serious frame of mind and reflects on the meaning of life and the ways of rational living; when the truth that his real happiness does consist in so acting as to attain his last end appears clearly to his mind, he there and then forms the intention of acting in this way, and then, without actually recalling it to mind again, except perhaps at rare intervals, he goes on about his business. Thus his actions are performed under the influence of this intention which, not having been recalled, still persists. He acts *virtually* for his last end, that is, in virtue of the actual intention he had formerly made and not retracted.

But what if one should act without either any explicit advertence to his last end or without having had any such intention beforehand? Even in this case one could still be said to intend the last end, provided that what he did was something that of its very nature was ordained to the last end or happiness. This would be the case if, for instance, one merely intended to perform his duty, to be just, to keep the Commandments, and the like. He would then *implicitly* seek his last end or perfect happiness.

It is not, certainly, the usual thing for one to act explicitly for the ultimate end; neither can it be proved that in all moral acts the virtual intention is present. But the will in all its deliberate acts, implicitly at least, does look for happiness. For "happiness is the satisfaction of desire by which men are drawn toward the good, because through that desire of good they think they are able to gain at least some satisfaction. Whatever, therefore, they desire, they try to grasp some measure of happiness. And thus from the very nature of the act of desire man always seeks something that is referred to happiness."

The Desire for Happiness Not Illusory. That perfect happiness is a real good for whose attainment man has been ordained by his Creator follows from the very nature of the creative act. That act was an intelligent act, and hence of necessity must have been performed with some end in view. And since God has created all, He must likewise have given to each of His creatures an end proportionate to its nature. So He must have given to man also a final end, which can be nothing short of perfect happiness. For otherwise, (a) the natural desire for it which resides in the heart of every man would be vain and useless; (b) God's wisdom would be impugned, since He would have put in men a real tendency toward happiness without providing anything to secure that happiness; (c) His goodness would be unintelligible, since in that case the very brutes of the field would be better off than men. For brute animals are able to satisfy their natural desires with sensible goods.

We may fitly quote the following striking passage from Monsabré:

"God is just. It is not possible that He should be pleased to make Himself the persecutor of His creature, to fill him with desires which will never be satisfied, to urge him violently toward an end which he is destined never to attain. Why this universal desire for happiness that torments our poor hearts if human life is to cease at the grave? Has anyone ever been quite satisfied at any moment between birth and death? Alas! the ephemeral pleasures of the world do nothing but deceive the divine languor of our souls. Even the joys afforded by the possession of truth and of virtue have been constantly disturbed by base tendencies, overshadowed by incessant contradictions. Our nature is so constituted that it wishes, it demands necessarily the true without obscurity, the good without mixture of evil, the active repose of all our faculties in peace; and still some would have it that God pitilessly casts that nature into the darkness, the void, and eternal nothingness. Such an idea is atrocious, and consequently incredible." [3]

OBJECTIVE HAPPINESS. A distinction has been made between objective and subjective happiness. The latter consists in the possession of some desired good, the former is the good which is possessed, and from whose possession happiness results. We have seen that rational nature craves for and strives for the possession of an object whose possession will completely satisfy its desires, render it perfectly happy, and that man is ordained by his Creator for the attainment of such a good, which must therefore exist.

We now ask, What, specifically and in the concrete, is that object in whose possession alone perfect happiness can be found? Obviously if we can discover such an object, if we can become certain that there is one such object among all the things that men strive for, we shall have found something which will be of inestimable value; something which will enable us to understand alike the wisdom of the lives of those men who, judged by certain standards, were little short of fools and madmen, and the folly of those who, though possessing all that wealth and power can supply, come to feel that life is hardly worth the living. Best of all, we shall have found something which, if pursued with constancy, will guarantee for us the only kind of success that possesses any lasting value.

THEORIES OF OBJECTIVE FINAL END. What men think this object to be may be discovered by taking account of their words and actions, of their ideals of a successful life. For a successful man is supposed to be one that has interpreted life correctly and to have achieved in it that which is most worth while. He is one whom others are urged to imitate in method and in aim. To achieve what he has achieved is assumed to be worthy of our best efforts.

A glance at contemporary literature shows that the highest aim, the all-absorbing passion, of many men is to amass a fortune through business enterprise. "Captains of industry" are acclaimed successful men. Their lot is envied because it is believed that they surely, of all men, must be perfectly happy. So also is adjudged the state of those who by unremitting effort have raised themselves to the

---

[3] Apud Lortie, *Elementa Phil. Christ.*, vol. iii, p. 20.

highest positions of honor and power in the State, to pinnacles of fame in art or science, or even of those who have acquired a singular degree of culture, or perfection of physical development and beauty and grace of form and action. Each of these classes of men has its coterie of admirers and imitators, to whom their lives are the embodiment of that which they think will bring perfect satisfaction. Besides these, there are of course those who merely live to eat and drink and indulge in all manner of sensuous gratification.

The point we wish to make here is not a puritanical condemnation of these so-called successful men, for in a sense they are rightly called successful, their achievements are rightly admired, their methods profitably imitated. What we mean is that the possession of none of these things taken singly, nor all of them taken together, can render a man perfectly happy, and hence are not and cannot be the prime object of life. In taking this position we are opposing those Schools of Philosophy known as Epicureans, Sensists, Materialists and Utilitarians who contend that men's final end and perfect happiness is to be found in goods of fortune, such as riches, honors, fame, power; the Rationalists, with Zeno and Kant, who posit this end in goods of the mind, such as virtue and knowledge; the Pantheists, who conceive it to be natural goods in general; the Evolutionists, who maintain that it can be found in nothing short of the complete evolution of man.

We maintain that the only object whose possession can render man perfectly happy is the Uncreated Good, or God Himself.

Reasons for This Position. The notion of a perfect good connotes something which can be desired in and for itself, but not as a means to something else; something which of itself is able totally to satisfy one's desires; something devoid of any defect, and which may be tranquilly and permanently possessed. But in vain shall we try to discover these attributes in the objects mentioned: not in riches, honor, fame, power, for they are either but means to the acquisition of further goods, or their possession is subject to so many conditions beyond our control that the fear of losing them is never absent, or the effect of their possession is such as to whet our desire for still more.

The transient character of health or strength or beauty of body rules them out at once. Human knowledge and wisdom, however great, are always miserably imperfect, and the insistence of the desire for yet greater knowledge is strictly commensurate with its increase. Finally virtue, if considered as a habit, is valued for the sake of the acts it renders easier and more perfect; if considered as an act, it is valued merely as a means to rational living.

Hence it follows that no created good can yield perfect happiness. Each is relative, defective. However much their possession may be multiplied, they must ever remain insufficient, for mere multiplication does not change their nature.

As to evolution, it should be noted that it in no way connotes an end, but merely a series of changes toward an end, which end is completely shrouded in mystery. It cannot be known, at least here and now. But since any change brought about in a given series must get its worth and significance from the end toward which it is a step, it is quite evident that evolution offers nothing by way of a perfect good according to which men may interpret life and regulate their acts.

"Happiness is a perfect good which totally satisfies rational desire. Otherwise it would not be the final end. . . . But the object of the will, or of human desire, is the universal good, just as the object of the intellect is the universal truth. Hence nothing can satisfy the will short of the universal good. But the universal good is found only in God; since all the goodness that there is in creatures is a result of the Divine Goodness. Therefore God alone is able to fully satisfy the will of man, and objective happiness is found in Him alone." [4]

In God we find all the requisites for a perfect good, for perfect happiness. For by nature He is the Supreme and Infinite Being. In Him exist eminently all the perfections of His creatures. In Him there is no limitation, no defect, no vestige of change. Being the Supreme Good, the possession of Him will render all ulterior desire impossible, and therefore render the possessor perfectly happy.

THE ACT OF POSSESSION (SUBJECTIVE HAPPINESS). God is neither a mere fiction of the mind nor a material entity

---

[4] Saint Thomas, *Summa Theol.*, ii, i, q. 2, a. 8.

that can be apprehended by one's hands. He is a spiritual Being, and consequently the act or acts by which He is to be possessed, the acts in which subjective happiness consists, must be spiritual or immaterial acts. Now, Psychology teaches us that the great obstacle to the understanding of anything is its materiality. Intellectual knowledge is, for the most part at least, abstractive in character. Concepts are formed by stripping things of their material conditions. In itself therefore the less material a thing is the more knowable it is, and the easier it is known. God, being absolutely immaterial, is the most knowable of all things. The immaterial or spiritual faculties of man are his intellect and his will. Hence it is by acts of knowledge and of will that God will be possessed. And since nothing can be desired before it is known, it follows that subjective happiness will consist primarily in the knowledge of God, and secondarily in the love of Him.

PRACTICAL CONCLUSIONS. I. If the above reasoning be true, it follows that it is vain to look for perfect happiness in this life. For it is evident that God, Who is our objective happiness, cannot be perfectly known here, and hence not perfectly loved. We have no intuition of Him; our knowledge of Him is analogical, imperfect, more negative than positive. The good things of this life, in however great measure possessed, cannot fully satisfy our wants. For in themselves they are corruptible, transitory, unstable. Moreover, we tire of them quickly. "We weary of everything—of labor, of rest, of pleasure, of success, of the company of friends, and of our own, but not of the divine presence uttering itself in hope and love, in peace and joy." So long as life lasts we shall be subject to ignorance, to passion, to infirmities from within, to annoyances from without.

Possibly this might lead some to think that our view of life must be a gloomy, pessimistic one. But such is far from being the case. We have stated only half of it. The other half is that God's universe is a rational universe; that God Himself does not lack either wisdom or justice; that this desire for perfect happiness which He implanted in the heart of every man will find its complete and permanent satisfaction in the life that is to come.

Moreover, the fact that we cannot attain to perfect happiness in this life does not mean that we cannot attain to a large measure of it, and that, in spite of whatever our lot or condition may be. God has created the universe for Himself, but He has given it to man, given it to him, that is, to use rationally and to enjoy. It would be folly to say that the possession of its treasures does not bring us happiness, and sometimes great happiness, albeit not perfect happiness. And if it is true that we cannot know God perfectly, it is equally true that there is immense joy in the knowledge that we can and do have of Him, in the firm hope that we shall one day possess Him.

Pitiable indeed is the man without this hope. For him life can have little meaning beyond an animal existence. But the undying conviction of immortality, of that reign of endless blessedness with God—this it is that robs the burdens of our present life of half their weight, and puts peace into the heart and song upon the lips even when the tides of adversity are sweeping away all that we hold of greatest value. There is no room for gloom or pessimism in the man in whom flames this hope.

II. Life is hereby given a definite meaning. "If we do not know what we want," some one has asked, "how shall anything be made to serve us?" It is the aim, the end we have in view, which alone is able to give any meaning to our acts. Hence if God is the end of all, the end of life, then it is He alone, the striving for Him, that can give any meaning to life. Every man not only needs God, but also in his own way wants God, in wanting to be perfectly happy. And every man, with the assistance of the moral law and his own free acts, can attain God.

The present life therefore must be looked upon as a journey toward God, man's last end and perfect happiness, and so lived that he may constantly prepare for life with God. The goods of this life he is not asked to spurn; he is merely asked to use them in a rational way, that is, to seek in them, not perfect happiness, for this they do not contain, but a means to his ultimate end, God, their Creator and his.

Before every man lie two roads. Over the one he may be led by right reason, guided always aright by the signposts of law. Over the other he may allow himself to travel wherever his fancy or his feelings entice him, ignoring all law. None will force him upon one road or the other. The choice is left entirely with him. But it would be absurdity itself to maintain that both roads will lead to the same land of promise. For this would be to make a mockery of God, and to delete the distinction between right and wrong, good and evil. It would amount to saying that whether we seek the object of perfect happiness or not we cannot fail to attain it. Our life is our actions, and the business of life is so to regulate them that each will conduct us toward that one supreme object in which life's full perfection is alone found.

26

HINDRANCES TO ACCOUNTABILITY

Michael Cronin [1]

The effect of the passions on the voluntariness of an act is set forth by St. Thomas Aquinas in a number of propositions which have now come to be looked upon as necessary formulae for the solution of practical questions on voluntariness and responsibility. We give them here with the briefest possible explanation:

(1) *Concupiscentia antecedens auget voluntarium sed minuit liberum*—that is, where passion is not itself consciously worked up, where it precedes an act, it increases voluntariness in the sense of increasing the onward movement of the will, but it lessens liberty since it brings the act under the control of the sense and not of the will.

(2) *Concupiscentia consequens auget voluntarium*—that is, where passion is consciously worked up, it increases voluntariness, for it increases the onward movement of the will. It also increases liberty in increasing the amount of free action.

(3) *Concupiscentia consequens et totaliter tollens usum rationis non tollit voluntarium.* Passion when directly worked up, may completely take away the use of reason, and still the act is voluntary and free.

(4) *Concupiscentia antecedens totaliter tollens usum rationis tollit voluntarium.* Passion which we do not our-

[1] *Science of Ethics*, Vol. I, pp. 43-46. (Benziger Brothers, New York.)

selves cause, and which completely takes away the use of reason, completely destroys voluntariness and freedom.

(5) *Concupiscentia non totaliter tollens usum rationis, et antecedens, minuit liberum.* Passion which we do not ourselves cause, if it should interfere with the use of reason, lessens freedom for the reason given above.

These five propositions, in so far as they relate to voluntariness, yield the following resultant which Aquinas gives as expressing the general relation subsisting between passion and voluntariness—*concupiscentia magis facit voluntarium quam involuntarium*—the general effect of passion is to increase voluntariness in the sense of intensifying the onward movement of the will to any object.

It is usual in works on moral science to pay some special attention to the passion of fear. Fear is the recoiling of the mind from some impending evil. It has this distinctive characteristic, that it induces the will to do an act which the will of itself would not do—that is, which it would not do were it not under the influence of fear. Thus the captain of a ship will, in order to save his vessel, throw out even valuable goods which it is of no pleasure for him to lose. And though the throwing out of these goods is *secundum quid* involuntary—that is, would not be willed, did ordinary circumstances prevail, yet absolutely (*simpliciter*) the loss of them is voluntary since *de facto* these circumstances do prevail and the goods are thrown over. When an act is done *from* fear, its voluntariness is lessened, but not when done merely *with* fear.

Fear, like the other passions, may be so strong as totally to destroy one's liberty, and the act so done is not a human act. It is an *actus hominis,* not an *actus humanus.* But if fear be not so strong as to destroy freedom, the act done under its influence is free and human, in the degree in which reason is allowed to play its part. If the evil feared be grave, then the fear is grave; if the evil be light, then the fear is light. But these terms must be understood as relative to the person affected, for what would be grave fear for one person may be light for another.

But the positive law often invalidates an act which is done from fear, not because the act which a person does from fear is not voluntary in itself, but because it is for the common good that an act so done should be invalidated in certain cases. The conditions generally required for such "invalidation" depend upon particular forms of legislation and the kind of act that is being legislated for. There is, however, one condition that is pretty generally regarded as necessary in all such cases—namely, that the fear which invalidates an act must be excited by someone directly and wrongfully, and for the express purpose of obtaining consent to the act in question—*"directe et injuste incussus ad extorquendum consensum."*

These are the principal elements that lessen the human character of acts: ignorance, violence and passion—and it is for the moralist to compute in individual cases how far an act done under their influence is voluntary and human and within the range of Ethical Science.

27

DOES THE END JUSTIFY THE MEANS?

JOHN GERARD [1]

REVISED BY HERBERT THURSTON

Although every other weapon in their armory should fail them, proving when put to the proof but a fragile reed with a perverse habit of running into the hand that uses it, yet upon one point anti-Jesuit writers and speakers feel quite secure; of the truth of one charge, they are persuaded, there can be no possible doubt. Do not Jesuits, as everybody knows, profess and practice the doctrine that "the end justifies the means"? And is it not the acknowledged signification of this atrocious maxim that when any advantage is to be gained for the Church, or the Pope, or, most especially, for their own unprincipled Order, any means however bad in itself becomes good, in view of the goodness of the purpose which it can be made to serve—so that it is lawful and even meritorious to lie, or perjure oneself, or steal, or commit suicide, as the particular case requires?

Here, thinks the controversialist, is something like an argument, something sound, solid, and compendious, port-

[1] The Catholic Truth Society, London.

able and ever ready for use—warranted to give his quietus at a moment's notice to any Papist or Jesuit that threatens to be troublesome, like the "Protestant flail" which men carried about their persons in the panic days of the Popish Plot.

Such a belief is undoubtedly very general, and if the man in the street entertains it, we can scarcely be surprised, for it comes to him upon the word of those whom he probably regards as authorities of the first rank, beyond whom it would be idle, if not impious, to attempt to mount. Has not, for instance, Mr. H. E. M. Stutfield said it quite recently in the *National Review*,[2] without any refutation appearing in the pages of that periodical? Has not the Count von Hoensbrœch, who was himself a Jesuit for fourteen years, maintained the same before a German court of law?[3] Has not the late Dr. Littledale put the matter on record in the ninth edition of the *Encyclopædia Britannica?* And did not one Mr. Cartwright, M. P., insist upon this point in a couple of articles in the *Quarterly Review*, subsequently expanded into a book which has been quoted again and again? In that book he solemnly declared[4]: "We believe it to be demonstrable that the maxim has been broached by an unbroken chain of Jesuit divines of first-rank standing, from Busenbaum down to Gury and Liberatore;" which assertion he proceeds to substantiate by "a series of quotations from writers whose authority cannot be disowned by the Order."—What more, it will be said, can be desired than evidence such as this?

And yet are there not some considerations on the very surface which the merest common-sense ought at once to suggest? Why should the Jesuits thus persist in spreading their nets before the eyes of those whom they wish to inveigle? Why, if they propose to impose upon men, should they be at such pains to let all the world know that they are imposters, that all their pretence of sanctity is a sham,

[2] September, 1921. The article is entitled, "Are you a Jesuit?" and forms a chapter in Mr. Stutfield's volume, *Priestcraft*. An answer written by Father Vassall-Phillips, C. SS. R., was refused insertion by *The National Review*, but may be read in *The Month* for October, 1921.

[3] Further reference to this German *cause celèbre* will be found at the close of the present article.

[4] Cartwright, *The Jesuits*, p. 167.

and that none should venture to sup with them unless provided with a very long-handled spoon? Is it usual for swindlers to commence operations by advertising the particulars of the tricks they mean to play? Yet this is precisely what these proverbially cunning and crafty tricksters are represented as doing.

When we turn to an examination of facts, another difficulty still more serious at once confronts us. Whether Jesuit writers have or have not taught, as Mr. Cartwright and the others declare, that "the end justifies the means" —a question to be considered presently—there can be no manner of doubt that these same Jesuits, in common with all Catholic theologians, have taught as a fundamental principle at the outset of their treatises, and in the plainest terms, the exact opposite,—that the end, however good, does not and cannot justify the means, if those means themselves are bad.

Before proceeding to establish this assertion, a word must be said concerning the terms employed, so that there may be no mistake as to what we are talking about—a point which those who treat of the subject frequently omit to determine.

In a human action three elements are distinguished: (1) The *end*, or that for the sake of which the action is undertaken. (2) The *means*, or the thing done to attain the end. (3) The *circumstances*, or conditions of time, place, and surroundings, under which the action is performed. The means, as being an objective act, while the end is but a subjective motive in the agent's mind, is frequently termed the *object*, not in the sense in which we now commonly use the word (viz., "The end and object") but to signify the deed actually done,—that to the doing of which the agent applies himself. It is only in its relation to the end that such action is a "means."

The *end* and the *means* alike may be good, bad, or indifferent. Confining our attention to the means, with which we are mainly concerned, some things are good in themselves, as love of God and our neighbour; some are bad in themselves, as blasphemy, injustice, impurity and untruth; some are indifferent, neither morally good nor morally evil, as reading, writing, art, and sport; and some, finally, though not intrinsically evil, are permissible only under conditions of exceptional gravity,—as the shedding of human blood, or mutilation of the human person. The *circumstances* may impart a positive character, for good or ill, to an action otherwise indifferent; thus Nero is rightly blamed for fiddling whilst Rome was burning.

It will thus be understood that a man who gives an alms out of charity, uses a good means for a good end. If he give the alms intending it as a bribe, he perverts the good means to a bad end. If he steal in order to give the alms, he endeavours to serve a good end with a bad means. If he sound a trumpet whilst giving his alms, he introduces a circumstance calculated to deprive him of his merit.

This being premised, let us turn to some Jesuit authors and examine their doctrine, selecting those by preference whom Mr. Cartwright proposes to put in the witness-box as representing his unbroken chain of Jesuit writers of first-rank standing.

Busenbaum [5] writes:
"A precept forbidding what is wrong in itself must never be violated, not even through fear of death."
[Things thus wrong in themselves being, for example, blasphemy, idolatry, impurity, slander,—as said above.][6]

Laymann: [7]
"The circumstance of a good end nowise benefits an action objectively bad, but leaves it simply and wholly bad —*e. g.*, He who steals to give an alms commits a bad action on the score of injustice, and does not perform a good action on the score of charity. . . . The reason is to be sought in the difference between moral good and moral evil: for, as St. Denis says, 'An action is good if all its constituent parts are good; it is bad if any one of them is bad,' [8] which means that for an action to be morally good both the *object* [*i. e.*, the deed done], and the end, and the circumstances must be good: whereas, if any one of them be defective, it will not be a good action, but vicious and evil."

This doctrine Laymann confirms by the following quotation from St. Augustine's *Enchiridion:*

---

[5] *Medulla,* lib. i. tract. 2, c. 4, dub. 2, n. 1.
[6] v. ibid. dub. 2.
[7] *Theol. mor.* lib. i. tract. ii. c. 9, n. 7. Mayence edition, 1654, 27.
[8] *"Bonum ex integra causa est, malum ex quocumque defectu."*

"What is known to be sinful must not be done under any pretext of a good cause, nor for any end as being a good one, nor with any intention professing to be good."

And he thus sums the matter up:

"Whenever the choice [of means] is bad, the intention [*i. e.,* the end] is also bad. In other words, a vicious choice [of means] makes the intention also vicious."

Escobar[9] speaks in terms almost identical:

"The circumstance of a good end nowise benefits an act objectively bad, but leaves it simply and utterly bad; *v. g.,* to steal in order to gives an alms. Because, a bad act is incapable of any moral goodness; for what is anywise bereft of the good it ought to have is simply bad."[1]

The doctrine taught by *Wagemann* is in exact agreement with that we have heard from his brethren, namely, that for an action to be good, end, means, and circumstances must *severally* be good, while the badness of any one of these makes the whole action bad. His words, which must presently be textually cited and, therefore, need not be set down here, will serve also to declare the teaching of *Voit,* who adopted and incorporated with his own work the treatise of Wagemann, in which they are found.[2]

Gury says:

"Three sources of morality are reckoned—1. The *object* of the act. 2. Its circumstances. 3. The end of the person acting. All of these are absolutely required for a good action. If even one of them be bad, the action will become bad. Hence the well-known maxim, 'Bonum ex integra causa,' &c."[3]

---

[9] *Theol. mor.* Lyons, 1652, p. 81.
[1] "Cf. D. Tho. 1-2. q. 8. a. 1."
[2] *Theologia Moralis, Wurzburg,* 1769. *Tractatus prodomus de actibus humanis.* With the exception of the first nine lines, the substance of which he gives in another form, the whole of Wagemann's treatise *de actibus* is printed *verbatim et literatim* by Voit, whose marginal numbering of sections is, however, less by one in each case than Wagemann's. The treatise thus reproduced terminates with section 34, in Voit 33, but the latter continues, adding four sections more (34-37), apparently borrowed from some other author, since, like what goes before, they are marked with inverted commas down the margins.
Compendium theologiæ moralis, tract. i. c. iii. art. 2.

It would be easy to multiply such testimonies indefinitely, but there can be no advantage in doing so, for all Catholic authors, whether Jesuit or not, lay down precisely the same doctrine, and usually in very much the same words, a clear, crisp statement once made being constantly adopted and repeated by subsequent writers.[4]

This, it must be allowed, is a strange method of teaching that a good end justifies the employment of bad means. Yet it is *these very same men* whom we have quoted, who are cited as laying down a doctrine diametrically opposite to that which we have heard from them. How can this be?

It comes about, we must reply, solely because certain writers, sedulously ignoring such plain and unambiguous declarations as the above, have fastened upon other phrases a meaning which, in the light of the principles thus ignored, they could not possibly bear, and have given forth the phrases so misinterpreted as being the sum and substance of Jesuit teaching. That they should have found an opportunity of so doing, is due to the circumstance that there is a sense in which we may truly say that certain means *are* justified or even sanctified by the end for which they are employed. It is by misrepresenting the scope and significance of utterances dealing with this particular class of cases that the slanderous charge we are examining has been trumped up.

It is, for instance, quite obvious that such things as acting, or singing, or hunting, or fishing, are, in themselves, absolutely "indifferent." But they may become unquestionably virtuous if undertaken from a motive of charity, to obtain funds for a hospital, or food for the starving poor.

---

[4] Father E. R. Hull, S. J., communicates the following information:
"I have made a *catena* of about thirty Jesuit authors, from Vasquez to Génicot, all expressly teaching that a good end does *not* justify an evil means. The indirect evidence from this clears the whole body of scholastic theologians—not merely Jesuits—since from beginning to end not a single scholastic writer is cited as an opponent of the doctrine which they all clearly and consistently teach—none, in fact, are cited as antagonists, but ancient authors of the early centuries,—Cassian, an anonymous Greek commentator on Chrysostom, and some ambiguous phrases of Saint Ambrose, Saint Augustine, and Abulensis. Had there been any scholastics to quote in this sense, they would not have gone so far back to look for objections."

They may even be heroic, if heavy sacrifices or great hardships be entailed. These are instances of the end sanctifying the means, or of the means being elevated and ennobled by the end; which, however, can only be when the means are capable of being sanctified, that is to say, as we have been told, when they are not intrinsically bad.

It is no less evident that certain actions which, though not intrinsically wrong, are not usually lawful, become lawful in view of a good end sufficiently serious to warrant their performance. Thus, for the purposes of a just war, it is allowed to kill men in battle: to save life, surgeons amputate legs and arms: for the protection of society, magistrates deprive burglars of their liberty: though it were wrong to support every trivial statement with an oath, we rightly speak on oath in a court of law. In such instances, and in such alone, can there be any question of the end justifying the means; that is to say, when the end is of serious importance, and when the means which it demands are capable of being justified, as not being intrinsically wrong, and being, moreover, proportionate to the end. No end whatsoever could possibly justify apostasy, or blasphemy, or theft, or adultery, or perjury.

It is of such cases, and only of such, that theologians speak when they lay down, as a mere *obiter dictum,* the maxim which has aroused so much horror, that "the end being lawful the means also are lawful," or that "for whom the end is licit, for him are means also licit." This does not signify, *as they are careful to explain*, any or every means, but means which are not intrinsically wrong, and which the end necessarily or naturally postulates. The end, in fact, cannot possibly be lawful, unless there be lawful means proper for its attainment. No theologian in the world, Jesuit or other, ever said that the end being *good* the means are lawful.[5] To style it *lawful* is to imply that the means needed for its attainment are not immoral.

---

[5] Boethius, who wrote in the fifth century, and who certainly was not a theologian, still less a Jesuit, and of whom it is not absolutely certain that he was even a Christian, incidentally, as an example of the *major* of a syllogism, gives the proposition, *cujus finis est bonus ipsum est quoque bonum* (*De differentiis topicis,* lib. ii.). The few moral theologians who comment upon this utterance, observe that the means are assumed not to be evil, *e. g.,* Silvius, Bonacina, and Loth.

The case considered by almost all the Jesuit theologians "of first-rank standing," cited by Mr. Cartwright—viz., Busenbaum,[6] Laymann,[7] Voit,[8] Gury,[9]—is that of a criminal lying in prison under sentence, or with the certain prospect of death or mutilation or torture. Such a one, they assume, is entitled, if he can, to make his escape, for every man, however guilty, has a right to secure his own life and liberty; just as, if condemned to death by starvation, he would not be bound to refuse food which his friends might manage to convey. Therefore, *within certain limits,* he may have recourse to the requisite means, that is to say, to such as, not being intrinsically wrong, the gravity of his situation warrants. He must not, indeed, say the doctors, offer violence to his keepers, nor injure them, nor tempt them to sinful neglect of duty by bribery or intoxication. But he may have them provided with a good dinner in the hope that they will be less vigilant after it; or he may play a trick upon them to get them out of the way; and though he foresee that they will get into trouble for their negligence in letting him escape, he is not on that account bound to forgo the chance of freedom, as it is not he but they themselves that directly bring their troubles upon them. Also, he may lawfully injure the property of the State, by breaking through bolts and bars and walls; though he may not, to secure his liberty, arrange to have his prison stormed and all those confined in it let loose; for in such a case his private gain would not be commensurate with the public loss. Nor can he rightly attempt to escape if he has given his parole that he will not do so.

This case, as being somewhat extreme, is a favourite with authors who wish to convey an idea as to how far the principle upon which their solution rests will go. It is, in fact, as I have said, the stock instance; and it is the decisions pronounced regarding it, as indicated above, that have evoked so much obloquy from those who would not

---

[6] *Medulla theologiæ moralis,* 1. iv. c. 3, d. 7, a. 2.
[7] *Theol. mor.* Mayence, 1654, p. 75.
[8] *Theol. mor.* Wurzburg, 1769, n. 191.
[9] *Cas. Consc.* pt. ii. n. 14. Edit. Ratisbon, 1865. Gury expressly limits the liceity to *"media per se indifferentia."* Mr. Cartwright endeavours to explain that this limitation means little or nothing (p. 170).

or could not understand them in the only sense in which they can reasonably be understood.

There is, however, another example which must not be omitted, affording, as it does, a prime illustration of the method according to which some controversialists can fashion for themselves arguments out of materials the most unpromising.

Amongst the Jesuit theologians called as witnesses by Dr. Littledale and Mr. Cartwright, quite singular importance is attributed to Wagemann, of whom we heard above but whose name will be unfamiliar to many students tolerably well versed in the literature of the schools. Of this book, *Synopsis Theologiæ Moralis,* there seems to be no copy, or at least none accessible, within the British Isles.[1] Yet Dr. Littledale and Mr. Cartwright both quote it, and quote it in such a manner as to suggest that, unless the former has borrowed from the latter, who was first in the field, they have both drawn upon one common source: while in view of their usual practice in regard of evidence, it might with some confidence be assumed that this source is not the original book. Fortunately, however, it is possible to identify this fountain-head of their information. More fortunately still, it has been possible to consult Wagemann's own work, a copy of which is found in the Royal Library at Munich, with the result that a highly instructive and edifying chapter in the history of literary evolution stands revealed.

Dealing with the question of the morality of human actions, Wagemann writes as follows:

"*Question.* Is the intention of a good end vitiated by the employment of a bad means?

"*Answer.* I distinguish. If the end be intended with direct reference to a bad means, the action becomes absolutely bad: not so if the end be intended without any reference to the means. For example: Titus steals in order to give an alms out of his theft: and Caius intends to give an alms, thinking nothing at the moment of a means. *Afterwards,* through avarice, he determines to give it out of a

---

[1] It is not found in the Catalogue of the British Museum, nor of the Bodleian, nor of Trinity College, Dublin, nor of Sion College, nor of any other library where I have inquired.

theft, which he, therefore, commits. The *first intention of almsgiving* was good in Caius."²

Here, it might seem, we have a mere harmless truism, too obvious to merit utterance; yet from such a harmless germ has been evolved an immoral paradox shocking and scandalous to all honest men. In this wise—

In 1874 there was published at Celle, in Hanover, a book entitled *Doctrina moralis Jesuitorum,* compiled by an "Old Catholic" in a spirit of bitter hostility to the Society of Jesus, as we learn from the preface, dated on the hundredth anniversary of its suppression. In this work are collected a number of extracts from the writings of Jesuits,³ frequently mutilated, always shorn of their context, and calculated, as they stand, to create a bad impression. Hence, undoubtedly, have Dr. Littledale and Mr. Cartwright drawn the information concerning Wagemann, which readers will naturally suppose to have been derived from his own writings. On p. 212 of the *Doctrina* the passage of his which we have already seen, is given in its first stage of transmutation, with a few particulars prefixed concerning the author himself—as follows:

"LEWIS WAGEMANN: Professor of Moral, in the University of Innspruck: born 1713, died 1792. *Synopsis Theologiæ Moralis,* Augsburg and Innspruck, 1762: *Permissu Superiorum.* 'Is the intention of a good end vitiated by the choice of bad means? Not if the end be intended without any reference to the means, . . . *e. g.,* Caius intends to give an alms, thinking nothing at the moment of a means: afterwards, through avarice, he determines to give it out of a theft, which he, therefore, commits.'"

That is all. The phrase containing the whole point of the solution is quietly burked, and the reader is left to conclude that because Caius did not at first intend to steal, Wagemann pronounces his conduct meritorious after he has stolen.

Next comes Mr. Cartwright. He manifestly betrays his entire dependence upon the information about Wagemann supplied above, though he does what he can by circumlocution and amplification to invest it with an air of originality. In particular he tries to improve upon the material

² *Synopsis,* i. 26. *Apud* Voit, i. 19. The italics are mine.
³ In Latin and German.

supplied him, finishing off its obviously ragged end into such a point as he conceives it ought to have. Accordingly, he informs us as follows:[4]

"In 1762 the Jesuit Wagemann, Professor of Morals (*sic*) at the University of Innspruck, published a Synopsis of Moral Theology, duly authenticated by official approbation, in which occurs this passage: 'Is the intention of a good end rendered vicious by the choice of bad means? Not if the end itself be intended irrespective of the means:' a proposition which he thus exemplifies, 'Caius is minded to bestow alms, without at the time taking thought as to the means; subsequently, from avarice, he elects to give them out of the proceeds of theft, which to that end he consequently commits;' *and so Caius is declared entitled to the merits of charity though he has aggravated the offence of violence by the motive of avarice.*"

Here is, undoubtedly, a particularly fine specimen of the maxim we are considering, as exhibited in practice. In order to fasten upon a Jesuit author the stigma of so immoral a doctrine, it is considered right and proper to falsify his words, and so make him say the opposite of what he actually says. Such an end, in the judgment of our rigorous moralists, justifies such means.

We have, however, by no means finished with Wagemann, who is made to supply another example even more remarkable. Going back to the point at which we left him, we find that Mr. Cartwright thus continues:

"Wagemann is not a doctor who deals in obscure words, for he says, *Finis determinat probitatem actus* ['The end determines the righteousness of the deed'], a definition of neat preciseness."

The same neatly precise phrase is fastened upon by Dr. Littledale,[5] who exhibits it as the most terse form in which the doctrine is "laid down" that the end justifies the means. It may, in fact, be now considered as the crucial piece of evidence committing Wagemann himself and the Society whose authorities approved his work to the doctrine they would fain repudiate.

Here again, however, it is abundantly clear that the neat and terse proposition to which such supreme importance

---

[4] *The Jesuits*, p. 168. Italics mine.
[5] *Encyclopædia Britannica*, Ninth Edition, art. *Jesuits*.

is attributed, has been supplied, not by Wagemann himself, but by the same hostile writer who was previously requisitioned. But hostile as he is, he is found to utter a note of warning which should have saved our learned friends from the trap in which they have both been caught. The terrible phrase, "Finis determinat moralitatem [6] actus," occurs only in the *Index* at the end of Wagemann's book, and, accordingly, lays down no doctrine whatever, good, bad, or indifferent, but merely refers the reader to the place where the doctrine may be obtained: if we go to that place, this is what we find: [7]

"The goodness or badness of actions is chiefly to be sought under three heads: namely, the *object* [or means], the end, and the circumstances. For an act to be good, it is required that these three should *all* be good: for it to be bad, it is sufficient that *one of them* be bad, according to the principle—*Bonum est ex integra causa, malum ex singulis defectibus.*"

A little further on,[8] Wagemann writes:

"All employment of an evil means is evil; but, on the other hand, it does not follow that all employment of a good means is actually good."

Such is the evidence which is triumphantly cited as proving beyond question that Jesuits hold the vile doctrine imputed to them, and such is the kind of erudition for which Dr. Littledale has found so imposing a vehicle as the *Encyclopædia Britannica*.

It is, of course, manifest, that even the phrase, as it stands in the Index, contains a large measure of truth. The end with which a person acts must always be *one* determinant of his merit, and in a vast number of instances it alone exerts any positive determination for good or evil, the other elements being purely "indifferent."

A homely instance in which the end thus determines the moral quality of the action is given by a German writer.[9] A schoolmaster flogs a boy. If he does so because the boy deserves a flogging, and it is likely to do him good, the master's action is good and praiseworthy. If, on the other

---

[6] Not *probitatem*, as Mr. Cartwright and Dr. Littledale have it.
[7] *Synopsis*, i. 17, 18. *Apud* Voit, i. 12. Italics mine.
[8] Ibid. i. 25. Voit, i. 18.
[9] Dr. Peter Henn. *Das schwarze Buch*, 173.

hand, he chastise the boy with precisely equal severity, because he has a grudge against one, who, being poor, brings him no present at the New Year or on his birthday, the action is unprincipled and tyrannical. It is its end or motive that determines its morality.

Such are positively *the only grounds* upon which Jesuits are said to hold and teach that "the end justifies the means." Such in particular are the "classical instances" by which, as we are sometimes assured, Dr. Littledale and Mr. Cartwright have put the truth of the allegation beyond dispute.

There are, moreover, some extraneous pieces of evidence that should weigh with every fair-minded inquirer. The most bitter and determined assailants of Jesuits and all concerning them who, having been trained in the methods and terminology of the schools, were well qualified to judge of such a matter, have invariably shown what they thought of this particular charge, by entirely ignoring it. In the seventeenth century, we find no word concerning any such teaching in Pascal's *Provincial Letters,*—and Pascal was not the man to neglect such a weapon had he thought it of any possible value. For how little it counted in the storm of obloquy which in the eighteenth century presaged and facilitated the temporary destruction of the Society, may be judged from this, that it is not even mentioned as an accusation in Pope Clement XIV.'s Brief of Suppression —that document which some would regard as the last word on the iniquities of Jesuits. In the nineteenth century, who were more fierce anti-Jesuits than Dr. Döllinger and Dr. Reusch, after their revolt against the Church? They specifically and in detail attacked the moral teaching of the Society; but they knew something of what they were talking about, and the idea that any Jesuit ever held or taught that the end justifies immoral means they left severely alone.

So we find an eminent Catholic writer, but no Jesuit— Mr. W. S. Lilly, in his *Claims of Christianity*—treating the whole matter as too absurd for serious discussion, and intimating that the idea we have been considering is a vulgar error which only the ignorant or the dishonest can entertain.

Finally, in the year 1852, the German Jesuit, Father Roh, issued a public challenge, offering to pay the sum of

1,000 Rhenish guilders to any one who, in the judgment of the faculty of law in the University of Heidelberg or of Bonn, should establish the fact that any Jesuit had ever taught the doctrine that the end justifies the means, or any doctrine equivalent to it. The challenge has been before the world for fifty years; but the thousand guilders have never yet been awarded.[1]

Count Paul von Hoensbrœch, who, after becoming a Jesuit, quarrelled with his superiors and then left both the Order and the Catholic Church, himself speaks of this matter. He tells us further that in April, 1903, one of the deputies of the Centre Party, Dasbach, repeated Roh's challenge, increasing the sum to 2,000 florins. "I took Herr Dasbach at his word," writes Hoensbrœch, "published the proofs from Jesuit writings, which appeared to me convincing, in the magazine *Deutschland* (July, 1903), edited by myself, and called on the challenger, Herr Dasbach, to pay the 2,000 florins. He refused." The Court of first instance decided the case in Dasbach's favour and Hoensbrœch appealed to a higher tribunal. According to the appellant's own statement, the High Court of Appeal at Cologne dismissed the case (March 30th, 1905) "on the ground that the passages adduced from Jesuit authors did not contain the sentence 'the end sanctifies the means' either formally or materially." [2]

Count von Hoensbrœch was advised by his counsel not to carry the appeal any further, and contents himself with the assertion that the judgment delivered by the Court had been drawn up with the assistance of the Jesuits. But the very quotations from Jesuit moralists adduced by Hoensbrœch in proof of his own contention may confidently be left to the judgment of all fair-minded readers.

Finally, we may note that many honest critics who in all good faith have repeated this charge on imperfect evidence, have afterwards upon fuller enquiry withdrawn it unconditionally. Such was the straightforward course adopted quite recently by General Sir Frederick Maurice. In a letter to the *Liverpool Daily Post* of August 30th, 1919, Sir Frederick wrote: "Loyola taught his followers

---

[1] See Father Roh's pamphlet, *Das alte Lied: Der Zweck heiligt die Mittel.*

[2] *Fourteen Years a Jesuit.* (Eng. trans.) II, p. 320.

that the end justifies the means, and Ludendorff and his colleagues in other times and for other purposes adopted the principles of the Jesuits." The statement was at once challenged by the late Father Garrold, who demanded an apology, but was warmly defended by the Rev. W. A. Limbrick, Secretary of the Protestant Reformation Society, who, in the *English Churchman* of October 2nd in the same year, implored Sir Frederick not to be "too hasty" in apologising, and proceeded to cite the ex-Jesuit quoted above and an author notoriously anti-Jesuit in support of the allegation. Sir Frederick, however, acted as a gentleman might be expected to do when he has made a charge which has been shown to be inaccurate, and in the *Daily News* of October 23rd published the letter from which the following is an extract. Having cited the passage in which the charge was made, he continues:

"I wrote this passage with my mind upon Ludendorff rather than upon the Jesuits, and I did not verify my references, as I should have done. I have now investigated, to the best of my ability, the long controversy which has raged between the Jesuits and their opponents on this question, and I have been unable to find that there is any evidence that Loyola taught his followers that the end justifies the means. I, therefore, desire to withdraw that statement and to apologise for having made it."

28

THE PASSIONS

Arthur Devine [1]

By passions we are to understand here motions of the sensitive appetite in man which tend toward the attainment of some real or apparent good or the avoidance of some evil. The more intensely the object is desired or abhorred, the more vehement is the passion. St. Paul thus speaks of them: "When we were in the flesh, the passions of sin, which were by the law, did work in our members, to bring forth fruit unto death" (Rom., vii, 5). They are called passions because they cause a transformation of the normal

---

[1] *Catholic Encyclopedia,* Vol. XI, pp. 534, 535.

condition of the body and its organs which often appears externally. It may also be noted that there is in man a rational appetite as well as a sensitive appetite. The rational appetite is the will; and its acts of love, joy, and sorrow are only called passions metaphorically, because of their likeness to the acts of the sensitive appetite. They are classified by St. Thomas and the Schoolmen as follows: The sensitive appetite is twofold, concupiscible and irascible, specifically distinct because of their objects. The object of the concupiscible is real or apparent good, and suitable to the sensitive inclination. The object of the irascible appetite is good qualified by some specific difficulty in its attainment. The chief passions are eleven in number: Six in the concupiscible appetite—namely, joy or delight, and sadness, desire and aversion or abhorrence, love and hatred—and five in the irascible—hope and despair, courage and fear, and anger.

To explain the passions in their relation to virtue it is necessary to consider them first in the moral order. Some moralists have taught that all passions are good if kept under subjection, and all bad if unrestrained. The truth is, that as regards morality, the passions are indifferent, that is, neither good nor bad in themselves. Only in so far as they are voluntary do they come under the moral law. Their motions may sometimes be antecedent to any act of the will; or they may be so strong as to resist every command of the will. The feelings in connection with the passions may be lasting, and not always under the control of the will, as for example the feelings of love, sorrow, fear, and anger as experienced in the sensitive appetite; but they can never be so strong as to force the consent of our free will unless they first run away with our reason.

These involuntary motions of the passions are neither morally good nor morally bad. They become voluntary in two ways: (1) by the command of the will, which can command the inferior powers of the sensitive appetite and excite its motions; (2) by non-resistance, for the will can resist by refusing its consent to their promptings, and it is bound to resist when their promptings are irrational and inordinate. When voluntary, the passions may increase the intensity of the acts of the will, but they may also lessen their morality by affecting its freedom.

In regard to virtue the passions may be considered in the three stages of the spiritual life: first, its acquisition, secondly, its increase; thirdly, its perfection. When regulated by reason, and subjected to the control of the will, the passions may be considered good and used as means of acquiring and exercising virtue. Christ Himself, in whom there could be no sin nor shadow of imperfection, admitted their influence, for we read that He was sorrowful unto death (Mark, xiv, 34), that He wept over Jerusalem (Luke, xix, 41), and at the tomb of Lazarus He groaned in the spirit, and troubled Himself (John, xi, 33). St. Paul bids us rejoice with them that rejoice, and weep with them that weep (Rom. xii, 15). The sensitive appetite is given to man by God, and therefore its acts have to be employed in His service. Fear of death, judgment, and hell prompts one to repentance, and to the first efforts in acquiring virtue. Thoughts of the mercy of God produce hope, gratitude, and correspondence. Reflection on the sufferings of Christ moves to sorrow for sin, and to compassion and love for Him in His suffering.

The moral virtues are to regulate the passions and employ them as aids in the progress of spiritual life. A just man at times experiences great joy, great hope and confidence, and other feelings in performing duties of piety, and also great sensible sorrow, as well as sorrow of soul, for his sins, and he is thus confirmed in his justice. He can also merit constantly by restraining and purifying his passions. The saints who have reached the exalted state of perfection, have retained their capacity for all human emotions and their sensibility has remained subject to the ordinary laws; but in them the love of God has controlled the mental images which excite the passions and directed all their emotions to His active service. It has been justly said that the saint dies, and is born again; he dies to an agitated, distracted, and sensual life, by temperance, continency, and austerity, and is born to a new and transformed life. He passes through what St. John calls "the night of the senses," after which his eyes are opened to a clearer light. "The saint will return later on to sensible objects to enjoy them in his own way, but far more intensely than other men" (H. Joly, "Psychology of the Saints," 128). Accordingly we can understand how the passions and the emotions of the sensitive appetite may be directed and devoted to the service of God, and to the acquisition, increase and perfection of virtue.

All admit that the passions, unless restrained, will carry a man beyond the bounds of duty and honesty, and plunge him into sinful excesses. Unbridled passions cause all the moral ruin and most of the physical and social evils which afflict men. There are two adverse elements in man contending for the mastery, and designated by St. Paul as "the flesh" and "the spirit" (Gal. v, 17). These two are often at variance with each other in inclinations and desires. To establish and preserve harmony in the individual, it is necessary that the spirit rule, and that the flesh be made obedient to it. The spirit must set itself free from the tyranny of the passions in the flesh. It must free itself by the renunciation of all those unlawful things which our lower nature craves, that right order may be established and preserved in the relations of our higher and lower nature. The flesh and its appetites, if allowed, will throw everything into confusion and vitiate our whole nature by sin and its consequences. It is therefore man's duty to control and regulate it by reason and a strong will aided by God's grace.

29

FEAR AND ANGER

Michael Maher [1]

Fear and anger are ordinarily classified as *self-regarding* emotions, but may be aroused in behalf of other beings. Both are manifested throughout the entire animal kingdom. Both seem to be instinctive, at least in a vague form, in the infant; and both exhibit themselves at a very early age. Their general utility for the protection of the individual is obvious; but when excessive they are directly injurious. *Fear* is purely painful. It may be defined as *the pain of anticipated pain*. Anger may be in part pleasant. It includes both the pain of felt injury and the agreeable con-

---

[1] *Psychology*, pg. 430. (Longmans, Green and Company.) With permission.

sciousness of reacting against the cause of our pain. The intensity and power of the evil pleasure of revenge are only too well known. Physically, *fear,* apart from the exertion of flight, which it may excite, causes depression, lowering of vitality, derangement of the digestive organs. If the fear be great the imagination is excited, impressions are exaggerated, the faculty of judgment and reasoning is disordered, and control of attention is impaired. Consequently, from an educationalist standpoint, fear, though at times a necessary instrument, is always an imperfect motive. Its efficiency is deterrent from evil rather than promotive of genuinely good effort; and especially in the very young it may conflict with the very self-composure and steady concentrated energy needed for study.

Anger is amongst the most exciting of the emotions. It stirs up activity and arouses to energetic action. It seeks relief by injuring the cause of its pain. Like fear, though in a different way, it heightens the sensibility of the imagination and obscures the power of judgment and reflexion. When combined with fear, anger if fostered rapidly passes into *hatred.* In the form of virtuous indignation it may be an elevated moral force; but it is always a dangerous impulse, and needs watchful control from the earliest stages.

30

ANGER

St. Frances de Sales [1]

That holy and illustrious patriarch Joseph, sending back his brethren from Egypt to his father's house, gave them this only advice: "Be not angry with one another by the way." Gen. xlv. 29. I say the same to you, Philothea; this wretched life is but a journey to the happy life to come; let us not, then, be angry with each other by the way, but rather march on with the troop of our brethren and companions meekly, peaceably, and lovingly; nay, I say to you, absolutely and without exception, be not angry at all if it be possible, and admit no pretext whatsoever to open the

---

[1] *Introduction to a Devout Life,* pp. 154, 155. (F. Pustet and Company, New York.)

gate of your heart to so destructive a passion; for St. James tells us positively, and without reservation, "The anger of man works not the justice of God." St. James ii. 20. We must, indeed, resist evil, and restrain the vices of those that are under our charge constantly and courageously, but yet with meekness and compassion. Nothing so soon appeases the enraged elephant as the sight of a little lamb, and nothing so easily breaks the force of a canon-shot as wool. We do not value so much the correction which proceeds from passion, though it be accompanied with reason, as that which proceeds from reason alone; for the reasonable soul, being naturally subject to reason, is never subject to passion but through tyranny; and, therefore, when reason is accompanied by passion, she makes herself odious, her just government being debased by the fellowship of tyranny. Princes do honor to their people, and make them rejoice exceedingly, when they visit them with a peaceable train; but when they come at the head of armies, though it be for the common good, their visits are always disagreeable; for although they cause military discipline to be rigorously observed among their soldiers, yet they can never do it so effectually but that some disorders will always happen, by which the peasant will be a sufferer. In like manner, as long as reason rules, and peaceably exercises chastisements, corrections, and reprehensions, although severely and exactly, every one loves and approves it; but when she brings anger, passion, and rage, which St. Augustine calls her soldiers, along with her, she rather makes herself feared than loved, and even her own disordered heart is always the sufferer. "It is better," says the same St. Augustine, writing to Profuturus, "to deny entrance to just and reasonable anger, than to admit it, be it ever so little; because, being once admitted, it is with difficulty driven out again; for it enters as a little twig, and in a moment becomes a beam." And if it can but once gain the night of us, and the sun set upon it, which the apostle forbids, it turns into a hatred, from which we have scarce any means to rid ourselves; for it nourishes itself under a thousand false pretexts, since there was never an angry man that thought his anger unjust.

31

VIRTUE

Augustine Waldron [1]

According to its etymology the word *virtue* (Latin *virtus*) signifies manliness or courage. "Appelata est enim a viro virtus: viri autem propria maxime est fortitudo" ("the term is from the word that signifies man; a man's chief quality is fortitude"; Cicero, "Tuscul." 1, xi, 18). Taken in its widest sense, virtue means the excellence or perfection of a thing, just as vice, its contrary, denotes a defect or absence of perfection due to a thing. In its strictest meaning, however, as used by moral philosophers and theologians, it signifies a habit superadded to a faculty of the soul, disposing it to elicit with readiness acts conformable to our rational nature. "Virtue," says St. Augustine, "is a good habit consonant with our nature." From St. Thomas's entire question on the essence of virtue may be gathered his brief but complete definition of virtue: "habitus operativus bonus," an operative habit essentially good, as distinguished from vice, an operative habit essentially evil. Now a habit is a quality in itself difficult to change, disposing well or ill the subject in which it resides, either directly in itself or in its relation to its operation. An operative habit is a quality residing in a power or faculty in itself indifferent to this or that line of action, but determined by the habit to this rather than to that kind of acts. Virtue, then, has this in common with vice, that it disposes a potency to a certain determined activity; but it differs specifically from it in that it disposes it to good acts, i. e., acts in consonance with right reason. Thus, temperance inclines the sensuous appetite to acts of moderation conformable to right reason just as intemperance impels the same appetite to acts of excess contrary to the dictates of our rational reason.

Before determining the potencies or subjects in which the different virtues reside, it will be necessary to distinguish two kinds of virtues: those which are virtues absolutely (*simpliciter*) and those which are virtues only in a

---

[1] *Catholic Encyclopedia*, Vol. XV, pp. 472-475.

restricted sense (*secundum quid*). The latter confer only a faculty for well-doing, and render the possessor good only in a restricted sense, e. g., a good logician. The former, in addition to the facility for well-doing, cause one to use the facility rightly, and render the possessor unqualifiedly good. Now the intellect may be the subject of those habits which are called virtues in a restricted sense, such as science and art. But the will only, or any other faculty only in so far as it is moved by the will, can be the subject of habits, which are called virtues in the absolute sense. For it is the proper function of the will to move to their respective acts all the other powers which are in any way rational. Thus the intellect and the sensuous appetite as moved by the will are the subjects of prudence and temperance, while the will itself is the subject of justice, a virtue in the absolute sense.

Virtues may be divided into intellectual, moral, and theological. Intellectual virtue may be defined as a habit perfecting the intellect to elicit with readiness acts which are good in reference to their proper object, namely, truth. As the intellect is called speculative or practical according as it confines itself to the sole contemplation of truth or considers truth in reference to action, the intellectual virtues may be classified according to their twofold function of the mental faculty. The speculative intellectual virtues are wisdom, science, and understanding. Wisdom is the knowledge of conclusions through their highest causes. Thus philosophy, and particularly metaphysics, is properly designated as wisdom, since it considers truth of the natural order according to its highest principles. Science is the knowledge of conclusions acquired by demonstration through causes or principles which are final in one class or other. Thus, there are different sciences, mathematics, physics, etc., but only one wisdom, the supreme judge of all. Understanding is defined as the habit of first principles; as a habit or virtue it is to be distinguished, at least logically, from the faculty of intelligence. It is also called intuition, as it has for its object truths that are self-evident, the perception of which requires no discursive process. It is to be observed that these virtues differ from the gifts of the Holy Ghost, designated by the same name, inasmuch as they are qualities of the natural order, while the gifts are intrinsically supernatural. The practical intellectual virtues are two, namely, art and prudence. Art, according to the Schoolmen, signifies the right method with regard to external productions (*recta ratio factibilium*). Just as science perfects and directs the intellect to reason correctly with regard to its proper object in view of the attainment of truth, so also art perfects and directs the intellect in the application of certain rules in view of the production of external works, whether these be of a useful or aesthetic character. Hence the division into useful and fine arts. Art has this in common with the three speculative intellectual habits, that they are all virtues only in a restricted sense. Hence they constitute a man good only in a qualified sense, e. g., a good geometrician or a good sculptor. For the proper function of science and art, as such, is not to confer moral goodness, but to direct the intellect in its scientific or artistic processes.

As art is the right method of production, so prudence, as defined by St. Thomas, is the right method of conduct (*recta ratio agibilium*). It differs from all the other intellectual virtues in this, that it is a virtue in the absolute sense, not only conferring a readiness for well-doing, but causing one to use that readiness rightly. Considered more specifically, it is that virtue which directs one in the choice of means most apt, under existing circumstances, for the attainment of a due end. It differs from the moral virtues as it resides not in the appetitive powers but in the intellect, its proper act being not the choice of apt means but the direction of that choice. But although prudence is essentially an intellectual virtue, nevertheless, under a certain respect (*materialiter*) it may be considered a moral virtue, since it has as its subject matter the acts of the moral virtues. For that alone is true prudence which is directive of means in pursuit of a good in accordance with right reason, which good is the proper object of the moral virtues. For if the end be vicious, though a certain astuteness be manifested in the discernment of means, such astuteness is not real prudence, but the semblance of prudence.

Moral virtues are those which perfect the appetitive faculties of the soul, namely, the will and the sensuous appetite. Moral virtue is so called from the word *mos*, which signifies a certain natural or quasi-natural inclination to do a thing. But the inclination to act is properly attributed to the appetitive faculty, whose function it is to move the other powers to action. Consequently that virtue is called moral which perfects the appetitive faculty. For as appetite and reason have distinct activities, it is necessary that not only reason be well disposed by the habit of intellectual virtue, but that the appetitive powers also be well disposed by the habit of moral virtue. From this necessity of the moral virtues we see the falsity of the theory of Socrates, who held that all virtue was knowledge, as he held that all vice was ignorance. Moreover, the moral virtues excel the intellectual, prudence excepted, in this, that they give not only the facility, but also the right use of the facility, for well-doing. Hence moral virtues are virtues absolutely; and when we say without qualification that a man is good, we mean morally good. As the proper function of the moral virtues is to rectify the appetitive powers, i. e., to dispose them to act in accordance with right reason, there are principally three moral virtues: justice, which perfects the rational appetite or will; fortitude and temperance, which moderate the lower or sensuous appetite. Prudence, as we have observed, is called a moral virtue, not indeed essentially but by reason of its subject matter, inasmuch as it is directive of the acts of the moral virtues. Justice, an essentially moral virtue, regulates man in relation with his fellow men. It disposes us to respect the rights of others, to give each man his due. Among the virtues annexed to justice are: (1) religion, which regulates man in his relations to God, disposing him to pay due worship to his Creator; (2) piety, which disposes to the fulfilment of duties which one owes to parents and country (patriotism); (3) gratitude, which inclines one to recognition of benefits received; (4) liberality, which restrains the immoderate affection for wealth from withholding seasonable gifts or expenses; (5) affability, by which one is suitably adapted to his fellow-men in social intercourse so as to behave towards each appropriately.

All these moral virtues, as well as justice itself, regulate man in his dealings with others. But besides these there are moral virtues which regulate man with regard to his own inner passions. Now there are passions which impel man to desire that which reason forbids and those which hold him back when reason impels him forward; hence there are principally two moral virtues, namely, temperance and fortitude, whose function it is to regulate those lower appetites. Temperance it is which restrains the undue impulse of concupiscence for sensible pleasure, while fortitude causes man to be brave when he could otherwise shrink, contrary to reason, from dangers or difficulties. Temperance, then, to consider it more particularly, is that moral virtue which moderates in accordance with reason the desires and pleasures of the sensuous appetite attendant on those acts by which human nature is preserved in the individual or propagated in the species. The subordinate species of temperance are: (1) abstinence, which disposes to moderation in the use of food; (2) sobriety, which inclines to moderation in the use of spirituous liquors; (3) chastity, which regulates the appetite in regard to sexual pleasures; to chastity may be reduced modesty, which is concerned with acts subordinate to the act of reproduction. The virtues annexed to temperance are: (1) continence, which according to the Scholastics restrains the will from consenting to violent movements of concupiscence; (2) humility, which restrains inordinate desires of one's own excellence; (3) meekness, which checks inordinate movements of anger; (4) modesty or decorum, which consists in duly ordering the external movements of the body according to the direction of reason. To this virtue may be reduced what Aristotle designated as *eutrapelia,* or good cheer, which disposes to moderation in sports, games, and jests, in accordance with the dictates of reason, taking into consideration the circumstances of person, season, and place. As temperance and its annexed virtues remove from the will hindrances to rational good arising from sensuous pleasure, so fortitude removes from the will those obstacles arising from the difficulties of doing what reason requires. Hence fortitude, which implies a certain moral strength and courage, is the virtue by which one meets and sustains dangers and difficulties, even death itself, and is never through fear of these, deterred from the pursuit of good which reason dictates. The virtues annexed to fortitude are: (1) Patience, which disposes us to bear present evils with equanimity; for as the brave man is one who represses those fears which make him shrink from meeting dangers which reason dictates he should encounter, so also the patient man is one who endures present evils in such a way as not to be inordinately cast down by them. (2) Munificence, which disposes one to incur great expenses for the suitable doing of a great work. It differs from mere liberality, as it has reference not to ordinary expenses and donations, but to those that are great. Hence the munificent man is one who gives with royal generosity, who does things not on a cheap but magnificent scale, always, however, in accordance with right reason. (3) Magnanimity, which implies a reaching out of the soul to great things, is the virtue which regulates man with regard to honors. The magnanimous man aims at great works in every line of virtue, making it his purpose to do things worthy of great honor. Nor is magnanimity incompatible with true humility. "Magnanimity," says St. Thomas, "makes a man deem himself worthy of great honors in consideration of the Divine gifts he possesses; whilst humility makes him think little of himself in consideration of his own shortcomings." (4) Perseverance, the virtue which disposes to continuance in the accomplishment of good works in spite of the difficulties attendant upon them. As a moral virtue it is not to be taken precisely for what is designated as final perseverance, that special gift of the predestined by which one is found in the state of grace at the moment of death. It is used here to designate that virtue which disposes one in continuance in any virtuous work whatsoever. . . .

To the human intellect the first principles of knowledge, both speculative and moral, are connatural; to the human will the tendency to rational good is connatural. Now these naturally knowable principles and these natural tendencies to good constitute the seeds or germs whence the intellectual and moral virtues spring. Moreover, by reason of individual natural temperament, resulting from physiological conditions, particular individuals are better disposed than others to particular virtues. Thus certain persons have a natural aptitude with regard to science, others to temperance, and others to fortitude. Hence nature itself may be assigned as the radical cause of the intellectual and moral virtues, or the cause of those virtues viewed in their embryonic state. In their perfect and fully developed state, however, the aforesaid virtues are caused or acquired by frequently repeated acts. Thus by multiplied acts the moral virtues are generated in the appetitive faculties in so far as they are acted upon by reason, and the habit of science is generated in the intellect under the determination of the first principles. The supernatural virtues are immediately first principles. . . .

One of the properties of virtues is that they consist in the golden mean, that is to say, in what lies between excess and defect. For as the perfection of things subject to rule consists in conformity with that rule, so also evil in those same things results from deviation from that rule either by excess or defect. Hence the perfection of the moral virtues consists in rendering the movements of the appetitive powers conformable to their proper rule, which is reason, neither going beyond nor falling short of it. Thus fortitude, which makes one brave to meet dangers, avoids on the one hand reckless daring and on the other undue timidity. This golden mean, which consists in conformity with right reason, sometimes coincides with the mean of the objective thing (*medium rei*), as in the case of the virtue of justice, which renders to every man his due, no more and no less. The golden mean, however, is sometimes taken in reference to ourselves, as in the case of the other moral virtues, viz., fortitude and temperance. For these virtues are concerned with the inner passions, in which the standard of right cannot be fixed invariably, as different individuals vary with regard to the passions. Thus what would be moderation in one would be excess in another. Here also it is to be observed that the mean and extremes in actions and passions must be determined according to circumstances, which may vary. Hence with regard to a certain virtue, what may be an extreme according to one circumstance may be a mean according to another. Thus perpetual chastity, which renounces all sexual pleasures, and voluntary poverty, which renounces all temporal possessions, are true virtues when exercised for the motive of more surely securing life everlasting. With regard to the intellectual virtues, their golden mean is truth or conformity to reality, whilst excess consists in false affirmation, and defect in false negation.

Another property of virtues is their connection with one

another. This mutual connection exists between the moral virtues in their perfect state. "The virtues," says St. Gregory, "if separated, cannot be perfect in the nature of virtue; for that is no true prudence which is not just and temperate and brave." The reason of this connection is that no moral virtue can be had without prudence; because it is the function of moral virtue, being an elective habit, to make a right choice, which rectitude of choice must be directed by prudence. On the other hand prudence cannot exist without the moral virtues; because prudence being a right method of conduct has as principles whence it proceeds the ends of conduct, to which ends one becomes duly affected through the moral virtues. Imperfect moral virtues, however, that is to say, those inclinations to virtue resulting from natural temperament, are not necessarily connected with one another. Thus we see a man from natural temperament prompt to acts of liberality and not prompt to acts of chastity, nor are the natural or acquired moral virtues necessarily connected with charity, though they may be so occasionally.

From the doctrine of nature and properties of virtues it is abundantly clear how important a rôle they play in man's true and real perfection. In the economy of Divine providence all creatures by the exercise of their proper activity must tend to that end destined for them by the wisdom of an infinite intelligence. But as Divine Wisdom governs creatures conformably to their nature, man must tend to his destined end, not by blind instinct, but by the exercise of reason and free will. But as these faculties, as well as the faculties subject to them, may be exercised for good or evil, the proper function of the virtues is to dispose these various psychical activities to acts conducive to man's true ultimate end, just as the part which vice plays in man's rational life is to make him swerve from his final destiny. If then the excellence of a thing is to be measured by the end for which it is destined, without doubt, among man's highest perfections must be enumerated those principles of action which play so important a part in his rational, spiritual, supernatural life, and which in the truest sense of the word are justly called virtues.

32

VIRTUE, THE SOUL'S GREATNESS

Dom Anscar Vonier [1]

Virtues are the ornament of the soul, its greatness, its royal priesthood, its nobility; virtues, from the very fact of being virtues, are what we might call the most subjective portion of the spirit; they become part and parcel of the spirit itself.

It is true that some virtues are given to the soul by God, but the gift does not make them less the soul's property residing in the innermost sources of its being; for it is in the power of God, who created the spirit, and gave it its individuality, to bestow on it new and higher qualities that make it greater and stronger; God is able, and He alone is able, to give new things to a spirit, which yet are part of what is most vital in the spirit. God alone can enter into the sources of our soul, and there deposit new seeds of life that spring up into the soul's own life.

A great man said that to him the *Summa* of St. Thomas was a greater epic than Homer's Odyssey; so likewise the workings of virtue in a soul are the only dramas and tragedies worth our interest. It is there where the spirit stands and falls, and where the World is eternally divided.

33

CHARITY

John A. Ryan [2]

In its widest and highest sense, charity includes love of God as well as love of man. The latter kind of love is so closely connected with, and dependent upon the former, that neither it nor its fruits, under the Christian dispensation, can be adequately set forth without a brief preliminary glance at the relations existing between the two kinds.

As a virtue, charity is that habit or power which dis-

---

[1] *The Human Soul*, pp. 119-120. (B. Herder Book Company, St. Louis.)
[2] *The Catholic Encyclopedia*, Vol. III, pp. 592, 593.

poses us to love God above all creatures for Himself, and to love ourselves and our neighbors for the sake of God. When this power or habit is directly infused into the soul by God, the virtue is supernatural; when it is acquired through repeated personal acts, it is natural. If, in the last sentence but one, for the words "power or habit which disposes us to" we substitute the words "act by which we," the definition will fit the *act* of charity. Such an act will be supernatural if it proceeds from the infused virtue of charity, and if its motive (God lovable because of His infinite perfections) is apprehended through revelation; if either of these conditions is wanting the act is only natural. Thus, when a person with the virtue of charity in his soul assists a needy neighbor on account of the words of Christ, "as long as you did it to one of these my least brethren, you did it to Me," or simply because his Christian training tells him that the one in need is a child of God, the act is one of supernatural charity. It is likewise meritorious of eternal life. The same act performed by one who had never heard of the Christian revelation, and from the same motive of the love of God, would be one of natural charity. When charity towards the neighbor is based upon love of God, it belongs to the same virtue (natural or supernatural, according to circumstances) as charity towards God. However, it is not necessary that acts of brotherly love should rest upon this high motive in order to deserve a place under the head of charity. It is enough that they be prompted by consideration of the individual's dignity, qualities, or needs. Even when motived by some purely extrinsic end, as popular approval or the ultimate injury of the recipient, they are in essence acts of charity. The definition given above is at present scarcely ever used outside of Catholic religious and ethical treatises. In current speech and literature, the term is restricted to love of neighbor. Accordingly, charity may be popularly defined as the habit, desire or act of relieving the physical, mental, moral, or spiritual needs of one's fellows.

The obligation to perform acts of charity is taught both by revelation and by reason. Under the former head may be cited the words of Christ: "thou shalt love thy neighbor as thyself"; "as you would that men do to you, do you also to them in like manner"; and particularly the description in St. Matthew (xxv) of the separation of the good from the bad at the Final Judgment. Reason tells us that we ought to love our neighbors, since they are children of God; since they are our brothers, members of the same human family; and since they have the same nature, dignity, destiny, and needs as ourselves. This love, or charity, should be both internal and external. The former wishes the neighbor well, and rejoices in his good fortune; the latter comprises all those actions by which any of his needs are supplied. Charity differs from justice, inasmuch as it conceives its object, i. e., the neighbor, as a brother and is based on the union existing between man and man; whereas justice regards him as a separate individual, and is based on his independent personal dignity and rights. The spirit of the Gospel as regards charity is far superior to that of any of the other great religions. Its excellence appears in the following points: love of the neighbor is akin to love of God; the neighbor is to be loved even as the self; men are brothers, members of the same family; the law of charity extends to the whole human race, thus making all persons equal; men are obliged to love even their enemies; the neighbor is not merely a rational creature made in the image and likeness of God, but also the supernaturally adopted son of the Father, and the brother of the Father's Only-Begotten Son; finally, the Gospel presents the supreme exemplification of brotherly love in the death of Christ on the Cross. In no other religion are all these characteristics found; in most they are totally wanting.

34

THE PLACE OF CHARITY IN PRESENT SOCIETY

John A. Ryan [1]

Before the Reformation all charities were administered by the Church; to-day most of them are under the control of the State. Nevertheless the field still open to Catholic charity is neither small nor likely to become smaller. The limitations and defects of public charity are well known;

[1] *The Catholic Encyclopedia*, Vol. III, pp. 603, 604.

it is almost inevitably more mechanical and less sympathetic than private charity; it is more wasteful, not only because it is less carefully administered, but also on account of the readiness of many persons to claim public relief as a right; and, inasmuch as it supplants appeals to the individual conscience by the imposition of a tax it inflicts a mortal injury upon the spontaneity of charity and the sense of personal responsibility towards the unfortunate. The inferiority of state-administered charity, so far as outdoor relief is concerned, has received striking illustration in the achievements of Dr. Chalmers in Glasgow more than half a century ago, in the experiment of substituting voluntary for public relief in Whitechapel and Stepney, London, and in the policy of refusing public outdoor relief which prevails in Brooklyn and Philadelphia (cf. Bliss, Encyclopedia, s. v. Chalmers; Mackay, The State and Charity, pp. 164 sq; and Warner, American Charities, pp. 162-176). The general principles underlying the whole problem of state charity would seem to be these: instead of assuring every person a living, the State ought so to regulate economic conditions that every person able to obtain a livelihood by labor should have that opportunity; that it should have charge of certain extreme forms of distress, such as a virulent disease and insanity; and that in general it should co-operate with voluntary charitable agencies, and stand ready to relieve all serious want which is not met by them. At any rate, students and workers in the field of charity seem to be practically unanimous in the belief that the scope of private charity ought to be extended rather than restricted. In this field Catholic charity should occupy the foremost place, and do by far the largest and most effective work. The principles of Catholic charity, concerning the ownership and use of goods, the true equality and brotherhood of men, spontaneity in giving, and the motives for giving, are supremely great. Especially is this true of the motives. The neighbor ought to be assisted out of love of God. As the highest form of this is to love God for His own sake, so the highest form of fraternal charity is that which is motived by the thought that the neighbor is the creature, the image, the child of God, and the brother of Christ. Inasmuch as this motive points to a worth and sacredness in the individual which is higher than anything that he possesses when considered in himself, it is more effective and more comprehensive than the motive which is restricted to love of the neighbor for his own sake. Many needy individuals are in themselves repellent rather than sympathy-compelling. While the second form of fraternal charity for love of God, namely, to obtain the spiritual rewards which God has annexed to this form of good works, is lower than the first, it is entirely natural, entirely praiseworthy, and has the approval of Christ Himself. This motive appeals to multitudes who would rarely be able to rise to the higher one, and is occasionally effective in the case of the least selfish. Warner declares that "of all the churches the one that still induces the largest amount of giving in proportion to the means of those who give is no doubt the Roman Catholic" (op. cit., p. 316). To a large extent this fact is due to the Church's practice of insisting upon both motives, and thus touching all the springs of charity in man's complex nature. At the same time it is a patent fact that large numbers of men and women devote themselves and their means to works of charity solely out of love for the neighbor regarded in himself. This motive is likewise in harmony with the promptings of human nature. It is particularly effective in lofty souls who, lacking any positive religious faith, find in works of charity satisfaction of the desire to serve and worship something outside of themselves. While the number of such persons will in all probability be largely augmented in the near future, neither in numbers nor in achievements will they be worthy of comparison with those who come under the influence of the motives supplied by Christianity.

The second advantage possessed by Catholics in the work of charity lies in their ecclesiastical organization. Relief can be individualized by means of the parish, and centralized by means of the diocese. In many places Catholics are, moreover, co-operating with non-Catholics through the charity organization societies. This is entirely fitting, for two reasons: First, because the methods and purposes of what has come to be called organized charity—namely, investigation, attention to causes, specific treatment, self-help, record-keeping, and co-operation among the different charitable agencies in order to eliminate duplicated and misdirected effort—are entirely sound. Second, because Catholics have a prior claim upon all these principles and practices. The general principles were first formulated by the theologian Vives in 1526, and received their first application about the same time in the Catholic cities of the Netherlands and Germany. They were developed and applied along the specific lines of present practice by Frederic Ozanam in 1833 (cf. O'Meara, Life of Ozanam). The first non-Catholic to exemplify these modern methods was Chalmers in 1850, while the first charity organization society did not come into existence until 1868 (cf. Warner, op. cit., pp. 377-392). True, these methods are liable to abuse—the work may become too formal, too mechanical, too much given to investigation, and the results may be waste of money, lack of sympathy, and unnecessary hardship to the deserving poor. Nevertheless, time and experience seem, in most places, to have reduced these evils to the lowest proportions that can reasonably be expected in a human institution. In many localities it is desirable that Catholic charitable agencies should make a fuller use of these methods, and in general become better organized and better systematized. Where the St. Vincent de Paul Society lives up to the standard set by its founder in this matter, it is the most effective relief society in existence. Some of the American conferences of the association have in recent years begun to employ paid agents with gratifying results. This is a wise feature, inasmuch as voluntary workers cannot always be obtained in sufficient numbers who possess the time, ability, and experience essential to the largest achievement. Again, Catholic charity-workers will follow the best traditions of Catholic charity by co-operating with the tendency, which is every day becoming stronger in the circles of organized charity, to attack the social causes of distress (cf. Proceedings of the Thirty-third National Conference of Charities and Correction, pp. 1-10). This is of course the wisest, most effective, most difficult, and, therefore, most meritorious form of charitable effort. In the Middle Ages the social causes of poverty were much better controlled than at present, because the Church had infused into all classes the doctrine that social power carries with it social responsibility. To-day the chief social causes of poverty are the worship of money, and the lack of social responsibility in those who possess social power, i. e., economic power. Only within the Catholic Church can be found the principles, resources, organization, and authority through which these causes can be repressed.

Finally, the opportunities of private charity, the direct assistance of individuals by individuals, are still and will continue to be large. This form of charity has always been encouraged by the Church, and when wisely administered it has advantages which are not attainable by the organized form. It makes possible that exchange and that equalization between giver and receiver spoken of by St. Paul, and promotes that mutual understanding and mutual sympathy which are especially necessary in our day, when the gulf separating those who have and those who have not has become so wide and so ominous. Individual charity also increases vastly the total amount that passes from the more to the less fortunate, thereby producing a more equitable distribution of the earth's bounty than would take place if all cases of distress were referred to the already overburdened organizations. Dr. Devine, who is one of the foremost authorities in the field of organized charity, speaks in the highest terms of rightly administered individual charity, and declares that "it is a question whether the unmeasured but certainly large amount of neighborly assistance given in the tenement houses of the city, precisely as in a New England village or in a frontier settlement, does not rank first of all among the means for the alleviation of distress" ("The Principles of Relief," p. 332, and the entire chapter).

35

WHO IS MY NEIGHBOR?

William J. Kerby [1]

When the young man asked Our Lord the question "Who is my neighbor?" he sought a definition. He had been told that he should love his neighbor as himself but he was at a loss as to the indentity of the neighbor. In reply to the question Our Lord narrated the parable of the Good Sa-

---

[1] *The Social Mission of Charity*, pp. 101-110. (The Macmillan Company, New York.) Reprinted with permission of the publishers.

maritan and asked, "Who was neighbor to him that fell among the robbers?" "He that showed mercy," was the reply. Whereupon Our Lord said, "Go and do thou in like manner." When we undertake today to show mercy to our neighbor we are at a loss for a definition that will guide us in determining the neighbor that we would serve. He may not be picked at hazard. We may not show mercy in a thoughtless manner. The Good Samaritan was confronted by no complexities. He was guided wisely and without confusion. In our day, however, when there are thousands of good samaritans who wish to serve from whatsoever motive and tens of thousands of others in need of help the problem becomes difficult. When society is divided along economic, religious and race lines; when conflicting philosophies meet in the service of the poor and the utmost of our endeavors will fail of what is required, careful thought and thorough organization become necessary to our endeavor whose aim it is to find the needy neighbor.

The law of love is imperative and universal in the Christian life. The law of service prompted by love is conditioned on our resources. The legitimate claims of duty, efficiency and development on our time and means and sympathy must be respected. The fallacies urged upon us by ease, luxury, mistaken ambition, imaginary needs and excessive solicitudes for self-protection must be recognized and conquered. The claims of charity relate in varying degrees to the resources left available for the reasonable service of others after our own legitimate claims have met their satisfaction. When one has arrived at a Christian judgment of these claims upon one's resources, one is called upon to weigh the claims of idealistic interests. Community welfare, religion, education, and other culture interests appeal to us for support and their successful maintenance depends upon our generosity. Devotion to these interests is praiseworthy in the extreme, but it does not appear to excuse us from the specific claims of charity. The measurement and sanction of these claims are beyond the scope of this study. Assuming that they are established and recognized, we are called upon to undertake to find the neighbors to whom we should show mercy.

As life is organized those of approximately the same income live in the same neighborhood. The rich live among the rich. The well-to-do live among their own kind. The poor tend to be segregated to such a degree that the needy know only the needy. While common experience shows us that the most noble instances of neighborly service are found in the reciprocal relations of the poor, these are exceptional. They in no way interfere with the general process of our definition. This tendency to distribute population according to income extends so far that we find more or less exclusive circles in the laboring class itself. If he who needs me is my neighbor in the Christian sense, when I live among those who have no need of me, I have no neighbors. Were I to live among many who had immediate need of me I would have so many neighbors that I would be utterly helpless in presence of them. We are thus enabled to eliminate proximity in attempting to find our neighbors.

The processes of life perpetuate this condition. The strong know only the strong and the weak know only the weak. Friendships, intermarriage, acquaintanceship and association follow along those lines and make this condition self-perpetuating. Normal social relations follow the plans fixed by income and culture. Association among those of different income and culture planes occurs only by exception. It does not occur frequently enough to become a factor in our thought. There is, fortunately, a certain progress upward from lower to higher social and cultural planes found among those who are exceptionally gifted in mind or character. We pretend to be surprised, if not shocked, when one marries "beneath" one's social station. In fact, we do not know our neighbors whatsoever our social class. Complete indifference and lack of all information are not only possible but probable among the inhabitants of a modern city block. Locality fails altogether, then, to indicate the neighbor whom we would serve according to the command of Christ.

Since we are compelled to live in close physical proximity with large numbers of persons civilization has developed the forms of conventional privacy by which we protect ourselves against undue invasion of our lives by others. Those who are near us physically are kept at a distance socially. Life would be scarcely possible in a modern city except for the protection that we gain through respect for privacy.

The customs of privacy prevent strangers from speaking to one another, prevent us from asking impudent personal questions, forbid us to look at the book or the letter in the hands of those near us in a street car. The more closely we approach one another the more insistent are the obligations of privacy in order that we may live at all. The cultured man or woman holds curiosity about others in complete control. The result must be a shrinkage in human sympathy, cautious approach to social intercourse with others, a mental habit that leads us to mind our own business and not to interfere without reason in the affairs of others. Thus the free and spontaneous appeal of sympathy and interest in one another's affairs is practically forbidden. Even among the poor there is a form of self-respect, an appreciation of privacy that leads them to hide their distress against the inquiry of those who would serve them. One of the tasks of the friends of the poor is to find out how to serve these without giving offense, without breaking down that refined self-respect which is one of the flowers of culture. There can be no doubt that many carry the principle of respect for privacy too far and lose interest in seeking the neighbor who may be in need of mercy.

Those who enjoy the finding of fault with social workers express their sarcasm by calling these "busybodies," "meddlers," and the like. There is no doubt that the problem here hinted at is one of the most delicate to be met in the service of the poor. We do feel warranted in asking them questions concerning intimate personal life which we would never dare to ask of others. And yet information of this kind is necessary if we are to be of assistance at all. The inertia of the poor prevents them from helping themselves. The assistance that comes to them comes from a class alien in social standing, association and experience. The nobler the type among the poor the more delicate is their sense of privacy and their reluctance to see that privacy invaded. Much of the argument made against so-called systematic charity rests upon the assumption that office records are an unpardonable invasion of privacy. At the same time, many of those who are careless as to the results of their work among the poor are apt to hide faulty methods behind an exaggerated alleged respect for the feelings, that is, for the sense of privacy that the standards of civilization permit us to cherish.

Proximity does not define neighbor for us. The customs of conventional privacy interfere greatly with the processes by which we might find and serve our neighbor. One might be led to conclude, then, that contact in the organized service of life would furnish the definition of neighbor whom we would love and serve. But we are disappointed again. Not even the essential service of life that brings us into close contact with one another serves this purpose.

Life is fractioned. One life touches another in one way, but the relations are confined to that one contact. No one can come closer to us than the servant in the home. She comes from the weaker social class. Only too often has she need of neighborly service in the Christian sense, whether it relate to physical, mental or moral distress. But conventional privacy places a barrier between her and those whom she serves. She does her work, receives her wages and goes her way. Now and then kindly human relations are established, but the modern type of servant possesses a degree of dignity and shows an insistence on privacy and independence that keeps her mistress in her place. The newsboy, the milkman, the messenger boy, the drivers of the grocery and laundry wagons who come to our doors daily and minister to our recurring wants are in many, if not all, cases in need of some kind of neighborly interest and service relating to either health, home life or wage conditions. And yet we do not know their names. We know nothing about them. No human relations are created between them and us although the orderly movement of our intimate daily life is conditioned on their service. Life is fractioned here and relations remain entirely impersonal.

Nor can the condition be otherwise. Each one of those who render service of this kind comes into touch with a multitude of homes. Attempt on the part of any one to engage them in conversation would disorganize their service and disrupt the neighborhood. Not choice but the fixed demands of life force these relations upon us, bring us together in economic intimacy and separate us in complete social estrangement. And, again, we ourselves come into touch with so many of these in our daily life that it would be impractical for us to attempt to take a human interest in every one of them. Unless we discipline our sympathies we shall scarcely survive at all. Thus we gain no assistance in seeking the definition of neighbor from the economic services rendered to us in the most direct way daily by representatives of the weaker social classes, many of whom are probably in need of friendly service.

We might expect the bond of industrial employment to have some effect in determining Christian relations between strong and weak, in defining the neighbor in the friendly serving of whom the employer might obey the obligations of Christian charity. But again we are disappointed. The mental outlook of the employer is primarily economic. He belongs to his class. He thinks and feels with his class. That class embraces a philosophy and follows a practice that result generally in the fractioning of life again. Relations remain impersonal. Labor is performed. Wages are paid. Relations are ended. The historical antagonisms that have developed between employer and employed so dominate the mental attitudes of both that the holier relation of neighbor seems unbusinesslike and out of place. The competitive struggle dominates the outlook of the employer. As the number of those who work for him increases he takes refuge to his economic advantage against the human sympathy that might be his undoing. Furthermore, the typical modern employer is ordinarily not an owner. He is rather a manager. Generally speaking, the owners of an industry do not manage it and the managers of the industry do not own it.

The scattered owners who enjoy dividends have no knowledge of conditions under which business is conducted. So long as generosity of impulse increases cost of operation and reduces dividends, affects credit and the values of stock, business rules sympathy and generosity out. A broad view of our industrial history shows the horrible and inhuman extremes to which separation of employer and employed have led. Capital has asked labor to carry uncompensated the frightful risks to life, to limb and to health that have been associated with the feverish development of industrial processes. Hundreds of thousands of industrial accidents that resulted in death; hundreds of thousands of instances of occupational hazards that robbed working men of their health, deprived families of their breadwinners; robbed children of their parents and hurled helpless, maimed and broken, men, women and children into the pit of dependency declare the failure of Christian relationship, sympathy and love between employer and employed.

We may take into account all of the types of noble-minded employers that have endeavored to foster human relations with employees. We may take into account all of the instances wherein the distress of the weak is due to their own fault, sin, treachery and indifference. After making most generous allowance in both directions the facts of our industrial history still write a full indictment of the strong ones of the earth. They have builded an economic empire that gave them an imperial sway over uncounted thousands of lives which they used with pagan indifference to the claims of humanity and Christianity. Much of this is due to the exactions of the competitive system and the mental outlook that resulted from them. Much of it is due to the general conditions which the single employer could scarcely master. Whatever the circumstances the harvest of disaster, death, disease and dependency that resulted challenges the human and Christian sympathy of the world. While employers in individual cases find it possible to be neighbors in the fullest sense of the term to those who labor for them, the bond of employment has not operated and does not operate generally to unite strong and weak in bonds of Christian love and kindly service.

We might expect the bond of faith to define neighbor for us. Religion continues to teach the doctrine and foster the spirit of the charity of Christ. But every one of the factors already mentioned interferes in one way or another with the social relations of Christians. The complexities and mandates of social organizations, the social cleavage between strong and weak, between cultured and uncultured follow us into the house of God itself and affect mind and sympathy in varying degrees. While religious charities, particularly those of the Catholic Church, have done wonderful things in the way of service, these charities represent a reaction made necessary because the bond of faith does not automatically and directly define neighbor for us.

None of the social bonds described have, of themselves, operated to furnish automatically definitions of neighbor which enable strong and weak to cultivate the spirit of love and service that stands out in unparalleled grandeur in the ideal of Christian life. Again we must allow for exceptions. But these do not impair the truth of the general statement as made. We are confronted in this way by social classes and class estrangement, unequal distribution of strength and weakness, lack of normal definitions of neighbor by the ordinary processes of life. But the law of Christ's love has not remained inoperative. Christian sympathy has been sufficiently strong in Christian hearts to do in one way what has been found impossible in another. In this way the relation of neighbor in the Christian life has been made vicarious and service has become indirect. It has become necessary to seek out the poor. They have been found in such multitudes and in so many types that their condition has offered a challenge to Christian sympathy and the intelligence of the world.

Poverty has become so complex and the helplessness of the poor is so many sided that the service of them has become exacting and technical. We have been compelled, therefore, to specialize in the service of them and to become systematic and thoughtful in that service. The relief organization which assembles those who are skilful in the service of the poor and gathers their sources available for this service represents the combined typical Christian sympathies of the community and gives promise of most effective neighborly service of the poor. We turn, therefore, to the modern relief organization for the answer to our question, "Who is my neighbor?" We give our personal service and our means to the organization and ask it to administer these for the most effective service of the poor. Service becomes, to a great extent, vicarious and indirect.

Whenever it is possible for one who is strong to find a family or a person in need of whatsoever kind, the definition of neighbor is admirably supplied by the circumstances. This will remain for all time the ideal relation. In as far as the service is given intelligently and with sympathetic personal touch nothing is left to be desired. But there are so many of the poor who cannot hope for such direct and intimate relationship with the strong, and there are so many of the strong to whom the ordinary course of life does not make known particular instances of need that can be adequately met in this way we may not represent this method as either adequate or satisfactory.

When we look upon poverty as the plight of the individual or family we find dependents in such numbers that organization of relief work becomes imperative. As we gain insight into the forces that have made them dependent, and as we gain understanding of the processes that kept them so, we find need of foresight, thought and system. It is difficult to see how any lover of the poor can doubt this. If we look upon poverty as a plight of society rather than of the individual we find it necessary to organize the forces that can act upon society, strengthen its conscience and remedy conditions. If we look upon poverty as a phase of injustice and a plight of the State we find need again of concerted action, unceasing effort and sacrifice in order to adjust the institutions of law and the processes of its administrations to the requirements of the poor. From whatsoever standpoint we look upon the problem we find organization, insight, training, system and principle necessary in order to restore relations between strong and weak which will temper the former and encourage the latter in the spirit of Christian love.

Organization, training and system are required in order that we may find our neighbor and serve him well. In addition to the reasons alleged there are others which it may be well to mention.

The law of Christian charity rests in a supernatural attitude, expresses itself in an impulse and reaches its termination in a service. Insistence upon truth, impulse and motive without regard to outcome would be a mistake, an offense at least against the exalted dignity of love. If love may lead parents to err in dealing with their children, love may lead the strong to err in dealing with the weak. Giving to a neighbor and serving him hurriedly, thoughtlessly and without intelligent attention cannot be the fine flower of Christianity. We are compelled to discipline our love in order that we may serve and not harm the poor. This is true in all cases, but notably true in these days.

The tendency to insist upon motive without due regard to outcome in dealing with the poor is aggravated somewhat by the habit of over-idealizing them. By first intention pity and love lead us to see in them only their suffering. We resent the insinuation that there may be among them tricksters, deceivers, sinful men and women, bold, defiant and tricky children, those who are willing to trade on our sympathy and lie and cheat to gain their purposes. Again, we are disposed not to think that the poor suffer the penalties of ignorance and bad judgment. When our sympathies are aroused our critical habits retire. Love prefers to live in the present and not to take long outlooks. It is made to appear cold, inhuman and calculating, to favor investigation, to distinguish between worthy and unworthy poor, to serve the former with care and the latter with sternness. Now, training, system, method, are intended to meet these problems; to overcome the difficulties of multitudes, to seek out all who suffer and serve them well; to seek out the unworthy and deal with them as they deserve, and, above all, to protect the poor against the mistakes of their friends, whether trained or untrained.

36

THE CARDINAL VIRTUES

Joseph Rickaby [1]

We speak of a "cardinal of the Holy Roman Church" and of the "principal of the college." Both words have originally the same meaning. *Cardinal* is from *cardo,* a hinge. The college may be said to *hinge* upon its principal; and again a cardinal was originally and is to this day the principal priest of some parish-church in Rome. The cardinal virtues, then, are the principal virtues—and that in two ways. Either they are taken as the main virtues, to which all other virtues approximate and can be ultimately reduced, or they are taken for the chief *component elements* of every virtue whatsoever. In the latter sense they are spoken of as *integral* parts of virtue, their union going to make up virtue in its entirety. We will consider them in this latter sense first.

We owe the enumeration of the cardinal virtues, not to the Hebrew Scriptures, but to the Greek philosophers. Prudence, temperance, fortitude, justice, were already enumerated at Athens as far back as B. C. 400. The root idea of justice is the rendering to every man of his own.

[1] *Four-Square,* pp. 9-15. (Joseph Wagner, New York.)

But what is a man's own? That may be said to be determined by law. Let every man have what the law allows him. Justice, therefore, is conformity to law. But the law may be said to prescribe all virtues. The saying is debatable, but it is not worth while debating it here. Every virtue, therefore, is conformable to law, and in practising any virtue a man is observing the law, and is, therefore, *just*. Hence in Scripture the "just" or "righteous" man is the law-abiding man; the virtuous man simply the "good man," in contrast with the sinner, who is a law-breaker. Again, virtue moves a man to do good steadily, regularly and constantly, even in face of difficulties. But constancy under difficulties belongs to fortitude. There is, therefore, an element of fortitude in every virtue, by the mere fact of virtue being a habit. Once more, every virtue is a habit of doing things in moderation, holding on to the golden mean, neither overdoing the thing nor underdoing it, but doing exactly what is fit and proper under the circumstances. Such is the great Aristotelian doctrine, that all virtue lies in a mean between two vicious extremes. Liberality, for instance, observes the mean between prodigality and stinginess; fortitude between rashness and cowardice; humility between haughtiness and meanness of spirit. But moderation is the equivalent of temperance, which is thus shown to be an essential element in every virtue. It is not easy to discern the golden mean, *e. g.*, in government between remissness and over-indulgence, when to punish and when to condone, when to forbid and when to allow. Such discernment is the part of prudence. Prudence is the eye of every virtue. No virtue goes blind. Thus, to be virtuous in any department is to be at once prudent, just, courageous and temperate.

More usually, however, the four cardinal virtues are taken as four distinct virtues and main heads of virtue, under which the other virtues are severally enumerated. Under prudence come prudence in one's own affairs and prudence in the affairs of others whom one has to govern. Justice includes *distributive* (of rewards), *vindictive* (punishing), and *commutative* (enforcing contracts); it is further taken to include the virtues of religion, obedience, truthfulness, liberality and gratitude. Under fortitude come magnanimity, patience and perseverance. Temperance includes abstinence (in food), sobriety (in drink), chastity, also modesty, humility, meekness, clemency. The theological virtues are distinct from the cardinal, and are not considered here, as being not "acquired" but "infused."

Every habit, as we have seen, resides in some faculty or power. The habit does not make the power, any more than the school-master makes the child. It presupposes it as a thing given; then taking it in hand it disciplines and trains it and teaches it to act to good purpose; whereas, away from the good habit engendered in it by training, the power would have acted fitfully and at random. Virtue being a habit, it is possible to assign for every virtue the power in which it resides and which it perfects. We shall find the four cardinal virtues residing in the powers of the human soul. All these several powers want virtues to train them and guide them to orderly behaviour.

You sometimes hear people, who know no better, saying that all virtue is in the will. That is a mistake. Virtue is the discipline of the soul. It is not enough for the will alone to be disciplined, the subordinates must be disciplined as well as the chief, else you have no ready and regular action. Not only must the rider be skilled in horsemanship, but the horse also must be broken in. Virtue, therefore, resides even in appetite. It is put there (under God) by reason, and consists in the appetite's being habitually *broken in* to the obedience of reason. That habitual state is the result of many acts of conflict, in which reason has subdued appetite, as a trainer subdues a wild horse. Plato expresses it in these terms: "The driver (reason), laying himself back, tugs with all his might at bit and bridle in the teeth of the wanton horse, embruing in blood his foul-mouthed tongue and jaws, forcing him back on his haunches till his legs and hindquarters almost touch the ground, and putting him to pain." Plato thought, and thought rightly, that the discipline of the lower appetites, otherwise known as the virtue of temperance, is not established without strong and repeated efforts on the part of reason, or the rational appetite, that is, the will to enforce obedience to its commands. It may be added that the obedience of appetite to reason is never quite complete. Temperance is like a sovereign insecurely seated on his throne, and needing, when rebellion waxes high, to call in the aid of a superior power. The habit will not work automatically: it is not self-sufficient.

Justice regulates our dealings with other persons. Fortitude and temperance work within the self, and secure order at home. As for prudence, there is no department of human action which prudence should not pervade. Therefore, it has been said: "Temperance and fortitude in the home department; justice for foreign affairs; with prudence for premier."

The question has been asked whether the virtues are separable one from another, whether, for instance, one can be courageous without being temperate, or exercise liberality while neglecting religion? If the four cardinal virtues are taken, not as distinct virtues, but as common elements of all virtue, it is clear that they cannot be separated. In all virtue discretion (prudence), rectitude (justice), moderation (temperance), and firmness (fortitude) are inseparably conjoined. The question can be raised only when the virtues are considered as distinct from one another. One cardinal virtue is not another, e. g., justice is not fortitude, that we allow. May not in the same person one of these virtues flourish in the absence of one or more of the other three? Does not plain experience evince that the sailor is brave, but not temperate; and that many a man is temperate, and just to fellowmen, but not just to God in that he wholly discards the virtue of religion? In answer to this somewhat intricate question we must distinguish between a virtue and the good acts which that virtue is apt to elicit. Those acts, as we have seen, may be done in the absence of the virtue: a man may show liberality once in a while without having the virtue of liberality. Much more may he do acts of liberality here and there, without having some other virtue, as temperance or religion. A man of no religion may subscribe handsomely to a hospital—it may be, I allow, out of the virtue of liberality, but his mere subscription is no certain argument of that virtue. The act may be motived by ostentation or human respect and fear of public opinion; or he may give out of a certain native predisposition to fling his money about, a predisposition which makes excellent material for virtue, but is not of itself the virtue of liberality before it has been trained according to reason. What seems to be virtue may be a mere chance combination of good nature with happy circumstances. What seems to be virtue may keep up the semblance only because it has never been tried by temptation. It may be a keeping up of appearance out of love of respectability and desire to make one's way in society; and that is not virtue. Still I would not deny that a man may have one virtue and not another —liberality, for instance, and not religion—provided his lack of that second virtue be due wholly or chiefly to ignorance, misapprehension, weakness and frailty. But if a man casts any one virtue which carries duties in its train —casts it out wilfully and against his conscience—I should gravely doubt his possession of any other virtue. However much he did the acts, I should doubt whether they were motived by the motive of the virtue. A man who spurns conscience upon one ground is not likely to be really conscientious upon another. Henry VIII affected zeal for religion and for the sanctity of marriage. His loose and dissolute life gave the lie to his zeal. What shall we say of Louis XIV? We must be cautious in judging of individuals. But this we may observe in general. Virtues are like the timbers of a roof. Dry rot, set in on one beam, does not at once bring the whole roof down. Nor does the decay of one particular virtue work the immediate ruin of a man's whole moral character and destroy all his other virtues, the gradual growth of years of well-doing. They may remain some considerable time uninjured. But evil spreads, and things move from bad to worse.

By doing our duty we do acts, from which acts virtues are apt to result. Nor is a sinner condemned precisely for his vices, but for those sinful acts which have engendered vices in his soul. We are not bound to do all good acts possible, else there would be no difference between counsel and commandment. Good acts, indeed, are often inconsistent one with another. It is good to marry, good to receive holy orders; but you can not do both. In every good man, grown up, there will be found the cardinal virtues, but not every subordinate virtue which ranks under those general heads. Some virtues he may not have been in a position to practise. You can not practise clemency if you have no authority to punish; nor munificence if you are not a rich man. Some virtues grow out of acts which are rarely practicable or obligatory—magnanimity, for example, which is the maintenance of a proper attitude of mind in reference to high honors. Some virtues are as the garments of the soul, covering its nakedness and its shame; others are as jewelry; now no one is obliged to wear jewelry.

The ancient Greeks, who first made out the list of cardinal virtues, also enumerated four corresponding goods of man. They were health, strength, beauty, and what we may call a competence, or a competent position in society. Fortitude and temperance evidently answer to strength and beauty respectively: they are spiritual strength and beauty. The drunkard, or the unchaste youth, is morally and spiritually ugly, though he perceive it not: higher powers perceive it. The Greeks said: "Vice is unknown to itself." Prudence is the being of sound mind and sound judgment in matters of primary importance. Prudence takes "a healthy view" of the general situation. Justice is the moral attribute that fits us to be members of human society; for no society, not even that of thieves, could hold together, were the members all unjust to one another. In this, justice is like a "competence," which means a place in the social organism, with associates and friends to converse with, and sufficient pecuniary substances to maintain the position honorably.

Or we may put the relation in this way. Prudence is the safeguard of health; fortitude keeps up strength; temperance, which includes chastity, is the defender of beauty; while justice prevents a man abusing his worldly wealth and position. So that, without the cardinal virtues, health, strength, beauty and social competence, may prove a curse rather than a blessing to the owner. And the same of all other corporal and material advantages.

37

PERFECT VIRTUES ARE NEVER ONE WITHOUT THE OTHER

St. Francis de Sales [1]

All the virtues are not acquired together in an instant, but one after another, in proportion as reason, which is like the soul of our heart, takes possession first of one

---

[1] *Love of God,* pp. 481-485. (Burns and Oates, London.)

passion then of another to moderate and govern them; and, ordinarily, this life of our soul begins in the heart of our passions, which is love, and spreading itself over all the rest, it quickens at last the very understanding by contemplation; as on the contrary, moral or spiritual death makes its entry into the soul by the want of reflection—*death enters by the windows*, says the sacred text—and its last effect is to destroy good love, which once perishing, all our moral life is dead in us. So, then, although we may possess some virtues without others, yet are they but languishing, imperfect, and weak virtues, since reason, which is the life of our soul, is never satisfied nor at ease in a soul unless it occupy and possess all the faculties and passions; and when it is aggrieved and wounded in some one of our passions or affections, all the rest lose their force and vigor, and grow exceedingly weak.

You see, Theotimus, all the virtues are virtues by the proportion or conformity they have with reason, and an action cannot be called virtuous if it proceed not from the affection which the heart bears to the excellence and beauty of reason. Now if the love of reason possess and animate a soul, it will be obedient to reason in all occurrences, and, consequently, will practise all the virtues. If Jacob loved Rachel in consideration of her being Laban's daughter, why did he despise Lia, who was not only the daughter, but the eldest daughter of the same Laban? But because he loved Rachel by reason of her beauty, he could never equally love poor Lia, though a fruitful and wise maid, because, to his mind, she was not so fair. He who loves one virtue for the love of the reason and comeliness which shine in it, will love all the virtues, since he will find the same motive in them all, and he will love each of them more or less, as reason shall appear in them more or less resplendent. He who loves liberality and not chastity, shows sufficiently that he loves not liberality for reason's sake, because reason is still more radiant in chastity, and where the cause is more strong the effects ought, also, to be more strong. It is, therefore, an evident sign that such a heart is not moved to liberality by the motive and consideration of reason; whence it follows that this liberality which seemed to be virtue is but an appearance of it, since it proceeds not from reason, which is the true motive of virtues, but from some other and foreign motive. It is sufficient for a child to be born in marriage to bear in the world the name, the arms, and the titles of his mother's husband, but to have his blood and nature he must not only be born in the marriage but of the marriage. Actions have the name, arms and badges of the virtues, because being born of a heart endowed with reason, we presume them to be reasonable, yet they have neither the substance nor the vigor of virtue when they proceed from a foreign and illegitimate motive, and not from reason. It may happen, then, that a man may have some virtues and lack others; but they will either be virtues newly springing and as yet tender, like flowers in blossom; or else perishing and dying virtues, like fading flowers; for, in conclusion, virtues cannot have their true integrity and sufficiency unless they be all together, as all philosophy and divinity assure us. What prudence, I pray you, Theotimus, can an intemperate, unjust and cowardly man have, since he makes choice of vice and forsakes virtue? And how can one be just without being prudent, strong and temperate, since justice is no other thing than a perpetual, strong and constant will to render to every one his own, and since the science by which right is done is called jurisprudence, and since to give each one his own, we must live wisely and moderately, and hinder the disorders of intemperance in ourselves so as to give ourselves what belongs to us? And the word virtue, does it not signify a force and vigor belonging to the soul as a quality, even as we say that herbs and precious stones have such and such a virtue and property?

But is not prudence itself imprudent in an intemperate man? Fortitude, without prudence, justice and temperance is not fortitude but folly; and justice is unjust in the weak man who dares not do it, in the intemperate man who permits himself to be carried away with passion, and in the imprudent man who is not able to discern between the right and the wrong. Justice is not justice unless it be strong, prudent and temperate; nor is prudence prudence unless it be temperate, just and strong; nor fortitude fortitude unless it be just, prudent and temperate; nor temperance temperance unless it be prudent, strong and just. In fine, a virtue is not perfect virtue unless it be accompanied by all the rest.

It is true that one cannot exercise all the virtues at once, because the occasions are not all presented at once; yea, there are virtues which some of God's greatest saints had never occasion to practise: for St. Paul, the first hermit, for example, what occasion could he have to exercise the pardoning of injuries, affability, magnificence, and mildness? Nevertheless, such souls stand so affected to the rectitude of reason that though they have not all the virtues in effect, yet they have them all in affection, being ready and prepared to follow and obey reason in all occurrences, without exception or reservation.

There are certain inclinations which are esteemed virtues and are not so, but favors and advantages of nature. How many are there who are naturally sober, mild, silent, chaste and modest? Now all these seem to be virtues, and yet have no more the merit thereof than bad inclinations are blameworthy before we have given free and voluntary consent to such natural dispositions. It is no virtue to be by nature a man of little meat, yet to abstain by choice is a virtue. It is no virtue to be silent by nature, though it is a virtue to bridle one's tongue by reason. Many consider they have the virtues as long as they do not practise the contrary vices. One who has never been assaulted may truly boast that he was never a runaway, yet he has no ground to boast of his valor. He that has never been afflicted may boast of not being impatient, but not of being patient. In like manner, some think they have virtues who have only good inclinations, and as those inclinations are some without others, they suppose that virtues may be so too.

In truth, the great St. Augustine shows, in an epistle which he wrote to St. Jerome, that we may have some sort of virtue without having the rest, but that we cannot have perfect ones without having them all; whilst, as for vices, we may have some without having others; yea, it is even impossible to have them all together: so that it does not follow that he who has lost all the virtues has by consequence all the vices, since almost every virtue has two opposite vices, which are not only contrary to the virtue but also to one another. He who has forfeited valor by rashness cannot at the same time be taxed with cowardice; nor he who has lost liberality by prodigality, be at the same time reproached with niggardliness. Catiline, says St. Augustine, was sober, vigilant, patient in suffering cold, heat, and hunger; so that both himself and his accomplices deemed him marvellously constant; but this constancy wanted prudence, since it made choice of bad instead of good; it was not temperate, for it gave the bridle to repulsive uncleanness; it was not just, since he conspired against his country; it was not then constancy, but obstinacy, which to deceive fools bore the name of constancy.

38

TRUE CONCEPTIONS OF WELFARE

JOHN A. RYAN [1]

We speak much about the duty of avoiding excessive attachment to and misuse of wealth, but our utterances are mostly of the nature of platitudes. We do not often think into them any concrete meaning as to what precisely constitutes excessive attachment or misuse in the matter of food, clothing, houses, amusements, and "social" activities. Or, when our concepts are more specific, they are generally so liberal and lax as to fit only the very few whose offences under these heads are striking, notorious, and universally condemned. As a contribution toward more definite views and estimates, the present paper will attempt "to apply the Christian conception to the actual life of today and to indicate more precisely the content of a reasonable standard of life."

According to the Christian teaching, man's chief business on earth is to fit himself for the Life Beyond. This task he fulfils by living up to the commandments of Christ and the moral law of nature. As applying to the use of material goods and the satisfaction of material wants, the moral law may be summarized in the following sentences. The soul, its life, and its needs are intrinsically superior to the life and needs of the body. The intellect and the disinterested will are essentially higher faculties than the senses and the selfish will. Hence right human life con-

---

[1] *The Church and Socialism,* pp. 197-216. (The University Press, Washington, D. C.)

sists, not in the indefinite satisfaction of material wants, but in striving to know more and more, and to love more and more, the best that is to be known and loved, namely, God, and, in proportion to their resemblance to Him, His creatures. It demands that man shall satisfy the cravings of his animal and lower nature only to the extent that is compatible with a reasonable attention to the things of the mind and spirit. The senses and their demands are not on the same moral level as the reason; they are of subordinate worth and importance; they perform the function of instruments. Whenever they are made coordinate with, or superior to, the reason, whenever they are indulged so far as to interfere with the normal life and activity of the reason, there occur moral disorder, perversion of function, and unrighteous conduct. Similarly, whenever the selfish encroaches upon the disinterested will—as when we satisfy our senses with goods that ought to go to the neighbor, when we indulge such passions as envy and hatred, or when we expend upon our minds the time and energy that ought to be given to family, neighbor, or country—the moral order is inverted and violated.

Thus far the moral law of reason and nature. The supernatural, the Christian, moral law is frankly ascetic; not in the sense that it imposes upon all persons the Evangelical Counsels of poverty, chastity, and obedience, but in as much as it requires men to wage a continuous struggle against many of the cravings of appetite, and to deny many desires and ambitions which are dear to self. Unless the child subordinate his will to that of his parents, his love of play to the demands of school, his desire of possession to reasonable self-discipline, his selfishness and cruelty to the just claims of his playmates, he will grow into a self-willed, passionate, and unlovable youth. He will be the antithesis of the Christian type. The Christian young man or young woman enters into a series of relations in which the need of self-denial is intensified and widened. Purity demands rigid control of the desires of the flesh; temperance requires careful self-restraint in eating and drinking; justice enjoins respect for the rights and goods of others, notwithstanding the powerful, manifold, and insidious impulses that make for the violation of this precept; the law of labor forbids indulging the tendency of idleness and slothfulness; charity commands the denial of that self-satisfaction, self-comfort, and self-assertion which are incompatible with the claims of Christian brotherhood. Christianity is ascetic in the stricter sense of the term when it urges, nay, requires men to do without many things which are in themselves lawful, in order that they may be the better able to pass by the things that are unlawful. The words of St. Paul concerning the athlete who "refrains himself from all things" express the true Christian theory and practice.

Both the natural and the Christian laws of conduct are, consequently, opposed to the current ideals of life and welfare. Both demand that the power to do without shall be cultivated to such a degree that the lower nature in man shall be kept in constant subjection to the higher. Both deny that it is lawful for man to satisfy all wants indifferently or to seek the indefinite expansion and satisfaction of his material wants.

Concerning the value of material goods, the teaching of the Divine Founder of Christianity is clear and forcible. Consider a few of his pronouncements: "It is easier for a camel to pass through the eye of a needle than for a rich man to enter into the kingdom of heaven." "Woe to you rich." "Blessed are you poor." "Lay not up for yourselves treasures on earth." "For a man's life consisteth not in the abundance of things that he possesseth." "Be not solicitous as to what you shall eat, or what you shall drink, or what you shall put on." "Seek ye first the kingdom of God and his justice, and all these things shall be added unto you." "You cannot serve God and mammon." "If thou wouldst be perfect, go sell what thou hast and give to the poor, and come follow me." The doctrine of these texts is remote, indeed, from the theory that right life consists in the ever-widening and varying of material wants, and the ever fuller and more diversified satisfaction of them. In many places, and under many different forms, Christ insists that material possessions are unimportant for the child of God, and that those who have much wealth will find it almost impossible to get into His kingdom.

The great Fathers of the Church used strong, almost extreme language in describing the dangers of riches and denouncing the men of wealth of their time. Many of them are so severe that they have been, incorrectly however, classified as socialists. St. Thomas Aquinas declared that although man cannot entirely disregard the pursuit and the possession of external goods, he ought to seek them with moderation, and in conformity with the demands of a simple life. Essentially the same views have been held and taught by all the representative authorities of the Church throughout the Middle Ages and down to the present hour. Neither Christ nor His Church has ever sanctioned the theory that right and reasonable life requires magnificent houses, furnishings, equipage, and entertainment, sumptuous food and splendid apparel, costly recreation and luxurious amusements.

Let us apply these general truths and principles to the use of material goods and the process of satisfying material wants, and with a view to more definite and particular conclusions. To begin with, we can enclose the field of material welfare by certain upper and lower limits, within which ninety-nine of every hundred persons must have a place if they are to enjoy satisfactory conditions of Christian living. It would seem that these conditions are lacking whenever an average-sized family in one of the larger American cities receives an annual income of less than $1,500. When the family income falls below that amount per year, the quality and amount of food; the size, appearance, adornment, and equipment of the home; the kind of clothes; the scant provision for sickness, accidents, and old age; the lack of sufficient means for recreation, books, newspapers, charity, and religion; and the oppressively real fear of want, will subject the members of the family to severe temptations that would be unfelt, or much less keenly felt, if the income were above the figure named. Insufficient and monotonous food increases the craving for strong drink; shabby clothes make persons ashamed to appear among their fellows, and lead to loss of self-respect, discouragement, and discontent; an unattractive home produces similar results and impels some members of the family to seek outside associations, perhaps in the saloon; lack of provision for the untoward contingencies of life fosters discouragement and discontent which are harmful to thrift and industry, and productive of irreligion and envy of the neighbor; inability to contribute to religion causes men to remain away from church, while the absence of reading matter leaves the mind barren; insufficiency of recreation is injurious to health, efficiency, and contentment. All these evils are, indeed, relative. They are felt by families above as well as by those below the $1,500 limit. Nevertheless, they inflict serious, objective injury upon one hundred of the latter to one of the former.

How shall we define the upper limit of family expenditure that is compatible with decent Christian living? The question may at first sight seem preposterous, inasmuch as reasonable life is possible at many different stages above the decent minimum. Yet if the Christian view of life is correct, the maximum as well as the minimum ought to be susceptible of concrete statement. If expenditures for material goods begin to be harmful as soon as the limits of moderation are passed and the satisfaction of the senses comes into conflict with the life of the spirit, those limits ought to be capable of definition in terms of goods and of money. To deny this is implicitly to defend the theory that right life consists in the indefinite satisfaction of indefinitely expanding wants.

In the matter of shelter the maximum for an average-sized family—husband and wife and four or five children—would seem to be a house of about twelve rooms. Obviously the mere fact that the residence contains a larger number of rooms does not constitute a serious impediment to reasonable living. Not the quantity of housing, but its accidentals and accessories, is the important consideration. Not the rooms in excess of twelve, but what they generally bring in their train, makes the difference. When the limit here set down is passed, it is not additional comfort in the legitimate sense of that term that is desired, but rather accommodations for numerous servants, facilities for elaborate social functions, and the consciousness of occupying as large or as imposing a dwelling as some neighbor or neighbors. Such a house will usually involve adornment, furnishings, and equipment which will be distinguished more for costliness, richness, and magnificence than simply for beauty.

All these and many other ends, which assume prominence about the time that the twelve-room limit is exceeded, do create real and serious hindrances to decent Christian living. Chief among these hindrances are: a great waste of time, energy, thought, and money; many other demoralizing conditions that seem to be inseparable from sumptuous dwellings and the individual and social life therein fostered; the inevitable intensification of the passion of envy; the desire to outdo one's neighbors in the splendor of material possessions and in outward show generally; a diminution of sincerity in social relations; a lessened consciousness of the reality and the universality of Christian brotherhood; and, finally, immersion to such a degree in the things of matter that the higher realities of life are easily forgotten or ignored.

Satisfaction of the food want becomes excessive when the appetite is stimulated or pampered to the injury of health, and when victuals come to be prized for their capacity to please the palate rather than for their power to nourish. These conditions are reached sooner than most persons realize. Habitually to pass by plain food, and to seek the tenderest and most delicate grades, implies a condition in which the digestive organs are being overtaxed. Mere variety in the articles of diet, when extended beyond moderate bounds, produces the same result. A liberal use of the accidentals, such as condiments, relishes, exquisite desserts, is likewise harmful. Even a nice attention to the preparation and serving of the food easily produces undue and injurious stimulation of the appetite. These physical excesses, or extravagances, are generally accompanied by evils of the moral order. The pleasure-giving aspects of diet and of eating become too prominent and are too carefully sought. There is an excessive attention to the satisfaction of the food want which constitutes one form of the vice of gluttony. From it follows a lessening of control over other appetites; for the power of governing the senses is a unified thing which becomes weakened as a whole whenever it suffers injury in any part. Failure to control the food appetite, for example, reduces the ability to govern the sex appetite. Finally, the limits of reason are exceeded when the accessories of eating, as the service, the dishes, the dining-room furniture, are distinguished chiefly for their costliness, richness, and magnificence.

With regard to clothing, there is excess as soon as the desire to be dressed comfortably and decently becomes less prominent than the desire for conspicuousness, richness, elaborateness, splendor. All these are refinements, artificial complications, of the process of satisfying the clothing want. When they come to be regularly sought after, they cause a waste of money and a deterioration of character. There is waste of money, inasmuch as these ends are relatively—indeed, we might say, absolutely—of no importance to reasonable living. The character suffers through the indulgence of the passion for distinction in mere possessions and the passions of pride, vanity, and envy. It is obviously impossible to draw with precision the line which separates comfort, decency, and simple beauty from conspicuousness, richness, elaborateness, splendor; but the several estimates of a carefully selected committee would probably show a fairly close agreement.

The tests of simplicity, moderation, and comparative inexpensiveness mark off the reasonable from the unreasonable in the matter of amusement and recreation. When these conditions are present all the legitimate demands of these wants are abundantly supplied. The spirits are refreshed, the energies are relaxed, the faculties are recreated. When these bounds are exceeded, when amusements and recreation become elaborate, manifold, and costly, or when they are elevated to a place among the important aims of life, there occurs a perversion which is injurious both physically and morally. Time and money are wasted, energy is expended in the feverish pursuit of new forms of amusement, satiety and disappointment increase, and the temptations to unrighteous conduct are multiplied. Even the practice of making extensive and frequent sojourns in foreign countries, while possessing some educational advantages, consumes time and money out of all proportion to the resulting benefits. In many cases its chief effect is to satisfy jaded curiosity, fill up heavy-hanging time, or feed the passions of vanity and conscious superiority.

The activities that are denominated "social" afford perhaps the most striking indication of the distinction between the reasonable and the meretricious in the satisfaction of material wants. There is a certain moderate scale of social activity and entertainment in which the exercises, the dress, the refreshments, and all the other accessories, are distinguished by a certain naturalness and simplicity. Where these conditions (which are more easily recognized than described) are verified, the usual result is a maximum of enjoyment and right human feeling. When these limits are passed; when the chief concern is about the accessories of the entertainment rather than the promotion of kindly human intercourse and enjoyment; when the main object is to emulate the elaborateness, costliness, or magnificence of some other "function"—genuine enjoyment and kindly feeling are generally less than in the simpler conditions, while the damage to purse, health, nerves, and character is almost invariably greater.

The foregoing paragraphs may be correctly summarized in the statement that the annual expenditure for material goods in the case of the overwhelming majority of moderately sized families, ought not to exceed $10,000. Probably the range of expenditure which would afford the best conditions of Christian life for a considerable majority of all American families lies between $3,000 and $5,000 per annum.

The attempt to state so precisely and to define so narrowly the cost of living according to the Christian rule of life will probably strike many as presumptuous, preposterous, artificial, arbitrary. Nevertheless, if one is sincere, if one wishes to write to any serious purpose, if one intends to get beyond empty platitudes, one must make some such attempt and in some such terms. And the writer is perfectly willing to have his estimate subjected to criticism, to criticism as definite and concrete as the estimate itself. He is quite confident that, with very rare exceptions, $10,000 will seem ample to cover all reasonable family expenditures for material goods. When families go beyond this figure they are satisfying wants which in the interests of the best Christian life ought to be denied. In so far as the added amount is spent on a house, its principal effect is to increase not legitimate comfort, but pride, vanity, waste of time, and unsocial feelings of superiority. In so far as it is expended for dress it produces the same results, and makes persons unduly attendant to and dependent upon wants that are unnecessary, artificial, and fundamentally ignoble. In so far as it goes for food, it does not mean more nourishment, but some injury to health and an undue attachment to the lower or animal self. In so far as it is exchanged for amusements, recreation, or social activities, the same and other vices are fostered without any counterbalancing good result.

Where the family expends more than $10,000 for material goods, the results, except in a few cases, will be harmful to Christian life, inasmuch as the senses will be exalted to the detriment of the higher will and the reason, the altruistic qualities will be unable to obtain reasonable development in the midst of so many influences making for selfishness, and the character will grow soft, while the power to do without will grow weak.

The belief that men can live noble, religious, and intellectual lives in the presence of abundant material satisfaction, is well called by the economist, Charles Perin, "the most terrible seduction of our time." It counts among its adherents even the majority of Catholics. Whether they have little or much of this satisfaction, they long for more, and are willing to run the risk of the resulting demoralization. Nay, there are Catholics, both clerical and lay, who realize that the majority of their co-religionists whose expenditures are above the level described in these pages would be "better off" in the true, the Catholic, sense of these words, below that level; yet these same Catholics rejoice when their friends reach that scale of expenditure. So great is the power of a dominant popular fallacy!

Perhaps the strongest objection against the maximum set down here will be made on behalf of "social position." Larger, much larger expenditures seem to many persons to be justified and necessary in order to maintain that rank in society, that place among their fellows, that standard of living to which they have become accustomed. To sink below this scale would be a hardship and a departure from what they and their friends have come to regard as decent living. Now the requirements of social rank are among the legitimate needs that ought to be regularly met, for, as St. Thomas expresses it, "no one ought to live unbecomingly." In their discussions concerning the duties of almsgiving and of restitution, the theologians have always made definite and liberal allowance for this class of needs. Let us remember, however, that their estimates and conclusions reflect the social conditions of the Middle Ages, when the higher conveniences and the luxuries which absorb the greater part of the expenditures of the well-to-do classes today were practically all unknown; when most of the exceptional outlay was for servants, attendance, and the other accompaniments of public power; and when high social rank had its basis less in wealth than in public or quasi-public authority and functions. Reference was for the most part to rulers, members of the nobility, and public officials. Large concessions were made to their demands on behalf of social position, in order to safe-guard their functions and influence among the people. In other words, the chief reason was a social one; the people demanded a certain magnificence in the lives of their rulers and of the other wielders of social authority.

No such considerations can be urged in favor of the rich in a country like ours. Neither popular welfare, nor popular sentiment, nor any sane interpretation of decent or becoming living will justify expenditures in excess of $10,000 per year. If any serious defense of them is to be attempted, it must be based upon the assumption that any reduction of them would injure the morals or the self-respect of persons who had long been accustomed to this scale of living. That any permanent deterioration in conduct or character would overtake any considerable fraction of those who would descend to the $10,000 level, is a supposition that may be summarily dismissed. It is overwhelmingly probable that after a short time of adjustment to the new conditions, the "descenders," with rare exceptions, would be stronger morally than before. The hypothetical injury to self-respect does not deserve serious consideration, inasmuch as it refers to a false self-respect, a fear of being looked down upon by those who have false standards of worth, dignity, and decency. The self-respect which is based upon the extravagant satisfaction of material wants, and conditioned by the approval of those who believe in that sort of thing, ought to be trampled upon and eradicated.

Suppose that Mr. Carnegie, who has declared that the duty of the man of wealth is "to set an example of modest, unostentatious living, shunning display or extravagance," were to take these words seriously, interpreting them according to their ordinary acceptation, and to move from his sumptuous Fifth Avenue mansion into a comfortable, medium-sized house in a respectable, middle-class neighborhood, there to live on a scale of simple and moderate comfort. Does anyone think that he would suffer any real loss of self-respect, honor, reputation, public appreciation, or influence for good? On the contrary, he would gain in all these regards. Not the least of his gains would be his enhanced credit for seriousness and sincerity. And his experience would be duplicated by every rich man and rich woman who would make the experiment.

Those who would take this step would be better off, not only in character and public esteem, but even as regards contentment and happiness. At least, this would be the result if practically all who are now above the $10,000 level were to place themselves below it; for the principal factor impelling men to believe in the worth of luxurious living, namely, the social worship of luxury, would have disappeared. It is the popular faith in the happiness-producing power of abundant material satisfaction that leads the possessor of such satisfaction to cling to it. In reality it causes a greater slavery of the mind to the senses, and increases anxiety, worry, and satiety. "In proportion as a man strives to exalt and secure himself through external goods, he falls back wretchedly upon himself, and experiences an increase of dissatisfaction and *ennui*" (Perin, "De la Richesse," p. 11).

If only a few were to make the experiment, they would undoubtedly suffer considerable mental anguish, but it would be only temporary. Besides, it would be more than offset by the increase of mental and moral freedom, by a deeper and truer self-respect, and by the genuine approval of the larger and saner part of the community.

The foregoing discussion may be profitably supplemented by a word on the social aspects of excessive living expenditures. Beyond doubt, a scale of living in excess of the maximum limit defined in these pages renders the overwhelming majority of those who adopt it less able and less willing to make sacrifices for the public good, whether on the field of battle, in public life, or through any other form of social service. It makes great achievements in art, science, or literature morally impossible, for the simple reason that it reduces to a minimum the power to abstain, to endure, to wait patiently for large results. Nor is this all. For every person who lives according to this pernicious standard, there are thousands who are unable to do so, yet who adopt it as their ideal and strive to imitate it so far as they are able. Hence these, too, suffer immeasurable hurt in their capacity for self-sacrifice, generosity, and disinterested social service. All the lessons of history point unhesitatingly to the conclusion that social no less than individual welfare, is best promoted by moderate living. Colonel Roosevelt stated this truth in terms that ought to be committed to memory and constantly pondered by every one of his countrymen: "In the last analysis a healthy state can exist only when the men and women who make it lead clean, vigorous, healthy lives; when the children are so trained that they shall endeavor, not to shirk difficulties, but to overcome them, not to seek ease, but to know how to wrest triumph from toil and risk. The man must be glad to do a man's work, to dare and endure, and to labor; to keep himself, and to keep those dependent upon him. The woman must be the housewife, the helpmeet of the homemaker, the wise and fearless mother of many children" ("The Strenuous Life," p. 5). In the opinion of the writer, there are five hundred chances to one that a family will realize these conditions much more fully below than above the $10,000 level.

A stock objection to the doctrine here defended rests on the assertion that every community needs some examples of life on a scale of material magnificence, in order to prevent the dulling and deadening effect of monotonous mediocrity. Precisely why all the real and solid effects of variety could not be had within the limits set in this paper is not easily seen. The satisfaction and the uplifting influence that are derived by the masses from the contemplation of palatial residences, splendid raiment and equipages, and the other public manifestations of excessive expenditure, would be vastly overtopped by the benefits that would follow the investment of this money in decent habitations for the poor, schools, hospitals, parks, play-grounds, art galleries, and public concerts. There would also be a decrease of social hatred, envy, and discontent. At any rate a reduction of 90 per cent in the number of the existing instances of magnificent living would, owing to the comparative rarity of the phenomenon, increase the impression made upon the minds and imaginations of the masses.

The argument on behalf of lavish expenditures for works of art in private residences is likewise of little value. The assistance and encouragement given to artists would be equally great if these purchases were made for the benefit of public galleries.

It must be admitted that luxurious living benefits industry in so far as it prevents an excessive accumulation of capital and increases the demand for the products of capital and industry, but the money thus spent would be doubly beneficial if it were employed in works of public and private benevolence.

No direct reference has been made in the present paper to the question of great private fortunes. While these are a necessary condition of excessive standards of living, they are separable, at least in theory, from the latter, and present a distinct problem. The sole object of these pages has been to define as precisely as possible the range of expenditure which is most compatible with—which, indeed, may be called normal for—Christian living. Describing this in terms of dollars may, at first sight, seem ridiculous. Nevertheless, those who admit the soundness of the underlying principles cannot set aside the estimate with a wave of the hand. Possibly they will find that it is not easily overthrown by concrete argument. Throughout the article the writer has had chiefly in mind Catholics. For they, too, are, to a deplorable extent, under the delusion that valuable life consists in the indefinite satisfaction of material wants. This delusion injures those who are below as well as those who are above the reasonable maximum. The former are discontented where they ought to be well satisfied, and envious where they ought to be thankful because of the temptations that they have escaped. The latter frequently see their children grow weak in faith and character, while they themselves become worldly, cold, and ungenerous. The contributions to religion, charity, or education by Catholics who live sumptuously, by all Catholics, indeed, who exceed the bounds of simple and moderate living—are, generally speaking, utterly inadequate as compared with their income. Herein consists the *inordinate attachment* to wealth which is contrary to the Christian principle. It is no longer that ridiculous passion for gold which obsessed the misers of our nursery tales; it is simply the striving for and indulgence in excessive amounts of material satisfaction.

39

FALSE CONCEPTIONS OF WELFARE

John A. Ryan [1]

Between the ages of sixteen and fifty, the great majority of Americans unceasingly strive and hope to "better their position" by increasing their incomes, and thereby raising themselves above the social and economic plane upon which they have hitherto stood. In so far as they are successful in this aim, they obtain an increased satisfaction of their material wants. Increased satisfaction is immediately followed by a still larger increase, both numerically and intensively, of the wants themselves. It becomes literally true that "the more men have, the more they want." In proof of this statement, all that is necessary is to make a rapid survey of the chief ways in which material wants call for satisfaction.

The man who occupies a plain house of seven or eight rooms will expend a part of his larger income for a better house. A better house means, in the first place, a larger house. A larger house will, usually, be built of more costly materials. In addition, it will demand a greater quantity and a more expensive quality of equipment, furniture, and utensils—woodwork, wall paper, carpets, chairs, beds, tables, chinaware, etc. It means a larger outlay for "help." It implies also a more "select" neighborhood where land and, consequently, rents are higher. The cost of the new house and furnishings may be, let us say, $20,000, while the old one was built and equipped for $5,000; yet when the occupier's income is still further and in a considerable degree increased, there will emerge in his consciousness, or in that of his family, the want of a still better house. This will necessitate a considerably larger expenditure for all the items above enumerated, as well as an additional outlay for several others that have hitherto been unthought-of or disregarded.

[1] *The Church and Socialism*, pp. 180-197. (The University Press, Washington, D. C.)

When income permits a change men are no longer content with plain and nourishing food. They must have more tender meats, more select vegetables, richer and more varied desserts, older and more costly wines, and complicated mixtures instead of plain beverages. The manner in which the food is served becomes more formal, elaborate, and expensive; there must be many courses, more and dearer chinaware, and much cut glass. The same process appears in relation to clothing. After the demands of reasonable comfort have been met, there will rise the desire for a greater number of suits, a more frequent replacement to conform to the fashions, a better quality of materials, and a more high-priced tailor. All these and many other expansions of the clothing want become operative in the case of men, and to a ten-fold degree in the case of women. Witness the single item of jewelry.

Intimately connected with and dependent upon the standard of shelter, food, and clothing is that class of wants that is somewhat inadequately called "social." With increased expenditure for the former, the last-named want inevitably becomes more complicated and more costly. Entertainments and "functions" become more frequent and more elaborate; a notable increase takes place in the accessories of entertaining, such as decorations, flowers, attendants, etc.; and there is a considerable additional outlay for food and clothing. Finally, the desire for amusement and recreation is also capable of indefinite expansion. The person of moderate means goes to the theater occasionally and occupies a cheap seat. The rich or well-to-do person goes more frequently, rides to and from the theater in a carriage, pays much more for a seat, and not infrequently buys an elaborate luncheon after the performance. The pleasure trips and vacations of the poor and the moderately situated consist of trolley rides and a few days spent in some nearby town or country district; those who are rich enough to afford it possess carriages and automobiles, spend months at the seaside or in the mountains, take long ocean voyages, and make extended sojourns in Europe.

In the case of all but the few extremely rich, these five wants or classes of wants, comprised under the head of shelter, food, clothing, "society," and amusement, can be expanded indefinitely and can absorb all of a man's income.

No matter how much a person spends in meeting these wants, he can still maintain, in accordance with the language and standards of the day, that he has merely "bettered his social position."

Now this indefinite striving after indefinite amounts of material satisfaction is not an accidental feature of modern existence. It is but the natural outcome of the prevailing theory of life. "The old Christianity," says Paulsen, who is not medieval in his sympathies, "raised its eyes from the earth, which offered nothing and promised nothing, to heaven and its supersensuous glory. The new age is looking for heaven upon earth; it hopes to attain to the perfect civilization through *science,* and expects that this will make life healthy, long, rich, beautiful, and happy" ("A System of Ethics," pp. 139, 140). According to the dominant view, the loftiest object that man can pursue is the scientific knowledge of nature—not, indeed, for itself, but because of the abundance of material goods that it will put at his disposal. Hence the practical conclusion of the practical man is that he should seek to enjoy as much of these goods as possible. "It is a favorite principle of the ethical materialism of our days that a man is all the happier the more wants he has, if he has at the same time sufficient means for their satisfaction" (Lange's "History of Materialism," p. 239). Such is the prevailing conception of "wider and fuller life." Since life is merely, or at any rate chiefly, an aggregate of sensations, more abundant life means the multiplication of sensations, possessions, and pleasurable experiences.

This theory of life is evidently false. Not the number but the kind of wants that a man satisfies is the important thing. Reasonable human life is primarily *qualitative*. It consists in thinking, knowing, communing, loving, serving, and giving, rather than in having or enjoying. When the demands of health and *moderate* comfort have been supplied, additional sense-satisfactions contribute little or nothing to the development of body, heart, or mind. They necessitate an expenditure of time, energy, and resources that might be employed in building up the higher and rational side of man. They exert a damaging influence upon morals, mind, health, and happiness. Let us view the situation in some detail.

First, as to morals and character. The qualities that are fostered through the activities of "society" are, in great part, undesirable and ignoble. This assertion applies not only to the doings of the most wealthy and exclusive "set," but to all of those more or less formal and pretentious "functions" whose participants regard themselves as "in society," though they may belong within the middle class. Except in a very small proportion of cases, the functions and gatherings of "society" do not make for true culture or for intellectual improvement. Their primary object is to entertain, but they have come to include so many factitious elements in the matter of dress, decorations, feasting, and other accessories, that one of their most common by-products is a group of unlovely and unchristian qualities. One of the most marked of these qualities is the desire for social preeminence, the passion for distinction, the wish to be thought at least as prominent as any other person in one's social set. Thus the desire to excel, which is in itself laudable and useful, becomes, in the case of a large number of society persons, an ambition to outdo one's neighbors in the splendor of gowns, the elaborateness of feasting, and not infrequently in the ostentation and costliness of the entertainment generally. In the pursuit of this ambition are developed the vices of envy, hypocrisy, vanity, and snobbishness.

The realm of the animal appetites presents another instance of the damaging effects of the excessive pursuit of material satisfactions. In the matter of food and drink the line between sufficiency and gluttony is easily passed. Immoral indulgence takes place under the name of a more thorough, more discriminating, and more refined satisfaction of the desire for nourishment. Those who are guilty of this inordinate indulgence often do not realize that they are acting the part of animals rather than of rational beings, in whom the higher nature ought to exercise a controlling influence. Again, violations of the precept of chastity are apt to increase rather than diminish when the personal expenditures of the individual pass beyond the limits of moderate and reasonable comfort. Excessive satisfaction of the other senses creates increased cravings in the sex appetite. And these cravings are less likely to be resisted, precisely because the persons who experience them have become unaccustomed to deny the demands of the other appetites.

Another evil effect is the weakening of the religious sense and of the altruistic sense. It is a fact of general observation that after the stage of moderate income and plain living has been passed, there follows in probably the majority of instances a decay of religious fervor and of deep and vital faith. The things of God are crowded out, "choked by the cares and riches and pleasures of life." Owing to the essential selfishness of the process, inordinate satisfaction of material wants also weakens the feelings of disinterestedness and generosity. Hence the rule is almost universally valid that persons above the line of moderate comfort give a smaller proportion of their income to charitable and religious causes than those who are at or somewhat below that level.

Did men put a true valuation upon material goods, they would increase the *proportion* of their income given to these causes whenever an increase took place in the income itself. For example, if the man with an income of $2,000 per year contributed 3 per cent of this sum, the man who received $4,000 ought to give more than 3 per cent. The bulk of the extra thousand dollars goes, in most cases, to satisfy less important material wants; consequently, a larger proportion of it ought to be expended in meeting the higher want, that is, benevolence. What generally happens, however, is that the proportion decreases. The explanation is obvious; the receivers of the larger incomes become dominated by a false idea of the relative values of things, holding the goods of the senses in higher esteem than when their income was smaller.

Moreover, there are certain of the higher comforts and conveniences whose net effect upon human welfare is probably good, which involve no self-indulgence that is actually immoral, and yet which are in a considerable degree injurious to character. For example, the habit of using parlor cars, electric bells, and street cars, in season and out of season, makes us *dependent* upon them, and renders us less capable of that measure of self-denial and of endurance which is indispensable to the highest achievement. These and many other contrivances of modern life are undoubtedly an obstacle to the development of that invaluable ingredient of character which consists in the *power to do without*. They contribute insensibly, yet effectively, to a certain softness of mind, will, and body which is no advantage in life's many-sided struggle. It does not follow that these conveniences ought not to be utilized at all; it follows that they are not the unmixed blessing which they are commonly assumed to be.

Nowhere are the harmful effects of this materialistic conception of life that we are considering more manifest than in the phenomena associated with the reduced birth rate. The deliberate limitation of offspring is as yet chiefly confined to the middle and upper classes, to the persons whose elementary and reasonable wants are already fairly well supplied. They wish to be in a position to satisfy a larger number of material wants in themselves and to ensure the satisfaction of a still larger number in their children—if they have any. They speak much of aiming at quality rather than quantity in offspring. They do not realize that the special qualities developed in the artificially restricted family are almost entirely materialistic, while the qualities that go to make up strong and virtuous characters are almost inevitably neglected. In one word, the theory of life-values, which impels men and women to decline the burdens of a normal family, makes for enervating self-indulgence and perverted moral notions in parents, a morally and physically enfeebled generation of children, a diminishing population, and a decadent race.

So much for some of the damaging results to morals and character. It seems inevitable that mental powers and activities must likewise suffer. A people devoted to the pursuit of material things, of ease, and of pleasure does not seem to possess the best conditions for achievement in the higher and more arduous fields of mental effort. Even today an ever-increasing proportion of our college and university students choose those courses of study that have a "practical" rather than a theoretical or academic object and outcome. Whether or not this training is as effective as the "liberal" branches in developing the mental powers, those who select it will almost all devote their energies in after life to the business of money-getting. This means the exercise of the lower powers of the brain and intellect. The products of their mental activity will be material things and mechanical progress, rather than the thoughts and ideas and knowledge that make for the intellectual, moral, or spiritual improvement of the race. While the proportion of our population that is educated has greatly increased, there is reason to doubt that the proportion which reads serious, solid, and uplifting literature is any greater today than it was fifty years ago. The great mass of the reading public is now satisfied with the newspaper, the cheap magazine, and books of fiction, good, bad, and indifferent. Half a century ago the majority of those who read had access to only a few books, which were read again and again. It is maintained by some that the general quality of literature itself has deteriorated. Thus, Mr. Frederick Harrison, whose Positivism would naturally dispose him in favor of the present age and spirit, recently wrote: "As I look back over the sixty years since I first began to read for myself, English literature has never been so flat as it is now. . . . In my student days, say, the mid-40's and mid-50's, our poets were Tennyson, the two Brownings, Fitzgerald, Rosseti—all at their zenith. So were Dickens, Thackeray, Bulwer-Lytton, Kingsley, Disraeli. The Brontës, Trollope, George Eliot, Swinburne, Morris, were just coming into line. Year after year Ruskin poured out resounding fugues in every form of melodious art. Our historians were Carlyle, Grote, Milman, Macaulay, Kinglake—then Froude and Newman. Our philosophers were Mill, Buckle, Newman, Hamilton, Mansel. As I look back over these sixty years, it seems to me as if English literature had been slowly sinking, as they say our eastern counties are sinking, below the level of the sea. . . . Railroads, telegrams, telephones, motors, games, 'week ends,' have made life one long scramble, which wealth, luxury, and the 'smart world' have debauched. The result is six-penny magazines, four-and-six-penny novels, 'short stories' in every half-penny rag—print, print, print—everywhere, and 'not a drop to drink'—sheets of picture advertisements, but of literature not an ounce." Among the forces responsible for this decadence Mr. Harrison mentions "the increase of material appliances, vulgarizing life and making it a scramble for good things" (quoted in the *Literary Digest*, March 9, 1907).

The indefinite pursuit of material satisfaction is, in considerable measure, injurious to health. Rich and varied food is not always more nourishing and healthful food. Usually it perverts the taste and artificially stimulates the appetite to such an extent as to produce serious ailments of the digestive organs. The inordinate and feverish endeavor to increase income, the mad race for social distinction, and the unceasing quest of new enjoyments, new ways of satisfying tyrannical and jaded appetites, is disastrous to the nervous system. As a consequence of this twofold abuse of their physical and mental faculties, a large section of the American people are already confirmed dyspeptics or confirmed neurasthenics. The injurious physical effects of unchastity and intemperance are too obvious to need extended comment.

Even the claim that a larger volume of happiness will result from the development and satisfaction of a larger volume of wants is unfounded. For the greater the number of wants that have become active, the greater must be the pain or inconvenience suffered while these wants are unsatisfied. The more numerous the wants that clamor for satisfaction, the greater is the likelihood of disappointment, the greater is the care and worry needed to meet them, and the more numerous are the instances in which satisfaction leads inevitably to satiety. The more frequent and the more varied the satisfaction accorded to any want, the more must the stimulus or satisfying object be increased in order to produce the former measure of enjoyment. In a sense, we are all slaves to the wants that we habitually satisfy; consequently, the greater the number of indulged wants, the greater is the slavery. Socrates thanked the gods because they had given him but a few wants; both Epicurus and Diogenes sought happiness in freedom from wants. As the author of the "Simple Life" says: "The question of food and shelter has never been sharper or more absorbing than since we are better nourished, clothed, and housed than ever. It is not the woman of one dress who asks most insistently how she shall be clothed. Hunger has never driven men to such baseness as the superfluous needs, envy, avarice, and the thirst for pleasure."

Not only the rich but the middle classes experience increased discontent as a result of yielding to the "higher-standard-of-living" fallacy. An effective illustration of this fact is contained in an article by Annie Webster Noel in the New York *Independent*, October 26, 1905. Following are some of its most pertinent passages: "We married in New York City on twelve a week. . . . If our friends would only be happy our great trouble would be removed. They do enjoy staying with us. It is the plunge (into a cheaper house and neighborhood) that is hard. The fact is that our happiness, without so many of the things being striven for, is a slap in the face. . . . We kept house on twelve dollars a week for three months, on fourteen a week for six months. Then we had twenty a week. We have come to the conclusion that *twenty a week is about where poverty commences.* Below that contentment is found in meeting living expenses. But above that new wants begin to take shape. If one hasn't a dollar, one stays at home and is content. But whoever went out to buy something for a dollar and did not see just what she wanted for two? . . . We have reached the critical stage in our *ménage.* We are spending a little more here, a little more there. We are entertaining a little more. We are mixing more with people of larger means. . . . Through a gradual increase in our income we have been reduced to poverty." In other words, the increase of income brought into practical consideration new but purely material wants, whose satisfaction or attempted satisfaction not only did not make for improvement of mind or character, but left this woman and her husband less contented than before.

The worst effect of the failure to find increased happiness in the increased satisfaction of material wants is the realization of this fact by the seekers. The disillusion and disappointment not infrequently make them pessimists in their view of life as a whole. Having cherished for such a long time a false conception of what constitutes true worth and rational living, they do not readily return to saner views. In this connection the work of Paulsen, already quoted, furnishes some significant passages. After citing a document which was placed in the steeple-knob of St. Margaret's Church at Gotha in 1784, and which glorifies the modern age, with its freedom, its arts, and its sciences, and its useful knowledge—all pointing to greater material enjoyment and greater happiness—the author makes this comment: "When we compare the self-confidence of the dying eighteenth century, as expressed in these lines, with the opinion which the dying nineteenth century has of itself, we note a strong contrast. Instead of the proud consciousness of having reached a pinnacle, a feeling that we are on the decline; instead of joyful pride in the successes achieved and joyful hope of new and greater things, a feeling of disappointment and weariness, and a premonition of a coming catastrophe; . . . but one fundamental note running through the awful confusion of voices: *pessimism!* Indignation and disappointment; these seem to be the two strings to which the emotional life of the present is attuned. . . . What Rousseau hurled into the face of his times as an unheard-of paradox, namely, that culture and civilization do not make men better and happier, Schopenhauer teaches as a philosophical theorem: Civilization increases our misery, civilization is the one great *faux pas*" ("A System of Ethics," pp. 147, 148).

This doleful picture is truer of Europe than of America. We have not yet adopted the philosophy of Schopenhauer. We are younger than the European peoples, and have less experience; consequently, we have more enthusiasm, more illusions, more hope, more faith in ourselves and in the satisfying qualities of the material riches that we will secure from a land lavishly endowed by nature. And yet the rapidly increasing numbers of persons among us whose creed is pessimism, indicates that with the coming of more years, more experience, and more mature knowledge, we, too, shall be of the opinion that "culture"—so-called—"and civilization"—so-called—"do not make men better and happier."

It is sometimes asserted that the indefinite pursuit of material goods is necessary for the sake of beauty and refinement. Undoubtedly these have a legitimate place in any complete theory of right living, but their importance is only secondary. They ought not to be sought or obtained to the detriment of the primary goods of life, such as health, mentality, virility, good morals, contentment. Besides, much of the so-called refinement, that is so much prized and sought, is not genuine. It is largely imitation, effeminacy, artifice, vulgarity. True refinement includes not merely elegance, polish, and delicacy—which often appear in very artificial forms—but purity of mind, feelings, and tastes. In the endeavor to satisfy minutely one's material wants, the latter qualities are often weakened instead of being developed. The search for beauty and magnificence also leads frequently to grave perversions. Professor Veblen maintains that the expenditures of the richer classes in America are governed by "the principle of conspicuous waste." This means that a man or woman —especially the latter—must strive in the matter of dress, entertainment, and equipage, to show that he or she is able to command the most costly articles that money can buy, and then must treat them with such recklessness as to indicate that they could be immediately replaced. And Mrs. Charlotte Perkins Stetson tells us in *The Home* that, "woman puts upon her body, without criticism or objection, every excess, distortion, discord, and contradiction that can be sewed together. . . . The esthetic sense of woman has never interfered with her acceptance of ugliness if ugliness were the fashion."

This superficial survey of a field that is so broad as to demand a volume for adequate treatment, and so difficult as to be nearly incapable of definite description, no doubt appears fragmentary, vague, and possibly exaggerated. Nevertheless, the hope is entertained that two or three points have been made more or less clear. First, that the theory of values and of life which impels men to multiply and vary and develop and satisfy *indefinitely* those wants that are grouped under the heads of shelter, food, clothing, social intercourse, and amusement, is false, and makes, as a rule, for physical, mental, and moral decadence. To those persons—and their number is legion—who explicitly or implicitly adopt and pursue this materialistic ideal, money is literally "everything." Money does, indeed, "enslave" them. And it is difficult to say which class receives the greater hurt—those who succeed to a considerable degree in realizing their aim, or those who utterly fail. Although the latter do not attain to that excessive satisfaction of material wants which is demoralizing, their incessant striving for it prevents them from adopting reasonable views of life, and their failure leaves them discontented and pessimistic. In the second place, ninety-nine out of every hundred persons are morally certain to lead healthier, cleaner, nobler, more intellectual, and more useful lives if they neither pass nor attempt to pass beyond the line of moderate comfort in the matter of material satisfactions. Lest this statement be accounted too vague, let us hazard the assertion that the majority of families that expend more than $10,000 per year for the *material goods* of life would be better off in mind and character if they had kept below that figure. Because of this general fact, reflecting and discriminating persons have but scant sympathy with the ambitions of the mass of comfortably situated country people who come to the city to "better their position," or with the desire of the highest paid sections of the laboring classes to increase their remuneration. Today, as of old, the prayer of the Wise Man represents the highest practical wisdom: "Give me neither poverty nor riches; give me only the necessaries of life." In this connection the hope may be expressed that the foregoing pages will have shown the "indefinite-satisfaction-of-indefinite-wants" theory to be directly at variance with the Christian conception of wealth and of life. Even the majority of Catholics seem to hold to the Christian conceptions only theoretically and vaguely, not clearly and practically.[1]

40

VICE

Joseph F. Delany [2]

Vice (Lat. *vitium,* any sort of defect) is here regarded as a habit inclining one to sin. It is the product of repeated sinful acts of a given kind and when formed is in some sense also their cause. Its specific characterization in any instance must be gathered from the opposition it implies to a particular virtue. It is manifest that its employ-

---

[1] In order to make more concrete the argument set forth above, let us suggest that if one-fourth of the most costly houses in any large city were to disappear, to be replaced by dwellings costing one-third as much, and if the general standard of living of the occupants were reduced accordingly, practically all of them would be better off, and their example of sane living would have a very beneficial effect on the rest of the community.

[2] *Catholic Encyclopedia,* Vol. 15, pp. 403, 404.

ment to designate the individual wicked act is entirely improper. They differ as the habit of doing anything is distinguished from the act of that thing. Hence a man may have vices and yet be at times guilty of no sin, and conversely the commission of isolated sins does not make him vicious. Such guilt as he may have contracted in any case is charged directly to the sinful act, not to the vice. Hence the teaching of St. Thomas Aquinas that, absolutely speaking, the sin surpasses the vice in wickedness. Even though the sin be removed by God, the vice, if there was one, may still remain, just as failure to act in any direction does not necessarily and straightway destroy the habit which perchance existed. The habit of sinful indulgence of any sort is to be extirpated by unrelenting vigilance and the performance of contrary acts over a space more or less protracted according as the vice was more or less inveterate. Obviously this applies to vices antagonistic to acquired virtues, for so far as the infused virtues are concerned they can be recovered only as they were originally obtained, through the gratuitous bounty of God. It is interesting to note that according to St. Thomas after one has been rehabilitated in the state of grace and has received, let us say, the infused virtue of temperance, the vice of intemperance does not continue formally as a habit but only as a sort of disposition and as something which is in process of destruction (*in via corruptionis*).

41

PUNITIVE SANCTION

JOSEPH C. SASIA [1]

The justice and necessity of a place of punishment in the world to come may be demonstrated by arguing from what men exact from the civil authorities in the case of offenders against the laws.

Let us suppose that a man is found guilty of high treason or of some other abominable crime which makes him amenable to the penalty of death. But the chief ruler of the nation, wishing to exercise his right of clemency, pardons

---

[1] *The Future Life,* pp. 306, 307. (Benziger Brothers, New York.)

that criminal. What would happen in the commonwealth, if the same outrageous crime were to be repeated several times by the ungrateful wretch and as many times forgiven by the ruler? What would be the attitude of the people in such an event? They would demand the immediate infliction of the extreme penalty prescribed by the law on that incorrigible traitor. In their eyes any further exhibition of clemency would be a travesty of justice, imperilling the well-being of the State and affording encouragement to evil doers. The application of this to the transgressors of God's commandments is easy enough. What if they repeatedly break the divine law, insult and defy the majesty of the Lord, of whose universal governing power all earthly kings are but shadows? Shall there be no punishment for such criminals? Obstinately persevering in sin, they outrage God's patient, long-suffering mercy by refusing to submit to the easy and most reasonable condition on which full pardon would be granted. Yet they deliberately choose to die in open rebellion against their Maker, preferring to remain His perpetual enemies, forever separated from Him. Now, this is hell, for the eternal loss of God alone, independently of other penalties, is the greatest punishment which the omnipotent Judge of mankind could inflict. For any human being that should treat Almighty God as the reckless sinner described above, the mystery should be not that there is a hell, but that there were no hell to punish him as he deserves.

In this our mortal life there is nothing that strikes greater terror into the mind and heart of the wicked, and is more powerful in restraining men from sin than the fear of that punishment, which the Lord, the Supreme Judge, has threatened to inflict on the transgressors of His holy laws. Though virtue shows itself amiable and attractive by its natural beauty and grace, yet, as experience teaches, the majority of men are more deeply impressed by motives of fear than by those of love. In other words, the dread of punishment influences men's moral conduct more powerfully than the hope of reward.

42

ETHICAL IMPLICATIONS OF THE LAW OF HABIT

William James [1]

"Habit a second nature! Habit is ten times nature," the Duke of Wellington is said to have exclaimed; and the degree to which this is true no one probably can appreciate as well as one who is a veteran soldier himself. The daily drill and the years of discipline end by fashioning a man completely over again, as to most of the possibilities of his conduct.

"There is a story," says Prof. Huxley, "which is credible enough, though it may not be true, of a practical joker who, seeing a discharged veteran carrying home his dinner, suddenly called out, 'Attention!' whereupon the man instantly brought his hands down, and lost his mutton and potatoes in the gutter. The drill had been thorough, and its effects had become embodied in the man's nervous structure."

Riderless cavalry-horses, at many a battle, have been seen to come together and go through their customary evolutions at the sound of the bugle-call. Most domestic beasts seem machines almost pure and simple, undoubtedly, unhesitatingly doing from minute to minute the duties they have been taught, and giving no sign that the possibility of an alternative ever suggests itself to their mind. Men grown old in prison have asked to be readmitted after being once set free. In a railroad accident a menagerie-tiger, whose cage had broken open, is said to have emerged, but presently crept back again, as if too much bewildered by his new responsibilities, so that he was without difficulty secured.

Habit is thus the enormous fly-wheel of society, its most precious conservative agent. It alone is what keeps us all within the bounds of ordinance, and saves the children of fortune from the envious uprisings of the poor. It alone prevents the hardest and most repulsive walks of life from being deserted by those brought up to tread therein. It

[1] *Psychology*, Vol. I, pp. 120-127. (Henry Holt and Company, New York.)

keeps the fisherman and the deck-hand at sea through the winter; it holds the miner in his darkness, and nails the countryman to his log-cabin and his lonely farm through all the months of snow; it protects us from invasion by the natives of the desert and the frozen zone. It dooms us all to fight out the battle of life upon the lines of our nurture or our early choice, and to make the best of a pursuit that disagrees, because there is no other for which we are fitted, and it is too late to begin again. It keeps different social strata from mixing. Already at the age of twenty-five you see the professional mannerism settling down on the young commercial traveller, on the young doctor, on the young minister, on the young counsellor-at-law. You see the little lines of cleavage running through the character, the tricks of thought, the prejudices, the ways of the "shop," in a word, from which the man can by-and-by no more escape than his coat-sleeve can suddenly fall into a new set of folds. On the whole, it is best he should not escape. It is well for the world that in most of us, by the age of thirty, the character has set like plaster, and will never soften again.

If the period between twenty and thirty is the critical one in the formation of intellectual and professional habits, the period below twenty is more important still for the fixing of *personal* habits, properly so called, such as vocalization and pronunciation, gesture, motion, and address. Hardly ever is a language learned after twenty spoken without a foreign accent; hardly ever can a youth transferred to the society of his betters unlearn the nasality and other vices of speech bred in him by the associations of his growing years. Hardly ever, indeed, no matter how much money there be in his pocket, can he ever learn to *dress* like a gentleman-born. The merchants offer their wares as eagerly to him as to the veriest "swell," but he simply *cannot* buy the right things. An invisible law, as strong as gravitation, keeps him within his orbit, arrayed this year as he was the last; and how his better-clad acquaintances contrive to get the things they wear will be for him a mystery till his dying day.

The great thing, then, in all education, is to *make our nervous system our ally instead of our enemy.* It is to fund and capitalize our acquisitions, and live at ease upon the interest of the fund. *For this we must make automatic and habitual, as early as possible, as many useful actions as we can*, and guard against the growing into ways that are likely to be disadvantageous to us, as we should guard against the plague. The more of the details of our daily life we can hand over to the effortless custody of automatism, the more our higher powers of mind will be set free for their own proper work. There is no more miserable human being than one in whom nothing is habitual but indecision, and for whom the lighting of every cigar, the drinking of every cup, the time of rising and going to bed every day, and the beginning of every bit of work, are subjects of express volitional deliberation. Full half the time of such a man goes to the deciding, or regretting, of matters which ought to be so ingrained in him as practically not to exist for his consciousness at all. If there be such daily duties not yet ingrained in any one of my readers, let him begin this very hour to set the matter right.

In Professor Bain's chapter on "The Moral Habits" there are some admirable practical remarks laid down. Two great maxims emerge from his statement. The first is that in the acquisition of a new habit, or the leaving off of an old one, we must take care to *launch ourselves with as strong and decided an initiative as possible*. Accumulate all the possible circumstances which shall re-enforce the right motives; put yourself assiduously in conditions that encourage the new way; make engagements incompatible with the old; take a public pledge, if the case allows; in short, envelop your resolution with every aid you know. This will give your new beginning such a momentum that the temptation to break down will not occur as soon as it otherwise might; and every day during which a breakdown is postponed adds to the chances of its not occurring at all.

The second maxim is: *Never suffer an exception to occur till the new habit is securely rooted in your life.* Each lapse is like the letting fall of a ball of string which one is carefully winding up; a single slip undoes more than a great many turns will wind again. *Continuity* of training is the great means of making the nervous system act infallibly right. As Professor Bain says:

"The peculiarity of the moral habits, contradistinguishing them from the intellectual acquisitions, is the presence of two hostile powers, one to be gradually raised into the ascendant over the other. It is necessary, above all things, in such a situation, never to lose a battle. Every gain on the wrong side undoes the effect of many conquests on the right. The essential precaution, therefore, is so to regulate the two opposing powers that the one may have a series of uninterrupted successes, until repetition has fortified it to such a degree as to enable it to cope with the opposition, under any circumstances. This is the theoretically best career of mental progress."

The need of securing success at the *outset* is imperative. Failure at first is apt to damp the energy of all future attempts, whereas past experiences of success nerve one to future vigor. Goethe says to a man who consulted him about an enterprise but mistrusted his own powers: "Ach! you need only blow on your hands!" And the remark illustrates the effect on Goethe's spirits of his own habitually successful career.

The question of "tapering-off," in abandoning such habits as drink and opium-indulgence comes in here, and is a question about which experts differ within certain limits, and in regard to what may be best for an individual case. In the main, however, all expert opinion would agree that abrupt acquisition of the new habit is the best way, *if there be a real possibility of carrying it out.* We must be careful not to give the will so stiff a task as to insure its defeat at the very outset; but, *provided one can stand it,* a sharp period of suffering, and then a free time, is the best thing to aim at, whether in giving up a habit like that of opium, or in simply changing one's hours of rising or of work. It is surprising how soon a desire will die of inanition if it be *never* fed.

"One must first learn, unmoved, looking neither to the right nor left, to walk firmly on the strait and narrow path, before one can begin 'to make one's self over again.' He who every day makes a fresh resolve is like one who, arriving at the edge of the ditch he is to leap, forever stops and returns for a fresh run. Without *unbroken* advance there is no such thing as *accumulation* of the ethical forces possible, and to make this possible, and to exercise us and habituate us in it, is the sovereign blessing of regular work." [2]

A third maxim may be added to the preceding pair: *Seize the very first possible opportunity to act on every resolution you make, and on every emotional prompting you may experience in the direction of the habits you aspire to gain.* It is not in the moment of their forming, but in the moment of their producing *motor effects,* that resolves and aspirations communicate the new "set" to the brain. As the author last quoted remarks:

"The actual presence of the practical opportunity alone furnishes the fulcrum upon which the lever can rest, by means of which the moral will may multiply its strength, and raise itself aloft. He who has no solid ground to press against will never get beyond the stage of empty gesture-making."

No matter how full a reservoir of *maxims* one may possess, and no matter how good one's *sentiments* may be, if one have not taken advantage of every concrete opportunity to *act,* one's character may remain entirely unaffected for the better. With mere good intentions, hell is proverbially paved. And this is an obvious consequence of the principles we have laid down. "A character," as J. S. Mill says, "is a completely fashioned will;" and a will, in the sense in which he means it, is an aggregate of tendencies to act in a firm and prompt and definite way upon all the principal emergencies of life. A tendency to act only becomes effectively ingrained in us in proportion to the uninterrupted frequency with which the actions actually occur, and the brain "grows" to their use. When a resolve or a fine glow of feeling is allowed to evaporate without bearing practical fruit it is worse than a chance lost; it works so as positively to hinder future resolutions and emotions from taking the normal path of discharge. There is no more contemptible type of human character than that of the nerveless sentimentalist and dreamer, who spends his life in a weltering sea of sensibility and emotion, but who never does a manly concrete deed. Rousseau, inflaming all the mothers of France, by his eloquence, to follow Nature and nurse their babies themselves, while he sends

---

[2] J. Bahnsen: "Beiträge zu Charakterologie" (1867), Vol. I, p. 209.

his own children to the foundling hospital, is the classical example of what I mean. But every one of us in his measure, whenever, after glowing for an abstractly formulated Good, he practically ignores some actual case, among the squalid "other particulars" of which that same Good lurks disguised, treads straight on Rousseau's path. All Goods are disguised by the vulgarity of their concomitants, in this work-a-day world; but woe to him who can only recognize them when he thinks them in their pure and abstract form! The habit of excessive novel-reading and theatre-going will produce true monsters in this line. The weeping of the Russian lady over the fictitious personages in the play, while her coachman is freezing to death on his seat outside, is the sort of thing that everywhere happens on a less glaring scale. Even the habit of excessive indulgence in music, for those who are neither performers themselves nor musically gifted enough to take it in a purely intellectual way, has probably a relaxing effect upon the character. One becomes filled with emotions which habitually pass without prompting to any deed, and so the inertly sentimental condition is kept up. The remedy would be, never to suffer one's self to have an emotion at a concert, without expressing it afterwards in *some* active way. Let the expression be the least thing in the world—speaking genially to one's grandmother, or giving up one's seat in a horse-car, if nothing more heroic offers —but let it not fail to take place.

These latter cases make us aware that it is not simply *particular lines of discharge,* but also *general forms* of discharge, that seem to be grooved out by habit in the brain. Just as, if we let our emotions evaporate, they get into a way of evaporating; so there is reason to suppose that if we often flinch from making an effort, before we know it the effort-making capacity will be gone; and that, if we suffer the wandering of our attention, presently it will wander all the time. Attention and effort are, as we shall see later, but two names for the same psychic fact. To what brain-processes they correspond we do not know. The strongest reason for believing that they do depend on brain-processes at all, and are not pure acts of the spirit, is just this fact, that they seem in some degree subject to the law of habit, which is a material law. As a final practical maxim, relative to these habits of the will, we may, then, offer something like this: *keep the faculty of effort alive in you by a little gratuitous exercise every day.* That is, be systematically ascetic or heroic in little unnecessary points, do every day or two something for no other reason than that you would rather not do it, so that when the hour of dire need draws nigh, it may find you not unnerved and untrained to stand the test. Asceticism of this sort is like the insurance which a man pays on his house and goods. The tax does him no good at the time, and possibly may never bring him a return. But if the fire *does* come, his having paid it will be his salvation from ruin. So with the man who has daily inured himself to habits of concentrated attention, energetic volition, and self-denial in unnecessary things. He will stand like a tower when everything rocks around him, and when his softer fellow-mortals are winnowed like chaff in the blast.

The physiological study of mental conditions is thus the most powerful ally of hortatory ethics. The hell to be endured hereafter, of which theology tells, is no worse than the hell we make for ourselves in this world by habitually fashioning our characters in the wrong way. Could the young realize how soon they will become mere walking bundles of habits, they would give more heed to their conduct while in the plastic state. We are spinning our own fates, good or evil, and never to be undone. Every smallest stroke of virtue or of vice leaves its never so little scar. The drunken Rip Van Winkle, in Jefferson's play, excuses himself for every fresh dereliction by saying, "I won't count this time!" Well! he may not count it, and a kind Heaven may not count it; but it is being counted none the less. Down among his nerve-cells and fibres the molecules are counting it, registering and storing it up to be used against him when the next temptation comes. Nothing we ever do is, in strict scientific literalness, wiped out. Of course this has its good side as well as its bad one. As we become permanent drunkards by so many separate drinks, so we become saints in the moral, and authorities and experts in the practical and scientific spheres, by so many separate acts and hours of work. Let no youth have any anxiety about the upshot of his education, whatever the line of it may be. If he keep faithfully busy each hour of the working day, he may safely leave the final result to itself. He can with perfect certainty count on waking up some fine morning, to find himself one of the competent ones of his generation, in whatever pursuit he may have singled out. Silently, between all the details of his business, the *power of judging* in all that class of matter will have built itself up within him as a possession that will never pass away. Young people should know this truth in advance. The ignorance of it has probably engendered more discouragement and faint-heartedness in youths embarking on arduous careers than all other causes put together.

43

THE LIMITATIONS OF HABIT

John MacCunn

It is time to turn to the other side of the shield and to read there that habit has its perversions and its limitations.

In the first place, it is a double-edged instrument. For the reasons given, it can make virtue secure; but it may take the wrong side, thereby making vice incurable. Every reader of Aristotle must remember that upon his view there is a class of persons who have made themselves, by habitual profligacy, morally "incurable." And though there are those hopeful enough to believe that the word incurable ought to be expunged from the vocabulary of morals, even they must admit that what is sometimes called a moral "conversion" is, by law of habit, but the beginning of the long task that has to lay stone to stone in the rebuilding of a dismantled life.

A second possibility—need the familiar warning be repeated?—is that habit may easily end by producing the rigid and wooden type that is unequal to the demands of life. Life, of course, brings its changes, and the day comes when experience presents new situations. It may be when a boy leaves home for school, or school for college, or goes out into the world, or it may be simply one or other of the hundred lesser variations of which even a monotonous lot

[1] *The Making of Character*, pp. 63-68. (Macmillan Company, New York.) Reprinted with permission of the publishers.

has its share. The pathetic fact is that often enough, just in proportion as he has been trained up not wisely but too well in the habits of a sequestered home, the model youth may lamentably fail. Nor will he ever be equal to the demands of an environment that changes even in repeating itself, till among his habits he can number "the habit"— if it be not a contradiction so to call it—"of constantly rehabituating himself." This holds not only of the passage from old virtues to new. It holds within the sphere of every single virtue. It is not courage, for example, to be habituated to face, however steadfastly, only a given kind of danger. At best this is a wooden courage, compatible with lamentable failure in the hour of emergency. Genuine courage must include the flexibility that turns and adapts itself to novel circumstance.

It is easy to pass from these considerations to the further possibility that habit uncorrected by the "habit of rehabituation," may blunt the sensibilities and blind the intelligence.

In a sense it is not to be lamented that habit blunts the sensibilities. It was said of a great surgeon that, with him, pity as an emotion had to cease in order that pity as a motive might begin. And we may generalize the remark to the full length of the statement that few of our duties but would suffer if we tried to live from day to day in full emotional consciousness of all that they involve. Not that we have become automata, as, indeed, we know when the inhibition of habitual duties shows that latent feeling still burns; but simply that in order to get work done, it is needful to secure some measure of calm in the soul.

But there is another side,

"It is to spend long days
And not once feel that we were ever young,"

not to feel it because we have become case-hardened. It is here that Butler's analysis is so substantially sound. When impressions issue in action, he says, our aptitudes for acting are increased; when impressions are passive, that is, do not issue in action, they gradually issue in insensibility. This, to be sure, has been questioned. Granting that the indulgence of these sentimental passive impressions weakens the practical tendencies, they do not, so runs the criticism, diminish the susceptibility to the sentimental pleasure. But is it the fact that sentimental pity, for example, softens the heart even to sentimental pity? Does it not rather wear itself out, till it passes into the apathetic end, not to be disguised though it may still repeat, from the lips outward, the over-worn sentimental phrases; if, indeed it do not throw off all disguise, and pass into the sneer of the cynic? It is thus that habitual indulgence in sensibility issues in insensibility.

The same result may happen in the case of every habit. Acts done at first with a beating heart or a moistened eye, may come to be done without the stirring of a pulse; and this not because feeling is latent but because it is as good as dead. Hence, not unnaturally, feeling and habit have been set in antagonism, and habit branded as a kind of death in life.

It is of even more serious moment that the acquired facility to act in familiar ways, which ought to leave the mind free to deal with unfamiliar difficulties, may easily beget the indolent habit of acting without thinking at all. No result could be more fatal. Moral action, it is never to be forgotten is by its very nature immersed in circumstance. There are conditions of time and place, of manner and aim. And these are so far from being fixed once for all that, in the changeful scene of human activity, they are endlessly with the man and the occasion. Hence the need for that perpetual rehabituation without which, as we have seen, habit will degenerate into a stupid automatism. But such rehabituation will never come where there is not the wakeful, alert intelligence that is quick to read the changeful face of circumstance, and to note the peculiar requirements of the peculiar emergency. This is what Aristotle saw so clearly. No one has insisted more emphatically that the moral indeterminateness of natural desires must be superseded by habits; and no one has seen with more unerring perspicacity that this is never enough. The habits he magnifies are in truth not genuine virtues at all unless, as "habits of deliberate choice," they carry in them the resourceful vitality that can meet and adapt itself to new situations. For it is not the crowning merit of Aristotle to have seen that virtue is habit. This is, perhaps, the lesser part of his message. More pregnant, far, is his doctrine that, in any fully developed character, habit must be found side by side with a sound, practical judgment. For though, of course, there is a long probation during which our actions are chosen for us by those who are wiser than ourselves, this cannot go on forever. The time comes when the individual must face his own problems and find his own solutions, and this he will never do, unless to the habits that run in the ruts of use and wont he have added that sagacity, shrewdness, practical wisdom, sound judgment (call it what we may) which is nothing less than the crowning virtue of a good character.

It follows that the man of habits, however excellent these be, may still be far from being what can be fitly called a man of character. In two respects especially he may fall short. His habits, severally good, may lack the organic unity and the just relative proportion which are among the touchstones of character. It is not enough to give the young good habits: the habits must be co-ordinated in view of the functions which the man has to fulfil in the social economy, and built into a character that is permeated by the unity of coherent plan and purpose. And, as a second shortcoming, the man of habits may still be without that practical good judgment, in the absence of which no one need hope either to face successfully the complex changefulness of life's problems, or even to carry to their full development the habits that have been given him in the days of his tutelage.

Thus there are three main requirements to be satisfied before moral character can come to its full maturity. The first is good habits rooted in strong and promising instincts; the second, that co-ordination of habits that fits the man for his life's work; the third, the sound judgment which enables its possessor, when the days of leading strings are at an end, to stand alone and confront the world in his own independent strength.

44
ETHICS AND CHARACTER
Michael Maher [1]

Whilst psychology investigates the growth of different types of character, ethics considers the relative value of such types and the virtues which constitute them. The problem of the true moral ideal is, in some ethical systems mainly, and in all systems partially, a question of the relative value of the different types of character. The effect on the agent's character of a particular form of conduct is a universally accepted test of its moral quality. Different systems of ethics emphasize the importance of different virtues in the constitution of the ideal moral character. With the Utilitarian, who places the ethical end in the maximum of temporal happiness for the whole community, benevolence will form the primary element in the ideal character. For the Stoic, fortitude and self-control are the chief excellences. The egoistic Hedonist would seem bound to praise enlightened prudence as the highest virtue. For the Christian, Christ is, of course, the true example of ideal character. The vast multitude of varied types of moral perfection presented to us in the lives of the saints who have striven to copy Him show the infinite many-sidedness and rich fruitfulness of that ideal. In all conceptions of ideal character strength forms an essential feature. Firmness of will, fortitude, constancy in adhering to principle or in pursuit of a noble aim hold so important a place that, in common language, to be a man of character is frequently equivalent to being capable of adhering to a fixed purpose. But strength of this kind may easily degenerate into irrational obstinacy or narrow fanaticism. Another essential is the virtue of justice, the constant, practical recognition of the rights and claims of others—involving, of course, all our duties towards Almighty God. In addition to these, habits of charity and magnanimity, with temperance and self-restraint in the control of our lower appentencies will be included. Finally, the richer the culture of the mind, the larger the intellectual horizon, the broader the sympa-

---

[1] *Catholic Encyclopedia,* Vol. III, pg. 586.

thies, and the more balanced the springs of action in the soul, the more will the character approximate to the ideal of human perfection.

The true aim of education is not merely the cultivation of the intellect, but also the formation of moral character. Increased intelligence or physical skill may as easily be employed to the detriment as to the benefit of the community if not accompanied by improved will. Both do not necessarily go together. As it is the function of ethics to determine the ideal of human character, so it is the business of the theory or science of education to study the processes by which that end may be attained and to estimate the relative efficiency of different educational systems and methods in the prosecution of that end. Finally, it is the duty of the art of education to apply the conclusions thus reached to practice and to adapt the available machinery to the realization of the true purpose of education in the formation of the highest type of ideal human character.

45

CHARACTER

Timothy Brosnahan [1]

Etymologically, character means a significant mark stamped or cut on a hard material. Thence it was applied to a combination of qualities distinguishing one individual or group of individuals from others. The notion, therefore, varies with the science that employs it. Ethically it means the sum of moral traits or qualities which distinguish a person or class of persons from others, and by reason of which they receive a special moral designation.

The qualities which individuate personality coalesce in two syntheses: temperament due to nature and character due to nurture.

Temperament is the fusion of the various dispositions of our composite nature into a resultant disposition of the whole man. Disposition is a native bent towards action of a certain kind, and capacity for a certain form of develop-

---

[1] *Digests of Lectures on Ethics*, pp. 55, 56. (John Murphy Company, Baltimore.)

ment. In a secondary sense it is a tendency that has been awakened by previous workings of bent, without, however, giving formed capacity; so understood it is the initial factor of habit in formation.

Habit is a quality superinduced in a faculty by repeated performance of its functions, giving an impulse to and an ease in the exercise of these functions. Dispositions are congenital and plastic, i. e., receptive of form through use, and liable to degeneracy from disuse; habits are acquired and stable, i. e., once fixed, they can be thrown off only by the continued exercise of contrary acts. Habits of our rational nature are of two kinds: habits of thought, i. e., of intellect, and habits of conduct, i. e., of will. The latter may be either good or bad. We are concerned with habits of good conduct. Habits of thought invigorate intellectual dispositions and determine them in a particular direction, and are the products of disposition and training. Habits of conduct confer impulse and ease in the active determination of the will to appropriate ends, and are the product of will freely exercised on disposition, thought, emotion and action.

What dispositions are to temperament, that habits of conduct are to character. As the mental constitution due to the fusion of the former is temperament, so the blending of the latter into an unitary principle is character. Character, therefore, is an integration of habits of conduct superimposed on temperament.

46

THE NATURE OF CHARACTER

Robert Swickerath

We are now in a position to give a definition of character by saying that it is the sum of the inherited and chiefly the acquired ethical traits which give a person his moral individuality. As the acquired habits are based on the inherited traits, we may say that character is a person's inheritance of tendencies trained and shaped by the will. Its "form," to use a term of scholastic philosophy, is in the will. So long as the predominant natural dispositions sway the conduct unchecked, moral character is not yet formed. Whatever be the type of character it is the result of habits voluntarily cherished. It is therefore not a single act, but consists in established acts of self-government, in habitual exercise of the will in a certain direction. A good character is good will exercised habitually, or the best and highest development of the will in the pursuit of goodness. A Christian character is the dedication or consecration of the will to goodness, as put before us in the teaching and example of Christ. There is precious material for a beautiful character in many a child, but if the will does not exercise its influence over this material in the right direction, it will at best remain a diamond in the rough, but will never be the precious cut jewel. Of course there are persons who think they are diamonds, just because they always remained in the rough.

To show that character consists in habitual exercise of the will in a certain direction, let us take a few examples. A person has made a promise, but finds it difficult to keep it; a little "story," as they call it, would help him out of the trouble, but this he does not want to use: he keeps his promise. Another time he has made a mistake, he is ashamed of admitting it; he sees that a lie would save him the humiliation, but he tells the truth, however difficult it may be for him, and no matter what the consequences may be. In an examination he sees that others cheat, and he too has an opportunity of doing so, but he resists the temptation, he is determined to be honest. Again, he applies for a desirable position; he knows that he can obtain it by some misrepresentation with regard to age, studies, former occupation, or by some rather crooked intriguing; but no, he rejects all that, he will not tell a lie even if he should fail to get the position. This is a truthful character, the ideally truthful man. He habitually and deliberately tells the truth, although it often requires great interior struggle. We could similarly illustrate our proposition by the example of those who habitually are honest, kind and charitable, patient in trials, persevering, constant. He who in his actions habitually follows high moral principles, is the perfect, ideal character. If, on the other hand, a person habitually seeks his own gratification, trifles with truth, is inconstant and fickle, he is considered a selfish, deceitful, fickle character. The sum of the moral traits is a person's character, and we call his character after that trait which is most prominent. The perfect character, a rare and precious thing, is that in which the various qualities are beautifully and harmoniously balanced, so that it is difficult to single out one of them as the most pronounced.

Character, therefore, is good will exercised habitually:

> Sow a thought and reap a deed,
> Sow a deed and reap a habit,
> Sow a habit and reap character,
> Sow character and reap destiny.

From this follows an important conclusion, namely, that the formation of character is not the quick result of some energetic efforts; the "get-rich-quick" system has no place in character training. Character formation is a growth, a living process, and the growth of solid trees is invariably slow; it is an unfolding, a moral evolution, sprouting into blades, growing into stalks, budding into flowers, ripening into fruits. Here is a salutary warning for teachers who sometimes get impatient, because there seems to be no progress in the development, moral as well as intellectual, of the children. One can bake an apple in a few minutes; but it takes months to ripen it. Similarly, it takes years before the fruits of character become mature. Perhaps we are inclined to lose courage because, in the formation of our own characters, there is so little advancement. Since it is a growth we should not be surprised at not noticing much progress. In spring the trees are growing luxuriantly and yet we hardly notice it. Children are growing constantly and it is only after a long time that we perceive the fact. The progress in character formation escapes our notice much more, because so many different and even obscure elements are to be taken into consideration. But there is no doubt that every action contributes in some way to this formation, and if honest efforts are made there is surely progress.

> We have not wings, we cannot soar;
> But we have feet to scale and climb
> By slow degrees, by more and more,
> The cloudy summits of our time.
> —*Longfellow.*

47

THE VALUE OF CHARACTER

Ernest R. Hull [1]

It is of great importance to be a man of character; and to be a man of *good* character. For such a man can regulate his whole life according to reason, right and duty, and is not tossed about either by impulses from within or by influences from without. Such a man can steadily work his way towards his final happiness; whereas in case of a man of no character, his whole life and future destiny become a matter of chance.

Character helps a man in the general management of life. The grasp of principles causes him to realize his defects and imperfections, and makes him prompt and energetic in rooting them out. It rids him of many faults which spring from weakness and want of grit. A man of character will be prompt in keeping his appointments, true to his promises, accurate and efficient in his work, clear in his decisions and firm in keeping them. He will be the same to your face and behind your back, and will not give you away or leave you in the lurch. In short, everybody will find him satisfactory to deal with in every department of life.

A man of weak character or no character will be quite the contrary; a creature of impulse, neither at harmony with himself nor with others; unstable and unreliable, so that no one can know what he will be doing next. Such a man is altogether unsatisfactory to deal with, a nuisance to himself and to everybody else.

There is a very close connection between character and carrying out the law of life; because the law of right and wrong is the foundation of every good character, the one general rule which guides the whole of life. All other good principles are merely detailed applications of this one. Having a firm grasp of this first principle, a man of character will always be ready to carry it out, whereas a man of weak character or no character will forget it half the

[1] *Man's Great Concern*, pp. 82-85. (P. J. Kenedy and Sons, New York.)

time, and take no notice of it unless it happens to appeal to his fancy.

Character strengthens a man both against evil impulses from within and evil influences from without. When a man's intellect is filled with good principles and his will is always ready to apply them, he will be quick to notice the first rise of his passions and to check them as soon as they rise. So also he will be on his guard against bad example and the evil influence of others, and will have enough grit and backbone to stand against them.

We can form our character, first, by having a strong wish to do so, and then by exercising both our will and intellect in certain ways. We exercise our intellect (a) by learning the sound principles of a good life, and making much of them, and taking a pride in them; (b) by driving out of the mind all bad thoughts or principles, and learning to dislike and to avoid them; (c) by thinking often about God and our duty to him, and feeling that it is well worth while to become a really good man. We are to exercise our will, even in the ordinary affairs of life, by being prompt, firm and regular in doing the right and proper thing, and doing it as well as we can; by trying hard to do well, and allowing no pleasure or pain, like or dislike, to stand in our way. This exercise of the will in ordinary affairs will form a habit of strong and prompt choice and action, and will help us greatly to do the same in matters of religion and morality, which we must look upon as still more important.

"The secret of success in life is for a man to be ready for his opportunity when it comes."—Disraeli.

48

THE IMPORTANCE OF CHARACTER

Robert Swickerath

Intellectually and ethically man is essentially superior to the brute animal creation. What we admire most in him lies on the ethical side. It is not his talents nor his endowments, nor his powers, nor his attainments, that we respect most, that count most. The more character, the more a man. Knowledge is power, they say, and say rightly; but character is far more a source of power than knowledge. A man's success in life and the extent of his influence over his fellow-men, depend much more on character than on either intellect or fortune. Since the war with Spain, it has become a common expression to speak of "the man behind the gun." In truth, not that army is expected to be victorious which has the greatest number of combatants, the latest pattern of battleships and guns, but that which has the best men behind the guns, which has the best soldiers and the ablest leaders, the best character from the military point of view. In teaching, the most important factor is not the system, nor the curriculum, nor the school building, nor the equipment of the class-rooms, but the man and woman behind the desk—the teacher; and not so much the teacher's learning and knowledge, however important and indispensable these may be, as the teacher's character. The noblest teaching is a noble teacher, and "the teacher's value lies more in what he is than in what he knows" (Spalding).

The same great truth is confirmed by what we see in the family, in the home. There, in particular, we find that character is a source of power and the mainspring of happiness. What father is most respected by his children: he who possesses great wealth and brilliant talents, or he who has a noble character? What mother is loved most: the woman of fashion, of striking beauty, of exceptional culture, or the woman who has the most beautiful character? The answer to these questions is obvious. Again, who are the parents that exercise the most wholesome, the most lasting influence on their children? Are they those who bequeath to them a distinguished name and a large fortune, or those who leave them the memory of an exalted character? Such a memory will accompany the children through life, will be to them a guide and an inspiration, will warn them of dangerous shoals and rocks, will beckon them onward in the paths of moral excellence; such a memory will have more power and ennobling influence over them than the best system of school education can ever exercise. Thus it is clear that character is power. It is, besides, the chief source of happiness, not only to him who possesses it, but to all who come in contact with the happy possessor. What is the mainspring of happiness in a home;

in married life? Is it abundance of earthly goods, or physical attractions, or political power, or social prestige? If any one should be of such an opinion he might learn a different lesson from what is so prominent in the press of this country. How often do we read of the marriage of a young millionaire, the scion of an ancient, distinguished family, with a wealthy, beautiful, highly cultured young lady; or of the daughter of an American millionaire with a titled foreigner, an aristocrat of the highest rank, perhaps a duke or prince—and after a few years we read that the romance, the international romance, as it was called, has turned into an international scandal, and has come to a sad end in the divorce court. And yet they possessed whatever superficial people think necessary to secure all earthly happiness; they had wealth, social position, education; but happiness they did not enjoy. What was the cause of failure? Lack of real character, in one of them, or more commonly in both parties. Indeed, wealth cannot give happiness, beauty will fade, social success may please the vain, but all these things leave the heart empty and do not satisfy the deeper, nobler cravings of human nature. Whithersoever we turn we find that character is the most valuable asset in life. It is, indeed, our narrow word for the better, nobler life of man, for the truly human life. All other things—wealth, health, beauty, professional skill, political influence, literary reputation—all these are of secondary value as compared with character; they are the accidentals, not the essentials, in human life.

49

PERSONALITY

Howard C. Warren [1]

Personality is the *general rating* of an individual. It embraces all the various phases of one's character—temperament, intellectuality, skill, and morality. Personality sums up the total mental constitution of a human being at any stage of his development; in other words, it is the man's "general character."

[1] *Human Psychology*, pp. 383-385. (Houghton-Mifflin Company, New York.) Reprinted with permission of the publishers.

We may distinguish between *personality* and *individuality*. The study of a man's personality is an attempt to measure or rate him according to the standards which are common to human beings generally. The study of his individuality is an attempt to bring out the differential characteristics which mark him off from others. If we investigate a man's handwriting as an index to his temperament, intellectuality, and skill, we are studying this particular man's personality. On the other hand, if our object is merely to note the idiosyncrasies of his script, the study becomes one of individuality. The same is true of any similar investigation.

As a psychological term, personality denotes the man's combined rating in the several phases of mental life, while individuality is the sum total of his variations from the average. *Personality* and *individuality*, taken together, constitute the *self*.

Psychology as a science is not particularly interested in individual differences, except so far as they may be traced to the influence of heredity, organic defects, specific training, social environment and occupation, and other general factors. To this extent they are investigated in the branch called *individual psychology*. General psychology is the investigation of the common features of mental life, which are summed up in personality.

The self, or mind, or personality, is not to be regarded as an abstract being, an entity distinct from the specific phenomena of mental life. Man's self or personality is the sum total of his specific experiences insofar as they represent the results of organization. Each new experience modifies our personality. It is not merely an accretion to the sum of our mental data, but it alters our attitude toward the external world and makes a permanent impression, small or great, upon our general character. This permanent modification of the individual through experience is characteristic of all the higher organic species, but pre-eminently of man.

So far the attempts at a scientific measurement of human personality have met with little success. Most of the essays and books on personality are written by amateur psychologists, who have no appreciation of the real problems involved. They emphasize certain *striking individual* features, or deal merely with a few distinctive traits of character. The trained psychologist is apt to avoid the problem altogether.

The reason for this is plain. Measurement of personality involves determination of the relative importance of the several distinct phases of character. In a general scale of human "mentality" what proportion should be allowed to intellect? How much should temperament, skill, and morality count? Where such disparate factors are concerned the only satisfactory criterion, apparently, is the amount which each factor contributes toward the adaptation of our active processes to the conditions of our environment. It is readily seen that intellect is a highly important factor in promoting adaptation, and that temperamental growth is detrimental to smooth adjustment unless subjected to careful control by training. Up to the present psychologists have not advanced very far toward a quantitative expression of the relations between the several factors.[1]

50

PERSONALITY IN LIFE

ROBERT KANE [2]

While in the actual living of his own actual life, a man will take each day as it comes, and face each event as it happens, and fix his onward course step by step according to the circumstances in which he finds himself, yet he will not be content to allow his whole existence to be merely made up of a succession of human acts occasioned by chance or by opportunity; but if like a rational man he really means to live his own life for himself, he will know where he is going, and, above all, what sort of a man he is growing into; for before his thought there will be one great object of his whole ambition, one great end of his whole being, one purpose that gives a higher meaning and

---

[1] It should also be remembered that as yet we have made little headway toward explaining the *very complex* phenomena which enter into personality in terms of neural operations.

[2] *Worth*, pp. 134-140. (Longmans, Green and Company, New York.) With permission.

a more ultimate influence to each trifling act of each passing hour, a desired worth that beckons him onward, clearing his horizon, directing his views, guiding his efforts, stimulating his energies, overcoming his difficulties, consolidating his successes, until from what at first was potency, then dream, then definite object, then vital growth, then mature fruitfulness, and happy harvest, he shall have lived himself *into* the realization of his own noble self, the worth which is his own personal reproduction of his own personal likeness to his own personal ideal.

Much of this may appear to be vague. It is fundamental; and what is fundamental is vague. We have now to crystallize it into definite shape, and it will become more clear. What definitely are we to understand by one's own self? One's own self is expressed in one's own character. Character may be defined to be that special grouping, harmonizing, and unifying of intellectual and moral qualities and powers which stamp and seal the individual man with a distinctiveness and a personality that mark him out as only typical of himself.

The blending into one human life of soul and body, of clay and spirit, brings with it the vital association in being, and therefore the vital interdependence in action and reaction of many different needs and powers, of many various aims and impulses which by their fusion into the resultant force and effect produce a personality whose characteristics reflect the manner, mode and measure in which its different elements have been combined, and its various energies balance. As the possible kinds and degrees of harmony amongst this complexity of qualities are indefinite, it must follow that the variety of personal character is practically endless. Thus in one character, strength will be conspicuous, in another gentleness will predominate, in another a soaring towards the ideal will excel, in another a practical bent will hold chief sway. In each and all of these broad general types the other subordinate qualities will be heightened or lessened, toned down or intensified in corresponding scale. Where the harmony is not true, or the balancing not accurate, there will be flaws of character. Thus owing to some lack, or owing to some wrench, a character may be crippled, or it may be maimed. Where there is too much or too little own-thought, a character may be isolated, or it may be a dupe. Where there is too much or too little own-will, a character may suffer from mental deafness, or it may become a moral weather-cock. But we are not now concerned with the vices of character, but rather with its ideal virtues.

In human character, if it be truly human, there will be found "that one touch of nature which makes the whole world kin." All cynics and many ascetics are wont to rail fiercely and contemptuously against the depravity and worthlessness of poor human nature. But it is their own inhuman bitterness, or their own inhuman narrowness, which distorts the judgments of these people and tips their lips with poison or with prejudice. Both the great saints who were always angelic, and the great saints who were one time sinners, were as true and as broad in their appreciation of others as their hearts were merciful towards weakness, and generous towards worth. Indeed, even sinners themselves, who are only sinners, and have not been tainted with the venom of Satan or stupefied with his pride, recognize that in our frail, faultful nature there is after all more good than there is evil, and that while whatever evil there is, is unto the likeness of man, all that is good is unto the likeness of God.

That there is often such a thing as "honor amongst thieves" is not a mere mocking phrase. That there is such a thing as devotedness amongst wantons and self-sacrifice amongst criminals is a fairly frequent fact. When one thinks of the terrible circumstances of birth and bringing up in dens of vice and slums of shame of those who never breathe any atmosphere, or see any sight, or hear any sound, or learn any lesson but such as is infected, tainted, polluted, with sin, how can we dare to throw the stone while there is still something left in that life which is truly and even nobly human? Oh, God! surely thine infinite truthfulness of pity saw something good still left in human nature when Thou thyself didst stoop to be born of our flesh and blood in order to become our own true brother-man.

Beyond that very vague far likeness in character which is to be found in every man or woman who is truly human, there may also be found a closer although still vague likeness amongst characters who have the kinship of the same race, or of the some country, or of the same ancestry, or of the same home. Such likenesses as these are natural and inevitable. They are in the blood and they are never drained or fused or evaporated out of it unless by the intermingling of another blood. Most people are indeed well aware that likeness in character is in a great degree hereditary. The old saying "like father like son" is frequently verified. Few people understand the real and fundamental reason of this. Man, as you know, is composed of both body and soul united into one life. That soul is spiritual, and therefore comes directly and immediately from the Creator's hand. But while in its substance it is purely spiritual, it is yet merely potential as regards its evolution into definite kind or intensity or actuality, and it is of such nature as to require that this evolution should be determined by its living presence and action in matter and through matter. Now, on the other hand, the kind of the actual body which is united to that soul will have come from its parents, and will have been much determined in its actual influence on its spiritual counterpart by the conditions realized within it through its parentage and blood and birth. Hence as truly as the seeds of sickness or of health are dormant in that infant frame to be developed with its growth, so truly are the germs of evil influence or of good quiescent within that same material shrine, until they, too, exert their living action upon the passive potency of its indwelling spirit. Wherefore, in the first stage of life, the babe's material and moral character depends in a measure that is almost unimaginable, upon the likeness impressed upon it by those from whom it has received its life. Much of this influence, and of this likeness, will remain in its material and physical aspects throughout life, but as reason dawns and gradually grows from instinct into self-consciousness and self-ownership, it may assert its own mastery over its own self, and it may therefore with its own knowledge and its own will mould its own character in moral matters unto the likeness of an ideal which it has itself chosen and desired.

At last we turn to think of individual personal character. As we have just seen, this may be in great measure inborn; but it will also be, in some measure at least, and often, in very great measure, acquired or self-evolved.

Hence it is evident that the highest function of personality in life is in the taking of one's own character into one's own hands, and evolving it into the actual realization of one's own ideal self. Mark with absolute distinctness that this evolution must be all and utterly from within. There is no such thing as transmigration of souls. You can never cease to be your own self. Do not stupidly suppose, or madly dream, that you can become anybody else. This may sound like a truism. So, indeed, it is; but it is a truism which is unknown or ignored by very many people, and by almost all little ascetics who prose or prattle about the near possibility of a character being obliterated and its exact contrary character being set in its stead. That would not be an evolution of life, but the substitution of an impostor in the place of a murdered man.

Furthermore as self-evolution, which is moral life, is absolutely opposed to self-obliteration, which is moral death, so it is also opposed to the crushing or maiming of natural character. There is a system held, if not in theory, yet most certainly in practice, by writers on moral matters, which is a sort of spiritual nihilism. It aims in the first place, and above all, at destruction. Before it sets to build, it knocks down whatever stands. Before it plants, it roots up whatever grows. It will not try to sow the seed of virtue until it has plucked up every root of vice. That system is suited to dead matter. It is not suited to living things. You cannot improve a tree by cutting it down. You may improve it by pruning; but that is because you direct the life of the tree toward bearing fruit rather than towards straggling into useless shoots. The only true and sound system of cultivating the garden of the soul is to use positive means towards positive ends. Evil qualities in character are in reality good qualities that are stunted, or they are good qualities that are extravagant. It is by careful positive culture that the good is made to supersede the bad.

You will begin by accepting the advice of the wise old Socrates: "know thyself." You will commence this study of yourself by examining, analyzing and grouping your good qualities. Try to find out fully and accurately every atom of good that is in you. This you will do very honestly and very frankly. It is more important that you should know your advantages than that you should know your shortcomings, because the good in you is what is positive and real, while the evil in you is what is negative or defective. Now the good is to be cherished and perfected, while the evil is to be evolved into the good of which it is the want, or to which it is opposed. Are you tall with sturdy shoulders and graceful figure? If so, you should recognize the fact, and thank God for it. Are you good-natured, unselfish and self-controlled? If so, you will also recognize that fact, and you will also thank God for it. The recognition of your natural good qualities will give you confidence and courage to acquire what is still better and nobler. True humility recognizes facts. False humility is either a subtle and insincere form of pride, or it is a depression arising from foolishness, and tending to degenerate into creeping paralysis of the will. When you have studied all the positive and excellent aspects of your character you will turn to look carefully at the aspects which are dark or defective or faultful. Here also you will be quite fair and candid with yourself. See whether your drawbacks may not be the overstraining or the insufficiency of something which of itself is good. Examine whether your very sins or vices may not be an unwise direction or a wrong use of natural good impulse which should be controlled, or of natural, healthful energy which should be otherwise applied. If you suffer from gout, or be threatened with consumption, you will endeavor to remove the germs of disease by wholesome means of developing sound tissue and sturdy flesh. If you are liable to fits of anger, or to attacks of obstinacy, you will exercise yourself calmly but constantly so as to develop the muscles of self-control.

To sum up briefly: on the one hand you will aim at evolving all the sound, sturdy, select elements of good in your own natural character; and in the second place you will aim at toning, blending, harmonizing all these into the unity, symmetry, grace and beauty of that ideal type which is the mirror of your own perfect personal self.

LAW

51

THE NATURE OF LAW

Thomas Slater [1]

A law in general is a rule of conduct, but the term needs to be defined more exactly in order to mark it off from *precepts* and *counsels*.

A law then, in the strict sense of the word, is, according to St. Thomas, an ordinance of the practical reason for the common good, promulgated by him who has care of a society.

It is said to be *an ordinance of the practical reason,* for a law orders human actions with a view to a certain end, but to order and select proper means to an end belongs to the reason, and since the ordering in question has reference to practice, and is imposed by authority, it is attributed to the practical reason. Law then begets an obligation in the subject, and in this differs from a *counsel.*

For the common good indicates the end of all good laws.

By him who has care suggests the source of law which can only be one who has authority over the whole community. Regulations made by subordinate authorities are called in English *by-laws,* in ecclesiastical language, *statutes.*

Of the society.—These words imply that the subject of law is not a single person or family; a law is made for a community more or less numerous.

Promulgated.—Promulgation is the publication of the law by legitimate authority with a view to imposing an obligation. Some sort of promulgation is required in order that subjects may know of the existence of the law and the time when it begins to bind. In English legislation the time when a law will begin to take effect is often set down in the law itself; otherwise it begins to oblige when it receives the royal assent, by which act it is also promulgated. . . .

[1] *A Manual of Moral Theology,* Vol. I, pp. 81-83. (B. Herder Book Company, St. Louis.)

From what has been said, it will be clear how a law differs from a precept. A law is a regulation made by a public authority for the common good, and directly affects a definite territory, and indirectly those who live therein. It is stable and permanent, as is the society for whose good it is made. A precept, on the other hand, is imposed also by private authority for the good of the individual, and directly affects the person—*haeret ossibus.* Regularly a precept is limited in time and expires with the death or removal from office of him who gave it.

52

THE EFFECTS OF LAW

St. Thomas Aquinas [1]

If the intention of the lawgiver is fixed upon true good, which is public good regulated according to divine justice, it follows that the working of the law is toward making men good absolutely. But if the lawgiver's intention is carried to that which is not absolutely good, but is expedient or pleasurable to himself, even in opposition to divine justice, then the law does not make men good absolutely, but only in a restricted sense—good, that is, for the purposes of such a government. In this way good is found even in what is to be styled properly bad, as one is called a *good robber,* because he operates in a manner calculated to gain his end.[2]

Virtue is twofold, *acquired* and *infused.* Habituation contributes to both, but in different ways. It *causes* acquired virtue; it *disposes to* infused virtue, and where infused virtue exists, it preserves it and advances it. Hence the Philosopher says that "legislators make people good by habituating them."

The goodness of every part is estimated in reference to the whole to which it belongs. Hence Augustine says:

---

[1] *Aquinas Ethicus,* Vol. I, pp. 271-273. Translated by Joseph Rickaby, S. J. (Burns, Oates and Washbourne, London.)

[2] It follows that where the mass of the citizens are not good, democracy makes an unhappy government. So, of course, does oligarchy also, where the ruling few are unprincipled men.—*Translator.*

"Unseemly is every part that befits not the whole." Since then every man is a part of the State, it is impossible for any man to be good unless his behavior is well calculated to serve the common good; nor can the whole be in a good condition, unless it is made up of parts well adapted to it. Hence it is impossible for the common weal to flourish unless the citizens are virtuous, at least they who exercise the sovereignty. But it is enough for the good of the community that the others be virtuous to the extent of obeying the commands of those in power. And, therefore, the Philosopher says: "The virtue of a sovereign and of a good man is the same; but the virtue of any common citizen and of a good man is not the same."

A tyrannical law, not being according to reason, is not absolutely speaking a law, but rather a perversion of law; and yet inasmuch as it has something of a law about it, it intends that the citizens should be good, its aim being to make them obedient, or good for the purposes of such a government.

It is a saying of the Philosopher that "the wish of every legislator is to make men good."

To Augustine's words, "Of servile fear, which is the fear of punishment, though one do good, yet he does not do it well," it is to be said that from becoming accustomed to avoid evil and fulfil what is good through fear of punishment, a man is sometimes led on to do the same with delight and of his own will; and in this way the law even by punishment leads men on to goodness.

53

CLASSIFICATION OF LAWS

Victor Cathrein [1]

The actual, direct effect of law is obligation. According to the varieties of duties imposed, law is classified as: commanding, prohibitive, permissive, and penal. Commanding laws (*leges affirmativae*) make the performance of an action, of something positive, obligatory; prohibitive laws (*leges negativae*), on the other hand, make obligatory an

---

[1] *Catholic Encyclopedia*, Vol. IV, p. 56.

omission. The principle holds good for prohibitive laws, at least if they are absolute, like the commands of the natural moral law, ("Thou shalt not bear false witness," "Thou shalt not commit adultery," etc.) that they are always and forever obligatory (*leges negativae obligant semper et pro semper*—negative laws bind always and forever), i. e., it is never permissible to perform the forbidden action. Commanding laws, however, as the law that debts must be paid, always impose an obligation, it is true, but not forever (*leges affimativae obligant semper, sed non pro semper*—affirmative laws are always binding, but not forever), that is, they continue always to be laws, but they do not oblige one at every moment to the performance of the action commanded, but only at a certain time and under certain conditions. All laws which inflict penalties for violation of the law are called penal, whether they themselves directly define the manner and amount of penalty, or make it the duty of the judge to inflict, according to his judgment, a just punishment. Laws purely penal (*leges mere paenales*) are those which do not make an action absolutely obligatory, but simply impose penalty in case one is convicted of transgression. Thus, they leave it, in a certain sense, to the choice of the subject whether he will abstain from the penal action, or whether, if the violation is proved against him, he will submit to the penalty. The objection cannot be raised that purely penal laws are not actual laws because they create no bounden duty, for they oblige the violator of the law to bear the punishment if the authorities apprehend and convict him. Whether a law is a purely penal law or not is not so easy to decide in an individual case. The decision depends on the will of the lawgiver and also upon the general opinion and custom of a community.

In treating of promulgation a distinction has to be made between natural moral law and positive law. The first is proclaimed to all men by the natural light of reason; positive laws are made known by special outward signs (word of mouth or writing). The natural moral law is a law inseparable from the nature of men; positive law, on the contrary, is not. In regard to the origin or source of law, a distinction is made between Divine and human laws according as they are issued directly by God Himself or by men in virtue of the power granted them by God. If man in issuing a law is simply the herald or messenger of God, the law is not human but Divine. Thus the laws which Moses received from God on Mount Sinai and proclaimed to the people of Israel were not human but Divine laws. A distinction is further made between the laws of Church and State according as they are issued by the authorities of the State or of the Church. Laws are divided as to origin into prescriptive and statute laws. Prescriptive, or customary, law includes those laws which do not come into existence by direct decree of the lawgiving power, but by long continued custom of the community. Yet every custom does not give rise to a law or a right. In order to become a law a custom must be universal or, at least, be followed freely and with the intention of raising it to law by a considerable part of the population. It must further be a custom of long standing. Finally, it must be useful to the common welfare, because this is an essential requisite to every law. Custom receives its binding, obligatory force from the tacit or legal approval of the lawgiver, for every true law binds those upon whom it is imposed. Only he can impose a binding obligation on a community on whom the supervision of it or the power of jurisdiction over it devolves. If the legislative power of it belongs to a people itself, it can impose obligation on itself as a whole; if it has not this power, the obligation can only be formed with the consent of the lawgiver.

A classification of law, as limited to law administered in the courts, and familiar to Roman jurisprudence, is that of law in the strict sense and equity. Equity is often taken as synonymous with natural justice. In this sense we say that equity forbids that any one be judged unheard. Frequently, however, we speak of equity only in reference to positive laws. A human lawgiver is never able to foresee all the individual cases to which his law will be applied. Consequently, a law though just in general, may, taken literally, lead in some unforeseen cases to results which agree neither with the intent of the lawgiver nor with natural justice, but rather contravene them. In such cases the law must be expounded not according to its wording but according to the intent of the lawgiver and the general principles of natural justice. A reasonable lawgiver could not desire this law to be followed literally in cases where this would entail a violation of the principles of natural justice. Law in the strict sense (*jus strictum*) is, therefore, positive law in its literal interpretation; equity, on the contrary, consists of the principles of natural justice so far as they are used to explain or correct a positive human law if this is not in harmony with the former. For this reason Aristotle calls equity the correction of written or statute law.

54

MAJOR DIVISIONS OF LAW

Francis P. Le Buffe [1]

All law outside of Natural Law is called positive law. The derivation of the word gives us the doctrine contained in the name. Positive is from the Latin word *pono,* meaning I place or put; past participle *positus*—placed or put. Positive law, then, is law that is freely made or freely enacted and thus is contrasted with Natural Law, which is inevitably based on the very nature of things and which, therefore, God Himself necessarily enjoined, else He would have been untrue to His own perfect nature.

Positive Law, therefore, is a rule of action, mandatory in form, freely established and promulgated by competent authority for the common good.

According to the nature of this competent authority we have the following divisions:

1. Divine Positive Law;
2. Human Positive Law;
    a) Jus Gentium;
    b) Civil (or Municipal) Law;
    c) International Law;
    d) Ecclesiastical (Church) Law.

This was the original meaning of the term, i. e., any law freely put by any superior, and there is no reason for departing from it. However, it has been customary to narrow positive law to human positive law. So Austin accepts the

---

[1] *Outlines of Pure Jurisprudence,* pp. 49-56. (Fordham University Press, New York.)

term (Jurisprudence I, No. 189, p. 116): "Every positive law or every law simply and strictly so called is set by a sovereign person, or a sovereign body of persons, to a member or members of the independent political society wherein that person or body is sovereign or supreme." (See also I, Nos. 135-137, 143; Holland, Jurisprudence, Ch. IV, p. 43.) Bouvier (Law Dict., *sub voce*) says that positive law is — "Law actually ordained and established, under human sanctions, as distinguished from the law of nature or natural law, which comprises those considerations of justice, right and universal expediency that are announced by the voice of reason or of revelation." (Be careful of the last incorrect statement of Natural Law as due to revelation.)

Divine Positive Law.—A rule of action, mandatory in form, freely established and promulgated by God for mankind.

N. B. 1. A divine revealed law is a law imposed directly by God on man by a revelation. This revelation may be—
    a) revelation of Natural Law, i. e., its revelation immediately by God Himself. In this case the revelation is a re-affirmation of the Natural Law.
    b) revelation of positive law, i. e., of laws freely imposed by God. Hence "divine revealed law" includes both Natural Law and divine positive law.

2. There are few who deny the fact that God has made some positive laws, no matter how much various folks of various religions may dispute as to the content of those laws, i. e., as to what positive laws He has actually passed. Blackstone (Introd., Sect. 2, p. 41) says: "This has given manifold occasion for the benign interposition of divine Providence, which, in compassion to the frailty, the imperfections and the blindness of human reason, hath been pleased, at sundry times and in diverse manners, to discover and enforce its laws by an immediate and direct revelation."

"Even as regards those truths about God which human reason could have discovered, it was necessary that man should be taught by a divine revelation; because the truth about God, such as reason could discover, would be known only by a few, and after a long time, and with the admixture of many errors. . . . Therefore, in order that the salvation of men might be brought about more fitly and more surely, it was necessary that they should be taught divine truths by divine revelation."—St. Thomas, 1-1-1. (See Rickaby, "Of God and His Creatures," Bk. IV, Ch. 1.)

"With regard to the laws which God is pleased to reveal, the way wherein they are manifested is easily conceived. They are express commands; portions of the word of God; commands signified to men through the medium of human language; and uttered by God directly, or by servants whom He sends to announce them."—Austin, I, Lect. II, No. 41.

"Divine (Positive) Law is the rule presented directly to His rational creatures by the Creator Himself. It is a communication to them of such otherwise undiscoverable or unintelligible portions of the eternal law as may be necessary to enable them to govern their mental, moral and physical operations in accordance with the attributes of their own natures and the end for which they were created. That such a communication should be made whenever it becomes necessary, and so far as it is necessary, is inevitable, since otherwise the supreme reason would contradict itself and defeat its own designs."—Robinson, El. of Am. Jur., Sect. 5. (See Markby, El. of Law, Sect. 105, and ff.)

There is a natural obligation (i. e., an obligation based on the Natural Law) of assenting to revealed truths and of obeying revealed divine positive law once we are certain of the fact of such revelation and of the existence of such laws. This natural obligation is stated simply: "We must obey God when we learn of His commands."

Human Positive Law.—A rule of action, mandatory in form, freely established and promulgated by human superiors for the common good.

Jus Gentium.—This is of great historical importance. When the Romans attempted to manage cases between individuals of different subject nations or between a Roman citizen and an individual of a subject nation, they could not apply Roman Law to such cases, because Roman law was identified with the Roman religion which was exclusive of foreigners. They then proceeded to study the laws and customs of all subject peoples and to find the common elements therein contained. This common element or, to speak mathematically, this higher common factor was called Jus Gentium.

"When the jurists came to examine different systems of laws, they found much in each that was common to all. The common part they termed the Jus Gentium; and the residue, the part peculiar to each state, they called Jus Civile."—Sandar's Justinian (Hammond) 71 notes.

N. B. 1. Jus Gentium was not a parallel to international law, which exists between nations, but a law which was general within all nations, and, therefore, rightfully applied to all subjects of all nations. Historically, too, it would have been foreign to the Romans to regard it as international law, since they were the "lords of the world" and subject nations had what the Romans chose to leave them. (See Lorimer, Institutes, Introd. IX.)

2. Jus Gentium is not the same as Natural Law (Sect. IV), for it was positive law and custom, actually existing among the various peoples. By reason, however, of its universality, it necessarily approximated to the Natural Law and was in part an embodiment of it.

3. In later writers the term Jus Gentium was variable and sometimes did mean the same as Jus Naturale or Natural Law.

The clear distinction between Natural Law and Jus Gentium appears for the first time with Christianity. The influence of Christianity on the law in the early development of mediaeval law in so far as this law departed from Roman tradition, has been well stated by de Coulanges (The Ancient City, pp. 527-528): "Christianity is the first religion that did not claim to be the source of law. It occupied itself with the duties of men, not with their interests. Men saw it regulate neither the laws of property, nor the order of succession, nor obligations, nor legal proceedings. It placed itself outside the law, and outside all things purely terrestrial. Law was independent; it could draw its rules from nature, from the human conscience, from the powerful idea of the just that is in men's minds. It could develop in complete liberty; could be reformed and improved without obstacle; could follow the progress of morals, and could conform itself to the interests and social needs of every generation.

The happy influence of the new idea is easily seen in the history of Roman law. During several centuries preceding the triumph of Christianity, Roman law had already been striving to disengage itself from religion, and to approach natural equity; but it proceeded only by shifts and devices, which enervated and enfeebled its moral authority. The work of regenerating legislation announced by the Stoic philosophers, pursued by the noble efforts of Roman jurisconsults, outlined by the artifices and expedients of the pretor, could not completely succeed except by favor of the independence which the new religion allowed to the law. We can see, as Christianity gained ground, that the Roman codes admitted new rules no longer by subterfuges, but openly and without hesitation."

In view of this historical fact stated correctly by de Coulanges, such statements as the one subjoined from Bryce (Studies, XI, p. 596) will be seen to be thoroughly erroneous and misleading: "One can hardly say that the idea [of the Natural Law] emerges as an independently formative power in the growth . . . of the Canon Law . . . for the obvious reason that ecclesiastical systems do not need it. The Bible in Christendom . . . supplied all the philosophical basis and all such indications of the Divine Will as were needed to give law a moral character. So, although the term is, indeed, frequently used by mediaeval writers of all types, it is generally used with a theological or ethical bearing. Nature, except in such a sense as was given to it by St. Paul, or in such expressions as were sanctioned by Aristotle or by the texts of the Jurists, would have sounded strange, and might have savoured of heterodoxy."

Though this distinction came in with Christianity and is recognizable in the writings of the Fathers of the Church, the earliest statement of this very important position is found in Isidore of Seville (Etymology, Bk. 5, ch. 4) wherein, by the use of the phrase *"by* an instinct of nature," he indicates the departure from the Stoic idea of the Natural Law as a matter of mere instinct. He writes: "Natural law is common to all peoples in that it is had by an instinct of nature, not by any human agreement, as the marriage of man and woman, the begetting and rearing of children, the common possession of all, the one freedom of all, the acquisition of those things that are taken in the air or sea or on land; likewise the restoring of property entrusted or lent, the repelling of violence by force. For this, or whatever is like this could never constitute an injustice, but must be considered in accord with natural equity."

On the other hand Jus Gentium is clearly recognized as one form of positive law, as is plain from his phrase "nearly all nations" (Etymology, Bk. 5, ch. 6): "The law of nations (Jus Gentium) is the occupation of territory, the building and fortification of cities and castles, wars, captivities, enslavements, the recovery or rights of postliminy, treaties of peace and others, the scruple which protects ambassadors from violence and prohibitions of marriage between persons of different nationality. This is, therefore, called the law of nations because nearly all nations have made such things their custom."

It should be noted how far this statement differs from the position stated by Gaius, where the confusion of Jus Gentium with the Natural Law is clearly in evidence (Digest, 1, 4, 5): "The law which natural reason appoints for all mankind obtains equally among all nations, and is called the *law of nations* because all nations make use of it."

References for Jus Gentium: Bryce, Studies, XI, pp. 570 and ff.; Kinkead, Lecture VII, pp. 90-91; Lorimer, Institutes, Introd., pp. 12-14; Blackstone, Comm., Introd., p. 43; Suarez, De Legibus, Lib. II, c. XVII; St. Thomas, Summa Theologica, 1-2-95-4; Pollock, First Book, Ch. I, pp. 13-14; Kent, Commentaries, Vol. I, Lect. I; Ryan and Millar, The State and the Church, Ch. V, p. 105.

Civil or Municipal Law.—A rule of action, mandatory in form, established and promulgated by the competent authority of the State for the common good.

Blackstone (Introd., Sect. 2, p. 44) says: "I call it municipal law, in compliance with common speech; for, though strictly that expression denoted the particular customs of one single municipium or free town, yet it may with sufficient propriety be applied to any one state or nation, which is governed by the same laws and customs."

Blackstone's definition about which there has been a deal of dispute, reads (Introd., Sect. 2, p. 44): "A rule of civil conduct prescribed by the supreme power in a state, commanding what is right and prohibiting what is wrong."

This definition is correct and the final words, which give offence to so many, are understandable in the only sense in which Blackstone could logically, with his admission of Natural Law, understand them, i. e., commanding that which is objectively befitting and prohibiting that which is objectively unbefitting. Prof. Hammond (1 Bl. p. 125), commenting on this section, says correctly: "That the rights and wrongs of municipal law must necessarily be consistent with the law of nature is merely a logical corollary to the doctrine of this section." (Read Kinkead, pp. 184-187, Ch. XII.)

The root difficulty of those who misread Blackstone is that they divorce Jurisprudence from Ethics or deny Natural Law. (See Christian's confused note to 1 Bl. p. 44.)

International Law.—A rule of action, mandatory in form, established and promulgated by the competent authorities of two or more States for the common welfare of their relations.

Pollock (Essays, p. 64) writes: "For all practical purposes we may define International Law, with the late Lord Russel of Killowen, as 'the sum of the rules or usages which civilized States have agreed shall be binding upon them in their dealings with one another,' remembering, however, that the agreement need not be formal or express. Such rules may, of course, be modified, generally or partially, by convention or usage, in any manner consistent with the objects for which the law of nations exists. This is not only required by convenience, but wholly in accordance with the doctrine of the Law of Nature as received in the Middle Ages, which expressly admitted the validity of positive rules and conventions not contrary to fundamental principle. If any one ever did want to lay down a dogmatic and immutable code of Naturrecht it was not the schoolmen, but the utilitarians."

The first to define international law in this sense was the Jesuit Suarez who resorted to Isidore of Seville. Isidore, consequent upon his distinction between Natural Law and Jus Gentium, was in a position, at the time of the disruption of the Roman Empire, to use the term Jus Gentium in the strict sense of jus inter gentes, i. e., international law.

Ecclesiastical Law.—A rule of action, mandatory in form, established and promulgated by the competent authority of a Church for the spiritual welfare of its subjects.

55

THE ETERNAL LAW

JOSEPH RICKABY [1]

1. A law is defined to be: A precept just and abiding, given for promulgation to a perfect community. A law is primarily a rule of action. The first attribute of a law is that it be *just:* just to the subject on whom it is imposed, as being no harmful abridgment of his rights: just, also, to other men, as not moving him to injustice against them. An unjust law is no law at all, for it is not a rule of action. Still, we may sometimes be bound, when only our own rights are infringed, to submit to such an imposition, not as a law, for it is none, but on the score of prudence, to escape direr evils. A law is no fleeting, occasional rule of conduct, suited to meet some passing emergency or superficial disturbance. The reason of a law lies deep down, lasting and widespread in the nature of the governed. A law, then, has these two further attributes of permanence in duration and amplitude in area. Every law is made for all time, and lives on with the life of the community for whom it is enacted, forever, unless it be either expressly or implicitly repealed. A law in a community is like a habit in an individual, an accretion to nature, which abides as part of the natural being, and guides henceforth the course of natural action. This analogy holds especially of those laws, which are not enacted all of a sudden—and such are rarely the best laws—but grow upon the people with gradual growth unmarked, like a habit by the repetition of acts, in the way of immemorial custom. I have said that a law is for a community, that it requires amplitude and large area. A law is not laid down for an individual, except so far as his action is of importance to the community. The private concerns of one man do not afford

---

[1] *Moral Philosophy,* pp. 126-132. (Longmans, Green and Company, New York.) With permission.

scope and room enough for a law. Neither do the domestic affairs of one family. A father is not a legislator. A law aims at a deep, far-reaching, primary good. But the private good of an individual, and the domestic good of a family, are not primary goods, inasmuch as the individual and the family are not primary but subordinate beings: not complete and independent, but dependent and partial; not wholes but parts. The individual is part of the family, and the family is part of a higher community. It is only when we are come to some community which is not part of any higher, that we have found the being, the good of which is primary good, the aim of law. Such a community, not being part of any higher community in the same order, is in its own order a perfect community. Thus, in the temporal order, the individual is part of the State. The State is a perfect community; and the good of the State is of more consequence than the temporal well-being of any individual citizen. The temporal good of the individual, then, is matter of law, in so far as it is subservient to the good of the State. We have, then, to hold that a law is given to the members of a perfect community for the good of the whole. Not every precept, therefore, is a law; nor every superior a lawgiver; for it is not every superior that has charge of the good of a perfect community. Many a precept is given to an individual, either for his private good, as when a father commands his child, or for the private good of him that issues the precept, as when a master commands a servant. But every law is a precept; for a law is an imperative rule of action, in view of a good that is necessary, at least with the necessity of convenience. To every law there are counsels attached. A law may be said to be a *nucleus* of precept, having an *envelope* of counsel. Every law has, also, a pendent called punishment for those who break it; this is called the *sanction* of the law. A law is also for *promulgation,* as a birch rod for *application.* The promulgation, or application, brings the law home to the subject, but is not part of the law itself. So much for the definition of Law.

2. We have to learn to look upon the whole created universe, and the fulness thereof, angels, man, earth, sun, planets, fixed stars, all things visible and invisible, as one great and perfect community, whose King and Lawgiver

is God. He is King, because He is Creator and Lord. But lordship and kingship are different things, even in God. It is one thing to be lord and master, owner and proprietor of a chattel, property and domain; it is another thing to be king and governor, lawgiver and judge of political subjects. The former is called *power of dominion,* or right of ownership, the latter is *power of jurisdiction.* Power of dominion is for the good of him who wields it; but power of jurisdiction is for the good of the governed. As God is Lord of the universe, He directs all its operations to His own glory. As He is King, He governs as a king should govern, for the good of His subjects. In intellectual creatures, whose will is not set in opposition to God, the subject's good and the glory of the Lord finally coincide. God's power of dominion is the concern of theologians; the moralist is taken up with His power of jurisdiction, from whence emanates the moral law.

3. In the last chapter we stated the moral law in these terms, that *God wills to bind His creatures to certain lines of action,* not arbitrary lines, as we saw, but the natural lines of each creature's being. The law thus stated takes in manifestly a wider field than that of moral action. There is, in fact, no action of created things that is not comprehended under this statement. It comprises the laws of physical nature and the action of physical causes, no less than the moral law and human acts. It is the one primeval law of the universe, antecedent to all actual creation, and co-eternal with God. And yet not necessary as God; for had God not decreed from all eternity to create—and He need not have decreed it—neither would He have passed in His own Divine Mind this second decree, necessarily consequent as it is upon the decree of creation, namely, that every creature should act in the mode of action proper of its kind. This decree, supervening from eternity upon the creative decree, is called the Eternal Law.

4. This law does not govern the acts of God Himself. God ever does what is wise and good, not because He binds Himself by the decree of His own will so to act, but because of His all-perfect nature. His own decrees have not for Him the force of a precept: that is impossible in any case: yet He cannot act against them, as His nature allows not of irresolution, change of mind, and inconsistency.

5. Emanating from the will of God, and resting upon the nature of the creature, it would seem that the Eternal Law must be irresistible. "Who resisteth His will?" asks the Apostle (Rom. ix. 19). "The streams of sacred rivers are flowing upwards, and justice and the universal order is wrenched back." (Euripides, *Medea*, 499.) It is only the perversion spoken of by the poet, that can anywise supply the instance asked for by the Apostle. The thing is impossible in the physical order. The rivers cannot flow upwards, under the conditions under which rivers usually flow; but justice and purity, truth and religion may be wrenched back, in violation of nature and of the law eternal. The one thing that breaks this law is sin. Sin alone is properly unnatural. The world is full of physical evils, pain, famine, blindness, disease, decay and death. But herein is nothing against nature; the several agents act up to their nature, so far as it goes; it is the defect of nature that makes the evil. But sin is no mere shortcoming; it is a turning round and going against nature, as though the July sun should freeze a man, or the summer air suffocate him. Physical evil comes by the defect of nature, and by permission of the Eternal Law. But the moral evil of sin is a breach of that law.

6. A great point with modern thinkers is the inviolability of the laws of physical nature, *e. g.*, of gravitation or of electrical induction. If these laws are represented, as J. S. Mill said they should be, as *tendencies* only, they are truly inviolable. The law of gravitation is equally fulfilled in a falling body, in a body suspended by a string, and in a body borne up by the ministry of an angel. There is no law of nature to the effect that a supernatural force shall never intervene. Even if, as may be done perhaps in the greatest miracles, God suspends His concurrence, so that the creature acts not at all, even that would be no violation of the physical law of the creature's action; for all that such a law provides is, that the creature, if it acts at all, shall act in a certain way, not that God shall always give the concurrence which is the necessary condition of its acting at all. The laws of physical nature then are, strictly speaking, never violated, although the *course* of nature is occasionally altered by supernatural interference, and continually by free human volition. But the laws of physical

nature, in the highest generality, are identified with the moral law. The one Eternal Law embraces all the laws of creation. It has a physical and a moral side. On the former it *effects,* on the latter it *obliges,* but on both sides it is imperative; and though in moral matters it be temporarily defeated by sin, still the moral behest must in the end be fulfilled as surely as the physical behest. The defeat of the law must be made good, the sin must be punished.

7. It is important to hold this conception of the Eternal Law as embracing physical nature along with rational agents. To confine the law, as modern writers do, to rational agents alone, is sadly to abridge the view of its binding force. The rigid application of physical laws is brought home to us daily by science and by experience; it is a point gained, to come to understand that the moral law, being ultimately one with those physical laws, is no less absolute and indefeasible, though in a different manner, than they.

It is hard for us to conceive of laws being given to senseless things. We cannot ourselves prescribe to iron or to sulphur the manner of its action. As Bacon says (*Novum Organum,* i., Aphorism 4): "Man can only put natural bodies together or asunder; nature does the rest within." That is, man cannot make the laws of nature; he can only arrange collocations of materials so as to avail himself of those laws. But God makes the law, issuing His command, the warrant without which no creature could do anything, that every creature, rational and irrational, shall act each according to its kind or nature. Such is the Eternal Law.

56

THE NATURAL LAW

Walter McDonald [1]

As I understand the term "natural law," it denotes, not so much an enactment of a ruling will,—a law in the strict sense,—as an order or relation objectively existing, and capable of being expressed in a general formula akin to

---

[1] *The Principles of Moral Science,* pp. 93-95. (B. Herder Book Company, St. Louis.)

the laws of motion and other such principles of which we read in physics. It is, for instance, in accordance with the natural law that murder is inordinate; the meaning being that the moral order existing objectively between any two men whatsoever, is such as is expressed in the formula: murder is wrong. Just as the laws of motion are not communications or enactments of any ruling will, but merely general propositions representing the order in which the phenomena of motion take place; so the natural law regarding murder, or theft, or lying, is not an enactment, but merely a general truth regarding the objective relations that should subsist between the essences that are implied by murder, theft, and lying, and which may be in order and right or out of order and wrong.

I am aware that the general law is often represented by Catholic writers as some kind of participation of the eternal law, possessed by rational creatures; as some kind of impression on man of the divine light, whereby he may be able to discern good from evil, and as a natural intimate conception, whereby a man may direct his acts in accordance with right reason. All this may be true, if it is understood metaphorically or analogically. Strictly speaking, the natural law is neither an impression of the divine light on the soul of man, nor a conception of any kind, nor anything like a participation of the act of intellect or will in which the eternal law formally consists. It is an order, not merely between individual essences, but between all essences of definite types or species—an order, therefore, which may be expressed by a universal proposition, like those in which the relations of moving bodies are expressed, or like the rules and canons of art. These latter expressions also—the laws of motion and the rules of art—are laws of nature, in the physical and aesthetic orders. What is called natural law in the moral order is to be understood in the same way, allowance being made for the difference of order to which it belongs.

The foregoing explanation, in substance, corresponds to the idea of natural law which is set forth by the Jesuit theologian, Gabriel Vasquez, and to which his brother Jesuit, Suarez, objects on the ground that it does not make out the natural law to be a law in the strict sense, such as, he asserts, it has always been regarded by the great Scholastic writers. When, however, in the next chapter he undertakes to prove, against quite a number of theologians of the highest character, that the natural law is a law in the strict sense, he does not seem to be very successful. He admits that, strictly speaking, a law should emanate from the will of a superior; and if we distinguish, as he does, between the law of nature and the eternal law of God —the latter alone being the binding will of God, the former residing somehow in, and emanating from, those who are bound by its enactments—it is difficult to find the superior from whose will the natural law may emanate. No one is superior to himself, or can make for himself a law in the strict sense of the word. Hence I find that the French canonist, Bouix, states that the natural law, as distinguished from the eternal law of God, is not a law in the strict sense—which agrees exactly with the explanation set forth in the last paragraph.

I am aware also that the natural law is often represented as a dictate of reason with regard to the moral quality of certain acts, according to which it would seem to be not so much the objective general truth which is known by the reason as the subjective act by which the intellect perceives the objective truth. This, also, seems to be a very loose conception. For just as the laws of motion existed objectively before ever there was any created reason to become aware of their existence, and would continue to exist even though all men and angels were annihilated next instant; so, even though there were only one man in the world, and he a lunatic or an infant, and therefore proximately incapable of any act of reason, it would be for him a real, though material, violation of the natural law, to get drunk or to commit suicide. Nay, even though there were no man in existence actually, as long as men are possible, sin is possible, and these possible sins must be conceived as being against the natural law. This proves that the natural law of morals, just like the natural laws of motion or of the refraction of light, are objective truths and not merely subjective perceptions. They are, therefore, general truths based on nature—that is, on the relations between things which are capable of being governed by law, either towards one another or towards other beings. These general truths are capable of being known by human reason, which intues these essences and discovers the order between them, deducing conclusions from these primary intuitions. It is, therefore, only in a less strict sense, as so many theologians and jurists have taught, that the natural law of morals can be called a law.

57

THE NATURAL LAW

Victor Cathrein [1]

All created things have implanted in their natures certain guiding principles, necessary to their corresponding activities. Man must be no exception to this rule. He must be led by a natural inborn light, manifesting to him what he is to do or not to do. This natural light is the natural law. When we speak of man as possessing a natural, inborn light, it is not to be understood in the sense that man has innate ideas. Innate ideas do not exist. It is true, nevertheless, that the Creator has endowed man with the ability and the inclination to form many concepts and develop principles. As soon as he comes to the use of reason, he forms, by a natural necessity, on the basis of experience, certain general concepts of theoretical reason—e. g., those of being and not being, of cause and effect, of space and time—and so he arrives at universal principles, e. g., that "nothing can exist and not exist at the same time," that "every effect has its cause," etc. As it is in the theoretical, so, also, in the practical order. As soon as reason has been sufficiently developed, and the individual can somehow or other practically judge that he is something more than a mere animal, by an intrinsic necessity of his nature he forms the concept of good and evil, i. e., of something which is proper to the rational nature which distinguishes him from the brute, and which is, therefore, worth striving for, and something which is unbecoming and, therefore, to be avoided. And as by nature he feels himself attracted by what is good and repelled by what is evil, he naturally forms the judgments, that "good is to be done and evil avoided," that "man ought to live according to the dictates

---

[1] *Catholic Encyclopedia*, Vol. V, p. 562.

of reason," etc. From his own reflections, especially when assisted by instruction from others, he easily comes to the conclusion that in these judgments the will of a superior being, of the Creator and Designer of nature, has its expression. Around about him he perceives that all things are well ordered, so that it is very easy for him to discern in him the handiwork of a superior and all-wise power. He himself has been appointed to occupy in the domain of nature the position of lord and master; he, too, must lead a well-regulated life, as befits a rational being, not merely because he himself chooses to do so, but also in obedience to his Creator. Man did not give himself his nature with all its faculties and inclinations; he received it from a superior being, whose wisdom and power are everywhere manifest to him in creation.

The general practical judgments and principles: "Do good and avoid evil," "Lead a life regulated according to reason," etc., from which all the Commandments of the Decalogue are derived, are the basis of the natural law, of which St. Paul (Rom., ii, 14) says, that it is written in the hearts of all men. This law is an emanation of the Divine law, made known to all men by nature herself; it is the expression of the will of nature's Author, a participation of the created rational being in the eternal law of God. Hence the obligation it imposes does not arise from man's own autonomy, as Kant held, nor from any other human authority, but from the Will of the Creator; and man cannot violate it without rebelling against God, his Master, offending Him, and becoming amenable to His justice. How deeply rooted among all nations this conviction of the higher origin of the natural law was, is shown by the fact that for various violations of it (as murder, adultery, perjury, etc.), they did their utmost to propitiate the angered deity by means of prayers and sacrifices. Hence they looked upon the deity as the guardian and protector of the moral order, who would not allow the contempt of it to go unpunished. The same conviction is manifested by the value all nations have attached to the moral order, a value far surpassing that of all other earthly goods. The noblest among the nations maintained that it was better to undergo any hardship, even death itself, rather than prove recreant to one's duty. They understood, therefore, that, over and above earthly treasures, there were higher and more lasting goods whose attainment was dependent upon the observance of the moral order, and this not by reason of any ordinance of man, but because of the law of God. This being premised, it is clearly impossible to divorce morality from religion without robbing it of its true obligation and sanction, of its sanctity and inviolability and of its importance as transcending every other earthly consideration.

The natural law consists of general practical principles (commands and prohibitions) and the conclusions necessarily flowing therefrom. It is the peculiar function of man to formulate these conclusions himself, though instruction and training are to assist him in doing so. Besides this, each individual has to take these principles as the guide of his conduct and apply them to his particular actions. This, to a certain extent, everybody does spontaneously, by virtue of an innate tendency. As in the case of all practical things, so in regard to what concerns the moral order, reason uses syllogistic processes. When a person, e. g., is on the point of telling a lie, or saying what is contrary to his convictions, there rises before his mental vision the general precept of the natural law: "Lying is wrong and forbidden." Hence he avails himself, at least virtually, of the following syllogism: "Lying is forbidden; what you are about to say is a lie; therefore, what you are about to say is forbidden." The conclusion thus arrived at is our conscience, the proximate norm of our conduct. Conscience, therefore, is not an obscure feeling or a sort of moral instinct, but a practical judgment of our reason on the moral character of individual acts. If we follow the voice of conscience, our reward is peace and calm of soul; if we resist this voice, we experience disquiet and remorse.

The natural law is the foundation of all human laws and precepts. It is only because we recognize the necessity of authority for human society, and because the natural law enjoins obedience to regularly constituted authority, that it is possible for a human superior to impose laws and commands binding in conscience. Indeed, all human laws and precepts are fundamentally the conclusions, or more minute determinations, of the general principles of the natural law, and for this very reason every deliberate infraction of a law or precept binding in conscience is a sin, i. e., the violation of a Divine commandment, a rebellion against God, an offence against Him, which will not escape punishment in this life or in the next, unless duly repented of before death.

58

THE PRECEPTS OF THE NATURAL LAW

Joseph Rickaby [1]

Of the precepts of the Natural Law, some are more simple and of wider extension; others are derivative, complex, and extend to fewer cases. It is a question of more and less, and no hard and fast line of demarkation can be drawn between them. The former, however, are called *primary,* the latter *secondary* precepts. Again the nature of man is the same in all men and at all periods of history for its essential elements, but admits of wide accidental variation and declension for the worse. Thirdly, it is clear that Natural Law is a law good and suitable for human nature to observe. Starting from these three axioms, we apply the reasoning of St. Thomas, 1a, 2ae, q. 96, art. 2, not to human law alone, of which he is speaking, but to sundry secondary precepts of Natural Law. These are his words:

"A law is laid down as a rule or measure of human acts. Now a measure ought to be homogeneous with the thing measured. Hence laws also must be imposed upon men according to their condition. As Isidore says: 'A law ought to be possible both according to nature and according to the custom of the country.' Now the power or faculty of action proceeds from interior habit or disposition. The same thing is not possible to him who has no habit of virtue, that is possible to a virtuous man; as the same thing is not possible to a boy and to a grown man, and therefore the same rule is not laid down for children as for adults. Many things are allowed to children, that in adults are

---

[1] *Moral Philosophy,* pp. 371-373. (Longmans, Green and Company, New York.) With permission.

visited with legal punishment or with blame, and in like manner many things must be allowed to men not perfect in virtue, which would be intolerable in virtuous men."

This reasoning leads us up to a conclusion, which St. Thomas states thus (1a, 2ae, q. 94, art. 5):

"A conceivable way in which the Natural Law might be changed is the way of subtraction, that something should cease to be of the Natural Law that was of it before. Understanding change in this sense, the Natural Law is absolutely immutable in its first principles; but as to secondary precepts, which are certain detailed conclusions closely related to the first principles, the Natural Law is not so changed as that its dictate is not right in most cases steadily to abide by; it may, however, be changed in some particular case, and in rare instances, through some special causes impeding the observance of these secondary precepts."

The reason for this conclusion, more pregnant, it may be, than St. Thomas himself discerned, is given briefly as follows (2a, 2ae, q. 57, art. 2, ad 1):

"Human nature is changeable; and therefore what is natural to man may sometimes fail to hold good."

The precepts of Natural Law that fail to be applicable when human nature sinks below par, are only secondary precepts, and few even of them. Christianity brings human nature up to par, and *fulfils* the Natural Law (St. Matt. v. 17), enjoining the observance of it in its integrity. This is the meaning of St. John Chrysostom's saying: "Of old not such an ample measure of virtue was proposed to us; . . . but since the coming of Christ the way has been made much narrower." (*De Virginitate*, c. 44: cf. his 17th Homily on St. Matt. v. 37; indeed the doctrine is familiar in his pages.) Thus the prohibition of polygamy, being a secondary precept of the natural law, failed in its application in that age of lapsed humanity, when a woman was better one of many wives, protected by one husband, than exposed to promiscuous violence and lust. (Isaias iv. 1.)

59

MORAL LAW

Timothy Brosnahan [1]

The moral necessity inherent in law is imposed by self, by one's equal, or by one's superior. The first empties the concept of obligation of all content; one cannot have authority over oneself and be subject to oneself in the same respect. The control of reason, and of will over lower faculties is not authoritative. Kant's distinction between the noumenal and phenomenal man, and the subjection of one to the other is futile. The second is untenable; as moral beings, all men are equal, and no man or body of men has original jurisdiction over another man or can bind him in conscience. Such jurisdiction as they have must be derived from an authority that is superior to them and their subjects.

Reason makes known to us a moral law: (a) that between good and evil actions there is a difference which is intrinsic to the nature of things, which is founded in the three essential relations of man, i. e., to self, to others, and to the Creator, which consequently arises from a necessary connection or opposition to man's ultimate end and absolute good; (b) that the former are unconditionally prescribed and the latter in like manner prohibited. These imperatives of reason have the attributes of law; they are universal, i. e., experienced by all men; objective, i. e., not produced, but perceived by reason; constant, i. e., independent of the variations of times, places, and persons. Therefore there is a moral law. But it must exist somewhere. It cannot exist in material things; it can exist nowhere or nohow but in a Mind. An absolute and objective moral law must exist in a Mind which is the source and archetype of whatever is true in our moral judgments. The true in our moral judgments is the expression of our essential relations to reality. Therefore, the absolute moral ideal of right exists in a Mind that is the source of all reality, other than itself.

Though in form law is an ordination of superior reason

---

[1] *Digests of Lectures on Ethics*, pp. 35-37. (John Murphy Company, Baltimore.)

directing subject reason, it is in effect a necessity put by a superior will on a subject will to follow the direction of the ordinating reason. An act of legislation, therefore, is from reason presupposing an act of will in virtue of which it directs and moves through reason. The source of moral law, therefore, is the Will of a being which is the source of all reality, and which has supreme authority over every created will—the Divine Will.

All law supposes subjects or a community. Logically prior to the decree of creation, there could be no subjects of moral law. The Divine Will imposing moral law presupposes, therefore, the decree of creation. Now God was free to create or not create, but having decreed to create, He must necessarily create beings which in varying degrees of perfection were analogues of His Divine Essence and Nature. But such being must be in nature vestigial or imitative manifestations of the Divine activity, and have modes of operations which are to be conformed to the archetypal ideas of God. Therefore, the Divine Will, supposing the decree of creation, necessarily willed that all creatures should act in accord with their natures, necessarily, if they are irrational, freely if they are rational. The moral law, or the decree of the Divine Will obliging all free agents to act in a defined way, is necessary, universal, and immutable, since it is on God's part the expression of the Divine Practical Reason, and on man's part written in his reason in so far as that reason is an analogue of Divine Reason.

60

THE MORAL OBLIGATION OF CIVIL LAW

John A. Ryan [1]

The State performs its functions by means of law. Through the direct or indirect authorization of law, taxes are collected, public money is expended, public services, such as, the post office, the public schools, the department of justice, the fire department, the police department, are administered, and the various regulatory measures affecting

---

[1] *The Church and State*, pp. 244-259. (The Macmillan Company, New York.) Reprinted with permission of the publishers.

individuals and associations are ordained and enforced. It is law that warrants and supports every civil act performed by any official in any of the three great departments of government, the executive, the legislative and the judiciary. When a public official proceeds without the authorization of law or exceeds the scope of the law, his action has no civil validity.

The authority of the State to make laws is derived from God.[2] He has endowed men with such qualities and needs that they cannot live reasonable lives without the State. Therefore, He wishes the State to exist and to function in such a way as to attain this end, to promote man's temporal welfare. It does so by means of law. Hence civil law is genuine moral law, not merely a kind of legal or physical coercion. It binds in conscience. Herein it differs from the rules of a social club. The latter do not produce moral obligation. Even though they should be disregarded to such an extent as to destroy the club, its members would suffer no vital injury. On the other hand, men are deprived of a necessary means to human life and development when there is general disobedience of the laws of the State. The moral law which binds men to live reasonable lives, obliges them to adopt one of the essential means to this end, that is, to maintain the State and to obey its laws.

Such is the rational basis of the doctrine laid down in Holy Scripture, and taught without variation by the Catholic Church. According to this doctrine, the civil law binds in conscience, as such; not because it includes, nor only in so far as it includes, natural, or supernatural, or ecclesiastical law.[3]

No declaration of any Church authority can be cited in favor of the contrary opinion. A few individual writers have held it, but the overwhelming majority of theologians teach that the civil law is morally binding on its own account, because of the moral authority possessed by the State.[4]

[2] Cf. Pope Leo XIII, *The Christian Constitution of States*.
[3] Cf. Bouquillon, *Theologia Moralis Fundamentalis*, no. 223.
[4] The greatest authority on law among Catholic theologians, Francisco Suarez, S. J., declares that this is the "common opinion of Catholics." His own defense of the proposition is summed up in three declarations: The civil legislator makes laws as the minister of God; the legislator is required by the divine and natural

Of course, all ethically valid civil laws must be in harmony with the moral law of nature. A statute which is contrary to a precept of the natural law, has no moral force, however solemnly it may have been enacted, or formidably sanctioned, or vigorously enforced. Such an enactment is not law at all, but, as St. Thomas calls it, "a species of violence."

CIVIL LAW BASED ON NATURAL LAW

Indeed, all civil law may properly be regarded as either a reaffirmation of the natural law, or as an application of its precepts, principles or derived conclusions.[5] Of the former kind are the statutes forbidding theft, assault, and adultery. To the latter class belong the laws which determine individual property rights and prescribe the imposition and collection of taxes, and ordinances for the regulation of traffic on streets and roads. The natural law dictates that men should acquire and use external goods with a just regard to the rights of their fellows, but it does not inform them just how this requirement is to be observed and applied in particular cases. In virtue of the natural law, men are obliged to maintain the government, but there is no specific precept requiring this end to be attained through a certain form of taxation. We are enjoined by the natural law to refrain from inflicting physical injury upon the neighbor in our common use of the public streets, as well as in other relations, but we are not told whether the speed limit should be ten miles an hour or twenty. In all such cases, the general provisions and precepts of the natural law stand in need of specific and precise determination by the positive law. Civil statutes for this purpose derive their immediate moral authority and validity from the State itself. Their binding force cannot come directly from the natural law, since the latter is so general in its provisions that other specific determinations, for example, other property regulations and traffic regulations, might be equally in harmony with these general provisions. Natural law cannot oblige men to comply with its general provisions in a particular way, when another way would be

law to pass laws; this power and its exercise are necessary for the common good. *De Legibus*, lib. III, cap. 21.

[5] Cf. Cronin, *The Science of Ethics*, II, 599, 600.

equally efficacious. The function of prescribing one method rather than another belongs to the State. Its right to make such a prescription flows from the fact that it is the authorized and the only competent agency to determine and enforce necessary and uniform methods of carrying into effect the general principles of the natural law in all such matters. The obligation of the citizens to observe these methods and regulations is based ultimately on the natural law, but its immediate and formal basis is the State.[6]

The objection might be raised that all the foregoing instances and the reasoning that they are intended to illustrate, refer only to civil ordinances which are *necessary*. The moral obligation to obey such statutes is as clear as the obligation to maintain an effective political organization. In both cases we can trace the compelling and obligatory influence of the natural law. Its precepts require men to deal justly and charitably with one another, and to make and obey whatever civil regulations are necessary to attain this end. But the case seems to be different with those civil statutes which prescribe and administer things that are merely *useful*. Government regulation of street traffic is necessary, but government ownership of railroads is not necessary. Whence comes the moral obligation upon the citizens to obey the law which forbids them to own a railroad?

The answer is that the obligation is derived ultimately from the natural law, precisely as in the case of the traffic ordinance. Just as the State has the authority to prescribe one maximum rate of speed rather than another, so it has the right to determine that goods and passengers shall be carried by the government rather than by private corporations. In both cases the end is the common welfare. In both cases the State must adopt some means to attain this

[6] It is in this sense that St. Thomas speaks of civil law as a "participation in the eternal and natural law." Suarez draws the distinction clearly between a civil law conceived as obligatory because and when it contains or applies a *specific precept* of the natural law, or a necessary conclusion therefrom, and a civil law, or the whole body of civil law, conceived as obligatory because it is based on the *general principle* of the natural law which requires ordinances to be obeyed. He declares that if those who deny that the civil law binds in conscience hold to the latter instead of the former conception, the dispute is perhaps merely one of language. They agree with him in principle. *Idem, loc. cit.*

end. In each case more than one means would be adequate. Some speed limit must be prescribed, but it need not be fifteen miles per hour rather than twenty. As compared with the latter, the former is merely useful, and *vice versa*. The case of the railroads is exactly parallel. They are necessary for the common welfare. They can attain this end substantially under either private or public ownership. The issue between the two methods is merely one of utility, and the State is not clearly obliged to choose one rather than the other. But it must authorize some one of the two. When it adopts government ownership, its action is morally binding on the citizens for the same reason that makes its traffic regulations morally binding. That is, it is determining a method of promoting the common good, in virtue of its authority as the only competent determinant of such matters. The obligation of the citizens to accept the determination actually made, *i. e.*, government ownership, comes immediately from the authority of the State, but ultimately from that principle of the natural law which dictates that men should support all the legitimate activities of the State.

Individual citizens may think, and their opinion may be correct, that government ownership of railroads is less useful, less conducive to the common good, than private ownership. Nevertheless, they are morally obliged to accept the former for the sake of that same common good. Their refusal to do so would cause greater injury to the community than the continuation of and their acquiescence in the duly established arrangement. It would imply that a group of individuals may at any time reject any civil ordinance with which they do not agree. The contradiction is obvious between this position and the requirements of right reason, of the natural law, of the common good, and of individual welfare.

The sum of the matter is that every law enacted by a legitimate government, and not contrary to any provision of the natural law, whether its prescriptions are evidently necessary or merely useful, is in some degree morally binding on the citizens. The fundamental reason is the necessity, according to the divine plan, of an effectively functioning State for human welfare.

It has just been said that every genuine civil enactment is morally binding "in some degree." This phrase brings up for consideration certain modifications, or qualifications, of the general principle. It suggests these questions: Do civil laws bind under pain of mortal sin? Does their obligatory character depend upon the will of the legislator? Are some civil statutes "purely penal"? Does the validity of civil laws depend upon their acceptance by the people?

CIVIL LAWS OF GRAVE OBLIGATION

To the first of these questions the answer of the great majority of Catholic writers is in the affirmative. The reason is tersely stated by Suarez: Inasmuch as civil law binds in conscience, it necessarily produces a degree of obligation proportionate to its subject matter; if the latter is of grave importance, the obligation of obeying the law will likewise be grave.[7] Generally speaking, the person who violates a civil statute which prescribes some action of great importance for the commonwealth, is guilty of mortal sin. This proposition can be logically rejected only on the assumption that no civil law can be of great importance.

Such is the obligatory force of a momentous law, considered in itself. But we are confronted with the second question raised above. Does the obligation depend upon the will of the legislator? It is the unanimous, or practically unanimous, teaching of Catholic authorities that the intention of creating a moral obligation is of the essence of law, so that, a prescription by legislators who positively and explicitly intended that it should not bind in conscience, would not be a true law. It would be merely a direction, a counsel, or an expression of legislative preference. If the *existence* of moral obligation depends upon the will of the legislator, the same dependence must logically be predicated of the *degree* of obligation. Hence, the general opinion among Catholic moral theologians is that the legislator has the authority to render grave laws only slightly obligatory.[8] That is, a law which of itself would bind under pain of mortal sin, brings upon the transgressor merely venial guilt when this is the desire and intention of the legislator.

In order that a civil law should become obligatory to a grave degree two conditions are, therefore, necessary: First,

---

[7] Op. cit., lib. 3, cap. 24, no. 2.
[8] Cf. Suarez, op. cit., lib. 3, cap. 27.

that the subject matter be of great importance; second, that the legislator should intend the law to have this effect in the forum of conscience. Either of these conditions lacking, the law binds only under pain of venial sin. If the subject matter is of slight importance the legislator cannot perform the inherently contradictory feat of making the obligation grave; if the legislator does not wish a gravely important law to bind under pain of mortal sin it will not be obligatory in this degree.

THE INTENTION OF THE LEGISLATOR

A very important question arises here concerning the form which the legislator's intention must take in order to make an obligation slight which from the nature of the subject matter would be grave. Suppose he does not think about moral obligation at all, but merely has in mind the enactment of a law. In that case the law will bind in conscience, and the degree of the obligation will be determined by the importance of the subject matter. This is the normal effect of a true law, and it is always produced, so long as it is not positively excluded by the intention of the legislator. Suppose that the legislator explicitly desires that the law should be obligatory, but does not think about the degree of obligation. As in the former case, the obligation will be determined by the subject matter. If the latter is gravely important the law will be gravely obligatory. Therefore, a civil law of great importance always binds under pain of mortal sin, unless the legislator forms a positive intention to the contrary. A merely negative attitude toward the obligation will have no effect upon the obligation.[9]

The opponents of the doctrine that the legislator can render slight the obligation of a grave law, contend that the degree of binding force carried by a civil law depends exclusively upon the subject matter. The legislator's power is merely that of making or not making the statute.[1] This argument would lead logically to the conclusion that the existence of any obligation at all is entirely independent of the will of the legislator. Should the members of a legislative body explicitly will that their enactments should not be binding in conscience this reservation would be without

[9] Cf. Suarez, loc. cit.
[1] Cf. Suarez, *ibidem*.

effect. Suarez declares that such an enactment is not a true law; but this seems to be mostly a question of language.

Consider an ordinance which is clearly necessary for the common good, as, that which regulates the speed of vehicles. Does not the very necessity of this measure make it binding in conscience? It is true that a different law might be equally adapted to meet this necessity; and the inference might be drawn that the citizen who observed the provisions of this alternative and hypothetical rule would be under no obligation to obey the existing law. The reply is that the common good requires the enactment and the observance of *one* ordinance. Human welfare is not safeguarded through a kind of private interpretation by the citizens themselves of what constitutes a reasonable rule or standard. Now it is the proper and necessary function of the legislators to enact this uniform regulation. Once it has been chosen out of several possible ordinances, it becomes morally binding because of its necessity for the common good, no matter what the legislators may think of obligation. It is reasonable and necessary that they determine the provisions of the law, but it is neither reasonable nor necessary that they have power to determine the question of its moral obligation.

Even laws which are not necessary for the common welfare may conceivably be obligatory against the desires of the legislators. For the common good may require that a law of this sort, even though no more useful than the alternative arrangement, be obeyed for the sake of social order. Violations of it might be detrimental to the public good merely because they were violations of duly enacted law. In such a situation, why should the unwillingness of the legislator to impose moral obligation have any moral effect or significance?

Whatever may be thought of the foregoing argument, the question whether the legislator has power to render a grave law only slightly obligatory, has no practical importance in modern communities. No legislative body ever thinks of exercising such power. Therefore, modern civil laws dealing with gravely important matters always produce their normal effect of binding under pain of mortal sin.[2]

[2] Cf. Meyer, *Institutiones Juris Naturalis*, II, p. 569.

The doctrine that the moral obligation of civil law depends to some extent upon the intention of the legislator, is sometimes made the basis of an extraordinary view of modern civil legislation. It is nothing less than the conclusion that the ordinances of practically all modern legislative bodies have no binding force in conscience. Laws do not bind in conscience unless the legislator intends them so to bind; now contemporary lawmakers cannot have such an intention since they do not believe in the existence of genuine moral obligation. Such is the argument. Tanquerey rejects it on the ground that whatever may be their general and theoretical attitude toward the reality of moral obligation, modern legislators do desire their enactments to have the utmost possible force and authority; hence they *implicitly* intend them to be morally binding.[3] Bouquillon takes a similar position, declaring that the legislator need not expressly intend to impose an obligation in conscience, that it is insufficient for him to have the intention of issuing a genuine command.[4] Lehmkuhl holds the same view as Tanquerey and Bouquillon, and points out that if explicit intention to bind the conscience were indispensable, the laws enacted by Pagan rulers would be without obligatory force, which is surely contrary to the teaching of Holy Scripture.[5] Suarez declares that the design of the legislator to make a true law suffices, and that the formal intention to bind in conscience is not necessary. He notes that legislators, particularly unbelievers, rarely advert to the question of moral obligation.[6] Indeed, it seems to be the general opinion of the moral theologians that an implicit intention suffices; that is, the intention that the enactment should have all the moral authority which attaches to a genuine law.

This conclusion seems to be entirely consistent with the "necessity of intention" doctrine, as regards two classes of lawmakers who have no explicit desire to bind in conscience; namely, those who believe that civil law is morally obligatory but do not advert to this fact at the moment of legislating, and those who theoretically disbelieve in genuine moral obligation, but who are willing that if perchance it

[3] *Theologia Moralis Fundamentalis*, no. 343.
[4] *Theologia Moralis Fundamentalis*, no. 223.
[5] *Theologia Moralis*, I, no. 211.
[6] Op. cit., lib. 3, cap. 27, no. 7.

does exist it should attach to their ordinances. In the minds of both these classes, there is inherent a true implicit intention to make the law binding in conscience.

As regards those lawmakers who are firmly persuaded that civil laws are not obligatory in the proper sense, for example, those who, with the English jurist, John Austin, reduce the moral obligation of legal statutes to the evil chance of incurring the penalty for violation,—it is not clear that there exists even an implicit intention to produce moral obligation.[7] Tanquerey contends for the reality of such an intention on the ground that the legislator desires his laws to exercise all possible compelling force upon the will of the citizens, and, therefore, is quite willing that the latter should feel bound in conscience. Nevertheless, this is not an implicit intention to impose *objective* moral obligation. It does not recognize the objective bond which is the essence of genuine obligation, the bond between the will of the law giver and the will of the law receiver. The only thing covered by such an intention is the state of mind of the citizen. That this should be affected by a persuasion of obligation, the lawmaker is perfectly willing; that the objective moral bond constituting obligation should extend from his will to the will of the citizen, the lawmaker has not even an implicit intention, for he totally rejects the possibility of such a bond. His intention comprises only a subjective condition, not an objective relation. It is hard to see how such legislators can have even an implicit intention, either to make a true law, or to impose moral obligation.

As a matter of fact, it is very doubtful that many contemporary legislators deny to civil laws the possibility of moral obligation in the absolute and comprehensive manner supposed in the preceding paragraph. Probably the great majority of them accept, at least in some vague way, the existence, or at any rate, the possibility of a juristic moral bond between law giver and law receiver. This is a sufficient basis for an implicit intention to bind in conscience. Therefore, the general opinion of moral theologians that modern civil laws bind in conscience, is consistent with their teaching that this moral force is, in some degree, dependent upon the will of the legislator. To be sure, the case for the

---

[7] Cf. Slater, *Questions of Moral Theology*, pp. 279-288.

moral obligation of contemporary laws becomes clearer and simpler if we accept the theory that their obligatory character is independent of the legislator's will and is inherent in the laws themselves.

PURELY PENAL LAWS

The third question raised above concerns those laws which jurists and theologians call "purely penal," or "merely penal," or "distinctive." They are defined as laws which oblige the citizen either to obey them or to accept the penalty appointed for their violation. The obligation is not absolute, but conditional. If the citizen is ready to submit to the penalty he can licitly disobey the provisions of the law. Generally speaking, however, he is not bound in conscience to undergo the penalty until it has been formally imposed by the court. He is not obliged to give himself up, nor to forego his civil right of legal defence.

The great majority of moral theologians hold that the legislator has authority to enact laws of this sort. In the first place, it is contended that the object of the law and the common good may sometimes be more effectively promoted by a statute which leaves the citizen free to disobey the law and become morally liable to the penalty, than by one which gives no such choice but entails moral guilt every time it is violated. Such are laws which men transgress with uncommon frequency, but whose object can be adequately attained through the infliction of penalties upon their violators. A purely penal law is, in some sense, a concession to human weakness. The second reason given by the theologians to support the proposition under consideration is the legislator's power over the obligatory character of his enactments. Just as he can determine that a gravely important law shall bind only under pain of venial sin, so he can make the obligation of certain laws disjunctive. That is, he may attach the obligation either to the observance of the law or to the acceptance of the penalty, so that the citizen has the option of being bound to the latter instead of the former.

It is to be observed that a purely penal law must carry some obligation. The legislator cannot enact a statute which would bind the citizen neither to obey its provisions nor to accept its penalties.[8] Such an enactment would not be a true law, inasmuch as it would lack an essential element, namely, moral binding force. Hence the legislator must have at least the implicit intention of morally obliging the citizen to accept the penalty in case of violation.

It seems, however, that the practical obligation of a purely penal law is attenuated almost to the vanishing point. If the violator of the law is not obliged to make known his transgression, nor to waive his legal right of defence, his duty of "accepting the penalty" is merely that of submitting to the sentence of the court. That is, he must not break jail nor evade payment of a fine. When the offender evades apprehension, he escapes all moral obligation; when he successfully contests prosecution, he, likewise, remains free from moral accountability; when he is convicted, his moral obligation is merely that of omitting actions from which, in most cases, he is physically restrained by the sheriff or the policeman. In a word, the moral obligation of a purely penal law is next to nothing, its moral sanction, *i. e.*, the effectiveness of the moral element in preventing violations, is practically nothing.

These facts create a strong presumption that the field of purely penal law is extremely limited. The objective reason why civil law carries moral obligation is found ultimately in human welfare. If the law be deprived, or all but deprived, of its moral element its efficacy for the promotion of human welfare is greatly, even fatally, weakened. Nevertheless, the assertion is sometimes made that in our day all civil laws are merely penal.

Some who use this language, do not mean what they seem to mean. They wish to assert the theory, sufficiently discussed above, that modern laws do not bind in conscience, inasmuch as modern legislators have not the proper intention. If this contention were sound civil legislation would not even rise to the dignity of purely penal enactments; for the latter do entail some moral obligation. Those who, using the phrase in its proper sense, declare that all modern civil legislation is purely penal, are, happily, neither numerous nor authoritative. According to the common opinion of moral theologians, the presumption is always in favor

---

[8] Cf. Suarez, op. cit., lib. 3, cap. 27, no. 3.

of complete obligation.[9] Like all other presumptions, this one can be overcome only by positive facts and arguments. With regard to any particular law, the burden of proof rests upon him who contends that it is purely penal.

As commonly given by theologians, there are three tests by which a civil law may be adjudged purely penal: First, the declaration of the legislator; second, the attitude of popular tradition and custom; third, the enactment of a penalty so severe that it is out of all proportion to the law's importance. However, the second and third of these criteria are not valid universally; for the custom may be socially injurious, and the heavy penalty may be designed to prevent unusual frequency of violation, not to indicate that the law is to be regarded as purely penal.

Bouquillon adds another restriction which seems to be fundamental. It is that no law can be reasonably regarded as purely penal unless the burden or penalty attached to its violation is *specifically* adapted to attain the end of the law.[1] The penalty must be such as to compensate for the failure of the law; it may not be merely coercive. Thus, heavy fines may offset the loss to the public treasury through the non-observance of tax laws. In such a case, the law might fairly be interpreted as purely penal. But fines and imprisonment would not adequately achieve the end of a traffic ordinance, *i. e.*, safeguarding life and property. It is not easy to controvert this argument.

POPULAR ACCEPTANCE

The final question concerning the degree of obligation attaching to civil laws, is whether their binding force depends upon popular acceptance or ratification. At first sight, an affirmative answer would seem to contradict the general doctrine of the foregoing pages, namely, that civil legislation binds in conscience. However, there is no necessary contradiction; for civil ordinances might conceivably not attain the complete character of laws until they had been ratified by the people. In that supposition, the people would constitute an essential part of the legislative authority. The obligation of individual citizens to obey a statute would begin when the latter had been formally accepted by

---

[9] Cf. Tanquerey, op. cit., no. 347.
[1] Op. cit., p. 353.

the people as a whole. Only then would "the will of the legislator" have become fully manifest and formally effective.

Suarez informs us that in his time this was the commonly held opinion of the jurists.[2] He cites eight or ten important names, and admits that their view seems to have been anticipated by Aristotle. Their argument was briefly as follows: In order to make binding laws, the legislator must have both the authority and the will. In fact, he has neither. That he lacks moral *power* to legislate validly without the people's consent, is shown by the fact that his authority to govern and to make any laws at all is derived from the people; and they have given him legislative authority on condition that his ordinances shall become binding only when accepted by the people. That this condition is attached to the grant of authority, is evident from the "most ancient usage of the Roman people," and from the fact that popular acceptation is the best indication that a law really promotes the common good, just as the contrary attitude of the people proves the law to be socially harmful and thus without validity. The *will* to make binding laws without the consent of the people is wanting to the legislator because he cannot have a genuine intention of doing something for which he lacks authority.

In passing it is worthy of note that these ultra-democratic jurists all wrote before the beginning of the seventeenth century. This was the period when Catholic teaching supported political absolutism and political oppression generally, according to the perverted notions that still pass in many quarters as history. Major, one of the writers cited by Suarez, declared that the community is superior to the prince in all things that pertain to sovereignty; yet this doctrine gives many of us a disagreeable shock when it falls upon our ears in such a modernized version as "the people are the masters, the public official is their servant." It is likewise noteworthy that in support of their theory of popular acceptance of laws, these writers appeal to a principle which no one disputed in their day, namely, that rulers and legislators derive their authority from the people. The inference drawn from this principle by the jurists was not

---

[2] Op. cit., lib. 3, cap. 19, no. 7.

admitted by the moral theologians, but the principle itself was universally received.

Generally and *per se*, popular acceptance is not necessary for the validity of a civil law. Such is the unanimous teaching of the moral theologians. As stated by Suarez, the following are the main reasons which support this principle.[3] In every State that is not a pure democracy, the people have transferred supreme political power to the rulers and legislators, and have not retained the right of accepting or rejecting legislation. Secondly, the authority to legislate would be plainly futile if the people were morally free to obey or not to obey. Thirdly, usage shows that laws are held to be binding as soon as they have been regularly enacted and promulgated. In short, civil laws are obligatory without popular ratification, on account of the original grant of power to the rulers, on account of universal custom, and because this is necessary for the common good. It is not possible to overthrow this argument.

The general principle is subject, however, to certain qualifications and exceptions. Suarez notes that popular acceptance of the law is essential to its binding force when the people have attached that condition to the grant of legislative power. In the kingdom of Aragonia (a part of Medieval and benighted Spain, be it noted!) he says, the laws of the monarch do not become binding until they are ratified in public assemblies. On the same principle, certain enactments of legislative bodies in Switzerland, the United States, and New Zealand obtain the full force of law only when they have been approved by a popular referendum. Even in these States, the great majority of laws are recognized as valid as soon as they have been promulgated by the supreme legislative authority.

In the second place, Suarez points out that when a law is very frequently disregarded by the greater part of the people, the legislator may, through tacit consent, permit the law to be deprived of binding force. However, this is not an instance of direct popular authority over the law, but rather of revocation by the legislator. His tacit repeal of the law is indeed, occasioned by popular refusal to accept. In the third place, the law does not bind if it is not

---

[3] Op. cit., lib. 3, cap. 19, no. 7.

just, for an unjust law is no law at all. Fourthly, a law which is unreasonably burdensome to the people may sometimes lack obligatory force,—at least when it is so harsh that it is tantamount to an unjust enactment. Finally, when the majority of the people disregard the law to such an extent and in such a way that its observance by a minority becomes detrimental to the State, it ceases to bind the individual citizen.

To sum up: The Catholic Church, as well as natural reason, teaches that civil law binds in conscience. The ultimate basis of this obligation is the natural law; the immediate basis is the authority of the State. Civil laws of grave importance are gravely obligatory, unless the legislator formally intends their binding force to be slight. The general teaching of moral theologians is that a law is not binding without at least the implicit intention of the legislator. Some civil laws may be purely penal, but their number is probably small. In general, civil laws are binding without popular ratification.

61

SYNDERESIS

Thomas Slater [1]

Synderesis, or more correctly *synteresis,* is a term used by the Scholastic theologians to signify the habitual knowledge of the universal practical principles of moral action. The reasoning process in the field of speculative science presupposes certain fundamental axioms on which all science rests. Such are the principle of contradiction, "a thing can not be and not be at the same time," and self-evident truths like "the whole is greater than its part." These are the first principles of the speculative intellect. In the field of moral conduct there are similar first principles of action, such as, "evil must be avoided, good done"; "do not to others what you do not wish to be done to yourself"; "parents should be honored"; "we should live temperately and act justly." Such as these are self-evident truths in the field of moral conduct which any sane person

---

[1] *Catholic Encyclopedia,* Vol. XIV, pp. 384-385.

will admit if he understands them. According to the Scholastics, the readiness with which such moral truths are apprehended by the practical intellect is due to the natural habit impressed on the cognitive faculty which they call synderesis. While conscience is a dictate of the practical reason deciding that any particular action which I am contemplating is right or wrong, synderesis is a dictate of the same practical reason which has for its object the first general truths of moral action.

62

THE MORAL FACULTY
MICHAEL CRONIN [1]

By the Moral Faculty is meant that faculty by which we know the moral character of human acts. The expression "Moral Faculty" is sometimes, though not commonly, used to indicate the faculty in which good and evil reside, or that faculty which elicits good and evil *acts*—namely, the will. But at present we are dealing with the faculty which elicits *judgments* about good and evil—or, as it is called, the faculty of moral judgment. If we have not headed the present chapter with the title "the faculty of moral judgment," and thereby prevented all possibility of ambiguity, the reason is that by such an expression we might seem to anticipate a conclusion which we shall have to establish in the present chapter—viz., that the moral faculty is one of judgment and not a sense or instinct. This, we think, is sufficient reason for speaking of the present chapter as an inquiry into the "moral faculty" simply. We have said that by moral goodness is meant conformity between the human act and man's ultimate end, or between our acts and the law that is imposed upon us by our final end. And as the ultimate end of man and the law which that end imposes are known only through Intellect, so Intellect or Reason is the faculty by which the human mind judges of morality. Laws are not presented to the human mind as facts are, immediately and intuitively. Neither is the human mind directed to

[1] *Science of Ethics*, Vol. I, pp. 448-451. (Benziger Brothers, New York.)

the fulfilment of law as animals are b ythe compulsion of inner instinct. In the case of man, the knowledge of a law and direction of conduct by means of law always imply reasoning, and therefore, the Moral Faculty will be that faculty by which we are enabled to elicit reasoned judgments about good and evil.

And the truth of this proposition should be abundantly evident to us even from experience. For in ordinary life determination of morality involves, as we know, the reasoned application of one or many general laws to an individual case, and these laws are even quoted in justification of our action whenever we are questioned about it. The same laws which we give in justification of our action are the premises by which we reason that we are right in performing them. Reason, then, is the faculty by which the human mind determines what is right and wrong in human action.

Now, we need not say that in regarding Reason as the moral faculty we are far from claiming infallibility for this faculty. For Reason may go wrong in the sphere of morals just as it may in the sphere of physical science. But reason in the sphere of morals is as reliable as in any other sphere, and can lead the mind to certitude in simple as well as in complex cases, unless indeed the case be exceedingly complex, in which case the fault lies not with Reason, but either with the way in which the materials of our moral judgments are presented to us, or with the will, since often the will forces the Reason to issue judgments on only a slender examination of the case, judgments which of itself the Reason would not have issued.

The moral faculty is therefore the faculty of Reason or intellect. It is fundamentally that very faculty by which we carry on our deductions in mathematics or in any other science outside the sphere of morals. And what is called *Conscience* is merely the act which is elicited when we use this faculty on moral matters—the act, namely, by which we judge whether an act is good or bad. Moral judgments, therefore, are nothing but the judgments of our ordinary reason and intellect. But conscience is a particular function of our intellect, for in morals we have to do not with speculative truth, but with human actions. Hence, conscience is called an act not of the speculative but of the practical intellect. But the practical intellect of which conscience is a function is the ordinary practical intellect—the very same intellect which tells a man what to do or to avoid in ordinary extra-moral questions of the business of life—how, for instance, he ought to invest his money, or carry on a business, or preserve his health. Some Ethicians, indeed, speak of the act of Conscience as if it were a different thing subjectively from all other acts of the practical intellect, as if Conscience possessed a certain sacredness and authority based on the nature of the faculty itself which are present in no other intellectual act. The fact is that the sacredness which attaches to the act of conscience comes to it not from the faculty which elicits the act but from the object to which the act refers—viz., the "good" and duty. From the object of the moral faculty, indeed, there comes an element of sacredness which is not to be found in the object of any other faculty. But the act of conscience, as an act, or the faculty in which that act resides, and from which it springs, is not more sacred, *taken in itself,* than the common practical or speculative Reason which we use in mathematics or the other sciences. Conscience is an act of the "sicca lux intellectus" and no more.

The moral faculty then, we repeat, is the faculty of Reason or the practical intellect—the same faculty as that which guides us in business matters—in matters of ordinary human prudence.

63

CONSCIENCE

CARDINAL NEWMAN [1]

I assume, then, that Conscience has a legitimate place among our mental acts; as really so, as the action of memory, of reasoning, of imagination, or as the sense of the beautiful; that, as there are objects which, when presented to the mind, cause it to feel grief, regret, joy, or desire, so there are things which excite in us approbation or blame,

---

[1] *Grammar of Assent,* pp. 105-112. (Longmans, Green and Company, New York.)

and which we in consequence call right or wrong; and which, experienced in ourselves, kindle in us that specific sense of pleasure or pain, which goes by the name of a good or bad conscience. This being taken for granted, I shall attempt to show that in this special feeling, which follows on the commission of what we call right and wrong, lie the materials for the real apprehension of a Divine Sovereign and Judge.

The feeling of conscience being, I repeat, a certain keen sensibility, pleasant or painful,—self-approval and hope, or compunction and fear,—attendant on certain of our actions, which in consequence we call right or wrong, is twofold:— it is a moral sense, and a sense of duty; a judgment of the reason and a magisterial dictate. Of course its act is indivisible; still it has these two aspects, distinct from each other, and admitting of a separate consideration. Though I lost my sense of the obligation which I lie under to abstain from acts of dishonesty, I should not in consequence lose my sense that such actions were an outrage offered to my moral nature. Again; though I lost my sense of their moral deformity, I should not therefore lose my sense that they were forbidden to me. Thus conscience has both a critical and a judicial office, and though its promptings, in the breasts of the millions of human beings to whom it is given, are not in all cases correct, that does not necessarily interfere with the force of its testimony and of its sanction; its testimony that there is a right and a wrong, and its sanction to that testimony conveyed in the feelings which attend on right or wrong conduct. Here I have to speak of conscience in the latter point of view, not as supplying us, by means of its various acts, with the elements of morals, which may be developed by the intellect into an ethical code, but simply as the dictate of an authoritative monitor bearing upon the details of conduct as they come before us, and complete in its several acts, one by one.

Let us thus consider conscience, then, not as a rule of right conduct, but as a sanction of right conduct. This is its primary and most authoritative aspect; it is the ordinary sense of the word. Half the world would be puzzled to know what was meant by the moral sense; but every one knows what is meant by a good or bad conscience. Conscience is ever forcing on us by threats and by promises that we must follow the right and avoid the wrong; so far it is one and the same in the mind of every one, whatever be its particular errors in particular minds as to the acts which it orders to be done or to be avoided; and in this respect it corresponds to our perception of the beautiful and deformed. As we have naturally a sense of the beautiful and graceful in nature and art, though tastes proverbially differ, so we have a sense of duty and obligation, whether we all associate it with the same particular actions or not. Here, however, Taste and Conscience part company: for the sense of beautifulness, as, indeed, the Moral Sense, has no special relations to persons, but contemplates objects in themselves; conscience, on the other hand, is concerned with persons primarily, and with actions mainly as viewed in their doers, or rather with self alone and one's own actions, and with others only indirectly and as if in association with self. And further, taste is its own evidence, appealing to nothing beyond its own sense of the beautiful or the ugly, and enjoying the specimens of the beautiful simply for their own sake; but conscience does not repose on itself, but vaguely reaches forward to something beyond self, and dimly discerns a sanction higher than self for its decisions, as evidenced in that keen sense of obligation and responsibility which informs them. And hence it is that we are accustomed to speak of conscience as a voice,—a term which we should never think of applying to the sense of the beautiful; and, moreover, a voice, or the echo of a voice, imperative and constraining, like no other dictate in the whole of our experience.

And, again, in consequence of this prerogative of dictating and commanding, which is of its essence, Conscience has an intimate bearing on our affections and emotions, leading us to reverence and awe, hope and fear, especially fear, a feeling which is foreign for the most part, not only to Taste, but even to the Moral Sense, except in consequence of accidental associations. No fear is felt by any one who recognizes that his conduct has not been beautiful, though he may be mortified at himself, if, perhaps, he has thereby forfeited some advantage; but, if he has been betrayed into any kind of immorality, he has a lively sense of responsibility and guilt, though the act be no offence against society,—of distress and apprehension, even though it may be of present service to him,—of compunction and regret, though in itself it be most pleasurable,—of confusion of face, though it may have no witnesses. These various perturbations of mind, which are characteristic of a bad conscience, and may be very considerable,—self-reproach, poignant shame, haunting remorse, chill dismay at the prospect of the future,—and their contraries, when the conscience is good, as real though less forcible, self-approval, inward peace, lightness of heart, and the like,—these emotions constitute a generic difference between conscience and our other intellectual senses,—common sense, good sense, sense of expedience, taste, sense of honor, and the like,—as, indeed, they would also create between conscience and the moral sense, supposing these two were not aspects of one and the same feeling, exercised upon one and the same subject-matter.

So much for the characteristic phenomena, which conscience presents, nor is it difficult to determine what they imply. I refer once more to our sense of the beautiful. This sense is attended by an intellectual enjoyment, and is free from whatever is of the nature of emotion, except in one case, viz., when it is excited by personal objects; then it is that the tranquil feeling of admiration is exchanged for the excitement of affection and passion. Conscience, too, considered as a moral sense, an intellectual sentiment, is a sense of admiration and disgust, of approbation and blame; but it is something more than a moral sense; it is always what the sense of the beautiful is only in certain cases; it is always emotional. No wonder then that it always implies what that sense only sometimes implies; that it always involves the recognition of a living object, towards which it is directed. Inanimate things cannot stir our affections; these are correlative with persons. If, as is the case, we feel responsibility, are ashamed, are frightened, at transgressing the voice of conscience, this implies that there is One to whom we are responsible, before whom we are ashamed, whose claims upon us we fear. If, on doing wrong, we feel the same tearful, broken-hearted sorrow which overwhelms us on hurting a mother; if, on doing right, we enjoy the same sunny serenity of mind, the same soothing, satisfactory delight which follows on our receiving praise from a father, we certainly have within us the image of some person, to whom our love and veneration look, in whose smile we find our happiness, for whom we yearn, towards whom we direct our pleadings, in whose anger we are troubled and waste away. These feelings in us are such as require for their exciting cause an intelligent being; we are not affectionate towards a stone, nor do we feel shame before a horse or a dog; we have no remorse or compunction on breaking mere human law; yet, so it is, conscience excites all these painful emotions, confusion, foreboding, self-condemnation; and on the other hand it sheds upon us a deep peace, a sense of security, a resignation, and a hope, which there is no sensible, no earthly object to elicit. "The wicked flees, when no one pursueth"; then why does he flee? whence his terror? Who is it that he sees in solitude, in darkness, in the hidden chambers of his heart? If the cause of these emotions does not belong to this visible world, the Object to which his perception is directed must be Supernatural and Divine; and thus the phenomena of Conscience, as a dictate, avail to impress the imagination with the picture of a Supreme Governor, a Judge, holy, just, powerful, all-seeing, retributive, and is the creative principle of religion, as the moral sense is the principle of ethics.

And let me here refer again to the fact, to which I have already drawn attention, that this instinct of the mind recognizing an external Master in the dictate of conscience, and imaging the thought of Him in the definite impressions which conscience creates, is parallel to that other law of, not only human, but of brute nature, by which the presence of unseen individual beings is discerned under the shifting shapes and colors of the visible world. Is it by sense, or by reason, that brutes understand the real unities, material and spiritual, which are signified by the lights and shadows, the brilliant ever-changing kaleidoscope, as it may be called, which plays upon their *retina?* Not by reason, for they have not reason; not by sense, because they are transcending sense; therefore it is an instinct. This faculty on the part of brutes, unless we were used to it, would strike us as a great mystery. It is one peculiarity of animal natures to be susceptible of phenomena through the channels of sense; it is another to have in those sensible phenomena a perception of the individuals to which certain groups of them belong. This perception of individual things is given to brutes in large measures, and that, apparently from the moment of their birth. It is by no mere physical instinct, such as that which leads him to his mother for milk, that the new-dropped lamb recognizes each of his fellow-lambkins as a whole, consisting of many parts bound up in one, and, before he is an hour old, makes experience of his and their rival individualities. And much more distinctly do the horse and dog recognize even the personality of their masters. How are we to explain this apprehension of things, which are one and individual, in the midst of a world of pluralities and transmutations, whether in the instance of brutes or of children? But until we account for the knowledge which an infant has of its mother or his nurse, what reason have we to take exception at the doctrine, as strange and difficult, that in the dictate of conscience, without previous experiences or analogical reasoning, he is able gradually to perceive the voice, or the echoes of the voice, of a Master, living, personal, and sovereign?

64

CONSCIENCE

Ernest R. Hull [1]

If we view the universe as a self-made, self-existing system of things, and man as the most developed and exalted member of it—then we must recognize him as self-contained, autonomous, supreme, capable of self-determination, limited indeed in executive power by external forces, but otherwise absolute master of his own actions. And viewed in this light, there is no reason why he should not exercise complete liberty in self-determination—yielding to any suggestion of instinct or feeling or expediency, and determining his course accordingly if it seems well to do so; but still capable of rejecting all such suggestions, and taking the contrary course out of pure self-will, without fear and without reproach—since there is no assignable being outside himself who can claim the right of intruding upon his autonomy.

[1] *Why Should I Be Moral?* pp. 96-98. (Examiner Press, Bombay.)

But then comes the anomaly of conscience, which, although in itself a mere faculty, and therefore subordinate to the supremacy of the absolute self, assumes a tone of command which is absent from the other faculties, and seeks to impose its dictates even upon the autonomy of the free-will—not in such a way as to deprive it of its power of choice, but in such a way as to claim obedience as right, and to censure and condemn disobedience as wrong. How is this anomaly to be explained? Not surely by the weak expedient of explaining it away, as a disorder born of delusion; but rather by suspecting at least that it half conceals, half reveals an underlying mystery. And how can we penetrate into this mystery? Let us assume for the moment that there does exist—to adopt the beautiful expression of Matthew Arnold—"a something within us, not ourselves, which makes for righteousness"; and that the "something" is not merely something but *somebody*—a person other than ourselves, intimately present but still objective to us; a person ineffably superior to ourselves; a person on whom our very existence perhaps depends; a person who is himself the absolute embodiment of perfection or "righteousness," a person whose righteousness is the exemplar and model for the universe; a person possessed not only of intellect but of will, who has the right to impose upon us that will; who does so by commanding us to reproduce in ourselves a reflection of that righteousness which has its immeasurable fulness in him, thus imposing on us a law of righteousness which we are bound to obey; and finally, that in order to make this law known to us, he brands it indelibly on our mind as the categorical imperative of conscience.

I put this view forward for the moment not as an assertion but as a theory; as a hypothesis which may be provisionally accepted with a view of seeing how it solves our problem. And the least reflection will show that *as a hypothesis* it solves the problem entirely. Everything is now explained—the absolute nature of the dictate, its legitimacy and validity, its basis of right, its corollary of duty. Man retains his own absolute nature, in that he remains still in possession of the power to disobey; but he now finds his *inferior* and relative right restricted by a *superior* and absolute right, to which he ought in justice to yield. Hence there arises a restraint which is productive, not of disorder between the faculties but, on the contrary, of harmony between right and duty. Only when the free-will asserts itself against this right does a state of discord arise. But for this the free-will itself is responsible—because, being bound by a strict obligation to obey, it will not acknowledge its duty and prefers to disobey.

The outcome of this hypothesis can therefore be summed up as follows: So long as we look at man solely in himself, and in relation to his *immediate* environment—which is the universe—we are bound to regard him as an independent being, the supreme master of himself, and owing no absolute subjection to any other. But as soon as we extend our view to his *total* environment, we find that this includes not only the universe but something, or rather *somebody* at the back of the universe, who is man's supreme master, to whom man is subject, and whom he is bound to obey. And therefore, *in relation to this being,* man is no longer independent but intimately dependent. For if we ask what sort of a being it is who could have the power and the right to impose himself upon the autonomy of man, he can only be one who is the source and origin of the universe; one to whom the very existence and capabilities of man are due; to whom man belongs as so much *living property,* so that he can exercise supreme dominion over him with a far more complete title than that of a watchmaker over a watch or of a master over a slave. Among those who believe in his existence, this being is called God. By the name "God" we mean *the* infinitely perfect one, the source and cause of all that is, the creator, preserver and governor of the world, the moral exemplar and lawgiver to man, his ruler and ultimate judge. He it is who, after having founded the material universe, has furnished it with life, first of the lower order and then of the higher order. He has expressly made man in His own image and likeness—that is to say, a creature of intellect to seek *the true,* and of will to seek *the good.* Nay more, He has endowed him with the still higher perfection of internal autonomy, so that he may be the arbiter of his own actions and of his own destiny. Thus He has made man capable of evil, in order that his acceptance of good may not be the outcome of necessity but of free choice—that it may be man's *own* work. Corresponding to these two alternatives of good and evil, He has marked out for man a twofold destiny—a finality of happiness if he chooses the right, and a finality of evil if he chooses the wrong. He has therefore established man, thus equipped, in a state of probation, responsible to his Maker for the use made of his liberty—to be called rigorously to account at the close of his term, and then to be rewarded and punished according to his works. For this reason he has placed man under the reign not only of physical but also of moral law, of which the divine righteousness is the supreme exemplar, the natural code of morality its formulation, and the dictate of conscience its concrete expression. This is the doctrine of theism.

65

CAN CONSCIENCE DEVELOP AND DECAY?

Michael Cronin [1]

"Can conscience develop?" is a question which we shall find no difficulty in answering. Since conscience is nothing more than the practical reason, it can be educated and developed in two ways—(1) By the attainment of new truths, (2) by increase of power—*i. e.*, of energy and acuteness—in the reasoning faculty itself. These things require no elucidation; for the moral faculty is exactly on a par with the mathematical or the commercial reason, both of which can grow in the two ways mentioned—*i. e.*, objectively, by enlarging the sphere of knowledge, and subjectively, by developing one's inner power of observation and thought.

But a question of much more practical importance for ethicians, and of much greater difficulty as well, is the reverse of that just put—namely, (1) Can conscience decay, and if so (2) can it be lost altogether?—*i. e.*, can reason become partially blinded on moral matters, and if so can it wholly lose sight of morality?

(1) We answer, first, that conscience can decay in two ways—(a) By the weakening of the *general* faculty of rea-

[1] *Science of Ethics*, Vol. I, pp. 519-521. (Benziger Brothers, New York.)

son itself, (b) by loss of perceptive power within the special sphere of morals. (a) Of the first there is very little necessity to speak here. If the general faculty of Reason becomes impaired our power of moral judgment, like that of the mathematical judgment, must be to some extent adversely affected. We can no more trust the judgment of a madman on moral matters than we can trust his memory or his imagination on the facts of sense. But we must speak more at length of the possibility of decay in Conscience itself, or of Reason within the special department of morals. (b) May it happen that whilst in every other department the Reason retains its strength and balance, yet in the particular department of morals, of moral good and evil, the reason may become blurred and untrustworthy? That conscience does decay to some extent is a fact to which no observer of men can close his eyes. There are men in whom the moral faculty has become so irresponsive that they fail to see many truths that once were clear to their minds, and obvious and unmistakable. And this has come about, not because of any explicit or formal process of reasoning that they have gone through, but simply because conscience has lost its edge, because it has been blunted by one or more of the thousand and one influences that are wont to affect the practical reason. The first of these influences is the *constant misuse of conscience;* the second is the influence of desire upon thought. By the misuse of conscience we mean the use of conscience against one's better judgment. We rarely do evil without excusing ourselves in some way, and making up our minds that what we do is lawful—that it is well not to be too strict—that to err is human—that sin must be condoned, etc. All this is against our better judgment. The still small voice warns us that we are in the wrong. But the still small voice being constantly unheeded soon goes below the threshold of our moral consciousness, and ceases to be heard. Then, secondly, there is the general effect of desire on conscience and on the reason generally. Prejudice and desire are capable of warping the judgment not only in morals but in every kind of belief. Scientists often err unconsciously in their account of the laws of nature, because of some hobby or fancy for which they want to find support in the facts of nature. In politics, too, our views are influenced very much by our prejudices arising out of environment, or by the prevailing fashions of thought and speech. And just as our political and scientific views, so also our moral judgments are affected by our own desires or passions, and particularly by the views of that society in which we live. And we are affected in varying degrees according as our character is weaker or stronger, compromising or independent. Conscience, therefore, may decay, and even well-reasoned judgments be reversed through a variety of causes of which the cases just given are only a few prominent instances.

(2) But though conscience may decay there is still a limit to the reversibility or variability of our moral judgments. Our views on Political Philosophy may change, so far as to make us think that that particular system of taxation is the better one which suits our own business and requirements. But we cannot imagine a thinking man *genuinely* believing that there should be no such thing as government or "law and order" at all. So in morals, a man could never come to believe that indiscriminate murder and the complete neglect of children were lawful, or that the natural was the thing to be avoided, and the unnatural to be done. No, the first principles of Ethics and what has been called their proximate conclusions can never vanish from our minds, however much an evil life or prejudice or passion may affect us. We can imagine a man holding that in certain very exaggerated circumstances even murder would be lawful, though to the cold, unprejudiced, developed reason it could never seem so. But no developed mind could ever believe that wanton murder was the good thing and to be done, and its opposite the bad thing and to be avoided. Hence, whilst the faculty of conscience is quite capable of partial decadence, it can never be wholly lost. A man can never despoil himself of his first principles or of a knowledge of his main duties, and as long as these remain they will not only keep up a claim on their own account, but will also act as an incentive in bringing back to his mind even those discarded truths which crime and passion have eliminated.

66

THE PROHIBITION LAWS AND CONSCIENCE

John A. Ryan [1]

The Eighteenth Amendment and those provisions of the Volstead Act which forbid the sale of intoxicating liquor and which prohibit actions involved in, or immediately connected with, the sale of intoxicating liquor, are binding in conscience. The most important element in both the Amendment and the Volstead Act is the liquor selling. The manufacture of intoxicating beverages to be sold is so intimately connected with the sale itself that such manufacture may quite reasonably and properly be prohibited. The same is true of importation and transportation for purposes of sale. Hence, the provisions of the law prohibiting these actions are as obligatory as the prohibition of selling. All these prohibitions are binding in conscience because they are neither unjust nor construable as "purely penal" legislation.

On the other hand, the non-commercial and private manufacture, possession, and transportation of liquor for consumption by one's self or one's friends, remain lawful in the field of conscience and morality. The provisions of the Volstead Act which prohibit these actions are not binding in conscience because they constitute unjust interferences with personal liberty; nor are they justified on the theory that they are necessary or even useful means for attaining the end of the law, which is the abolition of the liquor traffic and the evils therewith connected.

What, precisely, is implied in the proposition that the provisions described in the second last paragraph are binding in conscience? Whose actions, or what actions, fall under this sentence? Primarily, the actions of the sellers of intoxicating liquor, such as saloon-keepers and "bootleggers." They are the chief offenders. In as much as the law which they violate has to do with a grave matter, it is difficult to see how they can carry on their traffic without committing a sin which is grave. The person who manufactures or transports liquor for purposes of sale is

[1] *The Catholic World*, May, 1925.

almost, if not quite, equally guilty. It is likewise gravely sinful to bribe the public enforcement officials.

What about the purchaser? While the act of purchase is not expressly forbidden in the Eighteenth Amendment, it is prohibited by the Volstead Act. The purchaser cooperates so closely with the seller that his action may rightfully be put under the ban of the law. He performs one part of the unlawful transaction, of which the other part is the sale. Nevertheless, the person who buys liquor only occasionally and for his own use cannot be held to cooperate so gravely in the evil traffic that each purchase renders him guilty of grave sin. On the other hand, it is difficult to see how these actions can be regarded as entirely free from moral guilt.

The only possible, or plausible, argument for entirely exculpating the purchaser would be drawn from the theory that the conscientious minority are not obliged to observe a law which is disregarded by the majority. This theory is defended by many moral theologians on the ground that it is not fair or equitable to compel a minority to submit to the burdens of a law which the majority evade.[2] It is difficult to see how this theory can be applied to the case of those who would like to purchase intoxicating liquor but who do not want to commit a sin; for the majority of Americans do not buy liquor. The more reasonable conclusion seems to be that the citizens are under some degree of moral obligation to observe that provision of the law which prohibits purchase.

67

IS NATIONAL PROHIBITION IN ACCORD WITH SOUND ETHICS?

PHILIP H. BURKETT [1]

There is perhaps no principle of ethics which is of such paramount importance in its application today among all nations as that which expresses the correct judicial relation between State and citizen. On perusing the writings of the

---

[2] Cf. Ballerini-Palmieri, *Opus Theologicum Morale*, I. 292; Vermeersch, *Theologia Moralis*, 253.

[1] *The Catholic Charities Review*, June, 1918.

sociologists and economists of the materialistic school we are continually confronted with the teaching of State omnipotence. The State has the duty, they say, to safeguard and promote the common welfare. Hence it has the power to make any laws whatsoever or to restrict or annul any rights of the citizens as it thinks fit. The laws it may enact become, by that very act, good and just laws; any rights it may deem fit to abolish cease to exist and any duty it may impose becomes a grave obligation. This is evidently wrong ethics. The individual and the family with their respective rights exist prior to the State. Moreover, the State is a natural society, whose whole *raison d'etre* is the temporal prosperity of the community, or, in other words, the State is a natural necessity for man's social nature, since man cannot defend his rights efficiently or procure the material and spiritual goods that social life demands without the intervention of the State. Hence we must conclude that the sphere of action of the State begins only where that of the individual or the family, its units, terminates by reason of their individuality, and that the State acts beyond the charter that nature has given it when, under cover of the "common good," it invades the natural rights of the individual, the family, or any factitious society, civil or religious, except where the invasion of such rights is necessary to safeguard the social good. In the latter case, the State evidently must be equipped with the means to the end, else nature has left it helpless.

Can the State then interfere in the exercise of rights given by nature? This question brings us to the second distinction, namely that of alienable and inalienable rights. Inalienable rights are those which cannot be renounced by the individual because they are a necessary means to fulfil an unconditional duty, *e. g.*, the right of life as a means to pursue one's ultimate end, or the right of parents to the respect of their children. Alienable rights can be ceded, *e. g.*, the right to marry, to the use of any particular food or drink, to all but the necessary goods of life, etc. If these rights may be freely ceded by the individual, some of them may in case of necessity be suspended against the individual's will by an authority having jurisdiction in that sphere. Putting the question more specifically, we now ask: "Can the State prohibit the use of intoxicating drinks?" There can be no doubt about the answer. The State can do so whenever such prohibition is absolutely necessary for the temporal welfare of the community. I say "community" and not a relatively small number; for it does not lie within the province of the State to provide individuals or a numerically small class of them with the means of temporal prosperity, or to remove the dangers thereto, when, by so doing, it curtails the reasonable liberties of the vast majority. A distinction must also be made between the prohibition of a thing wrong in itself or to the unrestricted use of which there is almost invariably linked a grave abuse or a serious danger to health, as for example, opium, and a thing lawful in itself but subject to occasional abuse. Secondly, the evil which the State seeks to remove must have assumed such enormous proportions as to render imperative the radical interference with the liberty of its citizens. For sane government would develop into tyranny were it to forbid the indulgence of any legitimate pleasure on account of a relatively moderate abuse. "Keep the use and correct the abuse," we should say. The activity of the State must not be exercised to restrict personal liberty but to extend it as far as consistent with its duties. It must not check initiative but defend and promote it. Only when all other ways and means not destructive of human liberty have been tried and found utterly ineffective, may the State proceed to such a serious operation as total prohibition.

We have now the principle to aid us in the solution of our question: Is national prohibition in accord with sound ethics? It is, if, first, the drink evil is so deep rooted and widespread as to seriously jeopardize the temporal prosperity of all, or at least a vast majority of this community of one hundred millions of citizens; and if, secondly, it is the only remedy which will keep the evil within narrow limits. We venture to deny both assumptions.

As regards the first point it is to be noted that prohibitionists have made little effort to prove their contention from reliable statistics. For the most part they belong to the class of ultra-Puritans who are shocked at the sight of gambling, card playing, theatre going, and baseball games on Sunday. It is a crime to drink, no matter how moderately, of any intoxicating beverage. The guilty person is to be ostracized, like a leper. But they will never raise their voice in protest against the unspeakable evils of birth control, divorce, and numerous other forms of immorality that threaten to undermine the foundation of the State. . . . But after all it remains true, first, that the extent of the evil and its consequences are rhetorically exaggerated, and, secondly, that we are still far from that stage where it becomes an imperative necessity for government to interfere with the liberty of the whole community. How many individuals in the country frequently drink to excess when compared to those who drink moderately or not at all? How many of the evils ascribed by the zealots to drink are due exclusively to that vice? Is crime less prevalent perhaps among the Mohammedans for that reason? . . . Even if man would be healthier and better prepared to resist the inroads of disease by observing total abstinence, the State would not be justified in legislating him into that condition. It would do so only at the expense of the greatest natural prerogative that man possesses, namely the freedom of choice. This is of priceless value. Society would gradually become unbearable in proportion to its restriction. Hence we must jealously safeguard it.

The second question to be answered is whether national prohibition would be an efficacious remedy against drunkenness. . . . "Our general conclusion seems unavoidable in the light of the evidence adduced. It is that State prohibition never has prohibited nor has it restrained the use of liquor to a degree that a sound basis of evolution may be said to have been made for the operation of national prohibition." . . . The laws will never be effective unless they have the staunch support of a great majority of those concerned. This approval does not exist despite the apparent popular vote in some States. It is a known fact that many ardent prohibitionists are equally ardent private consumers of alcohol. Besides, the prohibitionists have consistently worked against a referendum to the people.

Is national prohibition the only possible remedy for the evil? Of course, advocates of prohibition assert that years of trial and experience have proved that other remedies are useless. The writer is inclined to doubt very much whether concerted effort, such as is now made for prohibition, has ever been made in the use of the available remedies. These remedies have achieved a most encouraging success wherever they have been correctly applied. If the evil exists in certain States only, or in certain counties of those States, for example military or mining districts, local prohibition when rigidly enforced will sufficiently remedy the evil. The States with their own sovereign rights have ample powers to cope with it. Catholic societies, the National Temperance Society and others have enrolled thousands of members who promote the good cause by word and example, and who are constantly spreading sound literature on the question. Education in the character of the evil given to the young in the schools and to adults from pulpit, platform and press has already achieved wonderful results. Example and education are two wonderful factors for good and for evil. Medical science has contributed largely to the proper enlightenment. The Catholic Church, too, has exerted her influence most beneficially. Her moral motives and discipline in self-control based on religion have either protected many or saved them when endangered, from ruin. Other remedies, to which greater attention might be paid, are the following. The correction of the iniquitous industrial system of today which says the laborers' strength compels him to turn to some stimulant as the only prop for his failing strength or the only available recreation. The supply of opportunities for healthy diversion on the rest day of the week. There exists a puritanical tendency to suppress all such remedies. The State might also raise its high license and enact even stricter laws. . . . The Church has never countenanced universal prohibition and probably never will; for she respects human liberty—though her enemies do not admit it—and like her divine Founder, she warns us not to uproot the tares lest we also uproot the wheat.

68

PROBABILISM

JOSEPH RICKABY [1]

1. Sometimes conscience returns a clear, positive answer as to the morality of an act contemplated. True or false

---

[1] *Moral Philosophy*, pp. 153-158. (Longmans, Green and Company, New York.) With permission.

the answer may be, but the ring of it has no uncertain sound. At other times conscience is perplexed, and her answer is, *perhaps,* and *perhaps not.* When the woman hid Achimaas and Jonathan in the well, and said to Absalom's servants, "They passed on in haste" (2 Kings xvii. 17—21), did she do right in speaking thus to save their lives? A point that has perplexed consciences for centuries. A man's hesitation is sometimes subjective and peculiar to himself. It turns on a matter of fact, which others know full well, though he doubts; or on a point of law, dark to him, but clearly ruled by the consent of the learned. In such cases it is his duty to seek information from people about him, taking so much trouble to procure it as the importance of the matter warrants, not consulting ten doctors as to the ownership of one hen. But it may be that all due enquiries fail. The fact remains obscure; or about the law, doctors differ, and arguments conflict indecisively. What is the man to do? Take the *safe* course: suppose there is an obligation, and act accordingly? This principle, put as a command, would make human life intolerable. It is, moreover, false, when so put, as we shall presently prove. Take the *easy* course, and leave the obligation out of count? This principle is more nearly correct than the other; but it needs interpretation, else it may prove dangerously lax.

2. To return to Achimaas and Jonathan and their hostess. Some such reckoning as this may have passed through her mind: "Lying lips are an abomination to the Lord; but is it a lie to put murders off the scent of blood?" To that question finding no answer, she may have made up her mind in this way: "Well, I don't know, but I'll risk it." If that were her procedure, she did not walk by the scientific lines of Probabilism. The probabilist runs no risk, enters upon no uncertainty, and yet he by no means always follows what is technically termed the *safe* course, that is, the course which supposes the obligation, *e. g.,* in the case in point, to have said simply where the men were. How then does the probabilist contrive to extract certainty out of a case of insoluble doubt? By aid of what is called a *reflex* principle. A *reflex* is opposed to a *direct* principle. A direct principle lays down an obligation, as it would bind one who had a perfect discernment of the law and of the facts of the case, and of the application of the one to the

other, and who was perfectly able to keep the law. By a *reflex* principle, a man judges of his own act, taking account of the imperfection of his knowledge and the limitations of his power. Probabilism steps in, only where a case is practically insoluble to an agent upon direct principles. The probabilist thereupon leaves the direct speculative doubt unsolved. He relinquishes the attempt of determining what a man should do in the case in question, who had a thorough insight into the lie of the law. He leaves that aside, and considers what is his duty, or not his duty, in the deficiency of his knowledge. Then he strikes upon the principle, which is the root of Probabilism, that *a doubtful law has no binding power*. It will be observed that this is a *reflex principle*. For objectively nothing is doubtful, but everything is or is not in point of fact. To a mind that had a full grasp of the objective order of things, there would be no doubtful law: such a mind would discern the law in every case as holding or not holding. But no human mind is so perfect. Every man has to take account of his own limitations of vision in judging of his duty. The question for me is, not the law absolutely, but the law as far as I can make it out. Our proposition, then, states that when an individual, using such moral diligence of enquiry as the gravity of the matter calls for, still remains in a state of honest doubt as to whether the law binds, in that mental condition it does not bind *him*.

3. What the law does not forbid, it leaves open. Aristotle indeed (*Eth.*, V., xi., 1) says the contrary, that what the law does not command (he instances suicide), it forbids. All that he seems to mean is that if there be an act which at times might appear advantageous, and yet is never commanded, there is a presumption of the legislator being averse to that act. Again, there are special occasions, in view of which the legislator undertakes to regulate the whole outward conduct of a man by positive enactment, as with a soldier on parade: what is not there commanded, is forbidden. But these instances do not derogate from our general proposition, which is proved in this way. The office of law is not to loose, but to bind. It declares, not what the subject may do, but what he must or must not. It does not bring liberty, but restriction. Therefore, if any one wishes to assert a restriction, he must go to a law to

prove it. If he can find none, liberty remains. The law is laid on liberty. Liberty is not the outcome of law, but prior to it. Liberty is in possession. The burden of proof rests with those who would abridge liberty and impose an obligation. It is an axiom of law itself, a natural, not an arbitrary axiom, that *better is the condition of the possessor:* which amounts in this matter to another statement, also axiomatic, that *a law binds not till it is promulgated.* But a law of which I have serious outstanding doubts whether it exists at all, or, if existent, whether it reaches my case, is for this occasion a law not duly promulgated to me. Therefore it binds me not, and my liberty remains.

4. It remains to consider what constitutes a *serious outstanding doubt.* The word *outstanding* has been already explained. It means that we have sought for certain information, and cannot procure it. Now what is a *serious* doubt? It is a doubt founded on a *positive* opinion against the existence of the law, or its applicability to the case in point, an opinion fraught with probability, *solid, comparative, practical probability.* The doubt must not be mere negative doubt, or ignorance that cannot tell why it doubts; not a vague suspicion, or sentimental impression that defies all intellectual analysis; not a mere subjective inability to make up one's mind, but some counter-reason that admits of positive statement, as we say, *in black and white.* It is true that many minds cannot define their grounds of doubt, even when these are real. Such minds are unfit to apply the doctrine of Probabilism to themselves, but must seek its application from others. The opinion against the law, when explicitly drawn out, must be found to possess a *solid* probability. It may be either an intrinsic argument from reason and the nature of the case, or an extrinsic argument from the word of some authority; but the reason or the authority must be grave. The opinion is thus said to be *intrinsically* or *extrinsically* probable. The probability must also be *comparative.* There is many an argument, in itself a very good one, that perishes when we come to consider the crushing weight of evidence on the other side. An opinion is *comparatively* probable, when after hearing all the reasons and all the authorities on the other side, the said opinion still remains *not unlikely,* which is all that we mean to say of an opinion here, when we call it *probable.*

In ordinary English, the word *probable* means *more likely than otherwise,* which is not the signification of the Latin *opinio probabilis.* Lastly, the probability must be *practical;* it must take account of all the circumstances of the case. Practical probability is opposed to *speculative,* which leaves out of count certain circumstances, which are pretty sure to be present, and to make all the difference in the issue. Thus it is speculatively probable that a Catholic might without sin remain years without confession, never having any grievous sins to confess, grievous sin alone being necessary matter for that sacrament. There is no downright cogent reason why a man might not do so. And yet, if he neglected such ordinary means of grace as confession of venial sin, having it within reach, month after month, no one, considering "the sin which surrounds us," would expect that man to go without grievous scathe. In mechanics, there are many machines that work prettily enough in speculation and on paper, where the inventors do not consider the difficulties of imperfect material, careless handling, climate, and other influences, that render the invention of no practical avail.

5. The safest use of Probabilism is in the field of property transactions and of positive law. There is greatest risk of using it amiss in remaining in a false religion. All turns upon the varying amount of trouble involved in *moral diligence* of enquiry, according as the matter at issue is a point of mere observance or of vital interest.

6. The point on which the probability turns must be the lawfulness or unlawfulness of the action, not any other issue, as that of the physical consequences. Before rolling boulder-stones down a hill to amuse myself, it is not enough to have formed a probable opinion that there is no one coming up. That would be Probabilism misapplied. The correct enquiry is: Does any intrinsic reason or extrinsic authority make the opinion probable, that it is lawful for mere amusement to roll down rocks with any belief short of certainty that no one will be crushed thereby? The probability, thus turned on to the lawfulness of the action, breaks down altogether. This explanation, borne in mind, will save much misapprehension.

69

THE NATURE OF SIN

Thomas Slater [1]

A sin is nothing but a bad human act, and it may be defined as a free transgression of the law of God. For a bad human act is a disturbance of right order either because in itself it is against right reason, as murder or suicide, or because it is against the command of a legitimate superior, which imposes a strict obligation, and which right reason bids us obey. But such a disturbance of right order is against the law of God.

Every voluntary act against right reason is an offense against God and a sin, for although the sinner in committing sin does not always think explicitly of God, yet he always apprehends that he is doing wrong action, an action which his conscience condemns, and in the condemnation of conscience is implicitly contained the condemnation of God Himself.

A sin must be distinguished from an imperfection, which is either negative or positive. A negative imperfection is merely the omission of a good action which is not of precept; and such an omission when grace moves one to perform the act, though not a sin, yet is a falling short of the perfection which was within one's reach. A positive imperfection is a violation of God's will made known to us, but which does not strictly oblige us. God wishes a religious to observe his rule, but frequently this does not bind under sin. A positive imperfection then is a falling short not only of the perfection which was offered to us and which we might have had, but also of that which God wishes us to have, though He did not oblige us to have it.

Sin in the sense defined is called *actual* sin; *habitual* sin is the state which follows the commission of actual sin until this be forgiven.

A *formal* sin is committed knowingly and willfully; a *material* sin is committed without knowledge or free consent.

---

[1] *A Manual of Moral Theology*, Vol. I, pp. 133-135. (Benziger Brothers, New York.)

Sin is said to be against God, our neighbor, or ourself, as it is against some virtue which immediately regards God, or our neighbor, or ourself. All sin is ultimately against God.

Sins of *ignorance* are committed through culpable ignorance; sins of *infirmity* through passion or bad habit; sins of *malice* with cool deliberation and forethought. The last, as is obvious, are the least excusable.

A sin of *commission* is an act against a negative precept; a sin of *omission* is the willful neglect of a positive precept.

The meaning of the terms, sins of thought, word, and deed, is obvious.

To commit sin there must be actual advertence to the malice of the action done, either when the action is performed, or when the cause is put. This follows from what was said above about human acts, which must be voluntary either in themselves or at any rate in their cause. But no act is voluntary without previous knowledge and advertence. It is not sufficient then for sin that a man could physically advert to the wrongfulness of his action and should have done so; if there was no advertence either at the time of the action or when its cause was put, there is no sin. However, advertence to what is likely to follow when the cause is put is sufficient to contract the malice of sin; and so wrong done through wilful negligence, or passion, or habit, or carelessness, is imputable to the agent.

Advertence to an evil thought or motion does not constitute sin without free consent of the will. The will consents when it voluntarily accepts an evil suggestion presented by the mind, and it is immaterial whether the evil originates in the will, or whether the will accedes to evil when suggested to it from without. For sin, then, there must be both advertence to the evil and free consent to it; a man who takes another's money, thinking it to be his own, does not commit theft, nor does the kleptomaniac who is powerless to refrain.

70

THE MALICE OF SIN

Cardinal Manning [1]

The malice of sin consists in this: that an intelligent creature, having power of will, deliberately and consciously opposes the will of its Maker. The malice of sin is essentially internal to the soul. The external action whereby the sinner perpetrates his sin adds indeed an accidental malice and an accidental increase of wickedness; but the essence, the life of the malice, consists in the state of the soul itself. We see, then, that sin is the conscious variation of our moral being from the will of God. We abuse our whole nature, we abuse our intellect by acting irrationally, in violation of the will of God which is written upon the conscience; we abuse our will, because we deliberately abuse the power of the will, whereby we originate our actions in opposition to the will of God who gave it. We apply our intellect and will, with our eyes open, and with freedom and choice, to the perpetration of acts, or the utterance of words, or the harboring of thoughts which are known to be contrary to the will of God. Therefore in every sin there is the knowledge of the intellect of what we are doing, the consent of the will in doing it, and the consciousness of the mind fixed upon the action with two objects before it—the law and the Lawgiver—the law of God known to us, and the Giver of that law, who is God himself; so that we deliberately, with our eyes open and of our own free will, break God's law in God's face. Now this is the plain definition and description of sin.

71

WHY MEN SIN

Ernest R. Hull [2]

By the light of reason mankind knows nothing of the supernatural sonship. Many races, both archaic and cultivated, have conceived God as the father of mankind [*Jupi-*

---

[1] *Sin and Its Consequences,* pp. 14-15. (D. and J. Sadlier and Company, New York.)
[2] *The Catholic Mind,* Sept. 22, 1918, New York.

ter = *Deus-pater,* "*pater deorum hominumque*"] in the broad sense that He has produced us and that He loves us and provides for us. There is no need to quarrel with the idea taken loosely, though it does not stand good in any strict sense of paternity. The fatherhood of God and the sonship of man, as it exists in the Christian system, is something altogether beyond this, and belongs to a totally different plane. Secondly, natural humanity knows nothing of the notion of habitual grace. If it is recognized that a man can be specially pleasing to God, this is solely on the ground of his natural virtue and piety taken on its own merits. Thirdly, natural humanity knows nothing of actual or operative grace. The idea of some kind of inspiration or mental stimulus coming from above is familiar to all races, and manifests itself in the quasi-instinctive belief in a future life, belief in God as the law-giver at the back of conscience, and in all markedly noble insight into religious truth or aspiration towards virtue. But this still lies within the natural order. If there is anything supernatural underlying such mental movements—and we have the saying of St. John that the Word "enlighteneth *every man* that cometh into the world"—at least the supernaturality of it falls beyond human perception, and, therefore, lies outside the cognizance of reason.

Hence it follows that if circumstances require us to teach moral truths to non-Christians in such a way as to avoid religious propaganda interfering with their actual creeds, it is necessary to confine ourselves to the principles of the natural order. We can tell them how they ought to try to be good, and to ask God to help them to be good, and to pray for forgiveness if they fall into sin, and hold up before them the goal of *natural* happiness as the fruit of their endeavors. If at the back of this natural system God is really elevating their good-will and good actions into the supernatural order with a view of giving them the supernatural destiny of heaven, all the better. But if we undertake professedly to teach them only that which is known to reason without revelation, we cannot consistently put before them the system of grace and the supernatural, because this is unknown to reason left to itself, and cannot be proposed to them except on the authority of the Catholic Church, which they from their very position do not recognize. In other words, we must in such a course ignore and pass over the supernatural system, without in any way intending to deny or exclude it.

The Natural Power of Free-Will

Next we come to a still more important question, and that is, man's power of securing final happiness by the natural use of his free-will alone. Prescinding from the system of grace altogether, and confining ourselves to the order of nature pure and simple, we are confronted with the axiomatic principle that sin is essentially a free act; for if the act is not free it cannot be sinful. Sin is essentially a voluntary transgression of the Divine law. The law must first of all be known, and when known it must be transgressed with free choice and deliberation. This being the case, it follows that in the order of pure nature every man can of his free-will avoid each and every single sin which comes before him, simply for the reason that if he cannot avoid it it is not a sin. For an act is a sin only just precisely so far as a man can avoid it, and so far as he commits it by pure and simple free-choice.

But in speaking of the order of nature, we must bear in mind a distinction familiar to theologians, who say that mankind left to itself is not in the state of "pure nature" but in the state of "fallen nature." The state of pure nature, they declare, never actually existed. In the beginning Adam was created in the state of "nature elevated to the supernatural," and, therefore, endowed with certain qualities and gifts superior to pure nature. By the fall these special qualities and gifts were lost; and fallen man was, they say, in some respects in a worse condition than if he had never been elevated. He was (in technical phrase) "despoiled of his supernatural qualities and wounded or damaged in his natural qualities." His damage consisted in a certain obscuration of the intellect and a certain debilitation of the will. It was not bad enough to destroy free choice, or the power of judgment between good and evil; but it took the edge off the keenness of the perception of good, and especially of its appreciation. Moreover, in the state of fallen nature the passions and natural inclinations tend to assert themselves more strongly than would be normal to pure nature. Hence while the power of resistance remained, it became much easier and more likely that the will would yield and make a bad choice under the impulsion and attraction of pleasure or the deterrent influence of pain. In this way the fall has induced a certain proneness to sin more emphatic than that of healthy pure nature.

However, we must be quite clear how far this proneness goes. Even fallen nature is not corrupted in its essential qualities. The inherent power of choosing good and avoiding evil still remains. Speaking in general a man can perform each single duty and avoid each single sin which comes before him; and his failures to do so in any given case do not come from want of absolute power, but from easiness of making evil choice, and the fact of experience that every man is practically sure to give way sometime or other.

In short we must carefully steer clear of the Lutheran theory. This theory is that human nature by the fall was rendered inherently corrupt, so that it must sin as a matter of course and as a matter of necessity; that the infusion of grace was not merely an elevation of nature but a canceling of it and a substitution for it; that all acts, precisely as proceeding from man as such, were bad, and it was only by the imputation of Christ's merits that God came to accept them as good. This doctrine was expressly condemned by the Church as soon as it was broached.

All Men Are Sinners

Nevertheless, there is one orthodox sense in which "all men are sinners." If we take mankind as it exists in the state of fallen nature, and in the light of practical experience ask the question: "Will any man by his free-will always avoid all sin all his life through?" We answer "No." Every man is sure to fall into some sin, one time or other. The best-disposed will at least fall occasionally into some smaller sin; while the run of mankind, even with general good dispositions, are practically sure to fall even into serious sin sometimes, especially under stress of painful and difficult temptation.

To Christians this truth is known by Divine revelation. "A man who saith he hath no sin is a liar, and the truth is not in him," says St. John; and St. James, "In many things we all offend." But even putting aside such revealed pronouncements, and taking human nature as we know it, we can make the same assertion with full confidence; and it would require a man of singularly pedantic, priggish and self-conceited mind to deny it. An absolutely sinless human being no one will believe in. We may take it as certain that every man sins occasionally at least; and it would be extremely rare to come across any individual man who has not sinned grievously sometime or other in his life.

Yet, although this may be taken as a universal truth, it is not a necessary or metaphysical truth. There is no strict necessity for any man whatever to sin any time—for the fundamental reason already given; namely, that if a sin were necessary it would not be sin. The lapse into sin is not a necessity at all. It is a fact of the concrete order, and it is a fact which follows from the practical limitations of human nature. To put it concretely: there is a certain limit beyond which a man's self-restraint will in point of fact break down, though absolutely it need not do so. If a dentist is drawing my teeth I can, absolutely speaking, bear the pain without shouting, and will do so. But if the tooth-drawing goes on long enough I am sure to give way some time, when the pain reaches a certain point. Even under that stress I could still resist; but in point of fact I shall not do so. So it is in general life, where all sorts of things are repeatedly tempting us to sin. We need not in any single case give way. But it will be safe to get a wager that some time or other each individual will give way to temptation, just when it takes him at a weak moment. The mind will be conscious of the power to hold out; but yet it will not hold out on that occasion, even though it may have held out on many former occasions. The exercise of control becomes so painful that the spirit breaks down. "I can't stand it any longer" means: "I *won't* because it hurts too much." The will could really hold out, and the giving way is a consent of the will, and not a physical collapse. Thus by way of illustration, the muscles will not snap under a certain weight; but long before we reach that weight the muscles do give way, because the will yields to the pain of holding them up.

But the Will Can Avoid Sin

While thus maintaining as a universal proposition the sinfulness of all men, we must, therefore, bear in mind that it is a concrete proposition; a point of fact, and not a point of metaphysical principle, or of physical necessity. We must still preach the power of the human will on each and every occasion to choose the right and avoid the wrong. We must, moreover, maintain this power of avoiding sin as part of the inherent constitution of the human will—for the reasons already given which cannot be too often repeated; namely, that sin is essentially a free transgression of the Divine law, and if it is not free it is not a sin. Or to put it another way: An act is a sin only when we can avoid it; and so far as we cannot avoid it, so far it is not a sin.

What, then, is the meaning of the teaching which is so often heard among us, namely, "Without the help of God we cannot avoid all sin" or "Without the help of God we cannot keep all the Commandments" or "We cannot of our own strength avoid all sin; we need the help of God," etc. The meaning is that already explained. It is a concrete and practical proposition, not an abstract metaphysical one. Expressed more exactly it would mean this: In general principle and in absolute power you can avoid each and every sin which tempts you. But in point of fact, no matter what your general good intentions and resolutions may be, you will not do so. Even with the help of God you are likely enough to fall now and then. But without the help of God you are sure to fall; and almost sure to fall badly and often. Therefore, practically the help of God is necessary for you if you are to avoid sin.

That this is the sound orthodox meaning of the proposition was shown by my old professor, Father Tepe. When dealing with the proposition that "All men are sinners" and that "No human being will go through life without committing sin," he said: "This is not a universal necessity; but it is a universal fact, vouched for by revelation and confirmed by experience." It is a great stab at self-confidence, a great destroyer of self-complacency, and a great sermon on the fallibility of man and his dependence on the Divine aid.

When we have explained how in the order of pure nature man would possess the power to avoid each and every sin, we must add to this the parallel proposition, that in the order of nature man must also possess the power to carry out each single duty imposed on him by the law of God—for the parallel reason that *"Nemo ad impossibile tenetur,"* or, in other words, a duty is a duty precisely because and so far as a man has the power to perform it, and it ceases to be a duty as soon as the power to perform it is absent. Secondly, in case a man feels temptation so difficult that he is practically sure of giving way, he can always ask God's help in prayer, and will be sure to obtain the necessary strength to resist, and so to avoid sin. Therefore, the general conclusion is this: that in the order of pure nature man would possess all the necessary equipment to fulfil the Divine law of right and wrong; and, therefore, to attain his final happiness thereby.

72

PHILOSOPHICAL SIN

Arthur Charles O'Neill [1]

Those who would construct a moral system independent of God and His law distinguish between theological and philosophical sin. Philosophical sin is a morally bad act which violates the order of reason, not the Divine law. Theological sin is a transgression of the eternal law. Those who are of atheistic tendencies and contend for this distinction, either deny the existence of God or maintain that He exercises no providence in regard to human acts. This position is destructive of sin in the theological sense, as God and His law, reward and punishment, are done away with. Those who admit the existence of God, His law, human liberty and responsibility, and still contend for a distinction between philosophical and theological sin, maintain that in the present order of God's providence there are morally bad acts, which, while violating the order of reason, are not offensive to God, and they base their contention on this that the sinner can be ignorant of the existence of God, or not actually think of Him and His law when he acts. Without the knowledge of God and consideration of Him, it is impossible to offend Him. This doctrine was censured as scandalous, temerarious, and erroneous by

[1] *Catholic Encyclopedia,* Vol. XIV, pg. 7.

Alexander VIII (24 Aug., 1690) in his condemnation of the following proposition: "Philosophical or moral sin is a human act not in agreement with rational nature and right reason; theological and mortal sin is a free transgression of the Divine law. However grievous it may be, philosophical sin in one who is either ignorant of God or does not actually think of God, is indeed a grievous sin, but not an offense to God, nor a mortal sin dissolving friendship with God, nor worthy of eternal punishment" (Denzinger-Bannwart, 1290).

This proposition is condemned because it does not distinguish between vincible and invincible ignorance, and further supposes invincible ignorance of God to be sufficiently common, instead of only metaphysically possible, and because in the present dispensation of God's providence we are clearly taught in Scripture that God will punish all evil coming from the free will of man (Rom., ii, 5-11). There is no morally bad act that does not include a transgression of Divine law. From the fact that an action is conceived of as morally evil it is conceived of as prohibited. A prohibition is unintelligible without the notion of some one prohibiting. The one prohibiting in this case and binding the conscience of man can be only God, who alone has power over man's free will and actions, so that from the fact that any act is perceived to be morally bad and prohibited by conscience, God and His law are perceived at least confusedly, and a wilful transgression of the dictate of conscience is necessarily also a transgression of God's law. Cardinal de Lugo (De incarnat., disp. 5, lect. 3) admits the possibility of philosophical sin in those who are inculpably ignorant of God, but he holds that it does not actually occur, because in the present order of God's providence there cannot be invincible ignorance of God and His law. This teaching does not necessarily fall under the condemnation of Alexander VIII, but it is commonly rejected by theologians for the reason that a dictate of conscience necessarily involves a knowledge of the Divine law as a principle of morality.

73

UTILITARIANISM

JAMES J. FOX [1]

Utilitarianism (Lat. *utilis,* useful) is a modern form of the Hedonistic ethical theory which teaches that the end of human conduct is happiness, and that consequently the discriminating norm which distinguishes conduct into right and wrong is pleasure and pain. In the words of one of its most distinguished advocates, John Stuart Mill, "the creed which accepts as the foundation of morals, utility or the greatest happiness principle, holds that actions are right in proportion as they tend to promote happiness, wrong as they tend to produce the reverse of happiness. By happiness is intended pleasure and the absence of pain; by unhappiness, pain and the privation of pleasure" (Utilitarianism, ii, 1863). Although the term Utilitarianism did not come into vogue until it had been adopted by Bentham, and until the essential tenets of the system had already been advocated by many English philosophers, it may be said that, with the important exception of Helvetius (De l'esprit, 1758), from whom Bentham seems to have borrowed, all the champions of this system have been English. The favor which it has enjoyed in English speculation may be ascribed in a great measure to the dominance of Locke's teaching, that all our ideas are derived exclusively from sense experience. This epistemological doctrine, hostile to all shades of intentionalism, finds its ethical complement in the theory that our moral ideas of right and wrong, our moral judgments, and conscience itself are derived originally from the experienced results of actions.

Tracing the stream of Utilitarian thought from its sources, we may start with Hobbes (Leviathan, 1651), whose fundamental ethical axiom is that right conduct is that which promotes our own welfare; and the social code of morals depends for its justification on whether or not it serves the well-being of those who observe it. A Protestant divine, Richard Cumberland (De legibus naturae, 1672), engaged in the refutation of Hobbes's doctrine, that

[1] *Catholic Encyclopedia,* Vol. XV, pp. 241-243.

morality depends on civil enactment, sought to show that the greatest happiness principle is a law of the Gospel and a law of nature: "The greatest possible benevolence of every rational agent towards all the rest constitutes the happiest state of each and all. Accordingly common good will be the supreme law." This view was further developed by some other theologians of whom the last and most conspicuous was Paley (Principles of Moral and Political Philosophy, 1785), who reasoned that since God wills the happiness of all men it follows that if we would conform our conduct to God's will we must act so as to promote the common happiness; and virtue consists in doing good to all mankind in obedience to the will of God and for the sake of everlasting happiness. Moral obligation he conceived to be the pressure of the Divine will upon our wills urging us to right action. More in harmony with the spirit of the later Utilitarians was Hume, the slightest of whose preoccupations was to find any religious source or sanction of morality. In his "Inquiry concerning the Principles of Morals" (1751) he carried out an extensive analysis of the various judgments which we pass upon our own character and conduct and on those of others, and from this study drew the conclusion that virtue and personal merit consist in those qualities which are useful to ourselves and others. In the course of his speculation he encounters the question which is the irremovable stumbling block in the path of the Utilitarian theorist: How is the motive of self-interest to be reconciled with the motive of benevolence; if every man necessarily pursues his own happiness, how can the happiness of all be the end of conduct? Unlike the later thinkers of this school, Hume did not discuss or attempt systematically to solve the difficulty; he dismissed it by resting on the assumption that benevolence is the supreme virtue.

In Hartley (Observations of Man, 1748) we find the first methodical effort to justify the Utilitarian principle by means of the theory of association to which so large a part in the genesis of our moral judgments is assigned by subsequent speculators, especially those of the Evolutionist party. From sensations and the lower elementary or primary emotions, according to Hartley, result higher feelings and emotions, different in kind from the processes out of

which they have arisen. The altruistic motives, sympathy and benevolence, are then accounted for. With Bentham arises the group of thinkers who have appropriated the name of Utilitarians as their distinctive badge. The leaders after Bentham were the two Mills, the two Austins, and Godwin, who are also known as the Philosophic Radicals. While the members of this party devoted considerable thought to the defense and development of theoretical Utilitarianism and made it the starting point of their political activity, they became remarkable less as philosophic speculators than as active reformers of social and economic conditions and of legislation. The keynote of their doctrine and policy is struck by Bentham in the opening of his "Principles of Morals and Legislation" (1789) : "Nature has placed mankind under the governance of two sovereign masters, pain and pleasure. It is for them alone to point out what we ought to do as well as what we shall do. On the one hand the standard of right and wrong, on the other the chain of cause and effect are linked to their throne. They govern us in all we do; every effort we can make to throw off their subjection will serve but to demonstrate and confirm it. In a word man may pretend to abjure their empire; but in reality he will remain subject to it all the while. The principle of utility recognizes this subjection, and assumes it for the foundation of that system the object of which is to rear the fabric of felicity by the hand of reason and law." Staunchly standing by the principle of unqualified egoism, Bentham rids himself of the task of reconciling self-interest and altruism: "Dream not that men will move their little finger to serve you, unless their advantage in doing so is obvious to them. Men never did so and never will while human nature is made of its present materials. But they will desire to serve you when by so doing they can serve themselves; and the occasions on which they can serve themselves by serving you are multitudinous (Deontology, ii, 1834; posthumous work).

In the hands of Bentham and his disciples Utilitarianism dissociates morality from its religious basis and, incorporating Determinism with its other tenets, becomes pronouncedly Positivistic, and moral obligation is resolved into a prejudice or a feeling resulting from a long-continued association of disagreeable consequences attending some kinds of actions, and advantages following others. The word *ought* Bentham characterizes as an authoritative impostor, the talisman of arrogance, indolence, and ignorance. It is the condemnation of Utilitarianism that this estimate of duty is thoroughly consistent with the system; and no defender of the theory has been able, though some have tried, to indicate the claims of moral obligation on Positivistic Utilitarian grounds. Bentham drew up a curious scheme for computing the worth or weight to be assigned to all sorts of pleasures and pains, as a practical norm to determine in the concrete the moral value of any action. He assumes that all pleasures are alike in kind, and differ only in quantity, that is, in intensity, certainty, duration, etc. His psychological analysis, besides the original defect of making self-interest the sole motive of human action, contains many errors. Subsequent writers have abandoned it as worthless for the very good reason that to calculate, as its employment would demand, all the results of every action, and to strike a balance between the advantages and disadvantages attendant upon it, would require an intellect much more powerful than that with which man is endowed.

The classic expression of the system is John Stuart Mill's "Utilitarianism," which endeavors to raise the Utilitarian ideal to a higher plane than that of the undisguised selfishness upon which Bentham rested it. As the foundation of his structure Mill asserts that every man necessarily acts in order to obtain his own happiness, but finding this ground logically insufficient to furnish a basis for an adequate criterion of conduct, and prompted by his own large sympathies, he quickly endeavors to substitute "the happiness of all concerned" for "the agent's own happiness." The argument over which he, the author of a formidable work on logic, endeavors to pass from the first to the second position, may serve as an example suitable to submit to the beginner in logic when he is engaged in the detection of sophisms. The argument, in brief, is that, as each one desires and pursues his own happiness, and the sum total of these individual ends makes up the general happiness, it follows that the general happiness is the one thing desirable by all and provides the Utilitarian standard of what is right in conduct. "As well might you argue," says Martineau, "that because of a hundred men each one's hunger is satisfied by his dinner, the hunger of all must be satisfied by the dinner of each." To escape some of the criticisms urged against the doctrine as stated by Bentham, who made no distinction in the various kinds of pleasure, Mill claimed that Utilitarianism notes that pleasures differ in quality as well as quantity; that in the judgment of those that have experience of different pleasures, some are preferable to others, that it is better to be a human being dissatisfied than a pig satisfied, better to be Socrates dissatisfied than a fool satisfied. Then he slips from "preferable" to "higher," thus surreptitiously introducing a moral classification among pleasures. The only legitimate grounds for attaching higher and lower moral values to various pleasures, is to estimate them according to the rank of the faculties or of the kinds of action to which they belong as results. But to do this is to assume some moral standard by which we can measure the right and wrong of action, independently of its pleasurable or painful consequences. To answer the objection that virtue is desired for its own sake, and men do right frequently without any calculation of the happiness to be derived from their action, Mill enlists the association theory; as the result of experience, actions that have been approved or condemned on account of their pleasurable or disagreeable consequences at length come to be looked upon by us as good or bad, without our actually adverting to their pleasant or painful result.

Since Mill's time the only writer who has introduced any modification into strictly Utilitarian thought is Sidgwick (Methods of Ethics, 1874), who acknowledged that the pleasure-and-pain standard is incapable of serving universally as the criterion of morality, but believes it to be valuable as an instrument for the correction of the received moral code. The general happiness principle he defends as the norm of conduct; but he treats it rather as a primary than a demonstrable one. Although he vigorously denounced Utilitarianism, Herbert Spencer's ethical construction (Data of Ethics, 1879), which may be taken as the type of the Evolutionist school, is fundamentally Utilitarian. True, instead of happiness, he makes the increase of life, that is, a fuller and more intensive life, the end of human conduct, because it is the end of the entire cosmic activity of which human conduct is a part. But he holds pleasure and pain to be the standard which discriminates right from wrong, so that in reality he looks upon the moral value of actions as entirely dependent upon their utility. His account of the genesis of our moral ideas, of conscience, and of our moral judgments is too lengthy and complicated to enter into here. Suffice it to say that in it he sets forth the influence of association with that of heredity as the source of our moral standards and judgments. Our sense of moral obligation is but a transitory feeling, generated by the confluence of our inherited racial experience of the results of action with another feeling that the remote present themselves to our consciousness as possessing more "authoritativeness" than the immediate results. The arguments urged against Hedonism in general are effective against Utilitarianism. Its own peculiar weakness lies in its failure to find a passage from egoism to altruism: its identification of self-interest and benevolence as a motive of conduct, and its claim that the ideas *morally right* and *useful* are identical at bottom.

74

ALTRUISM

Timothy Brosnahan [1]

The representative exponent of English altruism is Herbert Spencer. The leading features of his system are these: (1) Conduct becomes ethical in the latest stages of evolution, when it assumes social aspects, when namely its tendency is to raise the aggregate happiness of the community. (2) The sense of duty originates in egoistic feelings of utility. But these in the process of evolution are modified by experience which associates personal happiness with social, political and religious well-being and their sanctions. These associated experiences are recorded in the brain, and by hereditary transmission, and accumulation in successive generations they finally become certain factors or moral intuitions, which we mistake for the voice of a superhuman authority. (3) The conflict between egoism and altruism

[1] *Catholic Encyclopedia*, Vol. I, pp. 369-370.

is not to be removed by giving preponderance to either, since pure egoism and pure altruism are both fatal to society; but by compromise of their respective claims such that the final result will be general altruism, as distinguished from the altruism that ministers to the egoistic satisfaction of others only, whether these others be individuals, or the community impersonally conceived. (4) This reconciliation can only be reached when society is perfectly evolved; when namely we are so constituted that our spontaneous activities are congruous with conditions imposed by our social environments, and social relations are so complete in their adjustments that altruism will not be associated with self-sacrifice, nor egoism with disregard for others. (5) Hence the distinction between Absolute Ethics which formulates the behavior of the completely adapted man in completely evolved society, and Relative Ethics which enjoins only what is relatively right, or least wrong. The former serves as a standard by which we estimate divergences from right; the latter by which we guide ourselves, as well as we can, in solving the problems of real conduct. By absolutely right conduct is understood, of course, that which produces pleasure unalloyed with pain; by relatively right conduct, that which has any painful concomitants or consequences.

Spencer's system is eudaemonistic and, therefore, subject to defects. Moreover, he reduces the moral imperative to a psychological constraint not differing in kind from other natural impluses. At best, even granting his evolutionary premises, he has only presented us with the genesis of conscience. He has not revealed the nature or source of its peculiar imperative. The fact that I know how conscience was evolved from lower instincts may be a reason, but is not a motive for obeying it. Lastly, the solution of the difficulty arising from the conflict between egoism and altruism is deferred to a future ideal state in which egoism, though transfigured, will be supreme. For the present we must be content to compromise, as best we may, on a relative morality. Spencer's own judgment on his system may be accepted. "The doctrine of evolution," he says, "has not furnished guidance to the extent I had hoped . . . some such result might have been foreseen."

The Catholic teaching on love of others is summed up in the precept of Christ: Love thy neighbor as thyself. The love due to oneself is the exemplar of the love due to others, though not the measure of it. Disinterested love of others, or the love of benevolence, the outward expression of which is beneficence, implies a union proximately based on likeness. All men are alike in this that they partake of the same rational nature made to the image and likeness of their Creator; have by nature the same social aptitudes, inclinations, and needs; and are destined for the same final union with God by which the likeness received through creation is perfected. By supernatural grace the natural likeness of man to man is exalted, changing fellowship into brotherhood. All likeness of whatever grade is founded ultimately in likeness with God. Love, therefore, whether of oneself or of others, is in its last analysis love of God, by partaking of whose perfections we become lovable.

The conflict between self-love and benevolence, which is inevitable in all systems that determine the morality of an act by its relation to an agreeable psychological state, need not arise in systems that make the ethical norm of action objective; the ethically desirable and the psychologically desirable are not identified. Catholic ethics does not deny that happiness of some kind is the necessary consequence of good conduct, or that the desire to attain or confer it is lawful, but it does deny that the pursuit of it for its own sake is the ultimate aim of conduct. Apparent conflict, however, may arise between duties to self and to others, when only mediately known. But these arise from defective limitations of the range of one or other duty, or of both. They do not inhere in the duties themselves. The general rules for determining the prevailing duty given by Catholic moralists are these: (1) Absolutely speaking there is no obligation to love others more than self. (2) There is an obligation, which admits of no exceptions, to love self more than others, whenever beneficence to others entails moral guilt. (3) In certain circumstances it may be obligatory, or at least a counsel of perfection, to love others more than self. Apart from cases in which one's profession or state of life, or justice imposes duties, these circumstances are determined by comparing the relative needs of self and others. (4) These needs may be spiritual or temporal; the need of the community or of the individual; the need of one in extreme, serious, or ordinary want; the need of those who are near to us by natural or social ties, and of those whose claims are only union in a common humanity. The first class in each group has precedence over the second.

Catholic ethics reconciles self-love and benevolence by subordinating both to the supreme purpose of creation and the providential ends of the Creator. It teaches that acts of self-love may have a moral quality; that sacrifice of self for the good of others may sometimes be a duty, and when not a duty may oftentimes be an act of virtue. It distinguishes between precept and counsel. The Positivist can only give counsel, and in his effort by emphasis and appeal to sentiment to make it imperative, he destroys all ethical proportion. Because the Catholic doctrine does not confound moral obligations with the perfection of moral goodness it is often charged with laxity by those whose teaching undermines all moral obligation.

75

THE KANTIAN OUGHT

Timothy Brosnahan [1]

Within the last twenty-five years ethical controversies—so far at least as they are confined to the English language—have come to range more and more around the meaning and the nature of the idea expressed by the word "ought." English Ethics since the times of Hobbes, that is to say, since the time that the England of the Reformation began to form for itself a systematized philosophy of conduct, has been distinctively hedonistic and utilitarian. It constituted pleasure and pain the ultimate norms of morality toward which man must of psychological necessity tend, "quite apart from any sense of *duty*" as Spencer says (*Principles of Ethics*, vol. 2, app. c); and made good and evil consist in the external consequences of his actions. The few examples of intuitional ethics that appeared as protests,

---

[1] *Report of the Proceedings and Addresses of the Seventh Annual Meeting of the Catholic Education Association*, Vol. VII, pp. 240-257.

like one or two bright colored flowers in a monochrome field of green, only served to bring into greater prominence the hedonistic character of English Ethics. Now utilitarianism, when egoistic, must repudiate the word "ought" and the underlying idea. It is unmeaning—if it is not absurd— to say that *I ought* to seek pleasure in all my actions, if psychologically I can do nothing else, and if no motive of mine to act is or can be otherwise than good. In fact, Bentham, the most straightforward and logical of English Hedonists tells us in a spurt of hedonistic fury that "the talisman of arrogancy, indolence and ignorance, is to be found in a single word, an authoritative imposter. . . . It is the word 'ought'—'ought' or 'ought not,' as circumstances may be. . . . If the use of the word be admissible at all, it *ought* to be banished from the vocabulary of morals." (*Deontology*, vol. 1, p. 31.) Nor does the concept of ought find any legitimate place in altruistic utilitarianism. If it is not always repudiated, it is so emptied of content as to be a merely larval symbol of itself. All such theories trace the origin of the idea to the individual's experience of pleasure and pain, and attempt to account for its non-hedonistic manifestations either by association of ideas or by the theory of evolution; and assume that in accounting for the genesis of the idea they have assigned the reason why it has moral force. "There is no distinction which has to be kept more steadily in view," says Sir Arthur Balfour, "than this between the causes or antecedents which produce a belief, and the grounds or reasons which justify one" (*Philosophic Doubt*, Chap. 1, p. 3). But there is no distinction which is more steadily ignored by altruistic utilitarians. The fact, for instance, that certain emotions responding to right conduct have, as Spencer informs us (Bain's *Mental* and *Moral Sciences, app.* Spencer's *letter*) arisen from ancestral experiences of pleasure and pain transmitted through cerebral modifications and accumulating through successive generations, would, if it were a fact, simply assign the psychological cause of those emotions, but would not tell me why I *ought* to obey them.

Today, however, Bentham's wild diatribe against the word "ought," would create either amusement or amazement, or raise the suspicion that he was suffering from an utilitarian brainstorm. Spencer's manufactured moral emotions are, like clothing that has gone out of fashion, now offered in the markets of thought only to inexperienced college or university students by secondhand professors. Huxley's taste for good conduct belonging to the same category as an ear for music, now serves no other purpose than to give a spice of intellectual deviltry to ethical discussions. English moralists have been going to school—mostly in Germany. They have learned from Kant, or from his disciples or from the systems derived from his, that the idea behind the word "ought" cannot be eliminated from the human mind. It may be obscured, misinterpreted, assigned this or that origin. It may, as Bentham says, have "in it something disagreeable and repulsive"; nevertheless, we cannot get rid of the consciousness that there are some actions that we *ought* to do, and some others that we *ought* not to do; that there resides within our breasts an authoritative law that prescribes or proscribes certain forms of conduct; that there is indwelling in our minds an internal monitor who has an exclusive right to the verb "ought." Whatever bones of contention there are between us and Kant—and they are neither few nor unimportant—we are indebted to him for the reinstatement of the verb of conscience in the English ethical thought of today. Even utilitarianism has felt his influence. Sidgwick, who began by being an out-and-out follower of John Stuart Mill, finally, as he acknowledges in the preface of the last edition of his *Methods of Ethics,* written shortly before his death, admitted the intuitional character of the concept of "ought;" though with that curious weakness of the English mind for compromise in principles which affect conduct, he tried to eat his bread and have it, and, accordingly, enriched the catalogue of ethical systems, which vex professors of ethics, with Rationalistic Utilitarianism.

But if the concept of "ought" is again accepted with practical unanimity by those who philosophize on morals—it was never absent from the minds of those unsophisticated by theories—the source of the idea and the ground of the obligation which it signifies, are matters on which conflicting schools still widely differ.

There are, in fact, but two possible theories; that of the Schoolmen who find the origin of the moral law in the archetypal ideas of God and the ground of obligation in the necessary will of God; and that of German rationalism which makes reason the origin and ground of obligation, whether that supreme law-giving reason be our individual reason as Kant taught, or in a *quasi* pantheistical sense the reason of the universal ethical substance, as Hegel taught and as derivative Hegelian schools teach with various modifications.

Now I propose to confine myself during the time at my disposal to an examination of Kant's theory. I do this for two reasons: First, he is the father of modern rationalists. They have lighted their tapers at his torch and have not illumined what he left obscure. And, secondly, because I think Paulsen (*Kantstudien,* May, 1899), has put his finger on the intellectual pulse of the times when he declared that there was no philosophic alternative between Neoscholasticism and Kantianism, and that as the ethics of Catholicism is based on Thomism, so the ethics of Protestantism is based on Kantianism. The conflict is between authority and private judgment pushed to their legitimate conclusions.

We are all acquainted with the formulas in which Kant's theory is succinctly presented, namely, that practical reason gives laws *a priori* to man as a rational being, or in other words, that man as a rational being is autonomous or a law unto himself. There is, of course, a sense in which we may affirm that man is a law unto himself. St. Paul, for instance, tells us (Rom. 2, 14) that "when the Gentiles who have not the law, do by nature those things that are of the law; these not having the law are a law unto themselves." It is a psychological fact that man finds within him a faculty by which he is self-compelled to recognize that certain modes of action are good and others evil, and to acknowledge that he ought to do the one and to avoid the other. We can no more deny that reason declares to us a moral law than we can deny that our senses declare to us the existence of an external world. "To deny the deliverances of our own reason," says Rashdall (*The Theory of Good and Evil,* vol. 1, p. 103), "is to deprive ourselves of any ground for believing anything whatsoever. To admit that our reason assures us that there are some things which we ought to do, and yet to ask why we should believe that those things ought to be done, is to ask why we should believe what we see to be true." Assuredly, we cannot ask why we should believe what we see to be true; but we can ask why we ought to do what we believe ought to be done. We need not, in other words, confound the psychological or the logical question with the ethical one. Psychologically I cannot help believing, that is to say, I *must* believe that I ought not to do evil; logically, or in order that my conduct be rational, I *should* do what I believe ought to be done; but ethically why *ought* I, or what binds my will to act in accordance with the deliverances of my reason? Man is, therefore, a law unto himself, first in the sense that his reason is so framed that he perceives of necessity certain truths of conduct; secondly, in the sense that he is conscious of the obligation of conforming his conduct to the dictates of his reason; but he is not a law to himself in the sense that his reason is the supreme lawgiver and the ultimate source of obligation. It is in this last sense that Kant and those who confound "ought" with an ultimate "should" of reason, or a psychological "must," declare that man is a law unto himself, and as a consequence, denude "ought" of any ethical authoritativeness.

The word "ought" is the *copula* of every ethical judgment either directly or indirectly. It is for a practical proposition regarding conduct what the substantive verb is for a speculative proposition. It may not be without significance that it is timeless and moodless. The word is sometimes, it is true, used in other than its ethical sense. By a loose and inexact usage it expresses a reasonable anticipation of what should take place, or a conjectured necessity the frustration of which is not deemed impossible; as when a weather-wise farmer gazing on the sky, says: It ought to rain tomorrow. Again it is used in an appropriated sense to denote a necessity of acting conditioned on expediency, propriety, or an end conceived to be the ideal of an enterprise, profession or state of life. In this derivative sense we say that a politician ought to be a "good mixer," that a gentleman ought to yield his seat in a trolley-car to a lady, or that all of us after our years of study ought to know more than we do. Furthermore, it is used analogously instead of "should" to signify the ultimate reasonableness of a mode of acting. I may say, for instance, that a scientific mind ought not to give unwavering assent to a mere theory, meaning that such assent is in opposition to the unconditioned laws of reason. But the "ought" of ethics has a meaning different from any of these three.

It is, in the first place, *objective;* it declares a truth that has validity independently of the perceiving mind. Human reason, individual or universal, is not the source from which truths of conduct spring as Minervas from the mind of Jove, nor the matrix into which the data of experience is cast, and out of which they are moulded, nor the alembic from which they are distilled as pragmatic values out of the raw material of thought. They do not become true, because reason is so constituted that under given conditions it pronounces them to be true; but because they are true, reason, which has been fitted for their perception by Him who framed it, inevitably assents to them. They would still be true if all the university professors and intellectualists of the country became paranoiacs and denied them. They do not become true because they are the expression of the *Ethos* of the race produced by a traditional or hereditary way of looking at conduct; but because they are true, and because human reason is framed to recognize them and the human will by an innate tendency feels their appeal, they have formed the moral customs of civilization, which, when embodied into a system, have received by historical usage a name that distinguishes it from customs of an inferior kind and designates it as preeminently the ethics or distinctive custom of mankind. They do not become true because they have a utilitarian or pragmatic value, or because by assenting to them we avoid the indignity of intellectual contradiction, but because they are true, they subserve our highest utility, give the finest practical meaning to life and action, and save us from intellectual suicide.

In a word, they are objective in the sense that they are neither mere subjective convictions, nor objective projections on a background of nothingness of the individual, collective, or if such a thing were given, the universal human reason.

In the second place, the "ought" of ethics is *absolute* in the sense that its cogency is not conditioned on any further purpose on which one may have resolved, or by any rational ideal at which one may aim. When I affirm that a politician ought to be a "good mixer," my meaning is that a man who has chosen a political career should, if he would succeed, be approachable by all, and able to adapt himself to the views and moods of others; but I do not assert that he ought to be a successful politician. When, however, I affirm that a reasonable man ought to worship his Creator, I assert not only the duty of worship, but also of the condition being fulfilled on which the duty is predicated. The incidence of oughtness is ultimate, and comprehensive of cognate and implied conditions.

In the third place the "ought" of ethics is *final;* its bond is ultimately on the will, not on the reason; it directly affects the faculty that is moved by good, not the faculty that is determined by truth. It is not the cognoscitive faculty that ought or ought not to do, but the faculty which is the first and efficient principle of all rational movement and action for which man is responsible. A false psychology of this faculty will necessarily involve a false conception of ought. If "will is nothing but practical reason," (p. 29),[2] then it is not an appetitive but at most a conative faculty. An appetitive faculty is drawn to an object, a conative faculty makes a *conatus* or effort to do something. Conation denotes the efficient causality of the will; appetence its response to an object external and congruous to it, and perfective of the being of which it is a faculty. If we ignore the appetitive side of will, as is widely done— not so much in expression as in thought—by modern ethicians who have been influenced by Kant, "ought" no longer expresses final causality; and in spite of verbal protestations we are committed either to determinism and the destruction of morality, or to sheer indeterminism and its meaninglessness.

Lastly, the "ought" of ethics regards an ideal that is *realizable.* I can be morally bound to do only that which it is possible for me to do. The end itself of conduct cannot be obligatory, if it be an ideal term of perfection towards which we can tend, but which we can never attain, though we may continuously approach it. There may be an obligation to tend towards such an end, but there cannot be an obligation to attempt the end itself. The ethical "ought,"

---

[2] See Abbott's "Kant's Theory of Ethics," 5th Ed., for this and subsequent page references.

therefore, declares an obligation which can be fulfilled, not as the poet says, a golden lure

> "to sway
> The heart of man; and teach him to attain
> By shadowing forth the Unattainable."

What, then, is the nature and source of the objective, absolute and final realizable reality which ought signifies to us? We are told today with some insistence and iteration that "ought" is "an ultimate category" of ethics, and that the notion itself is unanalyzable. The inferential suggestion being that we should be content to accept "ought" as an averment of reason and should not too curiously attempt to seek its origin. Minds which have hitherto done their thinking in terms of hedonism and empiricism, cannot wholly cast off their positivist caution, even after they have made profession of intuitionism. The timidity of the novice yet clings to them. They seem to fear that if they are not on their guard against the leadings of thought they might actually discover that there is a God behind all morality and that without Him its binding force is a delusion or a convention. Some of them who do admit God as a *ratio essendi* of morality, do so with a chariness that is apologetic, as though they wished to escape, as far as may be, the censure of being metaphysical or theological. But, after all, ought simply signifies obligation, or the necessity imposed on will by a superior; and, undoubtedly, we can analyze obligation. We have only to invoke the four causes so familiar to the Schoolmen, and we shall have an efficient cause of obligation, or one who obliges, a material cause or the subject obliged, a final cause or that to which the subject of obligation is obliged, and a formal cause, or the moral necessity actually and intrinsically affecting the subject of obligation.

In the first place, then, who is it that imposes obligation on us? It must necessarily be one who is superior to us. Kant in a well known passage (p. 321)[3] puts the problem with sufficient clearness: "Every man has a conscience, finds himself observed by an inward judge which threatens and keeps him in awe. ... Now this original intellectual and moral capacity, called *Conscience,* has this peculiarity

---

[3] All italics in citations from Kant are his own.

in it, that although its business is a business of man with himself, yet he finds himself compelled by his reason to transact it, as if at the command *of another person.* For the transaction here is the conduct of a *trial* before a tribunal. But that he who is accused by his conscience should be *one* and *the same person* with the judge is an absurd conception of a judicial court. . . . Therefore, in all duties the conscience must regard *another* than himself as the judge, if it is to avoid self-contradiction. Now this other may be an actual or merely an ideal person which reason frames to itself. Such an idealized person must be one who knows the heart; . . . at the same time he must also be *all-obliging,* that is, must be or be conceived to be a person in respect of whom all duties are to be regarded as commands. Now, since such a moral being must at the same time possess all power (in heaven and earth) . . . since such a moral being possessing power over all is called *God,* hence conscience must be conceived as the subjective principle of responsibility for one's deeds before God."

An incautious reader might be led to conclude from this passage that the Kantian and Scholastic systems were one on the ultimate source of obligation. But he would in the first place overlook a fundamental tenet of Kant's philosophy, namely, that we can have no theoretical knowledge of God, that even for practical reason He is an assumption, a necessary one, it is true, but not a condition of morality. And, in the second place, he would fail to notice that in the passage cited it is "merely an ideal person which reason frames to itself," which "is called God," in fact, not objectively different from Hobbes "power invisible framed by the mind." The actual person who dictates to us regarding conduct and hales us before a tribunal is the noumenal man, or man as he is in himself, the object of pure intellect and not at all cognizable through experience. The difficulty that arises from the twofold aspect of conscience Kant solved by conferring on man a twofold personality. In each of us there is the noumenal man, and, what is specifically distinct from it, the rationally endowed *homo sensibilis,* or the phenomenal man. The noumenal man is the author of obligation, and the rationally endowed phenomenal man is the subject thereof. The former is the sovereign judge, the latter is the accused. Presumably, too, the noumenal man possesses all power in heaven and earth over the phenomenal man, and knows the secrets of his heart. It is by recourse to some such arbitrary dualism of human personality that Kant avoids the contradiction that is not very far below the surface of every ethical system except that of the Scholastics, and which gives them their provokingly shallow and turbid character.

If Kant would adhere to this theory of a dual personality in man, we might acquit him of the contradiction involved in the idea of the same individual being at the same time sovereign over himself, and a liegeman under himself; a supreme lawgiver imposing laws on himself and a subject who finds that he is bound in conscience by his own laws; a judge who presides in a tribunal of last resort, and a culprit who stands in awe of his *alter ego*. On psychological grounds we might find such a theory untenable. We have no consciousness from which we could infer that there were two persons in our unitary nature. If a case of duplicity could be made out against us at all, some disagreeable moral experiences might lead us to think that we had two clashing natures welded to one person. Medical men, it may be suggested, tell us that those who suffer from some functional nervous diseases, and a consequent disorganization of memory, manifest a double personality. But in these cases the personalities alternate, and the conditions that induce the manifestations are pathological. To save Kant's ethical theory from contradiction our two selves, that is, our over-self and our under-self, should be simultaneous and our personal duplicity should be normal —unless, of course, we are willing to concede that the sense of moral obligation is due to a nervously diseased condition of the race engendered by some obliquity of evolutionary processes. Moreover, there are jural difficulties, besides the psychological ones. If the rationally endowed phenomenal man should challenge the authority of the noumenal man, the latter would have no way of enforcing his authority except to threaten himself with the loss of his own dignity. The sovereign would incur the penalty of being immoral when the subject disobeys. There is a sense, as we know, familiar to asceticism, in which the higher man is said to exercise rule over the lower man, and in default of which a rational nature does suffer personal degradation.

But this sense does not regard our lower nature as the personal subject of moral law. The rule of the higher faculties over the lower is psychological control, not merely supremacy. Morality enters only in so far as man, through his higher faculties of reason and will, is commanded by an authority other than himself, to govern himself in the use of his lower faculties in accordance with a moral law of which he is not the independent and original source. But this is not Kant's sense. His theory, if it has any moral significance, necessarily entails in man the existence of a supreme lawgiving power specifically distinct from the rationally endowed sensitive nature on which it imposes moral obligation. His "ought" if it is not purely psychological in meaning necessarily implies the contrast between sovereign and subject which the mandates of conscience disclose.

Although the passage regarding conscience which I have just quoted appears in one of the last works of Kant, published nine years after the *Critique of Practical Reason,* it does not seem to convey his true meaning on the source of moral obligation, if it is understood literally to assert a real personal distinction between the noumenal man and the phenomenal man. Both in *Fundamental Principles of the Metaphysics of Morality* and the *Critique of Pure Reason* he repeatedly, and in different formulas, declares that the laws to which a rational being is subject are only those of his own giving; that his will, or what is the same thing, his practical reason, is morally good only when it is autonomous. In the former work he presents us with an argument to prove this which is characteristic, inasmuch as from premises luminously clear, we have suddenly flashed upon us a conclusion that seems not only not to follow, but even to contradict the premises themselves. "Everyone must admit," he says, "that if a law is to have moral force, i. e., to be the basis of obligation, it must carry with it absolute necessity; that, for example, the precept, Thou shalt not lie, is not valid for men alone, as if other rational beings had no need to observe it; . . . that, therefore, the basis of obligation must not be sought in the nature of man or in the circumstances in which he is placed" (pp. 3 and 4).

We may indulgently ignore the example by which Kant seeks to conciliate assent to a principle, which he says, every one must admit, for though the precept, Thou shalt not lie, is valid for every being that has an intellect and can communicate thought, that is not the reason but the consequence of its absolute necessity. A precept of the moral law may have absolute necessity, even though it were valid for man alone, as for instance, Thou shalt not commit suicide. Its absolute character is not determined *a posteriori* by its extension, and its extension may vary with the nature of the beings for whom it is absolute. Apart from the illustration, then, which only obscures what it was meant to illumine, every one must admit, who admits any real morality at all, that a law to have moral force must carry with it absolute necessity; it cannot be conditioned by any wish, desire or inclination of the being whom it obliges. Admitting this premise, we should naturally conclude that the basis of morality is to be found only in a being who transcends all rational beings that are themselves subject to law. A moral ideal of goodness and duty can exist only in a mind, as Rashdall truly observes, and an absolute ideal can exist primordially only in an absolute mind, one, namely, that is the origin of all reality subject to law. Our moral ideal, therefore, can claim absolute validity only in so far as it is the impression on our minds of a conception eternally existing in the Divine Mind—*"participatio legis aeternae in rationali creatura,"* says St. Thomas. This, however, is not Kant's conclusion. The basis of obligation, he immediately infers, is to be sought *"a priori"* in the conception of pure reason. But we ask, In the conception of whose pure reason or what pure reason? If in that pure reason which is superior to all limitations and conceptually excludes all imperfections, we again revert to the doctrine of the Schoolmen. But Kant clearly and expressly denies that God is a condition or *ratio essendi* of morality, and puts between himself and Scholasticism a chasm which it is impossible to bridge. If in a pure reason that is neither God's nor creature's we have as a basis of moral obligation a chimerical and nondescript being, which, like the *intellectus agens* of Avicenna or the etnical substance of Hegel, is a cross between a figmental abstraction and a supposititious reality.

But Kant was never quite so absurd as those who improved on his theory. The pure reason in whose *a priori* conception he finds the basis of obligation is a faculty with which each individual rational being is endowed. Yet it may, furthermore, be asked: Does not the pure reason that is an endowment of a rational being belong to his nature, and if in this pure reason is found the ultimate source of morality, why may not the basis of morality be sought in the nature of man? The only answer that can be given is, that Kant arbitrarily restricts the meaning of nature to the physical or phenomenal nature. His argument simply concludes that man's phenomenal nature is not the basis of obligation—a rather ridiculous bantling to be the issue of such ostentatious intellectual gestation. Straightway and by immediate inference he adopts the only alternative that his theory of cognition permits him to entertain. If the origin of morality is not the phenomenal man there is no other origin left for it in Kant's universe but the noumenal man.

In the *Analytic of Pure Practical Reason* he indulges in a loose, rambling rhapsody on Duty. "Thou sublime and mighty name," be exclaims, and with much propriety, since in his system it is nothing but a name. "Thou sublime and mighty name, that dost embrace nothing charming or insinuating, but requirest submission, and yet seekest not to move the will by threatening aught that would arouse natural aversion or terror, but merely holdest forth a law which of itself finds entrance into the mind, and yet gains reluctant reverence (though not always obedience), a law before which all inclinations are dumb, even though they secretly counterwork it; what origin is there worthy of thee, and where is to be found the root of thy noble descent which proudly rejects all kindred with the inclinations; a root to be deprived from which is the indispensable condition of the only worth which men can give themselves?" (p. 180)

Answering his question, he continues: "It can be nothing else but a power which elevates man above himself (as a part of the world of sense), a power which connects him with an order of things that only the understanding can conceive with a world which, at the same time, commands the whole sensible world, and with it the empirically determined existence of man in time, as well as the sum total of all ends.... This power is nothing but personality, that is, freedom and independence of the mechanism of nature, yet regarded also as a faculty of a being which is subject to special laws, namely, pure practical laws given by his own reason, so that the person as belonging to the sensible world is subject to his own personality as belonging to the intelligible world."

The origin, therefore, of the sublime and mighty thing named duty to which man pays reluctant reverence, before which his inclinations are dumb, is man himself. He is the root of its noble descent. This peculiar posture of man standing in dumb reluctant reverence before himself, seems the very sublimity of pathos. As a philosophic concept it seems akin to the viewpoint of a Bowery metaphysician who expresses his moral disgust at another's presence in the curt advice: Go chase yourself. The feat of chasing one's self does not seem more unthinkable than the manoeuvre of standing in reluctant reverence in one's own presence. I venture to say that there are but two conceivable interpretations of this ethical posture. Either we must frankly admit that there are two distinct personalities in man, one of which reluctantly reverences the other as his sovereign lawgiver; or that there is but one and that this one reluctantly reverences himself as a sovereign lawgiver to himself, somewhat, I presume, after the fashion of the character who loved nobody but himself, and loved himself with regret. Which of these interpretations gives Kant's meaning let Paulsen or other loyal commentators decide.

Perhaps the well known passage in *The Fundamental Principles of the Metaphysics of Morals* (p. 51) on "the Kingdom of Ends" will throw some additional obscurity on the subject. Kant writes: "By a kingdom I understand the union of different rational beings in a system of laws. Now, since it is by laws that ends are determined as regards their universal validity, hence, if we abstract from the personal differences of rational beings, and, likewise, from all the content of their private ends, we shall be able to conceive all ends combined in a systematic whole . . . that is to say, we can conceive a kingdom of ends. . . ."

Thereafter he continues: "A rational being belongs *as a member* to the kingdom of ends, when, although giving universal laws in it, he is himself subject to those laws. He belongs to it as a *sovereign,* when, while giving laws he is not subject to the will of any other. A rational being must always regard himself as giving universal laws either as a member or as a sovereign in a Kingdom of Ends." This sovereign man Kant, furthermore, tells us, "is a completely independent being, without wants and with unrestricted power adequate to his will" (p. 52).

Now the main thing that concerns us all in this intellectual prestidigitation is that man in the world of morality is a completely independent being; that he is not bound by the will of any other being in the universe; that he is subject only to the laws of his own giving; that the sovereign obliging and the subject obliged are one and the same.

If this is the last word on the source of obligation of that system of ethics which is to supersede Scholasticism, what, we may ask, is the meaning of "Ought," what is obligation or the moral necessity actually and intrinsically affecting the subject of obligation?

Obligation, as defined by Kant, is "the dependence of a will, not absolutely good, on the principle of autonomy" (p. 58). An absolutely good will is one whose maxims or subjective reasons for acting always and inherently coincide with the laws of autonomy; such a will is not subject to obligation. But the human will is not inherently good, is not in itself in accord with reason; it becomes so when it is autonomous. Autonomy of the will is that property of the will by which it becomes a law unto itself, or acts independently of any property in the objects of volition (p. 59). A law should of its nature be universal, applicable, namely, to every member of the Kingdom of Ends, and it should also be absolute, binding unconditionally and without exceptions. The will is autonomous, therefore, when it is determined by imperatives of conduct that are universal and absolute, and that are of its own giving.

Kant maintains, then, that every rational being gives laws that are universal, to which, as a member of the Kingdom of Ends, he himself is subject, while as a sovereign in the same kingdom he is not subject to any other will. This may sound like a contradiction. For if each rational being who is not subject to any other will could give laws that are universal, it would seem to follow that each will is at the same time autonomous and heteronomous—autonomous, in so far as it would be subject only to the laws of its own giving; heteronomous, in so far as it would be subject to a universal law given by every other will. The contradiction, however, is only apparent, and arises from the fact that Kant uses the phrase, "to give universal laws" or "to legislate universally" in a sense that is his own and that is sophistical. No will in Kant's theory legislates in any proper sense of the word for any other will, nor could it do so without that other will becoming thereby heteronomous.

The universality of the Kantian law as proceeding from the will of a rational being does not regard its imposition, but the form that a personal reason for acting must take in the mind before it can become a law. It does not put an obligation on any will but the will from which it proceeds, and it is universal only in the sense that it can be conceived to be a principle of acting for every other rational being without thereupon contradicting or destroying itself. When it can be so conceived it is said by Kant to be objective. Its objectivity, therefore, like its universality, is conceptual, not ontological. An illustration of Kant may make his meaning clearer than his explanations do. Let the question be, for example: May I when in a difficulty make a promise with the intention of not keeping it? The answer is determined by my answer to a universal question: May every one make a deceitful promise when he finds himself in a difficulty from which he cannot otherwise extricate himself? "Then I presently become aware that while I can will the lie," says the sage of Königsberg, "I can by no means will that lying should be a universal law. For with such a law there would be no promises at all. . . . Hence my maxim, as soon as it should be made an universal law, would necessarily destroy itself" (p. 19).

Bearing in mind, therefore, that Kant makes no distinction whatsoever between will and practical reason, moral law is an *a priori* conception of consistency in action universally considered; and an obligation, the constraint put on the will by the rational necessity of avoiding contradiction in practical reason, or, in other words, it is the ultimate reasonableness of action determined negatively by the conceptual application of the principle of contradiction to universal volitional activity. Shakespeare discovered that consistency was a jewel, it was not till towards the end of the eighteenth century that it was proclaimed the only hall mark of absolute goodness.

The absoluteness that the Moralist of Pure Reason demands for his moral law is as characteristically his own as is its universality. It consists in this: *First,* that the law be given by a rational being who is an end to himself, whose existence has in itself a worth irrespective of its dependence on any other being, and unconditioned by any relation of whatever kind to any other being; and, *secondly,* that it be given through an *a priori* conception out of all relation to and independent of any inclination, desire, purpose or authority distinct from pure practical reason itself. Scholastic ethics admits, of course, and maintains that every rational being is *sui juris,* that is to say, not subordinated in worth to any other rational creature, but denies that his existence does not subserve the end and purposes of his Creator. Again, it admits that the obligation of the moral law is absolute in the sense that it is not contingent on our inclinations and desires, but it denies that it is out of all relation to our natural inclinations, to the primary impulses of our being, or the disinterested purposes of our existence. But Kant would have us admit more and deny less. The absoluteness which he claims for reason as a lawgiving faculty is an absoluteness which we can concede only to the infinite source and term of being, truth and goodness. Though protesting often and fervently against the inroads of self on our morality, and exacting its entire and positive exclusion from every moral motive, he bases his morality finally on the apotheosis of human personality.

But while thus exalting the noumenal self until it becomes like unto the Most High, the absoluteness that he prescribes as an essential condition of formal obligation would compel us to regard our phenomenal self or our rationally endowed sensitive nature, as poisoned in root and branch by a more than Calvinistic depravity. There is no action of ours, the spring of which is any inclination however noble, but is immoral on the principles of this magniloquent and denaturalized morality. When the Psalmist prayed, "Incline my heart unto Thy testimonies" (Ps. 118, 36), he asked for a grace, which, if granted, would have made his will heteronomous, and a life lived in accord with those testimonies devoid of moral worth; and his later acknowledgment: "I have inclined my heart for a reward to do thy justification forever" (Ps. 118, 112), proclaimed him no saint but an exceedingly heteronomous man. He subjected himself to the will of another, he did so from inclination, and, worst of all, he did so for the hope of reward. Poor David, had he aimed at being an autonomous man, should have lived in accord with God's testimonies and done his justifications, moved thereto by no command of God, impelled by no love of Him or His rewards, prompted by no response of his nature to the attraction of any good distinct from himself, but solely by respect for the principle of contradiction as applicable to the world of volitional activity, or, as Kant sophistically calls it, the Kingdom of Ends. Instead of the saint and sinner of Christian morality, we have the autonomous man and the heteronomous man—the autonomous man who gives laws to himself by *a priori* conceptions of reason which are absolutely devoid of any relation, and the heteronomous man who obeys the will of another or acts according to the impulses of his rationally endowed nature.

This is the system of ethics between which and that of St. Thomas, the professor of Berlin invites the world of thought to choose, warning it that if it wishes to preserve unblemished its intellectual freedom, the sacrosanct purity of "ought," the fundamental principles of Protestantism, its choice must be made in favor of Kantianism. The specific grievance against the ethics of St. Thomas is that he makes God the supreme authoritative lawgiver of the universe, and reason on which the light of the eternal ideal has been impressed only His herald. The specific fascination of Kant's system is that it emancipates man from any supreme authority, and confers the supreme power of legislation on a *Deus ex machina* whom he has labeled Pure Practical Reason, and who utters its hollow mandates in categorical imperatives which conveniently have no more binding force than the commands of Alice's Queen in Wonderland, and which, as Kant himself concedes, no rational being, so far as we can possibly discover, ever did obey.

PART TWO
SPECIAL ETHICS

RIGHTS AND DUTIES

76

THE BASIS AND JUSTIFICATION OF RIGHTS

John A. Ryan

A right in the moral sense of the term may be defined as an inviolable moral claim to some personal good. When this claim is created, as it sometimes is, by civil authority it is a positive or legal right; when it is derived from man's rational nature it is a natural right. All rights are means, moral means, whereby the possessor of them is enabled to reach some end. Natural rights are the moral means or opportunities by which the individual attains the end appointed to him by nature. For the present it is sufficient to say that this end is right and reasonable life. The exigencies of right and reasonable living, therefore, determine the existence, and number, and extent of man's natural rights. Just as his intellectual, volitional, sensitive, nutritive and motive faculties are the positive, or physical, agencies by which he lives and acts as a human being, so his natural rights are the *moral* faculties requisite to the same end. He cannot attain this end adequately unless he is regarded by his fellows as morally immune from arbitrary interference. They must hold themselves morally restrained from hindering him in the reasonable exercise of his faculties. His powers of intellect, will, sense, nutrition and motion will be of little use to him if his neighbors may licitly deprive him, whenever it may suit their convenience, of his external goods, or his liberty, or his members, or his life. In addition to his positive powers, he stands in need of those moral powers which give to his claim upon certain personal goods that character of sacredness which restrains or tends to restrain arbitrary interference by his fellows.

Man's natural rights are absolute, not in the sense that they are subject to no limitations—which would be absurd

[1] *A Living Wage*, pp. 4-26. (The Macmillan Company, New York.) Reprinted with permission of the publishers.

—but in the sense that their validity is not dependent on the will of anyone except the person in whom they inhere. They are absolute in existence but not in extent. Within reasonable limits their sacredness and binding force can never cease. Outside of these limits, they may in certain contingencies disappear. If they were not absolute to this extent, if there were no circumstances in which they were secure against *all* attacks, they would not deserve the name of rights. The matter may be made somewhat clearer by one or two examples. The right to life is said to be absolute because no human power may licitly kill an innocent man as a mere means to the realization of any end whatever. The life of the individual person is so sacred that, as long as the right thereto has not been forfeited by the perverse conduct of the subject himself, it may not be subordinated to the welfare of any other individual or any number of individuals. Not even to preserve its own existence may the State directly and deliberately put an unoffending man to death. When, however, the individual is not innocent, when by such actions as murder or attempted murder he has forfeited his right to live, he may, of course, be rightfully executed by civil authority, or killed in self-defense by his fellow man. He may also be compelled to risk his life on behalf of his country, for that is a part of his duty; and he may with entire justice be deprived of life indirectly and incidentally, as when non-combatants are unavoidably killed in a city that is besieged in time of war. Again, the right to liberty and property are not absolute in the sense that the individual may have as much of these goods as he pleases and do with them as he pleases, but inasmuch as within reasonable limits—which are always determined by the essential needs of personal development—these rights are sacred and inviolable.

With respect to their natural rights, all men are equal, because all are equal in the rational nature from which such rights are derived. By nature every man is a person, that is, a rational, self-active, independent being. Every man is rational because endowed with the faculties of reason and will. His will impels him to seek the good, the end, of his being, and his reason enables him to find and adjust means to this end. Every man is self-active, inasmuch as he is master of his own faculties and able in all the essentials of conduct to direct his own actions. Every man is independent in the sense that he is morally complete in himself, is not a part of any other man, nor inferior to any man, either in the essential qualities of his being or in the end toward which he is morally bound to move. In short, every individual is an "end in himself," and has a personality of his own to develop through the exercise of his own faculties. Because of this equality in the essentials of personality, men are of equal intrinsic worth, have ends to attain that are of equal intrinsic importance, and, consequently, have equal natural rights to the means without which these ends cannot be achieved.

Only in the abstract, however, are men's natural rights equal. In the concrete they are unequal, just as are the concrete natures from which they spring.[2] This is not to say that equality of rights is an empty abstraction, without any vital meaning or force or consequences in actual life. Men are equal as regards the *number* of their natural rights. The most important of these are the rights to life, to liberty, to property, to a livelihood, to marriage, to religious worship, to intellectual and moral education. These inhere in all men without distinction of person, but they have not necessarily the same *extension,* or content, in all. Indeed, proportional justice requires that individuals endowed with different powers should possess rights that vary in degree. For example, the right to a livelihood and the right to an education will include a greater amount of the means of living and greater opportunities of self-improvement in the cases of those who have greater needs and greater capacities. But in *every* case the natural rights of the individual will embrace a certain minimum of the goods to which these rights refer, which minimum is determined by the reasonable needs of personality. The rights that any person will possess in excess of this minimum will depend upon a variety of circumstances, individual and social. Hence, instead of saying that the natural rights of all men are equal in the abstract but not in the concrete, it would, perhaps, be more correct, or at least less misleading, to describe them as equal in kind, number and sacredness, and in extension

[2] For an explanation of the distinction between abstract or specific and concrete or individual equality, see Taparelli, "Droit naturel," nos. 354-363, and Cronin, "The Science of Ethics," vol. I, ch. XX.

relatively to their particular subjects; but not in quantity nor in *absolute* content.

Such in bare outline is the theory of the character, purpose, and extent of natural rights. Do they really exist? Is the individual really endowed with moral prerogatives, inviolable claims, in virtue of which it is wrong, for instance, to take from him, so long as he is innocent of crime, his life or his liberty? Whence comes the validity and sacredness of these claims? The answers to these questions have already been briefly indicated in the statement of the *end* for which the claims exist. Natural rights are necessary means of right and reasonable living. They are essential to the welfare of a human being, a person. They exist and are sacred and inviolable because the welfare of the person exists—as a fact of the ideal order—and is a sacred and inviolable thing. It was Cicero who wrote: "Fine in philosophia constituto, constituta sunt omnia." In problems of philosophy, when we have established the end we have established all things else. Let us look more deeply, then, into the scope and character of this end to which natural rights are but means.

Right and reasonable life, the welfare of the person, consist in the development of man's personality through the harmonious and properly ordered exercise of his faculties. He should subordinate his sense-faculties to his rational faculties; exercise his rational faculties consistently with the claims of his Creator and the reasonable demands of his fellows; and seek the goods that minister to the senses and the selfish promptings of the spirit in subordination to the higher goods, namely, those of the intellect and of the disinterested will. In a word, a supreme earthly goal of conduct is to know in the highest degree the best that is to be known, and to love in the highest degree the best that is to be loved. These highest objects of knowledge and love are God, and, in proportion to the degrees of excellence that they possess, His creatures. To prove that these moral and spiritual values are facts, we have only to appeal to the consciousness of any normally constituted human being. The average man has an abiding conviction that the rational faculties are higher, nobler, more excellent, of greater intrinsic worth than the sense-faculties; that consequently the goods of the mind are to be preferred to those of the senses; and that among the activities of the rational powers those dictated by disinterested love are intrinsically better than those which make for selfishness. These primary and general moral intuitions produce in the mind of the person who heeds them the conviction that it is not only reasonable but *obligatory* for him to pursue the path of conduct thus dimly outlined. The immediate objective basis of this obligation is the intrinsic superiority of the higher faculties, the infinite worth of God, and the essential sacredness of human personality. The ultimate source of the obligation is the Will of God; just as the ultimate source of the distinction between the higher and lower faculties, activites, and goods is the Divine Essence; and just as the ultimate source of the intuitions by which we perceive these distinctions is the Divine Reason.

Since, therefore, the individual is obliged to live a moral and reasonable life in the manner just described, the means to this end, *i. e.,* natural rights, are so necessary and so sacred that all other persons than the one in whom they reside are morally restrained from interfering with or ignoring them. The dignity of personality imposes upon the individual the duty of self-perfection; he cannot fulfil this duty adequately unless he is endowed with natural rights. Such is the immediate basis of natural rights and the proximate source of their sacredness; their ultimate source is to be found in the Reason and Will of God, who has decreed that men shall pursue self-perfection and that they shall not arbitrarily deprive one another of the means essential to this purpose.

This method of basing the individual's natural rights upon his duties is perhaps the one most commonly employed by those writers who hold individual perfection to be the immediate end and rule of conduct. According to another mode of reasoning, they rest, not upon the duties of their possessor, but upon those duties of other men toward him which are called *juridical,* that is, the "other-regarding" duties that cover goods which in the strict sense *belong* to him as his own. Thus the fulfilment of lawful contracts is a juridical duty, while assisting the needy is only a duty of charity. All juridical duties may be summed up in the command, "thou shalt not arbitrarily interfere with the external liberty of thy fellow man," for external liberty comprises all those opportunities of activity, acquisition and possession that are essential to the pursuit of reasonable self-perfection. Corresponding to and implied by these juridical duties in one man are those moral prerogatives in other men that we call natural rights. The foundation and source of these duties is that precept of the natural law (understanding by natural law that portion of God's eternal law which applies to human conduct and is written in the human reason) which enjoins men to respect the dignity of human personality in one another.[3]

This line of argument, however, suggests that not even the juridical duties of men are formally necessary as a basis and justification of natural rights. These duties are, indeed, imposed upon man by the natural law, but the reason why this particular precept of the law exists, as well as the reason that constrains us to believe that it does exist, is to be found in the intrinsic and inviolable worth of the individual. That is the ultimate basis—on this side of God —of both juridical duties and natural rights. To prove the existence of the latter, it seems, therefore, logically sufficient to show that because of his intrinsic dignity a person is morally *privileged* to pursue self-perfection, and his fellows are morally restrained from hindering his exercise of the privilege. Natural rights may be likened to the legal right by which a man holds a piece of land that he has bought from the State. His claim thereto is founded neither upon his duty to support his family (to which end the produce of the land may be assumed to be the necessary means) nor upon the obligation which binds his neighbors to leave him in undisturbed possession. Similarly, the individual's natural rights may be regarded as independent both of his own duties and of the duties which these rights occasion in his fellows.[4]

Finally, natural rights can be logically defended on the principles of what may be called intuitive hedonism. There are men who maintain that the supreme end and rule of conduct is universal happiness. By this phrase they mean not "the greatest happiness of the greatest number, nor the

[3] Cf. Cronin, *loc. cit.*
[4] Cf. "The Theory of Morals," by Paul Janet, Book II, ch. IV, in which the author defends a doctrine very similar to the one just outlined, although he strangely calls a right a "responsibility."

general happiness of the group or of society—all of which are equivalent in the concrete to the happiness of the majority—but the happiness of each and every human being. They insist that, since human happiness is the good of a person, it has *intrinsic worth,* is in itself a sacred thing, and that all individuals have, therefore, essentially equal claims to the opportunity of pursuing it. This doctrine is hedonistic, inasmuch as it makes happiness the ultimate end, and intuitive, inasmuch as it postulates not merely the desirableness of personal happiness, but the intrinsic worth of all human happiness. The late Professor Sidgwick held substantially this view, although he admitted that it contains an inherent contradiction.[5] For if the intuition of "rational benevolence" be acknowledged as logically sufficient to compel me to forego my own happiness for the greater happiness of others, then the ultimate end, rule and determinant of right action is no longer *my* happiness—which is the only "desirable consciousness" that can have any meaning for me—but conformity to the dictates of reason. In other words, *reason* assures me that human happiness is valuable *per se,* while all my aspirations and experiences tell me happiness is a good only in so far as it provides *me* with agreeable states of consciousness. If, however, the general principle be admitted in spite of its inherent weakness, a system of natural rights can be logically deduced therefrom.

All of these methods, therefore, posit as the ultimate earthly basis of the individual's natural rights the inherent sacredness of his personality. This is true even of the argument which derives rights from the duty of perfecting one's self; for this duty is itself founded upon the intrinsic worth of the person, specifically of his higher faculties. Hence we find that those who reject the doctrine of natural rights, and who reason logically, reject likewise the principle of the essential and absolute dignity of every human being. They either deny that anything in the universe possesses intrinsic worth, or assert that social welfare is the highest good. To the former class belong the believers in egoistic hedonism; to the latter, the social utilitarians and the Hegelians.

[5] See his "Methods of Ethics," Book III, chapters XIII and XIV; and Book IV, concluding chapter, 6th ed.

For those who maintain that the supreme end of life and rule of conduct is one's own happiness, there can, of course, be no such thing as a right in the *moral* sense of the term. There is no sacredness, no intrinsic worth, no obligation-compelling force in either the concept or the fact of happiness unqualified and divorced from all consideration of the dignity of personality. The person who refuses to seek his own happiness can be condemned as unwise but not as immoral. And if he is not, in any true sense of the word, under moral obligation to procure happiness for himself, neither is he bound by any sort of duty to respect or refrain from hindering the happiness of others. As there is no sacredness in the end—happiness—and none in the persons pursuing it, so there can be no sacredness in the means—those opportunities of activity that we call rights— and no obligation to respect them. In such a system individual rights have neither logical foundation nor intelligible meaning. Again, if personal happiness be the ultimate aim and criterion of reasonable conduct it is altogether fitting and reasonable that each man should interpret happiness in his own way, and strive to obtain it by whatever means seem to him best, regardless of such unreasonable and unfounded restraints as rights and obligations.

This purely egoistic hedonism seems to be completely and consistently accepted by only a very small minority of the world's thinkers. Even with them it is a merely speculative belief. In practice they reject or at least modify it, in common with the overwhelming majority of the men and women who live outside of lunatic asylums. A formal refutation of it in the interest of the doctrine of natural rights is, therefore, unnecessary. Of much greater importance for our contention is the theory that all rights are positive, that is, derived from society, and conferred upon the individual primarily for the benefit of society and only secondarily for the sake of the individual.[6] Individual

[6] In substance this theory seems to be held by a majority of the non-Catholics of our time who write on justice and political philosophy. Not all state it in the same language nor restrict the concrete rights of the individual to the same extent, but all accept the principle that the individual has no right which society may not in certain contingencies annul for its own welfare. The sources of the theory are chiefly: (1) writers who opposed the doctrines of the French Revolution, such as, Edmund Burke in "Reflections

rights are valid in so far as they do not hinder the social weal. "By himself," says Mackenzie, "a man has no right to anything whatever. He is a part of the social whole; and he has a right only to that which it is for the good of the whole that he should have." [7] In this view the social organism becomes an end in itself; and its good becomes the final goal and rule of human conduct. Now society is, indeed, something more than an abstraction, something more than the sum of its component individuals. And its function is not simply to guarantee equal liberty to all its members, in the sense of Immanuel Kant and Herbert Spencer. It is a real entity, a moral body, an organism, whose purpose is to safeguard the rights and promote to a reasonable degree the welfare of every one of its members. It is an organism only by analogy, however; not literally or physically. It is an organism inasmuch as its members are mutually dependent, and have diverse functions; inasmuch as it persists amid continuous changes in its membership, and will retain its identity after all its present members shall have perished; and inasmuch as its health is

on the Revolution in France," and Joseph de Maistre in "Essai sur le principe générateur des constitutions politiques"; (2) juristic writers who, in opposition to the Eighteenth century teaching on natural rights, endeavored to place all rights on a basis of historical facts and development, the most prominent of whom were F. C. de Savigny in "System des roemischen Rechts," and F. C. Stahl in "Philosophie des Rechts"; (3) the Hegelian conception of the State as the highest manifestation of the Universal Reason and Will, the source of all rights, and the absolute end to which the individual must subordinate his particular aims and activity; see Hegel's "Grundlinien der Philosophie des Rechts," and Lasson's "System der Rechts-philosophie"; (4) and finally, the doctrine of evolutionist utilitarianism, which emphasizes the importance of race progress at the expense of the individual.

Some indications of common points in the last two sources will be found in chapter II of Ritchie's "Darwin and Hegel," while recent statements of the general positivistic theory of rights are contained in "Natural Rights," by the same author, in Hobson's "Social Problem," and in Willoughby's "Social Justice." Good presentations of the doctrine of natural rights defended in this chapter are made by Taparelli, "Droit naturel," and Cronin, "The Science of Ethics," I, xx. Finally Hegel's general concept of personality is successfully attacked in Andrew Seth's "Hegelianism and Personality," especially on pp. 67-69 and in the concluding chapter.

[7] "A Manual of Ethics," p. 296.

determined by the health of its members, and in turn reacts upon the latter. When this much has been said the analogy between society and a biological organism is about exhausted. Society is not an organism in the sense that it is a finality. Its members do not exist and function for its welfare; they possess intrinsic worth and sacredness. Hence it is not an organism in which the individual's personality is merged and lost, like the branch in the tree, to use the illustration of Hegel. Society has, indeed, rights that are distinct from the rights of the individuals composing it, and its scope and aims reach beyond the welfare of the men and women that live in it at any given time. It has the right, for example, to make war, which the individual has not; and to prevent the ruthless destruction of forests, which prohibition may be contrary to the interests and wishes of its present members. Nevertheless, every right that society possesses, every act that it performs, every assertion that it makes of its legitimate power over individuals, is ultimately for the sake of individuals. It cannot otherwise be justified, for it is not an end in itself.

Let us concede for the moment that society exists for its own sake, is its own highest good. All its powers, prerogatives and activities will be naturally used as a means to this end. Whenever individuals, however innocent of wrong doing, impede society's progress they are to be relentlessly blotted out of existence. Let us suppose that as a result of this social selection the general level of the race is much higher than it would have been had regard been paid to the "superstition" of natural rights. Society has been treated as an end in itself, and the result is a more excellent society.

It must be evident that the individuals who have been removed to bring about this result could not reasonably have been expected to make the sacrifice willingly. They could not have been satisfied to efface themselves for the sake of society as distinct from its members, since this would be to die for an abstraction. Nor is it likely that any considerable number of them were willing to forego existence in order that the individuals who were left behind might enjoy a more complete existence in the improved society; for the real meaning of this situation is that the former have been used as mere instruments to the welfare of the latter. It is not reasonable to expect men to devote themselves completely to any other end than their own highest good, and a superior society cannot be the highest good for those who must be annihilated as a condition of its realization. They will very naturally prefer to run the risk of securing their own welfare in a less perfect social organization. There is no duty constraining one section of the community—not simply to risk their lives, as in a just war—but to submit to be killed by the social authority, in order that the surviving citizens may have the benefit of a more efficient State. The same statement may be made concerning any other of the individual's natural and essential rights. And if the individuals whose rights are treated as non-existent are neither willing nor bound by moral obligation to make the sacrifice, the State has certainly no right, no *moral* power, to treat them as a means pure and simple to the welfare of those of its members who are permitted to survive. For, juggle as we will with the terms "social utility" and "social welfare," talk as obscurely as we may about regarding the individual from the viewpoint of society, the true meaning of the assertion that the rights of the individual are derived from and wholly subordinate to society, is that the lives of those who are less useful to society are essentially inferior to the lives of those who are more useful. And not until those who reject natural rights have succeeded in proving that some human lives are less sacred, have less intrinsic worth, stand on a lower grade of being than others, can they indulge the hope of winning over any considerable number of thinkers to the contention that the individual—even the poorest and lowliest person that breathes—has no rights that are indestructible by society.

The positivist theory of rights becomes more formidable, at least at first sight, when it is stated in terms of Hegelianism. The question is no longer one between the relative interests and importance of the stronger, wiser and more virtuous citizens on the one hand, and of the weaker, less intelligent and more vicious on the other. Organized society, or the State, is in this system regarded as a good in itself, the highest manifestation of the Universal Reason, which is the only final reality. The all-important consideration, then, is to see that this highest embodiment of the

Universal Reason or World-Spirit called the State, shall reach the fullest possible development. Compared with this purpose, the welfare of individuals, who are merely particular and imperfect realizations of the one great reality, is insignificant. Their importance is analogous to that of the individual trees in a beautiful grove; the totality called the grove is the supreme end, to which the existence and condition of any particular tree is entirely subordinate. The rights of the individual are, therefore, derived from the State and intended for the greater glory of the State. The late Professor Ritchie, one of the ablest of the Hegelians who wrote in English, describes the rights and dignity of the human person thus: "Every human being may claim a right to be considered as such, because he *potentially* shares in the consciousness of the Universal Reason." [8] Each individual is, as it were, a receptacle of the Universal Reason, and derives therefrom all his worth and sacredness. When, consequently, the life or liberty of the individual begins to be an obstacle to the activity or unfolding of the Universal Reason, whenever the interests of the Universal Reason demand that any given individual should cease to embody it, he may lawfully be put to death, just as a diseased limb may be severed from the body, or a leaking pot be consigned to the scrap heap. If the Pantheistic basis of this deification of the State be accepted the theory of rights reared upon it is entirely logical. It may well be doubted, however, whether this blind, impersonal entity known as the Universal Reason seems to any considerable number of persons to have the moral authority requisite to oblige them to surrender their particular existence for its aggrandizement. And of the few who may recognize the supreme rights of the Universal Reason, not all will acknowledge that its loftiest manifestation is to be found in the very fallible and very imperfect State in which they happen to live. An attempt to refute the metaphysical assumptions underlying the Hegelian theory of rights is, consequently, not much needed at this time.

One of the most frequent of the popular arguments against natural rights runs thus: All rights come into existence, become necessary, and obtain adequate protection only in society; hence they are derived from society,

---

[8] "Natural Rights," pp. 96, 97.

exist for a social end, and should be exercised chiefly for the social welfare. This presentation is vitiated by an incorrect analysis and by unwarranted inferences. Not all of man's rights require a social organization, or even social contact of any kind, in order that they should become existent. All that is necessary is that two men be alive at the same time. They may be thousands of miles apart, may not even know of each other's existence, yet each will possess in full validity such natural rights as those of life, liberty and property, and will be morally restrained from hindering his fellow in the reasonable exercise of these rights. As to the second contention, it is true that rights are not needed until men come into some form of social intercourse; for a right means the moral power of restraining others from interfering with one's personal goods, and if there is no one near enough to interfere the moral restraint is unnecessary and impracticable; but this does not prove that rights are created by society, any more than the fact that evening dress is worn only at certain "functions" proves that this form of apparel is created by or for the "functions." The clothes are intended for the individual wearers *on certain occasions*. In like manner, the individual's rights have for their primary purpose his own welfare *in society*. Finally, the fact that a man's rights can be sufficiently protected only in civil society is not a reason why they should be entirely subordinated to the ends of society, any more than the employer's dependence upon his employees puts him under obligation to turn over to them all his profits.

Academic opposition to the doctrine of natural rights is directed not so much against the moderate conception of them that has always prevailed in Catholic ethical teaching, as against the exaggerated and anti-social form in which they were proclaimed by the political philosophers of France, and even by some of those of England and America, in the latter half of the eighteenth century. The Catholic view, which is the one defended in this chapter, is, as already noted, that the individual's natural rights are derived from and determined by his nature, that is to say, his essential constitution, relations and end. They are also said to proceed from the natural law, which is simply that portion of God's eternal law that applies to actions of human beings. The natural law is so expressed in man's nature that its general precepts may readily be known, partly by intuition and partly by analyzing man's faculties, tendencies and destiny. In the view of the Revolutionary philosophers, however, "nature" and "natural" referred not to what is essential and permanent in man, but to that which is primitive and unconventional. Hence they laid more stress on the "state of nature" than on the "law of nature." [9] The natural law was merely that very simple and very primitive system of rules that would suffice for the state of nature, in which political restraints would be unknown, or at least reduced to a minimum. As the late Professor Ritchie has well said: "To the Thomist [1] the law of nature is an ideal *for* human law; to the Rousseauist it is an ideal to be reached by getting rid of human law altogether." [2] In the mind of the Revolutionist, therefore, to reestablish the law of nature meant to shake off the cumbersome and obstructive political regulations of the day, and get back to the simple state of nature, the semi-anarchical conditions of primitive times. This was, of course, a very inadequate interpretation of man's nature and of the natural law. No such "state of nature" ever existed or ever could exist compatibly with civilization. No valid conclusion regarding the individual's liberties, duties or rights could be deduced from his position and relations in this imaginary and irrational existence. Nevertheless, upon it were based and by it were measured men's natural rights in the Revolutionary system. As a consequence, the rights of the individual were exaggerated and the rights of society minimized. In practice this juristic liberalism has meant, and always will mean, that the State allows to the strong the legal right and power to oppress the weak. A good example of the evil is to be found in the results of the economic policy of *laissez-faire*. It is no wonder that there has been a reaction against this pernicious, anti-social and really *unnatural* theory of natural rights.

The doctrine of natural rights outlined in the foregoing pages holds, then, a middle ground between the Revolutionary and the positivistic theories of the origin and ex-

---

[9] Cf. Bonar, "Philosophy and Political Economy," p. 186.
[1] And the Catholic philosopher generally.
[2] "Natural Rights," p. 43.

tent of the rights of the individual. It insists that the individual is endowed by nature, or rather, by God, with the rights that are requisite to a reasonable development of his personality, and that these rights are, within due limits, sacred against the power even of the State; but it insists that no individual's rights extend so far as to prevent the State from adjusting the conflicting claims of individuals and safeguarding the just welfare of all its citizens. In other words, man's natural rights must not be so widely interpreted that the strong, and the cunning, and the unscrupulous will be able, under the pretext of individual liberty, to exploit and overreach the weak, and simple, and honest majority. The formula that correctly describes the limits of individual rights is not the one enounced by Kant and Fichte, namely, that a person has a right to do everything that does not interfere with the equal liberty of others.[3] Interpreted in one way, this formula is utterly incapable of application, since the doing of an action by one man means the limitation to that degree of the liberty of all other men. Understood in a completely subjective sense, it would justify and legalize theft, adultery and murder; for I may claim the right to steal if I am willing that others should enjoy the same liberty. The true formula is that the individual has a right to all things that are essential to the reasonable development of his personality, consistently with the rights of others and the complete observance of the moral law. Where this rule is enforced the rights of *all* individuals, and of society as well, are amply and reasonably protected. On the other hand, if the individual's rights are given a narrower interpretation, if on any plea of public welfare they are treated by the State as non-existent, there is an end to the dignity of personality and the sacredness of human life. Man becomes merely an instrument of the State's aggrandizement, instead of the final end of its solicitude and the justification of its existence. If all rights are derived from the State, and determined by the needs of the State, the laborer has no such thing as a natural right to a living wage, nor any kind of right to any measure of wages, except in so far as the community would thereby be benefited. President Hadley

---

[3] See Kant's "Metaphysik der Sitten," section C, and Fichte's "Science of Rights," p. 161, Kroeger's translation.

tells us that some workers are more profitable at a low wage than at a high one, that the "economy of high wages" is not a universal law. "There are some men whose maximum efficiency per unit of food is obtained with small consumption and small output. These go into lines requiring neither exceptional strength nor exceptional skill, and remain poor because the best commercial economy in such lines is obtained by a combination of low output and low consumption." [4] Those who would measure the rights of the individual by the social weal must logically conclude that whenever "the best commercial economy" is secured by "low consumption," in other words, by low wages, the underpaid worker, let him be never so cruelly "sweated," is not treated unjustly and has no right to a larger remuneration. Hence the importance of the doctrine of rights . . . for it cannot be shown that every laborer has an ethical claim to a living wage unless the teaching of Christianity be accepted, to wit: "That every individual by virtue of his eternal destination is at the core somewhat holy and indestructible; that the smallest part has a value of its own, and not merely because it is part of a whole; that every man is to be regarded by the community, never as a mere instrument, but also as an end." [5]

77

DUTY

JAMES J. FOX [1]

The path of activity proper and congenial to every being is fixed and dictated by the nature which the being possesses. The cosmic order which pervades all the non-human universe is predetermined in the natures of the innumerable variety of things which make up the universe. For man, too, the course of action proper to him is indicated by the constitution of his nature. A great part of his activity is, like the entire movements of the non-human world, under the iron grip of determinism; there are large

---

[4] "Economics," section 363.
[5] Gierke, "Political Theories of the Middle Age," p. 82.
[1] *Catholic Encyclopedia,* Vol. V, pp. 215-217.

classes of vital functions over which he has no volitional control; and his body is subject to the physical laws of matter. But, unlike all the lower world, he is himself the master of his actions over a wide range of life which we know as conduct. He is free to choose between two opposite courses; he can elect, in circumstances innumerable, to do or not to do; to do this action, or to do that other which is incompatible with it. Does, then, his nature furnish no index for conduct? Is every form of conduct equally congenial and equally indifferent to human nature? By no means. His nature indicates the line of action which is proper, and the line which is abhorrent to it. This demand of nature is delivered partly in that hierarchical order which exists in our feelings and desires as motives of action; partly through the reflective reason which decides what form of action is consonant with the dignity of a rational being; comprehensively, and with immediate practical application to action, in those moral judgments involving the "ought." This function of reason, aided thus by good will and practical experience, we call conscience.

We have now reached the first strand of the bond which we know as moral obligation, or duty. Duty is a debt owed to the rational nature of which the spokesman and representative is conscience, which imperatively calls for the satisfaction of the claim. But is this the be-all and the end-all of duty? The idea of duty, of indebtedness, involves another self or person to whom the debt is due. Conscience is not another self, it is an element of one's own personality. How can one be said, except through a figure of speech, to be indebted to one's self? Here we must take into consideration another characteristic of conscience. It is that conscience in a dim, undefinable, but very real way, seems to set itself over against the rest of our personality. Its intimations awake, as no other exercise of our reason does, feelings of awe, reverence, love, fear, shame, such as are called forth in us by other persons, and by persons only. The universality of this experience is testified to by the expressions men commonly employ when speaking of conscience; they call it a voice, a judge; they say that they must answer to conscience for their conduct. Their attitude towards it is as to something not completely identical with themselves; its whole genesis is not to be accounted for by describing it as one function of life. It is the effect of education and training, some say. Certainly education and training may do a great deal to develop this impression that in conscience there is another self implicated beyond ourselves. But the quickness with which the child responds to its instructor or educator on this point proves that he feels within himself something which confirms his teacher's lesson. Ethical philosophers, and conspicuously among them Newman, have argued that to him who listens reverently and obediently to the dictates of conscience, they inevitably reveal themselves as emanating originally from "a Supreme Governor, a Judge, holy, just, powerful, all-seeing, retributive." If, however, we accept Newman's view as universally true, we cannot easily admit that, as is generally asserted and believed, many men obey conscience and love righteousness, who nevertheless do not believe in a personal, moral ruler of the universe. Why may not the most uncompromising theist admit that the moral guide which the Creator has implanted in our nature is powerful enough successfully to discharge its function, at least in occasional cases, without fully unfolding its implications? One of the leading Unitarian moralists has eloquently expressed this opinion. "The profound sense of the authority and even sacredness of the moral law is often conspicuous among men whose thoughts apparently never turn to superhuman things, but who are penetrated by a secret worship of honor, truth, and right. Were this noble state of mind brought out of its impulsive state and made to unfold its implicit contents, it would indeed reveal a source higher than human nature for the august authority of righteousness. But it is undeniable that that authority may be felt where it is not seen—felt as if it were the mandate of a Perfect Will, while yet there is no overt recognition of such a Will, i. e., conscience may act as human, before it is discovered to be divine. To the agent himself its whole history may seem to lie in his own personality and his visible social relations; and it shall nevertheless serve as his oracle, though it be hid from him Who it is that utters it." (Martineau, A Study of Religion, Introduc, p. 21.) Nevertheless, it must be admitted that such persons are comparatively few; and they, too, testify to the implications of another self in the intimations of consciousness; for they, as Ladd says, "personify the conception of the sum total of ethical obligations, they are fain to spell the word with capitals and swear allegiance to this purely abstract conception. They hypostatize and deify an abstraction as though it were itself existent and divine." (Ladd, Philosophy of Conduct, p. 385.)

The doctrine that conscience is autonomous, sovereign, independent, a law-giver deriving its authority from no higher source, will neither, logically speaking, satisfy the idea of duty, nor sufficiently safeguard morality. One cannot, after all, owe a debt to himself; he cannot lay a command on himself. If moral judgments can claim no higher origin than one's own reason, then under close, severe inspection they must be considered as merely preferential. The portentous magisterial tone in which conscience speaks is a mere delusion; it can show no warrant or title to the authority which it pretends to exercise. When, under stress of temptation, a man who believes in no higher legislator than conscience, finds arising in his mind the inevitable question, Why am I bound to obey my conscience when my desires run in another direction? he is perilously tempted to adjust his moral code to his inclinations; and the device of spelling duty with a capital will prove but a slender support to it against the attack of passion.

Reason solves the problem of duty, and vindicates the sanctity of the laws of righteousness by tracing them to their source in God. As the cosmic order is a product and expression of the Divine Will, so, likewise is the moral law which is expressed in the rational nature. God wills that we shape our free action or conduct to that norm. Reason, recognizing our dependence on the Creator, and acknowledging His ineffable majesty, power, goodness, and sanctity, teaches us that we owe Him love, reverence, obedience, service, and consequently we owe it to Him to observe that law which He has implanted within us as the ideal of conduct. This is our first and all-comprehensive duty in which all other duties have their root. In the light of this truth conscience explains itself, and is transfigured. It is the accredited representative of the Eternal; He is the original Imponent of moral obligation, and disobedience to conscience is disobedience to Him. Infraction of the moral law is not merely a violence done to our rational nature;

it is also an offence to God, and this aspect of its malice is designated by calling it sin. The sanctions of conscience, self-approbation and self-reproach, are re-inforced by the supreme sanction, which, if one may use the expression, acts automatically. It consists in this, that by obedience to the law we reach our perfection and compass our supreme good; while, on the other hand, the transgressor condemns himself to miss that good in the attainment of which alone lies the happiness that is incorruptible. To obviate a possible misapprehension, it may be remarked here that the distinction between right and wrong hangs not upon any arbitrary decree of the Divine Will. Right is right and wrong is wrong because the prototype of the created order, of which the moral law forms a part, is the Divine Nature itself, the ultimate ground of all truth, intellectual and moral.

Erroneous Ethics.—We have already touched upon the main weakness of the Kantian theory, which is to treat conscience as autonomous. Another mistake of Kant is that in his system duty and right are made coterminous. A moment's reflection is sufficient to perceive that this is an error. There are many conceivable good actions which one can do, and which it would be highly praiseworthy to perform, yet which no reasonable person, however rigorous his ideal of conduct might be, would say one is bound to perform. Duty and right are two concentric circles. The inner one, duty, embraces all that is to be observed under penalty of failing to live rationally. The outer contains the inner, but stretching far beyond permits an indefinite extension to the paths of virtue that lead to consummate righteousness and sanctity. Every philosophic system which embraces as one of its tenets the doctrine of determinism thereby commits itself to the denial of the existence of moral obligation. Duty implies that the subject of it possesses the power to observe the law, or to disobey, and the power to choose between these alternatives. What reproach can a determinist mentor logically address to one who has committed a wrong action? "You ought not to have done so"? The culprit can reply: "But you have taught me that free will is a delusion; that no one can act otherwise than he does. So, under the circumstances in which I found myself, it was impossible for me to refrain from the action which you condemn. What, then, can you mean by saying that I ought not to have acted as I did? You reproach me; as well reproach a tiger for having eaten his man or a volcano for having ruined a village."

With regard to the existence of duty, every form of pantheism, or monism, logically finds itself in the camp of determinism. When man is looked upon as one with the Infinite, his actions are not really his own, but belong properly to the Universal Being. The part assigned to him, in his activities, is similar to that played by a carbon burner in relation to the electric current generated by a dynamo. The Divine power passing through him clothes itself with only a seeming individuality, while the whole course of action, the direction which it takes, and the results in which it culminates, belong to the Supreme Being. If this were true, then lying, debauchery, theft, murder were equally as worthy as truthfulness, chastity, honesty, benevolence; for all would be equally manifestations of the one universal Divinity. Then a classification of conduct into two opposite categories might still be made from a standpoint of results; but the idea of moral worth, which is the very core of moral life and the first postulate of duty, would have vanished. Hedonism of every shade—epicurean, utilitarian, egoistic, altruistic, evolutionary—which builds on one or other form of the "greatest happiness" principle and makes pleasure and pain the discriminating norm of right and wrong, is unable to vindicate any authority for duty, or even to acknowledge the existence of moral obligation. No combination of impulses, if they are estimated from the merely biological or purely empirical standpoint, can, by any juggling of words, be converted into a moral hierarchy. The hedonist is doomed to find all his endeavor to establish the basis of the moral order terminate in "is," but never in "ought," in a fact, but never in an ideal. Lecky has neatly summed up the hedonist solution of the problem of duty: "All that is meant by saying we ought to do an action is that if we do not do it we shall suffer."

Pleasure, say the epicurean and the egoist, is the only motive of action; and actions are good or bad accordingly as they produce a surplus of pleasure over pain, or contribute to or diminish welfare. Then, we ask, must I always pursue what seems to me the most pleasurable or the most remunerative? If the answer is yes, we are again landed in determinism. If the reply is that I can choose, but that I ought to choose what produces the most happiness, then I ask, why ought I to choose the course which produces the most happiness or pleasure if I prefer to do otherwise? To this question the epicurean and the egoist have no answer. Besides, the most pleasurable conduct may be one that all reasonable men condemn as wrong, because it is injurious to some one else. Here the egoist is compelled to hand the difficulty over to the altruist. The latter endeavors to dispose of it by pointing out that the object of good conduct is not merely the agent's own happiness, but that of everybody concerned. But again, why am I bound to take into account the welfare of others? and the altruist is silent. The evolutionist of the Spencerian type intervenes with a ponderous theory that in gauging the measure in which actions produce welfare or diminish it, not merely the immediate, but also and more especially the remote results must be considered. He then proceeds to show that, as an hereditary consequence of our ancestors' experience that remote results are more important than immediate, we have come to fancy that remote results have a certain authoritativeness. Also, from unpleasant experiences of our ancestors, we inherit a tendency, when thinking of injurious actions, to think too of the external penalties which were attached to such actions. These two elements, blending into one, give rise, we are told, to the feeling of moral obligation. So the common conviction that moral obligation has really any binding authority is a mere delusion. Spencer is honest enough to draw the inevitable corollary of this doctrine which is that our sense of duty and moral obligation is transitory and destined to disappear. Ethical writers of the "independent morality" schools have devised a beautifully simple way of escaping from the embarrassment of accounting for the validity of moral obligation. They ignore the subject altogether and refer the disappointed inquirer to the metaphysician. Ethics, they blandly declare, is a descriptive, not a normative science; hence that imposing array of works professing to treat scientifically of morals, yet calmly ignoring the pivotal factor of the moral life.

78

CONTRACT

Thomas Slater [1]

The canonical and moralist doctrine on this subject is a development of that contained in the Roman civil law. In Roman law a mere agreement between two parties to give, do, or refrain from doing something was a nude pact (*pactum nudum*) which gave rise to no civil obligation, and no action lay to enforce it. It needed to be clothed in some investitive fact which the law recognized in order to give rise to a civil obligation which should be enforced at law. Not that the nude pact was considered to be destitute of all binding force; it gave rise to a natural obligation, and it might afford ground for a legal exception. A man of honor would keep his engagements even if he knew that the law could not be invoked to impel him to do so. Moral theology, being the science of Christian conduct, could not be satisfied with the mere legal view of the effect of an agreement. If the agreement had all other requisites for a valid contract, moral theology must necessarily consider it to be binding, even though it was a nude pact and could not be enforced in the courts of law. Canon law made this moral attitude its own. In the Decretals of Gregory IX it is expressly laid down that pacts however nude must be kept, and that a strenuous endeavor must be made to put in execution what one has promised. It thus came to pass that nude pacts could be enforced in the Christian courts, and the Church's legislation served eventually to break down the rigid formalism of Roman law, and to prepare the way for the more equitable law of contract which all Christian nations now possess.

In the canonical and moral doctrine there is hardly room for the distinction between a nude pact, or mere agreement, and a contract. The Roman jurist's definition of the former is frequently used by canonists to define contract. They say that a contract is the consent of two or more persons to the same proposal; or, bringing out a little more definitely the effect and object of a contract, they define it to

[1] *Catholic Encyclopedia*, Vol. IV, pp. 332, 333.

be an agreement by which two or more persons mutually bind themselves to give, do, or abstain from something. From the moralist's point of view, then, every agreement seriously entered into by those who are capable of contracting with reference to some lawful object is a contract, whether such agreement can be enforced in the civil courts or not. The intention of the parties is looked at, and if they seriously intended to bind themselves, there is a contractual relation between them. This doctrine, however, gives rise to a question of some importance. The Church fully admits and defends the right of the State to make laws for the temporal well-being of its citizens. All States require certain formalities for the validity of certain actions. Last wills and testaments are a familiar example, and although they are not strictly contracts, yet the principle is the same, and they will serve for an example of what is meant. A deed, the only formal contract of English law, is another example. A will destitute of the requisite formalities is null and void at law; but what is the effect of such a voiding law in the forum of conscience? This question has been much debated among moralists. Some have maintained that such a law is binding in the internal as well as in the external forum, so that a formal contract, destitute of the formalities required by law, is null and void in conscience as it is in law. Others adopted the contrary opinion, and held that the want of formality only affected the external forum of civil law, and left intact the natural obligation arising from a contract. The common opinion takes a middle course. It holds that the want of formality, though it makes the contract void in the eyes of the law, renders it only voidable in the forum of conscience; so that, until one of the parties moves to set the contract aside, it remains valid, and anyone deriving benefit under it may enjoy his benefit in peace. If, however, the party interested moves to set it aside, and does so effectively, by having recourse to the court of law if necessary, both must then abide by the law which makes the contract void and of no effect.

There are four essential elements in a contract—consent of the parties, contractual capacity in them, determinate and lawful subject-matter, and a lawful consideration. The contract is formed by the mutual consent of the parties, which must be real, not feigned, and manifested so that each may know that the other party consents. There is no difficulty about the outward manifestation of consent when the parties enter into the contract in each other's presence. But when the parties are not present to each other, and the contract is made by letter or telegraph, it sometimes becomes a question of importance as to when and how the contract is effected. Is the contract entered into when the offeree signifies his consent by posting a letter of acceptance to the offeror, or is the knowledge of his acceptance required to complete the contract? All that is required by the nature of a contract is that there should be mutually manifested agreement of the two wills. There will be such agreement when one of the parties makes an offer to the other, and this one manifests his acceptance of the offer by posting a letter or by sending a telegram. There is then consent of two wills to the proposal, and so there is a contract. Mutual consent to the same proposal may be hindered by a mistake of one of the parties. Such mistakes are not infrequently caused by the fraud or misrepresentation of one of the parties. If the mistake is substantial, so that at least one of the parties thinks that the subject-matter of the contract is quite other than it really is, there will be no consent and no contract. Similarly, if there be a mistake about the nature of the contract proposed (as, if one party intends to sell while the other only means to borrow) there is no agreement of wills. Mistake about the mere quality of the subject-matter of the contract is accidental, not substantial, and in spite of it there may be substantial agreement between the parties. If, however, such a mistake has been caused by the fraud or misrepresentation of the other party to the contract, and the party deceived would not otherwise have entered into it, it is only fair that the deceived party should be able to protect himself from injury by retiring from the agreement. Contracts, then, entered into because of accidental mistake which was induced by the fraud or misrepresentation of the other party, will be rescindable at the option of the party deceived.

The consent of the parties must be deliberate and free, for a perfect and grave obligation cannot arise from consent which is not deliberate or free. Hence we must see what the influence of fear is upon the validity of a contract. If the fear goes to the length of depriving one of the parties of the use of reason, he cannot, while in that state, give a valid consent, and the contract will be null and void. Fear, however, does not ordinarily produce such extreme effects; it leaves a man with the natural use of his reason and capable of consenting or withholding his consent. Even grave fear then does not of itself invalidate a contract, but if it is unjustly caused by the other party to the contract, with a view to forcing him who is under its influence to consent, the injured party may withdraw from the contract. Some contracts, such as marriage, thus entered into under the influence of grave fear unjustly caused by the other party to the contract with the intention of compelling consent, are made invalid by canon law. Some authorities even hold that all such contracts are invalid by natural law, but the opinion is at most only probable. A person must have the use of reason in order to give valid consent to a contract, and his contractual capacity must not have been taken away by law. Those who have not yet attained the use of reason, imbeciles, and those who are perfectly drunk so that they do not know what they are doing, are incapable of contracting by the law of nature. Minors are to a certain extent restricted in their contractual capacity by English and American law. Practically, their contracts are voidable except those for necessaries. Married women were formerly incapable of entering into a valid contract, but in England since 1882 their disability has been removed, and in most of the States of the Union the same doctrine begins to prevail.[1] Religious persons are to a greater or less extent, according as they are under solemn or simple vows, incapable of entering into a binding contract. Corporations and companies are limited in their contractual capacity by their nature or by the articles of association.

The subject-matter of a contract must be definite and certain, it must be possible, and it must be honest. A contract cannot be a bond of iniquity, and so an agreement to commit sin is null and void. Some theologians maintain that when, in execution of a contract, a sinful action has

---

[1] EDITOR'S NOTE: The Nineteenth Amendment to the Constitution of the United States does not in any way affect the contractual rights of women. It merely gives them the right of suffrage.

been performed, a right is acquired to receive the price agreed upon. The opinion seems at any rate probable. If the contract is not sinful in itself, but voided by positive law, it will be valid until it is set aside by the party interested, as was said above concerning informal contracts. When persons enter into a contract, each party promises to give, do, or forbear something in favor of the other. The benefit which thus immediately arises from the contract, and which is the cause of it, is called the *consideration* in English law. It is a necessary element in a contract, and if it is wanting, the contract is null on account of the failure of a necessary condition in the agreement. The courts of civil law will not enforce a simple contract unless there be a valuable consideration in it; mere motives of affection or moral duty will not suffice. This rule, however, only effects legal obligations; it has nothing to do with obligations in conscience. A valid contract imposes on the contracting parties an obligation of justice to act conscientiously according to the terms of the agreement. They will be bound to perform not only what they expressly agreed to do, but whatever the law, or custom, or usage prescribes in the circumstances. The obligation arising from a contract will cease when the contract has been executed, when a new one has been substituted for the old one by the free consent of the parties, when the parties mutually and freely withdraw from the contract. When one of the parties fails in what he promised, the other will, as a rule, be free. A contract may be concluded not absolutely but conditionally on the happening of some uncertain and future event. In this case the conditional contract imposes on the parties the obligation of waiting for the event, and in case it happens the contract becomes binding on them without renewal of consent. On the other hand, a contract is sometimes entered into and begins to bind at once; but the parties agree that it shall cease to bind on the happening of a certain event. This is called a condition subsequent, while the former is a condition precedent.

79
REVELATION
Timothy Brosnahan [1]

Revelation, which is the unveiling of truths hitherto hidden, is either *natural,* when the unveiling is done by human reason, or *divine,* when done through the formal communication of thought by God. Divine revelation is not impossible (a) on the part of God. If man can communicate thought, his Creator can. (b) On the part of man. If man can receive a revelation from his fellow-man auricularly, he can receive one from God through intellectual illumination. (c) On the part of the truth revealed, for these are truths the existence of which could not be known by unaided reason, and which when revealed to an intelligence of finite compass may be relatively unintelligible. (d) On the part of its purpose, for obedience of intellect is as essential in a creature as other obedience.

The moral law obliges us to believe one, (a) who can neither deceive nor be deceived; (b) who speaks in order to be believed; (c) who has the right of speaking and of requiring intellectual assent to what he says. But when God reveals anything to man, and the fact of such revelation is known, these three conditions are present.

80
OBLIGATION TO WORSHIP GOD
A Truth of Pure Reason
Orestes A. Brownson [2]

You know that God is, for the invisible things of him, even his eternal power and divinity, are clearly seen from creation, being understood from the things that are made. You cannot then doubt that you are under an obligation to worship him, and an obligation from which neither you can withdraw yourselves, nor even he himself dispense you.

---
[1] *Digests of Lectures on Ethics,* pp. 61, 62. (John Murphy Company, Baltimore.)
[2] *Brownson's* "*Quarterly Review,*" April, 1848, pp. 137-143.

Is not this the common sense of mankind? In every age and nation, savage, barbarous, or civilized, do you not find the fact of your obligation to worship God acknowledged and asserted? Have not even those of your philosophers, who maintain that religion is a law or principle of human nature, universal, permanent, and indestructible, triumphantly proved that religious worship of some sort, is coeval and coextensive with the race? Assuredly, what is proved by all men, in all ages of the world, is a dictate of reason, and we cannot deny it without divesting ourselves of that which constitutes the peculiar dignity and glory of our nature, and as far as in our power, placing ourselves out of the category of men, and in that of irrational beings.

Moreover, the obligation of all men to worship God is not only certain from the common sense of mankind, from what Immanuel Kant calls the practical reason, but it is a truth of the pure reason itself, and as demonstrably certain as any truth of philosophy or mathematics. Certainly, the Creator has the sovereign right of property to the creature—the maker, to the thing made. Is not this what you assert, when you say, a man has a right to the produce of his own hands, or the laborer is worthy of his hire? Is not God our creator? Has he not made us and bestowed upon us all our original endowments? You cannot deny it; for we could not act before we were, or bestow what we had not. Then he has the sovereign right of property to us; then we are his, not our own; and then we are bound to render ourselves, with all our original endowments, unto him, for justice requires us, as is undeniable, to render unto every one his own.

To render ourselves, that is, the tribute of our whole being, unto God as his due is, in general terms, what is to be understood by worshipping him. If, then, justice, as it undeniably does, requires us to render unto every one his due, and if we are due to God, are his and not our own, assuredly we are bound to worship him. This you cannot deny.

Can we ever withdraw ourselves from this obligation, or can it, by any act of ours, ever become true that we are not bound to worship God? Certainly not, unless we are able to destroy the relation which we hold to God as his creatures. We are bound to worship him because we are his;

and we are his because he has made us. We are bound to render unto him the tribute of our being because he is its author, and of our whole being because he is the author of the whole. So long, then, as it remains true that he is the author of the whole, we must be bound to worship him. Can we ever make it true that he is not the author of our whole being, that he has not made us and bestowed upon us all our faculties? If not, and we cannot, for it is metaphysically impossible—we can never withdraw ourselves from the obligation to worship God, or be released from it by any act of ours.

But cannot God, if he chooses, dispense us from this obligation? The obligation to render unto every one his due, and therefore ourselves unto God, is an obligation of eternal justice. To deny it would be to deny justice itself, that which is essential to the very conception of justice. To dispense from it would, then, be to dispense from the obligations of eternal justice, and to authorize injustice. God cannot do this, or choose to do it; for he is essentially just, and it would be to contradict his own essential, eternal, and immutable nature. Then it must follow, that, as long as we exist, we are bound to render unto him, and he must exact the tribute of our whole being. Then are we under obligation to worship God, and an obligation from which neither we can withdraw ourselves nor he himself dispense us.

You must concede this, or deny all morals. A moral action is not merely one which it is agreeable, convenient, or useful to perform, but a debt which we owe and are obliged in justice to pay. All morality rests on the idea of duty, and all duty on the principle that we are bound in justice to give unto every one his own. If, then, you assert moral obligation at all, you must concede that we are bound to worship God; for, evidently, we cannot be less bound to render unto God what is his than unto others what is theirs. Then, if you deny the obligation to worship God, you must deny that we are bound to render unto every one his own, and then moral obligation itself, and with it all morals.

But the obligation to worship God, if conceded, includes all our obligations, and is the only obligation which can be asserted. It is obvious to every one that we can owe only on condition that, to the extent of our indebtedness, we are not our own; and equally obvious, that we can owe only him whose we are. We owe God, because we are his—our whole being, because our whole being is his. If we owe our whole being to him, we can owe only him; for we evidently cannot be indebted beyond our whole being. Owing our whole being to God, we are incompetent to contract debts to or from another. The earnings of property are the proprietor's. If God owns our whole being, as he must if the author of the whole, he owns our faculties, and then all that we can do or acquire by their exercise. We are, then, in the condition of the son under age, who is incompetent to acquire property or to contract debts. What is due to the services of the son is due to the father; what is due to services rendered by others to the son is due from him only in and through the father. So with us, we can bind or be bound only in and through God, whose we are. If we can bind only in and through him, others can be bound to us or owe us any thing only as they owe, and for the reason that they owe it to him; and if we can be bound only in and through him, we can owe others but as we owe, and for the reason that we owe him. Is it not undeniable, then, that our duty to God is our only duty, and that our obligation to worship him includes all our obligations?

Unquestionably, we are bound to take proper care of ourselves, and to do ourselves no harm. But to whom are we bound? To ourselves? That is absurd, for it implies that the binder and the bound are identical, and also that we are our own; but so far as our own, it is evident that we are not and cannot be bound at all. If our own, we are free to dispose of ourselves as we please. May I not do as I will with mine own? If our own, whose business is it, if we waste our strength and activity, destroy our health of mind or body, and kill ourselves, body and soul? But we are not our own; we belong, in our whole being, to God, who has the sovereign right to all that we are and have; therefore we are bound, not to ourselves, but to him;—and bound to him to take proper care of ourselves and to do ourselves no harm, because justice requires us to take proper care of what is intrusted to us, and to refrain from all injury to the property of another.

Unquestionably, again, we are bound to do as much for our neighbor, to love him as we love ourselves. But to whom are we bound? Not to him; for he is no more his own than we are our own. Not being his own, he cannot bind us; having nothing of his own, he cannot bring us in debt to him. The obligation, therefore, is not to him, but to God, whose he is, and whose is all that he has, or that we receive from him. He being the property of God, who is our owner, our master, as well as his, and being also our equal, we are bound to treat him as ourselves; for we must needs be as much bound to protect and not to injure the property of our master in another as in ourselves.

If this be so, it is evident that we cannot worship God, if we refuse to love, and serve our neighbor. The claim of God extends to our whole being, and covers every sphere of our activity. God is the author of our whole being, and of all our relations, whether relations of family, of neighborhood, of country, or of humanity; and therefore whatever is due to these is due to him, and must be paid, or we fail to discharge the debt we owe him. The duties growing out of these several relations are as integral in the worship of God as any other duties we do or can have. He who would love God must love his brother also; and he who would worship God must serve his neighbor. There is no such thing as being faithful Godward, and faithless manward.

But because the worship of God includes integrally all our duties, you must not suppose that this worship is resolvable into the love and service of humanity, as do your Socialists and Humanityists. The debt is due to God, and to him alone. As sovereign proprietor of it, he may transfer it, and make it payable to whom he pleases; but it must be paid to him, or his order, or it is not paid at all. It may be payable to our neighbor, but only because God appoints him his agent to receive it. The error of your Socialists and Humanityists is not in asserting our duty to love and serve our neighbor, nor in identifying this love and service with the worship of God; but in asserting that they are due to our neighbor in his own right, and that we pay it to God because we pay it to man. We are assuredly to love and serve humanity, but not for humanity's sake. We love and serve our neighbor for God, and when we do we worship God. But we cannot reverse it, and love and serve God for our neighbor; for our neighbor, not being the owner of God, cannot be the owner of the debt. The debt is not due to our neighbor, and to make it due to him is to deny it to be due to God,—is to put man in the place of God,—the very essence of idolatry, forbidden alike by reason and revelation, and which threatens, unless checked, to assume ere long an avowed and public form, as is not obscurely indicated in the "soul-worship" and "Hero-worship" of your Transcendentalists.

Nevertheless, do not start at the assertion of your obligation to render unto God the tribute of your whole being. Undoubtedly, it implies your absolute subjection, soul and body, to God,—but this is not, as some of you have alleged, slavery; for slavery is not in subjection, but in *unjust* subjection. The slave is not more subjected to his master than the wife to her husband, or the son, while he serves, to his father, and if equally due, his subjection would be no more a grievance, or slavery, than theirs. Absolute subjection to God, if just,—and it is just, if his due,—is, then, no slavery, no grievance, no infringement of man's natural right or freedom.

All men do and must concede their absolute subjection to God, for they all do and must concede their absolute subjection to justice. No man can pretend that he has the right to be unjust, the right to do wrong; for it is a contradiction in terms. Rights are founded in justice, or they are wrongs, not rights. The denial of justice is the denial of right, and the denial of right is the denial of rights; for *rights* are only by participation of *right*. The ground of all complaints is the real or supposed injustice of the matter complained of; and whatever men demand they demand it on the ground of its real or pretended justice. The highest conception of freedom is in absolute subjection to justice, and to justice alone; and authority, civil or ecclesiastical, is held to be tyrannical or oppressive only because it is held to be unjust in its origin or exactions. What is just all men feel they may exact, and are bound to give. It is clear, then, that they acknowledge the absolute sovereignty of justice. But justice is God, who in himself is eternally and essentially just. Absolute subjection to God is, then, simply absolute subjection to justice. All men, therefore, in admitting their absolute subjection to justice, admit their absolute subjection to God; and since no one ever regards it as a hardship to be subjected to justice, no one can feel it a hardship to be subjected to God.

The repugnance manifested by your Liberals to the doctrine which requires every man to render unto God the tribute of his whole being, results either from their hatred of justice or their supposition that justice and God are separable. If the former, they are clearly condemned; for no man hates justice, unless conscious that his deeds are unjust. The latter cannot be entertained. We are not permitted to suppose that justice may stand on one side, and God on the other; for that would be to suppose God without and opposed to justice. Reason is declarative, not legislative. In teaching that justice requires us to render unto every one his due, it declares the precept of justice, but does not create it. Justice itself must, then, be prior to and independent of reason, it must be something or nothing. It cannot be nothing; for that would deny both reason and justice. Then it must be something; and if something, since reason declares it to be universal, eternal, and supreme, it must be God. Then God is essentially just, and we cannot suppose him distinguished from justice without supposing his non-existence. But his non-existence is not supposable; for he is a necessary existence—*ens necessarium*. His existence, then, must be supposed always and everywhere; and then, always and everywhere, must he be supposed as essentially, infinitely, immutably, and eternally just—justice itself. It is, then, absurd, as well as impious and atheistical, to suppose him ever otherwise than just, or that we, in surrendering ourselves unreservedly to him, can possibly run any risk of losing our rights, or of being oppressed. Our rights have thus the guaranty of infinite justice.

Moreover, you must not fall into the error common to many of your number, that, though we are bound to worship God, we are nevertheless not bound to render him any outward or external service. The worship of God, exacted by eternal justice, is the tribute of our whole being. Our being consists of body and soul, and is at once external and internal. Consequently, we must be bound to render unto God both soul and body, and therefore both internal and external worship.

This much you must concede, or deny human reason itself. But human reason itself you cannot deny; for you have nothing but it on which to deny it, and to deny it on its own authority is to affirm it. That you are bound to worship God is as certain as any moral or even mathematical truth is or can be; for it combines in its favor both the practical reason, or common sense of mankind, as is historically provable, and the speculative or demonstrative reason, as you have just seen—the only two kinds of certainty which natural reason ever furnishes or demands. Let it be assumed, then, that we are under an obligation to worship God, from which neither we can withdraw ourselves, nor even he himself dispense us. This is, and must—let the consequences be what they may—be conceded to be, certain and undeniable.

81

RELIGIOUS INDIFFERENTISM

JAMES J. FOX [1]

Religious indifferentism is the term given in general to all those theories which, for one reason or another, deny that it is the duty of man to worship God by believing and practicing the one true religion. This religious indifferentism is to be distinguished from *political* indifferentism, which is applied to the policy of a state which treats all the religions within its borders as being on an equal footing before the law of the country. Indifferentism is not to be confounded with religious indifference. The former is primarily a theory disparaging the value of religion; the latter term designates the conduct of those who, whether they do or do not believe in the necessity and utility of religion, do in fact neglect to fulfil its duties.

I. *Absolute Indifferentism.*—Under the above general definition come those philosophic systems which reject the ultimate foundation of all religion, that is, man's acknowledgment of his dependence on a personal creator, whom, in consequence of this dependence, he is bound to reverence, obey and love. This error is common to all atheistic, ma-

---

[1] *The Catholic Encyclopedia*, Vol. VII, pp. 759-761.

terialistic, pantheistic, and agnostic philosophies. If there is no God, as the atheist professes to believe, or if God be but the sum of material forces, or if the Supreme Being is an all-embracing, all-confounding totality in which human individuality is lost, then the personal relationship in which religion takes its rise does not exist. Again, if the human mind is incapable of attaining certitude as to whether God exists or not, or is even unable to form any valid idea of God, it follows that religious worship is a mere futility. This error is shared also by the Deists, who, while they admit the existence of a personal God, deny that He demand any worship from His creatures. These systems are answered by the apologist who proves that every one is bound to practise religion as a duty toward God, and in order that he may attain the end for which he has been called into existence.

II. *Restricted Indifferentism.*—In distinction from this absolute Indifferentism, a restricted form of the error admits the necessity of religion on account, chiefly, of its salutary influence on human life. But it holds that all religions are equally worthy and profitable to man, and equally pleasing to God. The classic advocate of this theory is Rousseau, who maintains in his "Emile" that God looks only to the sincerity of intention, and that everybody can serve Him by remaining in the religion in which he has been brought up, or by changing it at will for any other that pleases him more (Emile, III). This doctrine is widely advocated to-day on the grounds that, beyond the truth of God's existence, we can attain to no certain religious knowledge; and that, since God has left us thus in uncertainty, He will be pleased with whatever form of worship we sincerely offer Him. The full reply to this error consists in the proof that God has vouchsafed to man a supernatural revelation, embodying a definite religion, which He desires that all should embrace and practise. Without appealing to this fact, however, a little consideration suffices to lay bare the inherent absurdity of this doctrine. All religions, indeed, may be said to contain some measure of truth; and God may accept the imperfect worship of ignorant sincerity. But it is injurious to God, who is truth itself, to assert that truth and falsehood are indifferent in His sight. Since various religions are in disagreement, it follows that wherever they conflict, if one possesses the truth, the others are in error. The constituent elements of a religion are beliefs to be held by the intellect, precepts to be observed, and a form of worship to be practised. Now—to confine ourselves to the great religions of the world—Judaism, Mohammedanism, Christianity, and the religions of India and the Orient are in direct antagonism by their respective creeds, moral codes, and cults. To say that all these irreconcilable beliefs and cults are equally pleasing to God is to say that the Divine Being has no predilection for truth over error; that the true and the false are alike congenial to His nature. Again, to hold that truth and falsehood equally satisfy and perfect the human intellect is to deny that reason has a native bent towards, and affinity for, truth. If we deny this, we deny that any trust is to be placed in our reason. Turn to the ethical side of the question. Here again there is conflict over almost all the great moral issues. Let an illustration or two suffice. Mohammedanism approves polygamy, Christianity uncompromisingly condemns it as immoral. If these two teachers are equally trustworthy guides of life, then there is no such thing as fixed moral values at all. If the obscene orgies of phallic worship are as pure in the sight of God as the austere worship that was conducted in the temple of Jerusalem, then we must hold the Deity to be destitute of all moral attributes, in which case there would be no grounds for religion at all. The fact is that this type of Indifferentism, though verbally acknowledging the excellence and utility of religion, nevertheless, when pressed by logic, recoils into absolute indifferentism. "All religions are equally good" comes to mean at bottom that religion is good for nothing.

III. *Liberal or Latitudinarian Indifferentism.*—The foregoing types of Indifferentism are conveniently called infidel, to distinguish them from a third, which, while acknowledging the unique Divine origin and character of Christianity, and its consequent immeasurable superiority over all rival religions, holds that what particular Christian Church or sect one belongs to is an indifferent matter; all forms of Christianity are on the same footing, all are equally pleasing to God, and serviceable to man. On approaching this third error one may advantageously inquire into the genesis of indifferentism in general. In doing so we shall find that liberal indifferentism, as the third type is called, although it arises in belief, is closely akin to that of infidelity, and this community of origin will account for the tendency which is to-day working towards the union of both in a common mire of scepticism. Indifferentism springs from Rationalism. By Rationalism here we understand the principle that reason is the sole judge and discoverer of religious truth as of all other kinds of truth. It is the antithesis of the principle of authority which asserts that God, by a supernatural revelation, has taught man religious truths that are inaccessible to our mere unaided reason, as well as other truths which, though not absolutely beyond the native powers of reason, yet could not by reason alone be brought home to the generality of men with the facility, certitude, and freedom from error required for the right ordering of life. From the earliest ages of the Church the rationalistic spirit manifested itself in various heresies. During the Middle Ages it infected the teachings of many notable philosophers and theologians of the schools, and reigned unchecked in the Moorish centers of learning. Its influence may be traced through the Renaissance to the rise of the Reformation.

From the beginning of the Reformation the rationalistic current flowed with ever-increasing volume through two distinct channels which, though rising apart, have been gradually approaching each other. The one operated through purely philosophic thought which, wherever it set itself free from the authority of the Church, has on the whole served to display what has been justly called the "all-corroding, all-dissolving scepticism of the intellect in religious matters." Rationalistic speculation gave rise successively to the English Deism of the eighteenth century, to the school of the French Encyclopedists and their descendants, and to the various German systems of anti-Christian thought. It has culminated in the prevalent materialistic, monistic, and agnostic philosophies of to-day. When the Reformers rejected the dogmatic authority of the living Church they substituted for it that of the Bible. But their rule of faith was the Bible, interpreted by private judgment. This doctrine introduced the principle of rationalism into the very structure of Protestantism. The history of that movement is a record of continually increasing divisions, multiplications of sects, with a steady tendency to reduce the contents of a fixed dogmatic creed. In a few words Cardinal Newman has summed up the lesson of that history: "Experience proves surely that the Bible does not answer a purpose for which it never was intended. It may be accidentally the means for converting individuals, but a book after all cannot make a stand against the wild living intellect of man, and in this day it begins to testify, as regards its own structure and contents, to the power of that universal solvent which is so successfully acting upon religious establishments." (Apologia pro Vita Sua, London, 1883, v, 245). As divisions increased in the general body of Protestantism, and as domestic dissensions arose in the bosom of particular denominations, some of the leaders endeavored to find a principle of harmony in the theory that the essential doctrines of Chistianity are summed up in a few great simple truths which are clearly expressed in Scripture, and that consequently whoever believes these and regulates his life accordingly is a true follower of Christ. This movement failed to stay the process of disintegration, and powerfully promoted the opinion that, provided one accepts Christianity as the true religion, it makes little difference to what denomination one adheres. The view spread that there is no creed definitely set forth in Scripture, therefore all are of equal value, and all profitable to salvation. Large numbers in the Church of England adopted this opinion, which came to be known as Liberalism or Latitudinarianism. It was not, however, confined to one form of Protestantism, but obtained adherents in almost every body inheriting from the Reformation. The effort was made to reconcile it with the official confessions by introducing the policy of permitting every one to interpret the compulsory formulae in his own sense.

Indifferentism, liberal and infidel, has been vigorously promoted during the past half century by dominance of Rationalism in all the lines of scientific inquiry which touch upon religion. The theory of evolution applied to the origin of man, Biblical criticism of the Old and the New Testament, the comparative study of religions, archaeology, and ethnology in the hands of men who assume as their primary postulate that there is no supernatural, and that all religions, Christianity included, are but the offspring of the feeling and thought of the natural man, have propagated a general atmosphere of doubt or positive unbelief. As a result, large numbers of Protestants have abandoned all distinctly Christian belief, while others, still clinging to the name, have emptied their creed of all its essential dogmatic contents. The doctrine of Scriptural inspiration and inerrancy is all but universally abandoned. It would not, perhaps, be incorrect to say that the prevalent view to-day is that Christ taught no dogmatic doctrine, that His teaching was purely ethical, and its only permanent and valuable content is summed up in the Fatherhood of God and the brotherhood of man. When this point is reached the Indifferentism which arose in belief joins hands with the Indifferentism of infidelity. The latter substitutes for religion, the former advocates as the only essential of religion, the broad fundamental principles of natural morality, such as justice, veracity, and benevolence that takes concrete form in social service. In some minds this theory of life is combined wtih Agnosticism, in others with a vague Theism, while in many it is still united with some vestiges of Christian Faith.

Along with the intellectual cause just noted, another has been what one might call the automatic influence proceeding from the existence of many religions side by side in the same country. This condition has given rise to the political indifferentism referred to in the opening of this article. Where this state of affairs prevails, when men of various creeds meet one another in political, commercial and social life, in order that they may carry on their relations harmoniously, they will not demand any special recognition of their own respective denominations. Personal intercourse fosters the spirit of tolerance, and whoever does not unflinchingly hold to the truth that there is but one true religion is apt to be guided in his judgments by the maxim, "From their fruits ye shall know them." On observing that probity and good intention mark the lives of some of his associates who differ in their religious beliefs, he may easily come to the conclusion that one religion is as good as another. Probably, however, many who speak thus would acknowledge the fallacy of this view if pushed by argument. On the other hand, great numbers of theoretical Indifferentists display unmistakable hostility to the Catholic Church; while again, persons devoid of all religious belief, favor the Church as an efficient element of police for the preservation of the social order.

It would be beyond the scope of this article to develop, or even briefly sketch, the argument contained in the Scriptures and in the history of the Church for the truth that, from the beginning, Christianity was a dogmatic religion with a rule of faith, a rule of conduct, a definite, if not fully developed system, with promises to be fulfilled for those who adhered to the creed, the discipline, and the system, and with anathemas for those who rejected them. The exposition and the proof of these facts constitute in theology, the treatise on the Church. One obvious consideration may be briefly pointed out which lays bare the inconsistency of liberal indifferentism. If, as this theory admits, God did reveal any truth to men, then He surely intended that it should be believed. He can not have meant that men should treat His revelation as of no importance, or that it should signify one thing to you and something entirely different to me, nor can He be indifferent as to whether men interpret it correctly or incorrectly. If He revealed a religion, reason certainly tells us that such a religion must be true, and all others that disagree with it false, and that He desires men to embrace it; otherwise, why should He have given any revelation at all? It is true that in many places the Scriptures are obscure and furnish to those who assume to interpret them by the light of private judgment alone many occasions of reaching irreconcilable conclusions. This fact, however, proves only the falseness of the Protestant rule of faith. The inference that flows from it is not that all interpretations are equally trustworthy, but that, since God has given us a revelation, which is not so clearly or fully expressed in the Scripture that reason can grasp it with certitude, He must have constituted some authority to teach us what is the burden of revelation.

The cogency of this reasoning when set forth at adequate length has led into the Catholic Church many sincere non-Catholics, who have observed how Rationalism is rapidly dissolving religious faith over wide areas once occupied by dogmatic Protestantism. Present signs seem to indicate that, in the near future, the religious struggle shall be, not between this or that form of religion, but between Catholicism and no religion at all. It is true of course that reason, as the Vatican Council teaches, can, by its own native powers, reach with certitude the truths which suffice to form the basis of a natural religion. But it is also true that, as Newman has said, the tendency of the human intellect, as such, has been historically towards simple unbelief in matters of religion: "No truth, however sacred, can stand against it in the long run; and hence it is that in the Pagan world, when Our Lord came, the last traces of the religious knowledge of former times were all but disappearing from those portions of the world in which the intellect had been active and had a career" (Apologia, chap. v). These words might stand with but little modification as a description of present-day conditions where the rationalistic spirit is in control. The only effective barrier to resist its triumphal march, leading scepticism in its train, is the principle of authority embodied in the Catholic Church.

82

AUTHORITY IN RELIGION

WILFRID PARSONS [1]

Freedom of thought and liberty of conscience are truths that brook no denial. People are accustomed to take the assertions of scientists on their word, for science, as the world knows, is king of modern thought. Everybody wants progress, and this enlightened age has thrown over many superstitions, and will throw away many more. Even a certain type of Catholic may possibly become a trifle worried that maybe his own Church has gone a little too far in imposing her own will, and maybe even has not kept up with modern thought.

It is clear that the modern discussions about religion are vastly different from old controversies. We used to argue whether the Bible meant this or that; now we argue about whether it really matters what the Bible means. We used to argue about which church was God's authoritative Church; now we argue whether God did after all found an

[1] The America Press, New York City.

authoritative church. We used to argue whether this or that doctrine had been really revealed by God; now we argue whether God ever revealed anything. The result of the modern argument is that we have two classes of people outside the Catholic Church, those who affirm that God gave a Revelation once for all, which it behooves us to find, and those who deny this assertion. Those who deny are the "liberals" and the Modernists, and those who affirm are the traditional Christians.

This situation puts a double burden on anyone who wishes to make people see the truth as Catholics see it. The Modernist must be shown that God really gave a Revelation and the ordinary Protestant must be made to see that if he believes that God gave a Revelation, then the only safeguard for that Revelation is the Catholic Church. There is, however, another way to proceed, and it is this. Modernism is a logical and necessary outcome of Protestantism itself. The first Protestants threw off the authority of the Church to which they belonged, and many of its doctrines as well, by invoking the so-called right of private judgment. The new Protestants, using the same right, are now throwing off doctrines to which the old Protestants still cling. There is no fundamental difference between the Modernists and the Fundamentalists. They both start from the same first principle. This principle, held by each, destroys the stand of the other, and is self-destructive as well. The disastrous thing about the Reformation is this very principle. To those who hold it there is no reason for stopping anywhere in the process of denial. Those who hold it, yet wish to defend Christianity against its enemies, can never do so, for they have cut the ground from under their feet.

A church which does not teach the world with authority cannot be the true Church of Christ. Christ did not intend His Church to be a Babel of conflicting doctrines. He did intend it to be one flock, one in faith, one in discipline, under one shepherd. Protestantism, looked at as a whole, whether in history or today, is a Babel of conflicting doctrines. Each sect of Protestantism is a Babel of conflicting doctrines. And the reason why these conflicting doctrines exist, is inherent in Protestantism itself. It carries its own self-destroying poison in itself. Protestantism has split up into ever new sects, and divisions of sects, because it is not a teaching church, and the church which is not a teaching church is not Christ's Church. This is said in no uncharitable or contentious spirit. It is time for plain speaking of the plain truth, even though it hurts, and the plain truth is that churches which owe their existence to a denial of authority in teaching religion, carry on them the stamp of sheep outside the flock of Christ. The Holy Spirit simply cannot be with those who announce as their fundamental charter a principle which destroys, has destroyed, and must destroy the unity of faith in Christendom. There is only one Church which from the beginning to now has kept itself one in faith and discipline, and that is the Church which is in union with Peter, and teaches with the authority of Peter, and Peter's Master.

The name of science has been invoked in this controversy, and to Catholics the invocation is welcome, for it throws light on the truth. That science has disproved any Christian truths can at once be dismissed as a gratuitous assertion. Science being from God, and Christian truths, coming, though in a different way, from the same God, can never be in any real conflict. But science enters in another way also. It is held by most Protestants, as a result of their principle of free thought, that the *methods* of science must be applied to Christian teachings. This is true, if it means that we must use the methods of science to find if God gave a Revelation, and having found this, to see where the Revelation is at present. Catholics do this as a reasonable approach to their faith. But to apply the methods of science to the revealed truths themselves is another matter. To do this shows a profound ignorance of what science is, and of what Christianity is. Science is in constant process of being remade. Science is founded on facts, and new facts are constantly being discovered, which show the old conceptions to be partly false, and force new conceptions more in accord with the facts. Christianity is founded on facts, too, and our reason works on them just as in science. But in this case the facts are "given" once for all. No new facts will come to show the old conceptions false. We constantly progress in our knowledge of what the facts imply; the world's keenest intellects have been unceasingly occupied in this highest of all the sciences, theology. But all the data of this science have existed known from the beginning; these data are Christ's Revelation, the deposit delivered once for all to the saints. "The Holy Ghost when he shall come shall teach you all truth," said Christ to the Apostles, referring to Pentecost.

To talk, therefore, of Protestantism or Modernism as bringing progress is to talk nonsense. Protestantism or Modernism, in so far as they have anything proper to themselves, are mere denials. Modernism, with its "new knowledge," has added nothing to knowledge. It has merely denied truths already known for centuries. . . . Modernism has contributed nothing positive to progress, no new truths for the consolation of souls hungrily seeking truth.

It is plain that we are here at the heart of the matter. The whole Protestant movement, culminating logically in Modernism, was vitiated from the beginning by a distorted notion of just what Christianity is, and of what is the proper function of the Church. The Church is not a mere body of men left to find out by themselves what is true. "What is true" was told, once for all by Christ Himself and by His Spirit, to the Apostles. The Apostles, unlettered men, were not left to find out by themselves what God wanted of us. Christ told them what God wanted of us. Their part was merely to be witnesses of what Christ told them. Christ brought from God Himself the whole body of the truths that make up what is called, after Him, Christianity. The first function of the Apostles was to *witness,* and to witness is the first function of the Church, the successor of the Twelve. To relate to others what Christ had told them in God's name, that was the duty and the mission of the Apostles. In an unbroken line from the Apostles, each generation in the teaching Church has handed on to the next generation the account of what the first generation heard from Christ.

Lack of progress? Progress has nothing to do with this part of the matter. It happens that all the data of this science have been known from the beginning. This is true of no other science, but it is true of this one. There is no use railing at it, saying it ought not to be, it is unheard of, and so forth. The fact is that God wanted the data of this science to be Divinely revealed all at once, while those of other sciences are revealed gradually. Nor is this a mere pious belief. It is perfectly clear from every page of the Gospels: Christ spoke with authority, and He commissioned His Apostles to speak with authority, and He, the gentlest of men, consigned to damnation all who refused to accept the witness of the Apostles.

But there is progress, too. The first generation did not see all that the data of Revelation implied, nor did the second or third. Each new generation to the present has progressed in the knowledge of what the first Revelation meant. Each new age sees more explicitly what was implicit in the message which Christ brought from God. This process of *defining* dogmas, together with the witnessing to the complete Revelation, is always watched over by Christ, making sure that it teaches what He taught. By His dwelling in the Church He makes it a living organism, which by reason of that indwelling, is Divine, and cannot err. There is no degradation in obeying that Church. "He who heareth you, heareth me," He said to the Apostles and their successors. The Modernists are logical in refusing obedience to their own churches, which by their own admission are man-made and governed by man. To submit our reason to God dwelling in His true Church, when he teaches us Divine truths that transcend our reason, is no disgrace but a glorious privilege.

83

THE MALICE OF SCANDAL

Achille Van der Heeren [1]

That active scandal is a mortal sin Christ Himself has taught (Matt. xviii, 6) and reason makes evident. If charity obliges us to assist our neighbor's temporal and spiritual necessities, it obliges us still more strongly not to be to him a cause of sin or spiritual ruin. Hence it follows that every sin of scandal is contrary to charity. Moreover, direct scandal is obviously contrary to the virtue against which another is induced to sin; in fact, every virtue forbids not only its violations by ourselves but also that we should desire its violation by another. Indirect scandal is

---

[1] *Catholic Encyclopedia*, Vol. XIII, p. 507.

also contrary to charity; but is it also opposed to the virtue violated by another? St. Alphonsus answers in the affirmative; others, and this seems the true opinion, deny this. In fact no one has hitherto proved this species of malice, and those who admit it are not consistent with themselves, for they should also maintain, which no one does, that anyone who is indirectly the cause of an injustice by another is also bound to restitution; what is true of justice should also hold for the other virtues.

84

THE RIGHT TO MORAL INTEGRITY

Timothy Brosnahan [1]

The neighbor has the right: (a) that no unbecoming word or deed of ours be to him an occasion of moral corruption; (b) that by no action of ours is he deprived of necessary or salutary means of preserving or promoting his moral integrity. The first violation is called scandal. Scandal may be *given* without being *taken,* or taken without being given. Scandal, when taken, though not given is: (a) Scandal of the little ones, i. e., a deed or word, which harmless in itself, is when uttered or done in presence of the young an occasion to them of moral injury. *Maxima reverentia debetur pueris.* (b) Pharisaical scandal, i. e., when through malice, what is harmless is taken as an occasion of evil. Scandal, properly so called, i. e., when given and taken is: (a) indirect, when the offensive word is uttered or deed done primarily for one's own pleasure with disregard of its effect on others; (b) direct or diabolical when the direct purpose is to lead others astray either as a means or end. Moral injury is done to the neighbor: (a) by depriving him of the means of leading his spiritual life—children, orphans, prisoners; (b) by failing to give him the example due him: parents, teachers, persons of exemplary prominence; (c) by putting one's employees in circumstances in which the employer's interests are furthered by frauds or dishonesty.

[1] *Digests of Lectures on Ethics,* p. 76. (John Murphy Company, Baltimore.)

85

VIRTUE AND VICE IN MATTERS OF TOILET

St. Thomas Aquinas [1]

In the exterior things that man uses there is no vice, but only on the part of man himself who uses them immoderately. This immoderation may appear in two ways: one way is in comparison with the standard of custom in the social circle in which the person moves. Hence Augustine says: "Offences against manners are to be avoided according to the different fashion of manners. The convention of society, sanctioned by custom or by law, is not to be violated by the private whim of any citizen or stranger: for ungainly is every part that is not in agreement with the whole to which it belongs." In another way there may be immoderation arising from the inordinate affection of him who uses exterior things, when a man comes to luxuriate too much in such things, whether his use of them be according to the custom of the society in which he lives, or go beyond that custom. Hence Augustine says: "In the use of things there must be no luxury: for luxury not only abuses wickedly the custom of society in the sphere in which it lives, but often even goes beyond that custom, and breaking out into the foulest excesses, openly shows the shame that it formerly concealed behind the veil of customary observance."

On the side of defect there may be a twofold inordination, one in the way of negligence and refusal to take any trouble to make one's outward man what it should be; the other in making these very deficiencies of toilet a matter of vainglory.

They who are in positions of dignity, or again the ministers of the altar, wear more costly robes than other men, not for their own glorification, but to signify the excellence of their office or of divine worship; and therefore there is no fault in their so doing. Nor yet does he who wears a meaner dress than his fellows always sin. For if he does it for the maceration of the flesh, or the humiliation of the

---

[1] *Aquinas Ethicus*, translated by Joseph Rickaby. Vol. II, pp. 380-385. (Burns, Oates and Washbourne, London.)

spirit, it is an act of the virtue of temperance. The wearing of a mean dress is particularly proper in those who exhort other men by word and example to penance, as the Prophets did, of whom the Apostle says: "They wandered about in sheepskins." [2]

As regards female dress the same points are to be attended to as have been noted above concerning toilet generally; and moreover there is one special fact to be observed that is given in the text: "And behold a woman meeteth him in harlot's attire, prepared to deceive souls." [3] However, a married woman may lawfully lay herself out to please her husband, lest he despise her and form other connections. Hence it is said: "She that is married thinketh on the things of the world, how she may please her husband." [4] And therefore, if a married woman dresses well to please her husband, she may do so without sin. But those women who neither have nor want to have husbands, or who are in a state that binds them not to marry, cannot without sin seek to please the eyes of men to make them fall in love with them, because that is to furnish their neighbor with an incentive to sin. And if they dress themselves with this express purpose, that people may fall in love with them, they sin mortally; but if it is done out of thoughtlessness, or vanity and love of display, it is not always a mortal sin, but venial sometimes. Some ladies, however, in this situation may be excused from sin, when their dressing is not done out of vanity, but in compliance with a fashion to the contrary of what has been laid down, though such a fashion is not praiseworthy.

Women's painting of themselves is a species of counterfeit that cannot be without sin. Such painting, however, is not always fraught with mortal sin, but only when it is done for lasciviousness or in contempt of God. It is further to be observed that it is one thing to counterfeit a beauty not possessed, and another thing to conceal an ugliness arising from any cause, as from sickness or other such incident, for that concealment is lawful.[5]

[2] Hebrews, XI, 37.
[3] Prov. VII, 10.
[4] I Cor. VII, 34.
[5] So, says the Angelic Doctor, the lady may paint—if she is ugly. (Translator.)

In any art of manufacturing articles that men cannot use without sin, workmen making such things would thereby sin, as directly supplying others with an occasion of sin; thus it would be if one were to manufacture idols or articles of idolatrous worship. But any art that there may be, the products of which can be used by men either for good or for evil, as in the case of swords and arrows, is not a sinful art to practise; and only such arts as this ought to be called *arts*. Where, however, the products of any art are for the most part turned to evil use, arts in that case, though not unlawful in themselves, are to be exterminated from the city by the official act of the Sovereign. Since then women may lawfully adorn themselves, either to maintain the becoming level of their state, or even somewhat to improve upon it, and please their husbands, it follows that the makers of finery for this purpose do not sin in the practice of their art, except it be possibly by inventing sundry superfluous and curious novelties.

86

MORALITY AND ART

Wilfrid Parsons [1]

A common position taken by many moderns is that art has nothing to do with morality. A work of art is neither moral nor immoral, it has to do solely with life, and if the slice of life under scrutiny is an immoral slice, the artist is not defiled; he merely considers, and presents, what he sees. The artist is free from, and above, morality. On the other side, we have the Puritans, for whom many things are immoral that the common sense of men tells us are not immoral, and who demand that a work of art be "moral" in their special sense, namely that it always preach some lesson of godliness. It is safe to say that the truth lies between these two extremes. It is a purely arbitrary thing to say that in this particular branch of human activity the artist is free from the moral restraints that govern all the human activities of all other men. The artist in his art is bound by the immutable precepts of the natural moral law

---

[1] *America,* March 7, 1925.

as well as all other men. Art is a human activity and the artist in practising it may not offend God any more than the rest of us. But the question is: Does an artist offend the moral law in an "immoral" work of art? In Catholic language does an artist "commit a sin" in creating, and the audience in viewing, a "bad" play? This raises the second question, namely, what is a bad or immoral book or play?

This question can only be answered by reference to the general ethical principle of responsibility, and the narrower one of the proximate occasion of sin. It is admitted as a truism of the natural law that we may not willingly place ourselves in the proximate occasion of sin. We may not knowingly and deliberately place ourselves in a situation where we know that we are practically certain to commit sin. This is not a mere personal opinion of the writer, but the general teaching of all Catholic moralists. Moreover, it is just as certain that the responsibility devolves on all of us not to be the occasion of sin to others. A typical example of this is in dancing, where the difference between bad and good lies precisely in the danger or absence of danger of sinning. Dancing in itself is indifferent; it becomes bad only when it is an occasion of sin for oneself, or is an occasion of sin to others.

The same is true of works of art, taking art in its broadest sense, including books, plays, painting and sculpture. The responsibility lies upon the artist not to be the occasion of sin to others, and the duty on the rest of mankind not to read, hear or view works which will be an occasion of sin to them. So much for the principle of the thing. It is clear and undeniable. It is based on the well known frailty of human nature and the dictates of human reason, and very little reflection is needed to convince one of the justice of it. A book or play is immoral when it is the occasion of sin to those who read or see it.

Here a whole flock of questions arises. Let us take them in order. How can I know it is an occasion of sin, until I have seen the play or read the book? Perhaps what is an occasion of sin to one will not be such to me. Is it not a matter for each one's conscience to settle for itself? Do not standards of what is an occasion of sin vary with different ages, and places, and even different individuals?

The difficulty of knowing beforehand that a certain play is an occasion of sin is a real one. It diminishes considerably, however, on examination. The look in the eyes, or the tone of the voice, or the comment of the one who recommends it to us will tell us much. Even the guarded remarks of the reviewer will warn us. Very few go to a play without knowing something of what they are going to see. Now in the matter of most of God's Commandments it is true that one rarely knows a thing to be a proximate occasion of sin except from bitter experience. But in the matter of sexual morality, the experience of mankind has taught the moralists that certain things are for the normal man a proximate occasion of sin. Certain words uttered, certain actions performed, in certain situations, normally are occasions of sin to normal people. The artist who creates them, the person who views or hears them, has fallen foul of the principles set forth above. Normally sins of thought, act or desire will follow. It will be clear from this, too, why offenses against other Commandments are viewed with toleration in a book or play. Thievery, cheating, cruelty, lying, drunkenness, murder, even when depicted on a stage, do not ordinarily move those who view them to sin. But even here the artist may err. For he may so depict those crimes that in the audience the love of goodness is lessened, their ideas of honor and fidelity soiled, their whole attitude toward morality warped and twisted. The artist has then been guilty of the sin of scandal, that is, of contributing to the moral downfall of others. No sophistry of "art for art's sake" can change that fact.

It will be well to remark here, in passing, a point on which the Catholic moralist and writers outside the Church are in profound disagreement. Our newspaper moralists, and even others more highly placed, ordinarily are not much moved except by the total downfall of a man or woman. They will easily allow whatever does not bring on that total downfall. But to the Catholic, even in the light of reason, one mortal sin is greater than all temporal evils combined. Even to gain the whole world, one may not commit even one mortal sin, no, nor to save the lives or even the souls of all living men. No end justifies a means that is sinful. Catholics are almost alone in upholding this truth.

To revert to the argument, is it not true then that what constitutes a proximate occasion of sin will vary with the place and age and the individual? Will not certain situations that at one time or place would certainly cause sin, in others have absolutely no effect? Is not the "shockpoint" higher or lower in different ages and climes, and with different people? Facts, and common sense, answer that this is true. Moralists, and especially those with great practical experience in directing consciences, such as priests, recognize this fact. They will allow that if one has rashly exposed himself, and found that there is not there any occasion of sin for him, that his temperament is such that he is unmoved by what he sees or hears, then there is no occasion of sin for him. But they will be very slow to allow any to make the experiment in the case of a certain irreducible minimum, or even to admit that that irreducible minimum is not for everybody an occasion of sin. The conscience of every normal individual will echo an emphatic agreement with this.

87

SUICIDE

Achille Van der Heeren [1]

Suicide is the act of one who causes his own death, either by positively destroying his own life, or by inflicting on himself a mortal wound or injury, or by omitting to do what is necessary to escape death, as by refusing to leave a burning house. From a moral standpoint we must treat therefore not only the prohibition of positive suicide, but also the obligation incumbent on man to preserve his life. Suicide is direct when a man has the intention of causing his own death, whether as an end to be attained, or as a means to another end, as when a man kills himself to escape condemnation, disgrace, ruin, etc. It is indirect, and not usually called by this name when a man does not desire it, either as an end or as a means, but when he nevertheless commits an act which in effect involves death, as when he devotes himself to the care of the plague-stricken, knowing that he will succumb under the task.

[1] *Catholic Encyclopedia*, Vol. XIV, pp. 326-328.

The teaching of the Catholic Church concerning the morality of suicide may be summarized as follows:

Positive and Direct Suicide perpetrated without God's consent always constitutes a grave injustice towards Him. To destroy a thing is to dispose of it as an absolute master and to act as one having full and independent dominion over it; but man does not possess this full and independent dominion over his life, since to be an owner one must be superior to his property. God has reserved to Himself direct dominion over life; He is the owner of its substance, and He has given man only the serviceable dominion, the right to use, with the charge of protecting and preserving the substance, that is life itself. Consequently suicide is an attempt against the dominion and right of ownership of the Creator. To this injustice is added a serious offence against the charity which man owes to himself, since by his act he deprives himself of the greatest good in his possession and the possibility of attaining his final end. Moreover, the sin may be aggravated by circumstances, such as failure in conjugal, paternal, or filial piety, failure in justice or charity, if by taking his life one eludes existing obligations of justice or acts of charity which he could and should perform. That suicide is unlawful is the teaching of Holy Scripture and of the Church, which condemns the act as a most atrocious crime and, in hatred of the sin, and to arouse the horror of its children, denies the suicide Christian burial. Moreover, suicide is directly opposed to the most powerful and invincible tendency of every creature and especially of man, the preservation of life. Finally, for a sane man deliberately to take his own life he must, as a general rule, first have annihilated in himself all that he possessed of spiritual life, since suicide is in absolute contradiction to everything that the Christian religion teaches us as to the end and object of life and, except in cases of insanity, is usually the natural termination of a life of disorder, weakness, and cowardice.

The reason we have advanced to prove the malice of suicide, namely, God's right and dominion, likewise justifies the modification of the general principle: God being the master of our life He may with His own consent remove from suicide whatever constitutes its disorder. Thus do some authorities justify the conduct of certain saints, who, impelled by the desire of martyrdom and especially to protect their chastity, did not wait for their executioners to put them to death, but sought it in one manner or other themselves; nevertheless, the Divine will should be certain and clearly manifested in each particular case. The question is asked: Can one who is condemned to death kill himself if ordered to do so by the judge? Some authors answer this question in the affirmative, basing their argument on the right which society possesses to punish certain malefactors with death and to commission any executioner, hence also the malefactor himself, to carry out the sentence. We share the most widely accepted opinion that this practice, prevalent in certain countries of the East, is not lawful. Vindictive, and for that matter all, justice requires a distinction between the subject of a right and that of a duty; hence in the present case between the one who punishes and the one who is punished. Finally, the same principle which forbids anyone to personally compass his own death also forbids him to advise, direct, or command, with the direct intention of suicide, that another should slay him.

Positive but Indirect Suicide committed without Divine consent is also unlawful unless, everything considered, there is sufficient reason for doing what will cause death to follow. Thus, it is not a sin, but an act of exalted virtue, to go into savage lands to preach the Gospel, or to the bedside of the plague-stricken to minister to them, although they who do so have before them the prospect of inevitable and speedy death; nor is it a sin for workmen in the discharge of duties to climb on roofs and buildings, thus exposing themselves to danger of death, etc. All this is lawful precisely because the act itself is good and upright, for in theory the persons in question have not in view either as end or means the evil result, that is, death, that will follow, and moreover if there be an evil result it is largely compensated for by the good and useful result which they seek. On the other hand there is sin in exposing oneself to danger of death to display courage, to win a wager, etc., because in all these cases the end does not in any way compensate for the danger of death that is run. To judge whether or not there is sufficient reason for an act which will apparently be followed by death, all the circumstances must be weighed, namely, the importance of the good result, the greater or less certainty of its being attained, the greater or less danger of death, etc., all questions which may in a specific case be very difficult to solve.

Negative and Direct Suicide without the consent of God constitutes the same sin as positive suicide. In fact man has over his life only the right of use with corresponding obligations to preserve the object of God's dominion, the substance of his life. Hence it follows obviously that he fails in this obligation of usufructuary who neglects the necessary means for the preservation of life, and this with the intention of destroying the latter, and consequently violates the rights of God.

Indirect and Negative Suicide without the consent of God is also an attempt against the rights of the Creator and an injustice towards Him whenever without sufficient cause a man neglects all the means of preservation of which he should make use. If a man as usufructuary is obliged in justice to preserve his life, it follows that he is equally bound to make use of all the ordinary means which are indicated in the usual course of things, viz.: (1) he should employ all the ordinary means which nature itself provides, such as to eat, drink, sleep, and so on; (2) moreover, he should avoid all dangers which he may easily avoid, e. g., to flee from a burning house, to escape from an infuriated animal when it may be done without difficulty. In fact to neglect the ordinary means of preserving life is equivalent to killing oneself, but the same is not true with regard to extraordinary means. Thus theologians teach that one is not bound in order to preserve life to employ remedies which, considering one's condition, are regarded as extraordinary and involving extraordinary expenditure; one is not obliged to undergo a very painful surgical operation, nor a considerable amputation, nor to go into exile in order to seek a more beneficial climate, etc. To use a comparison, the lessee of a house is bound to take care of it as becomes a good father of a family, to make use of the ordinary means for the preservation of the property, for instance, to extinguish a fire which he may easily extinguish, etc., but he is not bound to employ means considered extraordinary, such as to procure the latest novelties invented by science to prevent or extinguish fire.

The principles which have been outlined in the four propositions or divisions above given should serve for the solution of particular cases; however, the application may not always be equally easy, and thus a person may by an objectively unlawful act take his life and nevertheless consider it permissible and even an act of exalted virtue. It may be asked whether by performing or omitting a certain act a person may injure his health and shorten his life. To apply the foregoing principles, it is first of all clear that one may not have in view this hastening of death, but, this hypothesis aside, it may be said on the one hand that to expose oneself without sufficient reason to a considerable shortening of life constitutes a serious injury to the rights of the Creator; but on the other hand if the danger of death be not imminent, although it is to be feared that life may be shortened even by several years, it is not a grave but only a venial sin. This is the case of the drunkard who by his intemperance causes his premature death. Again it must be born in mind that with the addition of a reasonable motive the thing may be entirely lawful and even an act of virtue; thus the workman does not sin by devoting himself to the rough labor of the mines, glass-works, etc., and the saints performed a very meritorious and highly virtuous act when to overcome their passions they lacerated and tortured their flesh by penance and fasting and were thus the cause of their earlier death.

The plague of suicide belongs especially to the period of decadence of the civilized peoples of antiquity, Greeks, Romans, and Egyptians. The Christian Middle Ages were unacquainted with this morbid tendency, but it has reappeared at a more recent period, has developed constantly since the Renaissance, and at present has reached such an intensity among all civilized nations that it may be considered the special evil of our time. At present the increase in the tendency to suicide is, with that to mental alienation, the saddest and thereby the most important characteristic fact of our era. The officially established number of suicides during the nineteenth century was a million and a half, of which 1,300,000 were in Europe. Again Father Krose estimates the real number for Europe alone at two millions. During the last ten years of the nineteenth century there were 400,000 suicides, of which France and

Germany alone furnished half. The following details are given by Nieubarn and Jacquart. Taking the countries in the order of the frequency of the rate of suicides, and taking as a scale the number of the latter to the million of inhabitants, we have the following results for the last ten years of the nineteenth century: France, 239; Denmark, 234; Switzerland, 232; Germany, 206 (in Saxony especially the sinister rate was 308, which figure rose to 325 for 1901-1905); Austria, 158; Sweden, 147; Hungary, 145; Belgium, 124; England, 84; Norway, 63; Italy, 60; Scotland, 59; Low Countries, 56; Russia, 32; Ireland, 26; Spain, 21. But as is shown by the indications furnished by Jacquart for this period of 1901-05, this figure has risen in recent years to an alarming extent. For instance, England in 1905 has risen to 103 to the million inhabitants; Switzerland to 232; the Low Countries to 64, and Ireland to 33. In the United States the annual average of suicides from 1901-5 was 4,548 or 107 per million of population; in 1908 the number of suicides was 8,332, or 116 per million.

In this number must obviously be included the suicides attributable to madness, but we cannot accept the opinion of a large number of physicians, moralists, and jurists, who, led into error by a false philosophy, lay it down as a general rule that suicide is always due to dementia, so great is the horror which this act inspires in every man of sane mind. The Church rejects this theory and, while admitting exceptions, considers that those unfortunates who, impelled by despair or anger, attempt their life, often act through malice or culpable cowardice. In fact, despair and anger are not as a general thing movements of the soul which it is impossible to resist, especially if one does not neglect the helps offered by religion, confidence in God, belief in the immortality of the soul, and in a future life of rewards and punishments. Widely different reasons have been advanced to explain this frequency of suicide, but it is more correct to say that it does not depend on any one particular cause, but rather on an assemblage of factors, such as the social and economic situation, the misery of a great number, a more feverish pursuit of what is considered happiness, often ending in cruel deceptions, the ever more refined search for pleasure, a more precocious and intense stimulation of sexual life, intellectual overwork, the influence of the press and the sensational news with which it daily provides its readers, the influences of heredity, the ravages of alcoholism, etc. But it it undeniable that the religious factor is by far the most important, as statistics prove (cf. the detailed investigations of Jacquart); the proportion of suicides in Protestant countries being as a general rule greater than that in Catholic countries, and the increase in suicides keeping step with the de-Christianization of a country. France presents a painful example parallel to the systematic de-Christianization; the number of suicides for each 100,000 of population has increased from 8.32 in 1852 to 29 in 1900. The reason is obvious. Religion alone, and especially the Catholic religion, instructs us with regard to the true destiny of life and the importance of death; it alone furnishes a solution of the enigma of suffering, inasmuch as it shows man living in a land of exile and suffering as a means of acquiring the glory and happiness of a future life. By its doctrine of the efficacy of repentance and the practice of confession it relieves the moral suffering of man; it forbids and prevents to a large extent the disorders of life; in a word it is of a nature to prevent the causes which are calculated to impel a man to the extreme act.

88

DUTIES TOWARD THE BODY

Charles C. Miltner [1]

GROUNDS OF THESE DUTIES. Doubtless one may say: "My body is my own." But he may not, therefore, conclude that he may do as he likes with it. For though it may rightly be called *his*, it is not his in the same sense that his dog or his gun is his. He may abuse, mutilate, destroy or alienate his property, and the rights of others will not be violated. But not so with his body. He has no property right over it. It is his, but his only to use, and to use in a manner consonant with the intention of its donor. For it is a living thing, and "Life because the root

---

[1] *The Elements of Ethics*, pp. 199-214. (The Macmillan Company, New York. By permission of the publishers.)

of all succeeding favors, is Heaven's first and highest gift; ... and it never loses this quality of a gift."[2] Man's living body is a gift of the Creator, a gift to be used in accordance with the laws governing his rational nature, and, therefore, a gift which entails responsibilities, obligations, duties. Duties toward the body, therefore, spring from the natural law. This law is general, but the precepts that flow from it serve to regulate man's love of and care for himself in accordance with right reason.

CLASSIFICATION OF THESE DUTIES. Every duty imposes an obligation. Duty binds us either to do or not to do something. With regard to the body there are, accordingly, positive and negative duties. By positive duties we mean all those acts which we are morally bound to perform in order to preserve and to perfect integrity of health of body. By negative duties, those acts which right reason and experience warn us to avoid as injurious to health of body and the perfection of bodily life.

POSITIVE DUTIES. That one should feed and clothe his body needs, ordinarily, neither proof nor threat of reward or punishment. They are conditions necessary to life, and self-preservation is man's primary and strongest instinct. The difficulty lies rather in the proper mode of doing these things. As to food and drink, disorder results not only from taking too much or too little, but also from the kind that is taken. Two extremes are equally to be avoided: (1) One is not to make a religion out of care for his body, a cult of health, and thus, through over anxiety about health, nullify the very effort made to preserve it; nor (2) is he to cast all precaution to the winds and suffer himself to be guided by every passing fancy or carnal desire. Here, as elsewhere in the moral order, the axiom, *In medio stat virtus,* holds true. And that middle course in the use of food and drink, and in the care of one's body generally, is attained by the virtue of temperance, and maintained by the virtue of fortitude. In extreme cases, sumptuary laws on the part of the State may be necessary, and they may serve to emphasize the need of greater caution or of reform, but of themselves they can never effect a reform. Man is a free creature. And since this is so, all rational

[2] Hill, *Ethics,* p. 203.

use of food and drink and clothing must spring from an enlightened mind and a strong will. Law may guide to this end; it cannot drive. Legal prohibition, or total abstinence, may be good, but it should not be forgotten that the virtue to be cultivated in these matters is temperance, or the habitual use of the necessaries and legitimate luxuries of life with that moderation and order which right reason dictates. As neither food nor drink are primarily intended to be instruments of pleasure, so neither is clothing intended to be an instrument of vanity. Both are means to an end, never ends in themselves.

NEGATIVE DUTIES. If one has the positive duty to use one's body according to the intentions of the Creator who gave it, it follows that all actions at cross-purposes with these intentions or laws are morally forbidden. The moral obligation to avoid such actions is called negative duty. These actions are all such as are notably detrimental to health, or which involve abuse or mutilation of one's members, or the destruction of life itself by suicide. Of these we shall consider suicide first.

THE FACT OF SUICIDE. Suicide is a fact of daily occurrence. It is deplorable and deplored. Besides, its steady increase in the chief countries of the world, despite our much boasted civilization and culture, is no small cause of alarm to those charged with the promotion of social welfare, whether in the Church or in the State. The following statistics will give a fairly adequate idea of the extent of this revolting crime:

Suicide in the United States
		Per 100,000
1885	937	1.37
1895	5,759	8.27
1905	9,982	12.08
1906	10,155	12.05

1917 to 1921 the grand total was 49,820.

Suicide in England
Per 100,000
In 1904 .... 9.85

Suicide in Germany
Per 100,000
In 1904 .... 25.0

In France the growth of population since 1830 was 100%; the increase in suicide was 245%. In Belgium during the same time the suicides had quintupled, i. e., from 1830 to 1906.[3]

[3] *Ency. of Social Reform*, 1174.

According to the World Almanac (1922), p. 368, the number of suicides in 100 American cities from 1910 to 1914 was 23,421. From 1915 to 1919 it was 21,904.

MOTIVES OF SUICIDE (1890 TO 1900).

Motives	Totals	Males	Females
Despondency	2,207		
Business Loss	1,398		
Insanity	1,361		
Ill Health	1,309		
Disappointment in Love	900		
Domestic Trouble	773		
Fear of Disgrace	539		
Grief	427		
Alcoholism	413		
Chagrin	294		
Unknown	559		
Approximate	10,000	7,781	2,219

CONCLUSIONS OF STATISTICIANS.
a. Suicide is on the increase.
b. Civilization increases the suicide rate more rapidly than growth in population.
c. The urban suicide rate is greater than the country rate.
d. The influence of occupation on the rate is incongruous.
e. With one exception (disappointment in love) the rate of males is several times higher than that of females.
f. The rate is higher among the single than among the married, and still higher among the divorced and the widowed.
g. The rate rises in proportion to school pressure, education, etc.[4]

THE NATURE OF SUICIDE. The term means, literally, to kill oneself (*Seipsum occidere*). Yet not every self-inflicted violent action which results in the death of the agent can be called suicide. He commits suicide who freely and deliberately, directly, and designedly brings about the destruction of his own life. The agent must *intend* to accomplish his own destruction. Death must be the primary object of his act. He must aim at death, and effectively procure it. So far as the moral character of the act is concerned it does not matter essentially whether the means

---

[4] Figures and conclusions taken from *Enc. of Social Ref.*, 1174-5.

chosen be positive, as *v. g.*, shooting or drowning oneself, or negative, as *v. g.*, voluntarily refusing to make use of some ordinary remedy or precaution, without whose use death would follow, and *in order that* death may ensue. For in both instances means are employed *per se* capable of self-destruction, and in both there is positive aiming at death.

Direct suicide must not be confounded with indirect, which is:

"An action whose certain and foreseen effect is the death of the agent, without its being intentionally willed or aimed at as an end in itself. It is only permitted as a consequence in virtue of its union with another effect, legitimate in itself and sufficiently important, which is directly and formally intended. Such a death may constitute a great act of virtue; it may even be a duty." [5]

An example of indirect suicide would be the action of a soldier in battle who charges a strongly fortified position of the enemy, or of a man jumping off a raft in mid-ocean, to save the lives of many others.

DIRECT SUICIDE NEVER JUSTIFIABLE. Man stands to God in the essential relation of servant to Master. The very end of his existence, as has been shown, is to attain to God by the observance of His laws. Now no servant, by the very fact that he is such, has the right to determine the nature and duration of his servitude. Both are determined by him upon whom he depends for his life and sustenance. Therefore man does not possess supreme dominion over his life, and consequently may not terminate it at will. In other words, suicide is contrary to the law of man's nature, or the natural law.

"To kill oneself is altogether unlawful, for three reasons: First, because naturally everything loves itself, and consequently everything naturally preserves itself in being, and resists destroying agencies as much as it can. And therefore for any one to kill himself is against a natural inclination and against the charity wherewith he ought to love himself. And therefore the killing of one's self is always a mortal sin, as being against charity.

---

[5] A. Castelein, *Droit Naturel*, p. 95.

"Secondly, because all that any part is, is of the whole. But every man is of the community; and so what he is is of the community. Hence in killing himself he does an injury to the community." [6]

Doubt has been expressed as to the conclusiveness of these arguments. But, we think, without solid grounds.[7] It is argued that the fact of some seventy or eighty thousand suicides per year seems to indicate that one is not altogether logical in claiming that God has not given to men perfect dominion over their lives, that the argument thereby loses some of its force. But it should be noted that the principle of God's perfect dominion over human life is not incompatible with the fact of suicide, however frequently it may occur. For the truth of the principle rests not on the frequency or even upon the fact of suicide, but upon an essential relation existing between man and God. The frequency of suicide proves, in this connection, nothing more than the freedom of the human will and the perversity of the human heart.

Against the argument condemning suicide on the grounds of social injustice, Dr. Ross tells that:

"It may be just as advantageous to society to have a criminal commit suicide as to hang him. In fact, it would save the cost of a trial and the ill effects of the morbid publicity given such things. And if the act be done secretly, there is no bad example set, no encouragement given better people to do likewise." [8]

It seems to us that there is here a confusing of two distinct questions, that is, whether it may be as advantageous to society to allow all criminals, already justly condemned, to be their own executioners, as to go to the expense of hanging them, or whether society is injured less by allowing any feeble or evil-minded man to destroy himself rather than to go to the trouble of preventing such action and of punishing any unsuccessful attempt. If Dr. Ross means that, once a criminal has been sentenced to death, society has nothing to lose by allowing him to be his own executioner, one might let it pass—though the common opinion

---

[6] Rickaby, *Aquin. Ethic,* p. 43.
[7] Cf. Ross, *Ethics,* p. 179.
[8] *Op. cit.,* p. 180.

among moralists is against it.⁹ Moreover, such an action could not properly be called suicide. At any rate, the objection would be wholly beside the point, for it would have no necessary connection with the social argument.

On the other hand, if he means—and it is hard to think he does—that all who contemplate suicide deserve to be hanged by the State, his view is evidently erroneous. A poor wretch suffering excruciating pain from some incurable disease might in his agony contemplate suicide, but he would not forfeit thereby his right to life so that society would be justified in hanging him.

But even on the supposition that the objection be restricted to those whose life must be terminated either by suicide or by being hung, we see no force in it against our argument. Hanging, after judicial sentence of death based on a fair trial, is an act of vindictive civil justice. The publicity given such cases, far from having ill effects, is possibly the very best deterrent against further criminal acts. To complain of the expenditures of public monies necessary for such prosecution is little less than puerile when the social benefit gained therefrom is considered. But for society to allow her self-confessed criminals to commit suicide would be to put the seal of her approval upon a crime at least as repellent as any for which the suicidal action in question is intended to be the expiation. Surely the saving of a few dollars, or the scandal of some needlessly morbid journalistic accounts, cannot fairly be balanced against the toleration of intrinsically evil acts, on the plea of greater advantages to society.

REASONS ADVANCED IN JUSTIFICATION OF SUICIDE. (1) It is a courageous thing to do, an act of the virtue of fortitude. (2) It is reasonable when confronted with two evils to choose the lesser of the two, and suicide may be the lesser of the two. (3) Even though we are not the authors of our lives, they belong to us, for we have received them as a gift. (4) In certain circumstances one is allowed to destroy a member of his body, and he has the same dominion over the whole as of a part. (5) Useless members are but a burden and a hindrance to the social body. Hence to destroy such a member is to confer a benefit upon so-

⁹ Pruner, *Kirchen-lexicon*, Art., "Suicide."

ciety. (6) No man in his right mind ever commits suicide. It is the act of a person mentally unbalanced. It is therefore an irresponsible and hence a non-moral act. (7) Necessity knows no law. But suicide may be the only remedy against the miseries of life.

CRITICISM. The courage manifested by the suicide is a case of fools rushing in where Angels fear to tread. Courage is something more than a mere display of physical violence. It is a moral virtue by which a man is enabled constantly to endure the miseries and to confront the dangers of life, not only to enhance physical welfare, but also, and primarily, to safeguard the moral order. Such a virtue assuredly the suicide does not possess. The cool deliberation or the reckless abandon with which he takes his own life springs fundamentally from the weakness of a soul too cowardly to sustain the miseries which have fallen to his lot, and thus, though his act has the semblance of courage, it is in fact the opposite of courage. "In the face of adversity," says Martial, "it is easy to condemn life; he acts bravely who is able to be miserable."

To attempt to justify suicide on the score of choosing between two evils is not a case of choosing between the devil and the deep sea, but between the devil and the moral law. It is not a case of choosing the lesser of two physical evils—which one may certainly do—but of preferring a moral evil of the worst kind—for there is no possibility of atoning for it—to some physical evil which one is unwilling to sustain.

As to life being a gift, it should be noted that there are gifts made unconditionally, and gifts made with certain definite conditions attached to them. The gift of life carries with it the reservation of absolute dominion by the Creator. It is given on condition that it be used in accordance with the wishes of the giver. It cannot therefore be destroyed at will by its possessor without grave injury to the giver.

The fourth reason urged in justification of suicide deserves refutation. For the only legitimate excuse for the amputation of a bodily member is the necessity of so doing in order to save life. Parts are subordinate to the whole, and therefore their destruction is permissible for the conservation of the whole. This does not mean that man has perfect dominion over the parts taken singly and thus of the whole. He possesses the use-right of the whole and hence he must so administer the parts that the whole may be properly cared for.

Were any living member of society ever really useless, the contention that his self-destruction would be advantageous to society might be conceded. But what living person can be called useless, except in the merely economical sense of being a non-producer of wealth? Criminals, however depraved in character, so long as they are able-bodied can be compelled to work. Their incarceration and forced employment, aside from being a standing object-lesson to the criminal-minded outside prison walls, can be made profitable to the State. And as for the incurables and the feeble-minded, surely the example of heroic patience and fortitude manifested by the former, and the equally heroic patience and self-sacrifice and devotion of those who spend their lives in the care of the latter, are examples of virtues of which the effeminate society of the present time stands sorely in need.

As in the care of criminals, so in the attitude adopted toward suicides, the moral welfare of society suffers from ill-regulated sentiment. Doubtless it would rob suicide of its disgraceful quality if it could always be laid to the functioning of an unbalanced mind. But several stubborn facts stand in the way of this universal white-washing. That the act of suicide shows poor judgment goes without saying, but that it shows inability to judge normally at all is abundantly refuted by the elaborate precautions frequently taken by those who contemplate suicide, by the written "justifications" which they leave behind them, by the manner in which they calmly go about making disposition of their property and business affairs before striking the cowardly blow. Suicide is a sin, and every sinner is foolish, though he need not be a fool.

Finally, to say that death is the only remedy against the miseries of life is plainly to confess one's ignorance of the meaning of life, the worth of suffering, and one's want of religion. Supernatural religion alone can teach man the lesson of the value of human suffering, as it alone can give one an adequate explanation of the meaning and purpose of life. Were such a being as an utter atheist possible, then possibly death would be the only solution of a joyless life. But to all others religion is able to furnish an alternative which often leads to far greater joy than that experienced by those possessing a plethora of this world's goods and perfect health besides.

COGNATE QUESTIONS. (1) Can a man be his own executioner? May a man, justly condemned to death, and acting under the orders of competent public authority, execute his own death sentence? It is generally agreed that no judge has the power *to oblige* any malefactor to do so. But whether with the permission of the judge the criminal may execute a death sentence upon himself is a disputed point. Those who would permit it—and though they are few, they are not the least prominent among moralists—argue that since public authority may commission anyone to execute the sentence, the culprit himself is not to be excluded. Those who would not permit it—and their opinion is the common one—maintain that it is an action directly contrary to a universal natural inclination. For in no case does it appear that nature intends a thing to destroy itself. Moreover, unless cruelty and inhumanity are to be allowed, a distinction between suitable and unsuitable executors of death sentences must be made. For as it would be patently inhuman to allow anyone to be the executioner of his parents, so for a still greater reason would it be inhuman to allow him to take his own life.

(2) What obligation is there (a) to avoid mutilation, and (b) to avoid circumstances dangerous to life and limb? The principle governing mutilation has already been given. God alone is the absolute and direct master of human life. Man's dominion does not extend beyond its use. His right to dispose of his body, and hence of its members, is indirect, contingent upon the will of his Creator. But being his to use and to use so as to attain a definite end, he may when, through infection, for instance, or other untoward circumstance, they imperil life itself, permit their amputation. Parts exist for the whole. Hence they may be sacrificed for its preservation. But to amputate hand or foot to escape, *v. g.*, military service, or some less serious inconvenience, or, *a fortiori,* to submit to the removal of certain organs connected with the reproductive faculty in order to avoid the onerous consequences attendant upon its licit or

illicit exercise, is a direct violation of divine right, an injury to society, an irreparable loss to the individual. The skill of modern surgery, together with the frequent want of respect for divine rights on the part of surgeons and their patients, make this particular form of crime especially tempting to those who through an inordinate love of pleasure and a most contemptible fear of suffering would seek by this means to unfit themselves for the natural duties of conjugal life.

The second part of our question, or that which concerns the duty of avoiding dangers to life and limb, has reference to those habitual occupations and specific acts in which more than ordinary risk of losing one's life or injuring one's health is involved, in which, *v. g.*, the danger of grave injury or sudden death is such as to debar men engaged in them from taking out life insurance policies. It is not necessary to enumerate the various cases of this kind. One general principle governs the licitness of all. It is the principle applied to actions indirectly voluntary, or voluntary only in cause. Whenever, therefore, there is question of assuming such risks, provided that the action in itself is good or at least indifferent, and at least equally as liable to be safe as to be injurious; and provided one has an honest intention in undertaking the work and a reason for assuming the risk of injury, in some way proportionate to its gravity and the chances of incurring it, one may freely undertake such works. Thus miners or steel workers or employees in a munitions factory, for instance, since these occupations involve dangers to health and to life itself, may legitimately engage in them on the above conditions. The work in itself is not bad; the risk is not so great but what there are at least as good chances for safety as for injury; the intention governing their action, gaining a livelihood for themsevles and their families, is lawful, and the livelihood thus to be gained is of sufficient importance to warrant their taking the risks involved.

89

PRESERVATION OF LIFE

Thomas Slater [1]

We are obliged to take ordinary means to preserve our lives, for to do otherwise would be virtually to commit suicide. There is no obligation to take extraordinary, unusual, or very painful or expensive means to preserve our lives. And so one in feeble health, who will probably die if he spends the winter in England, is not bound to expatriate himself and go and live in a milder climate. Nor am I bound to undergo a painful and costly operation in order to save my life; I may if I like choose rather to die, unless my life is of great importance for the common good, for then the public good must be considered first. Except in such a case as this, a superior could not oblige a subject to undergo a very painful operation, or to submit to the amputation of a leg; obedience to human authority does not seem to extend to such matters as these.

90

THE ETHICS OF INTOXICATION

Ernest R. Hull [2]

It is far easier to perceive that drunkenness is a sin than to produce a scientific analysis of the reasons why it is a sin. The arguments are usually treated in too wooden a manner.

(1) *"Deprivation of consciousness"* or loss of the use of reason is particularly open to adverse criticism just because the loss of the use of reason is a thing which nature itself forces on us every time we fall asleep; and secondly, because deprivation of the use of reason is justified for any good reason, such as an operation, merely with the object of avoiding pain.

---

[1] *A Manual of Moral Theology,* Vol. I, p. 304. (Benziger Brothers, New York.)
[2] *The Catholic Mind,* June 22, 1921. (America Press, New York.)

(2) The loss of reason leading to lack of self-control, and therefore an opening of the door to misbehavior, makes the case a bit stronger. But on the other hand, this objection applies only to semi-drunkenness, and fails to apply to total drunkenness. For when a man is dead drunk he becomes like a log, and cannot either behave or misbehave.

(3) The argument is often put forward: "If you allow a man to deprive himself of consciousness for a good purpose by the use of chloroform, why not allow man to do the same by the use of alcohol?" At the mention of alcohol I have found moral professors getting quite alarmed and trying to find reasons why the one thing should be allowed and not the other. The real reason at the back of their mind was one of expediency. They will allow the use of chloroform because there is no likelihood of abuse; and as soon as you allow people to make use of alcohol for the same purpose, you are encouraging them to drink. The question of expediency, however, is somewhat irrelevant when it is a question of judging the intrinsic morality of acts.

(4) The argument from gluttony is also often unconvincing. Gluttony means undue sensuality in eating and drinking, and *ex genere* is only a venial sin. But the sin of drunkenness is not mere sensuality. The sin of drunkenness would be the same evil if all sensuality were absent. A man could take a dose of alcohol in a capsule without the least gratification of the sensual appetite, and the effects would be just the same.

The sin of drunkenness is a "sin against oneself," or an outrage of the law of self-preservation. It is an act of self-injury or incapacitation in body, mind or will. It stands on a par with self-mutilation, but of the functional and not of the organic order. The law of self-preservation imposes the duty of keeping our faculties and powers in that normally healthy and effective condition in which God Almighty has created them, so as to use our talents as God meant us to use them. Hence in the physiological order we are not allowed to cut off a limb or excise an organ unless the well being of the whole requires a sacrifice of the part. Again in the functional order we are forbidden to spoil our powers by under use tending to atrophy, or over use tending to break down. Under the same law of self-preservation we must furnish the body with sufficient and proper exercise without overdoing it, with proper beneficial food and drink without overdoing it; all with the same end of maintaining that physical, mental and moral health which lies at the back of true average efficiency in the conduct of life according to God's designs.

Let us now attend to the particular kind of injury which a man can do to himself by the use of poisonous drugs. Alcohol, nicotine, cocaine, opium, bang, all come together under this head, and no substantial distinction ought to be made between them. Each drug has its peculiar use which under certain circumstances is beneficial. It just happens that alcohol and nicotine in a mild form have come into general use for drinking and smoking. Their habitual use in due moderation is practically harmless. But this peculiarity about alcohol and nicotine must not obscure the fact that they both fall under the same category as those other more recondite drugs, and the ethical principles governing their use are throughout the same.

In the case of those other drugs the case is simple and clear. Except in closely restricted medical use, these drugs are highly dangerous to health and efficiency, physical, mental and moral. The habitué of cocaine or opium is doomed to become a wreck in some direction and ultimately in all directions. The injury lies not in the single act, but in the accumulation of acts; and the measure of the injury is the measure of the sin. The ultimate wreckage, contemplated as something incurred or seriously risked, is in itself a mortal sin. It becomes a mortal sin in *anticipation* as soon as a man realizes that he is drifting in that direction, and yet allows himself to go on. Indulgence in the single act can be justified for a proportionate reason. But as soon as a propensity begins to betray itself, a proximate occasion of sin arises. The sin thus occasioned consists in foreseeing what the end is practically sure to be, and yet going on instead of breaking off the habit.

Concretely, a man may escape the guilt of anticipative sin because his perversion is obscure, or because he feels confident that the habit can be kept in moderate compass, and need not issue in the ultimate ruin which is apprehended. Still, our ethical judgment must not be blurred by these subjective considerations. Objectively we are bound to say

that as soon as a man is launched on the downward grade of a drug habit, calculated by the nature of the case to issue in ruin, the conditions for a state of mortal sin are present. It is on this broad ground that we have to seek the inherent sinfulness which lies at the back of the drug habit, no matter whether the drug be opium or cocaine or alcohol or whatever else you like to name. To justify the use of such drugs the danger of ultimate ruin has to be guarded against and the single act requires a justifying reason proportional to the risk, wherever risk is incurred. To go now into closer detail:

(1) At one end of the list comes tobacco (nicotine), in which experience shows that ordinary use is not seriously harmful, and is at least thought to be more than compensatingly beneficial. Smoking can, however, be so definitely injurious to some individuals as to involve a grave responsibility in continuing the habit.

(2) The ordinary mild use of alcoholic beverages again has the same backing up of experience. The numerous cases in which use drifts almost inevitably into abuse, puts the same grave responsibility on a far larger number of persons. One may say in general that as soon as an individual finds by experience that drink is causing him bodily, mental or moral injury so soon is he on the threshold of sin. It is not here a matter of getting drunk occasionally, but a matter of regularly dosing the system with small quantities of poison which, by their accumulative effect, undermine and ruin the system, although the man is never "the worse for liquor," in the popular sense of the term.

(3) With regard to cocaine, opium, and other recondite drugs, it is clear that they can never be justified as habits, because they serve no general purpose like tobacco and alcoholic beverages. They work a definite amount of injury every time, and induce a craving which grows by a geometrical ratio, producing at once an accumulation of evil effect, and an increasing difficulty in breaking off.

The use of alcoholic drink taken in its moral aspect ranges through the following degrees: (1) *Harmless and innocent* in strict moderation, so long as there is no danger of a growing habit verging towards excess.

(2) *A remote occasion of sin* as soon as such dangers arise, which gradually develops into a proximate occasion of sin.

(3) *Objective sin* as soon as the danger becomes serious and certain. *Venial sin* if the danger is slight and can be averted in time; *Mortal sin* as soon as the danger is clearly proximate, imminent and unmistakable.

(4) *Subjective guilt* in the individual is determined by his realization of the cause and the response of his conscience to the facts realized. This will differ so much in individuals, that (except in marked cases) it is impossible for any one to sit in judgment on his neighbor.

(5) The sinfulness may be simplex or complex. In some cases there will be *simple sensuality* or love of the taste of drink. In other cases it may be *craving for a stimulus* rather than a sensation. But the *root sin* is the *sin of injury to self outraging* the law of self-preservation. Following on this are *external consequences;* for instance where a man incapacitates himself to perform his duties either to his employer or to his family; and in this respect the sin will be one against *justice or charity*. Lastly, there is the weakening of the moral judgment and the will, and the loss of power to foresee and resist temptations. In this case the sin will be specified by the kind of temptation yielded to. These rules apply to all cases where the injury is accumulative, even where the man never "gets drunk" in the ordinary sense of the term.

(6) *Getting drunk*, that is, partially or wholly losing the use of reason and self-control may be *occasional* or *habitual*. If *occasional* it is often unforeseen; and the sin in that single case may be simply one of gluttony. The heinousness of the sin lies in the temporary incapacitation rather than in an ultimate injury; and it might be defined as "a sin of temporary functional inhibition not justified by a reasonable cause." If the drunkenness is *frequent or habitual*, besides the sin of the single act there will be the sin of the accumulation foreseen and sanctioned. Except in cases of hereditary or acquired mania, which puts a man beside himself in this particular, the sin will be not only that of habitual gluttony, but of habitual self-injury, plus any evil consequences which issue to himself or others.

Such is our attempt to simplify a very complex problem. Its strength lies in its harmony with the broad moral instincts of mankind contemplating the pathetic victim of drink, rather than in any authoritative teaching of revelation, which so strongly condemns the drunkard but leaves it to our common sense to discover the reason why.

The common saying that by getting drunk a man "makes a beast of himself" is singularly incorrect. Just the one thing which a beast never does is to get drunk; except by accident, as when flies sip Indian ink, or drop into a wine glass. Moreover, when a beast does by any accident get drunk, he immediately ceases to behave like a beast, and begins to behave like a man under the same influence. Even regarded as an indulgence of the animal appetite, it is quite unsound to say that a gluttonous man makes a beast of himself. The animals in their normal circumstances never indulge in gluttony. They follow their healthy appetite, and when that is satisfied, they stop. Nature has provided for that; and it is only when animals are removed from their natural conditions and introduced into artificial ones, that they eat more than is good for them. For example, a cow put in a field of clover will eat till it bursts. But that is because clover is never meant to grow together in such quantities. Nature has scattered clover over the fields so that the cows may have a delicious nibble now and then. They take all the clover they can get, but nature takes care not to provide too much. No; the correct expression is to say that a man when drunk makes a madman of himself. He deprives himself of his rational faculties which are supposed to keep him in order, and then acts as an animal would if deprived of its well-ordered instincts. A drunken man is far below a beast; and it is an insult to the animals to mention the two in one breath.

91

HEALTH AND HOLINESS

Francis Thompson [1]

Holiness not merely energizes, not merely quickens; one might almost say it prolongs life. By its Divine reinforcement of the will and the energies, it wrings from the body the uttermost drop of service; so that, if it can postpone dissolution, it averts age, it secures vital vigor to the last. It prolongs that life of the faculties, without which age is the fore-shadow of the coming eclipse. These men, in whom is the indwelling of the Author of life, scarce know the meaning of decrepitude; they are constantly familiar with the suffering, but not the palsy, of mortality. Regard Manning, an unfaltering power, a pauseless energy, till the grave gripped him; yet a "bag of bones." That phrase, the reproach of emaciation, is the gibe flung at the saints; but these "bags of bones" have a vitality which sleek worldlings might envy. St. Francis of Assisi is a flame of active love to the end, despite his confessed ill-use of "Brother Ass," despite emaciation, despite ceaseless labor, despite the daily hemorrhage from his Stigmata. In all these men you witness the same striking spectacle; in all these men, nay, and in all these women. Sex and fragility matter not; these flames burn till the candle is consumed utterly. "We are always young," said the Egyptian priests to the Greek emissaries; and the saints might repeat the boast, did they not disdain boasting. It was on the instinctive knowledge of this, on the generous confidence they might trust the Creator with His creation, that the saints based the stern handling of the body which some of them afterwards allowed to have been excessive. For though the oil can immensely energize and prolong the life of the wick, it is on that corporeal wick, after all, that the flame of active energy depends. The fire is conditioned by the fleshly fuel. No energy can replace the substance of energy; and while some impoverishment is a necessity of ascetic preparation, waste is a costly waste. For, even as a beast of burthen, this sore-spent body is a Golden Ass.

[1] *Works of Francis Thompson*, Vol. III, pp. 279-281. (Burns, Oates and Washbourne, London.)

RIGHTS AND DUTIES

But with all tender and wise allowance (and in these pages I have not been slack of allowance) it remains as it was said: "He that loseth his life for Me shall find it." The remedy for modern lassitude of body, for modern weakness of will, is holiness. There alone is the energizing principle from which the modern world persists in divorcing itself. If "this body of death" be, in ways of hitherto undreamed subtlety, a clog upon the spirit, it is no less true that the spirit can lift up the body. In the knowledge of the body's endless interplay with the spirit, of the subtle inter-relations between this father and daughter, this husband and wife, this pair whose bond is at once filial and marital, we have grown paralysingly learned in late days. But our knowledge is paralysing because it is one-sided. Of the body's reactions and command upon the spirit we know far indeed from all, yet fearfully much. Of the potency, magisterial, benevolent, even tyrannous, which goes forth from the spirit upon the body we have but young knowledge. Nevertheless, it is in rapid act of blossoming. Hypnotism, faith-healing, radium—all these, of such seeming multiple divergence, are really concentrating their rays upon a common centre. When that centre is at length divined, we shall have scientific witness, demonstrated certification, to the commerce between body and spirit, the regality of will over matter. To the blind tyranny of flesh upon spirit will then visibly be opposed the serene and sapient awe of spirit upon flesh. Then will lie open the truth which now we can merely point to by plausibilities and fortify by instance: that Sanctity is medicinal, Holiness a healer, from Virtue goes out virtue, in the love of God is more than solely ethical sanity. For the feebleness of a world seeking some maternal hand to which it may cling a wise asceticism is remedial.

Health, I have well-nigh said, is Holiness. What if Holiness be Health? Two sides of one truth. In their co-ordination and embrace resides the rounded answer. It is that embrace of body and spirit, Seen and Unseen, to which mortality, sagging but pertinacious, unalterably tends.

92

GAMES AND SPORTS

St. Thomas Aquinas [1]

As man needs bodily rest to refresh his body, which cannot labour continually, because its strength is limited and proportioned to finite toil, so with the mind the case is the same for the same reason. And, therefore, when the mind exerts itself beyond its measure, it labours and is fatigued thereby, especially because in operations of the soul, the body labours also, inasmuch as the intellectual soul uses powers that work by means of bodily organs. But sensible goods are connatural to man; and, therefore, when the mind soars above the things of sense, and is intent upon the goods of reason, the result is a certain psychical fatigue, whether it be the works of practical or of speculative reason that the man is intent upon; more, however, if he be intent upon the works of contemplation, because thereby he soars higher above sensible things; though possibly in some exterior works of the practical reason greater labour of the body is involved. But as bodily fatigue is thrown off by rest of the body, so must psychical fatigue be thrown off by rest of the mind. Now, the mind's rest is pleasure or delight. And, therefore, a remedy must be applied to psychical fatigue by some pleasure, and the intense application to rational pursuits must be for the time intermitted. Thus we read of blessed John the Evangelist, that when some persons were scandalized to find him at play with his disciples, he told one of them who had a bow, to shoot an arrow, and so again and again, and then asked him if he could go on doing that always. The other answered that if he tried to do it always, the bow would break. Hence blessed John drew the moral, that in like manner man's head would break, if his mind was kept forever on the strain. But sayings or doings of this sort, wherein nothing is sought beyond amusement, are spoken of as things said or done in *sport* or *jest*. And, therefore, we must at times make use of such things to rest the mind. In doing so there

---

[1] *Aquinas Ethicus,* translated by Joseph Rickaby, Vol. II, pp. 376-378. (Burns, Oates and Washbourne, London.)

are three precautions to be observed. The first and principal is, that the aforesaid amusement be not sought for in actions or words that are unseemly or hurtful. The second is, that the gravity of the mind be not altogether relaxed. Hence Tully says: "In our very jest let some glimpse of a virtuous character shine out." The third precaution here as in all other human actions is, that whatever is said or done should be in keeping with the person, the season, and the place, as Tully says that it should be "worthy of the time and of the man." Now a habit working according to reason is a moral virtue; and, therefore, in the matter of games and sports there can be a virtue, which the Philosopher calls *eutrapelia* (sprightliness).

93

BODY TRAINING AND TEMPORAL WORLD-FORCES

William J. Lockington [1]

By a world-force I mean, a man who stands out from other men and has in an uncommon degree the power of moving and leading them. In all ages and nations the names of such men are honoured and remembered, their memories are cherished and reverenced by their fellow-men. Right through the centuries, as we read of these moulders of nations, we learn, from their own words or from those of their contemporaries, that one of the main factors in their success was a well-trained, strong body.

Among those intellectual giants, the ancient Greeks, we find Socrates, still a world-force, though living twenty-three hundred years ago. He was a man "who could bear the longest fasts and the soldier's fare; he had immense strength and health, and he surpassed all men in physical endurance." His pupil, Plato, who held that a man educated in mind only and not in body was a cripple, was "endowed with a robust frame, and exercised in gymnastics and attained such force and skill as to contend for the prize, wrestling at the Isthmian festival." [2] Of the fiery orator

---

[1] *Bodily Health and Spiritual Vigour*, pp. 28-34. (Longmans, Green and Company, New York.) With permission.
[2] Grote's *Plato*.

Demosthenes we have spoken elsewhere and shown how he strengthened his body by walking and running up-hill, when a friend showed him that he had failed because "you do not prepare your body by exercise for the labour of the rostrum but suffer your parts to wither away in negligence and indulgence."

Turning to their neighbours, the Romans, we find, standing in the front rank, Cicero, an orator of orators. In early life he was a delicate man with a weak voice, and his fiery, impetuous nature soon broke down his body. By systematic exercise he strengthened it, "and by this management of his constitution, gained a sufficient stock of health and strength for the great labours and fatigues which he afterwards underwent." We find in his writings this statement: "It is exercise alone that supports the spirits and keeps the mind in vigour." His voice still rings across the earth.

Julius Cæsar, his contemporary, was hampered by bodily weakness, but "sought in war a remedy for his infirmities, endeavouring to strengthen his body by long marches and by simple diet." How he succeeded is plain to read.

And in later days it is the same story. Napoleon, the modern Cæsar, was "a man of stone and iron, capable of sitting on horseback sixteen or seventeen hours; of going many days together without food or rest, and with the speed and spring of a tiger in action." Maitland describes him as "a remarkably strong, well-built man at five feet seven inches high." A dictum of Napoleon was "the first requisite of good generalship is good health." His great adversary, Wellington, was a small eater and a great walker.

Gladstone so trained his body daily, that he was governing a nation at an age when his compeers were either dead, or, with wasted bodies, were waiting for death. The magnificent speech which closed the second reading of the Home Rule Bill was made when he was in his eighty-third year, and electrified the House. He trained by walking, and by ordinary exercise. When at the House of Commons he took a walk of two hours, every day, wet or dry. At eighty, he cut down an oak four feet in diameter,—evidently being a believer in the truth of the saying of Horace Greeley: "The axe is the healthiest implement that man ever handled and is especially so for habitual writers and other sedentary workers, whose shoulders it throws back, expanding their chests and opening their lungs. If every youth and man from fifteen to fifty years old could wield an axe two hours per day, dyspepsia would vanish from the earth and rheumatism become decidedly scarce. I am a poor chopper, yet the axe is my doctor and my delight. Its use gives the mind just enough occupation to prevent it falling into reverie or absorbing trains of thought; while every muscle of the body receives sufficient yet not exhausting exercise."

To return to Mr. Gladstone. "He had enormous driving power and physical energy," says Stead, "and his keen enjoyment of rural life at Hawarden, his famed habit of felling trees, and his always being a great walker, are pointed out as causes of his rare staying power and surpassing accomplishments." Here are a few extracts from his diary: "August 31, 1863, Walked 24¾ miles." He was then fifty-three years of age. In his fifty-fourth year we find this entry: "September 29th, 6:30 P. M. I have just come in from a fine hill walk of over three hours, quite ready for another, were there light and opportunity." "September 30th: I am come in from a nineteen mile walk as fresh as a lark. Very wet. We climbed 3300 feet." "October: I have been out for a good seven hours to-day going up Lochnagar,—3800 feet. I walked it all and am not in the least tired, but quite ready if there were need to set out for it again."

During the next year at Balmoral he writes, "I have just come in from a sixteen mile walk, quite fresh and pleased with myself! for having in my old age walked a measured mile in twelve minutes." Evidently this was no user of cushioned chairs and consequent cathartics. In his seventy-first year he walked seven miles, travelled forty miles and delivered three speeches of from forty-five to fifty minutes each, all within the one day. The contemplation of such a day's work by an old man gives one cause for thought, if a few hours in the schools daily or the celebrating of a second Mass on Sunday is felt to be a burden.

Another famous Englishman, Lord Palmerston, who for sixty years was a leading statesman, tells us that "every other abstinence will not make up for abstinence from exercise."

John Ruskin insisted on his students taking vigorous physical exercise, and led his class out in person, armed with shovel and pick, to make roads. In Chapter VI of "The Stones of Venice," he writes: "Now it is only by labour that thought can be made healthy, and only by thought that labor can be made happy, and the two cannot be separated with impunity."

President Eliot of Harvard College writes: "To attain success and length of service in any one of the learned professions, including that of teaching, a vigorous body is well-nigh essential. A busy lawyer, editor, minister, physician or teacher has need of greater physical endurance than a farmer, trader, manufacturer or mechanic. All professional biography teaches that to attain lasting distinction in sedentary indoor occupations which task the brain and the nervous system, extraordinary toughness of body must accompany extraordinary mental powers."

Of Bismarck, the founder of modern Germany, we are told, "he never could have accomplished his work without that herculean frame and iron constitution." He wrote in the year 1878, when in his sixty-third year: "I always did what I had to do with all my might, whatever really succeeded I paid for with my health and strength," and he had amassed health and strength from his boyhood onward until it was colossal;—"what impresses everyone is his air of vast bodily strength."

Of that sterling Catholic, Garcia Moreno, we read: "Nature had given him all that eminent qualities that formed the man of action. Tall and upright, with a robust constitution, everything revealed a man of untiring energy. In troubles times he was on horseback from morning till night, and his iron constitution resisted all fatigue." This is the man of whom Pius IX said: "Ah, if he were but the king of some powerful nation the Pope would have someone to support him in this world."

Washington, the father of his country, was a man of tireless endurance, "few equalled him in strength of arm or power of endurance, and he was a man of most extraordinary physical strength."

One of the leaders of the American bar, speaking at Chicago, and enumerating the causes that make for success, said: "It is the same old story of the sound mind and the honest heart in the sound body. The sound body is at the bottom of it all. The stomach is, indeed, the key of all professional eminence. If that goes back on you, you might as well throw up your sponge."

These examples are but few and taken at random, but they are sufficient to show that physical vigour is a tremendous factor in giving power to man to move other men. How these men stand out high above unknown millions of their fellows! How they swayed them and drew them through the years in countless armies obedient to their wills, as the mighty tidal-wave is drawn by the all-compelling lunar force. Imagine such bodies tenanted by fighting Catholic souls! What work could they not have done in saving souls for Christ! St. Ignatius, looking at the great world-forces, who at their will moved nations and who trained hard and long before they got the requisite vigour of body, wishes us to learn from them a lesson. "A man incapable of succeeding in the world," says he, "is incapable of succeeding in the Society of Jesus, while those who have the qualities necessary to secure worldly advancement make excellent subjects for religion." Father Meyer has the same thought in the sentence: "The heroes of the Cross are cast in the same natural mould as the heroes of the world."

94

HOMICIDE

Joseph F. Delany [1]

Homicide signifies in general the killing of a human being. In practice, however, the word has come to mean the unjust taking away of human life, perpetrated by one distinct from the victim and acting in a private capacity. For the purpose of this article, therefore, account is not taken of suicide, nor of the carrying out of the penalty of death by due process of law. The direct killing of an innocent person is of course to be reckoned among the most grievous of sins. It is said to happen directly when the death of the person is viewed either as an end attractive in itself, or at any rate is chosen as a means to an end. The malice discernible in the sin is primarily chargeable to the violation of the supreme ownership of God over the lives

---

[1] *The Catholic Encyclopedia*, Vol. VII, pp. 441, 442.

of His creatures. It arises as well from the manifest outrage upon one of the most conspicuous and cherished rights enjoyed by man, namely the right to life. For the scope contemplated here, a person is regarded as innocent so long as he has not by any responsible act brought any hurt to the community or to an individual comparable with the loss of life. Homicide is said to be indirect when it is no part of the agent's plan to bring about the death which occurs, so that this latter is not intended as an end nor is it selected as a means to further any purpose. In this hypothesis, it is at most permitted on account of a reason commensurate with so great an evil as is the destruction of human life. Thus, for instance, a military commander may train his guns upon a fortified place, even though in the bombardment which follows, he knows perfectly well that many non-combatants will perish. The sufficient cause in the case is consideration of the highest public good to be subserved by the defeat of the enemy. When, however, the untoward death of a person is the outcome of an action prohibited precisely because of the founded likelihood of its having this fatal result, then in the court of conscience the doer is held to be guilty in spite of his disclaimer of all intention in the matter. Hence, for example, one who fires a shotgun into the public thoroughfare, whilst protesting that he has no wish to work any mischief, is, nevertheless, obviously to be reproached as a murderer if perchance his bullet has killed anybody.

For the protection of one's own or another's life, limb, chastity, or valuables of some moment, it is agreed on all sides that it is lawful for anyone to repel violence with violence, even to the point of taking away the life of the unjust assailant, provided always that in so doing the limits of a blameless defence be not exceeded. It is proper to note (1) that the danger apprehended for oneself or another must be actual and even, so to speak, imminent, not merely prospective. Hence, the teaching here propounded cannot be adduced to justify the use of force for purposes of reprisal or vengeance by a private individual. This latter is a function belonging to the public authority. (2) No more violence may be employed than is required to safeguard sufficiently the goods already enumerated upon which an unwarranted assault has been made. The right of self-defence so universally attributed does not necessarily pre-suppose in the aggressor an imputable malice. It is enough that one's life or some other possession comparable with life should be threatened outside of the proper channels of the law. One might, for instance, kill a lunatic, or one crazed with drink, although there is no malice on their part, if this were the only effective way to head off their onset. St. Thomas is careful to say that even in self-defence it is unlawful to kill another directly, that is, to intend immediately the death of that other. His mind is that the formal volition of the self-defender should entirely be to preserve his own life and repulse the onslaught, whilst, as to the loss of life, which, as a matter of fact ensues, he keeps himself in a purely permissive attitude. This contention is combated by De Lugo and some others, who believe it to be right to choose expressly the killing of another as a means to self-defence. In conformity with the Thomistic doctrine is the axiomatic utterance that a private individual may never lawfully kill anyone whatever, because in self-defence one does not, technically speaking, kill, but only endeavors to stop the trespasser. Hence, according to the Angelic Doctor, it would follow that only by due operation of law may a human being ever be directly done to death.

Unlike other instances of damage wrought, the murderer cannot offer an adequate indemnity. For one thing, he cannot restore the life he has destroyed. There is no doubt, however, that he is obliged to make good whatever expenses may have been incurred for medical attendance or hospital care, and this to the surviving heirs. He is likewise bound to furnish to the immediate relatives of his victim, such as wife, children, parents, the sustenance for which they depended on the latter. Should the murderer die before being able to satisfy these claims, they pass as a burden to be met by the inheritors of his estate. It is not easy to determine what obligation, if any, the slayer has to the creditors of the slain; but it seems equitable to say that he must at least reimburse them whenever it is clear that his aim in the perpetration of the deed of blood was to injure them.

95

HOMICIDE, EXCUSABLE AND FELONIOUS

J. Harding Fisher [1]

Just at present two spectacular moving-picture productions are occupying the attention, it is scarcely too much to say, of hundreds of thousands of people in many cities of the United States. In one, there is a case of what some people would erroneously call suicide; and in the other, a double murder and a homicide in self-defense occur. All three instances are presented to the spectator in such a way as to evoke approval, and in no case is there any criticism or comment either for or against the deed. The situation which results in the taking of human life is practically identical in all three cases, but is dealt with in three different ways. Virtue is endangered in each instance, but in one case the person endangered leaps from a cliff, with only one chance in a thousand of escaping death; in the second case the person endangered shoots the unjust aggressor; and in the third, a mother sends a bullet through the hearts of her two imperiled children, being goaded to her awful deed by the frenzied fear of a fate for them, which she regards as far worse than death. The widespread publicity which these vast scenic representations have enjoyed and are likely to enjoy for an indefinite time to come, makes a discussion of the homicides timely and even necessary.

There is no doubt whatever that homicide in general is forbidden by the natural law and by positive Divine command. The precept, "Thou shalt not kill," was not merely engraved on the tablets of Mt. Sinai; it is written unmistakably in every human heart. Directly, deliberately and on one's own authority, to take the life of another who is innocent, is an unjust invasion of the rights of the individual, of the State of which he is a member, and of God. Civilized society is unanimous in its reprobation of such a deed, and almost universally punishes it with death. The public executioner in the performance of his duty may put an end to the existence of a condemned criminal; and in a

---

[1] "The Catholic Mind," November 8, 1915.

just war, an individual may, at his country's bidding, do his best to disable his enemy even with the certain prospect of inflicting a mortal wound. But no man in his private capacity, may lawfully, by his direct action, seek to kill another, unless that other is unjustly, here and now, actually assailing or certainly about to assail his own or a third person's right to life and limb, or to property of great value, or to virtue.

"Lynch Law" therefore is an outrageous crime, being the usurpation of an authority over life and death, to which no private citizen, nor any group of private citizens has any claim. Similarly no motive, whether it be to prevent insult and shame, or to put an end to hopeless suffering, or to save the life of another, justifies the taking of an innocent life. Putting a mortally wounded comrade out of agony, therefore, as soldiers are sometimes asked to do on the battlefield, taking a child's life to preserve the mother's, or to save the child itself from disgrace, are all unjustifiable; such acts constitute murder. The mother, therefore, in the moving-picture is guilty of murder, although in her frenzied state she is not perhaps altogether responsible; thus, too, husbands and fathers who during the Boxer movement put pistols into their wives' hands with the counsel to use them against their daughters when all hope of saving the legations was gone, advised the commission of murder, pure and simple. The reason is that human life belongs to God alone, and in the above-mentioned cases He refuses to transfer His dominion over it to another. Even should the one who is killed consent to the killing, it would be murder none the less, because God's rights over that life would remain.

On the other hand, homicide, in the case where it is a necessity of self-defense, has always been held to be justifiable before the tribunal of God and excusable in the eyes of the law. Every man has a right, given him by nature itself, to his life; although not in the sense that he may keep it or terminate it at his pleasure, for being a gift of God that is intended primarily and essentially for the service of God, he is bound to take ordinary means to preserve it until it shall have run the course and rendered the service assigned to it by Divine Providence. Life, however, belongs to man in the limited sense that it is his to possess, to use, to enjoy and to defend against all unjust attacks. Individuals, therefore, who assail this right, so long as the one attacked is not himself guilty of unjust aggression on the rights of others, do so at their peril. Life is so precious a gift, that a man may take such means to save it as are necessary, even to the extent of causing the death of an unjust assailant. Of course, no man may licitly inflict more injury on his assailant than is required for legitimate self-defense; but jurists, ethicists and moral theologians are agreed that he may licitly proceed to any length that is necessary to resist murderous attacks, not excluding the infliction of death on the person by whom his own life is put in jeopardy.

The man attacked is not ordinarily obliged in conscience to take his adversary's life to save his own, for such an action is clearly not one of the ordinary means of preserving life which every man is bound to employ; but he is justified in doing so, whenever it is the only means of escaping death. For in the collision of the two rights, the right of the person attacked and the right of the assailant, the latter right gives way. It is abdicated so to speak by the free act of the wrong-doer. Nor is any injury done to the State, for it exists precisely to defend the rights of its citizens. God, too, in such cases signifies by the prompting of the natural law that He gives permission for what would otherwise be a usurpation of His dominion over life and death; for by the very fact that God gives a man a right to defend his life, which no one denies, He also gives him the right to use such means to that end as are necessary; in other words, to take the life of the unjust assailant, where without this, self-defense is impossible.

It is to be noted also that what one is justified in doing for himself in this matter, he may do for another. Provided he be certain that the attack on the third person's life is unjust, and that there is no other way of saving him except by killing his assailant, not only will he be free from blame, in saving the life of the person attacked by taking the life of the one who assails him, but he will perform an act of virtue.

Again, where an attempt is made on a person's virtue, not in the moral sense by temptation, but in the technical sense of an outrageous assault on chastity, the life of the person who makes the attempt, may be taken either by the person who is actually endangered or by another who comes to the rescue. The same is true of cases where goods of great value are in danger of being lost by robbery, and there is no hope of saving them except by killing the thief, although this last point, which relates to goods of value, is only probable and is not so easy of application. In both these cases, however, as in the former instances, no greater violence may be used than the case actually demands.

Save in very exceptional instances no one is obliged in conscience to resist. In circumstances, therefore, where there is felt a violent disinclination to the shedding of human blood, or where all efforts at resistance are seen to be fruitless, escape from the attack may be sought in other ways, as in the case of the leap from the cliff, even though the chances of not being killed by the means employed for escape, in the example, by the leap itself, are slight. Suicide indeed is always forbidden. No one may ever for any motive, directly, deliberately and on his own authority end his own life. But in cases of extreme peril to either life or virtue, one may take means to escape the pressing danger, even though these means *may* lead to death. The good which is directly sought being so great, it is deemed sufficient to justify the risk.

The examples referred to in this paper were chosen, not because they are strange and extraordinary, but because they are depicted in the most widely circulated and best attended of the moving-pictures of the day, and because they are typical of very many other instances, taken from fiction and life, and shown on the screen and in the papers, which call for an application of the elementary but not always understood principles which have been exposed. Human life is a sacred thing. It is not a mere chattel or a plaything to be used for a day or as long as it amuses, and then carelessly cast aside. Dominion over human life belongs exclusively to God. He who trifles with the life of man, trifles with one of God's exclusive possessions and will be held to a strict account. Its use, however, belongs to man, and is a precious gift, the foundation gift of all God's personal gifts to man. We must be on our guard, therefore, lest our appreciation of its worth be cheapened by the light estimation in which it is apparently held in the press, and in the film. Its rights and privileges must be learned from the basic character of human nature, not from the whim or fancy of scenario writers, whose concern is to create striking or thrilling situations, not to expose the truth.

96

SELF-DEFENCE

James J. Fox [1]

Ethically the subject of self-defence regards the right of a private person to employ force against any one who unjustly attacks his life or person, his property or good name. While differing among themselves on some of the more subtle and less practical points comprised in this topic, our moralists may be said to be unanimous on the main principles and their application regarding the right of self-defence. The teaching may be summarized as follows:

Defence of life and person.—Everyone has the right to defend his life against the attacks of an unjust aggressor. For this end he may employ whatever force is necessary and even take the life of an unjust assailant. As bodily integrity is included in the good of life, it may be defended in the same way as life itself. It must be observed, however, that no more injury may be inflicted on the assailant than is necessary to defeat his purpose. If, for example, he can be driven off by a call for help or by inflicting a slight wound on him, he may not lawfully be slain. Again the unjust attack must be actually begun, at least morally speaking, not merely planned or intended for some future time or occasion. Generally speaking one is not bound to preserve one's own life at the expense of the assailant's; one may, out of charity, forego one's right in the matter. Sometimes, however, one may be bound to defend one's own life to the utmost on account of one's duty of state or other obligations. The life of another person may be defended on the same conditions by us as our own. For since each person has the right to defend his life unjustly

[1] *Catholic Encyclopedia*, Vol. XIII, p. 691.

attacked, what he can lawfully do through his own efforts he may also do through the agency of others. Sometimes too, charity, natural affection, or official duty imposes the obligation of defending others. A father ought, for example, to defend the lives of his children; a husband, his wife; and all ought to defend the life of one whose death would be a serious loss to the community. Soldiers, policemen, and private guards hired for that purpose are bound in justice to safeguard the lives of those entrusted to them.

Defence of property.—It is lawful to defend one's material goods even at the expense of the aggressor's life; for neither justice nor charity require that one should sacrifice possessions, even though they be of less value than human life in order to preserve the life of a man who wantonly exposes it in order to do an injustice. Here, however, we must recall the principle that in extreme necessity every man has a right to appropriate what is necessary to preserve his life. The starving man who snatches a meal is not an unjust aggressor; consequently it is not lawful to use force against him. Again, the property which may be defended at the expense of the aggressor's life must be of considerable value; for charity forbids that in order to protect ourselves from a trivial loss we should deprive our neighbor of his life. Thefts or robberies, however, of small value, are to be considered not in their individual, but in their cumulative aspect. A thief may be slain in the act of carrying away stolen property provided that it cannot be recovered from him by any other means: if, for example, he can be made to abandon his spoil through fright, then it would not be lawful to shoot him. If he has carried the goods away to safety he cannot then be killed in order to recover them; but the owner may endeavor to take them from him, and if the thief resists with violence he may be killed in self-defence.

Honor.—Since it is lawful to take life in the legitimate defence of one's material goods, it is evidently also lawful to do so in defence of chastity which is a good of a much higher order. With regard to honor or reputation, it is not lawful to kill one to prevent an insult or an attack upon our reputation which we believe he intends or threatens. Nor may we take a life to avenge an insult already offered. This proceeding would not be defence of our honor or reputation, but revenge. Besides, in the general estimation honor and reputation may be sufficiently protected without taking the life of the offender.

97

ETHICS OF THE OUIJA BOARD

James F. Barrett [1]

From the standpoint of morality and ethics, occult practices, performed deliberately and sincerely, fall under the head of divination and are mortal sins. Frequently, however, they are only slight faults, because of the fact that they who indulge in them do not place implicit belief in the revelation of the future by such methods, and employ them oftentimes as a joke or out of curiosity. The immorality of the practices consists in the use of them for occult purposes with a sinful end in view, and under this caption are included all forms of crystal-gazing, table-turning, and the use of the planchette or ouija-board, when by such means the operators seek to discover what it is certain none of them know, either consciously or unconsciously. Such practices are declared specifically in Holy Scripture to be hateful to God; for we read in the eighteenth chapter of Deuteronomy, verses ten to twelve: "Neither let there be found among you anyone that shall expiate his son or daughter, making them to pass through the fire; or that consulteth soothsayers, or observeth dreams and omens, neither let there be any wizard, nor charmer, nor anyone that consulteth pythonic spirits, or fortune-tellers or that seeketh truth from the dead. For the Lord abhorreth all these things and for these abominations He will destroy them at thy coming."

Throughout the ages, moreover, this has been the teaching of the Church, solicitous as she is for the welfare of her children and careful to warn them against what is harmful. And such a position she finds well authenticated by the passage of the Sacred Text quoted above, by the plain words of Christ as they are recorded in the pages of the Scriptures, by the teachings of her Apostles and

[1] The America Press, New York.

Fathers and Doctors, and by facts carefully observed and studied throughout the centuries of her experience. But at the same time she has exercised the greatest care and the most prudent judgment in regard to the value of mystic phenomena, for with the same breath that she condemns the false and morbid mysticism, she recognizes and approves the true and the healthy.

Because of the compelling fact that many are accustomed to enter upon experiments with the supernatural, through the instrumentality of the ouija-board or the planchette or various other practices, solely for the mere amusement of it and with no sense of the seriousness of the undertaking or of the responsibilities which are being incurred, the Catholic Church has seen fit, in a recent decree, to forbid her children taking any part in Spiritistic seances of any kind. In a decree of the Congregation of the Holy Office, dated April 24, 1917, attendance is forbidden "at any Spiritistic communications or manifestations whatsoever," irrespective of the purpose in view, "whether in the capacity of an active participant or merely as an interested spectator." The reasonableness of this prohibition is apparent from the fact that activities of this nature are becoming day by day a graver source of moral peril to society. For with the practice of many forms of mind-passivity, of which the ouija-board is but one, the doors of the soul are being opened, thus giving to spirits an intimate and perilous access to the minds and souls of unwary men. In numerous instances this leads to the loss of all religious faith and to the moral and mental undoing of the victims.

Hence any participation in such performances is not permitted not only because of the dangers, physical and mental that may lurk beneath them, but because of the cataclysm which yawns imperceptibly at their very feet. Such has been the implicit belief of the Church throughout her centuries' history; such is her explicit teaching now in the voice of her sovereign Pontiff. For it has been her ordinances alone which, in the past, have succeeded in shutting out from men's souls those dangerous powers of darkness which have threatened to invade them, and it will be her ordinances alone which can do this effectively and consistently in the future. She has ever feared the powers of darkness and she fears them now in these spiritistic practices, for, as St. Thomas says, the devil wishes to excite among man a greater curiosity about occult matters, in order that, "being implicated in these observances, they may become more curious and get themselves more entangled in the manifold snares of pernicious error."

98

THE WRONGFULNESS OF DUELLING

Victor Cathrein [1]

There can be no doubt that duelling is contrary to the ordinances of the Catholic Church and of most civilized countries. By the wording of its ordinance against duelling, the Council of Trent plainly indicated that duelling was essentially wrong and since then theologians have almost universally characterized it as a sinful and reprehensible course of action. However there were always a few scholars who held the opinion that cases might arise in which the unlawfulness of duelling could not be proved with certainty by mere reason. But this opinion has not been tenable since Pope Benedict XIV in the Bull "Detestabilem" of the year 1752 condemned the following propositions: (1) "A soldier would be blameless and not liable to punishment for sending or accepting a challenge if he would be considered timid and cowardly, worthy of contempt, and unfit for military duty, were he not to send a challenge or accept such, and who would for this reason lose the position which supported himself and his family, or who would be obliged to give up forever the hope of befitting and well-earned advancement." (2) "Those persons are excusable who to defend their honor or to escape the contempt of men accept or send a challenge when they know positively that the duel will not take place but will be permitted by others." (3) "A general or officer who accepts a challenge through fear of the loss of his reputation and his position does not come under the ecclesiastical punishment decreed by the Church for duellists." (4) "It is permissible under the natural conditions of man to accept or send a challenge in order to save one's fortune, when the loss of it can not be

[1] *Catholic Encyclopedia*, Vol. V, pp. 185-186.

prevented by any other means." (5) "This permission claimed for natural conditions can also be applied to a badly guided state in which, especially, justice is openly denied by the remissness or malevolence of the authorities." Like his predecessors, Leo XIII in his letter "Pastoralis officii," of 12 September, 1891, to the German and Austro-Hungarian bishops, laid down the following principles: "From two points of view the Divine law forbids a man as a private person to wound or kill another, excepting when he is forced to it by self-defence. Both natural reason and the inspired Holy Scriptures proclaim this Divine law."

The intrinsic reason why duelling is in itself sinful and reprehensible is that it is an arbitrary attack on God's right of ownership as regards human life. Only the owner and master of a thing has the right at pleasure to destroy it or expose it to the danger of destruction. But man is not the owner and master of his life; it belongs instead to his Creator. Now man can only call that his property and treat it as such which is intended in the first instance for his benefit, so that he has the right to exclude others from the use of the same. Man, however, is not created primarily for himself but for the glory and service of God. Here below he is to serve his Creator and Lord as long as the Lord wills and thus attain his own salvation. For this end God has given man life, maintains it for him, and has bestowed on him the instinct of self-preservation. But if man is not the master of his life, he has not the right to expose it at pleasure to destruction or even deliberately to seek such danger. In order rightfully to expose the life to danger, there must be a justifiable reason, and even then the risking of life is only permissible, not the end to be sought in itself. What is said of one's own life applies also to the life of one's fellow-man. Every man has the right in case of necessity forcibly to defend himself against an unlawful attack on his life, even if it cost the life of the assailant; this is a requirement of public safety; but apart from such defence, no man has the right as a private individual to injure the life of his fellow-man or at pleasure to expose his own to similar danger. Hence it is easy to perceive that a duellist unjustifiably exposes both his own life and that of his fellow-man, consequently is guilty of a wrongful assumption of the right of God, the Lord of life and death. To make this clear it is only necessary to examine the pretexts used to palliate duelling, or, what is the same, to look into the aims sought to be attained by this custom. One of the principal reasons given in justification of duelling is the obtaining of satisfaction. A man is insulted or injured in reputation, and in order to obtain satisfaction challenges the defamer. But besides the offence against civil law in seeking to establish one's rights with weapons, thus evading the authority of the State, a duel is totally unsuited to the attainment of satisfaction, and in addition is wrongful. Satisfaction consists in the offender withdrawing his insult and treating the offended person with respect and honor. This end cannot, however, be attained by duelling. When the one who has given the provocation accepts the challenge he does not thereby withdraw the insult; he intends, rather, to maintain it by weapons and shows himself moreover ready to add other and greater wrong-doing to the first, inasmuch as he may severely wound or even kill the challenger. Moreover, who would allow to the man whom he wishes to compel to make good a wrong the chance of victory as to himself, i. e., who would give the offender the opportunity to add to the wrong he has already done an even more heinous injury? Yet this is what the challenger does in granting his adversary the same weapons and the same chance for success as he claims for himself.

Another reason offered in justification of duelling is self-defence. The duellist desires to avoid the loss of respect of his peers and thus to retain his office and his income, or, as is said, to defend his honor and his social position. It is unfortunately only too true that to-day the conscientious opponent of duelling, especially in the army, must often suffer great losses. Nevertheless duelling cannot be justified as self-defence. Honor and the respect of others cannot be preserved by the use of arms, nor in a duel is there any actual vindication of these. The duel implies that the honor of the challenger has already been injured, and consequently that this injury is an accomplished fact; besides, the duel takes place according to agreement, so that it is not a case of self-defence against sudden attack. But the word *self-defence* is used in a broader sense. According to the prejudice existing in certain circles, the person

who does not answer an insult by a challenge or who
declines a challenge is held to be dishonorable and cowardly; thus it may be that a man's entire social position is
at stake. Yet, from its very nature, a duel is an unsuitable
and illicit method of preserving or rehabilitating honor.
Look at a duel first from the point of view of the person
injured. He must, it is said, send a challenge because he
has been insulted. Two cases, however, are here possible.
Either his moral character and good name have been attacked, or the specific charge of cowardice has been made
against him. If the former be the case, the duel is manifestly unsuited to defend the injured man's honor. A duel
can never prove that the person attacked is a man of honor,
is not a simpleton, has not committed adultery, or the like.
A man without character or morals can be just as skillful
in handling weapons as his honorable opponent. If the
quarrel hinges on the charge of cowardice, a duel is apparently a proper means of disproving the same. But in this
instance the challenger directly endangers his life in order
to prove that he is no coward. Consequently he cannot say
that he only suffers his life to be endangered, he deliberately
seeks this danger in order to show his courage. And,
according to our former statements, this is to dispose of
one's life unlawfully. It cannot be said in reply that the
injured person merely intends the rehabilitation of his
honor. That is certainly the final aim of the duel, but the
first and direct aim is to prove one's courage by fighting
the duel. Is it permissible, however, to risk one's own life
and that of one's fellow-man merely as a means of proving
one's courage? If this be correct, it would be equally allowable to enter a lion's cage, sword in hand, if public opinion
demanded such proof of personal bravery. Hence it follows
that the duel is not in reality a proper means to demonstrate
one's courage, for true courage is a moral virtue which is
not blind and foolhardy, but exposes itself to danger only
if reason demand it. What has been said of the injured
party is applicable also to the party giving the provocation,
the one who is challenged. If he has acted unjustly, he
should as a man of honor offer reparation; that is his duty,
and the refusal to perform this duty plainly gives him no
right to fight a duel with his opponent. If he is not in the
wrong, he ought to refuse the challenge. The only ground

for which a challenge might be accepted would be fear of the accusation of cowardice; that this reason is, however, not tenable has already been shown. It surely is the basest cowardice to do, through fear of being accused of want of courage, what sober reflection would lead any man of sense to condemn as immoral and wrong.

The conclusion necessary to be drawn from the above is: whoever is killed in a duel is guilty of self-murder, because he has for no justifiable reason risked his life, and whoever slays his adversary in a duel is guilty of unjustifiable homicide, because he has taken the risk of causing death without any right to do so; this holds true even though he did not directly intend his opponent's death. The above applies not only to duels undertaken by private individuals of their own free will, but also to duels fought on account of personal grievances by order of State authorities. Those in authority have not the right to dispose at their pleasure of the life of the subject. Should a dispute be laid before them, they should examine the matter judiciously and punish the guilty party. If the guilt cannot be proved the accused should be acquitted; in such a case the authorities have no right to command a duel and thus expose the innocent to the same peril as the guilty. This has all the more force, as duels often take place on account of wrongs which are not to-day punished with death by civil law.

99

MAY THE STATE KILL?

PAUL L. BLAKELY [1]

In his "Criminal Sociology," Enrico Ferri writes that capital punishment is one of those complex questions which cannot be met with monosyllabic answers. Complex it is, especially at the present time when, at least in the United States, lawlessness and even disrespect for the principle of authority itself, appear to be increasing; yet, if it be divided, monosyllables will serve very well. Has civil society the right to inflict death? Must civil society always exercise this right? (For it is clear, I think, that there is a differ-

---

[1] *America,* May 16, 1925.

ence between a right, and the obligation to exercise that right wherever and whenever it may apply.) If we answer the first question with an affirmative and the second with a negative, I think we shall have a fairly accurate presentation of authoritative Catholic teaching on capital punishment.

Capital punishment may be defined as the taking of human life by the legitimate authority as an atonement for grievous crime and as a means for the preservation of public order and security. "The right to inflict this penalty is known as 'the right of the sword.' We call it the power of life and death." . . .

Both Scripture and tradition support the right of the State to inflict the penalty of death, and their teaching is shared by the *consensus gentium*. Dr. Koch makes a shrewd point when he observes, "Surely men would not have so willingly admitted the right of their rulers to deprive them of their most precious possession, i. e., life, for certain grievous crimes committed against the public order, had not this right been universally regarded as a corollary of the natural law and a postulate of right reason." It may also be noted in this connection that no nation, so far as can be ascertained, has ever renounced this right. Italy which has done away with the death penalty for murder is a seeming exception. Yet there can be no doubt that the authorities would shoot down rioters in the streets, without the formality of a trial, did they refuse to disperse, and Italy still has an army to defend the Kingdom by putting its enemies, internal or external, to death, should that extreme treatment be found necessary. In other countries, too, where capital punishment has been apparently abolished, an exception has been made for time of war, and in some instances the death penalty has been retained even in peace time for certain infractions of military law.

The arguments for capital punishment, drawn from natural reason, are many and varied, but the most convincing may be reduced, it seems to me, to the principle of the State's right to self-defense. "To kill a man," writes St. Thomas, "is not lawful, except it be done by public authority for the common good." (*Summa*, 2a, 2ae, qu. 64, art. 7). "The slaying of an evildoer is lawful inasmuch as it is directed to the welfare of the whole community" (*Ib. art* 3).

Every part [of an organism] is directed to the whole, as imperfect to perfect, and therefore every part is naturally for the sake of the whole. For this reason we observe that if the health of the whole body demands the excision of a member, on account of its being decayed or infectious to the other members, it is both praiseworthy and advantageous to have it cut away. Now every individual is to the whole community as a part to the whole. Therefore, if a man be dangerous and infectious to the community, on account of some sin, it is praiseworthy and advantageous that he be killed in order to safeguard the common good. (*Summa Theol.* 2a, 2ae, qu. 64, *art.* 2).

Anticipating the objection frequently heard today, "Capital punishment is nothing but murder done by the State," St. Thomas argues that "the slaying of a man is forbidden in the Decalogue, only insofar as it bears the character of *something undue,* for in this sense the precept contains the very essence of justice. Human law cannot make it lawful for a man to be slain unduly. But it is not undue for all evil-doers or foes of the common weal to be slain, and hence this is not contrary to the precept of the Decalogue . . ." (*Summa Theol.* 1a, 2ae, qu. 100, *art.* 8, *ad* 31).

Other arguments, drawn, for instance, from the notion and purpose of punishment in general, or from reasons of social utility, are frequently cited, but Dr. Koch is justified, I think, in his contention that the right of the State to inflict capital punishment can be best shown from its right of self-defense. He argues that as a State may be attacked by foreign enemies, so it may also be attacked by those guilty of a violence which undermines the very foundations of the social order. "Against these—radical Socialists, anarchists, Bolsheviki, or whatever else they may be called—the authorities frequently have no other effective means of preserving or restoring law and order and securing peace than capital punishment." This argument does not show, indeed, that the State may lawfully put to death for *this* or *that* violation, or supposed violation, of public order. But it does show that the State may rightly inflict the penalty for such violations as here and now make impossible the due preservation of peace and good order in the community, and threaten its own existence.

100

KILLING THE WOUNDED

Ernest R. Hull [1]

An English military Chaplain made the following inquiry: "In defending outposts of the Empire, our soldiers are often engaged with savage frontier tribes, who invariably torture, mutilate, and kill prisoners of war. There is a general feeling in military circles that it is in keeping with the noblest instinct of humanity, mercifully to put an end to wounded comrades who are in danger of being taken alive. Also, it is felt that self-destruction is justifiable and better than having to face the certain prospect of a cruel and lingering death. What should be the attitude of Catholic soldiers under these circumstances?"

This cannot be done. The teaching of the Church is unequivocal, that God is the supreme master of life and death; and that no human being is allowed to usurp His dominion so as deliberately to put an end to life, either his own or any one else's without an authorization or delegation of God, either direct or indirect, expressed or implied.

The Church recognizes this kind of authorization or delegation in certain instances, especially in the Old Testament: (1) In specific and individual cases, as for instance the command to Abraham to sacrifice his son Isaac, or where God ordered Saul to "utterly destroy Amalec," and so on. (2) In case of certain crimes, as where God attached a death penalty to adultery, etc., in the Mosaic law. (3) Where God instructs the Chosen People to wage certain wars against their enemies. Apart from explicit authorization, the Church also interprets the law of nature as allowing the act of killing: (1) To a nation engaged in a just war. (2) The execution of criminals by the Government. (3) The killing of an unjust aggressor by the innocent individual in self-defence.

But the Church never has allowed, and never will allow, the killing of individuals on the grounds of private expediency: for instance to escape torture or mutilation; or to

---

[1] Reprinted from the Bombay *Examiner*, in *The Catholic Mind*, May 8, 1919.

put an end to prolonged suffering or hopeless sickness; or to rid the community of decayed and useless members who are a burden to themselves and to others, The modern outsider often looks upon this prohibition as very unpractical and also very inhumane. They say: It would be a positive mercy to the sufferer and to everybody else to put this or that wretch out of his pain; and the sufferer himself would in many cases be glad of it.

The argument is plausible enough, and it is not the only instance of the kind. Take for example divorce. There are cases in which the maintenance of the marriage bond is a source of life-long misery, to which divorce would at once put an end. There are cases in which divorce would not only be a relief and benefit to the two parties, but it would also be free from all evil or injurious consequences to any third party. And yet even in the single clear case, the Church sticks inexorably to its principle: "A Christian marriage (we put aside the more complex case of non-Christian marriage) is a life-long bond soluble only by death"—and there is an end of it. It may be "hard lines" in a particular case. But the hard lines must be accepted as part of the inevitable, and made the best of.

It may be difficult to find any convincing intrinsic reason why these rigid doctrines should be maintained as admitting of no exception. But there is at least one indirect reason which, when stated clearly, can hardly be gainsaid. If the Church did once relax the rigor of the universal law by allowing divorce under certain distressful circumstances, the effect would be disastrous to the whole system. The human mind, once given an opening, would take appalling advantage of it. As soon as divorce looms on the horizon, the foundations of the stability of marriage are shaken. Every quarrel, or disagreement, or weariness will at once suggest the idea of separation. Every illicit attraction felt for another person will be indulged in with impunity, on the ground that if the new *laison* "comes off," the old marriage bond need not stand in the way. The mere fact that the marriage bond is soluble at option will make married people far less careful to keep up their affection and agreeableness with their partners. The occasions justifying divorce will be multiplied; and designing people will actually lay themselves out to create those occasions in order to secure their liberty and marry elsewhere.

In much the same way, as soon as a case of prolonged suffering occurred, immediately the thought of *euthanasia* would also arise as a feasible means of escape. The victim of the suffering would merely have to feel "This is intolerable" and he would be tempted to add "I had better make away with myself, or get somebody else to do so." Nurses would fall under the temptation of quietly smothering an agonizing patient with a pillow. Burdened relatives would begin to think of doing the same. The practice of killing the wounded in fires, in railway collisions and in war would come into vogue. The same principle would next be applied to mental troubles. Suicide would become an ordinary refuge for the distressed or dependent, and all conscience about the solemn sacredness of life would disappear.

A French philosopher once said "If there were no God we should have to invent one" in order to keep the vicious inclinations of humanity in check. In the same way we might say "If the Catholic doctrine regarding the sacredness of life and of the marriage-bond did not exist, we should have to invent it," in order to keep life and marriage safe from the inroads of laxity and ruin. The very fact that a departure from the strict principles of the Church at once opens the doors to wholesale and widespread disorder is not altogether a *direct* proof of the truth of the Catholic position. But it is at least a very persuasive argument, which tends to show that the constitution of humanity itself requires such absolute restraining laws; and that therefore the laws themselves must be founded in the nature of things, and belong to the natural law as stamped by God on the world.

101

VIVISECTION

John S. Vaughan [1]

The special purpose of this paper is to consider the much debated question of vivisection, about which a vast deal of

[1] *Thoughts for All Times*, pp. 371-379. (O'Shea & Co., New York.)

nonsense is written, and a vast deal of unnecessary acrimony and abuse is expended.

We must begin by anticipating a very common and specious objection. How is it possible that any verdict upon the point can be gathered—it is objected—from the great theologians, considering that vivisection is a thing of modern date, and could never have come under their notice, nor have commanded their attention? Now as a matter of fact, vivisection "has been practiced since the dawn of history, and flourished extensively all through the Middle Ages." [2] This at once disposes of the objection. But, since it is quite obvious that it was never practiced in the precise manner, nor on the same scale as obtains at the present day, we will, for the sake of argument, allow the objection to remain, and give our answer.

Vivisection, as such, is evidently nothing more than a mode of action. It can neither create nor can it evolve new principles of morality, for the simple reason that principles are eternal and rooted in the very nature of things. At most, vivisection can but present itself as a new case which falls under the application of moral principles already in existence. Now, all these principles have met with a full and exhaustive treatment at the hands of the schoolmen. Of course, it is as clear as noonday that the ancient theologians could not have anticipated modern progress in *medicine* by treating explicitly of the actual case of vivisection, any more than they could have anticipated the results of modern progress in *acoustics* by discussing the validity of a confession heard, or of an absolution conferred, through the telephone. Such applications are, as they would have termed it, *in infima specie;* and their solution, and that of others as well, is to be sought and found in the ordinary and acknowledged determining principles of which the schoolmen have bequeathed us a most searching and careful statement. It would, indeed, be difficult to discover any

---

[2] "A toutes les époques, on a pratiqué des vivisections. On raconte que les rois de Perse livraient les condamnés à mort aux médecins, afin qu'ils fissent sur eux des vivisections utiles à la médecine. Selon Galien, Attale III. Philométor, qui regnait 137 ans av. J. C. à Pergame, experimentait les poisons et les contre-poisons sur des criminels condamnés à mort. . . On peut considérer Galien comme le fondateur des vivisections sur les animaux."—*Vide* Pierre Larousse. Tome 15.

vital consideration which enters into the question of vivisection, of which the principles of solution are not to be found in the *Summa* of the great St. Thomas, either where he treats of the vice of cruelty, or where he speaks of animals and their place and use in the economy of creation.

The objection founded upon the modernness of the practice of vivisection—even supposing it to be quite modern, which we have seen it is not—is utterly baseless and imaginary. One might as well argue that a newly discovered metal would not fall under the ordinary rules of gravitation, as that a new case of conscience could not be disposed of by an application of the ordinary principles of morality.

In vivisection man inflicts a certain amount of pain upon the beasts, not indeed for the sake of causing pain, which *ex hypothesi* he regrets, but solely for the sake of some advantage or some gain to himself or to his fellow man. Now the question arises—Is this lawful or not? Here, I take it, lies the whole kernel of the matter, so we must put the point as clearly as we can, and as logically. Thus, of two things, one. Either it is lawful for man to inflict pain upon beasts for his own advantage and profit, or it is not. To cause such an amount of pain as is unavoidable for the obtaining of the end he has in view is evidently either a sin or not a sin. There is no middle term; it must necessarily be one or the other. Take the first alternative. Say it is a sin. Very well. Then it necessarily follows that to drive a horse in a cab; or to imprison a thrush in a cage; or to hunt the fox or the hare; or to put a worm on a fish-hook; or to add a butterfly to a collection, and thousands of similar common practices, are all actual sins. And if sins, then not to be committed for any consideration whatsoever —no! Not even to save a thousand worlds could one dig one's spurs into a horse's flanks, or chain up a dog in one's backyard, or spit a worm upon a hook. This is the absurdity to which the one alternative binds us.

Then let us assume the other, and only remaining alternative, and grant that none of the foregoing practices are sins. What then? To concede so much is to evacuate one's position altogether. It is to establish the important and far-reaching principle that beasts may be made to suffer, at least in so far as it may be necessary or conducive to the well-being of man, for whose use and rational service they have been made; or, as St. Thomas expresses it, "propter quam sunt."³

Now, observe the *degree* of suffering inflicted does not enter into the essence of the matter at all. Whether the pain be greater or less cannot affect the principle one jot. The theological axiom, "magis et minus non variant speciem," is as true and as universally admitted among theologians as the geometrical axiom, "the part can never equal the whole," is among mathematicians. Thus the whole matter at once reduces itself to a question of adjustment and proportion. For the sake of a trifling gain, but a moderate degree of pain may reasonably be inflicted. But, as the importance of the end to be obtained increases, so may the amount of pain that is inflicted increase.

Thus, merely for the pleasure and recreation of a spin through the open country, I may harness my horse, and compel him, *nolens volens*, to drag my carriage over hill and down dale, and to turn now to the right, and now to the left, as fancy may suggest. If, however, I am anxious to catch a train, and can do so only by putting spurs to my beast, and by pressing him, somewhat beyond his accustomed pace, there is a sufficient motive to justify my conduct. But if I am traveling among some hostile tribe of savages, and I find myself so situated that escape will be impossible unless I use much greater violence, and so urge on my mettlesome steed that he does himself serious damage, and finally falls exhausted and dying by my camp fire, I am still guilty of no sin whatever. For I may most justly save my own life at the sacrifice of my horse's, even though its death be accompanied with the greatest agony.

Cardinal Newman, with his customary accuracy, states the relation between man and beast thus:

---

³ Consult also: "*Omnia subjecisti sub pedibus ejus,* scilicet hominis. Est homini rerum exteriorum aliqua naturalis possessio, quantum ad usum, quo ipsis secundum rationem et voluntatem uti potest ad suum commodum et utilitatem. . . . Hoc autem naturale dominium super ceteras creaturas, quod competit homini secundum rationem, in qua imago Dei consistit, manifestatur in ipsa hominis creatione (Gen. i. 26), ubi dicitur: Faciamus hominem ad imaginem et similitudinem nostram; et præsit piscibus maris, etc. (2ª 2ᵃᵉ q. lxvi, a. 1., ad. c., p. 386)." N. B.—Dominium, apud jurisconsultos definitur, "jus vel facultas re propria utendi ad quemlibet usum lege permissum, idque in commodum proprium."

"You know *we have no duties towards the brute creation;* there is no relation of justice between them and us. Of course, we are bound not to treat them ill, for cruelty is an offence against that holy law which our Maker has written on our hearts, and it is displeasing to Him. But they can claim nothing at our hand; into our hands they are *absolutely* delivered. We may use them, we may destroy them at our pleasure, not our wanton pleasure, but still for our own ends, for our own benefit and satisfaction, *provided that we can give a rational account of what we do.*" [4]

Such is the clear exposition of the doctrine by, perhaps, the profoundest and greatest thinker of the present century. But here some may be inclined to ask: Is man, then, allowed to abuse and maltreat the dumb beasts *just as he pleases?* Does this doctrine afford him license to inflict the most hideous torture for any purpose, however trivial and insignificant? Most certainly not. And this brings us face to face with another important principle—a principle which corrects and controls and moderates the first, and keeps it within due bounds. This second principle is, that "Man, being a rational creature, must act in a rational manner." God alone is the absolute Master and Lord of the irrational creation, and though He has given man dominion over every living thing, He requires that this dominion should be exercised in accordance with the rational nature which man possesses, and which should hold all his lower and animal appetites in subjection. Man has no right to act in an arbitrary and irresponsible way towards any creature whatsoever, not even towards himself. "You are not your own" (1 Cor. vi. 19). Hence the authority over the beasts, communicated to him by God, though a very real authority, must be exercised in a reasonable manner. Reason, not passion, not cruelty, not lust, must guide his actions and superintend his conduct. Hence St. Thomas teaches: "Ratio est primum principium omnium actuum humanorum, et omnia alia principia eorum obediunt rationi, sed diversimode."[5]

[4] Vide *Omnipotence in Bonds,* sermon preached before the Catholic University of Dublin.

[5] Consult 1. 2, q. 58, 2. 0.; et q. 90, 2 c.; et 100, 1 c.; et q. 102, 1 ad 3.

Who orders his life and action according to sound reason, acts justly, uprightly, and in a virtuous manner, as all theologians agree.[6]

Hence it follows that before utilising the beasts in any way that may cause them pain, reason must be consulted. Reason must assign the conditions and the degree of pain permissible under different circumstances. Now, reason demands three conditions. Firstly, that there be a *motive;* secondly, that there be a *just* motive; and, thirdly, that there be some *proportion* between the end to be gained and the means employed in reaching that end, thus *e. g.,* in the matter of vivisection, the amount of suffering inflicted must bear some relation to the result to be obtained.

If important results are obtained by certain experiments on rabbits, cats, dogs and other beasts, then such experiments are certainly not, in themselves, contrary to the law of God. Such experiments should, of course, be conducted with all the gentleness and humanity that is possible; anæsthetics should be used where they are applicable, and no useless or unnecessary pain is to be tolerated. But under such conditions vivisection has always been, and is, tolerated by the Church.

"There is in the whole world no cruelty more cruel than ignorance, and it is this cruel ignorance which we, by experiment, seek to dispel."—Sir WILLIAM GULL.

"The results of experiments on living animals have been of *inestimable service* to man, and to the lower animals, and the continuance and extension of such investigations is *essential* to the progress of knowledge, the relief of suffering, and the saving of life."—The recorded opinion of the General Meeting of the British Medical Assocaition, 1892.

"The law of sacrifice is the law of life, which no one can escape; and, provided it is conducted with reverence, of neces-

---

[6] Thus, to select one among many, the Theologia Wirceburgensis lays down the following proposition:

"Quicumque deliberate agit, vel cognoscit id, quod hic et nunc facit, esse rectæ rationi conforme, et sic elicit actum *moraliter bonum:* vel. cognoscit esse rectæ rationi difforme, et sic elicit actum *moraliter malum:* vel cognoscit, illud nec esse positive conforme vel difforme, *i. e.,* nec sibi esse præceptum, nec prohibitum, sed permissum; et tunc agens *debet ulterius habere finem* extrinsecum, si ergo pro fine habeat honestum, actus erit bonus," etc. (*De Actibus Humanis,* cap. iii., artic. 2).

sity, and under supervision, I regard *experimental research* not as a mere privilege, but as a moral duty."—Sir ANDREW CLARK.

"Experiments on living animals are as necessary to the further progress of medical science and the healing art, as are experiments in test-tubes to the advancement of chemistry, theoretical and applied."—Sir JAMES CRICHTON BROWNE.

102

BETTING

THOMAS SLATER [1]

A bet may be defined as the backing of an affirmation or forecast by offering to forfeit, in case of an adverse issue, a sum of money or article of value to one who, by accepting, maintains the opposite and backs his opinion by a corresponding stipulation. Although there are no federal statutes in the United States on this matter, many of the States make it a penal offence when the bet is upon a horse-race, or an election, or a game of hazard. Betting contracts are also frequently made void. Similarly in Great Britain betting in streets and public places, and the keeping of betting houses are forbidden by law, and wagering contracts are null and void. Such laws are just and useful, inasmuch as they serve to keep within the bounds of decency the dangerous habit of gambling, and the many evils which are usually associated with it. Although betting is to be discouraged as being fraught with danger, and, although it may be morally wrong, still in particular cases it is not necessarily so. As I may give the money of which I have the free disposal to another, so there is nothing in sound morals to prevent me from entering into a contract with another to hand over to him a sum of money if an assertion be found to be true, or if a certain event come to pass, with the stipulation that he is to do the same in my favor if the event be otherwise.

This may be an innocent form of recreation, or a ready way of settling a dispute. However, the practice is very liable to abuse, and that it may be morally justifiable, theologians require the following conditions: The parties must

---

[1] *Catholic Encyclopedia*, Vol. 11, p. 539.

have the free disposal of what they stake, and both must bind themselves to stand by the event and pay in case of loss. Welshing is wrong in morals as it is in law. Both must understand the matter of the bet in the same sense, and it must be uncertain for them both. If, however, one has absolutely certain evidence of the truth of his contention, and says so to the other party, he is not precluded from betting if the latter remains obstinate. If a bet fulfils these conditions and the object of it is honest, so that the bet is not an incentive to sin, it will be a valid contract, and, therefore, obligatory in conscience. Debts of honor, then, are also debts that we are in conscience bound to pay if they fulfil the conditions just laid down. It follows that the avocation of the professional bookmaker need not be morally wrong. It is quite possible to keep the moral law and at the same time so to arrange one's bets with different people that, though in all probability there will be some loss, still there will be gain on the whole.

103

GAMBLING

Thomas Slater [1]

Gambling, or gaming, is the staking of money or other things of value on the issue of a game of chance. It thus belongs to the class of aleatory contracts in which the gain or loss of the parties depends on an uncertain event. It is not gaming, in the strict sense, if a bet is laid on the issue of a game of skill like billiards or football. The issue must depend on chance, as in dice, or partly on chance, partly on skill, as in whist. Moreover, in ordinary parlance, a person who plays for small stakes to give zest to the game is not said to gamble; gambling connotes playing for high stakes. In its moral aspect, although gambling usually has a bad meaning, yet we may apply to it what is said about betting. On certain conditions, and apart from excess or scandal, it is not sinful to stake money on the issue of a game of chance any more than it is sinful to insure one's property against risk, or to deal in futures on the produce market.

[1] *The Catholic Encyclopedia*, Vol. VI., pp. 375, 376.

As I may make a free gift of my own property to another if I choose, so I may agree with another to hand over to him a sum of money if the issue of a game of cards is other than I expect, while he agrees to do the same in my favor in the contrary event. Theologians commonly require four conditions so that gaming may not be illicit. What is staked must belong to the gambler and must be at his free disposal. It is wrong, therefore, for the lawyer to stake the money of his client, or for anyone to gamble with what is necessary for the maintenance of his wife and children. The gambler must act freely, without unjust compulsion. There must be no fraud in the transaction, although the usual ruses of the game may be allowed. It is unlawful, accordingly, to mark the cards, but it is permissible to conceal carefully from an opponent the number of trump cards one holds. Finally, there must be some sort of equality between the parties to make the contract equitable; it would be unfair for a combination of two expert whist players to take the money of a couple of mere novices at the game. If any of these conditions be wanting, gambling becomes more or less wrong; and, besides, there is generally an element of danger in it which is quite sufficient to account for the bad name it has. In most people gambling arouses keen excitement, and quickly develops into a passion which is difficult to control. If indulged in to excess it leads to loss of time, and usually of money; to an idle and useless life spent in the midst of bad company and unwholesome surroundings; and to scandal, which is a source of sin and ruin to others. It panders to the craving for excitement, and in many countries it has become so prevalent that it rivals drunkenness in its destructive effects on the lives of the people. It is obvious that the moral aspect of the question is not essentially different if for a game of chance is substituted a horserace, a football or cricket match, or the price of stock or produce at some future date. Although the issue in these cases seldom depends on chance, still the moral aspect of betting upon it is the same in so far as the issue is unknown or uncertain to the parties who make the contract. Time bargains, difference transactions, options, and other speculative dealings on the exchanges, which are so common nowadays, add to the malice of gambling special evils of their own. They lead to the disturbance of the natural prices of commodities and securities, do grave injury to producers and consumers of these commodities, and are frequently attended by such unlawful methods of influencing prices as the dissemination of false reports, cornering, and the fierce contests of "bulls" and "bears," i. e., of the dealers who wish, respectively, to raise or lower prices.

Hitherto we have prescinded from positive law in our treatment of the question of gambling. It is, however, a matter on which both the civil and the canon law have much to say. In the United States the subject lies outside the province of the Federal Government, but many of the States make gambling a penal offence when the bet is upon an election, a horserace, or a game of chance. Betting contracts and securities given upon a bet are often made void. In England the Gambling Act, 1845, voids contracts made by way of gaming and wagering; and the Gaming Act, 1892, renders null and void any promise, express or implied, to pay any person any sum of money under, or in respect of, any contract or agreement rendered null and void by the Gaming Act, 1845, or to pay any sum of money by way of commission, fee, reward, or otherwise, in respect of any such contract or agreement, or of any services in relation thereto, or in connection therewith. From very early times gambling was forbidden by canon law. Two of the oldest (41, 42) among the so-called canons of the Apostles forbade games of chance under pain of excommunication to clergy and laity alike. The 79th canon of the Council Elvira (306) decreed that one of the faithful who had been guilty of gambling might be, on amendment, restored to communion on the lapse of a year. A homily (the famous "de Aleatoribus") long ascribed to St. Cyprian, but by modern scholars variously attributed to Popes Victor I, Callistus I, and Melchiades, and which, undoubtedly, is a very early and interesting monument of Christian antiquity, is a vigorous denunciation of gambling. The Fourth Lateran Council (1215), by a decree subsequently inserted in the "Corpus Juris," forbade clerics to play or to be present at games of chance. Some authorities, as Aubespine, have attempted to explain the severity of the ancient canons against gambling by supposing that idolatry was often connected with it in practice. The pieces that were played with were small-sized idols or images of the gods, which were invoked by the players for good luck. However, as Benedict XIV remarks, this can hardly be true, as in that case the penalties would have been still more severe. Profane writers of antiquity are almost as severe in their condemnation of gambling as are the councils of the Christian Church. Tacitus and Ammianus Marcellinus tell us that by gambling men are led into fraud, cheating, lying, perjury, theft, and other enormities; while Peter of Blois says that dice is the mother of perjury, theft, and sacrilege. The old canonists and theologians remark that although the canons only mention dice by name, yet under this appellation must be understood all games of chance; and even those that require skill, if they are played for money.

The Council of Trent contented itself with ordering all the ancient canons on the the subject to be observed, and, in general, prescribed that the clergy were to abstain from unlawful games. As Benedict XIV remarks, it was left to the judgment of the bishops to decide what games should be held to be unlawful according to the different circumstances of person, place, and time.

104

THE MORAL ASPECTS OF SPECULATION

John A. Ryan [1]

Taken in its narrowest sense, the word *speculation* describes transactions that are made for the sole purpose of getting a profit from changes in price. This is the sense in which it will be used in this paper. Furthermore, the discussion will be confined to operations on the stock and produce exchanges. The speculator, then, buys and sells property because he expects to realize a gain from changes in its price, not because he expects to be a sharer in its earnings. The reason that he does not intend to profit by the earnings of the property that he ostensibly buys and sells is to be found in the fact that his control of the property will be either too brief to secure the actual earnings or too indefinite to create earnings. The former is the

---

[1] *The Church and Socialism*, pp. 163-179. (The University Press, Washington, D. C.)

usual case of speculation in stock, the latter, of speculation in produce.

Some examples will make clearer this distinction between the speculator and the ordinary investor or trader. The man who buys railway stocks merely to sell them in a few days at an expected advance is a speculator; the man who buys them to hold permanently for the sake of the dividends that they will yield is not a speculator. The former looks to price changes for his gains, the latter to property earnings. Again, two men buy wheat on the board of trade: the first is a miller who wants wheat to grind; the second is a speculator who has no particular use for wheat. He does not intend to change its form in any way or bring it nearer to the consumer; his interest in it is confined solely to its fluctuations in price. From these he expects to make his profit. The miller, on the other hand, will add utility to the wheat by converting it into flour. His profit will be in the nature of a payment for this productive and social service. In like manner, the dividends received by the genuine investor in railway stocks will be a return for the use of his capital in a productive business. Both he and the miller are producers of utility, while the speculative buyer of stocks and the speculative buyer of wheat add nothing to the utility of any property—make no contribution to production.

Pure speculation on the exchanges differs, therefore, from ordinary trade and investment in its effect upon the production of utility and in the source of its gains. These are, in reality, two aspects of the same economic fact. It is also unique in the manner in which its contracts are completed, or "settled." I have spoken of the speculator as *ostensibly* buying and selling. In purely speculative purchases and sales there is no genuine *transfer* of goods. The stocks bought are not, in any adequate sense, brought into the possession and control of the purchaser, but are usually "carried" by his broker until they are sold. The exceptions to this rule are not of great importance and need not concern us here. The produce bought—wheat, cotton, petroleum, etc.—is not moved an inch in any direction. When the buyer completes one of these transactions he merely receives or pays out a sum based on the extent to which the price of the goods in question has risen or fallen. The mechanism of these settlements falls outside the scope of this paper. It suffices to point out that speculative contracts are settled by a payment of price differences instead of by a genuine delivery of goods. In effect and intention they are substantially wagers on the course of prices.

Indiscriminate apologists for speculation and the exchanges are fond of insisting on the productive services of so-called speculators who gather and store up goods during a period of plenty and dispose of them during a period of scarcity, or who carry goods from a place where they are abundant to a place where they are in greater demand. Hence they conclude that speculation, *i. e.*, all speculation, is useful. Such reasoning betrays confusion of thought. With speculators in the sense just mentioned we have nothing to do in this place. Besides, their social worth is obvious. Nor are we concerned with the exchanges, as such. Their original function was a very necessary one, namely, to serve as meeting places for those who wished to buy and sell real goods. They still retain that function in so far as they constitute a market place for permanent investors and for manufacturers and productive traders. These productive transactions, however, have become subordinated to purely speculative operations, so that, according to conservative estimates, fully 90 per cent of the business done on the exchanges is of the latter character.

Now this kind of speculation, as already pointed out, is non-productive. It creates no utility, either of time, place, or form; that is to say, it neither distributes goods over intervals of time or space nor puts them through any process of manufacture. Does it perform a social service of any kind? If it does, there will arise a presumption that it is morally good.

Prof. Henry C. Emery ("Speculation on the Stock and Produce Exchanges of the United States," Macmillan) strongly maintains that organized speculation, of the kind that we are discussing, is of great service to legitimate trade. Since the market for great staples, like grain and cotton, so runs his argument, has become a world-market, the large dealers in these goods must not only buy, store, and move them, but also take extraordinary risks of changing prices. These risks are extraordinary because they extend over a long period of time and are subject to world-wide trade conditions. What the dealers need, then, is "a distinct body of men to relieve them of the speculative element of their business." The professional operators on the produce exchanges constitute just such a class. The wheat merchant buys a quantity of wheat in the northwest for shipment to Liverpool, where he intends to sell it some time later. But the price of wheat may fall before that time arrives. Here arises the element of risk. To avoid it, he immediately sells to a speculator, for future delivery, an equal quantity of "paper" wheat. The delivery of this "paper" wheat, or, rather, the settlement contract, is to take place about the same time that his cargo of actual wheat is to be delivered and sold in Liverpool. If, in the meantime, the price of wheat falls he will lose on his actual wheat, but he will gain on his "paper" wheat. For, when a man sells any commodity in the speculative market for future delivery, his interest is to have the price of that commodity fall. Thus he gains the difference between the price of the article when he sold it and its price at the time of delivery, or settlement. Hence, by means of this "hedge" sale the wheat merchant is secured against loss on his cargo of actual wheat. Sales of this kind are a sort of insurance that lessen both the possibilities of great profit and the risks of great loss. It is said that nine-tenths of the wheat stored in the elevators of the northwest is "sold against" in this way ("Proceedings of Twelfth Annual Meeting of American Economic Association," p. 110).

So much for speculation in produce: speculation in stocks, it is maintained, enables the small investor to have within reach a class of men "ready to assume all the risk of buying and selling his security, and a market that fixes prices by which he can intelligently invest." The army of professional speculators stand prepared at any time to buy or sell any kind of stocks that are at all marketable, while their incessant buying and selling keeps the market active and the quotations of the different securities at their proper level. The whole function of organized speculation is summed up to be: taking the great risks of fluctuating values, reducing these fluctuations to a minimum, and providing an active market for produce and securities.

The obvious answer to the above argument is that traders in produce should take the risks of fluctuating prices themselves. At present, indeed, they seem unwilling to do so, because the speculators stand ready to do it for them. But it is difficult to see how the public would suffer if traders, importers, and manufacturers were compelled to take all the risks incident to their business, instead of handing them over to a special class. Under such an arrangement many of them would doubtless go to the wall, but the community would be the gainer through the elimination of the unfit. Besides, there is reason to believe that the superior knowledge of market conditions possessed by the professional speculators, and their work in reducing the range of price fluctuations, is very much overestimated. At any rate, there seems to be no good reason why the capable dealer or manufacturer could not acquire a sufficient amount of this same knowledge and foresight. To set apart a body of men for the sole purpose of *dealing in risks* seems to be carrying the principle of division of labor unnecessarily far, especially when these men manage to charge the high price for their services that is obtained by the professional speculators of our produce exchanges.

As to stock speculators, it may be reasonably admitted that they know the true value of the various securities more accurately than the small investors, and that they are able to fix more correct prices than would be possible without their activity. Yet if there were no dealing in stocks, except for permanent investment, there would still be a stock market. That is to say, if there were no speculators, and if stocks were bought solely for the sake of their dividends, it would still be possible for an investor to buy them at quotations sufficiently correct and stable. This fact is exemplified today in the case of numerous securities that are not dealt in by speculators nor listed on the exchanges. It is worthy of note that two prominent German economists, who maintain that the produce exchange is a necessary institution, declare that the stock exchange is "an unnecessary and injurious one."

The institution of organized speculation is not only of doubtful benefit to the community, but produces serious public evils. Only those who have expert knowledge of market conditions can, in the long run, make money on the exchanges. These are the prominent professional speculators, the "big operators," as they are often called. The great majority of all the others who speculate, namely, the outside public, either know nothing of the intricacies of the market, or rely on "inside information" that is worse than useless because misleading. Out of the losses of this class comes the greater part of the gains of the big operators. One proof of this is seen in the fact that, when the general public and the small operators desert the exchanges after being fleeced, speculative activity is checked until such time as the "small fry" begin operations anew. And yet the general public continues to patronize the centers of speculation in ever-increasing numbers, notwithstanding the lessons of the past. Thus the chief losses of speculation are borne by those who can least afford to bear them.

Speculation absorbs a considerable amount of the community's capital and directive energy. It diverts money from productive enterprises and engages the activity of men who, if removed from the unhealthy atmosphere of the exchanges, would be of great service to the world of industry. By holding out to its votaries the hope of getting rich quickly, it discourages industry and thrift and makes men worshipers of the goddess of chance. It imbues thousands with the persuasion that acquiring wealth is a colossal game in which they are to be fortune's favorites. The career of the "Franklin Syndicate" in Brooklyn, in 1899, is a typical instance of the way in which those who have caught the speculative fever disregard the laws of probability and the laws of wealth. The promoters of this company agreed to pay 10 per cent per week on all deposits, pretending that they were enabled to do so through their "inside information" of the stock market. Within a few weeks they took in nearly one million dollars, showing how large is the number of people who regard the stock exchange as an institution that creates wealth without labor.

To the question that was asked above—Does speculation perform any social service?—the correct answer, then, would seem to be in the negative. At any rate, its good features, which are problematical, are more than offset by its bad features, which are grave and unmistakable. Hence there is no reason to regard organized speculation as morally good because of any economic or social function that it exercises.

If the *institution* of speculation is at best of doubtful moral and social worth, what are we to say concerning the moral character of the *individual act* of speculating in stocks or produce? According to Funck-Brentano, speculation on the exchanges, although not highway robbery, is "robbery according to the rules of an art so refined that the keenest lawyer cannot exactly determine the point where fraud begins and legality ceases." This condemnation, however, seems too sweeping; for many of the transactions on the exchanges are made by men who have no intention of acting dishonestly. At the worst, they are actuated merely by the spirit of the gambler. But it is true that moral and immoral operations are often inextricably mingled, so that it is extremely difficult, no less for the moralist than the lawyer, to separate the good from the bad. For our purpose it will be best, perhaps, to point out the dishonesty of some of the more notorious practices and the extent to which they are followed, and then discuss the morality of speculative transactions that are entered into with the most upright intentions.

A favorite method of manipulating values is to disseminate false reports concerning property or market conditions. A description of the various ways in which this scheme is practiced is not possible nor necessary here, but a typical instance may be given. In the spring of 1900 a prominent manufacturing company, having its headquarters in New York, sent out a report that a dividend was to be immediately declared on its stock. This caused the stock to rise several points, and the directors and their friends then "sold for a fall." Next the report concerning the dividend was denounced as false, and official announcement was made that the company's condition did not warrant the payment of a dividend. Immediately values began to fall, and those who had sold "short" bought in at a profit, while the small holders of stock became panic-stricken and sold their holdings to the larger ones. This last phase of manipulation, which consists in depressing values for the purpose of getting possession of the stock of the small holders, is expressively termed "shaking out."

The industrious circulation of false reports is an essential part of the process known as "supporting." The owners of some stock that is worth little send out glowing accounts of its desirability as an investment, and of the earning capacity of the property that it represents. At the same time they begin to make purely speculative purchases on a large scale. The intention is to deceive the public into the belief that the owners have confidence in the future of their property. The result is that the price of the stock rises. When it has reached what the conspirators regard as its maximum, they sell both their cash stock and their purely speculative purchases to a confiding public. Then the stock rapidly sinks to its proper level.

Another way of manipulating is by "wash sales." One or more operators scheme to depress the quotations of a particular stock by making a show of enormous sales. The natural effect of such wholesale selling when reported on the stock market is to cause a fall, but the peculiarity of these transactions is that they are not sales at all, for the same person is both buyer and seller. He employs two brokers, one of whom sells to the other. Thus the supposed sales are all counterfeit, since the supposed buyers have no existence. The same principle can be carried out in attempts to *inflate* values, and in the case of produce as well as stock.

A simpler form of manipulation is the attempt to raise or depress the value of a stock by extensive genuine buying or selling. Where several operators act together the operation is called a "pool." An extreme instance of continued buying for a rise is the "corner." If it is successful, the result is that one or a few men get control of sufficient of the available supply of a certain produce or stock to create what is practically a monopoly, and thus force up prices almost at will. The corner, however, is rarely successful.

The schemes above described are some of the more common forms of manipulation. Clearly they are all immoral, and the gains accruing from them dishonest. Closely allied to false rumors as a source of unjust profit is the special and secret information that is so often turned to account on the exchanges. When this special information concerns a movement of prices that will come about naturally, not artificially, and when the information is acquired by the expenditure of some labor, either intellectual or physical, or when the information is not entirely certain—there would seem to be nothing wrong in making use of it for profit. But it is difficult to see how the profit will be honest if any of these conditions be wanting. Suppose that a certain stock is about to be manipulated upward. Now if an "outsider" is apprised of this fact, and buys some of the stock to sell at the advance, he is simply realizing unique possibilities of stealing. He defrauds the other party to the contract; for artificially produced gains for one man mean, in the long run, artificially produced losses for another. But suppose that an advance in the price of a certain property is due to the natural laws and conditions of trade. In that case a man who foresees the advance, by reason of exceptional skill and diligence in studying the conditions of the market, may rightfully invest in the property and reap a profit that will be in some sense the reward of ability. Again, if a man without exercising labor or skill obtains special information that is not entirely trustworthy, his gains from a speculation made on this basis might be regarded as the reward of risk-taking. But if the information is practically certain, and got without any personal expenditure of any kind, the morality of gains coming even from a natural movement in prices will usually be very questionable. Obtained as they are from differences in price, their source will, in most cases, be the pocket of some one who is not possessed of this special knowledge. The transaction is substantially a wager in which one party takes the other at a disadvantage. These are the principles: in practice it would seem that most of the profits arising from secret information on the exchanges are unlawful.

To what extent do manipulation and the various other forms of immoral speculation prevail? A precise and definite answer to this question is, of course, not obtainable, but it is safe to say that on the more prominent exchanges of the country questionable methods are in very common use. "Schaeffle, who is not only an eminent political economist, but has been minister of commerce to one of the great political powers of Europe, says that when he became acquainted with the bourse he gave up believing any longer in the economic harmonies, and declared theft to be the principle of modern European commerce" (John Rae, "Contemporary Socialism," p. 326). A member of the New York Stock Exchange declared a few years ago that 50 per cent of the operations in that institution were attempts to manipulate prices. The maneuvers of the great operators have often been compared to a game in which the successful players use loaded dice or marked cards. Indeed, many close observers of the speculative market assert that, in the long run, money is made only by those who resort to questionable devices. This is probably an exaggeration, but we can readily see that when men having great power, the big operators, are engaged in operations whose success depends solely on the movement of prices, they will be strongly tempted to use their power in order to influence this movement. It is impossible to watch their tactics for any length of time without concluding that they regard manipulation in some form as an essential feature of speculative operations. The stock market columns of almost any morning newspaper will show that on the preceding day there was "an assault by the bears" on this or that stock, and that under "constant hammering" the stock fell one or more points. Or, we are informed that, "after a rally by the bulls," such a stock "went skyward."

So far, at least, as the big operators are concerned, the exchange is a battlefield on which two opposing armies, the bulls and the bears, are constantly engaged at close range. "All is fair in war," and it is not surprising that in the speculators' warfare nice ethical discriminations as to methods should be overlooked. Manipulation is regarded as lawful, since it is merely fighting the enemy with his own weapons. The intellectual atmosphere of the bourse is so befogged that the moral vision of its habitués becomes easily dulled. The mental qualities that are most frequently called into play among professional speculators are those that characterize the activities of the professional gambler. "A man's nerve is put to the highest tension; his mind is always on the stretch; not guiding the policy of a great commercial venture, but bearing up under, and watching over, the fluctuations of some stock, in the opinion of the majority, and by virtue of what has been paid for it at the outset, is worth only so much, and which he has estimated at a different value. The trade is not a noble one, and there are few noble men engaged in it" (*Frazer's Magazine*, vol. 94, p. 84).

So much for practices of speculation that are certainly dishonest; what about the acts of a speculator who has no desire to take advantage of any unlawful practice? Is it wrong to make a purchase or sale on the exchange solely for the purpose of realizing a profit out of a change in prices? The purchaser or seller, we will suppose, seeks no dishonest advantage, but is willing to take all the risks of an unfavorable turn in prices. We cannot say that such a transaction is, in itself, wrong. At the worst it is merely a wager on prices, and wagers are not immoral, provided: (1) that those who take part in them have the right to dispose of the property that they hazard; (2) that neither fraud nor violence be used; (3) that the chances for winning be approximately equal, so far as the knowledge of the participants is concerned; (4) that the parties risk no more than they can afford consistently with the duties of their condition and calling; and (5) that the transaction in question is not forbidden by the positive law. All of these conditions may easily be present in a speculative deal; consequently, there may be nothing in it contrary to the moral law. This statement applies to an act of speculation in the abstract, not in the actual conditions of to-day.

For we have seen that from the side of economic welfare the whole institution of non-productive speculation is in all probability useless; that from the side of social welfare it involves many grave evils; and that from the side of morality its transactions are to an alarming extent carried on by dishonest methods. In the light of these facts, we may safely conclude that, so far as the principal exchanges of the country are concerned, it is morally impossible for a man who spends all or the greater part of his time speculating, to avoid all the dishonest practices of speculation. Secondly, we would seem to be justified in asserting that men who, even without any intention to be dishonest, participate to *any* extent in speculative transactions on these exchanges, are engaging in actions that may easily be *morally questionable*. As we said above, the isolated act of speculation may in itself be without censure—may be no worse than the placing of a wager—but because of its connection with a questionable institution, and because of its grave danger to the individual himself, it can never be pronounced licit in the sense that the transactions of ordinary trade are licit. The shadow of immorality is over it always. Every speculative deal is a participation, remote and insignificant, perhaps, in what can without exaggeration be regarded as a social and moral evil, namely, the institution of organized speculation.[1] Every anticipated profit, almost, is in danger of being promoted by illicit manipulation; for the well-meaning outsider can seldom be certain, even if he tries, that movements of price by which he is the gainer have not been artificially produced. Every man who yields to the seductive temptation to speculate feeds the passion of avarice, strengthens the ignoble desire to profit by the losses of his fellows, cultivates a dislike for honest, productive labor, and exposes himself to financial ruin. Hence, no man who is fully acquainted with the character and effects of speculation, and who is possessed of a fine moral nature, will ever participate in the purely speculative operations of either the stock or the produce exchanges of our largest cities.

The question—"Is speculation wrong?"—cannot, therefore, be answered categorically. The phenomena with which it deals are too complex. But, with the help of the distinctions above drawn, an answer may be obtained that is fairly definite. To resume, then: speculation as an institution is *economically* of doubtful utility; *socially,* it is productive of great and widespread evils; and *morally,* it is vitiated by a very considerable amount of dishonest "deals" and practices.

105

THE MALICE OF A LIE

J. HARDING FISHER [2]

The malice of the lie is one of those obvious things which everyone recognizes but which, in spite of their obviousness, seem more or less to defy accurate analysis. So true is this that, although no one doubts a lie when he is confronted with it, there is still today, after many centuries of speculation on the subject, considerable disagreement not only as regards its definition but also as to the source of its malice.

---

[1] For a strong confirmation of this view, see A. Crump's well-known work, *The Theory of Stock Speculation.*
[2] *America,* May 12, 1923.

The ancient Greeks regarded lying with abhorrence, but set up the god Hermes as its patron; Sophocles stigmatized it as dishonorable, but in certain grave contingencies pardoned its use; Plato characterized it as pernicious and harmful to the commonwealth but permitted it to be employed occasionally in the interests of the State, by those who had wisdom and self-restraint. Aristotle with his usual clarity proclaimed it intrinsically wrong and blameworthy. The Romans were more unanimous in their condemnation of lying. The Jews with their vivid realization of Divine Revelation held it up to unquestioned reprobation. It belonged, however, to Christianity to develop gradually a universal sense of its intrinsic and unvarying wickedness. Unfortunately Grotius and his followers introduced elements of discord into the discussion, by distinguishing between lies, which he condemned, and falsehoods, which he permitted for grave reasons. From the time of the sixteenth century there has not been unanimity among writers on ethics as to the elements that go to make up a lie, or as to the reasons which underlie its condemnation.

The confusion of mind, which practically every one at times experiences, arises from the fact that it is the common persuasion of mankind that a lie on the one hand is illicit, but that on the other hand there are circumstances in which it is not only permissible but imperative to conceal the truth. In the solution of this difficulty ethical theories have taken different ways. Among the doctrines that prevail two stand out clearly: the one defines the lie as the denial of the truth to one who has the right to know it, derives the lie's malice from extrinsic circumstances such as the injustice and malevolence shown to another, and permits falsehoods for considerations of grave private or public utility in cases where the questioner has no strict right to the truth; the other doctrine holds that a lie is the deliberate utterance of what one thinks to be false, finds its malice in the very nature of the lie apart from all external circumstances, declares that such elements of wrong as the violation of the hearer's right to the truth are added and concomitant, but only accessory, modifications of the essential inward malice, lays it down as a principle that a lie may never be told either to avert great evil or compass great good, and for the safeguarding of secrets sanctions the use of what are technically called broad mental restrictions. The latter view is the one held with practical unanimity by Catholics.

The moral law, of which every man, whether he admits it or not, is acutely conscious, is the pressure of the Divine will on the will of man. Human nature is not left to its own fancies and caprices; it was created for a definite end, and is rightly directed when it moves steadily towards the attainment of this end. Nor is man left in ignorance either as to his general destiny or as to the purpose of his various faculties. Both one and the other are written in the very nature of his being and therefore of his faculties. To find out the use destined for any faculty by God, man has but to study the nature of that faculty, and once having discovered it, to employ it according to its God-ordained purpose. That he has the obligation so to employ it he realizes perfectly. For one of the finest of his moral perceptions is that he must work out, as far as in him lies, the Divine plan; that he ought to live and act according to the order of things established by the Creator. The critical analysis of the notion of "oughtness" is somewhat baffling to the untrained mind, but the fact that he is subject to rule and to law is patent to every one whose mind functions normally.

Acting on this principle, the Catholic writers on ethics have studied the nature of speech in order to determine its proper use. Speech, they find, is by its very nature the complement of the mental life of the soul. Man is evidently destined to social life, to communion with his fellow-man. This need demands some means of communicating to others his hidden thoughts. The means for so doing is obviously the faculty of speech. Speech is the instrument by which mind is brought into contact with mind; by which the thoughts of one are conveyed to another. This is so patent that it is idle to insist on it. The right use of speech, therefore, as determined by its very nature, is to make known the thoughts of the mind, to manifest one's knowledge, to signify what one thinks to be true.

By its very nature, therefore, speech should be veracious, that is, possess moral truth. There are three kinds of truth: ontological, or conformity between objects and the thought of God; logical, or conformity between the intellect and objects, and moral, or conformity between speech and the mind. It is the lack of moral truth that constitutes the lie.

Speech is a gift conferred on man by God for the express purpose of manifesting his thoughts to others; this is its essential and primary end; this is the order established by the Divine intellect and commanded by the Divine will. To use speech, therefore, to manifest as the thought of the mind what is not the thought of the mind, is to use the faculty given by God in a way that is contrary to the Divine intention, in a way that violates its primary purpose. When a man knowingly and willingly uses words, actions or gestures which belie his inner convictions, he does violence to his own nature, he outrages his own dignity, he misuses his God-given faculty, he introduces into his soul elements of discord. All this is forbidden by the natural law. Due order requires that there be harmony between the internal judgment and the external expression of it. This harmony the lie destroys. It also destroys the harmony that should exist between the intellect and the will. The intellect accepts the truth, and the will, by moving the faculty of speech to express the false, repudiates the truth. This involves disorder in the soul, which is thus set at variance with itself. The lie, also, by its very nature introduces disorder in the mind of the hearer. It is disorder in the intellect to assent to what is false. This, however, is the direct effect of the lie. Moreover, the lie runs counter to man's social nature for it tends to break down mutual confidence and weakens the bonds of society. And, most fundamental of all, it misrepresents the truth as expressed in the mind of God.

The lie, therefore, is intrinsically wrong, because of its very nature it is a violation of the Divine law commanding the preservation of natural order and forbidding its disturbance. The gravity of its malice is to be judged by the seriousness of the disturbance it causes. Viewed in itself and apart from external circumstances, solely as an offense against veracity, the lie does not cause grave inordination. Considered in the speaker himself, it leaves the hierarchy of the faculties substantially intact, for the will, though it commands the inordination, remains in control. The inordination caused in the hearer's mind is not serious, because the latter is deprived only of the knowledge of the speaker's mind, a deprivation of no grave character. The harm done to society is light in character, for the effect of a single lie on human relations is not such as to involve marked derangement of human relations. The intrinsic malice of the lie, therefore, does not exceed a venial sin. There are, of course, grades in the malice of venial sin, but the lie does not pass into the category of mortal sin unless its offense against truth be linked to some other offense. That it can be linked with other offenses is clear from a moment's consideration of the determinants of morality.

The right and wrong of an action are differentiated primarily by the conformity or difformity of the action with the natural purpose of the faculty from which it proceeds; if the action is in accord with the nature of the agent, it is good; if it is not in accord with the nature of the agent, it is bad. This relation constitutes the foremost objective constituent of morality. But over and above this element, there are others which differentiate the action secondarily. Thus the end which the agent has in view, in so far as it is independent of the normal result of the action, if it be evil, adds a new element of malice. The same is true of the circumstances of the act, for although circumstances do not enter intrinsically into the nature of the act, if it be considered only in its physical entity, they have an essential bearing on its morality.

Applying these principles to the lie, it becomes apparent at once that an untruth may take on the character of serious evil, if the intention of the person who tells it is to compass some seriously evil purpose, for example, the ruin of a person's character, and this whether or not his evil intention has its effect. Similarly a lie takes on the character of serious sin, if the circumstances which attend it clothe it with grave malice. Suppose a person tells under oath a lie from which results considerable loss of property to an innocent person. In such a case, there is not merely the inordination involved in the contradiction between the liar's words and thoughts, but the grave indignity put upon God by calling the Divinity to witness the truth of what he knows to be false, and the grave injury done to persons he maligns. A lie is, then, intrinsically wrong, but its malice may be increased in a most serious way by the end desired and by circumstances attendant on the act. From this it appears that there is no difficulty about accounting for the various degrees of malice in the lie.

106

THE DOCTRINE OF LYING AND EQUIVOCATION

Joseph Rickaby [1]

There is a question often put, and probably never answered in the negative: "Can you keep a secret?" No woman certainly ever avowed that she could not. We all profess to know how to keep secrets; we all profess likewise to speak the truth; yet how to keep a secret in the face of an impertinent questioner, and still tell no lie to put him off, is a delicate moral operation that baffles many people's skill. There is one rough way of doing it, which I suppose is the common way. It begins by assuming that the essence of a lie consists in a violation of a hearer's right to the truth. Then the consequence is drawn, that where an inquirer has no right to know the truth about which he inquires, and an untruth is necessary to keep the truth from him, there an untruth may be told which will be no lie. "If all killing be not murder," demands Milton, "nor all taking of another man's property stealing, why should all untruths be lies?" I will not call this doctrine un-Catholic, held as it is by many loyal children of the Church, but I submit that it is unphilosophical, and may be brought to bear bitter fruit in theology. For if truthfulness is a matter of strict justice and the hearer's right, and we have, as the best theologians teach, no strict rights against our Creator, where is the guarantee of the truthfulness of God in revelation?

Another way, amusingly described by Cardinal Newman, is the way of those who will have it through thick and thin, that all lies and untruths, and all manner of equivocation and lack of sincerity in speech, are radically wrong, extremely wrong and shameful; still that a man would not be man, if he did not tell a lie now and then at a hard

[1] *Moral and Political Essays*, pp. 215-234. (Benziger Brothers, New York.)

pinch; and that the best thing he can do is to come out with the lie, and have done with it, and forget it, and rail louder than before against casuists and Jesuits, lying lips, and all who speak leasing.

Both these ways are objectionable. We must not lie to keep a secret, neither may we tell an untruth, for all formal untruth is lying. Are we then to use equivocation? Equivocation is a word formed from the Latin *æquivocatio*. Many good theologians writing in Latin have advocated what they call *æquivocatio*. English Catholic authors, treading in their footsteps, and literally translating their words, have argued in favor of equivocation as being, in case of need, a lawful means for preserving what ought to be preserved secret. But English is unfortunately not the language of a Catholic people. Words mean, not what we would have them mean, not what the corresponding word means in the language of the Church, but their meaning is that which they commonly bear in educated English society. Now the ordinary educated Englishman takes equivocation to denote a practice which is certainly wrong, and carries all the guilt of lying, as, if being asked whether Antony is in the house, I privately press my foot on the ground, and say, "No, he is not here," meaning he is not in the cellar; or if I deny that I have any Spanish letters about me, understanding that such letters are not in my pockets, but in my portmanteau, which is lying beside me on the pavement. The answer *No* in these cases may be a lie, or it may not, but it is not saved from being a lie by such subterfuges as these, which are purely mental and confined to the mind of the speaker.

What ordinary Englishmen call equivocation corresponds to that which Catholic divines know as *pure mental reservation*, and that is a cowardly fashion of lying. Where *æquivocatio* is mentioned with approval in a page of Latin casuistry, the word ought to be translated, *broad mental reservation*. To render it *equivocation* is to create confusion, just as much as if one should render the canonical appeal, *peto apostolos* "I ask for the apostles," or the old French, *entre chien et loup*, "between a dog and a wolf." On this understanding I venture to assert that the Catholic doctrine condemns, absolutely and under all circumstances, all lying and all equivocation.

And likewise all mental reservation? No, not all mental reservation. One form of that is lawful, when it is necessary to baffle an impertinent enquirer and keep a secret.

Mental reservation is an act of the mind, limiting the spoken phrase that it may not bear the full sense which at first hearing it seems to bear. The reservation, or limitation of the spoken sense, is said to be *broad* or *pure,* according as it is, or is not, indicated externally. A *pure mental reservation,* where the speaker uses words in a limited meaning, without giving any outward clue to the limitation, is, as I have said already, in nothing different from a lie, and is wrong as a lie is always wrong. Is then a *broad mental reservation* always right? May we amuse ourselves, trying the quickness of our friends' perceptions, meaning less than we seem to say, and leaving them to guess the "economy of truth" by some delicate hint thrown out thereof? Such sharp practice is by no means to be permitted promiscuously. Mental reservation, even on the *broad* gauge, is permissible only as a last resource, when no other means are available for the preservation of some secret, which one has a duty to others, or a right to oneself, to keep.

Here I must explain the Catholic doctrine concerning secrets. We distinguish *natural* secrets, secrets of *promise* (*secretum promissum*), and secrets of *trust* (*secretum commissum*). A natural secret is all a man's own private history, which he would not have made public, as also all that he discovers of the private history of his neighbors by his own lawful observation without being told, supposing the thing discovered to be one that requires concealment. If I find out something about my neighbor, and after I have found it out for myself, he gets me to promise not to publish it, that is a secret of promise. Lastly, if one man comes to another, as to a lawyer, or a surgeon, for professional advice, or simply to a friend, for moral counsel, and in order thereto imparts to him some of his natural secrets, those secrets, as they are received and held by the person consulted, are called secrets of trust. This latter kind of secret is privileged above the other two. A natural secret, and also a secret of promise, must be delivered up on the demand of an authority empowered to enquire in the department in which the secret lies. A counsel cross-examining a witness would not be put off with the answer, "I promised not to tell." But a secret of trust is to be given up to no enquirer. Such a secret is to be kept against all who seek to come by it, except where the matter bodes mischief and wrong to a third party, or to the community, and where at the same time the owner of the secret cannot be persuaded to desist from the wrong. In particular cases it is often extremely difficult to decide whether this exception holds or not. But some cases are plain. If Father Garnet had known of the Gunpowder Plot under a secret of trust—and not under the seal of confession, which makes a secret supernatural, and absolutely inviolable—he ought certainly either to have turned the conspirators from their purpose, or, failing that, to have given information to the government.

Therefore a secret of promise is to be kept against all enquirers other than official. A secret of trust is to be kept even against official enquiries, under the limitations that I have laid down. The keeping of a secret of promise is an obligation at least of fidelity: that of a secret of trust is matter of strict justice. Both are obligations binding under sin. It is a sin to lie, no doubt; but it is a greater sin, usually, to divulge your neighbor's secret.

The difficulty now comes round again, how to keep a secret against an impertinent questioner, without lying. The main art of keeping a secret is not to talk about it. If a man is asked an awkward question, and sees no alternative but to let out or lie, it is usually his own fault for having encouraged the questioner up to that point. A wise man lets drop in time topics of conversation which he is unwilling to have pressed. He is never the first to introduce such topics. It is said of the ploughman in Ecclesiasticus, that his story is of the sons of bulls—*enarratio ejus in filiis taurorum*. After all, cattle have no secrets, but men and women have. Of that class of persons whose profession lies in the way of hearing them, doctors, lawyers, priests, none would altogether like to hear it said of him: His stories are of his penitents, his clients, or his patients.

But there are unconscionable people, ἀναιδεῖς, who will not be put off, and who, either out of malice or out of stupidity, ply you with questions against all rules of good breeding. This direct assault may sometimes be retaliated, and a rude question met by a rough answer. But such a reply is not always prudent, and would not unfrequently convey the very information required. Silence would serve no better, for silence gives consent, and is eloquent at times. There is nothing left for it in such cases but to lock your secret up, as it were, in a separate compartment of your breast, and answer according to the remainder of your information, which is not secret, private, and confidential. This looks very much like lying, but it is not lying, it is speaking the truth under a broad mental reservation.

"What news, my lord, from France?" some one asked of a cabinet minister. "I don't know," was the reply, "I have not read the papers." The story is Cardinal Newman's. Here the sense of the *I don't know* is restricted and reserved, internally in the mind of the speaker, and externally by the words added about the newspapers. It is a mental reservation of the broadest, such as no Pharisee could call a lie. Now suppose the reference to the papers omitted. It would still be very hard to call the *don't know* a lie. The reservation of official knowledge is still sufficiently apparent; no sensible man would expect that to be communicated by way of ordinary chit-chat. Above all, when a topic has been forced upon one, and questions put that admit of no evasion, by an enquirer who has no right to ask, then surely any denial or disclaimer that may be elicited, however direct the form of words, must be qualified by the outward circumstances in which it is spoken. This qualification, unspoken, but not unsignified, will be, "secrets apart."

Indeed, this qualification may be said to go along with all human replies to human questions. But in nine hundred and ninety-nine cases out of a thousand, the facts of the position indicate that the value of the qualification comes to zero: there can or ought to be no secrets about the matter. "Porter, what time does the night mail leave for Paris?" "At a quarter to nine." "You mean, of course, *secrets apart?*" "Well, I do; but who dreams of secrets about the train service?" On my way to Paris I come across a garrulous Frenchman, who pesters me with politics when I want to sleep. I conclude there are no political secrets in that man's brain; if there are, he has no business to be so free with his tongue. But as I show a resolute unwillingness to talk politics, the reserve of *secrets apart* has an appreciable value in the *yes's* and *no's* which he contrives to wring out of me: how does he know that he has not to do with a confidential diplomatic agent? This at least he ought to know, that a man who is honored with the confidence of the government will not part with it to the first puppy who sets upon him to worry him, but will either hold his peace, or when that cannot be, will return an answer for which his interrogator shall be none the wiser. In other words, he will answer out of his communicable, and not out of his incommunicable knowledge. The qualification, *secrets apart,* should be borne in mind by persons who are in the habit of asking indiscreet and unwarrantable questions.

Dr. Johnson said: "I should have considered Burke to be Junius, but Burke spontaneously denied it to me. The case would have been different had I asked him if he were the author: a man so questioned as to an anonymous publication may think that he has a right to deny it" (Boswell's *Life of Johnson*, ed. Croker, IV. 246). Sir Walter Scott considered that he had such a right, while he chose to remain the anonymous author of the Novels (*General Preface to the Waverley Novels,* 1829, pp. 21, 22, ed. Black, 1865). *The Spectator* for July 23, 1898, allows this right where there is question of other people's secrets, not where there is question of your own. The distinction seems arbitrary, and too favorable to busybodies. In practice the difficulty is to decide when a secret is important enough to give the clause, *secrets apart,* a positive value. No general rule can be assigned. The clause is not available, and should not be presumed to hold, for the protection of any and every trumpery secret. We must not make mysteries of trifles.

But also it must be borne in mind that a question which would be unwarrantable, put by equal to equal, may be perfectly fair and proper in the mouth of a parent, or of a cross-examining counsel who has the support of a court of law. There are few secrets that one has a right to hold against every enquirer. Knowledge that is incommunicable here is communicable there: absolutely incommunicable knowledge is a rare possession.

Mental reservation is allowable only when we are driven into a corner by captious questions about a matter which we have a grave reason and a right to keep secret, and where we have no other escape. This doctrine will not justify the setting of false or equivocal statements afloat where no one has questioned you. It will not justify the practice of lying to children as such. But, of course, in meeting their demands, we may present the information in a childish dress, so that they may learn only that which a good and reasonable child would wish to know. In replying to a sick person, I suppose a piece of news highly dangerous for him to hear might be treated as a natural secret. But I cannot comprehend the morality, nor, indeed, the wisdom, of inventing gratuitous fictions for the comfort of the sick. As for lies in jest, they remain lies, unless it be tolerably manifest that we are "drawing the long bow." Words may be explained away by looks or other outward circumstances, sometimes by the very grotesqueness or absurdity of the statement itself. Friend addressing friend does not mean all he says to be taken *au pied de la lettre:* it is part of knowing a man to understand his jokes.

It will add very much to clearness of notions in all this matter, to define wherein the essential wrongness of lying consists. What is there cleaving to a lie that makes it always wrong, so that one must never lie, no, not for worlds? A lie is made up of two elements, one in the utterer, and one in the hearer. There is the deception begotten in the mind of the hearer, and in the speaker there is the discord between what he says and what he thinks to be true—not necessarily, be it observed, between what he says and what is true. Both these elements are evil; the former, the deception, obviously so. Human society cannot go on, if men are to be allowed promiscuously to deceive one another. Then, no one likes to be deceived, and we are not to do to our neighbor what we would not have done to ourselves. The laws of good fellowship require that we should speak the truth to one another in ordinary circumstances, as they likewise require that in ordinary circumstances we should respect the life and property of our fellow-men. But to take life and to seize upon property is lawful in certain emergencies, in self-defense and for self-preservation, or with the sanction of authority. These exceptions stand very well with the well-being of society, or rather are required by it: the lives of brigands and assassins must not be sacrosanct as the lives of other men. No man is reasonably unwilling that, if taken red-handed, he may himself be slain. The law against deceiving our neighbor, so far as it is founded on the prejudice done to society and the annoyance of the person deceived, seems to admit of similar exceptions. Whoever has no reasonable objection to have life and property taken from him in certain circumstances, cannot reasonably complain of any hurt or inconvenience that he may suffer in being sometimes deceived. There is a well-known story told by the younger Pliny of the Roman matron Arria, who, having lost her son by sickness, and all but lost her husband, used to tell the latter in his convalescence, when he enquired about the boy: "Oh, he has slept well; he had quite an appetite." Then she would rush out of the room to conceal her tears. I will not vouch for the objective morality of these replies: they may or may not be justified as broad mental reservations. But they are much more easily justified, if the whole harm of lying consists in the hearer's unwillingness to be deceived, by saying that the sick man was not unwilling to suffer a deception rendered necessary by his state of health. The same doctrine would justify other speeches of a much more objectionable character. It would, in fact, contain the reaffirmation of the old Greek position, that deceit is a medicine and a drug, and may be administered, ἐν φαρμάκου εἴδει, especially by persons in authority, wherever they judge that it will work a wholesome effect, and wherever the person deceived is not unwilling, or at least ought not to be surprised or complain, considering the circumstances. But this would be to throw the door open wide to the whole crowd of official, officious, and jocose lies. Untruths told for a purpose to enemies, to children, to subjects, to servants; pleasant fictions to gratify a friend; hoaxes unlimited, where we think the victim ought not much to mind—these will be withdrawn from the category of lying, or will be registered as white lies and lawful.

Worst of all, if the whole harm of lying is in the unpleasant effect wrought upon the deceived hearer, or in the scandal and bad consequences to society at large, it is not clear that lying is impossible to God; and our faith, based on the divine veracity, is shaken to the foundation. God, as Master, might bid the deceived listener bear the mortification and shame of being duped. He might by His providence prevent any scandal or general bad consequences to society; or, as Sovereign, He might impose or permit such consequences, as He sends or permits a pestilence. The Lord of life and death, who commanded Isaac to be slain, and who daily "taketh away the spirit of princes," is not to be restrained from being a deceiver by the mere reluctance of His creatures, unless there be some element in the divine nature itself which makes it utterly impossible for God to deceive and speak false.

Undoubtedly there is such an element. It lies even at the root of the sanctity of God. God is holy in that, being by essence the fulness of all Being and all Goodness, He is ever true to Himself in every act of His understanding, of His will, and of His power. By His understanding He abidingly covers, grasps, and comprehends His whole Being. With His will He loves Himself supremely. His power is exercised entirely for His glory—entirely, but not exclusively, for God's last and best external glory is in the consummated happiness of His creatures. Whatever God makes, He makes in His own likeness, more or less so according to the degree of being which He imparts to the creature. And as whatever God does is like Him, and whatever God makes is like Him, so whatever God says is like Him. His spoken word answers to His inward word and thought. It holds of God, as of every being who has a thought to think and a word to utter:—

> To thine own self be true,
> And it must follow, as the night the day,
> Thou canst not then be false to any man.

God's sanctity is in His being true to Himself. His veracity is a part of His sanctity. He cannot in His speech, or revelation of Himself, contradict what He really has in His mind, without ceasing to be holy and being no longer God.

But the sanctity of intellectual creatures must be, like their every other attribute and perfection, modelled on the corresponding perfection of their Maker. Holiness must mean truthfulness in man, for it means truthfulness in God.

God's words cannot be at variance with His thought, for God is essential holiness. Nor can man speak otherwise than as he thinks without marring the attribute of holiness in himself, that is, without doing wrong. And this is the real, intrinsic, primary, and inseparable reason, why lying, or speech in contradiction with the thought of the speaker, is everywhere and always wrong.

This is the simple reason assigned by St. Thomas Aquinas:—

"A lie is wrong in its kind, for it is an act falling on undue matter. For whereas words are naturally signs of thoughts, it is unnatural and undue that any one should signify by word that which he has not in his mind."

He admits as a secondary reason of the evil of lying, that:—

"Because man is a social animal, naturally one man owes another that without which human society could not be preserved. But men could not mutually dwell together, unless they mutually trusted one another as mutually declaring to each other the truth."

But when he faces the objection, that "the lesser evil is to be chosen for the avoidance of the greater; but it is less harm that one should engender a false opinion in the mind of another than that a man should slay or be slain; therefore a man may lawfully lie to keep one party from committing murder and to save another's blood"—in face of this objection he falls back upon the main argument already alleged, and replies:—

"A lie is a sin, not merely for the damage done thereby to a neighbor, but for its own inordinateness, as has been explained. But it is not lawful to use any unlawful inordinateness to hinder the harm and prejudice of others. And therefore it is not lawful to tell a lie for the purpose of delivering another from any danger whatsoever. It is lawful, however, to hide the truth prudently under some dissembling."

I believe that this doctrine of the Angel of the Schools has never been departed from without danger to theology and to morality, to the one in the matter of the divine veracity, and to the other in the matter of officious lying. Never must any intellectual being, not even the highest and most exalted of all, be permitted to use signs in contradiction to his thought whereof they are signs. If for the keeping of a secret, and under sore pressure, a man may speak by his communicable knowledge alone, and ignore what he has of incommunicable knowledge, circumstances must outwardly suggest that reservation to a prudent listener. The whole man speaks, the situation speaks; the words must not be considered by themselves and in the abstract; they are a text to be taken in conjunction with the note and comment which accompany them. This annotated text, so to speak, answers to the thought of the author; there is then no clash of sign and thing signified, there is no lie. What is required is that the comment and reservation be not all inscribed within the mind of the speaker, but be legible outwardly; likewise, that the modifying clause be not resorted to without reason. The reservation must not be needless, and it must be *broad*, not *pure*. Thus we are to take St. Thomas's hint, "It is lawful to hide the truth prudently under some dissembling." [1]

107

LYING AND EQUIVOCATION

Cardinal Newman [2]

Almost all authors, Catholic and Protestant, admit that *when a just cause is present,* there is some kind or other of verbal misleading, which is not sin. Even silence is in certain cases virtually such a misleading, according to the Proverb, "Silence gives consent." Again, silence is absolutely forbidden to a Catholic, as a mortal sin, under certain circumstances, e. g., to keep silence, when it is a duty to make a profession of faith.

Another mode of verbal misleading, and the most direct, is actually saying the thing that is not; and it is defended on the principle that such words are not a lie, when there

---

[1] See *Summa Theologiæ,* 2^a-2^{ae}, q. 109, art. 3, ad. 1; and q. 110, art. 3, corp. and ad. 4. See, too, q. 110, art. 1, corp., where lying is accurately defined. The passages are in my *Aquinas Ethicus,* II, pp. 214-221.

[2] *Apologia pro Vita Sua,* pp. 348-363. (Longmans, Green & Co., New York.)

is a "justa causa," as killing is not murder in the case of an executioner.

Another ground of certain authors for saying that an untruth is not a lie where there is a just cause is that veracity is a kind of justice, and therefore, when we have no duty of justice to tell truth to another, it is no sin not to do so. Hence we may say the thing that is not, to children, to madmen, to men who ask impertinent questions, to those whom we hope to benefit by misleading.

Another ground, taken in defending certain untruths, *ex justâ causâ*, as if not lies, is, that veracity is for the sake of society, and that, if in no case whatever we might lawfully mislead others, we should actually be doing society great harm.

Another mode of verbal misleading is equivocation or a play upon words; and it is defended on the theory that to lie is to use words in a sense which they will not bear. But an equivocator uses them in a received sense, though there is another received sense, and therefore, according to this definition, he does not lie.

Others say that all equivocations are, after all, a kind of lying—faint lies or awkward lies, but still lies; and some of these disputants infer that therefore we must not equivocate, and others that equivocation is but a half-measure, and that it is better to say at once that in certain cases untruths are not lies.

Others will try to distinguish between evasions and equivocations; but though there are evasions which are clearly not equivocations, yet it is very difficult scientifically to draw the line between the one and the other.

To these must be added the unscientific way of dealing with lies:—viz., that on a great or cruel occasion a man cannot help telling a lie, and he would not be a man, did he not tell it, but still it is very wrong, and he ought not to do it, and he must trust that the sin will be forgiven him, though he goes about to commit it ever so deliberately, and is sure to commit it again under similar circumstances. It is a necessary frailty, and had better not be thought about before it is incurred, and not thought of again, after it is well over. This view cannot for a moment be defended, but, I suppose, it is very common.

I think the historical course of thought upon the matter has been this: the Greek Fathers thought that, when there was a *justa causa,* an untruth need not be a lie. St. Augustine took another view, though with great misgiving; and, whether he is rightly interpreted or not, is the doctor of the great and common view that all untruths are lies, and that there can be *no* just cause of untruth. In these later times, this doctrine has been found difficult to work, and it has been largely taught that, though all untruths are lies, yet that certain equivocations, when given in a just cause, are not untruths.

Further, there have been and all along through these later ages, other schools, running parallel with the above mentioned, one of which says that equivocations, etc., after all *are* lies, and another which says that there are untruths which are not lies.

And now as to the "just cause," which is the condition, *sine quâ non.* The Greek Fathers make it such as these, self-defence, charity, zeal for God's honor, and the like.

St. Augustine seems to deal with the same "just causes" as the Greek Fathers, even though he does not allow of their availableness as depriving untruths, spoken on such occasions, of their sinfulness. He mentions defence of life and of honor, and the safe custody of a secret. Also the great Anglican writers, who have followed the Greek Fathers, in defending untruths when there is the "just cause," consider that "just cause" to be such as the preservation of life and property, defence of law, the good of others. Moreover, their moral rights, e. g., defence against the inquisitive, etc.

St. Alfonso, I consider, would take the same view of the "justa causa" as the Anglican divines; he speaks of it as "quicunque finis *honestus,* ad servanda bona spiritui vel corpori utilia;" which is very much the view which they take of it, judging by the instances which they give.

In all cases, however, and as contemplated by all authors, Clement of Alexandria, or Milton, or St. Alfonso, such a causa is, in fact, extreme, rare, great, or at least special. Thus the writer in the *Mélanges Théologiques* (Liège, 1852-3, p. 453) quotes Lessius: "Si absque justa causa fiat, est abusio orationis contra virtutem veritatis, et civilem consuetudinem, etsi proprie non sit mendacium." That is, the virtue of truth, and the civil custom, are the *measure* of the just cause. And so Voit, "If a man has used a reservation (restrictione non purè mentali) without a *grave cause*, he has sinned gravely." And so the author himself, from whom I quote, and who defends the Patristic and Anglican doctrine that there *are* untruths which are not lies, says, "Under the name of mental reservation theologians authorize many lies, *when there is for them a grave reason and proportionate*," i. e., to their character—p. 459. And so St. Alfonso, in another Treatise, quotes St. Thomas to the effect that if from one cause two immediate effects follow, and, if the good effect of that cause is *equal in value* to the bad effect (bonus *æquivalet* malo), then nothing hinders the speaker's intending the good and only permitting the evil. From which it will follow that, since the evil to society from lying is very great, the just cause which is to make it allowable must be very great also. And so Kenrick: "It is confessed by all Catholics that, in the common intercourse of life, all ambiguity of language is to be avoided; but it is debated whether such ambiguity is *ever* lawful. Most theologians answer in the affirmative, supposing a *grave cause* urges, and the (true) mind of the speaker can be collected from the adjuncts, though in fact it be not collected."

However, there are cases, I have already said, of another kind, in which Anglican authors would think a lie allowable, such as when a question is *impertinent*. Of such a case Walter Scott, if I mistake not, supplied a very distinct example, in his denying so long the authorship of his novels.

What I have been saying shows what different schools of opinion there are in the Church in the treatment of this difficult doctrine; and, by consequence, that a given individual, such as I am, *cannot* agree with all of them, works in too large a sense. Before a Saint is canonized, his works are examined, and a judgment pronounced upon them. Pope Benedict XIV says, "The *end* or *scope* of this judgment is, that it may appear, whether the doctrine of the servant of God, which he has brought out in his writings, is free from any soever *theological censure*." And he remarks in addition, "It never can be said that the doctrine of a servant of God is *approved* by the Holy See, but at most it can (only) be said that it is *not disapproved* (non reprobatam) in case that the Revisers had reported that there is nothing found by them in his works, which is adverse to the decrees of Urban VIII, and that the judgment of the Revisers has been approved by the sacred Congregation, and confirmed by the Supreme Pontiff." The Decree of Urban VIII here referred to is, "Let works be examined, whether they contain errors against faith or good morals (bonos mores), or any new doctrine, or a doctrine foreign and alien to the common sense and custom of the Church." The author from whom I quote this (M. Vandenbroeck, of the diocese of Malines) observes, "It is therefore clear that the approbation of the works of the Holy Bishop touches not the truth of every proposition, adds nothing to them, nor even gives them by consequence a degree of intrinsic probability." He adds that it gives St. Alfonso's theology an extrinsic probability, from the fact that, in the judgment of the Holy See, no proposition deserves to receive a censure; but that "that probability will cease nevertheless in a particular case, for any one who should be convinced, whether by evident arguments, or by a decree of the Holy See, or otherwise, that the doctrine of the Saint deviates from the truth." He adds, "From the fact that the approbation of the works of St. Alfonso does not decide the truth of each proposition, it follows, as Benedict XIV has remarked, that we may combat the doctrine which they contain; only, since a canonized saint is in question, who is honored by a solemn *culte* in the Church, we ought not to speak except with respect, nor to attack his opinions except with temper and modesty."

2. Then, as to the meaning of the word *censura:* Benedict XIV enumerates a number of "Notes" which come under that name; he says, "Out of propositions which are to be noted with theological censure, some are heretical, some erroneous, some close upon error, some savouring of heresy," and so on; and each of these terms has its own definite meaning. Thus by "erroneous" is meant, according to Viva, a proposition which is not *immediately* opposed to a revealed proposition, but only to a theological *conclusion* drawn from premisses which are *de fide;* "savouring of heresy" is a proposition, which is opposed to a theological conclusion not evidently drawn from premisses which are *de fide,* but most probably and according to the common

mode of theologizing; and so with the rest. Therefore when it was said by the Revisers of St. Alfonso's works that they were not "worthy of *censure*," it was only meant that they did not fall under these particular Notes.

But the answer from Rome to the Archbishop of Besançon went further than this; it actually took pains to declare that any one who pleased might follow other theologians instead of St. Alfonso. After saying that no Priest was to be interfered with who followed St. Alfonso in the Confessional, it added, "This is said, however, without on that account judging that they are reprehended who follow opinions handed down by other approved authors."

And this, too, I will observe,—that St. Alfonso made many changes of opinion himself in the course of his writings; and it could not for an instant be supposed that we were bound to every one of his opinions, when he did not feel himself bound to them in his own person. And, what is more to the purpose still, there are opinions, or some opinion, of his which actually have been proscribed by the Church since, and cannot now be put forward or used. I do not pretend to be a well-read theologian myself, but I say this on the authority of a theological professor of Breda, quoted in the *Mélanges Théol.* for 1850-1. He says: "It may happen, that, in the course of time, errors may be found in the works of St. Alfonso and be proscribed by the Church, *a thing which in fact has already occurred.*"

In not ranging myself then with those who consider that it is justifiable to use words in a double sense, that is, to equivocate, I put myself under the protection of such authors as Cardinal Gerdil, Natalis Alexander, Contenson, Concina, and others. Under the protection of these authorities, I say as follows:

Casuistry is a noble science, but it is one to which I am led, neither by my abilities nor my turn of mind. Independently, then, of the difficulties of the subject, and the necessity, before forming an opinion, of knowing more of the arguments of theologians upon it than I do, I am very unwilling to say a word here on the subject of Lying and Equivocation. But I consider myself bound to speak; and therefore, in this strait, I can do nothing better, even for my own relief, than submit myself, and what I shall say, to the judgment of the Church, and to the consent, so far as in this matter there be a consent, of the Schola Theologorum.

Now in the case of one of those special and rare exigencies or emergencies, which constitute the *justa causa* of dissembling or misleading, whether it be extreme as the defence of life, or a duty as the cutsody of a secret, or of a personal nature as to repel an impertinent inquirer, or a matter too trivial to provoke question, as in dealing with children or madmen, there seem to be four courses:—

1. *To say the thing that is not.* Here I draw the reader's attention to the words *material* and *formal*. "Thou shalt not kill"; *murder* is the *formal* transgression of this commandment, but *accidental homicide* is the *material* transgression. The *matter* of the act is the same in both cases; but in the *homicide,* there is nothing more than the act, whereas in *murder* there must be the intention, etc., which constitutes the formal sin. So, again, an executioner commits the material act, but not that formal killing which is a breach of the commandment. So a man, who simply to save himself from starving takes a loaf which is not his own, commits only the material, not the formal act of stealing, that is, he does not commit a sin. And so a baptized Christian, external to the Church, who is in invincible ignorance, is a material heretic, and not a formal. And in like manner, if to say the thing which is not be in special cases lawful, it may be called a *material lie.*

The first mode then which has been suggested of meeting those special cases, in which to mislead by words has a sufficient occasion, or has a *just cause,* is by a material lie.

The second mode is by an *æquivocatio,* which is not equivalent to the English word "equivocation," but means sometimes a *play upon words,* sometimes an *evasion:* we must take these two modes of misleading separately.

2. *A play upon words.* St. Alfonso certainly says that a play upon words is allowable; and, speaking under correction, I should say that he does so on the ground that lying is *not* a sin against justice, that is, against our neighbour, but a sin against God. God has made words the signs of ideas, and, therefore, if a word denotes two ideas, we are at liberty to use it in either of its senses; but I think I must be incorrect in some respect in supposing that the Saint does not recognize a lie as an injustice, because the

Catechism of the Council, as I have quoted it at p. 281, says, "Vanitate et mendacio fides ac veritas tolluntur, arctissima vincula *societatis humanæ;* quibus sublatis, sequitur summa vitæ *confusio,* ut *homines nihil a dæmonibus differre videantur.*"

3. *Evasion;*—when, for instance, the speaker diverts the attention of the hearer to another subject; suggests an irrelevant fact or makes a remark, which confuses him and gives him something to think about; throws dust into his eyes; states some truth, from which he is quite sure his hearer will draw an illogical and untrue conclusion, and the like.

The greatest school of evasion, I speak seriously, is the House of Commons; and necessarily so, from the nature of the case. And the hustings is another.

An instance is supplied in the history of St. Athanasius: he was in a boat on the Nile, flying persecution; and he found himself pursued. On this he ordered his men to turn his boat round, and ran right to meet the satellites of Julian. They asked him, "Have you seen Athanasius?" and he told his followers to answer, "Yes, he is close to you." *They* went on their course as if they were sure to come up to him, while *he* ran back into Alexandria, and there lay hid till the end of the persecution.

I gave another instance above, in reference to a doctrine of religion. The early Christians did their best to conceal their Creed on account of the misconceptions of the heathen about it. Were the question asked of them, "Do you worship a Trinity?" and did they answer, "We worship one God, and none else"; the inquirer might, or would, infer that they did not acknowledge the Trinity of Divine Persons.

It is very difficult to draw the line between these evasions and what are commonly called in English *equivocations;* and of this difficulty, again, I think, the scenes in the House of Commons supply us with illustrations.

4. The fourth method is *silence.* For instance, not giving the *whole* truth in a court of law. If St. Alban, after dressing himself in the Priest's clothes, and, being taken before the persecutor, had been able to pass off for his friend, and so gone to martyrdom without being discovered; and had he in the course of examination answered all questions

truly, but not given the whole truth, the most important truth, that he was the wrong person, he would have come very near to telling a lie, for half-truth is often a falsehood. And his defence must have been the *justa causa*, viz., either that he might in charity or for religion's sake save a priest, or, again, that the judge had no right to interrogate him on the subject.

Now, of these four modes of misleading others by the tongue, when there is a *justa causa* (supposing there can be such),—(1) a material lie, that is, an untruth which is not a lie, (2) an equivocation, (3) an evasion, and (4) silence,—First, I have no difficulty whatever in recognizing as allowable the method of *silence*.

Secondly, But, if I allow of *silence*, why not of the method of *material lying*, since half of a truth *is* often a lie? And, again, if all killing be not murder, nor all taking from another stealing, why must all untruths be lies? Now, I will say freely that I think it difficult to answer this question, whether it be urged by St. Clement or by Milton; at the same time, I never have acted, and I think, when it came to the point, I never should act upon such a theory myself, except in one case, stated below. This I say for the benefit of those who speak hardly of Catholic theologians, on the ground that they admit text-books which allow of equivocation. They are asked, how can we trust you, when such are your views? But such views, as I already have said, need not have anything to do with their own practice, merely from the circumstance that they are contained in their text-books. A theologian draws out a system; he does it partly as a scientific speculation; but much more for the sake of others. He is lax for the sake of others, not of himself. His own standard of action is much higher than that which he imposes upon men in general. One special reason why religious men, after drawing out a theory, are unwilling to act upon it themselves, is this: that they practically acknowledge a broad distinction between their reason and their conscience; and that they feel the latter to be the safer guide, though the former may be the clearer, nay, even though it be the truer. They would rather be in error with the sanction of their conscience, than be right with the mere judgment of their reason. And, again, here is this more tangible difficulty in the case of exceptions to the rule of Veracity, that so very little external help is given us in drawing the line, as to when untruths are allowable and when not; whereas, that sort of killing which is not murder, is most definitely marked off by legal enactments, so that it cannot possibly be mistaken for such killing as *is* murder. On the other hand the cases of exemption from the rule of Veracity are left to the private judgment of the individual, and he may easily be led on from acts which are allowable to acts which are not. Now this remark does *not* apply to such acts as are related in Scripture, as being done by a particular inspiration, for in such cases there *is* a command. If I had my own way, I would oblige society, that is, its great men, its lawyers, its divines, its literature, publicly to acknowledge as such, those instances of untruth which are not lies, as, for instance, untruths in war; and then there could be no perplexity to the individual Catholic, for he would not be taking the law into his own hands.

Thirdly, as to playing upon words, or equivocation, I suppose it is from the English habit, but, without meaning any disrespect to a great Saint, or wishing to set myself up, or taking my conscience for more than it is worth, I can only say as a fact, that I admit it as little as the rest of my countrymen; and, without any reference to the right and the wrong of the matter, of this I am sure, that, if there is one thing more than another which prejudices Englishmen against the Catholic Church, it is the doctrine of great authorities on the subject of equivocation. For myself, I can fancy myself thinking it was allowable in extreme cases for me to lie, but never to equivocate. Luther said, "Pecca fortiter." I anathematize his formal sentiment, but there is a truth in it, when spoken of material acts.

Fourthly, I think *evasion,* as I have described it, to be perfectly allowable; indeed, I do not know, who does not use it, under circumstances; but that a good deal of moral danger is attached to its use; and that, the cleverer a man is, the more likely he is to pass the line of Christian duty.

But it may be said, that such decisions do not meet the particular difficulties for which provision is required; let us, then, take some instances.

1. I do not think it right to tell lies to children, even on this account, that they are sharper than we think them, and will soon find out what we are doing; and our example will be a very bad training for them. And so of equivocation: it is easy of imitation, and we ourselves shall be sure to get the worst of it in the end.

2. If an early Father defends the patriarch Jacob in his mode of gaining his father's blessing, on the ground that the blessing was divinely pledged to him already, that it was his, and that his father and brother were acting at once against his own rights and the divine will, it does not follow from this that such conduct is a pattern to us, who have no supernatural means of determining *when* an untruth becomes a *material,* and not a *formal* lie. It seems to me very dangerous, be it ever allowable or not, to lie or equivocate in order to preserve some great temporal or spiritual benefit; nor does St. Alfonso here say anything to the contrary, for he is not discussing the question of danger or expedience.

3. As to Johnson's case of a murderer asking you which way a man had gone, I should have anticipated that, had such a difficulty happened to him, his first act would have been to knock the man down, and to call out for the police; and next, if he was worsted in the conflict, he would not have given the ruffian the information he asked, at whatever risk to himself. I think he would have let himself be killed first. I do not think that he would have told a lie.

4. A secret is a more difficult case. Supposing something has been confided to me in the strictest secrecy, which could not be revealed without great disadvantage to another, what am I to do? If I am a lawyer, I am protected by my profession. I have a right to treat with extreme indignation any question which trenches on the inviolability of my position; but, supposing I was driven up into a corner, I think I should have a right to say an untruth, or that, under such circumstances, a lie would be *material,* but it is almost an impossible case, for the law would defend me. In like manner, as a priest, I should think it lawful to speak as if I knew nothing of what passed in confession. And I think in these cases, I do in fact possess that guarantee, that I am not going by private judgment, which just now I demanded; for society would bear

me out, whether as a lawyer or as a priest, in holding that I had a duty to my client or penitent, such, that an untruth in the matter was not a lie. A common type of this permissible denial, be it *material lie* or *evasion,* is at the moment supplied to me. An artist asked a Prime Minister, who was sitting to him, "What news, my Lord, from France?" He answered, *"I do not know; I have not read the papers."*

5. A more difficult question is, when to accept confidence has not been a duty. Supposing a man wishes to keep a secret that he is the author of a book, and he is plainly asked on the subject. Here I should ask the previous question, whether anyone has a right to publish what he dare not avow. It requires to have traced the bearings and results of such a principle, before being sure of it; but certainly, for myself, I am no friend of strictly anonymous writing. Next, supposing another has confided to you the secret of his authorship:—there are persons who would have no scruple at all in giving a denial to impertinent questions asked them on the subject. I have heard a great man in his day at Oxford, warmly contend, as if he could not enter into any other view of the matter, that, if he had been trusted by a friend with the secret of his being author of a certain book, and he were asked by a third person, if his friend was not (as he really was) the author of it, he ought, without any scruple and distinctly, to answer that he did not know. He had an existing duty towards the author; he had none towards his inquirer. The author had a claim on him; an impertinent questioner had none at all. But here, again, I desiderate some leave, recognized by society, as in the case of the formulas, "Not at home," and "Not guilty," in order to give me the right of saying what is a *material* untruth. And, moreover, I should here also ask the previous question, Have I any right to accept such a confidence? have I any right to make such a promise? and, if it be an unlawful promise, is it binding when it cannot be kept without a lie? I am not attempting to solve these difficult questions, but they have to be carefully examined.

108

THE OBLIGATION OF VERACITY

Reginald Middleton [1]

Truthfulness is one of the most important social virtues, but there are times when it is a duty to conceal the truth. A member of the Government, for instance, may have knowledge which, if published, would cause a war or a revolution; so, too, a confidential clerk might ruin his employers by an untimely revelation; lawyers, doctors, priests, and others are often the depositaries of important secrets confided to them by those who seek their help or advice. In all these cases it is a duty to conceal the truth, and if hard pressed by an impertinent questioner, the denial of all knowledge of the fact or of the fact itself may be not only lawful but of obligation, when this is the only means of concealment.

Is such a denial a lie? When and on what principles is it justifiable?

There is some difference of opinion as to what a lie is and why it is wrong, though all right-thinking people will agree in condemning it.

Some writers distinguish a lie from a falsehood, making the former an offence against justice—a *"privatio veri debiti"*—though assigning different reasons for the truth being due. Paley, for instance, held it a breach of promise (to speak the truth) "which is tacitly given in all conversation because we know it is expected of us"; Grotius, a violation of our neighbor's right "to form a true judgment of the conception of our mind, which by a silent contract we are presumed to owe him."

St. Augustine defined a lie as untruth spoken with intent to deceive; this definition, however, though more comprehensive, does not include all forms of falsehood, for it is quite possible to speak untruthfully without intending to deceive; exaggeration, for instance, is untruthful, though sometimes there may be no intention to deceive; so, too, the habitual liar does not always intend to deceive.

[1] *The American Ecclesiastical Review*, August, 1898.

St. Thomas held every deliberate falsehood to be a lie, and defined it simply as *"locutio contra mentem,"* distinguishing three elements: the untrue statement, which constitutes the *material* falsehood and may be due to ignorance, error, want of reflection, etc.; the will to utter what the mind knows to be false, which constitutes the *formal* lie, and is present in every deliberate falsehood, giving it its specific character; and the intention to deceive, which completes and perfects, but is not essential to a lie and may in some cases be absent.

This, then, is the simplest and most comprehensive definition we may adopt; but it must be noticed that *"locutio"* here means speech in the strict sense, *i. e.*, a serious manifestation of our mind by words, writing or other *recognized* signs. So that rhetorical figures and ornaments of speech, fables, parables, recitations, etc., are not "speech" in this sense; neither can we lie by soliloquising or speaking to brutes or inanimate objects, for we do not manifest our mind to ourselves by outward signs, neither can we do so to beings incapable of understanding us. (We may, of course, deceive ourselves, but the act is a mental one quite independent of outward signs and of a totally different nature from the act of deceiving others.) Again, as words are arbitrary signs used by man to express his thoughts, there can be no *"locutio contra mentem"* in using phrases which have a generally understood meaning, such, for instance as "not at home," "not guilty," etc.; or to use ordinary expressions of civility, to sign one's self "your obedient servant" when writing to one held to be inferior, or to express "one's pleasure" in accepting a troublesome invitation—this last point, it may be remarked, explains what looks like gross flattery and untruthfulness in the writings of many eminent Christians living under the later Roman Empire. Living in a period of decaying and degraded civilization, they used phrases which at the time were considered ordinary expressions of civility, but would now be looked upon as the grossest flattery.

The question, then, is why is a lie in this sense, as embracing all forms of deliberate falsehood, wrong?

That it is *extrinsically* evil—evil on account of its injurious effects—is admitted by all.

When we consider the harm done to society by the loosening of the bonds of mutual trust and confidence and by the suspicions, misunderstandings, resentments, etc., to which lying gives rise, as well as the harm done to the individual, both the ignorance and error caused him and the specific injury the particular lie may do him; and when we further take into account all the remote consequences of lying, and its degrading and demoralizing effect on the character of the speaker, its tendency to foster moral cowardice and the other mean vices which usually accompany it, there can be no question about the moral evil of lying, or that it is rightly branded as disgraceful, the refuge of the coward and the knave.

But are these the only reasons? Is falsehood only *extrinsically* evil—evil from its circumstances and consequences, and not in itself?

If so, then just as homicide is lawful in war or self-defence, and the taking of food which does not belong to us when in danger of starvation, falsehood then, too, may be lawful when there is a grave reason to justify it, when the evil can be averted or compensated by some greater good; and on the ground that a lie is not *intrinsically* evil, we may use it as a means to an end, for although it is not lawful "to do evil that good may come of it" we may do that which is neither good nor evil in itself for the sake of some good and proportionately important object, even if we foresee that evil *we do not intend* will follow from it. Thus, it is lawful to build a factory even if it be certain that the vice of the neighborhood will be increased thereby; or to declare war in a just cause, though much misery to innocent persons will be caused thereby; or to hold fairs, markets, etc., though these may be the occasion of thieving, drunkenness, etc.

This view has been held by Plato and some of the early Fathers of the Church, by the majority of Protestant and many Catholic writers (of whom Cardinal Newman gives a list in the *Apologia*), as well as by the Utilitarian school of moralists. If we accept it, however, it is not easy to explain why God cannot lie, just as He can destroy life or property. That He never does so is an article of Catholic faith; that He absolutely could not do so is difficult to prove in this assumption (on the ground that a lie is *intrinsically* evil, it would of course be repugnant to the perfection of the Divine Nature); to say He has no need of such shifts is hardly an answer to the difficulty.

But is falsehood only *extrinsically* evil? Is it not also intrinsically evil, *i. e.*, evil in itself and not merely from its circumstances?

According to Aristotle, "Falsehood of any kind, considered entirely by itself, and without reference to consequences, is disgraceful and blamable." St. Augustine and St. Thomas, who have been followed by the great majority of Catholic theologians, are of the same opinion. Kant held this view very strongly, and would even forbid the use of accepted phrases.

The proof of this doctrine, though subtle, seems conclusive.

Whatever is contrary to reason is sinful; there may be acts which in themselves are not contrary to reason, which are wrong because they are forbidden, not forbidden because they are wrong, as servile work on Sunday; but there is no deliberate thought, word, or deed contrary to reason which is not, *ipso facto*, sinful. For, in ultimate analysis our reason is the impress of the Divine law given us to guide us through life. He who has made all things has made nothing without a purpose; but while irrational creatures play their part in the economy of the universe and attain their ends by acting according to their natures or their instincts, man knows his end and what actions are and what are not conducive to the attainment of it. Thus, chemical elements, for instance, unite and act according to their nature; a brute eats and drinks to satisfy the cravings of appetite; but man, while satisfying his appetite, knows that food and drink are to be used primarily for the sake of bodily health, and secondarily to enable him to discharge efficiently the duties of his state. The judgment of his practical reason, declaring that certain actions are or are not conducive to the attainment of the end intended by Nature in the particular case, is called the natural law. It may be sometimes lawful to forego the secondary for the sake of more perfectly attaining the primary end, *v. g.*, by a use of alcohol, drugs, etc., which incapacitate for mental work, for the sake of health; but an action which destroys the primary end can never be lawful, *v. g.*, an abuse of food or drink which destroys health. Such an action is said to be contrary to a primary precept of the natural law.

That falsehood, in itself and apart from all circumstances and consequences, is contrary to reason, follows from the fact that speech is a manifestation of thought, and is principally intended by nature as a means of communicating our mind to others—as our reason plainly tells us; consequently, falsehood, by which we outwardly signify what we do not inwardly think, and are thus in contradiction with ourselves, is discordant and inordinate, an abuse of speech by destroying the principal end intended by nature, and so contrary to the dictates of right reason and degrading to our nature.

It is this element of discord, present in every deliberate falsehood, that renders a lie impossible for Him to whom we pray, "who can neither deceive nor be deceived."

It may be said that this element of evil is not a very grave one; but it must be remembered that it seldom occurs by itself, and the *extrinsic* evil of a particular lie may make it a very grave matter indeed.

On the ground, then, that falsehood is *intrinsically* evil, no good end can justify its use. Thus, the *charitable* lie must be held illicit—it may be a duty to conceal bad news from a sick person, but it is not lawful to invent good news in order to cheer him up—much more so the *useful* lie told for our own sake; so, too, the *jocose* lie, unless it be evident from our manner that we are not speaking seriously, in which case our whole bearing, together with the words used, sufficiently manifest our meaning, our words by themselves being but part of the *"locutio."*

Extreme cases, where the good to be gained is enormously great, and the evil reduced to a minimum, can easily be imagined; but whatever their theoretical value may be as a test of principles, they are not of much practical importance. They hardly occur once in a lifetime, and when they do, can be solved as secrets, or there is some other alternative, and, finally, where none such exists 999 men out of 1,000 will lie and have done with it; and although such conduct cannot be justified (unless we are prepared to sacrifice the principle that "it is not lawful to do evil that good may come of it," and if we do so in an extreme case where can we draw the line?), it must be remembered that the evil by our supposition is originally small, and is further reduced though *not cancelled* by the goodness of the motive; that, in fact, the fault may be much less serious than many which even good people are in the habit of committing and think little of; this, of course, does not *justify*, but it does in great measure *excuse* it.

Secrecy, which we have now to deal with, is much more practical and important.

To return then to the question asked in the beginning of this paper—when the obligation of secrecy seems to clash with the obligation of veracity, when the only means of keeping a secret is the denial of the truth, is such a denial a lie? When and on what principles is it justifiable?

Without entering into a long discussion of the question of secrecy, it may be said generally that any knowledge which, if revealed, would injure our neighbor in his person, property, or good name, is by its own nature secret and unlawful to reveal, whether it has been acquired by chance, by fair means or by foul (as by eavesdropping, reading private letters, etc.). Of course, if the knowledge is public property, we do not injure our neighbor by speaking of it; neither may we conceal it when questioned by one who has a right to the information. Thus, the fact of a man's being a drunkard is a natural secret, but we may speak of it, if notorious, or if questioned by one, say, who wishes to employ him as a servant and asks us for a character. So, too, we may warn others to avoid the company of one whom we know to be a bad character, and give reaons for our warning.

If we have bound ourselves by promise, the obligation is evidently greater; but it must be remembered that no one can bind himself to that which is illicit, or when he has no right to do so; thus, a witness of a crime may be bound by promise not to reveal it to any chance person who has no right to the information; but he cannot bind himself not to reveal it when questioned in a court of justice, and if he does so his promise is, *ipso facto,* invalid.

The obligation of secrecy is still greater when the fact has not been discovered or witnessed by one's self, but has been communicated by one seeking advice or help. This is known as a *"secretum commissum,"* and under this head will come all secrets of counsel as well as all professional secrets, which lawyers, doctors, priests, etc., and speaking generally, all who hold an official position, may have. Nothing can justify the revelation of a secret except the free consent of the party concerned or the duty to preserve the State or an innocent person from grave injury, when this is the only means of doing so. Thus, for instance, had the knowledge of the gunpowder plot been revealed to Father Garnet as a mere *"secretum commissum,"* it would have been his duty to inform the Government, if he were unable to prevent it by other means; as a secret of the confessional it could not be revealed under any circumstances—nothing justifies the violation of the sacramental seal but the free and unsolicited consent of the penitent.

The obligation of secrecy *ceteris paribus* varies as the matter; the duty of concealing a lady's age is evidently not so grave as that of hiding the whereabouts of an innocent person from his would-be assassins, or of concealing a fact which, if revealed, would seriously injure another's character.

Few will question the duty of secrecy, though, it may be remarked, were it better understood and more generally acted upon, an almost incalculable amount of mischief would be prevented. It is not too much to say that the greater part of what may be called "tea-table gossip" is a direct violation of the obligation of secrecy.

The right way to keep a secret is not to speak of the matter, or, when questioned, by silence or evasion—throwing dust in the questioner's eyes by directing his attention to some other subject, or confusing him by a sharp answer, a question, or some similar device; but sometimes silence or evasion (in which there can be no question of falsehood) would be equivalent to a confession, and in such a case it may be a duty to preserve our secret even by a flat denial of the truth, or of our knowledge of it, when this is the only alternative left us.

And now to answer our original question—is such a denial a lie? Let us suppose, for argument's sake, that it is, and that it is a sin. If it be so we are liable to be involved in contradictory obligations of which the duty of secrecy may be by far the most important; so that on the principle that "of two evils it is a duty to choose the less," a lie might be of obligation if it were the only means of concealment. Here it must be noticed that we are not using a lie as a means to an end, but that we are, by supposition, driven into a corner and obliged to choose between two alternatives.

But is this denial a lie in the sense in which we have explained it—a *"locutio contra mentem?"* Is the exterior sign contrary to the interior thought it manifests?

It evidently is *"contra mentem,"* in the sense that our words are contrary to our *full knowledge* of the matter; but it is a true manifestation of our *communicable* knowledge; and, moreover, our audience can gather that we are thus restricting our answer. The words by themselves do not here constitute the full *"locutio";* the "manifestation of our mind" is given by the words taken together with the circumstances of the particular case; and read in this light, the meaning they convey to a prudent person is—*"secrets apart,* I know nothing about the matter," which is the true manifestation of our mind.

If our questioner has an average share of intelligence he is not deceived by our answer, but judges that whatever the facts or our knowledge of them may be, we have no information to give him. When a lawyer, a doctor, or a priest is questioned about a matter which may be a professional secret, and answers "I do not know," does anyone gifted with ordinary common sense understand him to mean more than that he has no knowledge of the matter which he is at liberty to reveal? We all know the story of Lord Palmerston answering a question about a secret treaty by "I do not know; I have not seen the paper yet." If he had omitted the qualifying phrase, would his answer have conveyed a different impression?

Similarly, if a question be asked which cannot be answered without injury to another, "No," or "I do not know," means plainly enough that the fact, whether known or not, is not public property.

This is known as "imperfect mental reservation" (*restrictio late vel non pure mentalis*), and it is essential that a prudent person should be able to gather from the circumstances of the case—the person speaking, the nature of the subject discussed, etc.—that we are restricting our answer to knowledge we are at liberty to reveal.

It is not contended that "imperfect mental reservation" may not have the *extrinsic* evil of a lie; but it is contended that it has not the *intrinsic* evil, i. e., the contradiction between our thought and its outward manifestation; for our verbal answer, taken together with the circumstances of the case, says plainly enough: "I have no knowledge of the matter which I am at liberty to reveal."

On the ground that this *"restrictio late mentalis"* is not *intrinsically* evil, evil in itself, it may be used as a means to an end (though it is difficult to think of an example of such use), or to conceal our own private affairs, when this is the only means of doing so, provided, always, we have some grave reason to justify its use; for it must be remembered that, though not evil in itself, it may have all the evil consequences of a lie.

Pure mental reservation, i. e., where the fact that an answer is being restricted, cannot be gathered from the circumstancs of the case (v. g., if asked whether a person be in the house, to answer "he is not here," meaning "in this room"), is only another name for a lie, and as such has been authoritatively condemned by the Church.

Many Catholic writers have defended *ambiguity* (*aequivocatio*) on the same ground as imperfect mental reservation, namely, that it is not *intrinsically evil,* and can therefore be used when there is a grave reason to justify it; though, like the latter, it may have all the *extrinsic* evil of a lie, its consequences may even be worse than those of a lie, because often more cowardly and more demoralizing from the danger there is of the speaker persuading himself that he is not doing evil, and also from its greater tendency than even lying to cause suspicion and distrust. It may be remarked, too, that when driven into a corner, a secret would probably be given away ten times over before a clever ambiguous answer could be thought of.

What, it may be asked, is the duty of truthfulness towards children and lunatics? The answer will depend on the capacity of the subject and the circumstances of the particular case. We evidently cannot reveal our thoughts to a raving lunatic or to an infant in arms, but we can do so to an intelligent child or to one slightly deranged.

Where are we to draw the line? Much more strictly probably than is usually the case. Much harm is certainly done, to children especially, by violating the obligation of veracity in this matter.

We must, of course, adapt our language to the capacity of the person we are speaking to; difficult matters have to be so explained as to be understood. Knowledge which would harm a child or excite a lunatic is a natural secret in their regard, and, as such, must be withheld.

We may sum up by saying there is no falsehood in the use of phrases which have a generally received meaning.

If falsehood be only *extrinsically* evil its use is lawful when there is a grave reason for it, when its evil consequences can be averted or compensated by some greater good.

If, however, it be *intrinsically* evil no good end can justify its use, and reason, supported by some of the greatest minds the world has produced, as well as by the majority of Catholic theologians, points to this as the true view.

Knowledge which, if revealed, would injure another in person, property, or good name, constitutes a natural secret, which it is of *obligation* to keep, even by a denial of the truth, or of our knowledge of it, when this is the only means of doing so.

Our own private affairs, etc., constitute a natural secret which we have a *right* to protect in the same way, provided this be the only alternative, and the matter be sufficiently important to justify its use.

Such a denial has not the *intrinsic* evil, but may have all the *extrinsic* evil of a lie, and so is lawful only when there is a grave reason for it (as homicide is lawful in war or self-defence). A secret should be kept by avoiding the subject, by silence or by evasion (in all which there is no question of falsehood), and only as a last resort by denial.

Whatever be the view taken of falsehood, all will agree that neither falsehood nor mental reservation nor ambiguity is lawful (1) when the reason for it is not good in itself and proportionately important; (2) when speaking to one who has a right to the truth; (3) when injury to our neighbor would result from it; (4) in all questions of contract, promise, etc.—a promise binds in the sense in which he who takes it knows that it is understood by him to whom it is made.

In this matter it is well to remember Aristotle's advice "not to try to be more accurate than the nature of the subject permits." It is easy to lay down general principles in the abstract, but the question whether they apply or not in a particular concrete case may be a very difficult one to answer.

109

THE LOAN OF MONEY

Michael Cronin [1]

Loan may occur in connection with two kinds of things: First, things that are consumed in their use; second, things that are not. Examples of the former are fruit, bread, wine; an example of the second is machinery of any kind. In the technical sense, however, a thing is said to be consumed in its use not only if it is necessarily destroyed by use, but also if the use of it necessarily entails its being lost to the owner, even though in its use it is not destroyed.

Now there is this great difference between the loan of things that are consumed in their use and the loan of a productive thing which is not consumed in its use, like a machine, that the former kind of a loan confers no right on the lender other than the right of recovering the equivalent of *the thing lent*—it confers no additional right of recovering something for the use of the thing lent; whilst the latter kind of loan confers not only a right of recovering what is lent but a right to charge something in addition for the use of what is lent. Let us compare the two cases.

A machine has two simultaneous values for its owner. First, there is the value of its use, the profit that arises from its use. A machine, for instance, produces saleable commodities of various kinds. Then since after the use the machine is still available, whole and unimpaired, there is also the value of the machine itself as a substance. For the owner the machine has always these two values, and to fail to take account of either of these in computing the total value of the machine to its owner would be to represent the value of the machine as lower than it really is. This doctrine that in productive things like a machine there are two distinct values, making up between them the full economic value of the machine, viz., the value of its use and the value of the machine itself, is briefly expressed by saying that in productive things *it is possible to distinguish between the use and the thing itself*. Suppose now that the owner

---

[1] *The Science of Ethics*, vol. II, pp. 328-333. (Benziger Brothers, New York.)

instead of using the machine himself lends it to another to be used, it becomes plain that the lender is depriving himself of the two values which we have distinguished, and that the borrower receives these two values. In justice, therefore, he should pay back these two values to the owner; first, he should return the machine itself, and, secondly, he should pay a charge upon its use.

The rights and obligations arising from the loan of fruits and such things are very different. Fruits and consumable goods generally have one value only for their owner, viz., the value of their use. Once used their value disappears, for they have themselves perished in their use. This was their only value for their original owner. This is their only value when lent. This, therefore, is the only value which the borrower should return; and the question arises—what is the extent of this value?

The question what is the value of things that are consumed in their use, may best be answered from an examination of a simple concrete case. What, for instance, is the value attaching to a pound of grapes or a loaf of bread? The man who eats a pound of grapes has had value to the extent of a pound of grapes. The man who eats a loaf has had value to the extent of a loaf. In general terms, *the value of anything, the use of which consists in its being consumed, is the value of the thing itself;* it has not, like the machine, two joint values, one arising out of its use, and one the continuing value of the thing itself after use; it has one value only, equal to the thing which is consumed. This, therefore, is the extent of the borrower's obligation in the case of things *primo usu consumptibilia*, viz., to return the equivalent of what has been lent. The lender in the case of loans of this kind (they are known as *mutuum*) has no right, *vi mutui*, in addition to demanding the return of the object lent, to impose any other additional charge. He has no right to look for a profit out of his loan. We say *vi mutui;* for though the contract of *mutuum* itself does not entitle an owner to more than the return of the equivalent of what has been lent, an owner may acquire a right to more on other titles. A man, for instance, has a right to compensate himself for any loss sustained by reason of the loan (*damnum emergens*), for cessation of previous profits (*lucrum cessans*), for risk or danger run (*periculum sortis*), and finally he may demand compensation for failure on the part of the borrower to pay within the stipulated time (*poena conventionalis*). These, however, are all extrinsic titles. They do not arise out of the nature of the contract itself. Granted that no losses are incurred, nor risk run, the loan of a thing *primo usu consumptibile* confers no title to special profit or to anything more than the return of the equivalent of what has been lent. Any such profit arising out of and based exclusively on the contract itself, and not on some other extrinsic title, **is wholly unjustified.**

We now come to the special question of the loan of money. Money is anything that serves as a **medium** of exchange. Whether money consists of gold and silver or paper or any other material, its one function *as money* is to serve as a means for buying and selling. *A* purchases goods from *B* by means of money. With that money *B* purchases goods from *C*. As money this is its one exclusive function, viz., to be a means of exchange. Now it is evident that a medium of exchange is something, the use of which is to be given away in exchange (*distractio, secundum quod in commutationes expenditur*), to be given for something received; it is, therefore, something which is necessarily lost to the owner in its use, something which an owner cannot use and at the same time keep, like machines and other productive things; it is, therefore, something which is consumed in its use in the technical use of this term. And since in the Middle Ages money had no other function than to serve as a medium of exchange, to charge interest for money at that period, demanding in return for money lent both the original sum and something additional for its use by the borrower, would be attributing to money a double value which it did not then possess.

Now all this reasoning of the Scholastic writers holds true to-day as in the Middle Ages. Money as money, i. e., as a mere medium of exchange, is still unproductive, still something, the use of which is its consumption, and therefore, as money, it confers on the owner no right to special profit arising out of its being lent. But money is now what it was not in the Middle Ages, something more than this. Money now is capital, it is productive, *for it can be turned into capital* at any moment by the simplest of processes, and at no cost. In the Middle Ages capital was not on the market. At that period the only kind of capital worth talking about was land, and land was not in the market. At that period, therefore, money could not be turned into capital. So easily on the other hand is money turned into capital at present that each is ordinarily spoken of in terms of the other. Although money is not, *in specie,* the same thing as a railway or a mine or a business concern or any of the other kinds of capital, yet he who has money is said to be possessed of capital; and on the other hand a railway or a mine is ordinarily spoken of as stock, i. e., it is spoken of in terms of its money-value just as if it consisted of so many sovereigns or pound notes. He, therefore, who at present has money has capital, and consequently when money is lent a charge can be made for the loan of it just as for the loan of any other productive thing.

110

THE CHURCH AND THE MONEY LENDER

Henry Irwin [1]

In former centuries the Church prohibited interest as a rule; she allowed it only as an exception. Now she prohibits it only as an exception, when it is excessive; she allows it as a rule. She forbade it when money generally was barren; she permits it now that money is virtually productive. Where is the inconsistency? There is here no contradiction; only another instance of the Church's wonderful sameness amid change, of her adaptability to circumstances, coupled with fidelity to principle. As she never has relaxed her severity with regard to divorce, however flattered or menaced she might be, so she will never sanction usury. . . .

From the end of the fifteenth century both Church and State accorded greater freedom of money contract. Rent charges on movable property and even on the general credit of persons in quest of capital (*census personalis*) received ecclesiastical sanction. The principle of partnership underwent an evolution which practically converted it into a loan of money in what was known as the Triple Contract. Both, however, were somewhat abused to cloak usurious bargains,

[1] *The Catholic Mind,* 1914.

and in so far as they did so, were condemned by the Church. The Triple Contract was initially a contract of partnership, attached to which were two subsidiary contracts of insurance, by which the capitalist bargained himself out of the risk of losing his capital and even his interest. He covenanted in fact to receive a smaller certain gain in preference to a larger but uncertain one. Each of these contracts was licit in itself. The whole difficulty arose when they were all made at once with the same person. It was, however, in itself no evasion of the usury prohibition, and, though provisionally forbidden by Sixtus V in 1586, it was set forth with evident approval by Benedict XIV at a later date. . . .

Even after capital had begun to be formed on a more extensive scale, the Church's motives for maintaining the usury prohibition for the protection of the weak remained as valid as before. Agriculture continued long to be the great employment of the bulk of the population. To have given money-lenders a free hand in dealing with an ignorant peasantry too often harassed by drought, blight, pestilence, famine and war "would have meant delivering them into the hands of the spoiler." (*Ashley*, p. 438.)

The State is preoccupied, to judge by her action in the past, rather with the *production* of wealth; the Church is concerned far more with its *distribution*. The bursting of the South Sea Bubble in 1720 ruined many, but enriched a few. English historians draw comfort from the fact that the blow, looked at from a national standpoint, was less severe than it seemed. Money changed hands; it did not leave the country. That is the kind of view a Chancellor of the Exchequer might be tempted to take, whose task as tax-collector is much easier and less invidious when money is concentrated in the hands of a small minority, and revenue can be raised by directly taxing them on income and inheritance. From the statesman's point of view *national wealth* is paramount; from the philanthropist's, *individual well-being*. Clearly it is for the greater good of the greater number that capital should be spread thinner over a broader area. This was the tendency of the action of the usury prohibition. It was designed partly to protect ignorance and necessity from being exploited for the benefit of those who, in dealing with them, had the powerful lever of an economic advantage.

111

THE JUST PRICE

PATRICK CLEARY [1]

I take it that the Marxian theory of price is manifestly false: the price of a rich vein of iron ore is out of all proportion to the labor expended in unearthing it; on the other hand a manufacturer of wooden pots will never make a fortune.

Nor does price seem to be determined by the objective or physical utility of the object which is sold; since if it were, the price of a pound of bread must remain constant, seeing that the feeding power of bread is invariable—I suppose, of course, that the quality of the bread remains the same.

What then constitutes just price? Utility is necessary, for otherwise our pot-manufacturer would not fare so badly. Yet it is not mere physical utility that counts. What is it then? Why will a community give more for one object than for another? Evidently because one object meets the wants of the community better than another. Why will people give more at one time than at another for the same object? Because, again, it is more useful to them at one time than at another. The measure of any object's usefulness is determined by its capacity for meeting the desires of the community in the varied circumstances of the moment. Thus if a man desires a motor more than a carriage, the former is more useful for him since it satisfies his desires in a greater degree. So too that which best satisfies the desires of the community is most useful for the community. Again as the desire of the community for a particular object may vary in intensity from time to time, the usefulness of that object will vary in a corresponding degree. This capacity for satisfying the wants of the community at a particular moment may be called social utility. Articles have the same social utility when they satisfy the social wants to an equal degree; and I lay it down as a principle that articles which have the same social utility are

---

[1] *The Church and Usury,* a Thesis, pp. 186-188. (M. H. Gill & Son, Dublin.)

interchangeable in that community; and if the articles are exchanged, one is the just price of the other.

This position—which is substantially that of Jevons—will not yield any results differing in practice from the conclusions of the theologians. These are indeed inclined to regard social utility—or, as they prefer to speak of it, common estimation—as a regulative rather than as a constitutive principle of just price; but this difference of theory does not lead to any difference in practice. Common estimation is a test of value; but it is more than a test, for it is the true constituent of value. Just price is but an equivalent of value, hence the constituent of the latter is also the constituent of just price.

Working together our principles that loans of money are true sales, and that just price is determined by social utility, we draw the conclusion that for a "loan" of money—when there is no intention of making a donation—one may demand the just price, viz., whatever has the same social utility. If one gets paid in coin, he may demand coin which has the same social utility; if, as usually happens, he gets merely a right to coin, that right should have the same social utility. Now if society thinks that a right to present coin, or ownership of present coin, possesses a higher rate of utility than is possessed by the same quantity of coin when payable at a future date, then clearly it is not a just sale when the same physical quantity of coin is returned for a loan. In the concrete: if society thinks that £100 ready cash is as valuable as £105 payable twelve months hence, the true equivalent and consequently the just price of £100 is £105 payable at the end of a year.

The question of the legality of usury becomes therefore one of fact. Is the social utility of a sum of money whose payment is deferred, less than the social utility of the same sum when paid immediately? When it is less, one may take an "increment" to place the social utilities on an equality. It is plain that the amount of the increment may vary with circumstances, since the social estimate of the value of deferred payments may vary. The face value of the coins, and indeed their purchasing-power also, may remain quite constant; but we may not thence infer that the social utility is invariable: a pound of bread will always do the same amount of work, yet everybody admits that its price may rise or fall. Hence the just increment—the just rate of interest—may sink to zero, or may rise (I speak of possibilities) above 100 per cent.

112

THE ETHICS OF JUST PRICES

JOSEPH HUSSLEIN [1]

The question of prices is of universal interest. For the poor it is a matter of daily and often of anxious consideration. Just prices and fair wages are two hinges on which revolves the economic welfare of the world. On the proper solution of these two cardinal problems depends far more than the mere material prosperity of a nation, for extortionate prices and unfair wages form together one of the most serious social and moral perils of our age. They are not indeed the fatalistic cause of radicalism and vice, as non-Catholic sociologists often teach, but they are the fruitful occasion of these evils.

The ethics of modern "commercialism" are familiar to us all. "Demand for your product the highest returns you can prudently hope to gain," is the pithy counsel of the worldly-wise. "Eliminate competition by all expedient means that you may safely increase your demands. There is no Decalogue in trade. Keep within the bounds of the law, wherever it is effective, and do not exasperate the people to the danger point; but multiply your profits in the surest way you can. This is the golden rule."

Far other are the principles of the Church. They permit a margin of profits which will enable commerce to flourish in a healthy state, but at the same time they provide that the life-blood of trade may circulate freely through the veins and arteries of the social body for the common good. They forbid excessive charges, a source of wealth to a few, a cause of hunger to many. They neither allow the cancer of capitalistic selfishness to fasten itself upon the social body, nor suffer the paralysis of Socialism to afflict society. The principle of just prices is thus expressed by the greatest of theologians, St. Thomas:

[1] *America*, March 31, 1917.

"Buying and selling were introduced for the common benefit of both purchaser and vender, since each stands in need of what belongs to the other. The exchange, however, intended for the common benefit of both, ought not to impose a greater hardship upon one than upon the other party to the contract, which should be objectively equal (*secundum aequalitatem rei*). But the worth of the article applied to human use is measured by the price paid for it, and for this purpose money was invented. Wherefore, the equality of justice is destroyed if either the price exceeds the complete value of the article, or the article exceeds the price in value. Whence it follows that to sell an article at a higher, or to buy it at a lower price than its worth is in itself unjust and illicit." (*Sum. Theol.*, 2, 2, 9, 77, a. 1.)

There is, consequently, an obligation in conscience of neither selling above the just price, which represents the value of an article at a given time and place, nor forcing a sale beneath it. But how is this just price to be determined? Is it mathematically defined for any period and locality, or is it sufficiently elastic to expand and contract within fixed limits?

From what has already been said it is clear that the Church will not admit as a general principle that a price is just simply because it has been agreed upon between seller and buyer. So, likewise, she will not admit that wages are just simply because they were determined by a "free" contract between employer and employed. On this principle the stronger in wealth or the more cunning in wit could always take advantage of his weaker and more innocent brother. Such is the theory of liberalism and modern commercialism, but such is not the doctrine of the Church of Christ. Yet neither is she extreme in any of her views, and her teachers readily concede that in exceptional instances, where no other standard can be applied, prices must be based upon free agreement between purchaser and seller. Such is the case where there is question of curios, rarities, masterpieces of art or other articles of extraordinary value, or objects whose real worth neither party is able rightly to appraise. Such is the case, likewise, where articles are sold that have already been worn by use. The price then determined by free agreement is technically known as the "conventional" price. So, too, the price at an auction sale is that which an article can bring according to honest bidding.

Aside from such rare exceptions, however, the just price will be either the "legal" or the "common" price. The former is the price definitely prescribed by the law, where such exists. Thus in the Middle Ages the prices of the principal commodities were determined by the gilds, and strict adherence to these rulings was enforced by the gild officials supported by the civic authorities. Legal prices are always binding in conscience, unless obviously unjust.

Where legal regulations do not exist, there remains but one way in which the just price can ordinarily be determined, and that is by the common estimation of men setting the value of any article in a given time and place. This is known as the "common" or "natural" price.

The common price, as we can readily understand, is not to be determined, like the legal price, with mathematical precision. Catholic moralists, therefore, acknowledge a highest, a lowest, and an average or mean common price, all of which remain within the strict limits of justice, according to the popular estimation of men. They indicate respectively the highest price at which truly honest men would try to sell an article, the lowest at which they might try to purchase it from others, and the average at which it would be ordinarily sold by such bargainers. The margin between the highest and lowest just price is greatest in commodities that minister to mere pleasure and luxury, and least in those that pertain to the necessities of life. St. Alphonsus has laid down a rule which is accepted as applicable in the sale of ordinary articles. Thus if the mean just price is five, he says, then the highest price might rise to six, and the lowest fall to four; if the mean common price is ten, the extremes will be eight and eleven; if the mean is 100, the extremes may be 95 and 105. Others admit that these prices might reach to 90 and 110 without injustice. The proportion naturally cannot remain the same as when the sum is small.

In determining the just price there is question not of an individual judgment, but of a social judgment formed by the great body of buyers and sellers, who together sufficiently take into account all the factors that can reasonably enter into the process of production, transportation and sale. The estimate to be followed is the common estimate of the place in which the sale is made even though this should differ widely from that obtaining in other lands.

While the highest as well as the lowest common prices are just, yet an injustice is committed whenever either the highest or lowest just prices are secured in place of a less favorable just price by real fraud. We can readily understand, therefore, how criminally unjust it is to raise or depress by unrighteous means the common or natural market price, which may be said to coincide with the common or natural price of moral theologians. We thus see how practical is the teaching of the Church upon this as upon all other questions.

Accidentally, however, the price may be raised above the normal value of the article, according to St. Thomas, when the person who sells it suffers some special loss by parting with it. This principle is further developed by Catholic moralists who mention various exceptional instances in which the highest common just price may be exceeded, as when the seller has a particular affection for the article which, for example, might be an heirloom in his family; or when he sacrifices opportunities of future gains by parting with it at a certain time. Similarly an article may be bought below the lowest common just price when the seller comes of his own accord in order to dispose of it. Even here, however, no undue advantage may be taken when poverty or necessity urge such a step.

St. Thomas, and so likewise St. Alphonsus, would not permit any article to be sold above the highest common just price because of any special value it might have for the purchaser. "If any one," writes the Angelic Doctor, "derives great advantage from what he buys, but he who sells the article suffers no loss by parting with it, then the latter may not sell it at a higher price (than the highest common price). The reason is because the special advantage which the object possesses for the purchaser does not arise from the seller, but solely from the condition of the buyer. But no one may sell to another what is not his own." It is, however, considered quite proper that the purchaser should freely give a donation over and above the just price which he pays.

Father Noldin, with some other modern moralists, is of opinion that there is, nevertheless, reason for charging above the highest common just price in such a case, but he would not, of course, permit this charge to become exorbitant. In common with all other theologians he, moreover, expressly states that such an exception can apply only where the purchaser has in view his own convenience and pleasure. All Catholic moralists agree, with perfect unanimity, that it would be an injustice to charge more than the normally just price because another stands in real need of any object: "The mere want and necessity which force a person to buy are not ratable at a price."

How vastly different this from the doctrine and practice of the unjust commercialism of our day!

113

MORALITY OF MONOPOLISTIC PRICES

Joseph Husslein [1]

We are living in an age of corporations, trusts and monopolies. As a consequence the vexed problem of prices cannot be considered without direct reference to them. In fact this problem is intimately connected with the question of exacting justice from the powerful interests which now control the wealth, the industry, and the resources of the country.

That gigantic organizations, once they have assumed the proportions of actual or virtual monopolies, are in reality a condition for obtaining the greatest efficiency, and hence for reducing prices in spite of enormous profits, is a contention often made in the past. Competition can no doubt become excessive, but the conviction is growing that corporations can reach a magnitude at which they become economically wasteful. There is no evidence to prove that efficiency increases in proportion to the vastness of a monopolistic enterprise. In the opinion of competent judges the same, or even a higher degree of efficiency, can be attained under a competitive system which combines the

[1] *America,* April 7, 1917.

advantages of moderately large-scale production with the benefits of competitive prices.

The huge profits accumulated by some of our monopolistic business ventures are, therefore, not due to superior efficiency, but to the power of inflicting extravagant prices upon the people. Declarations of dividends which seem to justify the prices charged for products are not necessarily a safe index of conditions. The cost of production can be raised, actually or fictitiously, to the great personal aggrandizement of the initiated, while the consumer is made to pay the entire false surplus gain, where it is not taken out of the wages of the laborers and the dividends of the petty shareholders.

As an example, rich contracts, resulting in a needless increase in the cost of production, can be given out to firms in which the directors of the monopoly have large vested interests. Or the familiar device of stock-watering may be resorted to, which affects the consumers' prices as well as the dividends of the small stock owners. Profits can in this way be drawn by the inner circle upon a presumed capitalization of $1,000,000 where only $500,000 were actually invested. The published figures, based upon this fictitious capital, may delude purchasers into paying an entirely unwarranted price, while minor shareholders receive precisely one-half of the dividends that would otherwise fall to them.

A monopoly may, in the first place, be legal and public in its nature, established and conducted by the Government itself as in the case of the postal system. Kept within proper limits such monopolies are entirely licit and may be made a source of public revenue. The reason is because they are intended solely for the common good. Even should prices be raised above normal competitive rates in order to secure larger incomes, such an increase would be merely another form of indirect taxation, and is to be judged upon that basis. But public authority may also, *for the common good,* give certain monopolistic rights and privileges to private individuals, as in the case of patents which are granted to encourage inventions, on the principle that such encouragement will benefit the community. Although the holders of legal monopolies can commit injustice by excessive prices, moralists admit that it is difficult to set definite limits, particularly where new inventions are placed upon the market. Such a monopoly is not granted in commodities necessary for life.

The great suffering of the people, due to high prices, is not caused by these forms of monopoly. We are mainly concerned, therefore, with purely private monopolies, and with all large enterprises or combinations which become powerful enough to control market prices or influence them sufficiently to exceed the competitive rate which else would have existed. Under this head come, likewise, the agreements among merchants not to sell an article below a set price, and particularly the practice of buying up commodities of any kind with the purpose of creating a "corner."

Before determining the rules which must govern the regulation of just prices under these various conditions it is well to premise that justice is not violated where surplus gains are due to special efficiency without any undue raising of prices. Neither is it wrong for merchants to combine in order that they may more readily procure their own benefits. Independent firms may, furthermore, agree, one with the other, upon a price, provided it violates neither justice nor charity. This is particularly the case when its purpose is to enable them to pay fitting wages to their employees. Experience, however, has taught that "rings" are likely to end in seeking to extort excessive prices from the helpless public.

We thus come to the general laws which are laid down for private monopolies and for all other private enterprises that gain control of the market. These rules are not spun out of the brain of any individual writer, but are the common teaching of Catholic moralists at the present day. They can be briefly stated as follows:

(1) The prices established by private monopolies, "rings," and similar business ventures are just, if they do not exceed the highest common price which an article would bring if these undertakings did not exist and the market were left open to fair competition. It is supposed, however, that just wages are paid to labor under both systems. (2) Prices which in themselves are not exorbitant, because they do not exceed the highest common price which would have obtained had these monopolistic conditions not been created,

may, nevertheless, be seriously sinful when they impose a notable hardship upon the poor. They then constitute an offense, not indeed against justice, but against the great and vital law of Christian charity. This takes place when the poor, in consequence of such conditions, are constrained to buy the necessaries of life at the highest common just price, whereas otherwise they might have bought them at the mean or lowest competitive price, and are thus made to suffer seriously. (3) The same strict laws are not to be laid down where an article merely ministers to pleasure. The reason is because purchasers can simply refuse to buy it. In such cases even the highest common price may more readily be exceeded.

The technical term frequently used here, "the highest common price," is defined in Reading No. 112, "The Ethics of Just Prices." It is in practice the highest market price for any commodity, determined by free competition for any given time and place, if the market is not tampered with. Theoretically it represents the just cost of production and sale, including the honest profit of employer and merchant, no less than the fair wages paid to labor. Finally, it also includes the surplus gain which may come to any individual or corporation because of superior efficiency.

There is another phase of monopolistic prices. This results from the effort to undersell an opponent. If a firm can permanently dispose of an article at a lower price than any of its competitors, because of a greater efficiency, there is at least no injustice committed. But such is not the purpose of modern underselling. The prices of a commodity are ruinously depressed in a certain locality or for a certain period, until the competitor has been crushed to the earth. They are then systematically raised above the former competitive rate. By this method injustice has been done to the man ruined in business, since trade has been taken from him under false pretenses, while an added injustice is inflicted on the consumer who has been led into a snare and is now forced to pay extortionate prices.

Crimes against justice and charity are committed in our day that cry to Heaven. Prices are arbitrarily fixed and supply is regulated according to whim. The weaker are driven to the wall and the poor are made to starve in order that a few may hoard up unjust profits. Labor, when it gains supremacy, too often follows the same principles freely employed by the unjust element in capitalism. The rights of the consumer are then equally disregarded by both parties. True principles are lost to sight because there is no one to declare them with precision and authority, except the Church of Christ, whose voice is disregarded. She alone can bring harmony out of all this discord, and order out of our modern economic and social chaos.

PROPERTY

114

THE DOCTRINE OF PROPERTY

John A. Ryan [1]

All the great radical movements for industrial reform involve the institution of private property. Socialism would abolish private ownership of the instruments of production; the Single Tax system would substantially abolish private ownership of land. Public ownership of such things as railroads, telegraphs, and municipal utilities would restrict very considerably the scope of private ownership, and even such milder proposals as profit-sharing and labor participation in management would cause a redistribution of the existing powers and functions of ownership.

The relations between capital and labor and the manner in which the product is distributed are what we find them today mainly because our industrial system is based upon a certain form of private property. The instruments of production are owned and managed by private individuals and organizations. The conditions and terms of employment and the distribution of the industrial product, are likewise determined by the fact that capital is private property, not the property of the State. Both these matters are arranged by agreement between the workers on the one hand, and the owners of capital on the other. Hence, both capitalist and laborer are vitally interested in the institution of private property. The former prizes the institution as a means of livelihood and a source of social and industrial power; the latter is no less keenly interested, although in a somewhat different way, and for somewhat different reasons. The worker wishes to own his wages and the things that his wages will buy, and he frequently desires to restrict the social and industrial power which ownership confers upon the capitalist.

[1] Reprinted from the *Quarterly Bulletin* of the Meadville Theological School, April, 1922.

All the efforts of revolutionists and reformers for the abolition or for a reorganization of the system of private property, and all the disputes between labor and capital concerning employment conditions and the distribution of the product, assume that there is involved an ethical principle, a principle of justice. To that supreme principle all make their final appeal. Inasmuch as the Church is the teacher and interpreter of morals, in economic no less than in the other relations of life, her doctrine of property is of the highest importance.

The founder of Christianity is sometimes represented as a revolutionist, a communist, or at least as one who did not believe in private property. No such claim can be substantiated by any fair study of the Gospels. Christ nowhere condemned the private ownership of goods as unjust or unlawful. Probably the nearest approach to such a declaration is found in His reply to the rich young man who asked what he should do in order to have life everlasting. When Christ enumerated the principal commandments, the young man replied: "All these have I kept from my youth, what is yet wanting to me?" The answer of Jesus was: "If thou wilt be perfect, go sell what thou hast and give to the poor. . . ." In these statements Our Lord drew quite clearly the distinction between what is necessary and what is of counsel. The young man was not required to divest himself of his goods unless he wished to be *perfect,* but he was not *commanded* to be perfect. Moreover, the fact that Christ counseled the young man to "sell" his goods, shows that He did not regard private ownership as unlawful in itself. Had He meant to teach such a doctrine, He would have required the young man to give away his goods, not to convey the title of ownership to another by a sale. The young man could not have sold what was not his. Again, Christ became a guest in the house of the rich man, Zacheus, and assured him, "this day is salvation come to this house." Zacheus had said: "Behold, Lord, the half of my goods I give to the poor." Christ did not command him to give away the other half as a condition of salvation.

Our Divine Lord did, indeed, emphasize the dangers of riches and denounce the rich in severe terms. "It is easier for a camel to pass through the eye of a needle, than for a rich man to enter into the Kingdom of Heaven." Nevertheless, He immediately added: "With men this is impossible, but with God all things are possible." The rich man who had rejected the plea of the beggar Lazarus is pictured in hell. The poor widow who contributed two brass mites to the treasury is praised above the rich men who had given of their abundance.

What Christ required was not that men should refrain from calling external goods their own, but that they should make a right use of such goods. He declared that salvation was come to the house of Zacheus when He heard that the latter was in the habit of giving half of his wealth to the poor. In His description of the last judgment He promised heaven to those who would feed the hungry, give drink to the thirsty, and clothe the naked. These are only a few of the Gospel indications that Christ made the right use and the proper distribution of private property one of the most binding and important of His commandments.

There is another element of Christ's teaching which has a very important bearing upon the doctrine of property. That is His insistence upon the intrinsic worth and sacredness of the human individual, and the essential equality of all human persons. From the fact that every human being has intrinsic worth, it follows that he has a moral claim upon the common means of life and of livelihood; from the fact that all persons are equal in the eyes of God and equally destined for eternal life, it follows that they have equal claims upon God's earthly bounty for at least the essentials of right and Christian living. It is true, indeed, that Christ nowhere formulated these propositions in the terms just used; nevertheless, they are a correct rendering of His teaching on these subjects. Because of this teaching, St. Paul could adjure Philemon to take back his runaway slave, Onesimus, "not now as a servant, but instead of a servant a most dear brother." Christ's teaching concerning the intrinsic worth and the essential equality of all human beings has important implications, not only with regard to spiritual goods and welfare, but also with respect to all things necessary for Christian living, including access to material goods. These implications have been recognized and applied by the authorities of the Church from the beginning until the present hour.

The most radical application of the doctrine of equality was made by the first Christians of Jerusalem who sold their individual possessions and "had all things in common, . . . and divided them to all, according as everyone had need." This was the Christian Communism which Socialists and other extremists sometimes point to as exemplifying the normal and necessary Christian attitude toward property. However, this contention is unsound, for two very good reasons. First, the arrangement was entirely voluntary, as we see from the words of St. Peter to Ananias: "Whilst it remained, did it not remain to thee? And after it was sold, was it not in thy power?" Here is a clear indication that none of the early Christians was morally bound to contribute his private property to the common store. In the second place, there is no evidence that community of goods was continued more than a few years among the early Christians. Apparently, it was due to the peculiar conditions of the faithful in Jerusalem, and possibly to the first fervor of new converts.

It is in the writings of some of the great Fathers of the Church in the fourth and fifth centuries that we find the most striking recognition of the claims of all men upon the bounty of the earth, and of the obligations of proprietors to make a right and social use of their goods. St. John Chrysostom exclaimed: "Are not the earth and the fullness thereof the Lord's? If, therefore, our possessions are the common gift of the Lord, they belong also to our fellows; for all the things of the Lord are common." Speaking to the rich of his day, St. Basil declared: "That bread which you keep belongs to the hungry; that coat which you preserve in your wardrobe, to the naked; those shoes which are rotting in your possession, to the barefooted; that gold which you have hidden in the ground, to the needy." According to St. Augustine: "The superfluities of the rich are the necessaries of the poor. They who possess superfluities, possess the goods of others." St. Ambrose declared that God intended the earth to be "the common possession of all," and that "the earth belongs to all, not to the rich." In the words of St. Gregory the Great: "When we give necessaries to the needy, we do not bestow upon them our goods; we return to them their own; we pay a debt of justice, rather than fulfill a work of mercy." St. Jerome quoted with approval a saying that was common in his time: "All riches come from iniquity, and unless one has lost, another cannot gain."

While very few subsequent writers or teachers of the Church used quite such strong language as that just quoted, they all taught the same doctrine in substance. According to St. Thomas Aquinas, it is right that property should be private with respect to the power of acquisition and disposal, but that it should be common as regards its use; the abundance of the rich belongs by natural right to the poor; the order of reason requires that a man should possess justly what he owns, and use it in a proper manner for himself and others; and finally the man who takes the goods of another to save himself from starvation is not guilty of theft. When Cardinal Manning, some thirty-five years ago, reiterated this doctrine of the right of the starving man to appropriate alien goods to save himself from starvation, he was denounced as an anarchist by some of the newspapers of that day. These journals showed that they were ignorant of the traditional Christian teaching of property rights; they knew only a false ethics of property.

According to the Christian conception, and according to the law of nature and of reason, the primary right of property is not the right of exclusive control, but the right of use. In other words, the common right of use is superior to the private right of ownership. God created the goods of the earth for the sustenance of all the people of the earth; consequently, the common right of all to enjoy these goods takes precedence of the particular right of any individual to hold them as his exclusive possession. To deny this subordination of the private to the common right, is to assert in effect that nature and nature's God have discriminated against some individuals, and in favor of others. Obviously, this assertion cannot be proved by any evidence drawn either from revelation or from reason. The fact that the State sometimes violates this order, exaggerating the privileges of private owners to such an extent as to deny the common right of all the general heritage, merely shows that the State can sometimes do wrong.

Nevertheless, this common right of property, the right of use, is not a sufficient provision for human welfare. Men need not only the general opportunity to use goods, the general right of access to the bounty of nature, but also the power of holding some goods as their own continuously. They require the power of excluding others from interference with those goods that they call their own. Without such a right and such powers, personal development, personal security, and adequate provision for family life are impossible. All this is evident with regard to those things which economists call "consumptive goods;" that is, those goods which are necessary for the direct and immediate satisfaction of human wants; such as food, clothing, shelter, household furniture, and some means of amusement, recreation, and moral, religious, and intellectual activities. The necessity of private ownership in these articles is not denied by anyone today, not even by Socialists.

As the term is ordinarily understood, private ownership means more than ownership of consumptive goods. It embraces more particularly productive goods, the natural and artificial means of production; such as lands, mines, railroads, factories, stores and banks. Today, all these are owned by private individuals or by corporations. With regard to this kind of private property, the Catholic Church, especially through Pope Leo XIII and his successors, has laid down positive and specific doctrine. Socialism, that is, State ownership of all the means of production, was condemned by Pope Leo XIII as detrimental to the working people and to society, and as contrary to the natural rights of the individual. According to the Catholic doctrine, therefore, the right of the individual or of a group of individuals to acquire and hold in private ownership some of the means of production, is in harmony with, and required by, the moral law of nature. The institution of private ownership, even in the means of production, is declared to be necessary for human welfare. Therefore, the State would injure human welfare and violate the moral law if it were to abolish all private property in the instruments of production.

However, care must be taken not to exaggerate the implications of this doctrine. All that it asserts is that the institution of private property in some of the means of production is morally lawful and morally necessary; all that it condemns is the contradictory system which would put the State in the position of owner and manager of all, or practically all, natural and artificial capital.

Therefore, the Catholic teaching does not condemn public ownership of what are called public utilities, such as railroads, telegraphs, street railways, and lighting concerns. It does not even condemn public ownership of one or more of the great instruments of production which are not included in the field of public utilities. For example, it has nothing to say against State ownership of mines, or State ownership of any other particular industry if this were a necessary means of preventing monopolistic extortion to the great detriment of the public welfare. Where the line should be drawn between State ownership of industries which is morally lawful and State ownership which encroaches upon the right of private property, cannot be exactly described beforehand. The question is entirely one of expediency and human welfare. In any case, the State is obliged to respect the right of the private owner to compensation for any of his goods that may be appropriated to the uses of the public.

Another caution concerns the actual distribution and the actual enjoyment of private property. While the Church opposes Socialism, it does not look with favor upon the restriction of capital ownership to a small minority of the population. Indeed, the considerations which move the Church to oppose the Socialist concentration of ownership, are an argument against a concentration in the hands of individuals and corporations. Every argument which Pope Leo XIII uses against Socialism is virtually a plea for a wide diffusion of capital ownership. The individual security and the provision for one's family which a man derives from private property, are obviously benefits which it is desirable to extend to the great majority of the citizens. It is not enough that private ownership should be maintained as a social institution. The institution should be so managed and regulated that its benefits will be directly shared by the largest possible number of individuals. Therefore, Pope Leo XIII declared explicitly that it is the duty of the State "to multiply property owners."

Therefore, those ultra conservative beneficiaries of the present order who see in the Church's condemnation of Socialism approval of the existing system with all its inequities, are utterly mistaken. They have missed the fundamental principles and aims of the Church's teaching. The Church advocates private ownership indeed, but she does not defend the present unnatural and anti-social concentration of ownership. She is interested in the welfare of all the people, and wishes that all should share directly in the benefits which private property provides.

So much for the *right* of private ownership. The *duties* of the proprietor occupy a no less important place in the Christian teaching. In general, they are a limitation upon the right of property. The right is exclusive as regards other individuals; that is to say, it excludes others than the proprietor from exercising the essential control which is conferred upon the proprietor. As regards God, the right of the proprietor is limited. Neither Christian teaching nor sound philosophy regards this right as absolute. The private owner is a steward of his goods rather than an irresponsible master. It is from the pagan code of Roman law, from the virtually pagan Code Napoleon, and from the unmoral and immoral principles of economic liberalism that has arisen the pernicious doctrine that "one may do what one pleases with one's own." The so-called "right of use and abuse" which has obtained such wide currency in industrial thought and practice, is in fundamental opposition to the Christian teaching.

The limitations set by that teaching to the powers and rights of the private owner follow logically from the Christian doctrine concerning the common bounty of nature, the common right of access to that bounty, and the recognition of the right of use as the primary right of property. Some of the duties of the private owner have already been pointed out by implication in our discussion of the teaching of the Fathers of the Church. In a general way, the obligations of the proprietor with regard to the right use of his goods may be thus formulated: He must so use and administer his property that other men shall enjoy the benefit of it on just terms and conditions. Only thus can the private right of property be reconciled with the superior common right of access to the bounty of the earth. One inference from the general principle was drawn by St. Thomas Aquinas, when he declared that a man's superfluous goods belong by natural right to the poor. For the time and society in which

St. Thomas wrote, this was probably the most important particular application of the principle. In the present social and industrial system, with its immense aggregations of capital and its enormous numbers of people whose livelihood depends upon their relation and access to these industrial enterprises, right use of property and the sharing of its benefits "on just terms and conditions," have different and far wider applications. Chief among these applications is the right of the worker to a living wage, and the right of the consumer to just prices. So much is certain. Right use, reasonable access to the common bounty, and participation in the benefits of property on just and reasonable conditions, may also require, and sometimes they do require, the recognition of labor unions, sharing by the workers in industrial management and in profits, and the limitation of rates of industrial interest by the State.

In any case, the general principles are clear: The earth is intended by God for the children of men; individuals or corporations that have appropriated any portion of the common bounty to their exclusive control and disposition hold it subject to this primary and fundamental social purpose; therefore, they are morally obliged to administer it in such a way that all who live by it, or depend upon it, shall enjoy the economic opportunity of a reasonable and normal life.

Although Pope Leo XIII condemns State ownership and management of *all* the instruments of production, he did not reject State regulation of private property. On the contrary, he laid down a principle which would give to the State all the power and authority which any reasonable person could desire over industrial relations, and for enforcing the limitations of ownership: "Whenever the general interest or any particular class suffers or is threatened with injury which can in no other way be met or prevented, it is the duty of the public authority to intervene." This principle would justify legislation of many kinds for a better use of private property and for a wider distribution of its benefits.

The Christian doctrine of property is sufficient, on the one hand, to protect the common interest and claims of all human beings, and on the other hand, to safeguard all the reasonable rights of individual proprietors. The evils which have existed and still exist in connection with private property are not inherent in the institution, as that institution is understood and defended by the Christian teaching. The most dangerous enemies of the institution are neither the exponents of the Christian teaching nor the social reformer generally, but those extreme upholders of the present system who cling to an autocratic and irresponsible theory of ownership which is as inconsistent with human welfare as it is contrary to the ideals of democracy.

115

PROPERTY AND SOCIALISM

Pope Leo XIII [1]

But all agree, and there can be no question whatever, that some remedy must be found, and found quickly, for the misery and wretchedness which press so heavily at this moment on the large majority of the very poor. The ancient workmen's Guilds were destroyed in the last century, and no other organization took their place. Public institutions and the laws have repudiated the ancient religion. Hence by degrees it has come to pass that working men have been given over, isolated and defenceless, to the callousness of employers and the greed of unrestrained competition. The evil has been increased by rapacious usury, which, although more than once condemned by the Church, is, nevertheless, under a different form but with the same guilt, still practiced by avaricious and grasping men. And to this must be added the custom of working by contract, and the concentration of so many branches of trade in the hands of a few individuals, so that a small number of very rich men have been able to lay upon the masses of the poor a yoke little better than slavery itself.

To remedy these evils the *Socialists,* working on the poor man's envy of the rich, endeavor to destroy private property, and maintain that individual possessions should become the common property of all, to be administered by the State or by municipal bodies. They hold that, by thus

---

[1] *The Great Encyclicals of Leo XIII,* pp. 209-216. (Benziger Brothers, New York.)

transferring property from private persons to the community, the present evil state of things will be set to rights, because each citizen will then have his equal share of whatever there is to enjoy. But their proposals are so clearly futile for all practical purposes, that if they were carried out the working man himself would be among the first to suffer. Moreover they are emphatically unjust, because they would rob the lawful possessor, bring the State into a sphere that is not its own, and cause complete confusion in the community.

It is surely undeniable that, when a man engages in remunerative labor, the very reason and motive of his work is to obtain property, and to hold it as his own private possession. If one man hires out to another his strength or his industry, he does this for the purpose of receiving in return what is necessary for food and living; he thereby expressly proposes to acquire a full and real right, not only to the remuneration, but also to the disposal of that remuneration as he pleases. Thus, if he lives sparingly, saves money, and invests his savings, for greater security, in land, the land in such a case is only his wages in another form; and, consequently, a working man's little estate thus purchased should be as completely at his own disposal as the wages he receives for his labor. But it is precisely in this power of disposal that ownership consists, whether the property be land or movable goods. The *Socialists*, therefore, in endeavoring to transfer the possessions of individuals to the community, strike at the interests of every wage earner, for they deprive him of the liberty of disposing of his wages, and thus of all hope and possibility of increasing his stock and of bettering his condition in life.

What is of still greater importance, however, is that the remedy they propose is manifestly against justice. For every man has by nature the right to possess property as his own. This is one of the chief points of distinction between man and the animal creation. For the brute has no power of self-direction, but is governed by two chief instincts, which keep his powers alert, move him to use his strength, and determine him to action without the power of choice. These instincts are self-preservation and the propagation of the species. Both can attain their purpose by means of things which are close at hand; beyond their surroundings the brute creation cannot go, for they are moved to action by sensibility alone, and by the things which sense perceives. But with man it is different indeed. He possesses, on the one hand, the full perfection of animal nature, and therefore he enjoys, at least, as much as the rest of the animal race, the fruition of the things of the body. But animality, however perfect, is far from being the whole of humanity, and is indeed humanity's humble handmaid, made to serve and obey. It is the mind, or the reason, which is the chief thing in us who are human beings; it is this which makes a human being human, and distinguishes him essentially and completely from the brute. And on this account—viz., that man alone among animals possesses reason—it must be within his right to have things not merely for temporary and momentary use, as other living beings have them, but in stable and permanent possession; he must have not only things which perish in the using, but also those which, though used, remain for use in the future.

This becomes still more clearly evident if we consider man's nature a little more deeply. For man, comprehending by the power of his reason things innumerable, and joining the future with the present—being, moreover, the master of his own acts—governs himself by the foresight of his counsel, under the eternal law and the power of God, Whose Providence governs all things. Wherefore it is in his power to exercise his choice not only on things which regard his present welfare, but also on those which will be for his advantage in time to come. Hence man not only can possess the fruits of the earth, but also the earth itself; for of the products of the earth he can make provision for the future. Man's needs do not die out, but recur; satisfied to-day, they demand new supplies to-morrow. Nature, therefore, owes to man a storehouse that shall never fail, the daily supply of his daily wants. And this he finds only in the inexhaustible fertility of the earth.

Nor must we, at this stage, have recourse to the State.

Man is older than the State and he holds the right of providing for the life of his body prior to the formation of any State. And to say that God has given the earth to the use and enjoyment of the universal human race is not to deny that there can be private property. For God has granted the earth to mankind in general; not in the sense that all without distinction can deal with it as they please, but rather that no part of it has been assigned to any one in particular, and that the limits of private possession have been left to be fixed by man's own industry and the laws of individual peoples. Moreover, the earth, though divided among private owners, ceases not thereby to minister to the needs of all; for there is no one who does not live on what the land brings forth. Those who do not possess the soil, contribute their labor; so that it may be truly said that all human subsistence is derived either from labor on one's own land, or from some laborious industry which is paid for either in the produce of the land itself or in that which is exchanged for what the land brings forth.

Here, again, we have another proof that private ownership is according to nature's law. For that which is required for the preservation of life and for life's well-being, is produced in great abundance by the earth, but not until man has brought it into cultivation and lavished upon it his care and skill. Now, when man thus spends the industry of his mind and the strength of his body in procuring the fruits of nature, by that act he makes his own that portion of nature's field which he cultivates—that portion on which he leaves, as it were, the impress of his own personality; and it cannot but be just that he should possess that portion as his own, and should have a right to keep it without molestation.

These arguments are so strong and convincing that it seems surprising that certain obsolete opinions should now be raised in opposition to what is here laid down. We are told that it is right for private persons to have the use of the soil and the fruits of the land, but that it is unjust for anyone to possess as owner either the land on which he has built or the estate which he has cultivated. But those who assert this do not perceive that they are robbing man of what his own labor has produced. For the soil which is tilled and cultivated with toil and skill utterly changes its condition; it was wild before, it is now fruitful; it was barren, and now it brings forth in abundance. That which has thus altered and improved it becomes so truly part of itself as to be in a great measure indistinguishable and inseparable from it. Is it just that the fruit of a man's sweat and labor should be enjoyed by another? As effects follow their cause, so it is just and right that the results of labor should belong to him who has labored.

With reason, therefore, the common opinion of mankind, little affected by the few dissentients who have maintained the opposite view, has found in the study of nature, and in the law of nature herself, the foundations of the division of property, and has consecrated by the practice of all ages the principle of private ownership, as being pre-eminently in conformity with human nature, and as conducing in the most unmistakable manner to the peace and tranquility of human life. The same principle is confirmed and enforced by the civil laws—laws which, as long as they are just, derive their binding force from the law of nature. The authority of the Divine Law adds its sanction, forbidding us in the gravest terms even to covet that which is another's: *Thou shalt not covet thy neighbor's wife; nor his house, nor his field, nor his man-servant, nor his maid-servant, nor his ox, nor his ass, nor anything which is his.*[2]

The rights here spoken of belonging to each individual man, are seen in a much stronger light if they are considered in relation to man's social and domestic obligations.

In choosing a state of life, it is indisputable that all are at full liberty either to follow the counsel of Jesus Christ as to virginity, or to enter into the bonds of marriage. No human law can abolish the natural and primitive right of marriage, or in any way limit the chief and principal purpose of marriage, ordained by God's authority from the beginning. *Increase and multiply.*[3] Thus we have the family; the "society" of a man's own household; a society limited indeed in numbers, but a true "society," anterior to every kind of State or nation, with rights and duties of its own, totally independent of the commonwealth.

That right of property, therefore, which has been proved to belong naturally to individual persons must also belong to a man in his capacity of head of a family; nay, such a person must possess this right so much the more clearly in proportion as his position multiplies his duties. For it is a most sacred law of nature that a father must provide food and all necessaries for those whom he has begotten; and,

---

[2] Deuteronomy v. 21.
[3] Genesis i. 28.

similarly, nature dictates that a man's children, who carry on, as it were, and continue his own personality, should be provided by him with all that is needful to enable them honorably to keep themselves from want and misery in the uncertainties of this mortal life. Now, in no other way can a father effect this except by the ownership of profitable property, which he can transmit to his children by inheritance. A family, no less than a State, is, as we have said, a true society, governed by a power within itself, that is to say, by the father. Wherefore, provided the limits be not transgressed which are prescribed by the very purposes for which it exists, the family has, at least, equal rights with the State in the choice and pursuit of those things which are needful to its preservation and its just liberty.

We say, at least equal rights; for since the domestic household is anterior both in idea and in fact to the gathering of men into a commonwealth, the former must necessarily have rights and duties which are prior to those of the latter, and which rest more immediately on nature. If the citizens of a State—that is to say, the families—on entering into association and fellowship, experienced at the hands of the State hindrance instead of help, and found their rights attacked instead of being protected, such association were rather to be repudiated than sought after.

The idea, then, that the civil government should, at its own discretion, penetrate and pervade the family and the household, is a great and pernicious mistake. True, if a family finds itself in great difficulty, utterly friendless, and without prospect of help, it is right that extreme necessity be met by public aid; for each family is a part of the commonwealth. In like manner, if within the walls of the household there occur grave disturbance of mutual rights, the public power must interfere to force each party to give the other what is due; for this is not to rob citizens of their rights, but justly and properly to safeguard and strengthen them. But the rulers of the State must go no further: nature bids them stop here. Paternal authority can neither be abolished by the State nor absorbed; for it has the same source as human life itself; "the child belongs to the father," and is, as it were, the continuation of the father's personality; and, to speak with strictness, the child takes its place in civil society not in its own right, but in its quality as a member of the family in which it is begotten. And it is for the very reason that "the child belongs to the father," that, as St. Thomas of Aquin says, "before it attains the use of free-will, it is in the power and care of its parent."[4] The Socialists, therefore, in setting aside the parent and introducing the providence of the State, act *against natural justice,* and threaten the very existence of family life.

And such interference is not only unjust, but is quite certain to harass and disturb all classes of citizens, and to subject them to odious and intolerable slavery. It would open the door to envy, to evil speaking, and to quarreling; the sources of wealth would themselves run dry, for no one would have any interest in exerting his talents or his industry; and that ideal equality of which so much is said would, in reality, be the leveling down of all to the same condition of misery and dishonor.

Thus it is clear that the main tenet of *Socialism,* the community of goods, must be utterly rejected; for it would injure those whom it is intended to benefit, it would be contrary to the natural rights of mankind, and it would introduce confusion and disorder into the commonwealth. Our first and most fundamental principle, therefore, when we undertake to alleviate the condition of the masses, must be the inviolability of private property.

116

SOCIALISM

Peter Finlay [1]

I.—The deadly plague which is tainting society to its very core, and bringing it to a state of extreme peril. . . . We are alluding to that sect of men who, under the motley and all but barbarous terms and titles of Socialists, Communists, and Nihilists are spread abroad throughout the world, and . . . strive to carry out the purpose long resolved upon, of uprooting the foundations of civilized society. . . . From the heads of States to whom, as the Apostle admonishes, all owe submission, and on whom the rights of authority are bestowed by God

---

[4] St. Thomas, *Summa Theologica* 2a 2æ Q. x. Art. 12.
[1] *Studies,* September, 1919.

Himself, these sectaries withhold obedience, and preach the perfect equality of all men, in regard to rights alike and duties. The natural union of man and woman, which is held sacred even among barbarous nations, they hold in scorn; and its bond, whereby family life is chiefly maintained, they weaken or yield up to the sway of lust. And finally, spurred on by greedy hankering after things present . . . they attack the right of property, sanctioned by the law of nature, and . . . strain every nerve to seize upon and hold in common all that has been individually acquired by title of lawful inheritance, through intellectual and manual labor, or economy in living. —Leo XIII: Encycl. *Quod Apost. Muneris,* 1878. (*The Great Encyclical Letters,* pp. 22-23—Benziger.)

The Church recognizes the existence of inequality amongst men . . . and she enjoins that the right of property and of its disposal, derived from nature, should, in the case of every individual, remain intact and inviolate.—Leo XIII: *Ibid,* p. 30.

Every man has by nature the right to possess property as his own. This is one of the chief points of difference between man and the animal creation. . . . Man not only can possess the fruits of the earth, but also the very soil, inasmuch as from the produce of the earth he has to lay by provision for the future . . . for God has granted the earth to mankind in general, not in the sense that all without distinction can deal with it as they like, but rather that no part of it has been assigned to any one in particular, and that the limits of private possession have been left to be fixed by man's own industry and by the laws of individual races.—Leo XIII: Encycl.: *Rerum Novarum,* 1891. (*The Great Encycl. Letters,* pp. 210, 212.)

Hence it is clear that the main tenet of Socialism, community of goods, must be utterly rejected, since it . . . is directly contrary to the natural rights of mankind, and would introduce confusion and disorder into the commonwealth.—Leo XIII: *Ibid.,* p. 216.

II.—It is a suggestive and amusing fact that in the motley ranks of the defenders of capitalism the professional propagandists of freethought are comrades-in-arms of His Holiness the Pope: the ill-reasoned and inconclusive Encyclical lately issued against Socialism makes of the hierarchy of the Catholic Church belated camp followers in the armies marching under the banners raised by the agnostic exponents of the individualist philosophy.—James Connolly: *The New Evangel preached to Irish Toilers,* p. 4. (Published by the Socialist Party of Ireland, Liberty Hall, Dublin.)

Would you confiscate the property of the capitalist class and rob men of that which they have, perhaps, worked a whole lifetime to accumulate? Yes, sir, and certainly not. . . . Socialism will confiscate the property of the capitalist and in return will secure the individual against poverty and oppression; it, in return for so confiscating, will assure to all men and women a free, happy, and unanxious human life.—James Connolly: *Socialism Made Easy, pp.* 5-6. (Socialist Labour Press, Glasgow.)

The capital of the master class is not their property; it is the unpaid labor of the working class—the hire of the laborer kept back by fraud.—James Connolly: *Ibid.,* p. 7.

Law, morality, religion are for him (the proletarian) merely so many bourgeois prejudices, behind which as many bourgeois interests are concealed. . . .

The proletarians have nothing of their own to secure. They must destroy all previous securities for and insurances of individual property. . . .

The Communists can condense their theory into one sentence: abolition of private property.—Karl Marx and Friedrich Engels: *Manifesto of the Communist Party,* pp. 14, 16. (Socialist Labour Press, Glasgow.)

Nothing is more ridiculous than the virtuous horror of our bourgeois at the community of women, which he pretends will be officially established by the Communists. The Communists have no need to introduce community of women; it has nearly always existed . . . Bourgeois marriage is in reality community of wives. The Communists could at most be accused of wishing to replace a hypocritical and concealed community of women by an official and open community of women.—Marx and Engels: *Ibid.,* p. 19.

The first act wherein the State appears as the real representative of the whole body social—the seizure of the means of production in the name of society—is also its last independent act as State. The interference of the State in social relations becomes superfluous in one domain after another, and falls of itself into desuetude. . . . The State is not "abolished" —*it dies out.*—Frederick Engels: *The Development of Socialism from Utopia to Science,* p. 26. (Socialist Labour Press, Glasgow.)

III.—Russian Soviet Constitution. Adopted by the fifth All-Russian Congress of Soviets at its sitting of July 10, 1918. Chapter II, 3:—

(*a*) All private property in land is abrogated and all land is declared to be the common property of the people, and is handed over to the workers without compensation to its previous owners, on the basis of equalised use.

(*b*) All forests, mines, and waters of national importance, as well as all live stock and fixtures, model estates and agricultural concerns are declared to be the property of the nation.

(c) As a first step towards the complete transference to the Soviet Republic of Workers and Peasants of all factories, works, mines, railways, and other means of production and transport. . . .

(e) The nationalisation of all banks is hereby confirmed.

Chap. V., 13.—With a view to ensuring to the workers true liberty of conscience, the Church is disestablished in the State and in the school, and freedom of religious and anti-religious propaganda is granted to all citizens.—*New Russia,* pp. 7, 9. (The Socialist Party of Ireland, Room 3, Liberty Hall, Dublin.)

Greetings to the Bolshevik Republic! Greetings and heartiest congratulations on this the first anniversary of its birth. . . .

New Russia appeals to all to stand by her, or at least to give her a sympathetic understanding. She appeals especially to the young men and women of Ireland, who are still full of hope and faith, and who have not yet outlived their ideals, who are strong and brave of heart, and who can thrill to noble deeds, etc., etc.—"From an Irish Socialist" in *New Russia,* pp. 19, 21.

These extracts—and many similar ones might be added—prove conclusively that:—

(a) There is a form of Socialism which Leo XIII, the supreme teaching authority of the Catholic Church, has explicitly condemned.

(b) That form is the one preached by Marx and Engels, and at present seeking expression in the Soviet Republic of Russia;

(c) It is the form which the Socialist Labour Party in England and Scotland are preparing to set up; and which the Socialist Party of Ireland recommend to Irish workers, from their headquarters in Liberty Hall.

And there is no need to discuss at any length the Socialism which the Pope condemns, or to argue that it contradicts the plain and perpetual teaching of the Catholic Church. Indeed, the three chief doctrines which it involves—injustice of private ownership, particularly in land; community of women; abolition of all civil authority—are so clearly at variance with divinely revealed truth that they never came into prominence in either Jewish or Christian Church, or called for any formal condemnation. The moral law, imposed or approved by God Himself, in both Testaments, emphatically condemns them. There is no place in the Marxian system for the Ten Commandments, or the

Sermon on the Mount, or the Christian Sacraments, or the Gospel Counsels. Socialism, as propounded by Marx, Engels, Lassalle, and their disciples, and as it has taken hold on large numbers of the workers throughout Europe and America, is wholly materialistic: it knows nothing of God or of a future life. It is even actively and bitterly hostile to Christianity, and especially to that Catholic religion which we ourselves profess. We see it in operation in the Russia of our own day, where it tramples on the Greek Church with a ferocity only equalled by Turkish misrule in Asia. There are many among us who remember the anti-Catholic excesses of the Paris Communards in 1871. And we have grown accustomed during the last half century to the anti-clerical and irreligious legislation, and attempts at such legislation, by the Socialist parties in Italy, France, Belgium, Spain, England—wherever Socialism has gained political power. Hence adherents of the Socialism condemned by the three last Popes—that international socialism which is formulated in the extracts from propagandist pamphlets which I have quoted, and which James Connolly and his friends laboured strenuously to introduce into Ireland—are excommunicate. They are assuredly members of "an association which is plotting against the Church or lawful civil authorities." (J. C.: Can. 2335.)

But the name Socialism is not limited to the doctrines and movements just described. It is applied frequently to theories which have little in common with those that have been adopted by the Socialist Labour Parties. There is a Socialism—State or Municipal—which seeks to withhold the ownership or at least the control of sources of production and means of distribution from private individuals, while it makes no attack on religion or on civil governments.

"The result of civil change and revolution," says Leo XIII (*Rerum Novarum,* p. 237), "has been to divide society into two widely differing classes. On the one side there is the party which holds power because it holds wealth; which has in its grasp the whole of labour and trade; which manipulates for its own benefit and its own purposes all the sources of supply, and which is represented in the councils of the State itself. On the other side there is the needy and powerless multitude, broken down and suffering, and ever ready for disturbance." And again: "By degrees it has come to pass that workingmen have been surrendered, all isolated and helpless, to the hard-heartedness of employers and the greed of unchecked competition. The mischief has been increased by rapacious usury. ... To this must be added the custom of working by contract, and the concentration of so many branches of trade in the hands of a few individuals; so that a small number of very rich men have been able to lay upon the teeming masses of the labouring poor a yoke little better than that of slavery itself" (p. 209). And he adds: "Whenever the general interest or any particular class suffers, or is threatened with mischief which can in no other way be met or prevented, the public authority must step in to deal with it. ... Limits must be determined by the nature of the occasion which calls for the law's interference: the principle being that the law must not undertake more, nor proceed further, than is required for the remedy of the evil or the removal of the mischief" (pp. 230-1).

Few will be disposed to question the accuracy of the Pope's statements. Whatever may be the precise influence of the various causes which can be assigned—the destruction of the guild system, the growth of large industrial towns, the increasing use of perfected machinery and its substitution for human labour, the conditions of land tenure, the change from individual to company employers, facilities of communication, the setting aside of religion in public life—the fact is beyond controversy that never before in Christian history has there been such a contrast between rich and poor; such a concentration of the material good things of life in the hands of a few, and such utter destitution among the many. Never did the toil of the worker bring him a smaller share of the riches he produces. Never were the profits of the employer and the income of the wage earner so plainly in opposition. Never was class enmity so widespread and so bitter. "The teeming masses of the labouring poor," as Leo XIII says, bear "a yoke little better than slavery." Surely we have here an evil which, as the Pope adds, "the public authority must step in to deal with." Experience of human nature proves that nowhere else can any remedy be looked for.

But what remedy can the State apply? No one, except the revolutionary socialists, whom, as we have seen, all Catholic teaching condemns, has suggested the total abolition of private property. Community of goods has been tried in various voluntary societies, more particularly in the United States. It has succeeded nowhere, unless in the Religious Orders of the Catholic Church and in the Jesuit Reductions of Paraguay, and there under conditions which ordinarily civil society can never reproduce. The theory even has been maintained by some Catholic writers upon ethics that private ownership is commanded by the Law of Nature, and, therefore, by God Himself: that a man has not only the right but the duty to make provision for both his present and his future wants; and that, to do so, he must have not only the use but the ownership of property. The argument is not convincing. If it were, the Catholic Church would have greatly erred in encouraging a Vow of Poverty which forbids all private ownership, and in permitting her ministers to establish community of goods in Paraguay. Besides, even when we admit that man is bound to provide for present and future needs, and not for himself only but for those as well who are dependent on him, it nowise follows that, to make provision, he must acquire ownership of property: a right of use is abundantly sufficient.

Nor, indeed, if we distinguish between use and ownership, will it be easy to bring satisfactory proof that man has a natural right to own the necessary means of subsistence. Under normal conditions, he has a natural right to live, or rather to the usual and necessary requisites for the preservation of life. But if the use of such requisites, as distinct from their ownership, be sufficient for his purpose, it may be argued that his right extends no further.

On the other hand, it is evident that Catholic teaching lends no support to the theory that private ownership is essentially immoral. Not many will be found to maintain it, as regards the things which perish in our very use of them—food, drink, clothing, and the like; but not a few accept it, when applied to more permanent things—ways of communication, sources of production, coal, minerals, the very land itself; and in this latter sense the theory has met with considerable favour in recent times. We became to some extent familiar with it, when Mr. Henry George in America and Mr. Michael Davitt in Ireland sought to popularise their views on a Single Tax and Land Nationalisation. We hear much more of it to-day, when it has been largely adopted by a section of socialist and labour leaders. At the moment there is question only or mainly of coal and minerals; though there is no valid ground for the limitation. The miners are told that the earth is the common property of all mankind; that what individual man has not produced he can have neither natural nor God-given right to; that appropriation by individuals is a mere theft of inalienable public property: the nation may, or rather must, resume its ownership—and without compensation to the thieves.

Now, on this theory so put forward, it should be observed, in the first place, that it rests on simple assertions unaccompanied by any proof. There is, there can be, no proof that the earth—the whole or any portion of it—is the common property of all mankind. No proof has ever been given, indeed it is demonstrably false, that production is either the sole or the sufficient ground of ownership. And, further, the theory is halting and illogical. Are we to be told that all other peoples—the Germans, the Chinese, the Kaffirs—have the same right to the soil of Ireland, and to all which it contains, that our Irish farmers have? And if not, why not? If the whole earth belongs inalienably to all mankind, how can any portion of it—a field, a province, a country—belong to any group of men? If the land and mines of Ireland are to be nationalised, why should it be for the advantage of Irishmen only? What valid reason can be suggested, in the theory we are considering, for thinking that God or nature has given the soil and minerals of Ireland to the present inhabitants of the island collectively, and not also to those of Great Britain and of the wide world generally? Finally, the theory is contradicted by the whole current of divine revelation and of Church teaching down to our own day. In the Old Testament we find no trace of communal ownership either of land or of other goods; nor does God manifest any disapproval of the Jewish social system; rather, He Himself (Levit. xxv.) expressly confirms and sanctions the rights of private owners. In the New Testament—as in the parable of the vineyard (Matt. xxi.) and elsewhere—Our Lord assumes the justice of individual property in land, and emphasizes the rights that attach to it. Of the "piece of land" which Ananias sold (Acts v.) St. Peter says to him: "While it remained, did it not remain thine own? And, after it was sold, was it not in thy power?" In the Patristic writings and in the schools of theology we meet frequently with discussion on the nature of the right by which individual property in land is held; but that such property is in itself legitimate, in full accord with divine and natural law, is never called in question: it is taken for granted, when not expressly and positively asserted. And Leo XIII, as is plain from our quotations, teaches authoritatively that private ownership of land, as of other things, so far from being in opposition to the principles of reason and of religion, is in perfect harmony with both, and is based on the rights of the individual and the welfare of civil society.

It is not, therefore, lawful for a Catholic to embrace that form of Socialism which holds all the sources of production—land, coal, minerals, waterpower, and the rest—to be of right the inalienable property of the collective people, state, or province, and denies that in these things there can be any just private ownership. Such a form of socialism is in contradiction with revealed religion, and is condemned by the perpetual teaching, implicit and express, of the Catholic Church.

But there remains a further and more important, because more practical, question for examination: admitting the entire lawfulness of private ownership in all the sources of production and distribution, is it obligatory on the State to permit such ownership; or, may the State forbid or abolish it, when the common welfare appears to require its abolition? May the State, for instance, without violation of natural or divine law, nationalize all the coal, iron, copper and other minerals of the country; all the means of communication by land and air and water; and the whole soil itself? And, for the very reason that the question is practical, it is not concerned with an abstract right of ownership, as distinct from right of use and administration. The nationalization of the coal mines, which so many English miners demand to-day, is one under which the people, through the government, is to own the mines, and work them, and bear whatever loss or appropriate whatever profit may result from the working. Under land-nationalization, the State would be the sole landlord, would impose upon its tenants whatever burthens the land could carry; and would absorb all but the minimum of profit, without which no tenants could be found to cultivate it.

Now, it is no part of our purpose to determine here if a convincing case has been made out for nationalizing land or mines. Nationalization of Irish land is not even discussed in Ireland to-day. The tendency of legislation for the last fifty years, and the ceaseless struggle of our people to become individual owners of their farms, make it unlikely that any scheme of State ownership will gain favor amongst us. It is otherwise with the mines; no large body of the people can ever hope to become mining proprietors, unless under a nationalization scheme. They see in it no sacrifice of present or prospective personal rights. They would generally regard the experiment with indifference. But the ethical principles which underlie all schemes of nationalization are identical; it cannot be unjust or immoral to nationalize land, if it be not unjust and immoral to nationalize coal and minerals.

That any scheme of nationalization will be of benefit to the people, or to the workers in particular, is far from certain. Experiments have been already made in various of the public services; and the result seems generally to be less efficiency at greater cost. On the 1st of August last the United States Government relinquished control of telephone and telegraph lines, and the "Postal and Telegraph Co.," which took them over, at once announced a reduction of twenty per cent in the rates and a considerable improvement in their working. Among ourselves, no one will allow that the telephone system is as satisfactory as when in the hands of a private company; and it is now worked at a serious loss, while before its purchase by the Government it made a handsome profit. In France, before the war, the worst managed railways were State-owned; and we see what State control has done, and at what a cost, for the railways of the United Kingdom. But there is no need to quote further from the long list of admitted failures in attempts at nationalization. Such attempts can only benefit the workers and the nation generally, if they increase the output of labor, or lessen the cost of production, or prevent strife between employers and employed. And already a considerable experience seems to show that the State, as owner or employer, can scarcely hope to secure all or any of these things. In every branch of industrialism in which comparison can be made, private enterprise appears to produce better results than the State is able to produce, at less cost and with at least an equal share of profits to the workers.

But, as we have already noted, it is no part of our present purpose to discuss at any length a question which is the subject of much and warm controversy. Whatever may be the economic aspect of nationalization, we are here concerned solely with its lawfulness; and with its lawfulness, only in the hypothesis of its being to the advantage, certainly not to the detriment, of the State. So formulated, under such limitations, is there anything in Catholic teaching to prevent Catholics from accepting the theory of nationalization, and from furthering its application to all merely material sources of production and distribution? May they, in this sense, be State Socialists? If State Socialists, they may, of course, be Municipal Socialists as well.

To this question only one answer appears possible: there is nothing in Catholic teaching opposed to State or Municipal Socialism, as we have just explained it. No Catholic, lay or clerical, would dream of intervening in the present controversy on coal mines with a declaration that their nationalization must be regarded by Catholics as absolutely immoral, that under all circumstances it is contrary to the law of God. Under the pressure of war necessities the State became the owner of vast industries, and took over the control of many more; and no one questioned the State's right to do so. In peace time the State owns great tracts of Irish land, and it is part owner of many thousands of other acres. It owns and manages the posts, telegraphs, and telephones, which it acquired, by Act of Parliament and purchase, from private companies. We have already advanced not a little way on the road of State Socialism; and it is one and the same principle which underlies and justifies much of what has been already done, and which is believed to recommend the further developments we are considering. There is no essential difference between telegraphs and railways; between ownership of coal mines and ownership of factories; between land owned by the Congested Districts Board or the Land Commission and any other land. If the public need or public welfare can justify nationalization in any of these cases, it can justify it in all; the only issue reasonably open to doubt or controversy will be one of facts and circumstances.

Besides, it has never been a teaching of the Church, or a common doctrine of her schools, that private ownership of property such as coal and other minerals, railways and other high roads, the very soil itself, is prescribed by any natural or divine law. The great Catholic theologians have always held, with one or other exception, that private ownership is of natural right in the sense that it is allowed by nature; that it is singularly helpful to the well-being of civil society; that, under ordinary social conditions, it is necessary for social peace and progress; and that, under those conditions, and while they last, "division of goods" (*divisio bonorum*), and specifically "division of land" (*divisio agrorum*), should be the rule amongst mankind. But the rule is not absolute, as we have already pointed out: not independent of time and place and other circumstances. It is based upon considerations of general usefulness: and if the welfare of the people requires, it may be set aside.

As, then, in time of war the State may expropriate and control private owners, in so far as may be necessary for its existence and welfare, so too may it, in time of peace, if and in so far as the welfare of the people makes expropriation necessary.

But not without fitting compensation, if compensation be possible. If it were true, as some labor leaders assert, that private ownership of land and mines and railways is essentially unjust, then confiscation would be a lawful remedy; you cannot in justice be bound to make compensation to a thief or to the heirs of a thief, when you claim the restoration of your own property. But there is no warrant for the assertion, and no Catholic may allow it. Private ownership of land and mines may be as lawful as private ownership of the bread I eat and the water that I drink. And, if I am in lawful possession of any of these things, there is no authority on earth which may justly deprive me of it, unless for the common weal, and with due compensation. I stand in need of food and clothing; but I may not deprive others, the lawful owners, of them without payment, if I have the means to pay. And the argument of Pope Leo XIII, in a letter quoted at the beginning of this article, is conclusive: If a workman "lives sparingly, saves money, and invests his savings in land, the land in such case is only his wages under another form." (*Great Encyclicals*, p. 210.) The Pope does not say that the workman has necessarily a right to invest his savings in land; there may be no land available, and, even were there, there is no greater natural right to invest savings in land than in any other security—for instance, in Government telegraphs and telephones. But the Pope does teach that, if he do put his savings into land, because he so chooses, and there is no lack of the commodity, State monopoly, or dearth of vendors, to prevent him, then the workman owns the land as he had owned his wages; it is as much robbery to deprive him, without compensation, of the one as of the other. And there are many other titles by which land may lawfully be held as well as by the investment of a worker's wages. If, therefore, the State should judge it necessary or expedient, in the interest of the whole people, to nationalize the property of individuals or of private corporations, it can justly do so only by purchasing the property, by making compensation to the lawful owners.

Nationalization, then, of all a country's sources of production and means of distribution, Socialism so defined and limited, presents no difficulty in principle to a Catholic. If the manual workers, who form, and must always form, the great majority of our populations, whose toil is generally so hopeless, whose privations are so many and so intense, whose share is so insignificant in all the wealth which they produce—if they are to find in it a remedy for the evils that oppress them, the Church and her teaching will place no hindrance in their way. That it is likely to prove a remedy is believed to be improbable by many of those best qualified to judge; past experience gives little ground for hope. But Catholic teaching sets no obstacle in the way of further and larger experiments.

117
SOCIALISM AND RELIGIOUS ORDERS
BERNARD VAUGHAN [1]

Socialists are fond of pointing to the religious orders, and claiming them as concrete examples of Socialism.

It is true that from some points of view a religious order may be called socialistic, or rather communistic. But it differs from Socialism, as commonly propounded, in several important particulars, with the result that it forms no precedent from which the modern Socialist may argue. The religious rule is based upon the religious vows, and is quite incapable of general application. Religious orders consist of men and women who *voluntarily* cut themselves off from family life, commercial pursuits, and the like, in order to devote themselves to the sanctification of themselves and their neighbors. Comparatively few make suitable candidates for a religious order. A long and severe training tests the capacity of each. Those who, after such training, voluntarily elect to join the order, find the life tolerable, not because it is naturally pleasant, but because it is supernaturally satisfying. Even these may sometimes discover that community life is, after all, too great a strain upon them, and may apply to the Holy See for a dispensation from their vows, and return once more to a life in which not so much is required of them.

True, there is much happiness in religious orders. Those who have had a glimpse of the life, and do not form their estimate of it from sensational paragraphs in the gutter press about "escaped nuns," often look wistfully and half enviously at the serene and satisfying atmosphere of a monastery or of a convent, the delicate charity, the absence of sordid cares, the security, and the hope to be found there. That is all true. But the secret of this happiness does not lie in the economic arrangements of religious orders. It comes from their spirit of renunciation and loving service, without which life in religion would be unendurable. To attempt to force men who have not this spirit into the

---

[1] *Socialism from the Christian Standpoint,* pp. 233-236. (The Macmillan Company, New York.)

severe discipline of a monastic institution would be the most outrageous tyranny. It would be impossible of achievement. Nothing but strong ambition for God's glory, and zeal for the sanctification of souls; nothing but a community of spirit, and a tremendous personal love of Jesus Christ could make it possible for religious communities to live together under the discipline of rule, bearing one another's burdens, and exercising mutual patience and charity.

We have seen therefore that the attempt to base Socialism on Christianity breaks down all along the line. It can only be made by perverting the plain sense of the Gospels, misinterpreting history, and ignoring the very marked characteristics of Socialism as an actual movement.

The position of the Catholic Church in the matter has been clear and consistent. She has watched the socialist movement in its growth (as she has watched every political and social movement in its growth for nineteen centuries), and she has seen it developing along lines which are incompatible with Christian beliefs and standards. She definitely tells her children to keep clear of it. Unlike the Bishop of Durham, she will not "venture to use the word apart from its historical associations"—for she knows well to what confusion of ideas such a twisting of terminology may lead. Eager as she is to take her part in social reform, and to establish a Christian Democracy, she will not call her efforts by the name of Socialism or allow her children to join socialist bodies. For the name now stands for a definite movement with anti-Christian implications. It is idle to urge that the name denotes an economic theory only and that the movement might have proceeded on Christian lines. As a matter of fact it has not done so, and we must accept the facts as we find them. For the same reason the Church does not favor the use of the term "Christian Socialism," since it is productive of misunderstandings. Leo XIII ("Graves de Communi") observed that it had "justly fallen into desuetude." Let us define our terms and know what we are speaking about. Let us not forget that Christianity is one thing and Socialism another. The two systems work in opposite directions, and flow into different termini. Socialism makes for a Paradise beneath the moon; Christianity leads to a Heaven beyond the stars.

118

HENRY GEORGE AND THE SINGLE-TAX THEORY

Charles S. Devas [1]

Henry George (1839-1897) set forth most attractively in his "Progress and Poverty" (1897) the theory that not merely all future, but all actual unearned increment should be intercepted, the method being the total appropriation of rent by taxation, a single tax on land values replacing all other taxes. This "simple yet sovereign remedy" would raise wages and profits, abolish poverty, lessen crime, elevate morals, and purify government. Indeed this single-tax theory appeared to its author so self-evident that he reproached the Pope for not having, in his Labor Encyclical (Rerum Novarum, 1891), accepted its reasoning (Open Letter to Pope Leo XIII, New York, 1891). "Progress and Poverty" was translated into eleven languages; a Land-Nationalization Society, still existent (1906), was founded in England under Dr. A. Russel Wallace (author of "Land Nationalization," London, 1882), who, indeed, allowed to actual landlords what George calls "the impudent plea" of compensation; the single-tax was advocated by Flurscheim in Germany, and, under the persistent misnomer of "land reform," still has a German Society to support it (Adolf Damaschke, "Die Bodenreform," Berlin, 1902).

Henry George has been criticized from the economic, the juridical, and the socialist standpoint on the following grounds: (a) That "rent," in the sense of an unearned increment, is not confined to land, but is seen in all forms of production, wherever a common market price yields a surplus to those who can produce more cheaply than their competitors. (b) That we can separate "the original powers of the soil from the land as transformed by culture" (e. g., drainage or accessibility), or separate "property in things created by God" from "property in things made by man," much of so-called "rent" being merely interest on previous expenditure, and the part that is really unearned increment rarely ascertainable. (c) That neither theoreti-

---

[1] *Catholic Encyclopedia*, Vol. 1, pp. 228, 229.

cally nor historically true is the alleged tendency to a perpetual rise of rent; the amount depending on differential advantages, the difference incessantly fluctuating up and down, according to every change in production, consumption, and communication; and the final twenty years of George's life witnessing a serious decline in the value of farming-land in the United Kingdom and in New England. (d) That in one vast section of British India, where for many years the State has attempted by periodical land-settlements to absorb the unearned increment, and the single-tax system is in great measure in force, the population is no better off, but rather more penurious than in the other vast section, where no such system is in force, but the Permanent Settlement of Bengal instead. (e) That a great unmerited loss is inflicted on those who have recently bought land, or have received land as their part of a testamentary estate, while those who have recently sold land, or have received cash as their part of a testamentary estate, escape scot-free. (f) That if individuals may not take to themselves the land that God has given to all, no more may nations; and the Irish soil no more belongs to the Celts than to the Saxons, the United States no more to the Americans than to the Chinese. Further, from the socialistic standpoint (g) that George offers an illogical half measure, recovering for the workers only one portion of the "surplus product," and leaving competitive anarchy and capitalist exploitation untouched; whereas incomes, in the shape of dividends, and interest, are just as much "unearned income" as incomes in the shape of rent.

But though there is discord between revolutionary agrarianism and collectivism, they are alike in opposition to the uniform teaching and tradition of the Catholic Church on the lawfulness of private ownership of income-yielding property, whether it be named "land" or "capital." And they are alike in opposition to the idea of all great statesmen from Solon to Leo XIII, namely, flourishing populations of small farmers or peasants. Thus George attacks any wide distribution of landed property, asserts the productivity of large farms to be the greatest, the tendency of small farms to disappear, the misery of their holders, the pity of multiplying them (Progress and Poverty). Neither George nor Kautsky are true to facts, but both are good witnesses to the importance of agrarian reform as fatal to agrarian socialism. The misuse of the rights of property, such as the misdeeds of Scotch and Irish landlordism, and of the tenement owners of Europe and America, are the food that feeds agrarian socialism. To make such misdeeds impossible is the task of social reform under a wise government. Nor is it accidental that the Encyclicals of Leo XIII form a manual of social politics. For as grace rests on nature, the religion that is alone truly divine, must also *ipso facto*, be truly human. But the instinct of private property is truly human; and the proper unfolding of human liberty and personality is historically bound up with it, and cannot develop where each person is only a sharer in a compulsory partnership, or, on the other hand, where property is confined to a privileged few. Suitably, therefore, the same Pope who had defended the true dignity and the true liberty of man urged the diffusion of property as the mean between Socialism and Individualism, and that where possible each citizen should dwell secure in a homestead which, however humble, was his own.

119

THE ETHICS OF LABOR

Father Cuthbert [1]

In considering the industrial restlessness of today, it is well to bear in mind that the question of wages no longer constitutes the fundamental problem of the Labor aspiration. What the working-class is claiming as its right and what it is restlessly seeking to achieve, is not merely nor primarily a just wage, but that its labor and the conditions of labor shall be an expression of human personality. The worker wants not merely to exist, but to live a human life and to find in his work the freedom to express and develop himself. A man may receive just and generous wages and yet be a mere tool or machine in the hands of his employer; a mere *thing*, industrially considered, and not a human being with personal interests clamoring to be recognized. The motive underlying the movement of organized Labor

---

[1] The Paulist Press, New York.

today is to obtain such recognition both for the personality of the worker and for his human interests. The organized workers now demand economic freedom as well as a just remuneration. As one writer puts it: "They want greater security as regards employment and better provision for their old age; the opportunity of taking a greater interest in their work; and more freedom as to the ordering of their own lives." [2] Nothing less than that will satisfy the more intelligent worker; and we may all add, nothing less will satisfy the awakened Christian conscience.

It need hardly be said that the Catholic Church in its ethical teaching is at one with this new development in the Labor movement, with its claim that every man shall have as his natural due the *status* of a free agent in the disposal of his labor and the ordering of his own life, and in asserting the principle that the ultimate object of labor is not the acquisition of wages, but the development of human life and character. Thus, for instance, Leo XIII, in his Encyclical, *Rerum novarum,* on the condition of the working class, declares: "If the owners of property should be made secure, the workingman in like manner has property and belongings in respect to which he should be protected; and foremost of all, his soul and mind. . . . No man may with impunity outrage that human dignity which God Himself treats with reverence, nor stand in the way of that higher life which is the preparation of the eternal life of heaven. Nay, more; no man has in this matter power over himself. To consent to any treatment which is calculated to defeat the end and purpose of his being is beyond his right; he cannot give up his soul to servitude; for it is not man's own rights which are here in question, but the rights of God, the most sacred and inviolable of rights." [3] Hence, the Pope continues: "It is neither just nor human so to grind men down with excessive labor as to stupefy their minds and wear out their bodies." [4] Further, having regard to the same principle, he lays down that the employer who exploits the necessity of the worker, to enforce an insuffi-

---

[2] H. Sanderson Furniss, in *The Industrial Outlook* (London, 1917), Introductory, p. 16.
[3] See *The Pope and the People* (Catholic Truth Society. Edit. 1912), pp. 203, 204.
[4] *Ibid.,* p. 204.

cient wage or inhuman conditions of labor, infringes the "dictates of natural justice (which is) more imperious and ancient than any bargain between man and man." [5] And he suggests that "in these and similar questions, such as, for example, the hours of labor in different trades, the sanitary precautions to be observed in factories and workshops," etc., society or boards either of the workers themselves or of employers and employed should be formed "to safeguard the interests of the wage-earners"—an anticipation of that demand for a share in the control of labor, which is now generally adopted by labor organizations.

Throughout, the keynote of the Encyclical is the principle that conditions of labor shall be made more human and less servile, and for that reason that the worker be placed in a condition of greater economic freedom both as regards his security against want and the conditions of his labor. The worker is to be regarded as a human agent and not a mere tool; and as one who has the right *by means of his labor* to achieve a wholesome human existence, since, as the Pope says, it is only by his labor that he can preserve and develop himself. His necessity gives him the right to such conditions of labor as will enable him to achieve a complete human existence. Moreover, the same necessity demands that he should claim this right;[6] since, as the Pope says, "a man cannot give up his soul to servitude." Yet that is just what he was required to do under the economic system hitherto prevalent in modern industry. Nor is he relieved of that servitude merely by receiving a higher wage; he simply sells his soul at a higher rate, unless the essential conditions of servitude are abolished. To continue to blunt his mind and soul by excessive bodily labor, to go through the continuous monotony of a machine-existence, to be perpetually harassed by the insecurity of labor dependent on the arbitrary will of an employer; to have to work in circumstances degrading to body and soul—under such conditions labor cannot but be demoralizing, however high the rate of wage might be.

The new conscious aim in labor organization, which puts human personality in the foreground and explicitly regards wages and material advantages as mere means to an end,

[5] *Ibid.*, p. 207.
[6] *Ibid.*, p. 206.

has undoubtedly a higher human and ethical quality than was found in the purely materialistic schools of economics, and for that reason deserves the sympathetic attention of all Catholics.

The fact that this new purpose on the part of the labor organizations is associated among certain sections with a policy of expropriation, hardly distinguished, if at all, from confiscation of the capitalist's property, must not blind us to the justice of the main purpose itself; nor is it helpful to the cause of the Catholic Church to regard merely the extravagances and more violently revolutionary forms of the movement and to ignore the saner teaching of those who regard an economic revolution as inevitable, but believe that, with reasonableness on all sides, a just and peaceful solution of the problem is possible. That the economic system must be radically changed in many ways, few will be found to doubt, who have given any serious attention to the subject. Capitalism in the forms in which it has hitherto dominated the industrial world, is bound sooner or later to give way before the growing unity and consciousness of power among the workers; just as in the latter Middle Ages, feudalism had to give way before the growing power of the commercial class.

The only question today is whether this radical economic change can be brought about peacefully by a mutual recognition of reasonable claims on the part of the employer and the worker, or whether a violent solution is inevitable. If either party refuses to treat with the other in a spirit of reasonableness and with intent to recognize the fundamental principles of justice underlying the situation, then violent revolution, in the opinion of sane and impartial observers, will surely come: and unfortunately on both sides there are those who are prepared to stake their all upon a violent issue. If that issue is to be avoided, it is needful that all who wish for a peaceful solution should unite in a careful and sympathetic consideration of the ethical questions involved. For, after all, the problem as it presents itself today, is primarily and ultimately an ethical problem. "It is not merely discontent as to wages, but dissatisfaction with their lives as wage-earners, that lies at the heart of the trouble." [7]

[7] H. Sanderson Furniss, in *The Industrial Outlook*, Introductory, p. 16.

Undoubtedly the question of wages is the first practical consideration, since a man must have sufficient to provide for his bodily sustenance, if he is to cultivate mind and soul; and as connected with wages, come proper housing and whatever is needful for a healthy bodily existence. But beyond a just wage, there are other conditions to which the worker has a rightful claim, if he is to live a properly human life and not be degraded to the level of a mere tool or to a condition of servitude. As we have seen, these conditions are mainly three: security against unemployment, a larger control in the management of his work, and a greater liberty in the ordering of his own life. Ethically, his right to these conditions is undeniable, provided, of course, that he is capable of fulfilling the duties which go with the rights; since every right has a corresponding duty with which it is indissolubly connected in the sphere of morals.

The first of these conditions, then, is security against unemployment. The ethical right to this security is derived from the fact that the worker's labor is a necessity. He must work in order to live. In the words of Leo XIII: "The preservation of life is the bounden duty of one and all, and to be wanting therein is a crime. It follows that each one has a right to procure what is required in order to live; and the poor can procure it in no other way than through work and wages." [8] If this be so, it follows that every worker, dependent on his work, has a certain right to employment and to security against unemployment. Employment is for him a necessity of life. It may be said, of course, that his moral claim is not so much to employment as to the means of living, and that, consequently, so long as he is otherwise provided for, for instance by charity, he has no claim to employment. That might be so if merely bodily subsistence had to be thought of; but in dealing with human life one has to consider a man's self-respect and the general well-being of society at large.

No honest man willingly submits to be a drone in the community or to receive from others the wages of work whilst remaining unemployed, when he is capable of doing useful work. To force any man into a position in which

---

[8] *The Pope and the People*, p. 207.

his self-respect suffers, is to degrade him. St. Paul's words: "If a man will not work neither let him eat," expresses at once a social obligation and a proper sense of personal dignity. Every man, thus, has a right as well as a duty to some sort of useful employment; it is a condition of an honorable human existence. But in the case of the worker whose only honorable means of subsistence depends upon marketable labor, the rightful claim to employment and security against unemployment has a specific significance. But his ethical right in this matter of security is further derived from the fact that without a reasonable certainty of being able to maintain himself and those dependent on him, the anxiety about merely material things must take away his due liberty in the cultivation of his mental and spiritual interests. A normal healthy cultivation of mind and soul can with difficulty be achieved without a reasonable security against material want.

Indeed, there can be hardly any question as to the moral right underlying the worker's claim to security against unemployment. Less clear, perhaps, is the determination as to the incidence of the obligation to provide such security. There are those who would put the entire obligation upon the State; others would share the obligation between the State and the employer. But to put the entire obligation on the State is to assume a sphere of activity and responsibility on the part of the State towards the individual, which logically leads to a servile State. The wider the responsibility taken over by the State in the ordering of the individual's life, the less individual liberty there will be. In a free community ethical responsibilities must fall in the first place upon the individuals concerned, and only secondarily upon the State as the protector of the rights of the community and of the freedom of individuals. Doubtless in a matter which affects the general well-being of the community so vitally as does the labor problem, the State must necessarily intervene very largely, especially during a transitional period such as the present. That necessity of State intervention, however, will be less in proportion as employers of labor regard security against unemployment not merely as a matter of national expediency, but as a principle of inherent justice in the status of the worker which directly enters into the moral character of the contract between employer and worker.

The worker, dependent as he is upon his work, has a moral claim to security against unemployment, and that claim must enter into the contract between himself and his employer. When, for instance, a professional teacher demands "security of tenure" as well as a fixed salary, the demand is not merely arbitrary, but is based in a true sense of moral right. He may be forced by necessity to accept a position in a school which leaves him in constant danger of being arbitrarily dismissed to suit the convenience of the school manager, perhaps at a time when further employment may be difficult to obtain. But in accepting such a position through force of necessity, "he is made the victim of force and injustice," [9] just as truly as when he is forced to accept an unjust wage. Arbitrary dismissal, which takes into consideration merely the convenience or advantage of the employer without consideration for the well-being of the worker, is thus a real injustice. We are, of course, assuming that the worker is fulfilling his part of the "national bargain" by honestly discharging the duties he has undertaken; as otherwise he himself has broken his contract and has forfeited his claim upon the employer. Cases may indeed arise in which, through no fault of his own, the worker may be incapable of continuing in the service of the employer through a change of conditions which are of general advantage, as well as to the employer's interest, as for instance when new machinery or methods of higher scientific value are introduced into a manufactory. Yet in such cases there can be no doubt that the employer is under an obligation to do what he can to secure new employment to the honest worker; he cannot, without a violation of justice, dismiss him with no regard for the future, just because in the worker he is dealing with a human life and not with a mere tool.

But if this is true, then the worker has surely a right to take due measures that his just claim shall be safeguarded against the employer's arbitrary decision and, if need be, to invoke the intervention of the State. Whether the actual methods proposed by Trade Unions for enforcing this right are commendable or not, is another question. They have

---

[9] *Cf. The Pope and the People,* p. 207.

been accused of thinking too exclusively of the workers' rights and too little of their duties. If that be so, they will, in the long run, defeat their own ends. There is, however, evidence that amongst the leaders of the labor propaganda, a keen sense of the workers' responsibilities is manifesting itself, and that an increasing insistence is being laid upon the workers' efficiency in labor and upon self-discipline. Without efficiency and self-discipline on the workers' part, it is felt that no real progress can be made towards the further achievement of the new labor ideal, and this should go far towards bringing about a peaceful understanding between the employers and employed.

Here, however, we are concerned with the essential claim itself that the worker should have security against unemployment, and on ethical grounds the claim cannot be denied. At the same time the duty of safeguarding the worker against unemployment does not rest with the employer alone.[1] The worker himself has his coordinate share in the responsibility. Everyone will admit that no employer is obliged to keep in employment an idle or dishonest worker; nor can any individual employer be justly forced to employ or to retain in employment the inefficient who is incapable of earning his wage at least, when the incapability is not brought about by the employer's own act. These limitations of the employer's responsibility point to a corresponding duty on the part of the worker and of those upon whom the worker is naturally dependent. It is at once clear that if the worker has an ethical right to employment, he has a duty to fit himself for employment and to do what in him lies to justify his claim to be employed. Not only must he be honest and willing to work; he must also do his part in fitting himself for the work demanded of him by the needs of the community. This is a duty he owes at once to himself and to the community at large: he owes it to himself since work is an essential necessity in his life; he owes it to the community since otherwise he runs

---

[1] We are not considering here the duty of the employer to provide for those who have given good service and are incapacitated by age or sickness. Such provision is part of the question of wages. Nor are we referring here to the accidental inefficiency of the worker, caused by some action of the employer, as when a change of method is introduced. In such a case, as already noticed, a certain responsibility lies on the employer.

the risk of becoming a mere burden upon his fellow-men, and of fulfilling no useful part in the life of the community upon which he must ultimately fall back for his maintenance.

This duty of fitting oneself for useful employment is the one, perhaps, which the worker has most consistently ignored, or concerning which he has been too frequently left in ignorance. The fault is not altogether his, nor primarily his; it lies chiefly in the apathy or thoughtlessness of those who are responsible for his education.

Yet efficiency in labor is an integral element in the full moral claim to employment. No man who deliberately ignores his duty to fit himself for employment, can justly claim, on his own merits, security against unemployment, simply because he has not fulfilled his proper part as regards that anterior dictate of justice upon which all particular bargaining depends for its ethical obligation. The State may indeed, in the public interest, intervene to give him employment; but in such a case he becomes a dependent on the State rather than a free worker. Liberty, it must be remembered, is essentially bound up with capacity and duty; economic freedom in the fullest sense is for those who are capable and willing to do their part in the community's economic life.

And here, it would seem, comes in one of the more abiding duties of the State in the matter of securing the freedom of the worker and that security against unemployment which is part of that freedom. Allowing that the moral obligation towards efficiency of labor lies primarily with the individual and those immediately responsible for his early education, and, not least, to the Trade Unions which take the responsibility of enforcing his rights—allowing this, it yet remains for the State in the interest of the community at large, to give due opportunity for the worker's education and training, such as will fit him for his future work; and not only to give the opportunity, but to take such means as will best secure that the opportunity is not neglected. Further, it is the duty of the State to see that this security against unemployment enters into the bargain between employers and employed, and is not jeopardized by merely arbitrary action of either employer or worker. Thus, for instance, when new processes or methods are introduced into any industry, the State should insist that the change be made so as to minimize the danger of the worker finding himself without employment as a consequence of the change.

The proper action of the State is, however, limited. It cannot so control the conditions of industry as to leave no personal freedom to either employer or worker in the control of labor; for that would cut at the very root of personal responsibility and consequently of real personal liberty. But it can protect both employer and worker against the mere arbitrariness of physical or moral force, and it can also give opportunities which conduce to the fulfillment of moral obligations. The giving of these opportunities is indeed its most positive contribution to economic freedom, and more directly constructive than any restrictive or "police" intervention.

Such action the worker and the community at large can justly claim from the State. Thus education in the broadest sense, and such an education as will best develop the capacity of the worker to earn his living, is the worker's most urgent claim upon the State, since it is intimately bound up with the whole claim of the worker to economic freedom; without it the worker will always be in a servile condition either towards the individual employer or the State, just because the uneducated and inefficient worker is unable to stand upon his own merits, and is forced to depend upon the bounty either of the individual employer or of the community at large. As we have said, security against unemployment may be guaranteed by the State even to the inefficient on grounds of public policy; yet it is well for the worker clearly to recognize that his indefeasible moral right to security is ultimately bound up with his personal capacity and efficiency.

We come now to the second of the three claims put forward by the labor organizations, "a larger control in the management of his work." The term "larger control" needs, perhaps, definition. To the Syndicalist, it signifies the expropriation of the capitalist and the entire management of industry by the workers. The ordinary Trade Unionist demand has, however, been thus expressed by one of their representatives: "Would it not be possible for the employers of this country to agree to put their business on a new footing by admitting the workman to some participation, not in profits, but in control? We workmen do not ask that we should be admitted to any share in what is essentially the employer's own business—that is, in those matters which do not concern us directly in the industry or employment in which we may be engaged. But in the daily management of the employment in which we spend our working lives, we feel that we, as workmen, have a right to a voice—even an equal voice—with the management itself."[2] This seems to be the general demand at the present moment; and it has already been accepted by some employers with some acknowledged measure of success.

So far neither Syndicalism nor Guild-Socialism have secured the adherence of any large number of workers; and that for two reasons. The average worker has no wish to concern himself with what is outside the sphere of his labor itself. "They have no wish to be responsible for the purchase of raw material, for the raising of capital, the marketing of produce," etc.[3] Moreover, the workingmen as a body are well aware that they have not the training which will fit them to discharge the function in industry at present discharged by the employer. This does not mean that the Syndicalist or Guild-Socialist ideals may not yet gain a larger support. Much will depend upon the general attitude of employers, whether Collectivism or Syndicalism and kindred systems will further draw to themselves the allegiance of the workers, as an escape from conditions against which they now revolt. As they stand at present, all these systems are ethically objectionable inasmuch as they unduly curtail personal liberty;[4] at the best they propose to substitute one form of servitude for another, and that, doubtless, is what the common sense of the majority of the workers is aware of.

At the same time, however, whilst rejecting on ethical grounds the Socialist systems as generally propounded, there is no ethical reason why, under new economic conditions, the worker should not aim at becoming a part owner

---

[2] Mr. Gosling, at the Trade Union Congress, 1916, quoted in *The Industrial Outlook*, p. 398.
[3] H. Sanderson Furniss, in *The Industrial Outlook*, p. 17.
[4] On this point see the Encyclical, *Rerum novarum*, in *The Pope and the People*, p. 189, et. seq.

in industry, provided that the transfer of ownership is brought about without injustice to others and that due regard is had to individual liberty. What is true of a wider division of property in land, as advocated by Leo XIII, equally applies to a wider extension of property in industry. "Many excellent results," says the Pope, "will follow upon this; and, first of all, property will certainly become more equitably divided. For the result of civil change and revolution has been to divide society into two widely differing castes. On the one side there is the party which holds power because it holds wealth; which has in its grasp the whole of labor and trade; which manipulates for its own benefit and its own purposes all the sources of supply, and which is even represented in the councils of the State itself. On the other side there is the needy and the powerless multitude, broken-down and suffering, and ever ready for disturbance. If working people can be encouraged to look forward to obtaining a share in the land, the consequence will be that the gulf between vast wealth and sheer poverty will be bridged over and the respective classes will be brought nearer to each other. A further consequence will result in the greater abundance of the fruits of the earth. Men always work harder and more readily when they work on that which belongs to them. . . . That such a spirit of willing labor would add to the produce of the earth and to the wealth of the community is self-evident. And a third advantage would spring from this: men would cling to the country in which they were born; for no one would exchange his country for a foreign land if his own afforded him the means of living a decent and happy life."[5] The same economic and human results, we take it, would follow were the workers to be given some ownership in any industry in which they are employed; and such ownership would meet with the blessing of the Church, equally with ownership in land.

But at present the vast body of workers are not claiming such ownership; what they do claim is a greater control over their labor itself, or rather over the conditions under which they are required to labor.[6] It may be pointed out

---

[5] *The Pope and the People,* p. 208.
[6] What is wanted is that the work people should have a greater opportunity of participating in the discussion about and adjustment

that here again they have the approval and encouragement of Pope Leo XIII, when he says, speaking of the function of labor associations: "Should it happen that either a master or a workman believe himself injured, nothing would be more desirable than a committee should be appointed, composed of reliable and capable members of the association, whose duty would be, conformably with the rules of the association, to settle the dispute." Already he had declared that the purpose of these associations should be to help "each individual member to better his condition to the utmost in body, mind and property."[7]

Here we have in principle an acknowledgment of the right of the worker to a share in the control of the conditions which govern his labor. And the right flows from the same fundamental fact which, in the mind of the Pope and of the labor organizations, is the cardinal principle of economic reform, that the worker is a human being and not a tool. As such he has a right to a certain control over his own activity, so far at least that his activity shall conduce to his proper welfare and not be a means of degrading him in body or mind. This applies not merely to the material conditions of his labor; it applies even more urgently to the mental and spiritual conditions. Even granting that the conditions which directly affect his bodily welfare—wages, sanitation, etc.—are what they should be, there is yet the further consideration of his mental and spiritual development to which his labor should rightly conduce. One of the curses of labor under the modern industrial régime has been its tendency to stunt the mind and character of the worker; and this has been due not merely to overwork and an insufficient wage, but to the atmosphere of servitude, the dull monotony and the sense that the worker has no voice in the control of his labor.

Thus, under the prevailing system, he is not consulted about matters which directly concern his convenience or comfort; it is not considered necessary to give him any reasonable explanation of the cause which renders expedient changes of routine or method which directly affect him. If new processes are adopted, the change is made

of those parts of industry by which they are most affected (Whetley Interim Report).
[7] *The Pope and the People,* pp. 214-216.

with little or no consideration for the worker himself, though the worker may have given the best years of his life to building up the industry, and has thereby acquired a vested interest in the industry, in virtue of his labor, equally with the vested interest of the owner. Still less has the worker been encouraged to develop any personal thought or initiative in his labor. Under such a system men naturally tend to become mere machines instead of intelligent, responsible beings; and with perfect justice they may refuse to continue in such servitude, provided they are willing to accept the responsibilities which their new freedom entails.[8] For, it may be well to repeat, in all cases it is true: the greater the freedom, the greater the moral responsibility, and there is no right without its corresponding duty.

How far a greater control in the arrangement in the conditions of his labor, will tend to relieve the monotony and mechanism of the industrial world, is a question difficult to answer. There are those who claim that the mechanical industry of the present day is radically soul-killing; that with the over-development of machinery and the narrow limitations imposed by specialist labor in the modern manufactory, no workman can be otherwise than part of the machinery itself, nor be other than a servile worker. Those who hold this view, plead for a revival of handcrafts and the simpler forms of labor. Be that as it may—and there is much to be said in favor of it—it yet remains true that a greater control over the conditions of his labor will give the worker a sense of greater freedom, and open out to him an opportunity of developing a greater sense of responsibility in his work; so far it will create a more human atmosphere in industry. Very rightly the worker regards outside arbitration, except as an occasional necessity, with repugnance; it is but shifting to other shoulders the responsibility which he, equally with the employer, should take upon himself. That is the feeling of the more

---

[8] One is glad to know that in practice where this greater control has been granted, the result has usually been greater efficiency and orderliness. Much depends upon the spirit in which it is granted. An employer who is sympathetic to the new system, will gain more from it than one who is unsympathetic and so fails to gain the confidence of the workers.

serious thinkers amongst the advocates of "greater control"; and it is a right moral feeling, if the worker is to be raised economically to the status of a human being.

With this claim to greater control over the conditions of labor goes the still wider claim that the workers should have "a larger freedom as to the ordering of their own lives." This claim is social rather than economic, though it is intimately bound up with economic conditions. What it signifies is that the worker shall be given the opportunities for the development of those human interests which make for the fuller enjoyment of life; or, in the current phrase, for "the expression of personality, individual and collective," not merely in the workshop, but in social life generally. With the majority of the workers this "larger liberty" is probably an indefinite quantity; it expresses an opportunity of doing what they like with themselves outside the daily routine of their work; it is a more or less blind revolt against the feeling of servitude. But with the more thoughtful section of the labor class, however, it means a fuller enjoyment of family life, education in the true sense of the word, a wider extension of personal interests, a greater freedom for mental and spiritual betterment. All these things under the old economic *régime* have been made difficult for the worker; and who will say that he has not a right to them?

The candid recognition of these rights will doubtless mean a radical change in the conditions of labor and, to some extent, a remodeling of the whole economic system. Wages will have to be based, not upon the necessity of mere bodily subsistence, but upon the right of the worker to the enjoyment of a fuller human existence; the hours of paid employment will have to be restricted to allow leisure and opportunity for other interests. But further than that, the mental atmosphere in which employer and worker meet, will have to be radically changed. Employment will have to be no longer dominated by the idea of material profit—whether in the form of dividends or of wages—but by the idea of human welfare; and it is here that the real *crux* of the situation lies, for it means a conversion from the material outlook on life to the ethical, and without this change there can be no hope of a peaceful solution of the difficulties involved in the new labor demands.

Two things, it would seem, render a peaceful solution problematical. The one is the natural cupidity of men, fostered and intensified by the materialist social economy of the past three or four centuries, and especially intensified by the industrial system of the nineteenth century. The other is the blind acceptance of that system as a law of public life by the general body of Christian men and women, who, in their private personal affairs, are guided by high ethical ideals. This blind acquiescence on the part of otherwise high-minded people, is, perhaps, the greatest danger of the two, since it tends, in the eyes of those who are demanding a more ethical system, to identify the present materialist economy with the Christian life, and to throw a glamour of ethical respectability over the recalcitrance of those who uphold that economy. That way lies religious and class warfare. What we shall all be wise to recognize is that a fundamental change in the economic and social system lies before us and is, in fact, already taking place; and if it is to be brought about without violence and a disruption of society, it will only be by an unprejudiced and candid acknowledgment of what is right and just in the aspirations of the workers.

Frequently enough, the claims put forward by this or that section of organized labor, are as unethical and materialist in outlook as are those of the employers who exploit labor for their own selfish ends. The worker is still, to a great extent, the child of the unethical and irreligious system against which he revolts; yet that must not blind us to what is his just right, and only as he becomes conscious of a willingness on the part of the employers and of the public generally, to consider his claims in the spirit of justice and equity, will he be effectually convinced that others have rights too. Until then he will stand in an attitude of suspicion and revolt. The present is a time for taking the larger view, which looks not to a selfish and narrow material advantage, but to that ethical value which determines the rights and wrongs of human life.

120

SOCIAL REFORM

WILLIAM VON KETTELER [1]

We will examine one by one the reforms which the laboring classes wish to realize by their united efforts. Step by step we shall see that religion is intimately bound up with the labor question, with every demand made by the workingman, and that godlessness is the greatest enemy of the working classes.

The *first* demand of the working classes is: increase of wages corresponding to the true value of labor. This is, on the whole, a very fair demand; religion also insists that human labor be not treated like an article of merchandise and appraised simply according to the fluctuations of offer and demand.

Economic Liberalism, making abstraction of all religion and morality, not only degraded labor to the level of a commodity, but looked on man himself, with his capacity for work, simply as a machine bought as cheaply as possible and driven until it will go no more. To combat the dreadful consequences which resulted from the application of such principles the Trade Unions arose in England and, in time, spread into other countries. . . . The chief weapon of the Trade Unions against capital and the *grande industrie* is the strike, by means of which, in spite of many reverses and seeming defeats, they have succeeded.

Just as these efforts may be to reclaim for human labor and the laborer the human dignity of which economic Liberalism had robbed them, it is evident that they will not procure any real advantages, and will not be crowned with any lasting success unless they go hand in hand with religion and morality. Two considerations will make this clear.

---

[1] *Ketteler's Social Reform*, pp. 160-170, by George Metlake. (The Dolphin Press, Philadelphia.)

EDITOR'S NOTE: Leo XIII regarded this "fighting bishop" of the Rhineland as his precursor in his efforts to solve the social question. An ardent friend of the laboring classes, Bishop von Ketteler helped his folk by word and example. He died in 1877, loved and venerated for the holiness and austerity of his life.

In the first place, you cannot close your eyes to the fact that there must be a limit to wage increase, and that even the highest wages attainable under favorable conditions cannot do more than provide you with a decent subsistence. The natural limits of wages are determined by the productiveness of the business in which you are employed. The intellectual and material capital sunk in the business will be withdrawn and diverted into other channels the moment wages become so high that the investment ceases to pay. In that case work is at an end. Hence, in spite of combinations among workmen, there is a limit to wages, and it would be a fatal mistake if you did not make this clear to yourselves and if you allowed yourselves to be misled by exaggerated promises into the belief that an indefinite increase of wages is possible.

The highest wages you can hope for will, therefore, merely assure you a respectable competency provided you make temperance and economy the rule of your life. And these priceless goods—temperance and economy—the working classes will be possessed of only if their lives are guided by the spirit of religion. It is a fact absolutely beyond dispute that the welfare of the working classes is not merely a matter of wages. There are factory districts where wages are very high, but the prosperity of the people very low, while in others, where wages are by no means so high, the blessings of life are far more in evidence.

One of the greatest dangers for the workingman in this respect is drunkenness and pleasure seeking. . . . A few brief months given up to intemperance amply suffice to absorb the highest pay. Of what use then are high wages to one who is the slave of intemperance? And yet, on the other hand, what moral power is not required to keep the workman from debauchery and intemperance? Perhaps no labor to which toiling man has ever been condemned on earth is so exacting, so unintermitting, so fatiguing as mill or factory work. How easy for a man who is tied down without respite for the same number of hours to the same mechanical work every day of his life to be tempted, when released at last from this deadening toil, to seek compensation in intemperance and dissipation! Unusual moral energy is required to be sober and thrifty under such circumstances. Religion alone can infuse this high moral sense into the workman. If therefore higher wages are to profit you indeed, you must above all be true Christians.

Secondly, in your efforts to obtain higher wages, you have need of religion and morality in order not to carry your demands too far. We have already seen that there is a limit to the increase of wages. Hence, in our time, when the movements among the working classes for amelioration of their material condition are assuming larger proportions from day to day, it is of the highest importance not to exaggerate this demand. The working man can be only too easily imposed upon and the power of organization used to wrong purposes. *The object of the labor movement must not be war between the workman and the employer, but peace on equitable terms between both.*

The impiety of capital which would treat the workman like a machine, must be broken. It is a crime against the working classes; it degrades them. It fits in with the theory of those who would trace man's descent to the ape. But the impiety of labor must also be guarded against. If the movement in favor of higher wages overlaps the bounds of justice, catastrophes must necessarily ensue, the whole weight of which will recoil on the working classes. Capitalists are seldom at a loss for lucrative investments. When it comes to the worst, they can speculate in government securities. But the workman is in a far different position. When the business in which he is employed comes to a standstill, unemployment stares him in the face. Besides, exorbitant wage demands affect not only the large business concerns controlled by the capitalists, but also the smaller ones in the hands of the middle classes and the daily earnings of master workmen and handicraftsmen. But if the working classes are to observe just moderation in their demands, if they are to escape the danger of becoming mere tools in the hands of ambitious and unscrupulous demagogues, if they wish to keep clear of the inordinate selfishness which they condemn so severely in the capitalist, they must be filled with a lofty moral sense, their ranks must be made up of courageous, Christian, religious men. The power of money without religion is an evil, but the power of organized labor without religion is just as great an evil. Both lead to destruction.

The *second* claim put forward by the working classes is for shorter hours of labor. One thing is certain: working hours and wages have shared the same fate. Wherever capitalists, ignoring the dignity of man, have acted on the principles of modern political economy, wages have been reduced to a minimum and working hours have been prolonged to the limits of human endurance—and beyond them. Day and night, like a machine, the workman cannot be kept going; but for all that the impossible was expected of him. Hence, wherever the hours of work are lengthened beyond the limits fixed by nature, the workingmen have an indisputable right to combat this abuse of the power of wealth by well-directed concerted action.

But here again, the real value of efforts depends on religion and morality. If the workman uses the hour thus put at his disposal to fulfil in the bosom of his family the duties of a good father or a dutiful son, to tend to the affairs of the home, to cultivate the plot of ground he calls his own, then this hour will be of untold value to himself and his family. If, on the contrary, he throws it away in bad company, on the streets, in the tavern, it will profit neither his health nor his temporal and spiritual prosperity. It will simply serve to undermine his constitution, to disfigure the image of God in his soul, and to dissipate his wages all the more quickly and surely.

The *third* demand of the working classes is for days of rest. This claim also is perfectly legitimate. Religion is not only with you here, but, long before you, it vindicated the necessity of regularly recurring days of repose. God Himself inscribed them on the Tables of the Law: "Remember thou keep holy the Sabbath Day."

In this respect too our modern economists have committed, and still commit, a crime against the human race that cries to Heaven for vengeance. The culprits are not merely the wealthy *entrepreneurs* who force their workmen to work on Sundays, but also all tradesmen, land owners and masters generally who deprive their servants, hands or clerks of their well-earned Sunday rest. A number of labor leaders have quite recently openly exposed the hypocrisy of Liberalism in this matter. It has always been a favorite trick of the capitalists to throw the veil of the tenderest philanthropy over their ruthless abuse of the workman and to hold up the urgent demand of the Church for days of rest as prejudicial to the interests of the working classes. With what minute exactness were not the Sundays and holidays counted up, and with what a sugared mien was not the grand total of possible gain calculated if these days were given up to work! From this the inference was drawn that the money magnates were animated by the purest feelings of charity and that the Church was hard hearted and cruel and hostile to the prosperity of the people. To this the organs of the labor party replied that there was another means of securing these advantages for the laboring man without having to work him to death. This means would be to give him as much pay for six days' work as he now receives for seven. The profit to the laborer would remain the same, and he would not sacrifice his human dignity, into the bargain. Who can deny the truth of this observation? If the capitalists were right, it would be inhuman to allow the workman even the indulgence of sleep. The immense profit to be derived from night work would be demonstrated with the same hypocritical mien as the benefit of Sunday work. Just as man has need of a certain number of hours for repose out of the twenty-four which make up the day, so also has he need of one day of rest out of the seven which make up the week. He has a right to this for the sake of his soul, in order that he may have leisure to think of his relationship to God, to recollect that he is not merely a son of toil, but a child of God as well. He has a right to this for the sake of his body, for whose health and vigor he must have a care. Just as a master who employs a workman a whole day is obliged to give him time for the necessary night rest and to calculate his wages accordingly, in the same way the factory owner, who uses up the brawn and muscle and brain of a workman for a whole week, is bound to give him the necessary weekly day of rest and to estimate his wages accordingly. The time devoted to repose must be added to the time spent at work, inasmuch as it has become necessary by reason of the work done and is a prerequisite of the work to be done.

But it is not enough that the labor leaders and the labor organs insist on days of rest. Each one must work to this end by scrupulously keeping holy the Sabbath Day. There are still unfortunately very many workmen who, without being obliged, and for filthy lucre's sake simply, work on Sundays. Such men sin not merely against God and His commandments, but really and truly against the whole body of workpeople, because by their base cupidity they furnish the employers with a ready-made excuse for refusing days of rest to all without exception. May all the workpeople, not excepting the servant girl whom a heartless mistress overburdens with work, and the humble railway employee for whom wealthy corporations have made Sunday a dead letter, with one voice reclaim this right as a right of man. To what purpose have the so-called rights of man been laid down in our Constitutions so long as capital is free to trample them under foot?

It is certain that you have religion on your side in your demand for days of rest. It is certain also that all the efforts of the working classes would be of no avail if they were not sustained by the power of religion and the divine precept: "Remember thou keep holy the Sabbath day." But it is no less certain that this weekly day of rest will profit you, your health, your soul, your families, from whom your work keeps you away so much during the week, only if you remain intimately united with the Church. Without religion the days of rest will serve no other purpose than to bring ruin on the workman and his family. What is called "blue Monday" is nothing else but Sunday spent without religion. . . . Your own experience is able to furnish you with examples enough of the vast difference of the workingman's family in which the day of rest is spent in harmony with the principles of religion and one in which religion is ignored. A Christian Sunday is a blessing.

A *fourth* demand of the working classes is the prohibition of child labor in factories. I regret to say that this demand is not as general as it ought to be, and that many workmen send their children to the mills and factories in order to increase their income. It would be more correct to say that it is a demand made by certain spokesmen of the labor organizations. . . . Child labor is restricted but not forbidden. I deplore this action of the legislature profoundly, and look on it as a victory of materialism over moral principles. My own observations are in full accord with the statements on the bad effects of factory labor on children. I know right well what arguments are brought forward to excuse it, and I am also aware that even some who are well disposed toward the working classes wish to see child labor tolerated to a certain extent. Children are in duty bound, these men argue, to help their parents in the house and the field, why debar them from the factory? These people forget that there is a vast difference between work at home and work in a factory. Factory work quenches, as it were, the family spirit in the child, and this is the greatest danger that threatens the working classes in our day. Moreover, it robs the child of the time it should devote to innocent, joyous recreation so necessary at this period of life. Lastly, the factory undermines the bodily and spiritual health of the child. I regard child labor in factories as a monstrous cruelty of our time, a cruelty committed against the child by the spirit of the age and the selfishness of parents. I look on it as a slow poisoning of the body and the soul of the child. With the sacrifice of the joys of childhood, with the sacrifice of health, with the sacrifice of innocence, the child is condemned to increase the profits of the *entrepreneur* and oftentimes to earn bread for parents whose dissolute life has made them incapable of doing so themselves. Hence I rejoice at every good word spoken in favor of the workingman's child. Religion in its great love for children cannot but support the demand for the prohibition of child labor in factories.

The *fifth* demand made by the working classes is that women, especially the mothers of families, be prohibited from working in factories. Jules Simon says in his warmly conceived and highly instructive book *L'ouvrière*: "Our whole economic organization is suffering from a dreadful malady which is the cause of the misery of the working classes and must be overcome at all costs if dissolution is to be checked—I mean the slow destruction of family life." After describing conditions prevailing in many industrial districts in France repeatedly visited by him, where women work in the factories, and family life is but an idle word, he comes to the conclusion that higher wages for workpeople are useless so long as they are not accompanied by a thorough regeneration of morals, and that, on the other hand, all moral reform must begin with the restoration of family life.

Two things must follow from what has been said thus far: the workpeople are beginning to understand more and more the supreme importance of the family for their own prosperity, and the close connection between religion and the urgent reforms demanded by the working classes—reforms which will never be fully realized except in and through religion. Religion also wants the mother to pass the day at home in order that she may fulfil her high and holy mission toward her husband and her children. All that Jules Simon, all that the friends of the workman have ever said concerning the significance of the family, is infinitely surpassed by what you heard in your youth and still hear out of the mouth of the Church on the sanctity of the Christian family. There is no doubt that the labor question is above all a question of morality and religion. The more intimately you are united with the Church, the better wives you will have for yourselves, the better mothers for your children, the more cheering will your home life be, the more effectually will the ties of family keep you from dangers.

A *sixth* demand made by many and which follows as a corollary from the previous one is, that young girls should not in future be employed in factory work. Various reasons have been urged in favor of this demand. Thus, it has been pointed out that, as a general rule, girls can work for far lower wages because they require less to live on, and that therefore, wholesale girl labor must of necessity have a damaging effect on the wages of men.

But the principal argument against the employment of girls in factories is the prejudicial influence of factory work on the morals of the working girls and consequently on the families of the future. Workmen themselves have repeatedly called attention to these sad consequences. In their meetings such striking argumentation as the following has been heard: "We want good and happy families. But to have good and happy families we must have pure and virtuous mothers. Now, where can we find these if our young girls are lured into the factories and are there inoculated with the germs of impudence and immorality?" I cannot tell you how deeply such words coming from the ranks of the working classes touched and gladdened my heart. When the labor movement was still in its infancy, such sentiments were hardly heard anywhere except from our Christian pulpits. The Liberals were insensible to the moral dangers to which the daughters of the workman were exposed. When these poor creatures were utterly corrupted in the factory, their employers still had the effrontery to pose as their benefactors—because, thanks to them, they were earning so many cents a day. The dangers of factory life to the morals of the young working girls and therefore to the family of the workman are beginning to be recognized more and more even by the factory owners themselves. This is a happy symptom and shows once more that the labor question, like all the other great social questions, is in the last analysis a question of religion and morality.

121

THE CONDITION OF LABOR

Pope Leo XIII

Neither must it be supposed that the solicitude of the Church is so occupied with the spiritual concerns of its children as to neglect their interests temporal and earthly. Its desire is that the poor, for example, should rise above poverty and wretchedness, and should better their condition in life; and for this it strives. By the very fact that it calls men to virtue and forms them to its practice, it promotes this in no slight degree. Christian morality, when it is adequately and completely practiced, conduces of itself to temporal prosperity, for it merits the blessing of that God who is the source of all blessings; it powerfully restrains the lust of possession and the lust of pleasure—twin plagues which too often make a man without self-restraint miserable in the midst of abundance;[1] it makes men supply by economy for the want of means, teaching them to be content with frugal living, and keeping them out of the reach of those vices which eat up not only merely small incomes, but large fortunes, and dissipate many a goodly inheritance. . . . We have insisted that, since it is the end of Society to make men better, the chief good that Society can be possessed of is Virtue. Nevertheless, in all well-constituted States it is a by no means unimportant matter to provide those bodily and external commodities, *the use of which is necessary to virtuous action.*[2] And in the provision of material well-being, the labor of the poor—the exercise of

---

[1] St. Thomas of Aquin, *Summa Theologica,* 2a 2ae Q. lxi. Art. 1 and 2.

[2] St. Thomas of Aquin. *De Regimine Principum,* I cap. 15.

their skill and the employment of their strength in the culture of the land and the workshops of trade—is most efficacious and altogether indispensable. Indeed, their cooperation in this respect is so important that it may be truly said that *it is only by the labor of the working man that States grow rich.*

Justice, therefore, demands that the interests of the poorer population be carefully watched over by the Administration, so that they who contribute so largely to the advantage of the community may themselves share in the benefits they create—that being housed, clothed, and enabled to support life, they may find their existence less hard and more endurable. It follows that whatever shall appear to to be conducive to the well-being of those who work, should receive favorable consideration. Let it not be feared that solicitude of this kind will injure any interest; on the contrary, it will be to the advantage of all; for it cannot but be good for the commonwealth to secure from misery those on whom it so largely depends.

Whenever the general interest or any particular class suffers or is threatened with evils, which can in no other way be met, the public authority must step in to meet them. Now among the interests of the public, as of private individuals, are these: that peace and good order should be maintained; that family life should be carried on in accordance with God's laws and those of nature; that religion should be reverenced and obeyed; that a high standard of morality should prevail in public and private life; that the sanctity of justice should be respected, and that no one should injure another with impunity; that the members of the commonwealth should grow up to man's estate strong and robust, and capable, if need be, of guarding and defending their country. If by a strike, or other combination of workmen, there should be imminent danger of disturbance to the public peace; or if circumstances were such that among the laboring population the ties of family life were relaxed; if religion were found to suffer through the workmen not having time and opportunity to practice it; if in workshops and factories there were danger to morals through the mixing of the sexes or from any occasion of evil; or if employers laid burdens upon the workmen which were unjust, or degraded them with conditions that were repugnant to their dignity as human beings; finally, if health were endangered by excessive labor, or by work unsuited to sex or age—in these cases there can be no question that, within certain limits, it would be right to call in the help and authority of the law. The limits must be determined by the nature of the occasion which calls for the law's interference—the principle being this, that the law must not undertake more, nor go further, than is required for the remedy of the evil or the removal of the danger.

Rights must be religiously respected wherever they are found; and it is the duty of the public authority to prevent and punish injury, and to protect each one in the possession of his own. Still, when there is question of protecting the rights of individuals, the poor and helpless have a claim to special consideration. The richer population have many ways of protecting themselves, and stand less in need of help from the State; those who are badly off have no resources of their own to fall back upon, and must chiefly rely upon the assistance of the State. And it is for this reason that wage-earners, who are, undoubtedly, among the weak and necessitous, should be specially cared for and protected by the commonwealth.

Here, however, it will be advisable to advert expressly to one or two of the more important details.

It must be borne in mind that the chief thing to be secured is the safeguarding, by legal enactment and policy, of private property. Most of all it is essential in these times of covetous greed, to keep the multitude within the line of duty; for if all may justly strive to better their condition, yet neither justice nor the common good allows anyone to seize that which belongs to another, or under the pretext of futile and ridiculous equality, to lay hands on other people's fortunes. It is most true that by far the greater part of the people who work prefer to improve themselves by honest labor rather than by doing wrong to others. But there are not a few who are imbued with bad principles and are anxious for revolutionary change, and whose great purpose it is to stir up tumult and bring about a policy of violence. The authority of the State should intervene to put restraint upon these disturbers, to save the workmen from their seditious arts, and to protect lawful owners from spoliation.

When work-people have recourse to a strike, it is frequently because the hours of labor are too long, or the work too hard, or because they consider their wages insufficient. The grave inconvenience of this not uncommon occurrence should be obviated by public remedial measures; for such paralysis of labor not only affects the masters and their work-people, but is extremely injurious to trade, and to the general interests of the public; moreover, on such occasions, violence and disorder are not far off, and thus it frequently happens that the public peace is threatened. The laws should be beforehand and prevent these troubles from arising; they should lend their influence and authority to the removal in good time of the causes which lead to conflicts between masters and those whom they employ. . . .

If we turn now to things exterior and corporeal, the first concern of all is to save the poor workers from the cruelty of grasping speculators, who use human beings as mere instruments for making money. It is neither justice nor humanity so to grind men down with excessive labor as to stupefy their minds and wear out their bodies. Man's powers, like his general nature, are limited, and beyond these limits he cannot go. His strength is developed and increased by use and exercise, but only on condition of due intermission and proper rest. Daily labor, therefore, must be so regulated that it may not be protracted during longer hours than strength admits. How many and how long the intervals of rest should be, will depend upon the nature of the work, on circumstances of time and place, and on the health and strength of the workman. Those who labor in mines and quarries, and in work within the bowels of the earth, should have shorter hours in proportion as their labor is more severe and more trying to health. Then, again, the season of the year must be taken into account; for not unfrequently a kind of labor is easy at one time which at another is intolerable or very difficult. Finally, work which is suitable for a strong man cannot reasonably be required from a woman or a child.

And, in regard to children, great care should be taken not to place them in workshops and factories until their bodies and minds are sufficiently mature. For just as rough weather destroys the buds of spring, so too early an experience of life's hard work blights the young promise of a child's powers, and makes any real education impossible. Women, again, are not suited to certain trades; for a woman is by nature fitted for home-work, and it is that which is best adapted at once to preserve her modesty, and to promote the good bringing up of children and the well-being of the family. As a general principle, it may be laid down, that a workman ought to have leisure and rest in proportion to the wear and tear of his strength; for the waste of strength must be repaired by the cessation of work.

In all agreements between masters and work-people, there is always the condition, expressed or understood, that there be allowed proper rest for soul and body. To agree in any other sense would be against what is right and just; for it can never be right or just to require on the one side, or to promise on the other, the giving up of those duties which a man owes to his God and to himself. . . .

Let it be granted, then, that as a rule, workman and employer should make free engagements, and in particular should freely agree as to wages; nevertheless, there is a dictate of nature more imperious and more ancient than any bargain between man and man, that the remuneration must be enough to support the wage earner in reasonable and frugal comfort. If, through necessity, or fear of a worse evil, the workman accepts harder conditions because an employer or contractor will give him no better, he is the victim of force and injustice. In these and similar questions, however—such as, for example, the hours of labor in different trades, the sanitary precautions to be observed in factories and workshops, etc.,—in order to supersede undue interference on the part of the State, especially as circumstances, times, and localities differ so widely, it is advisable that recourse be had to Societies or Boards such as we shall mention presently, or to some other method of safeguarding the interests of wage earners; the State to be asked for approval and protection.

If a workman's wages be sufficient to enable him to maintain himself, his wife, and his children in reasonable comfort, he will not find it difficult, if he is a sensible man, to study economy; and he will not fail, by cutting down expenses, to put by a little property; nature and reason would urge him to do this. We have seen that this great labor question cannot be solved except by assuming as a principle that private ownership must be held sacred and inviolable. The law, therefore, should favor ownership, and its policy should be to induce as many people as possible to become owners.

Many excellent results will follow from this; and, first of all, property will certainly become more equitably divided. For the effect of civil change and revolution has been to divide society into two widely different castes. On the one side there is the party which holds the power because it holds the wealth; which has in its grasp all labor and all trade; which manipulates for its own benefit and its own purposes all the resources of supply, and which is powerfully represented in the councils of the State itself. On the other side there is the needy and powerless multitude, sore and suffering, always ready for disturbance. If working people can be encouraged to look forward to obtaining a share in the land, the result will be that the gulf between vast wealth and deep poverty will be bridged over, and the two orders will be brought nearer together. Another consequence will be the greater abundance of the fruits of the earth. Men always work harder and more readily when they work on that which is their own; nay, they learn to love the very soil which yields in response to the labor of their hands, not only food to eat, but an abundance of the good things for themselves and those that are dear to them. It is evident how such a spirit of willing labor would add to the produce of the earth and to the wealth of the community. And a third advantage would arise from this: men would cling to the country in which they were born; for no one would exchange his country for a foreign land if his own afforded him the means of living a tolerable and happy life. These three important benefits, however, can only be expected on the condition that a man's means be not drained and exhausted by excessive taxation. The right to possess private property is from nature, not from man; and the State has only the right to regulate its use in the interests of the public good, but by no means to abolish it altogether. The State is, therefore, unjust and cruel, if, in the name of taxation, it deprives the private owner of more than is just. . . .

The most important of all are Workmen's Associations; for these virtually include all the rest. History attests what excellent results were effected by the Artificers' Guilds of a former day. They were the means not only of many advantages to the workmen, but in no small degree of the advancement of art, as numerous monuments remain to prove. Such associations should be adapted to the requirements of the age in which we live—an age of greater instruction, of different customs, and of more numerous requirements in daily life. It is gratifying to know that there are already in existence not a few societies of this nature, consisting either of workmen alone, or of workmen and employers together; but it were greatly to be desired that they should multiply and become more effective. We have spoken of them more than once; but it will be well here to explain how much they are needed, to show that they exist by their own right, and to enter into their organization and their work. . . .

Particular societies, then, although they exist within the State, and are each a part of the State, nevertheless, cannot be prohibited by the State absolutely and as such. For to enter into "society" of this kind is the natural right of man; and the State must protect natural rights, not destroy them; and if it forbids its citizens to form associations, it contradicts the very principle of its own existence; for both they and it exist in virtue of the same principle, viz., the natural propensity of man to live in society.

There are times, no doubt, when it is right that the law should interfere to prevent association; as when men join together for purposes which are evidently bad, unjust, or dangerous to the State. In such cases the public authority may justly forbid the formation of associations, and may dissolve them when they already exist. But every precaution should be taken not to violate the rights of individuals, and not to make unreasonable regulations under the pretense of public benefit. For laws only bind when they are in accordance with right reason, and, therefore, with the eternal law of God.[3]

---

[3] "Human law is law only in virtue of its accordance with right reason; and thus it is manifest that it flows from the eternal law. And in so far as it deviates from right reason it is called an unjust law; in such case it is not law at all, but rather a species of violence."—St. Thomas of Aquin, *Summa Theologica*, 1a 2æ Q. xciii. Art. iii.

Speaking summarily, we may lay it down as a general and perpetual law, that Workmen's Associations should be so organized and governed as to furnish the best and most suitable means for attaining what is aimed at, that is to say, for helping each individual member to better his condition to the utmost, in body, mind and property. It is clear that they must pay special and principal attention to piety and morality, and that their internal discipline must be directed precisely by these considerations; otherwise they entirely lose their special character, and come to be very little better than those societies which take no account of religion at all. What advantage can it be to a workman to obtain by means of a society all that he requires, and to endanger his soul for want of spiritual food? *What doth it profit a man if he gain the whole world and suffer the loss of his own soul?*

122

INDUSTRIAL DEMOCRACY

JOHN A. RYAN [1]

Democracy means rule by the people. As we all know, it generally describes popular rule in political government. A democratic state is one in which the people make and execute the laws, either directly, or through elected representatives. Its opposite is an autocratic state, in which government is in the hands of a king, who either rules alone, or with the assistance of a small, privileged class. Both the king and the privileged, or aristocratic, group obtain their political power by inheritance, not by commission from the people.

Democracy in industry, or industrial democracy, carries over the idea of popular rule from the political field to the industrial field. In general, it means direction and control of industry by the people. At least, that is the significance of the words themselves. In actual use, the phrase has many and various significations. At the one extreme, it has been used as a synonym of Socialism, or Collectivism; at the other extreme, it has been applied to collective bar-

[1] Published by The Rossi-Bryn Company, 1925. Washington, D. C.

gaining. In other words, some persons understand by industrial democracy the ownership and operation of the instruments of production by the democratic state, the democratic government, the people acting through their political representatives; while other persons apply the phrase to that arrangement by which the workers, through their chosen representatives, have a share in making the labor contract, and in determining the conditions of employment. Those who use the term in the former sense are Socialists; those who use it in the latter sense are trade unionists.

Neither of these uses of industrial democracy is necessarily wrong. A Socialist organization of industry would be government of industry by the people, at least ultimately and fundamentally. Determination of wages, hours, and other employment conditions, is partial popular government of industry within certain limits; that is, with regard to the labor contract. Such popular control through the labor union does not touch the ownership of the instruments of production, nor the direction of industrial operations. Nevertheless, it includes a degree of industrial democracy.

As the term has come to be used, therefore, industrial democracy is a relative thing. It means, or may mean, simply a greater degree of popular control than has heretofore existed in our industrial system. In every use of the phrase, however, popular control means control by the employees, or wage-earners. This is seen even in the mildest acceptation of the phrase, namely, the sense in which it is used by trade unionists.

The industrial democracy that I intend to discuss is considerably less than Socialism, and considerably more than collective bargaining, or trade union agreements. Socialism is impracticable and undesirable. Collective bargaining is insufficient. Socialism is now accepted by such a small number of persons that it does not come within the scope of practical consideration. The vast majority of American wage-earners do not believe in Socialism, and are very unlikely to accept it in the near future. On the other hand, a considerable proportion of the members of trade unions are apparently satisfied with that degree of industrial democracy which is embraced in the concept of collective bargaining. In my opinion, this amount of industrial democracy is inadequate, either to protect the interests of the wage-earners, to secure industrial efficiency, or to safeguard industrial peace. It is not a solution, even a temporary solution, of our greatest industrial problem.

Trade unionism, even though it include all the control which the most thorough conception of collective bargaining can comprehend, cannot give adequate protection to the masses of the wage-earners. It has never been extended to more than a small minority of all those who work for wages, and it is not likely to take in the majority for a long time to come. At least there is nothing in the present trend of industrial relations to indicate that the majority will become members of the labor unions in the next twenty-five years.

Even if all the wage-earners were now organized, the methods and policies of the labor union would not bring about industrial efficiency or industrial peace. The reason for this is to be found in the industrial antagonisms which would necessarily follow complete organization of labor into unions. From its very nature, the labor union is a fighting organization. Its primary aim is to secure for its members a larger share of the product of industry, and better working conditions in the matter of hours, shop arrangements, etc. On the other hand, the employer finds it to his interest, or thinks so, to oppose the efforts of the union in all these directions. Higher wages, a shorter working day, and improvement in working conditions mean for the employer reduced profits. At any rate, that is what he believes, and very often rightly believes. We need not stop here to consider the "economy of high wages," nor the general contention that the shorter working day and improved shop conditions are for the interest of employer, as well as employee. This theory is true only within certain limits. Anyhow, it is not accepted by more than a small per cent of employers.

Therefore, the trade union meets the employer, or the association of employers, on a basis and in a spirit of combat, not of co-operation. When the two groups come together for the purpose of making a trade agreement, each strives to gain as much and to concede as little as it can. Employer and employee have, indeed, certain common interests. In general, it is good for both that industrial operations should go on without interruption and that the joint product should be as large as possible. The greater the product, the larger will be the amount to be divided. Nevertheless, the diversity of interests is more important, or at least always seems so, than the community of interests. The manner in which the product shall be divided between the two groups seems of much greater consequence than the size of the product. Hence, when the groups are making a bargain both lay stress upon the division of the product, both emphasize diversity of interests rather than community of interests. If they fail to agree, there is a strike, with consequent loss to both parties. If they effect an agreement, one or the other, or both, very often believe that they have not obtained all that was their due. This condition does not make for industrial contentment, or industrial peace.

From the viewpoint of industrial efficiency, the whole condition may be summed up in the statement that the worker is not interested in his work. In very many industries, particularly in the great industries owned by corporations, the majority of the employees have little or no thought of the prosperity of the concern that employs them. What they are interested in, primarily, is their jobs. The fear that if they do not turn out a reasonable amount of work the product will be insufficient to afford them the wages which have been agreed upon, seldom affects them, or determines the rate or quality of their efforts. They assume that the product will be sufficient to provide their remuneration, and they scarcely ever fear that the employing concern will have to shut down because of their failure to turn out a larger daily product. The thought that they are fundamentally co-operating with the employer in a common enterprise does not often enter the minds of the workers, or if it does, it has very little influence over their attitude toward their tasks.

The worker's lack of interest in his work may be considered with advantage from another viewpoint. In our great urban industries, on the railroads, and in the mines, the industrial population is rather sharply divided into two groups. On the one hand is a small number of persons who own the instruments of production, and direct their operation. On the other hand is the vast majority who neither own nor direct. They merely carry out orders.

Since they do not own and do not direct, they have little or no conscious interest in the fortunes of the concern that employs them. They are interested only in holding their jobs, and in obtaining the best conditions of employment that they can get from the employer.

If all wage-earners had some hope of becoming owners, or partial owners, of the instruments of production, they would necessarily be interested in something more than their jobs and their working conditions. If they looked forward to a time when they would share in the ownership of the concern that employs them, they would necessarily be interested in the prosperity of that concern. If each worker expected to become the owner and director of a business of his own, he would be interested in the success of his employer's business, because he would be moved by business considerations, and would be acquiring the business man's viewpoint. He would look upon his employee function as temporary, as subordinate to, and as a preparation for his function as director of industry. In such conditions, the diversity of interests between employer and employee would be minimized in the consciousness of both. Most of the emphasis would be placed upon their common interests. The employee would be more interested in saving his money, in turning out a larger product, and in acquiring the knowledge necessary for his later activity as an owner and operator of some industry or business.

Many years ago, that psychology and that hope were possessed by a large proportion of American wage-earners. Indeed, the American industrial tradition has, until comparatively recent years, included the belief that almost any wage-earner, who worked hard, tried to acquire industrial knowledge, and saved his money, had a solid hope of becoming something more than a wage-earner, long before he reached the end of his working days. Some twenty years ago, John Mitchell, who was for many years the successful leader of the Mine Workers' Union, declared that 90 per cent of American wage-earners had reconciled themselves to the prospect of remaining such all their lives. In effect, Mr. Mitchell declared that the American industrial traditions had ceased to be in accord with the facts. He was sharply criticised for this statement by many of our metropolitan newspapers, by many men who prided themselves on being self-made, and by many other men who never took the trouble to examine the trend of industrial change or the actual facts concerning industrial opportunities. As everyone who is acquainted with these facts now knows, the proportion of wage-earners in urban industries, in the mines, and on the railroads, that can expect to become owners or directors of industry, is very small. Certainly, it is not greater than 10 per cent. This is simply the expression of a mathematical relation. If not more than 10 per cent of those engaged in industry occupy, or tend to occupy, proprietary and directive positions, it is obvious that the other 90 per cent must, at any given time, occupy a subordinate and wage-earning position.

It is true that a large proportion, or even all of the wage-earners, might, until past middle age, indulge the hope of some day being included in the fortunate minority who rise to positions of ownership and direction. So long as they cling to this hope, they would have the viewpoint, and practice the industrial virtues of persons who had the certain assurance of reaching that goal. Even though the hope were an illusion, it would, so long as it were cherished, produce the beneficent effects in the mind of the wage-earner.

However, the fact is that no such hope or thought affects, for any considerable time, or to any effective extent, the minds of the great majority of wage-earners. It is only the exceptionally energetic, the exceptionally able, and the exceptionally ambitious, who look forward to the time when they will become business men, and whose activities and consciousness during their wage-earning period are notably determined by this prospect. The great majority think of themselves as likely to continue as wage-earners during all their working lives. Their attitude toward their jobs and toward the industrial system is determined accordingly.

Obviously, the average worker would be interested in his work if our industrial system were reorganized in such a fashion that the majority were owners of the instruments of production. The most desirable and the most democratic arrangement would be that in which the workers owned and carried on the industry in which they were engaged. They would be at once capitalists, business men, and laborers. This would be what is known as co-operative production, or productive co-operation. However, such a reorganization of industry, or of any considerable part of industry, cannot be hoped for in the near future. It would necessarily be a matter of very slow growth and accomplishment.

In the meantime, there is another method of getting the workers interested in their work, improving their status, and promoting industrial efficiency and industrial peace. It includes a certain degree of industrial democracy. Various names have been used to designate it, but the one which seems most appropriate is, "labor sharing in management." That the workers be given a share in the management of industry, means at once something more and something less than might be understood from that phrase. Those who have studied most intelligently the problem of management sharing by labor, do not think that the average wage-earner is now capable of taking any part in either the commercial or financial operations of a business. Buying materials, marketing the product, borrowing money, making extensions of a business enterprise, and many other of the commercial and financial activities of an industrial concern, are at present beyond the competence of the great majority of wage-earners. Indeed, the masses of the workers have no desire to undertake such responsibilities. On the other hand, labor sharing in management extends beyond collective bargaining and welfare activities. To take part in determining the labor contract as regards wages, hours, and other working conditions, is an already recognized function of the trade union. To have something to say about welfare activities, is a recognized function of those who are employed in a given shop or establishment. Neither of these forms of control is within the field of management sharing.

The nature of the field can be most clearly indicated through one or two examples. The American Multigraph Company of Cleveland, Ohio, has, or at any rate had a few years ago, an organization of employees which was subdivided into fifteen working committees. Each of the committees had charge of a task which involved a certain measure of workers' control. Some of them had to do with one or other phase of the labor contract; others, with shop conditions; still others, with entertainment and welfare activities. Other sub-committees dealt with production control, improvements in the company product, time and motion study, spoiled work, machinery and tools, sales co-operation, and the economy of the eight hour day. All subjects specified in the last sentence come properly under the head of labor sharing in management. They deal with the management of production, with the production department of the industry. They are all matters in which the employees have a direct interest, and about which they may be assumed to have some knowledge which could be utilized with advantage by the responsible management of the enterprise.

Another example is found in the experiment inaugurated some three or four years ago in the Baltimore and Ohio Railroad shops at Glenwood, Pa. A committee representing the Machinists' Union met regularly and frequently with a committee representing the management of the shops. The arrangement was entered into as an experiment in co-operation between employer and employee for the benefit of both. The two primary ends were to increase the number of days' employment per year, and to reduce waste in production. The precise method by which these aims were pursued is necessarily technical and need not be described here. What is important to note, is the spirit and the results. It is to be kept in mind that the co-operating committee representing the workers was drawn from, and selected by the regular trade union. No "employee representation" plan, nor "company union" plan was thought necessary to the success of the project. It was the regular union, which embraced most of the employees in the shops, that joined with the management in the experiment. Indeed, the initiative came from the union, which employed an industrial engineer to work out the plan of co-operation with the management. When the plan was put into operation, it naturally had the good will of the workers. The two committees, therefore, met in a spirit of co-operation, not in a spirit of opposition. And they have continued to meet in that spirit.

With regard to the results, the experience at Glenwood proved so satisfactory that it has been extended to all the forty-five shop centers on the B. & O. system. It has also been adopted by the Canadian National Railways. In an address delivered a few months ago, Mr. Daniel Willard, President of the Baltimore and Ohio Company, said: "I believe that it has now been fully demonstrated that the co-operative plan which the Baltimore and Ohio Railroad has put into effect, in co-operation with its shop employees, and with the support of their respective unions, is no longer an experiment. It has more than justified itself from many different angles. It is now a part of the definitely adopted policy of the Baltimore and Ohio Company, and I have a feeling that we have yet not begun to realize the potential possibilities of the plan."

Some idea of the possibilities of labor participation in the operative, or productive side of industrial management can be obtained from certain figures submitted by Mr. Willard. The number of suggestions concerning various phases of management, which were brought into the meetings of the joint committee, was 5272. Of these, no less than 3800 were adopted. All this happened within a space of eight months. While Mr. Willard did not specify what proportion of the five thousand and odd suggestions came from the employees, we may safely assume that it was at least one-half of the total number. This fact alone is convincing testimony of the amount of interest which the plan has aroused in the workers.

The theory of labor sharing in management rests upon some of the most fundamental desires and capacities of human nature. A vast majority of persons desire to exercise some controlling influence over their environment. There is some directive, initiative, creative capacity in every normal human being. The industrial population is not sharply divided into two classes, one possessing all the directive capacity, the other possessing merely the capacity to carry out orders. The wage-earners have directive talents as well as talents to obey. They have potencies to become something more than animated instruments of production. If their directive capacities do not obtain some opportunity for expression, they naturally remain relatively uninterested in their work. When their directive and creative faculties are exercised, their interest is necessarily aroused, and their efficiency increased.

This does not mean that the average wage-earner is as capable of directing industry, or any of its operations, as the average employer, or industrial superintendent. It is not necessary to prove or disprove this hypothesis. All that is here contended is that the majority of workers possess *some* directive capacity, and have some desire to exercise that capacity.

These facts have been strangely ignored by the majority of employers. Thus, they have deprived themselves of the benefits which they might have obtained through the assistance and co-operation of the rank and file of their employees. The statement of Dr. Royal Meeker, for many years United States Commissioner of the Bureau of Labor Statistics, is worth quoting on this point: "I insist that the management, even scientific management, has not a monopoly of all the brains in an establishment. . . . As a worker and a student, I feel that there is a tremendous, latent, creative force in the workers of today, which is not being utilized at all. . . . Here is a vast source of industrial power, which has been cut off, isolated, by the transformation of little business into big business. It will be difficult to tap this source, but tap it we must, if we are to continue anything resembling the present organization, with its large scale production. The good will of the workers is a much more potent force in making for industrial efficiency than all the scientific management formulas and systems of production."

We may sum up as follows the benefits that may reasonably be looked for from labor sharing in management: through the exercise of their directive and creative faculties, the workers will acquire greater consciousness of their dignity, and greater self-respect; out of this will necessarily come interest in their work, and a sense of responsibility for the welfare of the employing concern. The merely business relation, the "cash nexus" between employer and employee will be supplanted by a human relation, which will make the latter feel more like a partner, and less like an antagonist of the former. The employer will gain in pecuniary welfare and peace of mind; while the whole community will be benefited through a larger and more efficient production.

So much for that measure of industrial democracy which is possible in the productive operations of industry. All that has been said in the last few pages refers to the shop.

Is it possible to carry industrial democracy into the wider field of commercial and financial management? Undoubtedly it is, but the method by which, and the extent to which this can be accomplished, are matters upon which it is impossible to speak with any degree of confidence. The reason is lack of experience. Very few industrial corporations have admitted the wage-earners to membership in the board of directors. Even where this policy has been adopted, the employee numbers have always been in a small minority. Nevertheless, it is correct to say that the presence of even one wage-earner on the board of directors of a corporation, exemplifies to some degree the principle of industrial democracy in the supreme management.

More ambitious and thoroughgoing plans of democracy in the supreme direction of industry have been advocated by various persons and organizations. The one which is best known in the United States is the so-called Plumb Plan. In its original form, it was proposed by the late Mr. Glenn E. Plumb for the solution of the railway problem. Its main features can be stated very briefly. The ownership of the railroads should be vested in the government of the United States. Their operation should be conducted by a board consisting of fifteen persons, five of whom should represent the federal government; five, the executive employees; and five, the subordinate employees. All matters of policy, including the determination of wages and salaries and the fixing of charges for carrying freight and passengers, would be in the control of this board. The annual surplus which remained after wages, salaries, interest on the government's investment, and all other charges had been paid, would be divided into two equal parts, one-half going to the treasury of the railroad management, and one-half to be distributed as a dividend to both classes of employees. The share going into the railroad treasury would be used for betterments and extensions. If, in any year, the railroad's share of the surplus should exceed 5 per cent of operating revenues, the excess would be utilized for the reduction of freight and passenger rates. In this way, the interests of the consumers would receive consideration.

Many who believe in government ownership and operation of the railroads have objected to this plan on the ground that it provides, in effect, too much industrial democracy. The employees, executive and subordinate, would have two-thirds of the membership of the board of directors. Therefore, they would be in a position to raise wages and salaries indefinitely. In reply to this objection, Mr. Plumb contended that he had provided against this danger by the provision that the executive, or managerial, employees should receive a larger share of the surplus profits than the subordinate employees. Now it is conceivable that the share of the former should be so much greater than the share of the latter, that the former would be more interested in bringing about a surplus than they would in raising their salaries. But this contention supposes such a great discrepancy between the rates at which the two classes would participate in the surplus, that the proposal would seem to be unworkable. It is practically certain that the executive employees would be more interested in joining with the subordinate employees to vote both classes higher pay than they would in keeping down wages and salaries for the sake of providing a surplus in which their share would be proportionately greater than that of the subordinate employees.

Here, then, we have the difficulty which confronts any plan of industrial democracy in the supreme direction of a business concern. Either capital or labor must have the majority of the membership in the board of directors; or the two factors must be equally represented; or representatives of the public must be admitted as an impartial element to hold the balance even between the groups representing, respectively, capital and labor. If labor controls the board of directors, it will be tempted to raise wages and salaries at the expense of interest and dividends, and even at the expense of the consumer. If capital is in control, it strives to keep down wages and salaries, and to get as much as possible from the consumer for the sake of interest, dividends and profits. The supposition that the power of labor and capital might be equal on the board of directors, does not seem to be practicable, at least as a permanent arrangement. The introduction of a mediating and balancing element in the form of members appointed by public authority, would seem to meet the difficulty. And it would have the very important advantage of so directing the policies of the corporation as to take some account of the interests of the consumer.

So far as government-owned industries are concerned, the problem is comparatively simple. In the case of the railroads, for example, the board of directors proposed by Mr. Plumb should be reorganized. Since government members represent at the same time the government as capitalist, and the people as consumers, they should comprise a majority of the board. To be sure, the objection may be made that the interest of consumer plus the interest of the government as investor, would outweigh in the minds of the government members, the welfare of the employees. Quite true; nevertheless, the employees would be likely to get far more consideration from such a group than they would obtain from the capitalist majority in a board of directors having control of a private corporation. At any rate, the only alternative is that of giving the majority control to labor. Some day in the future that may be wise, but at present it seems to us, to say the least, premature.

Mr. Plumb's proposal for industrial democracy in privately owned corporations has many excellent features, not the least of which is recognizing that the employees have a substantial claim upon, and interest in the concern by which they are employed. Nevertheless, the plan has the same defect as that which inheres in his plan for the railroads. That is, it would give majority control and, indeed, overwhelming majority control to the employees. In the nature of things, and in the nature of industry, there may, indeed, be no decisive reason why dominant labor control is any worse than dominant capitalist control. Each will be tempted to use its power for its own ends. The interests of the investor are no more important than the interests of the laborer. Possibly human welfare would suffer no more as a result of labor control than as a result of capitalist control. Nevertheless, any scheme of industrial democracy which proposes to transfer the dominant control from capital to labor, has no hope of realization in the near future. If it comes, it will appear as a development of a gradual process.

It is worth while to repeat, at this point, the statement that in private corporations, capital, as well as labor, might be prevented from exercising dominant control through the presence on the board of directors of persons appointed by public authority. It is likewise worth while to stress again the fact that this public group would have an important function to perform in safeguarding the interests of the consumers.

So long as capital remains in the hands of persons who are distinct from the wage-earners, there is no likelihood that the latter will obtain dominant control of industry. The greatest degree of industrial democracy that can be hoped for is the presence on the board of directors of a sufficient number of labor representatives to form, in conjunction with the representatives of the public, a majority of the board. If the public is unrepresented, then the labor members will undoubtedly remain a minority for a long time to come, in any experiment that is likely to be made. Even this minority representation would constitute a degree of industrial democracy. And it would be a vast improvement over the existing condition, in which labor is scarcely ever represented on boards of directors. In any deliberative body, the presence of even one person who can set forth intelligently the needs and viewpoint of an important group of persons, is a great advantage to that group.

It has been asserted above that in private corporations, whose boards of directors include no representatives of the public, capitalist control will remain dominant. However, it is possible to make this control ultimate and conditional, instead of immediate and continuous. In that case, the general and normal control of the business would be in the hands of the employees. Something of this kind is exemplified in the operation of the Dennison Manufacturing Company, at Framingham, Mass. In that arrangement, the immediate control is carried on by those managerial employees who have been with the Company at least five years. The capitalist shareholders exercise no immediate control, but they receive a guarantee and cumulative dividend of 8 per cent. If, at the end of any three-year period, their dividends have not averaged 8 per cent, they resume active control.

The theory of this arrangement seems to be that capital, as such, has no right to more than that rate of interest which is sufficient to induce men to invest their money in, and take the risk of a given industrial enterprise. The profits which remain after interest, wages, and all other charges have been met, are distributed among the managerial employees. This plan relates rewards to functions, distributes surplus profits among those whose labor or ability is responsible for creating the profits. The stockholder who is also a member of the managerial group shares in the profits, but as a worker, not as an owner of capital.

This seems to be a more scientific and more efficient plan of industrial government than that which exists in the ordinary corporations. It gives to the capitalist, as such, all that is necessary to induce him to continue his function as capitalist, and it gives the contingent and variable surplus to those who have the power to produce the surplus. Thus it provides the strongest incentive to productiveness and efficiency. It exemplifies the principle of industrial democracy to a safe and practicable degree. While the control of the Dennison Company is exercised by only a small proportion of the employees, there is no reason why it should not be extended, according as conditions warrant, to the majority, or even to the entire body of employees.

The Catholic viewpoint of industrial democracy has received no explicit mention in the foregoing pages. Nevertheless, it has been implicit in the whole discussion. No feature of industrial democracy, advocated or discussed in the foregoing paragraphs, is contrary to Catholic ethical or social principles. The complete, or even the dominant, control of industry by the capitalistic element is not an article of Catholic faith or morals. Government ownership and operation of the railroads is not opposed to Catholic doctrine. The presence of government representatives on the boards of directors of corporations runs counter to no principle of Catholic moral teaching. The same may be said of the proposal to limit the reward of the capitalist, as such, to a fair rate of interest. According to Catholic moral teaching, the money lender has a right to only a fair, or moderate, rate of interest. Why then, should the money investor have a right to any greater rate, except to the extent necessary to protect him against the greater risk?

Indeed, one might go further, and say that the spirit which animates many of the current proposals for industrial democracy is more in harmony with Catholic teaching than the theory and practice of complete capitalist control. The system of industry and industrial control which flourished in the Middle Ages, was the Guild System. In that period, Catholic social principles exercised a greater influence over economic arrangements than they have exercised at any other time in history. The Guild System arose and flourished, not merely in a society which was dominated by Catholic principles, but under the positive guidance and fostering care of the Church. Now the Guild System was essentially a system of labor control. The instruments of production were not owned by a separate, capitalist class, nor by any class that could properly be called capitalistic. They were owned by the men who operated them. Whatever of negotiation and trading was involved in carrying on productive enterprises, was conducted by the artisan-owners. Appropriate here is the characterization of that system, and that time, by Professor E. R. A. Seligman: "It was a period of supremacy of labor over capital, and the master worked beside the artisan."

The industrial democracy of the guild system cannot be restored in this day of greater machinery and greater corporations. But the spirit of that earlier and saner period can be made to function again in the modern system. It can express itself through labor sharing in shop management, through labor membership in boards of directors, through labor control which protects adequately the interests of the capitalists, as in the Dennison plan, and through co-operative ownership and management of the instruments of production. While the last named system has received no mention in the foregoing pages, it would realize a higher form of industrial democracy than any of the plans that have been discussed. And it would be in accord with the dictum of Pope Leo XIII: "The law, therefore, should favor ownership, and its policy should be to induce as many people as possible to become owners."

123

A MODERN GILD PROGRAM
Joseph Husslein [1]

Of all the constructive labor movements that at the close of the war are sweeping over the world in a mighty wave of industrial unrest, there is not one whose leaders are not inspired by the supreme idea of labor organization. Trade unionism and the cooperative movement, Syndicalism and the groupings of the I. W. W., gild Socialism and the Soviet system are but different and often hostile phases of the same world-wide labor agitation that is steadily gathering to a crest and moving on with impetuous force. Law-abiding or opposed to all authority, Christian or relentlessly determined on the destruction of all religious beliefs, these various movements still conform with one another in a vague acceptance of the gild idea.

Anarchism cannot be reckoned among the world's constructive forces. Though it may blend with other movements and even for the time adopt their purposes, it remains, as its name implies, a pure negation. Its immediate object is neither more nor less than the annihilation of the entire existing order of society. Out of the ashes of the old world, sunk in flame and ruin, a new order is phenix-like to arise in liberty, youth and beauty. Destruction is sufficient for today. The morrow will provide for itself. Such was the principle of its founder, Bakounin. The constructive ideas that its ardent champions claim for it are nothing more than a mere general license, with no authority of God or man to hold it in restraint.

Socialism, too, while allied with a thousand plans that are not of its own origin or being, contains but one vague constructive thought: The more or less common ownership of the means of production and distribution. How far this shall be effected, how it shall be carried out, and what shall be its future details, no one is qualified to say. We do not marvel, therefore, that Socialism has been the prolific breeding place of every variety of radical thought.

[1] *Democratic Industry*, pp. 285-293. (P. J. Kenedy & Sons, New York.)

Countless numbers of its leaders, and of its rank and file have steadily drifted to the gild idea, which many of its own members now conceive to be the only practical working plan.

Men realize that the outcome of Socialism can be nothing but tyranny. This was again fully evinced in its ultimate development, Bolshevism. Speaking of the philosophy of the Russian Bolshevists, the American Secretary of Labor, the Hon. William B. Wilson, rightly said:

"The will of the majority is as objectionable to them as it was to the Kaiser or the Tsar. It establishes a dictatorship on the plea that the autocrat knows better what is best for the people than they themselves know. It sets up a close dictatorship which demands obligatory labor service. The worker sacrifices his own free will. Whether he likes his employment or not—whatever may be his desire to move, he cannot do so, without permission of the dictator. He cannot change the conditions of his employment, he must not quit, because of the merciless 'dictatorship of individuals for definite processes of work.'

"This dictatorship would control the courts which are to be used as a means of discipline that will consider responsibility for the 'pangs of famine and unemployment to be visited upon those who fail to produce bread for men and fuel for industry.'

"The public press is to be systematically repressed or controlled. Nothing is to reach the attention of the masses except that which has been prepared for them."

The gild system, then, under one form or another, is doubtless the most important social suggestion for our own time, and indeed for any stage of industrial development. It is the one unfailing means of self-help that labor possesses. The first true conception of the craft-gild idea was given to the world by the Catholic Church. We are not therefore surprised that in assigning the causes of our modern social disorders Pope Leo XIII significantly singled out before all others the abolition of the gilds: "For the ancient workingmen's gilds were abolished in the last century, and no other organization took their place."[2] So,

---

[2] "On the Condition of the Working Classes." See A. C. Breig, *Papal Program of Social Reform,* p. 10.

too, in the work of reconstruction he naturally placed the greatest stress upon their speedy restoration. It will be easy for working men to solve aright the question of the hour, he tells them, "if they will form associations, choose wise guides and follow on the path which with so much advantage to themselves and the commonwealth was trodden by their fathers before them." [3] The utmost betterment of the condition of each individual member "in body, mind and property," [4] is the purpose for which these gilds are to be founded. But for their success religion is as essential today as in the days of old. It is true that the outline of these new organizations drawn by Pope Leo in his Encyclical on "The Condition of the Working Classes," is suggestive merely of an ideal Christian labor unionism, such as alone was practical at the time of his writing. This does not preclude a far closer approximation to the medieval gild system. He purposely refrains from adding more specific details, since the latter, as he wisely remarks, must of necessity vary with time, and place, and circumstances:

"We do not judge it expedient to enter into minute particulars touching the subject of organization; this must depend on national character, on practice and experience, on the nature and aim of the work to be done, on the scope of the various trades and employments, and on other circumstances of fact and of time; all of which should be carefully considered." [5]

Following the example of his predecessor, Pope Piux X, too, called attention above all to the need of workingmen's unions. He, too, reminded men that social science is not of yesterday, that no new civilization is to be invented and no city to be built in the clouds; that the successful organizations established in the past, under the wise cooperation of Church and State, are of far more than historic interest. Writing to the Archbishops and Bishops of France, he thus instructed them in this regard:

"It will be enough to take up again, with the help of true workers for social restoration, the organisms broken by the Revolution, and to adapt them to the new situation created by the material evolution of contemporary society in the

[3] *Ibid.*, p. 56.
[4] *Ibid.*, pp. 53, 54.
[5] *Ibid.*, p. 53.

same Christian spirit which of old inspired them. For the true friends of the people are neither revolutionists, nor innovators, but traditionalists." [6]

Urgently as he recommends the gild ideal, his greatest stress is placed upon the need of adaptation, the need of carefully availing ourselves of "all the practical methods furnished at the present day by progress in social and economic studies." This thought is even more clearly expressed in his letter to the Bishops of Italy, June 11, 1905:

"It is impossible at the present day to reestablish in the same form all the institutions which may have been useful, and were even the only efficient ones in past centuries, so numerous are the radical modifications which time has brought to society and life, and so many are the fresh needs which changing circumstances cease not to call forth. But the Church throughout her long history has always and on every occasion luminously shown that she possesses a wonderful power of adaptation to the varying conditions of civil society, without injury to the integrity or immutability of faith or morals." [7]

For a brief but complete summary of all that has hitherto been said we may turn to the Encyclical of Leo XIII on "The Condition of the Working Classes." Referring to the various associations and organizations that can be created for the benefit of the laborer, he concludes:

"The most important of all are workingmen's unions, for these virtually include all the rest. History attests what excellent results were brought about by the craft gilds of olden times. They were the means of affording not only many advantages to the workingmen, but in no small degree of promoting the advancement of art, as numerous monuments remain to bear witness. Such unions should be suited to the requirements of this, our age, an age of wider education, of different habits, and of far more numerous requirements in daily life." [8]

But neither Leo XIII nor Pius X could have foreseen the rapidity with which social developments were accelerated by the stirring events of the World War. The slow

---

[6] Letter to Archbishops and Bishops of France, August 25, 1910.
[7] *On Christian Social Reform*, Catholic Social Guild Pamphlets, pp. 18, 19.
[8] Cnf. Breig, p. 48.

material evolution of centuries was then compressed within as many years of energetic, throbbing life, of revolutionary and often misdirected social action. Yet it was all finally to aid in bringing the world nearer to the ideals of the Middle Ages, in making possible a closer approximation of the Catholic gild system than even Leo XIII, with all his marvelous insight into the social developments of the future, could have considered feasible. He has not, however, failed to leave provision for even this situation. We need but turn again to the final norm by which, as he says, every labor organization of the future must be tested and found true or wanting:

"To sum up, then, we may lay it down as a general and lasting law that workingmen's associations should be so organized and governed as to furnish the best and most suitable means for attaining what is aimed at, that is to say, for helping each individual member to better his condition to the utmost in body, mind and property." [9]

This ideal was strictly kept in view in the program of social reconstruction drawn up by the Administrative Committee of the National Catholic War Council, January, 1919, and later incorporated in the *Congressional Record* of the United States. That suggestions occur here which were never formally included in the Encyclicals of Leo XIII or Pius X need not startle anyone. They are not the less surely contained in that "general and lasting law" of the great "Pope of the Workingmen" which was just quoted. In the reconstructive program, stamped with the seal of the Hierarchy of the United States, can be found the consummation of the gild idea. In their most vital passage the Bishops say:

"The full possibilities of increased production will not be realized so long as the majority of the workers remain mere wage-earners. The majority must somehow become owners, or at least in part, of the means of production. They can be enabled to reach this stage gradually through cooperative productive societies and copartnership arrangements. In the former the workers own and manage the industries themselves; in the latter they own a substantial part of the corporate stock and exercise a reasonable share in the management. However slow the attainment of these

[9] *Ibid.*, pp. 53, 54.

ends they will have to be reached before we can have a thoroughly efficient system of production, or an industrial social order that will be secure from the danger of revolution." [1]

Such is the aim of the new Catholic gild system. No one maintains that these developments are possible without wisely directed labor organizations, both where there is question of establishing cooperative productive societies— a true gild ideal—or of merely sharing in the management of industries, obviously through the representatives of craft gilds. Such, too, is clearly the meaning of the Bishops, who strongly vindicate the right of labor "to organize and to deal with employers through representatives," and heartily approve of the establishment of shop committees, "working wherever possible with the trade union." [2] That such methods will imply "to a great extent the abolition of the wage-system," they candidly confess, but their main purpose is the increase of private productive ownership and so the most perfect attainment of the supreme gild ideal proposed by Leo XIII: the betterment of the condition of each individual member "to the utmost in body, mind and property." In the words of Pope Pius X, they are "neither revolutionists, nor innovators, but traditionalists." And with these great Pontiffs they, too, understand that no program of labor can be finally successful that is not inspired by true religious ideals. Here is the great need of the future.

124

INDUSTRIAL RELATIONS [3]

In 1891, Pope Leo XIII published his Encyclical *Rerum Novarum*, a document which shows the insight of that great Pontiff into the industrial conditions of the time, and his wisdom in pointing out the principles needed for the solving of economic problems. "That the spirit of revolutionary change which has long been disturbing the nations

---

[1] *Social Reconstruction.* Reconstruction Pamphlets, No. 1, p. 22.
[2] *Ibid.*, p. 19.
[3] *Pastoral Letter of the Archbishops and Bishops of the United States,* 1919.

of the world, should have passed beyond the sphere of practical economics, is not surprising. The elements of the conflict now raging are unmistakable, in vast expansion of industrial pursuits and the marvelous discoveries of science; in the changed relations between masters and workmen; in the enormous fortunes of some few individuals and the utter poverty of the masses; in the increased self-reliance and closer mutual combination of the working classes; as also, finally in the prevailing moral degeneracy. The momentous gravity of the state of things now obtaining fills every mind with painful apprehension; wise men are discussing it; practical men are proposing schemes; popular meetings, legislatures and rulers of nations are all busied with it—and actually there is no question that has taken a deeper hold on the public mind."

How fully these statements apply to our present situation, must be clear to all who have noted the course of events during the year just elapsed. The War indeed has sharpened the issues and intensified the conflict that rages in the world of industry; but the elements, the parties and their respective attitudes are practically unchanged. Unchanged also are the principles which must be applied, if order is to be restored and placed on such a permanent basis that our people may continue their peaceful pursuits without dread of further disturbance. So far as men are willing to accept those principles as the common ground on which all parties may meet and adjust their several claims, there is hope of a settlement without the more radical measures which the situation seemed but lately to be forcing on public authority. But in any event, the agitation of the last few months should convince us that something more is needed than temporary arrangements or local readjustments. The atmosphere must be cleared so that, however great the difficulties which presently block the way, men of good will may not, through erroneous preconceptions, go stumbling on from one detail to another, thus adding confusion to darkness of counsel.

"It is the opinion of some," says Pope Leo XIII, "and the error is already very common, that the social question is merely an economic one, whereas in point of fact, it is first of all a moral and religious matter, and for that reason its settlement is to be sought mainly in the moral law and the pronouncements of religion" (Apostolic Letter, *Graves de communi*, January 18, 1901). These words are as pertinent and their teaching as necessary today as they were nineteen years ago. Their meaning, substantially, has been reaffirmed by Pope Benedict XV in his recent statement that "without justice and charity there will be no social progress." The fact that men are striving for what they consider to be their rights, puts their dispute on a moral basis; and wherever justice may lie, whichever of the opposing claims may have the better foundation, it is justice that all demand.

In the prosecution of their respective claims, the parties have, apparently, disregarded the fact that the people as a whole have a prior claim. The great number of unnecessary strikes which have occurred within the last few months is evidence that justice has been widely violated as regards the rights and needs of the public. To assume that the only rights involved in an industrial dispute are those of capital and labor, is a radical error. It leads, practically, to the conclusion that at any time and for an indefinite period, even the most necessary products can be withheld from general use until the controversy is settled. In fact, while it lasts, millions of persons are compelled to suffer hardship for want of goods and services which they require for reasonable living. The first step, therefore, toward correcting the evil is to insist that the rights of the community shall prevail, and that no individual claim conflicting with those rights shall be valid.

Among those rights is that which entitles the people to order and tranquillity as the necessary condition for social existence. Industrial disturbance invariably spreads beyond the sphere in which it originates, and interferes, more or less seriously, with other occupations. The whole economic system is so compacted together and its parts are so dependent one upon the other, that the failure of a single element, especially if this be of vital importance, must affect all the rest. The disorder which ensues is an injustice inflicted upon the community; and the wrong is the greater because, usually, there is no redress. Those who are responsible for it pursue their own ends without regard for moral consequences and, in some cases, with no concern for the provisions of law. When such a temper asserts itself, indignation is aroused throughout the country and the authorities are urged to take action. This, under given circumstances, may be the only possible course; but, as experience shows, it does not eradicate the evil. A further diagnosis is needed. The causes of industrial trouble are generally known, as are also the various phases through which it develops and the positions which the several parties assume. The more serious problem is to ascertain why, in such conditions, men fail to see their obligations to one another and to the public, or seeing them, refuse to fulfil them except under threat and compulsion.

"The great mistake in regard to the matter now under consideration is to take up with the notion that class is naturally hostile to class, and that the wealthy and the workingmen are intended by nature to live in mutual conflict." (*Rerum Novarum*). On the contrary, as Pope Leo adds, "each needs the other: Capital cannot do without Labor, nor Labor without Capital. Religion is a powerful agency in drawing the rich and the bread-winner together, by reminding each class of its duties to the other and especially of the obligation of justice. Religion teaches the laboring man and the artisan to carry out honestly and fairly all equitable agreements freely arranged, to refrain from injuring person or property, from using violence and creating disorder. It teaches the owner and employer that the laborer is not their bondsman, that in every man they must respect his dignity and worth as a man and as a Christian; that labor is not a thing to be ashamed of, if we listen to right reason and to Christian philosophy, but is an honorable calling, enabling a man to sustain his life in a way upright and creditable; and that it is shameful and inhuman to treat men like chattels, as means for making money, or as machines for grinding out work." The moral value of man and the dignity of human labor are cardinal points in this whole question. Let them be the directive principles in industry, and they will go far toward preventing disputes. By treating the laborer first of all as a man, the employer will make him a better workingman; by respecting his own moral dignity as a man, the laborer will compel the respect of his employer and of the community.

The settlement of our industrial problems would offer less difficulty if, while upholding its rights, each party were disposed to meet the other in a friendly spirit. The strict requirements of justice can be fulfilled without creating animosity; in fact, where this arises, it is apt to obscure the whole issue. On the contrary, a manifest desire to win over, rather than drive, the opponent to the acceptance of equitable terms, would facilitate the recognition of claims which are founded in justice. The evidence of such a disposition would break down the barriers of mistrust and set up in their stead the bond of good will. Not an armistice but a conciliation would result; and this would establish all parties in the exercise of their rights and the cheerful performance of their duties.

The right of labor to organize, and the great benefit to be derived from workingmen's associations, was plainly set forth by Pope Leo XIII. In this connection, we would call attention to two rights, one of employees and the other of employers, the violation of which contributes largely to the existing unrest and suffering. The first is the right of the workers to form and maintain the kind of organization that is necessary and that will be most effectual in securing their welfare. The second is the right of employers to the faithful observance by the labor unions of all contracts and agreements. The unreasonableness of denying either of these rights is too obvious to require proof or explanation.

A dispute that cannot be adjusted by direct negotiation between the parties concerned, should always be submitted to arbitration. Neither employer nor employee may reasonably reject this method on the ground that it does not bring about perfect justice. No human institution is perfect or infallible; even our courts of law are sometimes in error. Like the law court, the tribunal of industrial arbitration provides the nearest approach to justice that is practically attainable; for the only alternative is economic force, and its decisions have no necessary relation to the decrees of justice. They show which party is economically stronger, not which is in the right.

The right of labor to a living wage, authoritatively and eloquently reasserted more than a quarter of a century ago by Pope Leo XIII, is happily no longer denied by any considerable number of persons. What is principally needed now is that its content should be adequately defined, and that it should be made universal in practice, through whatever means will be at once legitimate and effective. In particular, it is to be kept in mind that a living wage includes not merely decent maintenance for the present, but also a reasonable provision for such future needs as sickness, invalidity and old age. Capital likewise has its rights. Among them is the right to "a fair day's work for a fair day's pay," and the right to returns which will be sufficient to stimulate thrift, saving, initiative, enterprise, and all those directive and productive energies which promote social welfare.

In his pronouncement on Labor (*Rerum Novarum*) Pope Leo XIII describes the advantages to be derived by both employer and employee from "associations and organizations which draw the two classes more closely together." Such associations are especially needed at the present time. While the labor union or trade union has been, and still is, necessary in the struggle of the workers for fair wages and fair conditions of employment, we have to recognize that its history, methods and objects have made it essentially a militant organization. The time seems now to have arrived when it should be, not supplanted, but supplemented by associations or conferences, composed jointly of employers and employees, which will place emphasis upon the common interests rather than the divergent aims of the two parties, upon cooperation rather than conflict. Through such arrangements, all classes would be greatly benefited. The worker would participate in those matters of industrial management which directly concern him and about which he possesses helpful knowledge; he would acquire an increased sense of personal dignity and personal responsibility, take greater interest and pride in his work, and become more efficient and more contented. The employer would have the benefit of willing cooperation from, and harmonious relations with, his employees. The consumer, in common with employer and employee, would share in the advantages of larger and steadier production. In a word, industry would be carried on as a cooperative enterprise for the common good, and not as a contest between two parties for a restricted product.

Deploring the social changes which have divided "society into two widely different castes," of which one "holds power because it holds wealth," while the other is "the needy and powerless multitude," Pope Leo XIII declared that the remedy is "to induce as many as possible of the humbler classes to become owners" (*Rerum Novarum*). This recommendation is in exact accord with the traditional teaching and practice of the Church. When her social influence was greatest, in the later Middle Ages, the prevailing economic system was such that the workers were gradually obtaining a larger share in the ownership of the lands upon which, and the tools with which, they labored. Though the economic arrangements of that time cannot be restored, the underlying principle is of permanent application, and is the only one that will give stability to industrial society. It should be applied to our present system as rapidly as conditions will permit.

Whatever may be the industrial and social remedies which will approve themselves to the American people, there is one that, we feel confident, they will never adopt. That is the method of revolution. For it there is neither justification nor excuse under our form of government. Through the ordinary and orderly processes of education, organization and legislation, all social wrongs can be righted. While these processes may at times seem distressingly slow, they will achieve more in the final result than violence or revolution. The radicalism, and worse than radicalism, of the labor movement in some of the countries of Europe, has no lesson for the workers of the United States, except as an example of methods to be detested and avoided.

Pope Benedict has recently expressed a desire that the people should study the great encyclicals on the social question of his predecessor, Leo XIII. We heartily commend this advice to the faithful and, indeed, to all the people of the United States. They will find in these documents the practical wisdom which the experience of centuries has stored up in the Holy See and, moreover, that solicitude for the welfare of mankind which fitly characterizes the Head of the Catholic Church.

125

RIGHTS AND DUTIES OF THE UNIONS

J. Alfred Lane [1]

Labor has at last come into its own. Thank God that it has! Your improved status is not due to any voluntary concessions on the part of capital, but to your own brain and brawn and united strength. You have had to fight your way for every new foothold you have gained from serfdom up to freedom. The secret of your success has been a steady adherence to the principle that "in union there is strength." The workingman today, impelled by the instinct of self-preservation, has been merging his own individual self in the membership of a mighty and vast organization. Employers have to deal now mostly with labor unions instead of individual workmen. There is less chance for deception, there is less room for fraud, and thus any laboring man who refuses to join his brothers in united organization fails to understand his real interests, he weakens his own cause.

Let no man tell me that labor unions are radical. Individual labor leaders may be, but labor unions themselves are not. They are sound, they are sane. They violate no just law; they imperil no legitimate interest; they are opposed to no honest claim; they act within the sphere of social justice; they constitute the greatest economic necessity of today. They have given the laboring man a greater independence of character, they have offered him a greater self-respect, they have brought about a juster remuneration in his wages, they have won a higher appreciation of his dignity. They have lifted him up, they have elevated him, they have raised his labor to its proper place as a potent factor in the economic life of today. Hence I say to you, members of this convention, that no greater evil could possibly come to you as a class or as individuals than to sink back into that helpless individualism from which trade unionism has delivered you.

[1] Reprinted from *The Catholic Mind* for Dec. 22, 1922. An address delivered at the opening of the fortieth convention of the Bricklayers, Masons and Plasterers International Union, Springfield, Mass.

But for the very fact that you are so powerful, you must be careful. In union there is strength, but strength abused is just as bad as no strength at all. It is tempting to descend to the unfair, unjust, unscrupulous methods of the past, if you have the necessary physical strength to enforce them. But that would be employing the principle that "might makes right," and that is ethically unsound for labor as well as for capital. If a thing is right, uphold it, and with all your united strength enforce its recognition. If it is wrong, condemn it, and with equal strength seek to suppress it. The wrongs of the past can never be righted by wrongs of the present. The laws of God never change. Justice comes through charity, not injustice; and "charity is patient, is kind . . . dealeth not perversely . . . rejoiceth not in iniquity, but rejoiceth in the truth." It is only the little man who will allow himself to harbor hatred and seek revenge. The big, broad man is above that. Anyone can remember wrongs; it takes a man to forget them. A spirit of animosity never got anyone anywhere; a spirit of kindliness has. Vindictiveness may execute a temporary win, but it is always a win that finally loses.

Where you find that men are not on the level with you, where you feel that they are not square, be armed to meet them—but not on their own ground. Make them honest with you if you can, but under no circumstances allow them to make you dishonest, too. Overcome evil by good. In the long run you will find that the advice you have given to your own sons more than once is true. "Honesty is always the best policy that any man or union of men can pursue."

Let no man tell you that labor is necessarily opposed to capital. That is a lie. The greatest mistake that could possibly be made at the present is to act on the supposition and assumption that these two factors of production are hostile one to the other naturally, and that the wealthy and the workingman are intended by nature to live in mutual conflict. Nothing could be further from the truth. There may be, and there are, dishonest and unjust employers among the wealthy, just as there may be and are extremists among the workingmen. But capital itself is all right, and labor itself is all right. They are, in very truth, the two poles of the great dynamo of business. If one is injured, the other suffers. Capital needs labor, labor needs capital.

Society needs them both. Each one has what the other has not. One completes the other, and is in turn completed by it, and the peace, prosperity and happiness of every community depends upon the one asking and receiving from the other what the other alone can give.

Neither capital nor labor can be unmindful of each other. Each has its rights. They both have their duties. In demanding the recognition of one they may not, they must not, they cannot be unmindful of the other. The mere assertion of their rights on the part of either capital or labor without a fulfilment of their duties, can end only in the demoralization of the body politic. In such an assertion lies the root of all economic selfishness and the source of all economic strife. Remember, gentlemen, unions have their duties as well as their rights; and the exercise of one should never be allowed to interfere with the fulfilment of the other. If you ask for an honest wage, insist that you get it. You have a right to that, a right that God gave you and no man or set of men should be allowed to take it away from you. Your children should not be forced to quit school at a tender age and work because the family really needs their support. They are entitled to an education that will fit them to take their proper place as self-respecting citizens of the community in which they live. The boys and girls of today are the men and women of tomorrow. The future of this country demands that the workingman receive a fair, honest wage for his labor, not all he can get, providing he takes it; nor all he can take either, providing he gets it; but a decent, living wage, sufficient to support himself and family and reasonably educate his children. But remember that a fair wage implies fair labor. If you get one, you are in justice bound to give the other, and any man of your organization who would idle on the job because he felt the union would stand behind him in a tilt with his employer is not worthy of a man's place in a union of honest men. "Liberty is born" it is true, "in a recognition of personal rights; but it flourishes in a recognition of personal duties."

You are a mighty organization; you wield a tremendous power. What you have done in the past is but an earnest of the things you can do in the future. Ask not the impossible; seek not the unfair; demand not the unjust; but ask,

seek, demand what you would wish others under similar circumstances to ask, seek and demand of you. Put yourself in the other fellow's position, and do unto him as you would have him do unto you. For that constitutes the summary of all law, the abridgement of all justice, the root of all truth and sincerity.

We are passing through strange times, gentlemen, times that to many older minds than mine seem almost unprecedented. And just as there was need of Divine help, of Divine assistance, of Divine guidance in the days now past and gone to solve the difficult, intricate problems of life and save man from himself, so, too, there is need today of the same help, of the same assistance, of the same guidance from the self-same source and for the self-same purpose.

You and I know well that the world to-day seems utterly lost in the maze of reconstructive problems, and utterly dazed by the sudden turn which human events seem to have taken. It is one seething mass of discontent and unrest, the victim of the unbridled greed, avarice, ambition of a conscienceless few. It is sick and tired of panaceas, Utopian dreams and promises. It is sorely tried, disgusted and disappointed at the lack of candor, the lack of honor, the lack of sincerity, that has characterized many of the shapers of its destiny. It is becoming more and more receptive to the poisonous virus of human selfishness that is slowly but surely leading it into a political, social and economic cataclysm from which only God Himself will be able finally to extricate it and to save it.

Yes, there seems to be but one law governing the world today, and that the law of human selfishness. We have seen it in the conduct of the nations, who have as yet failed in their problems of readjustment and rehabilitation for no other reason than that the law of selfishness was allowed to enter into their counsels and deliberations and influence their supposed settlements of peace. We see it in the amazingly alarming increase of disrupted home lives, as couple after couple go before the courts of divorce and petition them to loose the bonds with which God has joined them together, so that unbridled self may have full, free rein to seek, satisfy, to satiate every whim and caprice of sensuous, selfish love. We see it in the individual, who today seems to be actuated by no other norm of human conduct than the norm of human selfishness. "What am I going to get out of it?" "What is there in it for me?" Do you think for one moment, gentlemen, that living conditions would be what they are today if those who are responsible for keeping them as they are today, thought a little more about others and a little less about themselves? What does the average man today care about others when it is a case of benefiting himself? You know I speak the truth when I say that most of them care nothing, absolutely nothing! It is a case of get what you can out of others, get all you can out of others, do not rest satisfied until you get practically all they have. No, the average individual today is not thinking about others; he is too busy thinking about himself. It is self, self, first—last—always.

If this is true, and it is true, in the political, domestic and social life of our times, it is equally true in the economic life. For too long a time was the laboring man kept in a position of inferiority and servitude. For too long a time were his nobler instincts stifled and his influence destroyed. For too long a time was he dispossessed of his God-given rights and burdened with oppressive duties. For too long a time did the law of human selfishness instead of the dictates of common justice regulate the actions of the wealthy in their dealings with the poor. The bigger the dam of patience, the worse the flood when the dam breaks. The reaction was bound to come. The reaction has come, and weighty, indeed, the consequences. The eyes of this country, for a long, long time, have been riveted on an industrial situation which threatened it with disaster. Momentarily the danger has been lessened, but optimistic indeed would that man be who would venture to say that it has been finally averted.

The capitalistic class is still looking out for capital, the laboring class is still all eyes on labor. One is not thinking of the interest of the other. Each is thinking of its own. But where human selfishness is allowed to rule the actions of men, human justice is very soon lost sight of. Where justice is lost sight of, honesty is little practiced. Where honesty is little practiced, confidence is destroyed. Where confidence is destroyed, suspicion, distrust and consequent unrest always follow. That is just what has happened. The selfishness and unconscionable greed in the world today has been productive of a seething mass of discontent and unrest that makes thoughtful men everywhere fearful of the consequences that may follow.

The world today is not the same as the world of the past. The men and women of today are not the same as the men and women of the past. Why, even the children of today are not the same as the children of the past. On September 17, 1796, the immortal founder of this country offered a piece of advice to his countrymen. In his farewell address to the American people, George Washington issued this solemn warning:

"Of all the dispositions and habits that lead to political prosperity, religion and morality are indispensable supports. The mere politician equally with the pious man, ought to respect and cherish them. A volume could not trace all their connections with private and public felicity. Where is the security for property, for reputation, for life, if the sense of religious obligation desert the oaths which are the instruments of investigation in courts of justice? And let us with caution indulge the supposition that morality can be maintained without religion. Reason and experience both forbid us to expect that national morality can prevail where religious principles are excluded."

Despite this historic warning, sixty-five per cent of the people of this country alone are said to be without religious affiliation of any kind. Thus we are reaping today in a whirlwind of carelessness, of recklessness, of downright selfishness and Godlessness the poisonous fruit of the irreligion that has been sowed among our people. A materialistic interpretation of the universe, with its attendant cult of the body, has been placed before man as the be-all and end-all of his existence, thus destroying his hope in a future life. But when you deprive a man of his belief in a future life, you deprive him of his religion. When you deprive him of his religion, you likewise deprive him of his morality. When you deprive him of his morality, you deprive him of virtue. When you deprive him of virtue, you deprive him of character. And when you deprive him of character, you have taken away the only real, permanent and stable foundation of a true and lasting citizenship.

History is once more repeating itself. The world is once more passing through another critical stage of its existence. God taught us a lesson in that last world war, but we have not fully learned it yet, and we never shall learn it probably until we realize that true human greatness does not consist in amassing great wealth and power, that it does not consist in the magnitude of great worldly achievement, that it does not consist, primarily and essentially, in an altruistic humanitarianism or in the law of extreme selfishness, but that true human greatness consists first, last, always, in being faithful to one's duties as well as to one's rights, one's duties to God and one's duties to one's neighbor, ever rendering to God the things that are God's and to one's neighbor that which is his.

Our modern reformers, gentlemen, may honestly strive to make this world a better place to live in; they may guarantee to all people, life, liberty and the pursuit of happiness; they may try to shake off from the throat of human society the clutching fangs of imperial finance; they may attempt to end the century-old difficulties between capital and labor; in a word, they may do their level best to restore and readjust the human scale in all things; but all their labors, all their efforts, all their pains will go for naught until they return to the principles of the Christian faith and the dynamic force of a Christian philosophy of life. For Christian principles alone can stem the dangerous tide of human events and bring peace and order out of chaos and unrest. Religion is their foundation. Religion is their safeguard. Religion is their guide. For religion means sacrifice; sacrifice means forgetfulness of self; forgetfulness of self means consideration for your neighbor; consideration for your neighbor means justice and honesty; it brings back confidence, it insures success.

The world today needs men, real men, consistent men, men with clearly defined Christian principles, who adjust their views to those principles, and then act in conformity with their views; men whose minds and hearts and souls are attuned to the harmony of their God's and their country's laws, who not only know what to do, but who have the strength, the courage, the manhood, the will to do it; men who are big enough, men who are brave enough, men who are bold enough to value principle above expediency and place honor above success.

We are sick and tired of the wishy-washy, will-o'-the-wisp type of double-dealing hypocrite, who tells you one thing and means another, who is always promising and never doing, who is going to give you everything and finally gives you nothing, who greets you to your face, with a golden smile, a glad shake, an outwardly hearty "How-do-you-do," but inwardly is plotting and planning and scheming to defraud you when he gets even half a chance. We are sick and tired of the showy seeming in lives that are half a lie. We want men, real men, real consistent men, real consistent men of character and of principle, in action faithful and in honor true, who hold their duty as they hold their soul.

Emerson, indeed, spoke well when he said that the truest test of a civilization is not to be found in the census, nor the size of cities, nor the crop its farms produce, but rather in the kind of men a country turns out. As the poet, John Boyle O'Reilly says: "Not power alone, can make a noble State; whate'er the land, tho' all things else concerning, unless it breed great men, it is not great." "A nation's greatness lies in men, not acres," in the men who control its political destiny, in the men who control its capitalistic fortunes, in the men who control its labor. Yes, we look for real men among God's workingmen.

126

RELATIONS BETWEEN EMPLOYERS AND THE EMPLOYED

Cardinal O'Connell [1]

The social problem of the relations between employers and employed appears to be the one most fraught with danger to our peaceful living. It has been many times in the past the source of widespread discord and disorder, and may in the future prove a danger to the public peace unless some remedy can be found to better our social conditions. The hostile attitude of one set of men against another is always prejudicial to the permanence of peaceful relations; but when two classes are arrayed in antagonism and dis-

---

[1] Pastoral Letter given at Boston, November 23, 1912.

trust, each against the other, the one with the resources of wealth and power behind it, the other with the force of numbers to make its influence felt, society is menaced by impending outbreaks, and the peace of families, the tranquillity of the State and the normal calm engendered by religion are imperilled.

To find a way out of these social dangers, to reconcile conflicting interests, to lay down a basis for the just and equitable settlement of differences between employers and workers is a call to an apostolate of the highest service, which every lover of his faith and of his country should heed, and to which every Christian and every patriot may well consecrate his best endeavors.

Justice and charity, two of the noblest Christian virtues, hold a foremost place in any genuine crusade for social betterment, and make the cause a holy one that appeals even more strongly to the churchman than to the statesman.

The proper consideration of the problem depends much on the way in which we approach it. The initial mistake that is made in trying to find a solution is in viewing the question as a merely economic one. The lives and happiness of millions of human beings are involved in the issue; and this gives it a moral aspect which cannot be ignored. It is much more than an economic problem. From the moment that the well-being of individuals and families is concerned in any question at issue, it is lifted out of the domain of mere economics. Bald political economy with its inflexible law of supply and demand can no longer cope with it. The reciprocal rights and duties inhering in the personality and position of those who are making claims and of those who are resisting them, enter in and create at once a moral issue. In the long run dollars and cents are powerless before a just human right and must give way in every community ruled by principles of justice.

The question of human rights that is involved in the issue between capital and labor goes deeper down than any legal enactment concerning them. In fact, much of the confusion of thought surrounding the problem springs from a faulty conception of the fundamental sources of human society. There is a tendency today to exalt unduly the State, and to regard it as the creator of all the rights and privileges which we enjoy, and to look to it for the solution of all our problems. Such a position is philosophically and historically false. The family is by nature and in fact anterior to the State. There are certain inherent individual and family rights that spring from nature itself and from the fundamental relations established by the Creator in the universe which antedate the constitution of States or the enactments of civil law. The authority of the parent over his child, his right to provide for his family, the choice of the kind of education his children shall receive—all these fundamental rights are rooted in the very nature of family life. So also the rights of conscience are inherent in the individual. They were not created by the State. They are anterior to it by nature and in fact. But if the State is not the creator of them, the State should be the conserver and respecter of them. For it was precisely to safeguard these primary rights of the individual and of the family that States were formed. To the fact that man is by nature a social being made so by his Creator and to the natural need of individuals and families of protecting their primary and natural rights, which alone and isolated they had not the strength to defend against unjust aggression, States owe their origin and formation. It is the province of the State in consonance with its origin to protect these fundamental, individual and family rights, not to invade them.

Now the right of a man to provide for his family is a natural one. In the exercise of this right he may sell his labor for what he considers just compensation, or may refuse his labor for what he deems an inadequate return. The measure which he must use in determining his decision is that imposed by nature itself. He must support his family; and the living wage which he has a right to demand according to the teaching of Leo XIII, of blessed memory, is the one which will maintain his family in decent and frugal comfort. The man who accepts less through necessity or fear of harder conditions is the victim of force and injustice. This general norm of wage does not exclude the special claims of labor, skilled and unskilled, which according to the degree of toil or danger incurred, has a right to greater compensation. It simply means that the lowest measure of compensation must be the decent maintenance of a man and his home.

This principle is based on sound political economy and the highest political wisdom. The safety of the State depends upon the integrity of its homes. To build up contented homes should be the aim of enlightened legislation as well as the scope of every movement for social betterment. The source of the nation's strength lies in the stable and well-ordered home, and without it, national greatness swiftly hastens to decay. The homeless man, free from the restraints of domestic life may easily become a menace, and to diminish such a danger becomes the duty of comprehensive patriotic statesmanship.

The maintenance of a home, then, is the standard of the minimum wage dictated by the law of nature, and prompted by the highest public policy. It is the clear right of the wage-earner, and to protect this right he may make use of all legitimate means. He may combine with others to enforce it and form a union with his fellow workers to exert the adequate moral power to maintain it or to better his condition within the limits of justice. To deny him this right is a tyranny and an injustice. He has no other way to safeguard his interests. The rich and the powerful have many ways which they do not hesitate to employ to protect their investments; the workingman has only the support of peaceful combination.

Moreover, workmen's associations may peacefully agitate and seek to mould public opinion in their favor to bring about a redress of real grievances. A campaign of this kind must, however, be legitimately conducted, free from violations of justice and of charity and of the public peace. Finally, the worker in the last resort has the right to refuse to work, that is to strike, and to induce by peaceful and lawful methods others to strike with him when this extreme measure becomes necessary to mitigate unendurable conditions, or to wrest from an unreasonable employer just compensation for his labor, after all other measures have failed.

All this is the teaching of the illustrious Pontiff Leo XIII in his now famous encyclical "On the Condition of the Workingmen." It has its root in the law of nature, which dictates that a man has a natural right to a wage which will maintain his home in frugal and reasonable comfort. All the other conclusions which we have laid down are but corollaries flowing from this fundamental principle, on the ground that any one who possesses a natural right may make use of all legitimate means to protect it, and to safeguard it from violation.

These are the objective principles which may serve as guiding ones in contests between workers and employers, and if loyally accepted by both sides, would undoubtedly mitigate the bitterness that often arises in labor disputes.

The principles governing the conduct of employers are well known and are generally accepted as the only safe ones which may be followed. They may be summed up as follows: Capital has a right to a just share of the profits, but only to a just share: Employers should treat those who work under them with humanity and justice; they should be solicitous for the healthful conditions of the places where workmen daily toil; they should use all reasonable means to promote the material and moral well-being of their employees. They should be kindly humane and just in all their relations with them.

We are well aware that some of these principles find no place in a political and commercial economy which has become wholly pagan. We are convinced, however, that the social problem of the relations between employers and workers can never be settled on any other than a Christian basis. The attitude of each towards the other must radically change round to a Christian one, else we shall have the spectacle of two opposing forces facing each other in a hostile spirit, each stubbornly insisting on its pound of flesh, with no thought of the Christian brotherhood which ought to bind them together.

The present deplorable situation in the world of labor has been brought about by a neglect of Christian principles, and by the attempt to put this question on a material basis only. On the other hand, riches and power bring danger in their train unless moral rectitude and moral standards are accepted as guiding sign posts along the way of life. Money gives power, and it may be sought after too anxiously without due regard to the principles of justice. . . .

Men with money should be careful to regard it as a means to do good rather than an end. They should beware lest its possession make them arrogant, tyrannical and despisers of their less fortunate brethren. The great restraining force against these natural tendencies is the spirit of religion, which subdues while it strengthens and sanctifies while it chastens. Whether as individuals or as members of corporate bodies, men of wealth must remember that the Christian law obliges them in one capacity as in the other. There is no double moral standard, no loop-hole of escape from the sanctions which the moral law of Christ imposes. Men of wealth should not buy that which is not sellable according to Christian ethics. It is an abuse of their wealth and an infraction of the moral code, and a crime against society.

The merely natural outlook has produced another idea of wealth which is a source of danger. Men regard themselves as absolute owners of what they possess, and claim the right to do with it what they please. In one sense this is true. They are owners, and exclusive owners. But there is a law higher than themselves, and there is a God above them. To stand stubbornly upon individual ground and because they are owners to absolve themselves from all obligations to society and their weaker brethren is paganism, pure and simple. In reality they are according to the Divine Word stewards of God. The greater their wealth, the greater their responsibilities.

Before the so-called Reformation, this was the Christian conception of wealth as any one who will read the records of history will readily see. There was poverty, but not pauperism. The rich man saw in the poor his brethren in Jesus Christ, and was well content to share his treasures on earth that he might lay up for himself treasures in heaven.

The individualistic principle of life was introduced by the revolt against the authority of the Church. The unity of faith was broken and Christendom ceased to be one great organic social body, one brotherhood in Christ. Once granted, the principle that man can choose, as he would a garment, his own religion, the most supreme issue of life, the way is open for him to have his own way in things of all moral import. The direct tendency of the spirit of individualism is to breed self-sufficiency and selfishness. That it does not always do so is owing solely to the fact that it is not always carried out to its logical outcome.

There is need of a return to old Catholic ideals. Men must learn to give to every cause of religion and charity and mutual help, in proportion to their means. Rich men should bear in mind that they shall one day hear the voice of the Master of all saying, "render an account of thy stewardship." There must be a generous recognition, on the part of those whom God has blessed with abundance, of their obligations to society and the poorer members of the human family. The Christian spirit must be enkindled in the soul and this will of itself arouse the noble and generous disposition to approach conflicts with a calm and balanced mind, and with a readiness to listen to higher impulses than the mere desire for victory over helpless and oftentimes maddened men, who alas too often have good reason to believe that the rich have lost all sense of kindly feeling and think only of themselves.

On the other hand, workers are just as much bound by the Christian law as their employers. This fact seems to be lost sight of at times, and men give way to their baser impulses. The spirit of envy generates discontent, and the attitude of the laborer towards his employer becomes un-Christian and pagan. There is a disposition, too, to regard work as an intolerable burden to be gotten rid of as soon as possible, and with as little effort as possible. This is contrary to Christian teaching. The Wise Man in Ecclesiastes who had tasted all the pleasures of life was forced to confess: "for I have found that there is nothing better for a man than to rejoice in his work." This natural discontent is fomented and intensified by the noisy agitators of Socialism, the enemies of God and man, who would overturn the foundations upon which human society is built, and exile God from His universe.

127

A LIVING WAGE BY LAW

John A. Ryan

The remuneration of the laborer is the most important single question in any scheme of social reform. Bernard

[1] *Social Reconstruction,* pp. 62-80. (The Macmillan Company, New York. Reprinted with permission of the publishers.)

Shaw declared a few years ago that the trouble with the poor was their poverty. Similarly we may say that the industrial question in so far as it relates to the less prosperous classes, is a question of wages almost entirely. If the working people have sufficient income, they will be able themselves to meet many of the problems for which reformers are trying to find remedies, such as insurance against sickness and accidents and old age. The objection might arise that the question of a living wage is not very pertinent at this particular time; that wages are now so high as to make irrelevant the question how a living wage shall be established, whether by law or by any other method; but I think that one or two statistical statements will indicate that the question is not altogether an antiquated one. Some of you will recall, perhaps, that in those twenty-eight industries in which a survey was made by the Bureau of Labor last year (1919), about 48 per cent of the male workers were getting less than fifty cents an hour, or less than five dollars per day on a ten hour basis, and less than four dollars on an eight hour basis; whereas, in cities at any rate, five dollars per day is not more than a living wage. So, the question is still pertinent, and may be more pertinent later on than it is now. . . .

The most famous and influential declaration concerning a living wage was that made by Leo XIII in his encyclical on the Condition of Labor, some thirty years ago. The substance of that statement was that, while it is proper for employer and employee to make free agreements concerning wages, still there is "a dictate of nature more ancient and more imperative than any bargain between man and man, namely, that the remuneration of the worker should be sufficient to enable him to live in reasonable and frugal comfort." A few lines further on in that document the Pope says, "if, through necessity or fear of a worse evil the worker accepts less than this measure of remuneration, he is the victim of force and injustice." That, I say, is the most famous and the most influential statement that has been made on this subject. It clearly places the laborer's claim for remuneration in the class of rights. The prevailing economic doctrine up to a few years ago was that a free contract is always a fair contract; that no matter how low a wage a worker agrees to accept, or how high a price the consumer agrees to pay, both are fair as long as the contract is free. In this theory free contract was made the determinant of justice. Now the statement of the Pope directly contradicts this. It asserts that, generally speaking, a free contract ought to govern, determine and fix wages, but that there is a limit to the moral lawfulness of a free contract in this matter; that the contract must not be of such a nature that it will deprive the worker of at least that amount of wages which will enable him to live in reasonable and frugal comfort. So, the Pope places the conception of a right over against the conception of a free contract. I shall return to this point presently.

Last week somebody asked the question, "What is a living wage?" particularly as regards women workers. The lady wanted to know whether it meant a fair wage or a mere subsistence wage. I answered that it was a compromise of some sort between the two. The living wage for male workers is generally understood to be a wage that will enable him and his family to have a decent livelihood. Well, what is a decent livelihood? We speak now of the minimum amount, the least amount of goods which will satisfy the demands of a decent livelihood. It means something more than a mere existence; it means something more than the necessaries which will enable a worker to function effectively as an instrument of production; it means something more than merely keeping him and his famliy in health. It means, in general, that amount of goods which will enable a human being to live as a human being rather than as an animal, even a well fed animal. It supposes that he shall have food, clothing, and shelter sufficient to maintain him and his family in health, and that they shall have the means of some recreation, at least sufficient recreation to enable them to be healthy and enjoy an elementary degree of contentment. It means some opportunity for social intercourse, the possibility of meeting their fellows, those of their class, in a social way without loss of self-respect. It means the requisites of a religious and moral life; therefore, the opportunities and conditions of being a member of a church, of living in a neighborhood in which the dangers to morals will not be unreasonably great. It means also some opportunities for intellectual development, some reading matter, and at least an elementary education for the children. In general, therefore, it comprises an elementary degree of physical, mental, moral, religious, social, and recreational welfare. That is about as clearly, I think, as the concept can be defined in general terms.

When men attempt to put that conception into terms of money, they naturally differ considerably one from the other, and yet whenever the thing has been systematically undertaken men have been able to come to an agreement. It is probably more easy for a group of fair-minded men, even drawn from different classes, to agree as to what constitutes the minimum requirements or minimum cost of a decent livelihood for a man and his family than it is for employer and employees to make a bargain that will be mutually satisfactory. Probably the amount now required is 1,400 to 1,500 dollars a year.

Pope Leo XIII says the worker has a *right* to a living wage; that it is not merely *desirable* that he should have this reasonable minimum of the good things of life, but that he has a *moral right* to this much,—a thing having the same moral force as the right which we assert to our money if somebody attempts to take it away from us. Why does a laborer have such a right—why do we say that he has a right to at least that much remuneration? In order to answer that in the shortest possible form, and to make it as clear as possible in a brief form, we have to keep in mind three important facts or factors. There is, first, the fact that this earth of ours, the nursing mother of us all, was created by God for all human beings. He did not pick out any certain class and hand it over to them. The second fact is that the goods of this earth become available, as a rule, only at the cost of labor. The command in the book of Genesis, "In the sweat of thy brow, thou shalt eat thy bread," announces not merely a law, but a fact, that men do not get a livelihood from the earth unless they work for it. And the third important fact to consider is that the earth does not, even for those who work, produce its fruits in unlimited abundance. Therefore, it is possible for a group of persons, large or small, to be in control in any given time and country of all the natural resources, and that group may be less than the whole number of the country's inhabitants.

As a result of these three factors: first, that God made the earth for all human beings; second, that men must get their livelihood from the earth by labor; and, third, that it is possible for a part of the people of any country to get possession of the earth,—it follows that the laborer has a right against the masters of the earth to a decent livelihood.

Every person has a right of access to the earth, an equal right with everybody else. There is nobody living—I do not care what his condition is—whether he be a multi-millionaire or whether he has any money at all, who can say to his fellow, "I have a better right to get my livelihood from the earth than you have." Men are equal in that respect. Of course, if one wants to say that there is no such thing as rights in this matter, that the man who gets possession of the earth first may properly exclude all others from any share in it, there is no possibility of answering such a person by reason, because he denies the existence of rights. He asserts, in effect, that he is of a superior nature to the rest of men, that he has all the right in this case, and that other men have no rights.

When a man has performed a reasonable amount of useful labor, his right of access to the earth becomes a right to a livelihood from the earth against the persons who have control of it. To put it in other terms, the persons who have control of the resources of the earth are bound so to exercise that control that the man who performs a reasonable amount of labor will be able to obtain at least a decent livelihood. Or, to put it still in another way, the persons who are in control of the earth are obliged to permit all persons to get a decent livelihood from it on reasonable terms, and the main element in "reasonable terms" is the performance of a reasonable amount of labor. Such is the ethical basis of the right to a living wage, or the right to a decent livelihood.

Suppose it be objected that the worker who performs a reasonable amount of labor has a right to a living or an existence from the earth, but not a right to so much of the earth's goods as are equivalent to a decent livelihood. The answer is that the human being is a person, not an animal; that he has intrinsic worth and sacredness; that he has faculties to be developed which are above his physical faculties; and that he has a free will and a rational soul. Since

God has imposed upon him the obligation of attaining his eternal end, his eternal salvation, God wishes him to have the means which are adequate for that purpose. Now, a human being will not have the means to attain his salvation, will not have the means to live a reasonable life, unless he has the minimum amount of the material things and opportunities which is equivalent to a decent livelihood.

Therefore, the persons in control of the goods of the earth have no more right to exclude the man who performs a reasonable amount of labor from this measure of the good things of life than they have to deprive him of his liberty, or to compel him to work as a slave. Suppose they say, "yes, we will give him a decent livelihood, but we will make a slave of him; we will give him a living just as a father gives a living to a child who is not able to care for himself." Everyone would say, "that is wrong; that is a violation of man's right to freedom"; yet it is no more of a violation of his rights than is this other action of conceding to him only the means of subsistence. His rights are violated in the latter case quite as certainly as in the former; it is a different kind of right, but it is a right that is essential to a reasonable life, and that is the end and purpose of all rights. Through all this conception of a living wage, a decent wage, a decent livelihood, we have the idea of man as a person of intrinsic worth, with faculties which he has a right to develop and which God wishes him to develop, which he must develop if he is to have the opportunity of working out his salvation and living his life as a person made in the image and likeness of God.

Now this language may seem elusive and vague, and yet it is not possible to justify human rights by anything like a mathematical argument. If the proposition that a man has a right to a better living than a well fed horse does not appeal to us as persuasive, there is no way of proving it that I know. Either the principle is self-evident or it is nothing. As a matter of fact, it is self-evident to most persons when they examine its elements, and it is more or less self-evident to all persons instinctively. I think the best proof that the proposition is self-evident is the fact that hardly any person any longer will publicly assert that a laborer ought to be paid less than a living wage.

It was not because some men were morally blind that they once denied the laborer's right to a living wage, but because they thought they had moral sanction for a different kind of conception, namely, the conception that in the wage agreement, as in every other bargain, a free contract is always a fair contract. Of course, there is no sacredness whatever about a free contract in itself; it may be unfair, brought about by economic force. There is no more sacredness in economic force as a determinant of a fair contract than there is in physical force. When a highwayman points a pistol at the wayfarer and says to him, "give me your money or I will shoot you," and the wayfarer hands over his money, no one pretends that the highwayman thereby gets title to this money, and yet it has been a free contract. The highwayman agrees not to shoot the traveler if the traveler hands over his money. The contract is free in a sense; for the traveler need not surrender the money;—he could wait and be shot. All admit that such a contract is not a determinant of justice. Neither is the contract which compels the worker to accept less than a living wage, because of the fear of starvation for himself or for his family. In this case it is an economic force that prevents the contract from being free, and an economic force has no more validity, no more moral worth as a determinant of justice or as a basis of a free contract than physical force, physical pressure and threats, as in the case of the highwayman with the pistol.

A right to a decent livelihood means a right to a living wage in the case of the laborer. Why? Because that is the kind of industrial system in which we live. The goods and products of the earth are controlled in our industrial system by the employer. If it were the State that managed and operated industry, the right of the laborer would be against the State, because the State would then have control of the means out of which wages must come. As a matter of fact, it is not the State that controls in our system; it is the employer. Therefore, the laborer's right to a decent livelihood from the fruits of the earth becomes a right against the employer for a living wage. The employer is bound to pay that because he has the product, and he is the paymaster of society. There is no other reasonable way to determine rights and obligations in our system of production and distribution. Who else could be reasonably charged with the obligation of paying living wages except the man who has the product?

Suppose the employer says, "but this product is mine. I think that the laborer should have only this much of it, less than a living wage. Since the product is mine, why may I not keep it all except the equivalent of a starvation wage?" Perhaps the most effective reply to that question is another question: "Whence did you get ownership of this product? Who made it yours? You have the power over it, yes; so has the highwayman the power over my purse—if he thrusts a gun against me he compels me to hand it over to him. Physical power, economic power, legal power, does not necessarily give you a moral right. The laborers have co-operated with you in producing the product. Why should you say that it is all yours except this amount you give to them which is less than a living wage?" It is impossible to prove that the product is the employer's, in the sense that he may agree to give less of it to his employees than will enable them to live decently. His control of that part of the earth's resources does not free him from the obligation of distributing it in such a way that the getting of a decent livelihood by those who work for him will not be unreasonably difficult. Otherwise he is setting himself up as having a superior claim to the goods of the earth as compared to those who work for him.

How shall the living wage be brought about universally? There was a time when economists thought that the laborers would get not only living wages but something more through the operation of competition and the free play of economic forces. The general theory was that capital is increasing so much faster than labor that labor will be able through competition to get an ever increasing share of the product, while capital will get a relatively decreasing share. I do not think that many economists hold that opinion now. Greater experience has shown that economic forces and the free play of competition do not of themselves increase wages. The period of the war is almost the first time since the industrial revolution that the theory of the economists in regard to the laborer's share increasing through the free play of economic forces has been verified; but we all realize that this is a temporary condition, that the normal situation is rather that which prevailed for twenty-five or thirty years before the war, when wages were not rising except very slightly. It is probable that there was no rise in real wages, wages measured by purchasing power, between 1900 and 1915.

So, we cannot look to economic forces to provide the laborers with living wages. We cannot rely upon the benevolence of the employers either, because the majority of employers in competitive industries cannot pay much more wages than they are paying, and the few who could pay more unfortunately will not do so. They will pay the same wages as their least efficient competitor. The labor unions will not be able to provide a guarantee of living wages to all the workers, because those groups of the laboring class that need living wages most are the ones that are least able to organize. As a matter of fact, the persons in the labor unions of this country, men and women, are not more than 15 per cent of the wage-earners.

The only method of bringing about living wages universally is that of legislation. That is to say, the State should make it illegal for any one to pay less than what competent authorities will determine to be a living wage. That means in the case of a man a wage sufficient for decent support of himself and family, and in the case of a woman, remuneration sufficient for decent individual support. In times past there have been a few Catholics who have declared that this was socialistic, or that it was not in accordance with Catholic doctrine. I do not know now of any Catholic of importance who is making such an assertion. It seems to me as clear as any proposition can be that this device of a legal minimum wage is a proper intervention by the State, according to the Catholic principles of political ethics. The Catholic theory of the State is not the *laissez faire* theory; it is not the theory that the State should keep its hands off industry, allowing individuals to have free play to compete with one another by cut-throat competition, and to pay men starvation wages if they can get them to work so cheaply. The Catholic doctrine is that the function of the State in this matter is two-fold: it must protect *all* natural rights, not merely the right of free contract, not merely the right of physical integrity, of protection against the thief and the burglar, but all natural rights; and the right to a living wage is one of the natural rights. Secondly, the State is obliged to do more, or at least may properly do more, than to protect rights; it may go further and promote the general welfare of the community or of a particular section of the community.

The general principle is expressed by Pope Leo XIII in the general encyclical on "The Condition of Labor," in very definite, clear and brief terms: "When the general interest or any particular class suffers or is threatened with mischief which can in no other way be met or prevented, the public authority must step in and deal with it." Now, that is about as sweeping a general pronouncement of the propriety of the State interfering in industrial matters as any one could desire. The only thing necessary to prove, according to this doctrine, that the State has a right to enact minimum living wages is to supply the monor proposition; "but a large class of the workers are threatened with, or rather are suffering grievous economic evils which cannot be met except through State intervention. Therefore, it is proper for the State to intervene and establish legal minimum wages."

The legal minimum wage is no longer among the novelties. It has existed in the State of Victoria, Australia, since 1896. It was applied in the beginning to only three trades; but it was extended gradually to trade after trade, and then from Victoria to the neighboring States in Australia, then to New Zealand and Tasmania, so that today they have the legal minimum wage throughout the whole of Australasia. Legal minimum wage laws were introduced into England in 1910 and now apply to a large proportion of the working population. Manitoba, and I think two or three other provinces in Canada, have minimum wage laws.

Fourteen States of the United States and the District of Columbia have such legislation; but in the United States the law applies to women and minors only, not to men. There are two or three reasons for that; the first is that the people are more willing to pass radical legislation where women and minors are concerned than where only men are concerned. The second is that the law compelling women to be paid living wages will more probably stand the test of constitutionality in the courts than would such a law applied to men. But when we who believe in a legal minimum wage speak of the desirability of its extension, we mean that it should be applied to men as well as to women. There is no fundamental reason why it should be confined to women and minors. For a good while it was feared that the minimum wage law for women and minors would be declared unconstitutional; but finally the United States Supreme Court refused to nullify the Oregon law. When that law came before the United States Supreme Court on appeal, four justices voted in favor of it and four against it. Since the Oregon Supreme Court had declared the law constitutional this equal division of the Federal Court had the effect of sustaining the law.

There is the greatest irony in the constitutional jeopardy to which legislation of this kind is subject. It is attacked under the Fourteenth Amendment to the Constitution. The Fourteenth Amendment declares that no one shall be deprived of life, liberty or property without due process of law. Those who oppose minimum wage legislation say that it deprives the citizen of the liberty of hiring persons for less than living wages, or less than a legally fixed wage, and also of his property, inasmuch as it makes his business less profitable by compelling him to pay a higher wage than he would be obliged to pay in the absence of the law. I say there is the greatest irony in that, because this amendment was adopted, put into the Constitution, for the protection of the Negroes of the South, for the protection of an oppressed class that would otherwise have been deprived of these rights by the States. Now we have this amendment which was adopted for the protection of the oppressed black race, turned against legislation for the protection of an oppressed section of the white race. It is one of the curiosities of the Constitution. The clause itself is all right, but it is perverted to uphold a liberty which is unreasonable, the liberty to use economic force in order to get men and women to work for less than decent wages.

There are many objections against the legal minimum wage which I do not intend to go into at any length, but I shall state the substance of most of them. It runs thus: if you raise the wages of any class artificially, as by legislation, you will compel the product which they make to be sold at a higher price in order to provide the additional wages. If it is sold at a higher price, the consumption of it will fall off, the demand will be less. If the demand for the product is less, the demand for the workers to make the product will correspondingly decline; therefore, some of the workers will be thrown out of employment. You will have a smaller number of workers employed at a higher wage, instead of having a larger number of persons employed at a lower wage. The second evil is worse than the first.

Such is the substance of most of the economic objections. The main defect of the argument is that it proves too much. If that reasoning were correct, it would be folly for any group of workers to try to get their wages raised by any method whatever, because they would forge the same fatal chain of events: a raise in wages and an increased cost of production which must be passed to the consumer in the form of higher prices, which higher prices will cause a falling off in demand, which lessened demand will reduce the demand for labor. That argument applies against every increase in wages, even that due to the benevolence of the employer. So, I say, it proves too much. The answer to it in brief is simply this: There are four sources from which the additional wages can come: first, from greater efficiency on the part of the workers. I do not say that this will always be forthcoming; but the general experience is that when persons who have been underpaid, getting less than living wages, are enabled to rise to that level, their productivity does increase somewhat. The second source is more efficient methods of production. Very often men employ cheap labor in place of machinery. It is cheaper to hire human beings than to put in a machine. It is easier to get on with antiquated methods of production, or with poor organization of productive processes so long as labor is cheap; but if more wages have to be paid, it becomes to the interests of the employer to improve the whole organization of his business and plant. There was a distinct manifestation of that in England in the tailoring trade after the legal minimum wage was established. The employing tailors put in improved machinery and improved the processes of production generally, which they had not thought worth while before. In the third place, some of the increased wages can come from profits, and from the elimination of the least efficient employees. Finally, a part of the increased wages will have to come out of prices. Will these increased prices, in so far as they are necessary to provide additional wages, cause a falling off in demand? Not at all. Demands will be increased instead of diminished, owing to the greater purchasing power of these workers whose remuneration has been increased. Why is it that there is such a great demand for everything now? that there is under-production in everything? One of the main reasons is that a large proportion of the working population has now a larger purchasing power than ever before. The workers are keeping industry going by providing a large and steady demand for goods in spite of the enormously high prices. It is probable that prices have increased since the beginning of the war three or four times as much as they would have to be increased if we had a legal minimum wage throughout the whole of this country for men, women and children.

128

FAMILY ENDOWMENT

J. E. Canavan [1]

Nearly every moralist admits, nowadays, that the worker's family is a legitimate charge upon the industry in which he is engaged. We have come to realise that the workman may not be treated like a piece of machinery, nor be reckoned as a wholly detached individual with a certain commodity, i. e., his labour, to sell in the open market, on the most favourable terms, to the highest bidder. We have abandoned the doctrines of the Manchester School in admitting that labour has a value independent of the Law of Supply and Demand. An able-bodied worker must be paid for his labour, not just what he is willing to take in the circumstances, but what is sufficient to satisfy his human needs. Among his natural rights is the right to marry and raise a family; and the industry in which he is employed is bound to recognise this right and supply, out of profits, the needs arising from the exercise of it. The worker should be paid a Family Wage. This is the first charge on industry.

However, not every industry could afford to pay each worker a family wage, and meet, at the same time, the

[1] *The Irish Tribune.*

expectations of shareholders. If dividends fall below a certain figure, or vanish entirely, or grow precarious, capital will be withdrawn, for capital is the most sensitive of things; and if capital is not provided, the industry dies out. It comes to this: if we put too heavy a strain on the cost of production, the very process of production ceases, and the workers lose their employment. You may say that an enterprise which cannot pay a reasonable dividend and a family wage as well is bankrupt. In a sense, it is; assuredly it is not flourishing; but we must make the best of conditions like these, lest worse fall upon us.

The dispute over the wages offered in the Shannon Scheme brought the whole question urgently before the Irish people. The State said it could not afford any more; the Labour leaders declared that the remuneration was insufficient to support a married workman and his family. I am presuming that both parties to the dispute were right. What could be done, if not in this venture, at least in others, where an offer of a rate of wages was made and challenged on the grounds advanced by the State and the Labour leaders in the Shannon dispute? We may, I think, address ourselves to this problem the more hopefully, since the difficulty is by no means a new one, nor peculiar to the present economic condition of Ireland. Others have had to face it and solve it as best they could. Europe had to meet the difficulty before and after the war. On the Continent capital was depleted, capital was shy, because the outlook was unsettled, markets were changing, and currency was disturbed and fluctuating. Europe, in other words, could not afford to pay a family wage, as its industries were languishing. Europe was, in a sense, bankrupt. How could industry be revived, wealth produced, without starving the children of the working classes? Europe solved the problem in the following way:

The solution commonly adopted is to remunerate labour, not according to a rigid, uniform rate, but according to need. In general, the scheme is this: The employer fixes a standard wage to be paid to all his workmen. This wage is lower than the normal wage in the industry, and may, perhaps, be little more than is needed for the support of a single man. In addition to this standard wage, an allowance is paid to each married man for the support of his wife, with a further allowance for each child under a certain age, say, under fourteen years. Employers pay the same total amount as they did under the old system, but the sum is distributed differently; bachelors receiving less than before, married men with families, more. The net result is that all have enough to live on.

For example: all employers in a certain industry, say, the mining industry, agree to establish a fund for family endowments. Let us suppose the standard wages, previously, were 40/- a week. The standard wage is now fixed at 30/- a week. The employers pay this wage to every man, and, in addition, they pay into the fund an additional 10/- for every man in their employment. Married men are entitled to draw from the fund, over and above the standard wage, 10/- a week for their wives, 5/- a week for each child under 14 years. Previously, all received 40/- a week; now single men get 30/-, married men with no families, 40/-; married men with one child, 45/-, and so on. The employers pay out the same amount as they paid before in total wages.

The system was first introduced into France by a few Catholic employers in Grenoble, and spread rapidly during the war. An attempt was made in 1921 to pass a Bill making the system compulsory throughout the country, but this was unsuccessful. As it was adopted first by private firms, so it has been developed by private enterprise. In June, 1924, there were in existence 151 pools or funds, either industrial or regional, 9,300 firms being represented. The total sum paid in family allowances amounted, that year, to 763,000,000 francs; and 2,700,000 workers, or 3-5ths of those engaged in industry were benefited. In June, 1925, the amount had increased to 1,000 million francs, and the workers to 3,500,000, or 78 per cent of the total number employed in France.

In Belgium in 1920, 5,000 workers were associated in a similar scheme; in 1925 they had increased to 540,000—truly a remarkable development. In Belgium, though the system generally is modelled on that of France, there is one important difference. Certain Trade Unions pay family allowances to members out of Union funds, providing thus for those workers who are not drawing benefits from Employer's Endowment Funds. At least the Catholic Trade

Unions support this policy, and mean to keep it, while the Socialist Trade Unions are strongly in favour of the State paying the allowances, as a kind of dole.

Introduced into Germany during the war, the payment of family allowances has since been maintained and extended. It is in full vogue now in practically all industries, and covers almost all the workers.

In Austria, the system was first introduced for State employees in 1916. In 1921 it was made compulsory. The compulsory allowances, however, were meant to cover the cost of food only, and not the total cost of living. Accordingly, many private schemes are in operation to secure the worker more liberal grants than those exacted by the law.

There is no need to continue this summary. It is sufficient to mention that the system of supplementing wages by family allowances has been adopted—with modifications of detail—in Czecho-Slovakia, Denmark, Holland, Finland, Italy, Jugo-Slavia, Norway, Poland, Sweden, and Switzerland. It is, therefore, practically universal throughout Europe.

Family endowments were first suggested by Catholics as a remedy for social ills, not according to an ideal formula alone, but with reference to economic facts. It was first put into practice by Catholics. In every country it owes its introduction to them, and in them it finds its warmest supporters. In the report of the Labour Commission of the League of Nations, it is referred to as the system first advocated by Roman Catholic sociologists, at least in the Netherlands; and the report remarks that it is the system commonly proposed by Catholics everywhere.

We may recognise in this the fruit of Leo XIII's Encyclicals, where he urged the clergy to interest themselves in the condition of the poor. The chief motive that weighs with Catholics is the need of caring for the children. They are fully alive to the fact that infant mortality is high when the family wage is too low; that insanity is prevalent, or, at least, that the seeds of it are sown, in conditions like these; and that, in any event, underfed children are not likely to grow up into good citizens. Further, poverty, discontent, smouldering resentment, are not a good background for the truths of religion and the spiritual life. Children, born and bred in dire want, are apt to be ignorant, intolerant, gross, and make poor subjects for an ordered community. It was noticed that children born during the war in the allied countries, were, on account of the high wages paid at the time, sturdier and more amenable to education and discipline, than those born immediately after the war. Give, therefore, say the Catholics, the worker with a family, a chance of providing decently for his children, even though the unmarried workers may have to make sacrifices. It will be better for the common good. Moreover, Catholics are opposed to the endowment being administered by the State, just as they are opposed to the dole, because they are suspicious of bureaucratic control over the homes of the poor.

It is, therefore, widely adopted, and Catholic. These are high credentials. The workers in general seem pleased with it. The Administrative Secretary of the "Confederation Generale du Travail" expresses his opinion of it thus: "What is certain is that the family wage makes possible a fairer distribution of the product of labour, and increases the well-being of the children. . . . As for the bachelors and married men without children it cannot be maintained that the family wage has no influence on their rates of pay, but, in reality an organisation which has for its aim equity and solidarity recognises that there are certain sacrifices which must be accepted. . . . I may add that we in France consider that the family wage is purely and simply a redistribution, on sounder and more humane lines, of the wage bill." . . .

As the ideal of the family wage for all cannot be attained in the present state of industry or of national finances, one must fall back on the endowment system. It is not perfect; it is not final; it is not a complete remedy; it is temporary and a palliative. But it is a solution on the right lines, as far as it goes; and it holds the promise of better things.

129
A NEW METHOD OF WAGE DISTRIBUTION
Virginia M. Crawford [1]

Catholic sociologists have paid more reasoned attention to the needs of the human family than those of either Liberal or Socialist schools of thought. By them, as we all know, the family, and not the individual, has been accepted as the unit on which to build up our social and economic structure. It is largely due to them that, on the continent, at least a theoretic recognition of a "living wage" as a fundamental right of the worker has been generally conceded. Curiously enough, far less attention has been paid to methods of wage distribution than to the amount of the wages fund, and it is probably true to say that most people still accept unquestioningly our individualistic method of wage-paying, based exclusively on the supposed value of the labor and skill of the worker as the only reasonable—indeed, as the only possible—method in modern industry. It is to France that we have to turn if we wish to find a tardy recognition of the importance, both to the worker and to the employer, of this problem of wage distribution, which is today being extensively met on the continent by the system known as *allocations familiales,* a term not very happily rendered in English by "family endowment."

To find the true origin of this innovation—for in practice it only dates from post-war years—we have to go back well-nigh half a century to the time when Count Albert de Mun was preaching Christian democracy throughout the length and breadth of France, and when Léon Harmel, the *bon père* of Val-des-Bois, was putting into practice in his cotton-mills those social doctrines which were soon to find the official sanction of the Church in Leo XIII's *Rerum Novarum.* Harmel, as is well known, established a whole network of *œuvres* at Val-des-Bois, all of them planned to raise the moral and material standard of the factory-worker and to give him a direct interest in his labor. This Harmel did, not as an act of charity, but as a duty imposed by

---
[1] *"Studies,"* June, 1925.

social justice, and undoubtedly the lot of the Val-des-Bois workers in regard to housing, sanitation, hours of labor, security and so forth was immeasurably superior to that of the average mill-hand. But M. Harmel, watching over his employees with paternal eyes, observed that in spite of all he had done to raise the standard of living of his workers, conditions of health and comfort still remained unsatisfactory in families where there were three or more children. Such households remained at a low level, the children ill-fed and ill-clad. M. Harmel could not persuade himself, so he explained to the present writer, that it was his actual duty as a *patron* to pay higher wages to a worker with many children—such a system seemed to him to run contrary to all the economic principles of industry—but still less could he, as a Christian, reconcile himself to any of his dependants lacking the necessaries of life. In this dilemma he constituted a small special fund out of which he was wont to grant, as a thing quite apart from the wages earned, weekly allowances to all parents of more than three children. In other words, he instituted, in a private way, what we now know as *allocations familiales*.

Many Catholic employers throughout France imitated the enlightened industrial policy that the Harmel firm pursued with marked success right up to the War (when the whole factory was destroyed during the German bombardment of Rheims), and, thanks to them, a great deal was done in individual factories which compensated in a measure for the comparative lack of social legislation in France. Moreover, all through these years the Catholic movement was in full swing, laymen and priests vying with one another in preaching the doctrines of the Leonine labor encyclicals. Thus it happened that early in the present century the Abbé Cetty, of Mulhouse, a priest of strong "social" sympathies, delivered a series of lectures at Grenoble on Christian industrial duties and responsibilities, and among his hearers was M. Romanet, manager of the great ironworks known as the Maison Joya, himself a devout Catholic and a man of energy and vision. Fired by what he heard from the Abbé Cetty, he proceeded to introduce bit by bit a series of beneficent reforms into the Joya foundries, including some form of consultative workers' councils, and in due course M. Romanet's attention was called by the men to the poverty and hardships endured by their comrades who happened to be the fathers of four or five children. Thus M. Romanet found himself faced with precisely the same problem as had confronted Léon Harmel thirty years earlier. Moreover, thoughtful men in France had by this time become alive to the national danger of a stationary population, while yet allowing the few prolific families to bear unaided a crushing financial burden. M. Romanet set himself resolutely to find a solution. Merely to pay higher wages to a workman because he was blessed with a large family was of no avail, for such a policy would quickly result in the exclusion of such men from industry altogether on the plea of economy. Yet to bring the wages of all workers, married and unmarried alike, up to a level sufficient to ensure comfort and well-being to the exceptional family of six or eight children appeared to him at once impracticable and unnecessary.

Allowances for children, therefore, seemed the only alternative, and M. Romanet first started them, under the name of *sursalaires familiales,* for his own men on a very small scale: 7.50 frs. a month for the first child, increasing up to 12 frs. a month for the fourth and each succeeding child. The plan "caught on" with amazing rapidity; other employers at Grenoble—a very large industrial centre for *métallurgie*—were anxious to follow suit and pay these popular allowances on an agreed scale. It was M. Romanet who devised a remedy for the first and most obvious obstacle to be overcome, by instituting a pool (or *caisse*) into which every federated employer paid a sum calculated on the whole number of his employees, and out of which the allowances were paid each month directly to the parents of dependant children. Thus no employer was tempted to discriminate against married men, while the sum required from each amounted to a very small percentage of his total wages bill. In this way there was founded in France (May, 1918) the first *Caisse de Compensation pour Allocations Familiales,* and the story of their rapid development throughout the country has been admirably told by Miss Eleanor Rathbone in her weighty volume, *The Disinherited Family.*[2]

[2] London: Arnold. 1924. 7s. 6d. net.

From her well-documented pages we learn that *Caisses de Compensation* have been springing up in all directions in the last six years, sometimes on a regional and sometimes on an occupational or professional basis. One of the most remarkable of the latter type is the Roubaix-Tourcoing *Caisse,* founded by the federation of textile manufacturers of the district. It gives larger benefits than any other, i. e., 2 frs. per day for the first child, 5 frs. for two children, 8 frs. for three, 12 frs. for four, and 15 frs. for five children. The amount distributed has steadily increased from 96,000 frs. in 1919 to 17,765,468 frs. in 1924. Nantes and Paris, on the other hand, each have flourishing regional *Caisses,* in which all branches of trade and industry are represented. Altogether there are today, according to the latest figures available (Jan., 1925), some 160 *Caisses* in operation in France, covering some 10,000 firms and paying varying benefits, which are roughly calculated at one-third of the cost of child-rearing. In addition, family allowances have been made compulsory for all government and municipal employees, railway servants, postmen, etc., so that the amount expended in allowances is now calculated at the enormous total of 900 million francs a year, distributed among three million wage-earners, or two-thirds of all the wage-earners of the country.

The reason of this truly amazing growth—though Miss Rathbone somewhat fails to appreciate this—lies surely in the fact that the scheme corresponds so exactly to the teaching of the French Catholic social school concerning the family, the relations of capital and labor, and so forth. The plan at the outset excited veritable enthusiasm. Every social-minded Catholic employer felt that here at last was a practical plan by which, without unduly burdening his industry, he could effectively relieve the poverty of his employees and do his share in building up a healthy Christian family life for the nation. A further motive was undoubtedly that of counteracting the devastating effects of birth-control propaganda concerning which Mr. Denis Gwynn has written an illuminating chapter in his recent volume, *The Catholic Reaction in France.* Many causes, apart from the decay of religious faith—the laws of inheritance, the housing shortage, the high cost of living— have all tended to popularize practices which have resulted in an alarmingly low birth-rate, the remedies for which proposed at times by the Government, such as medals and cheaper railway fares for large families, have been ludicrously inadequate. But it was believed with much show of reason that the institution of *allocations familiales,* by removing in some measure the economic obstacles to childbearing, would have effected an appreciable improvement in the birth-rate. It is with this object that the allowance has been almost invariably fixed on an ascending scale as the family increases. Thus in the French civil service the allowance, since a recent increase, has stood as follows: 540 frs. a year for first child, 720 frs. for second, 1,080 for third, and 1,060 frs. for fourth and any subsequent child. So strong, indeed, was the expectation of good results from allowances that the promoters of the *Caisses* found a fertile field of propaganda in the *congrès de natalité* held annually in different French towns. Unhappily this expectation has apparently not been fulfilled. According to the latest available statistics published (Feb., 1925) by the Family Endowment Society,[3] the birth-rate of the ten largest towns in France still shows a progressive diminution, while their excess of births over deaths, which in 1923 was 8,122, had fallen in 1924 to 7,391. It is, however, probably too soon to speak with certainty as to the effect of family allowances upon the birth-rate. What happily is beyond question is that they react most favourably on the health and welfare of the children on whose behalf they were instituted, and are proving a potent weapon in the campaign against infant mortality.

Family allowances have, indeed, been generally used by their originators as a means of developing infant welfare work. The money being paid solely in the interests of the children, it was natural, and indeed laudable, that steps should be taken to ensure that it fulfilled its purpose. It is with this object that most *Caisses,* in addition to the monthly allowances, pay a lump sum at birth (*prime de naissance*), and sometimes also a *prime d'allaitement* for all breast-fed infants. Unfortunately the welfare work has been accompanied by a certain amount of domestic supervision of the workers' families, and this in some dis-

---

[3] 50 Romney Street, London, S. W. 1.

tricts has been somewhat hotly resented, all the more that the intruding visitors have been regarded as the representatives of the employers. It seems certain that in some cases the visiting has been done in a tactless and inquisitorial manner, while it is admitted that certain firms have made use of the allowances as a means of bringing pressure to bear on the worker in order to discourage strikes and irregular time-keeping.

It is here that we come to the cause of most of the criticisms that have been levelled against the system. The Trade Unions of France were at the outset suspicious of the whole movement, where indeed they were not definitely hostile, seeing in it a fresh means of keeping the worker and his family in tutelage. By degrees, however, their attitude, even of those affiliated to the Socialist Confédération Générale du Travail, has become far more friendly. They now approve in principle of the allowances on the ground that "they enable a fairer distribution of the product of labour and a higher standard of life for children." Where a very wide division of opinion still prevails is as to the best practical methods of carrying the principle into effect. Hitherto the *Caisses,* having been organised by separate federations of industries, have varied greatly in many particulars—and in this way much useful experience has been gained—but they have practically all been directed by the employers, with no real co-operation from the side of the worker, who has had to accept whatever conditions and benefits his employer has been pleased to determine. Moreover, many large employers of labour still remain outside the system altogether. Hence a growing inequality between workers, even in the same industry or district, a state of affairs which Trade Unions specially exist to combat.

Today it is widely felt in industrial circles throughout France that private enterprise in a matter so vital to the workers' welfare can no longer be accepted as satisfactory. Summarising the various protests that have been made and resolutions adopted at trade union and other gatherings within the last two years, it would appear that the fathers of families receiving the allowances feel strongly and justifiably that they should have a voice in the framing and administration of the schemes by which they are to benefit.

and that allowances—being accepted as something apart from wages—should continue through periods of strike and unemployment. It would probably also assist in the peaceful development of the system if the monthly allowances were invariably paid by the Secretary of the *Caisse,* and not, as often happens, by the individual employer. Writing as a woman, I feel further that they should invariably be paid direct to the mother, a regulation which, in deference to paternal susceptibilities, is only slowly being adopted in France. The Confédération Générale du Travail and the federations of workers in various industries have, on many recent occasions, pronounced themselves definitely in favour of placing the whole organisation of *allocations familiales* under State control. Miss Rathbone relates (*The Disinherited Family,* p. 213) that at the annual conference of the C. G. T. in 1923 a long resolution was passed, declaring that "the service of family allowances, premiums at birth, and allowances to nursing mothers should be under the control of the State (*la collectivité*), managed by officially appointed committees, including representatives of the various interests concerned, and financed by compulsory contributions from employers and by subsidies from the public purse. The allowances should be completely separated from the question of labour, and should not be affected by its fluctuations, or by unemployment or illness."

Other leading Trade Union officials have declared that (p. 214): "In its existing form the institution of family allowances is aimed at undermining the freedom of the worker"; and, again, that as "it could not be destroyed without inconvenience, only one course remains open: to transform it by amending and perfecting it."

The employers, on the other hand, seem anxious to leave things as they are. They deprecate State control in any form; they protest against any enforced uniformity of method; they fear increased cost of administration and higher rates of contribution, which remain, with the exception of the Roubaix *Caisse,* at the very moderate sum of 2 per cent of the wages bill. In a word, like employers all over the world, they are opposed to any measures likely to lead to interference with their liberty of action in the industrial sphere.

An objection to the system that suggests itself to most people is that the unmarried men would resent it. In practice this has not proved to be the case, although reports from Germany mention the point as one of the difficulties to be contended with. In point of fact the majority of men of the working class not only marry, but marry young, and would therefore look forward to enjoying the advantages of the plan at no distant date. Moreover, nowhere has it been deemed necessary to cut down the basic wage of the industry, although admittedly it has sometimes happened that a *caisse de compensation* has been started by the employer in lieu of a general rise in wages asked for. It may also surely be argued with some reason that for a young unmarried man to be able for a brief period to spend on himself the wage which later on will have to suffice for a wife and several children in addition, is merely to encourage him to acquire tastes and habits which later on poverty will compel him to give up.

A more difficult question as far as France is concerned, or indeed any country where agriculture is still the staple industry, is how best to apply the scheme to agricultural workers. Already it has been suggested in France that one reason why young people flock to the towns in ever-increasing numbers is that the urban worker enjoys the advantages of family allowances. We gather from Miss Rathbone's pages that so far only three rural *Caisses* have been formed. Two of them assess their members according to the number of *hectares* of land they possess, and the third on the number of hands employed. But the problem of the peasant proprietor still remains, and unless he can be brought into the scheme it is obvious that no very great progress can be made in rural districts.

It must not for a moment be imagined that family allowances are confined to France, the land of their birth. They are spreading rapidly in Belgium, more especially in the mining districts, on lines very similar to those in France, and are warmly supported by the Catholic Trade Unions. Already 280,000 workers are covered by the allowances.[4] It is worth noting that a very important *Caisse* at Liége, on a regional basis, has adopted the excellent plan of send-

[4] See "Foreign and Colonial Experiments in Family Allowances." By Olive Vlasto. 1925. Price 3d.

ing the allowances monthly, by post, direct to the mother. In Germany the system is now firmly established in all important industries, more especially in mines, textiles and engineering, and allowances are also often paid by individual employers. In addition, they are compulsory in all public and municipal services. This is also true of Austria, but there the allowances are on a very small scale. At Geneva a number of Catholic manufacturers have recently organised the system in their works, and they profess themselves delighted with the results, and maintain that the plan makes for stability and contentment among the workers. In Holland and the Scandinavian countries the system is steadily making its way; indeed, the only countries in Europe where it has not yet penetrated are Italy, Spain, Portugal, Russia—and Great Britain and Ireland.

In England the atmosphere of the moment does not appear favourable to the innovation. The Trade Unions, in so far as they have grasped it at all, are both suspicious and scornful. Unemployment, the heart-breaking problem of the last four years, would be unalleviated by it. Moreover, the country has been so swept by birth-control propaganda and is so alarmed at the number of its children, in conjunction with the lack of work and the acute housing shortage, that anything that may be supposed likely to favour large families is looked at askance, even by the very women who, one would have imagined, would have been the first to welcome the proposals. It is organised labour that would normally profit by the scheme, and it is precisely in the ranks of organised labour that small families are becoming the rule.

In her warm advocacy of Family Endowment, Miss Rathbone has dwelt, to the British public, mainly on its advantages as a possible solution of the prevailing industrial unrest. Wages have fallen in the last four years down to or even below a pre-war level, and the men clamour for a higher standard of living. On the other hand, employers maintain that with the existing stagnation of trade even the present rates are higher than the industries can afford. Hence strikes and rumours of strikes and a prevailing sense of industrial insecurity which helps to perpetuate the very conditions from which it is essential to escape with all possible speed. Without entering into any controversy as to the proportion wages should bear to the total product of industry, Miss Rathbone asks the pertinent question whether the amount actually available is being distributed in the most economical and effective manner. We are all agreed, she points out, on the need for a "living wage" for men employed in industry, and by degrees a living wage has come to mean by common consent a sum equal to the support of an "average" family of five persons, i. e., father, mother, and three children. And we all talk loosely as though, in nine cases out of ten, such were indeed the case. But what are the facts? Taking the census figures of 1921, Miss Rathbone is able to establish—and her deductions remain unchallenged—the following startling statistics concerning men over twenty in England and Wales:

26.6 per cent are bachelors.
39 per cent are married, or widowers with no dependant children.
15 per cent have one dependant child.
10.5 per cent have two dependant children.
6.2 per cent have three dependant children.
6.7 per cent have four or more dependant children.[5]

Thus the truth is that the "average" family theory of wage-paying only fits about 6 per cent of the workers and their homes. For whereas 65 per cent enjoy an income, not indeed of excessive amount, but yet above what is strictly necessary, over 12 per cent of the families, and these with 1½ million children between them, are living in a state of poverty which not only inflicts much misery, but reacts lamentably on the health and capacity of all concerned. Yet in order to provide a decent maintenance for these children and their mothers, is it really necessary to increase the already adequate wage—comparatively speaking—of all the bachelors and childless families? Miss Rathbone comes to the conclusion that such a method would not only be in the highest degree uneconomical, but that it is "unachievable out of the present national income."

Miss Rathbone's argument is so clear and her logic so unassailable that she makes instant converts of many readers. Yet the fact remains that, for various reasons, as far

---

[5] See *Wages Plus Family Allowances* (March, 1925), 50 Romney St., London, S. W. 1. Price 2d.

as England is concerned, the question is still an academic one, outside the purview of Parliament and untouched by any political party. Moreover, the method of working Family Endowment that Miss Rathbone now appears to favour, i. e., by a great extension of Compulsory Contributory Insurance, is not likely, in my opinion, to bring about its early acceptance. Such a scheme would be very expensive and vastly unpopular with many people. In any case there appears for the present to be no likelihood of any experiments in Family Endowment being made in England.

The question I would rather put tentatively is whether a reform with so Catholic an origin and with all the prestige of a real success in France, might not commend itself more quickly to the Irish people With low wages, and large families, and fewer Trade Union restrictions than in England, the Irish worker would surely welcome an innovation which unquestionably goes a long way to build up family life while making for industrial peace and stability. As in France, experiments might be made piecemeal and the details worked out to suit national needs. The post-office, the railways and the Civil Service generally all offer favourable fields for experiment. Incidentally Family Allowances provide an easy—and perhaps the only—solution of the difficult sex-problem of "equal pay for equal work." The solution has already been adopted in Holland, where certified teachers, male and female, receive similar pay according to their class, supplemented for all married teachers by an allowance for each dependant child equal to 3 per cent of the salary enjoyed. The plan is said to work well, although the allowances appear inadequate, and it does remove a standing bone of contention between men and women teachers in all countries. For all these reasons the scheme, surely, is worthy the fullest consideration.[6]

[6] Apart from Miss Rathbone's standard work, *The Disinherited Family*, the Family Endowment Council, 50 Romney Street, London, S. W. 1, issues valuable pamphlets and leaflets at small cost bearing on the whole subject, and is always pleased to supply information.

130

CO-OPERATION A PARTIAL SOLVENT OF CAPITALISM

John A. Ryan [1]

Interest is not a return for labor. The majority of interest receivers are, indeed, regularly engaged at some active task, whether as day laborers, salaried employees, directors of industry, or members of the profession; but for these services they obtain specific and distinct compensation. The interest that they get comes to them solely in their capacity as owners of capital, independently of any personal activity. From the viewpoint of economic distribution, interest is a "workless" income. As such, it seems to challenge that ethical intuition which connects reward with effort and which inclines to regard income from any other source as not quite normal. Moreover, interest absorbs a large part of the national income, and perpetuates grave economic inequalities.[2]

---

[1] *Distributive Justice*, pp. 210-233. (The Macmillan Company, New York. Reprinted with permission of the publishers.)

[2] Professor Scott Nearing estimates the annual income derived from the ownership of property in the United States; that is, land and all forms of capital, at from six to nine billion dollars. Professor W. I. King gives the combined shares of the national income received by the landowners and the capitalists at more than six and three-quarter billions in 1910. According to the Census Bulletin on the *Estimated Valuation of National Wealth*, the capital goods of the country were in 1912 approximately $175,000,000,000.00 At four per cent this would mean an annual income of seven million dollars. The lowest of the three estimates, six billion dollars, is equivalent to more than sixty dollars a year for every man, woman, and child in the United States. If that sum were equally distributed among the whole population, it would mean an increase of between forty and sixty per cent in the income of the majority of workingmen's families! Nor do present tendencies hold out any hope of an automatic reduction of the interest-burden in the future. In the opinion of Professor Scott Nearing, "the present economic tendencies will greatly increase the amount of property inco c paid with each passing decade." *Income*, p. 199; New York, 1915. See especially ch. vii. According to Professor Taussig, "the absolute amount of income going to this [the capitalist] class tends to increase, and its share of the total income tends also to increase; whereas for the laborers, though their total income may increase, their share of income as a whole tends to decline." *Principles of Economics*, II, 205.

Nevertheless, interest cannot be wholy abolished. As long as capital remains in private hands, its owners will demand and obtain interest. The only way of escape is by the road of Socialism, and this would prove a blind alley. As we have seen in a preceding chapter, Socialism is ethically and economically impossible.

May not the burdens and disadvantages of interest be mitigated or minimised? Such a result could conceivably be reached in two ways: the sum total of interest might be reduced, and the incomes derived from interest might be more widely distributed.

Reducing the Rate of Interest

No considerable diminution of the interest-volume can be expected through a decline in the interest rate. As far back as the middle of the eighteenth century, England and Holland were able to borrow money at three per cent. During the period that has since intervened, the rate has varied from three to six per cent on this class of loans. Between 1870 and 1890 the general rate of interest declined about two per cent, but it has risen since the latter date about one per cent. The Great War now (1916) in action is destroying an enormous amount of capital, and it will, as in the case of all previous military conflicts of importance, undoubtedly be followed by a marked rise in the rate of interest.

On the other hand, the only definite grounds upon which a decline in the rate can be hoped for are either uncertain or unimportant. They are the rapid increase of capital, and the extension of government ownership and operation of natural monopolies.

The first is uncertain in its effects upon the rate of interest because the increased supply of capital is often neutralized by the process of substitution. That is, a large part of the new capital does not compete with and bring down the price of the old capital. Instead, it is absorbed in new inventions, new types of machinery, and new processes of production, all of which take the place of labor, thus tending to increase rather than diminish the demand for capital and the rate of interest. To be sure, the demand for capital thus arising has not always been sufficient to offset the enlarged supply. Since the Industrial Revolution capital has at certain periods and in certain regions increased so rapidly that it could not all find employment in new forms and in old forms at the old rate. In some instances a decline in the rate of interest can be clearly traced to the disproportionately quick growth of capital. But this phenomenon has been far from uniform, and there is no indication that it will become so in the future. The possibilities of the process of substitution have been by no means exhausted.

The effects of government ownership are even more problematical. States and cities are, indeed, able to obtain capital more cheaply than private corporations for such public utilities as railways, telegraphs, tramways, and street lighting; and public ownership of all such concerns will probably become general in the not remote future. Nevertheless, the social gain is not likely to be proportionate to the reduction of interest on this section of capital. A part, possibly a considerable part, of the saving in interest will be neutralized by the lower efficiency and greater cost of operation; for in this respect publicly managed are inferior to privately managed enterprises. Consequently, the charges to the public for the services rendered by these utilities cannot be reduced to the same degree as the rate of interest on the capital. On the other hand, the exclusion of private operating capital from this very large field of public utilities should increase competition among the various units of capital, and thus bring down its rewards. To what extent this would happen cannot be estimated even approximately. The only safe statement is that the decline in the general rate of interest would probably be slight.

Need for a Wider Distribution of Capital

The main hope of lightening the social burden of interest lies in the possible reduction in the necessary volume of capital, and especially in a wider distribution of interest-incomes. In many parts of the industrial field there is a considerable waste of capital through unnecessary duplication. This means that a large amount of unnecessary interest is paid by the consumer in the form of unnecessarily high prices. Again, the owners of capital and receivers of interest constitute only a minority of the population of all countries, with the possible exception of the United States. The great majority of the wage earners in all lands possess no capital, and obtain no interest. Not only are their incomes small, often pitiably small, but their lack of capital deprives them of the security, confidence, and independence which are required for comfortable existence and efficient citizenship. They have no income from productive property to protect them against the cessation of wages. During periods of unemployment they are frequently compelled to have recourse to charity, and to forego many of the necessary comforts of life. So long as the bulk of the means of production remains in the hands of a distinct capitalist class, this demoralizing insecurity of the workers must continue as an essential part of our industrial system. While it might conceivably be eliminated through a comprehensive scheme of State insurance, this arrangement would substitute dependence upon the State for dependence upon the capitalist, and be much less desirable than ownership of income-bearing property.

The workers who possess no capital do not enjoy a normal and reasonable degree of independence, self-respect, or self confidence. They have not sufficient control over the wage contract and the other conditions of employment, and they have nothing at all to say concerning the goods that they shall produce, or the persons to whom their product shall be sold. They lack the incentive to put forth their best efforts in production. They cannot satisfy adequately the instinct of property, the desire to control some of the determining forms of material possession. They are deprived of that consciousness of power which is generated exclusively by property, and which contributes so powerfully toward the making of a contended and efficient life. They do not possess a normal amount of freedom in politics, nor in those civic and social relations which lie outside the spheres of industry and politics. In a word, the worker without capital has not sufficient power over the ordering of his own life.

The Essence of Co-operative Enterprise

The most effective means of lessening the volume of interest, and bringing about a wider distribution of capital, is to be found in co-operative enterprise. Co-operation in general denotes the unified action of a group of persons for a common end. A church, a debating club, a joint stock company, exemplifies co-operation in this sense. In the strict and technical sense, it has received various definitions. Professor Taussig declares that it "consists essentially in getting rid of the managing employer"; but this description is applicable only to co-operatives of production. "A combination of individuals to economize by buying in common, or increase their profits by selling in common" (Encyclopedia Britannica) is likewise too narrow, since it fits only distributive and agricultural co-operation. According to C. R. Fay, a co-operative society is "an association for the purpose of joint trading, originating among the weak, and conducted always in an unselfish spirit." If the word "trading" be stretched to comprehend manufacturing as well as commercial activities, Fay's definition is fairly satisfactory. The distinguishing circumstance, "originating among the weak," is also emphasized by Father Pesch in his statement that the essence, aim, and meaning of co-operation are to be found in "a combination of the economically weak in common efforts for the security and betterment of their condition." [3] In order to give the proper connotation for our purpose, we shall define co-operation as that joint economic action which seeks to obtain for a relatively weak group all or part of the profits and interest which in the ordinary capitalist enterprise are taken by a smaller and different group. This formula puts in the foreground the important fact that in every form of co-operative effort, some interest or profits, or both, are diverted from those who would have received them under purely capitalistic arrangements, and distributed among a larger number of persons. Thus it indicates the bearing of co-operation upon the problem of lightening the social burden of interest.

From the viewpoint of economic function, co-operation may be divided into two general kinds, producers' and consumers'. The best example of the former is a wage earners' productive society; of the latter, a co-operative store. Credit co-operatives and agricultural co-operatives fall mainly under the former head, inasmuch as their principal object is to assist production, and to benefit men as pro-

[3] *Lehrbuch der Nationaloekonomie,* III, 517.

ducers rather than as consumers. Hence from the viewpoint of type, co-operation may be classified as credit, agricultural, distributive, and productive.

Co-operative Credit Societies

A co-operative credit society is a bank controlled by the persons who patronize it, and lending on personal rather than material security. Such banks are intended almost exclusively for the relatively helpless borrower, as, the small farmer, artisan, shopkeeper, and the small man generally. Fundamentally they are associations of neighbors who combine their resources and their credit in order to obtain loans on better terms than are accorded by the ordinary commercial banks. The capital is derived partly from the sale of shares of stock, partly from deposits, and partly from borrowed money. In Germany, where credit associations have been more widely extended and more highly developed than in any other country, they are of two kinds, named after their respective founders, Schulze-Delitzsch and Raiffeisen. The former operates chiefly in the cities, serves the middle classes rather than the very poor, requires all its members to subscribe for capital stock, commits them to a long course of saving, and thus develops their interest as lenders. The Raiffeisen societies have, as a rule, very little share capital, exist chiefly in the country districts, especially among the poorest of the peasantry, are based mostly on personal credit, and do not profess to encourage greatly the saving and lending activities of their members. Both forms of association loan money to their members at lower rates of interest than these persons could obtain elsewhere. Hence credit co-operation directly reduces the burden of interest.

The Schulze-Delitzsch societies have more than half a million members in the cities and towns of Germany, sixty per cent of whom take advantage of the borrowing facilities. The Raiffeisen banks comprise about one-half of all the independent German agriculturists. Some form of co-operative banking is well established in every important country of Europe, except Denmark and Great Britain. In the former country its place seems to be satisfactorily filled by the ordinary commercial banks. Its absence from Great Britain is apparently due to the credit system provided by the large landholders, to the scarcity of peasant proprietors, and to general lack of initiative. It is especially strong in Italy, Belgium, and Austria, and it has made a promising beginning in Ireland. In every country in which it has obtained a foothold, it gives indication of steady and continuous progress. Nevertheless it is subject to definite limits. It can never make much headway among that class of persons whose material resources are sufficiently large and palpable to command loans on the usual terms offered by the commercial banks. As a rule, these terms are quite as favorable as those available through the co-operative credit associations. It is only because the poorer men cannot obtain loans from the commercial banks on the prevailing conditions that they are impelled to have recourse to the co-operative associations.

Co-operative Agricultural Societies

The chief operations of agricultural co-operative societies are manufacturing, marketing, and purchasing. In the first named field the most important example is the co-operative dairy. The owners of cows hold the stock or shares of the concern, and in addition to dividends receive profits in proportion to the amount of milk that they supply. In Ireland and some other countries, a portion of the profits goes to the employees of the dairy as a dividend on wages. Other productive co-operatives of agriculture are found in cheese making, bacon curing, distilling, and wine making. All are conducted on the same general principles as the co-operative dairy.

Through the marketing societies and purchasing societies, the farmers are enabled to sell their products to better advantage, and to obtain materials needed for carrying on agricultural operations more cheaply than would be possible by isolated individual action. Some of the products marketed by the selling societies are eggs, milk, poultry, fruit, vegetables, live stock, and various kinds of grain. The purchasing societies supply for the most part manures, seeds, and machinery. Occasionally they buy the most costly machinery in such a way that the association becomes the corporate owner of the implements. In these cases the individual members have only the use of the machines, but they would be unable to enjoy even that advantage were it not for the intervention of the co-operative society.

Where such arrangements exist, the society exemplifies not only co-operative buying but co-operative ownership.

Agricultural co-operation has become most widely extended in Denmark, and has displayed its most striking possibilities in Ireland. Relatively to its population, the former country has more farmers in co-operative societies, and has derived more profit therefrom than any other nation. The rapid growth and achievements of agricultural co-operation in the peculiarly unfavorable circumstances of Ireland constitute the most convincing proof to be found anywhere of the essential soundness and efficacy of the movement. Various forms of rural co-operative societies are solidly established in Germany, France, Belgium, Italy, and Switzerland. In recent years the movement has made some progress in the United States, especially in relation to dairies, grain elevators, the marketing of live stock and fruit, the various forms of rural insurance. The co-operative insurance companies effect a saving to the Minnesota farmers of $700,000 annually, and the co-operative elevators handle about 30 per cent of the grain marketed in that state. In 1915 the business transacted by the co-operative marketing and purchasing organizations of the farmers of the United States amounted to $1,400,000,000.

The transformation in the rural life of more than one European community through co-operation has amounted to little less than a revolution. Higher standards of agricultural products and production have been set up and maintained, better methods of farming have been inculcated and enforced, and the whole social, moral, and civic life of the people has been raised to a higher level. From the viewpoint of material gain, the chief benefits of agricultural co-operation have been the elimination of unnecessary middlemen, and the economies of buying in large quantities, selling in the best markets, and employing the most efficient implements. As compared with farming conducted on a large scale, the small farm possesses certain advantages, and is subject to certain disadvantages. It is less wasteful, permits greater attention to details, and makes a greater appeal to the self interest of the cultivator; but the small farmer cannot afford to buy the best machinery, nor is he in a position to carry on to the best advantage the commercial features of his occupation, such as borrowing, buying, and marketing. Co-operation frees him from all these handicaps. "The co-operative community ... is one in which groups of humble men combine their efforts, and to some extent their resources, in order to secure for themselves those advantages in industry which the masters of capital derive from the organization of labor, from the use of costly machinery, and from the economies of business when done on a large scale. They apply in their industry the methods by which the fortunes of the magnates in commerce and manufacture are made." These words, uttered by a prominent member of the Irish co-operative movement, summarize the aims and achievements of agricultural co-operation in every country of Europe in which it has obtained a strong foothold. In every such community the small farm has gained at the expense of the large farm system. Finally, agricultural co-operation reduces the burden of interest by eliminating some unnecessary capital, stimulates saving among the tillers of the soil by providing a ready and safe means of investment, and in manifold ways contributes materially toward a better distribution of wealth.

Co-operative Mercantile Societies

Co-operative stores are organized by and for consumers. In every country they follow rather closely the Rochdale system, so called from the English town in which the first store of this kind was established in 1844. The members of the co-operative society furnish the capital, and receive thereon interest at the prevailing rate, usually five per cent. The stores sell goods at about the same prices as their privately owned competitors, but return a dividend on the purchases of all those customers who are members of the society. The dividends are provided from the surplus which remains after wages, interest on the capital stock, and all other expenses have been paid. In some co-operative stores non-members receive a dividend on their purchases at half the rate accorded to members of the society, but only on condition that these payments shall be invested in the capital stock of the enterprise. And the members themselves are strongly urged to make this disposition of their purchase-dividends. Since the latter are paid only quarterly, the co-operative store exercises a considerable influence toward inducing its patrons to save and to become small capitalists.

In Great Britain the vast majority of the retail stores have been federated into two great wholesale societies, one in England and the other in Scotland. The retail stores provide the capital, and participate in the profits according to the amounts purchased, just as the individual consumers furnish the capital and share the profits of the retail establishments. The Scottish Wholesale Society divides a part of the profits among its employees. Besides their operations as jobbers, the wholesale societies are bankers for the retail stores, and own and operate factories, farms, warehouses, and steamships. Many of the retail co-operatives likewise carry on productive enterprises, such as milling, tailoring, bread making, and the manufacture of boots, shoes, and other commodities, and some of them build, sell, and rent cottages, and lend money to members who desire to obtain homes.

The co-operative store movement has made greatest progress in its original home, Great Britain. In 1913 about one person in every three was to some degree interested in or a beneficiary of these institutions. The profits of the stores amounted to about $71,302,070, which was about 35 per cent on the capital. The employees numbered about 145,000, and the sales for the year aggregated $650,000,000. The English Wholesale Society was the largest flour miller and shoe manufacturer in Great Britain, and its total business amounted to $150,000,000. Outside of Great Britain, co-operative distribution has been most successful in Germany, Belgium, and Switzerland. It has had a fair measure of development in Italy, but has failed to assume any importance in France. "There is every sign that within the near future—except in France—the stores will come to include the great majority of the wage earning class, which is a constantly growing percentage of the total population." [4] Within recent years a respectable number of stores have been established on a sound basis in Canada and the United States. Owing, however, to the marked individualism and the better economic conditions of these two countries, the co-operative movement will continue for some time to be relatively slow.

[4] Fay, *Co-operation at Home and Abroad*, p. 340.

As in the case of agricultural co-operation, the money benefits accruing to the members of the co-operative stores consist mainly of profits rather than interest. In the absence of the store societies, these profits would have gone for the most part to middlemen as payments for the risks and labour of conducting privately owned establishments. Forty-seven of the sixty million dollars profits of the British co-operative stores in 1910 were divided among more than two and one-half million members of these institutions, instead of going to a comparatively small number of private merchants. The other thirteen million dollars were interest on the capital stock. Had the members invested an equal amount in other enterprises they could, indeed, have obtained about the same rate and amount of interest, but in the absence of the co-operative stores their inducements and opportunities to save would have been much smaller. For it must be kept in mind that a very large part of the capital stock in the co-operative stores is derived from the members' dividends on their purchases at such stores, and would not have come into existence at all without these establishments. The gains of the co-operative stores, whether classified as profits or as interest, are evidently a not inconsiderable indication of a better distribution of wealth.

Co-operation in Production

Co-operative production has occasionally been pronounced a failure. This judgment is too sweeping and too severe. "As a matter of fact," says a prominent London weekly, "the co-operators' success has been even more remarkable in production than in distribution. The co-operative movement runs five of the largest of our flour mills; it has, amongst others, the very largest of our boot factories; it makes cotton cloth and woollens, and all sorts of clothing; it has even a corset factory of its own; it turns out huge quantities of soap; it makes every article of household furniture; it produces cocoa and confectionery; it grows its own fruit and makes its own jams; it has one of the largest tobacco factories, and so on." Obviously this passage refers to that kind of productive co-operation which is carried on by the stores, not to productive concerns owned and managed by the workers therein employed. Nevertheless, the enterprises in question are co-operatively managed, and hence exemplify co-operation rather than private and competitive industry. They ought not to be left out of any statement of the field occupied by co-operative production. The limitations and possibilities of co-operation in production can best be set forth by considering its three different forms separately.

The "perfect" form occurs when all the workers engaged in a concern own all the share capital, control the entire management, and receive the whole of the wages, profits, and interest. In this field the failures have been much more numerous and conspicuous than the successes. Godin's stove works at Guise, France, is the only important enterprise of this kind that is now in existence. Great Britain has several establishments in which the workers own a large part of the capital, but apparently none in which they are the sole proprietors and managers. The "labour societies" of Italy, consisting mostly of diggers, masons, and bricklayers, co-operatively enter into contracts for the performance of public works, and share in the profits of the undertaking in addition to their wages; but the only capital that they provide consists of comparatively simple and inexpensive tools. The raw material and other capital is furnished by the public authority which gives the contract.

A second kind of productive co-operation is found in the arrangement known as co-partnership. This is "the system under which, in the first place, a substantial and known share of the profit of a business belongs to the workers in it, not by right of any shares they may hold, or any other title, but simply by right of the labour they have contributed to make the profit; and, in the second place, every worker is at liberty to invest his profit, or any other savings, in shares of the society or company, and so become a member entitled to vote on the affairs of the body which employs him."[5] So far as its first, or profit sharing, feature is concerned, co-partnership is not genuine co-operation, for it includes neither ownership of capital nor management of the business. Co-operative action begins only with the adoption of the second element. In most of the existing co-partnership concerns, all the employés are urged, and many of them required to invest at least a part of their profits in the capital stock. The most notable and successful

[5] Schloss, *Methods of Industrial Remuneration,* pp. 353, 354.

of these experiments is that carried on by the South Metropolitan Gas Company of London. Practically all the company's 6,000 employés are now among its stockholders. Although their combined holdings are only about one-twenty-eighth of the total, they are empowered to select two of the ten members of the board of directors. Essentially the same co-partnership arrangements have been adopted by about one-half the privately owned gas companies of Great Britain. In none of them, however, have the workers obtained as yet such a large percentage of either ownership or control as in the South Metropolitan. Co-partnership exists in several other enterprises in Great Britain, and is found in a considerable number of French concerns. There are a few instances in the United States, the most thoroughgoing being that of N. O. Nelson & Co. at Le Claire, Ill.

As already noted, the co-operative stores exemplify a third type of co-operative production. In some cases the productive concern is under the management of a local retail establishment, but the great majority of them are conducted by the English and Scottish Wholesale Societies. As regards the employés of these enterprises, the arrangement is not true co-operation, since they have no part in the ownership of the capital. The Scottish Wholesale Society, as we have seen, permits the employés of its productive works to share in the profits thereof; nevertheless, it does not admit them as stockholders, nor give them any voice in the management. In all cases the workers may, indeed, become owners of stock in their local retail stores. Since the latter are stockholders in the wholesale societies, which in turn own the productive enterprises, the workers have a certain indirect and attenuated proprietorship in the productive concerns. But they derive therefrom no dividends. All the interest and most of the profits of the productive establishments are taken by the wholesale and retail stores. For it is the theory of the wholesale societies that the employés in the works of production should share in the gains thereof only as consumers. They are to profit only in the same way and to the same extent as other consumer-members of the local retail establishments.

The most effective and beneficial form of co-operative production is evidently that which has been described as the "perfect" type. Were all production organised on this plan, the social burden of interest would be insignificant, industrial despotism would be ended, and industrial democracy realised. As things are, however, the establishments exemplifying this type are of small importance. Their increase and expansion are impeded by lack of directive ability and of capital, and the risk to the workers' savings. Yet none of these obstacles is necessarily insuperable. Directive ability can be developed in the course of time, just as it was in the co-operative stores. Capital can be obtained fast enough, perhaps, to keep pace with the supply of directive ability and the spirit of co-operation. The risk undertaken by workers who put their savings into productive concerns owned and managed by themselves need not be greater than that now borne by investors in private enterprises of the same kind. There is no essential reason why the former should not provide the same profits and insurance against business risks as the latter. While the employees assume none of the risks of capitalistic industry, neither do they receive any of the profits. If the co-operative factory exhibits the same degree of business efficiency as the private enterprise it will necessarily afford the workers adequate protection for their savings and capital. Indeed, if "perfect" co-operative production is to be successful at all its profits will be larger than those of the capitalistic concern, owing to the greater interest taken by the workers in their tasks, and in the management of the business.

For a long time to come, however, it is probable that "perfect" co-operative production will be confined to relatively small and local industries. The difficulty of finding sufficient workers' capital and ability to carry on, for example, a transcontinental railroad or a nationwide steel business, is not likely to be overcome for one or two generations.[6]

The labour co-partnership form of co-operation is susceptible of much wider and more rapid extension. It can be adapted readily to the very large as well as to the small and medium sized concerns. Since it requires the workers to own but a part of the capital, it can be established in any

[6] Cf., however, Mr. A. R. Orage's work, *National Guilds*, London, 1914.

enterprise in which the capitalists show themselves willing and sympathetic. In every industrial corporation there are some employés who possess savings, and these can be considerably increased through the profit sharing feature of co-partnership. A very long time must, indeed, elapse before the workers in any of the larger enterprises could get possession of all, or even of a controlling share of the capital, and a considerable time would be needed to educate and fit them for successful management.

Production under the direction of the co-operative stores can be extended faster than either of the other two forms, and it has before it a very wide, even though definitely limited field. The British wholesale societies have already shown themselves able to conduct with great success large manufacturing concerns, have trained and attracted an adequate number of competent leaders, and have accumulated so much capital that they have been obliged to invest several million pounds in other enterprises. The possible scope of the stores and their co-operative production has been well described by C. R. Fay: "distribution of goods for personal consumption, first, among the working class population; secondly, among the salaried classes who feel a homogeneity of professional interest; production by working class organisations alone (with rare exceptions in Italy) of all the goods which they distribute to their members. But this is its limit. Distribution among the remaining sections of the industrial population; production for distribution to these members; production of the instruments of production, and production for international trade; the services of transport and exchange. All these industrial departments are, so far as can be seen, permanently outside the domain of a store movement." [7]

The theory by which the stores attempt to justify the exclusion of the employés of their productive concerns from a share of the profits thereof is that all profits come ultimately from the pockets of the consumer, and should all return to that source. The defect in this theory is that it ignores the question whether the consumers ought not to be required to pay a sufficiently high price for their goods to provide the producers with profits in addition to wages. While the wholesale stores are the owners and

[7] Op. cit., p. 341.

managers of the capital in the productive enterprises, and, on the capitalistic principle, should obtain the profits, the question remains whether this is necessarily a sound principle, and whether it is in harmony with the theory and ideals of co-operation. In those concerns which have adopted the labour co-partnership scheme, the workers, even when they own none of the capital, are accorded a part of the profits. It is assumed that this is a fairer and wiser method of distribution than that which gives the labourer only wages, leaving all the profits to the manager-capitalist. This feature of co-partnership rests on the theory that the workers can, if they will, increase their efficiency and reduce the friction between themselves and their employer to such an extent as to make the profit-sharing arrangement a good thing for both parties. Consequently, the profits obtained by the workers are a payment for this specific contribution to the prosperity of the business. Why should not this theory find recognition in productive enterprises conducted by the co-operative stores?

In the second place, the workers in these concerns ought to be permitted to participate in the capital ownership and management. They would thus be strongly encouraged to become better workers, to save more money, and to increase their capacity for initiative and self-government. Moreover, this arrangement would go farther than any other system toward reconciling the interests of producer and consumer. As producer, the worker would obtain, besides his wages, interest and profits up to the limit set by the competition of private productive concerns. As consumer, he would share in the profits and interest which would otherwise have gone to the private distributive enterprises. In this way the producer and consumer would each get the gains that were due specifically and respectively to his activity and efficiency.

Advantages and Prospects of Co-operation

At this point it will, perhaps, be well to sum up the advantages and to estimate the prospects of the co-operative movement. In all its forms co-operation eliminates some waste of capital and energy, and, therefore, transfers some interest and profits from a special capitalist and undertaking class to a larger and economically weaker group of persons. For it must be borne in mind that all co-operative enterprises are conducted mainly by and for labourers or small farmers. Hence the system always makes directly for a better distribution of wealth. To a considerable extent it transfers capital ownership from those who do not themselves work with or upon capital to those who are so engaged, namely, the labourers and the farmers; thus it diminishes the unhealthy separation now existing between the owners and the users of the instruments of production. Co-operation has, in the second place, a very great educational value. It enables and induces the weaker members of economic society to combine and utilise energies and resources that would otherwise remain unused and undeveloped; and it greatly stimulates and fosters initiative, self-confidence, self-restraint, self-government and the capacity for democracy. In other words, it vastly increases the development and efficiency of the individual. It likewise induces him to practise thrift, and frequently provides better fields for investment than would be open to him outside the co-operative movement. It diminishes selfishness and inculcates altruism; for no co-operative enterprise can succeed in which the individual members are not willing to make greater sacrifices for the common good than are ordinarily evoked by private enterprise. Precisely because co-operation makes such heavy demands upon the capacity for altruism, its progress always has been and must always continue to be relatively slow. Its fundamental and, perhaps, chief merit is that it does provide the mechanism and the atmosphere for a greater development of the altruistic spirit than is possible under any other economic system that has ever been tried or devised.

By putting productive property into the hands of those who now possess little or nothing, co-operation promotes social stability and social progress. This statement is true in some degree of all forms of co-operation, but it applies with particular force to those forms which are carried on by the working classes. A steadily growing number of keen-sighted social students are coming to realise that an industrial system which permits a comparatively small section of society to own the means of production and the instrumentalities of distribution, leaving to the great majority of the workers nothing but their labour power, is fundamentaly unstable, and contains within itself the germs of inevitable dissolution. No mere adequacy of wages and other working conditions, and no mere security of the workers' livelihood, can permanently avert this danger, nor compensate the individual for the lack of power to determine those activities of life which depend upon the possession of property. Through co-operation this unnatural divorce of the users from the owners of capital can be minimised. The worker is converted from a mere wage earner to a wage earner plus a property owner, thus becoming a safer and more useful member of society. In a word, co-operation produces all the well recognised individual and social benefits which have in all ages been evoked by the "magic of property."

Finally, co-operation is a golden mean between individualism and Socialism. It includes all the good features and excludes all the evil features of both. On the one hand, it demands and develops individual initiative and self-reliance, makes the rewards of the individual depend upon his own efforts and efficiency, and gives him full ownership of specific pieces of property. On the other hand, it compels him to submerge much of the selfishness and indifference to the welfare of his fellows which characterise our individual economy. It embraces all the good that is claimed for Socialism because it induces men to consider and to work earnestly for the common good, eliminates much of the waste of competitive industry, reduces and redistributes the burdens of profits and interest, and puts the workers in control of capital and industry. At the same time, it avoids the evils of an industrial despotism, of bureaucratic inefficiency, of individual indifference, and of an all-pervading collective ownership. The resemblances that Socialists sometimes profess to see between their system and co-operation are superficial and far less important than the differences. Under both arrangements the workers would, we are told, own and control the means of production; but the members of a co-operative society directly own and immediately control a *definite amount of specific capital*, which is essentially *private* property. In a Socialist régime the workers' ownership of capital would be collective not private, general not specific, while their control of the productive instruments with which they worked would be shared with other citizens. The latter would vastly outnumber the workers in any particular industry, and would be interested therein not as producers but as consumers. No less obvious and fundamental are the differences in favour of co-operation as regards the vital matters of freedom, opportunity, and efficiency.

In so far as the future of co-operation can be predicted from its past, the outlook is distinctly encouraging. The success attained in credit, agriculture, and distribution, is a sufficient guarantee for these departments. While productive co-operation has experienced more failures than successes, it has finally shown itself to be sound in principle, and feasible in practice. Its extension will necessarily be slow, but this is exactly what should be expected by any one who is acquainted with the limitations of human nature and the history of human progress. If a movement that is capable of modifying so profoundly the condition of the workers as is co-operative production, gave indications of increasing rapidly, we should be inclined to question its soundness and permanence. Experience has given us abundant proof that no mere system or machinery can effect a revolutionary improvement in economic conditions. No social system can do more than provide a favourable environment for the development of those individual capacities and energies which are the true and the only causal forces of betterment.

Nor is it to be expected that any of the other three forms of co-operation will ever cover the entire field to which it might, absolutely speaking, be extended; or that co-operation as a whole will become the one industrial system of the future. Even if the latter contingency were possible it would not be desirable. The elements of our economic life, and the capacities of human nature, are too varied and too complex to be forced with advantage into any one system, whether capitalism, Socialism, or co-operation. Any single system or form of socio-economic organisation would prove an intolerable obstacle to individual opportunity and social progress. Multiplicity and variety in social and industrial orders are required for an effective range of choices, and an adequate scope for human effort. In a general way the limits of co-operation in relation to the other forms of economic organisation have been satisfactorily stated by Mr. Aneurin Williams: "I suggest, therefore, that where there are great monopolies, either natural or created by the combination of businesses, there you have a presumption in favour of State and municipal ownership. In those forms of industry where individuality is everything; where there are new inventions to make, or to develop or put on the market, or merely to adopt in some rapidly transformed industry; where the eye of the master is everything; where reference to a committee, or appeals from one official to another, would cause fatal delay: there is the natural sphere of individual enterprise pure and simple. Between these two extremes there is surely a great sphere for voluntary association to carry on commerce, manufacture, and retail trade, in circumstances where there is no natural monopoly, and where the routine of work is not rapidly changing, but, on the whole, fairly well established and constant."[8]

The province open to co-operation is, indeed, very large. If it were fully occupied the danger of a social revolution would be non-existent, and what remained of the socio-industrial problem would be relatively undisturbing and unimportant. The "specialisation of function" in industrial organisation, as outlined by Mr. Williams, would give a balanced economy in which the three great socio-economic systems and principles would have full play, and each would be required to do its best in fair competition with the other two. Economic life would exhibit a diversity making strongly for social satisfaction and stability, inasmuch as no very large section of the industrial population would desire to overthrow the existing order. Finally, the choice of three great systems of industry would offer the utmost opportunity and scope for the energies and the development of the individual. And this, when all is said, remains the supreme end of a just and efficient socio-industrial organisation.

[8] *Copartnership and Profit-Sharing*, p. 235.

131

THE ETHICS OF STRIKES

Joseph J. Ayd [1]

Strikes are not fresh pimples on the face of labor. Novels like Churchill's "The Dwelling Place of Light," Poole's "The Harbor," and Hedges' "Iron City" might incline one to imagine that this form of servile revolt is a twentieth-century addition to the world's civilization. History, however, unblushingly offers evidence to the contrary. As far back as 1767 we read of an organized weavers' strike in Dublin that very nearly took the wool out of the woolen industry. By 1835, in fact, strikes had become so numerous that a New York paper asserted that "Strikes are all the fashion." From 1881 to 1905 there were, on an average, 1,470 strikes yearly, that is, four strikes a day for every day of the year. And few of us, I am sure, were not filled with amazement by the estimates of the losses to labor and industry through strikes for the year 1919, published in the New York *Sun*, December 15, 1919: "Since January 1, this year, strikes in this country have cost labor about $723,478,300. Meanwhile and incidentally capital was suffering a loss approximating $1,266,357,450." In New York State alone there were, between January 1 and December 10, 1919, 278 strikes.

No honest student of industrial conditions will see in the labor agitators or professional malcontents the sole cause of these widespread and distressing upheavals. Unhappily, we have these agitators with us, and they certainly deliver smashing blows to industry, but to lay the whole blame of social disturbances at their door is a species of blind prejudice that engenders more harm than good. You could collect all these lurid figures into one great crowd, cast them into jail, and yet, sad to say, strikes would go merrily onward. "To see in the agitator the sole cause of a problem and a movement that girdles the planet is plain bankruptcy of intelligence."

Loosely speaking, a strike is any widespread quitting of work. Strictly considered, however, a strike may be defined

[1] *The Catholic Mind*, July 22, 1920.

as a concerted cessation of work on the part of a large number of workmen for the purpose of securing the assent of an employer to certain specific demands. In the twenty-first annual report of the United States Commissioner of Labor, published in 1906, a strike is defined as "a concerted withdrawal from work by a part or all of the employees of an establishment, or several establishments, to enforce a demand on the part of the employers." Hence a strike is an organized movement, involving a simultaneous cessation of work on the part of a number of workmen, not for the purpose of changing their place of employment, but rather with the purpose and the prospect of regaining their old positions on better terms.

Strikes may be distinguished into three classes: The direct strike, the sympathetic strike and the general strike. The direct strike is usually simple in form and is an organized cessation of work by a number of men laboring under the same industrial grievance. The late coal and steel strikes of unhappy memory are samples. A sympathetic strike, on the other hand, is not simple; it is hydra-headed. It is a strike of workers out of pure sympathy. It is, scientifically speaking, a concerted quitting of work by men justly treated for the removal of a grievance or grievances of other workmen who have "struck" for their "rights." As an example, suppose the brakemen of a roalroad quit their work simply and solely because the trackmen, on strike for a demand for fewer hours and less pay, are fighting a losing battle against the company. The strike of the brakemen would be sympathetic. A general strike, the apple of the eye of syndicalism, means a concerted and morally universal quitting of work on the part of all workmen (proletariat) for the avowed and sole purpose of exterminating capitalism root and branch and installing the State, or trades unions, or soviets as the owner of the sources and the means of production.

Are strikes ever morally justifiable? The answer to this question is a large order. To throw a whole community or a whole nation into chaos on the off-chance of benefiting one's self or one's class or combination is playing with vital issues and is not easily justified. No one will, however, dispute the workman's clear right to quit his job at any time he wishes, provided that he does not thereby violate the conditions of a contract voluntarily and freely entered into. But when there is a question of the right of a number of men to unite and formally agree to quit work simultaneously, involving by their action considerable inconvenience and financial loss to themselves, and especially to their employers, then we have another pair of sleeves, and the case assumes a serious aspect.

Let us study the simple or direct strike first. Moralists assert that this form of strike is not in itself an evil; that is to say, when considered apart from the circumstances that usually attend and follow it, it is not unjust or wrong. But because of the grave character of the evil consequences that dog the steps of strikes, their moral justification depends wholly on the fulfilment of certain obvious and necessary conditions. These conditions, which apply to any direct strike in any industrial center or plant, may be briefly stated thus: 1. There must be a sincere and genuine grievance to be remedied: such as deprivation of living wage. 2. The strike must be the last resort, that is to say, safer and less drastic measures must have proved inadequate. 3. Supposing a sound prospect of ultimate success, the good results to be obtained must be reasonably proportional to the unseemly consequences of the strike to the community.

The first of these conditions needs no comment. An action, in itself harmless, but accompanied by harmful effects, may not be placed unless a just cause makes it imperative. The second condition also seems clear. If a dispute between workmen and their masters can be settled by safer methods, then the parties thereto are morally bound to settle it accordingly. The third condition contributes the bone of contention. It is based upon some undeniable dictates of the natural law. When God formed man he gave him a social nature, thereby ordaining that he work out his destiny in society. Now society, as we know, would be utterly impossible unless its members willingly submitted to certain sacrifices for the common welfare. Therefore, when discussing the morality of a strike, entailing as it does the exercise of violent human passions, we must carefully consider just how far it will affect the common welfare.

When we come to study the sympathetic strike we find we are treading debatable and dangerous ground. Simply mention the sympathetic strike to some folk, and at once they begin to fashion thunderbolts. Even the authorities are at loggerheads. However, with a clear eye to complex, modern industrial conditions, we may distinguish two kinds of sympathetic strikes, and assert that one is wholly justifiable and the other doubtfully so, or not at all.

Let us suppose a strike has been declared in one of the various branches of labor controlled by a single firm. The workmen have been summarily refused, say, a living wage —that is, a wage sufficient to support themselves and families in reasonable comfort. Having failed to receive redress, and knowing from sad experience the impotence of courts and the strange unwillingness of the State to interfere, they have "struck" for their just demand. During the progress of a losing fight, they appeal for assistance to their fellow-workmen employed in other departments of the same plant. These latter, however, have no personal grivance, and yet, out of regard for the welfare of their less fortunate fellows, and after having made futile representations to the firm, they vote a sympathetic strike. Can such a strike be justified?

The answer is yes. The mere continuance at work of the more fortunate workmen would assist the firm in its unjust treatment of the supposedly enslaved section of workmen. In the case cited the firm has, in effect, constituted itself the unjust aggressor by endeavoring economically to force men to be parties to a contract which is ethically indefensible.

Suppose, now, that the unjustly treated workmen lodge their appeal for help with workmen hired by an entirely different firm. We take for granted that this latter firm is uniformly fair to its men. But, by extending its patronage to the unjust firm, it is, mayhap involuntarily, assisting it in its oppressive methods. Can we justify the workmen of the just firm in declaring a sympathetic strike against it, unless business relations with the unjust firm are severed?

The answer is no longer simple. This sort of sympathetic strike is based on the doctrine of "tainted goods," and, according to most moralists, seems to be ordinarily unlawful for several reasons. (cf. Cronin, *The Science of Ethics*, vol. II, p. 365.) In the first place, a strike of this kind is opposed to the nature of the labor contract. The workman hires out his labor to his employer, and by his contract gives the employer the full use and direction of his labor. It is the employer's business then to determine the nature and amount of the work to be performed and what goods are to be handled in the contract. Secondly, the immediate effect of this kind of strike is not the favorable ending of the original strike, but the spreading of the strike. Thirdly, a strike of this kind carried to its logical extreme would mean a universal quitting of work the country over for the sake of a comparatively small group of men. This militates against the principle that there must be a proportion between the means used and the effect to be obtained.

To the general strike, as defined above, we can give short shrift. It is the pet of the Reds and the Bolshevists. Its one sole purpose is to overthrow the so-called capital system and substitute sovietism, already shown to be unadulterated moonshine by the autocratic measures of the Russian "Dictatorship of the Proletariat." This kind of strike is wholly unjustifiable. Its aim, the total extinction of private ownership in capital, cannot be justified, and the means approved and adopted to accomplish this aim are strikingly unlawful. The capitalists of today, no matter how much we may wish to berate them, are *bona-fide* owners, and no one is justified in attempting to injure them, render their property useless and in myriad shady ways force them to surrender what is rightfully theirs.

SOCIETY

132
SOCIETY

CHARLES MACKSEY [1]

Society implies fellowship, company, and has always been conceived as signifying a human relation, and not a herding of sheep, a hiving of bees, or a mating of wild animals. The accepted definition of a society is a stable union of a plurality of persons co-operating for a common purpose of benefit to all. The fulness of co-operation involved naturally extends to all the activities of the mind, will, and external faculties, commensurate with the common purpose and the bond of union: this alone presents an adequate, human working-together.

This definition is as old as the Schoolmen, and embodies the historical concept as definitized by cogent reasoning. Under such reasoning it has become the essential idea of society and remains so still, notwithstanding the perversion of philosophical terms consequent upon later confusion of man with beast, stock, and stone. It is à priori only as far as chastened by restrictions put upon it by the necessities of known truth, and is a departure from the inductive method in vogue to-day only so far as to exclude rigidly the aberrations of uncivilized tribes and degenerate races from the requirements of reason and basic truth. Historical induction taken alone, while investigating efficient causes of society, may yet miss its essential idea, and is in peril of including irrational abuse with rational action and development.

The first obvious requisite in all society is authority. Without this there can be no secure co-ordination of effort nor permanency of co-operation. No secure co-ordination, for men's judgment will differ on the relative value of means for the common purpose, men's choice will vary on

[1] *Catholic Encyclopedia,* vol. XIV, pp. 74-78.

means of like value; and unless there is some headship, confusion will result. No permanence of co-operation, for the best of men relax in their initial resolutions, and to hold them at a co-ordinate task, a tight rein and a steady spur is needed. In fact, reluctant though man is to surrender the smallest tittle of independence and submit in the slightest his freedom to the bidding of another, there never has been in the history of the world a successful, nor even a serious attempt at co-operative effort without authoritative guidance. Starting with this definition and requirement, philosophy finds itself confronted with two kinds of society, the artificial or conventional, and the natural; and on pursuing the subject finds the latter differentiating itself into domestic society, or the family, civil society, or the State, and religious society, or the Church. Here we shall state the philosophic basis of each, and add thereto the theories which have had a vogue for the last three centuries, though breaking down now under the strain of modern problems before the bar of calm judgment.

Conventional Societies.—The plurality of persons, the community of aim, the stability of bond, authority, and some co-operation of effort, being elements common to every form of society, the differentiation must come from differences in the character of purpose, in the nature of the bond. Qualifications of authority as well as modifications in details of requisite co-operation will follow on changes in the purpose and the extent of the bond. As many then as there are objects of human desire attainable by common effort (and their name is legion, from the making of money, which is perhaps the commonest to-day, to the rendering of public workship to our Maker which is surely the most sacred), so manifold are the co-operative associations of men. The character, as well as the existence of most of them, is left in full freedom to human choice. These may be denominated conventional societies. Man is under no precept to establish them, nor in universal need of them. He makes or unmakes them at his pleasure. They serve a passing purpose, and in setting them up men give them the exact character which they judge at present suitable for their purpose, determining as they see fit the limits of authority, the choice of means, the extent of the bond holding them together, as well as their own individual reservations. Everything about such a society is of free election, barring the fact that the essential requisites of a society must be there. We find this type exemplified in a reading circle, a business partnership, or a private charitable organization. Of course in establishing such a society men are under the Natural Law of right and wrong, and there can be no moral bond, for example, where the common purpose is immoral. They also fall under the restrictions of the civil law, when the existence or action of such an organization comes to have a bearing, whether of promise or of menace, upon the common weal. In such case the State lays down its essential requirements for the formation of such bodies, and so we come to have what is known as a legal society, a society, namely, freely established under the sanction and according to the requirements of the civil law. Such are mercantile corporations and beneficial organizations with civil charter.

Natural Societies.—Standing apart from the foregoing in a class by themselves are the family, the State, and the Church. That these differ from all other societies in purpose and means, is clear and universally admitted. That they have a general application to the whole human race, history declares. That there is a difference between the bond holding them in existence and the bond of union in every other society has been disputed—with more enthusiasm and imagination, however, than logical force. The logical view of the matter brings us to the concept of a natural society, a society, that is to say, which men are in general under a mandate of the natural law to establish, a society by consequence whose essential requisites are firmly fixed by the same natural law. To get at this is simple enough, if the philosophical problems are taken in due order. Ethics may not be divided from psychology and theodicy, any more than from deductive logic. With the proper premisals then from one and the other here assumed, we say that the Creator could not have given man a fixed nature, as He has, without willing man to work out the purpose for which that nature is framed. He cannot act idly and without purpose, cannot form His creature discordantly with the purpose of His will. He cannot multiply men on the face of the earth without a plan for working out the destiny of mankind at large. This plan must contain all the elements necessary to His purpose, and these necessary details He must have willed men freely to accomplish, that is to say, He must have put upon man a strict obligation thereunto. Other details may be alternatives, or helpful but not necessary, and these He has left to man's free choice; though where one of these elements would of its nature be far more helpful than another, God's counsel to man will be in favor of the former. God's will directing man through his nature to his share in the full purpose of the cosmic plan, we know as the natural law, containing precept, permission and counsel, according to the necessity, helpfulness, or extraordinary value of an action to the achievement of the Divine purpose. We recognize these in the concrete by a rational study of the essential characteristics of human nature and its relations with the rest of the universe. If we find a natural aptitude in man for an action, not at variance with the general purpose of things, we recognize also the license of the natural law to that action. If we find a more urgent natural propensity to it, we recognize further the counsel of the law. If we find the use of a natural faculty, the following up of a natural propensity, inseparable from the rational fulfilment of the ultimate destiny of the individual or of the human race, we know that thereon lies a mandate of the natural law, obliging the conscience of man. We must not, however, miss the difference, that if the need of the action or effort is for the individual natural destiny, the mandate lies on each human being severally: but if the need be for the natural destiny of the race, the precept does not descend to this or that particular individual, so long as the necessary bulk of men accomplish the detail so intended in the plan for the natural destiny of the race. This is abstract reasoning, but necessary for the understanding of a natural society in the fulness of its idea.

A Society Natural by Mandate.—A society then is natural by mandate when the law of nature sets the precept upon mankind to establish that society. The precept is recognized by natural aptitude, propensity, and need in men for the establishment of such a union. From this point alone the gift of speech alone is sufficient to show man's aptitude for fellowship with his kind. It is emphasized by his manifold perfectibility through contact with others and through their permanent companionship. Furthermore, his normal shrinking from solitude, from working out the problems of life alone, is evidence of a social propensity to which mankind has always yielded. If again we consider his dependence and comfort on the multiplied products of co-ordinate human effort; and his dependence for the development of his physical, intellectual, and moral perfectibility on complex intercourse with others, we see a need, in view of man's ultimate destiny, that makes the actualization of man's capacity of organized social co-operation a stringent law upon mankind. Taking then the kinds of social organization universally existent among men, it is plain not only that they are the result of natural propensities, but that, as analysis shows, they are a human need and hence are prescribed in the code of the Natural Law.

A Society Natural in Essentials.—Furthermore, as we understand a legal contract to be one which, because of its abutment on common interests, the civil law hedges round with restrictions and reservations for their protection, similarly on examination we shall find that all agreements by which men enter into stable social union are fenced in with limitations set by the natural law guarding the essential interests of the good of mankind. When, moreover, we come to social unions prescribed for mankind by mandate of that law, we expect to find the purpose of the union set by the law (otherwise the law would not have prescribed the union), all the details morally necessary for the rational attainment of that purpose fixed by the law, and all obstacles threatening sure defeat to that purpose proscribed by the same. A natural society, then, besides being natural by mandate, will also be natural in all its essentials, for as much as these too shall be determined by law.

The Family a Natural Society.—Working along these lines upon the data given by experience, personal as well as through the proxy of history, the philosopher finds in man's nature, considered physiologically and psychologically, the aptitude, propensity, and, both as a general thing and for mankind at large, the need of the matrimonial relation. Seeing the natural and needful purpose to which this relation shapes itself to be in full the mutually perfecting compensation of common life between man and woman, as well as the procreation and education of the child, and keeping in mind that Nature's Lawgiver has in view the rational development of the race (or human nature at large), as well as of the individual, we conclude not only to abiding rational love, as its distinguishing characteristic, but to monogamy and a stability that is exclusive of absolute divorce. This gives us the essential requisites of domestic society, a stable union of man and wife bound together to work for a fixed common good to themselves and humanity. When this company is filled out with children and its incidental complement of household servants, we have domestic society in its fulness. It is created under mandate of the natural law, for though this or that individual may safely eschew matrimony for some good purpose, mankind may not. The individual in exception need not be concerned about the purpose of the Lawgiver, as human nature is so constituted that mankind will not fail of its fulfilment. The efficient cause of this domestic union in the concrete instance is the free consent of the initial couple, but the character of the judicial bond which they thus freely accept is determined for them by the natural law according to Nature's full purpose. Husband and wife may see to their personal benefit in choosing to establish a domestic community, but the interests of the child and of the future race are safeguarded by the law. The essential purpose of this society we have stated above. The essential requisite of authority takes on a divided character of partnership, because of the separate functions of husband and wife requiring authority as well as calling for harmonious agreement upon details of common interest; but the headship of final decision is put by the law, as a matter of ordinary course, in the man, as is shown by his natural characteristics marking him for the preference. The essential limitations forbid plural marriage, race-suicide, sexual excess, unnecessary separation, and absolute divorce.

The State a Natural Society.—On the same principle of human aptitude, propensity, and need for the individual and the race, we find the larger social unit of civil society manifested to us as part of the Divine set purpose with regard to human nature, and so under precept of the natural law. Again, the exceptional individual may take to solitude for some ennobling purpose; but he is an exception, and the bulk of mankind will not hesitate to fulfil Nature's bidding and accomplish Nature's purpose. In the concrete instance civil society, though morally incumbent on man to establish, still comes into existence by the exercise of his free activity. We have seen the same of domestic society, which begins by the mutual free consent of man and woman to the acceptance of the bond involving all the natural rights and duties of the permanent matrimonial relation. The beginning of civil society as an historical fact has taken on divers colors, far different at different times and places. It has arisen by peaceful expansion of a family into a widespread kindred eventually linked together in a civil union. It has sprung from the multiplication of independent families in the colonizing of undeveloped lands. It has come into being under the strong hand of conquest enforcing law, order, and civil organization, not always justly, upon a people. There have been rare instances of its birth through the tutoring efforts of the gentler type of civilizers, who came to spread the Gospel. But the juridical origin is not obviously identical with this. History alone exhibits only the manifold confluent causes which moved men into an organized civil unit. The juridical cause is quite another matter. This is the cause which of its character under the natural law puts the actual moral bond of civil union upon the many in the concrete, imposes the concrete obligation involving all the rights, duties, and powers native to a State, even as the mutual consent of the contracting parties creates the mutual bond of initial domestic society. This determinant has been under dispute among Catholic teachers.

The common view of Scholastic philosophy, so ably developed by Francis Suarez, S. J., sets it in the consent of the constituent members, whether given explicitly in the acceptance of a constitution, or tacitly by submitting to an organization of another's making, even if this consent be not given by immediate surrender, but by gradual process of slow and often reluctant acquiescence in the stability of a common union for the essential civil purpose. In the early fifties of the nineteenth century, Luigi Taparelli, S. J., borrowing an idea from C. de Haller of Berne, brilliantly developed a theory of the juridical origin of civil government, which has dominated in the Italian Catholic schools even to the present day, as well as in Catholic schools of Europe, whose professors of ethics have been of Italian training. In this theory civil society has grown into being from the natural multiplication of cognate families, and the gradual extension of parental power. The Patriarchal State is the primitive form, the normal type, though by accident of circumstances States may begin here or there from occupation of the same wide territory under feudal ownership; by organization consequent upon conquest; or in rarer instances by the common consent of independent colonial freeholders. These two Catholic views part company also in declaring the primitive juridical determinant of the concrete subject of supreme authority. To-day the Catholic schools are divided between these two positions. We shall subjoin below other theories of the juridical origin of the State, which have no place in Catholic thought for the simple reason that they exclude the natural character of civil society and throw to the winds the principles logically inseparable from the existing natural law.

With regard to the essential elements in civil society fixed by the natural law, it is first to be noted that the normal unit is the family: for not only has the family come historically before the commonwealth, but the natural needs of man lead him first to that social combination, in pursuit of a natural result only to be obtained thereby; and it is logically only subsequent that the purpose of civil society comes into human life. Of course this does not mean that individuals actually outside of the surroundings of family life cannot be constituent members of civil society with full civic rights and duties, but they are not the primary unit; they are in the nature of things the exception, however numerous they may be, and beyond the family limit of perfectibility it is in the interests of complementary development that civil authority is exercised. The State cannot eliminate the family; neither can it rob it of its inalienable rights, nor bar the fulfilment of its inseparable duties, though it may restrict the exercise of certain family activities so as to co-ordinate them to the benefit of the body politic.

Secondly, the natural object pursued by man in his ultimate social activity is perfect temporal happiness, the satisfaction, to wit, of his natural faculties to the full power of their development within his capacity, on his way, of course, to eternal felicity beyond earth. Man's happiness cannot be handed over to him, or thrust upon him by another here on earth; for his nature supposes that his possession of it, and so too in large measure his achievement of it, shall be by the exercise of his native faculties. Hence civil society is destined by the natural law to give him his opportunity, i. e., to give it to all who share its citizenship. This shows the proximate natural purpose of the State to be: first, to establish and preserve social order, a condition, namely, wherein every man, as far as may be, is secured in the possession and free exercise of his rights, natural and legal, and is held up to the fulfilment of his duties as far as they bear upon the commonweal; secondly, to put within reasonable reach of all citizens a fair allowance of the means of temporal happiness. This is what is known as external peace and prosperity, prosperity being also denominated the relatively perfect sufficiency of life. There are misconceptions enough about the generic purpose native to all civil society. De Haller thought that there is none such; that civil purposes are all specific, peculiar to each specific State. Kant limited it to external peace. The Manchester School did the same, leaving the citizen to work out his subsistence and development as best he may. The Evolutionist consistently makes it the survival of the fittest, on the way to developing a better type. The modern peril is to treat the citizen merely as an industrial unit, mistaking national material progress for the goal of civil energy; or as a military unit, looking to self-preservation as the nation's first if not only aim. Neither material progress nor martial power, nor merely intellectual civilization, can fill the requirements of existing and expanding human nature. The State, while protecting a man's rights, must put him in the way of opportunity for developing his entire nature, physical, mental, and moral.

Thirdly, the accomplishment of this calls for an authority which the Lawgiver of Nature, because of its reach, extending as it does to life and death, to reluctant subjects and to the posterity of its citizenship, surpasses the capacity of its citizenship to create out of any mere conventional surrender of natural rights. The question of the origin of civil power and its concentration in this or that subject is like the origin of society itself, a topic of debate. Catholic philosophy is agreed that it is conferred by Nature's Lawgiver directly upon the social depositary thereof, as parental supremacy is upon the father of a family. But the determination of the depositary is another matter. The doctrine of Suarez makes the community itself the depositary, immediately and naturally consequent upon its establishment of civil society, to be disposed of then by their consent, overt or tacit, at once or by degrees, according as they determine for themselves a form of government. This is the only true philosophical sense of the dictum that "governments derive their just powers from the consent of the governed." The Taparelli school makes the primitive determinant out of an existing prior right of another character, which passes naturally into this power. Primitively this is parental supremacy grown to patriarchal dimensions and resulting at the last in supreme civil power. Secondarily, it may arise from other rights, showing natural aptitude preferentially in one subject or another, as that of feudal ownership of the territory of the community, capacity to extricate order out of chaos in moments of civic confusion, military ability and success in case of just conquest, and, finally, in remote instances by the consent of the governed.

Finally, the means by which the commonwealth will work toward its ideal condition of the largest measure of peace and prosperity attainable are embraced in the just exercise, under direction of civil authority, of the physical, mental, and moral activities of the members of the community: and here the field of human endeavor is wide and expansive. However, the calls upon the individual by the governmental power are necessarily limited by the scope of the natural purpose of the State and by the inalienable prior rights and inseparable duties conferred or imposed upon the individual by the Natural Law.

Religious Society de facto a Supernatural Society.—If we analyze the moral development of man, we find looming large his obligation to worship his Creator, not only privately, but publicly, not only as an individual, but in social union. This opens up another kind of society ordered by the natural law, to wit, religious society. An examination of this in the natural order and by force of reason alone would seem to show that man, though morally obliged to social worship, was morally free to establish a parallel organization for such worship or to merge its functions with those of the State, giving a double character to the enlarged society, namely, civil and religious. Historically, among those who knew not divine revelation, men would seem to have been inclined more to the latter; but not always so. Of course, the purpose and means of this religious social duty are so related to those of a merely civil society that considerable care would have to be exercised in adjusting the balance of intersecting rights and duties, to define the relative domains of religious and civil authority, and, finally, to adjudicate supremacy in case of direct apparent conflict. The development of all this has been given an entirely different turn through the intervention of the Creator in His creation by positive law revealed to man, changing the natural status into a higher one, eliminating natural religious society, and at the last establishing through the mission of our Lord Jesus Christ an universal and unfailing religious society in the Church. This is a supernatural religious society.

Non-Catholic Theories.—Thomas Hobbes, starting from the assumption which Calvin had propagated that human nature is itself perverse and man essentially inept for consorting with his fellows, made the natural state of man to be one of universal and continuous warfare. This of course excludes the Maker of man from having destined him originally to society, since he would in Hobbes's view have given him a nature exactly the reverse of a proportioned means. Hobbes thought that he found in man such selfish rivalry, weak cowardice, and greed of self-glorification as to make him naturally prey upon his fellows and subdue them, if he could, to his wants, making might to be the only source of right. However, finding life intolerable (if not impossible) under such conditions, he resorted to a social pact with other men for the establishment of peace, and, as that was a prudent thing to do, man, adds Hobbes, was thus following the dictates of reason and in that sense the law of nature. On this basis Hobbes could and did make civil authority consist in nothing more than the sum of the physical might of the people massed in a chosen center of force. This theory was developed in the "Leviathan" of Hobbes to account for the existence of civil authority and civil society, but its author left his reader to apply the same perversity of nature and exercise of physical force for the taking of a wife or wives and establishing domestic society.

Jean-Jacques Rousseau, though borrowing largely from Hobbes and fearlessly carrying some of his principles to their most extreme issue, had a view in part his own. As for the family, he was content to leave it as a natural institution, with a stability, however, commensurate only with the need of putting the offspring within reach of self-preservation. Not so for the State. Man naturally, he contended, was sylvan and solitary, a fine type of indolent animal, mating with his like and living in the pleasant ease of shady retreats by running waters. He was virtuous, sufficient to himself for his own needs, essentially free, leaving others alone in their freedom, and desirous of being left alone in his. His life was not to be disturbed by the fever of ambitious desires, the burden of ideas, or the restriction of moral laws. Unfortunately he had a capacity and an itch for self-improvement, and his inventive genius, creating new conveniences, started new deeds, and, to meet these more readily, he entered into transitory agreements with other men. Then came differences, frauds, and quarrels, and so ended the tranquil ease and innocence of his native condition. Through sheer necessity of self-defence, as in the theory of Hobbes, he took to the establishment of civil society. To do so without loss of personal freedom, there was but one way, namely, that all the members should agree to merge all their rights, wills, and personalities in a unit moral person and will, leaving the subject member the satisfaction that he was obeying but his own will thus merged, and so in possession still of full liberty in every act. Thus civil authority was but the merger of all rights and wills in the one supreme right and will of the community. The merging agreement was Rousseau's "Social Contract." Unfortunately for its author, as he himself confessed, the condition of perfect, self-sufficient, lawless men was never seen on land or sea; and his social contract had no precedent in all the centuries of the history of man. His dream ignored man's inalienable rights, took no account of coercing wills that would not agree, nor of the unauthorized merging of the wills of posterity, and drained all the vitality as well out of authority as out of obedience. He left authority a power shorn of the requisites essential for the purpose of civil security.

The evolutionist, who has left the twisted turn of all his theories in much of the common language of the day, even after the theories themselves have died to all serious scientific acceptance, wished to make ethics a department of materialistic biology, and have the aggregate of human entities assemble by the same physical laws that mass cells into a living being. Man's native tendency to persist, pure egotism, made him shrink from the danger of destruction or injury at the hands of other individuals, and this timidity became a moving force driving him to compound with his peers into a unit force of strength without which he could not persist. From common life in this unit man's egoism began to take on a bit of altruism, and men acquired at the last a sense of the common good, which replaced their original timidity as the spring of merging activity. Later mutual sympathy put forth its tendrils, a sense of unity sprang up, and man had a civil society. Herein was latent the capacity for expressing the general will, which when developed became civil society. This evolutionary process is still in motion toward the last stand foreseen by the theorist, a universal democracy clad in a federation of the world. All this has been seriously and solemnly presented to our consideration with a naive absence of all sense of humor, with no suspicion that the human mind naturally refuses to confound the unchanging action of material attraction and repulsion with human choice; or to mistake the fruit of intellectual planning and execution for the fortuitous results of blind force. We are not cowards all, and have not fled to society from the sole promptings of fear, but from the natural desire we have of human development. Authority for mankind is not viewed as the necessary resultant of the necessary influx of all men's wills to one goal, but is recognized to be a power to loose and to bind in a moral sense the wills of innumerable freemen.

The neo-pagan theory, renewing the error of Plato, and in a measure of Aristotle also, has made the individual and the family mere creatures and chattels of the State, and, pushing the error further, wishes to orientate all moral good and evil, all right and duty from the authority of the State, whose good as a national unit is paramount. This theory sets up the State as an idol for human worship and eventually, if the theory were acted upon, though its authors dream it not, for human destruction.

The historical school, mistaking what men have done for what men should do, and while often missing the full induction of the past, scornfully rejecting as empty apriorism deductive reasoning from the nature of man, presents a materialistic, evolutionary, and positivistic view of human society, which in no way appeals to sane reason. No more does the theory of Kant, as applied to society in the Hegelian development of it; though, owing to its intellectual character and appearance of ultimate analysis, it has found favor with those who seek philosophic principles from sources of so-called pure metaphysics. It would be idle to present here with Kant an analysis of the assumption of the development of all human right from the conditions of the use of liberty consistent with the general law of universal liberty, and the creation of civil government as an embodiment of universal liberty in the unified will of all the constituents of the State.

133

THE THEORY OF HOBBES

Michael Cronin [1]

In his well-known work, the "Leviathan" (1651), Hobbes draws a picture of what he calls the "state of nature," i. e., the condition in which man found himself before the rise of the State, and he describes also the manner in which this condition of nature gave place to the social condition of man under the State. He describes first the psychical condition of man in the "state of nature," then his moral condition. The *psychical* characteristics of the community were as follows: in the State of nature all men were equal, not in the juridical sense of having equal rights, for at that period, according to Hobbes, there were no rights, but in the sense of possessing equal capacities and powers.

[1] *The Science of Ethics*, vol. II, p. 491-494. (Benziger Brothers, New York.)

There was no ruler then, and men took advantage of the absence of a controlling power to use their equal powers to the best advantage they could secure, even to the injuring of one another. In fact, the condition of nature was a condition of universal warfare—"such a war as is of every man against every man." This condition of warfare did not, indeed, entail continuous actual fighting. It consisted of actual fighting at times, a permanent known disposition to fight, and the absence of all assurances of peace. "For war consisteth not in battle only or the art of fighting, but in a tract of time wherein the will to contend by battle is sufficiently known, and, therefore, the notion of time is to be considered in the nature of war as it is in the nature of weather. For as the nature of foul weather lieth not in a shower or two of rain but in an inclination thereto of many days together, so the nature of war consisteth not in actual fighting but in the known disposition thereto during all the time there is no assurance to the contrary. . . . Whatsoever, therefore, is consequent to a time of war where every man is enemy to every man the same is consequent to the time wherein men live without other security than that which their own strength and their invention shall furnish them withal. In such condition there is no place for industry because the fruit thereof is uncertain, and consequently no culture of the earth, no navigation nor use of the commodities that may be imported by sea, no commodious building, no instruments of moving and removing such things as require much force, no knowledge of the face of the earth; no account of time, no arts, no letters, no society, and, which is worst of all, continual fear and danger of violent death, and the life of man solitary, poor, nasty, brutish, and short."

"It may, peradventure be thought," Hobbes continues, "that there was never such a time nor condition of war as this, and I believe it was never generally so all over the world, but there are many places where they live so now." Besides, "in all times kings and persons of sovereign authority, because of their independency, are in continual jealousies and in the state and posture of gladiators, having their weapons pointing, and their eyes fixed on one another."

Hobbes now proceeds to describe the *moral* condition of man in the "state of nature." "To this war of every man against every man this also is consequent that nothing can be unjust. The notions of right and wrong, justice and injustice have there no place. Where there is no common power there is no law; where no law, no injustice. Force and fraud are in war the two cardinal virtues. Justice and injustice are none of the faculties neither of the body nor mind. . . . They are qualities that relate to men in society not in solitude. It is consequent also to the same condition that there be no property, no dominion, no 'mine' and 'thine' distinct, but only that to be every man's that he can get, and for so long as he can keep it. . . . Thus much for the ill condition which man by mere nature is actually placed in, though with a possibility to come out of it."

In the state of nature, Hobbes proceeds to show, men are moved by a single all-powerful impulse, that, viz., of self-preservation; but with this impulse springs another which quickly reacts on the very condition of nature in which it rises, and leads on to another and opposed condition. This derived impulse is the impulse to seek for peace as a means to self-preservation. It is from this impulse that the social-contract sprang—a contract devised to end the condition of primitive warfare with all its attendant inconveniences. This contract was a covenant of every man with every other to place all their liberties in the hands of some one man or body of men to whom all should be subject and who should direct the destinies of all. Its terms were: "I authorize and give up my right of governing myself to this man or this assembly of men on the condition that thou give thy right to him and authorize all his actions in like manner." Thus, in Hobbes' theory, the power of the governing authorities is only the aggregate of the powers possessed by individuals, their power, namely, of governing themselves. The ruler as bearing their powers carries in himself the persons of all his subjects. In obeying him the subject really obeys himself as existent in the ruler. This social-compact, Hobbes remarks, being once effected, is irrevocable.

The qualities of the *sovereignty* enjoyed by the ruler are determined by the conditions of the social-contract. In one place Hobbes maintains that sovereignty is an absolute power in the sense that a ruler has no obligations towards his subjects, and consequently that rebellion against the sovereign could never be lawful. This doctrine of absoluteness, however, is modified elsewhere with, we consider, little care for consistency. Though the sovereign, he tells us, has absolute rights within the terms of the contract, yet these terms themselves impose limitations on him that are of immense importance in determining the juridical relations obtaining between ruler and subject. First, a sovereign may not interfere with his subjects beyond the terms of the convention: he may interfere, therefore, only for their preservation and defence; secondly, his sovereignty lasts only for as long as the end is attainable for which it was conferred, i. e., as long as he is in a position to protect his subjects. When that power ceases, all obligations to him have disappeared.

134

ROUSSEAU'S SOCIAL CONTRACT

Charles Macksey [1]

Rousseau's social contract gives judicial existence to the body politic as a distinct moral person by "the total alienation to the whole community of each associate with all his rights." The doctrine of that contract is primarily false because no man can, even juridically, alienate himself, i. e., his personality, nor all his rights. For a man's person is the subjective term of imputability. If a man could alienate that, he would no longer be responsible for his individual actions, nor for his individual part in carrying out God's plan of creation. A man cannot thus throw on civil society all his personal responsibility to his Maker. No more can a man surrender all his rights. For some of them are an inalienable accompaniment of natural Divinely-imposed duties which the individual cannot fulfil, if he be without the aforesaid rights. A surrender of these would be of a piece with a dishonest debtor's transfer of all his property to his wife. It is true that Rousseau further on in his work

[1] *Sovereignty and Consent*, pp. 3-8. (The America Press, New York.)

wishes to qualify that total and absolute surrender, so as to leave with the individual the rights for which the State has no use; but the withdrawal will not stand: for he has already gone the whole way and made the social contract the foundation of all right and duty, leaving no right or duty antecedent to it, and thus cutting the ground from under his own feet. For with all other prior duties of man he eliminates by necessity that of keeping a contract; so that the present one loses all binding force.

Secondly, the contract as described by Rousseau is purely conventional, i. e., arbitrary and artificial; it is not the result of any natural impulse nor under any precept of natural law; its content is not determined for it by the natural law. Yet civil society is as natural as the family; man's natural tendencies are equally strong towards it; it is equally necessary for God's full plan; it carries a like obligation upon mankind to establish it; its essential elements, juridical as well as others, are determined by the nature of the case, and hence are prescribed by the natural law, so that, if consent is to establish its existence, it cannot be the arbitrary and artificial consent of a conventional contract. Why, the thing would be revocable at will, and could give no stability at all to our political existence: whereas obviously civil society, if not as indissoluble as matrimony, must at least be fundamentally stable.

Moreover, if the social bond were Rousseau's contract only, it could bind no one not a party to the contract, and would have to be renewed by each successive generation—a consequence which does not escape Rousseau himself. Yet, the essential continuity of society would thus perish utterly.

Furthermore, the contract as explaining the origin of sovereignty destroys the very idea of sovereignty itself. Rousseau states that sovereignty is an absolute power in the body politic, i. e., in the moral person of the State as constituted by the civic compact, over all its members, when directed by the general will: that an act of sovereignty is an authentic act of the general will, an agreement of the body with each of its members, in a word a general convention. He had already laid down that there is no lawful authority among men except what is based on conventions. Now, with this concept of sovereignty as a blend of all the wills of the community, its binding force or obligation would come by way of each individual's consent to the original compact. This compact virtually enduring, every man, by his original consent, either antecedently bound himself by each law of sovereignty, or else bound himself, then, to consent anew to each law, in due course. But the human will properly never binds itself. It may consent to obligation, as it does in making a contract; but the obligation comes from the will of one higher up, from authority, from prior law. So just as the consent to the original contract does not itself properly bind, neither does it found an obligation, except in the supposition of prior existing law, right and duty. Moreover, if, in order to save obligation, we presume (as Russeau does not) the existence of the natural law and the authority of God binding us through the natural law to keep our just contracts, we still (in Rousseau's concept) eliminate all idea of authority (i. e., all superior right to bind the will even of the reluctant) resident in civil society itself. This is precisely what Rousseau wishes to do; but despite that, this higher power has been insisted upon in the past, and is insisted upon in the present by the common-sense and practice of mankind.

Nor is this all. Reason shows us the truth of the lesson of St. Paul that "there is no power but from God." Power over the free will of man is nugatory without obligation, and ultimately only the Maker of man, who gave him his freedom, can, of original right, limit its exercise. In point of fact He *must* limit the exercise of human freedom according to the exigencies of purpose for which man was made. All obligation is ultimately from God; all right to impose obligation (i. e., all power) is consequently from Him. No man can sanely deny the Creator absolute right of both property and jurisdiction over His creature. None other can rule that creature except with power derived from on high. Of course Rousseau might have said that the power which men have over their own wills comes from God, and that when these wills are merged, the merger is still from God. As a matter of fact he did not say it. Though doubtless he conceded man to be God's creature, he had no concept of God conceding, by law, to man his rights over his own will. However, even that modification in his concept would not save the entirety of philosophic truth in the question: for civil authority is something more than a complex of individual rights over individual wills, and, as we shall see later, must come from God to civil society immediately.

For the moment we must call attention to the fact that this combination of citizens' wills would have no power of life and death in the community: for no one puts into the merger what he has not got, the right namely of direct disposal of his own life, much less of that of his fellow. Rousseau realizes this difficulty and labors in vain both to make a man's prior consent to his own possible execution the only indirect disposal of his own life, and to turn a criminal into an enemy at war, in the hope of finding a right to kill him as an unjust aggressor inevitably to be killed to save one's own life as well as the lives of our fellow-citizens. Rousseau proves quite well that civil society should have the right of life and death: but he does not prove what he should prove and what he set out to prove, viz.: that individuals had that right and transferred it to the community.

The same difficulty arises with regard to all punishment for crime, as distinguished from reparation for damage. No individual can prove his right to punish his neighbor; and though Locke, to save the situation, insisted that in the state of man prior to civil society the right of necessary punishment was in every man's hands, he never proved the assertion. It is a right of God, which we cannot claim to share without showing clear and evident title, and there is none forthcoming to the individual, though there is for the State. To be accuser, witness, judge and executioner, all in one, against one's fellow-citizen is more than we can expect the wisdom and justice of God to have conceded to every poor, selfish, passionate man, even before civil society arose. Now if the individual never had the right, no number of them can confer it upon the State.

Finally, distinguishing between sovereignty, which is power, and administration, which is but the execution of sovereignty's law, Rousseau's sovereignty of permanently amalgamated wills leaves no civil power possible except in the moral person of the community. That reduces all just forms of government to one, that of absolute democracy; makes the authority of all officers of the State merely illusory, reducing them to mere agents of the popular will with no power to bind or to loose in any act whatever. Now though an absolute form of democracy is one of the just forms of government, and in a small community may be prudent and practical, the rejection of all serious entrusting of authority to any one distinct from the moral person of the whole community is an exaggeration, which would make political government on any extended scale merely nugatory. Even the subjection of princes and officers of State to the arbitrary recall of their commission and power, while more than the safety of the people from oppression requires, at the same time nullifies the possibility of stably preserving peace and promoting prosperity, the very purpose for which God ordains and man institutes civil society.

Summarily, our indictment comes to this, that the social contract of Rousseau as a juridical foundation of civil society is a juridical contradiction in terms, and that his concept of sovereignty contradicts common sense and common need, perverts political philosophy, ignores the supreme rights of God, while aiming to safeguard the rights of man, and makes insecure in civil society the very justice, peace, and prosperity which Rousseau was on fire to restore.

135

MARRIAGE

John A. Ryan [1]

History.—The word marriage may be taken to denote the action, contract, formality, or ceremony by which the conjugal union is formed, or the union itself as an enduring condition. In this article we deal for the most part with marriage as a condition, and with its moral and social aspects. It is usually defined as the legitimate union of husband and wife. "Legitimate" indicates the sanction of some kind of law, natural, evangelical, or civil, while the phrase, "husband and wife," implies mutual rights of sexual intercourse, life in common, and an enduring union. The last two characters distinguish marriage, respectively, from concubinage and fornication. The definition, however, is broad enough to comprehend polygamous and polyandrous

---

[1] *Catholic Encyclopedia,* vol. IX, pp. 693-698.

unions when they are permitted by the civil law; for in such relationships there are as many marriages as there are individuals of the numerically larger sex. Whether promiscuity, the condition in which all the men of a group maintain relations and live indiscriminately with all the women, can be properly called marriage, may well be doubted. In such a relation, cohabitation and domestic life are devoid of that exclusiveness which is commonly associated with the idea of conjugal union.

(1) *The Theory of Primitive Promiscuity.*—All authorities agree that during historical times promiscuity has been either non-existent or confined to a few small groups. Did it prevail to any extent during the prehistoric period of the race? Writing between 1860 and 1890, a considerable number of anthropologists, such as Bachofen, Morgan, McLennan, Lubboch, and Giraud-Teulon, maintained that this was the original relationship between the sexes among practically all peoples. So rapidly did the theory win favor that in 1891 it was, according to Westermarck, "treated by many writers as a demonstrated truth." (History of Human Marriage, p. 51.) It appealed strongly to those believers in organic evolution who assumed that the social customs of primitive man, including sex relations, must have differed but slightly from the corresponding usages among the brutes. It has been eagerly adopted by the Marxian Socialists, on account of its agreement with their theories of primitive common property and of economic determinism. According to the latter hypothesis, all other social institutions are, and have ever been, determined by the underlying economic institutions; hence in the original condition of common property, wives and husbands must likewise have been held in common (see Engels, "The Origin of the Family, Private Property, and the State," tr. from German, Chicago, 1902). Indeed, the vogue which the theory of promiscuity for a time enjoyed seems to have been due far more to a priori considerations of the kind just mentioned, and to the wish to believe in it, than to positive evidence.

About the only direct testimony in its favor is found in the fragmentary statements of some ancient writers, such as Herodotus and Strabo, concerning a few unimportant peoples, and in the accounts of some modern travelers regarding some uncivilized tribes of the present day. Neither of these classes of testimony clearly shows that the peoples to which they refer practised promiscuity, and both are entirely too few to justify the generalization that all peoples lived originally in the conditions which they described. As for the indirect evidence of the theory, consisting of inferences from such social customs as the tracing of kinship through the mother, religious prostitution, unrestrained sexual intercourse previous to marriage among some savage peoples, and primitive community of goods,—none of these conditions can be proved to have been universal at any stage of human development, and every one of them can be explained more easily and more naturally on other grounds than on the assumption of promiscuity. We may say that the positive arguments in favor of the theory of primitive promiscuity seem insufficient to give it any degree of probability, while the biological, economic, psychological, and historical arguments brought against it by many writers, e. g., Westermarck, seem to render it unworthy of serious consideration. The attitude of contemporary scholars is thus described by Howard: "The researches of several recent writers, notably those of Starcke and Westermarck, confirming in part and further developing the earlier conclusions of Darwin and Spencer, have established a probability that marriage or pairing between one man and one woman, though the union be often transitory and the rule frequently violated, is the typical form of sexual union from the infancy of the human race" (History of Matrimonial Institutions, I, pp. 90, 91).

(2) *Polyandry and Polygamy.*—One deviation from the typical form of sexual union which, however, is also called marriage, is polyandry, the union of several husbands with one wife. It has been practised at various times by a considerable number of peoples or tribes. It existed among the ancient Britons, the primitive Arabs, the inhabitants of the Canary Islands, the Aborigines of America, the Hottentots, the inhabitants of India, Ceylon, Thibet, Malabar, and New Zealand. In the great majority of these instances polyandry was the exceptional form of conjugal union. Monogamy and even polygamy were much more prevalent. The greater number of the polyandrous unions seem to have been of the kind called fraternal; that is, the husbands in each conjugal group were all brothers. Frequently, if not

generally, the first husband enjoyed conjugal and domestic rights superior to the others, was, in fact, the chief husband. The others were husbands only in a secondary and limited sense. Both these circumstances show that even in the comparatively few cases in which polyandry existed it was softened in the direction of monogamy; for the wife belonged not to several entirely independent men, but to a group united by the closest ties of blood; she was married to one family rather than to one person. And the fact that one of her consorts possessed superior marital privileges shows that she had only one husband in the full sense of the term. Some writers, e. g., McLennan (Studies in Ancient History, pp. 112, sq.) have asserted that the Levirate, the custom which compelled the brother of a deceased husband to marry his widow, had its origin in polyandry. But the Levirate can be explained without any such hypothesis. In many cases it merely indicated that the wife, as the property of her husband, was inherited by his nearest heir, i. e., his brother; in other instances, as among the ancient Hebrews, it was evidently a means of continuing the name, family, and individuality of the deceased husband. If the Levirate pointed in all cases to a previous condition of polyandry, the latter practice must have been much more common than it is shown to have been by direct evidence. It is certain that the Levirate existed among the New Caledonians, the Redskins, the Mongols, Afghans, Hebrews, and Abyssinians; yet none of these peoples shows any trace of polyandry. The principal causes of polyandry were the scarcity of women, due to female infanticide and to the appropriation of many women by polygamous chiefs and strong men in a tribe, and to the scarcity of the food supply, which made it impossible for every male member of a family to support a wife alone. Even to-day polyandry is not entirely unknown. It is found to some extent in Thibet, in the Aleutian Islands, among the Hottentots, and the Zaporogian Cossacks.

Polygamy (many marriages) or, more correctly, polygyny (many wives) has been, and is still much more common than polyandry. It existed among most of the ancient peoples known to history, and occurs at present in some civilized nations and in the majority of savage tribes. About the only important peoples of ancient times that showed little or no traces of it were the Greeks and the Romans. Nevertheless, concubinage, which may be regarded as a higher form of polygamy, or at least as nearer to pure monogamy, was for many centuries recognized by the customs and even by the legislation of these two nations. The principal peoples among whom the practice still exists are those under the sway of Mohammedanism, as those of Arabia, Turkey, and some of the peoples of India. Its chief home among uncivilized races is Africa. However widespread polygamy has been territorially, it has never been practised by more than a small minority of any people. Even where it has been sanctioned by custom or the civil law, the vast majority of the population have been monogamous. The reasons are obvious: there are not sufficient women to provide every man with several wives, nor are the majority of men able to support more than one. Hence polygamous marriages are found for the most part among the kings, chiefs, strong men, and rich men of the community; and its prevailing form seems to have been bigamy. Moreover, polygamous unions are as a rule, modified in the direction of monogamy, inasmuch as one of the wives, usually the first married, occupies a higher place in the household than the others, or one of them is the favorite, and has exceptional privileges of intercourse with the common husband.

Among the principal causes of polygamy are: the relative scarcity of males, arising sometimes from numerous destructive wars, and sometimes from an excess of female births; the unwillingness of the husband to remain continent when intercourse with one wife is undesirable or impossible; and unrestrained lustful cravings. Still another cause, or more properly a condition, is a certain degree of economic advancement in a people, and a certain amount of wealth accumulated by some individuals. In the rudest societies polygamy is almost unknown, because hunting and fishing are the chief means of livelihood, and female labor has not the value that attaches to it when a man's wives can be employed in tending flocks, cultivating fields, or exercising useful handicrafts. Before the pastoral stage of industry has been reached, scarcely any man can afford to support several women. When, however, some accumulation of wealth has taken place, polygamy becomes possible for the more wealthy, and for those who can utilize the productive labor of their wives. Hence the practice has been more frequent among the higher savages and barbarians than among the very lowest races. At a still higher stage it tends to give way to monogamy.

We may now sum up the whole historical situation concerning the forms of sexual union and of marriage in the words of one of the ablest living authorities in this field of investigation: "It is not, of course, impossible that, among some peoples, intercourse between the sexes may have been almost promiscuous. But there is not a shred of genuine evidence for the notion that promiscuity ever formed a general stage in the history of mankind . . . although polygamy occurs among most existing peoples, and polyandry among some, monogamy is by far the most common form of human marriage. It was so among the ancient peoples of whom we have any direct knowledge. Monogamy is the form which is generally recognized and permitted. The great majority of peoples are, as a rule, monogamous, and the other forms of marriage are usually modified in a monogamous direction. We may without hesitation assert that, if mankind advance in the same direction as hitherto; if, consequently, the causes to which monogamy in the most progressive societies owes its origin continue to operate with constantly growing force; if, especially, altruism increases, and the feeling of love becomes more refined, and more exclusively directed to one,—the laws of monogamy can never be changed, but must be followed much more strictly than they are now" (Westermarck, op. cit. pp. 133, 459, 510).

The experience of the race, particularly in its movement toward and its progress in civilization, has approved monogamy for the simple reason that monogamy is in harmony with the essential and immutable elements of human nature. Taking the word natural in its full sense, we may unhesitatingly affirm that monogamy is the only natural form of marriage. While promiscuity responds to certain elemental passions, and temporarily satisfies certain superficial wants, it contradicts the parental instinct, the welfare of children and of the race, and the overpowering forces of jealousy and individual preference in both men and women. While polyandry satisfied in some measure the temporary and exceptional wants arising from scarcity of food or scarcity of women, it finds an insuperable barrier in male jealousy, in the male sense of proprietorship, and is directly opposed to the welfare of the wife, and fatal to the fecundity of the race. While polygamy has prevailed among so many peoples and over so long a period of history as to suggest that it is in some sense natural, and, while it does seem to furnish a means of satisfying the stronger and more frequently recurring desires of the male, it conflicts with the numerical equality of the sexes, with the jealousy, sense of proprietorship, equality, dignity, and general welfare of the wife, and with the best interests of the offspring.

In all those regions in which polygamy has existed or still exists, the status of woman is extremely low; she is treated as man's property, not as his companion; her life is invariably one of great hardship, while her moral, spiritual, and intellectual qualities are almost utterly neglected. Even the male human being is, in the highest sense of the phrase, naturally monogamous. His moral, spiritual, and aesthetic faculties can obtain normal development only when his sexual relations are confined to one woman in the common life and enduring association provided by monogamy. The welfare of children, and, therefore, of the race, obviously demands that the offspring of each pair shall have the undivided attention and care of both their parents. When we speak of the naturalness of any social institution, we necessarily take as our standard, not nature in a superficial or one-sided sense, or in its savage state, or as exemplified in a few individuals, or in a single generation, but nature adequately considered, in all its needs and powers, in all the members of the present and of future generations, and as it appears in those tendencies which lead toward its highest development. The verdict of experience and the voice of nature reinforce, consequently, the Christian teaching on the unity of marriage. Moreover, the progress of the race toward monogamy, as well as toward a purer monogamy, during the last two thousand years, owes more to the influence of Christianity than to all other forces combined. Christianity has not only abolished or diminished polyandry and polygamy among the savage and barbarous peoples which it has converted, but it has preserved Europe from the polygamous civilization of Mohammedanism, has kept before the eyes of the more enlightened peoples the ideal of an unadulterated monogamy, and has given to the world its highest conception of the equality that should exist between the two parties in the marriage relation. And its influence on behalf of monogamy has extended, and continues to extend, far beyond the confines of those countries that call themselves Christian.

(3) *Deviations from Marriage.*—Our discussion of the various forms of marriage would be incomplete without some reference to those practices that have been more or less prevalent, and yet that are a transgression of every form of marriage. Sexual license amounting almost to promiscuity seems to have prevailed among a few peoples or tribes. Among some ancient peoples the women, especially the unmarried, practised prostitution as an act of religion. Some tribes, both ancient and relatively modern, have maintained the custom of yielding the newly married bride to the relatives and guests of the bridegroom. Unlimited sexual intercourse before marriage has been sanctioned by the customs of some uncivilized peoples. Among some savage tribes the husband permits his guests to have intercourse with his wife, or loans her for hire. Certain uncivilized peoples are known to have practised trial marriages, marriages that were binding only until the birth of a child, and marriages that bound the parties only for certain days of the week. Although any general exercise of the so-called *jus primae noctis* has no historical basis, and is now admitted to be an invention of the encyclopedists, at times serf women were required to submit to their overlords before assuming marital relations with their husbands (Schmidt, Karl, "Jus Primae Noctis, a historical examination"). Japanese maidens of the poorer classes frequently spend a portion of their youth as prostitutes, with the consent of their parents and the sanction of public opinion.

Concubinage, the practice of forming a somewhat enduring union with some other woman than the wife, or such union between two unmarried persons, has prevailed to some extent among most peoples, even among some that had attained a high degree of civilization, as the Greeks and Romans (for detailed proof of the foregoing statements, see Westermarck, op. cit., *passim*). In a word, fornication and adultery have been sufficiently common at all stages of the world's history and among almost all peoples, to arouse the anxiety of the moralists, the statesmen, and the sociologists. Owing to the growth of cities, the changed relations between the sexes in social and industrial life, the decay of religion, and the relaxation of parental control, these evils have increased very greatly within the last one hundred years. The extent to which prostitution and venereal disease are sapping the mental, moral, and physical health of the nations, is of itself abundant proof that the strict and lofty standards of purity set up by the Catholic Church, both within and without the marriage relation, constitute the only adequate safeguard of society.

(4) *Divorce.*—This is a modification of monogamy that seems to be less opposed to its spirit than polyandry, polygamy, or adultery. It requires, indeed, that the parties should await a certain time or a certain contingency before severing the unity of marriage, but it is essentially a violation of monogamy, of the enduring union of husband and wife. Yet it has obtained practically among all peoples, savage and civilized. About the only people that seem never to have practiced or recognized it are the inhabitants of the Andaman Islands, some of the Papuans of New Guinea, some tribes of the Indian Archipelago, and the Veddahs of Ceylon. Among the majority of uncivilized peoples the marital unions that endured until the death of one of the parties seem to have been in the minority. It is substantially true to say that the majority of savage races authorized the husband to divorce his wife whenever he felt so inclined. A majority of even the advanced peoples who remained outside the pale of Christianity restrict the right of divorce to the husband, although the reasons for which he could put away his wife are, as a rule, not so numerous as among the uncivilized races. In all those countries that adopted the Catholic religion, however, divorce was very soon abolished, and continued to be forbidden as long as that religion was recognized by the State. The early Christian emperors, as Constantine, Theodosius, and Justinian, did, indeed, legalize the practice, but before the tenth century the Catholic teaching on the indissolubility of marriage had become embodied in the civil legislation of

every Catholic country. The Oriental Churches separated from Rome, including the Greek Orthodox Church, and all the Protestant sects, permit divorce in varying degrees, and the practice prevails in every country in which any of these Churches exercise a considerable influence. In some of the non-Catholic countries divorce is extremely easy and scandalously frequent. Between 1890 and 1900 the divorces granted in the United States averaged 73 per 100,000 of the population annually. This was more than twice the rate in any other Western nation. The proportion in Switzerland was 32; in France, 23; in Saxony, 29; and in the majority of European countries, less than 15. So far as we are informed by statistics, only one country in the world, namely, Japan, had a worse record than the United States, the rate per 100,000 of the population in the Flowery Kingdom being 215. In most of the civilized countries the divorce rate is increasing, slowly in some, very rapidly in others. Relatively to the population, about two and one-half times as many divorces are granted now in the United States as were issued forty years ago.

But the practice of attempting to dissolve the bond of marriage by law is not confined to Protestant, schismatic, and pagan countries. It obtains to some extent in all the Catholic lands of Europe, except Italy, Portugal, and Spain. South America is freer from it than any other continent. The majority of the countries in this geographical division do not grant absolute divorce. A notable fact in the history of divorce is that those countries which have never been Christianized, and those which remained faithful to the Christian teaching for only a short time (e. g., the regions that fell under the sway of Mohammedanism) conducted the practice on terms more favorable to the husband than to the wife. About the only important exception to this rule was pagan Rome in the later centuries of her existence. In modern countries which permit divorce, and yet call themselves Christian, the wife can take advantage of the practice about as easily as the husband; but this is undoubtedly due to the previous influence of Christianity in raising the social and civil status of woman during the long period in which divorce was forbidden. In the long run divorce must be inevitably more injurious to women than to men. If the divorced woman remains single, she generally has greater difficulty in supporting herself than the divorced man; if she is young, her opportunities for marrying again may, indeed, be about as good as those of the divorced man who is young; but if she is at or beyond middle age the probability that she will find a suitable spouse is decidedly smaller than in the case of her separated husband.

The fact that in the United States more women than men apply for divorces proves nothing as yet against the statements just set down; for we do not know whether these women have generally found it easy to get other husbands, or whether their new condition was better than the old. The frequent appeal to the divorce courts by American women is a comparatively recent phenomenon, and is undoubtedly due more to emotion, imaginary hopes, and a hasty use of newly acquired freedom, than to calm and adequate study of the experiences of other divorced women. If the present facility of divorce should continue fifty years longer, the disproportionate hardship to women from the practice will probably have become so evident that the number of them taking advantage of it, or approving it, will be much smaller than to-day.

The social evils of easy divorce are so obvious that the majority of Americans undoubtedly are in favor of a stricter policy. One of the most far-reaching of these evils is the encouragement of lower conceptions of conjugal fidelity; for when a person regards the taking of a new spouse as entirely lawful for a multitude of more or less slight reasons, his sense of obligation toward his present partner cannot be very strong or very deep. Simultaneous cannot seem much worse than successive plurality of sexual relations. The average husband and wife who become divorced for a trivial cause are less faithful to each other during their temporary union than the average couple who do not believe in divorce. Similarly, easy divorce gives an impetus to illicit relations between the unmarried, inasmuch as it tends to destroy the association in the popular consciousness between sexual intercourse and the enduring union of one man with one woman. Another evil is the increase in the number of hasty and unfortunate marriages among persons who look forward to divorce as an easy remedy for present mistakes. Inasmuch as the children of a divorced couple are deprived of their normal heritage, which is education and care by both father and mother in the same household, they almost always suffer grave and varied disadvantages. Finally, there is the injury done to the moral character generally. Indissoluble marriage is one of the most effective means of developing self-control and mutual self-sacrifice. Many salutary inconveniences are endured because they cannot be avoided, and many imperfections of temper and character are corrected because the husband and wife realize that thus only is conjugal happiness possible. On the other hand, when divorce is easily obtained there is no sufficient motive for undergoing those inconveniences which are so essential to self-discipline, self-development, and the practice of altruism.

All the objections just noted are valid against frequent divorce, against the abuse of divorce, but not against divorce so far as it implies separation from bed and board without the right to contract another marriage. The Church permits limited separation in certain cases, chiefly, when one of the parties has been guilty of adultery, and when further cohabitation would cause grave injury to soul or body. If divorce were restricted to these two cases some pretend that it would be socially preferable to mere separation without the right to remarry, at least for the innocent spouse. But it would surely be less advantageous to society than a regime of no divorce. Where mere separation is permitted, it will, in a considerable proportion of instances, need to be only temporary, and the welfare of parents and children will be better promoted by reconciliation than if one of the parties formed another matrimonial union. When there is no hope of another marriage, the offences that justify separation are less likely to be provoked or committed by either party, and separation is less likely to be sought on insufficient grounds, or obtained through fraudulent methods. Moreover, experience shows that when divorce is permitted for a few causes, there is an almost irresistible tendency to increase the number of legal grounds, and to make the administration of the law less strict. Finally, the absolute prohibition of divorce has certain moral effects which contribute in a fundamental and far-reaching way to the social welfare. The popular mind is impressed with the thought that marriage is an exclusive relation between two persons, and that sexual intercourse of itself and normally calls for a life-long union of the persons entering upon such intercourse.

The obligation of self-control, and of subordinating the animal in human nature to the reason and the spirit, as well as the possibility of fulfilling this obligation, are likewise taught in a most striking and practical manner. Humanity is thus aided and encouraged to reach a higher moral plane. In the matter of the indissolubility, as well as in that of the unity of marriage, therefore, the Christian teaching is in harmony with nature at her best, and with the deepest needs of civilization. "There is abundant evidence," says Westermarck, "that marriage has, upon the whole, become more durable in proportion as the human race has risen to higher degrees of civilization, and that a certain amount of civilization is an essential condition of the formation of lifelong unions" (op. cit., p. 535). This statement suggests two tolerably safe generalizations: first, that the prohibition of divorce during many centuries has been a cause as well as an effect of those "higher degrees of civilization" that have been already attained; and, second, that the same policy will be found essential to the highest degree of civilization.

(5) *Abstention from Marriage.*—With a very few unimportant exceptions, all peoples, savage and civilized, that have not accepted the Catholic religion, have looked with some disdain upon celibacy. Savage races marry much earlier, and have a smaller proportion of celibates than civilized nations. During the last century the proportion of unmarried persons has increased in the United States and in Europe. The causes of this change are partly economic, inasmuch as it has become more difficult to support a family in accordance with contemporary standards of living; partly social, inasmuch as the increased social pleasure and opportunities have displaced to some degree domestic desires and interests; and partly moral, inasmuch as laxer notions of chastity have increased the number of those who satisfy their sexual desires outside of marriage. From the viewpoint of social morality and social welfare, this modern celibacy is an almost unmixed evil. On the other hand, the religious celibacy taught and encouraged by the Church is socially beneficial, since it shows that continence is practicable, and since religious celibates exemplify a higher degree

of altruism than any other section of society. The assertion that celibacy tends to make the married state seem low or unworthy, is contradicted by the public opinion and practice of every country in which celibacy is held in highest honor. For it is precisely in such places that the marriage relation, and the relations between the sexes generally, are purest.

(6) *Marriage as a Ceremony or Contract.*—The act, formality, or ceremony by which the marriage union is created, has differed widely at different times and among different peoples. One of the earliest and most frequent customs associated with the entrance into marriage was the capture of the woman by her intended husband, usually from another tribe than that to which he himself belonged. Among most primitive peoples this act seems to have been regarded rather as a means of getting a wife, than as the formation of the marriage union itself. The latter was subsequent to the capture, and was generally devoid of any formality whatever, beyond mere cohabitation. But the symbolic seizure of wives continued in many places long after the reality had ceased. It still exists among some of the lower races, and, until quite recently, was not unknown in some parts of Eastern Europe. After the practice had become simulated instead of actual, it was frequently looked upon as either the whole of the marriage ceremony or an essential accompaniment of the marriage. Symbolic capture has largely given way to wife purchase, which seems to prevail among most uncivilized peoples to-day. It has assumed various forms. Sometimes the man desiring a wife gave one of his kinswomen in exchange; sometimes he served for a period his intended bride's father, which was a frequent custom among the ancient Hebrews; but most often the bride was paid for in money or some form of property. Like capture, purchase became after a time among many peoples a symbol to signify the taking of a wife and the formation of the marriage union. Sometimes, however, it was merely an accompanying ceremony. Various other ceremonial forms have accompanied or constituted the entrance upon the marriage relation, the most common of which was some kind of feast; yet among many uncivilized peoples marriage has taken place, and still takes place, without any formal ceremony whatever.

By many uncivilized races, and by most civilized ones, the marriage ceremony is regarded as a religious rite or includes religious features, although the religious element is not always regarded as necessary to the validity of the union. Under the Christian dispensation marriage is a religious act of the very highest kind, namely, one of the seven sacraments. Although Luther declared that marriage was not a sacrament, but "a worldly thing," all the Protestant sects have continued to regard it as religious in the sense that it ought normally to be contracted in the presence of a clergyman. Owing to the influence of the Lutheran view and of the French Revolution, civil marriage has been instituted in almost all the countries of Europe and North America, as well as in some of the States of South America. In some countries it is essential to the validity of the union before the civil law, while in others, e. g., in the United States, it is merely one of the ways in which marriage may be contracted. Civil marriage is not, however, a post-Reformation institution, for it existed among the ancient Peruvians, and among the Aborigines of North America.

Whether as a state or as a contract, whether from the viewpoint of religion and morals or from that of social welfare, marriage appears in its highest form in the teaching and practice of the Catholic Church. The fact that the contract is a sacrament impresses the popular mind with the importance and sacredness of the relation thus begun. The fact that the union is indissoluble and monogamous promotes in the highest degree the welfare of parents and children, and stimulates in the whole community the practice of those qualities of self-restraint and altruism which are essential to social well-being, physical, mental, and moral.

136

THE PRINCIPLE OF THE MARRIAGE BOND

CHARLES MACKSEY [1]

Pursuant of his way towards the natural development of his life powers, man comes to recognize that the family relation has place in the fulness of the Divine plan of

---

[1] *Sovereignty and Consent,* pp. 14, 15. (The American Press, New York.)

human life; and when he enters into that relation, he is normally conscious both of an obligation of the natural law binding him to all the necessary conditions of that relation as bearing on the purposes of human life, and is conscious at the same time of rights which the natural law gives him unto the fulfilment of that obligation and the promotion of life's purposes. We know this definite, specific compound of obligations and rights as the marriage bond: its obligations give it the name; but its obligations on the one side involve rights on the other, and vice versa, and the two combined integrate the juridical connection. As a set of duties and rights, of obligations and moral powers, it has its source in God, whence it descends through the natural law. As incumbent on any man and wife in the concrete, no one denies today that it comes into existence by consent. As to the nature and force of its obligations and rights, it is of Divine right; as to concrete existence it is of human right. The principle of the bond is the natural law; but the foundation of its presence in this or that concrete couple is consent.

137

THE EVILS THAT FLOW FROM DIVORCE

Leo XIII [1]

Truly, it is hardly possible to describe how great are the evils that flow from divorce. Matrimonial contracts are by it made variable; mutual kindness is weakened; deplorable inducements to unfaithfulness are supplied; harm is done to the education and training of children; occasion is offered for the breaking up of homes; the seeds of dissension are sown among families; the dignity of womanhood is lessened and brought low, and women run the risk of being deserted after having ministered to the pleasures of men. Since, then, nothing has such power to lay waste families and destroy the mainstay of kingdoms as the corruption of morals, it is easily seen that divorces are in the highest degree hostile to the prosperity of families and States,

---

[1] *Great Encyclicals of Leo XIII*, pp. 74, 75. (Benziger Brothers, New York.)

springing as they do from the depraved morals of the people, and, as experience shows us, opening out a way to every kind of evil-doing in public and in private life alike.

Further still, if the matter be duly pondered, we shall clearly see these evils to be the more especially dangerous because, divorce, once being tolerated, there will be no restraint powerful enough to keep it within the bounds marked out or presurmised. Great, indeed, is the force of example, and even greater still the might of passion. With such incitements it must needs follow that the eagerness for divorce, daily spreading by devious ways, will seize upon the minds of many like a virulent contagious disease, or like a flood of water bursting through every barrier. These are truths that doubtlessly are all clear in themselves; but they will become clearer yet if we call to mind the teachings of experience. So soon as the road to divorce began to be made smooth by law, at once quarrels, jealousies, and judicial separations largely increased; and such shamelessness of life followed, that men who had been in favor of these divorces repented of what they had done, and feared that, if they did not carefully seek a remedy by repealing the law, the State itself might come to ruin.

138

DIVORCE [1]

Of itself and under normal conditions, marital love endures through life, growing in strength as time passes and renewing its tenderness in the children that are its pledges. The thought of separation even by death is repugnant, and nothing less than death can weaken the bond. No sane man or woman regards divorce as a good thing; the most that can be said in its favor is that, under given circumstances, it affords relief from intolerable evil.

Reluctantly, the Church permits limited divorce: the parties are allowed for certain causes to separate, though the bond continues in force and neither may contract a new marriage while the other is living. But absolute divorce

---

[1] *Pastoral Letter of the Archbishops and Bishops of the United States,* 1919.

which severs the bond, the Church does not and will not permit.

We consider the growth of the divorce evil an evidence of moral decay and a present danger to the best elements in our American life. In its causes and their revelation by process of law, in its results for those who are immediately concerned and its suggestion to the minds of the entire community, divorce is our national scandal. It not only disrupts the home of the separated parties, but it also leads others who are not yet married, to look upon the bond as a trivial circumstance. Thus, through the ease and frequency with which it is granted, divorce increases with an evil momentum until it passes the limits of decency and reduces the sexual relation to the level of animal instinct.

This degradation of marriage, once considered the holiest of human relations, naturally tends to the injury of other things whose efficacy ought to be secured, not by coercion but by the freely given respect of a free people. Public authority, individual rights and even the institutions on which liberty depends, must inevitably weaken. Hence the importance of measures and movements which aim at checking the spread of divorce. It is to be hoped that they will succeed; but an effectual remedy cannot be found or applied, unless we aim at purity in all matters of sex, restore the dignity of marriage and emphasize its obligations.

139

DIVORCE LEGISLATION IN THE UNITED STATES

John A. Ryan [1]

This article does not pretend to be an adequate study of the topic with which it deals. All that is here attempted is to present in outline the most interesting and important facts concerning the institution of divorce in the United States.

During the colonial period, divorces were granted by the courts only in those areas which composed New England. In one or two of the other colonies the bond of matrimony

---

[1] *Studies,* December, 1924.

could be dissolved by the legislature, but this power was very rarely exercised. The Constitution of the United States does not give the federal government any general power over the subject of divorce. The Congress of the United States can legislate concerning marriage and divorce only for those parts of the country which have not become States. At present there are only two such jurisdictions, the Territory of Alaska and the federal District of Columbia. All the States of the Union have enacted divorce laws, with the single exception of South Calolina.

The divorce statutes of the various States differ very greatly one from the other. At one extreme is New York which permits dissolution of the marriage bond for only two causes, adultery and a continuous desertion of five years; at the other extreme is the State of New Hampshire with fourteen causes. The State of Washington recognises nine causes, the last of which reads substantially as follows: "or any other cause which the court may in its discretion regard as sufficient." In the great majority of States the recognized causes for divorce are six: adultery, bigamy, conviction of crimes in certain classes of cases, intolerable cruelty, wilful desertion for two years, habitual drunkenness. In all cases of absolute divorce re-marriage is permitted, but in a few States that right is denied to the guilty party.

The *theory* of the law in all the States is that marriage is a permanent status to be ended only by the death of one of the parties. But the theory also provides that this permanent status can be changed by divorce when the purpose of the marriage relation has been thwarted, by the fault of the guilty party, to such an extent that greater evil will follow from maintaining than from terminating the marriage relation. In theory, divorce is granted only for such causes as are sufficient to defeat the ends for which the marriage was contracted. Almost every element of this curious theory has been set at naught in the State divorce statutes; for some of them refuse to regard, as sufficient, causes which others assume to be destructive of the purpose of marriage. At any rate, the variation among the States in recognizing causes for divorce is an interesting commentary on the different judgments of legislative bodies concerning the "permanence" of the marriage status. As the theory has been applied, it does not include the proposition that marriage is a *permanent* status, but only that it is *more or less* permanent.

The increase in both the absolute and the proportional number of divorces which has taken place in the United States in the last two decades is notorious. Here are some of the outstanding figures:

In 1890 there were 53 divorces per 100,000 of population.
In 1916 there were 112 divorces per 100,000 of population.
In 1922 there were 136 divorces per 100,000 of population.
To state the increase in another way:
In 1890 there were 13 marriages for each divorce.
In 1916 there were 9.3 marriages for each divorce.
In 1922 there were 7.3 marriages for each divorce.

As we might expect, the divorce rate varies greatly among the different States. In 1922 Nevada had only .9 of a marriage for each divorce; the ratio in Oregon was 2.6; in Wyoming, 3.9; Kansas, 5.7; Indiana, 5.4; New Hampshire, 7.5; Kentucky, 6.7; Illinois, 6.8. The best record, or rather the least deplorable, is held by the District of Columbia with 35.8 marriages to one divorce. The next place is occupied by New York with 22.6 marriages to one divorce. Turning our attention for a moment to smaller political divisions, we find that in 1921 four counties in Oregon had more divorces than marriages, and one of these counties maintained that condition for four years.

At one time Japan had the highest divorce rate in the world, namely, 140 per 100,000 of population. This was only 4 per 100,000 above the figure which was attained in the United States in 1922. In view of the increase which took place in the United States between 1916 and 1922 (from 112 to 136) it is safe to say that our divorce rate in the year 1924 is worse than the worst record of Japan.

It may be of interest to compare the rate in the United States with that of some countries where divorce is rare. In 1904 the rate in England was 2 per 100,000 of population; in France, 28; in Germany, 18; in Norway, 8; in Finland, 5.

Some other statistics are worth noting. In the United States the proportions of divorces granted to the husband and wife respectively have not varied greatly in the last thirty-five years. In 1889 almost 65 per cent were obtained by the wife. That proportion has increased slightly but rather steadily until to-day it is about 70 per cent. These figures directly contradict the assumption sometimes made that the institution of divorce is to the advantage of the stronger sex. That assumption may be true when all the incidents, the long-run effects as well as the immediate circumstances, are considered. Nevertheless, it is quite clear that the women take advantage much oftener of the opportunities presented by our divorce laws for dissolution of their matrimonial relations. Possibly the husbands are more often to blame than the wives for the creation of those conditions which the law recognizes as sufficient for divorce. There is, however, another explanation: "In this country, in recent years, a feeling has undoubtedly grown up that if the separation of husband and wife becomes imperative, chivalrous motives should prompt the husband to permit the wife to institute divorce proceedings. It is realized that, socially speaking, a man who appears as defendant in a divorce case is injured far less than a woman is, and the general acceptance of this idea has had a great influence on litigation."[2]

Another interesting statistical statement is that 62 per cent of divorced couples in the United States had no children. This seems to be important testimony to the effect that children have in preventing parents from seeking to annul the marriage bond. Probably it also testifies to the intention of many couples at the time of the marriage to get a divorce upon slight provocation. Hence, they took care not to be encumbered with children. The economic independence of women is shown in the fact that in 1916 about three-fourths of those who were granted divorces did not ask for alimony; that is, sought no support from the husbands. Among the causes of divorce in that year drunkenness was least, operating in 3 per cent of the cases; "neglect to provide" was accountable for 6 per cent, while the two causes which ranked highest were "cruelty" at 33 per cent and desertion at 37 per cent. The last cause does

---

[2] William E. Carson: *The Marriage Revolt,* p. 141.

not stand in need of explanation, but "cruelty" receives a very elastic interpretation in the divorce courts, being in most instances synonymous with "incompatibility of temper."

Despite the laxity and even frivolity which characterize many of our State divorce statutes, and despite the fact that the law does not recognize matrimony as a sacrament, the marriage relation is not a mere civil contract. A civil contract can generally be ended by mutual consent. In none of our States is this possible with marriage. In fact, all our divorce proceedings assume that one of the parties opposes the suit brought by the other. Hence, where "collusion" comes to the notice of the court, that is, when it becomes evident that the party against whom the action is brought is somehow co-operating with the plaintiff, the court generally refuses to grant the divorce. The difference between the marriage relation and that of a contract is thus summarized by a prominent legal authority:

"Because the parties cannot mutually dissolve it; because an act of God incapacitating one to discharge its duties will not release it; because there is no accepted performance that will end it; because a minor of marriageable age can no more recede from it than an adult; because it is not dissolved by failure of the original consideration; because no suit for damages will lie for the non-fulfilment of its duties; because legislation may annul it at pleasure; and because none of its other elements are those of contract, but are all of status."

What is the attitude of the American people toward our scandalous divorce theories, laws and practices? What may be called the "social" attitude seems to be accurately described in the following paragraph by a well-known woman author in the *Atlantic Monthly* for October, 1923:

"I fancy it is still true that, in most sections of America, the fact that a man or a woman has been divorced—especially if he or she has remarried—is something to be set down, until further information comes in, on the debit side of the account. In some American worlds, people have achieved a state of mind in which one's divorce is of no more moral significance than the colour of one's eyes; but these worlds are still few, and, in comparison, small. The prejudice is lessening all the time; and I wonder if there is left any group of individuals, large enough to count as a social group, which does not know and receive and like certain divorced and remarried people. I fancy not. Yet it can still be said, I think, that divorce, as such, is looked at askance. Most people, if pinned down, would probably say that, in their opinion, certain circumstances justified divorce absolutely, but that promiscuous and light-minded divorcing shocked them. A good many people, too (apart from Roman Catholics, I mean), draw a definite distinction between a divorce which is a mere legal separation and a divorce with remarriage."

The attitude of the churches is pretty well known, at least in its more general phases. The Catholic Church, of course, opposes all divorce. The Protestant Episcopal denomination clings fairly well to the traditional Anglican position that divorce should be granted only for adultery. Sometimes a clergyman of that denomination disregards the tradition and performs a marriage ceremony where one of the parties has been divorced for some other cause. But such conduct is generally condemned by the church authorities. All the other denominations approve, or at least permit, annulment of the marriage bond for more than one cause, and as a rule their ministers do not hesitate to officiate at marriages, one of the parties to which has obtained a legal divorce in any State for any cause recognized in that State. It is true that a considerable number, apparently an increasing number, of non-Catholic clergymen are raising their voices against the divorce evil; but I am not aware that any of the non-Catholic denominations, outside of the Protestant Episcopal, have taken a very decisive official stand. So far as I know, none of them has officially defined or proposed a list of causes which would be small in number as compared with the causes recognized in our more lax statutes.

Of course, there is a great number of individuals outside of the Catholic Church who are alarmed by the great increase in divorces. These include clergymen, lawyers, physicians, social workers and representatives of other important groups in our population. Perhaps the most significant manifestations of this general feeling of alarm are seen in the proposal for a uniform divorce law, drawn up by the Conference of Commissioners on Uniform State

Laws some three years ago, and in the proposal for an amendment to the federal Constitution giving Congress exclusive legislative power over marriage and divorce. A bill for a constitutional amendment was introduced in Congress early in the present year. The Senate Committee having charge of the measure held some public hearings, at which a considerable number of prominent persons spoke in favor of the proposal. However, it is not likely that the amendment will become a part of the Constitution within the next ten or fifteen years.

The most significant aspect of the proposed uniform law for all the States is the number of causes which it sets forth as sufficient for divorce. It is to be kept in mind that those who drew up this uniform bill were eager to reduce, so far as practicable, the causes for and number of divorces in the country. Nevertheless, they thought it necessary, or desirable, to include five causes, namely—adultery, extreme cruelty, habitual drunkenness, whether arising from drugs or drink, conviction of felony, and continuous desertion for a number of years which the Committee did not agree upon. The same causes are apparently approved by the advocates of a constitutional amendment. Should the amendment be adopted and Congress proceed to enact a divorce law for the whole country the legislation would, in all probability, include all these causes.

Summing up the public attitude towards divorce in the United States, we may say that while the evil is arousing a steadily-increasing amount of attention and concern, it has not yet so alarmed the dominant element of the population that anything like a considerable reform or a rigid divorce law is within the realm of probability. A uniform law permitting divorce for the five causes specified above would still produce the highest divorce rate in the world except Japan.

The committee which drew up the proposed uniform law for the States included in its recommendations some important improvements in procedure. They recommended that no divorce should be granted to any person who had not been a resident of the State in which the action was brought for a considerably longer time than is now sufficient in some of our more lax jurisdictions. Another recommendation was that no divorce should be granted unless the defendant actually appears in court. On the other hand, the committee failed to recommend for all cases a waiting period between the granting of a divorce and the re-marriage of either party. This failure is very significant testimony to the laxity of the public attitude on the whole subject of divorce. A few of the State laws forbid a second marriage within one year after the divorce. This is obviously a very considerable discouragement to a certain class desiring to sever the marriage bond. Yet the committee did not feel justified in urging its adoption upon all the States.

Undoubtedly the main reason for the infrequency of divorces in England is the very high cost of the judicial process. An undefended divorce suit entails an expense of about 50 pounds, while in an action which is opposed the cost ranges from 70 pounds to 500 pounds. In recent years there has been considerable agitation in Great Britain for cheaper divorce proceedings in the interest of the poor. In the United States there is little or no complaint on that score. A divorce action is relatively no more costly to the poor person than it is to the rich person. That is to say, the poor person is at no greater disadvantage as compared with the rich person in a divorce action than in any other court proceeding.

The effects of our lax divorce laws and procedure constitute obviously a most interesting and important subject. Nevertheless, they are extremely difficult to describe either accurately or concretely. Here is one example of a concrete statement. In the year 1921, 30 per cent of the children who were brought into the Juvenile Court of Portland, Oregon, on account of misconduct were the offspring of divorced parents. This percentage is probably three to five times as great as it should have been when we consider the proportion which divorces bear to marriages and the proportion of divorced couples who have no children. Probably the figure given above does not differ materially from that which obtains in most of our large cities. Its significance as an evil effect of divorce is somewhat lessened, however, when we reflect that the children of parents who have been judicially separated, not absolutely divorced, would probably be in an equally bad condition. Hence the

Portland experience is about equally valid as an argument against limited separation.

Some of the more general and less concretely measurable effects of frequent and easy divorce are those that might antecedently be expected. Among them are a general weakening of the sense of sin or crime regarding illicit sexual relations. When an easy court process and formality render regular and permissible a new sexual relation, it is very easy for men and women to assume that other causes and excuses may be sufficient to justify entering such relations. Why wait for a divorce? To put it in another way: why is simultaneous polygamy any worse than successive polygamy? Again, the realization that divorce is easily obtained, impels many persons to enter upon hasty marriages which end in divorce, but which would not be contracted at all if divorce did not offer an easy way of correcting a mistake. The facility with which divorces are obtained frequently prevents married couples from composing differences which would readily disappear if divorce were impossible. When such persons form new unions they very often find the same differences recurring and learn too late that they are more or less inevitable in the marriage state. Divorce has increased rather than diminished their difficulties.

140

WOMAN'S INFLUENCE [1]

In society as in the home, the influence of woman is potent. She rules with the power of gentleness, and, where men are chivalrous, her will is the social law. To use this power and fashion this law in such wise that the world may be better because of her presence, is a worthy ambition. But it will not be achieved by devices that arouse the coarser instincts and gratify vanity at the expense of decency. There will be less ground to complain of the wrong inflicted on women, when women themselves maintain their true dignity. "Favor is deceitful and beauty is vain; the

[1] *Pastoral Letter of the Archbishops and Bishops of the United States*, 1919.

woman that feareth the Lord, she shall be praised" (Proverbs XXXI, 30).

The present tendency in all civilized countries is to give woman a larger share in pursuits and occupations that formerly were reserved to men. The sphere of her activity is no longer confined to the home or to her social environment; it includes the learned professions, the field of industry and the forum of political life. Her ability to meet the hardest of human conditions has been tested by the experience of war; and the world pays tribute, rightfully, to her patriotic spirit, her courage and her power of restoring what the havoc of war had well-nigh destroyed.

Those same qualities are now to undergo a different sort of trial; for woman by engaging in public affairs, accepts, with equal rights, an equal responsibility. So far as she may purify and elevate our political life, her use of the franchise will prove an advantage; and this will be greater if it involve no loss of the qualities in which woman excels. Such a loss would deprive her of the influence which she wields in the home, and eventually defeat the very purpose for which she has entered the public arena. The evils that result from wrong political practice must surely arouse apprehension, but what we have chiefly to fear is the growth of division that tends to breed hatred. The remedy for this lies not in the struggle of parties, but in the diffusion of good will. To reach the hearts of men and take away their bitterness that they may live henceforth in fellowship one with another—this is woman's vocation in respect to public affairs, and the service which she by nature is best fitted to render.

141

WOMAN IN SOCIETY

John L. Spalding [1]

The objection has often been urged that, in making man the head of the family, the Church is injust to woman. But the family is an organic unity, and cannot exist without

---

[1] *Socialism and Labor and Other Arguments,* pp. 111-116. (A. C. McClurg & Co., Chicago.)

subordination and authority. Either the husband or the wife must be the depository of domestic authority, and unless it can be shown that woman is better fitted than man to exercise this power, no injustice has been done. Physically, man is stronger than woman; he is better able to confront the world and to do the work by which the members of the family are maintained in health and comfort. Historically, society grows out of a warlike and barbarous state of life; and since women are less fitted for war than men, the defence of property and rights is naturally intrusted to those whose hands hold the sword. But it is not necessary to examine into the genesis and evolution of society to find reasons for giving the headship of the family to man; we need but look into the heart of woman to see there an impulse as strong as life to look up to and follow the man she loves. Between man and woman there ought to be no question of superiority and inferiority; they are unlike, and in nothing do they differ more than in their relative power to escape from their impressions. A woman understands only what she feels, whereas a man may grow to be able to look at things as they are in themselves, remaining the while indifferent to their relations to himself. Hence women are superior to men in those virtues in which the essential element is right feeling. They believe more, hope more, and love more than men. They are more compassionate, more capable of remaining faithful to those who are unworthy of their love, because they consider only the love they feel, and give comparatively little heed to its object. Men, on the other hand, are superior in the virtues that spring less from sentiment and depend rather on the nature of things—their eternal fitness—as justice, fortitude, equanimity, wisdom, prudence. This difference in character determines their position in domestic and social relations; nor would there be gain for either man or woman if they could be made less unlike. The charm, as well as the helpfulness, of their relations lies in their differences, and not in their likenesses. They are complementary; each needs the qualities of the other, and their wants are the bond of union. The opposition of men and women to so-called woman's rights comes doubtless in many instances from a belief that to throw woman into public life is to make her less womanly. Nor gods nor men love a mannish woman or a womanish man. The unfairness with which woman is treated in the legislation of the medieval epoch may be traced to the barbarous ideas concerning woman that partially survived in Europe centuries after our ancestors had been converted to Christianity; nor has this injustice even yet disappeared from the statute books of the civilized nations. The causes that have led to the improvement of woman's condition among the Christian nations are in general the same that have developed our civilization. Whatever influences have been active in the abolition of slavery, in securing popular rights, free government, protection for children and the poor, in bringing knowledge within the reach of all, and thereby spreading abroad juster and more humane principles of conduct, have also wrought for the welfare of woman; and it is not necessary to point out how intimately all this progress is associated with the social action of the Christian religion. The spirit of chivalry is the outgrowth of the Christian ideal of womanhood. To maintain that Christianity crushed out "the feminine element, and more than all other elements combined, plunged the world into the dark ages," is to indulge in a kind of declamation that, for the past half century at least, has become impossible to enlightened minds. To say that the doctrine of original sin throws the guilt exclusively or chiefly on woman is merely to affirm one's ignorance of Christian teaching. St. Ambrose, one of the four great doctors of the Western Church, declares that woman's fault in the original fall was less than that of man, as her bearing was beyond question more generous. And then the Catholic Church at least teaches that Mary has more than made good any wrong that Eve may have done. To assert that in the Christian religion "the godhead is a trinity of males," is to be at once ignorant and coarse. God is neither male nor female, as in Christ there is neither male nor female. To proclaim that the Christian religion teaches that "woman is an after thought in creation, sex a crime, marriage a condition of slavery for woman and defilement for man, and maternity a curse," is to mistake rant for reason, declamation for argument. In fact, the advocates for woman's rights too often take this false and therefore offensive tone. They speak like people who have grievances; and to have a grievance is to be a bore. They scold, and when women scold, whether in public or in private, men may not be able to answer them, but they grow sullen and cease to be helpful. To be persuasive, woman must be amiable. And to be strong, she must speak from a loving heart, and not from a sour mind. Whoever is thoroughly imbued with the spirit of Christianity must sympathize with all movements having as their object the giving to woman the full possession of her rights. No law that is unjust to her should exist in Christendom. She should not be shut out from any career that offers to her the means to an honest livelihood. For the same work she should receive the same wages as a man, and should hold her property in virtue of the same right that secures to him the possession of his own. For wrong doing of whatever kind she should not be made to suffer a severer punishment than is inflicted upon man. The world will continue to be unjust to her until public opinion makes the impure man as odious as it makes the impure woman.

The best interests of mankind, of the Church and the State will be served by widening and strengthening woman's influence. The ancient civilization perished because woman was degraded, and ours will be perpetuated by a pure, believing, self-reverent, and enlightened womanhood. Woman here in the United States is more religious, more moral, more intelligent than man; more intelligent in the sense of greater openness to ideas, greater flexibility of mind, and a wider acquaintance with literature; and whatever is really good for her must be good for our religion and civilization. She "stays all the fair young planet in her hands."

142

ONE MORAL LAW FOR MEN AND WOMEN

Margaret Fletcher [1]

From the fact that the human soul is a moral entity essentially the same whether it energizes a male or a female body, it follows that in either case it is subject to the same moral law.

[1] *Christian Feminism,* pp. 11, 12. (B. Herder Book Co., St Louis, Mo.)

But although there is one moral law, the entity composed of sexless spirit and sexed body may be so profoundly different according as that body is male or female, that the difficulty of obeying a given law in the complex code of Christian morality may be greater in the one case than in the other. Thus the proportion of guilt in disobedience can be adequately known only to the omniscient God. The most penetrating of human judges is hindered in his estimate by the essential limitation of human knowledge. Therefore the verdicts of a human tribunal may often differ from those of the Divine Tribunal. Only occasionally do we see what appear to be deviations from even justice (deviations in the direction of leniency) in the administration of human law. These seeming illegalities have in reality their source in equity, being an attempt to do justice by the verdict both to society outraged by crime and to the individual laboring under some exceptional handicap. This tendency is more often found in Continental countries than in our own.

If, on the one hand, we see in courts of law efforts to harmonize Divine and human justice, why on the other do we often find such unequal justice in *social* life in the matter of the same sin committed by a man or a woman, an inequality which bears hardly on the woman?

Because though the same sin, whether committed by a man or by a woman, may involve equal guilt before God it yet may have unequal social consequences according to the sex of the sinner. Even where the moral guilt is less the social injury may be greater. Mankind looks mainly to social consequences. *Human* laws must take into account these consequences of sin, for their aim is the welfare and protection of the social body as a whole.

143

THE ATTITUDE OF THE CHURCH TOWARD WOMEN

Margaret Fletcher [1]

It has frequently been urged by the revolutionary type of feminist that the Church's attitude toward women has

[1] *Christian Feminism,* p. 17. (B. Herder Book Co., St. Louis, Mo.)

been repressive and contemptuous. Although her attitude does not, strictly speaking, constitute a principle, it is well to say a word upon it here. These charges are based upon extracts from the writings of some early Fathers, isolated from their context, inaccurately translated and judged without sufficient knowledge of contemporary history or of the kind of woman against which they were mostly aimed—namely, pagan women, the declared enemies of the new Christian virtue of chastity.

That the Church's attitude is the contrary of repressive is easily established by authenticated facts—women are canonized as saints, are accepted as doctors of mystical theology, installed as rulers over large communities, in some cases (such as in that of St. Hilda) over men. They have been encouraged to undertake the highest studies, and have filled professorial chairs in papal universities. It would be an easy matter to cite the names of Catholic women eminent for learning and distinguished in the arts, who were illustrious for their virtue and were faithful daughters of the Church. Indeed, it might be difficult to find women in modern times outside the Church of the same intellectual and moral stature.

At the so-called Reformation women were deprived of all existing means of education, for which, until very recent times, nothing was substituted.

With the dishonor of the ideal of celibacy and the materialized view of marriage consequent upon it, women fell in the scale of freedom and consequently of dignity.

144

EQUAL RIGHTS AMENDMENT

NATIONAL COUNCIL CATHOLIC WOMEN [1]

The term "Equal Rights" as used by the advocates of the amendment is a palpable misnomer.

If the term is interpreted to mean "identical rights" for men and women (and this is the interpretation put upon it by its friends) then the amendment flies in the face of fact, science and philosophy. Men and women can have

[1] *The Senate Committee Hearing*, February 7, 1924.

identical rights only on the supposition that they are identical beings from every point of view. Such a conception of womanhood contradicts all the facts of physiology, psychology, economics and social science. The physiological differences between men and women, besides the obvious ones, are so many, so deeply laid, are so persistent that no law can wipe them out. These differences of function, the result of natural law, imply essential differences in rights and duties. Woman, because of her structure and consequent functions, has acquired in fact and in law certain definite rights. It would be as silly to argue that man should have the same rights as it would be unjust not to recognize that woman must have them, both for her personal protection and for the preservation of the race. What has been said of physiological function, must be repeated of psychological, economic, and social. These differences are innate, natural, the result of factors over which neither sex has any control. To say that they make woman the inferior of man is foolish; to contend that they make women different from man is to talk both common sense and science.

Woman, therefore, should have in law definite, specific rights as nature has conferred upon her definite, specific duties. It is neither justifiable nor reasonable to level down these rights for the attainment of a purely theoretical *identity*.

The history of civilization, especially in modern times is the record of the fight of womankind to have recognized in law these fundamental differences which divide her from man by the passage of legislation which will protect her in the peculiar functions which she possesses and which are so vital to the welfare and the continued existence of society itself. The Equal Rights Amendment would wipe all this out at one stroke of the pen.

That woman has been discriminated against, we are ready to admit. That her full position in society has not been recognized, we readily acknowledge. But that identity of rights will spell for her, in the last analysis, equality of rights is purely chimerical. Such an amendment negatives all history, science and philosophy. It erects into a principle the philosophy of extreme feminism. It is false precisely to that extent.

145

THE INDISPENSABILITY OF THE ASCETIC IDEAL

F. W. FOERSTER [1]

To secure the mastery of man's higher self over the whole world of animal desire is a task which demands a more systematic development of will-power and the cultivation of a deeper faith in the spiritual destiny of humanity than are to be found in the superficial intellectualistic civilization of today. To achieve such a result it will be necessary not only to have recourse to new methods and new ideals, but to make sure that we do not allow what is valuable and in any way worthy of imitation, in the old, to be forgotten. The ascetic principle, in particular, is today in danger of being undervalued.

Asceticism should be regarded, not as a negation of nature nor as an attempt to extirpate natural forces, but as practice in the art of self-discipline. Its object should be to show humanity what the human will is capable of performing, to serve as an encouraging example of the conquest of the spirit over the animal self. The contempt which has been poured upon the idea of asceticism in recent times has contributed more than anything else towards effeminacy. Nothing could be more effective in bringing humanity back to the best traditions of manhood than a respect for the spiritual strength and conquest which is symbolized in ascetic lives.

It may be true that in the history of asceticism there have been absurdities and abuses. But this must not blind us to the eternal value of complete self-conquest in the task of attaining true inner freedom. The orgies of the French Revolution do not discredit the principle of political freedom. Neither should the occasional excesses of individuals, or even the degenerate condition of whole epochs, prevent us from appreciating the educational value of the ascetic

---

[1] *Marriage and the Sex Problem"*; Published by F. A. Stokes Company, New York. This is perhaps the best chapter of the author's remarkable book. It was reprinted in *"The Catholic Mind"* for May 8-22, 1914.

principle and the inspiration and encouragement which come from contemplating the lives of the great saints.

In this chapter I propose to deal with the *social and psychological value* of the ascetic ideal. By the ascetic ideal is meant that view of life which does not simply regard self-conquest as a stage in self-development, but which assigns a definite and essential function in the evolution of humanity to men and women who shall demonstrate, in one sphere or another, the possibility of living a life of continual and complete abnegation—not in order to make a more natural life appear contemptible, but with the express purpose of enriching life and preserving it from degeneration by means of heroic examples of spiritual power. Properly to understand the significance of asceticism, it should be remembered that natural life does not flourish unless the spirit retains the upper hand; and since we are surrounded for the most part by striking examples of lives in which the spirit plays anything but a leading part, it is in the highest degree desirable that living and striking examples of men and women who have fully freed themselves from the distraction of the world and the domination of natural desires should be continually before our eyes. The vast majority of modern men will see nothing but matter for laughter in such an ideal as this. Even earnest and spiritually-minded people regard it as an obsolete and erroneous view, which must soon give place to a more harmonious conception of life. I am, however, profoundly convinced that this attitude is the product of a shallow understanding of actual human nature. Ignorance of the awful dangers latent in our weak nature is very commonly to be met with in epochs still powerfully influenced by great traditions of moral discipline. Those born in such periods are apt to be lacking in personal acquaintance with the darker side of human nature, owing to the very state of discipline into which their fellow-citizens have been brought. Hence they fail to realize what a laborious taming of passion has preceded the comparative security they find around them. Time will soon give us a demonstration on a large scale of what men can be like when undisciplined.

In the sphere of sex a rapid disintegration of character is already going on. The effect of the increasing laxity in this direction will make itself felt in other directions. A disrespect for definite moral standards in this region will tend to initiate a spirit of license in every other department of social and moral life. It is astounding with what rapidity all moral convictions are today breaking down in the minds of vast masses of the people. This would not occur if the deepest foundations of these convictions had not been long undermined. The suggestive force of tradition continues to be operative in an age which has largely abandoned the positive belief lying behind the tradition, and this deceives us as to the real extent of the disintegration. The first vigorous push shows us how far the process of undermining has gone.

Without most people being conscious of the fact, one of the main foundation-stones of our traditional moral culture has been the constant presence in our midst of great personalities illustrating in their own lives the highest possible degree of spiritual freedom, the complete conquest of the spirit over the world and the senses. The presence in society of such spiritually dedicated characters is a source of psychic inspiration for the whole community, and a constant and courageous protest against the smug Philistinism of the men of the world. The true building up of moral ideas and the chief stimulus towards their fulfilment come from the embodiment of the spiritual life in its most perfect form in heroic human life, and not from any kind of merely intellectual demonstration.

A belief in the spiritual destiny of man—no mere dream, but a belief confirmed and strengthened by the lives of great spiritual geniuses—is the first necessity in arousing and developing a spiritual conscience in the human race, a sense of the bounden duty of resisting the lower self. Unless this feeling has been brought into being, morality itself has no deep soil in which to take root. There could be no greater aid to its creation than the spectacle of men who can pursue spiritual things with a more powerful passion than that with which men of the world follow after gold, fame, and women.

These ultimate inspirations of all great self-mastery may be hidden from consciousness for generations; they nevertheless continue to perform their work and to supply the higher aspirations with their final authority and reality.

But one day the world of sensuous impulses will again raise itself in opposition to the dominion of the spirit, and a fresh sophistry will undermine the past foundations of spiritual dignity; then humanity will again discover the real bases of civilization and realize the impotence of all moral culture (in the absence of these inspirations) over against the influence of more tangible things. These spiritual factors grow more and more indispensable the greater becomes the disturbing influence of outer things, and the more the uniting communal nature of man gives way to individual instincts, feelings, interests and fancies, which carry in themselves no fixed norm.

It is from this point of view that we should consider the charge of retirement from the world and opposition to nature, which has always been brought against the ascetic ideal of life by those who regard it as a fruitless and weakening error. Every moral action is, in a certain sense, a resistance to nature and an overcoming of the world, and therefore needs the suggestive influence of elevated and perfect examples of self-mastery, in order, through a connection with such tangible embodiments of the spiritual life, to be equal to the power of the outer world, and the task of retaining faith in the right and possibility of resistance to mere nature.

There is an Indian saying: "Humanity waits upon the sacrifice of those who overcome the world, as the hungry young birds wait upon their mother." This is a very drastic expression of the manner in which the world depends upon those who can rise superior to it; it gives voice to the intense desire for spiritual strength on the part of those who are occupied with the tragedies and difficulties of their own lives—a desire which can be satisfied only by those who have attained to complete freedom. It is an eternal fact that humanity continually scorns and rejects the high, and yet at the same time dimly realizes that it cannot master its own life without the illumination and power coming from thence. Therefore the demonstration of a complete overcoming of the world is in no sense an attack upon life—rather is it a contribution towards life. In the face of the immense suggestive power of wealth, of ambition, and of every kind of sensuous temptation, humanity cannot dispense with the counteracting suggestion of a life which has made itself absolutely independent of all these things.

As is well known, it was the Franciscan movement which gave rise to the so-called Third Order: the members of this Order were permitted to live in the world, to carry on business and to marry; but they were required at the same time, through specific vows, to honor the saints to whom their Order was dedicated, and they were enjoined throughout their economic and family life never to lose sight of the spiritual destiny of man. This Third Order symbolizes the influence of the ascetic ideal upon real life; it shows the manner in which this ideal provides our earthly existence with an access of power—not the least of its services being the strengthening of the individual spirit against the confused world of human instincts and feelings.

From this point of view the saints are of imperishable importance in the world of education. They illuminate and demonstrate the teaching of Christ in many and varied directions, at the same time linking it up with human life. In order to avoid every misunderstanding, I must make it clear that I do not ask Protestant ministers or teachers simply to take over Catholic doctrines, customs, or institutions. They cannot, however, afford to neglect the *psychology and pedagogy* which lie behind the Catholic system; these must be thoroughly understood and valued, in order that the broader view of life which thus results should give rise to something of a corresponding nature within the framework of the Protestant tradition. With regard to the question of asceticism, I should not expect Protestants to undertake the worship of the saints, but they might well make the heroic lives and achievements of those men and women who dedicated themselves to the Church, fruitful for Christian worship and for the development of will and character. Indeed, we are driven in this direction by the simplest fundamental truth of all moral education—*the decisive importance of example.* "Thou shalt" is, indeed, great and important; but not less important is the "Thou canst," which is forced upon us by a mighty and consistent example. It is indeed true that we need in the first place the perfect example of Christ Himself, in which the higher is revealed in its entire purity; but in another sense we need also the encouragement of personalities more closely related to our weakness and error, and who have nevertheless attained to inner freedom in so impressive a manner. That the human soul should never be without a secret desire for absolute perfection bears witness to the divine light within us: even in a mistaken character, such as Nietzsche, this desire clamored for expression, and created the idea of the superman as a protest against a deadening materialism and a cheap and leveling education. This desire is enormously stimulated by the heroic consistency with which these great Christians worked out its possibilities, if one may use such an expression, and made into a complete whole all that which remains so weak and incomplete in our own Christian life. From the immense earnestness and decision of such heroes there radiates a suggestive influence of incomparable power, strengthening the shifting will of the ordinary man. On this point Hilty justly remarks:

From a fear of the "excesses" of the Catholic Church at the time of the Reformation, we have rejected the veneration of the saints, and in this manner have lost a powerful stimulus for good; for men learn more willingly and more easily from examples than from sermons. . . . But a time is coming in which the true saints of the Catholic Church will be better known to us than has been the case in the past.

From the fact that recent Protestant writers, like Sabatier and Thode, have devoted much thorough study to the life of St. Francis of Assisi, we may perceive that the period of mere neglect has come to an end. The Church of England has always attached a high value to the lives of the saints, both for sermons and for educational purposes, and has drawn no small inspiration from this source; it has recently paid peculiar attention to the legends of St. Francis, and has issued good editions of these works for its priests and educators. What reason is there, indeed, why our youth should be brought up upon legends and biographies from the antique world? Why should they be intimately acquainted with the deeds of Hercules, and yet be practically ignorant of the life of St. Francis or of St. Vincent de Paul, who stands incomparably nearer to our social and spiritual needs?

A modern philosopher, H. von Stein, whose too early death was so deplorable, has drawn attention in his later works to the imperishable significance of the lives of the saints. Attracted to their study through Schopenhauer, he discovered behind every negation their mighty positive element, their gift to the world and to those who live and struggle in it: "In the highest and noblest," he says, "our experience is unfortunately confined to what is limited and inadequate . . . they, however, experienced in themselves the absolute, and life is nothing when one has not in some fashion or another acquired this experience."

All such thoughts as these have to-day sunk into the background. In the last few centuries mankind has increasingly occupied itself with the question of external freedom, and the personalities of the saints have largely passed into oblivion; but they will again come into the forefront of our consciousness when the most important of all the problems of freedom has again become a central question: "How shall I become free from myself?" This question may from time to time be drowned through the clash of outward interests, but just as the great pyramid of Cheops always majestically reappears, even if it be temporarily veiled by the sandstorms of the desert, so, too, this great question of inner freedom will ever again raise its head above the dust and storm of daily existence, leading man back from all external things to the great problems of his own nature.

But is it not a fact that the lives of the saints abound in exaggerations and eccentricity? What would become of humanity if such types were raised to be authoritative ideals of life? We are quite prepared to admit that there is here much exaggeration and eccentricity, as indeed there is in the lives of all men of genius. But why should one prefer to allow the genius almost any moral laxity rather than an exaggerated attempt at securing spiritual power? Doubtless because in the first case we are encouraged in our own inadequacy, whereas in the latter the distressing gap between his intense spiritual endeavor and our easygoing lives becomes painfully evident! Moreover, the majority of men are restricted to normal conditions of life, and are able to develop their powers within these limits only. The genius of self-discipline, the saint, does not despise these conditions, nay, he may himself temporarily or wholly exist within them—like St. Louis of France or

St. Elizabeth—but in any case he attains to a superhuman inner freedom which cannot be imitated by any and everyone, but which even for the ordinary man remains an inexhaustible source of encouragement and a species of outer conscience. Rather than venture to call all that eccentric, or even morbid, which goes beyond our own moral power and does not fit within our scheme of life, we should rather acknowledge that throughout the whole of life the visible rests upon the invisible, the ordinary upon the extraordinary, and that we ourselves, in all our customs, our affections and our freedom, are reaping the benefit of these great spiritual conquests over the sensuous world.

It should never be forgotten that behind the purest and sweetest gifts of Nature there often lie the greatest dangers for the character of man—so soon, namely, as we become the slaves of these gifts instead of maintaining our freedom with regard to them. In family life, for example, there certainly lies a source of the finest human feeling; but this is not unaccompanied by the danger of family egoism and of the destruction of all higher *caritas* and all higher spiritual endeavor. Therefore there should be gifted personalities who know how to sacrifice not only the ugliest but even the most beautiful things in life—not in order to embitter earthly things for man, but in order to liberate them from the dangers of misuse, exaggeration, and overvaluation, which lie ready in man's nature. Of the great followers of Christ it may be said that they, too, take the guilt of the world upon themselves; they sacrifice so much because the others are able to sacrifice so little.

The spirit which animated the great saints was one of pure devotion to God. With the penetrating gaze of the purified soul, they saw that a family life not based upon anything higher than earthly love may be no more than a species of extended self-interest; they perceived that blunting of all higher needs which so often accompanies the mere worship of motherhood, that naïve self-expansion and self-reflection in the offspring, that character-destroying exaggeration of outward care, that growing indifference to everything except the welfare of one's own circle, that idolatrous cult of the work of human propagation, without any true and consistent worship of God. They knew, too, that children thus loved and thus brought up, in spite of all outer baptism, would never possess the true baptism; they are reared in the flesh and not in the spirit, and therefore they will be ruled by the flesh and not by the higher life of the spirit. Thus the separation of St. Elizabeth from her children, for example, was an extraordinary step; but it was the heroic action of a soul wholly devoted to God, who, through such an example, and in the face of the onesided worship of family life and children, aiming at *pointing out those high goals, in the absence of which family life itself lacks its commanding ideals and the true care of the soul is neglected.* For nothing allows children so to degenerate, and so shuts them out from all higher life, as the fact of being trained in an atmosphere of family egoism, and being brought up by a mother who knows nothing higher than her own offspring. And nothing educates and preserves the children so effectually as the example of a mother who shines with the inspiration of a higher love than that of the natural maternal instincts. Such rare examples of a completely self-forgetful approach to heavenly love, far removed from attacking or lowering human family life, act continually as a wonderful source of sacrificial strength and spiritual dignity, in this way enriching all earthly bonds. Characters like St. Elizabeth, even though, in their enthusiastic devotion to their Saviour, they burst the limits of ordinary family life, are *the protecting spirits of the family;* they bring into domestic life a *deeper loyalty,* a *more self-sacrificing devotion,* and a *more spiritual care,* and protect it from the connection with lower instincts, and thus from disintegration.

What has just been said with regard to the ascetic view of life in general must apply also to our valuation of the religious orders. In the lower Franciscan church in Assisi, we see a representation of the threefold sacrifice, poverty, chastity, and obedience, with which Christian asceticism opposes the strongest passions of humanity. These three sacrifices give those living in the world and struggling with the desire for material gain, with sensuality and with personal ambition, a continual reminder of their spiritual origin and a continual assistance against the over-valuation of external things. The earnestness and reality of the spiritual world is strengthened, in an altogether indispensable fashion, by the fact that there are and have been men who voluntarily denied themselves all these things, devoting themselves entirely to spiritual contemplation or Christian charity. And in face of the extraordinary tangibility of outward claims and temptations, what could be more necessary than such a strengthening? In the case of the energetic races of the Western World, occupied as they are so largely with outward and politico-economic activities, such an opposition—on the part of a whole class—to the over-valuation of material things is of the most imperative importance—not least for the health and true productivity of our worldly civilization itself. What is all *laborare* without the right *orare;* whither leads all creation without self-knowledge and self-recollection and uninspired by those high aims which first enable us to distinguish between primary and secondary things in life, nay, which first enable our whole work to acquire a deeper meaning? "We need seers and doers," a great American capitalist once said—the true seer, however, indispensably requires such a radical liberation from the goods and illusions of the world and from the turmoil of secular activity, and the ideal of such a liberation (in spite of all "progressive" blindness) will never perish, but will always acquire new strength from the necessities of our social life itself. A modern free-thinking criminalist, who stands entirely on the basis of scientific materialism, has very justly observed:

Only a view of the matter which overlooked the realities of human nature itself, and was blind both to historical and philosophical considerations, could fail to recognize the importance and justification of the religious orders from the point of view of human culture itself.

He does not doubt in the least that such retreats as these should play a very important rôle in the regeneration of weak and erring humanity, and in general in the liberation of the soul from the darkness of the past. So that even outside the Ancient Church itself there is again a feeling that it will be necessary to come back to these fundamental ideas and give them a new form. He says, for example:

Even in the oldest Oriental philosophy we see this spiritual instinct on the part of man, causing him to withdraw from the world and often from the corruption of society in order to seek protection against evil and temptation in solitude or in intercourse with similar souls, and, through a life of contemplation and asceticism, gradually to withdraw himself from the demands of the senses. . . . Not less ancient and universal is the conviction, which has become a regular dogma throughout the Eastern World, that one can best reconcile oneself with the Divine Power through such a retired existence devoted to spiritual elevation. . . . In the Nazarenes the Jews, too, possessed such a body of men, to whom Moses had already granted specific rights. There were also the flourishing Hebrew sects of the Essenes and the Therapeuteans, who were contemporaneous with Christ in Palestine and Egypt, and devoted themselves to a life of monastic piety.

In the structure of our book as a whole, these indications of the pedagogical value of the ascetic ideal and of the religious orders are of peculiar importance. Here we may perceive with the greatest clearness the relationship between such a retirement from the world and the needs of secular life itself. We shall thus be able to realize that in the future all these institutions will experience a development and fructification on a grand scale; the more the one-sided cultivation of merely worldly activity breaks down the nervous and psychic force of civilized man and coarsens his moral nature, and the more the increasing cult of the Ego destroys the capacity for true self-denial, the more their indispensability will be recognized.[2]

[2] In the nursing profession, too, the Orders with their vows are indispensable. The lack of power exhibited by the Protestant diaconal system (in Germany), as well as on the part of the secular nursing sisters, shows clearly that the supply of spiritual force has been inadequate to the very difficult demands of this kind of work. Hence it frequently occurs that doctors of great experience give the preference to Catholic sisters. There are, of course, numbers of self-sacrificing characters outside the Orders. But the Orders understand how to inspire *mediocre* characters, and to educate them in a magnificent fashion to an almost superhuman degree of self-sacrifice. And the main reason for this superiority on the part of the Catholic sisters is the vow of voluntary celibacy. In the first place, it puts the nurses in quite a different position with regard to the patients and doctors; they cease, indeed, to be women, and become sisters; and, moreover, they have put away the idea of leading lives of their own outside the hospital. This gives them a wholeness, dignity, and sacredness which they would not otherwise be able to acquire. Here, again, we perceive the deep relationship between social service and the ascetic ideal—the close connection between the capacity for the greatest sacrifice, and a form of retirement from the world; we see that only those who have left the "natural man" entirely behind are able to do the best work in many spheres of life.

There are a great many men and women who entirely fail to

The full and permanent resignation of that which for the majority of men alone makes life desirable, has a power of attraction only for the rarest natures, and for this very reason the ascetic type will never lose its honorable position among the people, but will be newly produced and newly honored in every age; and it is not the most enlightened but the darkest ages of history in which men so forget their own deeply hidden yearning for spiritual freedom and the torment of their actual lack of freedom that they fail to recognize those who overcome the world as social assets of the first rank. Degeneration and abuse of all kinds naturally await all institutions and ideals when they are translated into life, and the highest thoughts and customs will be the most liable to such misuse since they are the furthest removed from the ordinary level of human life. How can it be attempted to refute the institutions of religion, which are indeed the answer to the fundamental weaknesses of human nature, through a reference to abuses which are after all only a new proof of this weakness

realize the need for such ascetic examples, because their view of life is not sufficiently realistic to enable them to grasp the actual needs of our human life. Dostojewski once said: "He who does not understand the monk, does not understand the world." It is frequently asked to-day: "Is it not more useful to live in the midst of the world rather than withdraw from its keenest attractions and temptations and make vows of solitude?" But this question is quite irrelevant when we look upon these ascetic figures as *object lessons in spiritual earnestness,* and thus essential to our social and educational work. Certainly it is more difficult to remain pure and free in the midst of the world—and this was achieved only by a very few of the greatest saints. The Orders, however, assist men of a more ordinary stamp to attain to this condition of inner peace and of freedom from the fever of needs and passions, a state of mind which they would not achieve if they lived in the world, and one which is not achieved by those who, in the midst of comfortable worldly circumstances, contemplate with superiority this world of discipline and obedience, and feel themselves to be more developed and more useful personalities. There can be no manner of doubt that there are highly developed men and women worthy of the greatest honor who live exemplary lives in commerce, family relationships, and secular activities in general, in the midst of great conflicts and temptations; but along with their burdens and duties they also enjoy all the alleviations and satisfactions which accompany the cares and disappointments of secular life. We must on no account deceive ourselves as to this. Let one but approach these people with the veil or the monk's vow, and they would draw back in horror.

itself? What would the champions of democracy say if one met the ideal of self-government with a reference to the political corruption of the United States? The radicalism and individualism of our age has not the faintest idea how deeply all the victories of personal freedom over the omnipotence of the State, of the so-called "rights of man," are linked up with this much-scorned retirement from the world, which has brought personality to its highest concentration and raised spiritual life above all other aims. It was doubtless the fervor and intensity with which whole groups of individuals left domestic and social life, in order to come entirely to themselves, which first made men conscious, in the most impressive manner, that man has a right to himself—that there is a holiness of inner life and effort, in which society and the State have no right to interfere. Moreover, the right and dignity of the woman, apart from her mere valuation as a sexual being, is closely related to the existence and honorable recognition of bodies of women dedicated to God in which human personality found a safe refuge from the world and all its merely utilitarian aims. Thus these ascetic institutions, on closer study, reveal themselves as a most powerful support for everything which one may call *character,* and a pillar of that great and true resistance to all that is merely tangible and useful, upon which, ultimately, everything depends which makes life worth living and lends men real power over material things.

Very interesting from this point of view are the conclusions drawn by Frau Gnauck-Kühne in her penetrating book "Die deutsche Frau." The authoress here shows us that the deeper problems associated with the woman question cannot be solved without the help of the ideal of the Order, and she shows what a deep understanding of the heart of this question has been acquired by the Catholic Orders through the experience of centuries. One must not leave out of account, she says, that the modern tendencies within the woman's movement which aim at a breaking down of strict monogamy have their origin to no small extent in the fact that it is exceptional for a woman to feel her whole nature satisfied by any mere profession, and that the mere cult of her individuality leaves her deep desire for concrete human devotion and companionship unsatisfied. Thus, for those women who do not marry and who have no family circle, there remains only the following alternative: either one allows them that fulfilment of those natural and psychic needs which the merely professional life does not satisfy, through free love relationships (a tendency represented, for example, by those modern reformers who proclaim "the right of motherhood"), or one creates for them, along some other line, the social life, the fulfilment of maternal instincts, and the concrete human work, which they do not find in their abstract professional work. The latter is done, however, in the best and most definite manner by the Orders, with their close social life, their manifold tasks of love, and their work of personal education. At the same time, through their rules, their self-elected authority, and their religious self-discipline, these institutions best meet the great difficulties which follow upon the lasting communal life of women, when the individuals are without higher order and the calming influence of a dedicated life. And finally, it is these institutions alone which, by virtue of the solemn dignity which they assign to the virgin state, overcome the customary disparagement of the "old maid." This disparagement rests upon the idea that the one decisive question in a woman's life is whether or not she finds favor in the eyes of a man. Frau Gnauck-Kühne regards this view as the foundation of all feminine inferiority and lack of freedom, and observes with justice:

There can be no question of a choice between two courses, unless the condition of virginity offers the possibility of a life fully as happy and fully as valuable as that of the married woman. This choice is given by the Women's Orders, which, in the shape of a celibate life dedicated to God, provide an earthly existence which in happiness and value yields nothing to the married state. . . . There are two paths open to a woman, the path without a man and the path with a man. Of these two possibilities, the nuns are an example of the first, of the life without the man. Upon the summit of the other path, the life with the man, stands the happy mother. . . . From both these summits, and with an understanding for spiritual necessity, the right way must be sought by which to approach the solitary women in the world, the brave women workers of all classes. The matrons will have no difficulty in getting into touch with such women workers. The convents can become centres for whole classes of women workers, places of refuge, which release their charges in the morning and receive them again in the evening; they can be developed as institutions for mutual assistance and social work.

Frau Gnauck-Kühne is hence right when she asserts that for the *real* solution of this problem there is no alternative to the course which she suggests. This brings us around to a point of view to which we have already called attention: the development of our civilization is leading us to perceive, with more and more clearness, that the basis upon which our modern society has built its moral and spiritual structure is absolutely inadequate. Many deep needs, serious temptations, and severe conflicts have been entirely neglected. In every direction forces have been liberated and needs have been exposed or created—but there has been no corresponding provision of spiritual education, care, and leadership. The modern moralists, who wax so indignant over the "new ethic," should be mindful of the fact that it is very easy, on paper, to call whole classes of people to self-denial, but that one cannot reckon upon obedience and any enduring joy in life, if at the same time one deprives such people of their faith in another world, with its illuminating reminder of man's higher destiny, *and if at the same time one provides no spiritual equivalent for the painful vacuity which the non-fulfilment of natural instincts always leaves in the minds and hearts of the majority of women.* When a higher view of life is lacking, it must always seem a cruel accident that a particular individual should be deprived of the satisfaction of marriage—and this individaul is expected, merely for the sake of "ethics," to bow to this accident for a lifetime, while at the same time all the voluble culture of our age and all the ideals of everyday citizenship are unable to offer him or her anything which really satisfies the heart in the place of what has been missed. The authoress of the book to which we refer is undoubtedly right when she says that the increasing concentration of the modern world upon sensuous satisfaction, the more and more insistent cry of *carpe diem*, is no more than the necessary consequence of wide circles of people having abandoned all deep religious care of the soul and spiritual fulfilment of life.

It is indeed time to consider the great problems of our civilization more from this standpoint, instead of merely condemning, from the moral point of view, the whole modern revolt and desire for an enhancement of life. Who knows if among those in revolt we may not find the more gifted and deeper characters, who have been prevented from rising above their merely natural desires, in the first place on account of the frequently weak and uninspiring character of our modern Christianity and social morality? Under the influence of a greater inspiration these would perhaps be the very people to respond most eagerly to a higher view of life.

When the rejection of the ascetic principle has proceeded yet further, men will be forced to realize that in an atmosphere of indulgence even the simplest and most indispensable acts of self-mastery will give way to the tyranny of the desires. For even the most elementary act of self-mastery presupposes a certain acceptance and social recognition of the principle of abnegation. "Can you conceive of a moral reaction," Richard Wagner once asked, "otherwise than under the conception of abnegation?" Truthfulness, loyalty, honor—all these elements of character demand an overcoming of self. They therefore need a view of life which emphasizes the spiritual power of man over mere impulses and desire, a view in which this spiritual element is cultivated and practiced as the foundation of all moral reliability. In order to realize this, one should consider the intelligent hatred with which the more consistent anti-moralists regard the ascetic principle and look upon all our moral views as the consequences of this principle. In this sense, Nietzsche describes the insistence upon truthfulness as an ascetic principle, which cannot justify itself from the point of view of mere life expansion. Who cannot perceive that, from this point of view, all earnest sense of honor undoubtedly bears within itself an element of self-overcoming, and who could be so blind, in the face of all such consequences, as not to perceive whence the rejection of the ascetic principle would ultimately lead?

All the points of view which we have above justified are also applicable to the objections raised against *ecclesiastical celibacy,* as if it were a sort of treachery to the race and an entirely antiquated and fruitless form of asceticism.

To begin with, it seems to be quite forgotten that a class of persons who are not married, owing to natural causes, will always exist. Hence it is of great importance, in the interests of the happiness and vital energy of the unmarried, that their condition shall not be regarded as one of necessity, and as a frustrated form of existence, but as a hallowed state full of its own special advantages and blessings. This service is rendered by the voluntarily celibate life, dedicated to God, with all the glory of its heroic renunciation. By this means the state of the unmarried gains an altogether new dignity and meaning. The final trend of all arguments against celibacy dedicated to the service of religion is towards strengthening the view quite sufficiently strengthened by nature—that the real meaning of life lies in the fact of marriage, and that the unmarried are an inferior class. It can be cloaked with fine words, but it is nevertheless the logical outcome of this attitude towards life. But it should never be forgotten that family life itself degenerates, unless it is kept in subjection to higher aims. Now celibacy is an extremely valuable means of representing the independence of higher aims in life against the ascendancy of family impulses and family cares, thus safeguarding marriage against being degraded from a sacrament to a mere matter of gratification.

Moreover, the argument already propounded in favor of asceticism, by the side of worldly callings and situations, is also applicable to this question. The oath of voluntary celibacy, so far from degrading marriage, is a support to the holiness of the marital bond, since it gives material shape to the spiritual freedom of man in the face of natural impulses; it also acts like a conscience, in respect of all passing moods and encroachments of the sensual temperament. Celibacy is a protection of marriage in this sense, too, that its existence prevents married people, in their relations to one another, from feeling themselves as the mere slaves of obscure natural forces, and leads them to take their stand against nature as free beings able to command. Those who mock at celibacy as unnatural and impossible, know not, in very truth, what they do. They do not see that the attitude which induces them to speak thus must lead, as its logical consequence, to prostitution and to the dissolution of monogamy. For, if the compulsion of nature be so urgent, how can one demand continence before marriage? In fact, how can one demand a chaste life from the unmarried? And finally, do they not give a thought to the number of marriages which are for months, or years, or even for life, tantamount to celibacy for one of the partners, because the husband or wife has fallen a victim to illness? For this reason alone, consistent monogamy stands or falls with the esteem in which celibacy is held. It is no accident that Luther, by his fight against celibacy, was led to the secondary result that breach of marriage is permissible in cases where the physiological aim of the marriage cannot be fulfilled. He says, for instance:

If a healthy woman has an impotent husband, she is to say to him: See, dear husband, thou canst not take my virginity from me, and thou hast cheated me out of my young life, wherefore thine honor and hope of felicity are endangered, and there is no marriage between us in the sight of God. Grant that I may have a secret marriage with thy brother or nearest kinsman and thou shalt have the name, so that thy goods may not be inherited by strangers; and allow thyself to be willingly deceived in thy turn by me, as thou hast deceived me.

This position (taken up, consistently enough, by the Reformer personally) has checked further influence by the power of the deeper Christian tradition in this sphere. To-day Luther's strongly naturalistic view of these things revives again, and in modern writers it develops similar consequences. Forel, Ellen Key, and others, attack absolute monogamy for the same reasons which have been urged against celibacy; from which circumstance one only too clearly recognizes that celibacy is not a merely hierarchical institution, as has been assumed, but is at the same time an institution in favor of family life, a heroic taking of the offensive against the confident power of merely natural impulses—which make more and more demands the more concessions one makes to them, and whose despotism can be broken only by renunciation on the great scale.

Justly do the Protestants point to the great blessings which have issued from the evangelical manse; but they forget that truly Christian family life existed *before* Luther and exists still in both confessions, so that the married pastor is not unconditionally necessary for this side of

Christian culture. And they also forget that the Protestant manse itself, like the whole family of Christians, is still unconsciously nourished by the spiritual greatness of the institution of celibacy, of the mighty advance against the dominion of the senses which it represents. Marital fidelity is not in the least "natural," it is already an extraordinary conquest of Nature. Psychologically it is inextricably bound up with the demand that the spiritual man shall be stronger than his impulses and shall not be their obedient servant. Celibacy was the great sacrifice whose flame ever nourishes and irradiates this faith anew. And, in truth, how is one seriously to justify fidelity, if natural impulses are so unconquerable that celibacy must be pronounced to be folly and a sin against nature?

I have expressly drawn attention to the deeper consequences of the contempt of celibacy, because we have to deal in this book with the fundamental basis of all our pedagogic operation. In this connection I should not omit to point out that Schopenhauer characterized the rejection of celibacy as a fatal error on the part of Protestantism. Bähr, in his "Gesprächen mit Schopenhauer," reports that the latter said:

Protestantism killed one of the vital nerves of Christianity in combating the value of celibacy, which in the Catholic Church still finds its visible expression in the monasteries and nunneries. That Luther had by then entered into the state of matrimony, that he maintained the impossibility of a chaste life outside matrimony, is held to have decided the matter. "Wait!—that which thou hast said, that shall break thy neck." Continuing the conversation in a gentler tone, he admitted that Luther was a great man, a deep and powerful thinker, but that he was driven by the conditions of the times into too wide-reaching admissions.

These are very serious objections, but it is indeed the duty of our age to examine them and see if they are justified. It is an indisputable fact that Protestantism, with its objection on principle to the ascetic ideal of life, occupies an entirely isolated position amidst all the great religions, including those of the Ancient World. This should indeed give us pause. And the matter is not by any means settled by drawing attention to the unnatural character of asceticism, or by references to the abuses and exaggerations which naturally accompany such a great and difficult attempt to elevate man above himself. Protestantism should rather ask itself if, as a result of this position, it does not lend assistance to a species of naturalism which may some day prove disastrous to itself. When one bears in mind the remarkable reverence which was paid to the Vestals, and when one thinks of the saying *casta placent diis,* while remembering the almost universal rejection of the ascetic idea in Protestant literature, one is compelled to recall Schopenhauer's saying. One feels that Schopenhauer, in his elementary remark, gave expression to a sudden vision —namely, that such a position as this is absolutely incompatible with the essential foundations of a spiritual religion. In this respect Protestantism will be compelled to alter its position or to perish. The people itself *demands* a standpoint superior to the world. It pays no attention to a form of belief which leaves it too much upon the level of its natural and economic life. Precisely those very people who live and work amidst material things demand, consciously or unconsciously, an ideal of super-material freedom. As is well known, Christianity would not have become a universal religion but for its immense power of resistance to the world. For secular life pure and simple, indeed, a religion is not necessary! The turning away of the young generation is not merely the result of religious indifference; only too often it represents the rejection of a species of faith which no longer appears to possess a genuine inward belief in the superhuman, or which at any rate produces the impression that Christ only lived a superhuman life in order that we might be justified in remaining on the merely human level. For this reason Nietzsche sought to attain the superhuman by another road; he missed the heroic element in Christianity because it had fallen under the dominion of the domestic Philistine.

The rejection of every species of asceticism is, moreover, especially connected with the spirit of the great industrial community. Our economic system, with its unceasing pursuit of new opportunities for expansion, is wholly dependent upon an ever-increasing multiplication of human needs, not only in the case of the consumers, but also in the case of the workmen, who will work with greater intensity the more needs they and their womenfolk have to satisfy. W. von Siemens tells us in his "Recollections," how, when building a great electricity works in the Caucasus, he had in the first place to solve the problem of the workers; this he did by encouraging the workmen's wives to wish for increased luxuries, jewelry, etc., in consequence of which the men were compelled to work with increased diligence. Modern industrial society regards the multiplication of material needs as the basis of its entire existence and therefore perceives in the ascetic principle its deadliest enemy, as clearly as the brewer sees his ruin threatened by the temperance movement. In his "Asiatic Studies," Lyall has given a vivid picture of the conflict between the Eastern ascetic view of life and modern civilization in India; we see the incompatibility of the two points of view and the moral confusion of the younger generation of Indians which is growing up in the midst of this conflict. Japanese writers, in dealing with the fitness of the Asiatic races for modern industrial competition, have also drawn frequent attention to the fact that the whole view of life prevailing in the East is, so to speak, "anti-economical," and stands in diametrical opposition to that principle of industrial expansion which is the real motive power of the western world; it will be necessary, therefore, for the East, if it is to enter into successful competition with the West, to take over not only the *machines* but also the *philosophy* of modern civilization.

In the opinion of a typical modern thinker such as Fr. Naumann, the ascetic ideal has passed away, never to return. He cannot see that it has any relationship to the great forces which mould life, and he regards it as a childish answer to the great economic questions of the day. In the face of the great industrial tasks of modern life, of what use to us is the ideal of voluntary poverty? Do we not rather need the desire for wealth, the greatest possible exertion and expansion of material power, to enlarge the bounds of human life? From this standpoint are we not compelled to regard the simplification of life as a weakening of economic energy?

The Bible tells us we are to make the world subject to ourselves; but it also says, "Seek ye first the kingdom of God, and all these things shall be added unto you." There is a full realization of the fact that matter is only really organized by means of spirit. From this point of view even an apparently remote and other-worldly inward deepening of life provides, at the same time, an increment of energy for secular civilization, and the most consistent liberation from the world is at the same time an increase in power over the world. Thus in the face of the modern type of civilization we may well ask: Is economic progress really bound up with this blind and feverish multiplication of needs, or is not man's material civilization itself dependent, perhaps, for its inner health, upon a strong counteracting factor in the shape of ascetic ideals? This is a question of decisive importance, in answering which the western world may have occasion to realize anew the significance of the phrase *ex oriente lux*. In the midst of our apparently healthy and productive development of economical and technical energy who cannot perceive on every hand the symptoms of hidden disease? Consider, for example, the increasing brutality with which we pursue an aimless and meaningless struggle for life, the disintegration of will-power through the ever-increasing multiplication of the demands upon it, the disturbance of nervous equilibrium as a result of the creation of artificial needs, and the stimulus of more and more urgent claims, the deadening of spiritual power caused by the breathless pace of our machine-like system of life, in which all the inner needs of man are reckoned as no more than sand in the bearings! One day we shall come to ourselves and ask: What is the object of all this perpetual strain, all this restless activity; what is the ultimate aim of this soul-destroying haste and competition? Is it so important that men should travel more and more rapidly from St. Petersburg to Paris, or that one nation should outdo another in the manufacture of the best motor-cars? All deeper life, all sacred peace and solemnity, all humanity's higher goods, all quiet love, are sacrificed to the insatiable demands of our ever-increasing material needs. Every section of society is compelled to join in this acceleration of life and this restless mutiplication of needs. Is it absolutely indispensable that the cultivation of the earth and the technical mastery of nature should be accompanied by this destruction of the deeper life of humanity?

There can be no doubt that, either through its own downfall or through a timely regeneration, the civilized world will be compelled to abandon its present belief that the immeasurable increase of personal needs is the proper basis of its economic activity. An age will come when social thought will be deepened and purified, and when, even outside the Catholic Church, St. Francis of Assisi will raise up new disciples under new conditions. There can be no real love without great sacrifice, no true communal life without great abnegation, no renovation of society without a heroic struggle against selfishness. The creation of artificial necessities for personal life is, however, an incentive to the growth of selfishness; while our slavish dependence upon a recognized "standard of life" is the deepest cause of the bitter obstinacy of the opposing parties in our economic conflicts. The humanization of the economic struggle cannot come about except through the adoption of new values resulting from the ascent of new and higher ideals of life. On the other hand, the increase of the purely materialistic view of life, with its concentration upon outward things, will drive the struggle to a bitterness and intensity of which we can to-day form no conception.

Would it not be possible for the initiative of the individual and the total economic energy of humanity to accomplish much higher achievements, if we could succeed in freeing ourselves from the tyranny of a morbid individualism and in placing ourselves under the inspiration of great ideals and institutions in the service of justice and Christian charity, while at the same time not depriving natural human individualism of all its scope?

To-day all this sounds Utopian. It will appear less so when our civilization has proceeded a few more decades along its present line. It will be perceived that no merely socialistic machinery will be capable of controlling its impulse. Along this path there will be developed a corporative brutality and selfishness which will show only too clearly what socialization of the means of production signifies, when it is carried on by mere communities or political majorities, and not supported by superior ideals.

There will be no escape from this, except through the spirit, and there will be none without the aid of religion; for the latter has most clearly and purely embodied and exhibited the spiritual and has best shown us the significance of spiritual freedom. We feel inclined to remark at this point that St. Francis of Assisi has still much to say to our civilization. This is not meant in the sense that our industrial economics should take the form of an Italian idyll; on the contrary, there must be a full recognition of all the great accomplishments of modern technical science. But our economic life must in a great measure be subordinated to the development of the soul. In this manner alone our technical and economic activity will receive a counteracting force in face of the immense temptations which result from the ever-increasing power of man over the gifts and forces of the external world. Therefore, the principle of asceticism, as an educational method and as a way of life on the part of individual gifted natures, does not stand in opposition to economic development, but is rather the condition of its health. When there is no such active opposition to the tyrannical power of material interests, then economic development falls entirely into the hands of an ever-increasing desire for pleasure and a more and more unprincipled selfishness—and in this case there must come a catastrophe in comparison with which all the previous crises through which our civilization has passed will seem almost insignificant.

We should, at any rate, bear in mind that the passionate antipathy of the modern man to the ascetic principle is connected with the *laissez faire, laissez aller,* and other characteristic tendencies of our great industrial system of competition. The personal deepening of the social idea will doubtless also contribute towards the counteraction of the reckless and unscrupulous multiplication of needs and luxuries, towards awakening an understanding of the education for inner freedom, and towards destroying that false and misleading doctrine of freedom which encourages all our inclinations to run riot, while allowing our higher nature to pass into decay.

Auguste Comte, the founder of sociology and the first really consistent social philosopher of the nineteenth century, was also the first modern thinker who again assigned to asceticism its full rights. This he did in the name of social education. It was his regular custom to eat a piece of dry bread instead of dessert, in order that he might not fail to recollect those who had not even bread. We may take this as a symbol of the imperishable social value of the ascetic principle. It may serve to remind us that the limitless satisfaction of our personal needs and passions brings us into unavoidable conflict with all really deep social life, and that we do not become free to think of others, unless we are thoroughly practiced in our own emancipation from our own moods and instincts. Only the really free man is capable of true social conduct. Of freedom, however, we may say that it can be attained only by those "who must conquer it daily."

146

CELIBACY

C. KEGAN PAUL [1]

There can be no question that two principles contended for mastery in the primitive Church: the inherent sanctity for marriage, which was raised into a sacrament of the Church, the still greater holiness of the celibate life, decreed under the Gospel as a counsel of perfection for those who are able to receive it. No doubt under the Old Law there were virgins who consecrated themselves to God, as the daughter of Jephthe, but the celibate life was an accident, and not an essential part of holiness: it was a penitent privation rather than a higher privilege; the maidens went year by year to lament their virginity; it was not even a part of the Nazarite vows, for Samson was twice married.

It was reserved for St. John the Baptist that he should be the first hermit of the desert, and for our Lady that she should be the first consecrated nun, though living ostensibly the life of a Jewish woman in the world. Then first was seen the supernatural virtue of purity, and the development of the human consciousness sprang up to greet the new type of human dignity. Evolution played its part in the spiritual life, and the Church stamped the development with its own seal. And as it has been reserved to certain physiologists of these later days to justify and even extol the lower nature which they conceive man to have risen out of, but not to have laid aside, so in these days have heretics dared to deny the eternal virginity of Mary, and

[1] International Catholic Truth Society.

have declared that they found the true type of womanhood in her supposed bearing of children to Joseph, rather than in her virgin conception of the Eternal Word; and of manhood, not in St. John the Baptist, St. John the Evangelist, and St. Joseph, but rather in the domestic life of the patriarchs, or the married priesthood of the Jewish church.

Long before St. Gregory made the rule of celibacy absolute on the Church, the sporadic usage of the early centuries had become all but universal, and this for reasons easy to understand. The position of woman had been increasingly raised in the Jewish church. The wives of patriarchs and kings had often claimed an equality with, at times even manifested a superiority to, their husbands, though there is no lack of signs that the Oriental seclusion of the harem attempted to assert itself among the Israelites. But it had not done so, and the fact that women shared their husband's interests made a sacerdotal caste in the Church necessary, in which women could have no part. The Sacrament of Penance would of itself require a celibate and lonely priesthood, for even with no intention of betraying confidences a man reveals involuntarily the secrets of others to those with whom he lives much. The greater the share which any good wife takes in her husband's work the more does she discover what is in his mind, and read his thoughts about others, even when she does not agree with them. Nor is it possible that those who are much together and in sympathy with each other should constantly discuss abstract questions. So soon as personal matters come into conversation it is not possible but that hints, however veiled, should be given, and revelations implicitly if not explicitly made. Indeed, when considered from the merely human side, it might be well that the freedom from ties of relationship should be extended beyond the priesthood. The school-master and the physician would be the better if they were able to say, with St. Paul, that the unmarried were solicitous for the things that belong to the Lord, how they may please God, and not be solicitous for the things of the world, how to please their wives, and so be divided. To the one his boys, to the other his patients, should be the first care, and the principle is just as applicable to the other sex, now that the care of the sick is more and more in the hands of women, and the higher learning within the reach of girls. In the middle ages the teaching and healing professions were entrusted to clerics and monks, already vowed to celibacy, and therefore, as by accident, the very principle for which we contend was carried out and ratified by the conscience of mankind. So a rule of the Church grew up which even in these laxer days is maintained as far as the clergy are concerned, nor is it likely to be laid aside by those who rightly grasp the principles of a Church and a sacerdotal caste.

147

BIRTH CONTROL

JOHN M. COOPER [1]

Marriage has a threefold purpose. First and primarily, its purpose is the begetting and rearing of children. Secondly, it fosters conjugal love and mutual helpfulness between man and wife. Thirdly, it allays the dangers of incontinence.

Promiscuous or free love relations might conceivably maintain the existence or being of the race, but its well-being would, under such a régime, suffer beyond description. Marriage makes for the maximum well-being of the race by providing maximum and permanent care by both parents in the upbringing of children; it ensures the maximum protection of the mother by the father; it pins down responsibility on the father by determining clearly who the true father is.

Marriage and parenthood are sacred. Parents are in no figurative sense but literally the agents and representatives of God in rearing children to be worthwhile citizens of the commonwealth of man and the commonwealth of God. Their task is to train up souls for this life and for the next. Their mission is a trusteeship than which none is more exalted and sublime. The vocation of a father and of a mother is a sacrosanct and holy one, so sacred that Christ saw fit to re-consecrate marriage by raising it to the dignity of a sacrament. The Catholic Church extols vir-

---

[1] *Birth Control*, pp. 5-11. (National Catholic Welfare Council, Washington, D. C.)

ginity as holy, for those who can take it. She likewise honors parenthood as holy and sacred. And she holds aloft both ideals in her reverence for and devotion to Mary, Virgin and Mother.

Time and again, in the history of Christianity, heretical groups have maintained that marriage is unlawful, and that the exercise of marital relations and the begetting of children thereby is sinful. The Church has consistently condemned in the strongest terms this suicidal position. Sexual intercourse within the marriage union is the means divinely established for the propagation of the race. But such intercourse outside the marriage union strikes a deadly blow at all three values that marriage protects and that promiscuous mating would utterly blast. For extra-marital intercourse tends to bring children into the world without proper provision for permanent and maximum care of offspring, without proper protection of motherhood, and without definite determination of paternity and paternal responsibility.

Within, however, the marital union, intercourse is not only lawful. It is divinely planned and sanctioned. The vague feeling sometimes met with that even within the marriage union such relations are indecent, or little short of sinful, or only reluctantly tolerated by morality, is an outgrowth of various causes. This feeling is in no sense an outgrowth of Catholic teaching, and it can find no shadow of support therein.

Not only is the marital relation within the marriage union lawful, but it is of the nature of a strict right. In the marriage contract, by which man and woman take each other for wedded mates until death do them part, they mutually confer on each other the right to marital relations. The two parties enter into the agreement freely and the mutual right is conferred on an absolutely equal plane. The contract is between equals and binds each and both with democratic equality.

Such being the marriage agreement, the refusal on the part of either party to grant the marital right constitutes a breach of contract, an injustice, provided, of course, there be no serious or grave reason for the refusal. Such a grave reason would be, for instance, uncondoned adultery on the part of the requesting husband or wife, the state of insanity or intoxication, grave danger to life or health of mate or of offspring from contagion, serious illness, or extraordinary suffering and peril in childbirth. And there may be other grave exempting grounds.

Husband and wife may, however, by mutual consent, forego the exercise of their marital rights, whether for a time or even permanently, if moral and other danger is absent. They are not strictly obliged to exercise the right at any particular time, and, if they both elect to abstain during certain days of the month, as, for example, the midmenstrual period, they are free to do so. Such abstention on the one hand places no unnatural obstacle in the way of procreation, and in the main is not open to the gravely harmful consequences that follow the use of direct contraceptive measures, and on the other hand may be fairly looked upon as a corollary of the general liberty to abstain by mutual consent when the parties so choose.

The Catholic position on the limitation of offspring is frequently misinterpreted by non-Catholics and sometimes misunderstood by Catholics themselves. It does not hold that married couples are under obligation to bring into the world the maximum number of children, to exercise no foresight or prudence, to bear offspring up to the limit of physiological fertility, to labor for the maximum increase of the population, to bring on "an avalanche of babies"—all regardless alike of circumstances and consequences. It holds no brief for imprudence or intemperance. It does emphatically stand for marital chastity against artificial prevention of conception.

The question is not primarily, Is it ethical to limit the number of offspring? but rather, What method is ethically justified in the accomplishment of this end, the method of abstinence and continence, or the method of artificial prevention? The two questions open up profoundly different ethical issues. If a married couple elect to practise continence and thus limit the number of offspring, they will not be infringing on Catholic principles. Such limitation by continence may at times be distinctly to be advised, as, for instance, when the mother's health or life would be seriously jeopardized by further childbearing, or when real destitution may result from further additions to the family.

But limitation of offspring by artificial prevention of conception is of its very nature immoral, and immoral means are not justified by ends however good. Having marital relations while at the same time using physiological, mechanical, or other means to prevent conception is, in accordance with Catholic ethics, ever and always immoral, sinful, and grievously sinful.

This attitude on the part of the Catholic Church is not a mere matter of ecclesiastical legislation, as are, for instance, such laws as those of fasting during Lent or of abstaining from meat on Fridays. She has no power to dispense in the premises. Her standard is not merely a matter of Church law. It is a matter of divine law over which the Church has no authority except the authority of promulgating it and of standing by it, come what may. Artificial prevention of conception is ever and always gravely sinful, just as adultery is.

Such is the historic stand of the Catholic conscience. What are the ethical grounds therefor? It is to the consideration of the more important of these grounds that we may now address ourselves.

There is a widespread if not universal shrinking from and repulsion towards artificial tampering with the functions of procreation. Unsophisticated mankind more generally looks upon contraceptive methods as unnatural, unclean, immoral. Most simple peoples on the lower cultural levels are little addicted to such practices, even peoples who do not scruple much at abortion and infanticide. Among peoples on the higher civilized levels of material culture, individuals or groups may reason themselves into an ethical defence of such methods and may acquire a certain relative callousness in practising them, but even they do not always succeed in entirely quenching the disgust and repugnance that the personal use of contraceptive measures commonly arouses in refined and high-principled natures.

The dictates of unsophisticated conscience in the field of sex are not, it is true, necessarily the last word in morality. They are not necessarily infallible. But, on the other hand, to brush them aside lightly as superstitious inheritances from a dark and ignorant past is perilously foolhardy. "To disregard instinctive [?] repugnances in matters of sex-morality is exceedingly dangerous, and would lead logically to the toleration of acts which all decent persons condemn." What of the disgust at and condemnation of unnatural and solitary vice? And what of the seemingly universal sense of shame, modesty, reticence, and reserve in sex matters? We may be pardoned for not instancing more lurid examples.

The real reasons underlying the moral intuitions of sex are not always obvious to the casual observer. How often do we find otherwise intelligent folks overlooking the profound protective value of, for instance, reasonable sex conventions and reasonable sex reticences? Or take a more striking example, the prohibition of near kin marriage. The deep horror at and the draconian prohibition of incestuous sex relations or of incestuous marriage, particularly between parent and offspring and between brother and sister, is practically universal among both uncivilized and civilized peoples. Yet how few individuals, even among educated and highly intelligent Christians, are at all aware of the real reasons that are back of their own social, moral, and religious condemnation of such relations and marriages.

Such condemnation is commonly supposed to rest on an assumed danger of giving birth to degenerate offspring. It does not rest, however, and historically has not rested on such a ground. Recent biological discoveries in heredity, while seemingly discounting to a considerable extent the theories prevalent in the last century regarding direct degeneration of the offspring of near kin unions, nevertheless on account of the hazards of transmission of undesirable latent recessive traits, are very far from lending approval to indiscriminate human inbreeding.

But even were such hazards altogether absent, the Catholic position would be quite unaffected. This position rests on other grounds and has historically so rested. The two more important of these have been: first, the social value of checking family clannishness and exclusiveness and of multiplying social bonds in the community; secondly, and above all, the profound necessity of preserving from taint the sanctuary of the home wherein the members must live day and night under promiscuous conditions that might readily give rise to grave immoralities, were not the severest taboo on sex rigidly enforced within the family circle. Some of the data from the Freudian psychology have seemingly thrown new light on this second consideration. St. Thomas, by the way, who clearly and explicitly sets forth the foregoing grounds, makes no mention whatever of the danger of degenerate offspring.

We have given space to this apparent digression from our subject to illustrate a vital point, namely, that sex reaches down into unfathomed depths of human nature, that its moral intuitions are fraught with far-reaching, albeit subtle and silent, consequences, and that the moral grounds for the tenets of sex codes are very often far from being so obvious that he who runs may read.

Such is emphatically the case in regard to birth control. The Catholic position thereon certainly does not rest primarily on the widespread attitude of disgust at contraceptive methods as unclean and immoral, yet it would be worse than folly to waive aside such an emotional and ethical reaction as of no moment. The bare fact of the existence of such a social or moral intuition is at its lowest valuation significant, a "stop, look, listen" sign.

148

THE ESSENTIAL FALLACIES OF MALTHUSIAN TEACHING

HALLIDAY G. SUTHERLAND [1]

1. *Malthus and the Neo-Malthusians*

Birth control, in the sense of the prevention of pregnancy by chemical, mechanical, or other artificial means, is being widely advocated as a sure method of lessening poverty and of increasing the physical and mental health of the nation. It is, therefore, advisable to examine these claims and the grounds on which they are based. The following investigation will prove that the propaganda throughout Western Europe and America in favor of artificial birth control is based on a mere assumption, bolstered up by economic and statistical fallacies; that Malthusian teaching is contrary to reason and to fact; that Neo-Malthusian practices are disastrous alike to nations and to individuals; and those practices are in themselves an offence against the Law of Nature, whereby the Divine Will is expressed in creation.

[1] *Birth Control*, pp. 1-22. (P. J. Kenedy & Sons, New York.)

(a) *Malthus*

The Rev. Thomas Malthus, M. A., in 1798 published his *Essay on the Principle of Population.* His pamphlet was an answer to Condorcet and Godwin, who held that vice and poverty were the result of human institutions and could be remedied by an even distribution of property. Malthus, on the other hand, believed that population increased more rapidly than the means of subsistence, and consequently that vice and poverty were always due to overpopulation and not to any particular form of society or of government. He stated that owing to the relatively slow rate at which the food supply of countries was increased, a high birth-rate [2] inevitably led to all the evils of poverty, war, and high death-rates. In an infamous passage he wrote that there was no vacant place for the superfluous child at Nature's mighty feast; that Nature told the child to be gone; and that she quickly executed her own order. This passage was modified in the second, and deleted from the third edition of the Essay. In later editions he maintained that vice and misery had checked population, that the progress of society might have diminished rather than increased the "evils resulting from the principle of population," and that by "moral restraint" overpopulation could be prevented. As Cannan has pointed out,[3] this last suggestion destroyed the force of the argument against Godwin, who could have replied that in order to make "moral restraint" universal a socialist State was necessary. In order to avoid the evils of overpopulation, Malthus advised people not to marry, or, if they did, to marry late in life and to limit the number of their children by the exercise of self-restraint. He reprobated all artificial and unnatural methods of birth control as immoral, and as removing the necessary stimulus to industry; but he failed to grasp the whole truth that an increase of population is necessary as a stimulus not only to industry, but also as essential to man's moral and intellectual progress.

---

[2] The birth-rate is the number of births per 1,000 of the whole population. In order to make a fair comparison between one community and another, the birth-rate is often calculated as the number of births per 1,000 married women between 15 and 45 years of age, as these constitute the great majority of child-bearing mothers. This is called the *corrected birth-rate.*

[3] *Economic Review,* January, 1892.

(b) *The Neo-Malthusians*

The Malthusian League accept the theory of their revered teacher, but, curiously enough, they reject his advice "as being impracticable and productive of the greatest possible evils to health and morality."[4] On the contrary, they advise universal early marriage, combined with artificial birth control. Although their policy is thus in flat contradiction to the policy of Malthus, there are two things common to both. Each is based on the same fallacy, and the aim of both is wide of the mark. Indeed, the Neo-Malthusian, like Malthus, has "a mist of speculation over his facts, and a vapour of fact over his ideas."[5] Moreover, as will be shown here, the path of the Malthusian League, although at first glance an easy way out of many human difficulties, is in reality the broad road along which a man or a nation travels to destruction; and as guides the Neo-Malthusians are utterly unsafe, since they argue from (*a*) false premises to (*b*) false deductions. We shall deal with the former in this chapter.

§ 2. TEACHING BASED ON FALSE PREMISES

The theory of Malthus is based on three errors, namely (*a*) that the population increases in geometrical progression, a progression of 1, 2, 4, 8, 16, and so on upwards; (*b*) that the food supply increases in arithmetical progression, a progression of 1, 2, 3, 4, 5, and so on upwards; and (*c*) that overpopulation is the cause of poverty and disease. If we show that *de facto* there *is* no overpopulation it obviously cannot be a cause of anything, nor be itself caused by the joint operation of the first two causes. However, each of the errors can be severally refuted.

(*a*) In the first place, it is true that a population *might* increase in geometrical progression, and that a woman *might* bear thirty children in her lifetime; but it is wrong to assume that because a thing *might* happen, it, therefore, does happen. The population, as a matter of fact, does not increase in geometrical progression, because Nature[6] places

---

[4] So says the Secretary of the Malthusian League. Vide *The Declining Birth-Rate*, 1916, p. 88.

[5] Bagehot, *Economic Studies*, p. 193.

[6] To assign a personality to "Nature" is, of course, a mere *façon de parler*; the believer holds that the "course of Nature" is an expression of the Mind and Will of the Creator.

her own checks on the birth-rate, and no woman bears all the children she might theoretically bear, apart altogether from artificial birth control.

(*b*) Secondly, the food supply does not of necessity increase in arithmetical progression, because food is produced by human hands, and is, therefore, increased in proportion to the increase of workers, unless the food supply of a country or of the world has reached its limit. The food supply of the world *might* reach a limit beyond which it could not be increased; but as yet this event has not happened, and there is no indication whatsoever that it is likely to happen.

Human life is immediately sustained by food, clothing, shelter, and fuel. Food and clothing are principally derived from fish, fowl, sheep, cattle, and grain, all of which *tend*, more so than man, to increase in *geometrical* ratio, although actually their increase in this progression is checked by man or by Nature. As regards shelter there can be no increase at all, either arithmetical or geometrical, apart from the work of human hands. Again, the stock of fuel in or on the earth cannot increase of itself, and is gradually becoming exhausted. On the other hand, within living memory, new sources of fuel, such as petroleum, have been made available, and old varieties of fuel have been used to better advantage, as witness the internal-combustion engine driven by smoke from sawdust. Moreover, in the ocean tides is a vast energy that one day may take the place of fuel.

(*c*) Thirdly, before anyone can reasonably maintain that overpopulation is the cause of poverty and disease, it is necessary to prove that overpopulation actually exists or is likely to occur in the future. By overpopulation we mean the condition of a country in which there are so many inhabitants that the production of necessaries of livelihood is insufficient for the support of all, with the result that many people are overworked or ill-fed. Under these circumstances the population can be said to *press on the soil*: and, unless their methods of production could be improved, or resources secured from outside, the only possible remedy against the principle of diminishing returns would be a reduction of population; otherwise, the death-rate from want and starvation would gradually rise until it equalled the birth-rate in order to maintain an unhappy equilibrium.

§ 3. THE ROOT FALLACY

According to Malthusian doctrine overpopulation is the cause of poverty, disease, and war; and consequently, unless the growth of population is artificially restrained, all attempts to remedy social evils are futile. Malthusians claim that "if only the devastating torrent of children could be arrested for a few years, it would bring untold relief." They hold that overpopulation is the root of all social evil, and the truth or falsehood of that proposition is, therefore, the basis of all their teaching. Now, when Malthusians are asked to prove that this their basic proposition is true, they adopt one of two methods, not of proof, but of evasion. Their first method of evading the question is by asserting that the truth of their proposition is self-evident and needs no proof. To that we reply that the falsity of the proposition can and will be proved. Their second device is to put up a barrage of facts which merely show that all countries, and, indeed, the earth itself, would have been overpopulated long ago if the increase of population had not been limited by certain factors, ranging from celibacy and late marriages to famines, diseases, wars, and infanticide. The truth of these facts is indisputable, but it is, nevertheless, a manifest breach of logic to argue from the fact of poverty, disease, and war having checked an increase of population, that, therefore, poverty, disease, and war are due to an increase of population. It would be as reasonable to argue that, because an unlimited increase of insects is prevented by birds and by climatic changes, therefore, an increase of insects accounts for the existence of birds, and for variations of climate. Nor is it of any use for Malthusians to say that overpopulation *might* be the cause of poverty. They cannot prove that it *is* the cause of poverty, and, as will be shown in the following chapter, more obvious and probable causes are staring them in the face. For our present purpose it will suffice if we are able to prove that overpopulation has not occurred in the past and is unlikely to occur in the future.

§ 4. WHAT OVERPOPULATION MEANS

In the first place, the meaning of the word "overpopulation" should be clearly understood. The word does not mean a very large number of inhabitants in a country. If that were its meaning the Malthusian fallacy could be disproved by merely pointing out that poverty exists both in thinly populated and in thickly populated countries. Now, in reality, overpopulation would occur whenever the production of the necessities of life in a country was insufficient for the support of all the inhabitants. For example, a barren rock in the ocean would be overpopulated, even if it contained only one inhabitant. It follows that the term "overpopulation" should be applied only to an economic situation in which the population presses on the soil. The point may be illustrated by a simple example.

Let us assume that a fertile island of 100 acres is divided into 10 farms, each of 10 acres, and each capable of supporting a family of ten. Under these conditions the island could support a population of 1,000 people without being overpopulated. If, however, the numbers in each family increased to 20 the population would *press on the soil,* and the island, with 2,000 inhabitants, would be an example of overpopulation, and of poverty due to overpopulation.

On the other hand, let us assume that there are only 1,000 people on the island, but that one family of ten individuals has managed to gain possession of eight farms, in addition to their own, and that the other nine families are forced to live on one farm. Obviously, 900 people would be attempting to live under conditions of dire poverty, and the island, with its population of 1,000, would now offer an example, not of overpopulation, but of human selfishness.

My contentions are that poverty is neither solely nor, indeed, generally related to economic pressure on the soil; that there are many causes of poverty apart altogether from overpopulation; and that in reality overpopulation does not exist in those countries where Malthusians claim to find proofs of social misery due to a high birth-rate.

If overpopulation in the economic sense occurred in a closed country, whose inhabitants were either unable or unwilling to send out colonies, it is obvious that general poverty and misery would result. This *might* happen in small islands, but it is of greater interest to know what does happen.

§ 5. NO EVIDENCE OF OVERPOPULATION

In a closed country, producing all its own necessities of life and incapable of expansion, a high birth-rate would eventually increase the struggle for existence and would lead to overpopulation, always provided that, firstly, the high birth-rate is accompanied by a low death-rate, and, secondly, that the high birth-rate is maintained. For example, although a birth-rate was high, a population would not increase in numbers if the death-rate was equally high. Therefore, a high birth-rate does not of necessity imply that population will be increased or that overpopulation will occur. Again, if the birth-rate fell as the population increased, the danger of overpopulation would be avoided without the aid of a high death-rate. For a moment, however, let us assume that the Malthusian premise is correct, that a high birth-rate has led to overpopulation, and that the struggle for existence has, therefore, increased. Then, obviously, the death-rate would rise; the effect of the high birth-rate would be neutralised; and beyond a certain point neither the population nor the struggle for existence could be further increased. On these grounds Neo-Malthusians argue that birth-control is necessary precisely to obviate that cruel device whereby Nature strives to restore the balance upset by a reckless increase of births; and that the only alternative to frequent and premature deaths is regulation of the source of life. As a corollary to this proposition they claim that, if the death-rate be reduced, a country is bound to become overpopulated unless the births are artificially controlled. Fortunately it is possible to test the truth of this corollary, because certain definite observations on this very point have been recorded. These observations do not support the argument of birth controllers.

(a) *In the Suez Canal Zone*

In the Suez Canal Zone there was a high death-rate chiefly owing to fever. According to Malthus it would have been a great mistake to lower this death-rate, because, if social conditions were improved, the population would rapidly increase and exceed the resources of the country. Now, in fact, the social conditions were improved, the death-rate was lowered, and the subsequent events, utterly refuting the above contention, are thus noted by Dr. Halford Ross, who was medical officer in that region:

During the years 1901 to 1910, health measures in this zone produced a very considerable fall in the death-rate, from 30.2

per thousand to 19.6 per thousand; the infant mortality was also reduced very greatly, and it was expected that, after a lapse of time, the reduction of the death-rate would result in a rise of the birth-rate, and a corresponding increase of the population. *But such was not the case.* When the death-rate fell, the birth-rate fell too, and the number of the population remained the same as before, even after nearly a decade had passed, and notwithstanding the fact that the whole district had become much healthier, and one town, Port Said, was converted from an unhealthy, fever-stricken place into a seaside health resort.[7]

Moreover, Dr. Halford Ross has told me that artificial birth control was not practised in this region, and played no part in maintaining a stationary population. The majority of the people were strict Mohammedans, amongst whom the practice of birth control is forbidden by the Koran.

(b) *In "Closed Countries" like Japan*

But a much more striking example of the population in a closed country remaining stationary without the practice of birth control, thus refuting the contention of our birth controllers, is to be found in their own periodical, *The Malthusian.*[8] It would appear that in Japan from 1723 to 1846 the population remained almost stationary, only increasing from 26,065,422 to 26,907,625. In 1867 the Shogunate was abolished, the Emperor was restored, and Japan began to be a civilized power. Now from 1872 the population increased by 10,649,990 in twenty-seven years, and "during the period between 1897 and 1907 the population received an increment of 11.6 per cent, whereas the food-producing area increased by only 4.4 per cent.... According to Professor Morimoro, the cost of living is now so high in Japan that 98 per cent of the people do not get enough to eat." From these facts certain obvious deductions may be made. So long as Japan was a closed country her population remained stationary. When she became a civilised industrial power the mass of her people became poorer, the birth-rate rose, and the population increased, this last result being the real problem to-day in the Far East. In face of these facts it is sheer comedy to learn that our

[7] *Problems of Population*, p. 382.
[8] *The Malthusian*, July 15, 1921.

Malthusians are sending a woman to preach birth control amongst the Japanese! Do they really believe that for over a hundred years Japan, unlike most semi-barbaric countries, practised birth control, and that when she became civilised she refused, unlike most civilised countries, to continue this practice? There is surely a limit to human credulity.

The truth appears to be that in closed countries the population remains more or less stationary, that Nature herself checks the birth-rate without the aid of artificial birth control, and that birth-rates and death-rates are independently related to the means of subsistence.

§ 6. A NATURAL LAW CHECKING FERTILITY

During the past century the population of Europe increased by about 160,000,000, but it is utterly unreasonable to assume that this rate of increase will be maintained during the present century. It would be as sensible to argue that because a child is four feet high at the age of ten he will be eight feet high at the age of twenty. Moreover, there is evidence that, apart altogether from vice, the fertility of a nation is reduced at every step in civilisation. The cause of this reduction in fertility is unknown. It is probably a reaction to many complex influences, and possibly associated with the vast growth of great cities. This decline in the fertility of a community is a natural protection against the possibility of overpopulation; but, on the other hand, there is a point beyond which any further decline in fertility will bring a community within sight of depopulation and of extinction.

§ 7. OVERPOPULATION IN THE FUTURE

It is a fallacy to say that overpopulation is the cause of poverty and disease, and that for the simple reason that overpopulation has not yet occurred. For the growth of a nation we assume that the birth-rate should exceed the death-rate by from 10 to 20 per thousand, and it is obvious that in a *closed* country the evil of overpopulation might appear in a comparatively short time. The natural remedies in the past have been emigration and colonisation. According to the birth controllers these remedies are only temporary, because sooner or later all colonies and eventually the earth itself will be overpopulated. At the British Association meeting in 1890 the population of the earth was said to be 1,500 millions, and it was calculated that only 6,000 millions could live on the earth. This means that if the birth-rate throughout the world exceeded the death-rate by only 8 per thousand, the earth would be overpopulated within 200 years. It is probable that in these calculations the capacity of the earth to sustain human life has been underestimated; that the earth could support not four times but sixteen times its present population; and that the latter figure could be still further increased by the progress of inventions. But, apart altogether from the accuracy of these figures, the danger of overpopulation is nothing more or less than a myth. Indeed, the end of the world, a philosophic and scientific certitude, is a more imminent event than its overpopulation.

§ 8. HOW NATIONS HAVE PERISHED

Before speculating on what might happen in the future, it is well to recollect what has happened in the past. The earth has been inhabited for thousands of years, and modern research has revealed the remains of many ancient civilisations that have perished. For example, there were the great nations of Cambodia and of Guatemala. In Crete, about 2000 B. C., there existed a civilisation where women were dressed as are this evening the women of London and Paris. That civilisation perished, and even its language cannot now be deciphered. Why did these civilisations perish? Surely this momentous question should take precedence over barren discussions as to whether there will be sufficient food on the land or in the sea for the inhabitants of the world in 200 years' time. How came it about that these ancient nations did not double their numbers every fifty years and fill up the earth long ago?

The answer is that they were overcome and annihilated by the incidence of one or other of two dangers that threaten every civilisation, including our own. These dangers are certain physical and moral catastrophes, against which there is only one form of natural insurance, namely, a birth-rate that adequately exceeds the death-rate. They help to illustrate further the fallacy of the overpopulation scare.

The following is a general outline of these dangers.

§ 9. PHYSICAL CATASTROPHES

Deaths from famine, floods, earthquakes, and volcanic eruptions are confined to comparatively small areas, and the two physical catastrophes that may seriously threaten a civilisation may be reduced to endemic disease and war.

(a) *Disease*

Disease, in the form of malaria, contributed to the fall of ancient Greece and Rome. In the fourteenth century 25,000,000 people, one-quarter of the population of Europe, were exterminated by plague, the "Black Death," and in the sixteenth century smallpox depopulated Spanish America. Although these particular diseases have lost much of their power owing to the progress of medical science, we have no right to assume that disease in general has been conquered by our civilisation, or that a new pestilence may not appear. On the contrary, in 1805, a new disease, spotted fever, appeared in Geneva, and within half a century had become endemic throughout Europe and America. Of this fever during the Great War the late Sir William Osler wrote: "In cerebro-spinal fever we may be witnessing the struggle of a new disease to win a place among the great epidemics of the world." There was a mystery about this disease, because, although unknown in the Arctic Circle, it appeared in temperate climates during the coldest months of the year. As I was able to prove in 1915,[9] it is a disease of civilisation. I found that the causal organism was killed in thirty minutes by a temperature of 62° F. It was thus obvious that infection could never be carried by cold air. But in overcrowded rooms where windows are closed, and the temperature of warm, impure, saturated air was raised by the natural heat of the body to 80° F. or over, the life of the micro-organism, expelled from the mouths of infected people during the act of coughing, was prolonged. Infection is thus carried from one person to another by warm currents of moving air, and at the same time resistance against the disease is lowered. Cold air kills the organism, but cold weather favours the disease. In that paradox the ætiology of cerebro-spinal fever became as clear as the means of prevention. The story of spotted fever reveals the forces of nature fighting against the disease at

[9] *Lancet*, 1915, vol. ii, p. 862.

every turn, and implacably opposed to its existence, while man alone, of his own will and folly, harbours infection and creates the only conditions under which the malady can appear. For example, during two consecutive winters cerebro-spinal fever had appeared in barracks capable of housing 2,000 men. A simple and effective method of ventilation was then introduced. From that day to this not a single case of cerebro-spinal fever has occurred in these barracks, although there have been outbreaks of this disease in the town in which the barracks are situated.

There are many other diseases peculiar to civilisation, and concerning the wherefore and the why an apposite passage occurs in the works of Sir William Gull.

Causes affecting health and shortening life may be inappreciable in the individual, but sufficiently obvious when their effect is multiplied a thousandfold. If the conditions of society render us liable to many diseases, they in return enable us to establish the general laws of life and health, a knowledge of which soon becomes a distributive blessing. The cure of individual diseases, whilst we leave open the dark fountains from which they spring, is to labour like Sisyphus, and have our work continually returning upon our hands. And, again, there are diseases over which, directly, we have little or no control, as if Providence had set them as signs to direct us to wider fields of inquiry and exertion. Even partial success is often denied, lest we should rest satisfied with it, and forget the *truer and better means* of prevention.[1]

Medical and sanitary science have made great progress in the conquest of enteric fever, diphtheria, scarlet fever, measles, and whooping cough. The mortality from bronchitis and from pulmonary tuberculosis has also been reduced, but, nevertheless, tuberculosis still claims more victims in the prime of life than any other malady. It is a disease of civilisation and is intimately associated with economic conditions. The history of tuberculosis has yet to be written. On the other hand, deaths from certain other diseases are actually increasing, as witness the following figures from the Reports of the Registrar-General for England and Wales:

---

[1] *The New Sydenham Society,* vol. clvi, section viii, p. 12.

Disease	Number of Deaths in 1898	Number of Deaths in 1919
Diseases of the heart and circulatory system	50,492	69,637
Pneumonia	35,462	38,949
Cancer	25,196	42,144
Influenza	10,405	44,801

In view of these figures it is folly to suppose that the final conquest of disease is imminent.

(b) *War*

War, foreign or civil, is another sword hanging over civilisations, whereby the fruits of a long period of growth may be destroyed in a few years. After the Thirty Years War the recovery of Germany occupied a century and a half. During the fourteen years of the Taiping rebellion in China whole provinces were devastated and millions upon millions of people were killed or died. In spite of the Great War during the past decade, there are some who would delude themselves and others into the vain belief that, without a radical change in international relations and a determined effort to neutralise its causes, there will be no more war; but unless the nations learn through Christianity that justice is higher than self-interest the following brilliant passage by Devas is as true to-day as when it was written in 1901:

True, that the spread of humanitarianism and cosmopolitanism made many people think, towards the end of the nineteenth century, that bloodshed was at an end. But their hopes were dreams: the visible growth of national rivalry and gigantic armaments can only issue in desperate struggles; while not a few among the nations are troubled with the growth of internal dissensions and accumulations of social hatred that point to bloody catastrophes in the future; and the tremendous means of destruction that modern science puts in our hands offer frightful possibilities of slaughter, murderous anarchical outrages, and rivers of blood shed in pitiless repression.[2]

Malthusians may inveigh against wars waged to achieve the expansion of a nation, but so long as international rivalry disregards the moral law their words will neither stop war nor prevent a Malthusian country from falling an easy prey to a stronger people. On the contrary, a low

---

[2] Charles S. Devas, *Political Economy*, 1901, p. 191.

birth-rate, by reducing the potential force available for defence, is actually an incentive to a declaration of war from an envious neighbour, because it means that he will not hesitate so long when attempting to count the cost beforehand. In 1850 the population of France and Germany numbered practically the same, 35,500,000; in 1913 that of France was 39,600,000, that of Germany 67,000,000.[3] The bearing of these facts on the Great War is obvious. In 1919 the new Germany, including Silesia, had a population of just over 60,000,000; whereas, in 1921, France, including Alsace-Lorraine, had a population of 39,200,000. Thus, despite her victory in the war, the population of France is less to-day than it was seven years ago.

§ 10. MORAL CATASTROPHES

In view of past history only an ostrich with its head in the sand can profess to believe that there will be no calamities in the future to reduce the population of the earth. And apart from cataclysms of disease or of war, empires have perished by moral catastrophe. A disbelief in God results in selfishness, and in various moral catastrophes. In the terse phrase of Mr. Bernard Shaw, "Voluptuaries prosper and perish."[4] For example, during the second century B. C. the disease of rationalism[5] spread over Greece, and a rapid depopulation of the country began.

The facts were recorded by Polybius,[6] who expressly states that at the time of which he is writing serious pestilences did not occur, and that depopulation was caused by the selfishness of the Greeks, who, being addicted to pleasure, either did not marry at all or refused to rear more than one or two children, lest it should be impossible to bring them up in extravagant luxury. This ancient historian also noted that the death of a son in war or by pestilence is a serious matter when there are only one or two sons in a family. Greece fell to the conquering Romans, and they also in course of time were infected with

---

[3] *Revue Pratique d'Apologétique,* September 15, 1914.
[4] *Man and Superman,* p. 195.
[5] By rationalism we mean a denial of God and of responsibility for conduct to a Higher Being.
[6] Quoted by W. H. S. Jones, *Malaria and Greek History,* 1909, p. 95.

this evil canker. There came a day when over the battlements of Constantinople the blood-red Crescent was unfurled. Later on all Christendom was threatened, and the King of France appealed to the Pope for men and arms to resist the challenge to Europe of the Mohammedan world. The Empire of the Turk spread over the whole of South-Eastern Europe. But once more the evil poison spread, this time into the homes in many parts of Islam, and to-day the once triumphant foes of Christianity are decaying nations whose dominions are the appanage of Europe. In face of these facts it is sheer madness to assume that all the Great Powers now existing will maintain their population and prove immune from decay. Indeed, the very propaganda against which this Essay is directed is in itself positive proof that the seeds of decay have already been sown within the British Empire. Yet, in an age in which thought and reason are suppressed by systematised confusion and spiritless perplexity, the very simplicity of a truth will operate against its general acceptance.

From the theological point of view, the myth of overpopulation is definitely of anti-Christian growth, because it assumes that, owing to the operation of natural instincts implanted in mankind by the Creator, the only alternative offered to the race is a choice between misery and vice, an alternative utterly incompatible with Divine goodness in the government of the world.

149

DUTIES RESULTING FROM THE MARRIAGE RELATION

René I. Holaind [1]

The conjugal union of man and woman has for its natural consequence the continuance of the family and the permanency of human society. Hence the main purpose of matrimony is the raising and education of children till they have reached the fulness of manhood and womanhood. But this is not the only purpose of married life. Each sex is

---

[1] *Natural Law and Legal Practice*, pp. 183-189. (Benziger Brothers, New York.)

imperfect, insomuch as neither contains all the potentialities of human nature; as a consequence, the complete type of humanity unites both sexes in the bonds of conjugal love. When God created man, *Male and female He created them* (Gen. 1, 27).

Hence the secondary purpose of matrimony is the complement, physical and moral, of both sexes.

If we condense in a short formula what we have said of the nature of marriage, the result will be the following definition: Marriage is the union of one man and one woman in a community of life, hallowed by conjugal love, formed by the united consent of both parties to last until death part them, ordained by nature for the continuance and increase of the human race and the complement of both sexes.

It will be observed that we have not said, raised by Christ to the dignity of a sacrament. We have left out this important clause because it is theological in its character, and would prevent our definition from being universal. But we are not blind to the fact that to take away from marriage its character as a sacred rite is to tear down the strongest barrier that can be opposed to mere animal passions. Replying to those who said that pure and happy marriages were not dreams but facts, Count Tolstoi says somewhere: "All that was possible when marriage was a sacrament." There is more in this remark than a fling at modern society. When marriage is not a sacrament it is apt to become a mere temporary association, from which all sacredness has departed, and which is not secure enough to be the foundation of civil society.

Passing over in silence the reciprocal duties of married persons, duties which are commonly well known, if not always faithfuly observed, we shall come to the duties of parents to their children. By Blackstone they are reduced to three: maintenance, protection, education. Four evident reasons show that this threefold duty follows directly from natural law: 1st, every moral agent is accountable for the consequences of his own acts, so far as he can foresee them; on him it is incumbent to provide that those consequences be not hurtful, but beneficial. But the birth of children is the result of an act of the free will of their parents. Therefore, it is the bounden duty of the parents to see that the life which they have given be not a curse, but a blessing. It could not be a blessing were the duties mentioned, especially that of education, neglected; therefore, it is the duty for the parents to provide for the maintenance, protection, and *education* of their children; and that duty would exist of necessity even if positive law should fail to sanction it; for even in that case the natural relation of parents to children would remain essentially unchanged.

2nd. As we have seen, the end of nature in the marriage relation is to secure the continuance and perfection of the human race; but this purpose would evidently be defeated if the three obligations above mentioned were neglected by the parents; therefore, those obligations are laid upon them by nature itself. Blackstone says: "The last duty of parents to their children is that of giving them an education suitable to their station in life; a duty pointed out by reason, and of far the greatest importance of any. For, as Puffendorf very well observes, it is not easy to imagine or allow that a parent has conferred any considerable benefit upon his child by bringing him into the world, if he afterward entirely neglects his culture and education, and suffers him to grow up like a mere beast, to lead a life useless to others and shameful to himself."[2]

We must add that by this neglect the parent not only sins against the child and against society, but also thwarts the beneficent purpose of the Creator in instituting matrimony.

3d. A universal impulse which is not only rational and human, but which is reproduced in the instinct of animals, is, according to Roman jurisconsults and to reason itself, the unmistakable token of natural law. But such is the impulse of parents to accomplish the three duties mentioned, and it finds its counterpart even in the instinct of animals. Therefore, those duties are imposed by natural law. We quote in full the celebrated text of Ulpian: "Natural law is that which nature has taught all living beings, for it is not the exclusive property of man, but it reaches all the animals which live in the air, on the earth, or in the depths of the sea. Hence flow the union of man and woman, which we call matrimony; hence the procreation of children; hence their education."

---

[2] *Blackstone's Commentaries,* vol. I, n. 451.

4th. Where there is a special and natural fitness, there, also, is laid a special and natural duty; but parents have a special and natural fitness to educate their own children; hence it is their special and natural duty. The minor premise is evidenced by observation both of private and of social life. Nothing can supply the love of a mother or the mild firmness of a father. Young orphans are at a disadvantage at the start, as keen observers of human nature well know. After insisting on the duty of the parents to educate their children in a manner suitable to their station and calling, Chancellor Kent makes the following important observation: "Several of the States of antiquity were too solicitous to form their youth for the various duties of civil life, even to intrust their education solely to the parent; but this, as in Crete and Sparta, was upon the principle, totally inadmissible in the modern civilized world, of the absorption of the individual in the body politic, and of his entire subjection to the despotism of the State."

History has proved that it is unwise to depart from the natural law either by encroaching on parental rights, or by conferring on parents rights which natural law does not sanction. One of the Grecian States, Sparta, shifted the responsibility from the parents to the State. It interfered with nature's law, and the consequence was that Sparta did not produce a single poet, a single orator, a single statesman of superior ability, unless it be Lycurgus, who invented the system but was not reared according to it. For a time it had warriors, but even these at last were wanting, and Sparta was conquered by the other commonwealths, on which in the beginning she was wont to impose her will. Rome committed another fault, that of giving by law to the father an authority which had no warrant in nature; but although she paid the forfeit in the end, yet she can boast of a succession of great men down to the last period of decline.

"The father," says Blackstone, "may delegate part of his parental authority during his life to the tutor or schoolmaster of his child, who is then, *in loco parentis,* and has such a portion of the power of the parent committed to his charge, namely, that of restraint and correction, as may be necessary to answer the purpose for which he is employed.

... The power of the parents over their children is derived from ... their duty."

The duties of the children offer no serious ethical difficulty; they are often explained but seldom enforced sufficiently. They owe to their parents reverence, obedience, and love; they must help their parents to support the family, and give them maintenance when strength and resources fail them. To the performance of those duties they are bound in strict justice, but they have also their rights. They are not the *things* of their parents; they are human persons, holding the moral powers inherent to personality, and entitled to the necessary means to work out their destiny.

The family is a complete society, having its own organization, its own rights, and its own directing power; by nature itself its power is invested in the father, the head of the household, and in the mother, who has her own sphere of action, and must have her share of parental authority. Within its own sphere—that is, with regard to marriage, *to the raising and education of children*—the family does not depend on the State. The family, both in concept and in fact, existed before the commonwealth, and, therefore, cannot have derived its special rights and duties from the commonwealth. The *personal* rights of the individual must be respected by the family, and the special rights of the household must be protected by the State. In order to protect the family against all aggressions within and without the commonwealth, the State is armed with extensive powers which, according as they are used justly or unjustly, may secure liberty or crush it.

150

THE DUTY OF CARING FOR THE CHILD

Michael Cronin [1]

It is quite obvious that the child if left to itself in the first years of its existence must simply perish. For continuance in life it depends altogether on the ministrations of others. From itself it can obtain neither food nor

---

[1] *The Science of Ethics*, vol. II, pp. 394-397. (Benziger Brothers, New York.)

clothing or any other thing necessary for its life. And if the ministrations of others are necessary for the life, so also are they necessary for the development of the child. We are speaking here, not of those higher stages of human development which go to make up what is known as the higher or civilized life, and for which, as we shall show later on, much more is required than mere stability of union between man and woman, but merely of those simpler attainments which might legitimately be expected of the human race at any period of its development, and even these, we claim, the child is not capable of reaching by its own exertions. Even after the first couple of years of its life have passed away, during which the child is utterly helpless and dependent on others for its life, the child is still dependent on others for its growth and development, both in the physical and the mental order. A child of seven or eight years is in no condition to procure a living for itself, whilst the degree of development, mental and moral, attained at that age is not much higher than the level of ordinary animal perfection, and, such as it is, it would quickly be lost again were the child to be abandoned to its own resources.

These things will hardly be called in question by any sensible person, for they are obvious truths based upon ordinary reason and experience. But they assume a new significance and become more cogent and instructive when we go on to compare the provision which nature makes for the offspring of animals with the want of natural provision apparent in the case of the child. The young of most animals are, very early in their lives, enabled to dispense with the services of others. Their clothing is from nature; through their natural instincts and capacities they are soon fitted to acquire the necessary food and to live and move and develop fully from themselves. The bird that is only a short while out of its nest is physically and psychically almost as perfect as ever it will or could become; and whatever degree of perfection it may lack at that period will surely come to it later, but automatically as it were, and even without the need of its own co-operation. The child, on the other hand, even after the long period is over during which nutrition can be obtained only from another, is still only at the beginning of the period of growth and development, physical, mental, and moral. To abandon the child before it is physically mature would be equivalent almost to depriving it of food, whilst to abandon it even after physical growth is assured, and before at least the minimum degree of mental and moral training has been attained, would be to leave the child, as a human being, stunted and deformed, as truly so as if physically it had failed to grow for want of material nourishment. The child, therefore, is not in a position to live or develop of itself, but is naturally dependent on others, even for many years after it has attained the use of reason.

From what we have been saying it will be evident that by natural law there devolves on somebody other than the child a duty of caring for the child during a period extending over many years. And that this natural duty devolves in the first instance and essentially on the parent will readily be admitted by any one who considers the position of the parent in regard to the child. For it is the parents who have brought the child into existence, and, therefore, on the parent devolves the duty of providing those things that are necessary for its existence and for its development. A child might, indeed, for a number of reasons pass into the guardianship of another, and be nurtured and educated by that other. But it is on the parent that this duty devolves in the first instance; and even if others should take up this work, the parent must always be available, ready to aid it at any time, should the child call for his or her presence and assistance. For this is the primary and inalienable right of the child—to call upon those who have given it existence for aid and guidance in the infantine and, certainly, also during the early adult period.

And in this connection it is important to remember that nature knows nothing of any other guardian for the child than its own parents. The State, for instance, it knows in other capacities as necessary for the defence of the nation or for supplying the means of social progress. But of the State as nurse of the child nature knows nothing. Nature has set up the parents as the proper owners and guardians of the child, first, in the fact that the parents are its natural causes, and secondly by the thousand and one physical and mental ties by which it has bound parent and child into one distinctive natural group. To the mother it has given milk, naturally destined for her own child, beginning, as this fount of nurture does, with the life of the child, and continuing as long as the child requires. Also, both parents and child are supplied by nature with instincts of affection, one for the other, which no other relationship can satisfy or replace. The parent, therefore, is the only guardian known to nature, and, consequently, on the parent devolves the natural duty of rearing and caring for the child. Our argument may be thus briefly expressed: the parent is the cause of the child's existence and, therefore, is charged with caring for its welfare; the parent is supplied by nature with the essential means required for the rearing of the child, and is thus designated by nature herself as its proper and exclusive guardian.

151
DISCUSSION OF THE RIGHTS OF THE STATE TO EDUCATE

James A. Burns [1]

In connection with the practical plans for the settlement of the "school question" there has been frequent discussion among Catholic educators and apologists as to the rights of the State in respect to education. Dr. Brownson would deny to the State the right to educate, in the strict and proper sense of the term, although he conceded to it the right to establish and maintain public schools. This was the view more generally held by American Catholic educators. In the year 1891 the Rev. Thomas Bouquillon, D. D., professor of moral theology at the Catholic University, Washington, issued a pamphlet in which he maintained that the State has the right to educate in the sense that it has the right of "establishing schools, appointing teachers, prescribing methods and programs of study"; and that "education belongs to men taken individually and collectively in legitimate association, to the family, to the state, to the church, to all four together, and not to any one of these four factors separately." These views aroused a storm of controversy which lasted for several years, and engaged the

[1] *Catholic Encyclopedia*, vol. XIII, p. 583.

attention not only of Catholics of the United States but of the whole Catholic world. The efforts of Cardinal Satolli to settle the question by means of a series of fourteen propositions which he submitted to the board of archbishops at their meeting in New York, in the autumn of 1892, were futile; and the agitation subsided only when Pope Leo XIII addressed a letter to the American hierarchy through Cardinal Gibbons in May, 1893, in which, while appealing for the cessation of the controversy, he declared that the decrees of the Baltimore Councils were to be steadfastly observed in determining the attitude to be maintained by Catholics in respect both to parish and to public schools.

152

THE CATHOLIC ATTITUDE ON EDUCATION[1]

Inasmuch as permanent peace on a sound basis is the desire of all our people, it is necessary to provide for the future by shaping the thought and guiding the purpose of our children and youth toward a complete understanding and discharge of their duties. Herein lies the importance of education and the responsibility of those to whom it is entrusted. Serious at all times, the educational problem is now graver and more complex by reason of the manifold demands that are made on the school, the changes in our industrial conditions, and above all, by reason of the confusion and error which obscure the purpose of life and therefore of true education.

Nevertheless, it is mainly through education that our country will accomplish its task and perpetuate its free institutions. Such is the conviction that inspires much of the activity displayed in this field, whether by individuals or by organizations. Their confidence is naturally strengthened by the interest which is taken in the school, the enlarged facilities for instruction and the increased efficiency of educational work.

But these again are so many reasons for insisting that education shall move in the right direction. The more

[1] *Joint Pastoral of the Archbishops and Bishops of the United States,* 1919.

thorough it becomes, the greater is its power either for good or for evil. A trained intelligence is but a highly tempered instrument, whose use must depend on the character of its possessor. Of itself knowledge gives no guarantee that it will issue in righteous action, and much less that it will redound to the benefit of society. As experience too plainly shows, culture of the highest order, with abundance of knowledge at its command, may be employed for criminal ends and be turned to the ruin of the very institutions which gave it support and protection. While, therefore, it is useful to improve education by organizing the work of the schools, enriching the content of knowledge and refining the methods of teaching, it is still more necessary to insure that all educational activity shall be guided by sound principles toward the attainment of its true purpose.

The Church in our country is obliged, for the sake of principle, to maintain a system of education distinct and separate from other systems. It is supported by the voluntary contributions of Catholics who, at the same time, contribute as required by law to the maintenance of the public schools. It engages in the service of education a body of teachers who consecrate their lives to this high calling; and it prepares, without expense to the State, a considerable number of Americans to live worthily as citizens of the Republic.

Our system is based on certain convictions that grow stronger as we observe the testing of all education, not simply by calm theoretic discussion, but by the crucial experience of recent events. It should not have required the pitiless searching of war to determine the value of any theory or system, but since that rude test has been so drastically applied and with such unmistakable results, we judge it opportune to restate the principles which serve as the basis of Catholic education.

First: The right of the child to receive education and the correlative duty of providing it are established on the fact that man has a soul created by God and endowed with capacities which need to be developed, for the good of the individual and the good of society. In its highest meaning, therefore, education is a co-operation by human agencies with the Creator for the attainment of His purpose in regard to the individual who is to be educated, and in regard to the social order of which he is a member. Neither self-realization alone nor social service alone is the end of education, but rather these two in accordance with God's design, which gives to each of them its proportionate value. Hence it follows that education is essentially and inevitably a moral activity in the sense that it undertakes to satisfy certain claims through the fulfilment of certain obligations. This is true independently of the manner and means which constitute the actual process; and it remains true, whether recognized or disregarded in educational practice, whether this practice include the teaching of morality, or exclude it, or try to maintain a neutral position.

Second: Since the child is endowed with physical, intellectual and moral capacities, all these must be developed harmoniously. An education that quickens the intelligence and enriches the mind with knowledge, but fails to develop the will and direct it to the practice of virtue, may produce scholars, but it cannot produce good men. The exclusion of moral training from the educative process is more dangerous in proportion to the thoroughness with which the intellectual powers are developed, because it gives the impression that morality is of little importance, and thus sends the pupil into life with a false idea which is not easily corrected.

Third: Since the duties we owe our Creator take precedence of all other duties, moral training must accord the first place to religion, that is, to the knowledge of God and His law, and must cultivate a spirit of obedience to His commands. The performance, sincere and complete, of religious duties, ensures the fulfilment of other obligations.

Fourth: Moral and religious training is most efficacious when it is joined with instruction in other kinds of knowledge. It should so permeate these that its influence will be felt in every circumstance of life, and be strengthened as the mind advances to a fuller acquaintance with nature and a riper experience with the realities of human existence.

Fifth: An education that unites intellectual, moral and religious elements is the best training for citizenship. It inculcates a sense of responsibility, a respect for authority and a considerateness for the rights of others which are the necessary foundations of civic virtue—more necessary where, as in a democracy, the citizen, enjoying a larger freedom, has a greater obligation to govern himself. We are convinced that, as religion and morality are essential to right living and to the public welfare, both should be included in the work of education.

There is reason to believe that this conviction is shared by a considerable number of our fellow-citizens who are not of the Catholic faith. They realize that the omission of religious instruction is a defect in education and also a detriment to religion. But in their view the home and the church should give the needed training in morality and religion, leaving the school to provide only secular knowledge. Experience, however, confirms us in the belief that instead of dividing education among these several agencies, each of them should, in its own measure, contribute to the intellectual, moral and religious development of the child, and by this means become helpful to all the rest.

In order that the educative agencies may co-operate to the best effect, it is important to understand and safeguard their respective functions and rights. The office of the Church instituted by Christ is to "teach all nations," teaching them to observe whatsoever He commanded. This commission authorizes the Church to teach the truths of salvation to every human being, whether adult or child, rich or poor, private citizen or public official.

In the home with its limited sphere but intimate relations, the parent has both the right and the duty to educate his children; and he has both, not by any concession from an earthly power, but in virtue of a divine ordinance. Parenthood, because it means co-operation with God's design for the perpetuation of human kind, involves responsibility, and therefore implies a corresponding right to prepare for complete living those whom the parent brings into the world.

The school supplements and extends the educational function of the home. With its larger facilities and through the agency of teachers properly trained for the purpose, it accomplishes in a more effectual way the task of education for which the parent, as a rule, has neither the time, the means nor the requisite qualifications. But the school cannot deprive the parent of his right nor absolve him from his duty, in the matter of educating his children. It may properly supply for certain deficiencies of the home in the way of physical training and cultivation of manners; and it must, by its discipline as well as by explicit instruction, imbue its pupils with habits of virtue. But it should not, through any of its ministrations, lead the parent to believe that having placed his children in school, he is freed from responsibility, nor should it weaken the ties which attach the child to parent and home. On the contrary, the school should strengthen the home influence by developing in the child those traits of character which help to maintain the unity and happiness of family life. By this means it will co-operate effectually with the parent and worthily discharge its function.

Since the child is a member not only of the family, but also of the larger social group, his education must prepare him to fulfil his obligations to society. The community has the right to insist that those who as members share in its benefits shall possess the necessary qualifications. The school, therefore, whether private or public as regards maintenance and control, is an agency for social welfare, and as such it bears responsibility to the whole civic body.

While the social aspect of education is evidently important, it must be remembered that social righteousness depends upon individual morality. There are virtues, such as justice and charity, which are exercised in our relations with others; but there is no such thing as collective virtue which can be practiced by a community whose individual members do not possess it in any manner or degree. For this very reason the attempt to develop the qualities of citizenship without regard for personal virtue, or to make civic utility the one standard of moral excellence, is doomed to failure. Integrity of life in each citizen is the only sure guarantee of worthy citizenship.

As the public welfare is largely dependent upon the intelligence of the citizen, the State has a vital concern in education. This is implied in the original purpose of our government which, as set forth in the preamble to the Constitution, is "to form a more perfect union, establish justice, ensure domestic tranquility, provide for the common defense, promote the general welfare, and secure the blessings of liberty to ourselves and our posterity."

In accordance with these purposes, the State has a right to insist that its citizens shall be educated. It should encourage among the people such a love of learning that they will take the initiative and, without constraint, provide for the education of their children. Should they through negligence or lack of means fail to do so, the State has the right to establish schools and take every other legitimate means to safeguard its vital interests against the dangers that result from ignorance. In particular, it has both the right and the duty to exclude the teaching of doctrines which aim at the subversion of law and order and therefore at the destruction of the State itself.

The State is competent to do these things because its essential function is to promote the general welfare. But on the same principle it is bound to respect and protect the rights of the citizen and especially of the parent. So long as these rights are properly exercised, to encroach upon them is not to further the general welfare, but to put it in peril. If the function of government is to protect the liberty of the citizen, and if the aim of education is to prepare the individual for the rational use of his liberty, the State cannot rightfully or consistently make education a pretext for interfering with rights and liberties which the Creator, not the State, has conferred. Any advantage that might accrue even from a perfect system of State education would be more than offset by the wrong which the violation of parental rights would involve.

In our country, government thus far has wisely refrained from placing any other than absolutely necessary restrictions upon private initiative. The result is seen in the development of our resources, the products of inventive genius and the magnitude of our enterprises. But our most valuable resources are the minds of our children, and for their development at least the same scope should be allowed to individual effort as is secured to our undertakings in the material order.

The spirit of our people in general is adverse to State monopoly, and this for the obvious reason that such an absorption of control would mean the end of freedom and initiative. The same consequence is sure to follow when the State attempts to monopolize education; and the disaster will be greater inasmuch as it will affect, not simply the worldly interests of the citizen, but also his spiritual growth and salvation.

With great wisdom our American Constitution provides that every citizen shall be free to follow the dictates of his conscience in the matter of religious belief and observance. While the State gives no preference or advantage to any form of religion, its own best interests require that religion as well as education should flourish and exert its wholesome influence upon the lives of the people. And since education is so powerful an agency for the preservation of religion, equal freedom should be secured to both. This is the more needful where the State refuses religious instruction any place in its schools. To compel the attendance of all children at these schools would be practically equivalent to an invasion of the rights of conscience, in respect to those parents who believe that religion forms a necessary part of education.

Our Catholic schools are not established and maintained with any idea of holding our children apart from the general body and spirit of American citizenship. They are simply the concrete form in which we exercise our rights as free citizens, in conformity with the dictates of conscience. Their very existence is a great moral fact in American life. For while they aim, openly and avowedly, to preserve our Catholic faith, they offer to all our people an example of the use of freedom for the advancement of morality and religion.

153

THE RIGHT TO EDUCATE

Victor Cathrein [1]

A group of families under a common authoritative head, and not subject to any similar aggregation, forms the primitive State, however small it may be. By further development, or by coalition with other States, larger States gradually come into existence. It is not the purpose of the State to supplant the families, but to safeguard their rights, to protect them, and to supplement their efforts. It is not to forfeit their rights or to abandon their proper functions that individuals and families combine to form the State,

---

[1] *Catholic Encyclopedia,* vol. V, p. 564.

but to be secured in these rights, and to find support and encouragement in the discharge of the various duties assigned them. Hence the State may not deprive the family of its right to educate and instruct the children, but must simply lend its assistance by supplying, wherever needful, opportunities for the better accomplishment of this duty. Only so far as the order and prosperity of the body politic requires it, may the State circumscribe individual effort and activity. In other words, the State is to posit the conditions under which, provided private endeavor is not lacking, each individual and each family may attain to true earthly happiness. By true earthly happiness is meant such as not only does not interfere with the free performance of the individual's moral duties, but even upholds and encourages him therein.

154

THE STATE AND EDUCATION

MICHAEL CRONIN [1]

The end of the State is to provide for the higher or more developed "good" in so far as its attainment exceeds the capacity of individuals and the family. Let us see in the light of this principle what is the position of the State in regard to education. For the sake of simplicity we shall here confine our discussion to the case of primary education, or the education of children.

Education is essentially a part of the process of rearing. By rearing is meant the training of the child, both in body and mind, and education is that part of rearing which relates to mind. And since the rearing of the child is primarily and essentially a duty and a right of parents, so the education of the child is primarily and essentially their right. The parent may hand over the child to be nursed by another, or taught by another, whether a private teacher or the State, but the final responsibility to nature and to the Author of nature falls on the parent. The employed teacher is in nature's eyes only the deputy of the parent.

[1] *The Science of Ethics*, vol. II, pp. 486-491. (Benziger Brothers, New York.)

Now whereas, generally speaking, parents can by their own united efforts provide for the bodily welfare of their children and in some measure can provide also for their mental welfare or their education, to a great extent and normally this latter side of the process of rearing is something that exceeds the means, the capacities, and the opportunities of parents; and it is for parents exclusively to determine how their own efforts in these circumstances are to be supplemented by the aid of others. If by means of combination amongst many families it is possible to maintain a private school, conducted according to a program either drawn up or at least approved by themselves, then it is their right to maintain such a school and without interference from the State. In two cases only would interference be possible, viz., where it is evident that the child is not really being educated, for then an injustice is being done to the child, and the State could interfere on its behalf just as it can interefere if a child is not being properly fed. But such interference is, in general, invidious, and so far as education is concerned could be justified only on very rare occasions. The other case arises in connection with the requirements of the common good. The good of the State might require a certain standard of education, higher than that normally given, and the State could legitimately insist upon this standard being attained by all.

As a rule, however, parents cannot afford to maintain and equip schools like those just mentioned. The maintenance of an efficient school is costly and troublesome, and therefore, parents have a right to call upon the State to provide the opportunities for education which they themselves cannot afford to give, and the State is under an obligation to provide these opportunities, i. e., to build and equip schools, to pay the teachers, to maintain the schools, in so far at least as these things are beyond the means and the capacities of parents. But even where education is fully provided by the State, it has to be remembered that the first right and the final responsibility are the parents', and that in providing the means of education the State is only fulfilling its natural function of supplementing the efforts of parents in regard to the requirements of the developed life. The State, therefore, is not justified in wresting the child from the parent or ignoring the parent in the domain of education. It is not justified in forcing on the children a system of education which is unacceptable to parents, or a system to which they conscientiously object. In certain matters, of course, the State is free not to consult the parents, those matters, namely, in which the parents are not supposed to be capable of judging aright, as for instance, whether mathematics should be taught in the school, and to what extent, and according to what methods; but there are certain matters of which parents are quite competent judges, or at all events, of which the State and the public authorities are not the appointed judges, for instance, religion, and in these connections the advantageous position which the State occupies through being necessary to the parent, gives it no right to force a system of education or a set of principles on the children, of which their parents disapprove. What, therefore, is the duty of the State in the circumstances in question? The State may, of course, provide its own schools, conducted according to its own methods for all those who are willing to make use of them; but it should also provide schools approved of by parents, and equip and maintain them at the expense of the State, provided, of course, that the requisite number of families is present to constitute a school. In that case, as in every case in which public money is devoted to any work, the State enjoys a full right of inspection and examination so that the public may have some guarantee that its money is being properly applied. But the fact, we repeat, that the State does provide public money for education, and that consequently it is in the advantageous position of being necessary to parents, no more gives it a right to take the children out of the parents' hands and educate them according to its own ideas exclusively, than its necessity in the interests of public order bestows on the State a right of forcing a particular kind of dress or food or habitation on all those who are in the unhappy position of having to appeal to it for aid against thieves and robbers. Where reasonable aid is asked of the State, aid should be given; but in seeking for such aid men are not to be regarded as forfeiting or surrendering in any way the rights and liberties which nature bestows on them as human persons, or as parents entrusted with the duty of caring for their children. Nobody would, of course, expect the State to provide schools for every handful of children whose parents entertain conscientious objections to the system that is actually provided by the State. But wherever a multiplicity of schools has to be provided, the State is bound to make special provision for any large and important body of parents making common appeal to the State, and resting their appeal on the same group of conscientious principles or difficulties.

Nor should the State complain about the multiplicity of systems that may thus be generated. For, in the first place, the group requiring and deserving (from the point of view of numbers) special treatment are never many. And in the second place, it is a good thing that the whole educational system of a country should not be cast in a single mould. The single-mould system advocated by State monopolists in the domain of education is bound to hamper and repress initiative and originality, and even that spirit of freedom which every modern government either genuinely aims at, or pretends to aim at, encouraging amongst its subjects. Diversities of spirit are widely encouraged in modern times in the domain of university education. There is no reason in the world why similar encouragement, always, of course, supposing that the State is given the free exercise of its right of inspection and examination, should not be extended to the elementary sphere as well. Even such a strong advocate of governmental interference in matters moral as John Stuart Mill was fully alive to the advantages attaching to freedom of development in the sphere of elementary education. "All that has been said," he writes,[1] "of the importance of individuality of character, and diversity in opinions and modes of conduct involves, as of the same unspeakable importance, diversity of education. A general State education is a mere contrivance for moulding people to be exactly like one another; and as the mould in which it casts them is that which pleases the predominant power in the government . . . in the proportion as it is efficient and successful, it establishes a despotism over the mind leading by natural tendency to one over the body. An education established by the State should exist, if it exists at all, as one among many competing experiments, carried on for the purpose of example

[1] *On Liberty*, p. 63.

and stimulus to keep the others up to a certain standard of excellence." We do not consider that Mill has here succeeded in setting forth the entire obligation of the State in regard to education. The State should not merely set up a number of competing schools with others, leaving these others to depend upon themselves. The State should be prepared to extend encouragement and pecuniary aid to all those schools that need and deserve it. But the testimony of so great an authority is valuable as showing the injury done to the interests of education itself by any attempt to bring the whole education of the country under one rigid system, or (we may add) by declining to support in any way those schools in the case of which, whilst fully acknowledging a right of inspection and examination on the part of the State, parents still insist on exercising some discretion in matters that, to their mind, appertain not to the State, but to themselves and to the appointed guardians of religion.

155

RIGHTS AND DUTIES REGARDING EDUCATION

James Conway [1]

By the very fact of procreation there arises the strict obligation on the part of both parents to preserve the life and procure the spiritual and temporal welfare of their progeny. For this end the Creator has infused into the hearts of parents an inborn and indelible affection for their children. For this end He has inviolably sanctioned the unity and indissolubility of matrimony. For this end sacramental grace is dispensed to Christians who join in lawful wedlock. But in this sacramental contract they also undertake the sacred and strictly binding duty of procuring their offspring a physical, moral, and religious (Christian) education. From this obligation they cannot be dispensed. How far this duty extends cannot so easily be defined, as it depends a good deal on particular circumstances, and especially on the parents' position in life. Neither does it lie

[1] *The Respective Rights and Duties of Family, State and Church in Regard to Education*, pp. 9-15; 20-22; 41-44. (Fr. Pustet & Co., New York.)

within our present purpose to investigate the extent of this obligation in detail. So much, however, is certain, that parents are strictly bound to provide for their children such a physical development that they may be able at least to procure their living honestly by the work of their own hands, and such a mental development as to insure their possible success in the ordinary pursuits of life.

For this physical and mental training of their children, however, neither the study of pedagogy, as Herbert Spencer would recommend for intended parents, nor a course of hygiene such as is sometimes pleaded for with much pathos in American journals of education, is required for parents. That parental love and solicitude implanted in their hearts by the Creator, aided by common sense, is sufficient guide, as long as it is not stifled by vicious habits. Still greater care, however, must be bestowed by parents on the moral and religious education of their children than on their physical and mental development. They are obliged to watch over their innocence, to guard them against all demoralizing influences and associations, to imbue them practically with an early sense of modesty, truthfulness, filial piety, obedience, etc. But above all they must at an early age endeavor to imprint on their yet tender hearts religious sentiments—love of prayer, reverence for whatever is holy, fondness of the Christian doctrine, and of all religious practices, love of God, detestation of sin, etc. It is scarcely necessary to add that they are bound to procure them a sound religious instruction.

Those duties are common to all parents. The duties of a higher education, literary or scientific, vary according to particular circumstances and conditions of life. Here the question might be put whether parents in general are bound in conscience to have their children taught to read, write, and reckon. Certainly, if we abstract from particular circumstances, no such obligation can be proved; as such knowledge is necessary neither for the temporal nor spiritual welfare of man. Neither is it required for an ordinary mental, moral, and religious development, as may be seen in the case of many illiterate persons who have more moral grasp and a good deal more delicate and defined moral and religious sense than many of their comparatively well-informed brethren. We know that some of the poets of the

Middle Ages, whose works take the highest rank in literature, could neither read nor write. We need only recall the name of Wolfram von Eschenbach, the sweet minnesinger, who is known as the author of the famous "Parceval," one of the finest literary productions which have reached us. However, if we take the circumstances into consideration, such are the inconveniences of illiteracy in our days, in most places, and such the facility of acquiring those rudiments of knowledge, that the parents who, in normal social circumstances, brought up their children unlettered, could scarcely be considered blameless. Yet, reading, writing, etc., as may be readily seen, constitute the least important part of education. Such knowledge is only accessory to the true essentials. Whatever then may be said of those useful and ornamental requirements, with which civilized society in our days can hardly dispense, it is certain that parents are strictly bound to procure the essential physical, moral, and religious education of their children. The sense of this duty is so deeply impressed on the nature of man by the Creator that it cannot be wholly effaced, even by the grossest barbarism.

To facilitate the fulfilment of education, parents have been gifted by the Creator with the most wonderful educational talents. He has infused into their hearts an unspeakable love and tenderness for their offspring, an unwearied patience with their children's weaknesses, an unremitting watchfulness over their every step and movement. Who has taught the mother to enter into the very soul of her child, to read his thoughts and desires, to take the liveliest interest in his chldish pastimes? Yet no kindergartner of Fröbel's school has ever learned to penetrate into the secrets of the mystery of childhood as does the untutored mother, guided only by the voice of nature. Who is better adapted to make early and lasting impressions on the susceptible heart of the child, than his own mother? How often do we find that an early lesson of a mother, recalled to the mind of a wayward son, effects that which no other motive, however strong, can accomplish? It is true those natural gifts are not dispensed in like measure to all parents, and can be wholly or partially eliminated by vicious habits; but this does not weaken the force of the general fact, which evidently proves the intention of the Creator that parents should be the educators of their own children.

To this intent also God has infused into the hearts of children a love and reverence for, a confidence and docility toward their parents which they can rarely acquire toward others, and this dictate of filial piety has been sanctioned by the positive law of God: "Honor thy father and thy mother." It requires no small degree of depravity to stifle this voice of nature in the heart of the child. As the parent, then, is by divine institution the natural teacher of the child, so the child is the divinely appointed pupil of his parents. The family, therefore, is a divinely constituted school, with an inviolable charter, framed and written by the finger of the Almighty in the hearts of parents and children. This school has existed before all universities, and will survive them all, because it is a divine institution which forms part and portion of human nature.

Whoever, therefore, meddles with this divine creation, violates the most sacred rights of parents and children, and thwarts the intention of the Creator. For if parents have the strict duty of educating their children according to their own convictions, they have also the inviolable right to do so; and, if children are bound by the law of nature to submit themselves to that education which their parents are in conscience obliged to give them, they also have the right not to be impeded in the fulfilment of this duty. They may be arrested by truant officers, and dragged into the State schools against their own will and that of their parents; they may be submitted to educational tyranny worse than Spartan, but the voice of injured human nature cries up to the Creator for vengeance against that State which thus disregards the unprotected rights of its subjects.

Though the duty and right of parents to educate their offspring is inalienable, and though this obligation is personal, yet it does not follow that they may not make use of the assistance of others in discharging this office. As parents can employ a trusty servant to nurse their children, so they can appoint a reliable teacher to instruct them in reading, writing, good manners, Christian doctrine, and the various arts and sciences; to superintend their physical, mental, and religious development. And as parents frequently have not the necessary time and knowledge to give their children a complete education, there is nothing more natural than that they should call in the aid of others, to whom they should consign a share of their parental office, with a corresponding portion of their parental rights. But as it would involve too great inconvenience and expenditure for every family to employ one or more pedagogues, and one teacher can instruct and train several with the same or with greater facility than he could a single child, the suggestion is obvious that several families should unite and employ one or several trustworthy teachers, in common, to assist them in the education of their children.

This circumstance first gave rise to *schools,* which are nothing else in reality than supplementary institutions to assist parents in the work of education. Whatever then may be the lofty idea which the worthy pedagogue may have of his exalted calling, he has only a subsidiary office, and so much authority and jurisdiction, in the natural order, as parents choose to confer on him. But like every other employee, he too can contract with his employer. He can propose certain conditions on which alone his services are obtainable. Hence it is quite natural that schools should in course of time acquire a certain degree of autonomy, should have certain constitutions, certain laws and regulations to which parents and children should be obliged to submit if they wish to avail themselves of their advantages. Yet from the nature of things, schools should be ultimately at the mercy of parents; for on them should finally depend whether they send their children to such institutions or have them otherwise instructed and educated. . . .

Now, does this education fall within the scope of civil power? In other words, has civil authority been instituted by the Creator to teach the nations? Certainly education does not fall within the *protective* function of the State, for no right is thereby violated that parents educate their own children, or intrust them to private individuals or institutions to be educated, according to the dictates of their own conscience. On the contrary, this as we have seen, is the intention of the Creator, and the most perfect execution of the Divine order. The only case in which State interference can be warranted is that in which the necessary education of children is notably neglected, as in case of exposed infants and orphans, for whom provision is not otherwise made by the Church, or by private charity. Every child has a right to the necessary education, and if his claims are not satisfied in the natural divinely sanctioned order, it is the business of the State to take measures that the child may come to his right. By so doing, however, the State does not act as an educator more than it becomes the administrator of private property by punishing theft, or enforcing the restitution of stolen goods. It only defends the personal rights of its subjects within lawful bounds. But the State that takes education into its own hands and monopolizes schools, violates in the most glaring manner, personal, parental, and divine rights.

The child, under ordinary circumstances, has an inviolable right, though he may have no means of enforcing it, to be educated in the way intended by the Creator; not under the iron rod of the State official, but under the loving care of his parents, either in the bosom of the family, or in that place where parents believe him to be best cared for; not according to that manner of pedagogy which may seem to philosophers to make him an enlightened citizen and patriot, but in that way which will bring him nearer to his Creator, and guide him most effectually to his last end. Therefore, the child who is violently wrested from the arms of his parents and thrust into a public school, is injured in his most sacred *personal rights;* and this violence is the more crying in the sight of heaven because the child has no means of self-defence, nor even the consciousness of the wrongs inflicted upon him.

State education is, furthermore, a violation of *domestic rights;* nay, it frustrates the object of domestic society, which is not merely the procreation, but mainly the education of the human race. Procreation without the divinely intended education, is a curse rather than a blessing for the individual as well as for the race. It were better for that child not to be born who is not educated in the way of the commandments of God; and parents cannot be indifferent whether they are to be the cause of a blessing or of a curse to their children. They cannot, therefore, leave them a prey to the ambition of the State. It is their duty and their inalienable right to have their children brought up according to their conscientious convictions. Hence the State that compels parents to send their children to schools which in their minds do not direct, but impede them in the attainment of their last end, tramples their most sacred rights under foot.

But the State which monopolizes education goes still further in its injustice; it violates the *divine right;* for if God has both naturally and positively sanctioned the law of domestic education, He cannot be indifferent to its fulfilment. Whoever, then, conduces to, or connives at the upsetting of this divine ordination, not only violates the rights of men, but lifts his unhallowed hand in rebellion against the Creator Himself. He opposes himself to the teaching of Christ, and impedes His Church in the discharge of her teaching office; for, supposing even the best case, in which the minister of the Church has access to the schools, to teach the Christian doctrine; yet this is not the full exercise of the charge the Church has received from her Founder. Abstracting from the fact that primary education is essentially religious, and is, consequently, altogether subject to the jurisdiction of the Church, in virtue of the commission given her by Christ to teach, preserve, and defend His doctrine; the Church has the divine right of supervision over the teaching of the various branches of profane science, in this sense, that she can assure herself that those branches are taught in such a way as not to convey any error in faith, or anything manifestly leading to such error, nor to contain anything dangerous to morals. Hence a profession of faith is exacted by law, not only of the professors of sacred, but also of the teachers of profane sciences in ecclesiastical institutions. Therefore, the State that takes education into its own hands, though it may permit religious instruction, violates the most fundamental of the divine rights of the Church. Whatever view, then, we choose to take of State education, it is a most flagrant injustice, a most impious and sacrilegious violation of the holiest rights of God and man.

If State education subverts the natural order instituted by the Creator, we may justly expect that it entails the most serious *consequences for morality.* And, in fact, we need not go far to find the pernicious moral effects of State or secular education. The catalogue of crime which is daily and weekly chronicled in our newspapers bears ample testimony to the effects of our public education. And how could it be otherwise if the schools are secularized, religion not taught; if children are not impressed with the external maxims, which alone (though only aided by the interior grace of God) can restrain the impetuosity of the passions of man? History, sacred and profane, should have long since convinced the nations that man cannot be made moral without religion. "Whatever may be conceded to the influence of refined education on minds of peculiar structure," says George Washington, in his last injunction to his country, "reason and experience both forbid us to expect that national morality can prevail in exclusion of religious principle." . . .

The fact that the Church has from the very outset claimed and exercised the right of educating the Christian youth is a sufficient proof of the existence of such a right. Her rights may be violated. The youth may be wrested from her arms with brute force and driven into godless institutions. Concessions may be extorted from her, whereby, to prevent greater evils, she may yield a portion of her rights, provided only the principle be maintained. But the rights entrusted to her by her divine Spouse she can never abandon, because they imply the most serious and binding duties. Let us now enter somewhat more minutely into those rights and duties, and try as far as space permits to determine their extent more in detail.

And for the first we say: *The Church has the divinely constituted and inalienable right to provide for a complete religious education of all her children in all schools, of whatever kind or grade they may be.*

By *a religious education* we do not mean the mere instruction in the Christian doctrine. This, though an essential element, does not constitute a religious education. A religious education supposes knowledge of the Christian doctrine and consists mainly in a religious and moral training by the exercise of virtuous acts and all those practices of religion which, according to the principles of revelation, constitute or insure a Christian and supernatural life. This training the Church owes to all her children and she has an indisputable right, unmolested, to fulfil this duty through her lawful ministers, under all circumstances, and in all institutions—in the high school and university as well as in the elementary school.

This is manifest first from the duty which the Church has of directing the faithful by efficacious means to their supernatural end. With the exercise of this duty the Church cannot dispense at any instant of man's life, from the moment she has received him into her fold until she delivers him up to the Supreme Pastor, at the hour of his death. But toward no state of life is this duty so strictly incumbent upon her as toward that of youth and childhood. "As the twig is bent the tree's inclined." She must, therefore, exercise the greatest vigilance that, while the child and youth is growing physically and intellectually, his moral and religious development may keep pace with his bodily and mental growth. She must take care that the germ of supernatural life, which is deposited in his soul in the sacrament of Baptism, be nurtured and watered by instruction and appropriate devotional exercises in order that it may take deep root and wax strong into supernatural maturity. She must guard that principle against the evil influences of false doctrines and demoralizing associations, lest it may be blasted in the bud. And should the supernatural seedling become extinct by the blighting breath of sin, she must restore it by the regenerating virtue of the sacraments.

Such is the divine mission of the Church, such her indispensable duty. If, then, the Church has received this charge from her divine Spouse, she surely has the right to fulfil it without let or hindrance. But it cannot be fulfilled without free access to the schools; without a perfect freedom in teaching the children, in assembling them to daily exercises of devotion and, at stated times, to the sacraments; without the means of assuring herself of the moral and religious tone of the schools, of exercising the necessary supervision, to prevent anything being taught by word or example which might endanger the faith or morals of the children. Any institution which excludes the Church from those functions of education, or obstructs her in their free exercise, evidently violates her most sacred rights. That such an institution also infringes upon the natural rights of the individual, of the family, the parents and children, and tramples under foot the inborn claims of conscience, we have already shown.

Nor need the advocates of non-sectarian education point to the reading of the Scriptures "without note or comment," or to the compensation of the Sunday school. Abstracting from the fact that the reading of a disapproved version of the Scriptures will be against the convictions of a large fraction of the parents and children, no one will look upon such reading of the Scriptures "without note or comment," as part or portion of religious education, unless he indulge in the old-fashioned Protestant theory that the word of God acts immediately and directly on the soul by a quasi-inspiration. Nay, we are convinced that such mechanical reading and hearing of the Bible "without note or comment," in the schools, can only produce scepticism and generate contempt for the word of God in the minds of the children. The experiment has been so unsuccessful here in our own country that the practice is now all but abandoned in our public schools.

The Sunday school experiment, as far as non-Catholics are concerned in this country, has proved equally unsuccessful. This is evident from the complete disintegration of the Protestant sects, the gross ignorance in religious matters and the widespread religious indifference outside of the Catholic Church. How many of our go-to-meeting and Sunday-school young Americans know even those articles whose knowledge is absolutely necessary for salvation, to say nothing of the absolutely necessary means of salvation? Such is the drift at present, that unless our public educational system is changed, we shall in a few generations, have a nation of educated pagans, who will have retained of Christianity no more than a few conventional phrases. And how can it be otherwise if religion is ostracized from the schools and relegated into the Sunday school as a branch of knowledge and education that is not worth caring for, that does not deserve a place in the ordinary life of the child or man, but is merely a matter of private interest and taste?

Still less effectual will be the work of the Sunday school when, as is frequently the case, it is paralyzed during the week by the naturalistic or anti-Christian tone of the school and other demoralizing influences. So much has already been said and written on the influence of secular education on the Catholic youth, especially in our own country, that we prefer to pass it over in silence. The conviction has been brought home to every thinking Catholic worthy of the name, that only a complete religious education, such as is given in Catholic schools, can preserve our children from the drift of infidelity and the deluge of immorality which a godless system of education has brought upon the country.

Should the education be Christian, it is plain to all right-thinking Catholics that the schools must be Christian, that the children must move in a Christian atmosphere, not for one day of the week only, but all the year round. And this can be obtained only by the direct influence of the Church on the schools and their daily workings. If the child has an immortal soul to save, and his eternal weal or woe depends upon the issue of this affair of salvation, surely no less, but much more stress should be laid upon his training to success in this all important business, than to cleverness in the secular pursuits of life. If such is the case, why should the Church, the divinely appointed organ instituted by God for the salvation of mankind, be excluded from the domain of education? Such an exclusion is a crying iniquity against God and man, manifesting either the grossest ignorance of the most elementary Christian maxims or the most inconceivable and fiendish malice.

156

THE STATE'S POWER TO REGULATE EDUCATION [1]

As a rule, all the States encourage the assumption that the average parent is both able and willing to provide for the welfare of his child. They interfere only when it is clear that the assumption is contrary to fact.

But there need be no conflict between the rights of parents and the rights of the State in education. There has never been a conflict in this country which might not have been averted by mutual understanding and good will. The most determined defender of parental rights and duties must admit the rights and duties of the State. What he will be at pains to show, is that to subject parental prerogatives to the dictates of an omnipotent State is at variance both with right reason and with the letter and spirit of our organic law.

[1] The Editor of *America*, March 28, 1925.

Again and again have Catholic apologists admitted the right, and, indeed, the duty, of the State to exercise a reasonable degree of supervision over the education of the child. Obviously it would not contribute to the general good were any body of men or women permitted to set themselves up as teachers, and to conduct educational establishments at their own good pleasure. In a matter so intimately affecting society, it is the duty of the State to protect children and parents as well as itself. The State may insist that children be provided with the opportunity of obtaining a suitable education, and to effect this end, it may determine certain standards of training, examine the teachers and inspect the schools. The precise extent to which the State may go will depend largely upon circumstances. In this, it is not subject to a definite rule, except the fundamental rule that the essential rights of the parent, upon whom rests the first right and duty of educating the child, must not be infringed.

The hearings before the Supreme Court brought into clear relief the fact that chief proponents of the Oregon law were not actuated by zeal in the cause of education. The law was condemned by practically all educational bodies, non-Catholic as well as Catholic, throughout the country, and enthusiastically supported by the professed enemies of the Catholic Church. It is to be hoped that all American citizens will at last realize that Catholics are fighting not only for their schools, but for the constitutional rights of every American. When the State can invade the home, and place the child in a school which, in the conscientious judgment of the family, will not give the child a desirable training, it is difficult to understand what right can be placed beyond the power of the State.

157

THE EDUCATIONAL FACT

Timothy Brosnahan [1]

The adequate purpose of education, so far as it regards the present life, is to form citizens, that is to say, men and

[1] *The Catholic Educational Association Bulletin,* May, 1911, pp. 24-36; 61-64.

women capable of promoting progress and enriching civilization. If that be not the purpose of it, it is hard to see why the State should attach so much importance to it. It should aim, therefore, at procuring the development of powers and the formation of habits that secure and enlarge prosperity, and at evolving the faculties and virtues that humanize feeling, widen outlooks and elevate ideals. But undoubtedly its paramount aim should be to fit youth for civilization, that is to say, for life in a civil community. However adapted a young man may have become as the result of education to increase wealth, if he be unsuited to live in the fellowship of justice and benevolence with other men, his education is worse than a failure; it is likely to be a disaster to himself and a menace to society. If the scope of education is narrowed to the production of a highly efficient dollar-hunting animal, or if this be the predominant scope, the material well-being of the community is provided for at the sacrifice of its social well-being. A man so trained may observe the law of the land without being a *civis*. He may be legally a citizen with the right to vote and to be voted for; but he is not necessarily a citizen in the ethical sense. Men may be induced to observe the law from one of three motives: self-interest, fear of superior physical force, or love of righteousness. And unless observance of law springs from this last as the dominant motive, we may have "honored and respected citizens" who are clear-sighted enough to see that their business enterprises are more secure under the reign of law, and that it is on the whole to their advantage to avoid incurring the risk of legal penalties; but not men possessing the moral attributes of citizenship. Such men may be law-abiding in appearance and to the outward eye of the State. If circumstances arise, however, in which they may with impunity violate the law, and appropriate to themselves some of the fat of the land, there are in their code of ethics no principles prohibiting action. Take away the love of righteousness as a motive of conduct and a civil community becomes a pestilential congregation of freebooters, who have adopted some "laws of the game," keep up some appearances of well-behaved propriety, and publicly profess theoretic adherence to some principles of right. Now righteousness is a moral quality. An education, therefore, which does not primarily aim at the development of the child's moral nature and which does not ultimately effect this development, whatever other merits it may have, has this drawback, that it tends to produce a type of character against whom society must be constantly on its guard, and to whom the laws of God and man are tolerable only in so far as they subserve his personal interests, and failing in this are to be observed only when he cannot, through mental adroitness acquired from education, devise subterfuges and deceits to avoid their sanctions. Can this be the end to be attained through education?

A man whose moral nature has been undeveloped, or by defective educational processes impaired, is a social nonconformist whose unfitness for civil life, and, therefore, for civilization, increases in proportion as his intellectual powers are enlarged. A political controversy which has recently engaged the attention of the country will illustrate the principle which I have just enunciated. On the concrete merits of that controversy I have, of course, nothing to say. Under that aspect it has no bearing on my subject, belongs, moreover, to the domain of practical politics, and there it may remain so far as I am concerned. I am only using as an illustration the principles that underlie the controversy and which are assented to by both political parties. Whatever the political allegiance of an American citizen, he admits as a fundamental and essential characteristic of our government the distribution of supreme political power in three different departments, and accepts as final the advice of Washington, who warns us in his farewell address to see to it that those entrusted with the legislative, judicial, and executive powers confine themselves to their respective constitutional spheres, avoiding in the exercise of the power of one department encroachment upon that of another. When the legislature is wise and prudent, the judiciary just and fearless, the executive strong and temperate, we have good government. But if any of these supreme powers loses its proper virtue, or permits the usurpation of its functions by another, then the organic unity of the State is deranged, and a first step has been taken, the logical issue of which is either anarchy or despotism.

Now the human soul is a republic whose legislative power is intellect, whose judicial power is conscience, and whose executive power is the will. Each of these powers in the soul of a child demands a training in keeping with its own nature and its relation to the other powers. The enfeebling, defective unfolding or stunting of any of them will result as disastrously for the individual as the weakening of the analogous civil powers will for the State. If the result of education is to leave the republic of the soul with a conscience that is undeveloped or corrupted, or a will that is egotistic, arbitrary and overpowering, or an intellect that has become subservient to the lawless movements of the will, an individual has been produced who is unfit for citizenship in a civilized community and is suited only for anarchy or despotism. And if millions of such citizens are annually produced in a nation, it requires no vision of a seer to foresee the outcome. History tells us of no greater scourges of humanity, of no men less fit for social and civic life than those men who use their powers of intellect to contrive means of carrying into execution the mandates of a will uncontrolled by conscience. And experience teaches us that the social evils that threaten the peace and security of a people are rooted ultimately in the fact that the due balance between the powers of conscience, will, and intellect have been disturbed; that conscience has been corrupted or malformed, and intellect made the slave of lawless will. Any system of education, therefore, which does not aim at such a correlated development of the child's will, conscience and intellect as shall habituate it to confine these powers within "their respective constitutional spheres" is an education which has excluded the ideals of civilization from the scope of its attainment. We may train the intellect to cleverness, ingenuity and subtlety; we may inspire the will with an eager desire to compass material well-being, honor, seats in high places; but if we exclude from our school the systematic and rational training of conscience, no plethora of books or horde of pedagogical writers can obscure the fact that we do not know what education is. Unless, therefore, the child has been taught to regulate its desires and the movements of its will by the dictates of right reason and the judgments of a sound conscience, the man will subordinate righteousness to the prosecution of his personal purposes. He may as a result of education have acquired the sagacity that unerringly apprehends a remote and materially valuable end, skill in adapting means to its attainment, and energy and despatch in their use—and these qualities are undoubtedly worth acquiring; but without an inward sense of probity to rule and control his conduct in the employment of the natural and human agencies which he manipulates, they become the forces through which all that is finest within him grows coarse. He may attain a commanding position in commercial, financial, administrative or political arenas, but his very success creates for the community a civic ideal that is false and harmful.

I said that the child should be taught to govern itself by the dictates of right reason and the judgments of a sound conscience. The reason is not difficult to find. For the moral conduct of life we require, first, general principles of right and wrong, which the intellect recognizes as expressions of a supreme law to which unconditional obedience is due, and, secondly, rectitude of mind in applying these precepts of morality to the individual and concrete circumstances of life. There are as a consequence in the education of a child two elements—the inculcation of right principles of conduct and of solid grounds for the obligation of conforming daily actions to principles; and the formation of an intellectual habit whereby one so reverences moral laws as to make application of them unerringly, and on motives that are superior to though not necessarily independent of personal considerations. Therefore, knowledge not only of what is right and what is wrong, but also of the ultimate reasons why one ought to do the right and avoid the wrong; and reverence, or a sense of awe in the presence of moral obligation, are the essential elements in the education of a rational being and in the formation of a citizen in a civilized State. These two, knowledge and reverence, have been recognized by every clear thinker since the days of Plato as the cardinal forces of education. The need of reverence in education, its complementary character in relation to knowledge, its necessity for civic life, is an oft-repeated theme, especially of his dialogues on the Republic and on Laws. Tennyson utters the aim and the aspiration of every true teacher in the familiar verses:

> "Let knowledge grow from more to more,
>   But more of reverence in us dwell;
>   That mind and soul, according well,

> May make one music as before,
> But vaster."

With regard to the first element there is little difficulty so far as the content of morality is concerned. It is only when there is question of its form, of determining the why and wherefore of its obligatory character that confusion, vacillation and incertitude arise. The spirit of Christianity has so pervaded our moral atmosphere that the *zeitgeist*, though it distorts and rejects its doctrinal teachings, cannot cast off the moral precepts of which those teachings are the basis. The canons of right and wrong which Christianity has fixed have, in the main, become the principles of our civilization, and are accepted theoretically at least even by those to whom the dogmas of Christianity are foolishness and a stumbling-block. Even systems of morality which are thoroughly anti-Christian in substance and bent endeavor to adjust themselves to the common moral sentiment of the age. The very fact that they make the attempt at sacrifices of logical consistency, and of what they would call scientific precision proves that the spirit of Christianity has yet a hold on the soul, although in many quarters it has lost its influence over the reason. As a rule the ideals of righteousness which the religion of Christ presented to a world that unaided reason had betrayed into moral and religious degradation, are by subtle and informal inferences known and intellectually felt to be the substructure and support of our civilization. These ideals in their higher shape are not, it is true, received except as beautiful forms of religious poetry, counsels of perfection, which we contemplate with devout emotion, or with which we embellish our pulpit oratory; but which in stern practice that neoteric deity called the Spirit of the Age, with its triune feature of profit, honor, pleasure, declares offensive to modern ears. And it must, furthermore, be confessed that even the imperatives of that ideal are sometimes and with regard to some lines of conduct stammeringly and hesitatingly spoken by the exponents and advocates of the age's morality. The fervent discourse of many a preacher and the eloquent page of many a moralist, when looked at closely, will be found to resolve itself into the confession of Jeremiah, before the Lord put forth His hand and touched his mouth: "Ah, ah, ah, Lord God; behold I cannot speak, for I am a child."

Nevertheless, making these concessions, it must be admitted that the impress of Christianity is on our moral standards in so far as they exhibit precepts of conduct.

But when it comes to determining the ultimate and cogent reason of obedience to those precepts the failure of modern ethics is impressive, and would be appalling, if the law that is written in the heart of man could be wholly obliterated, and the "light which enlighteneth every man that cometh into this world" could be extinguished. The word "ought" has been either wholly or nearly emptied of significance by the ethical writers who represent this age. At best the reason advanced for declaring a given action or course of conduct good or just, and its omission bad or unjust, may be such as to compel assent of the intellect; but they cannot exact the unconditional obedience of the will. The necessity they produce is logical, not moral. If we demand why we ought to do what is just, humane, or virtuous, and why we ought not to do what is unjust, inhumane or vicious, we are given answers which show that either the nature of the question is not apprehended, or that the word "ought" has lost its distinctive meaning. Why ought I do what I know to be right? Why may I not, if I find it agreeable, profitable, and sometimes even respectable, indulge in wrong conduct, provided I am well-bred, prudent and temperate? Why must I, even when it is disagreeable or entails danger and sacrifice, walk in the narrow path of rectitude? No system of Eudaemonism gives an answer. He who tells me that the right conduct is obligatory because it promotes happiness, is ennobling, advances the interests of humanity or is required for the welfare of the State has simply failed to apprehend the initial problem of Ethics; he has not even assigned a universal and objective norm of right and wrong, let alone an ultimate ground of obligation. Nor does any system of rational Deontologism give an answer, though this may be said to the credit of such systems, they do not debase or nullify absolutely the concept of moral law. All of them, however, from Kant with his autonomous reason, which is endowed with the power of furnishing categorical imperatives when occasion demands, to Hegel, with his statolatry and pantheistic reconstruction of Hobbes' "great Leviathan," leave the superstructure of morality hanging like the Hindoo turtle in mid-air. They either invest man himself through some faculty with authority to command himself, or they create out of abstractions a figment which they christen Humanity, or the State, and whose mandates they ask us, after making an act of faith in its existence and sanctity, to accept as obligatory.

Now, it is a fact, I think, which conversation and observation will confirm, that most men outside of those whose inner life is governed by Christianity, are to-day utilitarians in their personal practice of morality, some of them actually Benthamites,[2] and Kantians or Hegelians in the principles they profess when on parade, and in the standards they set up for others. Many of them may never have read a page of Bentham, or Mill, or Kant, or Hegel; but they have imbibed the views and principles of those writers from newspapers, novels, and magazines and in the intercourse and competitions of business and social life. Yet, unless the precepts of morality impose an unconditional obligation on the will, and unless the source of that obligation is a being, real and actually existing, who is superior to man individually and collectively and on whom man is absolutely dependent, it is impossible to think of morality as anything else than a precarious scheme of behavior, somewhat more universal in its reach than the conventions of good society. It does not, of course, fall within the scope of this paper to discuss the value of modern systems of Ethics. Nor is such discussion really needed. The complete breakdown of these systems is known to everyone whose duty it is to become acquainted with them and is now nearly universally admitted by ethical scholars. They have multiplied books and, like the friends of Job, they "have wrapped up sentences in unskilled words" with the sole intention of establishing moral obligation without admitting the existence of

---

[2] Bentham in a posthumous work, curiously entitled Deontology, declares: "It is, in fact, idle to talk about duties; the word itself has in it something disagreeable and repulsive; and talk about it as we may, the word (sic) will not become a rule of conduct. . . . Every man is thinking about interests. It is a part of his very nature to think about interests. . . . To interest duty must and will be made subservient." And again: "The talisman of arrogancy, indolence and ignorance is to be found in a single word, an authoritative imposter, which in these papers it will be frequently necessary to unveil. It is the word, 'ought'—'ought' or 'ought not,' as circumstances may be. . . . If the use of the word be admissible at all, it ought to be banished from the vocabulary of morals."

One who alone can bind in conscience a human will, and the only success they have attained consists in confusing men's thoughts, and in preparing the way for moral skepticism, and in imposing intolerable burdens on those whose profession obliges them to keep acquainted with their adversaries' briefs. The modern spirit is like the children of some millionaire fathers who enjoy superbly the fruits of the wealth they did not produce, and would like to thrust the creator of it as far as possible into the social background. It is rather an ignoble spirit, immeasurably so when the object of its aversion is the infinite and ineffable Reality from whose all-bountiful goodness spring being and the dowries thereof. Being ignoble it cannot elaborate a morality that will appeal to the deep inherent instincts of the soul, or satisfy those primal cravings of it for holiness and righteousness that proclaim its kinship with the Deity.

It may be galling to the devotees of the modern spirit to base their morality on God and religion. But until they do it shall possess neither stability nor fruition. Until two fundamental positions are admitted there is no possibility of teaching morality effectively. These are: first, certain modes of conduct are the expressions of an absolute exemplar of conduct, the impress of which is found in our ratonal nature; and, secondly, the Being of whom our nature is an image, and on whom it depends primarily for its origin, and ultimately for its final perfection, necessarily wills and ordains that only actions fully in accord with the exigencies of our nature are lawful, or, what is the same thing, that conduct *ought* to be in conformity with the absolute exemplar. The concept of morality entails the admission of a supreme Legislator, to whom we owe absolute obedience, and involves Ethics with religion. It is, therefore, distasteful to the modern spirit which desires to construct a system of morality independent of God, and to inculcate duty without obtruding the disagreeable idea of obligation. But if there is any necessity of teaching morality to secure the true happiness of the individual, the safety of the State, and the well-being of the race, there is the same necessity of teaching religion, the existence, namely, of a Supreme Being, who manifests to us through our higher faculties the decrees of His eternal law.

Nor is it enough to know what is right or wrong, and why we ought to do the right and avoid the wrong, in order to render morality effective and enduring. Reverence must increase and consummate knowledge. Knowledge as such appeals only to the intellect; unless invested with something that touches the heart it has no motive power over the will. Bare truth of itself is incapable of arousing an emotion, of inspiring a purpose, or of impelling to action. Of whatever kind it may be it does not differ in its influence on the conative faculty from a perfectly demonstrated proposition of geometry. Man is more than a reasoner; he is a doer, and as such an emotional being. Unless a known truth, therefore, is clothed with a quality that approves it to the will, it cannot become a motive of action.

Now reverence is an intellectual emotion, complementing the knowledge of divine law and impelling to its observance. On its intellectual side it arises from a *quasi* intuitive apprehension of the excellence of another, when the elements of that excellence are superior power and worth. Power without worth we may fear, and worth without power we may respect and honor; but neither of them singly do we reverence. It is only when the two excellences are simultaneously perceived to be the conjoined attributes of another, that the rational ground of the emotion called reverence is present. Evidently, therefore, reverence primarily and directly regards a person, appreciation of whom does not spring from, but transcends the formal processes of deductive or inductive reasoning, although in balanced and receptive intellects it will often accompany the conclusions of such reasoning when concerned with the nature or character of a person. We do not feel reverence towards an abstraction nor toward a work of nature or art, however beautiful, imposing or sublime they may be, except in so far as contemplation of them excites to reverence for him whom they represent, or whose supremacy and excellence they attest. On its emotional side reverence is a mingled feeling, responding to the two personal attributes by which it is awakened. To reverence is to hold in awe because of superior power and in highest honor because of superior worthiness. The awe of reverence is not fear, since it arises from no threat or anticipation of impending evil, and is compatible with the highest degree of love. St. Paul tells us that Christ, as man, offered prayer and supplication to His Heavenly Father and "was heard for His reverence;" in Him, however, there could have been no fear of God. It may coexist with hope realized and a sense of spiritual elevation, as in the blessed who enjoy the beatific vision of God and adore Him in reverence. In fact, reverence necessarily includes some measure of love for the person reverenced, and some degree of spiritual elevation in the person reverencing. Yet a feeling akin to fear undoubtedly forms an element of this emotion. The very word by which it is denominated is borrowed from the Latin term which etymologically connotes fear. It is not, however, the fear of dread or terror, but the fear of humility and modesty, the rational self-abasement arising from conscious inferiority to another, mingled with care and prudent apprehension regarding the outcome of any act or course of conduct of which the person reverenced may become cognizant. Hence the word used by St. Paul in the original text of his Epistle to the Hebrews to designate the reverence of Christ for His Heavenly Father signifies cautious and scrupulous regard in conduct for the will of another.

In the human conscience reverence attains its holiest and most sacred expression. Through conscience man knows himself to be in presence of a Being of surpassing power and incomparable worthiness, of whom he stands in awe, for whom he feels the highest form of respect; knows, furthermore, that its dictates and injunctions are the authoritative voice of that Being. Conscience, therefore, does not simply apply the precepts of morality to individual cases, in much the same way, for instance, as reason might apply the general principles of a mechanical science to the solution of a particular problem of construction or engineering. It does this and more. It reveals the fact that these precepts are the ordinances of a supreme personal Legislator to whom unconditional obedience is due, not because of the sanctions decreed for observing or transgressing His commands, but because of His sovereign right to reverence. The need, therefore, of inculcating reverence for the formation of character is as evident as the necessity of training conscience for the same purpose. There are some who, without due analysis of their own thought, I think, and full realization of the consequences of their own theories, have denied this, in maintaining that the principle of authority should be excluded from the classroom. Yet no one acquainted with the psychology of the human soul can seriously contend that mere knowledge or intellectual development is of itself sufficient for the right formation of character. Such a thesis is, moreover, constantly disproved by the records of our criminal courts, and the efforts of our legislators to devise laws which will effectively restrain intelligent and expert lawlessness. Unless reverence be the result of education—reverence for God and the truths and commands and ways of God; reverence for all forms of authority, parental, civil and ecclesiastical; reverence for the family, the hallowed associations of home, the sanctity of the marriage bond and its sacred obligations; reverence for the neighbor, the dignity of his personality and the inviolability of his rights; reverence for ourselves, for our bodies that are the tabernacles of our souls and for our souls that are made to the image and likeness of God—unless, I say, reverence for all things worthy of reverence be so inculcated in childhood and youth as to become a habit of manhood, education is worse than a failure; it is an unparalleled misfortune. It has left the republic of the soul without a tribunal of right and wrong and without a judicial power to enjoin and compel execution. It has made wisdom, which is knowledge acquired under the elevating and vitalizing influence of reverence, an alien to science, and the higher ranges of truth an unknown or barren region.

But to fashion the minds of the young to habits of reverence conscience must be educated, since the reverence of conscience is the norm and exemplar of all reverence. Conscience cannot be educated without teaching morality. Morality cannot be taught unless religion is a part of the curriculum of the school. There is no more possibility of teaching moral obligation without teaching the existence of a supreme Legislator than there is of teaching the duty of filial love without admitting the fact of a father. There may be men, who from motives of worldly prudence or from temperament conform their lives in the main to those dictates of morality which regard their relations to other men, at least in so far as their lives are open to the inspection of the public. But men normally observe the whole law of morality only from motives of religion, and oftentimes in spite of temperament and the suggestions of worldly prudence. Unquestionably it is an historical fact that the morality of a people degenerates into some form of hedonism, utilitarianism or stoicism when not based on religion. It is equally certain that if religion is not taught in childhood and youth, its influence over conduct in later life will be problematic. Unless, therefore, religion supplies a fundamental law of constitution under which the republic of the soul lives, the intellect may know and proclaim, haltingly it is true and with some errors, the law of right and wrong which is inscribed in the heart, but there is no judicatory of conscience to keep the executive power of will from going outside its "constitutional sphere."

Briefly, if the paramount aim of education, so far as the State is concerned, is to fit the growing generation for future citizenship in a civilized community, the question proposed at the beginning of this paper reduces itself to this: What evidence is there in the disciplines and instructions of our schools and in the type of character which they develop that our voluminous educational literature has contributed to the ideals of civilization? If true citizens cannot be formed without inculcating morality, what indications are there that our copious pedagogical writers have aided in the formation of upright and conscientious citizens? If integrity of character and unselfish devotion to social responsibilities and civil duties are not normally found apart from religious convictions, what proofs are there that our schools through the persuasive wisdom of modern educators have furthered our religious life as a people? These are definite questions. It may be denied that it is the purpose of our schools to form citizens in the adequate sense of that term. It may be contended that the training of conscience is not an element in the education of a citizen. It may be maintained that conscience can be trained without moulding the soul of a child or youth to habits of reverence. And one or other of these positions is in fact concealed in the public proclamations of many who have discussed this question of education. But if none of them can be held, the question which I propose can be answered categorically by ingenuously looking at facts. . . .

Our public schools at the best are religious only in so far as the mere reading of the Bible is retained in them; and the tendency is to abolish this. The question of their relation to the morality of the country, space does not permit me to discuss; but the power that sustains morality is gone out of them. If we remember that the men and women of to-day were the school children of a generation since, and review the degrading, corrupt and lawless features of our national life which in recent years have become prominent, we may form our own judgment regarding the moral influence exerted by our public schools. What effect, therefore, has the educational literature of the last three-quarters of a century had on the moral and religious character of the training and instruction given under the ægis of the State? It would be a waste of time to show by citation that our organic and statute laws regarding education are a reflex of that literature. Occasionally a voice crying in the wilderness raised a protest against principles or practices that have led *recto tramite* to the present educational condition; but that voice was unheeded or drowned in the clamor of laudation and pseudo-patriotism that greets any criticism of defects in our public school system. To much of that laudation no one can reasonably demur; it would be easy to say with truth many things in praise of our public schools. One fundamental defect, however, obscures their good qualities in the eyes of those who still hold the conviction that the parables of the two houses, one of which was built on a rock and the other on sand, conveys a lesson of prudence and wisdom. However imposing the public school system may be in appearance, it is thousands of years behind the age in the foundation it lays for the upbuilding of an efficient type of character.

In many respects the interests and outlook of the age of Plato differ widely from those of our own time; but in nothing, I think, is the contrast stranger than in the respective views of Plato and many modern educators regarding the fundamental principles of education; and the contrast is not to the discredit of the pagan. Plato insisted with all the powers of his transcendent intellect that the first care of the rulers of his ideal republic should be an education providing primarily for morality and religion. Our modern educators, after so many centuries, during which the sublime doctrines of Christianity have held sway, refashioning the judgments of men, reforming their convictions, elevating their aspirations, hopes and ideals, have succeeded in excluding the formal teaching of religion from the common schools of every state and territory and in persuading a vast number of American citizens to accept, instead of the teaching of Christian morality, an umbral and emotional substitute based on no authority and secured by no adequate sanction. They have made the communication of religious instruction and the inculcation of Christian morality in those schools illegal. They have created a widespread conviction that this irreligious policy of education is the highest educational policy which the people of the United States are capable of attaining. It may seem strange, but it is an incontrovertible fact that so far as the fundamental aspects of education are concerned we have retrograded to principles that antedate Christianity and were disowned by pagan wisdom. This is a fact of curious significance—the most distinctive, notable and serious fact of our educational history.

To what causes are we to attribute it? Its origin, growth and lustihood are not to be explained by calling from the vast deep such impalpable entities as the genius of our people, the spirit of our national life, the secular idea, an atheistic figment, or the zeitgeist, an abstraction made in Germany; because these words so far as they have any ideas behind them, signify the prevailing convictions of men at a given time. And the dominating prevalence of certain convictions is not explained by giving it another and a more vague name, even though that name be written in capital letters. Historical facts are, of course, effects of antecedent causes acting as a rule steadily through a series of years, sometimes through secular periods. The progress of the movement by which they are produced may often be imperceptible to those who are carried onward by the current. It may be misunderstood by those who take their bearings from subjective impressions to be an advance towards a goal, when it is in fact a recession from it; or an ebbing tide when it may be flowing. The stream of an historical movement may seem retrograde, aberrant and lawless; or progressive, direct and uniform to him who fixes his eyes on small segments of its course, and never raises them to ascertain his direction by the light of a ruling luminary. But whatever the historical facts, they differ from other facts around us in that among their antecedent causes stand preeminently the co-operation of human activity and the directive power of human will. The primal impulses, intuitive wisdom and moral instincts of human nature may stay a social movement or deflect it from a course that leads to a haven of confusion; as, on the other hand, self-interest, estimated by the outlook of an economic day, the wisdom of unhumanizing philosophies or the dominance of great passions, may turn it into channels of degrading prosperity and demoralizing glory. The course of history may be changed, ennobled or depraved by the human agents that apparently drift along its surface, and its character at any given period is the resultant of the error or wisdom, the virtue or unrighteousness of preceding generations working through and with the present.

Furthermore, men do not act in unison unless under the influence of a common purpose and a common perception of the good to be obtained through the realization of that purpose; nor do they preserve over a long period of time continuously uniform action looking to the attainment of their purpose, unless under the guidance and government of a central directive power. The uninterrupted, methodical and progressive constancy with which the people of this vast nation have been working for nearly seventy-five years to get the least vestiges of religion out of their schools, would seem then to import the patient, tireless, determined and far-seeing efforts and direction of some hidden central power. The gradual but effective step by which this irreligious situation has been produced, the continuity with which social forces have been directed to bring it about, the steadiness and uniformity with which it has grown throughout every state of the Union, the fervor with which its apostles, however divergent and conflicting their views about details, have preached its fundamental principles, the subserviency with which it is accepted, even by those who loathe its tendency, the pæans of glorification of it that the slightest occasion will provoke from men of the most different temperaments, politics and religions, the ostrich-like blindness of all parts of the community to its concededly ruinous effect on religious, moral and civic character—these aspects of this significant fact would seem to suggest the activity and rule of some such central power. The human mind naturally attributes a constant, uniform and universal effect to a commensurate cause.

The educational fact, therefore, consists in this, that virtually there is a national alliance to cut out of the curricula of our public schools those disciplines and studies that are essential to the formation of citizenship and the preservation of civilization, and that this alliance, so far as we can see, is directed slowly, cautiously and progressively towards the accomplishment of this purpose by some central agency unknown to us.

158

THE CHRISTIAN HOME

Cardinal Gibbons [1]

The home is the primeval school. It is the best, the most hallowed, and the most potential of all the academies; and the parent, especially the mother, is the first, the most influential, and the most cherished of all teachers. No human ordinance can abrogate or annul the divine *right* of parents to rule their own household, neither can any vicarious instruction given in the day school or Sunday school exempt them from the obligation of a personal supervision over their offspring. If Christian training is eliminated from the home and relegated to the classroom, the child, when emancipated from his studies, may be tempted to regard religious knowledge as a mere detail of school work, and not, as it should be, a vital principal in his daily life and conduct.

And yet I fear there are many parents who imagine that they discharge their whole duty to their children by placing them under the zealous care of our Catholic teachers. These instructors may supplement and develop, but they were never intended to supplant the domestic tuition.

The education of a child should begin at its mother's knee. The mind of a child, like softened wax, receives first impressions with ease, and these impressions last longest. "Train up a child in the way he should go, and when he is

[1] *The Christian Home*, pp. 4-9. (The Columbus Press, New York.)

old he will not depart from it." A child is susceptible of instruction much earlier than parents commonly imagine. It has the capacity to perceive and apprehend the truth, though unable as yet to go through the process of reasoning and analysis. Mothers should watch with a zealous eye the first unfolding of the infant mind, and pour into it the seed of heavenly knowledge.

For various reasons mothers should be the first instructors of their children.

First, as nature ordains that mothers should be the first to feed their offspring with corporal nourishment of their own substance, so the God of nature ordains that mothers should be the first to impart to their little ones "the rational guileless milk" of heavenly knowledge, "whereby they may grow unto salvation" (I Peter ii 2).

Second, the children that are fed by their own mothers are usually more healthy and robust than those that are nurtured by wet-nurses. In like manner, the children who are instructed by their own mothers in the elements of Christian knowledge are commonly more sturdy in faith than those who are committed for instruction to strangers.

Third, the progress of a pupil in knowledge is in a great measure proportioned to the confidence he has in his preceptor. Now, in whom does a child place so much reliance as in his mother? She is his oracle and prophet. She is his guide, philosopher, and friend. He never doubts what his mother tells him. The lesson he receives acquires additional force because it proceeds from one to whom he gave his first love, and whose image, in after life, is indelibly stamped on his heart and memory. Mothers, do not lose the golden opportunity you have of training your children in faith and morals while their hearts are open to drink in your every word.

Fourth, you share the same home with your children, you frequently occupy the same apartment. You eat at the same table with them. They are habitually before your eyes. You are, therefore, the best fitted to instruct them, and you can avail yourself of every little incident that presents itself and draw from it some appropriate moral reflection.

The fruits of the realization amongst us of the divine beauties of the Home of Nazareth are not far to seek.

The most distinguished personages who have adorned the Church by their apostolic virtues, or who have served their country by fine patriotism, or who have shed a luster on the home by the integrity of their private lives, have usually been men who had the happiness of receiving from pious mothers early principles of moral rectitude.

Witness St. Augustine, the great Doctor of the Church in the fifth century. In his youth he had lost his faith, and with it purity of conscience. He was tainted with Manichæism, the most pernicious error of the times, and he became a prey to the fiercest passions. Monica, his saintly mother, prayed for him with a constancy which only a mother can exhibit. She hoped against hope; and before her death she had the consolation of seeing him restored to God and His Church. St. Augustine attributes his conversion to her, and in his matchless book, the *Confessions,* he speaks of her most tenderly.

St. Louis, King of France, is another example of what a mother may do. As a monarch and as a saint he owes his virtues, under God, to Queen Blanche, his mother: "I love you tenderly," she said to her child, "but sooner would I see you a corpse at my feet, and France bereft of an heir to the throne, than that you should tarnish your soul by a corrupt life."

If Queen Blanche could pay so much attention to her son's instruction, notwithstanding her engrossing administrative cares, surely the mothers of to-day, in private walks of life, should find leisure for a similar duty.

Nor need we look beyond our own country's first president for the fruition of that seed which was sown by a devoted mother. Washington was conspicuous for the natural virtues of frugality, industry, self-restraint, and respect for authority. Above all, he possessed a love of truth and an habitual recognition of the overruling Providence of God. And he gloried in declaring that these traits were impressed on his youthful mind by his mother, for whom he had a profound reverence, and whom in his letters he usually addressed as his "honored" mother.

If in our day we find the religion of Christ firmly rooted in the land; if the word of the Teacher of Men has quickened and brought forth good fruit; if we see about us homes spiritualized and sanctified by the radiance of the

Home of Nazareth, and lifted above the worldly and material by the memory of the Divine Exemplar—this happy condition is largely due to the faith and piety of Christian wives and mothers. This noble army of apostolic women "are the glory of Jerusalem, the joy of Israel, the honor of our people"; they are the saviors of society and a blessing to the nation.

It is true, indeed, that they are not clothed with the priestly character. They cannot offer the Holy Sacrifice or administer the Sacraments. But may we not apply to them the words of St. Peter: "Ye are a chosen generation, a holy nation, a royal priesthood"? Yes, we may in all truth. They are consecrated priestesses of the domestic temple, where they daily offer up in the sanctuary of their homes, and on the altar of their hearts, the sacrifice of praise and prayer, of supplication and thanksgiving to God. They cannot preach the word of God in public, but they are apostles by prayer, good deeds, and edifying example. They preach most effectually to the members of their households, and the word of God scattered from the pulpit would often bear little fruit if it were not watered and nurtured by the care of our pious mothers.

No more weighty obligation devolves upon Christian parents than that of recognizing and discharging conscientiously these fundamental duties of the home. It is a sublime task. "What is more noble," cries St. John Chrysostom, "than to form the minds of youth? He who fashions the morals of children performs a task in my judgment more sublime than that of any painter or sculptor." It is, indeed, a far more exalted task than that of sculptor or painter that is entrusted to fathers and mothers. They are creating living portraits, destined to adorn not only earthly temples, but also the Temple above, not fashioned of man's hand

And therefore built forever.

And mark well: home education does not mean merely those lessons in Christian Doctrine which are to be taught to children. The home should be pervaded by a religious atmosphere. It should be the sanctuary of domestic peace, sobriety, and parental love. Discontent and anger should be banished from it; and under these sweet influences the child will grow in virtue. Above all, let it be the asylum of daily prayer, and then the angels of God and the God of angels will be there.

It is to the mothers and fathers of to-day that we must look for the realization amongst us of this Christian ideal of the home—the Home of Nazareth. They are doubly bound to seek it, if need be "sorrowing"—as did Mary and Joseph. They are bound, on the one hand, by their Christian faith and the example of Christ; and, on the other, they owe a duty to the State. Thus shall they rear up for their country not scourges of society, but loyal, law-abiding citizens. "If any one," says the Apostle, "have not care of his own, and especially of his own household, he hath denied the faith, and is worse than an infidel" (1 Tim. v. 8; Prov. xxxi 28). Aye, more—he hath fallen short in his duty to his country.

THE STATE

159

ORIGIN AND RIGHTS OF SOVEREIGNTY

Charles Macksey [1]

When a multitude of people come to grasp, however dimly, the natural life-purposes incumbent upon them (purposes in themselves supremely desirable as well), come, moreover, to apprehend the obvious fact that only in civil union of a concrete society can these purposes be achieved; that this union implies a bond binding each of them, a bond bearing with it definite common civil duties and civil rights for all, they have certainly arrived at the threshold of a juridical union. In all other cases of juridical union contingent upon common action, in all other cases of natural and mutual obligation so contingent, as well as in the case of acquired natural rights over definite means to a natural end, the next step is a free act of the will, and the thing is done. In perfect parity, if the multitude there and then accept the bond in question, you there and then have in existence a new juridical entity, a juridical union, which men call civil society. They may have been entirely free to consent, or for one reason or other may have been morally bound to consent; they may have consented in written instrument or spoken word; in the cheerful enthusiasm of subordination and co-operation, with neither written nor spoken pledge, or in the silent omission of all protest and repudiation, when such protest would be efficient or a matter of duty; they may have consented all together, or group after group yielding in course of time; they may have consented to the entirety of the bond at once or by degrees to the different duties of its content. It matters not: the one substantial thing in the establishment of a State as of a family, in joining a civic unit together with

[1] *Sovereignty and Consent*, pp. 16-20; 30, 31; 32. (The America Press, New York.)

the civic bond as in joining a family unit with the marriage bond, is the voluntary and free consent of those who establish the union.

The consent of the community then is the fact which of its nature spells an exigency that the natural law should supply the essential juridical ingredient there and then necessary for the natural function and juridical cohesion of civil society: and that is, after all, what we understand by a foundation, a juridically determinant cause of the existence of that juridical effect, which is found in a multitude, when, instead of remaining an incoherent assembly of discrete atoms, it is bound together into the social union which we know as a body politic or a State. It is indeed the only fact that accounts juridically for that union, just as consent is the only juridical cause that accounts for the juridical existence of a marital union. Vicinage does not do it, nor kindred blood. Common needs may be a motive of consent, and even, in a conceivable case, extreme enough to give rise to an obligation to yield the consent; but of themselves they do not place the consent, nor sufficiently substitute for it in placing the social bond. Such conditions will not suffice in the case of the matrimonial union. Why should they in the case of the more extensive and complicated unit? Patriarchal descent, occupancy of the territory of one and the same landed proprietor, subjection by conquest, none of these are claimed to be sufficient juridically to make a discrete multitude into a civil community, except in so far as the patriarch, land-holder or conqueror has *ipso facto* sovereignty over those who fall under the respective categories correlative to each of them. But we shall proceed at once to show that sovereignty needs a firmer ground, lies originally with the people, and is found derivatively elsewhere only by the people's consent.

When men in the fulfilment of God's plan establish the juridical person of the body politic by their consent to this juridical union for the general welfare, the natural law necessarily concedes to that person in the very bond, which creates it, all the rights and powers necessary, and even those connaturally proportionate, to the purpose of the common weal. The powers essential to each and every State will be congenital rights of the body politic. If we conceive the thing as in a condition of juridical genesis, we ask ourselves, What are the first powers that body needs? The answer is the power to organize itself under a definite form of government of its choice; the power to choose the individuals in whom the governmental powers are stably to reside, to determine the stable limitation of these powers by reservation of power to the community itself, and the method of succession in their possession; the power to govern the community *ad interim* either directly or by the appointment of provisional governors; the power to reorganize the government, whenever its prior organization, whether from forces within or without, goes to pieces, or permanently fails to function *for the general welfare,* or in new times and circumstances fails to meet *the exigencies of the common weal;* the right, finally, to be the authentic judge of conditions requiring organization. I fancy we need not elaborate the point that substantially these powers are from the start requisite to the essential purpose of civil society; nor that by reason of God's ordering human society in His plan of human life, and by natural consequence of men putting one such into existence, this society has the above rights and powers. They are as obviously involved in the content of the civic bond as are all the rights and privileges necessary to the natural purpose of marital life involved in the marriage bond.

These powers may be and sometimes are called constituent powers, authority to enact a constitution or fundamental law, a law, namely, in which the organization of the government is provided for as above, and the reserved powers of the community declared. In point of fact that is what is meant by popular sovereignty, that is to say, the sum of supreme jurisdiction necessary to provide the organization and government of a State, as inherent in the community as a body politic, a moral person, from the first instant of its juridical existence; jurisdiction coming from God through the natural law in the civic bond which makes of a multitude a people, a community, a State. It is quite evident that such sovereign powers exist in some person or other within the range of the community, but the contention for popular sovereignty is that they are to be found in the moral person of the community itself.

It may appear that what is commonly known as sovereignty, the supreme powers, namely, in a sovereign, whether he be tsar, kaiser or king, a class of nobles or a republican president, is not quite the same as the constituent and other powers above enumerated. That is true, though not in a sense as mutually exclusive as might be apprehended. Sovereign powers, as they exist in actual rulers, are the sum of jurisdiction necessary for actual normal government, stably set indeed in the rulers in order so to govern. They suppose then a determinate form of government, definite rulers and definite powers and a determined mode of succession; and finally they imply the possession by the rulers of the fulness of authority necessary for their function: whereas on the other hand the sovereignty attributed to the people *seems* rather made up of preliminary powers of organization, and not of powers to govern at all. That is a mistake: popular sovereignty is both one and the other. As a matter of fact the community has in itself all the powers of governing provisionally in the interim of organization; may organize, if it so choose and the thing is expedient, a purely democratic form of government, and so retaining all its powers may stably govern the State. In one word original sovereignty as in the people includes the governing powers as well as the powers of organization. Outside of an absolute democracy the people entrust the governing powers to the rulers, retaining the organizing powers for the emergency of reorganization. . . .

Cardinal Bellarmine found no difficulty in maintaining both that governing sovereignty was first in the people and yet necessarily to be transferred to definite rulers under some legitimate form of government.[2] Sovereignty is held by no ruler except in trust for the general welfare, in trust for the accomplishment of the natural purpose of civil society; and certainly unless that trust were committed to the ruler by the community, the community itself would not have had original control over its own civil destiny, which the natural law not only supposes it to have had as a right, but has imposed as a duty.

The point is worth elaborating. To possess *per se* a right it is not necessary that the possessor be *per se* competent to exercise it by himself, but only that he be *per se* competent to exercise it either by himself or by others to whom

---

[2] Bellarmine, "De Laicis," Lib. III, cap. 6, not. 3.

he may entrust it for exercise. Thus the right to educate their children would still belong to the parents, even if parents were not *per se* fitted to exercise it by themselves, but were necessitated to seek competent substitutes, to whom they entrusted the right for execution. And the reason is that parents could not divest themselves of the duty and responsibility, even in the supposition that the duty was *per se* and of necessity to be fulfilled by others of their appointment. In like manner the community cannot escape the responsibility or divest itself of the duty of accomplishing the purpose for which governing sovereignty is given.

Just as the physical power of understanding belongs to the soul, though it cannot exercise it without an intellectual faculty, *which derives its power* from the soul; so too the moral power of tilling the soil of an immense estate which belongs to an individual owner, is his, even though he cannot exercise it by himself, but must needs invoke others to exercise it for his benefit. Even the civil law can grant a transitory right to an individual *per se* incompetent to exercise it, with the added obligation of transferring it to others at his choice, that they may exercise it for his benefit and for its civil purpose. . . .

To state by way of conclusion the Scholastic doctrine: the title for the juridical existence of an actual State is the consent of the people who constitute it. Immediately consequent upon this follows by Divine right of the natural law sovereignty in the people, now a juridical unit, a body politic, a moral person. Logically and juridically subsequent to this comes constitutional organization of a form of government and a determination of definite rulers, who constitute the government, the juridical and derivative title to whose sovereignty is the consent of the body politic, the people. In this sense lies the truth of the principle that "governments *derive* their just powers from the consent of the governed." [3]

[3] American "Declaration of Independence."

160

THE MORAL ORIGIN OF CIVIL AUTHORITY [1]

Louis Cardinal Billot [2]

The statement that political authority is immediately from the people, can be understood in two ways: Either from the people, as it were, abdicating and transferring by a donation or contract that authority to those who preside over the commonwealth; or from the people, creating organic law in virtue of which authority is embodied in such or such a governmental form, and given to such or such a possessor. . . . The difference between these two ways may be illustrated by an example taken from the law of property. I may receive dominion over a thing from another person, as the rightful possessor who now makes mine that which was his, as if Titius would donate to me his field; or from another, as from the immediate author of a law by which dominion is acquired, as if, in virtue of prescription enacted by the civil legislator, I begin to be the owner of a piece of land which before did not belong to me. That magistrates derive their power proximately from the people, is explained by most of the older scholastics according to the analogy of the former example. But we think that we should base the explanation rather on the second example. However, these points concern only the deeper understanding of the doctrine, and maybe this is a dispute more about words than things. In any case, forms of government and titles to exercise power, and power itself, as existing in its determinate possessors, are not immediately from God, but only through the medium of human consent, that is, the consent of the community.

An objection to the foregoing statement has been brought forward from the words of the Encyclical of Pope Leo XIII, *Diuturnum Illud:* "It is important to bear in mind that those who are to preside over the commonwealth can in some cases be selected by the will and judgment of the

---

[1] The paragraphs of this chapter are a free translation of the greater part of Propositions III and IV, section 1, question 12, chapter 3, *De Ecclesia Christi.*
[2] *The State and the Church,* by Ryan and Millar, pp. 62-67. (Macmillan Company, New York. With permission.)

multitude, without any opposition on the part of Catholic teaching. By this selection indeed the sovereign is designated, but the rights of sovereignty are not conferred; authority is not delegated, but the person who is to exercise it is designated." We reply that these words merely set forth the pure and simple doctrine of faith against the pernicious innovation with which very many were infatuated in the sixteenth century, and which in the eighteenth century led to the monstrous error of the Social Contract. . . . What the Pope denies is that the popular choice ever confers the rights of sovereignty in the sense of those who oppose Catholic doctrine; that is, in the sense that the right of sovereignty *in itself* comes from the people, after the manner of an instrumental power which flows from a supreme commissioner to one commissioned. In a word, the Pope denies what has been unanimously denied at all times by Catholic theologians. And the Pope agrees with the theologians likewise in his positive affirmations. Since authority in itself is constituted not by human but by divine natural right, there is nothing left for human will or action but the determination and designation of the ruler. . . . Through this designation the people become the proximate cause, not indeed of power as such, but of the conjunction of power with such a person, according to such or such a measure, and such or such conditions. Hence the Pope's statement does not remove from the community the power that is truly constitutive of government. . . .

Other objections are made by recent authors who hold that the power of sovereigns is derived immediately from God. One of these maintains that society cannot confer authority, since there is no constituted society prior to the institution of a government. I reply: At the moment before the institution of a government there exists a society constituted, not indeed ultimately and in perfect actuality, yet in potentiality, whenever there exists a determinate multitude of men assembled to help one another for a political end. Nor are the means wanting to produce the effect. Unless we fancy that civil societies have been immediately instituted by nature, we must recognize the existence of some constituting power in the community, in the first stage of political society. Before the institution of a government, therefore, there is already at hand a social power, not indeed for governing that society, but for constituting sovereignty from which the governing power is derived. . . .

According to the second objection, if political power is from God in any way whatsoever, it must be from God in some determinate and concrete subject or possessor. My reply is that political sovereignty, in so far as it is from God, exists immediately in a concrete subject or possessor, namely, in the community itself, by which it is afterwards retained, or is transferred to one monarch, or to a select group. Moreover, the power of jurisdiction is not to be likened entirely to physical forms which do not exist except in some determinate subject. If this were true, the Papal power would be extinct in the interval between the death of a Pope and the election of his successor. . . . If you ask where is political power, as immediately instituted by God? I reply: In the law of nature, or in the ordinance of the divine reason, which is manifested by human nature and written in the human mind. But this general ordinance must be determinated by men. Hence the actual holder of political authority, holds it by human law as its proximate source; but political authority as such does not come from men; they merely determine the form in which it will be actualized, and the person or persons by whom it will be exercised.

The third objection is that this doctrine of popular determination of government and selection of the ruler, provides a foundation for sedition and rebellion against the monarch. In reply, I would point out that there is no doctrine which cannot be abused. Yet no doctrine ought to be condemned for that reason alone. The view that authority is conferred by God immediately upon the ruler has likewise been abused, and it is hard to tell which abuse has been the greater or the more detestable. It is certain that the regalists have been led to conclude that kings as such may claim supreme indifference or irresponsibility, whence they extended the powers of civil society even over religion. . . . All that we can do is to abstract altogether from abuses, and to seek only what truly follows from principles. There is no foundation for rebellion in any doctrine which asserts the divine precept of obedience to constituted authority. This precept is neither taken away nor lessened by our doctrine. From the fact that the ruler does not derive his authority immediately from God, it does not follow that the precept of obeying constituted authority is destroyed or weakened.

Nor does it follow that one government can be deposed and another instantly substituted at the whim of the multitude. . . . A will which does not follow the order of reason neither has nor can have validity. However, let us not conjure up imaginary suppositions which have no place in our actual world. Let us remember that changes of government, whether licit or illicit, are humanly unavoidable, and that this instability can never be eradicated by any force or any theory. The practical question is, which of the two doctrines that we are considering is more conducive to the peace and prosperity of the commonwealth? Is it our doctrine? or is it forsooth that other doctrine which is based on a preposterous conception of legitimacy, and which would recognize in dynasties of kings a right as immovable as in the succession of the Pope to the Apostolic See? Let us consider this question at somewhat greater length.

The right of sovereignty is unlike the right of property, inasmuch as it is by nature ordained not for the benefit of him who holds it, but for the benefit of society. Hence if at any time the public good requires a new form of government and a new designation of rulers, no pre-existing right of any person or any family can validly prohibit this change. The right to create the new legitimate government inheres in the community habitually or potentially. However, it ought not to be used rashly and whimsically, but only when its use is demanded by the common good and social tranquility.

The question may be asked, when is the demand of social necessity evidently verified? For answer we do not need to go far away, nor to take refuge in metaphysics. The necessity of constituting a new government exists whenever the preceding government has been destroyed, and there has been introduced a new government which cannot be abolished without detriment to peace. In such a situation, the new government is legitimate, even though the preceding one was destroyed by iniquitous rebellion, for the only pertinent question concerns what is here and now required by the supreme law of the common good. By this supreme criterion it is evident that the community has the same right to constitute a new sovereignty as it had at the beginning of its political existence. Generally speaking, every civil government is to be held legitimate from the moment when it has been constituted and accepted and regularly exercised. . . .

This conclusion is confirmed by the ancient and immemorial practice of the Church. She has always recognized as legitimate governments of whatsoever origin, once they had been constituted and had been confirmed by the consent of peoples. . . . This perpetual practice and discipline of the Church has been illustrated by a doctrinal declaration of Pope Leo XIII in that memorable Encyclical to the French, *Au Milieu des Sollicitudes:*

However, here it must be carefully observed that whatever be the form of civil power in a nation, it cannot be considered so definitive as to have the right to remain immutable, even though such were the intention of those who, in the beginning, determined it. . . . Only the Church of Jesus Christ has been able to preserve, and surely will preserve unto the consummation of time, her form of government. Founded by Him who was, who is, and who will be forever, she has received from Him, since her very origin, all that she requires for the pursuing of her divine mission across the changeable ocean of human affairs. And, far from wishing to transform her essential constitution, she has not the power even to relinquish the conditions of true liberty and sovereign independence with which Providence has endowed her in the general interest of souls. . . . But, in regard to purely human societies, it is an oft-repeated historical fact that time, that great transformer of all things here below, operates great changes in their political institutions. On some occasions it limits itself to modifying something in the form of the established government; or, again, it will go so far as to substitute other forms for the primitive ones—forms totally different, even as regards the mode of transmitting sovereign power.

And how are these political changes of which we speak produced? They sometimes follow in the wake of violent crises, too often of a bloody character, in the midst of which pre-existing governments totally disappear; then anarchy holds sway, and soon public order is shaken to its very foundations and finally overthrown. From that time onward a social need obtrudes itself upon the nation; it must provide for itself without delay. Is it not its privilege—or, better still, its duty—to defend itself against a state of affairs troubling it so deeply, and to re-establish public peace in the tranquillity of order? Now, this social need justifies the creation and the existence of new governments, whatever form they take; since, in the hypothesis wherein we reason, these new governments are a requisite to public order, all public order being impossible without a government. Thence it follows that, in similar junctures, all the novelty is limited to the political form of civil power, or to its mode of transmission; it in no wise affects the power considered in itself. This continues to be immutable and worthy of respect, as, considered in its nature, it is constituted to provide for the common good, the supreme end which gives human society its origin. To put it otherwise, in all hypotheses, civil power, considered as such, is from God, always from God: "For there is no power but from God."

Consequently, when new governments representing this immutable power are constituted, their acceptance is not only permissible but even obligatory, being imposed by the need of the social good which has made and which upholds them. This is all the more imperative because an insurrection stirs up hatred among citizens, provokes civil war, and may throw a nation into chaos and anarchy, and this great duty of respect and dependence will endure as long as the exigencies of the common good shall demand it, since this good is, after God, the first and last law in society.

161

POLITICAL THEORIES OF ST. THOMAS

Leo E. Hughes [1]

The principal founder of political science was Aristotle. Before his time, politics as a distinct science had scarcely come into existence. By defining the best form of government, Aristotle's master, the sublime Plato, had assigned to politics the task of planning the ideal state.

The Stagyrite opposed Plato's theory, which was state absolution, and desired to offer men a better form of political organization. Unlike the poetic philosopher, Aristotle was always forced to remain with realities and necessities. Thus, all existing and defunct constitutions were investigated for the purpose of discovering the principles which gave them birth, helped them to thrive or ruined them.

[1] Adapted from *Dominicana*, June, 1919.

He was the first to assert the natural necessity of society, and, consequently, of government. The mission of the State, to him, was the advancement and development of its subjects; their elevation by the just administration of law to a higher plane of moral conduct. For this reason he sought a means of uniting the best elements in the various constitutions to establish a more perfect form of government, a type, however, which was not to be considered absolutely fixed. It should admit of applications and modifications instead of being an ideal but impracticable constitution.

So we may speak of the political pronouncements of the Angelic Doctor. The directing idea of his political doctrines pretends less to discover a model constitution than to set forth the constituent elements of good government, for his deepest consideration is ever for the welfare of the citizens rather than for the form of government under which they live.

Now, considered in itself, the origin of society is an isolated question and of no great practical importance. It becomes of grave significance, however, when we make our theories concerning it the basis of our doctrine of the foundation and legitimacy of authority in government.

On this capital point in political science we find the Prince of Schoolmen breaking away from the scholastic tradition of his day. Theologians of eminence, predecessors and contemporaries, cherished a radically different opinion. They maintained that the State has not a proper power which it holds in the nature of things and which in itself must be legitimate, always and everywhere. This power exists as such only in the Church and by the Church. Supernatural society alone confers on natural society the right to existence.

They justify these assertions by saying that the right of sovereignty was a consequence of the state of sinful nature. If man had not sinned he would not have been obliged to obey his own kind. This material authority of man over man, in itself merely the exercise of force, can become legitimate only as the reflection of a higher society which is qualified to lead man to salvation.

On the contrary, even in the state of innocence, the domination of man over man would have been exercised.

This is the declaration of St. Thomas and he gives the following reasons to support it: First, the condition of man in the state of innocence was not more worthy than that of the angels, and among them, some were governed by others; secondly, man is a social being, created to live in society, which necessitates a leader to direct all things to the common good; lastly, there was a disparity of gifts even in that state, and that one enjoyed greater wisdom or knowledge, would be inconvenient unless it were employed for the greatest benefit to the others. This means that the superior must command the inferior. In other words, the state of society is a necessary state.

St. Thomas comes to the same conclusion in the *De Regimine Principum* (book I, chap. I), where he treats professedly of the origin of society. And here, society is discussed *in abstracto* and not *in particulari*.

It is the nature of man, he says, to be a social and political being, living in community differently from all other animals. Nature has provided other animals with food, weapons for defense, such as claws, etc., the faculty of discerning the useful and injurious and means requisite for their development and self-preservation.

With man it is otherwise. He has not been blessed with these gifts. Reason and the labor of his hands are his instruments in the struggle for existence. Social life for man is required for his self-development, protection against enemies, the safe-guarding of his health, the advantages of the division of labor, his education and the promotion of friendship. Man left to himself would be seriously hampered, if not helpless, in these regards, and thus it is necessary that he live in society, applying himself to his own task; his neighbor doing the same, one helping the other.

Then a strengthening indication of this necessity is signed by his endowment, the faculty of speech, manifesting that he is destined to communicate with others and, consequently, to live in society.

This explanation of the origin of society is much better than the subtleties of covenants, explicit and implicit. It attributes to the Creator what Rousseau and others ascribe to the creature. Moreover, St. Thomas, with clearness of ideas, solidity of principles and exactness of deductions, puts forth in a few words all that can be said with respect to this question.

Political society is defined by St. Thomas as a community integrated of many members, whose activity is ordained to the welfare of all the members, in as much as they are parts of the society.

We have seen that society must be regarded as coeval with man; for man out of society is a solecism. And from this necessity the brilliant friar deduces that of power, as a corollary.

Thus, if it be natural for man to live in society, he says, it is necessary that some one should direct the multitude; for if many were united, and each one did as he thought proper, society would be sundered, unless somebody looked after the public good, as would be the case with the human body and that of any other animal if there did not exist a power to watch over the welfare of all the members. In man himself, the soul directs the body, and in the soul the feelings of anger and concupiscence are governed by the reason. Among the members of the body there is one principal member which directs all, as the heart or the head. There ought, then, to be in every multitude some governing power.

As St. Thomas differs from scholastic tradition on the natural existence of society and power, he gives added proof of his initiative in his doctrine of the origin of power. This problem has not been treated in one single tract, as it was not considered a live question in the thirteenth century, and, accordingly, did not receive the attention which other and more pressing problems demanded. So we are obliged to gather his doctrine from different passages of his various works where we find "the main lines of the solution drawn by him with more perfect design" than by writers who have since expounded on this point. His opinions so placed do not apparently agree. Hence, the differences of view among the interpreters of his thought. Some accept passages which assert intellectual sovereignty—favoring absolutism and sacrifice others which plainly make for popular sovereignty. We shall see that the Thomistic doctrine is rather a union of the two.

We must here remember that the key to the mind of St. Thomas is the Summa Theologica. This peerless work, written in more mature years must always be taken as the wonderful embodiment of his unparalleled mind.

The question of the origin of power is twofold: First, power considered in itself, i. e., the institution; secondly, the concrete realization of power as it is considered in the persons invested with it. All power comes from God. This is Catholic doctrine and has been stated by St. Thomas time and again. But to say that sovereignty in its source belongs to God alone because He is the Supreme Master of human society, and that worldly sovereigns are merely His instruments did not preclude his searching for the human source of this divine delegation.

God does not display authority directly. The authority which He alone possesses in its essence and perfection is participated in by man. It becomes incarnated in him. Thus, power comes at the same time from divine right and from human right. "Non est potestas nisi a Deo" the holy Doctor has repeated again and again after St. Paul. But he has also written "dominium a jure humano." Therefore, all power comes from God, but men exercise it. Sovereignty is of divine origin, but not necessarily the sovereigns. It may be mentioned here that nowhere does St. Thomas sustain the divine right of kings except in the Catholic sense that all lawfully constituted authority is the representative of divine authority. That doctrine was pagan, and has received its fullest and most systematic development since the so-called Reformation.

The question of the human origin of power resolves to this: Who of mankind is the depository of sovereignty? Aristotle establishes the true foundation of sovereignty upon intelligence and reason, making the intellectual chief leader by right. St. Thomas, strongly imbued with the value of intelligence, for he was ever its champion, readily assents to this thesis of the Master and agrees wtih him that political ability is the best title to the exercises of government; nevertheless, as we shall see, he does not accept the conclusion of the pagan philosopher as such.

For our answer to the question raised above, we must first go to the Treatise on Laws in the "Summa." Balmes calls this tract immortal, and defies any one to find a jurist or philosopher who expounds with more lucidity, wisdom, noble independence and generous dignity, the principles to which civil power ought to adhere, and further states that whoever fully comprehends it has no additional information to acquire respecting the principles which ought to guide the legislator.

Here studying legislative power, an essential attribute of sovereign dominion, he says: "Law properly regards, first and foremost, the order that is to be taken towards the general good. Now, to order anything towards the general good belongs either to the whole community or to some one who is vice-regent of the whole people. And, therefore, the framing of a law belongs either to the whole people or to a personage who has the care of the whole people, because in all things the ordering of the means to the end belongs to him to whom the end belongs as his special concern." If, therefore, to decree on the public order of the commonwealth is the right of society itself, or of some one acting in its place, whence would this last derive his authority but from society? This seems conclusive.

In another place he declares that if the people among whom a custom is introduced be "free and able to make their own laws, the consent of the whole people expressed by a custom counts for more in favor of a particular observance than does the authority of the sovereign who has not the power to frame laws except as representing the people."

In his commentary on the Sentences, when speaking of the usurpation of dominion by violence, he comes nearest to expressing that fundamental principle of American government—"governments derive their just powers from the consent of the governed"—which is true if correctly understood. He says the usurper may be lawfully repelled, unless, perchance, he becomes afterwards the recognized and legitimate ruler by consent of the subjects or through the authority of a superior.

Does this not sound like the principle of self-determination? We believe so. These citations seem clearly to assert that the primitive subject of sovereignty is the whole people; though from the last we perceive that dominion does not necessarily come from the deliberate and manifest choice of the people.

St. Thomas declares that the essential purpose of government is the welfare of the people. "The kingdom was not made for the king but the king for the kingdom." And here it is that we find the line of demarcation between the foundation of virtue of Aristotle and that of the Angelic Doctor. Good government demands the fullest promotion of the people's interests which are manifested by the aspirations of the national conscience, though they be obscure and latent. In other words, the foundation of sovereignty rests upon the demands of the people. Their demands will not always be expressed, but it suffices that the power satisfy them, no matter whence it comes, elective, hereditary or revolutionary.

Thus, in default of an election, or an explicit consent of the subjects, their implicit consent establishes a government which rightly responds to their wants. The popular will always exists, at least tacitly, to confirm the power of the ruler, even though it has not created him.

The principle of acquisition of every power is a contract or quasi-contract. St. Thomas hints at this very clearly. By this the ruler, on assuming the sovereignty, binds himself to forward the common weal with all his energy and efforts, while the subjects in return promise him obedience. The conditions of the contract are not always the same everywhere, hence the functions of sovereignty may be exercised in different ways which beget different types of government.

St. Thomas was acquainted with the diverse constitutions of government of ancient Rome and Greece and those of his own days. They were all examined by him. He admits the legitimacy of monarchy, aristocracy and democracy. However, no predilection is openly manifested for any particular constitution as ideal and fixed. For, unhesitatingly, and with profound wisdom he affirms that the happiness and prosperity of a nation depend not so much on their particular constitution, as upon the unwavering fidelity and constant adherence of the rulers to the purpose for which the government was instituted, and upon the moral fibre and integrity of the people.

He argues on general grounds that the rule of society is better secured by the rule of one than by that of the few or the many. But great danger lies in the supremacy of one. Power may be easily abused; the common interests perverted. Such conditions would be unsocial and tyrannical. Accordingly, the preventive and repressive measures against such a calamity; they are the limitation of power to remove the occasion and the right to depose the tyrant with very reasonable and wise restrictions.

The fear of tyranny is very marked in the writings of St. Thomas, and this seems to be the compelling reason for his sympathy with mixed government, i. e., a limited monarchy or a well-organized republic.

In his treatise on laws he says that the mixed polity is the best, i. e., the best elements of monarchy, aristocracy and democracy combined form the best type of government.

Aristotle emphasized the importance of the co-operation of all to maintain the State. St. Thomas accepts this when he states that one of the principal things to insure the stability and the peace of the State is that all should have some part in the government. Our attention is called to this in the 105 Question, article 1, 1a 2ae. We must here mention that some commentators deny its application to modern States; others interpret it in favor of a limited monarchy. Considering the principles contained therein, supported by what we have said concerning the origin of power, we feel justified in the opinion of a distinguished American Thomist, who is not alone in his thought, in our belief that the constitutional frame constructed by this eminent statesman fits very nicely that of our own Republic.

St. Thomas establishes a head, who is the unifying principle of power; confides the administration of affairs to enlightened citizens and confers the right of suffrage on the people; and says that "the best form of government is a mixture of kingdom, of aristocracy and of democracy, i. e., of the power of the people, inasmuch as the rulers can be chosen from the people and the election of the rulers belongs to the people." On the authority of the learned Thomist already quoted, we say that "there is a vast amount of good republicanism and sound democracy in these words."

In the ruler may be seen the president, the element of monarchy; the body of administrators, the element of aristocracy, corresponds to Congress, which, in the intention of the founders of our government, was to represent the intellectual nobility of the nation. Then, we have the element of democracy, the choice of ruler and administrators, of and by the people.

162

THE DEMOCRACY OF ST. THOMAS

Alfred O'Rahilly [1]

"A Churchman like Thomas Aquinas," declares a distinguished contemporary historian, "approaches nearer to the opinions of modern times than the generality of those who defended the claims of the emperor as against the pope, by a theory of the necessary, the indefeasible, the divine, basis of the imperial dignity." "Though a strong papalist," says Dr. A. J. Carlyle, "there is no trace in his writings of the mere partisan, and nothing is, perhaps, more remarkable than the entire absence of all trace of personal feeling in a man whose early life was passed in times of such violent conflict and in which his family suffered much."

Generalised and translated into modern terms, his view may be thus expressed. Every community which, as a fact of social psychology, acts as a moral whole—aided thereto by common race, tradition, language, religion or customs—is a complete society. For purposes of public order and international adjustment, it requires an organization known as the State. But this organization is a very incomplete and imperfect expression of the community or nation; it has no claim whatever to an entire monopoly of its human life and culture. "Man is not referred to the political community according to his whole self and all that he has." [2] With which dictum we may contrast the position of a contemporary philosopher, according to whom the State exists "for the special task of maintaining in a certain territory the external conditions of good life *as a whole*" and is the "*sole* organiser of rights and guardian of moral values." [3] This is correctly stated to represent "the Greek tradition as renewed by Hegel and by English thought," for it certainly contradicts the Catholic view; statolatry is very ancient and very modern, but it is not medieval; it can be found in Plato or in Hegel; there is not a trace of it in S. Thomas. For him there is an objective norm of right and wrong, not simply a set of abstract propositions but

---

[1] *Studies*, March, 1920. (Dublin.)
[2] 1-2, q. 21, a. 4, ad. 3.
[3] B. Bosanquet, *Social and International Ideals*, 1917, pp. 283f, 270.

truths and canons upheld by a living autonomous institution, whereby the State itself is to be judged. "Public power is committed to rulers that they may be the custodians of justice." "Man is bound to obey secular rulers only in so far as the order of justice requires."[4] The State has a limited authority to represent the community in certain aspects, and those not the deepest; outside this ambit its action is *ultra vires,* and within it its conduct is subject to moral criteria. There could be no greater contrast to the current theory of sovereignty, whether held by philosophers, so-colled constitutional lawyers or collectivist Socialists.

This emerges more closely from S. Thomas's remarks on legalized injustice. Laws, he says, are unjust in two ways.[5]

(1) Because contrary to human good:
    (*a*) From their object—for instance when a government imposes on subjects burdensome laws which are not connected with the common utility but rather with its own cupidity or glory.
    (*b*) From their author, as when anyone enacts a law outside the powers committed to him.
    (*c*) From their form—for example when burdens, even those ordained for the common good, are imposed unequally on the people.

These are rather acts of violence than laws. . . . Hence such laws have no obligation in conscience—unless, perhaps, for the avoidance of scandal or disturbance a man ought not to press his rights.

(2) Laws can also be unjust, because contrary to divine good —e. g., the laws of tyrants prescribing idolatry or anything else against the divine law. It is absolutely illicit to observe such laws.

In all this the emphasis is laid on the invalidity of laws which are contrary to human good; and even in the second possibility of injustice—contrariety to divine good—the reference is to natural religion. So far was this theory of State-limitation from being intended as a buttress to the Church, that it is admitted to be equally applicable to ecclesiastical and secular laws.[6] The essential point is that every

---

[4] 2-2, q. 66, a. 8; 2-2, q. 104, a. 6, ad. 3.
[5] 1-2, q. 96, a. 4.
[6] "An unjust civil law does not oblige, hence neither does an unjust ecclesiastical law."—Victoria, *Relect. theol.* iv. 18.

system of government is simply a means for securing the common good within a certain sphere; if it is perverted from this end it ceases to be a government binding in conscience and becomes a tyranny resting on physical force, resistance to which is a matter not for theoretical philosophy but for practical calculation. "A tyrannical government is not just, for it is worked not for the common good but for the private good of those governing. Hence to disturb such a government is not equivalent to sedition—unless, perhaps, when the tyrannical government is inordinately disturbed so that the people suffer more harm from the disturbance than from the tyranny. It is rather the tyrant that is seditious."[7] S. Thomas saw clearly that "sedition" is sometimes just a question of vocabulary. There are cases when the community is perfectly justified in seeking—and may even be bound to seek—by every effective means to oust an organised tyranny which has usurped the names of "government," "law" and "order" and has monopolized the charge of "sedition."

S. Thomas, however, does not confine himself to this extreme case which is the dissolution of all rule. He gives positive suggestions for obviating its occurrence.

Every effort should be made [he says[8]] to safeguard the people so that the ruler may not become a tyrant.

(1) It is necessary that only a man whose degeneracy into tyranny is improbable should be made ruler by those to whom the office pertains. . . .

(2) The government should be so arranged that there is no chance of tyranny left for a ruler already established; also his power should be so limited that he cannot easily lapse into tyranny. . . .

(3) Finally it should be settled how the case could be met if the ruler were to become tyrannical.

It is obvious that such advice could have been penned only by one who was an enemy to all autocracy whether regal or parliamentary. S. Thomas has in fact left us in no doubt concerning his ideal of government. This is his

---

[7] 2.2, q. 42, a. 2, ad. 3. In his commentary on the *Politics* (v. 1) he says: "If men have both a just cause and the power, and if the common good does not suffer, they would be right in promoting sedition and *they would sin if they did not do so.*"

[8] *De reg. princ.*, i. 6; Fretté 27, 342f. Cf. 1.2, q. 105, a. 1, ad. 2.

sketch of "the best arrangement of rulers in any city or kingdom." [9]

One man is, according to merit, set at the head to preside over all, and under him are other rulers according to merit. Yet such a regime is the concern of all, because the rulers are not only elected from all but also are elected by all. Such is every good polity combining monarchy inasmuch as one is at the head, aristocracy inasmuch as there are many rulers [elected] according to merit, and democracy, i. e., the power of the people, inasmuch as the rulers can be elected by the masses and the election of rulers is the business of the people.

This is surely a very uncompromising championship of democracy: *Ad populum pertinet electio principum.* And it is by no means an isolated dictum of S. Thomas.[1] There are many clear indications that he believed in the sovereignty of the people. Thus he holds that government, like private property, "was introduced by the *jus gentium* which is human law." [2] And concerning this so-called *jus gentium*—we might translate it people's right—he tells us that it is "by human agreement" and that men "consented easily" to its provisions.[3] "If, then," concludes an able modern commentator,[4] "S. Thomas holds that the designation of the holder of power is by the right of peoples, he holds that it is accomplished by the consent of men, and this is the

---

[9] 1.2, q. 105, a. 1. I have translated *secundum virtutem*—the Aristotelian κατ' ἀξίαν—by "according to merit."

[1] "When I began to read Catholic books," says Cardinal Manning (Purcell, *Life* ii, 630), "I found S. Thomas saying, *Reges propter regna, non regna propter reges.* And again that 'God gives sovereignty immediately to society and mediately (*mediante societate*) to the prince, president or consul, one or more, whom society may legitimately designate.'" I have been unable to discover either quotation in S. Thomas. In *De reg. princ.* iii 11 the sentence occurs: *Regnum non est propter regem sed rex propter regnum.*

[2] Dominium introductum est de iure gentium quod est ius humanum.—2.2, q. 12, a. 2. Dominium et praelatio introducta sunt ex iure humano.—2.2, q. 10, a. 10.

[3] Secundum humanum condictum.—2.2, q. 66, a. 2, ad. 1. De facili in huiusmodi homines consenserunt.—1.2, q. 95, a. 4, ad. 1. This raises the very important point of the meaning of the Scholastic term *ius gentium,* with which I propose to deal elsewhere.

[4] Père Schwalm, O. P., *Leçons de philosophie sociale,* ii 482. Owing to his mistaken interpretation of an Encyclical of Pope Leo XIII (cf. *Studies,* March, 1918, p. 9), Père Schwalm essays to read into S. Thomas the theory of "designation."

THE STATE 917

elective principle." So axiomatic is this to S. Thomas that he only admits one exception, the people of Israel. "That people," he says,[5] "was ruled by God's special care. . . . And hence the Lord did not entrust even the election of the king to the people but reserved it to Himself."

S. Thomas's argument would seem to be this[6]:

Primarily and principally law relates to order for the common good. But to order anything for the common good is the function either of the whole people or of someone taking the place of the whole people. Therefore, law-making pertains either to the whole people or to the public person who has charge of the whole people. For, as in everything else, to order for an end is the function of the being whose end it is.

The language might certainly be less ambiguous. But the commentators are unanimous in interpreting the passage to imply that political power resides primarily in the community and secondarily in one to whom the community has transferred the power and who is, therefore, the people's vicegerent.[7] This is confirmed by what S. Thomas says elsewhere. "In the case of a free people which can make law for itself," he remarks,[8] "the consent of the whole people for some observance, as shown by custom, is greater than the authority of the ruler, who possesses legislative power only in so far as he represents the people. Hence,

---

[5] 1.2, q. 105, a. 1, ad. 1.

[6] 1.2, q. 90, a. 3. This is Cajetan's comment (*Opera S. Thomae*, Leonine ed. vii 151): Seclusa namque divina lege. in multitudine generis humani nullus est princeps, sed ipsa multitudo commune bonum primo respicit per seipsam vel committit alteri; alioquin non princeps sed tyrannus esset qui multitudini praeesset. Every commentator I have read—I examined more than thirty—takes the same view. Compare also Cajetan on 2.2, q. 50, a. 1 (viii. 375): Regimen autem regium a populi quidem electione dependet, qui vota sua et potestatem in eum transtulerunt, et propterea vices populi gerere dicitur.

[7] The argument can be put thus. It is the function of a rational entity to take means towards its end. Therefore, as a particular case, it is the function of the community to enact laws for its good. And the community may for this purpose entrust its power to a vicegerent (*gerens vicem totius multitudinis*). Compare what S. Thomas says concerning the people's responsibility: Maiores omnia faciunt auctoritate et favore populi, et sic populus in favendo maioribus fuit in culpa.—*Quodl.* 12, a. 23, ad. 1.

[8] 1.2, q. 97, a. 3, ad. 3.

although individually the people cannot make law, they can do so as a whole."

To this very clear pronouncement it has been objected by some modern Scholastics that by "a free people" S. Thomas meant a direct democracy or at least a republic and that only in such a case does he suppose power to reside in the people. To this objection, however, there are two decisive replies. In the first place, the phrases which S. Thomas uses here to characterize the function and position of the ruler (*princeps*) are precisely those which he consistently applies to an ordinary monarchical government. In the second place, it is easily shown that by "a free people" is meant simply an autonomous political community. For S. Thomas always contrasts therewith a people having a higher superior, an expression which, in the circumstances of the thirteenth century compromise between feudalism and monarchy, aptly describes a partial or subordinate political community. Hence it is that S. Thomas recognises only two legitimate sources of political power: the will of the people or the authority of a superior or over-lord.[9] Thus he says that "when anyone seizes by force on the government, against the will or with the forced consent of the subjects, and when recourse cannot be had to a superior for a decision as to the usurper, then the man who, in order to free his country, slays the tyrant, deserves praise and reward."[1] Similarly in his more elaborate discussion of the right of resistance:

If any people has the right of providing a ruler for itself, then, after his appointment, the ruler can be justly deposed by the same people or his power may be checked, if he tyrannically abuses his power. Nor should such a people be regarded as disloyal in deposing the tyrant, even if it had previously submitted itself for ever to him. For inasmuch as he did not behave faithfully in his rule as his office requires, he did not deserve that the pact with him should be kept by the subjects. ... But if it is the right of some superior to provide a ruler for the people, it is from him that a remedy must be expected against the tyrant's wickedness.[2]

[9] *2 Sent.*, d. 44, q. 2, a. 2: vel per consensum subditorum vel per auctoritatem superioris.
[1] *Ibid.*, ad. 5.
[2] *De reg. principum* i. 6; Fretté 27, 343b. Fretté and other editors read *destrui*, but the correct reading seems to be *destitui*.—Zeiller,

This interesting passage expresses without ambiguity S. Thomas's view that all government is contractual or fiduciary and ultimately revocable by the people, and that even under a monarchy the community has not so transferred its authority that it does not retain very real power. This is what he calls "a free people," not in contrast to a people which has slavishly alienated all its power to an assembly or person (a type of government which he did not consider rational),[3] but rather as distinguished from a sub-community, one of those largely autonomous aggregations—duchy, fief, or town—which were commoner in the federalistic society of the middle ages than they are in these days of centralized despotism. This interpretation will also enable us to dispose of an objection which is based on a passage of the *Summa*,[4] wherein he says that "if a people is moderate, serious and carefully observant of the common utility, it is rightly established by law that such a people may create for itself magistrates for its administration," whereas if it is venal and corrupt it should be deprived of such power. "Whatever be the correct interpretation," says Dr. Carlyle,[5] "S. Thomas would certainly seem to indicate that the consent of the subjects is not always required to make a government lawful." A conclusion which is quite true for *local* government. And even if S. Thomas is referring to a politically autonomous people, his argument is that "different [polities] are expedient according to men's different conditions," that a democratic régime is unsuitable to a corrupt and unenlightened people; which is a very different proposition from the denial of the democratic basis of *every* form of government.[6] It is simply one of the

p. 40. I have translated *rex* as ruler; it would be incongruous to assign a 'superior' to a modern 'king.'

[3] Thus he says (*Pol.* ii 17; Fretté 26, 202*b*) : "Solon gave to the people only that power which is most necessary, namely, that of electing rulers and correcting their mistakes. He says this power of the people is necessary, for without it the people would be slaves—if rulers could be set up without their consent and if they could not remedy the evils which the rulers might do."

[4] 1.2, q. 97, a. 1.

[5] *Scottish Review*, 27 (1896) 138.

[6] It is worth noticing that though S. Thomas is really quoting S. Augustine [*De libero arbitrio* i 6, 14; Migne, P. L., 32, 1229], he modifies and tones down the original. S. Augustine says: Nonne item recte, si quis tunc exstiterit vir bonus qui plurimum possit,

many examples of S. Thomas's sturdy common sense and close contact with historical realities. "Justice," he says, "must indeed be always observed; but the determination of what is just must vary according to men's different states;" even "what is of natural law is diversified according to men's diverse states and conditions."[7] "In making laws," he holds, "men should not seek what was observed by their ancestors but what ought to be observed as good; hence it is advisable that old laws should be repealed if better ones are presented,"[8] But while thus making full allowance for progress, he, with that sane human kindliness which characterizes the best moral theologians, never forgot the nature of the human material on which legislation has to work. "The polity does not make men," he remarks,[9] "it receives them ready-made from nature and only thus does it make use of them." "Human law," he declares elsewhere,[1] "is for people among whom many are lacking in virtue, yet it is not intended solely for the virtuous. Hence human law could not prohibit everything that is contrary to virtue; it suffices for it to prohibit what is destructive of social existence." This perhaps explains why S. Thomas implies—if such be the meaning of his almost casual remark—that a democracy which results in hopeless venality and graft should be "deprived of its power of giving honours," lest it prove the undoing of society.

adimat huic populo potestatem dandi honores et in paucorum bonorum vel etiam unius redigat arbitrium? Which S. Thomas changes into: Recte adimitur populo tali potestas dandi honores et ad paucorum bonorum redit arbitrium. That S. Augustine's passing reference to the "vir bonus" is capable of very dangerous distortion, is shown by the use which anti-democratic writers made of it. Thus, De Dominis: Non igitur Augustino semper tyrannus est qui privata sua potestate eripit populo libertatem.—*De rep. eccles*, vi 2, 20.

[7] 1.2, q. 104, a. 3, ad. 1; *Suppl.* q. 41, a. 1, ad. 3.

[8] *Pol.* ii 12. See also 1.2, q. 97, a. 1: Primi qui intenderunt invenire aliquid utile communitati hominum, non valentes omnia considerare, instituerunt quaedam imperfecta in multis deficientia, quae posteriores mutaverunt.

[9] *Pol.* i 8.

[1] 2.2, q. 77, a. 1, ad. 1. Also 1.2, q. 96, a. 2, ad. 2: Lex humana intendit homines inducere ad virtutem, *non subito sed gradatim*. 1.2, q. 98, a. 2, ad. 1: Nihil prohibet aliquid non esse perfectum simpliciter quod tamen est perfectum secundum tempus.

THE STATE

This last objection concerning what Aquinas, using a phrase of S. Augustine's, calls the *potestas dandi honores*, really opens up a very big question which involves a real distinction between the medieval and the modern conception of democracy. This lies in the interpretation of "equality." In the eighteenth century the claims to equality —as used, for instance, in the American and French Revolutions—seems to have meant merely equality of burdens and abolition of special exemptions. Nowadays the idea of equality is made much more positive and comprehensive; it has come, in practice, to imply that men's opinions in public affairs are of equal value. So much so, that a shrewd observer has remarked that "the disregard of special fitness, combined with unwillingness to acknowledge that there can be anything special about any man, which is born of equality, constitutes the great defect of modern democracy." [2] No doubt, the problem has been to a certain extent faced. Non-elective elements of government have either been retained, for instance, the English House of Lords, which in theory consists of men of experience and ability; or have been actually introduced, for example, the competitive system for the civil service. If in the light of these experiences we turn back to S. Thomas's remark, which has been supposed to show lack of faith in the principle of government by consent, we shall see that it is peculiarly appropriate to modern conditions. "If people," he says, "gradually grow depraved, sell their votes, and entrust the administration to the vicious and unworthy, such people are rightly deprived of their power of bestowing offices, and this is restored to the decision of a select body of good men." Which is a very accurate description of, say, the Civil Service Commission. But while this latter is really an anomalous exception to the current conception of equality, it is quite consonant with the medieval view.

That all men are naturally equal is a commonplace of the Schoolmen.[3] And they meant by this natural equality

---

[2] E. L. Godkin, *Unforeseen Tendencies of Democracy*, p. 46.
[3] Omnes homines sunt natura pares.—2.2, q. 104, a. 5. Quantum ad naturalia omnes sunt pares.—4 *Sent.*, d. 36, q. 1, a. 2, ad. 1. The actual expression "omnes nascuntur liberi" does not seem to be used by S. Thomas, but it is very frequently used by Thomists, e. g., Soto, *De institia et iure*, v 2, 2. (Med. 1580, p. 280*b*).

something very definite, logical and practical, utterly unlike the slipshod sentimentalism which nowadays attaches to the phrase. "In what pertains to the interior motion of the will," says S. Thomas,[4] "man is not bound to obey man but only God. However, man is bound to obey man in the external bodily actions; but even in such of these as refer to the nature of the body—for example, whatever concerns the nourishment of the body and the generation of offspring—man is not bound to obey man but God alone, for all men are by nature equal." On which Cajetan comments thus: "When you hear that men are equal according to nature, understand this not of the equality of dignity or nobility, for one is found naturally superior to another in mind and body, but rather of the equality of power, for no man has any power over another in those things which relate to nature." We have here a clear doctrine of equal natural rights, which, while it is fruitful in social and political applications, is not based on any impossible or utopian hypotheses. Every man has the same inalienable imprescriptible right to spiritual freedom and to the exterior conditions of a human existence, whether proprietary, personal or marital. Within this sacred sphere no human organization can intrude. Hence S. Thomas strictly limits even serfdom. "A serf," he says,[5] "is his master's property in matters superadded to the natural, but in matters of nature all are equal."

It follows from this that there is no such thing as natural superiority in the strict sense.[6] The Aristotelian conception

---

[4] 2.2, q. 104, a. 5; Cajetan in Leonine ed. ix 391a.

[5] 2 *Sent.*, d. 36, q. 1, a. 2, ad. 1.

[6] Homines non sunt sibi invicem praeeminentes secundum ordinem naturae.—2 *Sent.*, d. 6, q. 1, a. 4, ad. 5. Dr. Carlyle (*op. cit.* p. 113) remarks on this: "The passage occurs in his earliest work, a commentary on the Sentences of Peter Lombard, and it is possible that he had not at that time so strong a conviction of the necessity of human government in this world, whether before or after the Fall, as later. It is perhaps more probable that S. Thomas merely means that men are not, like angels and devils, divided into orders rising one above the other." This is precisely what is meant; the rest of the sentence runs, "Even the damned are not ordered for the exercise of others or for punishment." As he says elsewhere (2 *Sent.*, d. 44, q. 1, a. 3): Creatura rationalis, quantum est de se, non ordinatur ut ad finem ad aliam, ut homo ad hominem. There is no contradiction whatever in S. Thomas, for he says in his last work

of a natural slave (φύσει δοῦλος) is as incompatible with Christianity as the Nietzschian ideal of a superman. No doubt, much of Aristotle's phraseology was accepted,[7] but this was at the price of christianizing his ideas. Thus the principle of natural inferiority and servitude was reduced to this axiom of competence: "Those who are pre-eminent in intellect naturally dominate, while those who are intellectually deficient but corporally strong seem by nature to be adapted for serving, as Aristotle says in his *Politics*."[8] This idea was also applied to politics. "In human government," continues S. Thomas, "inordination arises from the fact that someone rules not on account of intellectual pre-eminence, but usurps power for himself by brute force, or someone is appointed to government owing to sensual affection." That is, S. Thomas quietly substitutes the undeniable fact of accidental disparity for Aristotle's theory of natural superiority. "Wherever," says the philosopher,[9] "there happens to be a whole family or an individual superior in virtue to all the others, ... it is but just that this family should have the regal and supreme power or that this individual should be king." A condition of affairs which, as

(*Summa*, p. 1, q. 109, a. 2, ad. 3): Daemones non sunt aequales secundum naturam, unde in eis est naturalis praelatio. Quod in hominibus non contingit qui natura sunt pares.

[7] For S. Thomas, the pioneer defender of Aristotle, this acceptance was absolutely necessary—to have admitted anti-Christian elements in Aristotelianism would have been fatal—in order to defend Peripatetic study against the numerous attacks of the ultra-orthodox conservatives. Sometimes the defence of the Stagirite becomes very subtle casuistry. *Cf. Pol.* vii 12; Fretté 26, 484: Aristotles non dicit secundum intentionem suam quod debeant exterminari aliqui nati, sed secundum legem gentium.

[8] *Contra gentes* iii 81. In the actual commentaries the language is much more Aristotelian: a natural slave is one who lacks βουλευτικόν. Ille est naturaliter servus qui habet aptitudinem naturalem ut sit alterius, inquantum scilicet non potest regi propria ratione per quam homo est dominus sui, sed solum ratione alterius; propter quod naturaliter alterius est *quasi* servus.—*Pol.* i 3. I have noticed that when the Philosopher's language is particularly difficult to swallow, S. Thomas dexterously inserts a "quasi." Compare *Pol.* iii 16; Fretté 26, 274: Hoc enim est secundum naturam quod ille qui excedit secundum virtutem sit dominus aliorum. . . . Quare relinquitur istum debere principiari omnibus et semper et dominum esse, et omnes illi tali obedire *quasi* ex inclinatione naturali.

[9] *Politica* iii 17, 1288 a. 15.

even Aristotle had to admit, is "hard to realize";[1] for no man or set of men has a monopoly of ἀρετή and δύναμις πολιτική in a community of human beings. It is certainly a curious irony of history that a theory of quasi-natural designation, which is practically equivalent to this discredited Aristotelianism, should be found in many, if not most, contemporary expositions of Scholasticism.[2]

It is important to understand S. Thomas's position in this matter, for he was one of the first to modify the earlier and more unqualified medieval view of equality, by clearly emphasizing two other ideas: natural sociability and accidental inequalities.

> One person rules another as a free man [he says] when he directs him either to the good of him who is being directed or to the common good. And even in the state of innocence there would have been such a rule of man over man, for two reasons:
>
> (1) Because man is naturally a social being. . . .
> (2) Because if one man had over others supereminence in knowledge and justice, it would have been undesirable that this should not result in advantage to others.

Thus while it is true that men have equal natural rights, still some hierarchial gradation is essential for their social coexistence. And this gradation should be based on the existing distribution of disparities and aptitudes. "Those men who excel in active faculties ought to be directed by those who excel in mental faculties," says S. Thomas. And again, "It is impossible that the common good of the State should progress, unless there is virtue in the citizens, at least in those to whom the government is entrusted." It is thus definitely laid down that men, though equal in all

---

[1] Ibid vii 14, 1332 b. 23: οὐ ῥᾴδιον. *Cf.* S. Thomas (*Pol.* vii 10; Fretté 26, 468*b*.): Si inveniatur aliquis unus in civitate vel regno qui omnibus istis superexcellat alios, iustum est ipsum principari *solum quamdiu est talis.*

[2] For example, Cathrein, *Philosophia moralis*, 1925⁹, thesis 81, §587, p. 398: Determinatio originaria subiecti potestatis civilis fieri potest variis causis, quae alicui personae in concretis circumstantiis tantam moralem praeponderantiam et auctoritatem conferant, *ut ipsa sola ad regendam societatem idonea sit.* So also Schiffini, *Disputationes phil. moralis*, 1891, ii 412: Ex ipsa itaque exigentia ordinis naturalis constituitur [talis persona] totius reipublicae caput.

essential rights and fundamental claims, are unequal psychologically and politically. Democracy, in fact, if it is not to result in a chaos of mediocrity and incompetence, must be based on aristocracy in the strict and literal sense of the term—the rule of the best.

163

SUAREZ AND DEMOCRACY

Alfred O'Rahilly [1]

To the great Catholic protagonists of King James, especially to Bellarmine and Suarez, the world owes a real debt for their triumphant vindication of conscience and law. "The first step towards freedom of conscience," writes Dr. Neville Figgis,[2] "is to take away from the civil State . . . the right of deciding at its own pleasure what opinions shall be encouraged and what shall be suppressed. It is a real advance when anybody possessing purely moral authority claims to decide these questions, to make its decision binding on the State. Now this was the action of the Jesuits." By means of an oath skilfully devised by the apostate Perkins in 1606, James wished his Catholic subjects to declare that the international or supernatural authority—exercised by popes from Gregory VII to Boniface VIII—was not only incorrect or exaggerated or dangerous (as Gallicans would say), but actually "impious and heretical."[3] Both Bellarmine and Suarez upheld the *indirect* power of the Papacy in temporal matters;[4] and

---

[1] *Studies*, March, 1918. (Dublin.)

[2] *Trans. R. Hist. Society*, N. S., xi (1897), 110.

[3] On Sept. 22, 1606, and again on Aug. 22, 1607, Paul V condemned this oath of allegiance. In book 6 of his *Defensio* Suarez subjects the oath to complete analysis and refutation. But Dr. Figgis knows better. The oath, he says (*Transactions*, p. 99, *n*. 1), "was expressly framed so as to be admissible for Catholics." In 1608 two priests were executed for refusing to take the oath.

[4] Bellarmine, *De summo pontifice*: Pontificem ut pontificem non habere directe et immediate ullam temporalem potestatem sed solum spiritualem, tamen ratione spiritualis habere saltem indirecte potestatem quandam eamque summam in temporalibus.—*Opera*, i, 888a. Sixtus V, who personally held stronger views on papal power, put Bellarmine's work on the Index. But he died a month later (Aug.

in this they were true not only to the teaching of the Church but to the historical state of Europe, which was then, however, in a state of rapid transition. Nowadays, of course, we realize more fully that the coercive power of the Church is purely moral,[5] and that the international influence of the Papacy in a world which has ceased to be a Catholic hegemony is an ideal rather than a fact or a right. But we owe all honor to those pioneers who, amid the religious disaster and national development which shattered the old medieval union of Church and State, did not cling to impossible theories, and did not—like the Reformers or King James—with academic pedantry revert to a bygone theocracy. They refused to put any power on earth above the moral law, to hand men's consciences over to the State or to exempt international relations from the ethical judgment of the greatest spiritual tribunal in Christendom. It is not for us, in this age of brute force and sordid conflict, to say that they were wrong.[6]

I have deferred until now the consideration of the chief fallacy in James's assertion of divine right. His argument might run thus: All power is from God, therefore my power is from God. It is as if a capitalist argued: All

---

27, 1590). The new pope, Gregory XIV, gave Bellarmine's views his special approbation. See Couderc, *Le vén. Card. Bellarmin*, i, 133.

[5] Even Suarez (*De fide*, d. 20, n. 21) does not call this view heretical. Though it is beyond the scope of my article to examine the arguments adduced with such learning and skill by Bellarmine and Suarez to prove the indirect power of the Pope, I cannot refrain from vigorously protesting against Dr. Figgis's undignified attempts to be funny when writing history. After some humorous references to Jeremiah and Nimrod, he proceeds thus to give the Catholic arguments. "It is part of the jus gentium of Christian nations that the sovereign shall be a Catholic. Moreover, since St. Peter was ordered to feed the sheep of the Church, it is clear that the Pope has power to exclude the wolf from the State. Besides, Christ said that he came not to send peace on earth but a sword, and to divide sons from fathers, and that must include separating sovereigns from their subjects." Such, according to this witty writer, are "some political theories of the early Jesuits!" (*Trans. R. Hist. Soc.*, xi, 104.)

[6] Even Dr. Figgis admits that the Jesuits helped to make international law possible by "popularizing a way of looking at law which insisted on its ethical content and regarded it as the embodiment of reason."—*Trans. R. Hist. Soc.*, xi, 107.

property is from God, therefore my property is from God. All power, power in general, such authority as is essential for man's complete social life, comes from God. But not all powers are from God; the concrete apportionment of authority is a matter of human arrangement. Just so, any concrete distribution of property, though founded on a God-given right, cannot claim God's direct and immediate sanction. The objection to King James, therefore, and to all upholders of State-absolutism, is that they fail to distinguish between authority (undifferentiated) and its distribution, between generic power and its specific embodiments. In so far as James I exercised political authority at all, his right was divine; in so far as this authority was vested in him as king, his title was purely human. Whence, then, do kings and governments immediately derive their authority? The answer of Bellarmine and Suarez is clear and emphatic: *from the people*.[7] And indeed the answer could not be otherwise, once we grant the existence of the community as a corporate entity capable of moral relations with similar entities and with its constituent members. Political authority, therefore, being the unique prerogative of the social body, resides primarily in the community as an organic whole.[8] *De jure divino,* abstracting from positive law, men are equal; hence, as Suarez says,[9] "no one has

---

[7] Nota hanc potestatem immediate esse tamquam in subiecto in tota multitudine.—Bellarmine, *De controversiis,* v, 3, 6 (*Opera,* ii, 518c). Ex natura rei solum est haec potestas in communitate.—Suarez, *Defensio,* iii, 2, 7. So also Bannez and Molina—Quilliet, *De civilis potestatis origine theoria catholica* (Lille, 1893), pp. 190ff.

[8] It has been said that recent Papal pronouncements uphold the theory that political authority is conferred immediately by God in the sense that the people may designate but do not confer power on the recipient. Thus Pope Leo XIII, *Diuturnum,* 29 June, 1881 (*Lettres,* i, 142; cf. ii, 34, 41): Quo sane delectu designatur princeps, non conferuntur iura principatus; neque mandatur imperium sed statuitur a quo sit gerendum. The Pope, however, goes on to say: Ceterum ad politicum imperium quod attinet, illud a Deo proficisci recte docet Ecclesia. There is not the slightest doubt that such statements in these encyclicals are aimed at non-Catholic views; their reference is not to the collation of power through the intermediary of the community, but to the error of those who deny its divine origin. See P. Féret, *Le pouvoir civil devant l'enseignement catholique* (Paris, 1888), pp. 176f.; also Billot, *De ecclesia Christi,* 3 (1900), 23f.

[9] *De legibus,* iii, 2, 3.

political jurisdiction—no more than dominion—over another, nor is there any reason *ex natura rei* why it should be given to these men over those rather than conversely." Therefore the only natural subject of political power is not any individual or any number of individuals, but the juristic personality of the people. If then we find a particular man or set of men in legitimate possession of this power, they must have received it in trust from the people, they must have been authorized to act as executive, judicial or legislative organs of the will of the community.

Cardinal Bellarmine says distinctly that the community is bound so to transfer its power.[1] Suarez merely says that power is "rarely or never retained in the whole community so that it is immediately administered by it."[2] Indeed such a procedure would be hardly possible in any State larger than a commune or parish council. History knows of no such direct democracy; for even the city-states of Greece and Rome comprised slaves and helots. But the abstract possibility of such a primary civic administration is worth noticing. It is more important, however, to observe how Suarez treats what we should now call representative democracy. Not only does he admit its possibility, but he regards the republics of Venice and Genoa as concrete instances. These republics, he says,[3] "retain the supreme power in themselves; though they elect one doge or president, they do not transfer all power to him. In these cases the supreme power is neither in the president alone nor in the people alone apart from him, but in the whole body with its head." In such States, i. e., in those "which are free and retain the supreme power in themselves, while committing legislation to a senate or to a leader either alone

---

[1] Respublica non potest per se ipsam exercere hanc potestatem, ergo tenetur eam transferre in aliquem unum vel aliquos paucos.—*Op. cit.,* p. 518*d*.

[2] *De legibus,* iii, 4, 8. Taparelli (*Origine du pouvoir,* §125) argues that political power does not reside in the people on the ground that it is impossible for them to exercise. The impossibility is purely accidental, due to the large size of modern States, and is analogous to specialization in physiological organisms. Taparelli talks as if the right to decide or vote (such as exists in an elector or shareholder) is indiscerptible from the power of external execution and self-appointment.

[3] *De legibus,* iii, 9, 6.

or with a senate," the governments are "perhaps only delegates" of the people.⁴ Suarez, therefore, contemplates a form of democratic government in which all political authority is exercised by delegation from the community. But he also holds that the community has a power of absolutely or conditionally alienating its political power so that the government is no longer a mere delegacy. Thus "it is not altogether true to say that a king depends on the people for his power, even though he has received it from them, for he can depend on the people for his coming to have the power and not for its preservation if he has received it fully and absolutely." ⁵

What are we to think of this alienability of political power? In the first place, it must be noted that Suarez's argument is decidedly weak. It amounts to this: Just as an individual may by his own free will or by some just title be reduced to servitude, so may the community.⁶ This

⁴ *Ibid.*, iii, 4, 2. St. Thomas also contemplates this case: 1, 2, q. 97, a 3, ad. 3.

⁵ *Defensio,* iii, 3, 4. P. Janet (*Hist. de la philosophie morale,* ii, 95-97) is very severe on Suarez for his defence of the absolute alienability of political power. Mr. Figgis goes to the other extreme. Speaking of Sidney and Milton, he says: "All governments are in their view merely officials carrying out the will of the sovereign people, and they may therefore be removed at any time. This view is apparently also that of Mariana and Suarez."—*Divine Right,* p. 243. So also in *From Gerson to Grotius,* p. 201, he says that "the Jesuits emphasize" the idea that the king is a "delegate," the "mere creature of popular choice." On p. 199 he makes an illuminating remark: "The most interesting thing in Suarez's great book is its table of contents." The more I read Mr. Figgis the more convinced am I that his interest in the table of contents has been excessive. I have only space to note two more of his many egregious blunders concerning Suarez: (1) "The argument from the *lex regia* on which the Jesuits and others rely for their theory of popular sovereignty" (*ibid.,* p. 201). Suarez's reliance consists in one passing reference! Et *fortasse hoc* pactum nomine legis regiae significatur.—*Defensio,* iii, 2, 12. (2) "In spite of the recognized independence of States men like Suarez clearly regard the Corpus Juris as the common form of Law" (*ibid.,* p. 198). Suarez. *De legibus,* iii, 9, 3: In *paucis* provinciis Christianorum servatur ius civile; the Corpus Juris does not hold in France, Spain or Portugal. Apart from Dr. Figgis's strong point—sneers and insinuations—he is guilty of numerous downright errors of fact similar to those I have instanced.

⁶ *Defensio,* iii, 2, 9; *De legibus,* iii, 3, 7.

reasoning is not calculated to impress an age which has abolished chattel slavery and is beginning to criticize wage-slavery. In the next place, Suarez really corrects himself by holding that the transfer of power is never absolute and always by way of bilateral contract.[7] Hence not only are there in practice restrictions and exceptions reserved by the people, but even the power actually transferred is held only by virtue of a political contract binding on the ruler as well as on the people; and in certain circumstances the people may even revoke this power. This alienation, therefore, is not so anti-democratic as it might at first appear; for it never confers unlimited power on the government and it leaves the community the final arbiter in extreme cases. . . .

I have reserved until the last the consideration of the really basic discrepancy between the older and the newer Catholic theory of government. The theory that only the conscient will of the community can form the moral personality of the State and the theory which refuses to look further than the concrete existence of an external framework of order are most acutely at variance when it comes to the question of *de facto* government. "Whenever civil power," writes Suarez, "is found in one man or ruler by legitimate and ordinary right, it is proximately or remotely derived from the people and community; and it cannot be otherwise held if it is to be just (*nec posse aliter haberi ut iusta sit*)."[8] There is, he thinks, one apparent exception —when a people is conquered in a just war, it loses its independence; but even here the authority is quasi-contractual since "so far as regards the transfer of dominion and power, the just punishment of a crime is equivalent to a contract."[9] His argument in support of this contention is exceedingly weak. "Captives in a just war," he urges, "are deprived of their natural liberty and are truly made slaves as a just punishment." Already in the sixteenth

---

[7] Haec est veluti conventio quaedam inter communitatem et principem, et ideo potestas recepta non excedit modum donationis vel conventionis.—*De legibus*, iii, 9, 4. See also *Defensio*, iii, 3, 3.

[8] *De legibus*, iii, 4, 2. He adds: Haec est sententia communis iurisperitorum. He also cites S. Thomas, Cajetan, Victoria, Soto, Ledesma, Castro, Driedo.

[9] *Defensio*, iii, 2, 20.

century this argument was antiquated, as an ethical ideal, though rather useful to men of Cromwell's stamp. And Suarez himself felt the danger of licensing just wars—all wars are just!—for he adds: "It happens more often that a kingdom is occupied through an unjust war and in this way the great empires of the world were increased." In such a case of unjust invasion, the usurper has no true authority, though "it can happen that in course of time the people may consent and acknowledge such a government."[1] Then, and only then, according to Suarez, does the *de facto* government possess lawful authority. This very clear and strong position is the only one consistent with his general theory that government depends on the consent of the governed. The case becomes entirely altered once other titles to just power are admitted.[2] Thus Dr. Cronin[3] holds that "as soon as the old government has disappeared or is completely subdued, the natural law must be regarded as proceeding forthwith to legitimise the new government and to regularise its position in relation to the community." Whereas, on the Suaresian theory, no amount of objective external facts can abrogate the right of self-determination, no extrinsically imposed rule can ever become the government *de jure*. "In this case," asks Suarez,[4] "can subjects lawfully obey a ruler of this kind if he makes laws otherwise materially just?" "It is celar," he answers, that strictly speaking they are not bound, for these are not laws since they do not proceed from a legitimate power. But it would seem that they can obey, for they can do whatever is good or at least not bad, though they are not bound, thus yielding their right and patiently suffering the violence of an outsider." In this way the payment of taxes, etc., is licit, "because this is really not co-operation in, but toleration of, the aggression." But even here, he adds significantly,

---

[1] *De legibus*, iii, 4, 4.
[2] "We cannot base civil authority simply and solely upon the consent of the governed."—Fr. Rickaby, *op. cit.*, p. 49. "The view that there is only one possible title of political rule, viz., the consent of the governed, . . . is an essentially false idea."—Rev. Prof. M. Cronin, *Ethics*, ii, 538 note. Dr. Cronin (pp. 519ff.) enumerates the chief "natural titles of authority": (1) popular election, (2) the fact of possession, (3) conquest, (4) exclusive ability to govern.
[3] *Ethics*, ii, 529.
[4] *De legibus*, iii, 10, 8-9.

"scandal must be avoided and no occasion must be given to the tyrant of more firmly persevering in his injustice, but rather must he be opposed as much as can conveniently be done."

It is plain, then, that Suarez is quite prepared to concede the whole external apparatus of what is usually called government, and yet to refuse it all moral validity apart from such partial sanction as the community may itself give to some of its acts.[5] In this matter it is extremely important to distinguish between the extrinsic and accidental validity which the acts of such a *de facto* government may possess and the intrinsic political authority of a true *de jure* government. For a people may be bound to obey, i. e., in so far as relates to civil order, without thereby conferring authority on those who rule. The obligation to obey a *de facto* government rests not on the authentic and legitimate right of the constituted power, but on the moral necessity of public order and social continuity. So clear is this distinction that Catholic philosophy is unanimous in holding these two propositions: (1) that a government which exceeds its function by injustice or tyranny ceases *ipso facto* to be a government, and (2) that such a defunct, immoral government may nevertheless have a right to our obedience "lest the tranquillity of order be more and more disturbed or society should incur greater harm" by our refusal.[6] It would surely be monstrous to maintain that partial and temporary submission to a tyrannical or usurping government as the lesser of two evils—i. e., to avoid anarchy—thereby validated this so-called government.[7] A usurping government does not acquire any real authority or recognition, for such valid acts as it appears to perform receive their validity solely from the consent and public opinion of the downtrodden community. A rule of this kind is essentially unstable and conditional, it is politically and internationally violable. If it include any morality or utility

---

[5] Thus Suarez says that the punishment of felons may be lawful "quia reipublicae consensus supplet defectum potestatis tyranni."

[6] Pope Leo XIII, *Quod Apostolici*, 28 Dec., 1878 (*Lettres*, i, 34). Compare St. Thomas, 2, 2, q. 42, a. 2, ad. 3, and also 1-2, q. 96, a. 4.

[7] Quod si vere dicerent [liberalismi fautores], nullus esset tam immanis dominatus cui subesse et quem ferre non oporteret.—Leo XIII, *Libertas praestantissimum*, 20 June, 1888 (*Lettres*, ii, 202).

at all, it is merely in so far as it functions as an interim and partial instrument of the people's convenience and order; and it is sufferable only so long as its tyranny is a lesser evil than the trouble of removing it. "What will be safe here below," asks Balmez,[8] "if we admit the principle that success insures justice and that the conqueror is always the rightful ruler? ... In recommending prudence to the people, let us not disguise it under false doctrines, let us beware of calming the exasperation of misfortune by circulating errors subversive of all governments, of all society."

164

THE RIGHT OF SELF GOVERNMENT

JOHN A. RYAN [1]

While the Church has made no pronouncement for or against the right of national self government, her competent private teachers, the moral theologians and canonists, have discussed the question at considerable length. As we have just seen from the words of St. Paul and Leo XIII, the ruler derives his right to rule from God, Who is the source of all authority. Immediately, therefore, we face the questions: How does this governing authority descend from God to a ruler? How can we know that it has actually been conferred upon an existing king, president, or parliament? Theologians and canonists have dealt with these questions in considerable detail.

As regards the manner in which the right to govern reaches the first legitimate ruler of a State, the majority opinion among Catholic writers is that stated by Cardinal Bellarmine and Francisco Suarez. The work of the former on this subject was written in the last quarter of the sixteenth century; that of the latter in the first quarter of the seventeenth. Bellarmine's doctrine may be summarized as follows: Political authority in general comes directly from God to the whole community. Since God has not

---

[8] *European Civilization*, ch. 55, p. 316.
[1] *Catholic Doctrine on the Right of Self Government*, pp. 4-13, 31. (The Paulist Press, New York.)

given it to any one in particular, there is no natural reason why it should reside in one rather than another of many equal individuals. Inasmuch as the community is unable to exercise this authority directly, it must transfer the function to one or to a few persons. The community, the "multitude," also has the right to determine the form of government, whether it is to be a monarchy, an aristocracy, or a democracy, and, for a legitimate reason, to change any one of these forms into another. While the authority is, indeed, from God, it becomes particularized in one or more individuals through human counsel and choice.[2]

This doctrine was far from acceptable to the defenders of the "divine right of kings," which was claimed by more than one monarch in the days of Bellarmine. James I, of England, was so displeased and disturbed by the declarations of the Roman Cardinal that he took the trouble to write an attempted refutation. He contended that the king did not derive his authority from the people, but from God immediately. Against this assertion the Spanish theologian, Suarez, wrote several chapters in his *Defensio Fidei Catholicae*. He pointed out that the opinion enunciated by the King of England was "new and singular, invented to exaggerate the temporal and to minimize the spiritual power"; and that the doctrine of Bellarmine was "the ancient, commonly accepted, and true teaching." Supreme political authority, he maintains, is given by God directly to the political community as a whole, inasmuch as He made men of such a nature that they need to have a political organization. There is nothing in the nature of things to show that this organization should take the form of a monarchy or an aristocracy, nor that the ruling authority should be located in any given person or group of persons. Political authority resides in the community as a whole, and may be transferred by the community to one or more persons. Whence it follows that no monarch has ruling power immediately from God, but through the medium of the human will and human institution.[3]

Suarez concludes this part of his argument with the statement that this doctrine is not new, nor invented by Bellarmine, and he gives a long list of theological and

---

[2] *De Laicis*, ch. vi.
[3] Lib. III, cap. ii; cf. *De Legibus*, III, cap. ii.

canonical writers in proof of its universality and antiquity. Otto Gierke, a distinguished non-Catholic authority, tells us that, "an ancient and generally entertained opinion regarded the will of the people as the source of temporal power. . . . Indeed, that the legal title of all rulership lies in the voluntary and contracted submission of the ruled, could therefore be propounded as a philosophic axiom." [4] According to Dr. A. J. Carlyle, "the fact that in mediæval theory the authority of the king is founded upon the election or at least the recognition of the community, does not in truth require any serious demonstration." [5] Although Cathrein rejects the doctrine of his fellow Jesuits, Bellarmine and Suarez, he admits that it was held by almost all the Schoolmen.[6] Meyer concedes that "many Christian teachers" of the Middle Ages held that kings were not immediately appointed by God but mediately through the election or consent of the people; however, he maintains that these writers did not all clearly profess the opinion that the "mediating" act of the people consisted in transferring to the monarch political power; he contends that the expressions of some of them merely meant that the people have the right to determine the form of government and designate the person who is to rule." [7]

These qualifying observations are not of great practical importance. In the first place, he should have said "all Christian writers," for he does not mention a single exception to the general fact that mediæval opinion denied that political power comes to the ruler immediately from God. In the second place, if it be held that the consent of the people is always a necessary prerequisite to the assumption of political power by any person, it is of no practical significance whether the people be conceived as handing over to the ruler authority which God has deposited with them, or as designating the person upon whom God will confer the authority. In either supposition God does not bestow

---

[4] *Political Theories of the Middle Age,* pp. 38, 40.
[5] *History of Mediaeval Political Theory in the West,* vol. iii, p. 153.
[6] *Philosophia Moralis,* no. 496.
[7] *Institutiones Juris Naturalis,* II, 350, 351.

authority, nor does the ruler receive it, until the people have somehow given their consent.[8]

To sum up the historical situation: down to the nineteenth century, Catholic moralists and jurists, with the exception of certain adherents of Gallicanism, were unanimous in holding that the consent of the people was required to make the position of a ruler morally legitimate; and the majority of them maintained that the people had a right, not only to select the ruling person, but to confer the ruling authority.

The insistence of Suarez upon the doctrine that authority comes to the ruler only through the people, was to some extent due to the circumstances of his own time. Even before the Reformation, a tendency had appeared among some monarchs to claim authority directly from God. Kings who got into conflict with the Pope made this claim in the hope of strengthening their position; for if their authority was conferred upon them by a direct divine grant, it was on as high a plane as that of the Pope himself. This was the position taken, for example, by the rebellious imperial princes of Bavaria in a document addressed to the Pope toward the middle of the fourteenth century. In passing, it is worthy of notice that the monarchs who set up such a claim used it to exaggerate their own power, not only as against the authority of the Roman Pontiff, but as against the rights and liberties of their subjects. They were gradually approaching that claim of absolute power which was reached by many post-Reformation monarchs, but which "was wholly foreign to the Middle Age."[9] In resisting these pretensions, the Popes of the Middle Ages not only were defending their own spiritual and moral prerogatives, but in a very effective way protecting the rights of the people against royal encroachment and absolutism. Even Lecky admits that the power exercised by the mediæval Popes over secular princes was "on the whole favorable to liberty."[1]

This exaggeration of royal authority became much more general and more excessive after the Reformation; for the

---

[8] *Cf.* Balmez, *Protestantism and Catholicity in their Effects on the Civilization of Europe*, pp. 305-311.
[9] *Cf.* Gierke, *op. cit.*, pp. 35 *et seq.*
[1] *Rationalism in Europe*, vol. ii, p. 142.

Protestant monarchs were impelled by religious as well as political motives to exalt their power as compared with that of the Pope. In this they derived powerful assistance from the teachings of the Reformers, who declared that secular princes ruled by divine right. "In fact, the religion of the State superseded the religion of the Church. Its first form was the Divine Right of Kings. Luther and Machiavelli were two of the most important factors in the change."[2] Since they denied that their ruling authority was limited by either the Pope or the people, the Protestant monarchs naturally claimed that it came directly from God, quite in the same fashion as that of David and Saul. James I declared that his power was at once civil and ecclesiastical.

This doctrine, declared Suarez, is "new and singular, and invented to exaggerate the temporal and to minimize the spiritual power." He saw clearly that if the doctrine of James went uncontroverted it would have the effect of injuring the prestige of the Church in every nation whose ruler, whether Protestant or Catholic, made such a claim. Therefore, he stated the doctrine of the indirect derivation of civil authority, of its transfer to the king by the people, in the most systematic and convincing form that it had received up to his time. Fortunately he was able to show that such had been the traditional teaching of both theologians and jurists all through the Middle Ages; but the powerful religious motive that lay behind his argument cannot nor need not be denied.

In precisely the same way, the special circumstances of their time have been largely instrumental in determining many Catholic writers of the nineteenth century to depart from the doctrine of Bellarmine and Suarez. The superficial resemblances between this doctrine and the theories of popular sovereignty associated with the French Revolution and with subsequent revolutionary movements, seem to have impressed these nineteenth century writers as a grave danger to civil order and to the stability of royal dynasties. Hence they have turned their backs upon the traditional teaching that authority comes to the ruler only through the people. The principal names in this group are Haller,[3] Taparelli,[4] Liberatore,[5] Meyer,[6] Cathrein,[7] and

---

[2] *From Gerson to Grotius*, by John Neville Figgis, p. 71.
[3] *Restauration der Staatswissenschaften*, 1820.

Cronin.[8] All but the first and last of these are, like Bellarmine and Suarez, members of the Society of Jesus. On the other hand, one of the ablest recent defenders of the traditonal doctrine is likewise a Jesuit, Costa-Rosetti.[9]

That the apparent support given by the older doctrine to popular sovereignty and to the overthrow of monarchs has been a powerful motive in the rejection of that doctrine by the writers cited above, is clearly established by their own assertions and admissions. Taparelli intimates that Suarez and the other ancient exponents of the traditional doctrine would probably have modified their views had they lived two centuries later, in the midst of the havoc wrought by popular revolutions; and he expresses his astonishment that many should continue to boast of the sovereignty of the people and the inalienable rights of man to govern himself.[1] Meyer declares that in our age we ought to beware of defending doctrines which lend support to the ever increasing opposition to the monarchial form of government.[2]

Nevertheless, all these writers defend the traditional doctrine against the charge that it is equivalent to the social contract theory of Rousseau. They point out that the two doctrines are similar only superficially, inasmuch as both attribute the origin of civil society to a social compact, and teach that political authority resides primarily in the whole people. But these principles are very differently interpreted in the two doctrines. According to Suarez, political government is a natural necessity, and a community is not free to dispense with it; according to Rousseau, primitive men were under no moral obligation to organize themselves into a political society. According to Suarez, many of the individual's rights come from nature and from God; according to Rousseau, they all proceed from the social compact. Suarez maintained that political authority is derived ultimately from God who confers it upon the people, while Rousseau held that it rests in the people ultimately and

[4] *Saggio teoretico di diritto naturale*, 1856.
[5] *Institutiones Ethicae*, 1887.
[6] *Institutiones Juris Naturalis*, 1900.
[7] *Philosophia Moralis*, 1900.
[8] *The Science of Ethics*, 1917.
[9] *Philosophia Moralis*, 1886.
[1] *Op. cit.*, nota 79.
[2] *Op. cit.*, II, 375.

fundamentally. In the doctrine of Suarez, political authority rests in the people as an organic whole, or community; in the opinion of Rousseau, it is merely the sum of the rights of the individuals and is shared by each as an individual. There are other important differences, which need not be stated here.

Now the fact that the traditional doctrine may be misinterpreted and abused so as to give countenance to unsound revolutionary principles, or even to unjustified rebellions, is not a sufficient reason for discarding it, any more than the fact that the theory defended by the more recent Catholic writers can be, and has been, wrested to the support of despotism and absolutism, is a sufficient reason for adopting the older doctrine. Indeed, it is a fair question for debate whether the harm done to religion and to human welfare by the abuse of the more recent theory has not been greater than that resulting from the misapplication of the doctrine of Bellarmine and Suarez. In any case, the really important question is the objective soundness of either doctrine, and not its accidental consequences.

The Catholic writers who reject the theory of Suarez appeal in the first place to history, pointing to the well-known fact that the first rulers of many tribal and patriarchal societies did not owe their position to any sort of pact between themselves and the community, and contending that the latter gave no genuine consent to a transfer of political authority to the former. Nevertheless, Suarez declares that in such cases implicit consent sufficed, and that the people really gave this, inasmuch as they made no objection when the patriarchs gradually came to exercise political as well as domestic authority. This was surely effective, even though passive and informal, consent; for if the people had not been satisfied they would have offered opposition. The second historical argument used by the modern writers, is that in some primitive societies the ruler obtains authority by the simple fact that he is the only one that is capable of governing; therefore, it is unnecessary and unreasonable to suppose that the people have a right to give or withhold political power. Unfortunately this argument is sometimes presented in terms that would justify mere physical force as a determinant of the right to rule. Cathrein declares that in some communities the patriarch was the only one man fit to govern because he would not submit to any other ruler, and because he possessed sufficient physical power to make his refusal effective.[3] The German Kaiser need not go beyond this principle to justify his government of Belgium.

When, however, Cathrein lays stress upon the moral and intellectual prestige and qualifications of the patriarch, as the basis of the latter's exclusive right to govern, his argument is at least worthy of respect. If there have been, and the hypothesis seems not unhistorical, primitive societies in which only one man was capable of governing with even a minimum degree of efficiency, it seems reasonable to say that only that man had the right to exercise political authority, and therefore that the people had no right either to confer or withhold such authority. Since the sole purpose and justification of government and titles of authority is the welfare of the people, it would seem that when this end can be secured only through one man, the people have no reasonable choice in the matter. They have not even the right to make their consent decisive in the selection of the person.

The second or positive line of argument against the Suarezian theory takes the form of a direct attack upon the principle. It denies that the title of rulership is ever bestowed by God upon the whole people, except in the rare case in which they exercise the authority themselves; that is, in a pure democracy. Political authority, says Dr. Cronin, is an attribute of the ruler as such, just as domestic authority belongs to the position of the parent.[4] Where, then, did authority rest before it became attached to the patriarch, council or king? Nowhere. It is not like a physical entity that must have a local habitation before it can come into a person's possession. It is an attribute which attaches itself to the ruler through the occurrence of certain particular events, just as parental authority attaches itself to the father and mother by the fact that a child is born to them. They then receive the authority from God. In similar fashion the legitimate ruler receives his authority directly from God.

[3] *Op. cit.*, no. 502.
[4] *Op. cit.*, II, pp. 499-503.

This argument and the latter part of the second historical argument, summarized above, seem to be convincing. Moreover, there is another line of reasoning which seems to re-enforce these arguments and to weaken very seriously, if it does not entirely destroy, the cogency of the Suarezian doctrine. It leads to the conclusion that the central principle of the doctrine is gratuitous and unnecessary. Why should we assume that God gives authority to a king or a president through the people? Why should He not confer it upon the accredited ruler directly? Only one possible reason can be brought forward in support of the theory of indirect transmission. It is that this method is somehow required for the welfare of the people.

With the exception of the right to life, all natural rights are merely means to the attainment of some necessary personal or social end. Thus, private property and government are required for the reasonable life and development of the individual; hence he has a right to acquire goods and to have the benefit of a government. But the power to receive political authority from God and to transmit it thence to the ruler, is not necessary for the welfare of the community. Even if we were to assume that the consent of the people is, in every instance, a necessary condition to the legitimate reception and exercise of political authority by the ruler, we are not logically driven to the conclusion that the people must become the depositary and transmitter of that authority. It is enough to assume that they have the exclusive right to designate the ruling person, and that God invariably bestows the authority directly upon the person thus designated.

Some of the opponents of the Suarezian theory have contended that it was rejected by Pope Leo XIII in his encyclical "Diuturnum," and by Pope Pius X in his letter condemning the Sillon; but the contexts of the expressions used by both Popes show that they were refuting the eighteenth century theory of popular sovereignty. Neither of them makes any clear allusion to the doctrine of Bellarmine and Suarez. It is quite unfair and unscientific to read into two isolated sentences a condemnation of a doctrine which was taught by the great majority of Catholic moralists and jurists for upwards of seven centuries. Therefore, it cannot be seriously maintained that the traditional doctrine has been superseded by the official authority of the Church. We are still perfectly free to adopt it if we are convinced by the reasons urged in its favor.[5]

We have to admit that the traditional doctrine is very attractive to the believer in political democracy. It seems to provide a simple and obvious weapon for refuting the pretensions of autocracy. And it immensely enhances the dignity of the people, by making them the depositary of a most important moral prerogative. It is particularly pleasing to Americans, and above all to American Catholics. For the resemblance between it and certain well-known clauses in the Virginia Declaration of Rights, as well as in our national Declaration of Independence, is obvious and striking. These documents declare that governments derive their just powers from the consent of the governed, and that the people have the right to alter or abolish any political rule that becomes destructive of the true ends of government. Suarez declares that if the power of the ruler be not proximately or remotely derived from the people and community, it is not just [6] and that when the monarch converts his government into a tyranny, the people can revoke the grant of authority.[7]

Indeed, it may be persuasively argued that these two great Declarations have come more or less directly from Suarez or Bellarmine or both. Thus, Mr. Gaillard Hunt, of the Library of Congress, declares that Thomas Jefferson derived from Bellarmine substantially the wording in which he stated these famous doctrines. In the opinion of Mr. Hunt, "it should be a satisfaction to Catholics that the fundamental pronouncements upon which was built the greatest of modern revolutions found their best support in the writings of a Prince of the Church." [8] An Irishman, Professor Alfred O'Rahilly, goes further, declaring that, while Catholic scholars "have largely forgotten the great seventeenth century exposition of Christian Democracy, the influence of Suarez, working through English Whigs and Puritans and

---

[5] Cf. Costa-Rosetti, *op. cit.,* pp. 628-630; Meyer, *op. cit.,* pp. 370-372.
[6] *De Legibus,* III, cap. iv, par. 2.
[7] *Defensio,* III, 3, 7.
[8] *The Catholic Historical Review,* October, 1917, p. 289.

culminating in the American Declaration of Independence, is once again inspiring men toward freedom." [9] . . .

As a summary of this and the preceding article, we submit the following propositions: the official teaching of the Church is, that political government is a natural necessity for society; that the authority of the legitimate ruler comes from God, and that each of the three forms of government, the monarchic, the aristocratic, and the democratic, or any of the usual combinations of the three forms, is in itself morally lawful. According to the doctrine of Bellarmine and Suarez, which has in its favor more Catholic writers of authority than any other theory, political authority is derived directly from God by the people, and is by them transmitted, either explicitly or implicitly, to the ruler. But we have given reasons to show that the political rights of the people can be fully safeguarded by the theory that, instead of conferring authority upon the ruler, they merely designate him, and that the person so designated receives his authority directly from God. This right to choose their own form of government and ruler, is inherent in every people that has the capacity to provide for or maintain a fairly competent government.

As regards the right of a people to change the existing form of government, recent Catholic writers exaggerate the right of the actual or the recently deposed monarch. The reasonable conclusion seems to be that a politically competent people have the right to modify essentially their constitution and even, by passive resistance, to force a monarch to abdicate, when they are unwaveringly convinced that they can provide a better government, and when this conviction corresponds with the facts. The justification of this proposition is to be found in public welfare. Finally, the principles developed in our study indicate that substantially all the small nations of Europe are justified in their claims to "self-determination."

[9] *Studies*, March, 1918, p. 21.

165
THE SOVEREIGNTY OF THE PEOPLE
Alfred O'Rahilly [1]

I.—History of the Principle

The current Protestant view is that democracy was introduced by the Reformation; and unfortunately this travesty of history is nowadays accepted as a commonplace by many Catholics.[2] It is admitted, of course, that the Jesuits artfully "took a leaf from the Calvinistic book of political theory," [3] and thus for a century or so propagated alien democratic principles within the Church. This is the accepted thesis of contemporary non-Catholic Liberalism, and it is also held by a recent school of Catholic conservatives who, from the opposite standpoint, are equally desirous of repudiating any connection between Catholic teaching and democracy. One has but to open some recent manual to find the doctrine of popular supremacy referred to as "the doctrine of the ancients," the view upheld by "Bellarmine, Suarez, and not a few Scholastics," "the theory of social contract advocated by Cardinal Bellarmine and Francis Suarez," and so on.[4] It is plainly thereby insinuated that this democratic theory is a mere intrusion into Catholic political philosophy, due either to the inac-

---

[1] "*Studies*," March, 1921.

[2] I have attempted to refute this in two articles on "The Catholic Origin of Democracy" and "The Sources of English and American Democracy," in *Studies,* March and June, 1919.

[3] H. D. Forster, *American Hist. Review,* 21 (1915-16), 500. Ranke's statement is more accurate, for he wrote before the idea of Protestant democracy had become an established fiction. "The Jesuits," he complains (*History of the Popes,* vi. 1, Eng. trans., 1848, ii. 4), "made no scruple of deriving the power of the prince from the people." He correctly gives the Protestant theory of absolutism and passive obedience: "God alone, as the Protestants maintained, appoints princes over the human race; He reserves to Himself the office of exalting and abasing them, of apportioning and moderating the powers they are called on to exercise" (*ibid.* ii. 12). Cf. also L. von Ranke, *Sämtliche Werke,* 24 (1872), 227.

[4] Cathrein, *Phil. moralis,* 1915⁹, § 577, p. 391; Reinstadler *Elementa* 1913⁷ ii. 470; Vermeersch, *Quaestiones de iustitia,* 1904² § 559, p. 704; Cronin, *Science of Ethics,* 2 (1917); Pius La Scala, *Cursus phil.* (1910-11) ii. 251.

curate thinking of old writers such as St. Thomas, and their ignorance of the horrors of modern democracy,[5] or else to the mistaken zeal of Jesuit radicals such as Bellarmine and Suarez, who exalted the people simply as a dodge to depress the prince and to bring power to holy Mother Church.[6] It is quite in accordance wtih this idea that contemporary text-books of Catholic ethics usually dismiss as unworthy of serious or detailed refutation a theory which is assumed to be the temporary divagation of a few otherwise reliable Catholic thinkers.[7]

Now, as a matter of fact, this attitude of recent and contemporary writers is due to a twofold ignorance: firstly, of the very modern and rather dubious origin of the theory, or rather theories, which such writers confidently put forward as if in some way Catholic orthodoxy were bound up therewith; and secondly, of the continuous and practically unanimous adhesion which was given to the Scholastic theory ever since the thirteenth century. "In the later Middle Ages," admits Sidwick,[8] "from the end of

[5] Zigliara, *Phil. moralis,* 1912[15], p. 272; Comte de Vareilles-Sommières, *Les principes fond. du droit,* 1889, p. 113; Taparelli, *Saggio teoretico di dritto naturale,* note 79, ed. 1900, i. 269.

[6] L. von Ranke, *Sämtliche Werke,* 24 (1872), 230; Franck, *Réformateurs et publicistes de l'Europe: dix-septième siècle,* 1881, p. 47. Following the Protestants, several modern Jesuit followers of Taparelli have made similar insinuations against Suarez: Meyer, *Inst. iuris naturalis,* 1900, ii. 353 (§ 396); Vermeersch, *De iustitia,* 1904[2], § 559, p. 705; Rickaby, *Scholasticism,* 1908, pp. 113f; Schiffini, *Disp. phil. moralis,* 1891, § 450 (ii. 399).

[7] As examples of summary refutations: "Haec doctrina veterum . . . non, videtur esse vera. . . . Negamus principes saeculares a communitate accipere condendi leges potestatem."—Tepe, *Inst. theol. moralis* (1898), i. 337, 339. "Our criticism of this theory can only be of the briefest kind. In the first place, the theory of Suarez rests on a purely groundless supposition. . . ."—Cronin, *Ethics,* ii. 501. It is not unusually considered necessary to give any quotations, hardly even references. Thus Zigliara mentions less than six names and gives one short quotation from Victoria (torn from its context and ambiguous), on the strength of which he declares the theory obscure and its upholders excusable only because they were not faced by present-day questions.—*Phil. moralis,* 1912[15], p. 272. Even this meagre account is exploited at second-hand, *e. g.,* by Volpi, *Lectiones phil. moralis,* ii. (1900), 163, and Schiffini, *Disp. phil. moralis,* 1891, § 445 (ii. 387).

[8] *Development of European Policy,* 1903, p. 332. So also Viollet, *Histoire des institutions politiques et administratives de la France,* 2 (1898), pp. 2f. It is not really correct to say that the theory of

the thirteenth century onward, it is the most accepted doctrine, that secular government rests on the consent of the people, who have an original right to choose their own form of government." Such a doctrine, which for so many centuries, right down to our own times, has formed an integral part of Scholasticism, deserves a better fate than to be left quietly to drop into desuetude and oblivion, especially in these days when a favorite argument of our enemies is that the Church is opposed to the People. If it has to be abandoned, it merits more research into its history and meaning than it has hitherto received. Moreover, it is the clear duty of contemporary compilers of manuals, intended for young Catholic students, to give to the Scholastic theory of political power due consideration and tolerance, and to refrain from urging some newly invented anti-democratic reaction, as if it were the only view which a Catholic reader is entitled to hold. No doubt, in matters philosophical we must not argue solely or chiefly from authority; the Scholastic democratic theory does not become true merely because it was held by practically all Catholic philosophers and theologians for six centuries. But at the present time it is really necessary to appeal to this extrinsic authority to establish one's liberty of thought against what looks very like a concerted conspiracy on the part of most (but not all) text-books issued since the appearance of Taparelli's Essay (1840-41).[9] It is a common experience of every Catholic democrat to find half-a-dozen present-day manuals triumphantly quoted against him. The most effective retort is to point out that the argument from authority, if it is to be used at all, lies against those who have so lightly rejected the unanimous tradition of the School, not indeed in a thesis directly pertaining to faith, but concerning a matter where error may have very serious social and religious consequences.[1]

government by consent—except as consciously formulated and generalized political theory—began only in the thirteenth century. It can easily be proved, for instance, to underlie the Gothic rule in Spain, as well as the Carlovingian and Merovingian monarchy.

[9] As even de Vareilles-Sommières (p. 357) practically admits: "In our century, at least until the appearance of Taparelli's work, most theologians also accepted the thesis of the alienable sovereignty of the people."

[1] "Ex auctorum omnium scholasticorum communi sententia in re

THE STATE

It is obviously impossible within the limits of an article to outline the proof that popular sovereignty is the traditional political theory of Catholic philosophy. The only really satisfactory method is to make a tedious and exhaustive research by enumeration and citation. This has already been partially and imperfectly done;[2] a completer and more detailed investigation than has yet been made, I hope to publish in a long-delayed work on Catholic Democracy. It will suffice here to deal briefly with one point, namely, the rather common assumption that Suarez was an innovator and represents what may be called the left wing of Catholic politics. "Authority is a divine institution," says Father Joseph Rickaby,[3] "but kings are a human invention. The saying is a platitude in our time; three centuries ago, when Suarez wrote, it was a bold and startling pronouncement." "Before the time of Suarez," writes Schiffini,[4] "hardly a single writer can be cited for such a view." The most direct and conclusive refutation of this position is to give a brief list of some of the Catholic writers who, prior to the publication of the *De Legibus* of Suarez (in 1612), maintained the doctrine of popular supremacy and government by consent. I have personally and at first hand verified the doctrine in the following

---

quidem gravi, usque adeo probabilia sumuntur argumenta ut illis refragari temerarium sit. . . . Scholae igitur communem consensum non nisi impudenter et temere reiciemus."—Melchior Cano, *De locis theologicis*, viii. 4, 2 (ed. Migne, 1860, p. 400). "Quamquam controversia haec ad fidei dogmata directe non pertinet—nihil enim ex divina scriptura aut patrum traditione in illa definitum ostendi potest—nihilominus diligenter tractanda et explicanda est; tum quia potest esse occasio errandi in aliis dogmatibus. . . . tum denique quia sententiam illustrissimi Bellarmini antiquam, receptam, veram ac necessariam esse censemus."—Suarez, *Defensio Fidei*, iii. 2, 2. Cf. Mendive, *Ethica*, 1888, pp. 423f.

[2] Costa-Rosetti, *Philosophia moralis*, Innsbruck, 1886², Féret, *Le pouvoir civil devant l'enseignement catholique*, Paris, 1888; Quilliet, *De civilis potestatis origine theoria catholica*, Lille, 1893.

[3] Article "Authority," in *Cath. Enc.*, ii. 139b. The pronouncement was neither bold nor startling; it was the veriest commonplace in the Middle Ages and occurs quite formally in patristic commentaries on St. Paul's Epistle to the Romans, *e. g.*, Chrysostom, *In Rom.*, hom. 23, n. 1 (P.G. 60, 615), Theodoret, *Interpretatio ep. ad Rom.*, c. 13 v. 1 (P.G. 82, 193).

[4] *Disp. phil. mor.*, 1891, § 460, ii. 427.

among other Scholastic predecessors of Suarez, the date denoting the year of death where ascertainable:—

A. *Fourteenth Century* (i. e., writers who died before 1400).—John of Paris (1306), Enghelbert (1311), Aegidius Romanus (1316), William Durand (1332), Alvarez Pelayo (1340), Petrus de Palude (1342), Marsilius of Padua (after 1342), Cardinal P. Bertrand (1349), Lupold of Bebenburg (1363), Nicholas d'Oresme (1382).

B. *Fifteenth Century.*—Cardinal F. de Zabarellis, P. d'Ailly (1425), John Gerson (1429), St. Bernardino of Siena (1444), St. Antonino of Florence (1459), Alph Tostat (Abulensis, 1452), Petrus de Monte (1457), Card. Nicholas of Cusa (1564), Aeneas Sylvius (1464), John of Torquemada (1468).

C. *Sixteenth Century.*—James Almain (1515), Cajetan (1534), John Driedo (1535), Card. Gaspar Contarini (1542), Francis of Vitoria (1546), John of Medina (1547), John Major (1550), Ambrosius Catharinus (1553), Alf. de Castro (1558), Card. R. Pole (1558), Dom. de Soto (1560), Ferd. Vazquez Menchaca (1566), Diego Covarruvias (1577), Antonius Cordubensis (1578), Nicholas Sander (1581), Barth. of Medina (1581), Martin Azpilcueta (Navarrus, 1586), Peter of Navarre, Peter of Aragon, Michael de Palacios (1593).

D. *Seventeenth Century* (writers prior to 1612).—Barth. de Ledesma (1604), Dom. Bañes (1604), Luis Miranda, Gregory Sayr (1602), L. Carbo, Estius (Wm. Hessels van Est, 1613), Diego Cabezudo (1614), Ant. de Quintanadueñas (1628).

E. *Jesuit Predecessors of Suarez.* — James L a i n e z (1565), Alph. Salmeron (1585), Card. F. Toledo (1596), Luis de Molina (1600), John Azor (1603), Card. Robert Bellarmine (1621), Gregory of Valentia (1603), Robert Persons (1610), Juan de Salas (1612), James Gretser (1625), Juan de Mariana (1624), B. Giustiniani (1622).

An inspection of the above list of sixty names shows that it includes all the principal writers of the period. It could easily be extended by including writers prior to the fourteenth century—such as Hincmar of Rheims, Manegold of Lautenbach, William of Auvergne, St. Thomas, Duns Scotus—and canonists (such as Hostiensis), not to speak of legists. The significance of the list is further increased by the fact that among accepted Catholic writers during these centuries there is not a trace of any rival or alternative political theory; the only discordant expressions which occur are uttered by a few unorthodox partisans of Lewis of Bavaria. It may, therefore, be taken as certain that Suarez was perfectly justified in declaring that his teaching, so far from being an innovation, was commonly accepted by theologians and jurists.[5] That this was the case for two and a half centuries subsequent to Suarez, hardly needs to be proved.

No competent opponent has gone so far as to state that the Scholastic theory has now become obsolescent or obsolete; but the silence concerning recent defenders and the allusions to the theory as "the doctrine of the ancients," which characterize many widely-read text-books, are really tantamount to such an assertion. Even if it were true, there is no ground for surprise or discouragement at the decay of a theory which was once upheld by the Church's greatest philosophers and theologians. Three centuries ago Cartesianism almost completely ousted Scholastic philosophy from the Catholic schools; only in the latter half of the last century did Scholasticism again revive. In 1881 Liberatore recast his *Institutiones* and in his preface recounted that, when forty years before he started to restore the all but extinct philosophy of S. Thomas, he was considered mad. "There was once a time," wrote Dalgairns in 1861,[6] "when there reigned on earth a philosophy borrowed from an old heathen. . . . For hundreds of years it reigned paramount, if not alone, in the schools of Christendom. . . . It is now nearly forgotten."

It can be shown, however, that Scholastic political theory, thanks to moral theologians rather than to philosophers, survived even during the long interregnum of Scholastic

---

[5] *De legibus*, iii. 2, 3; *Defensio*, iii. 2, 2, 5, and 10.

[6] Holy Communion, ed. 1861, pp. 22, 35. Cf. Lemaire, *Le Cartésianisme chez les Bénédictins*, 1902. In the early 19th century Scholastic philosophy was unknown at Maynooth. In 1908 the only philosophical text-books used there were Locke and Seguy.—Healy, *Maynooth College*, 1895, p. 271. "One whole year is always devoted to logic and metaphysics upon Locke's system; and another to mathematics, physics and astronomy, in which Newton is the chief guide."—Milner, *An Inquiry into certain vulgar Opinions concerning the Catholic Inhabitants and the Antiquities of Ireland*, 1808, p. 19.

metaphysics; and at the present day is showing an ever increasing progress and vitality. It would be possible to add to the names of Suarez's sixty predecessors just given the names of sixty Catholic nineteenth-century writers who upheld and uphold the same doctrine. Cardinals such as Gonzalez, Hergenröther, Mazzella, Lavigerie, Manning, and Billot; Archbishops Maret, Ireland, Hughes and Spalding; Bishops Parisis, Guilbert, de Ségur, Hugonin [7]; Jesuits such as Draghetti, Chastel, Ramière, Costa-Rosetti, W. Hill, Watt, Van der Aa, Castelein, Mendive, Holaind, Brosnahan, Macksey,[8] Cavallera [9]; well known historical and critical writers like Marina, Rohrbacher, Balmes, Moulart, Féret, Quilliet; authors of widely-read text-books such as Dens, Scavini, Devoti, Brugère, Rutten, Vallet, Marcellus a Puero Iesu, Rodriguez de Cepeda, Gredt; philosophers and publicits like Bautain, Ventura, Raboisson, Desorges, Godard, Périn, Frémont, Ryan; these and many other distinguished writers have within the last century maintained, handed down and improved the Scholastic theory of political authority. With such exponents it is in no danger of premature obsolescence.[1]

II.—THE SCHOLASTIC THEORY

The Scholastic theory may be briefly stated; its underlying principles and arguments will emerge more clearly in considering some objections. The immediate and primary subject of political power is the people, not as a mere aggregate, but as forming a mystical body and as con-

---

[7] In 1848 nearly all the French Episcopate supported the democratic theory.—Bazin, *Vie de Mgr. Maret*, 1891, vol. i., ch. 15, pp. 190ff. Cf. Cabane, *Histoire du clergé de France pendant la révolution de 1843*, 1908.

[8] Professor of Ethics in the Gregorian University, 1911-1919. (See his *De Ethica Naturali*, 1914, p.. 527).

[9] Professor of Positive Theology in the Catholic Institute of Toulouse since 1909. (See his article on "Suarez et la doctrine catholique sur l'origine du pouvoir" in *Bulletin de Littérature ecclésiastique*, March, 1912).

[1] Since writing the above I have discovered the following information concerning the teaching in Rome: The Scholastic theory is taught in the Carmelite International College (Dr. Ronayne), the Benedictine Scholasticate of S. Anselmo (Dom Gredt), the Gregorian University (Canon Law Professors Ojetti, Vidal, Graziosi, Steiger, Capello).

stituting a corporate personality. This power resides in the people *ex natura rei,* not by any special concession of God, apart from creation and conservation, but rather by way of natural concomittance or immediate result.

This power is not in individual men taken separately, nor is it in the collection or aggregate of men taken in confusion and without order and union of members into one body. Hence the constitution of such a political body is prior to the existence of such power among men, since the subject of power must be prior, at least in the order of nature, to the power. But as soon as that body is constituted, this power is in it immediately by virtue of natural reason. Therefore it is rightly understood to exist by way of attribute resulting from such mystic body, constituted in such concrete existence.[2]

That is, assuming the consent of men to form a community, sovereignty by the very fact pertains to that community without further intervention of human wills. Men have power to delimit this political authority, to make contours and boundaries in its distribution, to determine the totalities in which it is localized; but they neither create such authority nor can they suppress it, for it is a moral fact, inevitably and immediately consequent on the existence even of a consent-formed community.[3] Sovereignty,

---

[2] Suarez, *De legibus,* iii. 3, 6. R. de Arriaga (following Salas, *De legibus,* vii. 2) puts this even more clearly: "Ea potestas non aliter a Deo provenit quam ut homines creat eosque conservat. ... Si intellegeremus homines existentes etiamsi Deus non esset, esset tamen in hominibus potestas constituendi unam rempublicam et elegendi suum caput a quo gubernarentur."—*De legibus,* xiii. 2, 7-8. This idea of the people as a corporate personality already appears in St. Thomas: "Condere legem vel pertinet ad totam multitudinem vel pertinet ad personam publicam quae totius multitudinis curam habet."—1, 2, q. 90, a. 3.

[3] Some Scholastics would not admit this, *e. g.,* Arriaga (*De legibus,* xiii. 3, 13): "Dico de iure naturae non esse ut actu sit aliqua potestas. ... Solum ergo est de iure naturae quod possint convenire homines." Cf. Bellarmine (*De laicis,* 6): "Non pendet ex consensu hominum; nam, velint nolint, debent regi ab aliquo." On which Vareilles-Sommières (*Principes fond. du droit,* p. 374) remarks: "The *nolint* is irreconcilable with the necessity of popular investiture which, nevertheless, the same Bellarmine requires for every government." This is a complete misunderstanding. The Scholastic analysis is: (1) consent to coexist as a community; (2) consequent authority as attribute of this community which, as Bellarmine

therefore, is essentially the attribute of the people as forming a juristic personality.

If supreme political authority is in any particular instance found to inhere in any other personality, sole or corporate, save that of the people, it is there only derivatively, and in virtue of communal consent. It is generally admitted by the Scholastics that this transfer of power to a "prince" may be either complete or partial; and this, as a matter of historical fact, is correct, for absolute monarchies have existed. But it is not at all clear that the *mere existence* of such instances of absolute alienation—apart from concomitant acquiescence—proves their moral validity, except such accidental, extrinsic and consequential validity as might follow from the actual functioning of such absolutism. The only argument adduced by some of the Schoolmen—that a nation as well as an individual may voluntarily enslave itself—is singularly weak.[4] Moreover, it is vehemently rejected by many writers, who deny the historical occurrence of any such absolute and permanent cession of power to a ruler; and these theologians also maintain that the prior consent of the people is necessary for the validation of a law.

I conclude (writes Alfonso de Castro)[5] that a law concerning a matter not necessary in virtue of divine law, which is passed by the prince or other magistrate in spite of the whole people, is of no force whatever—unless per-

---

says, "does not depend on the consent of men;" (3) concrete actualisation of this authority, which does depend on consent. "Supposita voluntate hominum conveniendi in una politica communitate, non est in potestate eorum impedire hanc iurisdictionem."—Suarez, *De legibus,* iii. 3, 2. So also Lessius, *De perfectionibus,* x. 2, 8.

[4] Suarez, *De legibus,* iii. 3, 7, *Defensio,* iii. 2, 9; Castro Palao, *De legibus,* i. 22, 4; Arriaga, *De legibus,* xiii. 3, 16; Neubauer, *De legibus,* 89.

[5] *De pot.* legis (1550), i. 1; *Opera* (1571), p. 1520. This must not be confused with the view—strangely liberal to modern ears—which the Scholastics and Canonists held with practical unanimity, namely, that any law which, though *per se* valid, was not accepted by the people, possessed no obligation. Other writers who reject complete alienation of power are Almain, *De suprema potestate,* q. 1, c. 16 (Goldast, *Monarchia,* i. 623); Major, 4 *Sent.,* d. 15, q. 10, also ap. Gerson, *Opera,* 1706, ii. 1139; Mariana, *De rege,* i. 5; Tanner, *Theol. schol.,* tom 2, disp. 5, q. dub. 4, n. 129 (ii. 1040); Becanus, *Summa theol.* schol., p. 2, tr. 3, c. 6, q. 8 (ii. 618f); Caramuel, *Theologia moralis fundamentalis,* §§ 673, 869, 926, (1657a, pp. 182, 238, 324).

chance the people may have without reservation transferred all their power to the prince or senate. But it can scarcely be believed that any people have made such a prodigal effusion of their power and liberty.

In any case even the absolute alienation, alleged as possible by some of the Scholastics, is not asserted to be unlimited and irrevocable; there are always reservations in virtue of natural law; there is an ultimate right of reassumption by the people in the interests of the common good.[6] This limitation of all derivative sovereignty is expressed in various ways by Catholic writers. The people retain authority *in habitu* or *in radice;* or they retain its possession and alienate only its exercise or use.[7]

The right of instituting a new form of government and a new investiture of power (says Cardinal Billot), is always in the community, so far as is required by necessity of the public good. Hence, generally speaking, every government to which the community peacefully adheres is to be considered legitimate. The proof is essentially this, that the right of rule is, unlike the right of property, not ordained for the good of the possessor, but simply and solely for the good of the society for which it is exercised. It follows at once, by an evident and clear dictate of natural

---

[6] Cf. *Irish Theol. Quarterly,* October, 1920, pp. 306f.

[7] *In habitu:* Almain, *De auct. ecclesia,* c. 1 (Gerson, *Opera,* ed. 1706, ii. 987); Azpilcueta (Navarrus), *Relectio cap. novit de iudic.,* notab. 3, n. 120 (*Opera,* Ven. 1602, iv. 595); Bellarmine, *Apologia,* 13; *Opera,* Naples, 1859, 4 (2), p. 399; Suarez, *Defensio,* iii. 3, 3; Dominic of St. Thomas, apud Rocaberti, *Bibliotheca,* x. 179a; Billot, *De ecclesia Christi,* 1903², p. 521. *In radice.* Lessius, *De perfectionibus moribusque divinis,* x. 2, 9. Only exercise or use alienated: Navarrus, op. cit.; Ventura, *Essai sur le pouvoir public,* 1859, pp. 431f; Rutten, *Ethicae seu phil. moralis elementa,* 1872², p. 253.

[8] Reference in previous note. Cf. Ryan, *Catholic Doctrine on the Right of Self-Government,* 1919, p. 31: "A politically competent people have the right to modify essentially their constitution, and even by passive resistance to force a monarch to abdicate, when they are unwaveringly convinced that they can provide a better government, and when this conviction corresponds with the facts." It may be observed (1) that the limitation of resistance to passivity is a question of expediency, not of principle; (2) that the final arbiter of the "correspondence with the facts" is the people, not the repudiated government; (3) that the most vital *fact* of all, perhaps the only really relevant one, is the conviction itself.

law, that in this matter only the public good is to be taken into account, so that if the necessity of the public good requires a new form of government and a new investiture of rulers, no pre-existing personal or family right can stand in the way. It follows also that this new constitution of a legitimate government pertains to the same as did the former; and thus the so-called constituent power always remains potentially (*in habitu*) in the community.

The Scholastic theory may now be fairly summarized as follows. Sovereignty is an essential attribute of the people, as constituting a corporate entity; it is radically and fundamentally inalienable, but for convenience and efficiency it may be transferred, by and with the consent of the community, for such time and under such conditions as the people deem expedient for the public good. The ultimate test of the juridical validity of any system of government is the consent of the governed.

III.—Some Objections

Several recent Catholic manuals have raised serious objections to the theory outlined above. A few of them will now be considered.

(A) Suarez and many other writers include just conquest as a primary title to sovereignty. It has been urged, and rightly urged, that this is not reconcilable with the principle that all sovereignty emanates from the people.[9] Suarez attempts to make it appear so by saying that in this case consent is *due* as a result of some crime. But this is a new and contradictory idea; it admits that the conqueror has a right prior to consent and not founded thereon; it further assumes that a moral obligation to consent is, from the objective juridical and political standpoint, synonymous with actual consent, just as one might assume that an obligation to marry is identical with marriage. Furthermore, it is supposed, on the antiquated analogy of the enslavement of prisoners of war, that the suppression and subjugation of nations is a legitimate function of "just" wars. Finally, it has been conclusively shown by history that without a supernational tribunal the Scholastic theory of

---

[9] Vareilles-Sommières, *Princ. fond. du droit*, pp. 374f; Liberatore, *Inst. ethicae*, 1884[8], p. 259.

a just war is quite unworkable. The conquered think it
unjust, the conqueror thinks it just. As Suarez himself
concedes,[1] "it happens more often that a kingdom is occupied through an unjust war, and in this way the more
famous empires of the world were extended. In that case
neither the kingdom nor the true power is acquired, for
the title of justice is lacking. But in course of time it may
happen that the people freely consent or that the kingdom
is acquired by prescription in good faith by the successors;
and then the tyranny will cease and true dominion and
power will begin."

The simplest answer to this objection is frankly to admit
its relevancy, to deny the assumptions of Suarez, and to
confess that it is only by the mere quibble of quasi-consent
that he subsumes enforced conquest under free consent.
This is the position of several among those modern Scholastics who adhere to the Scholastic theory.[2] In a just war
the victor *quâ* victor has no rights; but *quâ* just he has a
right to justice, i. e., to indemnity, reparation, and guaran-
tees. That justice necessitates the enslavement of peoples
is a false doctrine, whose refutation has been written in
blood; its falsity is intensified by the fact that all victors
deem their wars just; might likes to masquerade as right.[3]

(B) The quotation just given from Suarez seems to
justify the objection that the Scholastic theory is inconsistent inasmuch as it apparently admits that usurpation
may be legitimated either by consent or by prescription.
But it is certainly hazardous to father such a view on
Suarez merely on the ground that he *once* speaks of consent *or* prescription; especially as he distinctly declares elsewhere:[4]

"When a kingdom is possessed by mere unjust force,

---

[1] *Defensio*, iii. 2, 20. Cf. *De legibus*, iii. 4, 4.
[2] Zallinger, *Inst. iuris naturalis*, §207, Rome, 1832, i. 429; Macksey, *De ethica naturali*, 1914, p. 544; Macksey, *Sovereignty and Consent*, 1920, pp. 24f; Marcellus a Puero Iesu, *Phil. moralis*, 1913, p. 728.
[3] On reconsidering the above paragraph, I think it is too severe on Suarez. In admitting title by just conquest, Suarez probably did not abandon his criterion of consent; he merely superseded national consent by world-consent. This is his argument: Conquest in *just war* is based in the *ius gentium* (*Studies*, June, 1918, p. 230), which is based on world-consent (*Studies*, Dec. 1920, p. 585).
[4] *De legibus*, iii. 4, 4.

there is no true legislative power in the king. But it can happen that in course of time the people consent and admit such a rule; and then the (source of) power will be reduced to the transfer and donation of the people."

There is no doubt whatever that, consistently with its fundamental principle, the Scholastic theory has no place for prescription as a primary title to political power. Prescription, as such, has really no place in natural law at all; it is only in virtue of positive human law, for instance, that mere length of possession confers ownership. One of the propositions condemned in the Syllabus is that "an unjust fact, if crowned by success, does not injure the sanctity of right." [5] What modern opponents of the Scholastic theory mean by prescription is that social conditions and circumstances, which usually take time to mature (though this is quite irrelevant), may create, on the part of the people, a moral obligation to consent to an existing rule. This, as a mere matter of theory, may be conceded. But this concession is rather academic, inasmuch as usurpation is practically always an oppression also and thus incapable of any such rights, and when it is really not oppressive but for the people's good, it is almost sure to receive the community's consent. The real mistake in treating prescription as a primary title to political power lies in the confusion of moral obligation to consent, which may possibly occur in rare cases, with actual consent, which *ex hypothesi* is not given. Whereas the Scholastics hold that even a forced consent is insufficient to validate a government, a usurping rule becomes juridically valid only when the people give to it their free consent.[6]

But the Scholastics were well aware that this consent may be given tacitly and gradually; and they permitted prescription, in the sense of long-continued peaceful pros-

---

[5] No. 61: *Fortunata facti iniustitia nullum iuris sanctitati detrimentum affert.* Cf. Balmes, *El protestantismo* ii. 234 (ed. Paris, 1887), Eng. trans. ch. 55: "If Napoleon had succeeded in establishing his power amongst us, the Spanish nation would still have maintained the right on account of which it revolted in 1808; victory could not have rendered usurpation legitimate. . . . What will be safe here below if we admit the principle that success insures justice and that the conqueror is always the rightful ruler?"

[6] Cf. Navarrus, *Relectio* "Novit," notab. 3, n. 151; *Opera*, Venice, 1602, iv. 603a.

perous possession, not as *title* but as *evidence* of the people's acquiescence and consent. Thus Lessius says:[7]

"A tyrant cannot prescriptively acquire a right of rule against a free people when he holds them only by fear so that they are not presumed to consent freely to him. The reason is that in such cases of forceful usurpation prescription cannot confer a right, *except in so far as long-continued exercise and possession beget the presumption of the free consent of those concerned.*"

The admission of such a kind of prescription, so far from being inconsistent, is merely an application of the Scholastic theory of government with the consent of the governed.

(C) Perhaps the commonest objection of all is the statement, usually made rather bluntly and dogmatically, that the Scholastic theory is "at variance with historical fact."[8] To prove this we are told that "the first political rulers derived their authority at a time when such a compact would have been almost unthinkable, a period when any attempt to superimpose upon the family or tribal organization, based upon the tie of blood, another organization based upon a wholly different principle, viz., popular election to power, would have been exceedingly difficult, if not wholly impossible." This is merely an attempt to bury the problem in prehistoric darkness; one might with equal

---

[7] *De iustitia et iure* ii. 5, 8, 41 (Antv. 1612, p. 48a). He also says (*ibid.* ii. 29, 9, 70; p. 370b): The usurper "not only sinned by invading the country, but also continually sins (both himself and his heir) by keeping the country oppressed and subject to him; until at length he is spontaneously received by the kingdom—which can happen if it is *sui iuris* and subject to no other ruler—or after a long interval prescription arises." Lessius is here thinking of a town or province incapable of being *sui iuris*. The Schoolmen admitted—as do also their modern opponents, though these latter exaggerate the quasi-property rights of the expelled ruler or dynasty—prescription *against the ousted government,* i. e., the cessation of the community's obligation-to-consent to the vanquished ruler if still existent. Cf. Costa-Rossetti, *Phil. moralis,* 1886², pp. 662f; Van der Aa, *Ethica,* 1889, p. 203; Desorges, *De l'origine et de la nature du pouvoir,* 1869, pp. 131f; Raboisson, *Du pouvoir,* 1874, p. 297.

[8] Cronin, *Ethics,* ii. 503. So also Vareilles-Sommières, pp. 376f. Cathrein, § 584, p. 396; Vermeersch, § 559, p. 705; Reinstadler, *Elementa,* 1913⁷, ii. 472; Rickaby, *Moral Philosophy,* p. 337, and *Political and Moral Essays,* p. 109; Pius La Scala, loc. cit.

propriety and relevancy refute the civilized idea of marriage (prescinding from revelation) by referring to a time when such a marriage compact would have been almost unthinkable. Practically everything of the kind does become unthinkable if one accepts the modern conclusions about prehistoric man. The Scholastics, however, apparently took Adam more literally than do their successors. And also, with more science and prudence, they largely confined themselves to the verifiable history of civilized peoples— the Republic and Empire of Rome, the Jewish Kingdom, the Frankish Monarchy, the Holy Roman Empire—in whose constitutional theories consent and election were included.

But the real answer to this objection goes to the root of the matter; the problem is moral and juridical, not historical at all. "Judiciously explained and not driven home too rigidly," writes Father Rickaby,[9] "the Suarezian (he means Scholastic) theory of the origin of civil authority appears to be as accurate as any theory can be accurate under the vast variety of circumstances that have affected that origin in history." With all due respect it must be said that this distinguished Jesuit is confusing philosophy with history, politics and ethnology. Similarly, when another able critic [1] says that "to show what is general and invariable in the causes and in the formation of all civil societies is to indicate the philosophical origin of civil society," we must reply that it is nothing of the kind. Such an analysis is concerned solely with historical causative factors, whereas the philosophical origin of society and government means the ground of their validity. The problem has no connection with temporal priority or with antecedents in a historical process; it concerns the ethical justification, not only in the past but here and now, of a certain moral nexus between men. The Scholastic theory asserts that *consent* is the intrinsic essential moral factor which juridically validates these relationships. It may or may not

[9] *Political and Moral Essays*, 1902, p. 112.
[1] Comte de Vareilles-Sommières, p. 57. On p. 137 he inconsistently remarks that "it is impossible to understand how force can by itself alone create a valid society; force constrains but does not oblige." Precisely. But this introduces the idea of *moral validity*, on the strength of which the Count rejects force without examining if it is a general and invariable ingredient of nascent societies.

be true that such and such organizations originated in force or fraud or superstition. The genetic development of these institutions is quite irrelevant; at any given stage they are or are not ethically valid according as they are or are not founded on consent, however this consent be motived.

It is true indeed that this theory, like every claim based on the concept of self or person, whether natural law or moral responsibility or deliberate volition, is idealistic in the sense of becoming continually more applicable as personality and self-consciousness grow. We may, therefore, adopt as our own what an opponent has declared by way of objection: "The individual has not at first the government of his acts; he begins by obeying fatal laws and then paternal authority. It is only after long years that he is master of himself. Reasoning by analogy, if it has any value here, would therefore lead to this conclusion: that civil society ought not to begin but to end with the sovereignty of the people."[2] Precisely. There is the same, as much and as little, historical evolution in the sovereignty of the people as there is in natural law or the Ten Commandments. As a modern Scholastic says, in replying to the objection that this theory is unhistorical and unpractical:

"It exhibits the human ideal, of which the aristocratic or hereditary modes of designation are but imperfect approximations. And in our time it is specially urgent that we should consider this ideal. More and more the principle of heredity is becoming effaced in private and public posts; more and more the machinism of modern industry is necessitating and developing the effort towards personal life, in the private and public order; less and less do civilized men appear inclined to leave the supreme magistrate hereditary when any other is no longer so."[3]

(D) We are now in a better position to answer this query: "What is the necessity or opportuneness of this authority in the people, since the people, without exercising it, immediately transfer it to the ruler?"[4] That is,

---

[2] Vareilles-Sommières, pp. 367f.
[3] Schwalm, *Leçons de philosophie sociale,* ii. 502f. Cf. Bautain, *Philosophie morale,* 1842, ii. 542f.
[4] Vermeersch, *De iustitia,* 1904², § 559, p. 705. So also Taparelli, *Esame critico,* § § 88, 125 (i. pp. 70, 102); Zigliara, pp. 270f;

how can the people by natural right possess a sovereignty which they cannot retain or exercise? We might content ourselves with replying that if the people are unable to exercise sovereignty, they ought to be able; just as we might reply to an upholder of the divorce court that people ought to be able to observe monogamy. In other words, the alleged inability occurs *per accidens*. That is, we cannot have a real democracy because the individuals lack personality, religion and character; we cannot have direct democracy such as exists in the Swiss Landesgemeinden, because the natural small political units are absorbed into unwieldly centralized empires. But is it true as a matter of fact that the people cannot retain and exercise sovereignty, even in spite of these disabilities? The Scholastics not only freely admitted this possibility, but regarded republics like Venice and Genoa as being actual examples.[5] The horror of popular sovereignty, so noticeable in recent reactionary Catholic writers, is largely due to the delusion that it implies anarchy and instability; as if Switzerland, where the people are sovereign, is more unstable and anarchical than England, where the Parliament claims to be sovereign. Popular supremacy, it must not be forgotten, is quite compatible with ample delegation of power and full equipment of officials; it simply implies the possession of ultimate control by the people, exercised through referendum, initiative and suchlike. This is no more an objection to democracy than the existence of innumerable appointments and offices in which assistants, secretaries, and subordinates are indispensable, is an argument against all human organization.

Schiffini, § 447 (ii. 392-4); Vareilles-Sommières, p. 371; Cathrein, § 585, p. 397; O. Hill, *Ethics,* 1920, p. 380.

[5] Navarrus, *Novit,* notabile 3, n. 148 (*Opera,* iv. 602). Suarez, *De legibus,* iii. 4, 1: "Ex pura lege naturae non coguntur homines habere hanc potestatem in uno vel in pluribus vel in collectione omnium." Cf. *ibid.* iii. 9, 6. Bellarmine stands practically alone in maintaining that the people are bound by the law of nature to transfer their power, "for the nation cannot *by itself exercise* this power."—*De laicis,* 6: *Opera* (Naples ed.), ii. 317. But the nation can retain control, initiative, right of appointment, revocation, and ultimate decision. It is an utterly fallacious argument to say that a right does not exist because its detailed exercise and administration require the assistance and appointment of officials.

IV.—Transfer or Designation?

In the older Schoolmen, such as St. Thomas, we find the view that political power is in the people, or in a ruler in so far as he represents or takes the place of the people. But later on, under the influence of the famous *lex regia* of Roman law, the unanimous phraseology is that power is transferred by the people to the ruler. There is no doubt that many of the Scholastics took this to mean that the people first had the power and then despoiled themselves by handing it over, by way of donation or contract, to the ruler.[1] Now, this is not a very satisfactory position, inasmuch as it regards popular sovereignty as chronologically, rather than ethically, prior. Nor can the institution of government be viewed as the abdication of the community; it is rather the process whereby the community makes necessary provision for itself. In connection with the director or secretary of a company, a professor in a university, or the superintendent of an estate, we do not speak of a transfer of power, we use the word appointment. There does not seem any reason why we cannot similarly express the Scholastic theory by saying that the people *institute* the form of government and *appoint* the individual government or ruler.[2] It is really this communication or delegation of power which is meant by transfer, but which is, perhaps, less ambiguously expressed by appointment.

[1] This view was originated by certain legists, e.g., Baldus: "Populus Romanus . . . denudatus est generali potestate cum illa translata fuerit in principem."—*Commentarium in* i. ii. *et* iii. *codicis libros,* ed. Lugd., 1585, fol. 75c. But contrast Hugolinus (*Distinctiones,* 148, 34): "Certe non transtulit sic ut non remaneret apud eum, sed constituit eum quasi procuratorem ad hoc."

[2] "Instituere namque potestatem est ordinare quod in communitate sit aliqua potestas tanta et talis, ad tot casus, ad talem populum, et sic de similibus. Et talis institutio tempore praecedere potest communicationem certae personae."—Almain, *De auctoritate ecclesiae,* c. 2; Gerson, *Opera,* ed. 1706, ii. 980. Some modern upholders of the Scholastic theory prefer to avoid the idea of transfer. Quilliet, *De civilis potestatis origine theoria catholica,* 1893, p. 174: "ius naturaliter et divinitus populo competens elegendi ac determinandi politicum suum regimen." Billot, *De ecclesia Christi,* 1903², pp. 513, 515: "Non ipsa politica potestas sed solum ius determinandi legitimam regiminis formam, necnon et legitimam rationem investiturae gubernii, naturaliter in populo esse asseritur. . . . Sed haec ad penitiorem tantum doctrinae expositionem spectant, et forte lis esset magis de verbis quam de re."

There is, however, a school of thinkers who would not only improve terminology but entirely reject the whole idea of communication of power through the people. This theory, which assimilates the concession of political power to the collation of spiritual jurisdiction, was originated by the imperialist opponents of the papacy. "God alone elects," says Dante,[3] "hence electors should not be so called; they are rather to be regarded as declarers of divine providence." This view made no headway in Catholic philosophy, but after the Reformation it was adopted, as a moderate form of the theory of divine right, by many Protestants.

Between thirty and forty years since, when I was a young student in Cambridge (writes John Goodwin, in his *Obstructors of Justice,* 1649)[4], such doctrines and devises as these: . . . that the interest of the people extend only to the nomination or presentation of such a person unto God, who they desire might be their king, but that the regal power, by which he is properly and formally constituted a king, is, immediately and independently in respect of any act of the people, derived unto him by God—these, I say, or such like positions as these were the known preferment-divinity of the doctorate there, and (were) as the common air, taken in and breathed out by those who lived the life of hope in the king and sought the truth in matters of religion by the light of his countenance.

---

[3] *De monarchia,* iii. 16; *Opere,* ed. Moore, p. 376. Cf. the view cited by Ockham, *Octo quaestiones,* q. 2. c. 3 (Goldast, *Monarchia,* ii. 346f).

[4] § 26, pp. 28f. The pervert Archbishop De Dominis (died 1624) seems to have introduced this theory into England; it was at least an improvement on the divine right theory of Henry VIII and James I: "Non ergo qui mutat formam regiminis defert aut transfert potestatem rectivam, sed novas personarum facit vel electiones vel Deo ita disponente etiam legitimas inductiones; et tunc illis Deus dat immediate potestatem."—*De republica ecclesiastica,* ii. 919 (*Ostensio errorum P. F. Suarez,* § 6). In § 7 (p. 921) he uses the expression designation. The theory is also to be found in Maxwell, *Sacrosancta regum majestas,* ch. 12, 1686², pp. 190f. Baxter, *Holy Commonwealth* (1659), thesis 182, p. 190: "When the freest people choose a prince, they do not properly and efficiently give him his power as conveying it from them to him, but are only a *causa sine qua non,* and denominate or design the person that shall from God, and not from them, receive it."

That a theory with such an Imperialistic-Gallican-Protestant parentage should nowadays be expounded as the orthodox Catholic thesis, is somewhat of a shock. This particular contention is merely part of the general anti-democratic reaction to which reference has already been made. The chief argument in support of it is Pope Leo XIII's declaration[5]:

"Many more recent writers, following in the steps of those who in the last century gave themselves the title of philosophers, say that all power is from the people. . . . Catholics dissent from these men and seek the right to rule from God as its natural and necessary principle. It is important to note here that those who are to govern the State may, in certain cases, be selected by the will and judgement of the people, since Catholic doctrine is neither opposed nor repugnant thereto. *By which selection the ruler is designated, but the rights of rule are not conferred;* nor is the authority thereby constituted, but its wielder is determined. . . . As for political authority, the Church rightly teaches that it proceeds from God."

Now the very context, even as partially cited here, shows that the Pope is simply arguing against the anti-Christian theory which rejects the natural and divine law and makes the people the absolute creator of right and wrong.

In this passage (says Cardinal Billot[1]) there is really expounded the pure and simple teaching of the faith against

---

[5] *Diuturnum*, 29 June, 1881: *Lettres apostoliques*, i. 142. In Denzinger, *Enchiridion* (with context mutilated), nn. 1855-6. There are similar passages in other Encyclicals of Leo XIII and Pius X.

[1] *De ecclesia Christi*, 1903², pp. 515f. Similarly Hugonin, *Du droit ancien et droit nouveau*, 1887, p. 6; Costa-Rossetti, *Phil. moralis*, 1886², pp. 628, 630; Castelein, *Inst. phil. moralis*, 1899, p. 483; Quilliet, *De civilis potestatis origine theoria*, 1893, pp. 349-355; Moulart, *L'église et l'état*, 1895, pp. 87ff; Vermeersch, *Quaestiones de iustitia*, 1904⁴, § 559, p. 704; Macksey, *De ethica naturali*, 1914, pp. 550ff; Ireland, *The Church and Modern Society*, 1897², pp. 16f; Féret, *Le pouvoir civil devant l'enseignement catholique*, 1888, p. 177; Hickey, *Summula* 3 (1919¹), 501; Cavallera, *Bulletin de litt. eccles.* (Toulouse), March, 1912, p. 112; Sortais, *Les catholiques en face de la démocratie*, 1914, pp. 199-240; Gemelli, *Rivisa di Fil. Neoscol.* 10 (1918) 119; Choupin, *Valeur des décisions doctrinales et disciplinaires du Saint-Siège*, 1913². p. 358; Ryan, *Catholic Doctrine on the Right of Self-Government*, 1919, p. 12; Vallet, *Praelect. phil.*, 1890⁶, ii. 438; Marcellus a Puero Iesu, *Phil. moralis et socialis*, 1913, pp. 718f. B. Gaudeau, *La fausse démocratie et le droit naturel*, 1911,

hostile and novel views. . . . It is denied, then, that by the people's choice the rights of government are conferred, that is, in the sense of those opponents of Catholic doctrine who say that the right of government itself comes altogether from the people, and not merely according to its contingent and variable forms or the contingent and variable titles to its possession. It is also denied that authority is constituted by the people's choice. This again is against those who consider civil society as born of men's free consent and attribute the same origin to authority. . . . In one word, what is denied is what has always been denied with unanimous consent by Catholic theologians.

We are not dependent even on the clear interpretation of Cardinal Billot and a score of other eminent writers (including opponents of the Scholastic theory such as Vermeersch). For Pius X in his letter on the Sillon cites this very passage of Pope Leo as "a refutation of the attempt to reconcile Catholic teaching with the error of philosophism."[6] That Bellarmine and Suarez could be referred to as moderns following in the footsteps of (the 18th century) "philosophers" is chronologically impossible,

---

p. 55; T. Pégues, O. P., *Revue thomiste* 19 (1911) 607; L. Watt, S. J., *Irish Eccles. Record,* August, 1917, p. 97; P. Finlay, S. J., *Irish Catholic,* 19 Feb., 1921; L. Izaga, S. J., *Estudios de Deusto,* 10 (1918) 344f; E. Masterson, S. J., *Irish Theol. Quarterly,* April, 1921, p. 121. According to these twenty-four writers—and doubtless there are more—the Pope is simply combating atheistic individualism and makes no animadversion whatever on the Scholastic theory, which remains a perfectly tenable view supported by great authorities and strong arguments.

[6] *Acta Ap. Sedis* 2 (1910) 616. The reply of a Roman Cardinal to the Abbé Féret (reference in previous note) is worth citing in full: [Leo XIII] animo intendens non ad innocuas catholicae gentis opiniones sed ad pestiferas novatorum doctrinas, qui, inter terram caelum quodvis vinculum abrumpere pertentantes, civilis potestatis originem non a Deo sed ab hominum consilio emanare effutiunt, iure meritoque clamat: Potestas a Deo est. Hinc ipse dum profunde ac copiose suum edisserit argumentum, ea duo vocabula, *immediate, mediate,* silentio praeterit; quo sane incedendi modo ibi ecclesiae non filios sed perduelles corripi, hosque tantum ad meliora consilia amplectenda excitari liquido constat. . . . Evidenter eruitur sedem apostolicam haud torvis oculis conspecturam illorum librorum novas editiones, in quibus civilis potestatis origo mediate a Deo vindicatur. Et re quidem vera, cum ex Leonis XIII oraculo haec opinio nullam iacturam perpessa sit, eccur ipsa in damnatorum errorum censum enumeranda erit?

THE STATE 965

that the teaching of such great apologists should be characterized as "the error of philosophism" would be an utterly preposterous contention. But it passes all limits of our credulity and tolerance to be informed dogmatically, without reference to the score of authoritative writers who have emphatically repudiated the groundless suggestion, that a mere *obiter dictum* of a long papal letter, which is entirely devoted to upholding basic Christian principles, is to be construed as the official condemnation of a thesis which received the adhesion not only of Bellarmine and Suarez but of practically every Catholic philosopher and moral theologian for over five centuries; and this in favour of a view which was originally devised against the Papacy and has merely somersaulted into some recent Catholic books. "It is quite unfair and unscientific," says Dr. J. A. Ryan,[7] "to read into two isolated sentences a condemnation of a doctrine which was taught by the great majority of Catholic moralists and jurists for upwards of seven centuries. Therefore, it cannot be seriously maintained that the traditional doctrine has been superseded by the official authority of the Church." This alleged extraction of a concealed definition displays ignorance of those scientific rules of interpretation which, in the interest of justice and tolerance, should always be applied to such ecclesiastical documents, which, unless they contain formal mention and explicit reference, may not be presumed to intervene in controverted questions of the School.[8]

[7] *Catholic Doctrine on the Right of Self-Government*, 1919, p. 12.
[8] Many, if not most, writers since 1881 (*e. g.*, MacEvilly, *Expos. of the Ep. of S. Paul*, 1898⁵, i. 115) continue to regard the Scholastic theory as a perfectly free and very probable opinion, without referring at all to Pope Leo's Encyclicals. From 1911 to his death in 1919 Fr. Macksey, S. J., taught the Scholastic theory in the Gregorian University under the very shadow of the Vatican; his book, *De ethica naturali*, published in Rome in 1914, contains an able exposition of the theory and a detailed interpretation of the Encyclicals of Leo XIII and Pius X. I have been able to discover only two writers of repute who find a real discrepancy between the Scholastic theory and the Encyclicals: Archbishop Healy, who considered it "impossible to reconcile" Suarez with Leo XIII, though he admitted that the Suarezian was still "a perfectly free opinion" (*Irish Eccles. Record*, Dec. 1881, pp. 708, 704); and Père Schwalm, O. P., who (in his *Leçons de phil. sociale*, 1912², ii. 478) not only "extracts" from S. Thomas the designation-theory invented by later Gallicans and Protestants, but considers that Leo XIII has

This whole attempt to drag papal pronouncements into the midst of a philosophical discussion among Catholics is singularly irrelevant. As Cardinal Billot points out, the Pope is combating the atheistic individualism which was popularized by Rousseau and his successors. Here, as elsewhere, the Pope is engaged in refuting and condemning the sovereignty of the people solely and exclusively and formally in the sense in which this sovereignty denies the supremacy of God.[9] Every Catholic, whether he admits

made it "the Catholic thesis." (The absurdity of this is evidenced by the fact that only a small minority of Catholic writers uphold the theory of *designation* by the *people*). Cf. also Tepe, *Inst. theol. moralis,* 1898, i. 339; and note of editor in Zigliara, *Summa,* 1912[15], iii. 271. Most of those who misinterpret the Pope (*e. g.,* Schiffini, Bouquillon, Blanc, Farges and Barbedette) content themselves with saying that he seems to favour the idea of designation. Thus Vareilles-Sommières (pp. 379f): The Scholastic theory "does not seem to be exactly adapted to the indications given incidentally by Leo XIII. . . . But it would be going too far to say that this opinion is not conformed to the teachings of the Holy See." The *Leçons de philosophie sociale* of Père Schwalm (†1908) were published posthumously from his lecture-notes and never received his final revision. But in his later article on Democracy in the *Dictionnaire de Théologie* (tome 4, pp. 271-321) he makes no mention whatever of the designation-theory and states clearly (p. 304) that the encyclical *Diuturnum* was directed merely against Rousseau.

With reference to the teaching in the Gregorian University, I have before me copies of the highly laudatory letters sent to the Rector (P. Luigi Caterini, S. J.), together with three gold medals, by the Cardinal Secretary of State on behalf of Pius X., on 19 May, 1914, 30 Nov., 1915, 11 Nov., 1916.

[9] Cf. *Immortale Dei* (Denziger, n. 1868): Ortum publicae potestatis a Deo ipso, non a multitudine, repeti oportere. I have no space to deal with Pope Leo's two letters (*Au milieu des sollicitudes,* 16th Feb., 1892, and *Notre consolation,* 3rd May, 1892), whereby he sought to induce French Catholics to accept loyally the Republic. The letters are not really relevant and involve issues debated between Royalists and Republicans, which would require a whole article for adequate discussion. This is Archbishop Ireland's interpretation (*The Church and Modern Society,* 1897[2], pp. 395f): "The Pope declares that whatever be the form of government in a nation it cannot be considered so definite as to be unchangeable, even if this had been the intention of those who first constituted it. And when a nation has adopted a form of government however new, such form of government is binding upon citizens; for it is the expression of the will of the people, and the interests of social order demand that it be accepted and obeyed. Empires, monarchies, republics, are alike entitled to recognition and respect—the one

that power is transmitted mediately or immediately, must hold that political power comes from God, and is not simply a congeries of individual contributions over which the people have absolute control irrespective of moral principles. The Scholastic doctrine of the sovereignty of the people, so far from denying, actually presupposes the sovereignty of God.

If, then, both the Scholastics and their modern Catholic opponents admit the divine origin of civil power, are their differences so vitally important? Does it make any practical difference whether we speak of designation or transfer? In answering this question in the negative, many writers have failed to distinguish between designation-by-facts and designation-by-the-people. Probably a majority of contemporary Catholic writers advocate a theory, or rather various theories which agree in maintaining that certain *facts* (*e. g.*, occupancy) can designate and determine a sovereign immediately, *i. e.*, quite independently of the people's consent. And it is precisely these writers who have chiefly striven to eke out their arguments by quotations from encyclicals; quite forgetful of the fact that another important school of Catholic philosophers, who seek to modify rather than to oppose the Scholastic theory, also quote the Popes on *their* side. Thus Cavagnis, Schwalm, the editor of Zigliara, and others, think that Leo XIII's language favours the theory of designation, not by facts, but by the people. This serious division among the misinterpreters of the encyclicals may serve as a final *reductio ad absurdum* of this misplaced ingenuity which seeks to bury obnoxious Scholasticism beneath authoritative documents.

With the various, and often contradictory, theories of designation-by-facts we are not here concerned; they will be dealt with elsewhere. We are considering merely that modification in the Scholastic theory which consists in substituting designation-by-the-people for transfer-by-the-people. And at first sight the designation is more metaphysical than practical. For, if popular election is regarded as the *sole* medium of designation, then, in practice, it is tantamount to the theory of transfer or appointment.

condition for the legitimacy of any form of government being that it has been constituted by the people."

If it be held (says Dr. J. A. Ryan [1]) that the consent of the people is always a necessary prerequisite to the assumption of political power by any person, it is of no practical significance whether the people be conceived as handing over to the ruler authority which God has deposited with them or as designating the person upon whom God will confer the authority. In either supposition, God does not bestow authority nor does the ruler receive it, until the people have somehow given their consent.

Which is quite true, provided we add that God withdraws authority when the people validly revoke their consent. And if these conditions and limitations are inserted, the whole language and analysis of the designation-theory become highly artificial and unnecessarily subtle.[2]

The theory is, in fact, a particular application of a more general tendency, which, for convenience, may be termed moral occasionalism.[3] This is the view that moral obliga-

---

[1] *Catholic Doctrine on the Right of Self-Government*, 1919, pp. 6f. Cf. Balmes, *El protestantismo comparado con el catolicismo*, ed. Paris, 1887, ii. 431 (note 3): Eng. trans. (*European Civilization*), note 29. Cf. *Month*, Feb. 1921, p. 161: "There is little difference in practice between being the source and being the channel of authority." The following writers hold the theory of designation-by-the-people and so admit the general Scholastic thesis of government with the consent of the governed: Bailly, Audisio, Peltier, Cavagnis, Zigliara, de Belcastel, Schwalm, "M" (author of the Saint-Sulpice *Compendium philosophiae*), Deshayes, Farges et Barbedette, Blanc.

[2] Victoria (*Relectiones theologicae* iii. 8) is often incorrectly cited as holding the designation-theory. His language is certainly not clear and has been rejected by subsequent Scholastics: "Quamvis enim [rex] a republica constituatur—creat enim respublica regem—non potestatem sed propriam auctoritatem in regem transfert; nec sunt duae potestates una regia, altera communitatis." It seems clear that Victoria is merely trying to say that power in general (*potestas*) comes from God, while its concrete embodiment (*auctoritas*) comes from the people. Cf. Baldelli, *Disp. ex morali theologia*, v. 10, 6 (1637, p. 457a): "Si quis cum Victoria contendat potestatem regis esse a Deo, quia est illa ipsa quam Deus primo dedit communitati, . . . non est cum illo magnopere laborandum; dummodo constet quod translatio potestatis in regem et electio illius determinate in quem potestas est transferenda, sit ab ipsa communitate; et Deus non det regibus potestatem quasi primo et immediate, sed solum secundario et mediante communitate."

[3] This denial of all human causality and transient effectiveness in the moral order is strikingly apparent in some expositions of the

tion is something more than the direct result of the operation of our will or of a physical action; we merely *posit* the material conditions determining the creation or transfer of rights. Those who take this view deny what may be called secondary moral causality, that is, all direct efficient influx of secondary causes on moral obligations. The refutation of this theory is quite analogous to the disproof of physical occasionalism. It need not be here considered except to emphasize the principle, forgetfulness of which has led to many confusions, that the immediate moral causality of the people does not in the least contradict the equally immediate moral *concursus* of God.[4] In the natural order at least, secondary causes cannot be degraded into mere conditions without causal influence or efficiency.

designation-theory. Thus Fénelon: "Election, succession, just conquest, and all other means of attaining the sovereignty, are only canals through which it glides and not the fountain from whence it flows."—Ramsay, *Essay upon Civil Government,* 1722, ch. 17, p. 208. That is, in the moral order God alone is fountain, created beings are simply canals; what about the physical order—are there no fountains? "All authority comes essentially, uniquely, immediately from God. I say this, without exception of all authority, general, partial, sovereign or subordinate. I mean that at the very moment when authority begins to exist, no matter in what individual, of whatever nature it be . . . it is God which creates for him the duty and the right to govern me well and for me the right to be governed and the duty to obey."—Barruel, *Question nationale sur l'autorité et sur les droits du peuple dans le gouvernement* [1791], p. 100; cited in Féret, *Le pouvoir civil,* 188, pp. 411f.

[4] Catalano, *De legibus,* c. 3 (*Universi iuris theologico-moralis corpus integrum,* 1728, i. 18*b*): "Accipere immediate a Deo non facit quin etiam immediate accipiat a republica; sicuti non per hoc quod immediate accipiat respublica potestatem istam a natura, non immediate etiam accipiat a Deo." F. de Castro Palao, *De legibus,* i. 22, 4 (*Opus morale,* ed. 1700, i. 147): "Respondeo omnem protestatem regiam a Deo esse immediate; sed non inde infertur in alios prius immediate non fuisse, fuit quidem immediate in ipsa communitate a qua in regem translata fuit. Sed haec prioritas non obstat quominus in rege immediate a Deo sit potestas; tum quia non est alia potestas in rege quam illa potestas quae fuit in communitate, tum quia ipsemet Deus sua speciali providentia hanc translationem seu successionem ordinavit." Cf. also Miranda, *Manuale praelatorum,* tom. 2, q. 25, a. 14, concl. 2 (1630, p. 229*a*); and Navarrus, *Relectio "Novit,"* n. 147 (*Opera,* 1602, iv. 601): "Per Deum quidem regnant reges aetatis nostrae, quia regnant per potestatem quam habent ab ipso immediate creatam sed mediate acceptam."

Hence the distinction between the appointment of a governor or ruler and the designation of a priest or pope. To group all these together as examples of designation—as the moral-occasionalists do—is to neglect a clear existent distinction and to confuse diverse phenomena under a double-meaning phraseology. Hence the Schoolmen all but unanimously refused to identify transfer of political power with designation to ecclesiastical office.[5]

"Designation of a person," says Suarez,[6] is not enough, nor, if separated from donation or contract or quasi-contract, does it have the effect of conferring power; for natural reason alone does not sustain the translation of power from one man to another by mere designation of the person, without the consent and efficacious will of him by whom the power is to be transferred or conferred." That is, designation *per se,* apart from the deliberate efficacious will of God in case of supernatural jurisdiction and of man in natural appointments, is insufficient and ineffective; it must be conjoined with donation, trust or contract; it must, in other words, become transfer by agreement or consent. Such transfer implies both quantitative and qualitative control, *i. e.,* authority to decide both the specification and the individuation of the power; it assumes that the entire efficacy of the act of authorisation is derived from the will and consent of the transferor or appointer; it results in a contractual or fiduciary relation between the two parties. Not a single one of these characteristics is to be found in ecclesiastical ordination or canonical designa-

---

[5] The following, among others, reject the political designation-theory: Almain, *De suprema potestate,* q. 1, c. 16 (Goldcast, *Monarchia,* i. 623); Molina, *De iustitia* ii. 26 (1602, p. 124); Bellarmine, *Risposta alla difesa delle otto proposizioni, Opera,* Neap., 1859, 4 (2), 514; Navarrus, *Consiliorum sive responsorum libri quinque,* ii. 1. 3 (ed. 1602, i. 332f); Chastel, *De l'autorité et du respect qui lui est dû,* 1851, p. 196; Desorges, *De l'origine et de la nature du pouvoir,* 1869, p. 63f; Brugère, *De ecclesia Christi,* 1878[2], pp. 360f; Costa-Rossetti, *Phil. moralis,* 1886[2], pp. 62ff.; Mendive, *Ethica,* 1888, p. 329; Vander Aa, *Ethica,* 1889[2], pp. 192f.; R. Rodriguez de Cepeda, *Eléments de droit naturel,* 1890, p. 527; Billot, *De ecclesia Christi,* 1903[2], pp. 508f., 518. Also Suarez and Tanner, cited in next note; and Quilliet, Moulart, Macksey, Cavallera (p. 105), and Féret.

[6] *Defensio,* iii. 2, 17. Cf. Tanner, *Theol.* schol., tom. 2, disp., 5, dub. 1, n. 84 (ii. 10210).

tion. Hence, unless, with the Imperialist and Protestant absolutists of a former age, we wish to confound the spiritual and the temporal, we must reject as misleading and inaccurate the recently resuscitated theory that the people do not transfer power but merely designate its recipients.

166

THE BEST STATE

Michael Cronin [1]

The problem of the best kind of government may be raised in practical form in either of the two following senses: first, taking the circumstances of each State into account, what is the best form of government for that State? secondly, normally speaking, and comparing one State with another, what is the form of government that realizes the essential ends of the State in the fullest and highest way all round, or that is subject to the fewest and least important defects? To the first question, no general answer can be given, except, perhaps, the not very enlightening answer that the best form is the form that *works* in each case, the form that has proved itself both enduring and progressive, that has grown under the influence of the special needs of the people, and been gradually shaped to meet those needs. In the first setting up of a State it would be very difficult to anticipate future possibilities, and to declare that such and such a form is or is not suitable to, or best for, this people's requirements. Indeed, whatever form is finally set up, is sure to be found wanting, and to require modification in many respects, even by the admixture of other and opposed forms. Above all things, it would be rash to attempt to judge of the best form for a particular people by a consideration of the special character of that people, it being no easy thing to formulate the character of a whole people, and their character being itself to a large extent a result of the particular kind of government to which they have been subject. Aristotle made the attempt to assign the forms of government most suited to each kind of character, but his attempt can hardly be regarded as

[1] *The Science of Ethics*, vol. II, pp.584-587. (Benziger Brothers, New York.)

helpful in any way to the framers of constitutions. To the first of the two questions mentioned, therefore, it is hardly possible to return any other answer than that which we have given, viz., in particular circumstances, that form of government will be most suitable which has been found to work, that is, which has proved to be effective and enduring, and, to a certain degree progressive also, in those circumstances.

Our second question, however, admits of a completer and more definite answer. Put briefly, the question is this—of all the standard forms of government, which is the form that seems to fulfil the functions of government best, so that, *under average circumstances, and assuming that the character and history of the people favor all forms equally,* it could be predicted of it that it will be most promising in good results? That a strong democratic element will be present in this best constitution is certain from what we have already said. It will be democracy in at least the sense that the legislature will be appointed by the whole people, and the control of finance will be in their hands. There will also be an aristocratic element, in the sense that the educated and wealthy and virtuous (the social virtues being of more importance than the private in this connection) will be represented either by special provision or by force of circumstances. Thus, even in America, the aristocracy (in this case an aristocracy of wealth and education) is practically assured full representation, at least in the Upper House, not indeed by the constitution itself, but by the special economic circumstances of the country and by the manner in which elections take place to the Upper House.[2] In England the aristocracy has its privileges from the constitution. But in every community there must be some means devised of giving to the greater monied, and other prominent interests in the country a proper degree of representation. Any constitution in which the upper, and *even more particularly the great middle class,* are made completely subject, being allowed no share in the control of public affairs, the whole control being placed in the hands

---

[2] This guarantee was until recently more reliable than it is at present. Until recently, the State Legislatures appointed to the Senate; at present the people themselves appoint the representatives in the Senate.

of the masses, is doomed to failure from the beginning. As participants in sovereignty, the masses are an enduring source of strength and a guarantee of progress; as sole rulers the masses are wanting in balance, in skill, in capacity for continuous effort, in devotion to duty, in faith to others, and even to themselves. "If," says Maine, "the mass of mankind were to make an attempt at re-dividing the common stock of good things, they would resemble not a number of claimants insisting on a fair division of the funds, but a mutinous crew feasting on a ship's provisions, gorging themselves on the meat and intoxicating themselves with the liquors, but refusing to navigate the vessel to port." [3] As subjects and as part rulers it is the splendid virtues of the masses that come most into prominence; as sole rulers, their vices and shortcomings become effective competitors with their virtues, to the great detriment of the rest of the body politic and of themselves. But as we have said, and on this point we wish to lay most special emphasis, it is not to the masses, or to the higher aristocracy, but to what we might call the lower aristocracy, the great middle classes, that we must chiefly look for the greater ruling qualities—for stability and sound judgment, for sensibility in the domain of justice, for that exact balance of the two ideals of conservatism and progress, which, from all ages, are the chief acknowledged conditions of successful rule. Aristotle's well-known commendation, "Great is the good fortune of a State in which the (majority of the) citizens have a moderate and sufficient property," is as true of peoples and politics now as in his own far-distant age. It is through the great middle class (the class intermediate between the very wealthy and the poor), controlling as it does the chief department of politics, that America has proved itself a sound and stable government, in spite of the facilities offered by the constitution for rapid and revolutionary changes.

[3] *Popular Government*, p. 45.

167

PATRIOTISM

Thomas Slater [1]

There can be no doubt about the reality and universality of patriotism. Is it a blind, irrational impulse of our lower nature which should be curbed and corrected, or at least changed into a wider love for humanity in general? Or has it a rational and moral basis which requires that it should be esteemed and fostered? Is it a prejudice or is it a virtue which should be cultivated, though guarded from excess as well as from defect? Catholic teaching has no doubt about the answer to be given to such questions as these.

St. Thomas has no difficulty in showing that patriotism is a virtue. It is a virtue to pay one's debts, to give what is due to another. Such acts are prescribed by the general virtue of justice. But debts of general justice may be grounded on many different titles and reasons. A loan must be repaid because it is right that everyone should have his own. A contract should be fulfilled because a man should be faithful to his promises. Gratitude requires that we should make some return to those who have done us a favour. We owe all that we have and are to Almighty God, and so there is a special virtue called religion which prescribes the various acts of worship which are due to God in return for all that He has done for us. After God we owe most to our parents, of whom we were born and by whom we were reared, and to our country in which we were born and reared. There is, then, a special virtue which prescribes the acts due to our parents and to our country for all that we owe to them. That virtue is a natural virtue like justice, of which it is a part.[2] Cicero and the ancients called the virtue *pietas*.

Jesus Christ taught that He had not come to destroy the law, the Ten Commandments, but to perfect it. He did not abrogate natural obligations. And so, just as Christians are

---

[1] *Christ and Evolution*, pp. 162-168. (Burns, Oates & Washbourne, London.)

[2] St. Thomas, *Summa*, II, ii, q. 101, a. 3.

bound to show due honour, obedience, and love to their parents, so they are bound to fulfil all the obligations which they owe to their country. Accordingly, we find that St. Ambrose in his *De Officiis* adopts the teaching of Cicero on *pietas* in his work which bears the same title. And St. Thomas, too, has no scruple in borrowing his definition of *pietas* from the pagan philosopher.

Jesus Christ said that He came not to destroy, but to fulfil what was true and right in the moral teaching of the ancients. His teaching not only does not abrogate what was true and right in the doctrine of the ancients about patriotism, but it perfects it. Natural reason tells us what a heavy debt we owe to our native country. As a modern authority says:

To the happy conditions of soil, climate, configuration, and geographical position the inhabitants of Europe owe the honour of having been the first to obtain a knowledge of the earth in its entirety, and to have remained for so long a period at the head of mankind. Historical geographers are, therefore, right when they insist upon the influence which the configuration of a country exercises upon the nations who inhabit it. The extent of tablelands, the heights of mountain ranges, the direction and volume of rivers, the vicinity of the ocean, the indentation of the coastline, the temperature of the air, the abundance or rarity of rain, and the correlation between soil, air, and water, all these are pregnant with effects, and explain much of the character and mode of life of primitive nations. They account for most of the contrasts existing between nations subject to different conditions.[3]

If we owe so much to the external features of our native land, we owe still more to the spirit, history, institutions, common ideas, sentiments, and aims of its people, our progenitors. Natural reason prescribes that this huge debt which each of us owes to our native land should be paid by a devoted and enlightened patriotism. Christ taught us to fulfil it and make it perfect by the law of Charity.

The first precept of Charity is that we should love God for His own sake with our whole hearts, and the second precept is that we should love our neighbor as ourselves for God's sake. This does not mean that we should love all mankind with an evenly balanced affection. All men

---

[3] E. Reclus, *The Universal Geography*, i 4.

are not equally our neighbors, nor are all men equally dear to God and equally worthy of our affection. In formulating His precept Jesus Christ made the natural love which we all have for ourselves the rule and norm of the love which He commands us to bear towards our neighbor. We must do to others as we wish others to do to us. All men are not equally our neighbours, and we do not expect the same degree of love to be shown to us by everybody. With a general charity we are bound to love the inhabitants of China and Japan, whom we have never seen and who have few or no relations with ourselves. We are bound by a more particular obligation of charity to love our fellow countrymen, whose welfare is bound up with our own in many ways and whose help we need for the securing of a full and happy life.

Charity, then, as well as justice, sanctions and enforces the duty of patriotism.

It is true that Christianity modified and limited the teaching of the ancients about patriotism. According to the ancients the love of country was absolute and supreme. Cicero, for example, says:

When we have gone over all the relations that are in the world, and thoroughly considered the nature of each, we shall find that there is no one of greater obligation, no one that is dearer and nearer to us than that which we all of us bear to the Commonwealth. We have a tender concern and regard for our parents, for our children, our kindred, and acquaintance, but the love which we have for our native country swallows up all other loves whatsoever; for which there is no honest man but would die, if by his death he could do it any necessary service.[4]

The ancients deified their city and offered it divine worship. The individual was of small consequence, the State was everything; it domineered with absolute sway over both body and soul. Love for one's own country generally took the form of aggressive militarism. In famous lines the Roman poet tells Rome that it is her proud destiny to rule over the peoples with imperial sway, to spare those that submit, to war down those who proudly resist. Christianity modified this doctrine in many ways. It taught that supreme

[4] *De Officiis,* i, c. 17.

honour and obedience is due only to the one, true and living God, the Creator of all things and the Lord of the universe. According to pagan notions the very gods and goddesses in Olympus wrangled over the rival interests of the cities entrusted to their patronage. There is no room for such ideas as these in Christianity.

Christianity teaches that the individual is immortal, whereas the State is only temporary. Moreover, it withdraws the spiritual welfare of men from the authority of the State and commits it to the charge of a universal society founded by God which will last for ever. In religion and in all spiritual matters the Christian owes obedience and love to the Church; he belongs to a world-wide communion which transcends the limits of particular countries, and which will continue and attain its final development in heaven. His heavenly country should occupy his highest thoughts, desires, and aspirations. The love of his earthly country, though real and to be maintained, must of necessity take a subordinate place in his esteem and affections.

It is thus that Christianity curbs the excess and extravagance of the ancient patriotism. It sanctions and enforces the love of country with due moderation. Just as the traitor to his country was the blackest of criminals according to Cicero, and deserving of the lowest abyss of hell according to Virgil, so Dante places him in the lowest depths of his Inferno.

The Christian doctrine of patriotism is very necessary for the modern world. It provides a useful check for the dangerous views which are sometimes voiced by such expressions as "My country right or wrong."

There are signs that the spirit of nationality will not be satisfied with asserting itself and securing self-government for the nations. Under pretext of security, of the necessity of acquiring scientific frontiers, or because it is for their good, the stronger nations will inevitably strive to impose their yoke on the weaker. In many countries the State tends to usurp the rights of the individual and needs some strong influence to keep it in check, especially as it is often backed by modern philosophical theories. On the other hand the cosmopolitan and the conscientious objector require to be taught that the love of country is not only legitimate, but obligatory on every good man. The Catholic doctrine on patriotism provides us with the golden mean between the vices of excess and defect.

168
PRACTICAL PATRIOTISM

William Turner [1]

To begin at the very beginning, we ask "What is patriotism?" It is of course, "love of country." But that phrase is of little value until we have analyzed what it means. In the first place, love of country is an instinct which we share with all living things, an attachment to particular places and things developed largely by habit. It has its analogue in the tendencies of a plant to cling to a stake or a trellis on which it is, as we say, "trained." It is akin to the habit of life which bird and beast develop towards a particular tree or lair or corner of field or forest. It is, in a word, the home instinct extended to our larger home, which is our country. It is a fundamental thing in our lives, an interesting, curious, somewhat mysterious phenomenon which we pass over to the biologist and the psychologist for analysis. It does not concern us here.

In the next place, patriotism, love of country, is a sentiment; that is, a feeling exalted by emotion and clarified by ideas. It is like the love of home, of parents, of kindred, a distinctly human phenomenon, not shared by other living things. It is, I say, clarified by ideas, but its chief sentiment is idealism. Its object is not our country as a physical, geographical or political entity, "its rocks and rills, its woods and templed hills," but an entity transfigured in our emotions, beautified in our imaginations, colored by association with heroic deeds, noble national heroes. It is the stage, as it were, on which all the glorious deeds of our national history were enacted. It has its shrines of national interest, venerated spots on which sentiment is, so to speak, focused; its Mount Vernon, its Gettysburg, its Faneuil Hall, its Bunker Hill. It is symbolized in the flag, it is personified in its patriot soldiers and statesmen, its Washingtons, its Lincolns, its Roosevelts. This is the sentiment of which the poet sings: "Breathes there a man," etc.

[1] *The Catholic Mind*, May 22, 1921.

Like all idealized states of mind, it disregards realities, or rather beautifies them into something higher, nobler and sweeter. Our country need not be fair to the eye; it need not be great, or powerful, or prosperous; its soil need not be fertile; its climate need not be genial; its people need not be the best on earth, according to abstract standards. As the devoted son sees beauty in the graying locks, the warped, worked-worn fingers, the wrinkled, care-scarred face of the mother whom he loves, so the lover of his country idealizes, softening what is harsh, lighting what is dark, pouring the beauty of his own soul over all that is mean and drab and uninteresting in the country of his heart's devotion. It is a sentiment noble, elevating, and, in a sense, sanctifying the life of man. It inspires heroic deeds, it urges to the greatest sacrifices, it endures all trials; like charity itself, it "faileth not," but shall endure as long as human life itself endures on this planet, which would be so sad and cheerless without it.

I should like to dwell on this theme, the sentiment of patriotism, and show how it follows national and racial characteristics. For as men of different races are mingled differently of the ideal and the practical, so is there a different mingling of these in their love of country. Let me say merely this. As the Celt idealizes most, so that of him it is said that his real world is the world that he sees with his eyes closed, so his love of country is most ideal, most spiritual, less subject to the discouragement of hard facts, and therefore most enduring in circumstances that to another would be soul-killing.

We come, thirdly, to patriotism as a virtue. Now as this is to some of us, perhaps, an unaccustomed thought, let me offer proof of the statement that love of country is a virtue. The constituents of a virtue are principally two. First, a virtue is a fixed habit. He is not generous who once in a long while performs a generous deed. He is not obedient who at rare intervals submits to lawful authority. Generosity constantly inclines one to generous deeds, generous words, generous thoughts. I do not say that he who is generous may not become mean; for a virtue may be lost. My point is that a virtue is a habitual state, not a transitory phase of mind or soul. In the second place, virtue inclines to good, not to evil. When the habitual state of soul of which I have spoken results naturally, easily, and so to speak, gracefully, in good thoughts, good words and good deeds, it is called a virtue. There is, for example, the virtue of truthfulness. We do not consider a person truthful who tells the truth once in a long while. Nor do we consider a person untruthful who once in a long while departs from the truth under stress of fear or some other strong emotion. He is truthful who habitually strives to be truthful in word and deed.

Now it is evident that there is a habitual state of soul which inclines us to think and feel and speak and act in the interests of our country, and that is what I call the virtue of patriotism. It is more than mere instinct, although it may be related to instinctive love of country. It is more than sentiment, although in the sentiment of love of country it finds its chief source of inspiration. It has its definite duties and obligations, as we shall see. But first let us view it as we should view every virtue, in relation to our duty toward God. Is there any precept of God and His Church by which we are obliged to love our country?

Undoubtedly there is. First and most touching of all Scriptural references to this virtue is the scene in the Gospel where Christ wept over the city of Jerusalem. Here, it is true, we have the sentiment, not the virtue of patriotism. But we have a sentiment related to action. "Jerusalem, Jerusalem, . . . how often would I have gathered thy children as the hen gathers her chickens under her wings, and thou wouldst not." Surely He who was to show forth all human virtue, as the most perfect of the sons of men, spoke from a human soul that was not lacking in the greatest of the natural virtues, love of country. Throughout the Old Testament, Jerusalem the Holy City, is a symbol and a center of patriotic devotion, as well as of religious worship. By the waters of Babylon the exiled Jews bemoaned and lamented their exile, and the Sacred Text itself celebrates the beauty of this two-fold devotion. In the New Testament, the duty of obedience to lawful authority is emphasized over and over again, and that duty, as we shall see, is an obligation of the virtue of patriotism. St. Paul says, "Let every soul be subject to higher powers; for there is no power but from God. Therefore, he that resisteth the power, resisteth the ordinance of God." And surely the history of the Christian Church, with its patriot saints and its patriot martyrs, is eloquent testimony to the truth that love of country and love of God are closely related.

Moreover, if there is one virtue on which more than any other Christianity insists, it is charity, the love of one's neighbor. Now theologians teach that while the love of all, even of our enemies, is an obligation of charity, that love, like the physical law of attraction, should be inversely as the distance. The same law that binds us to love all, binds us to love more intensely those who are nearer to us in kinship, in spiritual or in temporal association; and, therefore, the love of our fellow citizens is a derivation from the law of charity itself.

Finally, and most important of all considerations, comes the reflection that God has created man not for himself alone, not for God alone, but also for his fellow human beings. We might, indeed, say that God has placed between himself and the human soul other souls, other human beings, so that we reach God by acts which, affecting others, have essentially a social character. The truth is that the unit of human nature is not the individual but the original divinely founded group of father, mother and children, the family. And the State, as we view it, is an aggregate of families. Our attitude, therefore, towards our fellow citizens, our duty towards them and our love of country, which is theirs and ours—all these are regulated by laws which are divine in their origin and have a divine sanction.

You see, then, how essentially practical the virtue of patriotism is. For it is a virtue. It is not transient sentiment, no spasmodic emotion that is evoked by war or revolution or some other crises. It is a virtue that belongs to our routine lives. Day in day out, the obligations of patriotism bind us. We are bound, first of all, to love our country, to infuse into the sentiment of patriotism that quality of permanence and stability which belong, as we said, to the very nature of virtue. We are bound to respect our country's laws and obey them; to reverence legitimate authority and sustain it. We are bound to pay our just share of the public burdens in taxes and other form of levy. We are bound to exercise our privilege as voters in a truly patriotic manner, to cast our ballot for him or her whom we believe to be best fitted for office. We are bound to do all in our power to promote good citizenship, to advance every patriotic cause, to encourage every enterprise that redounds to the benefit and credit of our country. All this is elementary. I only remind you here and now that such obligations are not vague and indefinite, but clear and concrete matters of civic responsibility, but also of individual conscience, and part of our duty to God as well as to our fellow man.

But, while we have duties, we have also rights. And to forego those rights or fail to claim them is contrary to the virtue of patriotism. As Catholics we ask for no privileges but we are accorded equal rights under the law and the Constitution. When these rights are denied in practice, when Catholics are, in fact, excluded from public office because they are Catholics, an injury is done, not only to us but to all citizens of whatever denomination, and it is the duty of all to protest. We labor under no civil disabilities, thank God, but our position is often misunderstood, our purposes misinterpreted and our best intentions misrepresented. That we cannot prevent perhaps. But one thing we can do. We can resolve that, as we have equal rights before the law, so by all lawful means we shall insist on our right to a fair estimate before the tribunal of public opinion. We are as good Americans as any, and better than some. Not only have we done our duty and borne our share of the burden in times of stress, but at all times we have upheld the law and order and reverence for authority; by our muscle and our brain, by hard labor and by skill, we have done our share to build up this great country; at tremendous cost to ourselves we are training millions of its children to fear God and love their country's institutions. If we do not possess a proportionate share of the country's wealth, we have at least done our share to make that wealth for others. We have contributed to make America greater, more productive, more prosperous and safer to live in. I take him to be a true American who has helped to make his country what it is, and judged by that standard, we can claim that our Americanism is as well proved as that of any other....

Woman is by nature intended to watch over the ideal in the home. After long ages of discrimination, she comes at last to take an active part in political life. Now she can be more than an inspiration, she can become a participant. Now she can not only teach love of country; she can practice it both in peace and in war. But now as always ideals are under her special guardianship, and she may be trusted here as in other matters to combine the ideal and the practical, to bring patriotism into our every day life and keep it pure and free from self-seeking and everything unworthy.

169

LEGISLATORS

RENÉ I. HOLAIND [1]

It may be said that in a democracy every citizen is something of a law-maker, but when we speak of legislators we speak of the men who are entrusted by the people with the special duty of framing laws for the community. Hence the term as we understand it comprises chiefly senators and congressmen. It applies also, though not in so strict a sense, to the magistrates who have such a right to interpret existing laws that their decisions practically determine what was indefinite in preceding legislation. Lastly, the President, when making use of the veto power, and the people, when using their right to approve or amend constitutions, may be said, in a broad sense, to legislate.

It is needless to say that all those who are called by special duties to help in framing laws or in carrying them out must have a fair amount of mental training, and more than an average eduction. *The blissful times of David Crockett have gone forever.* A man who should now attempt to deal with the highly complex organism of the commonwealth, though conscious of having but a half-trained and half-educated mind, would be guilty both against God and against society. Among other branches, the law-giver must be well acquainted with sociology, and political economy, besides Natural Law, Constitutional Law, International Law, and Statute Law. He need not be a *specialist* in any of these branches, but he must have mastered the principles sufficiently to be aware of his deficiency, when-

---

[1] *Natural Law and Legal Practice*, pp. 316-322. (Benziger Brothers, New York.)

ever his acquired knowledge is at fault, and to know where to go for more complete information.

A legislator must have made a conscientious study of history, especially of the history of his own people. General history will make him acquainted with human nature at large, and with the forces that determine the rise and fall of nations; the history of his own people will show the distinctive characteristics of the nation for which he will have to legislate.

He must know thoroughly the resources of his country, both in time of peace and in time of war; he must also be conversant with the wealth and strength of other nations with whom his own country may make treaties or come into conflict. It is true that excellent statistical abstracts are at his disposal, but he must at least be able to avail himself of these sources of information, and resort to them whenever occasion requires.

A man who does not know these things, and yet coolly asks the people to make him a senator or a congressman, is deceiving his constituents, and getting public money under false pretences.

In the framing of laws, the first standard to be held in view is natural equity for any law evidently unjust is by the very fact null and void; it is not a law, but an act of legislative tyranny. Next to justice, expediency must be considered, for many measures are just and good in theory, but prove impossible in practice, either because they are too burdensome to the community, or because they do more harm than good by provoking too many conflicts. Thus a law ordering a revision of all the title-deeds would not be against justice, but it would be the reverse of expedient; for it would bring about an immense amount of litigation and make property insecure. Let us bear in mind that legislators are not called upon to do all the good they can think of, or to prevent all the evils which may exist in a community, but that they must wield their power for the greatest good of all; not the greatest *ideal* good, but the greatest *practical* good. As a rule, a law which is not in accordance with enlightened public opinion should not be enacted. We say *enlightened* public opinion, because the whims and fads which become for a time popular cannot serve as guides of legislative action.

Legislators must beware of enacting laws which cannot be enforced. Whenever a law becomes a dead letter, especially when this happens a short time after it has been promulgated, the majesty of law is impaired, and the supreme civil power receives a check. No doubt, customs introduced *bona fide,* without protestation from the civil power, and with the implicit consent of the people, can abrogate pre-existing legislation, and it were absurd as well as inexpedient to revive obsolete legislation, which the people at large had discarded; but if such cases occur frequently, authors of those discarded laws must have been unwise, and their want of foresight may prove seriously injurious to social order. Let the line of Horace, which describes the caution of old age, be borne in mind by every law-maker: *Commisisse cavet, quod mox mutare laboret.* "He shall be wary of doing what he soon may labor to undo." Only men of ripe years and wide experience ought to try their hands at law-making. The same thing must be said of judges who have to give a new interpretation of existing laws, swerve from the precedents on record, or who themselves originate a precedent.

This brings us to say that laws must not be changed often, even under the pretence of improvement, reform, progress, and what not. We do not mean to say that they should *never* be changed, for it is evident that they must be adapted to the wants of the people, but we deplore the mania of changing for the sake of a change. We, moreover, aver that a slight improvement, especially if conjectural, is no compensation for the loss of stability caused by tinkering with existing laws. Let a State, for instance, adopt hanging as a way for disposing of criminals, then prefer death by electricity, afterwards choose the knife as more certain, later determine on chloroform or morphia as more humane, to come back at last to the rope as more appropriate. Would not such a legislation be a round of horrors? In legislating, beware of fads!

If it is not expedient to alter laws too often, much less is it advisable to multiply laws without necessity. We have already mentioned elsewhere that the multiplicity of laws was considered by Cicero as a token of national decline. Many statesmen have endorsed this opinion. One thing is certain: every law restrains liberty, and if we wish to prevent by legislation every possible evil, we shall at the same time prevent every individual good. We completely endorse the following declaration of Rutherford, as quoted by Sharswood: "Civil legislative power is not in the strict sense of the word, an absolute power of restraining or altering the rights of the subjects; it is limited in its own nature to its proper objects, to those rights only in which the common good of society or of its several parts requires some restraint or alteration. So that whenever we call the civil legislative power, either of society in general or of a particular legislative body within society, an absolute legislative body, we can only mean that it has no external check upon it in fact; for all civil legislative power is in its own nature under an internal check of right: it is a power of restraining or altering the rights of the subjects for the purpose of advancing or securing the general good, and not of restraining or altering them for any purpose whatever, and much less for no purpose at all." [2]

The modern tendency is to have recourse to legislation to cure all the evils of the body politic. It is as wise as binding a man hand and foot to prevent him from making a false step. It is an abuse that each incoming congressman should deem himself bound to have some law of his own passed by Congress, in order that his constituents may see that he earns his money.

Never enact retrospective laws, much less retrospective statutes; for, as Bacon says: *Non placet Janus in legibus*—the doublefaced god has no attraction in law. Of course this must not apply to retrospective laws which have for their object *the relief of some person or persons,* which relief may be due, but to *restraining* or *penal laws,* for such, when retroactive, are essentially unjust. A man is bound to obey the law as it stands, when he is yet free to act, not as it may stand when the act shall have been already consummated.

To sum up in a few words: laws must be both just and equitable; expedient, that is, practically useful; capable of being enforced; framed with prudence and foresight; not easily changed; not multiplied without necessity; not retroactive.

---

[2] *Professional Ethics,* Introduction, p. xiv; Rutherford, Inst. of Nat. law, book ii, chap. vi.

170

THE FUNCTIONS OF GOVERNMENT

Woodrow Wilson [1]

It will contribute to clearness of thought to observe the functions of government in two groups, 1. the *Constituent* Functions, 2. The *Ministrant*. Under the *Constituent* I would place that usual category of governmental function, the protection of life, liberty, and property, together with all other functions that are necessary to the civic organization of society,—functions which are *not optional* with governments, even in the eyes of strictest *laissez faire*,—which are, indeed, the very bonds of society. Under the *Ministrant* I would range those other functions (such as education, posts and telegraphs, and the care, say, of forests) which are undertaken not by way of *governing*, but by way of advancing the general interests of society,—functions which *are* optional, being necessary only according to standards of convenience or expediency, and not according to standards of existence; functions which must assist without constituting social organization.

171

THE DUTIES OF THE CITIZEN

John A. Ryan [2]

The obligations of the citizen to obey civil laws does not exhaust his duties to the State. So important is the State and its functions that it gives rise to a special kind of justice. This is called by the moral theologians legal justice, and it is commonly defined as that virtue which inclines the citizen to render to the community what is due it for the common good.[3] This means not only obedience to the laws, but all those actions, political and social, which are necessary for the common welfare. Legal justice binds both the ruler and the citizen. It obliges the former to make

---

[1] *The State*, p. 613. (D. C. Heath and Company, Boston.)
[2] *The Catholic World*, January, 1922.
[3] *Cf.* Vermeesch, *Questiones de Justitia*, pp. 39-49.

the common welfare the object of all his official acts. It obliges the citizen and the public official alike to comply with the laws, and to give due consideration to the needs of the State in all their actions and relationships.

The particular duties imposed upon public officials by the virtue of legal justice, can be stated summarily in a few paragraphs. The general obligation of promoting the social good implies, obviously, that the executive, the judge, the lawmaker are bound to prefer that end to their private advantage. The man who regards public office as an opportunity for private gain, except incidentally and as a necessary consequence of faithful public service, is false to his trust and violates legal justice. To accept a bribe for aid in the enactment of a bad law, for negligent or oppressive administration of the law, or for unjust judicial conduct, is an evident moral wrong. To obtain some advantage on the occasion of proper official actions, for example, through some form of "graft," is likewise a violation of legal justice. Such conduct is generally forbidden by the civil law; at any rate, it renders right judgment and adequate performance of official duties extremely difficult. Public officials are not justified in exposing themselves to such a grave temptation. What is true of their own private advantage applies likewise to that of their friends. In their enactment and administration of the law, they may not extend favors of any sort to any individual or class of individuals. The common good must be preferred to the good of individuals, and all individuals must be treated with exact justice.

Public officials are not only bound to refrain from promoting the interests of individuals at the expense of the common good, and to avoid favoritism toward certain individuals, but also to extend rigorous favoritism and proportionate justice to all social classes. This means that no class should be favored to the detriment of the general welfare, and that no class should receive less than its due proportion of public protection and assistance. For example, it is wrong to permit an industrial group to exploit its national resources, such as coal mines and timber, in such a way that present or future generations will suffer unnecessary hardship. It is wrong to give certain industrial interests the benefit of a public subsidy or a protective tariff, the effect of which is to impose extortionate costs upon the great body of the consumers. The possession of unregulated monopoly power is likewise a cause of injury to the public welfare, which will not be tolerated by public officials who habitually fulfill their public obligations.

On the other hand, every social class has a just claim against the State and its officials for that measure of governmental protection and assistance which is necessary to provide the conditions of right and reasonable life. Today, this principle receives its chief application in the weaker economic classes. As Pope Leo XIII observed: "The richer classes have many ways of shielding themselves, and stand less in need of help from the State; whereas, those who are badly off have no resources of their own to fall back upon, and must chiefly depend upon the assistance of the State. And it is for this reason that wage earners, who are undoubtedly among the weak and necessitous, should be specially cared for and protected by the government." [4] Therefore, legislators are morally bound to provide for minimum decent standards of life and labor. This means legislation to prevent child labor, an excessively long working day, oppressive conditions in work places, unduly low wages and the subjection of the workers to an inhumane insecurity as regards unemployment, sickness, accidents, invalidity and old age. Public officials are likewise under obligation to promote in due measure the prosperity of industrial enterprise, to levy taxes in proportion to ability and sacrifice, and in general to deal with all classes according to their actual needs and deserts, not according to some doctrinaire theory of *laissez-faire* or of opposition to class legislation. In the words of Pope Leo XIII: "Among the many and grave duties of rulers who would do their best for the people, the first and chief is to act with strict justice —with that justice which is called by the schoolmen *distributive*—towards each and every class alike." [5]

One of the primary duties of public officials is to possess an adequate knowledge of what constitutes the common welfare; and of the means by which it is best promoted. This obligation is disregarded by a large proportion of those who seek public office. Men, who are otherwise conscientious, assume that good will and right motives are a

---

[4] Encyclical, *On the Condition of Labor.*
[5] Encyclical, *On the Condition of Labor.*

sufficient equipment for public service. When we consider the enormously extended functions of the modern State, the numerous and profound ways in which its activities affect the welfare of all the people, and the consequent complexity of legislating and governing wisely, we see that this notion is utterly mistaken. Only in local governments and subordinate official positions is it true that common honesty plus common sense suffice for those who are charged with the duty of caring for the public welfare. In all the more important legislative and executive offices, a considerable amount of special knowledge is essential to an adequate discharge of official obligations.

So much for the nature and elements of the obligation resting upon public officials. The scope of their obligation is identical with the province of the State. This has been described in preceding articles on the State's end and functions. All of these functions, intellectual, moral, religious, political, civic and economic, public officials are morally bound to perform in accordance with the principles of strict and proportionate justice.

The statement is frequently made in the United States that public officials are merely public servants. It is incorrect. They are, indeed, the servants of the people, but they are also something more. Inasmuch as their function is that of public service, they may properly be regarded as public servants; inasmuch as their position gives them the authority to enact laws which are morally binding on the people, they are not servants but masters. Their character as public servants does not depend upon the fact that they are elected by the people; for hereditary kings are likewise bound to serve the common welfare. In a republic the members of legislatures may, in a special sense, be regarded as servants of the people, whenever they are instructed by the electors to carry out certain political policies. Their promise to pursue this course creates a particular responsibility to the people, and renders their position analogous to that of servants, or agents. Nevertheless, they are masters and rulers when they enact the legislation necessary to carry out the policies to which they have committed themselves.

The first duty of the citizen is obedience to law. It extends to the ordinances of every jurisdiction in which the citizen finds himself, national, state and municipal. The basis, nature and limits of this duty have been described in a previous article.[6]

A second duty is that of respect for public authority, and this means both public officials and their enactments. Of course, this duty can be exaggerated, but in our day and country the opposite perversion is much more frequent. Through false inferences drawn from the principles of democracy, men are inclined to minimize, or even to reject entirely, this obligation. Conscious that elected officials are human beings of the same clay as himself, and dependent upon him for an elevation that is only temporary, the citizen easily assumes that to show them respect is undemocratic and unworthy. The *Century Dictionary* defines respect as, "the feeling of esteem, regard or consideration excited by the contemplation of personal worth, dignity or power; also a similar feeling excited by corresponding attributes in things." While public officials are sometimes lacking in personal worth and dignity, they are always the possessors and custodians of political power, which of its nature demands esteem and consideration. Were this attitude habitually taken by the citizens, the problem of securing law observance would be greatly simplified. The man who refuses respect to civil authority because he fears that it would demean or degrade him, exhibits the slave mind and temper; for he has not sufficient confidence in his own worth to feel that he can afford to give honor where honor is due, or to recognize any kind of superiority. Such a man is not only a bad citizen, but a detriment to any social group.

Closely connected with obedience is the duty of loyalty. In essence, loyalty means faithfulness and constancy in allegiance and service. To the idea of obedience, which may be quite formal, mechanical, and even reluctant, it adds the notions of intensity, emotion, spontaneity and constancy. The genuinely loyal citizen is always ready and eager, not only to obey the laws, but to support and maintain the political institutions of his country. If the citizen merely refrains from seditious or treasonable conduct, his loyalty is negative and imperfect. Whether positive or negative, loyalty always implies a certain habitual spirit and

[6] *The Catholic World*, October, 1921.

attitude toward laws and institutions. It habitually recognizes that a presumption exists in favor of organic and statutory enactments and principles. The loyal citizen is always disposed to give his government and his political institutions "the benefit of the doubt," and to withhold obedience or support only when the doubt is converted into moral certainty that the laws or the government are in the wrong. In a word, the habitual attitude of the loyal citizen is that of sympathetic faith, not that of criticality and distrust.

The participation of the United States in the Great War made the subject of loyalty lively and very practical. As might have been expected, the discussion gave ignorant, prejudiced and selfish men the opportunity to exploit perverted notions of loyalty. During and since the War, various groups and organizations endeavored with considerable success to fasten the stigma of disloyalty upon many of their fellow citizens who were guilty of neither treason nor sedition. The conception of loyalty to the Constitution became perverted into the doctrine that any attempt to change the Constitution, even by legitimate means, is disloyal. Not only the method but the scope of loyalty was distorted. The demand was impudently and blatantly made that all citizens should show loyalty not only to our political and legal institutions, but also to our industrial institutions, specifically to the existing positions and relations of Capital and Labor. Any theory or movement which aimed at essentially modifying the industrial system or diminishing the power of Capital, whether through Socialism, Guildism, or co-operative enterprise, was denounced as seditious and un-American. It is significant that both these forms of exaggeration were, in the main, committed by the same persons. They denounced any effort to change the Constitution because they dislike changes which would facilitate industrial reforms and social justice; they strove to place industrial institutions on the same plane of authority as political institutions because they wish to perpetuate economic injustice. In short, the perversions and exaggerations of the notion and duty of loyalty were mainly determined by sordid economic motives.

Those corruptions of a noble sentiment and doctrine do not merit a formal refutation. Loyalty to political institutions does not exclude the desire or the effort to modify or even to abolish them by orderly and reasonable process. Loyalty to the State, to one's country, to the public weal, does not include belief in, love of or defence of existing private institutions, industrial or other. The loyalty which is incumbent upon the citizen, as citizen, concerns only political institutions and relations. The organized attempt to make it apply to the economic order, is one of the most extraordinary and brazen performances in the history of human selfishness. It was possible only in the vitiated atmosphere of war, and in the abnormal psychology of the years immediately following.

In his excellent brochure on *Christian Citizenship,* the Rev. Thomas Wright declares that obedience, respect and loyalty are the constituent elements of patriotism.[7] Probably, this is as satisfactory as any other analysis of the vague, though apparently elementary, sentiment that we call patriotism. The good citizen loves to be acclaimed a patriot, and the orator finds patriotism one of the most appealing and popular subjects. Nevertheless, it is very elusive. To the average man, it means love of country, but what does love of country mean? Not merely love of green fields, lofty mountains and winding rivers; not always love of existing political institutions. In time of actual or threatened war, the idea of patriotism is very simple. It means support and defence of one's country against armed attack.

In time of peace, the phrase, "love of country," means many things to many minds. The object of the love may be the physical characteristics of the country, or its economic and social opportunities, or its government, or its political ideals, or its history, or some combination of these entities. As commonly used, the term patriotism has almost always an international connotation. It appeals to the national consciousness. It brings before the mind the facts of national individuality, separateness, distinctness of interests. It lays stress upon the welfare of one's own country against the welfare of other countries. Too often, it takes the form of boasting, jingoism, contempt of foreign nations, and identifies the national welfare with national power, imperialism and aggression. The average citizen frequently

[7] Page 61.

confuses patriotism with national jealousy and provincialism. He does not regularly think of it as having anything to do with internal affairs.

Adequate and rational patriotism should be quite as active in peace as in war, and it should extend to every matter that affects the common good. If patriotism is love of country, its only rational and concrete meaning is love of the people who inhabit the country and compose the State, in other words, love of one's fellow citizens. Therefore, its ultimate object is the same as that of the State, namely, the common good. In time of peace, the common good is much more dependent upon domestic legislation and administration than upon foreign policies. The true patriot realizes this and strives to promote the common good in all his political activities. The man who participates in political corruption, or uses his political position or influence for the undue advantage of any social group or for the oppression of any social class, is not a patriot, no matter how loudly he may acclaim the glories of his country or how truculently he may proclaim his willingness to fight foreigners.

Taking up now the more specific duties of the citizen, we find that they may be conveniently grouped under two heads: those which are elementary and which exist under all forms of government; those which are complex and have place only in a State that possesses representative institutions. The most important of the specific elementary duties are concerned with taxation and military service.

According to Catholic teaching, statutes imposing taxes bind in conscience. The general reason is the same as that which attaches moral obligation to other civil laws. That is the common welfare. Since government cannot maintain itself nor perform its functions without revenues, and since it has not other means of obtaining them than taxation, the citizens are morally bound to provide the necessary revenues in this manner. Moreover, the obligation is not merely one of legal justice, that justice which requires citizens to promote the common good, but also of strict justice, that justice which requires restitution to be made when it is violated.[8] If the citizens fail to pay taxes, they sometimes inflict injury upon the State, injury which can be measured in terms of money and repaired by payments of money.

[8] *Cf.* Bouquillon, *Theologia Moralis Fundamentalis,* pp. 460-463.

When the evasion does not produce such injury, owing to the fact that the authorities increase the tax *rate,* or devise other and more effective forms of taxation, the obligation of making restitution will have a different object. The real beneficiaries of restitution will then be those citizens who have acted conscientiously and paid the full measure of taxes levied upon them.

Let us suppose that a tax rate of one and one-half per cent will yield sufficient revenue for a city if all the citizens contribute their proportionate share. Through various devices very many of them evade a considerable part of their obligation. In as far as the deficit is not made up through an increase in the tax rate, an injury is done the public welfare. If the rate is raised sufficiently to bring in all the necessary revenue, the conscientious taxpayers contribute more than their proper share, and, therefore, suffer injustice at the hands of the dishonest. If the evasions are so great as to require that the rate be raised to two per cent, it means that the honest citizens are paying one-third more than their fair quota. They pay one-third more than they would have to pay if all were as honest as they. The injustice done them by the evasive action of their fellow citizens is obvious. Hence, follows the obligation of restitution.

These are the general principles. Their application, however, is not entirely simple, owing to the complexity and injustice of our tax system, and the very large proportion of persons who habitually understate their taxable property. The principal form of taxation, at least in local and State jurisdictions, is what is known as the general property tax. Not only does this directly violate the ethical principle of taxation in proportion to ability to pay, as determined by comparative sacrifices, but it is apportioned and administered most inequitably, and it is evaded in wholesale fashion. In the words of Professor Seligman: "The general property tax, as actually administered, is beyond doubt one of the worst taxes known in the civilized world." [9] In these circumstances, the conscientious citizen cannot be required to do more than pay that proportion of the full amount which is paid by the majority. If the prevailing understatement of taxable property amounts to twenty-five per

---

[9] *Essays in Taxation,* p. 61.

cent, the citizen who pays on more than three-fourths of his goods, contributes more than his share.[1] This general rule of action may properly be applied to other kinds of taxes where evasion is considerable and notorious. Of course, the conscientious citizen will not take advantage of it until he is morally certain of the facts.

It is sometimes asserted that certain tax laws are purely penal, obliging the citizen only to submit to the penalty in case his evasion is detected. From our discussion on "The Moral Obligation of Civil Law,"[2] it seems fairly clear that this theory must be applied with great caution, and that the tax laws which fall under it are exceptional. Tariff duties are the taxes most commonly adduced. Probably, the laws prescribing these are purely penal, not only because of the common popular conviction, but because they are saturated with economic and ethical inequalities.

As a rule, the citizen is not bound to pay taxes until the amount due from him has been defined by the fiscal authorities. When he is legally required to furnish a statement of his property, he is obliged by legal justice to comply. Is he obliged to volunteer such information? For example, is a person morally bound to inform the authorities that his income is sufficiently large to subject him to the income tax? If he does not give this spontaneous information, he will escape. The income tax law requires the citizens to make such a statement, and penalizes them for failure to do so when their evasion of the tax has been detected. It seems clear, therefore, that the citizen is bound by legal justice to provide a statement of his taxable property, not only in response to an official requisition, but sometimes in the absence of such a requisition.

Another elementary obligation of the citizen is that of military service, when required by a law of conscription. The object of such a law is of the greatest importance to the public weal. As a rule, the obligation is gravely binding in conscience. Hence, all fraudulent methods of escaping its operation are a violation of legal justice.

The second class of duties incumbent on the citizen results from his electoral functions. In a republic, legislation and administration depend finally upon the intelligence

---

[1] *Cf.* Tanquerey, *De Justitia*, no. 597.
[2] *The Catholic World*, October, 1921.

and morality of the voters. They have it in their power to make the government a good one or a bad one. Whether the common good will be promoted or injured, depends upon the kind of laws enacted and the manner in which they are administered; but the character of the laws and the administration is primarily determined by the way in which the citizens discharge their function of choosing legislators and administrators. Therefore, this function is of the gravest importance and the obligation which it imposes is likewise grave.

It must be admitted that the importance and gravity of this obligation is frequently ignored by Catholics, as well as by other citizens. Writing of Great Britain, the Rev. Thomas Wright declares: "There are large numbers of Catholics in this land with but little appreciation of the strong inter-relation which exists between true citizenship and Christianity. . . . Many excuses, it must be owned, may be alleged in extenuation of the apathy of Catholics towards their civic obligations in these lands. Time, however, has undermined the substance of these apologetic pleas. Catholics are now able to appeal to no sufficient cause why they should stand aloof from public affairs, or why, participating in them, they need indiscriminately follow the policies of parties without thought or test of their moral justification."[3]

These observations may be applied in full measure to the Catholics of the United States. Like their co-religionists of Great Britain, they can show historical conditions to extenuate, if not to justify, their neglect of political obligations. Very many, if not the majority, of them are persons, or the descendants of persons, who came from countries whose Governments treated Catholics unfairly and allowed them very little participation in public affairs. As a consequence, a large proportion of American Catholics have been, until quite recently, possessed by what has been happily characterized "the psychology of persecution." They have looked upon government with a certain measure of distrust, and, therefore, have been predisposed to ignore or to minimize their electoral responsibility. Many of them have easily and complacently accepted the cynical judgment that "politics is a rotten business," and have either held aloof or

---

[3] *Christian Citizenship,* pp. 17, 18.

permitted their political influence to be utilized by special and unworthy interests.

The Catholic teaching on the duty of exercising the voting franchise, as stated in the authoritative manuals of moral theology, may be summed up as follows: [4]

The obligation of taking part in the election of candidates for civil offices is an obligation of legal justice. The citizens are bound to promote the common good in all reasonable ways. The franchise enables them to further or to hinder the common weal greatly and fundamentally, inasmuch as the quality of the government depends upon the kind of officials they elect. Not only questions of politics, but social, industrial, educational, moral and religious subjects are regulated by legislative bodies and administered by executives. Therefore, the matter is of grave importance, and the obligation of the citizen to participate in the election and to support fit candidates is correspondingly grave. According to Tanquerey, the elector cannot free himself from this obligation by any slight cause or reason, such as, going hunting, or criticism by his neighbors. The excusing cause needs to be of a grave nature, such as, loss of one's means of livelihood. A slight cause will relieve the citizen from the obligation of voting, only when he is morally certain that he cannot affect the immediate result. Even then, he ought to take part in the election to show good example, and to hasten the day when the cause which he supports will command a majority of the voters.[5]

Just as the official is obliged to refrain from promoting the interests of individuals as against the common good, so the elector is morally bound to cast his vote for the common welfare, instead of for the benefit of private persons or groups. This principle is very often forgotten by well-meaning citizens; for example, by giving their political support to a friend, or to a member of their own race or religion, when he has not the required moral or intellectual equipment, or when he is the upholder of socially harmful policies. Too often, in such situations, the honest citizen salves his conscience with the excuse that the opposing candidate "is just as bad." Were this the fact, it would be

---

[4] *Cf.* Tanquerey, *De Justitia,* pp. 475-477; Noldin, *De Praeceptis,* pp. 336-339.
[5] *Loc. cit.*

legitimate to determine one's choice on the basis of personal friendship, or racial or religious affiliation, or other extrinsic considerations; but the general fact is that voters who adopt this course do not take adequate care to find out whether the candidate of the opposition is in reality "just as bad." They too easily decide the question on the basis of their inclinations and predilections.

Closely connected with this unjustifiable practice is that of ignoring principles and policies in the exercise of the franchise. "Vote for a good man, regardless of party," is a plausible, but essentially inadequate, political rule. A distinction should be drawn between legislative positions and those which are merely administrative. In choosing a city treasurer or a county auditor, the only pertinent qualifications are honesty, intellectual capacity and technical equipment. There is involved no question of legislative policy. When the office to be filled is that of governor of a State, president of the United States, member of a State legislature or congressman, other qualifications are essential in addition to those just mentioned. The "good man" may have some very harmful views concerning political and industrial policies. He may sincerely favor national imperialism and jingoism, or legislation to promote the undue aggrandizement of one social class or the oppression of another social class. Obviously, the citizen does not fulfill his duty of promoting the common good when he votes for a "good man" of this sort. Sometimes the common welfare will suffer less through the election of a man whose political policies are right, but whose moral or intellectual equipment is deficient, than through the elevation of a "good man" who gives his adhesion to wrong policies.

It is sometimes said that the good man in other relations of life is always the best kind of a citizen. This statement is only half a truth. The unqualified proposition and acceptance of it is a serious obstacle to the improvement of citizenship. Fidelity to one's duties as husband, father, son, brother, neighbor, employer, employee, buyer, seller, debtor, creditor, professional man and client—does, indeed, contribute very greatly toward the common welfare. Actions performed under the direction of the domestic and social virtues necessarily promote individual and social happiness, just as the opposite actions are an injury to the commonwealth. Nevertheless, these virtues are not a complete equipment for all the duties of citizenship. They do not of themselves provide the citizen with that specific knowledge which he requires as a voter, nor with that civic consciousness which is essential to good citizenship.

An honest employer may treat his employees unjustly because he is unacquainted with those moral principles which apply specifically to industrial relations, or because he has an insufficient knowledge of the living conditions and needs of the workers, and the virtuous citizen may fail in his duties to the State because he does not realize the importance of this particular responsibility, or because he lacks the specific political knowledge which would enable him to exercise his suffrage for the best interests of the commonwealth. In this category are the man who does not realize how fundamentally good government depends upon the electors, the man who lazily assumes that politics is necessarily corrupt, and the man who thinks it sufficient to vote for good men, without any reference to the helpfulness or harmfulness of their political principles and policies.

In a word, the good man is not a good citizen unless he possesses the specific knowledge essential to good citizenship. This comprises adequate perception of the citizen's power and responsibility, and a reasonable degree of acquaintance with political institutions, personages and policies. The good citizen recognizes all these obligations and makes reasonable and continuous efforts to fulfill them. Such a man, and only such a man, possesses an adequate civic consciousness.

Worth quoting, are the following extracts from a letter addressed to his people, in the year 1921, by the late Cardinal Amette, Archbishop of Paris:

In the joint letter which they recently addressed to the French Catholics, the bishops of France said: "It is a duty of conscience for all citizens honored with the right of suffrage to vote honestly and wisely with the sole aim of benefiting the country. The citizen is subject to the Divine law as is the Christian. Of our votes, as of all our actions, God will demand an account. The duty of voting is so much the more binding upon conscience because on its good or evil exercise depend the gravest interests of the country and of religion.

It is your duty to vote: to neglect to do so would be a culpable abdication of duty on your part. It is your duty to vote *honestly;* that is to say, for men worthy of your esteem and trust. It is your duty to vote *wisely;* that is to say, in such a way as not to waste your votes. It would be better to cast them for candidates who, although not giving complete satisfaction to all our legitimate demands, would lead us to expect from them a line of conduct useful to the country, rather than to keep your votes for others whose programme would, indeed, be more perfect, but whose almost certain defeat might open the door to the enemies of religion and of the social order.

Tanquerey points out that, in order to be able to vote rightly and intelligently, in order to possess the specific knowledge requisite for this purpose, upright citizens should organize and participate in political associations.[6] This is obvious. Men unite in trade unions, manufacturers' associations, chambers of commerce and professional societies of various kinds for the promotion of their economic interests. Hundreds of thousands of good men, thus occupationally organized, fail to see the necessity of organizing politically for the protection of their civic interests and the effective performance of their duties to the commonwealth. The conduct of political organizations they leave to professional politicians, who are usually in the service of selfish private interests. When the inactive citizens see the evil results of this arrangement, they attempt to justify their aloofness by the reflection that politics is essentially corrupt. This lazy pessimism is not warranted by anything inherent in political affairs. It represents a vain attempt to evade moral responsibility. If politics is rotten, a large part of the responsibility rests upon well-meaning, but indolent, citizens.

In view of the fundamental and immense importance to the State of the voting function, and since the electors are in a practical sense the primary political authority, it would seem that the electoral duties of the citizens are not merely duties of legal justice. It would seem that, like the obligations of public officials, they also fall under the head of strict or commutative justice. A group of legislators inflict injury upon the community by a bad law, thereby violating strict justice: are not the citizens who elected them guilty

---

[6] *Loc. cit.*

of the same kind of injustice, in so far as they foresaw this possibility? The difference between their offence and that of the legislators seems to be one of degree, not one of kind.

Among the electoral duties of the citizen is that of becoming a candidate for public office in some circumstances. Of course, this applies only to that small minority who are competent. In certain situations, says Noldin, an upright Catholic is bound by a grave obligation to become a candidate for an administrative or legislative office; that is, when his election is certain, when he is able to avert grave evils from the community, when he can accept the office without grave inconvenience to himself, and when no other equally competent candidate is available.[7] Inasmuch as the issues involved in such a situation are of much graver consequence than those dependent upon the ballot of the private citizen, the man who refuses to become a candidate for office will need a much graver reason to excuse him than will the citizen who merely neglects to vote.

172

WOMAN SUFFRAGE

J. W. Dawson [1]

It is unnecessary to peer into the past to learn the universal truth of woman's love and inspiration and zeal for the better and nobler things of life. There is no son or daughter who will not testify to the affects of a mother's guidance, who will not say that he or she was influenced to higher things because of his or her mother. Nor is it merely by emotional inspiration that the mother works upon her children. Many times it is she who gives the practical common sense solution of a pressing problem proving too great for the other members of the family. In every crisis it is she who stands by, gentle yet firm, comforting but not weak, envisioned but not foolish. When the hour of sacrifice comes, she is always ready to take up the heavy burden so that another might go on into the light. Mothers are greater than governments and higher than law.

[7] *Loc. cit.*
[1] *The Catholic World,* November, 1920.

> *Quid leges sine moribus*
> *Vanæ proficiunt?*

To this question of Horace's we might ask: And how can we have morals and their observance without their inculcation by the mothers in the hearts of their children?

If this is true, some argue, that women have exerted and do exert an influence that elevates, that purifies, that fortifies for good, then the operation of that influence should be confined to where it belongs, within the circle of the home.

> *Quid terras alio calentes*
> *Sole mutamus?*

Where they accomplish the most, they say, there let them remain, rather than dissipate their energies upon the fruitless tasks of public life where all their efforts will turn to Dead Sea fruit, bringing only a sense of unattainment of their ideals and a loss of opportunity for doing real good in their homes.

But is the matter as simple as all that? Reduced to its simplest terms, their argument might be put into the following syllogism: Woman's greatest and best influence lies in the home. The extension of woman suffrage with its attendant obligations will tend to dissipate that influence. Therefore, women should prefer the home to exercising their political rights. Apparently this is sound reasoning, and once the premises are admitted as true, the conclusion necessarily follows. But the difficulty is not so elementary as conveyed in this syllogistic form, even were the truth of its mean premise conceded. There is still a very serious consideration to be kept in mind and one that must be met in a progressive spirit, with large foresight and courageous determination. It carries with it portentous consequences that must be guided and shaped correctly to rid them of evil. It may be summed up in the simple statement that *all* women *can* vote; *some* women *will* vote. Who are they to be? If this tremendous power is to be put into the hands of the women of our country to decide what our Government is to be, are we deliberately going to tell the best elements in that group of twenty-seven million people, the women who love their homes, the women who *do* exert that wonderful influence, the women who stand morally for the best in life, are we deliberately going to tell that wonderful body of voters not to vote? Are we going to counsel the women, who have inculcated beautiful ideals in their children and given them moral strength to live up to those ideals, to retire to the sanctity of their homes and leave the field free to those women who will insist upon voting?

The day when we can say that women do not need to vote; they are represented well enough by the men, has passed. Elections are based on mathematical results. Today the decent, forward-looking American who forms the bulwark against the destruction of our Republic cannot represent his wife by his vote alone. The radical and his wife will surely vote, and where only one votes where two should, the result cannot be disguised. As a question merely of defensive protection, it will be necessary for the women of the family to vote as well as the men members. Numbers will decide many grave questions of public policy which may affect our very homes. Numbers will spell success or defeat for the accomplishment of the ideals for which we stand. Numbers will cause us to be respected and our rights unmolested. Numbers are our weapons of offensive and defence. Do you, therefore, think it the part of wisdom to counsel our women not to vote?

Most of our citizens suffer from political myopia. They cannot see beyond their nose. In my experience in public life, I have been startled by the realization of the flux in our form of government. It is not a static condition. It is dynamic, living and, consequently, reactive to all influences brought to bear upon it. Our Government is ourselves and what we allow to predominate amongst us must have its effect upon our Government. Yet despite this patent fact, our citizens have been utterly apathetic in their scrutiny of the forces at work to accomplish their ends in our economic and political life. They shut their eyes to the efforts and, as in the case of prohibition, are dismayed at the results.

It is idle even to state that there are many propagandists in our public life whose philosophy is godless, whose morality is pagan, and whose vision is material. Their thoughts find translations in easy words that appeal to many minds. Those minds do and will translate these ideals into action.

The only action they can resort to at present is the use of the ballot. And, a conclusion that cannot be too seriously emphasized, they are going to make use of that opportunity with the ballot to make their ideas and their ideals a reality. And here again numbers count. Will the wives, the daughters and the sisters of such men vote? Will their women be told that their place is in the home, and to stay there? Of this be sure, the so-called liberal and the radical have agitated for years for woman suffrage, if for no other reason than that its extension would swell the ranks of their cohorts and add to their power.

A democracy is a nation of governing minorities. This is true because all the zeal, the energy, the force that can be obtained is centered upon the accomplishment of the aims and desires of the minority. They work day in and day out. The great mass of citizens are busy with other affairs; they are apathetic, and worse, unorganized. As a result, the minority succeeds in imposing its will upon the majority.

Recognizing this condition, it will be a serious mistake if we counsel our women to refrain from using their suffrage actively and vigilantly. We are adding to the forces that we know are plotting our destruction; we are increasing their power, for a vote withheld doubles the one that is cast. Into the conflicts that are to come we must not go unarmed or without adequate weapons, even if merely of defence. The world is slowly resolving itself into three great camps, the forces of greed and reaction, the forces of Christian conservation, and those of the revolutionists, the anarchists. The first are powerful; they are mighty in their resources of both money and brains. During, and since the unsatisfactory settlement of the recent War, they have used every opportunity to reach out for more power. If, in any great measure, they succeed, their progress spells the death of all Christian conservatism of thought and action, for then must come the terrible uprising of men, agitated to action by false leaders and goaded by social and industrial injustice, in a conflict against those who, forgetful of Christ and humanity, have intrenched themselves at the flesh-pots. The workingman will have pointed out to him the failure of any attempt to cure our social evils by calm, reasoned evolution, and will be taught that his only remedy lies in violence and revolution.

Will we, who have withheld a potent means for curing the evils in our present, social, political and economic systems, be able to blame him if this happens? Will we be able to stop him, when we might have prevented him from losing faith in our social institutions?

These are questions that are not far-fetched. By the proper use of the means now at our disposal we can help take away the causes of discontent and unrest. We know the futility of the Bolsheviki programme. We can render its menace futile and its meaning inane by removing the injustices that now irritate and that some day might infuriate. They are not so serious or deep-seated or intensive but that an intelligent understanding and a gentle but efficient treatment may remove them. They can be removed. And we who have the treasures of Jesus Christ as our heritage, we whose philosophy and ethics are based upon His Word, we who subscribe to the glorious Encyclical of Pope Leo XIII upon Labor, we who take pride in the Bishops' Programme, can be that power to check the encroachments of social greed and remove from among us the fear of Bolshevism by using our suffrage to promote social justice, and to insure for both laborer and capitalist their just deserts.

That to my mind is the meaning of universal woman suffrage. It is an opportunity to bring to the banners of Christian conversation a mighty force and a powerful ally. We know what women can do and have done. We know their idealism, their enthusiasm, their goodness, their sharp differentiation of right and wrong, their keen sense of justice. Let us use those gifts. Let us encourage them to join with us with their vote in fighting for the attainment of our ideals, which, after all, are theirs, too. Let them participate actively also in our social and political partnership. With them, we can succeed; without them, we must fail. Women may ask with Juvenal:

> *Quid Romæ faciam?*
> *Mentiri nescio.*

"What can I do at Rome? I cannot lie." Many feel, perhaps with some cause, that the political world is totally wicked, and if not wicked, debased with selfishness and corruption. If this be so, then it is time that woman enter that world, for if she will, she can do much to elevate politics, eliminate many of the abuses that now exist, and demand a higher standard of morals. Will she attain this? Not at once, perhaps, but she can accomplish this if she wills. A political leader owes his existence to his continuance in power. He continues to be a leader only as long as he is successful. Do you think that the political leaders view the advent of twenty-seven million new votes with unconcern? They want those votes. They will not be able to carry their elections without them. Therefore, they must please them. They are looking to see what the new voters want. And if the new electorate makes it clear that they will assist the better forces in the political struggles, if they show that they will not countenance chicanery and fraud, if they demand a newer and higher standard of action, they will get what they want. If they use their tremendous power for the accomplishment of the best ideals of womanhood, they will have the pleasure of seeing those ideals put into practice. But if, on the other hand, their coming into politics means merely a seeking for material advancement or personal gain they will pay the price of their venality and get what they give—and nothing more—though it be to their eternal shame.

The present-day political leaders are keen-witted men. They are watching for the women who exert a strong influence upon their fellows. They will quickly honor these women, for in doing so they hope to swing to their side the others who are their followers. They will bring forward and place in positions of importance the active, the competent, the popular women. They will place them in our Government where woman's work is most needed, as commissioners of charity, as commissioners of correction, as heads of school boards, as members of food and health boards—in short, in places where a definite policy must be formulated and put into action. Should our women stay in retirement and allow others who are active in public life, whose ideals are different, whose principles are different, whose lives are different, to step into these positions which carry with them such tremendous possibilities and opportunities for good or evil? Should our women who, by their training, their philosophy, their lives, are best fitted for true leadership in this kind of work stand aside for others whose leadership might be of another sort, whose principles might be indefensible and whose standards of life questionable?

The answer is a compelling one. We did not seek universal woman suffrage, perhaps. That is immaterial. Universal woman suffrage is here, and with it have come new obligations and new opportunities—obligations to vote and to participate actively in public matters so that our men may be sufficient in numbers to form an adequate bulwark against those enemies who would tear down and destroy, against those who would subtly substitute their principles of life in place of the ideals of home and country for which we stand—opportunities to do good in an affirmative way in applying our philosophy to the solution of our social and economic problems. This is a day for glorious leadership. The multitudes are listening for the call of some commander. They will follow at his word. Whither? That will depend upon the leader. Who will be that leader? He cannot come from our ranks if we retire from the struggle and lose by default. In the momentous hour of conflict, we will not be able to assist or resist when we willingly dissipate our forces now and vitiate our strength. If that time comes, it may be too late, with the strategic positions in the hands of the enemy, to call upon our auxiliaries for reënforcement. Powerful, we shall be powerless.

When Napoleon desired to honor his soldiers who fought with him in his great battles, he struck off a medal. On it was the name of the battle and the soldier's name and below the simple inscription: "I was there."

That reward should be the ambition of every citizen of this Republic, man and woman alike. The War has brought to our very doors problems fraught with great danger. They cannot be solved by expediency alone. The social readjustment that must come can be satisfactorily obtained only by the active participation of all those, regardless of sex, who stand for the better things in life, whose philosophy is sound, whose morality is above that of the pagan and the materialist. In that readjustment we must all take a hand, using all our influence to see that the principles of Christ form the warp and woof of the new social fabric. If we do not, the proper readjustment will not be made. From the failure there may spring a phoenix of force and revolution. The issue must be met. Our Government, our religion, our homes depend upon its outcome. In that struggle our men *and women* must participate or they shall be forever faithless to their trust. This is their duty, their sacred obligation, not only to themselves, but to posterity. They can be true to this only if they, too, can say, "I was there."

I have little patience with those who hold that women will lose their charm if they perform this necessary work; who believe that if they vote they will not find time to attend to their duties in the home; that in becoming participants in public affairs their influence in other and more sacred matters will wane. Surely those who hold to this view cannot be concerned with the actual casting of the ballot. This can be done at the cost of only an hour's time. One hour a year is not much. If they are grieved over women's more active participation in politics so called, let them be reassured. Most of our women are endowed with common sense. No appeal can be stronger than that of a happy home. When that call comes, the other interests that conflict are put aside. But in these days there are many of our women who are not married, who go daily to business. Let these take up the most active work. The other women in the homes find time to know the needs of the hour, to become conversant with current conditions and to be prepared to throw the weight of their numbers upon the side of justice and right. Surely, even if a small sacrifice be necessary, the outcome is so momentous as to warrant the making of it.

For bear this in mind, if the women who love their homes fail to use their powerful influence and allow others not so worthy to dictate the destiny of our nation, it may be that they shall live to see their homes destroyed and their hearths violated. "Eternal vigilance is the price of liberty."

173

INTERNATIONAL LAW

WALTER GEORGE SMITH [1]

International law has been defined to be "the rules which determine the conduct of the general body of civilized states in their dealings with each other" (American and English Ency. of Law). Different writers have given varying views of the foundation of the law of nations, some holding that it is founded merely upon consent and usage, and others that it is the same as the law of nature, applied to the conduct of nations in the character of moral persons susceptible of obligations and laws. Chancellor Kent holds that neither of these views is strictly true; that the law of nations is purely positive law founded on usage, consent, and agreement, but that it must not be separated entirely from natural jurisprudence, since it derives its force "from the same principles of right reason, the same views of the nature and constitution of man, and the same sanction of Divine revelation, as those from which the science of morality is deduced." It follows then that by the natural law every state is bound to conduct itself towards other states in accordance with the rules of justice, irrespective of the general rules that have arisen from long established custom and usage. International law is a part of the law of the land of which the courts take judicial notice, and municipal statutes are constructed so as not to infringe on its doctrines. The rules of international law are to be found in writers of recognized authority, in treaties between civilized nations, in the decisions of international tribunals, in state papers and diplomatic correspondence, and its application is to be sought especially in the decisions of the courts of different nations where the rules have been defined in litigated cases, arising especially in the admiralty where judgment has been sought in prize cases. The first great modern authority on the subject was Grotius. His works have been followed by those of Pufendorf, Burlamaqui, Bynkershoek, and Vattel. The works of these learned authors have been adapted and expanded by various writers,

[1] *Catholic Encyclopedia,* vol. IX, pp. 73-75.

so that now there is a vast body of literature upon the subject representing great learning and ability.

The law of nations is essentially the product of modern times. Ancient nations looked upon strangers as enemies, and upon their property as lawful prize. Among the Greeks prisoners of war might lawfully be put to death or sold into slavery with their wives and children, and there was no duty owed by the nation to a foreign nation. Some beginnings of diplomatic intercourse may be traced in the relations of the Greek states towards one another, by agreements relating to the burying of the dead and the exchange of prisoners, while the Amphictyonic Council affords an instance of an attempt to institute a law of nations among the Grecian States themselves. The Romans show stronger evidence of appreciation of international law, or at least of the beginnings of it. They had a college of heralds charged with the Fetial Law relating to declarations of war and treaties of peace, and as their power and civilization grew, there came an appreciation of the moral duty owed by the state to nations with which it was at war. After the establishment of the empire, especially in its later periods, the law of nations became recognized as part of the natural reason of mankind. After the fall of the empire there was a relapse into the barbarism of earlier ages, but, when in the ninth century Charlemagne consolidated his empire under the influence of Christianity, the law of nations took on a new growth. As commerce developed, the necessity of an international law providing for the enforcement of contracts, the protection of shipwrecked sailors and property, and the maintaining of harbors became more apparent. Various codes and regulations containing the laws of the sea gradually developed, the most famous of which are the "Judgments of Oléron," said to have been drawn up in the eleventh century and long recognized in the Atlantic ports of France and incorporated in part in the maritime ordinances of Louis XIV; the "Consolato del Mare," a collection of rules applicable to questions arising in commerce and navigation both in peace and war, probably drawn up in the twelfth century and founded upon the Roman maritime law and early maritime customs of the commercial cities of the Mediterranean; the "Guidon de la Mar," which dates from the close of the sixteenth century and deals with the law of maritime insurance, prize, and the regulations governing the issue of letters of marque and reprisal. In addition to these there were various bodies of sea laws, notably the maritime law of Wisby, the customs of Amsterdam, the laws of Antwerp, and the Hanseatic League. All of these codes contained provisions extracted from the earliest known maritime code, the Rhodian laws, which were incorporated into the general body of Roman law, and were recognized and sanctioned by Tibertius and Hadrian.

During the long period between the fall of the Roman Empire and the definitive beginning of modern European States the greatest influence working for a recognition of international law among all peoples was the Church. A common faith, imposing the same obligations upon the individual members of the Church among all nations, obviously tended to the establishment and recognition of rules of justice and morality as among the nations themselves; and, when the more general acceptance of the obligations of Christianity became the rule, it followed naturally that the head of the Church, the pope holding the Divine commission, should become the universal arbiter in disputes among nations. For centuries the great offices of state, especially those having to do with foreign relations, were held by bishops learned in canon law, and, as canon law was based upon Roman law, and especially adapted to the government of the Church whose jurisdiction was not bounded by State lines, it naturally suggested many of the rules that have found a place in international law. The pope became the natural arbitrator between nations, and the power to which appeals were made when the laws of justice and morality were flagrantly violated by sovereigns either in relation to their own subjects or to foreign nations.

As the empire founded by Charlemagne gained in power and extent, the controversies precipitated by the conflicting claims of civil and ecclesiastical jurisdiction developed still further the position of the pope as the highest representative of the moral power of Christendom. It has been justly said, therefore, that "of all the effects of Christianity in altering the political face of Europe throughout all its people, and which may, therefore, very fairly be denominated a part of its Law of Nations, none are so prominent to observation during these centuries as those which sprang from the influence and form of government of the Church" (Ward, "Law of Nations," 11, 31). At first, without territory or temporal power, on account of his spiritual influence alone the pope was recognized as the ultimate tribunal of Christendom, and as such was known as the Father of Christendom. Under the Holy Roman Empire from the time of Otho I, as is pointed out by Janssen, there was a close alliance between the Church and the State, though they were at no time identical. "Church and State," he says, "granting certain presupposed conditions, are two necessary embodiments of one and the same human society, the State taking charge of the temporal requirements, and the Church of the spiritual and supernatural. These two powers would, however, be in a state of continual contention were it not for a Divine Law of equilibrium keeping each within its own limits." He points out further that the original cause of the separation between the spiritual and temporal powers, as "taught by Pope Gelasius at the end of the fifth century, lies in the law established by the Divine Founder of the Church, Who, "cognizant of human weakness, was careful that the two powers should be kept separate, and each limited to its own province. Christian princes were to respect the priesthood in those things which relate to the soul, and the priests in their turn to obey the laws made for the preservation of order in worldly matters; so that the soldiers of God shall not mix in temporal affairs, and the worldly authorities shall have naught to say in spiritual things. The province of each being so marked out, neither power shall encroach on the prerogatives of the other, but confine itself to its own limit."

"While it is recognized that the kingdoms of this world, as opposed to the one universal Church, may exist and prosper while remaining separate and independent, yet it was thought that the bond with the Church would be of a higher nature if the partition walls between people and people were broken down, all nations joined together in one, and the unity of the human race under one lord and ruler acknowledged. It was this idea which inspired the popes with the desire to found the Holy Roman Empire, whose Emperor would deem it his highest prerogative to protect the Christian Church. . . . The Gospel was to be the law of nations. The State would consolidate the nations, while the Church would sow the seeds of revealed truth" (Janssen, "History of the German People," II, 110 sq.). In this ideal we find the medieval conception of the State. Although the ideal was never completely realized, yet it met such general acceptance that the emperor became the chief protector of law and order and the arbiter between lesser princes. The growth of the power of the State gradually diminished that of the feudal barons, whose petty contentions and the violence of whose lives were a hindrance to the development of international justice. Until this phase of the beginnings of civilization changed there was little to ameliorate the brutality of conduct between warring peoples, except as the individual education of knights in chivalry affected their conduct.

Another influence of great importance in the formation of international law were the general Councils of the Church, affecting as they did all Christian nations and laying down rules of faith and discipline binding alike upon individuals and governments. The history and development of rules of international law from these early beginnings have been traced to contemporary times, and, notwithstanding periods when the influence of a lofty and Christian ideal of the relations between nations seems almost to have been lost, it will appear that there has been a steady advance in the recognition of the existence of a moral law of nations whose sanction is the public opinion of the world. So far has this system progressed that its underlying principles are, in the main, well-defined, universally recognized, and constantly appealed to, both in times of war and in times of peace, by all civilized nations. Rules governing the acquisition of territorial property, jurisdiction over rivers and seas, protectorates over independent peoples; measures allowed to compel the rendering of justice, short of war; intervention in the affairs of foreign nations, have all been measurably settled; and so far as relates to the rights and duties of belligerents and of neutral States in declaring and carrying on war, the fixing of the character of property, the regulating of the effect of intercourse between individuals, many vexed points have also been carefully defined and to a large extent settled. Some of the most delicate questions, such as the right to visit and search the blockaded ports of the enemy, and the character of correspondence permitted between the subjects or citizens of neutral States and the belligerents, may be considered as well settled and recognized by decisions of the highest courts of all civilized nations as any of the rules of municipal law.

Earnest and intelligent efforts to bring about a permanent court of arbitration have resulted in the formation of an international tribunal at The Hague, which has already been accepted by the voluntary action of the various nations as a proper forum for the decision of many international questions specially referred to it. The principles of arbitration accepted by the United States and Great Britain in the settlement of the so-called Alabama Claims and the frequent agreement between the contending parties over questions of boundary, fisheries, and damages to private property of their respective citizens or subjects, have given emphasis to international law. Its rules have enforced respect for private property on the part of contending armies, and, under certain conditions, when such is carried by ships, have forbidden the use of certain destructive missles, and in very many ways have alleviated the horrors of war. While there must always remain questions that no self-respecting nation would be willing to submit to arbitration, yet the field for the exercise of the latter is indefinitely great, and, as the demands of modern civilization, the means of communication between nations, and the development of trade relations increase, questions more frequently arise requiring appeal to some tribunal, acceptable to both parties, whose decision shall be final and absolute.

174

INTERNATIONAL LAW

TIMOTHY BROSNAHAN [1]

International law is a body of duties and rights by which nations are mutually and morally bound. It must be distinguished from the *jus gentium* of the schoolmen. It is either natural or positive. Positive international law, like

---

[1] *Digests of Lectures on Ethics,* p. 135. (John Murphy Company, Baltimore.)

positive civil law, is either a more definite declaration of an already existing natural or moral law recognized by reason, or a determination of conditions required for the uniform and general practice of international intercourse and the practical safeguarding of international duties and rights. It comprises, therefore, principles which right reason perceives to be consonant with humanity and justice, and such definitions and determination of these as are established by general consent.

The primary duty of a nation toward other nations is to treat them with the benevolence, respect and justice due to an equal sovereign personality. Its primary rights are the rights of self-preservation, of self-development, of independence, and self-control, of territorial dominion and of a voice in matters affecting the community of nations.

175

THE LAW OF NATIONS

Alfred O'Rahilly [1]

(1) Roman Law

In the later days of the Roman Republic the Praetor Peregrinus acted as judge for Italian merchants and other strangers whose disputes had to be settled in Rome. In this praetorian court there grew up a code of jurisprudence, a loose collection of general principles of equity, largely untechnical and widely applicable. It is uncertain whether this law was originally merely a summary of the general customs of the Mediterranean world, or simply that portion of the positive law of Rome which, being in accordance with the private law of other nations, was applicable to the peregrini (probably all Roman subjects) who sought justice from the Praetor. It seems clear, however, that the technical term *ius gentium* (law of nations) had from the very start a theoretical and philosophical implication; it did not merely designate the precedents and principles upheld in a particular Roman court; it was employed to denote certain simple and universally accepted maxims of right which constituted a body of law approximating to the ideal natural

---

[1] *Studies*, December, 1920.

code of the Stoics. This is the meaning of *ius gentium* not only in Cicero's writings,[2] where the term first occurs, but also in the Corpus Iuris Civilis. Thus Gaius, writing about the middle of the second century, says that the laws and customs of any people can be analysed into (1) *ius civile* or state-law "set up by each people for itself," and (2) *ius gentium, commune omnium hominum ius,* world-law "set up by natural reason amongst all men."[3] This world-law is, according to Gaius, not only the common element in all particular systems of legislation and custom, but is the spontaneous outcome of natural reason, "conformable to natural equity," and, in a word, synonymous with "natural law."[4]

Yet side by side with this identification of natural law and world-law we find embedded in the Corpus Iuris the precise statement, made by three lawyers about the beginning of the third century, that liberty is of natural law, while servitude or domination was introduced by world-law.[5] We have here the first clear indication of a difference between the two terms which was destined to be developed by the Schoolmen. Still clearer is this quotation from the Institutes of Justinian (i, 2, 2): "The *ius gentium* is common to the entire human race. For, owing to the exigencies of custom and the needs of mankind, the nations set up certain things for themselves. Wars broke out, there fol-

[2] Cicero (*De officiis* iii, 17, 69) plainly equates *lex naturae* and *ius gentium*. *Cf.* also *Tusc.* i, 13, 30: Consensio omnium gentium lex naturae putanda est. In the phrase "natura id est iure gentium" (*De officiis* iii, 5, 23) it has been suggested by those who take a different view (e. g., Krueger, *Histoire des sources du droit romain,* 1894, p. 55, n. 2) that the words are either a gloss or else instead of *id est* we should read *et*.

[3] Gaius, *Inst.* i, 1 (p. 3, Krueger-Studemund); also *Digest* i, 1, 9. The version "world-law" is preferable to "law of nations," which nowadays means international law.

[4] Hae quoque res quae traditione nostrae fiunt, *iure gentium* nobis acquiruntur. Nihil enim tam *conveniens est naturali aequitati* quam voluntatem domini volentis rem suam in alium transferre ratam haberi.—*Digest,* 41.1, 9, (§ 3). Apparet quaedam *naturali iure* alienari, qualia sunt ea quae traditione alienantur.—Gaius, *Inst.* ii, 65. He also says that the ius gentium is the primitive law of mankind (in the golden age): Antiquius ius gentium cum ipso genere humano proditum est.—*Digest,* 41.1, 1.

[5] *Digest,* 12.6, 64 (Tryphoninus); *Digest* i, 5, 4 (Florentinus); *Digest* i, 1, 4 (Ulpian).

lowed captivity and servitude, which are contrary to natural law—for by natural law from the beginning all men were born equal. From this *ius gentium* also nearly all forms of contract were introduced." In this passage we have the germ of the later theory that world-law is an adaptation of natural law to corrupt humanity. But it is sufficient for the moment to observe that the two terms which elsewhere are treated as identical are here sharply contrasted. And so, when the study of Roman law was revived, the early jurists and schoolmen found no precise definitions or explanations of *ius naturae* and *ius gentium*.[6]

(2) ULPIAN'S DEFINITION

The ambiguity was still further increased by an unfortunate statement of Ulpian, which is not only philosophically untenable but also in contradiction with other pronouncements of the same lawyer. Influenced, no doubt, by the wide meaning of the Stoic *physis* or *natura,* and by the Cynic-Stoic idealising and moralising of animal life, Ulpian defined natural law as "that which nature taught all animals," e. g., the rearing of offspring; in contrast to which the *ius gentium* is applicable exclusively to mankind.[7] This would be a valid juristic distinction if Aesop's Fables were true, that is, if animals were formally as well as materially capable of ethical conduct. As it is, however, Ulpian's distinction merely served to spread confusion between the domains of physics and ethics.[8] This curious theory, that world-law is the specific human sub-division of nature-law, was, fortunately, ignored by S. Isidore, Gratian and the early Canonists.[9] It would probably have

[6] *Cf.* the Glossa Ordinaria on *Digest* i, 1, 3 (quod natura): Nota ius naturale quatuor modis dici—prima lex mosaica, secundo instinctus naturae, tertio ius gentium, quarto ius praetorium.

[7] *Justinian's Institutes* i.2 (procem.); also *Digest* i, 1, 3. This is repeated by the civilian jurists, e. g., Azo and Bracton—Maitland, *Select Passages from the Works of Bracton and Azo,* 1894, pp. 35, 38.

[8] Witness the Glossa Ordinaria: Animalia omnia iure naturali regi; quod regimen est in eo quod avis volat, quod piscis natat.—On *Digest* i, 1, 3 (omnium animalium).

[9] S. Isidore: "Ius naturale est commune omnium nationum, et quod ubique instinctu naturae non constitutione aliqua habeatur." Ius gentium is so called "quod eo iure omnes fere gentes utuntur." —*Etym.* v, 4 and 6; Migne, P.L. 82, 199; also Gratian, *Decretum,* p. 1, d. 1, c. 7 and 9. Rufinus, the first commentator on Gratian,

been regarded by all the Scholastics as an aberration of the Legists, had not S. Thomas, always tolerant and synthetic, sought to give an acceptable interpretation to Ulpian's remark.

Natural law, he says, is used in several different senses, because nature is capable of several interpretations. (1) Nature may mean an intrinsic or innate principle. Or (2) it may refer to a higher principle; thus the natural motion of the elements is induced by the influence of the celestial bodies; so also the divine law, impressed by God, is said to be natural. (3) It may be the matter and not the principle of the law which is natural. "And because nature is distinguished from reason, by which man is man, therefore, taking natural law in this strictest sense, what pertains to man, even though it be dictated by natural reason, is not said to be of natural law."[1] In this passage S. Thomas is merely dispassionately enumerating the senses in which (1) the Stoics and Cicero, (2) S. Isidore and Gratian, (3) Ulpian and other jurists, use the term natural law. He is engaged in explaining the terminology before answering the objection that monogamy, not being the rule among animals, cannot be of natural law. To this he replies that polygamy is against natural law in the first and second sense, though it is not against nature-law in the sense of Ulpian: a plain proof that he does not adopt this last sense as his own. Here, as elsewhere, he makes it clear that what certain jurists call *ius gentium,* i. e., those moral principles which are implied by man's nature as such, is really a part of the natural law.[2]

---

refuses to take any notice of the "legistica traditio."—*Summa Decretorum,* ed. Singer 1902, p. 6. But Hostiensis (*Summa aurea,* prooem., col. 5, Venice, 1574) and Bonaventure (4 *Sent.,* d. 33, a. 1, q. 2) repeat Ulpian's definition.

[1] *Suppl.,* q. 65, a. 1, ad 4; or 4 *Sent.,* d. 33, q. 1, a. 1, ad 4. It is quite inaccurate to cite the latter portion—section (3) translated in the text—as if it represented S. Thomas's own view, least of all to the exclusion of (1) and (2): as is done by Cathrein, *Philosophia moralis,* 1915⁹, p. 227, § 308. As a matter of fact, in the body of the article S. Thomas says that natural law applies *only* to man, other animals merely having *aestimatio naturalis* or instinct. Which shows the danger of partial quotations torn from their context.

[2] Thus *Ethica* v, 12, referring to Aristotle v, 10 (7), 1134*b*, 18: Illud autem quod consequitur propriam inclinationem naturae humanae, scilicet ut homo est rationale animal, vocant iuristae ius

This theory of Ulpian reappears in a much quoted and misquoted article of the Summa. S. Thomas decides here that the *ius gentium* is different from the *ius naturale*. What S. Thomas really means by world-law will be considered presently. Reference is now made to this article only because in it he once more deals with Ulpian's distinction and also makes an ingenious effort to give it a satisfactory meaning by identifying it with Aristotelianism. Natural law, he says, concerns the intrinsic harmony and purpose of things,[3] i. e., the primary functions of nature which animals execute instinctively and men consciously. World-law, on the contrary, deals with a certain extrinsic or consequential fittingness which is arrived at as the result of a reasoning process. The attempt to include animals in this scheme is more charitable to Ulpian than convincing to the reader. For, obviously, as S. Thomas himself admits when dealing with monogamy,[4] natural law covers those specifically human functions and destinies which—unlike the examples he adduces: generation and nourishment of offspring—man does not share even analogically and materially with the brutes.[5] Moreover, the ratiocination establishing the *ius gentium* must be a far different process from

gentium. . . . Utrumque autem horum comprehenditur sub iusto naturali prout hic a philosopho accipitur. That is the Aristotelian *politikon dikaion*—and the Scholastic natural law—includes both the nature-law and the world-law of Ulpian; an obvious remark repeated by later writers, e. g., Suarez, *De legibus* ii, 19, 1 and 17, 3. It shows extraordinary misunderstanding to cite this as proving that ius gentium, as used by S. Thomas himself, is part of the natural law; e. g., by Cathrein, *op. cit.;* Meyer, *Inst. iuris naturalis* i (1906²), 484, § 572.

[3] *Summa*, 2.2, q. 57, a. 3: commensuratio secundum absolutam sui considerationem. On this Aristotelian phraseology see Von Hertling, *Historische Beiträge zur Philosophie*, 1914, p. 83.

[4] Hoc modo matrimonium est naturale, quia ratio naturalis ad ipsum inclinat.—*Suppl.*, q. 41, a. 1. Pluralitas ergo uxorum [est] . . . contra ius naturale primo modo acceptum. . . . Quia natura dictat hoc cuilibet animali secundum modum convenientem speciei suae.—*Suppl.*, q. 65, a. 1, ad. 4.

[5] Sylvius, in loc. (*Commentarii*, 1697⁴, p. 274b): Advertendum autem quod B. Thomas hic sequatur iurisconsultos . . . Theologi et cum illis B. Thomas saepe aliter loquuntur tam de iure naturali quam de iure gentium. S. Thomas was followed by a few writers, e. g., Sylvester Prierias, Summa (1518), s. v. lex, ed. 1552, ii, 133b. But most subsequent Scholastics entirely reject Ulpian's view. See Suarez's attack: *De legibus* ii, 17, 5-7.

THE STATE

that working of the *naturalis ratio* which dictates the law of nature. It can hardly be supposed that S. Thomas expends a whole article in emphasising a mere subjective distinction, in differentiating world-law from natural law, not by means of any objective moral criterion or objectively valid characteristic, but by the duration and difficulty of the mental operations whereby we arrive at their recognition.[6] If at the end of either process of thought—whether "absolute apprehension" or reasoned "consideration by comparison with consequences"—we arrive at identically valid, binding, irrevocable, moral laws, then the difference in the method of human discovery of those laws is ethically and objectively irrelevant.[7] It has been left to some comparatively recent writers to suggest that S. Thomas, failing to perceive this irrelevancy, laboriously insisted on calling the same ethical concept by two different names, *ius naturale* and *ius gentium*.

(3) POSITIVE LAW

It must be admitted, however, that the terminology of this article of the Summa is rather ambiguous, owing to S. Thomas's well-meaning attempt to make Aristotle, Gaius and Ulpian speak the same language. It is, therefore, necessary to interpret this text of S. Thomas by the light of other passages and with the help of the tradition of the School. Amid many differences of detail there is one clear thesis which is accepted with practical unanimity by the Scholastics: The *ius gentium* is positive human law. According to S. Thomas positive law derives its essential validity from human consent (ex condicto sive ex communi placito), and "is divided into world-law and state-law."[8]

---

[6] In this same article (2.2, q. 57, a. 3) S. Thomas also unfortunately seeks to give a tolerable meaning to the *naturalis ratio* on which Gaius based his *ius gentium,* by identifying it with the reasoning whereby we establish the world-law—as if Gaius admitted *ius naturale* distinct from *ius gentium*.

[7] Non oportet ius gentium cum naturali confundere, nec propter solas illationes etiam plures ita vocare ius illud quod simpliciter naturale est. Nam discursus non excludit veram et naturalem necessitatem praecepti sic cogniti; et quod discursus sit per plures vel pauciores illationes magis vel minus notas, valde accidentarium est. Suarez, *De legibus* ii, 18, 8.

[8] 2.2, q. 57, a. 2. Dividitur ius positivum in ius gentium et ius civile.—1.2, q. 95, a. 4.

This unambiguous declaration is strengthened by the answers which on two separate occasions he makes to the objection that the *ius gentium* is not a positive law; the very placing of this statement as an objection shows, of course, without further proof, that he does not agree with it. His first reply is as follows:

The *ius gentium* is, indeed, in some way natural to man as a rational being, in so far as it is derived from the natural law by means of a conclusion which is not very remote from its principles—hence it is that men easily *consented* thereto. Still it is distinguished from natural law, *especially* from that which is common to all animals.[9]

The second time the objection recurs it is based on the argument that world-law cannot be positive since there never was a world-assembly to establish it by common consent. "Since world-law is dictated by natural reason," he replies,[1] "its justice being easily deduced (ex propinquo habentia aequitatem), therefore, it is that it does not need any special institution save that of natural reason." World-law, in other words, is largely customary and unwritten. This is the traditional thesis of the School. A few typical quotations will suffice:

World-law [says F. de Castro Palao[2]], which lies between natural law and state-law, is neither necessarily implanted by nature nor originated by any special ruler or kingdom; but it was introduced by almost all nations, not in writing but by usage and custom... Hence world-law, though it is in conformity with natural reason and is based thereon, is proximately and immediately positive and human, for it is originated by men who have thus established it by usage and custom.

The precepts of world-law [declares Suarez[3]] were introduced by men through their will and consent, whether in the whole community of men or in the greater part.

---

[9] 1.2, q. 95, a. 4, ad 1. Sylvius comments (*Commentarii in totam secundam secundae,* 1697⁴, p. 275*b*): Quibus verbis agnoscit ius gentium esse ex hominum consensu seu placito.

[1] 2.2, q. 57, a. 3, ad 3. Arauxo in loc. (*Lecturae,* 1638, p. 557*a*): Ibi nomine specialis institutionis intellegit illam quae fit immediate ex unius aut alterius populi beneplacito a quo dependet et constituitur ius civile.

[2] *De legibus* i, 3 (*Opus morale* i, 116*a*).

[3] *De legibus* ii, 17, 8.

Positive human law [according to Sylvius [4]] is divided into world-law, canon law and state-law. . . . Positive law is that which, without being from nature, is posited and constituted by some one possessing authority. . . . Law founded by human authority is called human law. World-law is human law used by nearly all the world, i. e., such as, without being from nature, was introduced by the common consent of peoples, whether it be observed among all or most nations. Such are the division of goods, individual possession of things, the principle that unpossessed objects cede to the first occupier, the non-violation of ambassadors, the enslavement of captives in war.

World-law is more clearly and accurately defined thus [says Neubauer [5]]: a free convention of peoples through tacit agreement, introduced by long-continued custom, to obtain and preserve the mutual intercourse and happiness of social life.

Many similar citations might be given. What has been quoted suffices to illustrate the practically unanimous teaching of the Scholastics that the *ius gentium* is positive human law, largely consuetudinary, deriving its authority from human consent.[6] Even the few writers who prefer to say that world-law is rather a mean between natural and positive law than actually positive, do not thereby mean to

---

[4] On 2.2, q. 57, a. 2: *Commentarii*, 1697[4], p. 272b.

[5] *De legibus*, 36: *Theologia Wiceburgensis*, Paris, 1880[3], v. 237.

[6] This is held by the following among others: Denis the Carthusian, *Summa fidei catholicae* ii. 101, 4; Covarruvias, *Rel. c. peccatum de reg.* xi. 4 (*Opera*, Francf. 1599-98, i. 538a.): propter reipublicae utilitatem . . . fere omnium hominum consensu; Soto, *De iustitia* i. 5, 4 and iii. 1, 3; Bannez on 2.2, q. 57, a. 3; Molina, *De iustitia* tr. 1, disp. 5 (i. 14): ius humanum hominum voluntate introductum; Valentia, 1.2, disp. 7, q. 5, punct. 2 (Commentaria, 1609, ii. 850); Vazques, 1.2, d. 157, c. 4, n. 24; Salas, *De legibus* ii. 3, 21; Arauxo, 1.2, q. 92, disp. 1. sect. 6, diff. 3 (*Lecturae*, 1638, p. 554 b.); Voit, *Theologia moralis*, 1769[6] i. 98 (§ 137): ius gentium respecit obiecta arbitraria in ordine ad maius commodum societatis humanae; Reding, *Theologia scholastica*, 1687, ii. 363 a.; Lacroix, *Theologia moralis*, ed. Ven. 1720, i. 58 (*de legibus* c. 1, dub. 2 § 606): vim obligandi habet per liberam consensionem; Michel, *Theologia canonico-moralis* (1707-12) i. 151; F. Schmier, *Iurisprudentia canonico-civilis*, ed. Avenione 1738, i. 87; Billuart, *De iure*, diss 1, a. 3 (*Summa*, Paris, 1895, vi. 12 a.); Dmowski, *Inst. phil.*, 1843[4], ii. 174; Schmalzgrueber, *Ius ecclesiasticum*, diss. proem. iv. 126 and 129 (Rome, 1843, i. pp. 59, 61); Solieri, *Iuris publici eccles. elementa*, 1900, pp. 21 f. I have also verified this thesis in Conradus, Victoria, Salmanticenses, Salon, Aragon, Lessius, Bonacina, Antoine, Viva, Reiffenstuel, Wiestner, Schwarz, P. Schmier, Huth, Roselli and many more.

deny that it owes its validity to human consent.[7] Moreover, there is not a single one of these writers who is not convinced that this was also the teaching of S. Thomas.[8]

(4) Constitutional World-Law

We are now in a better position for examining what S. Thomas means by the ratiocination on which world-law is based. There are two modes, he says[9] in which human positive law is derived from natural law: (1) by way of conclusion, as in the case of world-law; (2) by way of concrete determination, as in state-law. What is meant by determination—for example, the actual specification of a penalty or assignment of a contribution—is quite clear. But it is not so easy to analyze or illustrate the inference or conclusion on which world-law rests. Indeed it is most probable that S. Thomas, like all pioneers, failed to carry his own analysis far enough and omitted to make a vital distinction which first clearly appeared in the pages of Suarez. A few commentators regarded S. Thomas (in the article just cited) as merely speaking according to the language of the jurists. But the majority declared that the conclusions in question are not necessary but only probable.[1]

[7] Thus Bellarmine, *De clericis* 29 (*Opera,* Naples 1857, ii 206): Ius vero gentium partim est naturale, partim positivum; quia pendet quidem ab humana constitutione, i. e., a consensu omnium gentium, sed non pendet ab auctoritate principis vel magistratus particularis. Similarly Miranda, *Manuale praelatorum,* tom 2, q. 24, a. 2, concl. 5 (1630, p. 204): Ius gentium nec mere est de iure naturali nec mere de iure positivo . . . Ius gentium est ex hominum beneplacito institutum, quo fit ut respublica, iusta existente atque interveniente causa, potest illud abrogare et derogare.

[8] Sometimes after very close study and analysis of the relevant texts, e. g., J. Patuzzi, O. P., *Ethica christiana sive theol. moralis* (de legibus iii 1, 1) ed. 1790, i 61: Ut in tam ampla significatione ius gentium sumi posse minime diffitear, tamen pressius atque in arctiore sensu accipiendum existimo, adeo ut excludat tum leges naturales tum positivas civiles sitque speciale ius ab hisce distinctum. Hanc sententiam docuisse S. Thomam certum mihi est, eius mente accuratius expensa in pluribus locis ubi de hoc iure verba facit.

[9] 1.2, q. 95, a. 2 and 4.

[1] Quae doctrina . . . licet a Conrado intelligatur esse data iuxta modum loquendi iuristarum, melius cum Soto et aliis intellegimus praecepta iuris gentium vocari conclusiones iuris naturalis, non absolute et per necessariam illationem, sed comparatione facta ad determinationem iuris civilis et privati.—Suarez, *De legibus,* ii 20, 2. Intellegi debet de iis quae ex lege naturali derivantur tamquam

This is implied by S. Thomas himself, for he regards the result of such an inferential process as contingent and mutable and as requiring consent and agreement. "Human law," he says (1. 2, q. 97, a. 1), "may be justly changed owing to two causes: (1) on the part of reason, for it seems natural for human reason to advance gradually from imperfect to perfect; . . . (2) on the part of the subjects, for a law can be rightly changed owing to changes in men's conditions." Thus the inference of human reason does not necessarily make such ethico-legal conclusions absolute and certain. That is why they are not only liable to revision but require human consent for their validation.[2]

Now this seems clearly to imply that these deductions must somehow involve a contingent or variable supposition; they must be based on a doubtful or hypothetical premiss as well as on some principle of natural law. To this view Suarez makes the objection that in such a case the conclusion would also be of natural law. As examples he mentions the observance of a vow or promise, obedience to masters, the prohibition of theft and simony. These are admittedly of natural law; yet they suppose certain voluntary acts or contingent institutions—vows, slavery, private property, the consecration of some article. "Therefore," says Suarez,[3] "though the conclusion follows only if the supposition holds concerning the matter of the precept, yet if the inference is evident from clear principles, such a

conclusiones non omnino necessariae, sed valde probabiles; et ab hominum usu seu receptione dependent ad hoc ut vim obligandi sortiantur; cum alioquin non versentur circa materiam homini simpliciter necessariam in ordine ad ipsius finem.—Sylvius on 1.2, q. 94, a. 4: *Commentarii*, 1696[4], p. 521 a. Also Bellarmine, *De clericus* 29: Opera (1857) ii 205.

[2] De facili in huiusmodi [conclusiones] homines *consenserunt*.— 1.2, q. 95, a. 4, ad. 1. Secundum ius naturale non est distinctio possessionum, sed magis secundum humanum *condictum* . . . Unde proprietas possessionum non est contra ius naturale, sed iuri naturali superadditur per *adinventionem rationis* humanae.—2.2, q. 66, a. 2, ad. 1. Distinctio possessionum et servitus non sunt inductae a natura sed per hominum *rationem*,—1.2, q. 94, a. 5, ad. 3. The reference to slavery as due to "reason" is quite decisive proof that a "conclusion" may be entirely extirpated by human consent. Obligatio iuris gentium non oritur ex sola ratione sine aliquo modo obligationis humanae saltem per generalem consuetudinem introductae.—Suarez, *De legibus* ii 20, 6.

[3] *De legibus* ii 17, 9.

conclusion pertains to natural law and not to world-law. Hence that world-law may be distinguished from natural law, it is necessary that, even supposing such matter, [the formal conclusion] should follow by a sequence which is not evident but less certain, so that human decision and moral congruence rather than necessity may intervene."

We must, then, distinguish between the positing of a contingent moral and legal fact and the resulting obligation, between institution and observance. The latter is of natural law, it is only the former which is of positive law. "Though private property is not a precept of natural law," Suarez points out,[4] "yet after it has been instituted and properties have been assigned, natural law prohibits theft or the unlawful receiving of what belongs to another." In connection with another traditionally included precept of the *ius gentium,* the non-violation of envoys, Suarez makes a similar, more detailed analysis:[5]

Although, after the admission of envoys under an implied pact, it is against natural law not to respect their immunity, for it is contrary to justice and due fidelity, yet this supposition, and this pact under such a condition, was introduced by world-law.

The same consideration will apply to any contract or intercourse, in which three factors can be distinguished:

(1) The particular mode of contract. This ordinarily pertains to state-law and often, the law not being opposed, can be fixed by decision of the contracting parties.

(2) Observance of the contract after it has been completed. This, as is clear, pertains to natural law.

(3) Freedom of contract and intercourse with men who are not enemies. This is of world-law, for natural law of itself does not oblige thereto. For one state might live by itself and refuse intercourse even with another friendly state. But by world-law it was established that intercourse is free, and world-law

---

[4] *De legibus* ii 14, 17. Cf. Billuart, *De iure* diss. 4, a. 1 (*Summa,* Paris, 1895, vi 58): Ius naturae prohibet rem auferri alterius, quovis iure illam possideat. Hence the untenability of the argument: Observance of the rights of property is of natural law, just as theft is against it; therefore [the institution of] private property is of natural law.

[5] *De legibus* ii 19, 7.

would be violated if such were prohibited without reasonable cause.

Except for one point which will be noted presently, this analysis is perfect as applied to certain social schemes and arrangements of humanity. Their institution is due to world-law, their concrete details and working-out are determined by state-law, their observance after foundation is prescribed by natural law.

The *ius gentium*, according to this, is constitutional world-law. It is concerned solely with setting up certain world-wide social institutions such as private property and, we may add, capitalism. This setting up is, of course, not a definite chronological event, for as yet at least there is no world-parliament; world-law, in other words, is customary and unwritten, but by no means unreal. The legal validity of such institutions depends essentially on the tacit or formal consent of mankind; needless to say, there may be a moral obligation to yield such consent. But so long as such institutions validly exist, they claim our allegiance in virtue of natural law. It is owing to the absence of this distinction that confusion—S. Thomas himself is not exempt—occurs in expositions and explanations of world-law. A statement may be correct when interpreted as referring to institution, and wrong when taken as applying to observance.[6] It is admitted by S. Thomas and the Scholastics that the institution of private property is of world-law; they also admit that its observance is of natural law. Thus implicitly at least they hold that the *ius gentium* is—to use a convenient formula—constitutional world-law.

Reverting, then, to St. Thomas's statement, that world-law is added to natural law by human reasoning and con-

---

[6] Hence sometimes the difficulty of saying whether a particular author correctly or incorrectly describes the *ius gentium*. Toletus on 2.2, q. 57, a. 3 (*In summam theologiae enarratio,* ed. Paria, ii 241) and Wiggers on 1.2, q. 95, a. 4, n. 9 (*Commentaria,* 1634^2, p. 332), who take world-law as prescribing what is necessary, not absolutely but conditionally and by supposition, seem to be correct; for they are referring to institutions. Whereas Zigliara is thinking of observance and maintenance of an institution (e. g. private property) when he says: Ius gentium formaliter sumptum non est neque lex naturae neque lex positiva, sed infertur ex principio absoluto naturae et ex aliquo facto universali quidem sed in se contingenti.—*Phil. moralis,* 1912^{15}, p. 126.

sent, we can free it from all obscurity. "To world-law," he says (1. 2, q. 95, a. 4), "pertain all those things which are derived from natural law as conclusions from principles; such as just buying and selling and other such like without which men cannot live together—which living together is of natural law, for man is naturally sociable." The principle of natural law in this case is human social co-existence; the "conclusion." i. e., the practical deduction which in given concrete circumstances men draw from the law of sociability, is the institution of certain types of social and economic intercourse; without which—so it is reasoned with probability—social life is impracticable; the observance of which, so long as the institution holds, is of natural law.

(5) INTERNATIONAL LAW

On this last text of the *Summa* Sylvius makes a comment which will serve to illustrate a defect in the analysis of Suarez. "There is no difficulty," he says,[7] "in the fact that the holy doctor adduces as examples of world-law just exchange (buying and selling) and such like which seem to pertain to natural law. For though it be of natural law that whatever exchange does take place should take place justly, still it is not of natural law that exchange should take place between men of different nations; this is of world-law." It would seem from this that Sylvius, following Suarez, regarded the institution of exchange and intercourse as of natural law when between individuals within a nation, but as of world-law when international. The particular instance—namely, economic exchange—need not be here considered. But the distinction emphasized by Suarez in connection with it is extremely interesting as showing the transition from *ius gentium* to what is now called international law. "There are two ways," says Suarez,[8] "in which a thing is said to be of world-law. (1) Because it is the law which all peoples and nations ought to observe between themselves *(inter se)*. (2) Because it is a law which all individual states or kingdoms observe within themselves *(intra se)*, and by similarity and analogy is called world-law. But it is the first kind which seems to me most properly to contain world-law as really distinct

---
[7] Sylvius on 1.2, q. 95, a. 4; *Commentarii*, 1696⁴, p. 521 *b*.
[8] *De legibus* ii, 19,8. Cf. ii 20, 7.

from state-law." It is declarations such as these that have rightly merited for Suarez his claim to be one of the founders of international jurisprudence. And yet there is reason to believe that the merging of the *ius gentium* in international law has been a distinct loss to Catholic philosophy.

The very term "international" law is redolent of that disintegrating philosophy which refuses to regard either nation or humanity as natural law-creating entities; if we were consistent, we should also speak of state legislation as inter-individual law. Thus even our phraseology bears witness to our loss of faith in human solidarity and in the reality of world-law. Not of course that this was the view of the great Schoolmen, for whom the Church was a living world-wide reality and the Empire still a unifying influence on men's political ideals. "The whole world," says Francis of Victoria, "which is in some way one commonwealth, has the power of making just and suitable laws for all, such as are in the *ius gentium*. Hence those who violate the *ius gentium*, either in peace or war, sin mortally." "The human race," says Suarez, "though divided into various peoples and kingdoms, has a unity which is not only specific but also, as it were, political and moral. . . . Each complete community is also in a sense a member of this universe so far as it pertains to the human race." [9] Hence world-law is literally the law of the world, the law of nations regarded as forming the aggregate of humanity. The very title *ius gentium*, law of nations, shows that it includes more than law *between* nations; it envisages law not as relationships between autonomous disparate bodies but as moral precepts governing mankind as such; it is intra-world law rather than inter-national law.[1]

---

[9] Victoria, *Rel. theol.* iii 21. Suarez, *De legibus*, ii 20, 8. Cf. Martinez, *Commentaria super primam secundae,* q. 90, a. 3, dub. 4 (1637, iii 26a) : Haec potestas primo fuit in toto genere humana ex natura rei et forsitan modo durat.

[1] I have suggested above that the *ius gentium* should be restricted to constitutional world-law. For owing to the absence of any formal legislating world-assembly, it is only fundamental constitutional principles of society which can be regarded as having effective super-national ratification and validity. Much of what is termed international law—e. g., postal and coinage agreements, and all "private international law"—is merely the concurrent agreement or coincidence of several state legislatures and governments.

This is really the only theory which not only gives an account of present facts, but prepares for future ideals. The Scholastic view of law, and especially of consuetudinary law, enables us to see how far more deeply interconnected nations are than the very meagre and formal, and often very trivial, code of international agreements and laws seems to imply. If we look deeper we shall see that the relationship or community of peoples is far more dependent on, and much more clearly demonstrated by, world-wide social and economic institutions such as private property, wage-system, capitalism. To deal with the externalities of formal international law, while neglecting the inner and vital fact of this constitutional world-law based on tradition and custom, is to content oneself with superficiality. It is only by a reversion to, and an elaboration of, the Schoolmen's law-of-nations that we shall succeed in analyzing the realities of the world situation. Only thus, too, can we hope to solve adequately the ideals of humanity expressed by the attempt at a real league of nations (i. e., the effort to extend, improve and systematize the *ius gentium* by changing it from custom into formal law) and by the uprising against capitalism (i. e., the increasing withdrawal of consent from the present economic system).

(6) The Reaction

The gradual influence of the modern view of international law can easily be traced in the later Scholastics and is quite clear in most of the nineteenth-century writers of textbooks. R. de Arriaga, S. J. (1564-1662), denies the existence of the *ius gentium* altogether: "There are no real common laws such that one nation is bound to observe them with another." [2] But it is chiefly Protestant writers who, by their so-called separation of ethics and law, have succeeded in demolishing the entire basis of world-law. Hobbes's fundamental principle is that "where there is no common power, there is no law; where no law, no injustice." Pufendorf, Barbeyrac, Burlamaqui, and others deny the existence of any positive world-law. For them the *ius gentium* is merely the natural law applied to the intercourse of nations; and since their time natural law itself has been rejected as antiquated nonsense. "The law obtaining be-

[2] *De legibus* vii 8, 66: *Disput. theol.*, Lugd. 1647-54, iv 71 *a*.

tween nations," declares Austin, "is not positive law; for every positive law is set by a given sovereign to a person or persons in a state of subjection to its author."[3]

These non-Catholic writers, it should be observed, use the expression *ius gentium* solely in the modern sense of international law; and it was on this interpretation, and for the alleged reason that no supernatural "sovereign" existed, that they denied all *positive* law of nations. It has already been pointed out that early in the seventeenth century this restriction in the meaning of *ius gentium* is already noticeable in the Scholastics; this change is obviously connected with a contemporary process—the abolition of customary law and the cessation of all recognized jural facts save the authenticated decisions of some centralized sovereign body. Many Catholic writers, of course, formally retained the old concept of *ius gentium*; but, curiously enough, they came gradually to accept as applicable to the law-of-nations the decision of the Protestant jurists relative to law-between-nations, namely, the denial that it is positive. Thus it came to be generally admitted, though not until the latter half of the nineteenth century, that the *ius gentium* is natural law.[4]

It has therefore become necessary to re-interpret S. Thomas and all the older Scholastics: a task which has called forth much (sometimes amusing) ingenuity but no

---

[3] Hobbes, *Leviathan* i 13; cf. *De cive* xiv 4 (*Opera philos.*, Molesworth, ii 316): lex gentium = lex naturalis civitatum. Pufendorf, *De iure naturae* ii 3, 23; *Elementa* 24. Barbeyrac, note on Grotius, *De iure belli* i 1, 14 (Amst. 1720, p. 18). Burlamaqui, *Principles of Natural Law*, ii 6, 5 (Eng. trans., 1752, p. 195). Austin, *Jurisprudence*, 1869³, i 231. Cf. *Studies,* June, 1918, p. 232.

[4] The Protestant origin of this view is sometimes frankly admitted,—Dmowski, *Institutiones philosophicae*, 1843⁴, § 127 (ii 174); Meyer, *Inst. iuris naturalis*, 1906², i 484 (§572); A. de la Barre, *La morale*, 1911, p. 135. After a search through all the Scholastics accessible I have been able to discover only the following, among writers prior to 1850, who (with certain variations) seem to maintain that *ius gentium* is natural law: S. Antoninus, *Summa theologica* iv 5, 4 (ed. 1740, iv 186) seems to accept Ulpian's view here, but elsewhere (dealing with private property) speaks differently. Montesinus, *Commentaria in primam secundae,* disp. 23, q. 4 n. 57; 1622, ii 543b.; but he seems to admit that the current view is against him. Gamaches, *Summa,* 1634, ii 285. F. Mendoza, *De pactis* iii 1, 1. Devoti, *Institutiones canonicae,* proleg. § 30; 1842, i 22.

real scholarship. Many texts have had to be passed over with discreet silence; in other cases cautious interpolations have had to be made.[5] The plain fact that the unanimous teaching of the School regards the *ius gentium* as positive human law, has never been explained by these modern reactionary writers. "When the denomination of positive is given thereto," writes Liberatore,[6] "the epithet is not taken in the sense of being *ex condicto sive ex communi placito,* but only in the sense of being *posited* by man, though not of his own free will, but by deduction from the principles of the natural law. If any theologian—or even more than one—said the contrary, he is not to be followed." Thus, with a stroke of the pen, six centuries of Scholastic teaching are gracefully deleted: They either did not mean what they said, or else they are not to be followed. Why this eagerness to break with the past? "It must be confessed," says Zigliara,[7] "that among several there are not a few obscurities, which doubtless would not exist, if they lived in our times and heard the ravings of communism." That is, the old teaching concerning the *ius gentium* must be abandoned because it does not suit the new defence of private property.

176
WAR

Charles Macksey [1]

War, in its juridical sense, is a contention carried on by force of arms between sovereign states, or communities having in this regard the right of states. The term is often used for civil strife, sedition, rebellion properly so called, or even for the undertaking of a State to put down by force

---

[5] Thus "S. Thomas understands by *ius gentium* those positive laws which contain *necessary* [a mere interpolation] conclusions from natural law."—Cathrein, *Phil. moralis,* 1915⁹, thesis 43, p. 225. Cf. same writer in *Phil. Jahrbuch* 2 (1889) 373-388. Suarez (*De legibus* ii 17, 8) seems to attribute a similar view to "aliqui moderni Thomistae."

[6] *Principii de economia politica,* 1889, p. 171.

[7] *Phil. moralis,* 1912¹⁵, p. 194. Zigliara also rejects the Scholastic theory of political power and attributes (without proof) "obscurity" to it also (p. 272).

[1] *Catholic Encyclopedia,* vol. XV, pp. 546-550.

organized bodies of outlaws, and in fact there is no other proper word for the struggle as such; but as these are not juridically in the same class with contentions of force between sovereign states, the jurist may not so use the term. However, a people in revolution, in the rare instance of an effort to re-establish civil government which has practically vanished from the community except in name, or to vitalize constitutional rights reserved specifically or residuarily to the people, is conceded to be in like juridical case with a State, as far as protecting its fundamental rights by force of arms. Grote insisted that war was a more or less continuous condition of conflict between those contending by force; and so indeed it is; but even Grote, when seeking to determine the grounds of right and wrong in such a condition, necessarily moved the question back to the right of acts of force in either contending party, and so justified the more accepted juridical definition of a contest at arms between contending states. The juridical condition of the contending parties to the war is spoken of as a state of belligerency, while the term *war* more properly applies to the series of hostile acts of force exercised in the contention. To present here the position of Catholic philosophy in this regard, it will be convenient to discuss in sequence: I, The Existence of the Right of War; II, Its Juridical Source; III, Its Possessor; IV, Its Title and Purpose; V, Its Subject-matter; VI, Its Terms. From these we may gather the idea of a just war.

I. *The Existence of the Right of War.*—The right of war is the right of a sovereign state to wage a contention at arms against another, and is in its analysis an instance of the general moral power of coercion, i. e., to make use of physical force to conserve its rights inviolable. Every perfect right, i. e., every right involving in others an obligation in justice of deference thereto, to be efficacious, and consequently a real and not an illusory power, carries with it at the last appeal the subsidiary right of coercion. A perfect right, then, implies the right of physical force to defend itself against infringement, to recover the subject-matter of right unjustly withheld or to exact its equivalent, and to inflict damage in the exercise of this coercion wherever, as is almost universally the case, coercion cannot be exercised effectively without such damage. The limitations of the coercive right are: that its exercise be necessary; and that damage be not inflicted beyond measure—first of necessity and secondly of proportion with the subject-matter of right at issue. Furthermore, the exercise of coercion is restricted in civil communities to the public authority, for the reason that such restriction is a necessity of the common weal. In like manner the use of force beyond the region of defence and reparation, namely for the imposition of punishment to restore the balance of retributive justice by compensation for the mere violation of law and justice, as well as to assure the future security of the same, is reserved to public authority, for the reason that the State is the natural guardian of law and order, and to permit the individual, even in a matter of personal offence, to be witness, judge, and executioner all at once—human nature being what it is—would be a source of injustice rather than of equitable readjustment.

Now the State has corporate rights of its own which are perfect; it has also the duty to defend its citizens' rights; it consequently has the right of coercion in safeguarding its own and its citizens' rights in case of menace or violation from abroad as well as from at home, not only against foreign individuals, but also against foreign states. Otherwise the duty above indicated would be impossible of fulfilment; the corporate rights of the State would be nugatory, while the individual rights of the citizens would be at the mercy of the outside world. The pressure of such coercion, it is true, may be applied in certain circumstances without both parties going to the extreme of complete national conflict; but when the latter arises, as it commonly will, we have war pure and simple, even as the first application of force is initial warfare. Catholic philosophy, therefore, concedes to the State the full natural right of war, whether defensive, as in case of another's attack in force upon it; offensive (more properly, coercive), where it finds it necessary to take the initiative in the application of force; or punitive, in the infliction of punishment for evil done against itself or, in some determined cases, against others. International law views the punitive right of war with suspicion; but, though it is open to wide abuse, its original existence under the natural law cannot well be disputed.

II. *The Source of the Right of War* is the natural law, which confers upon states, as upon individuals, the moral powers or rights which are the necessary means to the essential purpose set by the natural law for the individual and the State to accomplish. Just as it is the natural law which, with a view to the natural purposes of mankind's creation, has granted its substantial rights to the State, so it is the same law which concedes the subsidiary right of physical coercion in their maintenance, without which none of its rights would be efficacious. The full truth, however, takes into consideration the limitations and extentions of the war-right set by international law in virtue of contract (either implicit in accepted customs or explicit in formal compact) among the nations which are party to international legal obligation. But it must be noted that civilized nations, in their effort to ameliorate the cruel conditions of warfare, have sometimes consented to allow, as the less of two imminent evils, that which is forbidden by the natural law. This is not strictly a right, though it is often so denominated, but an international toleration of a natural wrong. In the common territorial or commercial ambitions of great powers there may be an agreement of mutual toleration of what is pure and simple moral wrong by virtue of the natural law, and that without the excuse of its being a less evil than another to be avoided; in this case the unrighteousness is still more evident, for the toleration itself is wrong. The original determination of the right of war comes from the law of nature only; consent of mankind may manifest the existence of a phase of this law; it does not constitute it.

The agreement of nations may surrender in common a part of the full right and so qualify it; or it may tolerate a limited abuse of it; but such agreement does not confer a particle of the original right itself, nor can it take aught of it away, except by the consent of the nations so deprived. The usage of the better part of the world in such a matter may be argued to bind all nations, but the argument does not conclude convincingly. The decisions of American courts lean towards the proposition of universal obligation; English jurists are not so clearly or generally in its favor. Of course, for that part of the international law bearing on war, which may be justly said to be the natural law as binding nations in their dealings with one another, the existence of which is manifested by the common consent of mankind, there can be no controversy; here the international law is but a name for a part of the natural law. Suarez, it is true, is inclined to seek the right of war as a means not precisely of defence, but of reparation of right and of punishment of violation, from the international law, on the ground that it is not necessary in the nature of things that the power of such rehabilitation and punishment should rest with the aggrieved state (though it should be somewhere on earth), but that mankind has agreed to the individual state method rather than by formation of an international tribunal with adequate police powers. However, the argument given above shows with fair clearness that the power belongs to the aggrieved state, and that though it might have entrusted, and may yet entrust, its exercise to an international arbiter, it is not bound so to do, nor has it done so in the past save in some exceptional cases.

III. *The Possessor of the Right of War.*—The right of war lies solely with the sovereign authority of the State. As it flows from the efficacious character of other rights in peril, the coercive right must belong to the possessor, or to the natural guardian, of those rights. The rights in question may be directly corporate rights of the State, of which, of course, the State is itself the possessor, and of which there is no natural guardian but the sovereign authority of the State; or directly the rights of subordinate parts of the State or even of its individual citizens, and of these the sovereign authority is the natural guardian against foreign aggression. The sovereign authority is the guardian, because there is no higher power on earth to which appeal may be made; and, moreover, in the case of the individual citizen, the protection of his rights against foreign aggression will ordinarily become indirectly a matter of the good of the Commonwealth. It is clear that the right of war cannot become a prerogative of any subordinate power in the state, or of a section, a city, or an individual, for the several reasons: that none such can have the right to imperil the good of all the state (as happens in war) except the juridical guardian of the common good of all: that subordinate parts of the state, as well as the individual citizen, having the supreme authority of the state to which to make appeal, are not in the case of necessity required for the exercise of coercion; finally, that any such right in hands other than those of the sovereign power would upset the peace and order of the whole state. How sovereign authority in matter of war reverts back to the people as a whole in certain circumstances belongs for explanation to the question of revolution. With the supreme power lies also the judicial authority to determine when war is necessary, and what is the necessary and proportionate measure of damage it may therein inflict: there is no other natural tribunal to which recourse may be had, and without this judicial faculty the right of war would be vain.

IV. *The Title and Purpose of War.*—The primary title of a state to go to war is: first, the fact that the state's rights (either directly or indirectly through those of its citizens) are menaced by foreign aggression no otherwise to be prevented than by war; secondly, the fact of actual violation of right not otherwise reparable; thirdly, the need of punishing the threatening or infringing power for the security of the future. From the nature of the proved right these three facts are necessarily just titles, and the state, whose rights are in jeopardy, is itself the judge thereof. Secondary titles may come to a state, first, from the request of another state in peril (or of a people who happen themselves to be in possession of the right); secondly, from the fact of the oppression of the innocent, whose unjust suffering is proportionate to the gravity of war and whom it is impossible to rescue in any other way; in this latter case the innocent have the right to resist, charity calls for assistance, and the intervening state may justly assume the communication of the right of the innocent to exercise extreme coercion in their behalf. Whether a state may find title to interfere for punishment after the destruction of the innocent who were in no wise its own subjects, is not so clear, unless such punishment be a reasonable necessity for the future security of its own citizens and their rights. It has been argued that the extension of a state's punitive right outside of the field of its own subjects would seem to be a necessity of natural conditions; for the right must be somewhere, if we are to have law and order on earth, and there is no place to put it except in the hands of the state that is willing to undertake the punishment. Still, the matter is not so clear as the right to interfere in defence of the innocent.

The common good of the nation is a restricting condition upon the exercise of its right to go to war; but it is not itself a sufficient title for such exercise. Thus the mere expansion of trade, the acquisition of new territory, however beneficial or necessary for a developing state, gives no natural title to wage war upon another state to force that trade upon her, or to extort a measure of her surplus territory, as the common good of one state has no greater right than the common good of another, and each is the judge and guarantee of its own. Much less may a just title be found in the mere need of exercising a standing martial force, of reconciling a people to the tax for its maintenance, or to escape revolutionary trouble at home. Here also it is to be noted that nations cannot draw a parallel from Old-Testament titles. The Israelites lived under a theocracy; God, as supreme lord of all the earth, in specific instances, by the exercise of His supreme dominion, transferred the ownership of alien lands to the Israelites; by His command they waged war to obtain possession of it, and their title to war was the ownership (thus given them) of the land for which they fought. The privation thus wrought upon its prior owners and actual possessors had, moreover, the character of punishment visited upon them by God's order for offences committed against Him. No state can find such title existing for itself under the natural law.

Furthermore, a clear title is limited to the condition that war is necessary as a last appeal. Hence, if there is reasonable ground to think that the offending state will withdraw its menace, repair the injury done, and pay a penalty sufficient to satisfy retributive justice and give a fair guarantee of the future security of juridical order between the two states concerned—all in consequence of proper representation, judicious diplomacy, patient urgency, a mere threat of war, or any other means this side of actual war—then war itself cannot as yet be said to be a necessity, and so, in such premises, lacks full title. A fair opportunity of adjustment must be given, or a reasonable assurance had that the offence will not be rectified except under the stress of war, before the title is just. Whether the aggrieved state should consent to arbitrate differences of judgment before resorting to war, is within its own competency to decide, as the natural law has established no judge but the aggrieved state itself, and international law does not constrain it to transfer its judicial right to any other tribunal, except in so far forth as it has by prior agreement **bound itself so** to do. None the less, when the grievance is not clear, and the public authority has sound reason to think that it can arrange for a tribunal where justice will be done, it would seem that the necessity of war in that individual is not final, and even though international law may leave the state free to refuse all arbitration, the natural law would seem to commend if not to command it. Towards this solution of international differences, in spite of the difficulty of securing an unbiased tribunal, we have in the last fifty years made some progress.

Again, the question of proportion between the damages to be inflicted by war and the value of the national right menaced or violated must enter into consideration for the determination of the full justice of a title. Here we must take into account the consequences of such right being left unvindicated. Nations are prone to go to war for almost any violation of right and its reparation refused. This tendency argues the common conviction that such violation will go from bad to worse, and that, if sovereign right is not recognized in a small thing, it will be far less so in a great. The conviction is not without rational ground; and yet the pride of power and the sensitiveness of national vanity can readily lead, in the excitement of the moment, to a mistaken judgment of a gravity of offence proportionate to all the ills of war. Neither is force a successful means of securing honor, unless it be to assure the due recognition of the rights of the sovereign power behind that honor; while in the calm forum of deliberate reason the loss of one human life outweighs the mere offended vanity of a king or a people. The true proportion between the damage to be inflicted and the right violated is to be measured by whether the loss of right in itself or in its ordinary natural consequences would be morally as great a detriment to the common good of the state aggrieved as the damages which war conducted against the aggressor would entail upon the common good of the same, throwing into the balance against the latter the additional amount of damage due him as the punishment of retributive justice. Finally, a state going to war must weigh its own probable losses in blood and treasure, and its prospect of victory, before it may rightly enter upon a war; for the interests of the common good at home inhibit the exercise of force abroad, unless reasonably calculated not to be an ultimately graver loss to one's own community. This is not properly a limitation of title, but a prudential limitation upon the exercise of a right in the face of full title. The proper purpose of war is indicated by the title, and war conducted for a purpose beyond that contained in a just title is a moral wrong.

V. *The Subject-matter of the Right of War.*—This will cover what may be done by the warring power in exercise of its right. It embraces the infliction of all manner of damage to property and life of the other state and its contending subjects, up to the measure requisite to enforce submission, implying the acceptance of a final readjustment and proportionate penalty; it includes in general all acts that are necessary means to such damage, but is checked by the proviso that neither the damage inflicted nor the means taken involve actions that are intrinsically immoral. In the prosecution of the war, the killing or injuring of non-combatants (women, children, the aged and feeble, or even those capable of bearing arms but as a matter of fact not in any way participating in the war) is consequently barred, except where their simultaneous destruction is an unavoidable accident attending the attack upon the contending force. The wanton destruction of the property of such non-combatants, where it does not or will not minister maintenance or help to the state or its army, is likewise devoid of the requisite condition of necessity. In fact the wanton destruction of the property of the state or of combatants—i. e., where such destruction cannot make for their submission, reparation, or proportionate punishment—is beyond the pale of the just subject-matter of war. The burning of the Capitol and the White House at Washington in 1814, and the devastation of Georgia, South Carolina, and the Valley of the Shenandoah during the American Civil War have not escaped criticism in this category. That "war is hell," in the sense that it inevitably carries with it a maximum of human miseries, is true; in the sense that it justifies anything that makes for the suffering and punishment of a people at war, it cannot be ethically maintained. The defence, that it hastens the close of war through sympathy with the increased suffering of non-combatants, will not stand. The killing of the wounded or prisoners, who thereby have ceased to be combatants, and have rendered submission, is not only no necessity, but beyond the limits of right because of submission, while common charity requires that they be properly cared for.

A doubt might arise about the obligation to spare wounded and prisoners, the guardianship or care of whom would prevent immediate further prosecution of the war at perhaps its most auspicious moment, or their dismissal but replenish the forces of the enemy. The care of the wounded might be waived, as its obligation is not of justice but of charity, which yields to a superior claim of one's own benefit; but the killing of prisoners presents a different problem. All practical doubt in the matter has been removed among civilized nations by the agreements of international law. The canons of the natural law of necessity and proportion this side the limit of intrinsic moral wrong are so hard of application by the contending forces that the history of wars is full of excesses; hence international law has steadily moved towards hard and fast lines that will lessen the waste of human life and the miseries of warfare. Thus the use of ammunition causing excessive destruction of human life or excessive suffering, incurable wounds, or human defacement beyond the requirements for putting the combatants out of the conflict and so winning a battle are excluded by international agreement based upon the obvious limitation of the natural law. Poisoning, as imperilling the innocent beyond measure, and assassination, as associated with treachery and the personal assumption of the right of life and death (to say nothing of its want of a fair opportunity of defence and the cowardice commonly implied therein), have met with common condemnation, thus closing the loophole of obscurity in the natural law. The natural law is clear enough, however, in condemning as intrinsically immoral lying and the direct deception of another, as well as bad faith and treachery. The phrase, "All is fair in love and war," cannot be taken seriously; it is a loose by-word taken from the reckless practices of men, and runs counter to right reason, natural law, and justice. No end justifies an immoral means, and lying, perjury, bad faith, treachery, as well as the direct slaughter of the innocent, wanton destruction, and the lawless pillage and outrage of cruder times, are, as far as the worst of them go, a thing of the past among civilized nations. That states are not always nice in conscience about lying, deceit, and bad faith in war as in diplomacy is a fact to-day; and the defence of lying and deceit in the stratagems of war, where good faith or common convention is not violated, is a sequence of the erroneous doctrine of Grote that lying is not intrinsically immoral, but only wrong in as far as those with whom we deal have a right to demand the truth of us; but as such teaching is almost unanimously repudiated in Catholic philosophy, the practice has to-day in Catholic thought no ethical advocate. The hanging of spies, though commonly said to be merely a measure of menace against a peculiar peril of war, would seem to have behind it a remote suggestion of punishment of a form of deceit which is intrinsically wrong.

In the terms of readjustment after victory, the victorious state, if its cause is just, may exact full reparation of the original injustice suffered, full compensation for all its own losses by reason of the war, proportionate penalty to secure the future not only against the conquered state, but, through fear of such penalty, even against other possible hostile states. In the execution of such judgment the killing of surviving contestants or their enslavement, though, absolutely speaking, these might fall within the measure of just punishment, would to-day seem to be an extreme penalty, and the practice of civilization has abolished it. Here we are confronted with the appalling destruction of the vanquished in the Old Testament wars, where frequently all the adult males were slain after defeat and surrender, and sometimes even the women and children, unto utter extermination. But we cannot argue natural right from these instances, for, where justly done, this wholesale slaughter was the direct command of God, the sovereign Arbiter of life and death, as well as the just Judge of all reward and punishment. God by revelation made the Israelites but executioners of His supernatural sentence; the penalty was within God's right to assign, and within the Israelites' communicated right to enforce. The natural law gives man the right to no such measure. The appropriation of a part of the territory of the vanquished may quite readily be a necessity of payment for reparation of injury and loss, and even the entire subjection of the conquered state, as a part of, or tributary to, its conqueror, may possibly fall within the proportionate requirements for full reparation or for future security, and, if so, such subjection is within the competency of the last adjudication. The history of nations, however, would indicate that this exaction was enforced far oftener than it was justified by proportionate necessity.

VI. *The Term of the Right of War* is the nation against which war can justly be waged. It must be juridically in the wrong, i. e., it must have violated a perfect right of another state, or at least be involved in an attempt at such violation. Such a perfect right is one based upon strict justice between states, and so grounding an obligation in justice in the State against which war is to be waged. Here there is call for a distinction between the obligation of an ethical and a juridical duty. A juridical duty supposes a right in another which is violated by the State's neglect to fulfil that duty; not so a merely ethical duty, for this is one proceeding from some other foundation than justice, and so implies no right in another which is violated by the non-fulfilment of the duty. The foundation of the right of war is a right violated or threatened, not a mere ethical duty neglected. No State, any more than an individual, may use violence to enforce its neighbor's performance of the latter. Hence a foreign state may have a duty to develop its resources not for its own immediate or particular need alone, but out of universal comity to help the prosperity of other states, for one community is bound to another by charity as are individuals; but there is in another state no right to that development founded in justice. To assume that one state has the right to make war upon another to force it to develop its own resources is to assume that each state holds its own possessions in trust for the human race at large, with a strict right to share in its usufruct inhering in each other state in particular—an assumption that yet awaits proof. So, too, the need of one state of more territory for its overplus of population gives it no right to seize the superabundant and undeveloped territory of another.

In the case of extreme necessity, parallel to that of a starving man, where there is no other remedy except forced sale or seizure of the territory in question, there would be something upon which to base an argument, and the case may be conceived, but seems far from arising. Similarly, a government's neglect of a juridical duty towards its own people of itself gives no natural right to a foreign state to interfere, save only in the emergency, extreme and rare enough, where the people would have the right of force against its government and by asking aid from abroad would communicate in part the exercise of this coercive right to the succoring power. Lastly, in the case of a state's wholesale persecution of the innocent with death or unjust enslavement, a foreign power taking up their cause may fairly be said reasonably to assume the call of these and to make use of their right of resistance.

In conclusion, a war, to be just, must be waged by a sovereign power, for the security of a perfect right of its own (or of another justly invoking its protection) against foreign violation in a case where there is no other means available to secure or repair the right; and must be conducted with a moderation which, in the continuance and settlement of the struggle, commits no act intrinsically immoral, nor exceeds in damage done, or in payment and in penalty exacted, the measure of necessity and of proportion to the value of the right involved, the cost of the war, and the guarantee of future security.

177
WAR
Alfred O'Rahilly [1]

It were greatly to be desired that Catholic thinkers could be more successful in "popularising" the Catholic "way of looking at law," for the world would thereby regain a sound philosophy of war. So long as law is held to be essentially bounded by state-frontiers, so long as international forces such as the Church and Labour are regarded as inimical to states, so long as inter-state agreements merely concern the

[1] *Studies*, June, 1918. (Dublin.)

balance of power and the interest of trade, there is no room for the theory which represents war, not as the normal recognized institution for international adjustments and foreign policy, but as the ultimate procedure in supranational criminal procedure. The chief difference between the two views lies just in this that the medieval theory explains war as an extreme judicial act executed in accordance with principles sanctioned by humanity, whereas nowadays war has come to be regarded as the supreme assertion of sovereign power swayed not by laws but by prudential considerations.

This difference in outlook is not merely academic, it leads to a radical diversity of practical moral judgments. For instance, how many wars could be pronounced just if extension of territory were ruled out as justificatory motive? [2] if the sole licit cause be the infliction of a grave injustice not otherwise rectifiable? According to Suarez,[3] it is a pagan error "to think that the rights of kingdoms are based on arms and that war may be declared in order to win fame and riches." "The Romans," he remarks elsewhere, "believed that the wars which they waged against their enemies were just on both sides; for they wished to fight, as it were, with the tacit agreement that the winner should be master." Again, how would our present-day slaughter abide the test laid down by Victoria and other writers?

No war is just [he says [4]] if it is admitted that it involves more harm than good to the State, even though on other counts there are titles and reasons for a just war. . . . Indeed, since one State is a part of the whole, and especially a Christian province is part of the whole State, if a war is useful for one province or state, yet harmful to the world or to Christendom, then I believe that by that very fact the war is unjust.

Yet this seems not only a humane proposition but a logical conclusion from the Scholastic theory.

A still more important inference is the necessity for impartial investigation to justify war as a judicial act. "For a just war," says the great Spanish Dominican already

---

[2] Victoria, *Rel. theol.*, vi, 3, 2: Non est iusta causa belli amplificatio imperii. Contrast Dante, *De monarchia*, ii, 7-10.
[3] *De bello*, iv, *init.;* vii, 9.
[4] *Rel. theol.*, iii, 13. Also Navarro, *Manuale confessariorum*, xxv, 9; Vazquez, *disp.*, 64, *c.* 3, *n.* 10.

cited,[5] "the justice and causes of war must be examined with great diligence and also the reasons of the adversaries must be heard if they wish to discuss fairly." His disciple Bannez is still more emphatic.[6]

The ruler is bound to examine most carefully, by himself and through others, into the causes of a just war, also availing of the advice of wise men.

(1) A ruler who declares war is acting as the judge in a most serious case. . . . But the judge is bound to inquire and examine carefully into the case in order to pass sentence. . . . Therefore, the ruler is bound to inquire carefully into the case for the other ruler who is neither cited to judgment nor defends himself . . .

(2) In criminal charges against citizens the judge ought to proceed with the greatest care. But war is an act of vindicative justice in a most serious criminal case. Therefore, there ought to be a most careful examination . . .

If the ruler who declares war cannot by himself examine the justice of the war without consulting the other ruler, he is bound to send ambassadors to him to ask that the whole case be investigated by judicial arbitrators.

Again, all this is but a corollary from the Catholic theory —but how painfully unpractical and idealistic it sounds! The very idea of any such judicial procedure does not exist; whole nations rush to war without seeking to assure themselves that their cause is just or even what exactly that cause is. Contrast, for instance, the elaborate impartial proceedings which mark a great trial such as the Tichborne or even an investigation into some railway accident, with the secret machinations, underhand plotting and concocted frenzy which usher in a world-devastating war fraught with death and torture for millions of our fellow-men. The literal truth is, of course, that nowadays there is immeasurably more judicial and impartial investigation in trying the case of a single criminal than in declaring war on a whole people. The judicial concept of war is practically defunct.

It was not always thus. A slight acquaintance with English constitutional history—in this matter the precedent

---

[5] *Rel. theol.*, vi, 3, 21.
[6] In 2-2, q. 40, a. 1, *dub.* 5, *concl.* 1 and 2 (Duaci 1615, p. 528 *sq.*).

for other nations [7]—will show us the gradual transfer of questions concerning peace and war from the judiciary to the legislative assembly and finally to the all-powerful executive: in other words, from Privy Council to Parliament, from Parliament to Cabinet. We have almost forgotten that there was a time when the Lord Chancellor, as the highest legal authority, was responsible in transactions with foreign States, when the Privy Council, independent of political parties and of the Crown, exercised important functions of which a remnant still exists in its Judicial Committee.

In the Act of Settlement of 1701 there was an attempt to re-establish the Council by the enactment that "all matters and things relating to the well-governing of this kingdom, which are properly cognisable in the Privy Council by the laws and customs of this realm, shall be transacted there and all resolutions taken thereupon shall be signed by such of the Privy Council as shall advise and consent to the same." With the repeal of this provision six years later and with the gradual obsolescence of the right of impeaching ministers, the powers of peace and war finally fell into the hands of an irresponsible executive, where, in spite of much fine talk of democratic control, they still remain.[8] The most solemn and serious judicial act that any nation can perform—a declaration of war against another community of human beings—is still shrouded in the mists of secret diplomacy, is initiated by a handful of partisans, is

[7] For France the Ministry has no power to dissolve the House, and even for Foreign Affairs there is an independent Committee.

[8] What is called the collective responsibility of the English Cabinet—established since the second Rockingham ministry of 1782—is merely a euphemism for the threat or compact of collective resignation. Every member of the Privy Council signed his name to the minutes, and had to accept individual responsibility for his recommendations. Burnet (*History of My Own Time,* v 24) said of the Act of Settlement: "No man would be a privy councillor on those terms"—a remark which is eloquent testimony to the pleasant irresponsibility of Cabinet government. As to impeachment this is the opinion of Burke: "If the constitution should be deprived—I do not mean in form but virtually—of this resource, it is virtually deprived of everything else that is valuable in it. For this process is the cement which binds the whole together, this it is which makes England what England is." See D. Urquhart, *The Four Wars of the French Revolution,* 1874.

pursued for undiscoverable or unjustifiable objects, and is paid for by the sacrifice of all that is precious and noble in life. It is obvious that such summary and secret procedure is a mere travesty of international justice and is utterly at variance with the theory which assimilates war to an act of deliberate criminal jurisdiction.

How far, then, it may be asked, is the individual citizen responsible for the justice or injustice of war? This question was carefully discussed by the theologians of the sixteenth century. In his *Quaestiones quodlibeticae* (1521) Pope Hadrian VI laid down the principle that "no one can act against his own view at the command of a superior, even though he knows that there is a probable doubt that the command is licit." [9] This proposition, especially as applied to war, raised a storm of controversy; and its elucidation helped to fix those principles of probabilism which are now largely accepted in moral theology. It will suffice here to state the general conclusion that a merely speculative doubt does not render the conscience doubtful, and that in forming one's conscience practically the private individual can accept authority as a probable argument. Bannez thus sums up the result of the discussion: [1]

(1) If soldiers neither doubt of the justice of the war nor yet know the causes of its justice, they are not bound to investigate the matter; they can presume that their rulers are conscientious Christians, and have just reasons . . .

(2) Those soldiers who are ready for any war in any circumstances, without attending to the justice or injustice of the cause, but to where the pay is more or less, are in the state of mortal sin, and cannot be absolved by confessors . . .

(3) If soldiers are ready to engage only in a just war, whether they are subjects or not, they can follow a ruler whom they know to be a Christian man who is inflicting injustice on no one.

It is clear that there could be no discipline if every soldier had to make personal investigation into decisions of war; extrinsic authority must, to a large extent, guide the individual. As Bellarmine says:

Subjects must obey a superior and ought not to discuss his

---

[9] q. 2, *punct.* 3 (Lugd., 1546, p. 40a).
[1] In 2-2, q. 40, a. 1, *dub.* 6, *post concl.* 3 (Duaci 1615, p. 532).

commands, but rather they should presume that a good ruler
has a good cause, unless they clearly know the contrary; just
as when the guilt of an individual is doubtful, the judge who
condemns him sins, but not the executioner who puts the condemned man to death, for the executioner is not bound to
discuss the sentence of the judge.²

But it is important to observe that this case for submission is based entirely on the extrinsic moral authority of
the ruler; it is exactly proportional to the validity of the
assumption that the government is actuated by Christian
principles. Shatter this assumption and the entire case for
submission without personal investigation vanishes. The
argument for discipline and obedience is completely coun-
terbalanced by the presumption that the organisation is
being employed for unjustifiable ends. It would surely be
rather absurd to apply to a modern army a principle which
finds application only in a religious order,³ and this too
in a momentous decision concerning the lives of thousands.
In the present anti-Christian environment of war it is vital
to assert this right of conscience for that small minority
who take seriously the question of the liceity of war.

Moreover, this maxim—namely that the individual subject may take part in a doubtfully just war if lawfully
commanded to do so—was enunciated for the guidance of
soldiers and conscripts; it cannot be used by those who, as
officers or volunteers, freely elect to take part in a war.
"Those who are not obliged to fight," says Cardinal Bellarmine, "cannot with a safe conscience join in a war unless
they know it to be just." Their action being purely voluntary, they cannot transfer their individual responsibility to
anyone else. "If," says Suarez,⁴ "the reasons showing the

² *De laicis,* iii, 15. So also the Canon Law (in Sexto, de regulis
iuris, reg. 25): Quod quis mandato facit iudicis, dolo facere non
videtur cum habeat parere necesse.

³ *Summarium Constitutionum S. J.*, 31: voluntatem et iudicium
suum cum eo quod superior vult et sentit, in omnibus ubi peccatum
non cerneretur omnino conformantes.

⁴ *De bello,* vi, 9. With all due deference to the authority of Cardinal Wiseman, I am unable to reconcile a dictum of his with the
principles enunciated by canonists and schoolmen. The so-called
Chinese War of 1857 having broken out when a youth was on the
point of entering the English army, his father became uneasy
because, as he considered the war unjust, he did not know if he
should be doing right in allowing his son to enter. The Cardinal

war to be unjust are such that they cannot answer them, they are bound in some way to investigate the truth, though this burden must not be lightly imposed unless these reasons render the justice of the war very doubtful." The idea which has since become current, that men may join in a war simply for the sake of pay and allowances, without seriously considering the justice or injustice of the war, found no favour with the Schoolmen. Such men, says Cardinal Cajetan,[5] "are outside the range of conscience and are manifestly in a state of eternal damnation." It is clear, therefore, that no one can freely join in a war without having reasonably satisfied himself that the war is, in the strict canonical sense, a just war.[6]

Besides the supreme authority of the State (on which I have not deemed it necessary to dwell) and the justice of the cause in the sense explained, Catholic philosophy insists on a third condition for a justifiable war, namely, a right intention.[7] For, says Bellarmine,

was consulted, and replied as follows: "I do not see that you have anything to do with your private opinion about the justice of a particular war, in deciding your son's going into the army. You may freely let him obtain his commission as soon as possible." Similarly, Sir W. Butler wrote (*Autobiography*, p. 219): "The soldier of to-day has to be content with what he can get, and the gift war-horse which the Stock Exchange is now able to bestow upon him must not be examined too severely in the mouth."

[5] *Summula,* s.v. "bellum" (Duaci, 1627, p. 30).

[6] Suarez, *De bello,* iv, 9, points out that if a king has several kingdoms under him, he cannot declare war on behalf of one to the detriment of the other. "Not all States subject to the same king," he says (*ibid.,* ii, 4), "are incomplete in themselves, for their union may happen *per accidens*—as is shown by diversity of laws and taxes, etc. . . . If such a State is complete, it has power against its king." It follows that if one of such united kingdoms engages in a war, the other is not thereby bound, though its subjects may volunteer or the nation itself may join the war, after investigation into its justice. There is no need to consider here the question of conscription, for it follows from the principles explained in a former article, that this supreme political act requires the free consent of the whole community.

[7] St. Thomas, 2-2, q. 40, a. 1; also, for instance, Major, 4 sent., d. 15, q. 20 (fol. 117c) and Bellarmine, *De laicis,* iii, 15. John Major and Bellarmine have a fourth condition: *moderamen* or *modus debitus.* Suarez (*De bello,* i, 7) omits the intention, presumably as an internal element not falling under human judgment, and substitutes: ut servetur debitus modus et aequalitas in illius initio, prosecutione et victoria.

Since the end of war is public peace in tranquility, it is not lawful to wage war for any other end. Hence, not only kings but soldiers sin gravely, if they undertake war to injure others, to extend their empire, or to practice warlike courage, or for any other cause except the common good—even though neither legitimate authority nor a just cause be lacking.

A war may, therefore, be undertaken for a just cause and yet in course of time may cease to be a righteous war, inasmuch as it has become diverted to selfish ends, the wanton infliction of injury or the conquest of territory.[8] And a war, even though just in itself, may be waged unjustly, not only by the perpetration of cruelty and outrage but also by degeneracy into mere blood-lust. I am not here concerned with enumerating the brutalities and horrors of war, but it will be worth while to dwell for a moment on the *intentio bellantium recta* postulated by St. Thomas. How far is such a condition or criterion observed in practice? The long record of wars begun with generous enthusiasm and much parade of high principles but degenerating into orgies of hatred, greed and conquest, is an eloquent answer. And, as far as the individual combatants are concerned, one has but to read the memoirs of some soldier—Moltke, de Marbot, Roberts—or first-hand descriptions of some recent campaigns. In its lowest form the "intention" is merely the expression of savage passion,[9] in its highest it is the keen relish of the sportsman; but of any reference to high moral ideals we shall find singularly little trace. Here, for instance, are some typical citations from Wolseley's *Story of a Soldier's Life:*

Our whole battalion was composed of young men full of life and spirit, and impressed with the one idea that the world was specially created for their own wild pleasures, of which to most of us war, with all its sudden changes, and at times its maddening excitement, was the greatest (i, 228f).

When peace came in 1856, I may truthfully assert that very

---

[8] St. Thomas, *loc. cit.*: Potest autem contingere ut sit legitima auctoritas indicentis bellum et causa iusta, nihilominus propter pravam intentionem bellum reddatur illicitum.

[9] "Men will rob and pillage and rape and burn in war who would have lived very passable and decent lives in peace; many of them think that it is part of the business."—Sir W. Butler, *Autob.*, p. 199. To "the lower sort of the soldier mind . . . war means plunder, it has always done so, and it will always do so."—*ibid*, p. 236.

many in our army regretted it much, for we felt that whilst at the final assault the French had won . . . we had failed . . . I remember how sad I felt when the peace was announced (i, 212).

Running through the character of all the best soldiers I have known in our army, there is the love of national glory. . . . It becomes eventually a sort of national religion, and a veritable and powerful force in the character of a people. From this force springs the national ambition that makes all grades, the old and young, to wish their State to grow strong and powerful (ii, 374 f).

What a supremely delightful moment it was! . . . There can be nothing else in the world like it or that can approach its inspiration, its intense sense of pride. You are for the time being—and it is always short—lifted up from and out of all petty thoughts of self; and for the moment your whole existence, soul and body, seems to revel in a true sense of glory. . . . Oh! that I could again hope to experience such sensations! (i, 69 f—referring to his leading a storming party in Burmah, 1853).

It is only through experience of the sensation that we learn how intense, even in anticipation, is the rapture-giving delight which the attack upon an enemy affords (ii, 25).

These quotations, selected almost at random, give us a vivid idea of militarist psychology at its best. That such a mentality, however appropriate to salmon-fishing, motor-racing or big game hunting, is utterly unworthy of the dread responsibility of killing human beings, needs no proof to anyone who accepts the Catholic view of war outlined in this article. But, it may be asked, does the world seriously accept this idealistic theory so seemingly at variance with actual war? Perhaps not in its entirety; so much the worse for the world. I am not greatly concerned to prove that the theory does fit actual wars. Is it not an inspiring help to all lovers of humanity to find that the Church, even at the zenith of her political power, upheld such a high and noble ideal of a just war? Some there are, indeed, who go further and condemn all wars as essentially evil. But Catholic thinkers, ever in touch with the realities of human nature, have never condemned the use of physical coercion when necessary for the maintenance of justice. That does not mean that war is exalted as a positive ideal of unmixed good. The Scholastics' view, which relegates warfare to the region of criminal jurisdiction, attempts to control and sanctify what is necessary in our present stage of culture, without, however, forfeiting our claim to a higher and more Christian ideal. There was a time, let us not forget, when chattel slavery, albeit mitigated and reformed, was upheld by Christianity in so far as spasmodic individual revolt against the institution was not encouraged. The Catholic view of war is, like the Christian condonation of slavery, an *interim ethic*, a carefully limited permission of the lesser of two evils. It does not lie within the power of individuals to revolutionise fundamental social ideals and institutions. In such matters humanity must move as a whole; and, meanwhile, by striving towards a higher ideal in practice, the Church is sowing the seed-thoughts of a better age. There will come a time, let us hope, when the war of man with man will be replaced by an ideal, prematurely and partially imposed in the early middle ages—The Truce of God.[1]

178

AIR-RAIDS, THE SINKING OF MERCHANT VESSELS, AND REPRISALS

MICHAEL CRONIN [2]

Arising out of the distinction of combatants and non-combatants, is the question whether air-raids and the sinking of merchant and passenger vessels are lawful.

Air-raids upon fortifications, arsenals, military barracks, munition factories, and other belligerent institutions and places are lawful, provided every care is taken to spare the lives and property of non-combatants. But *indiscriminate* air-raids upon cities like London, Manchester, Cologne or

---

[1] In this brief article I have touched on so vast a subject that I cannot be sure of having made myself clear. I meant to convey the unanimous view of the Schoolmen that war is justifiable *only when unavoidable*, when the adversary is unwilling to negotiate and to discuss. Thus Suarez (*De bello,* iv i): Causa haec iusta et sufficiens est *gravis iniuria illata quae alia ratione vindicari aut reparari nequit.* The progress of civilisation consists in substituting *aliae rationes*—other means of redressing injustice.

[2] *The Science of Ethics,* vol. II, pp. 672-674. (Benziger Brothers, New York.)

Berlin are quite unlawful. For, first, such raids are obviously undertaken, not in order to kill enemy troops, but as a part of the general policy of "frightfulness," the policy, viz., of inspiring non-combatants with fear, and so undermining the *morale* of the enemy State. Such raids, therefore, are undertaken directly with a view to the death and destruction of non-combatants, their death being desired as a means to the lowering of the public *morale*. It is impossible to think that air-raids, which are always expensive and always dangerous to the raiders, would be undertaken for the mere off-chance of killing the few enemy soldiers that might happen to be abroad at the time of the raid. Secondly, lawful indirect killing always requires some proportion between the good expected from one's act and the deaths which occur. And, therefore, even if what is aimed at directly in these air-raids is the killing of a few soldiers, the *indiscriminate* air-raids are quite unlawful, for there is no justifying proportion between the chance killing of a few enemy soldiers on the one hand (a chance that can hardly ever be realized) and the certain death of many non-combatant citizens on the other.

The sinking of food ships destined for the enemy is not disallowed in natural law, since it is the soldiers in the field that have the first call upon all incoming supplies, and it is lawful to deprive them of these supplies. To sink passenger vessels or liners, carrying munitions of war or engaged in some other belligerent mission, is lawful, provided that all that is possible is done to save the lives of the passengers. To sink passenger vessels not engaged on any mission of war is wholly disallowed; and, if loss of life occurs, the act is to be regarded as an act of sheer and unadulterated murder.

We may define reprisals as any act of retaliation upon an enemy in which an equivalent evil is inflicted for damage sustained, for instance, an air-raid by the British on Cologne to balance the German air-raids on London and Scarborough. Are these acts of retaliation lawful? Our answer is that reprisals are lawful where the evil that is perpetrated on either side is evil by reason of treaty only and not by reason of natural law. If one party to a treaty ceases to abide by its terms it is no longer to be regarded as binding on the other party. Thus, the use of poisonous gases by one belligerent justifies their use by another opposed belligerent, these things being excluded by treaty only. But where the evil that is perpetrated by one of the belligerents is evil by reason of natural law, reprisals are wholly unlawful. What is evil by natural law remains evil, even though the natural law should be ignored, and the forbidden practices indulged, by one of the parties. It is forbidden, for instance, by natural law to kill non-combatants, and so, just as A could not kill B's child because B had killed A's child, so also it would be quite unlawful for England in the great war to make air-raids upon German cities because her own cities had been raided by Germany. Any satisfaction which is sought should be sought either at the expense of the enemy forces, they being the responsible parties, or by way of indemnity from the whole nation after the war.

179

THE BOMBARDMENT OF TOWNS AND REPRISALS

WALTER McDONALD [1]

1. *The Difficulty.*—On the supposition that war may be justly waged, there can be no scruple about killing those of the enemy who attack you—soldiers actually fighting or about to fight. They are aggressors; unjust, as we suppose; and, therefore, may be killed. It matters not that they are in good faith; as one may kill a lunatic, when there is no other way of saving oneself from his attack.

The difficulty about war arises from non-combatants, who suffer so much, in any case, many losing their lives. It is, no doubt, open to you to say that all who belong to the enemy nation co-operate in the unjust aggression, and so are liable to be killed. "The young men shall go to the battle,—it is their task to conquer; the married men shall forge arms, transport baggage and artillery, provide subsistence; the women shall work at soldiers' clothes, make tents, serve in the hospitals; the children shall scrape old linen into surgeon's lint; the aged men shall have themselves

---

[1] *Some Ethical Questions of Peace and War*, pp. 176-182. (Burns, Oates and Washbourne, London.)

carried into public places, and there by their words, excite the courage of the young, preach hatred to kings, and unity to the Republic." So wrote Barrère, in a Report that was afterwards embodied in a Decree, during the French Revolution; as may be seen in Carlyle.[2]

During the late war, everyone in the belligerent nations co-operated with the fighting men in some way. The ploughman who turned the glebe in Kerry, did so to grow potatoes or grain; which, if not sent to the British armies, served to feed those for whom Great Britain would have had to make provision otherwise. Your Kerry ploughman, therefore, was a belligerent; as surely,—though, perhaps, not so efficaciously or persistently,—as those who forged guns at Woolwich or Essen, or brought up shells to the batteries in the field.

2. *May Co-operators be Slain?*—Something like this was urged in *The Tablet*, in support of the view that it is in no way wrong to make air-raids on German towns. An Indian chief, it was argued, may be shot for attacking you; and why not the squaw who, in his tent, prepares his arrows; and his son, who is still too young to do more than carry the arrows from the tent to the fighting line? Why not, similarly, rain bombs on the women and children of Germany? We read this sort of reasoning in *The Tablet*.

The conscience of mankind is against it. Even the ex-Kaiser, Wilhelm, after an air-raid on Frankfurt, was reported to have written to the Mayor, to condole with the citizens, and protest against the barbarism of dropping bombs on open towns. London was always represented by the Germans as a fortress; wherein women and children stayed at their peril, and might be killed with safe conscience. One does not know which was the more inconsistent: the Catholic publicist who would bomb German cities, in reprisal for air-raids on London; or the Kaiser, who ordered or sanctioned the London raids, but protested that Frankfurt should be spared. When the danger approached themselves, both showed the true conscience of the race.

I deem it an enormity to say that, because a ploughman helps to grow corn that may feed those who supply an army; or because his little daughter knits or darns his stock-

---

[2] *French Revolution*, III, b. iv, ch. vi.

ings, his wife prepares his food, or his baby sucks taxed sugar; any or all of them may be put to death for co-operation in unjust aggression. If that were so, the citizens even of neutral states would not escape liability.

Accordingly, the principle that one may kill an unjust aggressor can be extended to co-operators only on condition that the co-operation is proximate and considerable.

3. *Grade of Proximity Difficult to Determine.*—So understood, the principle, I admit, is indeterminate; nor do I see any definite line whereat to draw the amount of co-operation that would or would not justify killing. Extreme cases are easily decided. You may, for instance, shell a train that is bringing supplies to the firing line; but may not kill the wife of the driver merely because in some far-off cottage she knits a comforter for her husband. You may drop bombs on the works at Essen or the arsenal at Woolwich; but should spare the home of the miner who helps to supply these places with coal or steel.

How near either mineral must be to the war zone and actual aggression, no man can say—with mathematical determination. I should not object to the bombing of a munition train leaving Calais, or even Woolwich; but I do not think you would be justified in bombing a train that leaves some Welsh mine with coal destined ultimately for the British fleet. There must necessarily be a belt of disputable territory between the extremes of certainty—lawful or unlawful—in matters of this kind.

4. *May such Non-Combatants be Killed Indirectly?*— There is, however, another principle on which, perhaps, one might be justified in taking the life of that Kerry ploughman or that knitting woman: indirectly, as it is phrased. An airman drops a bomb on plough or cottage, as is his right; even though, with either, ploughman or housewife should be blown to pieces. Though sorry for their fate, duty to his country requires the airman to proceed; to bomb the next cottage or plough, with whoever may, unfortunately, be near. You would not forbid a commander to fire on a fortress, even though some women or children should be killed therein.

I would not; and yet I would not allow him to fire on that plough, lest he should kill the ploughman; even though he might smash it to his heart's content, were there no danger for the man. There must be some proportion between the good you attain and the evil you do in attaining it; as also between the chances or danger of doing either. If an apple were so placed as, if shot at, to endanger merely a pane of glass, even an unskilled archer might take the risk; but, on the head of a child, it needed all the skill of Tell to justify the bowman. You may run down and kill a man to save your life, but not to save a trifling sum of money. I cannot believe the slaughter of a number of innocent London citizens justified by damage done to one of its railway termini: with the seat of war in Eastern France.

5. *Air-Raids and Long-Range Guns.*—Those who drop bombs on cities, from air-ships or aeroplanes, are often not justified in doing so, even though they aim at some arsenal or other legitimate object of attack; for lack of proportion between the good and the evil they are likely to do. Allow that the action would be right, if the airman was certain to hit the arsenal, or even if he had anything like a good chance of success. Often, however, they are up so high that, what with the rapidity of their motion, there is little or no chance of their hitting anything in particular beneath; and it takes a good deal to justify this. I do not say that it is never justifiable; if you suppose the good in view to be very great indeed, and the non-combatant population beneath sparse; as it often is near the front lines, where the probability of injury is proportionately small.

The same applies to bombardment with long-range guns, such as the Germans used against Paris. It is out of question, manifestly, to direct a shell from such great distances, —seventy miles or more,—so that there would be any real hope of injuring a combatant, or gun, or fort, or some one who, as proximate co-operator in the war, may be killed on that account. The most you can do is hit the city somewhere; with the practical certainty of taking innocent lives. Catholic ethics does not allow this, as I understand the science.

6. *Reprisals.*—When London and other English towns were being bombarded from the air, with no little loss of life and limb to the non-combatant citizens, a number of public men advocated reprisals in kind, as the only effectual way of bringing the Germans to anything like a sense of

the wickedness of their conduct. The French, I understand, threatened reprisals from the beginning; and carried out the threat. In time the English followed; claiming, as a rule, to direct their bombs only at legitimate objects of attack; but it is to be feared, letting them fall at times from heights at which it was impossible to give them any such direction. Others advocated slaughter of non-combatants by way of reprisal for the delight that was shown, as reported, even by the women of Germany, at the destruction wrought by the air-raids on English cities.

Here, again, it is not for ethical science to adjudicate on the fact—whether and how far the Germans rejoiced in this way. Let us suppose they did. The question is, how proximately they co-operated thereby in the raids, or in others that might follow. Was it so proximate as to justify the English in killing those German women, as unjust aggressors?

I find it hard to believe it; so that, in my opinion, neither the women of Germany nor the non-combatant men,—nor, above all, the children,—could be killed on that score. Reprisal, therefore, was unlawful, in so far as it meant killing such people by any shot or bomb that would not be otherwise justified.

It was hard, no doubt, on the French and English; but so it would be if one's house were attacked and one's wife and children slain by an armed band of robbers. Kill them in punishment if you can; but it were barbarous surely if, when you cannot reach the murderers themselves, you make it even with them by killing their wives and children; and not only morality but civilization would collapse.

180

INTERNATIONAL RELATIONS [1]

Though men are divided into various nationalities by reason of geographical position or historical vicissitude, the progress of civilization facilitates intercourse and, normally, brings about the exchange of good offices between people

[1] *Pastoral Letter of the Archbishops and Bishops of the United States,* 1919. (N. C. W. C., Washington, D. C.)

and people. War, for a time, suspends these friendly relations; but eventually it serves to focus attention upon them and to emphasize the need of readjustment. Having shared in the recent conflict, our country is now engaged with international problems and with the solution of these on a sound and permanent basis. Such a solution, however, can be reached only through the acceptance and application of moral principles. Without these, no form of agreement will avail to establish and maintain the order of the world.

Since God is the Ruler of nations no less than of individuals, His law is supreme over the external relations of states as well as in the internal affairs of each. The sovereignty that makes a nation independent of other nations, does not exempt it from its obligations toward God; nor can any covenant, however shrewdly arranged, guarantee peace and security, if it disregard the divine commands. These require that in their dealings with one another, nations shall observe both justice and charity. By the former, each nation is bound to respect the existence, integrity and rights of all other nations; by the latter, it is obliged to assist other nations with those acts of beneficence and good will which can be performed without undue inconvenience to itself. From these obligations a nation is not dispensed by reason of its superior civilization, its industrial activity or its commercial enterprise; least of all, by its military power. On the contrary, a state which possesses these advantages, is under a greater responsibility to exert its influence for the maintenance of justice and the diffusion of good will among all peoples. So far as it fulfills its obligation in this respect, a state contributes its share to the peace of the world: it disarms jealousy, removes all ground for suspicion and replaces intrigue with frank co-operation for the general welfare.

The growth of democracy implies that the people shall have a larger share in determining the form, attributions and policies of the government to which they look for the preservation of order. It should also imply that the calm deliberate judgment of the people, rather than the aims of the ambitious few, shall decide whether, in case of international disagreement, war will be the only solution. Knowing that the burdens of war will fall most heavily on them, the people will be slower in taking aggressive measures, and, with an adequate sense of what charity and justice require, they will refuse to be led or driven into conflict by false report or specious argument. Reluctance of this sort is entirely consistent with firmness for right and zeal for national honor. If it were developed in every people, it would prove a more effectual restraint than any craft of diplomacy or economic prudence. The wisest economy in fact would be exercised by making the principles of charity and justice an essential part of education. Instead of planning destruction, intelligence would then discover new methods of binding the nations together; and the good will which is now doing so much to relieve the distress produced by war, would be so strengthened and directed as to prevent the recurrence of international strife.

One of the most effectual means by which states can assist one another is the organization of international peace. The need of this is more generally felt at the present time when the meaning of war is so plainly before us. In former ages also the nations realized the necessity of compacts and agreements whereby the peace of the world would be secured. The success of these organized efforts was due, in large measure, to the influence of the Church. The position of the Holy See and the office of the Sovereign Pontiff as Father of Christendom, were recognized by the nations as powerful factors in any undertaking that had for its object the welfare of all. A "Truce of God" was not to be thought of without the Vicar of Christ; and no other truce could be of lasting effect. The Popes have been the chief exponents, both by word and act, of the principles which must underlie any successful agreement of this nature. Again and again they have united the nations of Europe, and history records the great services which they rendered in the field of international arbitration and in the development of international law.

The unbroken tradition of the Papacy with respect to international peace, has been worthily continued to the present by Pope Benedict XV. He not only made all possible efforts to bring the recent war to an end, but was also one of the first advocates of an organization for the preservation of peace. In his Letter to the American people on the last day of the year 1918, the Holy Father expressed his hope and desire for an international organization, "which by abolishing conscription will reduce armaments, by establishing international tribunals will eliminate or settle disputes, and by placing peace on a solid foundation will guarantee to all independence and equality of rights."

181

INTERNATIONAL PEACE

John A. Ryan [1]

There are persons who admit that the plight of Europe is due immediately to violations of charity by European statesmen, but who go back of the immediate cause and raise the question why the rulers of so many European states fell into such grossly uncharitable courses. Why did not Christian teaching prove sufficiently vital to impel the statesmen to avoid the war? Does not the conduct of European political leaders during the last century show that Christianity has failed?

Here we have the assumption that Christianity has been really tried. Condemnations on account of its supposed failure, either before, or during, or since the war, are usually formulated in terms which are too general and too simple. They do not make the necessary distinctions. The statement that Christianity failed with regard to the war may carry one or more of four positive meanings; that Christian principles sanctioned the war; or that Christian principles should have automatically prevented the war; or that the makers of the war had been conspicuous for their Christian practices; or that the teachers of Christianity had been negligent and inefficient.

It is obvious that Christianity did not fail in either of the first three acceptances. Far from sanctioning war as such, Christianity teaches that at least one of two opposing belligerents is always in the wrong. Nor are the principles of Christianity self-operating. They are addressed to free beings who have the power either to accept or reject. The statesmen responsible for the war did not even pretend that they were carrying out Christian principles.

[1] *Christian Charity and the Plight of Europe*, pp. 22-31. (The Paulist Press, New York.)

Therefore, the question is not whether Christianity failed, but whether its teachers failed. In other words, the only fair question to ask is whether the authorized teachers of Christianity did the utmost that might reasonably have been expected of them to prevent the war.

According to the Abbé Lugan, the instruction in our churches and schools, and particularly in our books of devotion, the last three centuries, dealt almost entirely with personal redemption and the salvation of the soul. The popular instruction did not portray the Gospel as providing light and guidance for social relations. Many of the spiritual writers exhibited tendencies that were too individualistic. While the ethical and Christian aspect of social and economic life was, indeed, set forth in our manuals of philosophy and theology, this teaching was not accessible to the masses.[2]

That there is considerable truth in this judgment, will be admitted by all Catholic scholars. Only since the appearance of the Encyclical of Pope Leo XIII, "On the Condition of Labor," has our practical teaching included anything like general attention to the moral side of industrial activities, to the ethical aspects of wages, profits, capital and labor. The reasons for this neglect of our rich heritage of social teaching cannot be adequately described in this place. Let it suffice to point out that they are to be found mainly in the Protestant Reformation. That disastrous event compelled Catholic teachers to concentrate most of their energies upon apologetics, upon the task of defending the faith; and it disseminated a pernicious and insidious individualism whose influence has not been entirely restricted to Protestants.

In such circumstances we should expect to find a similar lack of emphasis upon international relations. For these are but social relations under another and wider aspect. The individualistic viewpoint which prevents an adequate conception of man's social duties to his own countrymen is an even greater obstacle to a sufficient understanding of international obligations. "The true source of modern nationalism," says Professor A. W. Holcombe, "may be

[2] *L'Enseignement sociale de Jesus,* I, pp. 169, 188.

discovered in the period of the Protestant Reformation." [3] He refers to the philosophy and temper of individualism. What Professor Roscoe Pound calls "a maximum of individual self-assertion," easily and naturally passed from the social to the international field; individual egoism begot national egoism. It is not surprising that popular Catholic instruction did not remain unaffected by this modern nationalism, that it sometimes failed to lay sufficient emphasis upon the traditional Catholic doctrine of international obligations—that sane internationalism which knows neither bond nor free, neither Jew nor Gentile.

Unquestionably it is not an easy nor a simple task to apply the moral principles of Christianity to international affairs. Two methods are available; one general, the other particular. Using the first method, the religious teacher declares, expounds, interprets, illustrates and makes concrete Christ's commandment of love and the divine precept of justice. This teaching is imparted generally, to all groups and classes: in theological seminaries, in colleges and schools; in the pulpit and in catechetical instructions; in religious books and periodicals. Its efficacy depends mainly upon two pedagogical processes, namely, explication and repetition. By the former the truths and obligations implicit in a moral principle are made explicit. They are drawn out and exhibited in all their particular applications. The abstract is unfolded and made concrete. To proclaim the doctrine of brotherly love in general, no matter how solemnly or impressively, does not suffice. It is not enough to declare that "every human being is my neighbor." The meaning of this phrase must be explicitly and specifically set forth in relation to foreign races and nations. Insistence must be placed upon the fact that "every human being" includes Frenchmen, Germans, Italians, Englishmen. Particular stress should be laid upon the truth that the command of brotherly love is binding even with regard to the citizens of those states which are looked upon as rivals of the commonwealth of the persons who are being instructed. The inhabitants of every country should be explicitly instructed that the Golden Rule binds them in relation to foreigners, as well as in their relations to one another. And this unfolding process, this explicit and de-

---

[3] *The Foundations of the Modern Commonwealth*, p. 138.

tailed instruction in the duties of international charity, should be repeated and reiterated; for effective teaching and adequate assimilation are mainly dependent upon the simple process of repetition.

As we look back upon the century immediately preceding the war, we realize that the Christian principles of charity among nations were not adequately taught in any country of Europe. Catholic instruction, in the church, in the school and in the religious periodicals could have been occupied much more earnestly and intelligently with the task of refuting the monstrous theory that the conduct of states is exempt not only from the precept of charity but from every other precept of the moral law. It could have done more to make known in positive and concrete fashion the international aspects of the Golden Rule.

On the other hand, large concessions were made by religious teachers to a conception of patriotism which is essentially pagan. There was too much insistence upon the virtue of dying for one's country. Too frequently the words of the Roman poet were quoted with unqualified approval, *"dulce et decorum est pro patria mori."* There was not sufficient attention given to the fact that it is not "sweet and becoming to dies for one's country," when one's country is engaged in a war of aggression. It is not a becoming thing nor a righteous thing to kill somebody else for one's country in that kind of war. Too frequently, likewise, Christian teachers have advocated and glorified a jingoistic nationalism which is quite un-Catholic, and which arose from exactly the same source as the doctrine of unlimited individualism. The combination of too little explicit and detailed teaching of international charity and too much teaching of narrow patriotism and excessive nationalism, has left the Catholic masses unfortified against the pernicious and un-Christian political doctrines which beset them on every side. "They drink in the false doctrines of the Jingo press; they are misled by the fallacy of abstraction into conceiving vast nations as single entities; they do not realize that to hate or malign a whole people is just as sinful as to hate or malign an individual; their patriotism has lost sight of the necessary limits imposed by their Christianity." [4]

[4] Rev. Joseph Keating, S. J., in *The Month,* November, 1923.

The general method outlined and suggested in the last three paragraphs is less difficult than the one which has been designated as the "particular" method. This consists in applying the principles of international morality to current political events, policies and proposals. Moral teaching of this sort is addressed not only to the people but in an especial manner to statesmen. It is not easy to determine whether or how far contemporary international actions or policies are contrary to either justice or charity. Even when the moral aspect of the situation is clear, the question may arise whether religious teachers are not bound to remain silent from motives of Christian prudence.

The Triple Alliance and the Triple Entente were the main causes of the Great War. As we now know, many features of these agreements, and many courses of conduct undertaken because of them, were contrary to Christian morality. Should the authoritative religious teachers of Germany, Austria and Italy, of England, France and Russia have denounced these things at the time they were happening? In all probability bishops and priests could have done very little in this direction, owing to the secret character of the agreements and of the political movements therefrom resulting. Another potent cause of the war was the policy of excessive preparedness and competitive armaments. Should the religious teachers in the European countries have condemned this policy as carried on by their own governments? Obviously, this was a very delicate situation. Nevertheless, it does seem to us now that the religious authorities in each country could have done something to check this disastrous course. Something could surely have been accomplished through international action.

"Some years ago Chili and Argentina were on the verge of war. Ammunition factories were working day and night, and camps resounded to the tread of soldiers. Then at the instigation of the bishops of the two countries a conference was held. The leaders were reminded that they represented two Catholic nations; that both nations loved and served the God of peace. Why should such nations turn against each other in war and hatred? Why not consider the difficulties carefully? Why not arbitrate? Why not turn to the God of love and peace? The leaders prayed and asked light of God. They came to a satisfactory agreement and the war was averted. Cannons contributed by each nation were melted down and moulded into a statue of the Sacred Heart of Jesus Christ. High on the Andes Mountains this statue was placed, and under it today may be read the inscription: 'Sooner shall this mountain crumble away than will Chili and Argentina break the peace which they have made.' " [5]

A few months ago, a conference was held at Reading, England, attended by Catholics of some ten nationalities, to discuss the international as well as the national responsibilities of Catholic citizens. The main objects of the conference were to spread the Church's teaching in international relations, and to popularize the traditional Catholic law of nations. This is an important and a hopeful undertaking. What a pity that no such action was taken by the Catholics of the various European nations in the quarter of a century immediately preceding the fateful year of 1914!

Whatever deficiencies may be found in the teaching of international charity in Europe prior to the war, are attributable to the *subordinate teachers*. This is particularly true of the last half century. "Once more Popes have set forth —Leo, Pius, Benedict, and Pius again—clearly and emphatically the principles of Christian peace, but Catholics, immersed in their nationalistic preoccupations have not given due heed." [6] The Supreme Pontiffs who were nearest to the period of the war repeatedly proclaimed to the nations their moral obligations toward one another. Pope Leo XIII expounded the Christian doctrine of international relations in more than one majestic encyclical. One of the last acts of Piux X was to warn and rebuke the Emperor of Austria on account of his government's part in precipitating the awful conflict. At the outset of his pontificate, Benedict XV recalled to the minds of the belligerents the principles of international justice; later on he offered them a practical program for ending the war and setting up a stable peace. Pius XI condemned the French invasion of the Ruhr, and on other occasions urged the nations of Europe to abandon the methods of force in favor of the methods of Christian charity.

[5] Rev. Henry S. Spalding, S. J., in *The Queen's Work*.
[6] Rev. Joseph Keating, S. J.

That so much teaching of international charity as was humanly possible could have prevented the war, may well be doubted. Pertinent here is the ancient Scholastic axiom: "Whatever is received, is received according to the mode of the recipient." Neither the responsible statesmen nor the politically influential sections of the European peoples were in the proper attitude of mind and heart to give such teaching a sympathetic reception. At any rate, the question is now merely academic. The past is past. We have with us the present, and we are responsible for the future. We cannot too soon begin to take to heart the lessons of the devastating and unnecessary war. The first lesson is, that Christian charity is not only the way of individual righteousness, but the way of national salvation. The second is, that we are all under serious obligation not merely to accept this great principle, but to work earnestly for its realization in both national and international affairs.

"The Holy Father has recently stated that his conception of the 'Peace of Christ through the reign of Christ,' which alone can restore the shattered world, will be attained only if pastors, school-masters and catechists teach the catechism properly, and so cause the universality of the moral law to be adequately grasped. And just as important is it that national history should be read and taught in the light of Christian principles. Our text-books should be thoroughly purged of Jingoism and every sentiment that savours of racial pride. The crimes and follies of the past should be called by their right names, and not excused on plea of national exigencies; and justice should be done to other nations, at any rate, by not arrogating to ourselves rights which we deny to them. As no education which does not qualify its subject to be a good citizen can be thought adequate, so some training in the principles of true internationalism is essential." [7]

These obligations are incumbent not merely upon the authorized teachers of Christian charity and justice, but upon all Catholics, according to the form and measure of their opportunities. Now the opportunities lying before the Catholics of the United States are much greater than those within reach of our brethren in Europe. Happily we are far removed from the stifling atmosphere of European

[7] Rev. Joseph Keating, S. J.

feuds, jealousies and hatreds. Since we have within our fold a large representation from every one of the afflicted nations across the Atlantic, the doctrine, the meaning and the practice of international good-will ought to be much simpler and easier for us than it is for them.

With shame and regret we are compelled, nevertheless, to confess that we have not kept ourselves unspotted from the Jingoism and un-Christian nationalism which are not the least detestable elements in the war's miserable heritage. Some of us have given assistance to a cheap and blatant propaganda against veracious and judicious text-books of United States history, because they do not sufficiently glorify certain patriotic persons and events, nor paint in sufficiently hateful colors certain persons in the camp of the enemy. Some of us have opposed even the slightest and safest proposals of co-operation for the relief of the afflicted peoples of Europe, mainly because of dislike for some of the nations with whom we are asked to co-operate. Some of us defend an international policy of selfish isolation, unmindful that the law of brotherly love is not bounded by the western shore of the Atlantic Ocean.

A little reflection upon the implications of charity should be sufficient to show any intelligent and unprejudiced person that all this is un-Christian and un-Catholic. We are bound to assist nations in distress as well as individuals in distress. The principle and the determining considerations are the same. In both cases we are obliged to lend our help when we can do so without disproportionately grave inconvenience to ourselves. To be sure, it is not always easy to know whether a given form of co-operation would be unsafe for our country, but we are at least under solemn obligation to give every important proposal the benefit of sympathetic examination. We are not justified in prejudging the case, nor in acting upon the lazy assumption that no duty exists or that nothing can be done. The important preliminary is that we should approach the subject with a clear realization of the Catholic doctrine of international brotherhood, and in the spirit of charity rather than in the spirit of nationalistic superiority and selfishness. Hatred of a foreign country should not be mistaken for love of America.

Finally, there is urgent need of Catholic co-operation in the movement for world peace. This end cannot be attained without the assistance, indeed, the leadership, of the United States. Thousands upon thousands of earnest Americans are banded together to find means by which this assistance may be rendered and this leadership made effective. The number of Catholics enrolled in these organizations is insignificant. Nor have we any such associations of our own. We believe that the nations will have no lasting peace until they adopt and carry out the Christian principles of brotherhood, but we do nothing ourselves to give them direction or enlightenment. With justifiable pride, we dwell upon the peace teaching and the peace efforts of Benedict XV and Pius XI, but we do not lift a finger to carry their doctrine into practical effect. Surely it is high time for us to realize that we have obligations of our own under the law of charity; that we cannot escape these obligations by "pointing with pride" to the peace efforts of the Vicars of Christ; that we are in duty bound, not only to applaud their efforts, but to show our loyalty by active co-operation, by taking advantage of every practical opportunity to hasten the reign of "the Peace of Christ."

182

EFFORTS TOWARDS PEACE

CHARLES PLATER [1]

The first method of working towards peace, which, though remote, is of the greatest importance, is the education of public opinion with a view to securing:

(1) The subordination of international relations to the moral law.

(2) The right subordination of national interests.

(3) The cultivation of true as opposed to false nationalism.

(4) Increased popular control over foreign policy.

Nothing can resist steady, united, and enlightened public demand. It is now recognized in every country that the formation of public opinion is of more importance than appeals to princes or politicians. Legislation is of little

[1] *A Primer of Peace and War,* pp. 148-160. (P. S. King & Son, London.)

avail unless supported by public opinion. It might be thought that although public opinion is omnipotent within the nation, its influence does not extend to international relations. This is not the case. Given a healthy development of public opinion in all the great Powers, it will affect their mutual dealings. It will insist upon controlling foreign policy in accordance with justice and charity.

Professor Westlake has pointed out that the very vagueness of international law gives more scope for the influence of public opinion: "If a branch of law is still free to develop itself under the influence of public opinion, the student has the power, and with it the responsibility and the privilege, of assisting in its evolution. . International law being the science of what a State ought to do or may do with reference to other States and their subjects, every one should reflect on its principles who, in however limited a sphere of influence, helps to determine the action of his country by swelling the volume of its opinion."

There are, then, four directions in which public opinion needs to be educated:

(1) It must learn the need of *subordinating international relations* and politics generally to the moral law. The people must be convinced that the moral law binds States as well as individuals, and that its observance is the only way to secure international peace. Not only must public opinion regard a treaty as being as inviolable as a commercial contract, but it must be impressed with the truth, taught by reason and reinforced by Christianity, of the brotherhood of man.

(2) Secondly, the peoples of the world must be impressed with the fact that *various national interests* are to be *subordinated* to one another according to their true value. It is sometimes said that the interests of different nations are bound to conflict. But this is true only when nations put lower interests in the place of higher. If every nation aimed at its highest interests there would be no occasion for war; just as, if employers and workers aimed at their highest interests there would be no occasion for strikes and lock-outs.

There is a deplorable tendency among individuals and States alike, to lay the entire stress on those interests which are *capable of exact measurement*. They do not realize that even temporal welfare consists not in having many things but in having the right things. Just as the health of a man does not depend on his size or his money, so the welfare of a nation is not to be estimated by the extent of its territory or the amount of its wealth. The highest interests of a country cannot be reckoned in figures. Among them is peace, which is, moreover, a condition of the rest.

In this we have something to learn from the Stoic philosophers, whose fundamental principle was that man ought to live conformably to his reasonable nature. They equivalently reached the utilitarian maxim, "the greatest happiness of the greatest number." If happiness is not judged simply as quantity of pleasurable feeling or sentiment but as satisfaction in the good conscience which always seeks the right thing, then their principle is highly to be approved. . . .

(3) Thirdly, public opinion must be exerted in favour of a *true* as opposed to a false *patriotism*. It is no necessary part of patriotism to desire or to strive that our particular country should be at the head of the human race. We may rightly desire that our national virtues should win recognition and that our country should occupy that place in the assemblage of peoples to which her degree of civilization entitles her. But our estimate of that place must not be prejudiced nor oblivious of the claims of other nations; still less must we seek to occupy it otherwise than by fair means. Patriotism is one of the natural virtues, correcting to some extent the inborn selfishness of the individual but capable itself of ministering to that selfishness, unless in its turn spiritualized and otherwise conditioned by Christianity. Christianity reveals the true motive of patriotism—the love of our fellow-citizens precisely as such, people, i. e., associated with us by God's Providence either in racial origin or in the same social polity or in both ways. Catholic theology clearly states that patriotism, the love of the fatherland, consists chiefly in the "love of our fellow-citizens and of all the friends of our country." God has brought us into close relation with them for our mutual benefit and, therefore, has obliged us to show them a special regard.

But at the same time, Christianity, whilst spiritualizing this natural instinct, is also careful to mark its proper bounds. It emphasizes the fact of the common origin of mankind and still more of its common destiny. The sovereign States which now divide the allegiance of human beings on earth have no counterpart in the one eternal, heavenly Kingdom, where the essential brotherhood of men will find its full development in the light of the unclouded Fatherhood of God. Earthly patriotism, therefore, must take account of the fact that the whole human race are in God's design, potential citizens of the same abiding city. . . . Godless patriotism is merely the natural instinct binding men together on the merely natural grounds of mutual help and defence, and completely devoid of any supernatural check. Hence it easily degenerates into national pride, the fruits of which are militarism and jingoism.

(4) Fourthly, public opinion must be exerted in favor of *increased popular control over foreign policy.* There is a widespread feeling that the Foreign Offices of Europe do not sufficiently represent the better mind of the people, and that the public should control foreign policy as they control (or are supposed to control) domestic policy. This is all the more important since foreign and domestic affairs these days react so powerfully upon one another. . . . Lord Cromer is of opinion that "all the lessons of history go to show that the rule of Demos is no surer guarantee against war than that of oligarchs or despots," though he acknowledges that the present trend of democratic opinion is distinctly towards peace. . . .

It cannot be too often or too emphatically repeated that Christianity must take the leading part in the work of bringing international relations once more under the moral law. The moral law, it is true, is based on reason, but Christianity alone can make it prevail. . . . The task awaiting Christianity to-day is twofold; it comprises *study* and *teaching.*

INDEX

ST. THOMAS COLLEGE
LIBRARY

INDEX OF PROPER NAMES

Aa, Van der, 950, 953, 957, 960
Abraham, 151, 505
Abulensis, 198
Achimaas, 361
Adam, 151, 369, 958
Adler, Felix, 29
Ailly, d' P., 948
Alban, St., 550
Albert the Great, 23
Alexander VIII, 374
Alexander, Natalis, 548
Alexander, Prof., 98
Almain, 948, 952, 953, 961, 970
Alphonsus, St., 451, 545, 546, 547, 548, 549, 553, 575.
Ambrose, St., 22, 198, 586, 791, 975
Amette, Cardinal, 1000
Ananias, 586, 606
Anaxagoras, 48
Antoninus, St., 948, 1023, 1031
Apollonius, Tyaneus, 151
Apollos, 151
Aragon, 1023
Arauxo, 1022, 1023
Ariathenes, 21
Aristhenes, 21
Aristotle, 1, 2, 20, 42, 43, 44, 46, 47, 49, 66, 111, 112, 115, 129, 135, 136, 171, 217, 237, 279, 281, 310, 339, 362, 529, 558, 564, 755, 905, 909, 911, 912, 923, 924, 973, 1019, 1020, 1021
Arnold, Matthew, 350
Arria, 540
Arriaga, de, A., 951, 952, 1030
Ashley, 569
Ath, 31
Athanasius, St., 550
Attalus III, 508
Aubespine, 516
Audisio, 31, 968
Augustine, St., 12, 22, 23, 112, 182, 183, 196, 198, 212, 213, 244, 245, 302, 303, 308, 377, 452, 545, 555, 586, 889, 919, 920, 921
Austin, 308, 335, 377, 1031

Aurelius, Marcus, 21
Avicenna, 41, 394
Ayd, J. J., 735
Azo, 1018
Azor, J., 950
Azpilcueta, M., 948, 953

Bachofen, 764
Bacon, 49, 67, 317
Bailly, 968
Bain, A., 26, 115, 274, 384
Bakounin, 662
Bähr, 814
Baldelli, 968
Baldus, 961
Balfour, 77, 384
Balmes, J., 31, 950, 956, 968, 970
Balmez, 933, 936
Ballerini, 356
Banes, Dom., 950
Bannez, 927, 1023
Bantain, 950
Barbedette, 966, 968
Barbeyrac, 1030, 1031
Barrière, 1056
Barrett, J. F., 496
Barruel, 950, 969
Barre, de la, 1031
Barth. of Medina, 948
Basil, St., 586
Baxter, 962
Bayle, 124
Bellarmine, Cardinal, 898, 925, 926, 927, 928, 934, 935, 937, 938, 939, 942, 943, 944, 945, 950, 951, 953, 964, 965, 970, 1024, 1025, 1048, 1049, 1050
Benedict XIV, 498, 517, 546, 547, 569, 669, 673
Benedict XV, 1061, 1067, 1070
Beneke, F. E., 26
Benthan, 375, 377, 378, 379, 384, 878
Berkeley, 125
Bernardine of Siena, St., 948
Bertrand, P., Cardinal, 948

Billot, Cardinal, 900, 950, 953, 961, 963, 964, 966
Billuart, 1023, 1026
Bismark, 486
Blackstone, 307, 311, 842, 843, 844
Blanche, Queen, 889
Blakely, P. L., 502
Blanc, 966, 968
Boedder, Bernard, 48
Boethius, 182, 199
Bonacina, 1023
Bonald, 128
Bonar, 418
Bonaventure, St., 23
Boniface VIII, 925
Bouix, 319
Bouquillon, T., 327, 334, 338, 848, 966, 994
Bourget, 68
Boutain, 959
Bouvier, 307
Bracton, 1018
Brandis, 31
Breig, A. C., 663, 665
Brosnahan, Timothy, 36, 284, 325, 380, 383, 432, 451, 871, 1015
Browne, J. C., 513
Browning, 264
Browson, O., 432, 848
Bruhl, M. L., 15, 16
Brugere, 970
Brunetière, 67, 68
Bryce, 310, 311
Buchner, 85
Burke, E., 412, 1047
Burkett, P. H., 356
Burlamaqui, 1030, 1031
Burnet, 1047
Burns, J. A., 848
Busenbaum, 194, 196, 200
Butler, W., 60, 280, 1050, 1051
Byng, 115

Cabanis, 85
Cabezudo, D., 948, 950
Caesar, Julius, 484
Cajetan, 917, 922, 930, 948
Callistus I, Pope, 516
Calvin, 944
Canavan, J. E., 699
Cannan, 828
Cano. Melchior, 947

Capella, 95
Caramuel, 952
Carbane, 950
Carbo, L., 948, 950
Carlyle, Dr., 913, 919, 922, 935
Carlyle, Thomas, 1056
Carson, W. E., 783
Cartwright, 194, 195, 196, 200, 201, 202, 203, 204, 205
Carneades, 22
Carpenter, W. B., 50
Cassian, 198
Castelein, A., 31, 467, 950, 963
Castro, A., 930, 948, 952
Catalano, 969
Caterini, L., 966
Catharinus, A., 948
Cathrein, Victor, 3, 19, 156, 302, 303, 498, 855, 924, 937, 939, 940, 944, 957, 960, 1020, 1032
Cavagnis, 968
Cavallera, 950, 963, 970
Cepeda, de R., 31, 950, 970
Cetty, Abbé, 705
Chalmers, 224, 226
Charlemagne, 1012
Charron, 124
Chastel, 950, 970
Choupin, 963
Churchill, 735
Chrysippus, 21
Cicero, 21, 22, 48, 49, 62, 171, 182, 213, 408, 484, 974, 975, 976, 977, 985, 1017, 1018
Clark, Sir And., 513
Clarke, 14
Cleanthes, 21
Cleary, P., 570
Clement, 22, 545, 551
Clinton, 143, 144
Comte, August, 26, 819
Concina, 548
Condillac, 25
Confusius, 19
Connolly, James, 599, 600, 602
Conradus, 1023
Contarini, G., Cardinal, 948
Constantine, 771
Contenson, 548
Conway, James, 860
Cooper, J. M., 822
Coppée, 68

INDEX OF PROPER NAMES

Cordubensis, 948
Costa-Rosetti, 938, 942, 947, 950, 957, 963, 970
Cortés, Donoso, 31
Covarruvias, D., 948, 1023
Coulanges, de, 309, 310
Crawford, Virginia, 704
Cromer, Lord, 1073
Cromwell, 931
Cronin, M., 13, 165, 168, 191, 328, 342, 352, 407, 413, 565, 738, 756, 845, 856, 931, 938, 940, 945, 947, 951, 971, 1053
Conradus, 1023
Crump, A., 528
Cuthbert, 615
Cyprian, St., 516

Dalgairns, 949
Damascene, St. John, 48
Damaschke, A., 613
Dante, 977
Darmesteter, 69
Darwin, Charles, 26, 49, 52, 765
Dasbach, 205, 206
David, 400, 937
Davitt, M., 605
Dawson, J. W., 1002
Decius, 147
Delany, J. F., 269, 487
De Dominis, 962
Democritus, 20
Demos, 1073
Denis, St., 196
Denis, the Carthusian, 1023
Dennert, 68
Dens, 950
Denziger, 374, 963
Descartes, 24, 126, 127
Deshayes, 968
Desorges, 950, 957, 970
Devas, C. S., 11, 613, 839
Devine, A., 207, 227
Devoti, 950, 1031
Dickens, 264
Dinneen, M. F., 171
Disraeli, 289
Dmowski, 1023, 1031
Döllinger, 205
Dominic of St. Thomas, 953
Donedo, J., 948
Dostojewski, 807

Driedo, 930
Draghetti, 950
Durand, Wm., 948

Eliot, 486
Elizabeth, St., 803, 804
Emery, H. C., 519
Engels, F., 27, 600, 601, 602
Enghelbert, 948
Eschenbach, W. von, 862
Escobar, 197
Estius (Wm. Hessels van Est), 948
Euripedes, 316

Fabius, 147
Farges, 966, 968
Fay, C. R., 719, 724, 729
Faye, 50
Fechner, G. T., 26
Fénelon, 969
Féret, P., 927, 947, 950, 963, 964, 969, 970
Ferretti, 31
Ferri, Enrico, 502
Fichte, 17, 26, 419
Figgis, N. P., 925, 926, 929, 937
Finlay, P., 598, 964
Fisher, J. H., 490, 528
Fletcher, Margaret, 792, 793
Florentinus, 1017
Flurscheim, 613
Foerster, T. W., 796
Fonsegrive, G. L., 95
Forel, 813
Forster, H. D., 944
Fox, J. J., 375, 420, 439, 494
Francis, St. of Assisi, 480, 801, 818, 819
Francis St. de Sales, 211, 241
Francis of Victoria, 948, 1029
Franck, 69, 945
Fremont, 950
Freud, 113, 826
Frins, 31
Funck, 523
Furniss, H. S., 616, 618, 625

Gaius, 311, 1017, 1021
Galien, 508
Gamaches, 1031
Garnet, 536, 561
Garrold, 207

Gaudeau, B., 963
Gelasius, Pope, 1013
Gemelli, 963
Genicot, 198
George, Henry, 605, 613, 614
Gerard, John, 193
Gerdil, 548
Gerson, 929, 937, 952, 953, 961
Gibbon, 149
Gibbons, Cardinal, 849, 887
Gierke, 420, 935, 936
Gillon, 63
Gilson, E., 174
Giraud, 764
Giustiniani, B., 950
Gladstone, 484, 485
Gnauck - Kühne, Frau, 808, 809, 810
Godard, 950
Godwin, 377
Goethe, 275
Goldcast, 952, 970
Gonzalez, Cardinal, 950
Goodwin, J., 962
Gosling, 625
Gratian, 1018, 1019
Graziosi, 950
Gredt, 950
Greeley, Horace, 484
Green, 7
Gregory VII, St., 220, 586, 821, 925
Gregory IX, 427
Gregory XIV, 926
Gregory of Valencia, 950
Gretser, James, 948
Grote, 483, 1033, 1042
Grotius, Hugo, 24, 929, 937, 1031
Grumm, 68
Guilbert, 950
Gull, Sir Wm., 512, 838
Gutberlet, C., 31, 81
Gwynn, Denis, 707

Hadrian, 1012
Hadrian VI, Pope, 1048
Hale, 164
Haller, de C., 749, 751, 937
Hammond, 309, 312
Harmel, L., 704, 705, 706
Harrison, F., 264
Hartley, 376

Hartmann, E. von, 26, 29
Healy, Abp., 949, 965
Heeren, A. Van der, 450, 457
Hegel, 17, 394, 413, 756, 877, 878
Helvetius, 25, 375
Henn, Peter, 204
Henry VIII, 240, 962
Heraclius, 19
Herbart, 29
Hergenrother, Card., 950
Herodotus, 764
Hertling, von, 1020
Hickey, 963
Hill, W., 162, 464, 950, 960
Hilty, 801
Hincmar, 950
Hobbes, 24, 375, 383, 391, 753, 756, 757, 758, 877, 1030, 1031
Hobson, 413
Hoensbroech, von, 194, 206
Holaind, 31, 307, 841, 983, 950
Holbach, 25
Holcombe, 1063
Homer, 12, 221
Horace, 1003
Hostiensis, 948
Howard, 765
Huet, 125
Hughes, Abp., 950
Hughes, Leo F., 905
Hugonin, 950, 963
Hugolinus, 961
Hull, E. R., 198, 288, 349, 367, 474, 505
Hume, 125, 376
Hunt, G., 942
Husslein, J., 572, 576, 662
Huth, 1023
Huxley, 272, 385
Huysmans, 68

Ignatius Loyola, St., 206, 487
Ireland, Abp., 950, 966
Irenaeus, St., 22
Irwin, H., 568
Isaac, 505
Isidore, 310, 312, 323, 1018, 1019
Izaga, L., 964

Jacob, 553
Jacquart, 462
James, King, 925, 926, 927, 934, 937, 962

INDEX OF PROPER NAMES 1081

James, St., 212, 370
James, William, 90, 91, 94, 272
Janet, 410, 929
Janssen, 1014
Jeremiah, 876, 926
Jefferson, Thomas, 942
Jerome, St., 22, 244, 586
Jephthe, 820
Jevons, 571
Job, 878
John St., the Baptist, 820, 821
John St., 69, 71, 209, 370, 482, 820, 821
John Chrysostom, St., 198, 324, 586, 890, 947
John of Medina, 948
John, Major, 948
John of Paris, 948
John of Torquenada, 948
Johnson, Dr., 538, 553
Joly, H., 209
Jonathan, 361
Jones, W. H. S., 840
Joseph, St., 821
Jouin, 31
Jowett, 69
Joyce, G. H., 57
Juan de Mariana, 948, 950
Justin, St., 22
Justinian, 771, 1017, 1018

Kane, R., 293
Kant, 12, 25, 26, 29, 30, 50, 51, 60, 84, 92, 125, 187, 321, 325, 385, 386, 389, 390, 392, 393, 394, 395, 396, 397, 398, 399, 400, 413, 419, 424, 433, 558, 751, 756, 877, 878
Karl, 770
Kautsky, 614

Keating, J., 1065, 1067, 1068
Kelvin, Lord, 67, 68
Kenrick, 546
Kent, 311, 844, 1010
Kepler, 49
Kerby, W. J., 227
Ketteler, Wm. von, 631
Key, Ellen, 813
King, W. I., 715
Kinkead, 311, 312
Kleutgen, 31, 79
Koch, 503, 504

Krose, 461
Krueger, 1017

Lacroix, 1023
Lactantius, 62
Ladd, 86, 423
Lainez, J., 948
Lamennais, 129
Lane, J. A., 674
Lange, 260
Larousse, 508
Lassalle, 602
Lasson, 413
Lavigerie, Card., 950
Lavoisier, 110
Laymann, 196, 200
Lazarus, 585
Ledesma, 930
Lehen, de, 31
Lehmen, 31
Lehmkuhl, 334
Leibniz, 106, 107
Leibnitz, 49
Lemaire, 949
Leo XIII, Pope, 327, 499, 588, 589, 591, 592, 599, 601, 602, 603, 606, 610, 612, 613, 614, 615, 616, 617, 619, 620, 625, 626, 627, 631, 639, 661, 663, 664, 665, 666, 667, 668, 670, 671, 672, 673, 683, 684, 688, 690, 696, 702, 704, 778, 849, 900, 904, 916, 927, 932, 941, 963, 964, 965, 966, 967, 989, 1006, 1063, 1067
Lesbos, 136
Lessius, 24, 545, 952, 953, 957, 1023
Lewis, of Bavaria, 950
Lewis, Sir G., 143, 146, 147
Liberatore, 31, 194, 937, 949, 1032
Lilly, 205
Limbrick, 207
Lincoln, 978
Littledale, 194, 201, 202, 203, 204, 205
Locke, 375, 762, 949
Lockington, W. J., 483
Longfellow, 282
Lorimer, 309, 311
Lortie, 186
Louis, St., 802, 889
Louis XIV, 240, 1011

Lucretius, 85
Ludendorff, 207
Lugan, Abbé, 1063
Lugd, 1048
Lugo, De, 24, 374, 489
Lupold of Bebenburg, 948
Luther, 813, 814, 937
Lyall, 816
Lytton, Sir Bulwer, 264
MacCunn, J., 279
MacEvilly, 965
Machiavelli, 937
Mackay, 224
Mackenzie, 413
Macksey, C., 743, 759, 777, 895, 950, 955, 963, 965, 970, 1033
Maher, M., 71, 89, 210, 283
Maillard, 484
Maine, 973
Maistre, de, 413
Major, 339, 952, 1050
Mallock, 77
Malthus, 827, 828, 829, 831, 832, 833, 834, 835, 839
Manegold of Lautenbach, 948
Manning, Card., 367, 587, 916, 950
Marcellus a Puero Jesu, 950
Marcellinus, 517
Margerie, de, 31
Maret, Abp., 950
Mariana, 929, 952
Marina, 950
Markley, 308
Marsilius of Padua, 948
Martial, 470
Martineau, 75, 90, 91, 422
Martinez, 1029
Marx, Karl, 27, 570, 600, 601, 602
Masterson, E., 964
Matthew, St., 223, 324, 450
Maurice, Sir Frederick, 206, 207
Maxwell, 962
Mazzella, 950
McDonald, W., 317, 1055
McLennan, 764, 766
McNabb, V., 6
Meeker, R., 655
Melanchthon, 24
Melchiades, 516
Mendive, 31, 947, 950, 970
Mendoza, 1031
Mercier, Card., 106

Mettrie, de la, 25
Meyer, 31, 333, 487, 935, 937, 938, 945, 1020, 1031
Michel, 1023
Michell, J., 650
Middleton, R., 555
Mill, J. S., 26, 49, 59, 91, 92, 98, 276, 316, 375, 377, 378, 379, 385, 859, 878
Miltner, C., 182, 463
Milner, 949
Milton, J., 533, 545, 551, 929
Ming, J. J., 31
Miranda, 950, 969, 1024
Mivart, St. George, 49, 55
Molesworth, 1031
Molina, L., 24, 927, 950, 970, 1023, 1024
Monica, St., 889
Monsabré, 185
Montaigne, 124
More, Blessed Thomas, 17
Moreno, Garcia, 486
Morimoro, 834
Morgan, 764
Moulart, 31, 950, 963, 970
Moy de Sons, 31
Müller, 69
Mun, Albert de, 704
Mure, Col., 143, 144, 145, 146

Napoleon, 484, 590, 956, 1008
Naumann, 816
Navarrus, 953, 956, 969, 970
Nazarro, 1045
Nearing, Scott, 715
Neubauer, 952, 1023
Newman, Card., 61, 118, 129, 344, 422, 443, 446, 533, 537, 543, 557
Newton, 49, 949
Nicholas of Cusa, 124, 948
Nicholas d'Oresme, 948
Niebuhr, 143, 144, 147
Nieubarn, 462
Nietzsche, 28, 811, 815, 923
Nimrod, 926
Noël, 93
Nordau, 28

O'Connell, Card., 681
Ockham, 962
Ojetti, 950
O'Meara, 226

INDEX OF PROPER NAMES 1083

Onclair, 31
O'Neill, A. C., 373
Orage, 728
O'Rahilly, 913, 925, 942, 944, 1016, 1044
O'Reilly, J. B., 681
Origen, 22
Osler, Wm., 837
Ozanam, 226

Palacios, M., 950
Palao, de Castro, 952, 969, 1022
Paley, 376, 555
Palmerston, Lord, 485, 562
Parisis, 950
Parsons, W., 446, 454
Paschal, de, 31, 125
Pasteur, 55, 67, 68
Paul, C. Keegan, 820
Paul V, Pope, 925
Paul, St., 22, 70, 71, 207, 209, 210, 227, 244, 247, 310, 316, 321, 386, 453, 511, 585, 598, 620, 821, 880, 881, 891, 947, 980
Paulsen, 26, 29, 260, 386
Pégues, 964
Pelago, 948
Peltier, 968
Perkins, 925
Perin, C., 31, 253, 255, 950
Peregrinus, 1016
Persons, R., 950
Pesch, 31, 719
Peter of Aragon, 948
Peter of Blois, 517
Peter of Navarre, 950
Peter St., 448, 586, 606, 888, 890, 926
Petrus de Monte, 948
Petrus de Palude, 948
Phidias, 138
Philemon, 585
Pius IX, Pope, 486
Pius X, Pope, 963, 965, 966, 1067
Pius XI, Pope, 1067, 1068, 1069, 1070
Plater, C., 1070
Plato, 19, 20, 22, 41, 42, 43, 49, 111, 119, 171, 238, 483, 529, 557, 755, 884, 905, 909
Pliny, 540
Plumb, G. E., 656, 657, 658

Pole, Card., 948
Pollock, 311
Polybius, 840
Poole, 735
Porphyry, 12
Pound, R., 1064
Prichard, 68
Prierias, S., 1020
Pruner, 469
Pufendorf, 24, 843, 1030
Pythagoras, 19

Quilliet, 950, 961, 963, 970
Quintanadueñas, A., 948

Raboisson, 950, 957
Rae, J., 525
Rafael, 138
Raiffeisen, 720
Ramsay, 969
Ranke, von, 945
Rashdall, 386, 394
Rathbone, E., 706, 707, 710, 711, 712, 713, 714
Reding, 1023
Reid, T., 14, 25
Reiffenstuel, 1023
Reinstadler, 944, 957
Reisch, 205
Renninger, 31
Rickaby, J., 31, 69, 111, 122, 183, 236, 302, 308, 313, 323, 360, 452, 468, 482, 533, 931, 945, 947, 957, 958
Ritchie, 413, 416, 418
Robinson, 308
Rocaberti, 953
Roh, 205, 206
Rohrbacher, 950
Romanus, A., 948
Romanet, 705, 706
Roosevelt, 256, 978
Roselli, 31, 1023
Rosetti, 31
Rosmini, 31
Ross, J. E., 468
Ross, H., 833, 834
Rousseau, J. J., 267, 276, 440, 754, 759, 760, 761, 762, 938, 939, 966
Rufinus, 1018
Ruskin, 485
Russell, Lord, 312

Russo, N., 31
Rutherford, 986
Rutten, 950, 953
Ryan, J. A., 221, 223, 245, 258, 326, 355, 405, 517, 583, 646, 687, 715, 763, 780, 933, 950, 963, 965, 968, 987, 1062
Ryan, M. J., 120, 953
Sabatier, 801
Salas, de, 950, 951, 1023
Salmanticenses, 1023
Salmèron, A., 950
Salon, 1023
Salter, W. M., 29
Samson, 820
Sander, N., 948
Sanseverino, 31
Sasia, J. C., 270
Saul, 505, 937
Savigny, F. C. de, 413
Sayr, 948
Scala, Pius La, 944
Scavini, 950
Schaeffle, 525
Schiffini, 31, 924, 945, 947, 960, 966
Schleiermacher, 26
Schloss, 726
Schmalzgrueber, 1023
Schmidt, 770
Schmier, 1023
Schopenhauer, 267, 802, 814, 815
Schultze-Delitzsche, 720
Schwalm, 965, 966, 967, 968
Schwartz, I., 24, 1023
Scott, Sir W., 538
Scotus, Duns., 23, 168, 948
Ségur, 950
Seguy, 949
Seligman, E. R. A., 661
Seneca, 21
Seth, A., 413
Shaftesbury, 14, 25
Shakespeare, 398
Sharswood, 986
Shaw, B., 840
Sidgwick, H., 26, 76, 90, 91, 379, 385, 411
Sidwick, 945
Sidney, 929
Siemens, Sir Wm., 50, 815
Simon, Jules, 637, 638

Sixtus V, 569
Slater, T., 155, 301, 335, 341, 365, 427, 474, 513, 514, 974
Smith, W. G., 1010
Socrates, 19, 20, 22, 43, 111, 216, 265, 297, 379, 483
Solieri, 1023
Solomon, 151
Solon, 614, 919
Sophocles, 529
Sortais, 963
Soto, D., 24, 930, 948, 1023
Spalding, Abp., 950
Spalding, H. S., 35, 1067
Spalding, J. L., 789
Spencer, Herbert, 26, 59, 63, 379, 380, 381, 384, 413, 765, 861
Spinoza, 17, 25
Stahl, F. C., 413
Starcke, 765
Steiger, 950
Stein, H. von, 801
Stein, J., 31
Stetson, 268
Stirner, M., 28
Stöckl, A., 31
Strabo, 764
Stutfield, 194
Suarez, 24, 311, 312, 318, 327, 329, 331, 332, 333, 334, 337, 339, 340, 749, 925, 926, 927, 928, 929, 930, 931, 932, 934, 935, 936, 937, 938, 939, 941, 942, 943, 944, 945, 947, 948, 949, 950, 951, 952, 953, 954, 955, 958, 960, 962, 964, 965, 970, 1020, 1022, 2025, 1026, 1028, 1029, 1032, 1045, 1049, 1050, 1053
Swickerath, R., 285, 289
Sylvius Aeneas, 948, 1020, 1022, 1023, 1025, 1028

Talamo, 31
Tanner, 952, 970
Tanquerey, 334, 335, 338, 995, 998
Taparelli, 31, 413, 749, 937, 938, 945, 946, 959
Taussig, 715
Tennyson, 264
Tépe, 372, 945, 966
Tertullian, 22

INDEX OF PROPER NAMES

Thackeray, 264
Thales, 48
Theodore of Cyrene, 22
Theodoret, 947
Theodosius, 771
Thode, 801
Thomas of Aquin, St., 23, 301, 302, 308, 311, 323, 324, 328, 329, 394, 400, 452, 453, 482, 489, 498, 503, 504, 509, 510, 511, 542, 543, 546, 556, 558, 572, 575, 587, 590, 591, 598, 639, 645, 826, 908-924, 929, 930, 945, 948, 949, 951, 961, 965, 974, 975, 1019, 1020, 1021, 1024, 1025, 1027, 1032, 1050, 1051
Thompson, F., 480
Thomson, Sir W., 50
Thurston, H., 193
Tibertius, 1012
Tichborne, 1046
Toledo, Card. F., 948, 950
Toletus, 1027
Tostat, Alph., 948
Tolston, 842
Tully, 483
Turner, Wm., 978

Ulpian, 843, 1017, 1018, 1020, 1021, 1050, 1051
Urban VIII, Pope, 547
Urquhart, 1047

Valencia, 1023
Vallet, 31, 950, 963
Vance, J. G., 98
Vanderbroeck, 547
Vareilles-Sommières, de, 945, 946, 951, 954, 957, 958, 959, 960, 966
Vassall-Phillips, 194
Vasquez, 198, 318, 1048
Vaughan, B., 611
Vaughan, J. S., 507
Vazques, 1023
Veblen, 268
Ventura, 950, 953
Vermeersch, 944, 945, 957, 959, 963, 964, 987
Victor I, Pope, 516
Victoria, 24, 914, 930, 945, 1023, 1029, 1043, 1045
Vidal, 950

Vincent de Paul, St., 226, 801
Viollet, 945
Virgil, 977
Vivi, 547, 1023
Vives, 226
Vogt, 85
Voit, 200, 546, 1023
Voltaire, 115
Vonier, Dom A., 221

Wagemann, 197, 201, 202, 203, 204
Wagner, R., 811
Waldron, A., 213
Wallace, A. R., 50, 613
Walshe, T. J., 66
Walter, F., 31
Warburton, 149
Ward, 1013
Warner, 224, 225, 226
Warren, H. C., 291
Washington, George, 679, 873, 889, 978
Watt, L,. 950, 964
Watts, 116
Weiss, A. M., 31
Westermarck, 764, 765, 768, 770
Westlake, 1071
Wiestner, 1023
Wilhelm, 1056
Willard, D., 654
William of Auvergne, 950
Williams, 31, 734
Willoughby, 413
Wilson, Woodrow, 987
Wilson, Wm. B., 663
Wisby, 1012
Wiseman, Card., 1049, 1050
Wolseley, 1051
Wright, T., 973, 997
Wundt, 16, 26, 29

Xeno, 187

Zabarelli, Fr. de, 948
Zacheus, 584, 585
Zallinger, 955
Zeilier, 918
Zeno, 21
Ziegler, 29
Zigliara, 31, 121, 945, 959, 966, 967, 968, 1027, 1032

INDEX OF SUBJECTS

Acts, human, 162-165; indifferent, 168-171; moral, 156; 157; object of, 166; end of, 167; good, 168-169; 195; 281; bad, 365
Air-raids, 1053-1055; 1056; 1058; 1059
Altruism, 262; 380-383
Anger, 208; 210-211; 211-213
Appetite, 208; 210; 216; 250; 260-262
Asceticism, 246-248; 796-820
Authority, in religion, 446-450; 743-744; moral origin of civil, 900-905; 912; 918; 931; respect for, 991
Beatitude, 176-181
Benevolence, 382; 383
Betting, 513-514
Capital, 567; 568; 569; 583; 618; 633; 657; 659; 670; 676; 992; and co-operation, 715-734; wider distribution of, 717-720
Categorical imperative, and autonomy of pure reason, 383-400
Certitude, 120-129; metaphysical, 122; physical, 122; moral, 123; natural, 123; philosophical, 124; 129-130
Chance, 513-514; 514-517; 517-528
Character, ethics and, 283-284; nature of, 285-288; value of, 288-289; importance of, 289-291; 282; 294
Charity, 221-223; 223-227; 227-236; 975-976; 1060; 1062; 1065; 1066; 1067; 1068
Chastity, 217; 488; 492; 495
Children, 284; 286; 636; 637; 643; 706-708; 845-848; 865; 874-875; 887-889
Celibacy, 775-776; 796-820; 820-822
Circumstances, 165; 166; 169; 195; 196

Combatants, 1040; 1055-1059
Consent, 66-69; 895-897; 900; 916; 917
Conscience, 57-66; 156; 322; 343; 344-349; 349-352; 352-355; and prohibition, 355-356; 360-361; 381; 390; 421-423; 551; 881-883
Contract, 427-432; marriage, 776-777
Control, birth, 822-827; self, 796-820; 263
Co-operation, 715-735; for world peace, 1069-1070
Cosmology, postulate, 36
Culture, ethical, 29-30
Cynicism, 21
Democracy, industrial, 646-662; of St. Thomas, 913-925; Suarez on, 925-933; Christian, 704; 721; 944-945
Deontology, 172; 377; 384; 878
Determinants of an action, 165-168
Determinism. 91-92; 94; 96; 106-111; 112-120; 377; 420
Divorce, 506; 771-775; evils of, 778-779; 779-780; in the United States, 780-788
Duelling, 498-502
Duty, 75; 383; 395; 409; 464-465; 420-427; to worship God, 432-439; toward the body, 463-474; to preserve life, 474; of proprietors, 590-592; of trade-unions, 674-681; 878; toward our country, 981-982; of the citizen, 987-1002; to obey law, 990-991; of nations toward one another, 1016
Education, 284; right of State, 848-849; Catholic attitude on, 849-855; rights and duties regarding, 860-870; fact, 871-887; parents and, 843-844; of public opinion, 1071-1073

End, last, 174-182; and means, 193-207; of an act, 1-2; objective, final, 186-187

Ethics, purpose of, 1-3; definition and scope, 3-6; and life, 10; necessity of, 6-11; methods of, 13-19; history of, 19-35; and immortality, 75-78; and habits, 272-279; and character, 283-284; and prohibition, 356-360; of the ouija board, 496-498; of labor, 615-631

Eudaemonism, 172; 174; 381

Eutrapelia, 217; 483

Evolution, 15; 26; 27; 49; 54-55; 380; 381; 426; 443; 444; 755

Faculty, moral, 342-344

Family, 314; 747; 748; 789-790; 845; 855; 856; 863; endowment, 699-704

Fatalism, 91

Fear, 192; 193; 210-211; 303

Fortitude, 236-241

Freedom of will, 37-38; 89-98; 98-106; 107-108; 163-164; 208; 286; 349; 366; 369-370; 372; 389; 424-425; morality without, 111-120

Gambling, 514-517

Good, absolute, 19; highest, 171-174; 176

Government, righ of self, 933-944; functions of, 987; legitimate, 953-954; best kind of, 971-974

Guilds, 661; 662-667

Habit, 100; moral, 274-275; 285; law of, 272-279; limitation of, 279-283

Happiness, 20; 172; 173; 176; 182-191; in religious orders, 611

Health, 460; 472-473; 475-477; 480-483; 483-487; 838; 839

Hedonism, 15; 21; 174; 383; 384; 410-412; 883

Hindrances to accountability, 191-193

Holiness, 480-482; 541

Home, 290-291; 887-891; 1003; 1009

Homicide, 487-494; 505-507

Ignorance, 374

Immortality, 38; 71-89

Industrial, democracy, 646-662; relations, 667-674

Indifferentism, 439-446

Intention, 332-336; 440

Intoxication, 474-480

Judgments, 320-321; 342; 343; 353; 354

Justice, 237-238; 1060

Killing, the wounded, 505-507; 1041; combatants, 1056; non-combatants, 1057-1058

Labor, ethics of, 615-631; condition of, 639-646; child, 636-637; 657; 670; 674; 992; interest of, 715-717

Law, nature of, 301-302; effects of, 302-303; classification of, 303-306; major divisions of, 306-313; eternal, 313-317; natural, 60; 317-320; 323-325; 328-331; 418; 745-746; 1019; moral, 60; 325-326; 245-246; moral for men and women, 792-793; civil, 326-341; international, 1010-1016; 1028; of nations, 311; 1011-1012; 1016-1032; penal, 336-338; unjust, 914; positive, 1021-1024; constitutional world, 1024-1028; living wage by, 687-699

Legislation, 910; 983-987; 988-990; 996-1002; for a living wage, 684-699

Leviathan, 753-754; 756-759

Levirate, 766

Life, organic, 56; future, 82-87; 190; 191; 231; preservation of, 474

Lying, 528-564

Malthusianism, 827-841

Marriage, 596; 763-777; bond, 777-778; 822-824; duties of, 841-845

Mean, in philosophy, 11-13; in virtue, 219; 978

Mental reservation, 534-539; 560-564

Merit, 95-96

INDEX OF SUBJECTS

Method, in ethics, 13-19; intuitive, 13-17; inductive, 15; historic, 15; deductive, 17-19; geometric, 17; transcendental or abstract, 17; ideal, 17-18; Cartesian, 126-127

Money, 513-517; loan of, 565-568; the Church and, 568-570

Monogamy, 765; 768; 769; 770

Monopoly, 524; 576-580

Morality, of obligation, 59; without freewill, 111-120; norm of, 155-156; 159-160; 383; and art, 454-457; of monopolistic prices, 576-580; of speculation, 517-528; and catastrophies, 840-841; 876-877

Murder, 489-490

Nature, human, 158; laws of, 316-317

Obligation, 92-93; 308; 380; 385; 386; 390; 391; 392; 397; 431; of civil law, 326-341

Ought, Kantian, 383-400

Ownership, right of, 583-592; 594-596

Passion, 191-193; 207-210

Patriotism, 216; 974-978; practical, 978-983

Peace, international, 1061; 1062-1070; efforts towards, 1070-1073

People, sovereignty of, 944-971

Personality, 291-293; in life, 293-298

Pity, 281

Polyandry, 765-766

Polygamy, 441; 766-770

Positivism, 26; 377; 378; 415

Postulates, 36-39; necessity of, 35; anthropological, 38-39

Pragmatism, 27-28

Price, the just, 570-572; 572-576; monopolistic, 576-580

Prime Mover, 39-48

Probabilism, 360-365

Prohibition, 355-356; 356-360; 1004

Property, 583-592; and socialism, 592-596; 641

Prudence, 236-241

Relations, industrial, 667-674; between employers and employed, 681-687; international, 1059-1062

Remorse, 93-94

Reprisals, 1053-1055; 1055-1059

Responsibility, 96-98

Retribution, 96

Revelation, 22; 23; 69; 71; 125; 307; 370; 372; 432; 445

Right, basis of, 405-420; to moral integrity, 451; natural, 405-408; of private ownership, 587-590; 596-598; of trade unions, 674-681; 691-694; equal amendment, 794-796; to educate, 848-855; divine of kings, 934-937; of self-government, 933-943

Sanction, punitive, 270-272; of the illative sense, 130-134; imperfect, 77-78

Scandal, 450-451; 514

Scepticism, 28-29; 124-126; 442

Scholasticism, 23-24

Self-defence, 494-496; 500

Self-determination, 910; 933-943

Sense, illative, 129-152

Sex, 462; 480; 768-770; 764; 765; 776; 796-820; 820-822; 825; 826; 841-842

Sin, nature of, 365-367; malice of, 367; why men, 367-373; philosophical, 373-375; 450; 455-457

Social contract, 754; 759-763; 938

Social reform, 631-639

Socialism, 27; 592-598; 598-611; 662-664; in religious orders, 611-613

Society, 743-756; 907; 908

Sociology, and ethics, 5-6

Sophism, 22

Sovereignty, origin and rights of, 895-900; 903; of the people, 909-910; 944-971

Speculation, 517-528

State, 19-20; 24-25; duty of, 356-357; right to kill, 502-504; 748-752; and education, 848-849; 856-860; 870-871; the best, 971-974

Stoicism, 21-22; 883
Strikes, 642; 735-739
Suicide, 109; 457-463; 465-472; 474; 502
Synderesis, 341-342
Taxation, 613-615; 994-996
Teleological, proof, 48-57: argument, 71-74
Temperance, 236-241
Theory, moral sense, 25; Kant's "oughtness," 383-400; single-tax, 613-615; of labor, 654; laissez-faire, 619; 989; Malthusian, 827-841; political of St. Thomas, 905-913; scholastic political, 947-971
Trade Unions, 621; 644-646; 648; 665-667; 671-672; 674-681; 709-711
Traditionalism, 128
Transcentalism, 17
Utilitarianism, 15; 172; 375-380; 383; 385; 883

Values, 565-580
Vice, 269-270; in toilet, 452-454
Violence, 193
Virtue, 19; 137; 208-209; 213-221; intellectual, 214-215; moral, 216-218; cardinal, 236-241; relation of, 241-245; 302-303; 790; 974; 979-991; in toilet, 452-454
Vivisection, 507-513
Wages, 631-633; 644; earners of, 648-651; living, 687-699; family, 699-701; distribution of, 704-715
War, 930; 1032-1053
Welfare, false, 258-269; true, 245-258
Women, 637-638; in society, 789-792; influence of, 788-789; and Christianity, 791-792; attitude of the Church toward, 793-794; 982-983; suffrage of, 1002-1010